INTRODUCTION TO INFORMATION SYSTEMS

INTRODUCTION TO INFORMATION SYSTEMS

Fourteenth Edition

James A. O'Brien
College of Business Administration
Northern Arizona University

George M. Marakas
KU School of Business
University of Kansas

Boston Burr Ridge, IL Dubuque, IA New York San Francisco St. Louis
Bangkok Bogotá Caracas Kuala Lumpur Lisbon London Madrid Mexico City
Milan Montreal New Delhi Santiago Seoul Singapore Sydney Taipei Toronto

INTRODUCTION TO INFORMATION SYSTEMS

Published by McGraw-Hill/Irwin, a business unit of The McGraw-Hill Companies, Inc., 1221 Avenue of the Americas, New York, NY, 10020.

This book is printed on acid-free paper.

1 2 3 4 5 6 7 8 9 0 VNH/VNH 0 9 8 7

ISBN: 978-0-07-128326-7

MHID: 0-07-128326-9

www.mhhe.com

To your love, happiness, and success.

This edition represents both joy and sadness in the O'Brien and Marakas family. Jim and I have always found it a joyful experience to bring to our loyal adopters and students a new edition with fresh new information. This, the 14th edition of *Introduction to Information Systems,* represents the best we have to offer. We take pride in delivering this new edition to you and we thank all of you for your loyalty to the book and the input you provided that was instrumental in its development. Your continued support fills us with joy and a sense of both accomplishment and contribution.

The joy that we have experienced with the completion of each edition of the book this time comes tinged with sadness brought on by the loss of a good friend and talented author. My friend and co-author Jim O'Brien passed away during the final stages of our work on this edition. Our sense of loss is deep and our sadness for Jim's family and friends is profound. Jim O'Brien set the standard for excellence in everything he wrote and his legacy stands as a hallmark of achievement to which the rest of us aspire. I will always hear Jim's voice in the editions yet to come and will forever feel a void in the enjoyment we shared through our collaboration. I know I speak for all of the McGraw-Hill family who support us and make these books possible when I say Jim O'Brien will be greatly missed.

On behalf of Jim and myself, please accept our sincere appreciation for your support and loyalty. As always, we hope you enjoy and benefit from this book.

About the Authors

James A. O'Brien is an adjunct professor of Computer Information Systems in the College of Business Administration at Northern Arizona University. He completed his undergraduate studies at the University of Hawaii and Gonzaga University and earned an MS and Ph.D. in Business Administration from the University of Oregon. He has been professor and coordinator of the CIS area at Northern Arizona University, professor of Finance and Management Information Systems and chairman of the Department of Management at Eastern Washington University, and a visiting professor at the University of Alberta, the University of Hawaii, and Central Washington University.

Dr. O'Brien's business experience includes working in the Marketing Management Program of the IBM Corporation, as well as serving as a financial analyst for the General Electric Company. He is a graduate of General Electric's Financial Management Program. He also has served as an information systems consultant to several banks and computer services firms.

Jim's research interests lie in developing and testing basic conceptual frameworks used in information systems development and management. He has written eight books, including several that have been published in multiple editions, as well as in Chinese, Dutch, French, Japanese, or Spanish translations. He has also contributed to the field of information systems through the publication of many articles in business and academic journals, as well as through his participation in academic and industry associations in the field of information systems.

George M. Marakas is a professor of Information Systems at the School of Business at the University of Kansas. His teaching expertise includes Systems Analysis and Design, Technology-Assisted Decision Making, Electronic Commerce, Management of IS Resources, Behavioral IS Research Methods, and Data Visualization and Decision Support. In addition, George is an active researcher in the area of Systems Analysis Methods, Data Mining and Visualization, Creativity Enhancement, Conceptual Data Modeling, and Computer Self-Efficacy.

George received his Ph.D. in Information Systems from Florida International University in Miami and his MBA from Colorado State University. Prior to his position at the University of Kansas, he was a member of the faculties at the University of Maryland, Indiana University, and Helsinki School of Economics. Preceding his academic career, he enjoyed a highly successful career in the banking and real estate industries. His corporate experience includes senior management positions with Continental Illinois National Bank and the Federal Deposit Insurance Corporation. In addition, George served as president and CEO for CMC Group Inc., a major RTC management contractor in Miami, Florida, for three years. Throughout his academic career, George has distinguished himself both through his research and in the classroom. He has received numerous national teaching awards, and his research has appeared in the top journals in his field. In addition to this text, he is the author of three best-selling textbooks on information systems: *Decision Support Systems for the 21st Century*, *Systems Analysis and Design: An Active Approach*, and *Data Warehousing, Mining, and Visualization: Core Concepts.*

Beyond his academic endeavors, George is also an active consultant and has served as an advisor to a number of organizations, including the Central Intelligence Agency, Brown & Williamson, the Department of the Treasury, the Department of Defense, Xavier University, Citibank Asia-Pacific, Nokia Corporation, Professional Records Storage Inc., and United Information Systems, among many others. His consulting activities are concentrated primarily on electronic commerce strategy, the design and deployment of global IT strategy, workflow reengineering, e-business strategy, and ERP and CASE tool integration.

George is also an active member of a number of professional IS organizations and an avid golfer, second-degree Black Belt in Tae Kwon Do, a PADI master scuba diver trainer and IDC staff instructor, and a member of Pi Kappa Alpha fraternity.

The O'Brien Approach

A Business and Managerial Perspective

The Fourteenth Edition is designed for business students who are or who will soon become business professionals in the fast-changing business world of today. The goal of this text is to help business students learn how to use and manage information technologies to revitalize business processes, improve business decision making, and gain competitive advantage. Thus, it places a major emphasis on up-to-date coverage of the essential role of Internet technologies in providing a platform for business, commerce, and collaboration processes among all business stakeholders in today's networked enterprises and global markets. This is the business and managerial perspective that this text brings to the study of information systems. Of course, as in all O'Brien texts, this edition:

- Loads the text with **Real World Cases,** in-depth examples **(Blue Boxes),** and opportunities to learn about real people and companies in the business world (**Real World Activities, Case Study Questions, Discussion Questions,** and **Analysis Exercises**).
- Organizes the text around a simple **Five-Area Information Systems Framework** that emphasizes the IS knowledge a business professional needs to know.
- Places a **major emphasis on the strategic role of information technology** in providing business professionals with tools and resources for managing business operations, supporting decision making, enabling enterprise collaboration, and gaining competitive advantage.

Modular Structure of the Text

The text is organized into modules that reflect the five major areas of the framework for information systems knowledge. Each chapter is then organized into two or more distinct sections to provide the best possible conceptual organization of the text and each chapter. This organization increases instructor flexibility in assigning course material because it structures the text into modular levels (that is, modules, chapters, and sections) while reducing the number of chapters that need to be covered.

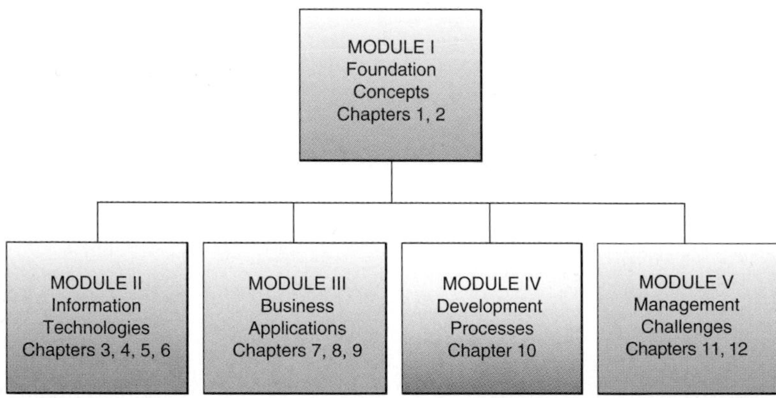

An Information Systems Framework

Business Applications

How businesses use the Internet and other information technologies to support their business processes, e-business and e-commerce initiatives, and business decision making (Chapters 7, 8, and 9).

Management Challenges

The challenges of business/IT technologies and strategies, including security and ethical challenges and global IT management (Chapters 11 and 12).

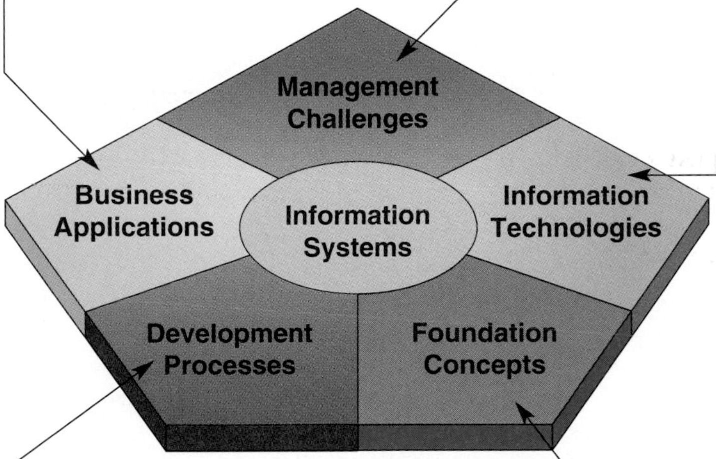

Management Challenges

Business Applications

Information Systems

Information Technologies

Development Processes

Foundation Concepts

Information Technologies

Includes major concepts, developments, and managerial issues involved in computer hardware, software, telecommunications networks, data resource management technologies, and other technologies (Chapters 3, 4, 5, and 6).

Development Processes

Developing and implementing business/IT strategies and systems using several strategic planning and application development approaches (Chapter 10).

Foundation Concepts

Fundamental business information systems concepts, including trends, components, and roles of information systems (Chapter 1) and competitive advantage concepts and applications (Chapter 2). Selective coverage of relevant behavioral, managerial, and technical concepts.

Real World Examples

Real World Cases

Each chapter provides three Real World Cases—in-depth examples that illustrate how prominent businesses and organizations have attempted to implement the theoretical concepts students have just learned.

A full list of cases is available inside the front cover.

REAL WORLD CASE 1

Amazon, eBay, and Google: Unlocking and Sharing Business Databases

The meeting had dragged on for more than an hour that rainy day in Seattle, and Jeff Bezos had heard enough. The CEO had rounded up 15 or so senior engineers and managers in one of Amazon's offices to tackle a question buzzing inside the company: Should Amazon bust open the doors of its most prized data warehouse, containing its myriad databases, and let an eager world of entrepreneurs scavenge through its data jewels?

For several years, scores of outsiders had been knocking on Amazon's door to gain access to the underlying data that powers the $7 billion retailer: product descriptions, prices, sales rankings, customer reviews, inventory figures, and countless other layers of content. In all, it was a data vault that Amazon had spent more than 10 years and a billion dollars to build, organize, and safeguard.

So why on earth would Bezos suddenly hand over the keys? Because in the hands of top Web innovators, some at the meeting argued, Amazon's data could be the dynamo of new Web sites and businesses that would expand the company's already gigantic online footprint and ultimately drive more sales. Others worried about the risks. A free-for-all, one manager warned, would "change our business in ways we don't understand."

Bezos ended the debate with characteristic gusto. He leaped from his seat, aping a flasher opening a trench coat. "We're going to aggressively expose ourselves!" he declared.

Today, there's considerable reason to cheer Bezos's exhibitionist move. Since the company opened up its data vaults in 2002, under the auspices of a project first called Amazon Web Services, more than 65,000 developers, businesses, and other entrepreneurs have tapped into the data. With it,

FIGURE 5.1

Amazon and eBay have opened up many of their databases to developers and entrepreneurs to broaden and facilitate the buying and selling process for their associates and customers.

they're building moneymaking Web sites, new online shopping interfaces, and innovative services for thousands of Amazon's independent sellers. Many have become Bezos's most ambitious business partners overnight. "Two years ago this was an experiment," says Amazon's engineering chief, Al Vermeulen. "Now it's a core part of our strategy."

And that's just at Amazon. A year after Bezos's decision to open Amazon's databases to developers and business partners, eBay chief executive Meg Whitman answered a similar cry from eBay's developer community, opening the $3 billion company's database of 33 million weekly auction items to the technorati. Some 15,000 developers and others have since registered to use that prized database and access other software features. Already, 41 percent of eBay's listings are uploaded to the site using software that takes advantage of these newly accessible resources.

At Google too, the concept is finding its legs: The company parcels out some of its search-results data and recently unlocked access to its desktop and paid-search products. Now dozens of Google-driven services are cropping up, from custom Web browsers to graphical search engines. Compared with Amazon and eBay however, Google is taking baby steps. Developers can grab 1,000 search results a day for free, but anything more than that requires special permission. In January 2005, Google finally opened up its AdWords paid-search service to outside applications, allowing marketers to automate their Google ad campaigns.

What's behind the open-door policies? True to their pioneering roots, Bezos, Whitman, and the Google boys are pushing their companies into what they believe is the Web's great new beyond: an era in which online businesses operate as open-ended software platforms that can accommodate thousands of other businesses selling symbiotic products and services. Says longtime tech-book publisher Tim O'Reilly, "We can finally rip, mix, and burn each other's Web sites."

Most people think of Amazon as the world's largest retailer, or "earth's biggest bookstore," as Bezos called it in its start-up days. Inside the company, those perceptions are decidedly old school. "We are at heart a technology company," Vermeulen says. He and Bezos have begun to view Amazon as simply a big piece of software available over the Web. "Amazon.com is just another application on the platform," Vermeulen asserts.

Eric von Hippel, a business professor at MIT's Sloan School of Management, explains the old rules: "We come from a culture where if you invested in it, you kept it. That was your competitive advantage." The rise of open-source software certainly challenged that notion. The rise of open databases and Web services goes even further, holding out the promise of automating the links between online businesses by applications that depend on companies sharing their vital data.

Real Life Lessons

Use Your Brain

Traditional case study questions promote and provide opportunity for critical thinking and classroom discussion.

As Vermeulen says, "Those that succeed have to think about removing walls instead of putting them up." For Amazon, there's some evidence to support that logic. Of the 65,000 people and companies that have signed up to use Amazon's free goodies, about one-third have been tinkering with software tools that help Amazon's 800,000 or so active sellers.

One of the most clever is ScoutPal, a service that turns cell phones into mobile bar-code scanners. "It's like a Geiger counter for books," founder Dave Anderson says. He came up with the idea a couple of years ago when his wife, Barbara, who sells books on Amazon, would lug home 50 pounds of titles from garage sales, only to discover that she'd paid too much for many of them to make any money. Anderson wrote an application that works in tandem with an attachable bar-code scanner. Barbara either scans in books' bar codes or punches in their 10-digit ID numbers. Then she can pull down the latest Amazon prices for the books and calculate her likely profit margin before she pays for the inventory. Anderson says his wife's sales have since tripled to about $100,000 a year, and her profit margins have jumped from 50 to 85 percent. And he's now bringing in six figures too: ScoutPal has more than 1,000 subscribers, each paying $10 a month.

Other tools are also gaining traction. Software programs like SellerEngine help merchants on the main site upload their inventory, check prices, and automate interactions such as adding new listings. Meanwhile, software from Associates Shop.com lets thousands of other Web site operators—there are more than 900,000 of these so-called Amazon associates—create customized storefronts that link back to Amazon, generating new sales for Bezos and commission revenue for the associates.

For the near term, maybe the biggest benefit to Amazon of letting folks like Anderson tinker with its platform is that it gets experimental R&D for free. "We can try to build all the applications for sellers ourselves," Vermeulen says, "or we can build a platform and let others build them." Adds Bezos, "Right now we just want to get people to use the guts of Amazon in ways that surprise us."

The experimentation at eBay has been just as ambitious. The company says that more than 1,000 new applications have emerged from its 15,000 or so registered developers. As with Amazon, the most popular are apps that help sellers automate the process of listing items on eBay or displaying them on other sites. Many of these outfits, such as ChannelAdvisor (itself a multimillion-dollar business), Marketworks, and Vendio, offer auction-listing software or services to eBay sellers. Jeff McManus, eBay's chief of platform evangelism, marvels at the benefits. "Sellers who use our APIs [application programming interfaces] become at least 50 percent more productive than those who use the Web site itself."

The data links also let companies create storefronts filled with their inventory while making transactions over eBay's network. One example is Las Vegas–based SuperPawn, which runs a chain of 46 pawnshops in Arizona, California, Nevada, Texas, and Washington. The company (recently acquired by the larger pawnshop operator Cash America International) uses eBay's APIs to automatically upload the latest pawned items from its physical stores to eBay. The system already generates more than 5 percent of SuperPawn's $40 million in annual sales and thousands more transactions for eBay.

Source: Erik Schonfeld, "The Great Giveaway," *Business 2.0*, April 2005, pp. 81–86.

CASE STUDY QUESTIONS

1. What are the business benefits to Amazon and eBay of opening up some of their databases to developers and entrepreneurs? Do you agree with this strategy? Why or why not?
2. What business factors are causing Google to move slowly in opening up its databases? Do you agree with its go-slow strategy? Why or why not?
3. Should other companies follow Amazon's and eBay's lead and open up some of their databases to developers and others? Defend your position with examples of the risks and benefits to an actual company.

REAL WORLD ACTIVITIES

1. The concept of opening up a company's product, inventory, and other databases to developers and entrepreneurs is a relatively new one. Use the Internet to find examples of companies that have adopted this strategy and the benefits they claim for doing so.
2. Opening up selective databases to outsiders is not a risk-free strategy for a company. What risks are involved? What safeguards should be put in place to guard against loss or misuse of a company's data? Break into small groups with your classmates to discuss and take a stand on these issues.

Use Your Hands

The Real World Activities section offers possibilities for hands-on exploration and learning.

Strategy, Ethics . . .

Competitive Advantage

Chapter 2 focuses on the use of IT as a way to surpass your competitor's performance.

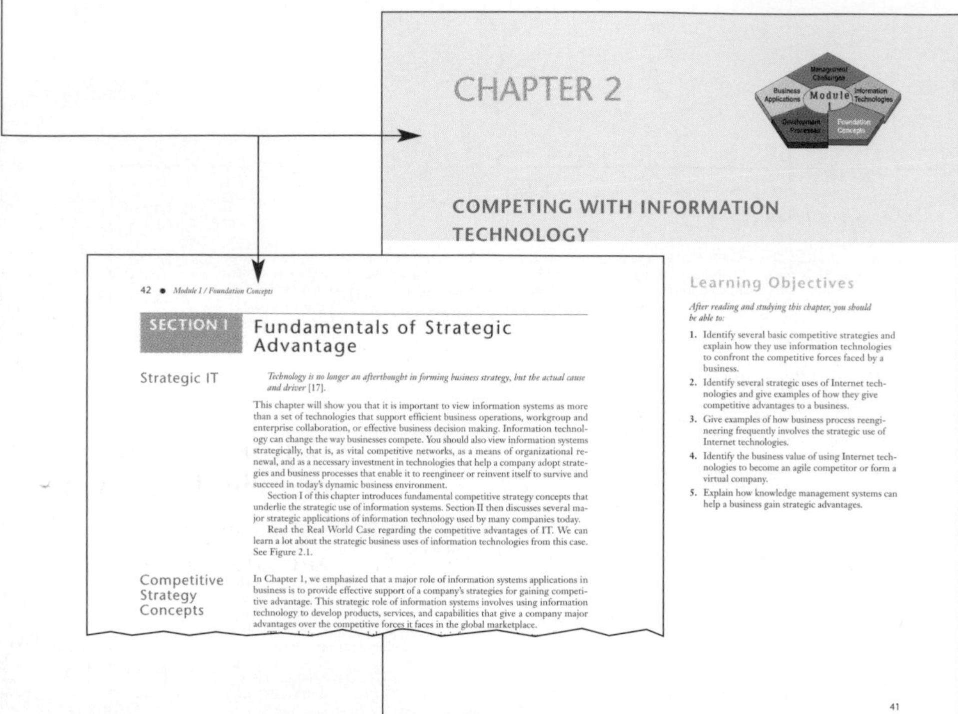

CHAPTER 2

COMPETING WITH INFORMATION TECHNOLOGY

Learning Objectives

After reading and studying this chapter, you should be able to:

1. Identify several basic competitive strategies and explain how they use information technologies to confront the competitive forces faced by a business.
2. Identify several strategic uses of Internet technologies and give examples of how they give competitive advantages to a business.
3. Give examples of how business process reengineering frequently involves the strategic use of Internet technologies.
4. Identify the business value of using Internet technologies to become an agile competitor or form a virtual company.
5. Explain how knowledge management systems can help a business gain strategic advantages.

41

42 ● *Module I / Foundation Concepts*

SECTION I Fundamentals of Strategic Advantage

Strategic IT

Technology is no longer an afterthought in forming business strategy, but the actual cause and driver [17].

This chapter will show you that it is important to view information systems as more than a set of technologies that support efficient business operations, workgroup and enterprise collaboration, or effective business decision making. Information technology can change the way businesses compete. You should also view information systems strategically, that is, as vital competitive networks, as a means of organizational renewal, and as a necessary investment in technologies that help a company adopt strategies and business processes that enable it to reengineer or reinvent itself to survive and succeed in today's dynamic business environment.

Section I of this chapter introduces fundamental competitive strategy concepts that underlie the strategic use of information systems. Section II then discusses several major strategic applications of information technology used by many companies today.

Read the Real World Case regarding the competitive advantages of IT. We can learn a lot about the strategic business uses of information technologies from this case. See Figure 2.1.

Competitive Strategy Concepts

In Chapter 1, we emphasized that a major role of information systems applications in business is to provide effective support of a company's strategies for gaining competitive advantage. This strategic role of information systems involves using information technology to develop products, services, and capabilities that give a company major advantages over the competitive forces it faces in the global marketplace.

Ethics & Security

Chapter 11 discusses the issues surrounding these topics and the challenges IT faces.

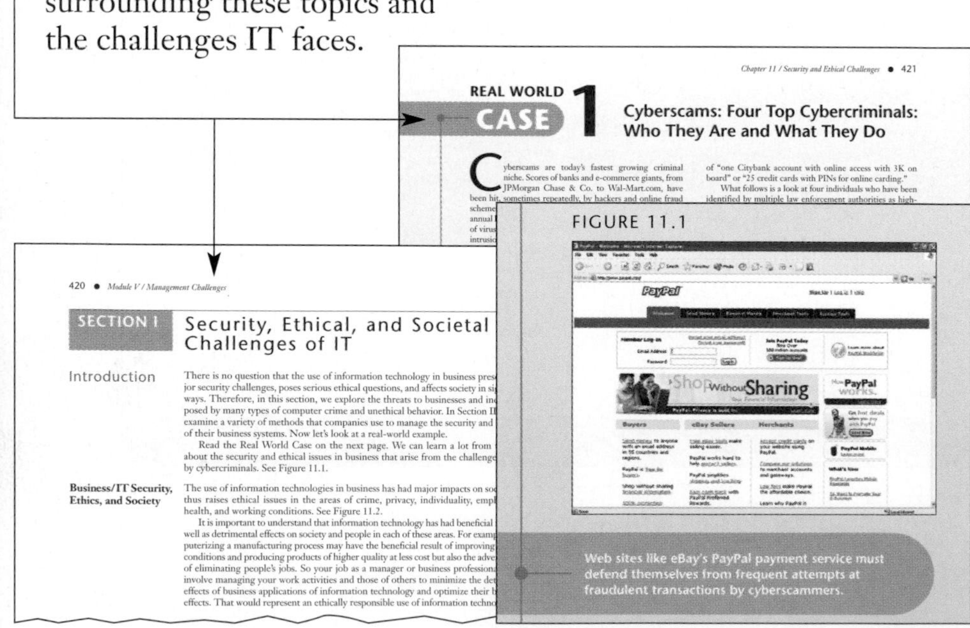

Chapter 11 / Security and Ethical Challenges ● 421

REAL WORLD CASE 1

Cyberscams: Four Top Cybercriminals: Who They Are and What They Do

Cyberscams are today's fastest growing criminal niche. Scores of banks and e-commerce giants, from JPMorgan Chase & Co. to Wal-Mart.com, have been hit, sometimes repeatedly, by hackers and online fraud scheme… annual… of virus… intrusi…

of "one Citybank account with online access with 3K on board" or "25 credit cards with PINs for online carding."

What follows is a look at four individuals who have been identified by multiple law enforcement authorities as high-

FIGURE 11.1

Web sites like eBay's PayPal payment service must defend themselves from frequent attempts at fraudulent transactions by cyberscammers.

420 ● *Module V / Management Challenges*

SECTION I Security, Ethical, and Societal Challenges of IT

Introduction

There is no question that the use of information technology in business pres… jor security challenges, poses serious ethical questions, and affects society in si… ways. Therefore, in this section, we explore the threats to businesses and in… posed by many types of computer crime and unethical behavior. In Section II… examine a variety of methods that companies use to manage the security and… of their business systems. Now let's look at a real-world example.

Read the Real World Case on the next page. We can learn a lot from… about the security and ethical issues in business that arise from the challenge… by cybercriminals. See Figure 11.1.

Business/IT Security, Ethics, and Society

The use of information technologies in business has had major impacts on so… thus raises ethical issues in the areas of crime, privacy, individuality, empl… health, and working conditions. See Figure 11.2.

It is important to understand that information technology has had beneficial… well as detrimental effects on society and people in each of these areas. For examp… puterizing a manufacturing process may have the beneficial result of improving… conditions and producing products of higher quality at less cost but also the adve… of eliminating people's jobs. So your job as a manager or business profession… involve managing your work activities and those of others to minimize the det… effects of business applications of information technology and optimize their b… effects. That would represent an ethically responsible use of information techno…

. . . and Beyond

SECTION II

Managing Global IT

The International Dimension

Whether they are in Berlin or Bombay, Kuala Lumpur or Kansas, San Francisco or Seoul, companies around the globe are developing new models to operate competitively in a digital economy. These models are structured, yet agile; global, yet local; and they concentrate on maximizing the risk-adjusted return from both knowledge and technology assets [10].

International dimensions have become a vital part of managing a business enterprise in the internetworked global economies and markets of today. Whether you become a manager in a large corporation or the owner of a small business, you will be affected by international business developments and deal in some way with people, products, or services whose origin is not your home country.

Read the Real World Case on the next page. We can learn a lot about the ways companies are responding to the challenges of the globalization of IT from this case. See Figure 12.11.

Global IT Management

Figure 12.9 illustrates the major dimensions of the job of managing global information technology that we cover in this section. Notice that all global IT activities must be adjusted to take into account the cultural, political, and geoeconomic challenges that exist in the international business community. Developing appropriate business and IT strategies for the global marketplace should be the first step in global information technology management. Once that is done, end users and IS managers can move on to developing the portfolio of business applications needed to support business/IT strategies; the hardware, software, and Internet-based technology platforms to support those applications; the data resource management methods to provide necessary databases; and finally the systems development projects that will produce the global information systems required.

Cendant Corp.: Global IT Management's Cultural, Political, and Geoeconomic Challenges

Lawrence Kinder faced a typical kind of global challenge. He is executive vice president and CIO with global responsibility for IT at Cendant Corp., which recently acquired Avis Group holdings. His company, a service and information provider for automotive transportation and vehicle management in Garden City, New York, grew internationally in 1999 by acquiring the United Kingdom's PHH Vehicle Management Services, the world's second-largest vehicle leasing and fleet management company, and Wright Express LLC, the world's largest credit card and information services provider.

"We grew organically in North America and built a solid and stable IT foundation that we have been able to leverage in Europe," Kinder says. The key is to take the time to understand the day-to-day workings of each local IT group, he claims, and to put strategic IT planning on the back burner until all groups can focus on leveraging their cultures and talents.

Kinder regularly brings together company leaders with similar roles from the United States, Canada, and Europe to "give each other a shot of adrenaline." He posits that developing and supporting global businesses is more demanding than even strategic planning. But, he says, "Giving my global IT leaders the opportunity to think more broadly about their applications and solve international business problems has created a true learning organization" [14].

Go Global with IT

This text closes with Chapter 12, an in-depth look at IT across borders.

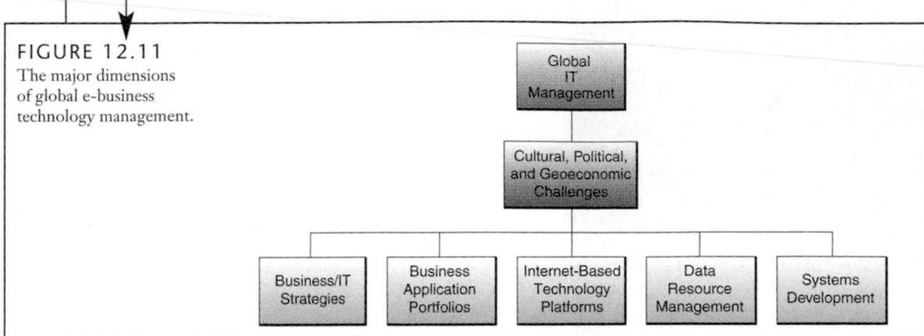

FIGURE 12.11
The major dimensions of global e-business technology management.

Expand Your Knowledge

Blue boxes in each chapter provide brief, in-depth examples of how corporations apply IS concepts and theories.

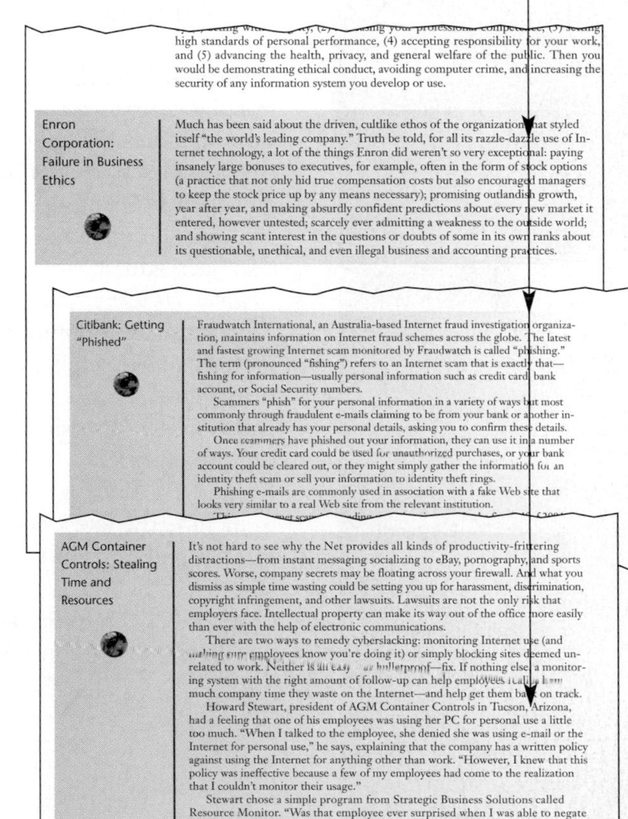

high standards of personal performance, (4) accepting responsibility for your work, and (5) advancing the health, privacy, and general welfare of the public. Then you would be demonstrating ethical conduct, avoiding computer crime, and increasing the security of any information system you develop or use.

Enron Corporation: Failure in Business Ethics

Much has been said about the driven, cultlike ethos of the organization that styled itself "the world's leading company." Truth be told, for all its razzle-dazzle use of Internet technology, a lot of the things Enron did weren't so very exceptional: paying insanely large bonuses to executives, for example, often in the form of stock options (a practice that not only hid true compensation costs but also encouraged managers to keep the stock price up by any means necessary); promising outlandish growth, year after year, and making absurdly confident predictions about every new market it entered, however untested; scarcely ever admitting a weakness to the outside world; and showing scant interest in the questions or doubts of some in its own ranks about its questionable, unethical, and even illegal business and accounting practices.

Citibank: Getting "Phished"

Fraudwatch International, an Australia-based Internet fraud investigation organization, maintains information on Internet fraud schemes across the globe. The latest and fastest growing Internet scam monitored by Fraudwatch is called "phishing." The term (pronounced "fishing") refers to an Internet scam that is exactly that—fishing for information—usually personal information such as credit card, bank account, or Social Security numbers.

Scammers "phish" for your personal information in a variety of ways but most commonly through fraudulent e-mails claiming to be from your bank or another institution that already has your personal details, asking you to confirm these details.

Once scammers have phished out your information, they can use it in a number of ways. Your credit card could be used for unauthorized purchases, or your bank account could be cleared out, or they might simply gather the information for an identity theft scam or sell your information to identity theft rings.

Phishing e-mails are commonly used in association with a fake Web site that looks very similar to a real Web site from the relevant institution.

AGM Container Controls: Stealing Time and Resources

It's not hard to see why the Net provides all kinds of productivity-frittering distractions—from instant messaging socializing to eBay, pornography, and sports scores. Worse, company secrets may be floating across your firewall. And what you dismiss as simple time wasting could be setting you up for harassment, discrimination, copyright infringement, and other lawsuits. Lawsuits are not the only risk that employers face. Intellectual property can make its way out of the office more easily than ever with the help of electronic communications.

There are two ways to remedy cyberslacking: monitoring Internet use (and making sure employees know you're doing it) or simply blocking sites deemed unrelated to work. Neither is an easy—or bulletproof—fix. If nothing else, a monitoring system with the right amount of follow-up can help employees realize how much company time they waste on the Internet—and help get them back on track.

Howard Stewart, president of AGM Container Controls in Tucson, Arizona, had a feeling that one of his employees was using her PC for personal use a little too much. "When I talked to the employee, she denied she was using e-mail or the Internet for personal use," he says, explaining that the company has a written policy against using the Internet for anything other than work. "However, I knew that this policy was ineffective because a few of my employees had come to the realization that I couldn't monitor their usage."

Stewart chose a simple program from Strategic Business Solutions called Resource Monitor. "Was that employee ever surprised when I was able to negate

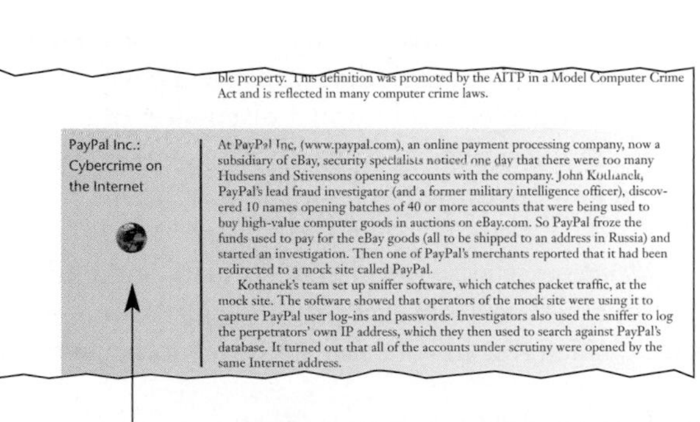

ble property. This definition was promoted by the AITP in a Model Computer Crime Act and is reflected in many computer crime laws.

PayPal Inc.: Cybercrime on the Internet

At PayPal Inc. (www.paypal.com), an online payment processing company, now a subsidiary of eBay, security specialists noticed one day that there were too many Hudsens and Stivensons opening accounts with the company. John Kothanek, PayPal's lead fraud investigator (and a former military intelligence officer), discovered 10 names opening batches of 40 or more accounts that were being used to buy high-value computer goods in auctions on eBay.com. So PayPal froze the funds used to pay for the eBay goods (all to be shipped to an address in Russia) and started an investigation. Then one of PayPal's merchants reported that it had been redirected to a mock site called PayPal.

Kothanek's team set up sniffer software, which catches packet traffic, at the mock site. The software showed that operators of the mock site were using it to capture PayPal user log-ins and passwords. Investigators also used the sniffer to log the perpetrators' own IP address, which they then used to search against PayPal's database. It turned out that all of the accounts under scrutiny were opened by the same Internet address.

Expand Your Horizons

Globe icons indicate examples with an international focus so that your knowledge makes you truly worldly.

What's New?

The Fourteenth Edition includes significant changes to the Thirteenth Edition's content that update and improve its coverage, many of them suggested by an extensive faculty review process. Highlights of key changes for this edition include the following:

- Real World Cases provide current, relevant, and in-depth examples of IS theory applications. A combination of *Case Study Questions* and *Real World Activities* allows you to engage students on a variety of levels.
- More new Real World Cases: More than two-thirds of the cases are new to the Fourteenth Edition. These up-to-date cases provide students with in-depth business examples of the successes and challenges companies are experiencing in implementing the information technology concepts covered in each chapter.
- Improved Analysis Exercises at the end of each chapter allow you to cover in class or assign as homework a wide variety of interesting projects that promote analysis and critical thinking.
- *Chapter 1: Foundations of Information Systems in Business* provides a discussion of the relationship between general systems theory and information systems. An expanded discussion on IT/IS careers has been added to Section I.
- *Chapter 2: Competing with Information Technology* has an expanded discussion of Porter's five force model of competition and provides added clarification of support versus primary processes and a more in-depth explanation of differentiation versus innovation.
- *Chapter 3: Computer Hardware* includes significant discussions of the history of computing and of Moore's law. It also provides a discussion of flash drives and new coverage on RFID technology, including a new in-depth blue box example.
- *Chapter 4: Computer Software* expands the discussion of open-source development and of Microsoft's .NET. A completely new discussion on weblogs has also been added.
- *Chapter 5: Data Resource Management* provides additional information about relational databases, a comparison of dynamic and static data, and a significant discussion on issues related to distributed databases.
- *Chapter 6: Telecommunications and Networks* now includes discussions of technologies such as Bluetooth and VoIP. Significant discussion of the difference between analog and digital technologies, as well as treatment of the last-mile problem, has also been added.
- *Chapter 10: Developing Business/IT Solutions* has a substantially improved presentation of the development of business/IT solutions, including expanded coverage of preliminary feasibility assessments of new projects; additional discussion of project management processes, tools, and techniques; new material on data conversion and system conversion strategies; and new coverage of change management and user involvement.
- *Chapter 11: Security and Ethical Challenges* expands coverage of security and ethics to include the latest developments: opt-in versus opt-out privacy legislation, HIPPA and Patriot Act compliance challenges, adware and spyware, and cyber law.
- *Chapter 12: Enterprise and Global Management of Information Technology* provides new in-depth coverage and business examples of outsourcing and offshoring.

Student Support

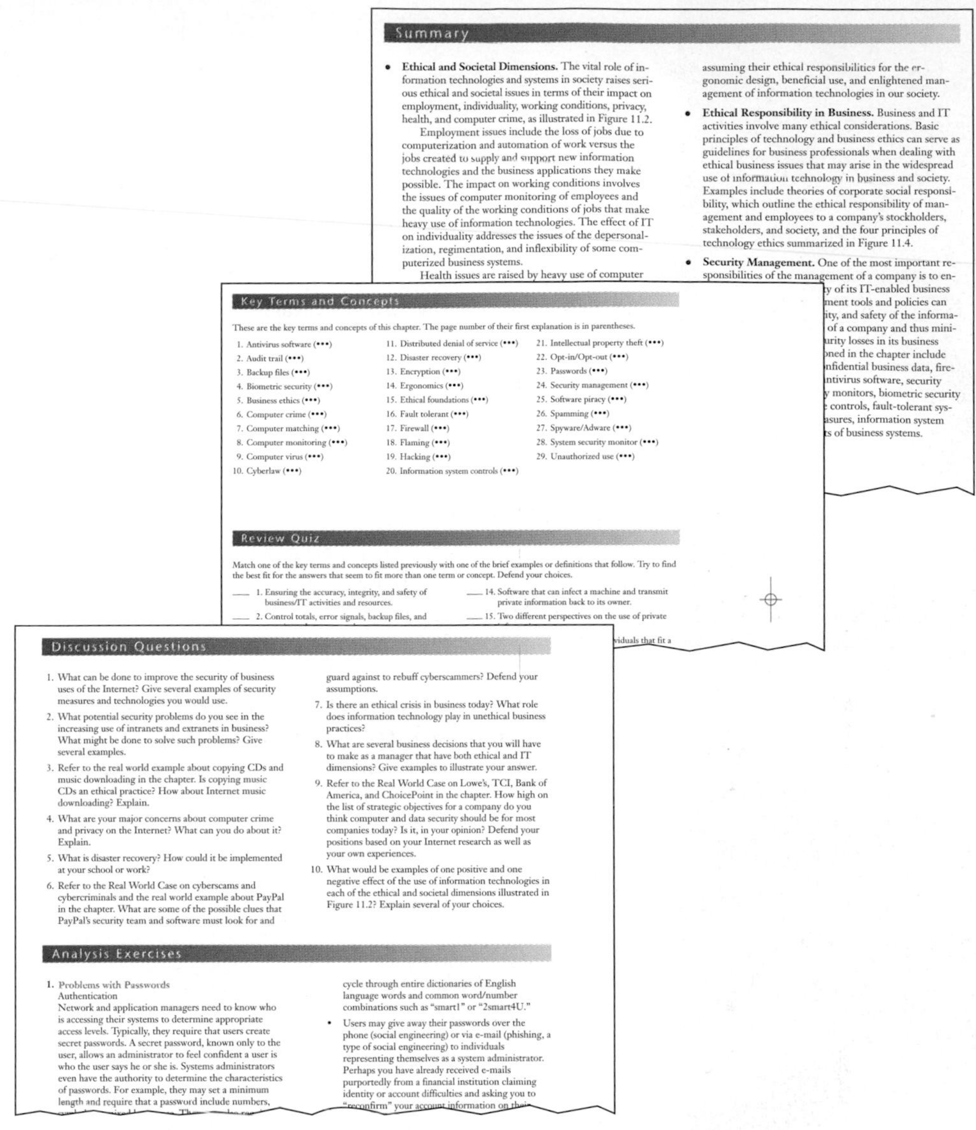

Summary

- **Ethical and Societal Dimensions.** The vital role of information technologies and systems in society raises serious ethical and societal issues in terms of their impact on employment, individuality, working conditions, privacy, health, and computer crime, as illustrated in Figure 11.2.
  Employment issues include the loss of jobs due to computerization and automation of work versus the jobs created to supply and support new information technologies and the business applications they make possible. The impact on working conditions involves the issues of computer monitoring of employees and the quality of the working conditions of jobs that make heavy use of information technologies. The effect of IT on individuality addresses the issues of the depersonalization, regimentation, and inflexibility of some computerized business systems.
  Health issues are raised by heavy use of computer

assuming their ethical responsibilities for the ergonomic design, beneficial use, and enlightened management of information technologies in our society.

- **Ethical Responsibility in Business.** Business and IT activities involve many ethical considerations. Basic principles of technology and business ethics can serve as guidelines for business professionals when dealing with ethical business issues that may arise in the widespread use of information technology in business and society. Examples include theories of corporate social responsibility, which outline the ethical responsibility of management and employees to a company's stockholders, stakeholders, and society, and the four principles of technology ethics summarized in Figure 11.4.
- **Security Management.** One of the most important responsibilities of the management of a company is to en-
  y of its IT-enabled business
  ment tools and policies can
  ity, and safety of the informa-
  of a company and thus mini-
  urity losses in its business
  oned in the chapter include
  nfidential business data, fire-
  ntivirus software, security
  y monitors, biometric security
  controls, fault-tolerant sys-
  asures, information system
  s of business systems.

Key Terms and Concepts

These are the key terms and concepts of this chapter. The page number of their first explanation is in parentheses.

1. Antivirus software (•••)
2. Audit trail (•••)
3. Backup files (•••)
4. Biometric security (•••)
5. Business ethics (•••)
6. Computer crime (•••)
7. Computer matching (•••)
8. Computer monitoring (•••)
9. Computer virus (•••)
10. Cyberlaw (•••)
11. Distributed denial of service (•••)
12. Disaster recovery (•••)
13. Encryption (•••)
14. Ergonomics (•••)
15. Ethical foundations (•••)
16. Fault tolerant (•••)
17. Firewall (•••)
18. Flaming (•••)
19. Hacking (•••)
20. Information system controls (•••)
21. Intellectual property theft (•••)
22. Opt-in/Opt-out (•••)
23. Passwords (•••)
24. Security management (•••)
25. Software piracy (•••)
26. Spamming (•••)
27. Spyware/Adware (•••)
28. System security monitor (•••)
29. Unauthorized use (•••)

Review Quiz

Match one of the key terms and concepts listed previously with one of the brief examples or definitions that follow. Try to find the best fit for the answers that seem to fit more than one term or concept. Defend your choices.

___ 1. Ensuring the accuracy, integrity, and safety of business/IT activities and resources.

___ 2. Control totals, error signals, backup files, and

___ 14. Software that can infect a machine and transmit private information back to its owner.

___ 15. Two different perspectives on the use of private

viduals that fit a

Discussion Questions

1. What can be done to improve the security of business uses of the Internet? Give several examples of security measures and technologies you would use.
2. What potential security problems do you see in the increasing use of intranets and extranets in business? What might be done to solve such problems? Give several examples.
3. Refer to the real world example about copying CDs and music downloading in the chapter. Is copying music CDs an ethical practice? How about Internet music downloading? Explain.
4. What are your major concerns about computer crime and privacy on the Internet? What can you do about it? Explain.
5. What is disaster recovery? How could it be implemented at your school or work?
6. Refer to the Real World Case on cyberscams and cybercriminals and the real world example about PayPal in the chapter. What are some of the possible clues that PayPal's security team and software must look for and guard against to rebuff cyberscammers? Defend your assumptions.
7. Is there an ethical crisis in business today? What role does information technology play in unethical business practices?
8. What are several business decisions that you will have to make as a manager that have both ethical and IT dimensions? Give examples to illustrate your answer.
9. Refer to the Real World Case on Lowe's, TCI, Bank of America, and ChoicePoint in the chapter. How high on the list of strategic objectives for a company do you think computer and data security should be for most companies today? Is it, in your opinion? Defend your positions based on your Internet research as well as your own experiences.
10. What would be examples of one positive and one negative effect of the use of information technologies in each of the ethical and societal dimensions illustrated in Figure 11.2? Explain several of your choices.

Analysis Exercises

1. Problems with Passwords
   Authentication
   Network and application managers need to know who is accessing their systems to determine appropriate access levels. Typically, they require that users create secret passwords. A secret password, known only to the user, allows an administrator to feel confident a user is who the user says he or she is. Systems administrators even have the authority to determine the characteristics of passwords. For example, they may set a minimum length and require that a password include numbers,

cycle through entire dictionaries of English language words and common word/number combinations such as "smart1" or "2smart4U."

- Users may give away their passwords over the phone (social engineering) or via e-mail (phishing, a type of social engineering) to individuals representing themselves as a system administrator. Perhaps you have already received e-mails purportedly from a financial institution claiming identity or account difficulties and asking you to "reconfirm" your account information on their

Each chapter contains *complete pedagogical support* in the form of:

- **Summary.** Revisiting key chapter concepts in a bullet-point summary.
- **Key Terms and Concepts.** Using page numbers to reference where terms are discussed in the text.
- **Review Quiz.** Providing a self-assessment for your students. Great for review before an important exam.
- **Discussion Questions.** Whether assigned as homework or used for in-class discussion, these complex questions will help your students develop critical thinking skills.
- **Analysis Exercises.** Each innovative scenario presents a business problem and asks students to use and test their IS knowledge through analytical, Web-based, spreadsheet, and/or database skills.
- **Closing Case Studies.** Reinforcing important concepts with prominent examples from businesses and organizations. Discussion questions follow each case study.

Instructor Support

Online Learning Center

Available to adopting faculty, the Online Learning Center provides one convenient place to access the Instructor's Manual, PowerPoint slides, and videos.

Instructor's Manual (IM)

To help ease your teaching burden, each chapter is supported by solutions to Real World Case questions, Discussion Questions, and Analysis Exercises.

Test Bank

Choose from over 1,800 true/false, multiple-choice, and fill-in-the-blank questions of varying levels of difficulty. Complete answers are provided for all test questions. By using the **EZ Test Computerized Test Bank** instructors can design, save, and generate custom tests. EZ Test also enables instructors to edit, add, or delete questions from the test bank; analyze test results; and organize a database of tests and student results.

PowerPoint Slides

A set of visually stimulating PowerPoint slides accompanies each chapter, providing a lecture outline and key figures and tables from the text. Slides can be edited to fit the needs of your course.

Videos

New videos will be downloadable from the instructor side of the OLC. Selections from our archive of videos from previous years will be delivered upon request.

MBA MIS Cases

Developed by Richard Perle of Loyola Marymount University, these 14 cases allow you to add MBA-level analysis to your course. See your McGraw-Hill Irwin sales representative for more information.

Online Course Formats

Content for the Fourteenth Edition is available in WebCT, Blackboard, and PageOut formats to accommodate virtually any online delivery platform.

Online Learning Center

Visit www.mhhe.com/obrien for additional instructor and student resources.

Use our EZ Test Online to help your students prepare to succeed with Apple iPod® iQuiz.

Using our EZ Test Online you can make test and quiz content available for a student's Apple iPod®.

Students must purchase the iQuiz game application from Apple for 99¢ in order to use the iQuiz content. It works on the iPod fifth generation iPods and better.

Instructors only need EZ Test Online to produce iQuiz ready content. Instructors take their existing tests and quizzes and export them to a file that can then be made available to the student to take as a self-quiz on their iPods. It's as simple as that.

Empower Your Students

MISOURCE

Mastery of Skills and Concepts

This student supplement provides animated tutorials and simulated practice of the core skills in Microsoft Office 2007 Excel, Access, and PowerPoint, as well as animation of 47 important computer concepts.

With MISource's three-pronged **Teach Me–Show Me–Let Me Try** approach, students of all learning styles can quickly master core MS Office skills—leaving you more classroom time to cover more important and more complex topics.

For those students who need it, MISource for Office 2007 is delivered online at www.mhhe.com/misource, while coverage of Office 2003 can be found on the MISource CD attached to this book.

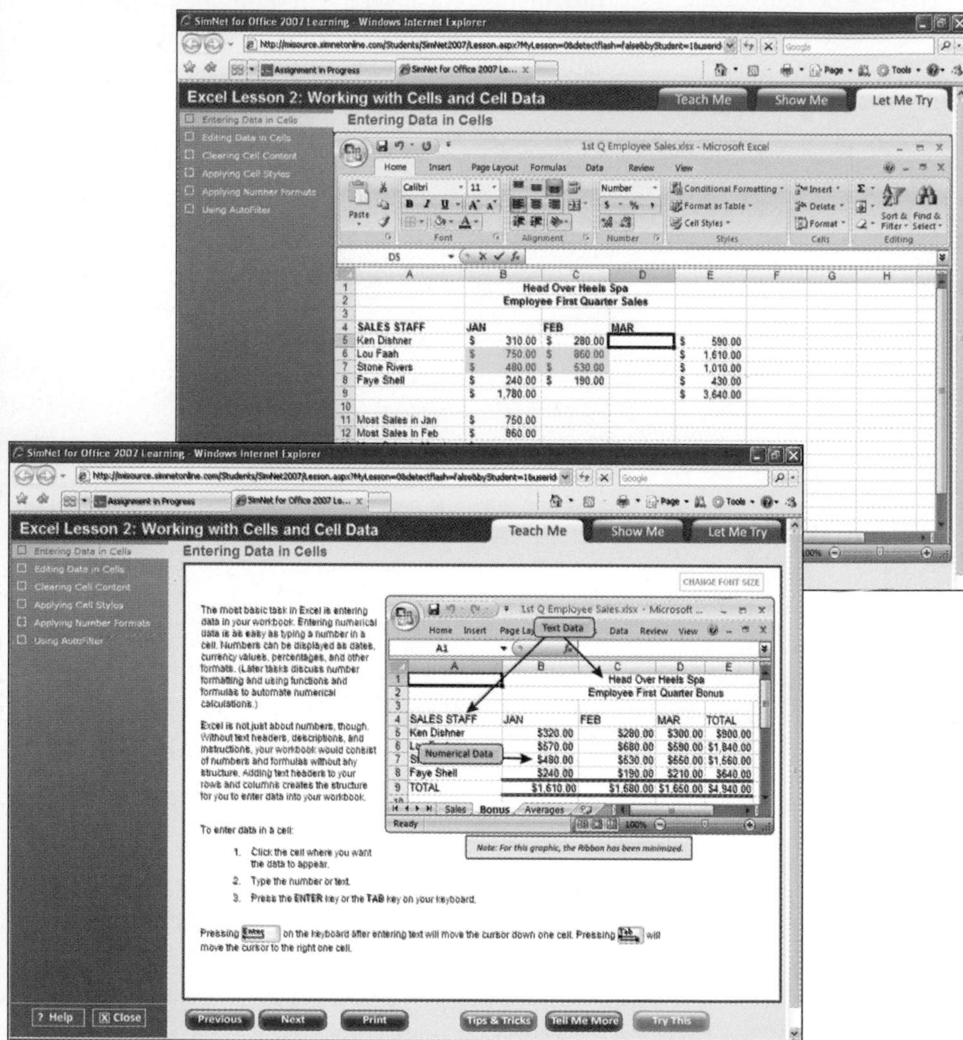

Empower Your Classroom

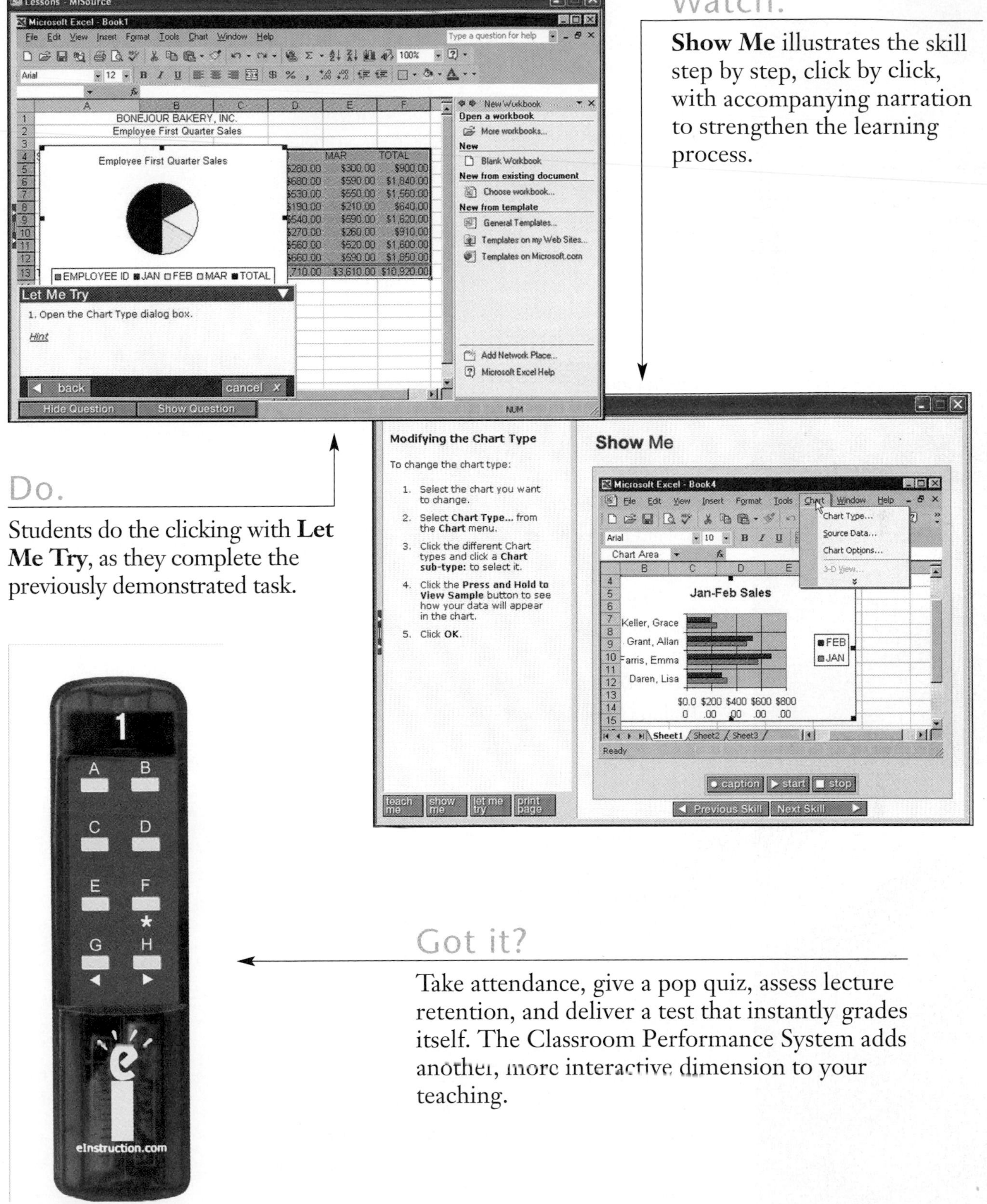

Watch.

Show Me illustrates the skill step by step, click by click, with accompanying narration to strengthen the learning process.

Do.

Students do the clicking with **Let Me Try**, as they complete the previously demonstrated task.

Got it?

Take attendance, give a pop quiz, assess lecture retention, and deliver a test that instantly grades itself. The Classroom Performance System adds another, more interactive dimension to your teaching.

Acknowledgments

The Fourteenth Edition represents an ongoing effort to improve and adapt this text to meet the needs of students and instructors. For this revision, we received the guidance of more than 50 reviewers over the course of several months of review work. We thank all of them for their insight and advice.

Adeyemi A. Adekoya, *Virginia State University*
Hans-Joachim Adler, *University of Texas—Dallas*
Noushin Ashrafi, *University of Massachusetts—Boston*
Bruce Bellak, *New Jersey Institute of Technology*
Jongbok Byun, *Point Loma Nazarene University*
Ralph J. Caputo, *Manhattan College*
Kala Chand Seal, *Loyola Marymount University*
Yong S. Choi, *California State University—Bakersfield*
Carey Cole, *James Madison University*
Susan Cooper, *Sam Houston State University*
Jeffrey P. Corcoran, *Lasell College*
Subhankar Dhar, *San Jose State University*
Thomas W. Dillon, *James Madison University*
David Dischiave, *Syracuse University*
Roland Eichelberger, *Baylor University*
Ray Eldridge, *Freed-Hardeman University*
Dr. Juan Esteva, *Eastern Michigan University*
Warren W. Fisher, *Stephen F. Austin State University*
Janos T. Fustos, *Metropolitan State College of Denver*
Gerald Gonsalves, *College of Charleston*
Phillip Gordon, *Mills College*
Dr. Vipul Gupta, *Saint Joseph's University*
Dr. Arie Halachmi, *Tennessee State University*
Dr. Judy D. Holmes, *Middle Tennessee State University*
Susan Hudgins, *East Central University*
Paramjit Kahai, *The University of Akron*
Betty Kleen, *Nicholls State University*
Kapil Ladha, *Drexel University*
Dr. Dick Larkin, *Central Washington University*
Robert Lawton, *Western Illinois University*
Diane Lending, *James Madison University*
Dr. Stan Lewis, *The University of Southern Mississippi*
Liping Liu, *The University of Akron*
Celia Romm Livermore, *Wayne State University*
Ronald Mashburn, *West Texas A&M University*
Richard McAndrew, *California Lutheran University*
Robert J. Mills, *Utah State University*

Luvai F. Motiwalla, *University of Massachusetts—Lowell*
Fawzi Noman, *Sam Houston State University*
Magnus Nystedt, *Francis Marion University*
Sandra O. Obilade, *Brescia University*
Denise Padavano, *Peirce College*
Dr. Richard G. Platt, *University of West Florida*
Ram Raghuraman, *Joliet Junior College*
Steve Rau, *Marquette University*
Randy Ryker, *Nicholls State University*
Dolly Samson, *Hawai'i Pacific University*
Matthew P. Schigur, *DeVry University—Milwaukee*
Morgan M. Shepherd, *University of Colorado at Colorado Springs*
John Smiley, *Penn State University—Abington*
Toni M. Somers, *Wayne State University*
Cheickna Sylla, *New Jersey Institute of Technology*
Nilmini Wickramasinghe, *Cleveland State University*
Jennifer Clark Williams, *University of Southern Indiana*
Mario Yanez, Jr., *University of Miami*
James E. Yao, *Montclair State University*
Vincent Yen, *Wright State University*

Our thanks also go to Robert Lawton of Western Illinois University for his contribution to the analysis exercises and Richard Perle of Loyola Marymount University for his MBA cases that so many instructors use in conjunction with this text.

Much credit should go to several individuals who played significant roles in this project. Thus, special thanks go to the editorial and production team at McGraw-Hill/Irwin: Scott Isenberg, executive editor; Trina Hauger, developmental editor; Sankha Basu, marketing manager; Bruce Gin, project manager; Lori Kramer, photo coordinator; and Cara David, designer. Their ideas and hard work were invaluable contributions to the successful completion of the project. The contributions of many authors, publishers, and firms in the computer industry that contributed case material, ideas, illustrations, and photographs used in this text are also thankfully acknowledged.

Acknowledging the Real World of Business

The unique contribution of the hundreds of business firms and other computer-using organizations that are the subjects of the Real World Cases, exercises, and examples in this text is gratefully acknowledged. The real-life situations faced by these firms and organizations provide readers of this text with valuable demonstrations of the benefits and limitations of using the Internet and other information technologies to enable electronic business and commerce, as well as enterprise communications and collaboration in support of the business processes, managerial decision making, and strategic advantage of the modern business enterprise.

James A. O'Brien
George M. Marakas

Assurance of Learning Ready

Many educational institutions today are focused on the notion of assurance of learning, an important element of some accreditation standards. *Introduction to Information Systems* is designed specifically to support your assurance of learning initiatives with a simple yet powerful solution.

Each test bank question for *Introduction to Information Systems* maps to a specific chapter learning outcome/objective listed in the text. You can use our test bank software, *EZ Test*, to query about learning outcomes/objectives that directly relate to the learning objectives for your course. You can then use the reporting features of *EZ Test* to aggregate student results in similar fashion, making the collection and presentation of assurance of learning data simple and easy.

AACSB Statement

McGraw-Hill Companies is a proud corporate member of AACSB International. Recognizing the importance and value of AACSB accreditation, the authors of *Introduction to Information Systems* 14e have sought to recognize the curricula guidelines detailed in AACSB standards for business accreditation by connecting selected questions in *Introduction to Information Systems* or its test bank with the general knowledge and skill guidelines found in the AACSB standards. It is important to note that the statements contained in *Introduction to Information Systems* 14e are provided only as a guide for the users of this text.

The statements contained in *Introduction to Information Systems* 14e are provided only as a guide for the users of this text. The AACSB leaves content coverage and assessment clearly within the realm and control of individual schools, the mission of the school, and the faculty. The AACSB charges schools with the obligation of doing assessment against their own content and learning goals. While *Introduction to Information Systems* 14e and its teaching package make no claim of any specific AACSB qualification or evaluation, we have, within *Introduction to Information Systems* 14e, labeled selected questions according to the six general knowledge and skills areas. The labels or tags within *Introduction to Information Systems* 14e are as indicated. There are of course, many more within the test bank, the text, and the teaching package, which might be used as a "standard" for your course. However, the labeled questions are suggested for your consideration.

Brief Contents

Module I Foundation Concepts

Module II Information Technologies

Module III Business Applications

Module IV Development Processes

Module V Management Challenges

Contents

Module I Foundation Concepts

Module II Information Technologies

Module III Business Applications

Module IV Development Processes

Chapter 10

Developing Business/ IT Solutions 373

Module V Management Challenges

INTRODUCTION TO INFORMATION SYSTEMS

MODULE I

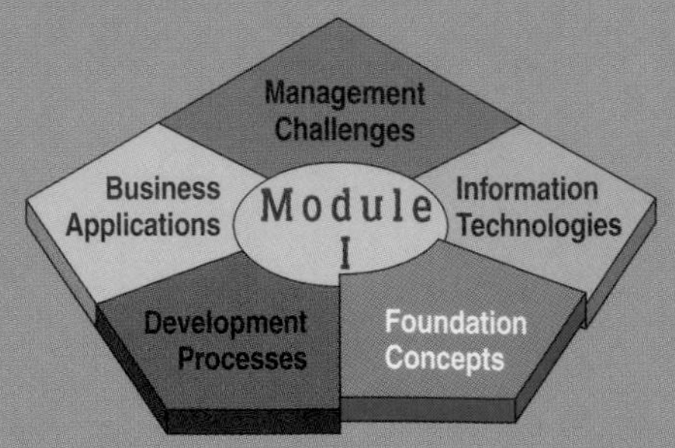

FOUNDATION CONCEPTS

Why study information systems? Why do businesses need information technology? What do you need to know about the use and management of information technologies in business? The introductory chapters of Module I are designed to answer these fundamental questions about the role of information systems in business.

- **Chapter 1: Foundations of Information Systems in Business** presents an overview of the five basic areas of information systems knowledge needed by business professionals, including the conceptual system components and major types of information systems. In addition, trends in information systems and an overview of the managerial challenges associated with information systems are presented.
- **Chapter 2: Competing with Information Technology** introduces fundamental concepts of competitive advantage through information technology and illustrates major strategic applications of information systems.

Completing these chapters will prepare you to move on to study chapters on information technologies (Module II), business applications (Module III), systems development processes (Module IV), and the management challenges of information systems (Module V).

CHAPTER 1

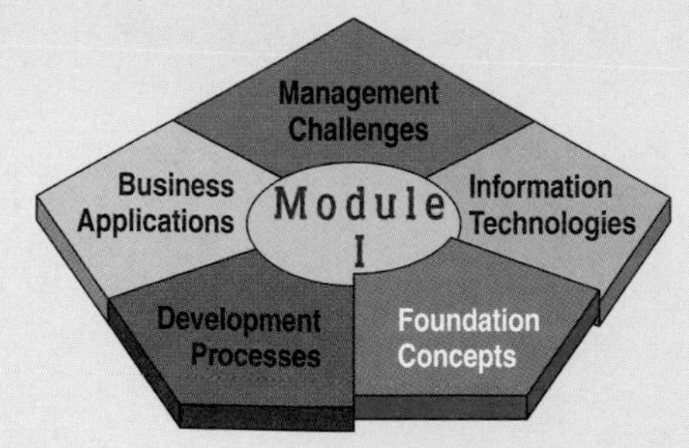

FOUNDATIONS OF INFORMATION SYSTEMS IN BUSINESS

Chapter Highlights

Section I
Foundation Concepts: Information Systems in Business

The Real World of Information Systems

Real World Case: Sew What? Inc.: The Role of Information Technology in Small Business Success

Information Technologies

What You Need to Know

The Fundamental Roles of IS in Business

Trends in Information Systems

The Role of e-Business in Business

Types of Information Systems

Managerial Challenges of Information Technology

Section II
Foundation Concepts: The Components of Information Systems

System Concepts: A Foundation

Real World Case: Autosystems: The Business Value of a Successful IT System for a Small Manufacturer

Components of an Information System

Information System Resources

Information System Activities

Recognizing Information Systems

Real World Case: Heidelberg, Honeywell, and Eaton: Using Information Technology to Build Smart Products and Services

Learning Objectives

After reading and studying this chapter, you should be able to:

1. Understand the concept of a system and how it relates to information systems.
2. Explain why knowledge of information systems is important for business professionals, and identify five areas of information systems knowledge they need.
3. Give examples to illustrate how the business applications of information systems can support a firm's business processes, managerial decision making, and strategies for competitive advantage.
4. Provide examples of several major types of information systems from your experiences with business organizations in the real world.
5. Identify several challenges that a business manager might face in managing the successful and ethical development and use of information technology in a business.
6. Provide examples of the components of real-world information systems. Illustrate that in an information system, people use hardware, software, data, and networks as resources to perform input, processing, output, storage, and control activities that transform data resources into information products.
7. Demonstrate familiarity with the myriad of career opportunities in information systems.

SECTION I Foundation Concepts: Information Systems in Business

Why study information systems and information technology? That's the same as asking why anyone should study accounting, finance, operations management, marketing, human resource management, or any other major business function. Information systems and technologies are vital components of successful businesses and organizations—some would say they are business imperatives. They thus constitute an essential field of study in business administration and management. That's why most business majors include a course in information systems. Since you probably intend to be a manager, entrepreneur, or business professional, it is just as important to have a basic understanding of information systems as it is to understand any other functional area in business.

Information technologies, including Internet-based information systems, are playing vital and expanding roles in business. Information technology can help all kinds of businesses improve the efficiency and effectiveness of their business processes, managerial decision making, and workgroup collaboration, which strengthens their competitive positions in rapidly changing marketplaces. This benefit occurs whether the information technology is used to support product development teams, customer support processes, electronic commerce transactions, or any other business activity. Information technologies and systems are, quite simply, a necessary ingredient for business success in today's dynamic global environment.

The Real World of Information Systems

Let's take a moment to bring the real world into our discussion of the importance of information systems (IS) and information technology (IT). See Figure 1.1, and read the Real World Case about using information technology to build smart products and services.

If we are to understand information systems and their functions, we first need to be clear on the concept of a system. In its simplest form, a system is a set of interrelated components, with a clearly defined boundary, working together to achieve a common set of objectives. Using this definition, it becomes easy to see that virtually everything you can think of is a system, and one system can be made up of other systems or be part of a bigger system. We will expand on this concept later in the next section, but for now, this definition gives us a good foundation for understanding the focus of this textbook: information systems.

What Is an Information System?

As we just did, we begin with a simple definition that we can expand upon later in the chapter. An **information system** (IS) can be any organized combination of people, hardware, software, communications networks, data resources, and policies and procedures that stores, retrieves, transforms, and disseminates information in an organization. People rely on modern information systems to communicate with one another using a variety of physical devices *(hardware)*, information processing instructions and procedures *(software)*, communications channels *(networks)*, and stored data *(data resources)*. Although today's information systems are typically thought of as having something to do with computers, we have been using information systems since the dawn of civilization. Even today we make regular use of information systems that have nothing to do with a computer. Consider some of the following examples of information systems:

- **Smoke signals for communication** were used as early as recorded history and can account for the human discovery of fire. The pattern of smoke transmitted valuable information to others who were too far to see or hear the sender.
- **Card catalogs in a library** are designed to store data about the books in an organized manner that allows readers to locate a particular book by its title, author name, subject, or a variety of other approaches.

REAL WORLD CASE 1 Sew What? Inc.: The Role of Information Technology in Small Business Success

What do Sting, Elton John, and Madonna have in common? Besides being international rock stars, they all use theatrical backdrops designed and manufactured by custom drapery maker Sew What? Inc. Based in Rancho Dominguez, California, Sew What? provides custom theatrical draperies and fabrics for stages, concerts, fashion shows, and special events worldwide and has become an industry leader in rock-and-roll staging.

Founded in 1992 by Australian-born Megan Duckett, Sew What? has grown from a tiny kitchen-and-garage operation to a multimillion dollar enterprise, thanks to Duckett's never-say-no approach to customer satisfaction. "When I see a problem, I just don't back down. I find a way to overcome it and I use everybody I know to help me," she says.

What made it possible for a one-woman business that started in a kitchen to evolve and grow into a multimillion dollar company with 35 employees? Megan Duckett attributes her success to hard work, quality workmanship—and information technology.

Sew What? has enjoyed explosive growth in recent years, reaching $4 million per year in sales by the end of 2006. Company president Duckett credits much of her firm's rapid growth to its ability to leverage information technology and the Internet to drive sales. "Before we put up our Web site, sewwhatinc.com, our business was almost all local," says Duckett. "But after launching the Web site three years ago, we now have clients all over the world. In fact, last year our revenue grew 45% on the previous year's sales, and this year we are on target to enjoy a 65% increase on 2005 sales. And nearly all that growth came from Web-driven sales."

FIGURE 1.1

Information technology is a vital component in the success of both large and small companies.

Although the company's Web site may take center stage, managing all the business the site brings in requires a lot of effort behind the scenes. In particular, Duckett relies on a solid IT infrastructure to help keep the company running smoothly. "We are a customer-centric company," notes Duckett. "It's critical that we have excellent back-office information technology to manage the business and deliver outstanding service to our customers."

Sew What? runs most of its business with Intuit's QuickBooks Enterprise Solutions Manufacturing and Wholesale Edition software and Microsoft's Windows Server operating system installed on a Dell PowerEdge 860 server, sporting an Intel Xeon processor and 146 gigabytes of disk storage. According to Duckett, "Running our business requires a lot of storage. In addition to customer information and vital operational and financial Quickbooks files, we need to store thousands of drapery and fabric image files, customer instruction document files, and other types of data." Sew What?'s additional computer support includes an older Dell PowerEdge 500 server dedicated to a few smaller applications and a variety of Dell desktop PC systems for employees.

Sew What? started in 1992 as a part-time endeavor, with Duckett cutting and sewing fabric on her kitchen table. She went full time in 1997 and incorporated in 1998. The important role technology plays in running a successful small business hit home when she lost a big contract. The potential client said that without a Web site, her company "lacked credibility."

"Before losing that contract, I thought, 'I run a sewing business, a cottage craft. I don't need a Web site'," she says. Duckett admits she was rather cocky, mainly because she had grown her business "quite well" by word of mouth alone. "I quickly learned the error of that thought process. You can't have that attitude and stick around," she acknowledges.

Losing the contract also coincided with a period of low growth between 2001 and 2002. That's when Duckett decided to embrace technology. Using Microsoft Publisher, she designed and built her own Web site. "You figure things out and learn how to do it yourself when budgets are thin," she admits.

Duckett kept working to improve the site and make it better for her customers. A year later, feeling that the site needed refreshing, she signed up for a 10-week course in Dreamweaver and again completely rebuilt the site. Yet another Web site reconstruction helped Sew What? grow into a company with customers around the world and a clientele list that includes international rock stars, Gucci, and *Rolling Stone* magazine.

In 2005, Duckett decided she needed to improve the site's navigation, because "I wanted it to be sleek and to provide a really good customer experience. That was beyond my abilities, so we hired a Web marketing consulting company to build a custom navigation system for the site."

She worked with the hired guns on branding, search engine optimization, overall design, and site layout. Duckett still provides all the content, including text and images. There's also a Spanish version of the site, and the professionals tuned up the main site's search features to include spelling variants for different English-speaking countries. For example, you can search for the American spelling of "theater" or the British and Australian "theatre."

The site also lets potential customers review all kinds of color swatches and teaches them how to calculate accurate measurements for their projects; the differences between a scrim, a tormentor, and a traveler curtain; the proper care and feeding of a variety of drape materials; and a lot more.

While perusing the Dell Web site one day, Duckett saw a news article about the Dell/NFIB Small Business Excellence Award. The National Federation of Independent Businesses (NFIB) and Dell Inc. present this annual prize to one small business in recognition of its innovative use of technology to improve its customers' experience. The winner receives $30,000 worth of Dell products and services, a lifetime membership to the NFIB, and a day at Dell's headquarters with Michael Dell and other senior executives.

"The description of the kinds of businesses they were looking for perfectly described Sew What?" Duckett realized. "Everything they were looking for, we'd done, so I decided to enter. My husband [and business partner] laughed and reminded me that I never win anything." Writing the essay for the contest caused Duckett to reflect on everything she and her employees had achieved over the years: "We got to sit back and feel really proud of ourselves. Just that process was enough to invigorate everyone in our weekly production meetings."

However, the contest judges also recognized Megan Duckett's passionate commitment to customer satisfaction and use of information technology for business success, so they awarded Sew What? the Small Business Excellence Award. Winning the award proved to be a very emotional experience. Looking at the caliber and achievements of the nine other finalists, Duckett figured Sew What? would remain just a top-ten finalist: "I could not believe that a big company like Dell—so entrepreneurial and advanced in every way—would look at our little company and recognize it."

Like other small business owners, Duckett puts an enormous amount of physical and emotional energy into her work. "Winning this award is so flattering on a personal level," she says. "This business is ingrained in every cell of my body, and to have someone saying, 'Good job,' well, in small business, nobody ever says that to you."

That may have been true previously, but Sew What?'s technology leadership and business success continue to earn recognition. In March 2007, the company received a Stevie Award for Women in Business for "most innovative company of the year" among those with up to 100 employees. A few months earlier, Sew What? had received a SMB 20 Award from *PC Magazine*, which honors 20 of the most technologically innovative small and medium-sized businesses (SMBs) each year. "Small and medium businesses drive today's economy. However, they often don't get the attention and recognition they deserve," said *PC Magazine*'s Editor-in-Chief, Jim Louderback. "We want to highlight the hard work, technological leadership and innovative spirit of thousands of SMB companies throughout the world."

Duckett plans to use her prize winnings to add a bar code system that can track the manufacturing process at the company's warehouse. In the drapery business, fabric is stored on a roll in the warehouse and then moves through different stages: receiving, cutting, sewing, shipping, and so forth. The scanning process will enable Duckett's team to track how long the fabric stays in any given stage. These data will give them a better idea of their costs, which then will help them produce more accurate price lists.

"We don't need to charge an hour and a half for labor if the cutting only takes an hour and 15 minutes," Duckett notes. Currently, the company uses a hand-written system of sign-in and sign-out sheets that she says takes too long and introduces too many errors. "The new system will also let us track the progress of individual orders," she promises. "We'll be able to provide better service by keeping the customer updated."

Source: Adapted from Lauren Simonds, "Pay Attention to the Woman Behind the Curtain," *Small Business Computing.com*, July 21, 2006, www.smallbusinesscomputing.com; Dell Inc., "Curtain Call," September 2006, www.dell.com; Alyson Mazzarelli, "Sew What? Recognized in PC Magazines SMB Awards," *PCmagazine.com*, October 17, 2006, www.pcmagazine.com; Chris Sandberg, "Sew What? Named Award Winner in Stevie Award for Women in Business," March 13, 2007; www.sewwhatinc.com.

CASE STUDY QUESTIONS

1. How do information technologies contribute to the business success of Sew What, Inc.? Give several examples from the case regarding the business value of information technology that demonstrate this conclusion.
2. If you were a management consultant to Sew What? Inc., what would you advise Megan Duckett to do at this point to be even more successful in her business? What role would information technology play in your proposals? Provide several specific recommendations.
3. How could the use of information technology help a small business you know be more successful? Provide several examples to support your answer.

REAL WORLD ACTIVITIES

1. Search the Internet to help you evaluate the business performance of Sew What? Inc. and its competitors at the present time. What conclusions can you draw from your research about Sew What?'s prospects for the future? Report your findings and recommendations for Sew What?'s continued business success to the class.
2. Small businesses have been slower to integrate information technology into their operations than larger companies. Break into small groups with your classmates to discuss the reasons for this state of affairs, identifying several possible IT solutions and their business benefits that could help small businesses be more successful.

- **Your book bag,** day planner, notebooks, and file folders are all part of an information system designed to assist you in organizing the inputs provided to you via handouts, lectures, presentations, and discussions. They also help you process these inputs into useful outputs: homework and good exam grades.
- **The cash register at your favorite fast-food restaurant** is part of a large information system that tracks the products sold, the time of a sale, inventory levels, and the amount of money in the cash drawer; it also contributes to the analysis of product sales in any combinations of locations anywhere in the world.

We will explore many more examples and types of information systems throughout this text. Suffice it to say that we are surrounded by information systems, and because of their importance in our everyday lives, we need to develop a clear understanding and appreciation of them.

Information Technologies

Business professionals rely on a variety of information systems that use various **information technologies** (ITs). Although the terms *information system* and *information technology* are sometimes used interchangeably, they are two distinct concepts. As defined previously, the term information system describes all of the components and resources necessary to deliver information and functions to the organization. In contrast, the term information technology refers to the various hardware, software, networking, and data management components necessary for the system to operate. In theory, an information system could use simple hardware components such as a pencil and paper or file folders to capture and store data. For our purposes however, we will concentrate on **computer-based information systems** and their use of the following information technologies:

- **Computer hardware technologies,** including microcomputers, midsize servers, and large mainframe systems, as well as the input, output, and storage devices that support them.
- **Computer software technologies,** including operating system software, Web browsers, software productivity suites, software drivers, database management systems, software for business applications like customer relationship management and supply chain management, and other software-based components and modules.
- **Telecommunications network technologies,** including the telecommunications media, processors, and software needed to provide wire-based and wireless access and support for the Internet and private Internet-based networks such as intranets and extranets.
- **Data resource management technologies,** including database management system software for the development, access, and maintenance of the databases of an organization.

What You Need to Know

> *There is no longer any distinction between an IT project and a business initiative. IT at Marriott is a key component of the products and services that we provide to our customers and guests at our properties. As such, there's very little that goes on within the company that either I personally or one of my top executives is not involved in* [7].

Those are the words of Carl Wilson, executive vice president and CIO of the Marriott International chain of hotels. Employees at all levels of business, including top executives and managers, must learn how to apply information systems and technologies to their unique business situations. In fact, business firms depend on all of their managers and employees to help them apply and manage their use of information technologies. So the important question for any business professional or manager is: What do you need to know to help manage the hardware, software, data, and network resources of your business so they are used for the strategic success of your company?

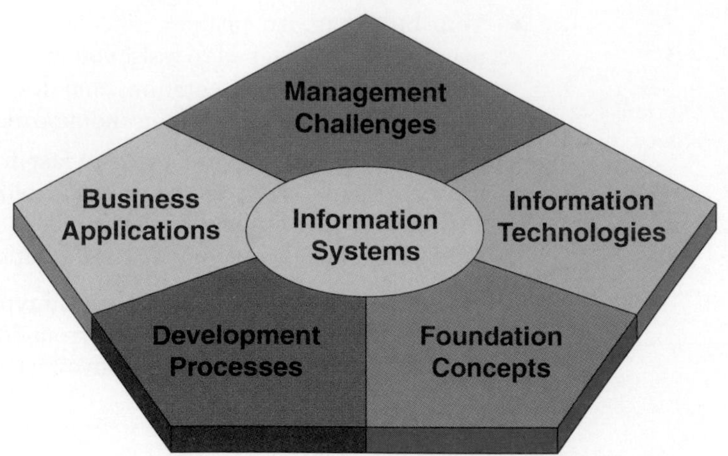

FIGURE 1.2
This framework outlines the major areas of information systems knowledge needed by business professionals.

An IS Knowledge Framework for Business Professionals

The field of information systems encompasses many complex technologies, abstract behavioral concepts, and specialized applications in countless business and non-business areas. As a manager or business professional, you do not have to absorb all of this knowledge. Figure 1.2 illustrates a useful conceptual framework that organizes the knowledge presented in this text and outlines areas of knowledge you need about information systems. It emphasizes that you should concentrate your efforts in the following five areas of IS knowledge:

- **Foundation Concepts.** Fundamental behavioral, technical, business, and managerial concepts about the components and roles of information systems. Examples include basic information system concepts derived from general systems theory or competitive strategy concepts used to develop business applications of information technology for competitive advantage. Chapters 1 and 2 and other chapters of the text support this area of IS knowledge.
- **Information Technologies.** Major concepts, developments, and management issues in information technology—that is, hardware, software, networks, data management, and many Internet-based technologies. Chapters 3 and 4 provide an overview of computer hardware and software technologies, and Chapters 5 and 6 cover key data resource management and telecommunications network technologies for business.
- **Business Applications.** The major uses of information systems for the operations, management, and competitive advantage of a business. Chapter 7 covers applications of information technology in functional areas of business such as marketing, manufacturing, and accounting. Chapter 8 focuses on electronic commerce applications that most companies use to buy and sell products on the Internet, and Chapter 9 covers the use of information systems and technologies to support decision making in business.
- **Development Processes.** How business professionals and information specialists plan, develop, and implement information systems to meet business opportunities. Several developmental methodologies are explored in Chapter 10, including the systems development life cycle and prototyping approaches to business application development.
- **Management Challenges.** The challenges of effectively and ethically managing information technology at the end-user, enterprise, and global levels of a business. Chapter 11 focuses on security challenges and security management issues in the use of information technology, whereas Chapter 12 covers some of the key methods business managers can use to manage the information systems function in a company with global business operations.

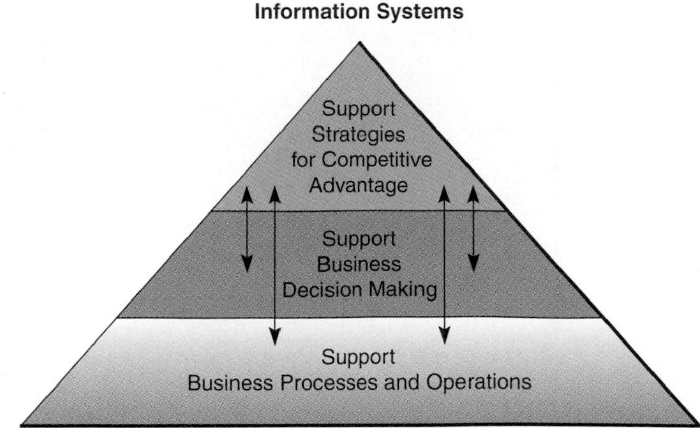

FIGURE 1.3
The three fundamental roles of the business applications of information systems. Information systems provide an organization with support for business processes and operations, decision making, and competitive advantage.

The Fundamental Roles of IS in Business

There are three fundamental reasons for all business applications of information technology. They are found in the three vital roles that information systems can perform for a business enterprise:

- Support of business processes and operations.
- Support of decision making by employees and managers.
- Support of strategies for competitive advantage.

Figure 1.3 illustrates how the fundamental roles interact in a typical organization. At any moment, information systems designed to support business processes and operations may also be providing data to, or accepting data from, systems focused on business decision making or achieving competitive advantage. The same is true for the other two fundamental roles of IS. Today's organizations constantly are striving to achieve integration of their systems to allow information to flow freely through them, which adds even greater flexibility and business support than any of the individual system roles could provide.

Let's look at a typical retail store as a good example of how these **roles of IS in business** can be implemented.

The Fundamental Roles of IS in Business: Examples

Support of Business Processes and Operations. As a consumer, you regularly encounter information systems that support the business processes and operations at the many retail stores where you shop. For example, most retail stores now use computer-based information systems to help their employees record customer purchases, keep track of inventory, pay employees, buy new merchandise, and evaluate sales trends. Store operations would grind to a halt without the support of such information systems.

Support of Business Decision Making. Information systems also help store managers and other business professionals make better decisions. For example, decisions about what lines of merchandise need to be added or discontinued and what kind of investments they require are typically made after an analysis provided by computer-based information systems. This function not only supports the decision making of store managers, buyers, and others but also helps them look for ways to gain an advantage over other retailers in the competition for customers.

Support of Strategies for Competitive Advantage. Gaining a strategic advantage over competitors requires the innovative application of information technologies. For example, store management might make a decision to install touchscreen kiosks in all stores, with links to the e-commerce Web site for online shopping. This offering might attract new customers and build customer loyalty because of the ease of shopping and buying merchandise provided by such information systems. Thus, strategic information systems can help provide products and services that give a business a comparative advantage over its competitors.

Information Technology Keeps the Boston Red Sox in the Game

An information storage system from EMC Corp. is scoring big points with the Boston Red Sox. The team is using high-density storage technologies to store several years of play footage and thus gain an edge in the highly competitive world of professional baseball.

"You may say, 'What is a baseball team doing with EMC?' but we have an ownership group and a baseball and business operation that's very committed to gaining a competitive advantage in the marketplace," notes Theo Epstein, Red Sox general manager. He believes that information is key to maintaining a competitive edge. Epstein points out that the Red Sox essentially are in competition with 29 other organizations to make better player decisions that revolve around access to and the use of information in their decision-making process.

"So, when I'm sitting at my desk and need to make a decision about a player, I need at my fingertips scouting reports, stats, medical information and contract information," says Epstein.

Epstein adds that he only has to be right 51% of the time in baseball— "You can use that information to get the smallest advantage, and in the end, you'll have a real competitive edge."

Steve Conley, the director of IT for the Red Sox, describes the organization's two large storage arrays: one used for services, including online editing of video for broadcast and news media, statistical archives, and a digital video system for home games, and another for the team's road games, which stores video of almost every at bat. This video is usually viewed before a series with a rival team to determine how they're going to pitch to someone, how often they bunt, and where they position their fielders.

Manny Ramirez, a star player for the Red Sox, is often seen sitting in front of the computer, watching game footage stored on the EMC technology.

"There's many times I'll go up to a plate and hit the first pitch. . . . I study the video very hard, and there's a lot of times where I can break the game wide open because I'm very prepared against the opposing pitcher," Ramirez says.

EMC's storage management software also has helped designated hitter David Ortiz improve his batting average, claims Epstein.

"He has the best progression of performance from his first to third at bat against the same pitcher. He's the best hitter in the league, third time around with the same pitcher in the same game, because of his ability to study and make adjustments," Epstein notes.

The IT director Conley argues that success by the team depends on mining and using data and video and that EMC storage helps deliver that information quickly, efficiently, and securely.

In addition to improving player's performances, an additional benefit is that it saves time, according to Epstein.

"That's key because those minutes and hours used up making phone calls, going back and getting files, waiting for an express package—that's time that could be used on the next decision, on gaining the next competitive advantage," he says. [11]

Trends in Information Systems

The business applications of information systems have expanded significantly over the years. Figure 1.4 summarizes these changes.

Until the 1960s, the role of most information systems was simple: transaction processing, record keeping, accounting, and other *electronic data processing* (EDP) applications. Then another role was added, namely, the processing of all these data into useful, informative reports. The concept of *management information systems* (MIS) thus was born. This new role focused on developing business applications that provided managerial end users with predefined management reports that would give managers the information they needed for decision-making purposes.

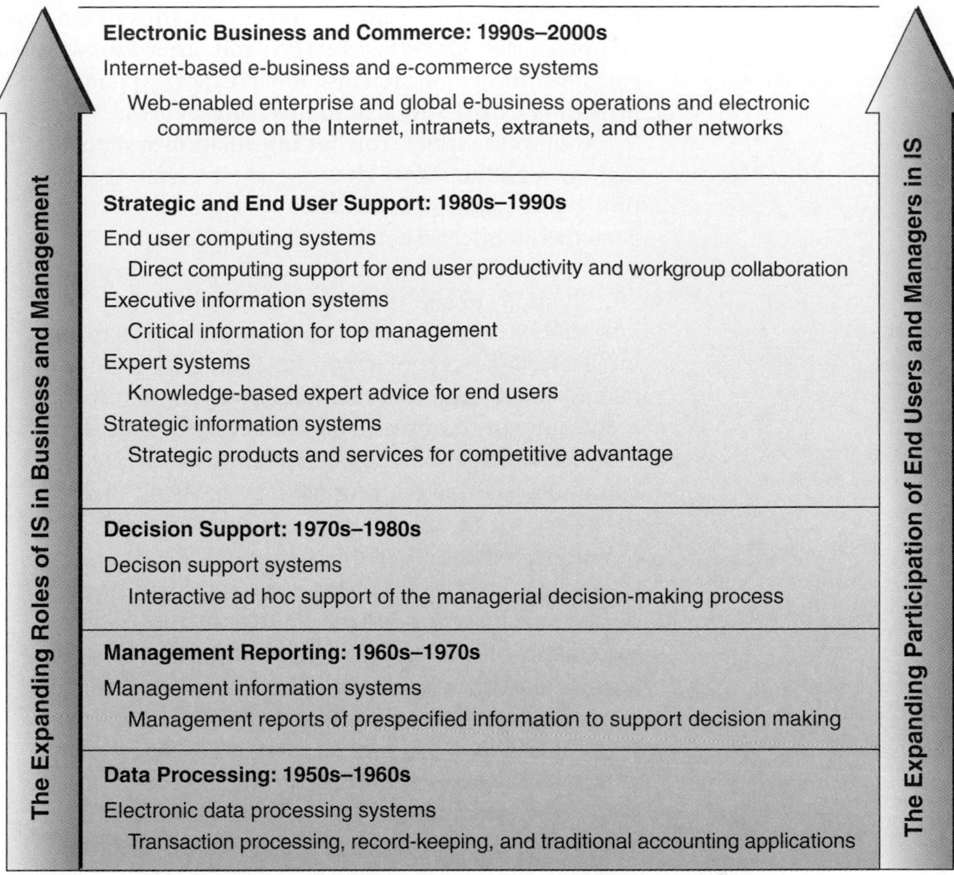

Electronic Business and Commerce: 1990s–2000s
Internet-based e-business and e-commerce systems
Web-enabled enterprise and global e-business operations and electronic commerce on the Internet, intranets, extranets, and other networks
Strategic and End User Support: 1980s–1990s
End user computing systems
Direct computing support for end user productivity and workgroup collaboration
Executive information systems
Critical information for top management
Expert systems
Knowledge-based expert advice for end users
Strategic information systems
Strategic products and services for competitive advantage
Decision Support: 1970s–1980s
Decison support systems
Interactive ad hoc support of the managerial decision-making process
Management Reporting: 1960s–1970s
Management information systems
Management reports of prespecified information to support decision making
Data Processing: 1950s–1960s
Electronic data processing systems
Transaction processing, record-keeping, and traditional accounting applications
The Expanding Roles of IS in Business and Management
The Expanding Participation of End Users and Managers in IS

FIGURE 1.4
The expanding roles of the business applications of information systems. Note how the roles of computer-based information systems have expanded over time. Also, note the impact of these changes on the end users and managers of an organization.

By the 1970s, it was evident that the prespecified information products produced by such management information systems were not meeting the decision-making needs of management adequately. So the concept of *decision support systems* (DSS) was born. The new role for information systems was to provide managerial end users with ad hoc, interactive support of their decision-making processes. This support would be tailored to the unique decisions, and decision-making styles, of managers as they confronted specific types of problems in the real world.

In the 1980s, several new roles for information systems appeared. First, the rapid development of microcomputer processing power, application software packages, and telecommunications networks gave birth to the phenomenon of *end-user computing*. End users could now use their own computing resources to support their job requirements instead of waiting for the indirect support of centralized corporate information services departments.

Second, it became evident that most top corporate executives did not directly use either the reports of management information systems or the analytical modeling capabilities of decision support systems, so the concept of *executive information systems* (EIS) developed. These information systems were created to give top executives an easy way to get the critical information they wanted, when they wanted it, and tailored to the formats they preferred.

Third, breakthroughs occurred in the development and application of artificial intelligence (AI) techniques to business information systems. Today's systems include intelligent software agents that can be programmed and deployed inside a system to act on behalf of their owner, system functions that can adapt themselves on the basis of the immediate needs of the user, virtual reality applications, advanced robotics, natural language processing, and a variety of applications for which artificial intelligence can replace the need for human intervention, thus freeing up knowledge workers for more complex tasks. *Expert systems* (ES) and other *knowledge-based systems* also forged a new role for information systems. Today, expert systems can serve as consultants to users by providing expert advice in limited subject areas.

An important new role for information systems appeared in the 1980s and continued through the 1990s: the concept of a strategic role for information systems, sometimes called *strategic information systems* (SIS). In this concept, information technology becomes an integral component of business processes, products, and services that help a company gain a competitive advantage in the global marketplace.

The mid- to late 1990s saw the revolutionary emergence of *enterprise resource planning* (ERP) systems. This organization-specific form of a strategic information system integrates all facets of a firm, including its planning, manufacturing, sales, resource management, customer relations, inventory control, order tracking, financial management, human resources, and marketing—virtually every business function. The primary advantage of these ERP systems lies in their common interface for all computer-based organizational functions and their tight integration and data sharing, necessary for flexible strategic decision making. We explore ERP and its associated functions in greater detail in Chapter 7.

Finally, the rapid growth of the Internet, intranets, extranets, and other interconnected global networks in the 1990s dramatically changed the capabilities of information systems in business at the beginning of the 21st century. Internet-based and Web-enabled enterprises and global electronic business and commerce systems are becoming commonplace in the operations and management of today's business enterprises.

A closer look at Figure 1.4 suggests that though we have expanded our abilities with regard to using information systems for conducting business, today's information systems are still doing the same basic things that they began doing more than 40 years ago. We still need to process transactions, keep records, provide management with useful and informative reports, and support the foundational accounting systems and processes of the organization. What has changed, however, is that we now enjoy a much higher level of integration of system functions across applications, greater connectivity across both similar and dissimilar system components, and the ability to reallocate critical computing tasks such as data storage, processing, and presentation to take maximum advantage of business and strategic opportunities. Because of these increased capabilities, the systems of tomorrow will be focused on increasing both the speed and reach of our systems to provide even tighter integration, combined with greater flexibility.

The Role of e-Business in Business

The Internet and related technologies and applications have changed the ways businesses operate and people work, as well as how information systems support business processes, decision making, and competitive advantage. Thus, many businesses today are using Internet technologies to Web-enable their business processes and create innovative **e-business applications**. See Figure 1.5.

In this text, we define **e-business** as the use of Internet technologies to work and empower business processes, electronic commerce, and enterprise collaboration within a company and with its customers, suppliers, and other business stakeholders. In essence, e-business can be more generally considered an *online exchange of value*. Any online exchange of information, money, resources, services, or any combination thereof falls under the e-business umbrella. The Internet and Internet-like networks—those inside the enterprise (**intranet**) and between an enterprise and its trading partners (**extranet**)—have become the primary information technology infrastructure that supports the e-business applications of many companies. These companies rely on e-business applications to (1) reengineer internal business processes, (2) implement electronic commerce systems with their customers and suppliers, and (3) promote enterprise collaboration among business teams and workgroups.

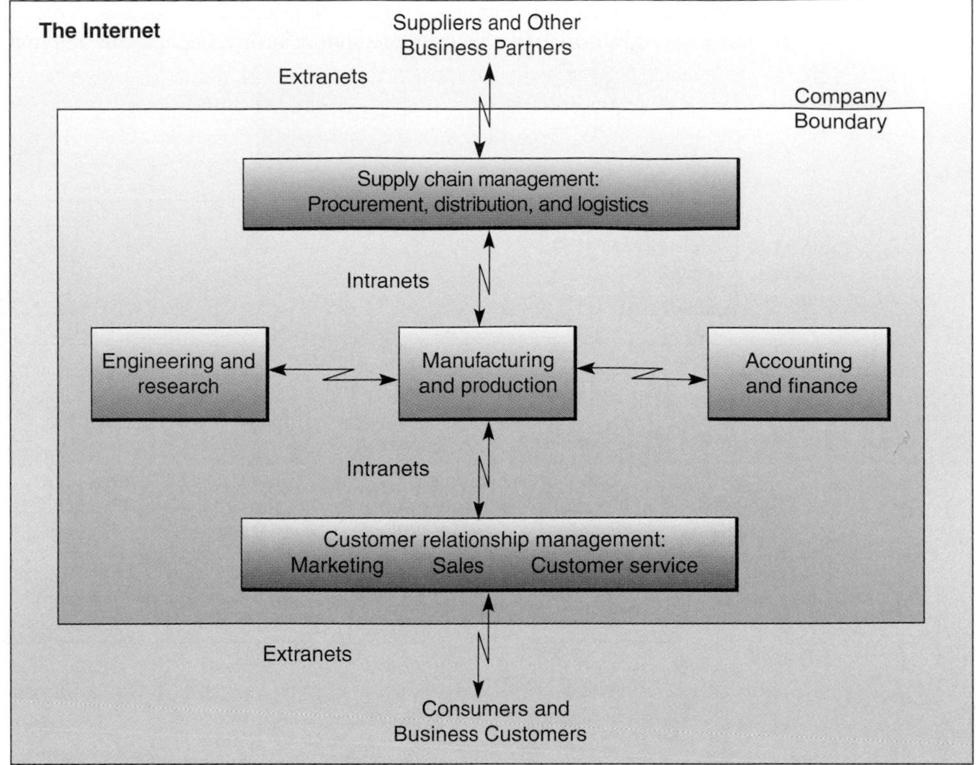

FIGURE 1.5
Businesses today depend on the Internet, intranets, and extranets to implement and manage innovative e-business applications.

Enterprise collaboration systems involve the use of software tools to support communication, coordination, and collaboration among the members of networked teams and workgroups. A business may use intranets, the Internet, extranets, and other networks to implement such systems. For example, employees and external consultants may form a *virtual team* that uses a corporate intranet and the Internet for electronic mail, videoconferencing, electronic discussion groups, and Web pages of work-in-progress information to collaborate on business projects.

Electronic commerce is the buying, selling, marketing, and servicing of products, services, and information over a variety of computer networks. Many businesses now use the Internet, intranets, extranets, and other networks to support every step of the commercial process, including everything from advertising, sales, and customer support on the World Wide Web to Internet security and payment mechanisms that ensure completion of delivery and payment processes. For example, electronic commerce systems include Internet Web sites for online sales, extranet access to inventory databases by large customers, and the use of corporate intranets by sales reps to access customer records for customer relationship management.

Types of Information Systems

Conceptually, the applications of information systems that are implemented in today's business world can be classified in several different ways. For example, several **types of information systems** can be classified as either operations or management information systems. Figure 1.6 illustrates this conceptual classification of information systems applications. Information systems are categorized this way to spotlight the major roles each plays in the operations and management of a business. Let's look briefly at some examples of such information systems categories.

Operations Support Systems

Information systems have always been needed to process data generated by, and used in, business operations. Such **operations support systems** produce a variety of information products for internal and external use. However, they do not emphasize the

FIGURE 1.6 Operations and management classifications of information systems. Note how this conceptual overview emphasizes the main purposes of information systems that support business operations and managerial decision making.

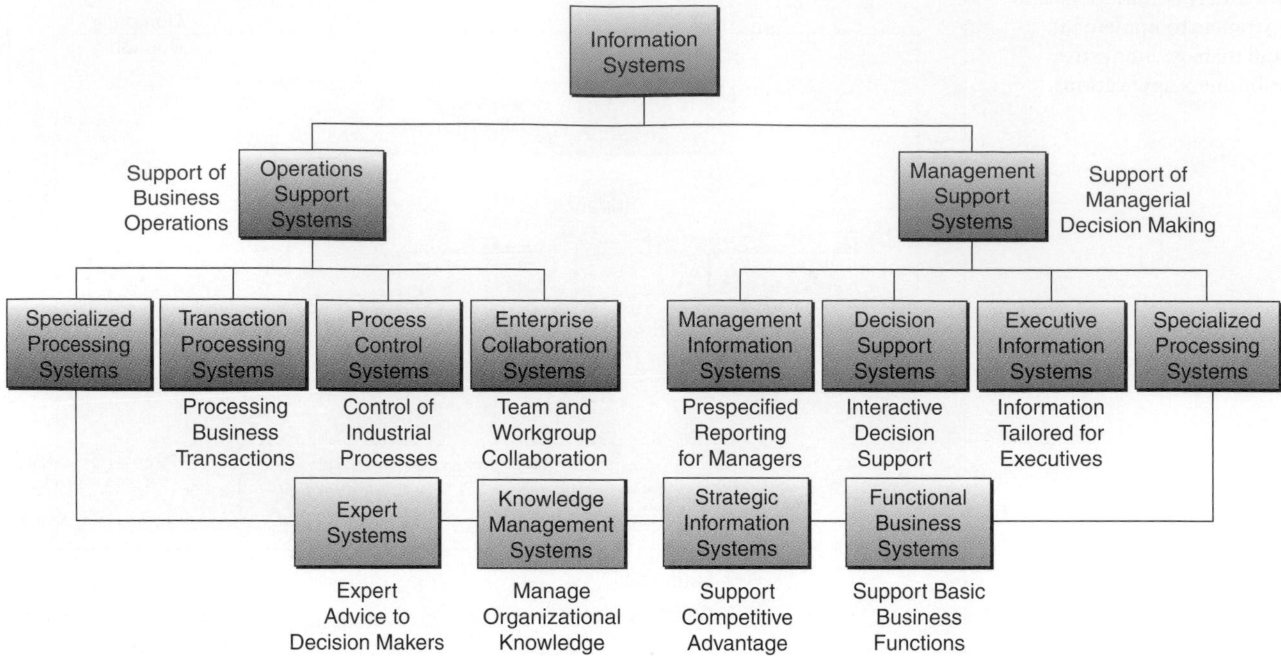

specific information products that can best be used by managers. Further processing by management information systems is usually required. The role of a business firm's operations support systems is to efficiently process business transactions, control industrial processes, support enterprise communications and collaborations, and update corporate databases. See Figure 1.7.

Transaction processing systems are important examples of operations support systems that record and process the data resulting from business transactions. They process transactions in two basic ways. In *batch processing*, transactions data are accumulated over a period of time and processed periodically. In *real-time* (or *online*) processing, data are processed immediately after a transaction occurs. For example, point-of-sale (POS) systems at many retail stores use electronic cash register terminals to electronically capture and transmit sales data over telecommunications links to regional computer centers for immediate (real-time) or nightly (batch) processing. Figure 1.8 is an example of software that automates accounting transaction processing.

FIGURE 1.7 A summary of operations support systems with examples.

Operations Support Systems
• **Transaction processing systems.** Process data resulting from business transactions, update operational databases, and produce business documents. Examples: sales and inventory processing and accounting systems.
• **Process control systems.** Monitor and control industrial processes. Examples: petroleum refining, power generation, and steel production systems.
• **Enterprise collaboration systems.** Support team, workgroup, and enterprise communications and collaborations. Examples: e-mail, chat, and videoconferencing groupware systems.

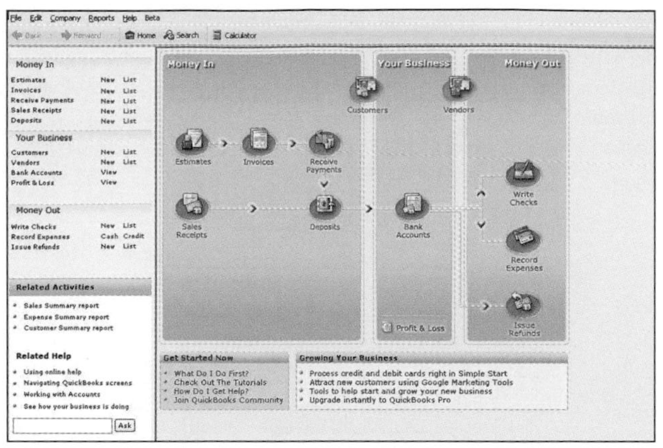

FIGURE 1.8
QuickBooks is a popular accounting package that automates small business accounting transaction processing while providing business owners with management reports.

Process control systems monitor and control physical processes. For example, a petroleum refinery uses electronic sensors linked to computers to continually monitor chemical processes and make instant (real-time) adjustments that control the refinery process. **Enterprise collaboration systems** enhance team and workgroup communications and productivity and include applications that are sometimes called *office automation systems*. For example, knowledge workers in a project team may use electronic mail to send and receive electronic messages or use videoconferencing to hold electronic meetings to coordinate their activities.

Management Support Systems

When information system applications focus on providing information and support for effective decision making by managers, they are called **management support systems**. Providing information and support for decision making by all types of managers and business professionals is a complex task. Conceptually, several major types of information systems support a variety of decision-making responsibilities: (1) management information systems, (2) decision support systems, and (3) executive information systems. See Figure 1.9.

Management information systems (MIS) provide information in the form of reports and displays to managers and many business professionals. For example, sales managers may use their networked computers and Web browsers to receive instantaneous displays about the sales results of their products and access their corporate intranet for daily sales analysis reports that evaluate sales made by each salesperson. **Decision support systems** (DSS) give direct computer support to managers during the decision-making process. For example, an advertising manager may use a DSS to perform a what-if analysis as part of the decision to determine how to spend advertising dollars. A production manager may use a DSS to decide

FIGURE 1.9 A summary of management support systems with examples.

Management Support Systems
• **Management information systems.** Provide information in the form of prespecified reports and displays to support business decision making. Examples: sales analysis, production performance, and cost trend reporting systems.
• **Decision support systems.** Provide interactive ad hoc support for the decision-making processes of managers and other business professionals. Examples: product pricing, profitability forecasting, and risk analysis systems.
• **Executive information systems.** Provide critical information from MIS, DSS, and other sources tailored to the information needs of executives. Examples: systems for easy access to analyses of business performance, actions of competitors, and economic developments to support strategic planning.

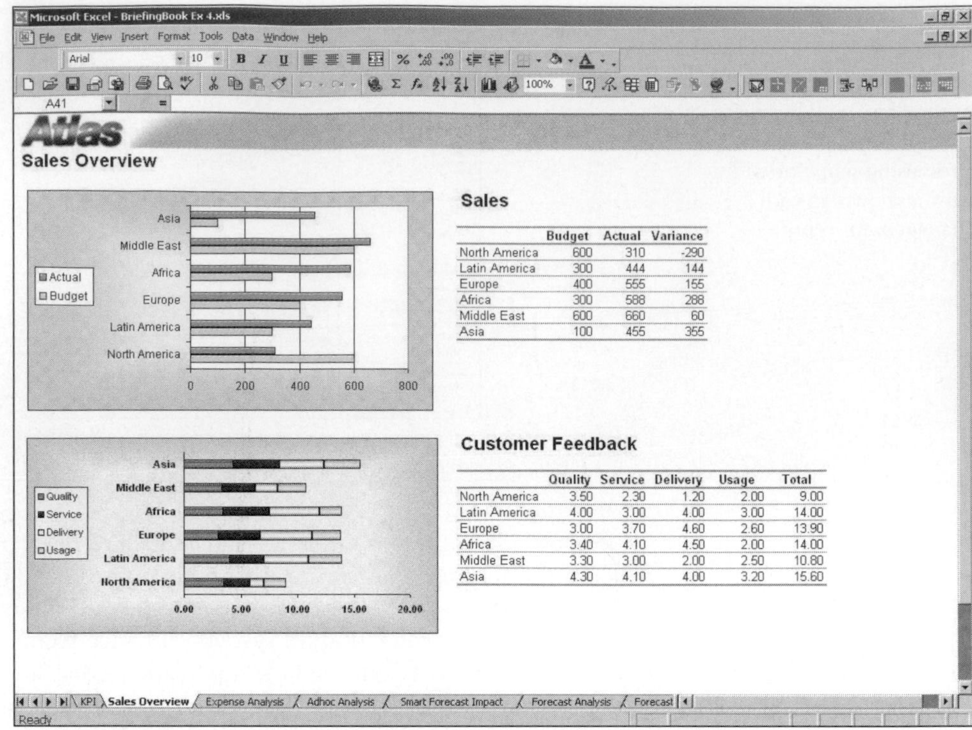

FIGURE 1.10
Management information systems provide information to business professionals in a variety of easy-to-use formats.

how much product to manufacture, based on the expected sales associated with a future promotion and the location and availability of the raw materials necessary to manufacture the product. **Executive information systems** (EIS) provide critical information from a wide variety of internal and external sources in easy-to-use displays to executives and managers. For example, top executives may use touchscreen terminals to instantly view text and graphics displays that highlight key areas of organizational and competitive performance. Figure 1.10 is an example of an MIS report display.

Other Classifications of Information Systems

Several other categories of information systems can support either operations or management applications. For example, **expert systems** can provide expert advice for operational chores like equipment diagnostics or managerial decisions such as loan portfolio management. **Knowledge management systems** are knowledge-based information systems that support the creation, organization, and dissemination of business knowledge to employees and managers throughout a company. Information systems that focus on operational and managerial applications in support of basic business functions such as accounting or marketing are known as **functional business systems**. Finally, **strategic information systems** apply information technology to a firm's products, services, or business processes to help it gain a strategic advantage over its competitors. See Figure 1.11.

It is also important to realize that business applications of information systems in the real world are typically integrated combinations of the several types of information systems just mentioned. That's because conceptual classifications of information systems are designed to emphasize the many different roles of information systems. In practice, these roles are combined into integrated or **cross-functional informational systems** that provide a variety of functions. Thus, most information systems are designed to produce information and support decision making for various levels of management and business functions, as well as perform record-keeping and transaction processing

FIGURE 1.11 A summary of other categories of information systems with examples.

Other Categories of Information Systems

- **Expert systems.** Knowledge-based systems that provide expert advice and act as expert consultants to users. Examples: credit application advisor, process monitor, and diagnostic maintenance systems.
- **Knowledge management systems.** Knowledge-based systems that support the creation, organization, and dissemination of business knowledge within the enterprise. Examples: intranet access to best business practices, sales proposal strategies, and customer problem resolution systems.
- **Strategic information systems.** Support operations or management processes that provide a firm with strategic products, services, and capabilities for competitive advantage. Examples: online stock trading, shipment tracking, and e-commerce Web systems.
- **Functional business systems.** Support a variety of operational and managerial applications of the basic business functions of a company. Examples: information systems that support applications in accounting, finance, marketing, operations management, and human resource management.

chores. Whenever you analyze an information system, you probably see that it provides information for a variety of managerial levels and business functions.

Managerial Challenges of Information Technology

Figure 1.12 illustrates the scope of the challenges and opportunities facing business managers and professionals in effectively managing information systems and technologies. Success in today's dynamic business environment depends heavily on maximizing the use of Internet-based technologies and Web-enabled information systems to meet the competitive requirements of customers, suppliers, and other business partners in a global marketplace. Figure 1.12 also emphasizes that information systems and their technologies must be managed to support the business strategies, business processes, and organizational structures and culture of a business enterprise. That's because computer-based information systems, though heavily dependent on information technologies, are designed, operated, and used by people in a variety of organizational settings and business environments. The goal of many companies today is to maximize their customer and business value by using information technology to support their employees in implementing cooperative business processes with customers, suppliers, and others.

FIGURE 1.12 Examples of the challenges and opportunities that business managers face in managing information systems and technologies to meet business goals.

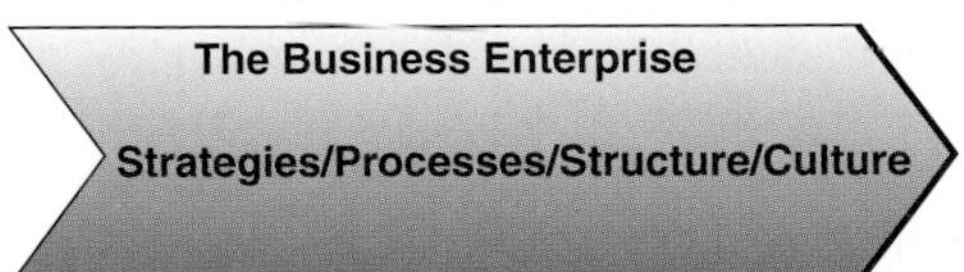

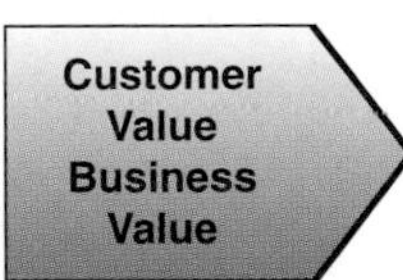

Business / IT Challenges

- Speed and flexibility requirements of product development, manufacturing, and delivery cycles.
- Reengineering and cross-functional integration of business processes using Internet technologies.
- Integration of e-business and e-commerce into the organization's strategies, processes, structure, and culture.

Business / IT Developments

- Use of the Internet, intranets, extranets, and the Web as the primary IT infrastructure.
- Diffusion of Web technology to internetwork employees, customers, and suppliers.
- Global networked computing, collaboration, and decision support systems.

Business / IT Goals

- Give customers what they want, when and how they want it, at the lowest cost.
- Coordination of manufacturing and business processes with suppliers and customers.
- Marketing channel partnerships with suppliers and distributors.

Success and Failure with IT

By now you should be able to see that the success of an information system should not be measured only by its *efficiency* in terms of minimizing costs, time, and the use of information resources. Success should also be measured by the *effectiveness* of the information technology in supporting an organization's business strategies, enabling its business processes, enhancing its organizational structures and culture, and increasing the customer and business value of the enterprise.

It is important to realize, however, that information technology and information systems can be mismanaged and misapplied in such a way that IS performance problems create both technological and business failures. Let's look at an example of how information technology contributed to business failure and success at a major corporation.

Hershey Foods: Failure and Success with IT

During the late 1990s, it was common to hear about major problems being faced by companies deploying enterprise resource planning (ERP) software.[1] Such deployments were both complex and extremely time consuming and often resulted in large productivity and resource losses early in the implementation—an outcome exactly the opposite of its goal. In 1999, Hershey Foods Corporation (www.hersheys.com) ran into many of the problems common to ERP deployments when it deployed SAP[2] AG's ERP software, along with several other mission-critical business applications. Despite this early failure however, the candy maker ultimately tasted sweet success with a major upgrade to the Web-enabled version of SAP's ERP software in 2002.

The Hershey, Pennsylvania, candy manufacturer lost a gamble in 1999 when it decided to install an ambitious number of SAP AG's R/3 ERP applications simultaneously with supporting software applications from two other software vendors. This decision was clearly risky, but the company dramatically increased its risk by targeting the completion of this daunting task for July 1999—one of its busiest times of the year. During this period each year, retailers begin ordering large amounts of candy for sales during their back-to-school days and Halloween. What was originally envisioned as a four-year project was rushed to completion in just 30 months in an effort to begin reaping the benefits of the new system as soon as possible. Industry sources and analysts generally classified Hershey's decision as a bad one and the initial project a failure.

However, Hershey finally realized success. It worked out the problems with the original deployment and pursued an upgrade of the ERP system to a new R/3 version in July 2001. By May 2002, the upgrade was completed at a cost 20 percent under budget and without any of the order-processing and product-shipment disruptions that marred the initial $112 million rollout in 1999.

More than 30 major improvements to its core business processes occurred within 60 days of going live with the system upgrade. Enhancements such as automated pick-list processing and materials management invoice verification, as well as credit processing for distributors to military customers, yielded measurable time and cost savings for Hershey. While greatly reducing product processing time, Hershey achieved nearly 100 percent quality in its production environment. Using the integrated business analysis tools in its ERP, Hershey has been able to effectively measure the impact of various sales and marketing programs as they happen. Despite its early failures, Hershey attributes its ultimate success to strong program management and executive leadership, diligent planning, and the development and implementation of an extensive testing and training plan. As they say, "Success is sweet" [8, 10].

[1]Recall that ERP stands for *enterprise resource planning*. This type of information system allows an organization to perform essentially all of its business functions by using a common interface, common data, and total connectivity across functions. We focus more on ERP in Chapter 7.

[2]SAP is a German company specializing in the development of ERP software.

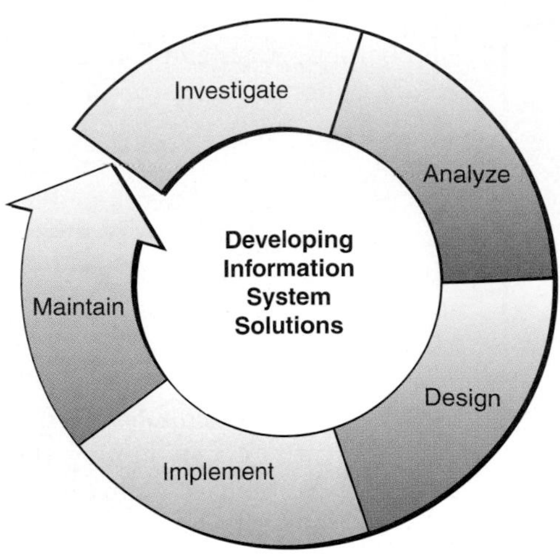

FIGURE 1.13
Developing information systems solutions to business problems can be implemented and managed as a multistep process or cycle.

Developing IS Solutions

Developing successful information system solutions to business problems is a major challenge for business managers and professionals today. As a business professional, you will be responsible for proposing or developing new or improved uses of information technologies for your company. As a business manager, you will frequently manage the development efforts of information systems specialists and other business end users.

Most computer-based information systems are conceived, designed, and implemented using some form of systematic development process. Figure 1.13 shows that several major activities must be accomplished and managed in a complete IS development cycle. In this development process, end users and information specialists *design* information system applications on the basis of an *analysis* of the business requirements of an organization. Examples of other activities include *investigating* the economic or technical feasibility of a proposed application, acquiring and learning how to use any software necessary to *implement* the new system, and making improvements to *maintain* the business value of a system.

We discuss the details of the information systems development process in Chapter 10. Many of the business and managerial challenges that arise in developing and implementing new uses of information technology will be explored in Chapter 12. Now let's look at an example of the challenges faced and overcome by a project team that developed and installed a major new information system application. This example emphasizes how important good systems development practices are to a business.

Frito-Lay: Challenges and Solutions in Systems Development

A few years ago, Frito-Lay created national sales teams to focus on top customers such as supermarket chains. But the teams, accustomed to working regionally, found nationwide collaboration difficult. Although Frito-Lay had rich stores of market research and other pertinent customer information housed in databases at its headquarters, there was no easy way for team members to find what they needed.

So Mike Marino, Frito-Lay's vice president for category and customer development, formed an IT portal development project team to develop a Web-based solution in cooperation with Frito-Lay's national supermarket sales team, because it had the most centralized and demanding customers. "We knew if we could deliver to those salespeople, we could satisfy any customer," Marino says. The supermarket sales team told the IT project team what kind of information they needed. The requests ranged from simple information, such as why Frito-Lay merchandises Lays and Ruffles products in one part of a store and Doritos in another, to more complex research about what motivates shoppers as they move through a store.

A few months later, the project team presented a working Web-based prototype system they had developed to the supermarket sales team, only to find that in the quest for speed, they had made a classic error. Because the project team had not involved any sales team members in the design of the proposed system, it did not provide information that was specific enough for the supermarket sales team to use.

"Conceptually, it was a great idea," says Frito-Lay sales team leader Joe Ackerman. "But when folks are not on the front line, their view of what is valuable is different from those running 100 miles an hour in the field." The project team needed to backtrack and plug in the missing features, but it also had to win back the sales force, which now suspected that even a revised system would be a waste of time.

The project team then spent the next four months working with salespeople to evolve the proposed Web-based system into one that the sales force finally embraced. For example, a call-reporting feature was added. "So many people want to know what happened on a sales call, the sales account manager involved can be on the phone for days," Ackerman explains. "Now, we're able to post that to a Web site. It frees up the account manager to document the call once and move on" [14].

Challenges and Ethics of IT

As a prospective manager, business professional, or knowledge worker, you will be challenged by the **ethical responsibilities** generated by the use of information technology. For example, what uses of information technology might be considered improper, irresponsible, or harmful to other people or society? What is the proper business use of the Internet and an organization's IT resources? What does it take to be a **responsible end user** of information technology? How can you protect yourself from computer crime and other risks of information technology? These are some of the questions that outline the ethical dimensions of information systems that we will discuss and illustrate with Real World Cases throughout this text. Figure 1.14 outlines some of the ethical risks that may arise in the use of several major applications of information technology. The following example illustrates some of the security challenges associated with conducting business over the Internet.

FIGURE 1.14 Examples of some of the ethical challenges that must be faced by business managers who implement major applications of information technology.

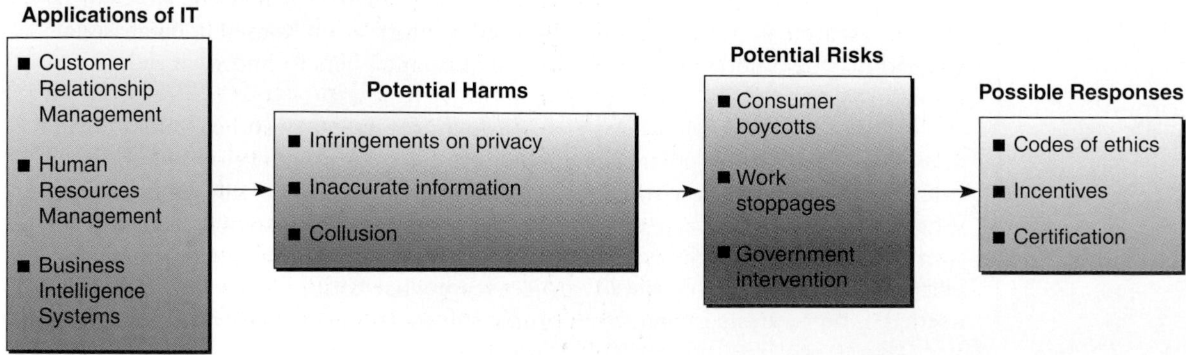

Citibank: Problems with e-Mail Scams

Citigroup Inc. (www.citigroup.com), one of the world's largest and most profitable financial services companies, has been in existence since 1812 and maintains some 200 million customer accounts in more than 100 countries. It would seem that such a large and prosperous organization would be protected from Internet scams as securely as a bank vault. Unfortunately, it is among the first to point out that no one is immune to these activities.

In November 2003, Citibank customers worldwide were being targeted by scam artists trying to get their confidential bank card numbers. The hoax was perpetrated via e-mails (a practice referred to as "phishing" and discussed in greater detail later in this text) that included links directing recipients to a Citibank Web site, where they were greeted with a pop-up box asking them for their full debit card numbers, their personal identification numbers (PINs), and their card expiration dates. However, the Web site was a fake, operated by someone trying to gain access to the information. It was eventually determined that the spoofed site was hosted by a Web-hosting company in Moscow.

Citibank network security officials were immediately alerted and posted a message to customers on their Web site, explaining the nature of the fraudulent e-mail and what customers should do if they received it, or worse, if they had responded to it.

The good news is that little actual damage or loss affected Citibank customers as a result of this potentially devastating fraud. However, customer confidence decreased, and Citibank incurred a significant cost in both money and time to secure its site, notify customers of the hoax, and investigate potential losses. The business potential of the Internet also brings with it the challenge of securing customer information and valuable corporate resources. This challenge grows each day, and all IT professionals must work toward improving the security and integrity of the Internet [4, 9].

Challenges of IT Careers

Both information technology and the myriad of information systems it supports have created interesting, challenging, and lucrative career opportunities for millions of men and women all over the globe. At this point in your life, you may still be uncertain about the career path you wish to follow, so learning more about information technology may help you decide if you want to pursue an IT-related career. In recent years, economic downturns have affected all job sectors, including IT. Furthermore, rising labor costs in North America, Canada, and Europe have resulted in large-scale movements to outsource basic software programming functions to India, the Middle East, and Asia-Pacific countries. Despite this move, employment opportunities in the information systems field are strong, with more new and exciting jobs emerging each day as organizations continue to expand their use of information technology. In addition, these new jobs pose constant human resource management challenges to all organizations because shortages of qualified information systems personnel frequently occur. The constantly changing job requirements in information systems, due to the dynamic developments in business and information technologies, will ensure that the long-term job outlook in IT remains both positive and exciting.

One major recruiter of IS professionals is the IT industry itself. Thousands of companies develop, manufacture, market, and service computer hardware, software, data, and network products and services or provide e-business and e-commerce applications and services, end-user training, and business systems consulting. However, the biggest need for qualified people comes from the millions of businesses, government agencies, and other organizations that use information technology. They need many types of IS professionals, such as systems analysts, software developers, and network managers, to help them plan, develop, implement, and manage today's Internet-based and Web-enabled business/IT applications.

Systems Analyst	System Consultant	Business Applications Consultant
Chief Information Officer	Computer Operator	Computer Serviceperson
Network Administrator	Data Dictionary Specialist	Network Manager
Database Administrator	Database Analyst	Documentation Specialist
IS Auditor	End-User Computer Manager	Equipment Manufacturer Representative
PC Sales Representative	Programmer	Program Librarian
Project Manager	Records Manager	Hardware Sales Representative
Scheduling and Control Person	Security Officer	Office Automation Specialist
Senior Project Leader	Service Sales Representative	Software Sales Representative
Technical Analyst	Software Quality Evaluator	Technical Writer
Telecommunications Specialist	Training & Standards Manager	User Interface Specialist

FIGURE 1.15
Careers in IS are as diverse and exciting as the technologies used in them; IS professionals have career opportunities in every business environment and activity throughout the world.

A more recent major recruiter of IS professionals is the accounting industry. Recent legislation, entitled the Sarbanes-Oxley Act of 2002, required major changes to auditing practices by public accounting firms and internal control processes by publicly held organizations of all sizes and industries. Many of these changes directly affect the IT/IS practices of all parties involved. To facilitate the execution of the covenants of Sarbanes-Oxley, the accounting industry is actively recruiting graduates from accounting programs that offer a significant emphasis on IS education. In addition, accounting firms are spending equal energy to recruit IS/IT professionals to work within the industry. In both cases, the result is a significant increase in demand for graduates with an IS/IT background or emphasis. Figure 1.15 lists just a few of the myriad of career roles available to the modern IT professional.

According to recent reports by the U.S. Department of Labor, computer systems analysts, database administrators, and other managerial-level IS positions are expected to be among the fastest growing occupations through 2012. Employment of IS professionals is expected to grow more than 36 percent (much higher than average) for all occupations as organizations continue to adopt and integrate increasingly sophisticated technologies. Job increases will be driven by very rapid growth in computer system design and related services, which is projected to be one of the fastest growing industries in the U.S. economy. In addition, many job openings will arise annually from the need to replace workers who move into managerial positions or other occupations or who leave the labor force.

Despite the recent economic downturn among information technology firms, IS professionals still enjoy favorable job prospects. The demand for networking to facilitate the sharing of information, the expansion of client/server environments, and the need for specialists to use their knowledge and skills in a problem-solving capacity will be major factors in the rising demand for computer systems analysts, database administrators, and other IS professionals. Moreover, falling prices of computer hardware and software should continue to induce more businesses to expand their computerized operations and integrate new technologies into them. To maintain a competitive edge and operate more efficiently, firms will keep demanding the services of professionals who are knowledgeable about the latest technologies and can apply them to meet the needs of businesses.

Increasingly, more sophisticated and complex technology is being implemented across all organizations, which should fuel the demand for these computer occupations. The demand for system analysts continues to grow to help firms maximize their efficiency with available technology. Expansion of electronic commerce—doing business on the Internet—and the continuing need to build and maintain databases that store critical information about customers, inventory, and projects are fueling demand for database administrators familiar with the latest technology. Finally, the increasing importance placed on "cybersecurity"—the protection of electronic information—will result in a need for workers skilled in information security. Let's take a look at IT career challenges at a leading Web company.

Want to Win in Vegas? Bet On an IT Job, Not the Super Bowl

To be sure, Las Vegas casinos were packed on the first weekend of 2007with Super Bowl bettors, but if you're looking for a sure bet, bring your resume, not your cash. In this fast growing city, IT workers are in high demand, a reflection of the dip in interest among college students in IT careers in the United States. "Anyone who can show up to work with a clean shirt is guaranteed a job," claims Ken Peffers, chairman of the MIS Department at the University of Nevada at Las Vegas (UNLV). There are now 200 students enrolled in the MIS undergraduate program at UNLV, but Peffers said the local labor market could easily support 400 students in his program.

If you are in IT and head to Las Vegas for work, Denny Frey, vice president of IT at Boyd Gaming Corp., suggests your luck will probably be very good. "Anybody who comes in here with any kind of information systems or technology background will definitely find a job," said Frey, whose company runs 17 casinos in Las Vegas and other states.

Frey and some of his IT peers advise UNLV on their training needs. He says a variety of technical skills is needed in this desert city, including telecommunications, networking, cabling, and program management. The gaming industry in particular needs database marketers, data warehouse skills, and business intelligence administrators, according to Frey.

Some IT skills in Vegas are system specific, whereas others focus on leveraging technology to achieve competitive advantages and advance corporate strategies.

The lack of IT workers is part of a national trend: College enrollments in computer science, information systems, and other related areas have been declining in recent years. For instance, the Computing Research Association (CRA) last year reported that the number of bachelor's degrees in computer science fell 17% in the 2004–05 academic year from the previous year, to 11,808, at Ph.D.-granting universities. Even greater declines have occurred in the numbers of information system degrees in major business schools. The decline is being blamed on the perception students have of the IT bubble crash earlier this decade, as well as concerns about offshoring.

Stephen Pickett, CIO at Bloomfield Hills, Michigan-based Penske Corp., is trying to do something about that. Pickett has spoken to undecided college students to talk about opportunities in IS and IT as part of an effort by the Chicago-based Society of Information Management (SIM) to encourage students to enter information technology–related fields. In addition, SIM plans to expand its academic outreach initiative this year, involve more of its chapters, and seek corporate support.

Many of SIM's members are also in the academic community, and "they are concerned about being able to retain professors because the class sizes are going down," says Pickett, the immediate past president of SIM. For IT managers, the implications of declining student enrollment mean increased wages, according to Pickett.

Pickett loves IT and began working on the technical side but ultimately moved into the business end of it. He encourages students to get training in both areas, because "You can't just have the technical part, you just can't have the business part—you really need to have both" [12].

The IS Function

The successful management of information systems and technologies presents major challenges to business managers and professionals. Thus, the information systems function represents:

- A major functional area of business equally as important to business success as the functions of accounting, finance, operations management, marketing, and human resource management.
- An important contributor to operational efficiency, employee productivity and morale, and customer service and satisfaction.
- A major source of information and support needed to promote effective decision making by managers and business professionals.
- A vital ingredient in developing competitive products and services that give an organization a strategic advantage in the global marketplace.
- A dynamic, rewarding, and challenging career opportunity for millions of men and women.
- A key component of the resources, infrastructure, and capabilities of today's networked business enterprises.

SECTION II Foundation Concepts: The Components of Information Systems

System Concepts: A Foundation

System concepts underlie all business processes, as well as our understanding of information systems and technologies. That's why we need to discuss how generic system concepts apply to business firms and the components and activities of information systems. Understanding system concepts will help you understand many other concepts in the technology, applications, development, and management of information systems that we cover in this text. For example, system concepts help us understand:

- **Technology.** Computer networks are systems of information processing components that use a variety of hardware, software, data management, and telecommunications network technologies.
- **Applications.** Electronic business and commerce applications involve interconnected business information systems.
- **Development.** Developing ways to use information technology in business includes designing the basic components of information systems.
- **Management.** Managing information technology emphasizes the quality, strategic business value, and security of an organization's information systems.

Read the Real World Case about an airline's use and management of mobile information systems. We can learn a lot from this case regarding the use of information technology to empower and support business professionals today. See Figure 1.16.

What Is a System?

We've used the term *system* well over 100 times already and will use it thousands more before we're done. It therefore seems reasonable that we focus our attention on exactly what a **system** is. As we discussed at the beginning of the chapter, a system is defined as *a set of interrelated components, with a clearly defined boundary, working together to achieve a common set of objectives by accepting inputs and producing outputs in an organized transformation process.* Many examples of systems can be found in the physical and biological sciences, in modern technology, and in human society. Thus, we can talk of the physical system of the sun and its planets, the biological system of the human body, the technological system of an oil refinery, and the socioeconomic system of a business organization.

Systems have three basic functions:

- **Input** involves capturing and assembling elements that enter the system to be processed. For example, raw materials, energy, data, and human effort must be secured and organized for processing.
- **Processing** involves transformation processes that convert input into output. Examples are manufacturing processes, the human breathing process, or mathematical calculations.
- **Output** involves transferring elements that have been produced by a transformation process to their ultimate destination. For example, finished products, human services, and management information must be transmitted to their human users.

Example. A manufacturing system accepts raw materials as input and produces finished goods as output. An information system is a system that accepts resources (data) as input and processes them into products (information) as output. A business organization is a system in which human and economic resources are transformed by various business processes into goods and services.

REAL WORLD CASE 2 Autosystems: The Business Value of a Successful IT System for a Small Manufacturer

Autosystems is an automotive lighting designer and manufacturer. Located in Belleville, Ontario, it employs approximately 800 people at three facilities. Autosystems' trading partners include General Motors, Visteon, Ford, Chrysler, Saturn, Harley-Davidson, Mack Truck, and Bombardier. Established in 1986, Autosystems manufactured its first headlamp assembly in 1987 and by 1997 had manufactured more than 10 million headlamp assemblies. In 1994, it received the Ford Q1 award, and it was the GM Supplier of the Year for headlamp assemblies in 1995 and 1996. For the first years of its existence, Autosystems concentrated only on manufacturing, then ventured into design by launching its design center, located in plant 3, 10 years later. The Impala and Monte Carlo headlamps were its first "black box" products, managed from design through production. Now, Autosystems is continuing its growth trends by consistently adding new customers.

Until a few years ago, Autosystems was still trying to manage its shop floor manufacturing process with a variety of paper documents. It previously had installed manufacturing planning and control software from Infor Global Solutions, called TRANS4M, but had not applied the software to shop floor processes. Finally, Autosystems management decided to consider installing the shop floor reporting module available for the TRANS4M manufacturing system, after asking themselves the following questions:

- Can the information usually written on shop documents be incorporated into our manufacturing system in a timely manner?

FIGURE 1.16

Manufacturing planning and reporting systems have become a vital business component of both large and small manufacturers.

- Do we want our shop floor employees accessing our manufacturing system?
- Is it worth the effort to train shop floor employees to use the system?
- Is there a way to get good, timely information into the system with low risk?
- Would the effort involved in implementing a shop floor reporting system have enough of a positive impact on the company to make it worthwhile?

After Autosystems management answered all those questions affirmatively, they installed the ActivEntry shop floor reporting system to move shop floor information into the TRANS4M system. Using ActivEntry, the information is now available, by work center, about labor efficiencies, cost of production, and scrap. Entering timely, accurate information into the system from the shop floor allows Autosystems to plan more efficiently, make production changes to avoid labor or scrap problems, and discuss these issues with production employees while they are still current and meaningful.

Lori Asbourne, a business systems analyst, and Peggy Shires, a cost accountant, handled the implementation of the ActivEntry system at Autosystems. Asbourne was responsible for the ActivEntry piece of the project, whereas Shires was responsible for finding what needed to be done with the TRANS4M system to make things work together smoothly. Asbourne and Shires conducted research to prepare for this implementation. They visited an ActivEntry user, looked at quotes for the costs of the software and hardware involved, and viewed product demonstrations.

Before implementing ActivEntry, Autosystems had no PCs on the shop floor. It now keeps 20 PCs throughout three plants, with plans to increase this number as necessary. It purchased three bar-code printers and 20 PCs and ran cable. The company also is looking into the future addition of scanning capabilities. The additional PCs required the upgrade of the telecommunications capacity of Autosystems' network.

Instead of just implementing ActivEntry, all aspects of the TRANS4M system that would interface with ActivEntry were considered and improved. By making process improvements, Autosystems hoped to make the use of ActivEntry easier for all employees involved.

One job, entitled "Production Analyst," was created as a result of the new system. Yvonne Millette is responsible for training, support, and continued assistance to production associates. She noted all the paperwork being used on the shop floor prior to the ActivEntry implementation. Each plant previously was using individual sets of paperwork; now, to reflect the information necessary to update the system, the work is standardized across all three plants. Not only did this change assist in training for the ActivEntry implementation, it also helps when staff members transfer among plants. In the long term, Autosystems would like these forms to go away. The plan therefore is to move to a fully electronic system.

Reporting occurs at the end of each shift. Team leaders stay until they have keyed in their shift data and looked at their audit information. "Our scrap rate has improved in all three plants by 2.7% in the last six months," reports Millette, the production analyst. "There is now visibility on the floor. The team leaders are responsible for keying in the data. Through team meetings, they are reporting to management and their teams, on a daily basis, their progress. By 8:30 a.m., everything is keyed in and reports are ready to discuss, by work centers—labor efficiencies, cost of production, and scrap—in the 9:00 a.m. meetings."

Other successes Millette likes to mention include that "Each employee is now more aware of what is costing the company money. They are more likely to shut down if there is a scrap problem because they realize how it affects the organization. Workers are more aware of crew sizes and how they can impact the comparison of actual to payroll dollars. This actual versus payroll number is getting really close."

"You can see everything! Before ActivEntry, you couldn't see it!" Millette explains. "The shop floor workers love it now. They are getting creative, coming up with ideas for improvements."

Autosystems' production managers have access to the supervisory mode of ActivEntry. They can review information from all three plants. Supervisors are trained to know if there is a problem and to check with the production manager to ensure information has been uploaded into the system quickly.

"We now have the ability to capture labor, efficiency, production, scrap, etc., on time and by work center, for every cell, and are able to talk about that every day in our team meetings. We can discuss what went well and what went wrong," Millette notes.

Asbourne and Shires like to share their successes with Autosystems' planners too: "It has helped our planners a lot with visibility. They have good, accurate data in the TRANS4M system to make their decisions. They are able to rely on the data, which means they are getting away from their separate spreadsheets for planning. There are no longer supposed to be any spreadsheets. We are temporarily running ActivEntry in parallel with their spreadsheets to confirm that the data is accurate."

Asbourne sums up the success of integrating ActivEntry into the manufacturing system: "My job was to find a tool that put the responsibility on the floor and we gained a lot more than that out of this project. We have some happy, happy people."

Source: "AUTOSYSTEMS: Bringing the Shop Floor into the 21st Century," Customer Success Story, Infor Global Solutions, 2006, www.infor.com; Scott Berinato, "The Post-PeopleSoft Landscape and the Future of ERP," *CIO Magazine*, June 1, 2005.

CASE STUDY QUESTIONS

1. Why did Autosystems decide to install the ActivEntry system? Why did the company feel it was necessary to integrate it with its TRANS4M system?
2. Which three business benefits, of the many that resulted from the use of ActivEntry, gave the company the most business value? Defend your choices.
3. What changes are already being planned to improve the use of ActivEntry? What other improvements should the company consider? Why?

REAL WORLD ACTIVITIES

1. Go to the Infor Global Solutions Web site, www.infor.com, to find other stories that describe the business value of manufacturing planning and control systems. Can you discover any common reasons for the success of these companies with their systems? Present your findings to the class.
2. Search the Internet for examples of problems that companies have had with manufacturing systems. Break into small groups with your classmates to discuss your findings and what solutions you can propose to help companies avoid the problems you discovered.

FIGURE 1.17 A common cybernetic system is a home temperature control system. The thermostat accepts the desired room temperature as input and sends voltage to open the gas valve, which fires the furnace. The resulting hot air goes into the room, and the thermometer in the thermostat provides feedback to shut the system down when the desired temperature is reached.

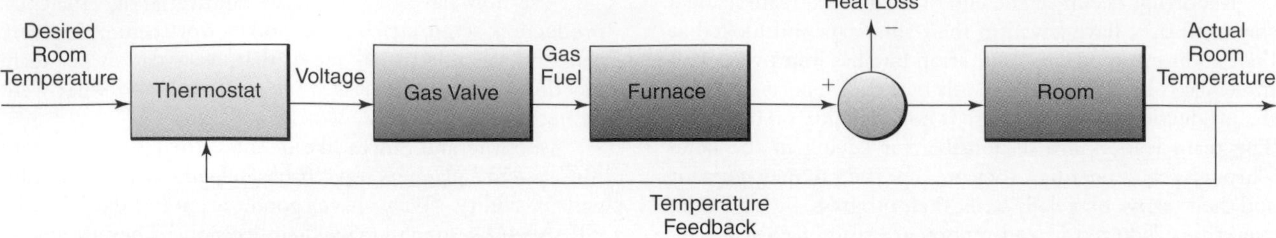

Feedback and Control

The system concept becomes even more useful by including two additional elements: feedback and control. A system with feedback and control functions is sometimes called a *cybernetic* system, that is, a self-monitoring, self-regulating system.

- **Feedback** is data about the performance of a system. For example, data about sales performance are feedback to a sales manager. Data about the speed, altitude, attitude, and direction of an aircraft are feedback to the aircraft's pilot or autopilot.
- **Control** involves monitoring and evaluating feedback to determine whether a system is moving toward the achievement of its goal. The control function then makes the necessary adjustments to a system's input and processing components to ensure that it produces proper output. For example, a sales manager exercises control when reassigning salespersons to new sales territories after evaluating feedback about their sales performance. An airline pilot, or the aircraft's autopilot, makes minute adjustments after evaluating the feedback from the instruments to ensure the plane is exactly where the pilot wants it to be.

Example. Figure 1.17 illustrates a familiar example of a self-monitoring, self-regulating, thermostat-controlled heating system found in many homes; it automatically monitors and regulates itself to maintain a desired temperature. Another example is the human body, which can be regarded as a cybernetic system that automatically monitors and adjusts many of its functions, such as temperature, heartbeat, and breathing. A business also has many control activities. For example, computers may monitor and control manufacturing processes, accounting procedures help control financial systems, data entry displays provide control of data entry activities, and sales quotas and sales bonuses attempt to control sales performance.

Other System Characteristics

Figure 1.18 uses a business organization to illustrate the fundamental components of a system, as well as several other system characteristics. Note that a system does not exist in a vacuum; rather, it exists and functions in an *environment* containing other systems. If a system is one of the components of a larger system, it is a *subsystem*, and the larger system is its environment.

Several systems may share the same environment. Some of these systems may be connected to one another by means of a shared boundary, or *interface*. Figure 1.18 also illustrates the concept of an *open system*, that is, a system that interacts with other systems in its environment. In this diagram, the system exchanges inputs and outputs with its environment. Thus, we could say that it is connected to its environment by input and output interfaces. Finally, a system that has the ability to change itself or its environment to survive is an *adaptive system*.

Example. Organizations such as businesses and government agencies are good examples of the systems in society, which is their environment. Society contains a multitude of such systems, including individuals and their social, political, and economic institutions.

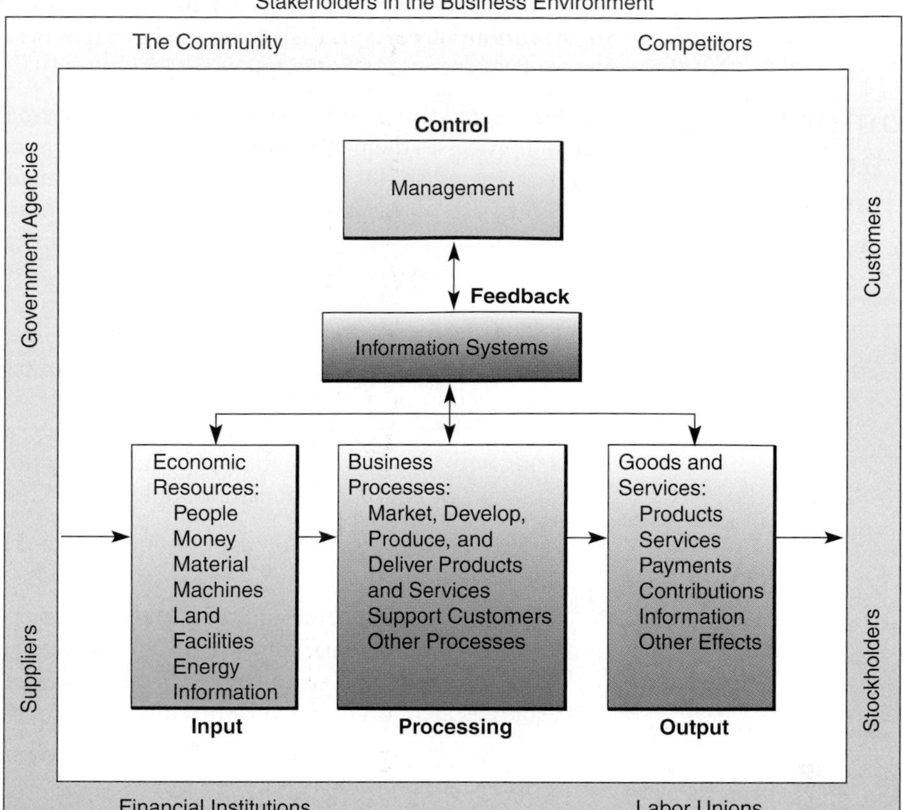

FIGURE 1.18
A business is an example of an organizational system in which economic resources (input) are transformed by various business processes (processing) into goods and services (output). Information systems provide information (feedback) about the operations of the system to management for the direction and maintenance of the system (control) as it exchanges inputs and outputs with its environment.

Organizations themselves consist of many subsystems, such as departments, divisions, process teams, and other workgroups. Organizations are examples of open systems because they interface and interact with other systems in their environment. Finally, organizations are examples of adaptive systems, because they can modify themselves to meet the demands of a changing environment.

If we apply our understanding of general system concepts to information systems, it should be easy to see the parallels.

Information systems are made up of interrelated components:

- People, hardware, software, peripherals, and networks.

They have clearly defined boundaries:

- Functions, modules, type of application, department, or end-user group.

All the interrelated components work together to achieve a common goal by accepting inputs and producing outputs in an organized transformation process:

- Using raw materials, hiring new people, manufacturing products for sale, and disseminating information to others.

Information systems make extensive use of feedback and control to improve their effectiveness:

- Error messages, dialog boxes, passwords, and user rights management.

Many information systems are designed to change in relation to their environments and are adaptive:

- Intelligent software agents, expert systems, and highly specialized decision support systems.

Information systems are systems just like any other system. Their value to the modern organization, however, is unlike any other system ever created.

Components of an Information System

We have noted that an information system is a system that accepts data resources as input and processes them into information products as output. How does an information system accomplish this task? What system components and activities are involved?

Figure 1.19 illustrates an **information system model** that expresses a fundamental conceptual framework for the major components and activities of information systems. An information system depends on the resources of people (end users and IS specialists), hardware (machines and media), software (programs and procedures), data (data and knowledge bases), and networks (communications media and network support) to perform input, processing, output, storage, and control activities that convert data resources into information products.

This information system model highlights the relationships among the components and activities of information systems. It also provides a framework that emphasizes four major concepts that can be applied to all types of information systems:

- People, hardware, software, data, and networks are the five basic resources of information systems.
- People resources include end users and IS specialists, hardware resources consist of machines and media, software resources include both programs and procedures, data resources can include data and knowledge bases, and network resources include communications media and networks.
- Data resources are transformed by information processing activities into a variety of information products for end users.
- Information processing consists of the system activities of input, processing, output, storage, and control.

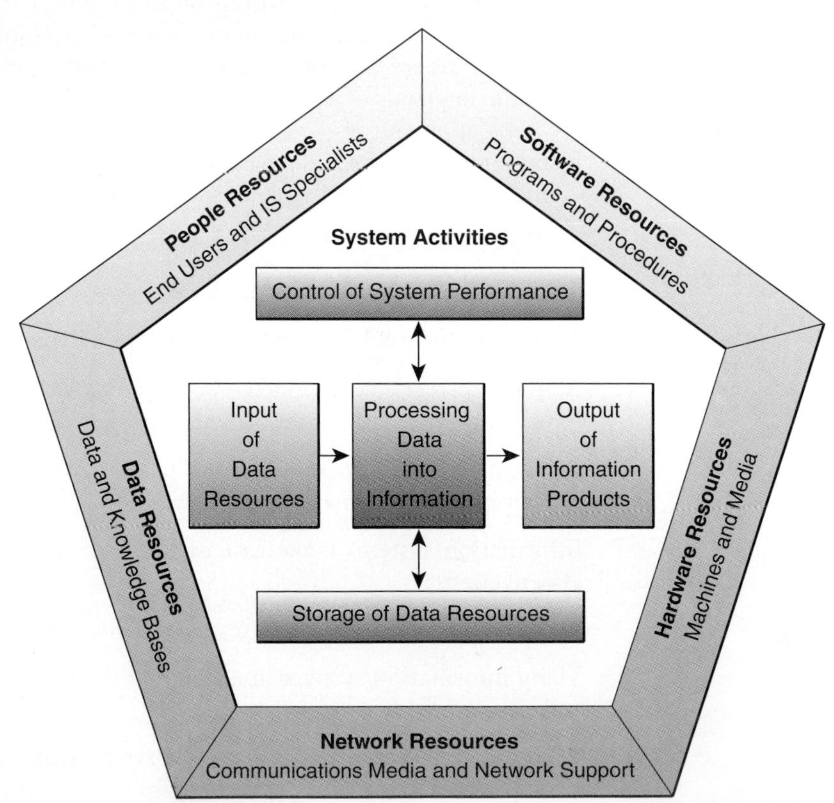

FIGURE 1.19
The components of an information system. All information systems use people, hardware, software, data, and network resources to perform input, processing, output, storage, and control activities that transform data resources into information products.

Information System Resources

Our basic IS model shows that an information system consists of five major resources: people, hardware, software, data, and networks. Let's briefly discuss several basic concepts and examples of the roles these resources play as the fundamental components of information systems. You should be able to recognize these five components at work in any type of information system you encounter in the real world. Figure 1.20 outlines several examples of typical information system resources and products.

People Resources

People are the essential ingredient for the successful operation of all information systems. These **people resources** include end users and IS specialists.

- **End users** (also called users or clients) are people who use an information system or the information it produces. They can be customers, salespersons, engineers, clerks, accountants, or managers and are found at all levels of an organization. In fact, most of us are information system end users. And most end users in business are **knowledge workers**, that is, people who spend most of their time communicating and collaborating in teams and workgroups and creating, using, and distributing information.
- **IS specialists** are people who develop and operate information systems. They include systems analysts, software developers, system operators, and other managerial, technical, and clerical IS personnel. Briefly, systems analysts design information systems based on the information requirements of end users, software developers create computer programs based on the specifications of systems analysts, and system operators help monitor and operate large computer systems and networks.

Hardware Resources

The concept of **hardware resources** includes all physical devices and materials used in information processing. Specifically, it includes not only **machines**, such as computers and other equipment, but also all data **media**, that is, tangible objects on which data are recorded, from sheets of paper to magnetic or optical disks. Examples of hardware in computer-based information systems are:

- **Computer systems,** which consist of central processing units containing microprocessors and a variety of interconnected peripheral devices such as printers, scanners, monitors, and so on. Examples are handheld, laptop, tablet, or desktop microcomputer systems, midrange computer systems, and large mainframe computer systems.

FIGURE 1.20
Examples of information system resources and products.

Information Systems Resources and Products
People Resources Specialists—systems analysts, software developers, systems operators. End Users—anyone else who uses information systems.
Hardware Resources Machines—computers, video monitors, magnetic disk drives, printers, optical scanners. Media—floppy disks, magnetic tape, optical disks, plastic cards, paper forms.
Software Resources Programs—operating system programs, spreadsheet programs, word processing programs, payroll programs. Procedures—data entry procedures, error correction procedures, paycheck distribution procedures.
Data Resources Product descriptions, customer records, employee files, inventory databases.
Network Resources Communications media, communications processors, network access and control software.
Information Products Management reports and business documents using text and graphics displays, audio responses, and paper forms.

- **Computer peripherals,** which are devices such as a keyboard, electronic mouse, trackball, or stylus for the input of data and commands, a video screen or printer for the output of information, and magnetic or optical disk drives for the storage of data resources.

Software Resources

The concept of **software resources** includes all sets of information processing instructions. This generic concept of software includes not only the sets of operating instructions called **programs**, which direct and control computer hardware, but also the sets of information processing instructions called **procedures** that people need.

It is important to understand that even information systems that do not use computers have a software resource component. This claim is true even for the information systems of ancient times or the manual and machine-supported information systems still used in the world today. They all require software resources in the form of information processing instructions and procedures to properly capture, process, and disseminate information to their users.

The following are examples of software resources:

- **System software,** such as an operating system program, which controls and supports the operations of a computer system. Microsoft Windows® and Unix are two examples of popular computer operating systems.
- **Application software,** which are programs that direct processing for a particular use of computers by end users. Examples are sales analysis, payroll, and word processing programs.
- **Procedures,** which are operating instructions for the people who will use an information system. Examples are instructions for filling out a paper form or using a software package.

Data Resources

Data are more than the raw material of information systems. The concept of **data resources** has been broadened by managers and information systems professionals. They realize that data constitute valuable organizational resources. Thus, you should view data just as you would any organizational resource that must be managed effectively to benefit all stakeholders in an organization.

The concept of data as an organizational resource has resulted in a variety of changes in the modern organization. Data that previously were captured as a result of a common transaction are now stored, processed, and analyzed using sophisticated software applications that can reveal complex relationships among sales, customers, competitors, and markets. In today's wired world, the data to create a simple list of an organization's customers are protected with the same energy as the cash in a bank vault. Data are the lifeblood of today's organizations, and the effective and efficient management of data is considered an integral part of organizational strategy.

Data can take many forms, including traditional alphanumeric data, composed of numbers, letters, and other characters that describe business transactions and other events and entities; text data, consisting of sentences and paragraphs used in written communications; image data, such as graphic shapes and figures or photographic and video images; and audio data, including the human voice and other sounds.

The data resources of information systems are typically organized, stored, and accessed by a variety of data resource management technologies into:

- Databases that hold processed and organized data.
- Knowledge bases that hold knowledge in a variety of forms, such as facts, rules, and case examples about successful business practices.

For example, data about sales transactions may be accumulated, processed, and stored in a Web-enabled sales database that can be accessed for sales analysis reports by managers and marketing professionals. Knowledge bases are used by knowledge management systems and expert systems to share knowledge or give expert advice on specific subjects. We explore these concepts further in subsequent chapters.

Data versus Information. The word **data** is the plural of *datum*, though *data* commonly represents both singular and plural forms. Data are raw facts or observations, typically about physical phenomena or business transactions. For example, a spacecraft launch or the sale of an automobile would generate a lot of data describing those events. More specifically, data are objective measurements of the *attributes* (the characteristics) of *entities* (e.g., people, places, things, events).

Example. Business transactions, such as buying a car or an airline ticket, can produce a lot of data. Just think of the hundreds of facts needed to describe the characteristics of the car you want and its financing or the intricate details for even the simplest airline reservation.

People often use the terms *data* and *information* interchangeably. However, it is better to view data as raw material resources that are processed into finished information products. Then we can define **information** as data that have been converted into a meaningful and useful context for specific end users. Thus, data are usually subjected to a value-added process (*data processing* or *information processing*) during which (1) their form is aggregated, manipulated, and organized; (2) their content is analyzed and evaluated; and (3) they are placed in a proper context for a human user.

The issue of context is really at the heart of understanding the difference between information and data. Data can be thought of as context independent: A list of numbers or names, by itself, does not provide any understanding of the context in which it was recorded. In fact, the same list could be recorded in a variety of contexts. In contrast, for data to become information, both the context of the data and the perspective of the person accessing the data become essential. The same data may be considered valuable information to one person and completely irrelevant to the next. Just think of data as potentially valuable to all and information as valuable relative to its user.

Example. Names, quantities, and dollar amounts recorded on sales forms represent data about sales transactions. However, a sales manager may not regard these as information. Only after such facts are properly organized and manipulated can meaningful sales information be furnished and specify, for example, the amount of sales by product type, sales territory, or salesperson.

Network Resources

Telecommunications technologies and networks like the Internet, intranets, and extranets are essential to the successful electronic business and commerce operations of all types of organizations and their computer-based information systems. Telecommunications networks consist of computers, communications processors, and other devices interconnected by communications media and controlled by communications software. The concept of **network resources** emphasizes that communications technologies and networks are fundamental resource components of all information systems. Network resources include:

- **Communications media.** Examples include twisted-pair wire, coaxial and fiber-optic cables, and microwave, cellular, and satellite wireless technologies.
- **Network infrastructure.** This generic category emphasizes that many hardware, software, and data technologies are needed to support the operation and use of a communications network. Examples include communications processors, such as modems and internetwork processors, and communications control software, such as network operating systems and Internet browser packages.

Information System Activities

Regardless of the type of information system, the same basic **information system activities** occur. Let's take a closer look now at each of the basic **data or information processing** activities. You should be able to recognize input, processing, output, storage, and control activities taking place in any information system you are studying. Figure 1.21 lists business examples that illustrate each of these information system activities.

FIGURE 1.21
Business examples of the basic activities of information systems.

Information System Activities
• **Input.** Optical scanning of bar-coded tags on merchandise.
• **Processing.** Calculating employee pay, taxes, and other payroll deductions.
• **Output.** Producing reports and displays about sales performance.
• **Storage.** Maintaining records on customers, employees, and products.
• **Control.** Generating audible signals to indicate proper entry of sales data.

Input of Data Resources

Data about business transactions and other events must be captured and prepared for processing by the **input** activity. Input typically takes the form of *data entry* activities such as recording and editing. End users usually enter data directly into a computer system or record data about transactions on some type of physical medium such as a paper form. This entry includes a variety of editing activities to ensure that they have recorded the data correctly. Once entered, data may be transferred onto a machine-readable medium, such as a magnetic disk, until needed for processing.

For example, data about sales transactions may be recorded on source documents such as paper order forms. (A **source document** is the original, formal record of a transaction.) Alternatively, salespersons might capture sales data using computer keyboards or optical scanning devices; they are visually prompted to enter data correctly by video displays. This method provides them with a more convenient and efficient **user interface,** that is, methods of end-user input and output with a computer system. Methods such as optical scanning and displays of menus, prompts, and fill-in-the-blank formats make it easier for end users to enter data correctly into an information system.

Processing of Data into Information

Data are typically subjected to **processing** activities, such as calculating, comparing, sorting, classifying, and summarizing. These activities organize, analyze, and manipulate data, thus converting them into information for end users. The quality of any data stored in an information system also must be maintained by a continual process of correcting and updating activities.

Example. Data received about a purchase can be (1) *added* to a running total of sales results, (2) *compared* to a standard to determine eligibility for a sales discount, (3) *sorted* in numerical order based on product identification numbers, (4) *classified* into product categories (e.g., food and nonfood items), (5) *summarized* to provide a sales manager with information about various product categories, and finally (6) used to *update* sales records.

Output of Information Products

Information in various forms is transmitted to end users and made available to them in the **output** activity. The goal of information systems is the production of appropriate **information products** for end users. Common information products include messages, reports, forms, and graphic images, which may be provided by video displays, audio responses, paper products, and multimedia. We routinely use the information provided by these products as we work in organizations and live in society. For example, a sales manager may view a video display to check on the performance of a salesperson, accept a computer-produced voice message by telephone, and receive a printout of monthly sales results.

Storage of Data Resources

Storage is a basic system component of information systems. Storage is the information system activity in which data are retained in an organized manner for later use. For example, just as written text material gets organized into words, sentences, paragraphs, and documents, stored data are commonly organized into a variety of data elements and databases. This organization facilitates their later use in processing or retrieval as output when needed by users of a system. Such data elements and databases are discussed further in Chapter 5, Data Resource Management.

Control of System Performance

An important information system activity is the **control** of system performance. An information system should produce feedback about its input, processing, output, and storage activities. This feedback must be monitored and evaluated to determine if the system is meeting established performance standards. Then appropriate system activities must be adjusted so that proper information products are produced for end users.

For example, a manager may discover that subtotals of sales amounts in a sales report do not add up to total sales. This conflict might mean that data entry or processing procedures need to be corrected. Then changes would have to be made to ensure that all sales transactions would be properly captured and processed by a sales information system.

Recognizing Information Systems

As a business professional, you should be able to recognize the fundamental components of information systems you encounter in the real world. This demand means that you should be able to identify:

- The people, hardware, software, data, and network resources they use.
- The types of information products they produce.
- The way they perform input, processing, output, storage, and control activities.

This kind of understanding will help you be a better user, developer, and manager of information systems. And that, as we have pointed out in this chapter, is important to your future success as a manager, entrepreneur, or professional in business.

Summary

- **IS Framework for Business Professionals.** The IS knowledge that a business manager or professional needs to know is illustrated in Figure 1.2 and covered in this chapter and text. This knowledge includes (1) *foundation concepts:* fundamental behavioral, technical, business, and managerial concepts like system components and functions, or competitive strategies; (2) *information technologies:* concepts, developments, or management issues regarding hardware, software, data management, networks, and other technologies; (3) *business applications:* major uses of IT for business processes, operations, decision making, and strategic/competitive advantage; (4) *development processes:* how end users and IS specialists develop and implement business/IT solutions to problems and opportunities arising in business; and (5) *management challenges:* how to effectively and ethically manage the IS function and IT resources to achieve top performance and business value in support of the business strategies of the enterprise.
- **Business Roles of Information Systems.** Information systems perform three vital roles in business firms. Business applications of IS support an organization's business processes and operations, business decision making, and strategic competitive advantage. Major application categories of information systems include operations support systems, such as transaction processing systems, process control systems, and enterprise collaboration systems, and management support systems, such as management information systems, decision support systems, and executive information systems. Other major categories are expert systems, knowledge management systems, strategic information systems, and functional business systems. However, in the real world, most application categories are combined into cross-functional information systems that provide information and support for decision making and also perform operational information processing activities. Refer to Figures 1.7, 1.9, and 1.11 for summaries of the major application categories of information systems.
- **System Concepts.** A system is a group of interrelated components, with a clearly defined boundary, working toward the attainment of a common goal by accepting inputs and producing outputs in an organized transformation process. Feedback is data about the performance of a system. Control is the component that monitors and evaluates feedback and makes any necessary adjustments to the input and processing components to ensure that proper output is produced.
- **Information System Model.** An information system uses the resources of people, hardware, software, data, and networks to perform input, processing, output, storage, and control activities that convert data resources into information products. Data are first collected and converted to a form that is suitable for processing (input). Then the data are manipulated and converted into information (processing), stored for future use (storage), or communicated to their ultimate user (output) according to correct processing procedures (control).
- **IS Resources and Products.** Hardware resources include machines and media used in information processing. Software resources include computerized

instructions (programs) and instructions for people (procedures). People resources include information systems specialists and users. Data resources include alphanumeric, text, image, video, audio, and other forms of data. Network resources include communications media and network support. Information products produced by an information system can take a variety of forms, including paper reports, visual displays, multimedia documents, electronic messages, graphics images, and audio responses.

Key Terms and Concepts

These are the key terms and concepts of this chapter. The page number of their first explanation appears in parentheses.

1. Computer-based information system (7)
2. Control (28)
3. Data (33)
4. Data or information processing (33)
5. Data resources (32)
6. Developing successful information system solutions (19)
7. E-business (12)
8. E-business applications (12)
9. Electronic commerce (13)
10. Enterprise collaboration systems (13)
11. Extranet (12)
12. Feedback (28)
13. Hardware resources (31)
    - *a.* Machines (31)
    - *b.* Media (31)
14. Information (33)
    - *a.* Information products (34)
15. Information system (4)
16. Information system activities (33)
    - *a.* Input (34)
    - *b.* Processing (34)
    - *c.* Output (34)
    - *d.* Storage (34)
    - *e.* Control (35)
17. Information system model (30)
18. Information technology (7)
19. Intranet (12)
20. Knowledge workers (31)
21. Management information systems (15)
22. Network resources (33)
23. People resources (31)
    - *a.* IS specialists (31)
    - *b.* End users (31)
24. Roles of IS in business (9)
    - *a.* Support of business processes and operations (9)
    - *b.* Support of business decision making (9)
    - *c.* Support of strategies for competitive advantage (9)
25. Software resources (32)
    - *a.* Programs (32)
    - *b.* Procedures (32)
26. System (25)
27. Types of information systems (13)
    - *a.* Cross-functional informational systems (16)
    - *b.* Management support systems (15)
    - *c.* Operations support systems (13)
    - *d.* Functional business systems (16)
    - *e.* Transaction processing systems (14)
    - *f.* Process control systems (15)
    - *g.* Enterprise collaboration systems (15)

Review Quiz

Match one of the previous key terms and concepts with one of the following brief examples or definitions. Look for the best fit for answers that seem to fit more than one key term or concept. Defend your choices.

____ 1. People who spend most of their workday creating, using, and distributing information.

____ 2. Computer hardware and software, networks, data management, and other technologies.

____ 3. Information systems support an organization's business processes, operations, decision making, and strategies for competitive advantage.

____ 4. Using IT to reengineer business processes to support e-business operations.

____ 5. Using Web-based decision support systems to support sales managers.

____ 6. Using information technology for electronic commerce to gain a strategic advantage over competitors.

____ 7. A system that uses people, hardware, software, and network resources to collect, transform, and disseminate information within an organization.

____ 8. An information system that uses computers and their hardware and software.

____ 9. Anyone who uses an information system or the information it produces.

____ 10. Applications using the Internet, corporate intranets, and interorganizational extranets for electronic business operations, e-commerce, and enterprise collaboration.

____ 11. The buying, selling, marketing, and servicing of products over the Internet and other networks.

____ 12. Groupware tools to support collaboration among networked teams.

____ 13. A group of interrelated components with a clearly defined boundary working together toward the attainment of a common goal.

____ 14. Data about a system's performance.

____ 15. Making adjustments to a system's components so that it operates properly.

____ 16. Facts or observations.

____ 17. Data that have been placed into a meaningful context for an end user.

____ 18. Converting data into information is a type of this kind of activity.

____ 19. An information system uses people, hardware, software, network, and data resources to perform input, processing, output, storage, and control activities that transform data resources into information products.

____ 20. Machines and media.

____ 21. Computers, disk drives, video monitors, and printers are examples.

____ 22. Magnetic disks, optical disks, and paper forms are examples.

____ 23. Programs and procedures.

____ 24. A set of instructions for a computer.

____ 25. A set of instructions for people.

____ 26. End users and information systems professionals.

____ 27. Using the keyboard of a computer to enter data.

____ 28. Computing loan payments.

____ 29. Printing a letter you wrote using a computer.

____ 30. Saving a copy of the letter on a magnetic disk.

____ 31. Having a sales receipt as proof of a purchase.

____ 32. Information systems can be classified into operations, management, and other categories.

____ 33. Includes transaction processing, process control, and end-user collaboration systems.

____ 34. Includes management information, decision support, and executive information systems.

____ 35. Information systems that perform transaction processing and provide information to managers across the boundaries of functional business areas.

____ 36. Internet-like networks and Web sites inside a company.

____ 37. Interorganizational Internet-like networks among trading partners.

____ 38. Using the Internet, intranets, and extranets to empower internal business operations, electronic commerce, and enterprise collaboration.

____ 39. Information systems that focus on operational and managerial applications in support of basic business functions such as accounting or marketing.

____ 40. Data should be viewed the same way as any organizational resource that must be managed effectively to benefit all stakeholders in an organization.

____ 41. A major challenge for business managers and professionals today in solving business problems.

____ 42. Examples include messages, reports, forms, and graphic images, which may be provided by video displays, audio responses, paper products, and multimedia.

____ 43. These include communications media and network infrastructure.

____ 44. People who develop and operate information systems.

Discussion Questions

1. How can information technology support a company's business processes and decision making and give it a competitive advantage? Give examples to illustrate your answer.
2. How does the use of the Internet, intranets, and extranets by companies today support their business processes and activities?
3. Refer to the Real World Case on Sew What? in the chapter. In the company's early years, Megan Duckett lost a major contract because a prospective client said that without a Web site, her business "lacked credibility." Does this hold true today for all businesses? Why or why not?
4. Why do big companies still fail in their use of information technology? What should they be doing differently?
5. How can a manager demonstrate that he or she is a responsible end user of information systems? Give several examples.
6. Refer to the Real World Case on Autosystems in the chapter. What should be the next step in business software implementation for a small manufacturer like Autosystems? Defend your proposal.
7. What are some of the toughest management challenges in developing IT solutions to solve business problems and meet new business opportunities?
8. Why are there so many conceptual classifications of information systems? Why are they typically integrated in the information systems found in the real world?
9. In what major ways have information systems in business changed during the last 40 years? What is one major change you think will happen in the next 10 years? Refer to Figure 1.4 to help you answer.
10. Refer to the real-world example of Hershey Foods in the chapter. Are the failure and success described due to managerial or technological challenges? Explain.

Analysis Exercises

Complete the following exercises as individual or group projects that apply chapter concepts to real world business situations.

1. **Understanding the Information System**
   The Library as an Information System
   A library makes an excellent information systems model. It serves as a very large information storage facility with text, audio, and video data archives. Look up the definitions for each term listed below and briefly explain a library's equivalents.
   a. Input
   b. Processing
   c. Output
   d. Storage
   e. Control
   f. Feedback

2. **Career Research on the Web**
   Comparing Information Sources
   Select a job title for a career you would like to pursue as a summer intern or new graduate. Use www.dogpile.com or www.monster.com and seek advice from your school's career services office to find and research four different job postings for your desired job title.
   a. Select four job listings most relevant to your desired job title. List the degrees, training, experience, and/or certifications these job postings share in common.
   b. Outline your plan for obtaining any requirements that you do not currently have.
   c. How did each of these information sources compare? Which source did you find most useful? Describe the attributes you found most important in making this determination.

3. **Skydive Chicago: Efficiency and Feedback**
   Digital Data
   Skydive Chicago (www.SkydiveChicago.com) is one of the United States' premier skydiving resorts, serving skydivers ranging in skills from first-time jumpers to internationally competitive freefly teams.

   Each student in Skydive Chicago's training program makes a series of progressive training jumps under the direct supervision of a United States Parachute Association–rated jumpmaster. The training program gears each jump in the series toward teaching one or two new skills. Jumpmasters video their students' jumps. Students use the feedback these videos provide to identify mistakes. They often copy their videos onto a personal tape for future reference.

   Jumpmasters may also copy well-executed student skydives to the facility's tape library. All students are given access to the dropzone's training room and are encouraged to watch video clips in preparation for their next training jump. This step saves jumpmasters, who are paid per jump, considerable time. Jumpmasters also use these videos to evaluate their training method's effectiveness.
   a. How can this information system benefit the skydiving student?
   b. How can this information system benefit Skydive Chicago?
   c. Draw an information systems model (Figure 1.18). Fill in your diagram with the information about people, hardware, software, and other resources from this exercise.

4. **Are Textbooks History?**
   Trends in Information Systems
   The wealth of free information available via the Internet continues to grow at incredible rates. Search engines such as Google make locating useful information practical. This textbook often explores the Internet's impact on various industries, and the textbook industry is no exception. Is it possible that free Internet content might one day replace textbooks?
   a. Go to www.google.com and use the search box to look up "End-user." Were any of Google's first five search results useful with respect to this course?
   b. Go to www.wikipedia.com and use the search box to look up "Knowledge worker." Compare Wikipedia's article with the information provided within this textbook. Which source did you find easiest to use? What advantages did Wikipedia provide? What advantages did this textbook provide?
   c. Among Google, Wikipedia, and this textbook, which source provides the most useful information about "Intranets"? Why?

5. **Careers in IS**
   Disaster Recovery
   "How important is your data to you?" "What would happen if…?" While business managers focus on solving business problems and determining what their information systems should do, disaster recovery consultants ask what would happen if things go wrong.

   With careful advance planning, disaster recovery specialists help their clients prevent calamity. Although this topic covers a wide variety of software issues, installation configuration issues, and security threats, examining common end user mistakes may also prove enlightening. Common end user mistakes include:
   - Failing to save work in progress frequently.
   - Failing to make a backup copy.
   - Storing original and backup copies in the same location.

   For each of the common end user mistakes listed above, answer the following questions.
   a. How might this mistake result in data loss?
   b. What procedures could you follow to this risk?

REAL WORLD CASE 3

Heidelberg, Honeywell, and Eaton: Using Information Technology to Build Smart Products and Services

In today's world, any manufacturing company that has not awakened to the fact that it must become a service business is in peril. Unfortunately, there are many businesses that still think of themselves as builders of things and state their measures of success solely in terms of "the product." But even their more enlightened competitors, the ones that have begun to wrap valuable services around their products and profit directly from those services, are enjoying only a temporary advantage. They may be improving their customer relationships by taking on various tasks such as maintenance and replenishment of supplies, but that will get them only so far. A select group of companies is already upping the ante. Soon, it will not be enough for a company to offer services; it will have to provide "smart services."

Smart services go beyond the kinds of upkeep and upgrades companies are bundling with their products in terms of both value to customers and cost efficiencies they generate for providers. To provide them, companies must use information technology to build "smart products"—products with awareness and connectivity—into the products themselves. And they must be prepared to act on what these smart products reveal about their use.

For example, maintenance is one of the key activities in the life cycle of a product, but forward-looking manufacturers are using information technology to intervene, assist, and gain the benefits of providing smart services to their customers. Typically, smart products can detect that a part is approaching failure and alert users, thus giving them the company opportunity to provide maintenance services and enjoy the resulting benefits.

Consider Heidelberger Druckmaschinen AG of Germany (commonly known as Heidelberg), the number-one maker of high-end printing presses for printers and print media producers throughout the world. For all of its long history, the company has offered repair services to customers. But several years ago, Heidelberg developed the ability to monitor its equipment remotely, using built-in sensors, networking microprocessors, and other information technologies. Heidelberg soon found that it could provide maintenance much more cost effectively with these smart products. Now with its machines communicating continuously over the Internet, relaying information about their status between the print shops and Heidelberg's regional and global technical support specialists, the company has the access and insight to optimize printing performance in customers' shops and minimize maintenance and repair costs for Heidelberg, as well as its customers.

With such smart services, Heidelberg now offers total support of its products—which can extend, for example, even to the removal and resale of its machines. Thus, the self-monitoring and networking capabilities built into its products provide a strategic opportunity for Heidelberg to use information technology to become a partner in the successful operations of its customers while reducing its costs and creating new sources of revenue from smart services.

Honeywell International is another prime example of a company that is benefiting from smart products and services. This global conglomerate is involved in many different industries, one of which is control and automation systems for petroleum refineries. Honeywell recognized that such systems represented just a small part of the cost involved in operating and maintaining a refinery. So its engineers developed a new suite of customer smart services called Experion Process Knowledge System, or PKS, a system of information and operations technologies deployed at a customer's refinery but controlled and monitored remotely via network connections by Honeywell. The PKS performs a variety of manufacturing equipment support and optimization tasks formerly performed by customer and Honeywell maintenance personnel.

With Honeywell's PKS smart services, customers experience fewer false alarms that a process is failing, less unanticipated downtime, and lower maintenance costs. They also work closely with Honeywell to learn from the knowledge the PKS provides regarding the performance of their refinery equipment and systems. The increased value provided by the PKS service enables Honeywell to charge a premium for its use, and in many cases, Honeywell has been able to increase the scope of other services it provides to its customers.

Our last example is the Cleveland-based Eaton Corp., which began making axles and other truck parts in 1911 and later diversified into other engineered components, including residential circuit breakers. With the end of its first century in business approaching, Eaton found itself in very mature businesses, fighting with established competitors over every point of market share. That's when a few visionary managers within the Electrical Products Division started to think about device connectivity and the broader solutions it could offer consumers. The system they envisioned, recently launched as Home Heartbeat, monitors the status of various home systems and alerts the homeowner when something is amiss. To do so, it uses water sensors, open/closed sensors, and power sensors, all of which communicate to a base station over a wireless network. That base station communicates with a key fob device carried by the homeowner or can send an e-mail or text message to a cell phone if there is a change in the state of a sensor.

Consider how useful this capability would be. You're commuting by car or train to work, and it occurs to you that a space heater might have been left on. You can check your key fob to be reassured instead of having to turn back. (The key fob device communicates only within a limited distance range but captures data about the status of your home when you left it.) Home Heartbeat also features a water shutoff valve that can be automatically activated by sensors. So if you're on vacation and you hear about an unexpected cold front, power outage, or burst pipe back home, you can check your e-mail. In the meantime, you can be confident that if the water needed to be shut off, it was.

Home Heartbeat is a good example of a smart product and service innovation. Eaton used information technology to build awareness and connectivity into devices it was already selling, turning them into smart products. Then it could position itself as not just a product vendor but a service provider. No longer consigned to an obscure corner of the industry, the Eaton brand now stands for total home awareness. Now the company is playing the role of new business aggregator as it courts an entirely new range of partners, from wireless carriers to insurance companies, to join with it in providing smart services to businesses and consumers.

Source: Adapted from Glen Allmendinger and Ralph Lombreglia, "Four Strategies for the Age of Smart Services," *Harvard Business Review*, October 2005; Peter Weill and Sinan Aral, "Generating Premium Returns on Your IT Investments," *MIT Sloan Management Review*, Winter 2006.

CASE STUDY QUESTIONS

1. Why should manufacturing companies build smart products and provide smart services? What business benefits can they gain? Provide several examples beyond those discussed in this case.
2. What information technologies are used by the companies in this case to build smart products and provide smart services? What other IT components might be used? Give examples of the capabilities they would provide.
3. What are some limitations of a smart products and smart services strategy? Give several examples of challenges that a business might encounter, and explain how it might overcome them.

REAL WORLD ACTIVITIES

1. Use the Internet to investigate how Heidelberg, Honeywell, and Eaton are proceeding in their use of smart products and services. Discover if they are expanding this approach and what benefits they are claiming for this strategy.
2. Now expand your Internet investigation to other manufacturing companies to find several that are building smart products and offering smart services. What business value are they claiming for themselves and their customers? If this search is fruitless, select several companies from your Internet research and explain how and why they might employ a smart products and services strategy.
3. What security and privacy concerns might consumers have about Eaton's Home Heartbeat service? Break into small groups with your classmates to discuss the rationale for these concerns, and consider what could be done to reduce any threats to security and privacy posed by such services while also improving the value of this new use of information technology.

CHAPTER 2

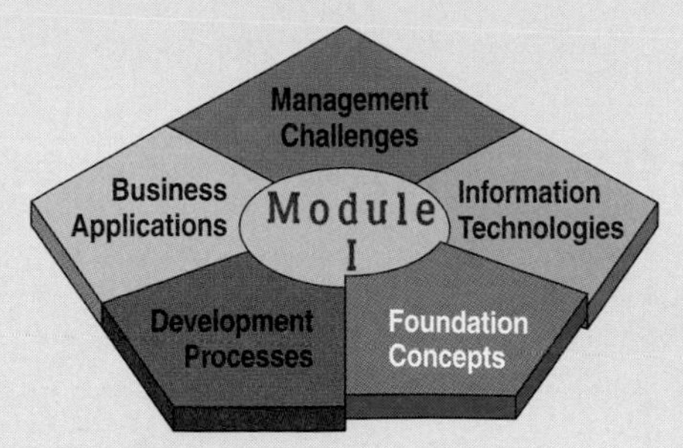

COMPETING WITH INFORMATION TECHNOLOGY

Chapter Highlights

Section I
Fundamentals of Strategic Advantage

Strategic IT

Competitive Strategy Concepts

Real World Case: FedEx Corporation: Investing in Information Technology for Competitive Advantage in a Dynamic Global Environment

Strategic Uses of Information Technology

Building a Customer-Focused Business

The Value Chain and Strategic IS

Section II
Using Information Technology for Strategic Advantage

Strategic Uses of IT

Reengineering Business Processes

Real World Case: GE Energy and GE Healthcare: Using Information Technology to Create Strategic Customer Relationships

Becoming an Agile Company

Creating a Virtual Company

Building a Knowledge-Creating Company

Real World Case: GE, Dell, Intel, GM, and Others: Debating the Competitive Advantage of Information Technology

Learning Objectives

After reading and studying this chapter, you should be able to:

1. Identify several basic competitive strategies and explain how they use information technologies to confront the competitive forces faced by a business.
2. Identify several strategic uses of Internet technologies and give examples of how they give competitive advantages to a business.
3. Give examples of how business process reengineering frequently involves the strategic use of Internet technologies.
4. Identify the business value of using Internet technologies to become an agile competitor or form a virtual company.
5. Explain how knowledge management systems can help a business gain strategic advantages.

SECTION I Fundamentals of Strategic Advantage

Strategic IT

Technology is no longer an afterthought in forming business strategy, but the actual cause and driver [17].

This chapter will show you that it is important to view information systems as more than a set of technologies that support efficient business operations, workgroup and enterprise collaboration, or effective business decision making. Information technology can change the way businesses compete. You should also view information systems strategically, that is, as vital competitive networks, as a means of organizational renewal, and as a necessary investment in technologies that help a company adopt strategies and business processes that enable it to reengineer or reinvent itself to survive and succeed in today's dynamic business environment.

Section I of this chapter introduces fundamental competitive strategy concepts that underlie the strategic use of information systems. Section II then discusses several major strategic applications of information technology used by many companies today.

Read the Real World Case regarding the competitive advantages of IT. We can learn a lot about the strategic business uses of information technologies from this case. See Figure 2.1.

Competitive Strategy Concepts

In Chapter 1, we emphasized that a major role of information systems applications in business is to provide effective support of a company's strategies for gaining competitive advantage. This strategic role of information systems involves using information technology to develop products, services, and capabilities that give a company major advantages over the competitive forces it faces in the global marketplace.

This role is accomplished through a strategic information architecture—the collection of **strategic information systems** that support or shape the competitive position and strategies of a business enterprise. So a strategic information system can be any kind of information system (TPS, MIS, DSS, etc.) that uses information technology to help an organization gain a competitive advantage, reduce a competitive disadvantage, or meet other strategic enterprise objectives.

Figure 2.2 illustrates the various competitive forces a business might encounter and the variety of competitive strategies that can be adopted to counteract such forces. Although not all strategies are used simultaneously by a single firm, each has value in certain circumstances. The key is to understand which strategy should be employed and why. For now, it's only important that you become familiar with the available strategic approaches. Let's look at several basic concepts that define the role of competitive strategy as it applies to information systems.

Competitive Forces and Strategies

How should a business professional think about competitive strategies? How can competitive strategies be applied to the use of information systems by a business? Figure 2.2 illustrates an important conceptual framework for understanding forces of competition and the various competitive strategies employed to balance them.

A company can survive and succeed in the long run only if it successfully develops strategies to confront five **competitive forces** that shape the structure of competition in its industry. In Michael Porter's classic model of competition, any business that wants to survive and succeed must develop and implement strategies to effectively counter (1) *the rivalry of competitors within its industry*, (2) *the threat of new entrants into an industry and its markets*, (3) *the threat posed by substitute products that might capture market share*, (4) *the bargaining power of customers*, and (5) *the bargaining power of suppliers* [21].

Competition is a positive characteristic in business, and competitors share a natural, and often healthy, rivalry. This rivalry encourages and sometimes requires a constant

REAL WORLD CASE 1

FedEx Corporation: Investing in Information Technology for Competitive Advantage in a Dynamic Global Environment

It's easy to feel a bit sorry for any company's chief information officer (CIO) these days. The pace of technology is accelerating, and costs seem to be going up just as fast. But for Rob Carter, the CIO of FedEx, the job may seem even more daunting. He's responsible for all the computer and communications systems that keep this staggeringly complex outfit running. He has to connect 39 hubs around the world with 677 airplanes, over 90,000 vehicles, and more than 200,000 employees delivering 6 million packages a day in 220 countries. Seconds count. The least glitch could cost millions of dollars and trigger a PR disaster. And if anything goes wrong, you know who takes the heat. Plus, FedEx's main competitor UPS and growing third-place provider DHL are continually trying to make the challenges harder for this on-the-spot CIO.

But don't feel all that sorry for him. Carter works for a boss, CEO and founder Fred Smith, who completely believes in the importance of infotech. He gives Carter a $1 billion annual budget. Most important, Carter is at the strategic heart of what makes FedEx successful. The company is America's second most admired and the world's fourth most admired, according to *Fortune*'s latest survey, and Carter knows he helped put it there and must keep it there. If you're in the field you love, a job doesn't get much better than that.

Rob Carter is a great example of a so-called C-suite member, one of those elite top execs whose titles start with "chief" and end with "officer." Increasingly, the C-suite is team managing companies in all kinds of industries. The

FIGURE 2.1

FedEx and many other companies know that the skillful management and use of their investment in information technology can give them a competitive advantage.

46-year-old Carter is widely regarded as America's preeminent CIO. (*Information Week* magazine recently named him CIO of the year, an honor he has shared twice before.) He joined FedEx 13 years ago and has been CIO since 2000.

Carter recently sat down with *Fortune* senior editor-at-large Geoffrey Colvin before an invited audience at the Time Warner Center in Manhattan. They discussed topics as varied as how FedEx encourages innovation, how it gains competitive advantage, competing with UPS, security measures, and the war on terror.

Colvin: Customers can track individual shipments on your Web site, which seems amazing, but they can do the same on UPS's site. You work hard, your competitors work hard. At the end of the day, is information technology a competitive advantage for you?

Carter: The answer is absolutely yes. UPS is a marvelous competitor. I'd say everybody needs a good competitor that keeps you on your toes, and I have tremendous respect for UPS and what they've accomplished with technology. There was a day when they didn't get this. It wasn't all that long ago, in the early '90s, when they really turned it around and said, "We're going to invest significantly."

From that point in time we've been in a battle on technology, no question about it, especially customer-based technology. We tend to focus slightly less on operational technology. We focus a little more on revenue-generating, customer-satisfaction–generating, strategic advantage technology. The key focus of my job is driving technology that increases the top line, and there are some terrific examples of that.

Colvin: Give me a good example.

Carter: A product we developed called Insight. The competition has now come close to doing this, but we took the whole tracking mechanism and turned it around so that as opposed to having to track a package, you say, "I want to know what's coming to me today." You can go out there now and see every inbound package, regardless of whether you knew someone was sending it to you.

In the Northeast there's a company that does bone marrow sample testing for bone marrow transplants. Getting those samples is a very painful process for the donors involved, and the viability of that sample is only about 24 hours. They'd send out kits to collection places, and they never knew exactly how many would be coming in on a given day. Using Insight, very early in the morning they can see every inbound kit that's heading to them and staff appropriately to get every one of those tests done, because the last thing you want to do is run out of hours in a day and have to recontact a potential donor and say, "Do the test again." Because it's not a fun test.

Colvin: So you figure you have an infotech competitive advantage over UPS. How long do you think it will last?

Carter: I think it's easier to copy than it is to innovate. There's no question about that. So when we launch something new, they're hot on our heels. That's why we simply have to keep moving. We have a philosophy—it came out of the Marine Corps—from the early days, that says, "Move, communicate, and shoot." That's one of our strategies. And in that order, by the way. It's not "Shoot, communicate, and stand still." So we move, communicate, and shoot, and it's a very important thing. We have an innovation team that does nothing but look for new opportunities to come out of the gate with something that'll be a whack on the side of the head to them.

Colvin: How much does FedEx spend on IT in a year, and how do you decide how much you need to spend to stay ahead of the competition?

Carter: We spend more than $1 billion a year on technology. So the technology budget is significant. Part of the idea, though, has been to manage the expense-to-revenue number down to help the company grow faster than the IT expense. You can do a lot with $1 billion. So I've been focused on saying we don't need to rapidly grow the staff and rapidly grow the footprint of IT at FedEx. Let's hold the line against the backdrop of a growing business and make that billion dollars more and more efficacious. We may not be able to outspend the Brown guys [UPS]. They're a larger company than us today, although we are hot on their heels. But we're going to come at it from a lot of different angles in trying to make those dollars really work for us, and people have fun doing that. We do get great accolades in the trade press too, for being one of the great places to work on hot, innovative IT projects.

Colvin: Let's switch gears a bit and talk about FedEx and the war on terror. I don't want to be macabre, but the reality is that your company is famous for delivering stuff to the right place at the right time. Isn't that awfully attractive to a terrorist who would want to make a bomb or other device and FedEx it someplace? And what's to stop him from doing that?

Carter: One of the things about our system compared with other systems is the visibility of every transaction. If you wanted to be anonymous about having something delivered, we're kind of the wrong place to start—especially to get something across borders. If you're not what the U.S. Transportation Administration [TSA] calls a known shipper, you go through a perimeter of control and inspection and those kinds of things to clear customs. So the "known shipper" phenomenon and related declarations make us a less attractive target for that.

Having said that, this is a very dangerous world. We take our responsibility very seriously. We work with the regulatory bodies, the defense agencies around the globe, and I think we're the best at deploying a security team and an intelligence team that works with the DEA, the FBI, the CIA, the Department of Defense, and various foreign agencies. We've had many arrests and stings that have not received any publicity. If I gave you examples, I'd have to shoot you.

Colvin: Security, the war on terror—not how most people would define your business. As Peter Drucker might say, What business are you in?

Carter: I believe we engineer time. I believe that as the world shrinks and changes, we offer solutions that allow you to engineer time to make things happen along time schedules that weren't possible before.

Source: Adapted from Geoffrey Colvin, "The FedEx Edge," *Fortune*, April 3, 2006.

CASE STUDY QUESTIONS

1. How do the IT investment strategies and focus of FedEx and its main competitor UPS differ? Which company has the better strategy? Why?
2. Is FedEx's "move, communicate, and shoot" IT strategy a good one for its competitive battle with UPS? Why or why not? Is it a good model of competitive IT strategy for other types of companies? Defend your position.
3. FedEx CIO Carter says his company is in the business of engineering time. Is this a good business vision for FedEx? Why or why not? How vital is IT to this definition of FedEx's business? Use examples from the case to illustrate your answer.

REAL WORLD ACTIVITIES

1. Use the Internet to compare the current status of FedEx, UPS, and DHL in terms of revenue, profitability, parcels delivered, and other measures of business success. Who is winning the competitive battle? Why? Check out what business commentators and financial analysts are reporting on the Web to help you answer.
2. Use the Internet to discover more about how FedEx is involved in fighting the war on terror, beyond what is reported in this case. For example, FedEx has made some controversial disclosures of customer information to intelligence agencies. Break into small groups with your classmates to discuss FedEx's corporate responsibility to assist in the war on terror while protecting the privacy of its customers, as well as any other issues uncovered in your research.

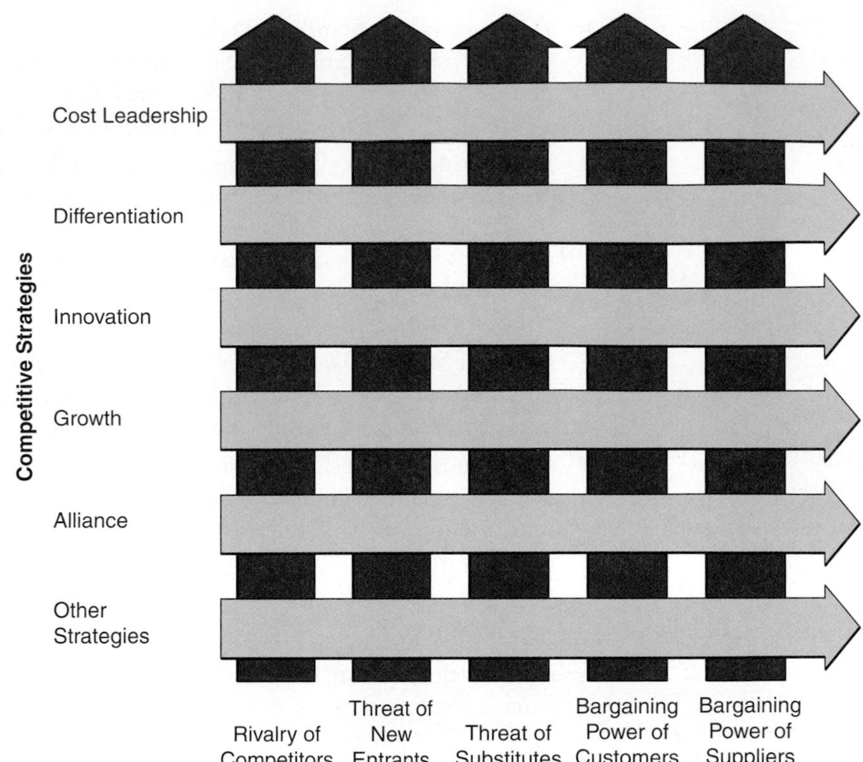

FIGURE 2.2
Businesses can develop competitive strategies to counter the actions of the competitive forces they confront in the marketplace.

effort to gain competitive advantage in the marketplace. This ever-present competitive force requires significant resources on the part of a firm.

Guarding against the threat of new entrants also requires the expenditure of significant organizational resources. Not only do firms need to compete with other firms in the marketplace, but they also must work to create significant barriers to the entry of new competition. This competitive force has always been difficult to manage, but it is even more so today. The Internet has created many ways for a new entrant to enter the marketplace quickly and with relatively low cost. In the Internet world, a firm's biggest potential competitor may be one that is not yet in the marketplace but could emerge almost overnight.

The threat of substitutes is another competitive force confronting a business. The effect of this force is seen almost daily in a wide variety of industries, often at its strongest during periods of rising costs or inflation. When airline prices get too high, people substitute car travel for their vacations. When the cost of steak gets too high, people eat more hamburger and fish. Most products or services have some sort of substitute available to the consumer.

Finally, a business must guard against the often opposing forces of customer and supplier bargaining powers. If customers' bargaining power gets too strong, they can drive prices to unmanageably low levels or simply refuse to buy the product or service. If a key supplier's bargaining power gets too strong, it can force the price of goods and services to unmanageably high levels or simply starve a business by controlling the flow of parts or raw materials essential to the manufacture of a product.

Figure 2.2 also illustrates that businesses can counter the threats of competitive forces that they face by implementing five basic **competitive strategies**.

- **Cost Leadership Strategy.** Becoming a low-cost producer of products and services in the industry or finding ways to help suppliers or customers reduce their costs or increase the costs of competitors.

- **Differentiation Strategy.** Developing ways to differentiate a firm's products and services from its competitors' or reduce the differentiation advantages of competitors. This strategy may allow a firm to focus its products or services to give it an advantage in particular segments or niches of a market.
- **Innovation Strategy.** Finding new ways of doing business. This strategy may involve developing unique products and services or entering unique markets or market niches. It may also involve making radical changes to the business processes for producing or distributing products and services that are so different from the way a business has been conducted that they alter the fundamental structure of an industry.
- **Growth Strategies.** Significantly expanding a company's capacity to produce goods and services, expanding into global markets, diversifying into new products and services, or integrating into related products and services.
- **Alliance Strategies.** Establishing new business linkages and alliances with customers, suppliers, competitors, consultants, and other companies. These linkages may include mergers, acquisitions, joint ventures, forming of "virtual companies," or other marketing, manufacturing, or distribution agreements between a business and its trading partners.

One additional point regarding these strategies is that they are not mutually exclusive. An organization may make use of one, some, or all of the strategies in varying degrees to manage the forces of competition. Therefore, a given activity could fall into one or more of the categories of competitive strategy. For example, implementing a system that allows customers to track their order or shipment online could be considered a form of differentiation if the other competitors in the marketplace do not offer this service. If they do offer the service however, online order tracking would not serve to differentiate one organization from another.

If an organization offers its online package tracking system in a manner that allows its customers to access shipment information via not only a computer but a mobile phone as well, then such an action could fall into both the differentiation and innovation strategy categories. Think of it this way: Not everything innovative will serve to differentiate one organization from another. Likewise, not everything that serves to differentiate organizations is necessarily viewed as innovative. These types of observations are true for any combination of the competitive strategies, thus making them complementary to each other rather than mutually exclusive.

Strategic Uses of Information Technology

How can business managers use investments in information technology to directly support a firm's competitive strategies? Figure 2.3 answers this question with a summary of the many ways that information technology can help a business implement the five basic competitive strategies. Figure 2.4 provides examples of how specific companies have used strategic information systems to implement each of these five basic strategies for competitive advantage. Note the major use of Internet technologies for electronic business and commerce applications. In the rest of this chapter, we discuss and provide examples of many strategic uses of information technology.

Other Competitive Strategies

There are many competitive strategies in addition to the five basic strategies of cost leadership, differentiation, innovation, growth, and alliance. Let's look at several key strategies that also can be implemented with information technology. They include locking in customers or suppliers, building switching costs, raising barriers to entry, and leveraging investment in information technology.

Investments in information technology can allow a business to **lock in customers and suppliers** (and lock out competitors) by building valuable new relationships with them. These business relationships can become so valuable to customers or suppliers that they deter them from abandoning a company for its competitors or intimidate

FIGURE 2.3
A summary of how information technology can be used to implement the five basic competitive strategies. Many companies are using Internet technologies as the foundation for such strategies.

Basic Strategies in the Business Use of Information Technology
Lower Costs • Use IT to substantially reduce the cost of business processes. • Use IT to lower the costs of customers or suppliers.
Differentiate • Develop new IT features to differentiate products and services. • Use IT features to reduce the differentiation advantages of competitors. • Use IT features to focus products and services on selected market niches.
Innovate • Create new products and services that include IT components. • Develop unique new markets or market niches with the help of IT. • Make radical changes to business processes with IT that dramatically cut costs; improve quality, efficiency, or customer service; or shorten time to market.
Promote Growth • Use IT to manage regional and global business expansion. • Use IT to diversify and integrate into other products and services.
Develop Alliances • Use IT to create virtual organizations of business partners. • Develop interenterprise information systems linked by the Internet and extranets that support strategic business relationships with customers, suppliers, subcontractors, and others.

them into accepting less profitable business arrangements. Early attempts to use information systems technology in these relationships focused on significantly improving the quality of service to customers and suppliers in a firm's distribution, marketing, sales, and service activities. More recent projects characterize a move toward more innovative uses of information technology.

A major emphasis in strategic information systems has been to find ways to **create switching costs** in the relationships between a firm and its customers or suppliers. That is, investments in information systems technology, such as those mentioned in the Wal-Mart example, can make customers or suppliers dependent on the continued use of innovative, mutually beneficial interenterprise information systems. Then they become reluctant to pay the costs in time, money, effort, and inconvenience that it would take to switch to a company's competitors.

By making investments in information technology to improve its operations or promote innovation, a firm could also **raise barriers to entry** that would discourage or delay other companies from entering a market. Typically, these barriers increase the amount of investment or the complexity of the technology required to compete in an industry or a market segment. Such actions tend to discourage firms already in the industry and deter external firms from entering the industry.

Investing in information technology enables a firm to build strategic IT capabilities that allow it to take advantage of strategic opportunities when they arise. In many cases, this ability results when a company invests in advanced computer-based information systems to improve the efficiency of its own business processes. Then, armed with this strategic technology platform, the firm can **leverage investment in IT** by developing new products and services that would not be possible without a strong IT capability. An important current example is the development of corporate intranets and extranets by many companies, which enables them to leverage their previous investments in Internet browsers, PCs, servers, and client/server networks. Figure 2.5 summarizes the additional strategic uses of IT we have just discussed.

FIGURE 2.4 Examples of how companies have used information technology to implement five competitive strategies for strategic advantage.

Strategy	Company	Strategic Use of Information Technology	Business Benefit
Cost Leadership	Dell Computer Priceline.com eBay.com	Online build to order Online seller bidding Online auctions	Lowest cost producer Buyer-set pricing Auction-set prices
Differentiation	AVNET Marshall Moen Inc. Consolidated Freightways	Customer/supplier e-commerce Online customer design Customer online shipment tracking	Increase in market share Increase in market share Increase in market share
Innovation	Charles Schwab & Co. Federal Express Amazon.com	Online discount stock trading Online package tracking and flight management Online full-service customer systems	Market leadership Market leadership Market leadership
Growth	Citicorp Wal-Mart Toys 'R' Us Inc.	Global intranet Merchandise ordering by global satellite network POS inventory tracking	Increase in global market Market leadership Market leadership
Alliance	Wal-Mart/Procter & Gamble Cisco Systems Staples Inc. and Partners	Automatic inventory replenishment by supplier Virtual manufacturing alliances Online one-stop shopping with partners	Reduced inventory cost/increased sales Agile market leadership Increase in market share

Wal-Mart and Others Get Innovative

Wal-Mart realized early on the benefits of using information technology to improve service. In 1983, it invested in an elaborate satellite network linking the point-of-sale terminals in all of its stores. In a few years, this system grew into a complex communication network that connected all Wal-Mart stores, its headquarters and distribution centers, and all its major suppliers. The most innovative aspect of the system was the facilitation of a modified just-in-time process of inventory control, a feat virtually unheard of in general merchandise retailing. When an item is sold by a store, a message is immediately sent to the supplier of that item. This message alerts the supplier to include a replacement in the next scheduled shipment (often the same day) to the nearest distribution hub. This tight connectivity allowed Wal-Mart's immediate response to inventory needs while significantly reducing the amount of inventory required. The innovation didn't stop there however. Wal-Mart realized the operational efficiency of its system and used it to offer lower-cost, better-quality products and services, as well as to differentiate itself from its competitors.

Companies have begun to follow Wal-Mart's example by extending their networks to customers and suppliers and adopting continuous inventory replenishment systems that serve to lock in business. These interenterprise information systems use the Internet and other networks to link the business processes of a company electronically with its customers and suppliers, resulting in new business alliances and partnerships. Extranets between a business and its suppliers are prime examples of such strategic linkages. One of the most innovative uses for these network linkages is the concept of *stockless* inventory replenishment systems. Such systems work for Wal-Mart and Procter & Gamble, a major supplier of personal care products. Using the network, Procter & Gamble automatically replenishes Wal-Mart's stock of all Procter & Gamble products [18, 29].

FIGURE 2.5 Additional ways that information technology can be used to implement competitive strategies.

Other Strategic Uses of Information Technology
• Develop interenterprise information systems whose convenience and efficiency create switching costs that lock in customers or suppliers.
• Make major investments in advanced IT applications that build barriers to entry against industry competitors or outsiders.
• Include IT components in products and services to make substitution of competing products or services more difficult.
• Leverage investments in IS people, hardware, software, databases, and networks from operational uses into strategic applications.

Competitive Advantage and Competitive Necessity

The constant struggle to achieve a measurable competitive advantage in an industry or marketplace occupies a significant portion of an organization's time and money. Creative and innovative marketing, research and development, and process reengineering, among many other activities, are used to gain that elusive and sometimes indescribable competitive advantage over rival firms. The real problem with a competitive advantage, however, is that it normally doesn't last very long and is generally not sustainable over the long term. Once a firm figures out how to gain an advantage over its competitors, the competitors figure out how it was done, and they do the same thing. What was once a competitive advantage is now a competitive necessity. Once a strategy or action becomes a competitive necessity, instead of it creating an advantage, the strategy or action becomes necessary simply to compete and do business in the industry. And when this happens, someone has to figure out a new way to gain a competitive edge, and the cycle starts over again.

Every organization is looking for a way to gain competitive advantage, and many have been successful in using strategic information systems to assist them in achieving it. The important point to remember is that competitive advantage doesn't last forever. Arie de Geus, head of strategic planning for Royal Dutch Shell, thinks there may be one way to sustain it, however: "The ability to learn faster than your competitors may be the only sustainable competitive advantage in the future."

Building a Customer-Focused Business

The driving force behind world economic growth has changed from manufacturing volume to improving customer value. As a result, the key success factor for many firms is maximizing customer value [6].

For many companies, the chief business value of becoming a customer-focused business lies in its ability to help them keep customers loyal, anticipate their future needs, respond to customer concerns, and provide top-quality customer service. This strategic focus on **customer value** recognizes that quality, rather than price, has become the primary determinant in a customer's perception of value. Companies that consistently offer the best value from the customer's perspective are those that keep track of their customers' individual preferences; keep up with market trends; supply products, services, and information anytime, anywhere, and provide customer services tailored to individual needs [6]. So Internet technologies have created a strategic opportunity for companies, large and small, to offer fast, responsive, high-quality products and services tailored to individual customer preferences.

Internet technologies can make customers the focal point of customer relationship management (CRM) and other e-business applications. In combination, CRM systems and Internet, intranet, and extranet Web sites create new channels for interactive communications within a company, with customers, and with suppliers, business partners, and others in the external environment. Such communications enable continual interaction with customers by most business functions and encourages cross-functional collaboration with customers in product development, marketing, delivery, service, and technical support [6]. We will discuss CRM systems in Chapter 7.

Typically, customers use the Internet to ask questions, lodge complaints, evaluate products, request support, and make and track their purchases. Using the Internet and corporate intranets, specialists in business functions throughout the enterprise can contribute to an effective response. This ability encourages the creation of cross-functional discussion groups and problem-solving teams dedicated to customer involvement, service, and support. Even the Internet and extranet links to suppliers and business partners can be used to enlist them in a way of doing business that ensures the prompt delivery of quality components and services to meet a company's commitments to its customers [13]. This process is how a business demonstrates its focus on customer value.

Figure 2.6 illustrates the interrelationships in a customer-focused business. Intranets, extranets, e-commerce Web sites, and Web-enabled internal business processes form the invisible IT platform that supports this e-business model. The platform enables the business to focus on targeting the kinds of customers it really wants and "owning" the customer's total business experience with the company. A successful

FIGURE 2.6 How a customer-focused business builds customer value and loyalty using Internet technologies.

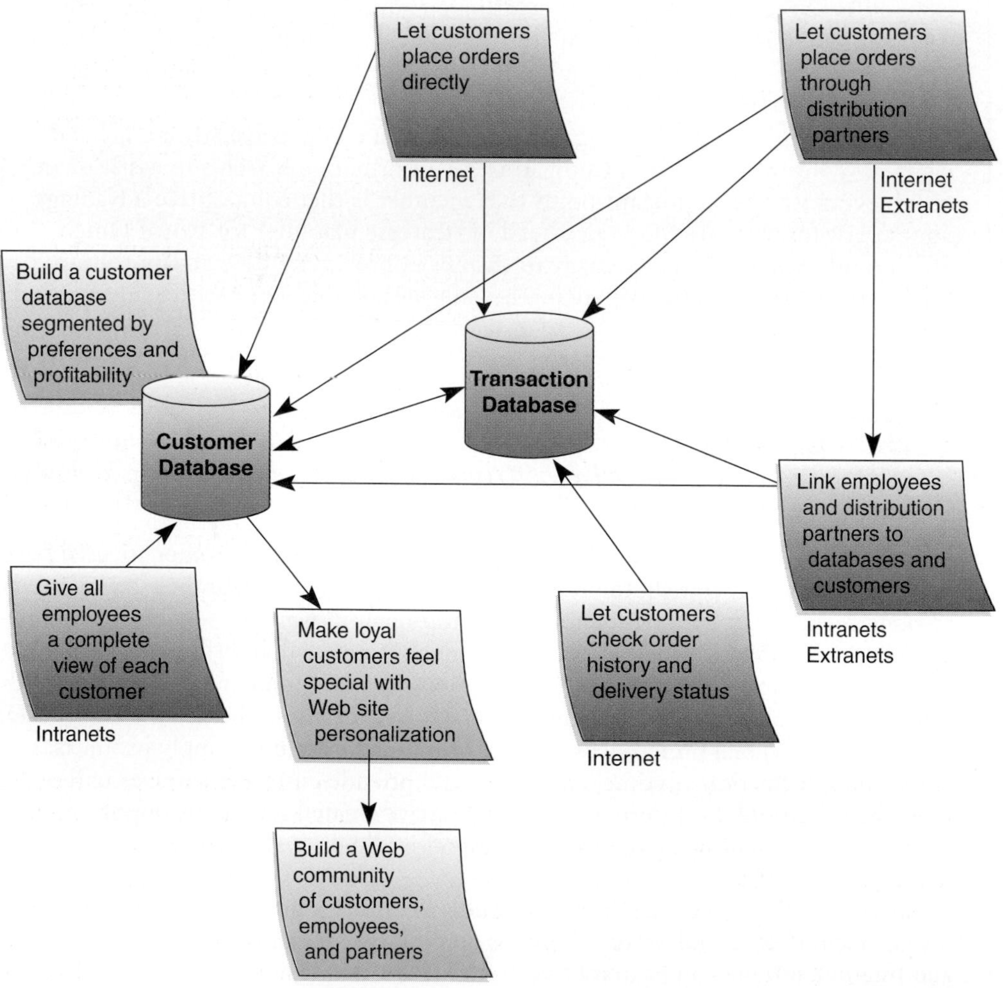

business streamlines all business processes systems that provide its employees with a have the information they need to offer th vice. A customer-focused business helps i while also helping them do their jobs. Fina community of customers, employees, and b loyalty while fostering cooperation to pr [24]. Let's review a real-world example.

Hilton Hotels: e-Business with the Customer in Mind

Hilton Hotels, via Carrolton, Texas-based Hil prides itself in having one of the fastest reservation s more than 2,400 hotels located in 65 countries worldwide, than 31 million calls and generates more than 9 million reserva Despite this incredible volume, the average time to complete a reser than two minutes. This high level of efficiency and customer service is the direct result of Hilton's innovative application of information technology.

Here's how the system works: When a call comes in to HRW, the Dialed Number Identification Services (DNIS) immediately identifies the Hilton brand that the customer is calling. The call is then passed to a reservation specialist for that brand, who uses Hilton's reservation front-end client to assist in locating the hotel brand reservation and room availability information. This information is immediately displayed on the reservation specialist's desktop as the call is being transferred. If accommodations are not available for the caller's choice of hotel, the specialist can click an onscreen button to start a search of other reservation databases. Within seconds, the reservation specialist can cross-sell an alternate Hilton property.

Innovative applications of IT have also been used to automate specific portions of the reservation system, further enabling agents to handle additional transactions and reducing the time and agent expense associated with each call. This point is where the interactive voice response (IVR) system enters the picture. Once an agent books the reservation, the customer is transferred to the IVR system. The IVR reads back and confirms the customer's reservation information, freeing the reservation specialist for the next customer. Callers can select their next option from the IVR—including being transferred back to an agent if required—or hang up to complete the transaction.

Hilton has also streamlined the reservation process for those who wish to use the Hilton.com Web site. Frequent guests have services automatically tailored to their last visit, and meeting planners access the Web site for group reservations and floor plans of venues. The Hilton Web site is designed for multiple customer segments as part of Hilton's direct-to-customer business model. Every customer segment—the business traveler, the tourist, the meeting planner, and the travel agent—has been accommodated.

To implement this e-business initiative, Hilton integrates workflows, a reservation system, call centers, and business processes with the common goal of obtaining more finely segmented customer data [16, 30].

The Value Chain and Strategic IS

Let's look at another important concept that can help you identify opportunities for strategic information systems. The **value chain** concept was developed by Michael Porter [21] and is illustrated in Figure 2.7. It views a firm as a series, chain, or network of basic activities that add value to its products and services and thus add a margin of value to both the firm and its customers. In the value chain conceptual framework, some business activities are primary processes; others are support processes. *Primary processes* are those business activities that are directly related to

...chain of a firm. Note the examples of the variety of strategic information systems that can ...business processes for competitive advantage.

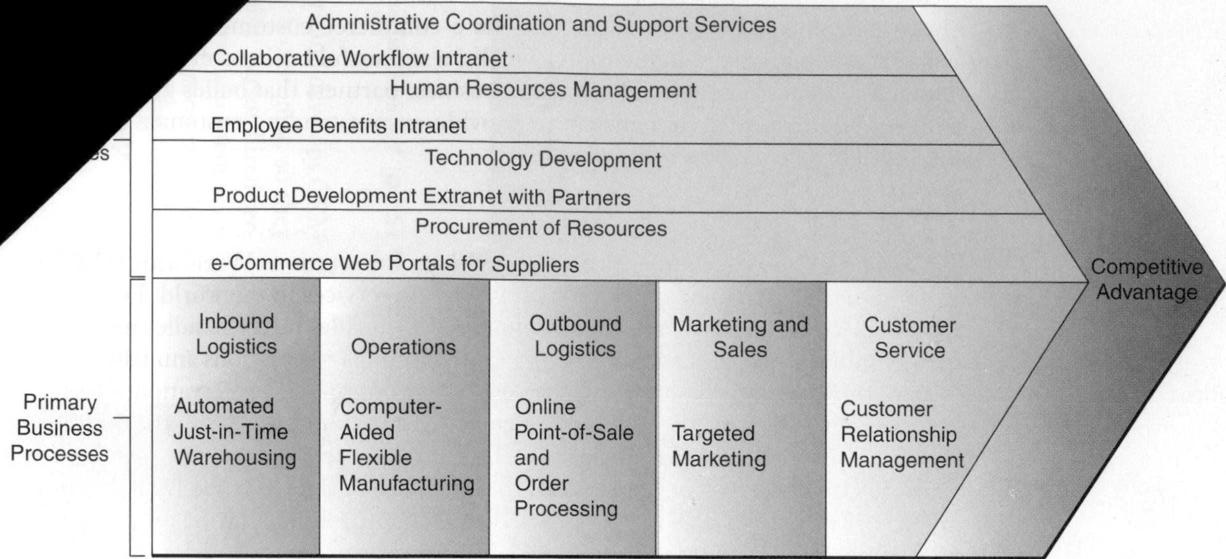

the manufacturing of products or the delivery of services to the customer. In contrast, *support processes* are those business activities that help support the day-to-day running of the business and that indirectly contribute to the products or services of the organization. This framework can highlight where competitive strategies can best be applied in a business. That is, managers and business professionals should try to develop a variety of strategic uses of the Internet and other technologies for those basic processes that add the most value to a company's products or services and thus to the overall business value of the company.

Value Chain Examples

Figure 2.7 provides examples of how and where information technologies can be applied to basic business processes using the value chain framework. For example, the figure illustrates that collaborative workflow intranets can increase the communications and collaboration required to improve administrative coordination and support services dramatically. An employee benefits intranet can help the human resources management function provide employees with easy, self-service access to their benefits information. Extranets enable a company and its global business partners to use the Web to jointly design products and processes. Finally, e-commerce Web portals can dramatically improve procurement of resources by providing online marketplaces for a firm's suppliers.

Examples of strategic applications of information systems technology to primary business processes are also identified by the value chain model in Figure 2.7. These include automated just-in-time warehousing systems to support inbound logistic processes involving the storage of inventory, computer-aided flexible manufacturing systems for manufacturing operations, and online point-of-sale and order processing systems to improve the outbound logistics processes that process customer orders. Information systems can also support marketing and sales processes by developing an interactive targeted marketing capability on the Internet and the Web. Finally, customer service can be dramatically improved by a coordinated and integrated customer relationship management system.

Thus, the value chain concept can help you identify where and how to apply the strategic capabilities of information technology. It shows how various types of information technologies might be applied to specific business processes to help a firm gain competitive advantages in the marketplace.

SECTION II Using Information Technology for Strategic Advantage

Strategic Uses of IT

Organizations may view and use information technology in many ways. For example, companies may choose to use information systems strategically, or they may be content to use IT to support efficient everyday operations. But if a company emphasized strategic business uses of information technology, its management would view IT as a major competitive differentiator. They would then devise business strategies that use IT to develop products, services, and capabilities that give the company major advantages in the markets in which it competes. In this section, we provide many examples of such strategic business applications of information technology. See Figure 2.8.

Read the Real World Case about using information technology to build strategic customer relationships. We can learn a lot about the competitive advantage gained through knowledge management systems.

Reengineering Business Processes

One of the most important implementations of competitive strategies is **business process reengineering** (BPR), often simply called *reengineering*. Reengineering is a fundamental rethinking and radical redesign of business processes to achieve dramatic improvements in cost, quality, speed, and service. So BPR combines a strategy of promoting business innovation with a strategy of making major improvements to business processes so that a company can become a much stronger and more successful competitor in the marketplace.

However, Figure 2.9 points out that though the potential payback of reengineering is high, so is its risk of failure and level of disruption to the organizational environment [10]. Making radical changes to business processes to dramatically improve efficiency and effectiveness is not an easy task. For example, many companies have used cross-functional enterprise resource planning (ERP) software to reengineer, automate, and integrate their manufacturing, distribution, finance, and human resource business processes. Although many companies have reported impressive gains with such ERP reengineering projects, many others have experienced dramatic failures or failed to achieve the improvements they sought (as we saw in the Real World Cases in Chapter 1).

Many companies have found that *organizational redesign* approaches are an important enabler of reengineering, along with the use of information technology. For example, one common approach is the use of self-directed cross-functional or multidisciplinary *process teams*. Employees from several departments or specialties, including engineering, marketing, customer service, and manufacturing, may work as a team on the product development process. Another example is the use of *case managers*, who handle almost all tasks in a business process instead of splitting tasks among many different specialists.

Evolve Business Processes, Don't Reengineer Them

For many people, discussing business-process-management is an academic exercise that doesn't lead to business results.

But Rosemary Baczewski, director of process and performance improvement at Horizon Blue Cross Blue Shield of N. J., sums up what it's all about when she tells the story of when her team identified a health care claims process that usually took 7.6 days to complete. In an experiment, two managers hand-carrying the same claim managed to push it past the right parties in only 45 minutes.

"This was a wakeup call to the company. The employees can't necessarily work harder. The process has to work harder," she says.

REAL WORLD CASE 2 GE Energy and GE Healthcare: Using Information Technology to Create Strategic Customer Relationships

When the global network that is the Internet arrived on the scene alongside rapidly advancing capabilities for large-scale storage and data analysis, most companies in the world were not aware of the strategic impact of the confluence of these information technologies. But a few proactive IT-savvy companies spotted the shift in the economics that these new IT developments provided. Now their products could be networked and accessed at their customers' sites, and this connectivity was cheap enough to permit continual monitoring of them anywhere in the world. Even a company like General Electric, already the premier model for downstream service expansion, saw unprecedented opportunities for strategic relationships and returns.

Look at GE's power turbine business, for instance. Its customers are major utilities, and they have good reason to hate equipment failures. At the least, any downtime creates huge opportunity costs for these customers; often it means they have to pay hefty regulatory compliance fines. To reduce that risk, GE (and its competition) invests heavily in information technologies for remote monitoring and diagnostics so it can deploy a technician or engineer ahead of a failure as opposed to on a planned schedule, based on assumptions about the maintenance needed by each type of turbine, or, even worse, after a turbine fails and the power has gone off.

This strategic investment in IT has a dramatic effect on the profitability of GE's maintenance services. Most manufacturers cannot charge more than $90 to $110 per hour for

FIGURE 2.8

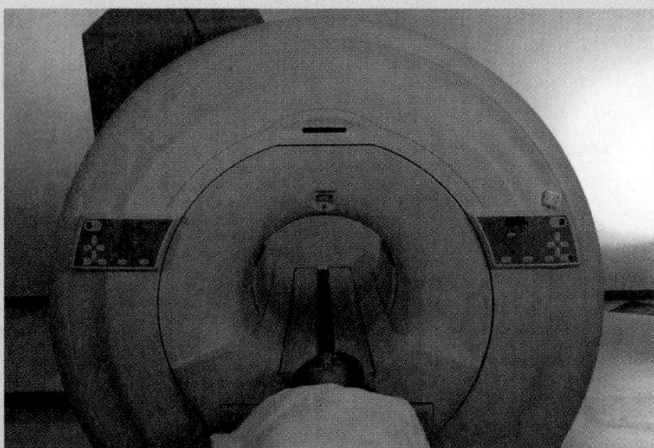

Networking and data storage and analysis technologies enable companies like GE Healthcare to gain a competitive advantage by becoming the sole provider of MRI scanners and all support services to their medical radiology customers.

their technical support because of price and benefit pressures from local competitors. But GE Energy, because of its efficient network-enabled remote servicing, can charge $500 to $600 per hour for the same technician. Even more important, the information generated by its continual monitoring allows GE to take on additional tasks, such as managing a customer's spare parts inventory or providing the customer's and GE's service and support personnel with complete access to unified data and knowledge about the status of the equipment.

Customers now look to GE not just for high-quality energy equipment but also for help in optimizing their ability to supply consistent and high-quality power to their customers. So GE has created a significant amount of customer dependency for its services, which has allowed GE to tie its pricing to the business benefits it provides ("power by the hour"), for instance, rather than the products themselves.

The same kinds of economics are at work at GE Healthcare. Its typical customer is a medical radiology clinic in the market for a new MRI (magnetic resonance imaging) machine. But these customers have not purchased such machines in years. Given the rapidly obsolescent technology involved and the quirks of hospital finances, they've tended to lease the machines. Now even conventional leasing has gone by the wayside as companies like GE offer to install the equipment at no upfront cost and instead charge for its ongoing upkeep and use. Think, for example, of all the activities associated with the life cycle of an MRI scanner:

1. Determining requirements and whether having a scanner is justified.
2. Financing the scanner.
3. Installing the scanner.
4. Testing, calibrating, and validating the scanner.
5. Maintaining and replacing parts.
6. Replenishing materials (gases and imaging media).
7. Training personnel to use the scanner.
8. Determining a patient's need for a scan (preliminary diagnosis).
9. Preparing the patient for a scan.
10. Scanning the patient.
11. Interpreting the scan.
12. Updating the software.
13. Upgrading the hardware.

Because of the high value, complexity, and cost of MRI scanning, most of these activities represent a business opportunity for a scanner manufacturer. (Only activities 8–11 are primarily medical matters and not the province of a manufacturer.) But that still leaves nine activities that are economic opportunities for scanner makers. This scenario is precisely the situation GE Healthcare has stepped into, positioning itself as a complete solution provider for its customers.

The strategic business result is a longer-term relationship than a traditional product sale would have yielded. Under the old model, a customer bought or leased a product and got some kind of warranty and support package with it. Then a salesperson would come back within a predictable amount of time to try to sell an upgrade or extension to the product or support services. Under the new model, the customer simply signs up, typically for a five-year-plus relationship with a major asset. All the support and replenishables related to that machine are handled, through individual transactions, as part of the managed service. By analogy, imagine not buying or leasing the car of your choice but instead paying for its use by the mile.

GE's ability to price those "miles" right is critical to its ongoing competitiveness. For an MRI machine, GE must estimate the number of images that will be required over the life of the contract based on the demographics of the customer's service area. Again, the company can make such estimates because of its investment in information technology for network monitoring, diagnostics, and data analysis of the use of its products at customer sites throughout the world.

Not long ago, we met with managers in GE's industrial capital equipment leasing division. These are the people responsible for those leased trailers you find at practically every construction site on earth. We were incredulous when we heard how much self-awareness the trailers have, even down to the number of times a particular door or window is opened in a given period. Why collect data on such seemingly minor events in the life of each trailer? "Because," we were told, "the business is actuarial science now."

Source: Adapted from Glen Allmendinger and Ralph Lombreglia, "Four Strategies for the Age of Smart Services," *Harvard Business Review*, October 2005; Peter Weill and Sinan Aral, "Generating Premium Returns on Your IT Investments," *MIT Sloan Management Review*, Winter 2006.

CASE STUDY QUESTIONS

1. What are the business benefits of using information technology to build strategic customer relationships for GE Energy and GE Healthcare? What are the business benefits for their customers?
2. What strategic uses of information technology discussed in this chapter and summarized in Figures 2.3 and 2.5 do you see implemented in this case? Explain the reasons for your choices.
3. How could other companies benefit from the use of IT to build strategic customer relationships? Provide or propose several examples of such uses. Explain how each benefits the business and its customers.

REAL WORLD ACTIVITIES

1. Use the Internet to discover if GE Energy and GE Healthcare are expanding or strengthening their uses of IT to build strategic customer relationships. What benefits are they gaining for themselves and claiming for their customers?
2. Use the Internet to discover other companies whose products are networked, monitored, diagnosed, and managed at customers' sites like the GE companies in this case. Alternatively, choose other companies you can research on the Internet and propose several ways they could implement and benefit from similar uses of information technology.
3. What business control and security concerns might a business customer have with the extent of its dependency on GE for the use and maintenance of assets that are vital to the operation of the business? Break into small groups to discuss the rationale for these concerns and what measures both the business and GE could take to reduce any security threats and improve a customer's secure control of the business assets it obtains from GE.

FIGURE 2.9
Some of the key ways that business process reengineering differs from business improvement.

	Business Improvement	Business Process Reengineering
Level of Change	Incremental	Radical
Process Change	Improved new version of process	Brand-new process
Starting Point	Existing processes	Clean slate
Frequency of Change	One-time or continuous	Periodic one-time change
Time Required	Short	Long
Typical Scope	Narrow, within functions	Broad, cross functional
Horizon	Past and present	Future
Participation	Bottom-up	Top-down
Path to Execution	Cultural	Cultural, structural
Primary Enabler	Statistical control	Information technology
Risk	Moderate	High

Source: Adapted from Howard Smith and Peter Fingar, *Business Process Management: The Third Wave* (Tampa, FL: Meghan-Kiffer Press, 2003), p. 118.

Baczewski said her business-process improvement team at Horizon tries to teach business-process managers to avoid excessive studying and defining of a business-process problem. "When you have 60% of the data you need, evaluate it and go with your gut" on how best to improve it, she said.

Many acknowledge that the field of business-process management, despite keen interest among managers inside companies, got something of a bad name during the 1990s when it was presented as business-process reengineering. Trying to reengineer many company processes at the same time proved disruptive and, in many cases, counterproductive. Now the goal is to improve business processes and capitalize on potential new efficiencies as a business evolves.

"CIOs are in their third year of relentless cost pressure to deliver more results, while meeting new requirements like those of the Sarbanes-Oxley Act. Improving business processes has to include collecting feedback on changes and using that feedback to further improve the overall business," says Robert Farrell, president of Metastorm Inc., a business-process-management software supplier. "We need round-trip business-process management."

Just as with Horizon, new systems at Agilent Technologies, Inc. (www.agilent.com) have enabled simplification and standardization of processes across the entire company. Real-time information about inventory and order status, easier-to-understand invoicing and pricing, and improved visibility in product delivery lead times are just some of the benefits being realized by Agilent customers, suppliers, and vendors.

Such approaches monitor and measure the results of business-process change, evaluate them, and try to further improve the process with that information. In other words, the job isn't over just because the process was changed. [1, 29]

The Role of Information Technology

Information technology plays a major role in reengineering most business processes. The speed, information processing capabilities, and connectivity of computers and Internet technologies can substantially increase the efficiency of business processes, as well as communications and collaboration among the people responsible for their

FIGURE 2.10 The order management process consists of several business processes and crosses the boundaries of traditional business functions.

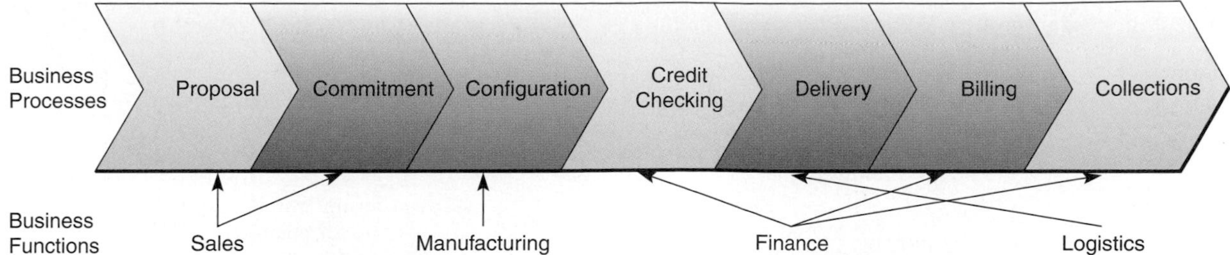

operation and management. For example, the order management process illustrated in Figure 2.10 is vital to the success of most companies [6]. Many of them are reengineering this process with ERP software and Web-enabled electronic business and commerce systems, as outlined in Figure 2.11. Let's take a look at an example.

Becoming an Agile Company

We are changing from a competitive environment in which mass-market products and services were standardized, long-lived, information-poor, and exchanged in one-time transactions, to an environment in which companies compete globally with niche market products and services that are individualized, short-lived, information-rich, and exchanged on an ongoing basis with customers [12].

Agility in business performance means the ability of a company to prosper in rapidly changing, continually fragmenting global markets for high-quality, high-performance, customer-configured products and services. An **agile company** can make a profit in markets with broad product ranges and short model lifetimes and can produce orders individually and in arbitrary lot sizes. It supports *mass customization* by offering individualized products while maintaining high volumes of production. Agile companies depend heavily on Internet technologies to integrate and manage their business processes while providing the information processing power to treat masses of customers as individuals.

To be an agile company, a business must implement four basic strategies. First, customers must perceive the products or services of an agile company as solutions to their individual problems. Thus, products can be priced on the basis of their value as solutions, not their cost to produce. Second, an agile company cooperates with customers, suppliers, and other companies—even with its competitors. This cooperation allows a business to bring products to market as rapidly and cost effectively as possible, no matter where resources are located or who owns them. Third, an agile company organizes so that it thrives on change and uncertainty. It uses flexible organizational structures keyed to the requirements of different and constantly changing customer opportunities.

FIGURE 2.11 Examples of information technologies that support reengineering the order management processes.

Reengineering Order Management
• Customer relationship management systems using corporate intranets and the Internet.
• Supplier-managed inventory systems using the Internet and extranets.
• Cross-functional ERP software for integrating manufacturing, distribution, finance, and human resource processes.
• Customer-accessible e-commerce Web sites for order entry, status checking, payment, and service.
• Customer, product, and order status databases accessed via intranets and extranets by employees and suppliers.

FIGURE 2.12 How information technology can help a company be an agile competitor, with the help of customers and business partners.

Type of Agility	Description	Role of IT	Example
Customer	Ability to co-opt customers in the exploitation of innovation opportunities • As sources of innovation ideas • As cocreators of innovation • As users in testing ideas or helping other users learn about the idea	Technologies for building and enhancing virtual customer communities for product design, feedback, and testing	eBay customers are its de facto product development team because they post an average of 10,000 messages each week to share tips, point out glitches, and lobby for changes.
Partnering	Ability to leverage assets, knowledge, and competencies of suppliers, distributors, contract manufacturers, and logistics providers in the exploration and exploitation of innovation opportunities	Technologies facilitating interfirm collaboration, such as collaborative platforms and portals, supply-chain systems, etc.	Yahoo! has accomplished a significant transformation of its service from a search engine into a portal by initiating numerous partnerships to provide content and other media-related services from its Web site.
Operational	Ability to accomplish speed, accuracy, and cost economy in the exploitation of innovation opportunities	Technologies for modularization and integration of business processes	Ingram Micro, a global wholesaler, has deployed an integrated trading system, allowing its customers and suppliers to connect directly to its procurement and ERP systems.

Source: Adapted from V. Sambamurthy, Anandhi Bhaharadwaj, and Varun Grover. "Shaping Agility Through Digital Options: Reconceptualizing the Role of Information Technology in Contemporary Firms," *MIS Quarterly* (June 2003), p. 246.

Fourth, an agile company leverages the impact of its people and the knowledge they possess. By nurturing an entrepreneurial spirit, an agile company provides powerful incentives for employee responsibility, adaptability, and innovation [12].

Figure 2.12 summarizes another useful way to think about agility in business. This framework emphasizes the roles customers, business partners, and information technology can play in developing and maintaining the strategic agility of a company. Notice how information technology can enable a company to develop relationships with its customers in virtual communities that help it be an agile innovator. And as we will see repeatedly throughout this text, information technologies enable a company to partner with its suppliers, distributors, contract manufacturers, and others via collaborative portals and other Web-based supply chain systems that significantly improve its agility in exploiting innovative business opportunities [23].

Creating a Virtual Company

In today's dynamic global business environment, forming a **virtual company** can be one of the most important strategic uses of information technology. A virtual company (also called a *virtual corporation* or *virtual organization*) is an organization that uses information technology to link people, organizations, assets, and ideas.

Figure 2.13 illustrates that virtual companies typically form virtual workgroups and alliances with business partners that are interlinked by the Internet, intranets, and extranets. Notice that this company has organized internally into clusters of process and cross-functional teams linked by intranets. It has also developed alliances and extranet links that form **interenterprise information systems** with suppliers,

FIGURE 2.13 A virtual company uses the Internet, intranets, and extranets to form virtual workgroups and support alliances with business partners.

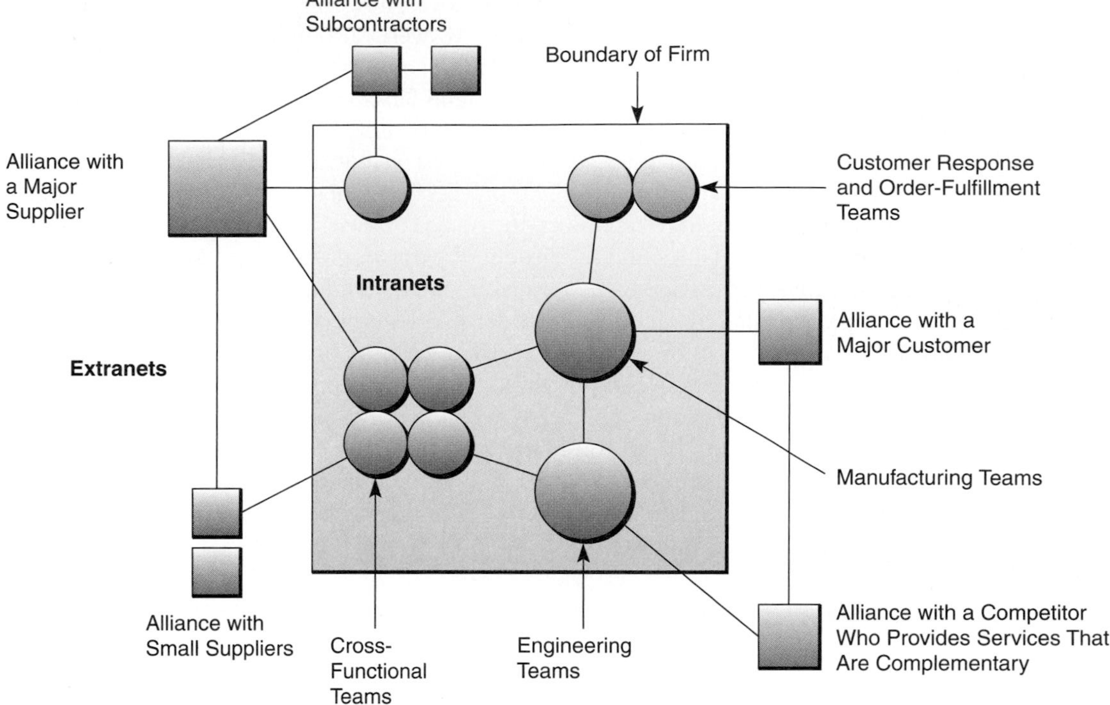

customers, subcontractors, and competitors. Thus, virtual companies create flexible and adaptable virtual workgroups and alliances keyed to exploit fast-changing business opportunities [2].

Virtual Company Strategies

Why are people forming virtual companies? Several major reasons stand out and are summarized in Figure 2.14. People and corporations are forming virtual companies as the best way to implement key business strategies and alliances that promise to ensure success in today's turbulent business climate.

For example, to quickly exploit a new market opportunity, a business may not have the time or resources to develop the manufacturing and distribution infrastructure, personnel competencies, and information technologies needed. Only by quickly forming a virtual company through a strategic alliance of all-star partners can it assemble the components it needs to provide a world-class solution for customers and capture the market opportunity. Of course, today, the Internet, intranets, extranets, and a variety of other Internet technologies are vital components in creating such successful solutions.

FIGURE 2.14 The basic business strategies of virtual companies.

Strategies of Virtual Companies
• Share infrastructure and risk with alliance partners.
• Link complementary core competencies.
• Reduce concept-to-cash time through sharing.
• Increase facilities and market coverage.
• Gain access to new markets and share market or customer loyalty.
• Migrate from selling products to selling solutions.

Cisco Systems: Virtual Manufacturing

Most people who have heard of Cisco Systems (www.cisco.com) would not be surprised to learn that Cisco is the world's largest supplier of telecommunications products. What they may be surprised to discover, however, is the answer to the question, "What does Cisco manufacture?" Answer: Absolutely nothing! Cisco sells solutions to their customers, but their products come from an innovative virtual manufacturing company arrangement with Jabil Circuit and Hamilton Standard, two large electronics suppliers and manufacturers. Let's look at an example of how these three companies collaborate to bring a Cisco solution to market.

An order placed for a Cisco product arrives simultaneously at Cisco in San Jose, California, and Jabil in St. Petersburg, Florida, via Cisco's online ordering system. Jabil immediately starts to build the product by drawing parts from any or all of three onsite inventories: one owned by Jabil, one belonging to Cisco, and one owned and controlled by Hamilton Standard. When the manufacturing process is complete, the product is tested and checked against the order in St. Petersburg by computers in San Jose, then shipped directly to the customer by Jabil. The shipment triggers the generation of a Cisco invoice sent to the customer and electronic bills from both Jabil and Hamilton Standard sent to Cisco in San Jose. Cisco's virtual manufacturing company alliance with Jabil Circuit and Hamilton Standard gives them an agile, build-to-order capability in the fiercely competitive telecommunications equipment industry [26].

Building a Knowledge-Creating Company

In an economy where the only certainty is uncertainty, the one sure source of lasting competitive advantage is knowledge. When markets shift, technologies proliferate, competitors multiply, and products become obsolete almost overnight, successful companies are those that consistently create new knowledge, disseminate it widely throughout the organization, and quickly embody it in new technologies and products. These activities define the "knowledge-creating" company, whose sole business is continuous innovation [20].

To many companies today, lasting competitive advantage can only be realized if they become **knowledge-creating companies** or *learning organizations.* That means consistently creating new business knowledge, disseminating it widely throughout the company, and quickly building the new knowledge into their products and services.

Knowledge-creating companies exploit two kinds of knowledge. One is *explicit knowledge*—data, documents, and things written down or stored on computers. The other kind is *tacit knowledge*—the "how-tos" of knowledge—which resides in workers. Tacit knowledge can often represent some of the most important information within an organization. Often, longtime employees of a company "know" many things about how to manufacture a product, deliver the service, deal with a particular vendor, or operate an essential piece of equipment. This tacit knowledge is not recorded or codified anywhere because it has evolved in the employee's mind through years of experience. Furthermore, much of this tacit knowledge is never shared with anyone who might be in a position to record it in a more formal way because there is often little incentive to do so or simply, "Nobody ever asked."

As illustrated in Figure 2.15, successful **knowledge management** creates techniques, technologies, systems, and rewards for getting employees to share what they know and make better use of accumulated workplace and enterprise knowledge. In that way, employees of a company are leveraging knowledge as they do their jobs [20].

Knowledge Management Systems

Making personal knowledge available to others is the central activity of the knowledge-creating company. It takes place continuously and at all levels of the organization [20].

Knowledge management has thus become one of the major strategic uses of information technology. Many companies are building **knowledge management systems** (KMS)

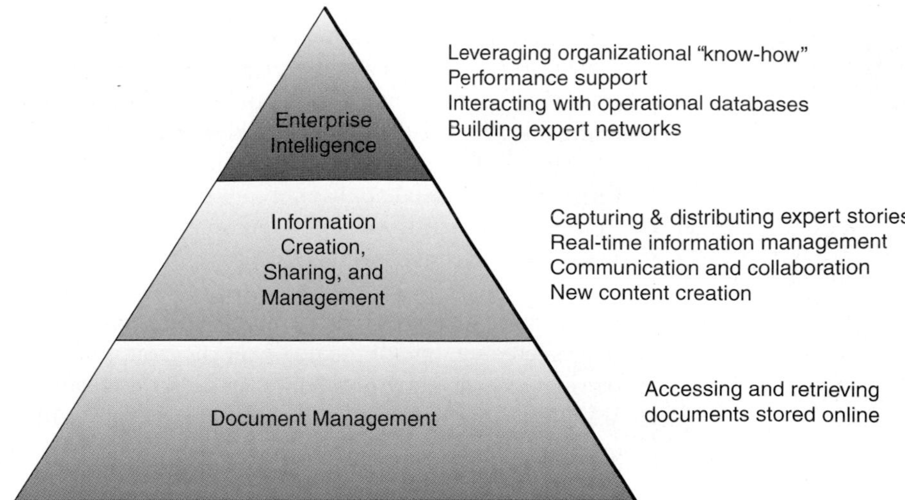

FIGURE 2.15
Knowledge management can be viewed as three levels of techniques, technologies, and systems that promote the collection, organization, access, sharing, and use of workplace and enterprise knowledge.

Source: Adapted from Marc Rosenberg, *e-Learning: Strategies for Delivering Knowledge in the Digital Age* (New York: McGraw-Hill, 2001), p. 70.

to manage organizational learning and business know-how. The goal of such systems is to help knowledge workers create, organize, and make available important business knowledge, wherever and whenever it's needed in an organization. This information includes processes, procedures, patents, reference works, formulas, "best practices," forecasts, and fixes. As you will see in Chapter 9, Internet and intranet Web sites, groupware, data mining, knowledge bases, and online discussion groups are some of the key technologies that may be used by a KMS.

Knowledge management systems also facilitate organizational learning and knowledge creation. They are designed to provide rapid feedback to knowledge workers, encourage behavior changes by employees, and significantly improve business performance. As the organizational learning process continues and its knowledge base expands, the knowledge-creating company works to integrate its knowledge into its business processes, products, and services. This integration helps the company become a more innovative and agile provider of high-quality products and customer services, as well as a formidable competitor in the marketplace [22]. Now let's close this chapter with an example of knowledge management strategies from the real world.

BAE Systems PLC: Managing Its Intellectual Capital

It's elusive, complex, and strategically essential to every modern organization: the capture of the seemingly infinite amount of intellectual capital carried by tens of thousands of employees around the world and then using it to achieve competitive advantage. London-based BAE Systems PLC, formerly British Aerospace, found its holy grail in its highly successful knowledge management (KM) intranet. The system is used by thousands of BAE engineers located in 110 offices across five continents to both search for vital information related to ongoing strategic initiatives and identify and eliminate redundant project work.

In early 1999, BAE Systems invested roughly $150,000 to study its global operations to determine whether it had the right information to support decision-making processes and if BAE employees had the right learning systems to help them support their daily activities. The results were remarkably revealing. The study showed that nearly two-thirds of BAE's top 120 decision makers didn't have the right information at key phases of the decision process. Furthermore, 80% of BAE employees were "wasting" an average of 30 minutes each day simply trying to locate the information they needed to do their jobs. Yet another 60% were spending an hour or more duplicating the work of others. Finally, one of the biggest problems revealed by the study was the large-scale information overload on the company intranets. The information itself was often unstructured, and the search engines were inadequate for conducting keyword searches to find information.

After testing several search engine technologies, BAE incorporated the best performer into the KM application on its corporate intranet. The system paid for itself in just seven months. The first demonstration of its effectiveness came in late 1999 when two different groups of BAE engineers in the United Kingdom were working on wing construction issues for the company's Harrier 2 military aircraft. After using the KM system to search for wing specification information across the company's intranet, one of the engineering groups discovered that the other group was working on the same problem. Catching this redundancy early in the cycle saved BAE millions—more than enough to pay for the entire new system! Within one year, BAE estimated the new KM system reduced the time needed to retrieve information from its intranet by 90%. Even a company that specializes in building things that go very fast above the ground can learn how to do things faster on the ground [15, 28].

Summary

- **Strategic Uses of Information Technology.** Information technologies can support many competitive strategies. They can help a business cut costs, differentiate and innovate in its products and services, promote growth, develop alliances, lock in customers and suppliers, create switching costs, raise barriers to entry, and leverage its investment in IT resources. Thus, information technology can help a business gain a competitive advantage in its relationships with customers, suppliers, competitors, new entrants, and producers of substitute products. Refer to Figures 2.3 and 2.5 for summaries of the uses of information technology for strategic advantage.
- **Building a Customer-Focused Business.** A key strategic use of Internet technologies is to build a company that develops its business value by making customer value its strategic focus. Customer-focused companies use Internet, intranet, and extranet e-commerce Web sites and services to keep track of their customers' preferences; to supply products, services, and information anytime, anywhere; and to provide services tailored to the individual needs of the customers.
- **Reengineering Business Processes.** Information technology is a key ingredient in reengineering business operations because it enables radical changes to business processes that dramatically improve their efficiency and effectiveness. Internet technologies can play a major role in supporting innovative changes in the design of workflows, job requirements, and organizational structures in a company.
- **Becoming an Agile Company.** A business can use information technology to help it become an agile company. Then it can prosper in rapidly changing markets with broad product ranges and short model lifetimes in which it must process orders in arbitrary lot sizes and can offer its customers customized products while maintaining high volumes of production. An agile company depends heavily on Internet technologies to help it be responsive to its customers with solutions customized to their needs and cooperate with its customers, suppliers, and other businesses to bring products to market as rapidly and cost effectively as possible.
- **Creating a Virtual Company.** Forming virtual companies has become an important competitive strategy in today's dynamic global markets. Internet and other information technologies play a key role in providing computing and telecommunications resources to support the communications, coordination, and information flows needed. Managers of a virtual company depend on IT to help them manage a network of people, knowledge, financial, and physical resources provided by many business partners to quickly take advantage of rapidly changing market opportunities.
- **Building a Knowledge-Creating Company.** Lasting competitive advantage today can only come from the innovative use and management of organizational knowledge by knowledge-creating companies and learning organizations. Internet technologies are widely used in knowledge management systems to support the creation and dissemination of business knowledge and its integration into new products, services, and business processes.

Key Terms and Concepts

These are the key terms and concepts of this chapter. The page number of their first explanation is in parentheses.

1. Agile company (57)
2. Business process reengineering (53)
3. Competitive forces (42)
4. Competitive strategies (45)
5. Create switching costs (47)
6. Customer value (49)
7. Interenterprise information systems (58)
8. Knowledge-creating company (60)
9. Knowledge management system (60)
10. Leverage investment in IT (47)
11. Lock in customers and suppliers (46)
12. Raise barriers to entry (47)
13. Strategic information systems (42)
14. Value chain (51)
15. Virtual company (58)

Review Quiz

Match one of the key terms and concepts listed previously with one of the brief examples or definitions that follow. Try to find the best fit for answers that seem to fit more than one term or concept. Defend your choices.

____ 1. A business must deal with customers, suppliers, competitors, new entrants, and substitutes.

____ 2. Cost leadership, differentiation of products, and new product innovation are examples.

____ 3. Using investments in technology to keep firms out of an industry.

____ 4. Making it unattractive for a firm's customers or suppliers to switch to its competitors.

____ 5. Time, money, and effort needed for customers or suppliers to change to a firm's competitors.

____ 6. Information systems that reengineer business processes or promote business innovation are examples.

____ 7. This strategic focus recognizes that quality, rather than price, has become the primary determinant in customers choosing a product or service.

____ 8. Highlights how strategic information systems can be applied to a firm's business processes and support activities for competitive advantage.

____ 9. A business finding strategic uses for the computing and telecommunications capabilities it has developed to run its operations.

____ 10. Information technology helping a business make radical improvements in business processes.

____ 11. A business can prosper in rapidly changing markets while offering its customers individualized solutions to their needs.

____ 12. A network of business partners formed to take advantage of rapidly changing market opportunities.

____ 13. Learning organizations that focus on creating, disseminating, and managing business knowledge.

____ 14. Information systems that manage the creation and dissemination of organizational knowledge.

____ 15. Using the Internet and extranets to link a company's information systems to those of its customers and suppliers.

Discussion Questions

1. Suppose you are a manager being asked to develop computer-based applications to gain a competitive advantage in an important market for your company. What reservations might you have about doing so? Why?
2. How could a business use information technology to increase switching costs and lock in its customers and suppliers? Use business examples to support your answers.
3. How could a business leverage its investment in information technology to build strategic IT capabilities that serve as a barrier to new entrants into its markets?
4. Refer to the Real World Case on FedEx Corporation in the chapter. Could any of FedEx's information technology strategies be copied by a small business to give it a competitive advantage? Why or why not? Use an example to illustrate your answer.

5. What strategic role can information play in business process reengineering?
6. How can Internet technologies help a business form strategic alliances with its customers, suppliers, and others?
7. How could a business use Internet technologies to form a virtual company or become an agile competitor?
8. Refer to the Real World Case on GE Energy and GE Healthcare in the chapter. Is it really necessary for GE's industrial capital leasing division to capture data each time a door or window is opened or closed in one of its leased trailers at construction sites all over the world? Is this overkill or a proper use of IT for competitive advantage? Defend your answer.
9. Information technology can't really give a company a strategic advantage, because most competitive advantages don't last more than a few years and soon become strategic necessities that just raise the stakes of the game. Discuss.
10. MIS author and consultant Peter Keen says: "We have learned that it is not technology that creates a competitive edge, but the management process that exploits technology." What does he mean? Do you agree or disagree? Why?

Analysis Exercises

1. End User Computing

Skill Assessment

Not all programs are written by dedicated programmers. Many knowledge workers write their own software using familiar word processing, spreadsheet, presentation, and database tools. This textbook contains end-user computing exercises representing a real-world programming challenge. This first exercise will allow your course instructor to assess the class. Assess your skills in each of the following areas:

- **a.** Word processing: Approximately how many words per minute can you type? Do you use styles to manage document formatting? Have you ever set up your own mail merge template and data source? Have you created your own macros to handle repetitive tasks? Have you ever added branching or looping logic in your macro programs?
- **b.** Spreadsheets: Do you know the order of operations your spreadsheet program uses (what does "55*2^2-10" equal)? Do you know how to automatically sort data in a spreadsheet? Do you know how to create graphs and charts from spreadsheet data? Can you build pivot tables from spreadsheet data? Do you know the difference between a relative and a fixed cell reference? Do you know how to use functions in your spreadsheet equations? Do you know how to use the IF function? Have you created your own macros to handle repetitive tasks? Have you ever added branching or looping logic in your macro programs?
- **c.** Presentations: Have you ever used presentation software to create presentation outlines? Have you added your own multimedia content to a presentation? Do you know how to add charts and graphs from spreadsheet software into your presentations so that they automatically update when the spreadsheet data change?
- **d.** Database: Have you ever imported data into a database from a text file? Have you ever written queries to sort or filter data stored in a database table? Have you built reports to format your data for output? Have you built forms to aid in manual data entry? Have you built functions or programs to manipulate data stored in database tables?

2. Marketing: Competitive Intelligence

Strategic Marketing

Marketing professionals use information systems to gather and analyze information about their competitors. They use this information to assess their product's position relative to the competition and make strategic marketing decisions about their product, its price, its distribution (place), and how to best manage its promotion. Michael Bloomberg, founder of Bloomberg (www.bloomberg.com), and others have made their fortunes gathering and selling data about businesses. Marketing professionals find information about a business's industry, location, employees, products, technologies, revenues, and market share useful when planning marketing initiatives.

During your senior year, you will find yourself in close competition for jobs. You can take the same intelligence-gathering approach used by professional marketers when planning how to sell your own skills. Use the following questions to help you prepare for your job search.

- **a.** Product: Which business majors are presently in greatest demand by employers? Use entry-level salaries as the primary indicator for demand.
- **b.** Product: What colleges or universities in your region pose the greatest competitive threat to students with your major?
- **c.** Price: What is the average salary for entry-level employees in your major and geographic region? Is salary your top concern? Why or why not?
- **d.** Place: What areas of the country are currently experiencing the greatest employment growth?
- **e.** Promotion: What is your marketing plan? Describe how you plan to get your name and qualifications in front of prospective employers. How can the Internet help you get noticed?

3. Competing against Free

Wikipedia Faces Down Encyclopedia Britannica

The record and movie industries are not the only industries to find themselves affected by free access to their products. Encyclopedia Britannica faces challenges by a nonprofit competitor that provides its services without charge or advertising, Wikipedia.org. Wikipedia depends on volunteers to create and edit original content under the condition that contributors provide their work without copyright.

Who would work for free? During the creation of the Oxford English Dictionary in the 19th century, the editors solicited word articles and references from the general public. In the 20th century, AOL.com found thousands of volunteers to monitor its chat rooms. Amazon.com coaxed over a hundred thousand readers to post book reviews on its retail Web site. Outdoing them all in the 21st century, Wikipedia published its one millionth English language article in March 2006. Wikipedia includes more than 2 million articles in over 200 languages, all created and edited by more than 1 million users.

Can Wikipedia compete on quality? Wikipedia provides its users both editing and monitoring tools, which allows users to self-police. Wikipedia also uses voluntary administrators who block vandals, temporarily protect articles, and manage arbitration processes when disputes arise. A paper published by *Nature* in December 2005 evaluated 50 Wikipedia articles and found an average of four factual errors per Wikipedia article compared with an average of three errors per article in the Encyclopedia Britannica. More significantly, Wikipedians (as the volunteers call themselves) corrected each error by January 2006. Alexa.com rated Wikipedia.com as the 17th most visited Web site on the Internet, while Britannica.com came in 2,858th place (Yahoo and Google ranked in the 1st and 2nd places).

Wikipedia has already built on its success. In addition to offering foreign language encyclopedias, it also provides a common media archive (commons.wikimedia.org), a multilingual dictionary (www.wiktionary.org), and a news service (www.wikinews.org).

a. How does the Wikimedia Foundation meet the criteria for an "agile" company?

b. How does the Wikimedia Foundation meet the criteria for a "virtual" company?

c. How does the Wikimedia Foundation meet the criteria for a "knowledge-creating" organization?

d. How would you recommend Encyclopedia Britannica adapt to this new threat?

4. Knowledge Management

Knowing What You Know

Employees often receive a great deal of unstructured information in the form of e-mails. For example, employees may receive policies, announcements, and daily operational information via e-mail. However, e-mail systems typically make poor enterprisewide knowledge management systems. New employees don't have access to e-mails predating their start date. Employees typically aren't permitted to search others' e-mail files for needed information. Organizations lose productivity when each employee spends time reviewing and organizing his or her e-mail files. Lastly, the same information may find itself saved across thousands of different e-mail files, thereby ballooning e-mail file storage space requirements.

Microsoft's Exchange server, IBM's Domino server, and Interwoven's WorkSite, along with a wide variety of open-standard Web-based products, aim to address an organization's need to share unstructured information. These products provide common repositories for various categories of information. For example, management may use a "Policy" folder in Microsoft Exchange to store all their policy decisions. Likewise, sales representatives may use a "Competitive Intelligence" database in IBM's Domino server to store information obtained during the sales process about competing products, prices, or marketplace rumors. WorkSite users categorize and store all their electronic documents in a large, searchable, secured common repository. Organizations using these systems can secure them, manage them, and make them available to the appropriate personnel. Managers can also appoint a few specific employees requiring little technical experience to manage the content.

However, these systems cannot benefit an organization if its employees fail to contribute their knowledge, if they fail to use the system to retrieve information, or if the system simply isn't available where and when needed. To help managers better understand how employees use these systems, knowledge management systems include usage statistics such as date/time, user name, reads, writes, and even specific document access information.

Research each of the products mentioned above and answer the following questions.

a. What steps might a manager take to encourage his or her employees to use their organization's knowledge management system?

b. Should managers set minimum quotas for system usage for each employee? Why or why not?

c. Aside from setting employee usage quotas, how might an organization benefit from knowledge management system usage statistics?

REAL WORLD CASE 3 GE, Dell, Intel, GM, and Others: Debating the Competitive Advantage of Information Technology

There's nothing like a punchy headline to get an article some attention. A piece in the *Harvard Business Review* (May 2003), shockingly labeled "IT Doesn't Matter," garnered the magazine more buzz than at any time since the Jack Welch affair. The article was approvingly cited in *The New York Times*, analyzed in Wall Street reports, and e-mailed around the world. But without such a dramatic and reckless title, the article probably would have received little notice. It's a sloppy mix of ersatz history, conventional wisdom, moderate insight, and unsupportable assertions. And it is dangerously wrong.

Author Nicholas Carr's main point is that information technology is nothing more than the infrastructure of modern business, similar to railroads, electricity, or the internal combustion engineering advances that have become too commonplace for any company to wangle a strategic advantage from them. Once innovative applications of information technology have now become merely a necessary cost. Thus, Carr thinks today's main risk is not underusing IT but overspending on it.

But before we get any further, let's have a reality check. First, let's ask Jeff Immelt, the CEO of General Electric Co., one of the premier business corporations in the world, "How important is information technology to GE?" Immelt's answer: "It's a business imperative. We're primarily a service-oriented company, and the lifeblood for productivity is more about tech than it is about investing in plants and equipment. We tend to get a 20 percent return on tech investments, and we tend to invest about $2.5 billion to $3 billion a year."

Then let's ask Dell Corp. CEO Michael Dell, "What's your take on Nick Carr's thesis that technology no longer gives corporate buyers a competitive advantage?" His answer: "Just about anything in business can be either a sinkhole or a competitive advantage if you do it really, really bad or you do it really, really well. And information technology is an often misunderstood field. You've got a lot of people who don't know what they're doing and don't do it very well. For us, IT is a huge advantage. For Wal-Mart, GE, and many other companies, technology is a huge advantage and will continue to be. Does that mean that you just pour money in and gold comes out? No, you can screw it up really bad."

Finally, let's ask Andy Grove, former CEO and now chairman of Intel Corp., "Nicholas Carr's recent *Harvard Business Review* article says: 'IT Doesn't Matter.' Is information technology so pervasive that it no longer offers companies a competitive advantage?" Grove says: "In any field, you can find segments that are close to maturation and draw a conclusion that the field is homogeneous. Carr is saying commercial-transaction processing in the United States and some parts of Europe has reached the top parts of an S-curve. But instead of talking about that segment, he put a provocative spin on it—that information technology doesn't matter—and suddenly the statement is grossly wrong. It couldn't be further from the truth. It's like saying: I have an old three-speed bike, and Lance Armstrong has a bike. So why should he have a competitive advantage?"

So, basically, Carr misunderstands what information technology is. He thinks it's merely a bunch of networks and computers. He notes, properly, that the price of those has plummeted and that companies bought way too much in recent years. He's also right that the hardware infrastructure of business is rapidly becoming commoditized and, even more important, standardized. Computers and networks per se are just infrastructure. However, one of the article's most glaring flaws is its complete disregard for the centrality of software and the fact that human knowledge or information can be mediated and managed by software.

Charles Fitzgerald, Microsoft's general manager for platform strategy, says that Carr doesn't put enough emphasis on the *I* in IT: "The source of competitive advantage in business is what you do with the information that technology gives you access to. How do you apply that to some particular business problem? To say IT doesn't matter is tantamount to saying that companies have enough information about their operations, customers, and employees. I have never heard a company make such a claim."

Paul Strassman, who has spent 42 years as a CIO—at General Foods, Xerox, the Pentagon, and most recently NASA—was more emphatic. "The hardware—the stuff everybody's fascinated with—isn't worth a damn," he says. "It's just disposable. Information technology today is a knowledge-capital issue. It's basically a huge amount of labor and software." He continues: "Look at the business powers—most of all Wal-Mart, but also companies like Pfizer or FedEx. They're all waging information warfare."

But one person with a truly unique set of qualifications with which to assess the article is Ralph Szygenda, CIO of General Motors. "Nicholas Carr may ultimately be correct when he says IT doesn't matter," Szygenda says. "Business-process improvement, competitive advantage, optimization, and business success do matter and they aren't commodities. To facilitate these business changes, IT can be considered a differentiator or a necessary evil. But today, it's a must in a real-time corporation."

Szygenda did concur with one of Carr's corollary recommendations: spend less. In the *HBR* article, Carr stated, "It's getting much harder to achieve a competitive advantage through an IT investment, but it is getting much easier to put your business at a cost disadvantage." Szygenda's reaction: "I also agree on spending the minimum on IT to reach desired business results. Precision investment on core infrastructure and process-differentiation IT systems is called for in today's intensely cost-conscious business versus the shotgun approach sometimes used in the past."

The real message: Spend what is required but no more to achieve essential differentiation via business processes and the IT systems that support them.

The CIO of GM continues with another agreement, though one with a significant qualification: "Yes, IT has aspects of commoditization. PCs, telecommunications, software components such as payroll, benefit programs, business-process outsourcing, and maybe even operating systems and database-management systems are examples. But the application of information systems in a corporation's product design, development, distribution, customer understanding, and cost-effective Internet services is probably at the fifth-grade level."

And, in conclusion, Szygenda's thoughts on the commodity claim: "After being a part of the IT industry for 35 years, I have heard similar pronouncements during the introduction of the integrated circuit, microprocessor, PCs, office systems, ERP systems, and the Internet. Nicholas Carr and others need to be careful not to overstate the speed of the information-management journey or they may make the same mistake that Charles H. Duell, the director of the U.S. Patent Office, did in 1899 when he said, 'Everything that can be invented has been invented.'"

Source: Adapted from David Kirkpatrick, "Stupid-Journal Alert: Why HBR's View of Tech Is Dangerous," *Fortune*, June 9, 2003, p. 190; Robert Hoff, "Andy Grove: We Can't Even Glimpse the Potential," *BusinessWeek*, August 25, 2003, pp. 86–88; "Speaking Out: View from the Top," *BusinessWeek*, August 25, 2003, pp. 108–13; Bob Evans, "Business Technology: IT Is a Must, No Matter How You View It," *InformationWeek*, May 19, 2003.

CASE STUDY QUESTIONS

1. Do you agree with the argument made by Nicholas Carr to support his position that IT no longer gives companies a competitive advantage? Why or why not?
2. Do you agree with the argument made by the business leaders in this case in support of the competitive advantage that IT can provide to a business? Why or why not?
3. What are several ways that IT could provide a competitive advantage to a business? Use some of the companies mentioned in this case as examples. Visit their Web sites to gather more information to help you answer.

REAL WORLD ACTIVITIES

1. Nicholas Carr's article created a storm of debate that is still raging. Using the Internet, see if you can find Carr's original article. Also, try to find some more opinions for and against Carr's arguments beyond those provided in the case.
2. The core of Carr's arguments has some significant implications for businesses. Break into small groups with your classmates and discuss your opinion of Carr's arguments. What are some of the implications of the argument that come to mind? How might they serve to change the way we use computers to support corporate strategy?

MODULE II

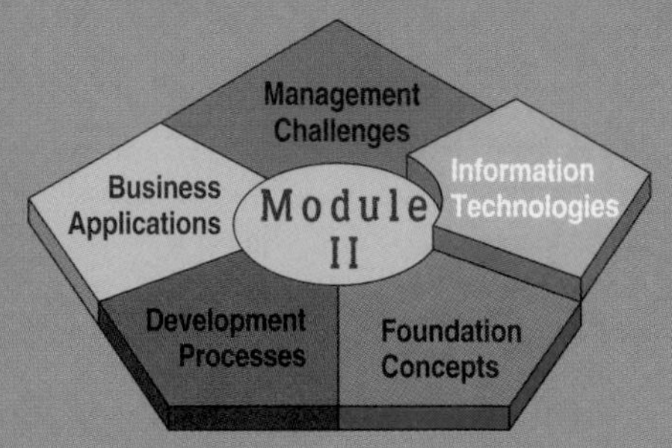

INFORMATION TECHNOLOGIES

What challenges do information system technologies pose for business professionals? What basic knowledge should you possess about information technology? The four chapters of this module give you an overview of the hardware, software, and data resource management and telecommunications network technologies used in information systems and their implications for business managers and professionals.

- **Chapter 3: Computer Hardware** reviews history, trends, and developments in microcomputer, midrange, and mainframe computer systems; basic computer system concepts; and the major types of technologies used in peripheral devices for computer input, output, and storage.
- **Chapter 4: Computer Software** reviews the basic features and trends in the major types of application software and system software used to support enterprise and end user computing.
- **Chapter 5: Data Resource Management** emphasizes management of the data resources of computer-using organizations. This chapter reviews key database management concepts and applications in business information systems.
- **Chapter 6: Telecommunications and Networks** presents an overview of the Internet and other telecommunications networks, business applications, and trends and reviews technical telecommunications alternatives.

CHAPTER 3

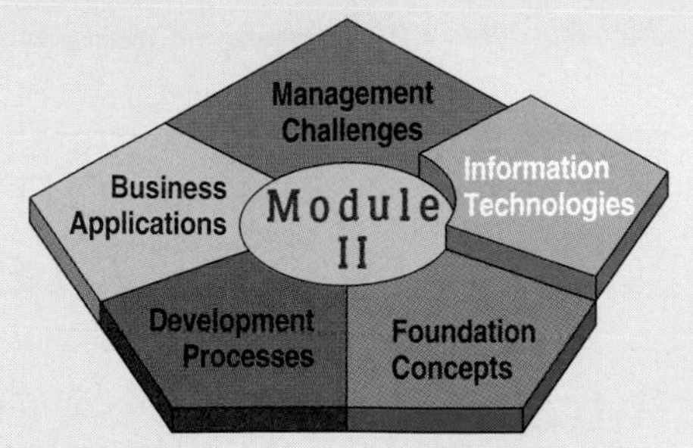

COMPUTER HARDWARE

Chapter Highlights

Learning Objectives

After reading and studying this chapter, you should be able to:

1. Understand the history and evolution of computer hardware.
2. Identify the major types and uses of microcomputer, midrange, and mainframe computer systems.
3. Outline the major technologies and uses of computer peripherals for input, output, and storage.
4. Identify and give examples of the components and functions of a computer system.
5. Identify the computer systems and peripherals you would acquire or recommend for a business of your choice, and explain the reasons for your selections.

SECTION I Computer Systems: End User and Enterprise Computing

Introduction

All computers are systems of input, processing, output, storage, and control components. In this section, we discuss the history, trends, applications, and some basic concepts of the many types of computer systems in use today. In Section II, we will cover the changing technologies for input, output, and storage that are provided by the peripheral devices that are part of modern computer systems.

Read the Real World Case regarding the business benefits and challenges of mobile computing systems. We can learn a lot about how businesses use mobile computing devices from this case. See Figure 3.1.

A Brief History of Computer Hardware

Today we are witnessing rapid technological changes on a broad scale. However, many centuries elapsed before technology was sufficiently advanced to develop computers. Without computers, many technological achievements of the past would not have been possible. To fully appreciate their contribution, however, we must understand their history and evolution. Whereas a thorough discussion of computing history is beyond the scope of this text, a brief consideration of the development of the computer is possible. Let's look quickly into the development of computers.

At the dawn of the human concept of numbers, humans used their fingers and toes to perform basic mathematical activities. Then our ancestors realized that by using some objects to represent digits, they could perform computations beyond the limited scope of their own fingers and toes.

Shells, chicken bones, or any number of objects could have been used, but the fact that the word *calculate* is derived from *calculus*, the Latin word for "small stone," suggests that pebbles or beads were arranged to form the familiar abacus, arguably the first human-made computing device. By manipulating the beads, it was possible with some skill and practice to make rapid calculations.

Blaise Pascal, a French mathematician, invented what is believed to be the first mechanical adding machine in 1642. The machine adopted partly the principles of the abacus but did away with the use of the hand to move the beads or counters. Instead, Pascal used wheels to move counters. The principle of Pascal's machine is still being used today, such as in the counters of tape recorders and odometers. In 1674, Gottfried Wilhelm Von Leibnitz improved Pascal's machine so that the machine could divide and multiply as easily as it could add and subtract.

When the age of industrialization spread throughout Europe, machines became fixtures in agricultural and production sites. An invention that made profound changes in the history of industrialization, and in the history of computing, was the mechanical loom, invented by a Frenchman named Joseph Jacquard. With the use of cards punched with holes, it was possible for the Jacquard loom to weave fabrics in a variety of patterns.

The idea of using punched cards to store a predetermined pattern to be woven by the loom clicked in the mind of Charles Babbage, an English mathematician who lived in the 19th century. He foresaw a machine that could perform all mathematical calculations, store values in its memory, and perform logical comparisons among values. He called it the *Analytical Engine*. Babbage's analytical engine, however, was never built. It lacked one thing—electronics. Herman Hollerith eventually adopted the punched card concept of Jacquard to record census data in the late 1880s. Census data were translated into a series of holes in a punched card to represent the digits and the letters of the alphabet. The card was then passed through a machine with a series of electrical contacts that were either turned off or on depending on the existence of holes in the punched cards. These different combinations of off/on situations were recorded by the machine and represented a

REAL WORLD CASE 1 Northrup Grumman, Boeing, and Others: Employee Connectivity Trumps ROI as Wireless Mobile Devices Change the Work Environment

It is usually the case that chief information officers (CIOs) need to be concerned with the return on investment (ROI) associated with the decision to deploy a particular technology solution. When it comes to wireless technologies used to empower a mobile workforce, the ROI seems a minor issue. Such technologies have become so ingrained in companies that return-on-investment concerns are often deemed less important than total connectivity of the workforce.

For example, Northrop Grumman Corp. CIO Keith Glennan claims the aerospace company views Research in Motion Ltd.'s BlackBerry handheld systems as essential to its global operations. At a CIO forum sponsored by the Wireless Internet for the Mobile Enterprise Consortium at the University of California, Los Angeles, Glennan noted that the Los Angeles–based company has rolled out 5,500 BlackBerry units to its employees, making it one of the largest users of the wireless devices.

In fact, every time RIM (Research in Motion) releases a new model, Northrop Grumman tests the technology in a corporate jet to ensure that it can provide mobile services to executives while they're in transit. Cost isn't the issue—connectivity is.

FIGURE 3.1

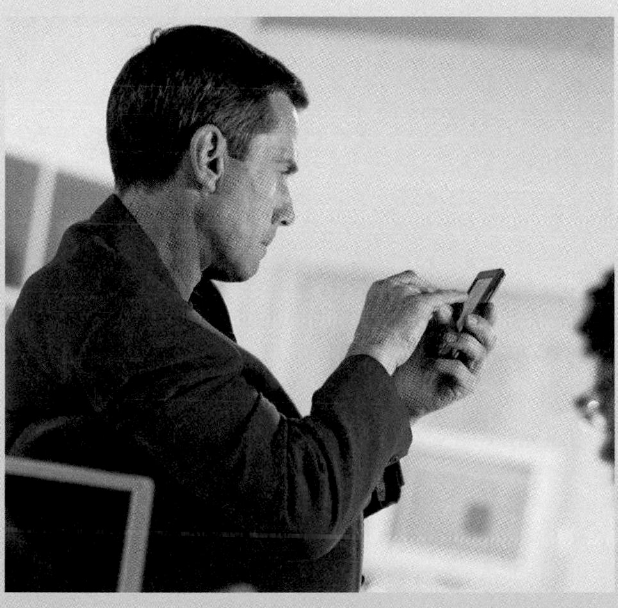

Mobile telecommunication devices allow us to conduct business anytime and virtually anywhere.

Scott Griffin, CIO at The Boeing Co. in Chicago, said his company also uses BlackBerry devices extensively with seemingly little regard to cost. Boeing does not do an ROI on mobility, he noted: "Some people simply must be connected, and then we figure out how much mobility they need."

According to Griffin, because Boeing seems to move each of its workers to new locations on an annual basis, building wireless connections into company facilities makes sense. It's easier and less expensive to hook up transplanted employees via wireless links than to install new Ethernet jacks, he said.

But Griffin adds that IT managers also have to think through the challenges of delivering all of Boeing's applications so they can be used on small LCD screens. That includes the applications now used by Boeing's engineers on high-end scientific workstations. The major challenge with this requirement is that to fully port an application to a smaller screen, a large portion of the application's interface must be recreated by IT software engineers. Often, this software development process can be more costly than the cost of acquiring or developing the original application.

The BlackBerry is the current product of choice in the U.S. corporate market for wireless devices, with over 3.7 million users in early 2007, though Windows Mobile handhelds like Palm's Treo, Motorola's Moto Q, and Samsung's Blackjack appear to have outsold Blackberry worldwide in 2006, and Nokia dominates the European and Japanese markets.

The BlackBerry provides users with phone, e-mail, text messaging, Web browser, and organizer applications in a compact and intuitive handheld. Features that most attract corporate users include the large, high-resolution screen and 65,000+ color display. In addition, integrated e-mail attachment viewing, the brightly backlit keyboard, and a battery life unrivaled among handheld wireless devices all contribute to BlackBerry's popularity.

Companies all over the world are moving to large-scale wireless solutions for their employees. Lance Perry, vice president of IT infrastructure at Cisco Systems, notes the networking vendor has about 30,000 remote users in 100 countries. "Even 9-to-5 workers have mobility needs when they go home," he pointed out. Corporate IT executives can't afford to ignore or dismiss mobility requirements because of ROI concerns, Perry advised. Mobile computing capabilities have become "a critical component of a company's success."

But Perry adds that companies can better manage their costs by using wireless technology to its fullest. For example, they could give end users IP-based "soft phones" built into

PCs for use in making international calls over public-access wireless networks.

Another example can be found at British Nuclear Fuels Limited (BNFL), a $4 billion provider of products to the nuclear energy industry. Operating in 16 countries with over 23,000 employees, BNFL recognizes that better management of e-mail and improved access to corporate data can have a dramatic impact on employee productivity. Part of BNFL's IT Manager Steve Davies's role is to keep abreast of the latest technology developments that could cut costs, maximize efficiency, and improve service.

Davies saw immediately the potential of the BlackBerry wireless solution, which would enable "downtime" to be converted into productive time. With the ability to integrate existing applications onto the BlackBerry, employees are not only able to receive and send e-mails, they can also manage their diaries instantly regardless of their physical location.

"A lot of our mobile employees are frustrated with the time it takes for a laptop to power up and dial in just to retrieve their mail. Timely communications do not just improve general communications; they are absolutely critical in some situations such as bids for major international projects or even in keeping our press officers up to speed," explains Davies.

Ken Venner, CIO at Broadcom Corp., an Irvine, California-based semiconductor maker, sees the growing ubiquity of public-access networks as a boon to Blackberry and laptop-toting mobile workers. He argues it's up to IT departments to ensure that business users have access to solid, secure connections, no matter where they're working.

But there are challenges in all this employee connectivity. It's true that mobile devices have proven themselves to be invaluable in ensuring timely communications among employees. Many managers view a Blackberry as a critical business tool, enabling them to handle any problem on the spot. But other users consider them as necessary evils, tying them to their work 24/7; still others see them as counterproductive irritants.

There's no question that the existence of the BlackBerry and similar devices has changed the way people do business. A message received on a BlackBerry—critical or not—seems to demand an immediate response, no matter the time of day. For instance, business clients and customers may expect replies to their wireless messages within minutes or question the customer-centricity of their vendors. Likewise, executives may measure the commitment of senior staff members by the speed of their wireless reply.

The downside of this instantaneous communication is that they give mobile device owners little time away from managerial concerns. Linked to senior managers via the BlackBerry, employees may have no peace from bosses who seem addicted to the mobile device and expect immediate replies to insignificant messages. Those who report to BlackBerry addicts who are also workaholics suffer the most, since they need to keep the device within reach to acknowledge messages even in the evening, while attending a social event, or when involved with their families.

Those who may be most annoyed with the BlackBerry movement, interestingly, usually don't own BlackBerries themselves. Rather, they work with people who think that any time is the right time to open their BlackBerry and attend to one or more messages. Imagine that you are in a team meeting, and suddenly one of the key participants pulls out his BlackBerry and begins to respond to an assortment of wireless messages. Too often, the group's work is interrupted as the person with a BlackBerry thumb (which comes from typing too much on the tiny keyboard) goes through each of his or her recent messages and acknowledges receipt or even replies to voice messages. The preoccupied BlackBerry user wastes the time of team members, interferes with team concentration, and may lead to hurried decisions by the user.

Like e-mail and cell phone overusers and abusers, mobile messaging can easily get in the way of effectively managing your time, both in and out of the office Mobile wireless devices have proven to be great connectivity and productivity tools, but overuse or misuse can be counterproductive to employee morale and business success.

Source: Adapted from Bob Brewin, "CIOs Say ROI on Mobile Devices Not a Big Concern: See Wireless Technology as a Must-Have," *Computerworld*, February 23, 2004; Jay Greene, "Surprise: That Mobile Is Running Windows," *BusinessWeek*, February 8, 2007; American Management Association International, "The Dark Side of the Blackberry," *AMA Seminars*, January–October 2007.

CASE STUDY QUESTIONS

1. What are several major business benefits that organizations can realize by connecting all of their employees with wireless mobile devices?
2. Are the CIOs in the case saying that ROI is not important when deploying mobile computing devices? Explain your response.
3. What are several challenges that employees and organizations face in connecting their employees with wireless mobile devices? Do these challenges outweigh the connectivity benefits you outlined earlier? Why or why not?

REAL WORLD ACTIVITIES

1. The BlackBerry mobile device, though extremely popular, is but one of several devices available for mobile communications and messaging. Using the Internet, see if you can find out who its major competitors are and what strategies they are using to advance their products into the marketplace. Is it features, price, brand, or something else? Who is the market leader? Why?
2. The case outlines several challenges to employee morale and productivity caused by overuse or misuse of wireless mobile devices. What are some of the potential problems that may arise in an organization from such challenges? What solutions can you propose? Break into small groups with your classmates to discuss these issues.

way of tabulating the result of the census. Hollerith's machine was highly successful. It cut by two-thirds the time it took to tabulate the result of the census, and it made money for the company that manufactured Hollerith's machine. In 1911 this company merged with its competitor to form International Business Machines (IBM).

The ENIAC (Electronic Numerical Integrator and Computer) was the first electronic digital computer. It was completed in 1946 at the Moore School of Electrical Engineering of the University of Pennsylvania. With no moving parts, ENIAC was programmable and had the capability to store problem calculations using vacuum tubes (about 18,000).

A computer that uses vacuum tube technology is called a first-generation computer. The ENIAC could add in 0.2 of a millisecond, or about 5,000 computations per second. The principal drawback of ENIAC was its size and processing ability. It occupied over 1,500 square feet of floor space and could process only one program or problem at a time. Figure 3.2 shows the ENIAC complex.

In the 1950s, Remington Rand manufactured the UNIVAC I (Universal Automatic Calculator). It could calculate at the rate of 10,000 additions per second. In 1957, IBM developed the IBM 704, which could perform 100,000 calculations per second.

In the late 1950s, transistors were invented and quickly replaced the thousands of vacuum tubes used in electronic computers. A transistor-based computer could perform 200,000–250,000 calculations per second. The transistorized computer represents the second generation of computer. It was not until the mid-1960s that the third generation of computers came into being. These were characterized by solid state technology and integrated circuitry coupled with extreme miniaturization.

In 1971 the fourth generation of computers was characterized by further miniaturization of circuits, increased multiprogramming, and virtual storage memory. In the 1980s the fifth generation of computers operated at speeds of 3–5 million calculations per second (for small-scale computers) and 10–15 million instructions per second (for large-scale computers).

The age of microcomputers began in 1975 when a company called MITS introduced the ALTAIR 8800. The computer was programmed by flicking switches on the front. It came as a kit and had to be soldered together. It had no software programs. But it was a personal computer available to the consumer for a few thousand dollars when most computer companies were charging tens of thousand of dollars. In 1977 both Commodore and Radio Shack announced that they were going to make personal computers. They did, and trotting along right beside them were Steve Jobs and Steve Wozniak, who invented their computer in a garage while in college. Mass production

FIGURE 3.2
ENIAC was the first digital computer. It is easy to see how far we have come in the evolution of computers.

of the APPLE began in 1979, and by the end of 1981, it was the fastest selling of all the personal computers. In August 1982 the IBM PC was born, and many would argue that the world changed forever as a result.

Following the introduction of the personal computer in the early 1980s, we used our knowledge of computer networks gained in the early days of computing and combined it with new and innovative technologies to create massive networks of people, computers, and data on which anyone can find almost anything: the Internet. Today we continue to see amazing advancements in computing technologies.

Okay, it's time to slow down a bit and begin our discussion of today's computer hardware.

Types of Computer Systems

Today's computer systems come in a variety of sizes, shapes, and computing capabilities. Rapid hardware and software developments and changing end-user needs continue to drive the emergence of new models of computers, from the smallest handheld personal digital assistant/cell phone combinations to the largest multiple-CPU mainframes for enterprises. See Figure 3.3.

Categories such as *mainframe*, *midrange*, and *microcomputer* systems are still used to help us express the relative processing power and number of end users that can be supported by different types of computers. But these are not precise classifications, and they do overlap each other. Thus, other names are commonly given to highlight the major uses of particular types of computers. Examples include personal computers, network servers, network computers, and technical workstations.

In addition, experts continue to predict the merging or disappearance of several computer categories. They feel, for example, that many midrange and mainframe systems have been made obsolete by the power and versatility of networks composed of microcomputers and servers. Other industry experts have predicted that the emergence of network computers and *information appliances* for applications on the Internet and corporate intranets will replace many personal computers, especially in large organizations and in the home computer market. Only time will tell whether such predictions will equal the expectations of industry forecasters.

FIGURE 3.3 Examples of computer system categories.

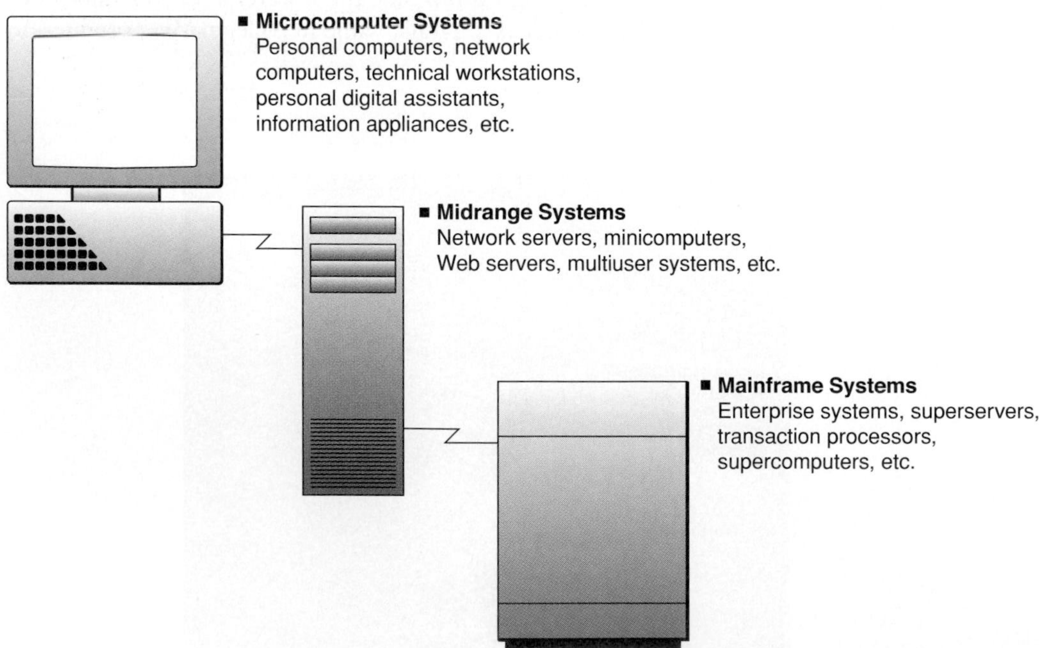

Microcomputer Systems

The entire center of gravity in computing has shifted. For millions of consumers and business users, the main function of desktop PCs is as a window to the Internet. Computers are now communications devices, and consumers want them to be as cheap as possible [4].

Microcomputers are the most important category of computer systems for both businesspeople and consumers. Although usually called a *personal computer*, or PC, a microcomputer is much more than a small computer for use by an individual. The computing power of microcomputers now exceeds that of the mainframes of previous computer generations, at a fraction of their cost. Thus, they have become powerful networked *professional workstations* for business professionals.

Microcomputers come in a variety of sizes and shapes for a variety of purposes, as Figure 3.4 illustrates. For example, PCs are available as handheld, notebook, laptop, tablet, portable, desktop, and floor-standing models. Or, based on their use, they include home, personal, professional, workstation, and multiuser systems. Most microcomputers are *desktops* designed to fit on an office desk or laptops for those who want a small, portable PC. Figure 3.5 offers advice on some of the key features you should consider in acquiring a high-end professional workstation, multimedia PC,

FIGURE 3.4 Examples of microcomputer systems.

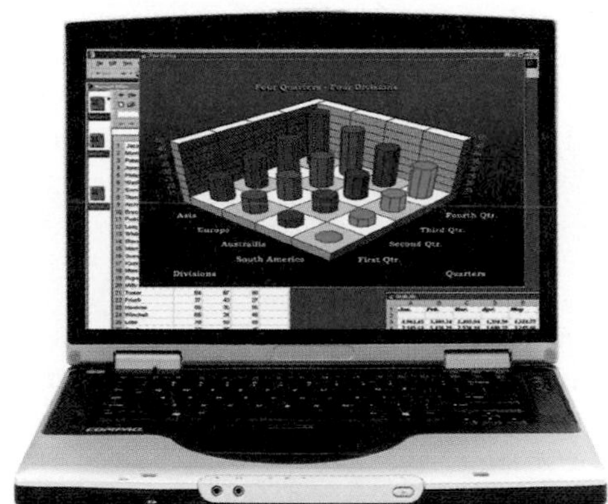

a. A notebook microcomputer.

b. The microcomputer as a professional workstation.

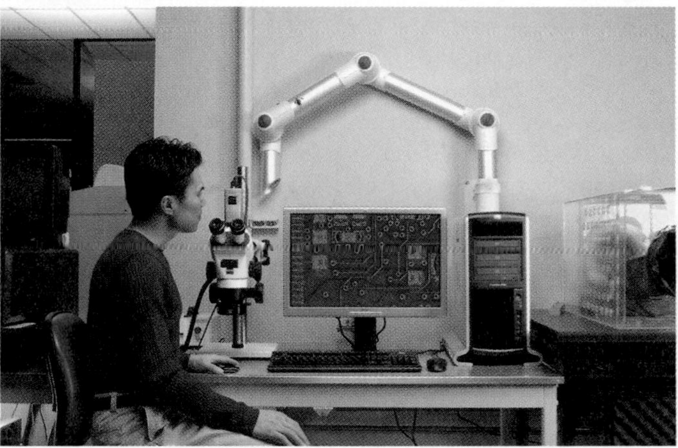

c. The microcomputer as a technical workstation.

FIGURE 3.5 Examples of recommended features for the three types of PC users. Note: www.dell.com and www.gateway.com are good sources for the latest PC features available.

Business Pro	Multimedia Heavy	Newcomer
To track your products, customers, and performance, you'll need more than just a fast machine:	Media pros and dedicated amateurs will want at least a Mac G4 or a 2–3GHz Intel chip, and:	Save money with a Celeron processor in the 1–2GHz range. Also look for:
• 2–3 Gigahertz processor	• 512MB RAM	• 256MB RAM
• 512MB RAM	• 120GB hard drive or more	• 40GB hard drive
• 80GB hard drive	• 18-inch or larger CRT, flat-panel LCD, or plasma display	• Internal 56K modem
• 18-inch flat-panel display	• High-end color printer	• CD–RW/DVD drive
• CD–RW/DVD drive or portable hard drives for backup	• CD–RW/DVD+RW drive	• 17-inch CRT or 15-inch flat panel LCD
• Network interface card (NIC)	• Deluxe speaker system	• Basic inkjet printer

or beginner's system. This breakdown should give you some idea of the range of features available in today's microcomputers.

Some microcomputers are powerful **workstation computers** (technical workstations) that support applications with heavy mathematical computing and graphics display demands such as computer-aided design (CAD) in engineering or investment and portfolio analysis in the securities industry. Other microcomputers are used as **network servers**. These are usually more powerful microcomputers that coordinate telecommunications and resource sharing in small local area networks (LANs) and in Internet and intranet Web sites.

Corporate PC Criteria

What do you look for in a new PC system? A big, bright screen? Zippy new processor? Capacious hard drive? Acres of RAM? Sorry, none of these is a top concern for corporate PC buyers. Numerous studies have shown that the price of a new computer is only a small part of the total cost of ownership (TCO). Support, maintenance, and other intangibles contribute far more heavily to the sum. Let's take a look at three top criteria.

Solid Performance at a Reasonable Price. Corporate buyers know that their users probably aren't mapping the human genome or plotting trajectories to Saturn. They're doing word processing, order entry, sales contact management, and other essential business tasks. They need a solid, competent machine at a reasonable price, not the latest whizbang.

Many organizations are adopting a laptop, rather than desktop, strategy. Using this approach, the employee uses his or her laptop while in the office and out in the field. With the proliferation of wireless Internet access, this strategy allows employees to take the desktop with them wherever they may be—at their desk, in a conference room, at a meeting offsite, or in a hotel room in another country.

One outcome of this strategy is the development and acquisition of more powerful laptops with larger and higher quality screens. This demand presents a challenge to laptop manufacturers to provide higher quality while continuing to make the laptop lightweight and portable.

Operating System Ready. A change in the operating system of a computer is the most disruptive upgrade an enterprise has to face. That's why many corporate buyers want their machines to be able to handle current operating systems and anticipated new ones. Although most organizations have adopted Windows XP, some enterprises still use Windows NT or operating systems of an even earlier vintage. Ultimately, they must be able to make the transition to Windows Vista (the newest OS from Microsoft) and even to OS versions expected three to five years hence. Primarily, that demand means deciding what hard disk space and RAM will be sufficient.

Connectivity. Networked machines are a given in corporate life, and Internet-ready machines are becoming a given. Buyers need machines equipped with reliable wireless capabilities. With fewer cables to worry about, wireless networks, especially when combined with laptop PCs, contribute to the flexibility of the workplace and the simplicity of PC deployment. Many organizations are planning for Internet-based applications and need machines ready to make fast, reliable, and secure connections.

Computer Terminals

Computer terminals, essentially any device that allows access to a computer, are undergoing a major conversion to networked computer devices. *Dumb terminals,* which are keyboard/video monitor devices with limited processing capabilities, are being replaced by *intelligent terminals,* which are modified networked PCs or network computers. Also included are network terminals, which may be *Windows terminals* that depend on network servers for Windows software, processing power, and storage, or *Internet terminals,* which depend on Internet or intranet Web site servers for their operating systems and application software.

Intelligent terminals take many forms and can perform data entry and some information processing tasks independently. These tasks include the widespread use of **transaction terminals** in banks, retail stores, factories, and other work sites. Examples are automated teller machines (ATMs), factory production recorders, airport check-in kiosks, and retail point-of-sale (POS) terminals. These intelligent terminals use keypads, touchscreens, bar code scanners, and other input methods to capture data and interact with end users during a transaction, while relying on servers or other computers in the network for further transaction processing.

Network Computers

Network computers (NCs) are a microcomputer category designed primarily for use with the Internet and corporate intranets by clerical workers, operational employees, and knowledge workers with specialized or limited computing applications. These NCs are low-cost, sealed microcomputers with no or minimal disk storage that are linked to the network. Users of NCs depend primarily on network servers for their operating system and Web browser, application software, and data access and storage.

One of the main attractions of network computers is their lower TCO (total cost of ownership; that is, the total of all costs associated with purchasing, installing, operating, and maintaining a computer). Purchase upgrades, maintenance, and support cost much less than for full-featured PCs. Other benefits to business include the ease of software distribution and licensing, computing platform standardization, reduced end-user support requirements, and improved manageability through centralized management and enterprisewide control of computer network resources [4]. See Figure 3.6.

Information Appliances

PCs aren't the only option: A host of smart gadgets and information appliances—from cellular phones and pagers to handheld PCs and Web-based game machines—promise Internet access and the ability to perform basic computational chores [4].

Handheld microcomputer devices known as **personal digital assistants** (PDAs) are some of the most popular devices in the information appliance category. Web-enabled PDAs use touchscreens, pen-based handwriting recognition, or keypads so that mobile workers can send and receive e-mail, access the Web, and exchange

FIGURE 3.6
An example of a network computer.

information such as appointments, to-do lists, and sales contacts with their desktop PCs or Web servers.

One of the latest entrants to PDA technology is the RIM BlackBerry, a small, pager-sized device that can perform all of the common PDA functions, plus act as a fully functional mobile telephone. What sets this device apart from other wireless PDA solutions is that it is always on and connected. A BlackBerry user doesn't need to retrieve e-mail; the e-mail finds the BlackBerry user. Because of this functionality, there is no need to dial in or initiate a connection. The BlackBerry doesn't even have a visible antenna. When a user wishes to send or reply to an e-mail, the small keyboard on the device allows text entry. Just like a mobile telephone, the BlackBerry is designed to remain on and continuously connected to the wireless network, allowing near real-time transfer of e-mail. Furthermore, because the BlackBerry uses the same network as most mobile telephone services, the unit can be used anywhere that a mobile phone can be used.

Another new entrant to this field is the Apple iPhone. iPhone combines three products—a revolutionary mobile phone, a widescreen iPod music and video player with touch controls, and a breakthrough Internet communications device with desktop-class e-mail, Web browsing, maps, and searching—into one small and lightweight handheld device. iPhone also introduces an entirely new user interface based on a large, multitouch display and pioneering new software, letting users control everything with just their fingers. Thus, it ushers in an era of software power and sophistication never before seen in a mobile device, completely redefining what people can do on a mobile phone. We can expect to see even more sophisticated mobile PDA-type devices in the future as Moore's Law continues to prevail and marketplace continues to demand more functionality (see the discussion on Moore's Law at the end of Section I for more details on this concept).

Information appliances may also take the form of video-game consoles and other devices that connect to your home TV set. These devices enable people to surf the World Wide Web or send and receive e-mail and watch TV programs or play video games at the same time. Other information appliances include wireless PDAs and Internet-enabled cellular and PCS phones, as well as wired, telephone-based home appliances that can send and receive e-mail and access the Web.

FIGURE 3.7
Midrange computer systems can handle large-scale processing without the high cost or space considerations of a large-scale mainframe.

Midrange Systems

Midrange systems are primarily high-end network servers and other types of servers that can handle the large-scale processing of many business applications. Although not as powerful as mainframe computers, they are less costly to buy, operate, and maintain than mainframe systems and thus meet the computing needs of many organizations. See Figure 3.7.

> *Burgeoning data warehouses and related applications such as data mining and online analytical processing are forcing IT shops into higher and higher levels of server configurations. Similarly, Internet-based applications, such as Web servers and electronic commerce, are forcing IT managers to push the envelope of processing speed and storage capacity and other [business] applications, fueling the growth of high-end servers* [14].

Midrange systems have become popular as powerful network servers (computers used to coordinate communications and manage resource sharing in network settings) to help manage large Internet Web sites, corporate intranets and extranets, and other networks. Internet functions and other applications are popular high-end server applications, as are integrated enterprisewide manufacturing, distribution, and financial applications. Other applications, like data warehouse management, data mining, and online analytical processing (which we discuss in Chapters 5 and 9), are contributing to the demand for high-end server systems [14].

Midrange systems first became popular as **minicomputers** for scientific research, instrumentation systems, engineering analysis, and industrial process monitoring and control. Minicomputers could easily handle such uses because these applications are narrow in scope and do not demand the processing versatility of mainframe systems. Today, midrange systems include servers used in industrial process-control and manufacturing plants and play major roles in computer-aided manufacturing (CAM). They can also take the form of powerful technical workstations for computer-aided design (CAD) and other computation- and graphics-intensive applications. Midrange systems are also used as *front-end servers* to assist mainframe computers in telecommunications processing and network management.

Los Alamos Laboratory and Others: Moving to Blade Servers

Los Alamos National Laboratory and Washington-based e-learning software and application service provider (ASP) Blackboard Inc. (www.blackboard.com) are finding that blade servers cost 30–50 percent less than traditional rack-mounted servers, with the biggest savings derived from their smaller size, low power-consumption costs, and reduced costs of cabling, power supply management, and integrated telecom switching.

A blade server is a thin, modular electronic circuit board. It contains one, two, or more microprocessors and memory and is intended for a single, dedicated application (e.g., serving Web pages). It can be easily inserted into a space-saving rack with many similar servers. One product offering, for example, makes it possible to install up to 280 blade server modules vertically in multiple racks or rows of a single floor-standing cabinet. Blade servers are designed to create less heat and thus save energy costs as well as space. Large data centers and Internet service providers (ISPs) that host Web sites are among companies most likely to buy blade servers.

Dollar Rent A Car Inc. (www.dollar.com) began using HP blade servers in 2002 to help speed the deployment of new Web and data center applications while keeping costs down, then expanded their use in 2003. Meanwhile, AOL (www.aol.com) began testing IBM BladeCenter servers running in 2002 as part of its goal of reducing IT costs by 30 percent in 2003.

Freed of the physical bulk and componentry of traditional servers, blade servers slide into slots on racks. In most cases, blade servers consist of microcomputer processing and storage assemblies that fit into slots in a rack unit that provides a common cooling fan, cabling, and network and external storage connections, reducing both cabling and space requirements. Analysts say cost savings increase the longer these systems are used. "Blade servers take up less space, generate less heat, use less power, and don't need the environment requirements of air conditioning or raised flooring, as larger servers require," says Tom Manter, research director at Aberdeen Group. The primary caveat in trying to achieve quick returns on investment for blade servers largely rests on how well the processing, networking, and storage features are integrated. "Any cost savings can quickly be eaten away if maintaining blade servers becomes complex and time-consuming," says John Humphreys, an analyst at IDC [13].

Mainframe Computer Systems

Several years after dire pronouncements that the mainframe was dead, quite the opposite is true: Mainframe usage is actually on the rise. And it's not just a short-term blip. One factor that's been driving mainframe sales is cost reductions [of 35 percent or more]. Price reductions aren't the only factor fueling mainframe acquisitions. IS organizations are teaching the old dog new tricks by putting mainframes at the center stage of emerging applications such as data mining and warehousing, decision support, and a variety of Internet-based applications, most notably electronic commerce [14].

Mainframe systems are large, fast, and powerful computer systems. For example, mainframes can process thousands of million instructions per second (MIPS). Mainframes can also have large primary storage capacities. Their main memory capacity can range from hundreds of gigabytes to many terabytes of primary storage. Mainframes have slimmed down drastically in the last few years, dramatically reducing their air-conditioning needs, electrical power consumption, and floor space requirements—and thus their acquisition and operating costs. Most of these improvements are the result of a move from cumbersome water-cooled mainframes to a newer air-cooled technology for mainframe systems [11]. See Figure 3.8.

Thus, mainframe computers continue to handle the information processing needs of major corporations and government agencies with high transaction processing volumes or complex computational problems. For example, major international banks,

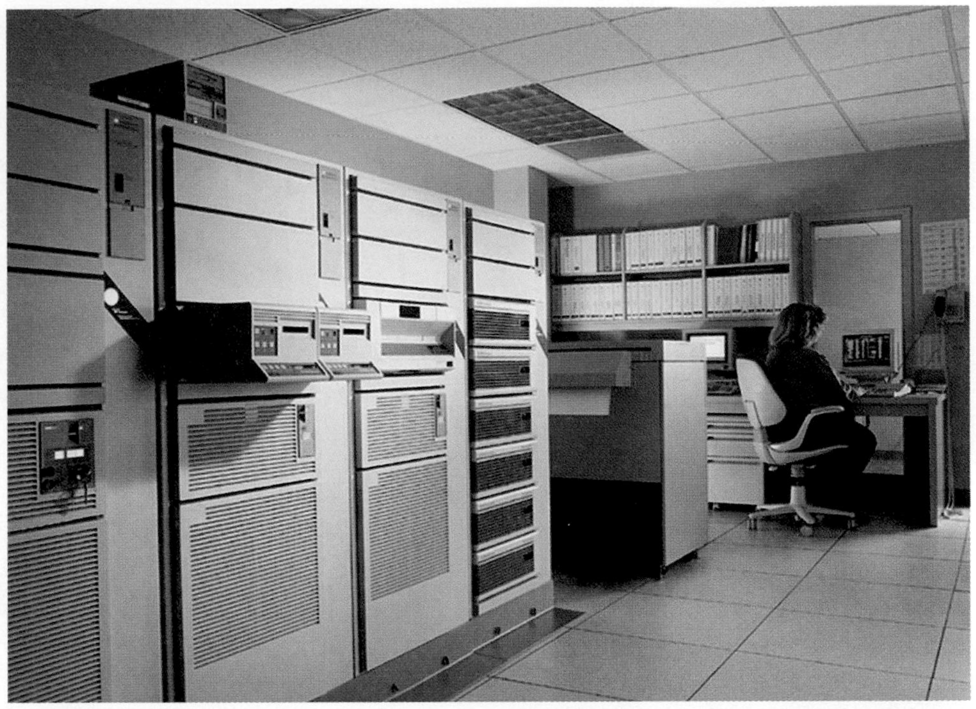

FIGURE 3.8
Mainframe computer systems are the heavy lifters of corporate computing.

airlines, oil companies, and other large corporations process millions of sales transactions and customer inquiries each day with the help of large mainframe systems. Mainframes are still used for computation-intensive applications such as analyzing seismic data from oil field explorations or simulating flight conditions in designing aircraft. Mainframes are also widely used as *superservers* for the large client/server networks and high-volume Internet Web sites of large companies. And as previously mentioned, mainframes are becoming a popular business computing platform for data mining and warehousing, as well as electronic commerce applications [11].

Supercomputer Systems

> *Supercomputers have now become "scalable servers" at the top end of the product lines that start with desktop workstations. Market-driven companies, like Silicon Graphics, Hewlett-Packard, and IBM, have a much broader focus than just building the world's fastest computer, and the software of the desktop computer has a much greater overlap with that of the supercomputer than it used to, because both are built from the same cache-based microprocessors* [9].

The term **supercomputer** describes a category of extremely powerful computer systems specifically designed for scientific, engineering, and business applications requiring extremely high speeds for massive numeric computations. The market for supercomputers includes government research agencies, large universities, and major corporations. They use supercomputers for applications such as global weather forecasting, military defense systems, computational cosmology and astronomy, microprocessor research and design, large-scale data mining, and so on.

Supercomputers use *parallel processing* architectures of interconnected microprocessors (which can execute many instructions at the same time in parallel). They can easily perform arithmetic calculations at speeds of billions of floating-point operations per second *(gigaflops)*. Supercomputers that can calculate in *teraflops* (trillions of floating-point operations per second), which use massive parallel processing (MPP) designs of thousands of microprocessors, are now in use. Purchase prices for large supercomputers are in the $5 million to $50 million range.

FIGURE 3.9
The ASCI White supercomputer system at Lawrence Livermore National Laboratory in Livermore, California.

However, the use of symmetric multiprocessing (SMP) and distributed shared memory (DSM) designs of smaller numbers of interconnected microprocessors has spawned a breed of *minisupercomputers* with prices that start in the hundreds of thousands of dollars. For example, IBM's RS/6000 SP starts at $150,000 for a one-processing-node SMP computer. However, it can be expanded to hundreds of processing nodes, which drives its price into the tens of millions of dollars.

The ASCI White supercomputer system, shown in Figure 3.9, consists of three IBM RS/6000 SP systems: White, Frost, and Ice. White, the largest of these systems, is a 512-node, 16-way symmetric multiprocessor (SMP) supercomputer with a peak performance of 12.3 teraflops. Frost is a 68-node, 16-way SMP system, and Ice is a 28-node, 16-way SMP system [15]. Supercomputers like these continue to advance the state of the art for the entire computer industry.

Technical Note: The Computer System Concept

As a business professional, you do not need detailed technical knowledge of computers. However, you do need to understand some basic concepts about computer systems, which should help you be an informed and productive user of computer system resources.

A computer is more than a high-powered collection of electronic devices performing a variety of information processing chores. A computer is a *system*, an interrelated combination of components that performs the basic system functions of input, processing, output, storage, and control, thus providing end users with a powerful information processing tool. Understanding the computer as a **computer system** is vital to the effective use and management of computers. You should be able to visualize any computer this way, from the smallest microcomputer device to the largest computer networks whose components are interconnected by telecommunications network links throughout a building complex or geographic area.

Figure 3.10 illustrates that a computer is a system of hardware devices organized according to the following system functions:

- **Input.** The input devices of a computer system include computer keyboards, touchscreens, pens, electronic mice, optical scanners, and so on. They convert data into electronic form for direct entry or through a telecommunications network into a computer system.

FIGURE 3.10 The computer system concept. A computer is a system of hardware components and functions.

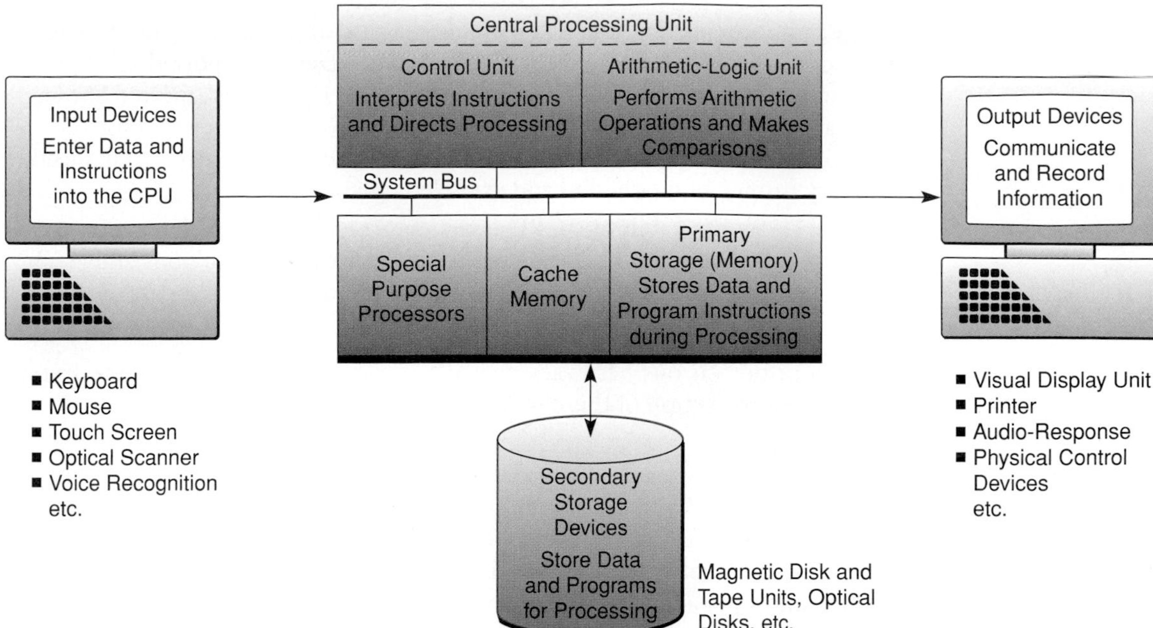

- **Processing.** The **central processing unit** (CPU) is the main processing component of a computer system. (In microcomputers, it is the main *microprocessor*. See Figure 3.11.) Conceptually, the circuitry of a CPU can be subdivided into two major subunits: the arithmetic-logic unit and the control unit. It is the electronic circuits (known as *registers*) of the *arithmetic-logic unit* that perform the arithmetic and logic functions required to execute software instructions.
- **Output.** The output devices of a computer system include video display units, printers, audio response units, and so on. They convert electronic information

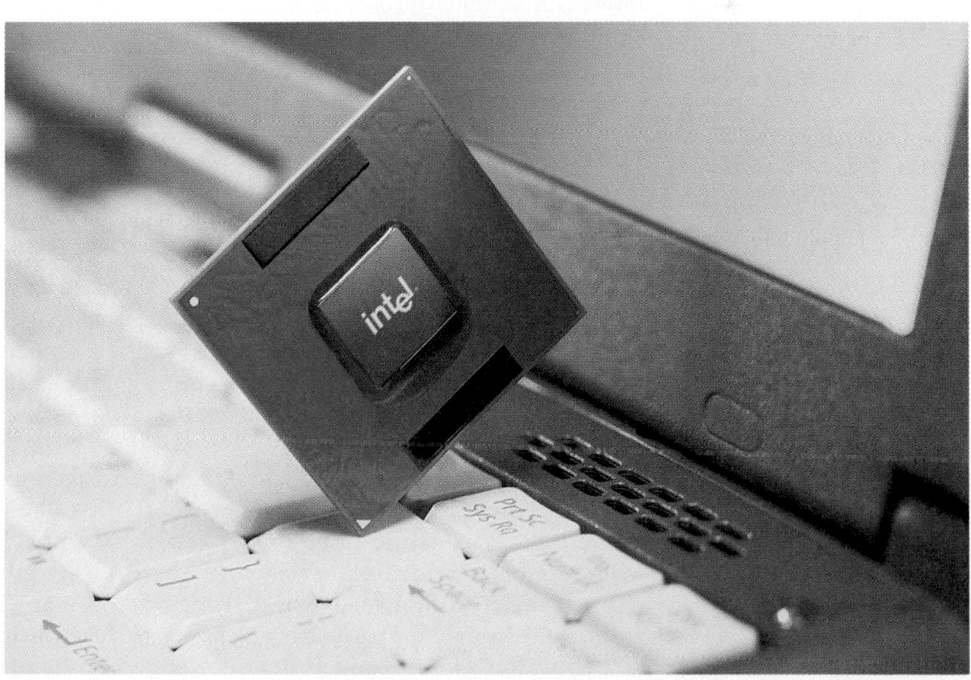

FIGURE 3.11 This Intel Mobile Pentium 4-M microprocessor operates at 3GHz clock speeds to bring desktop power to laptop PCs.

produced by the computer system into human-intelligible form for presentation to end users.

- **Storage.** The storage function of a computer system takes place in the storage circuits of the computer's **primary storage unit**, or *memory*, supported by **secondary storage** devices such as magnetic disk and optical disk drives. These devices store data and software instructions needed for processing. Computer processors may also include storage circuitry called *cache memory* for high-speed, temporary storage of instruction and data elements.
- **Control.** The control unit of a CPU is the control component of a computer system. Its registers and other circuits interpret software instructions and transmit directions that control the activities of the other components of the computer system.

We will explore the various hardware devices associated with each of these system functions in the next section of this chapter.

Computer Processing Speeds

How fast are computer systems? Early computer **processing speeds** were measured in **milliseconds** (thousandths of a second) and **microseconds** (millionths of a second). Now computers operate in the **nanosecond** (billionth of a second) range, with **picosecond** (trillionth of a second) speed being attained by some computers. Such speeds seem almost incomprehensible. For example, an average person taking one step each nanosecond would circle the earth about 20 times in one second!

We have already mentioned the *teraflop* speeds of some supercomputers. However, most computers can now process program instructions at **million instructions per second (MIPS)** speeds. Another measure of processing speed is *megahertz* (MHz), or millions of **cycles per second**, and *gigahertz* (GHz), or billions of cycles per second. This rating is commonly called the *clock speed* of a microprocessor, because it is used to rate microprocessors by the speed of their timing circuits or internal clock rather than by the number of specific instructions they can process in one second.

However, such ratings can be misleading indicators of the effective processing speed of microprocessors and their *throughput*, or ability to perform useful computation or data processing assignments during a given period. That's because processing speed depends on a variety of factors including the size of circuitry paths, or *buses*, that interconnect microprocessor components; the capacity of instruction-processing *registers;* the use of high-speed cache memory; and the use of specialized microprocessors such as a math coprocessor to do arithmetic calculations faster.

Moore's Law: Where Do We Go from Here?

Can computers get any faster? Can we afford the computers of the future? Both of these questions can be answered by understanding **Moore's law**. Gordon Moore, cofounder of Intel Corporation, made his famous observation in 1965, just four years after the first integrated circuit was commercialized. The press called it "Moore's law," and the name has stuck. In its form, Moore observed an exponential growth (doubling every 18 to 24 months) in the number of transistors per integrated circuit and predicted that this trend would continue. Through a number of advances in technology, Moore's law, the doubling of transistors every couple of years, has been maintained and still holds true today. Figure 3.12 illustrates Moore's law as it relates to the evolution of computing power.

Over the years, Moore's law has been interpreted and reinterpreted such that it is commonly defined in a much broader sense than it was originally offered. Nonetheless, its application, and its relative accuracy, is useful in understanding where we have been and in predicting where we are going. For example, one common corollary of Moore's law is that the price of a given level of computing power will be cut in half approximately every 18 to 24 months. While Moore didn't predict this effect specifically, it has been shown to be fairly consistently accurate as

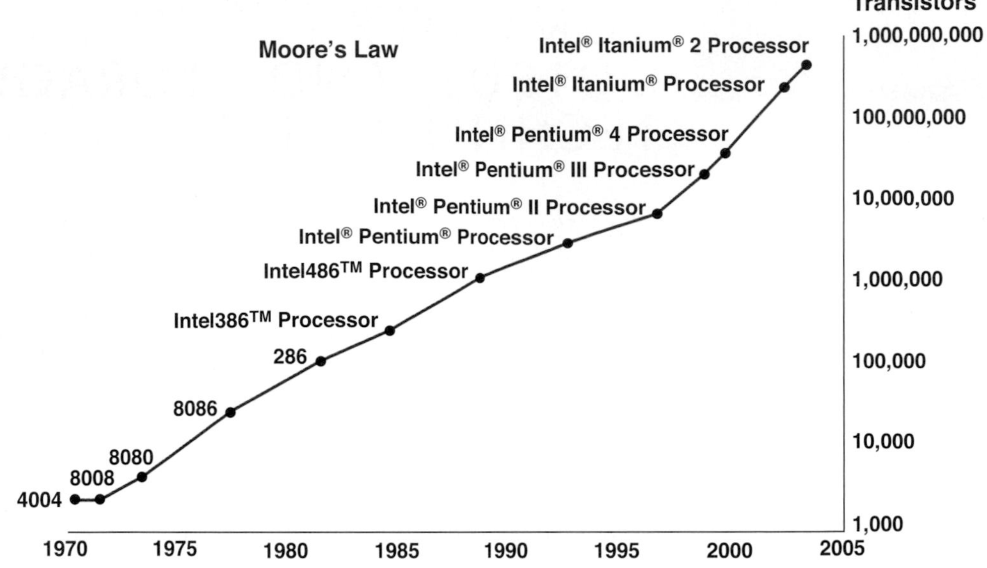

FIGURE 3.12
Moore's law suggests that computer power will double every 18 to 24 months. So far, it has.

well. This trend is also true for the cost of storage (we will explore this further in the next section).

Although Moore's law was initially made in the form of an observation and prediction, the more widely it became accepted, the more it served as a goal for an entire industry—driving both marketing and engineering departments of semiconductor manufacturers to focus enormous energy on the specified increase in processing power that it was presumed one or more of their competitors would soon actually attain. Expressed as "a doubling every 18 to 24 months," Moore's law suggests the phenomenal progress of technology in recent years. Expressed on a shorter timescale, however, Moore's law equates to an average performance improvement in the industry as a whole of more than 1 percent *per week*. For a manufacturer competing in the processor, storage, or memory markets, a new product that is expected to take three years to develop and is just two or three months late is 10–15 percent slower or larger than the directly competing products, thus rendering it harder to sell.

Recent computer industry studies predict that Moore's law will continue to hold for the next several chip generations (at least another decade). Depending on the doubling time used in the calculations, this progress could mean up to a 100-fold increase in transistor counts on a chip in the next 10 years. This rapid exponential improvement could put 100GHz personal computers in every home and 20GHz devices in every pocket. It seems reasonable to expect that sooner or later computers will meet or exceed any conceivable need for computation. Intel, however, suggests that it can sustain development in line with Moore's law for the next 20 years *without* any significant technological breakthroughs. Given the frequency of such breakthroughs in today's marketplace, it is conceivable that Moore's law can be sustained indefinitely. Regardless of what the end of Moore's law may look like, or when it may arrive, we are still moving along at a phenomenal rate of evolution, and the best may be yet to come.

SECTION II COMPUTER PERIPHERALS: INPUT, OUTPUT, AND STORAGE TECHNOLOGIES

The right peripherals can make all the difference in your computing experience. A top-quality monitor will be easier on your eyes—and may change the way you work. A scanner can edge you closer to that ever-elusive goal—the paperless office. Backup-storage systems can offer bank-vault security against losing your work. CD and DVD drives have become essential for many applications. Thus, the right choice of peripherals can make a big difference [6].

Read the Real World Case about Apple Computer on the next page. We can learn a lot about the business challenges and rewards of the strategic use of information technologies from this case. See Figure 3.13.

Peripherals

Peripherals is the generic name given to all input, output, and secondary storage devices that are part of a computer system but are not part of the CPU. Peripherals depend on direct connections or telecommunications links to the central processing unit of a computer system. Thus, all peripherals are **online** devices; that is, they are separate from, but can be electronically connected to and controlled by, a CPU. (This is the opposite of **offline** devices that are separate from and not under the control of the CPU.) The major types of peripherals and media that can be part of a computer system are discussed in this section. See Figure 3.14.

Input Technologies

Input technologies now provide a more **natural user interface** for computer users. You can enter data and commands directly and easily into a computer system through pointing devices like electronic mice and touchpads and with technologies like optical scanning, handwriting recognition, and voice recognition. These developments have made it unnecessary to record data on paper *source documents* (e.g., sales order forms) and then keyboard the data into a computer in an additional data-entry step. Further improvements in voice recognition and other technologies should enable an even more natural user interface in the future.

Pointing Devices

Keyboards are still the most widely used devices for entering data and text into computer systems. However, **pointing devices** are a better alternative for issuing commands, making choices, and responding to prompts displayed on your video screen. They work with your operating system's **graphical user interface** (GUI), which presents you with icons, menus, windows, buttons, bars, and so on for your selection. For example, pointing devices such as an electronic mouse, trackball, and touchpads allow you to choose easily from menu selections and icon displays using point-and-click or point-and-drag methods. See Figure 3.15.

The **electronic mouse** is the most popular pointing device used to move the cursor on the screen, as well as issue commands and make icon and menu selections. By moving the mouse on a desktop or pad, you can move the cursor onto an icon displayed on the screen. Pressing buttons on the mouse initiates various activities represented by the icon selected.

The trackball, pointing stick, and touchpad are other pointing devices most often used in place of the mouse. A **trackball** is a stationary device related to the mouse. You turn a roller ball with only its top exposed outside its case to move the cursor on the screen. A **pointing stick** (also called a *trackpoint*) is a small button-like device, sometimes likened to the eraser head of a pencil. It is usually centered one row above the space bar of a keyboard. The cursor moves in the direction of the pressure you place on the stick. The **touchpad** is a small rectangular touch-sensitive surface usually

REAL WORLD CASE 2 Apple Inc.: The iPod, the iMac, and the Business Lessons of Closed Systems

Seems like Steve Jobs always has something to celebrate. The Apple CEO dramatically announces new versions of the iPod every year, including revolutionary products like the iPhone, which combines the functions of an iPod music player with a video player, cell phone, Blackberry-type Internet communicator, and touchscreen color display into one cool small and thin package. Then Jobs underscores his success by noting that more than 90 million iPods were sold and two billion songs purchased from the iTunes Music Store by the beginning of 2007. Those measures of the iPod and iTunes' success are all the more impressive when you recall that Apple has numerous competitors in the digital music world. Microsoft, Yahoo, and the legal incarnation of Napster are gunning for iTunes customers, while Microsoft's Zune and SanDisks's Sansa lead the pack of supposed iPod killers.

Yet Apple's challengers all face the same problem: Jobs's company will probably dominate the digital music market for years to come because Apple has learned some of the hard lessons of closed systems.

In the microcomputer desktop market, Apple shrank from an industry leader to a niche player because it designed closed systems with proprietary hardware and software that were often incompatible with thousands of application software products that proliferated in the PC universe. Microsoft set out to replicate the basic features of the Macintosh operating system in each succeeding version of its Windows OS, encouraged software developers to write apps for it, and then licensed Windows to mass-market PC manufacturers like Dell, HP and IBM. When the technology dust settled, Apple ended up with barely 3.2 percent of the U.S. desktop market.

FIGURE 3.13

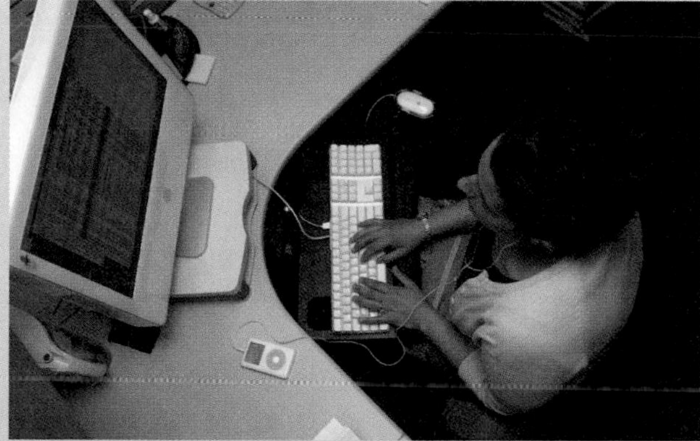

The runaway success of Apple's iPod has helped boost the market share of the iMac and other desktop and portable computers in Apple's Mac lineup.

And that's the way it was when Apple introduced the first iPod in October 2001. The iPod was another closed system, but this time Steve Jobs created a closed system with mass appeal. Fulcrum Global Partners estimated that iPods accounted for 73 percent of the 30 million MP3 players in use in the United States in 2006. That's partially because Apple released versions of the iPod and iTunes for Windows. But it's also because Jobs cut a deal with the Big Five record companies in 2003 that locked up his device. The music companies wanted to sell songs on iTunes, but they were afraid of Internet piracy. So Jobs promised to wrap their songs in Apple's FairPlay—the only copy-protection software that is iPod compatible.

Other digital music services such as Yahoo Music Unlimited and Napster reached similar deals with the big record labels. But Apple refused to license FairPlay to them. So those companies turned to Microsoft for copy protection. That satisfied fearful music companies, but it means none of the songs sold by those services can be played on the wildly popular iPod. Instead, users of the services had to rely on devices made by companies like Samsung, SanDisk, and Microsoft itself that use Microsoft's Windows Media format.

The situation has been a disaster for Apple's competitors. iTunes holds a commanding lead over its rivals, selling more than 75 percent of all digital songs, according to NPD Group, a company that provides tracking of consumer music purchases. The second-place digital music store, eMusic, can't sell any major-label hits because it refuses to copy-protect them. Instead, it relies on independent labels for content. But eMusic has a 9 percent share of the market, largely because you can play its unprotected MP3s on an iPod. Meanwhile, Microsoft, Rhapsody, Napster, Sony, Wal-Mart, AOL, and Yahoo—nearly all of which have deals with the major labels but are stuck with Microsoft's technology—are fighting over the remaining 16 percent of the digital music-store market.

Most of these music services argue that they have something to offer music lovers that Apple doesn't: digital music subscriptions providing customers the chance to listen to more than a million songs for a monthly fee of roughly $10. You can't burn these songs onto CDs, and they become unplayable if you don't pay your bill. But Napster argues that it is cheaper to listen to music this way than to buy thousands of iTunes.

True enough. But the software that Microsoft developed to allow this heavily protected music to be moved to portable devices has been so buggy that a lot of subscribers have given up and just listen to songs on their computers.

Poor Microsoft. Nearly every music service and MP3 player maker other than Apple supports Windows Media and its copy-protection software. But not enough music lovers want to use them. It's a far cry from what happened in the desktop wars. Now it's Bill Gates's turn to learn that it's no fun when you're outside a wildly successful closed system looking in.

But hold that iPhone. Apple has been coming under increasing pressure from European governments and consumer groups around the world to loosen up its Fairplay copy protection monopoly. What's a guy like Steve Jobs going to do? Simple. In a dramatic, 1,800-word turnaround statement entitled "Some Thoughts on Music," posted on Apple's Web site early in February 2007, Jobs took the onus for digital rights management (DRM) restrictions like copy protection and put it squarely on the shoulders of the music industry. Jobs said Apple is ready to "wholeheartedly" ditch copy protection and embrace an online "interoperable music marketplace" if the major record labels can be convinced to go along. Thus Jobs put the responsibility for continuing DRM in the online music market in the music industry's court.

But what about that poor market share of the iMac and other Apple desktop and portable PC products, you may ask? Well, a funny thing called the "halo effect" of the iPod, which Steve Jobs predicted, has happened, and this time he's laughing all the way to the bank. Since the arrival of the iPod, Apple's share of the desktop and portable computer market in the United States has almost doubled, reaching just under 6 percent in early 2006. Many analysts expect that trend will continue to inch upward as more iPods are sold and more iPod users turn to Apple's Mac computer lineup for their computing experience.

Even more growth is expected in the worldwide microcomputer market as iPod international sales continue to grow, driving more sales of iMac and other flavors of Macintosh desktop and portable computers. Apple's worldwide share of that market was estimated at 2.5 percent in 2005, with predictions of a jump in growth to 3.5 percent by the end of 2006 and another jump to 5.0 percent by the end of 2007, according to one computer industry forecaster.

Part of the reason for such lofty market share growth estimates was Apple's introduction of its Boot Camp software early in 2006. Boot Camp enables the newer iMac and other Mac models based on Intel's dual microprocessor chip to run applications software for both its own Mac OS X and the Windows operating system. Boot Camp will be folded into the upcoming Leopard version of Apple's OS X, further accelerating Apple's drive to lure corporate and business Windows users, as well as the iPod crowd, to its Mac lineup.

While Microsoft struggled with its five-year development of the new Vista version of Windows, Steve Jobs moved to seize the moment to regain the market share Apple lost to Windows PCs. Through his continuing innovations of the iPod, his willingness to consider alternatives to Apple's Fairplay monopoly, and the opening up of the Macs to run Windows applications, Jobs is proving that he has mastered the business lessons of how to successfully wield the two-edged sword of closed systems.

Source: Adapted from Devin Leonard, "The Player: Rivals Won't Find It Easy Competing with the iPod's Closed System," *Fortune*, March 20, 2006; Garry Barker, "Apple Makes Computer History—Windows on a Mac," *MacDailyNews*, April 8, 2006; Arik Hesseldahl, "Steve Jobs' Music Manifesto," *BusinessWeek.com*, February 7, 2007.

CASE STUDY QUESTIONS

1. Do you agree with the sources in this case that Apple will continue to dominate the digital music market for years to come? Why or why not?
2. Can the key technology and business strategies Steve Jobs implemented with the closed system of the iPod be applied successfully to the iMac and other Apple closed-system computer products? Defend your answer with several examples of what could or could not be accomplished for Apple's computer product line.
3. Will the cachet of the iPod and the capabilities of Boot Camp and the Leopard version of Apple's OS X continue to lure more first-time computer buyers and Windows PC users to the Mac lineup of desktops and portables? Why or why not?

REAL WORLD ACTIVITIES

1. Use the Internet to check out the claims of the iPod's dominance by the sources in this case. Research how the iPod's competitors are doing now, including new entrants like Microsoft's Zune, and what strategies they are employing to gain market share. Has the market changed since this case was written? Defend your view of the status of the battle for the digital music market.
2. What is your view of digital rights management tactics like copy protection that are used by Apple, its competitors, and the music industry? Is this capability a proper protection of the music companies' and artists' intellectual property rights? Is it an infringement on a purchaser's right to reproduce content? Is it an anti-competitive restraint of trade, especially for the closed system of the iPod? Break into small groups with your classmates to discuss these issues.

FIGURE 3.14
Some advice about peripherals for a business PC.

Peripherals Checklist
• **Monitors.** Bigger is better for computer screens. Consider a high-definition 19-inch or 21-inch flat screen CRT monitor, or LCD flat panel display. That gives you much more room to display spreadsheets, Web pages, lines of text, open windows, and so forth. An increasingly popular setup uses two monitors that allow multiple applications to be used simultaneously.
• **Printers.** Your choice is between laser printers or color inkjet printers. Lasers are better suited for high-volume business use. Moderately priced color inkjets provide high-quality images and are well suited for reproducing photographs. Per-page costs are higher than for laser printers.
• **Scanners.** You'll have to decide between a compact, sheet-fed scanner and a flatbed model. Sheet-fed scanners will save desktop space, while bulkier flatbed models provide higher speed and resolution.
• **Hard Disk Drives.** Bigger is better; as with closet space, you can always use the extra capacity. So go for 40 gigabytes at the minimum to 80 gigabytes and more.
• **CD and DVD Drives.** CD and DVD drives are a necessity for software installation and multimedia applications. Common today is a built-in CD-RW/DVD drive that both reads and writes CDs and plays DVDs.
• **Backup Systems.** Essential. Don't compute without them. Removable mag disk drives and even CD-RW and DVD-RW drives are convenient and versatile for backing up your hard drive's contents.

placed below the keyboard. The cursor moves in the direction your finger moves on the pad. Trackballs, pointing sticks, and touchpads are easier to use than a mouse for portable computer users and are thus built into most notebook computer keyboards.

Touchscreens are devices that allow you to use a computer by touching the surface of its video display screen. Some touchscreens emit a grid of infrared beams, sound waves, or a slight electric current that is broken when the screen is touched. The computer senses the point in the grid where the break occurs and responds with an appropriate action. For example, you can indicate your selection on a menu display by just touching the screen next to that menu item.

Pen-Based Computing

Handwriting-recognition systems convert script into text quickly and are friendly to shaky hands as well as those of block-printing draftsmen. The pen is more powerful than the keyboard in many vertical markets, as evidenced by the popularity of pen-based devices in the utilities, service, and medical trades [10].

FIGURE 3.15 Many choices exist for pointing devices including the trackball, mouse, pointing stick, and touchscreen.

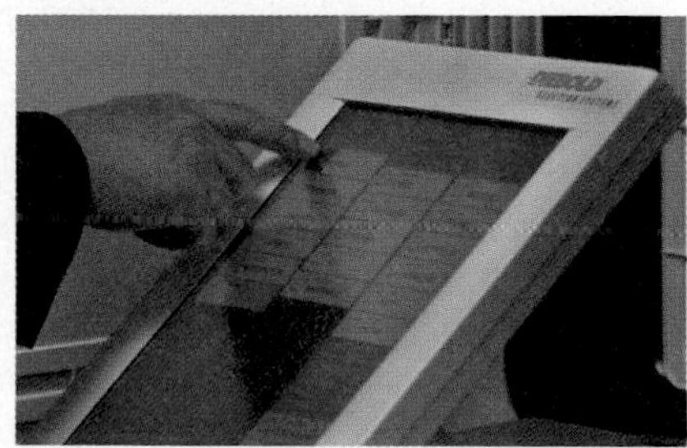

FIGURE 3.16
Many PDAs accept pen-based input.

Pen-based computing technologies are being used in many handheld computers and personal digital assistants. *Tablet* PCs and PDAs contain fast processors and software that recognizes and digitizes handwriting, handprinting, and hand drawing. They have a pressure-sensitive layer, similar to that of a touchscreen, under their slate-like liquid crystal display (LCD) screen. Instead of writing on a paper form fastened to a clipboard or using a keyboard device, you can use a pen to make selections, send e-mail, and enter handwritten data directly into a computer. See Figure 3.16.

Various pen-like devices are available. One example is the *digitizer pen* and *graphics tablet*. You can use the digitizer pen as a pointing device or to draw or write on the pressure-sensitive surface of the graphics tablet. Your handwriting or drawing is digitized by the computer, accepted as input, displayed on its video screen, and entered into your application.

Speech Recognition Systems

Speech recognition is gaining popularity in the corporate world among nontypists, people with disabilities, and business travelers, and is most frequently used for dictation, screen navigation, and Web browsing [3].

Speech recognition may be the future of data entry and certainly promises to be the easiest method for word processing, application navigation, and conversational computing, because speech is the easiest, most natural means of human communication. Speech input has now become technologically and economically feasible for a variety of applications. Early speech recognition products used *discrete speech recognition,* where you had to pause between each spoken word. New *continuous speech recognition* (CSR) software recognizes continuous, conversationally paced speech. See Figure 3.17.

Speech recognition systems digitize, analyze, and classify your speech and its sound patterns. The software compares your speech patterns to a database of sound patterns in its vocabulary and passes recognized words to your application software. Typically, speech recognition systems require training the computer to recognize your voice and its unique sound patterns to achieve a high degree of accuracy. Training such systems involves repeating a variety of words and phrases in a training session, as well as using the system extensively.

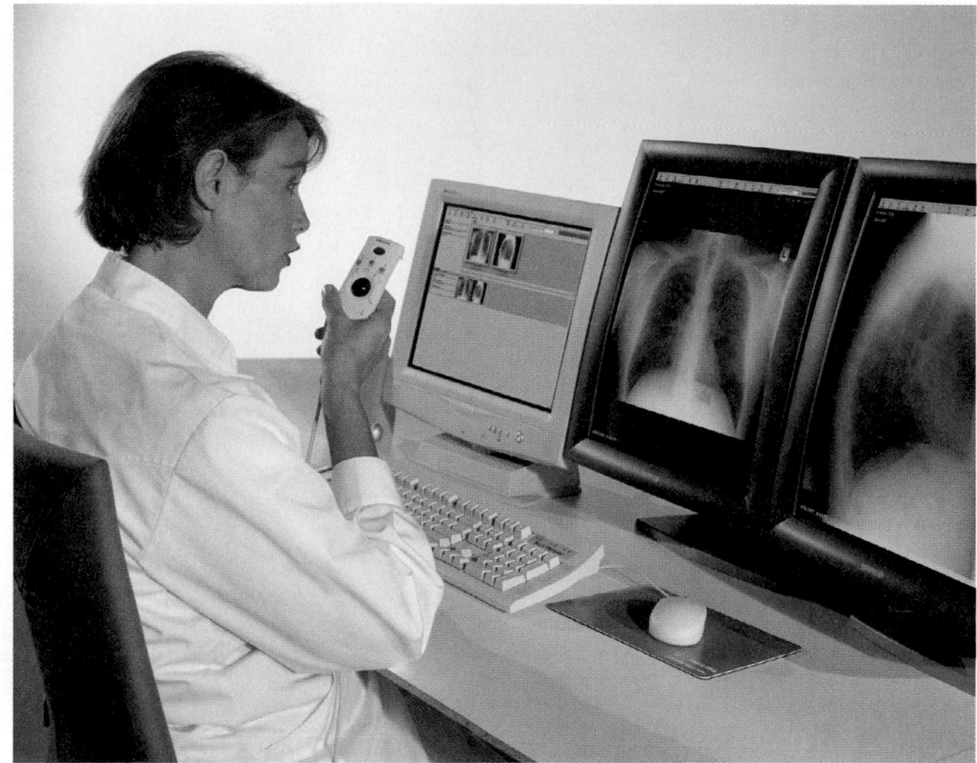

FIGURE 3.17
Using speech recognition technology for word processing.

Continuous speech recognition software products like Dragon NaturallySpeaking and ViaVoice by IBM have up to 300,000-word vocabularies. Training to 95 percent accuracy may take several hours. Longer use, faster processors, and more memory make 99 percent accuracy possible. In addition, Microsoft Office Suite 2003 and XP both have built-in speech recognition for dictation and voice commands of software processes.

Speech recognition devices in work situations allow operators to perform data entry without using their hands to key in data or instructions and to provide faster and more accurate input. For example, manufacturers use speech recognition systems for the inspection, inventory, and quality control of a variety of products; airlines and parcel delivery companies use them for voice-directed sorting of baggage and parcels. Speech recognition can also help you operate your computer's operating systems and software packages through voice input of data and commands. For example, such software can be voice-enabled so you can send e-mail and surf the World Wide Web.

Speaker-independent voice recognition systems, which allow a computer to understand a few words from a voice it has never heard before, are being built into products and used in a growing number of applications. Examples include *voice-messaging computers*, which use speech recognition and voice response software to guide an end user verbally through the steps of a task in many kinds of activities. Typically, they enable computers to respond to verbal and Touch-Tone input over the telephone. Examples of applications include computerized telephone call switching, telemarketing surveys, bank pay-by-phone bill-paying services, stock quotation services, university registration systems, and customer credit and account balance inquiries.

Optical Scanning

Few people understand how much scanners can improve a computer system and make your work easier. Their function is to get documents into your computer with a minimum of time and hassle, transforming just about anything on paper—a letter, a logo, or a photograph—into the digital format that your PC can make sense of. Scanners can be a big help in getting loads of paper off your desk and into your PC [6].

FIGURE 3.18
A modern document management system can serve as an optical scanner, copier, fax, and printer.

Optical scanning devices read text or graphics and convert them into digital input for your computer. Thus, optical scanning enables the direct entry of data from source documents into a computer system. For example, you can use a compact desktop scanner to scan pages of text and graphics into your computer for desktop publishing and Web publishing applications. Or you can scan documents of all kinds into your system and organize them into folders as part of a *document management* library system for easy reference or retrieval. See Figure 3.18.

There are many types of optical scanners, but all employ photoelectric devices to scan the characters being read. Reflected light patterns of the data are converted into electronic impulses that are then accepted as input to the computer system. Compact desktop scanners have become very popular due to their low cost and ease of use with personal computer systems. However, larger, more expensive *flatbed scanners* are faster and provide higher-resolution color scanning.

Another optical scanning technology is called **optical character recognition** (OCR). The OCR scanners can read the characters and codes on merchandise tags, product labels, credit card receipts, utility bills, insurance premiums, airline tickets, and other documents. In addition, OCR scanners are used to automatically sort mail, score tests, and process a wide variety of forms in business and government.

Devices such as handheld optical scanning **wands** are frequently used to read *bar codes*, codes that utilize bars to represent characters. One common example is the Universal Product Code (UPC) bar coding that you see on just about every product sold. For example, the automated checkout scanners found in supermarkets read UPC bar coding. Supermarket scanners emit laser beams that are reflected off a code. The reflected image is converted to electronic impulses that are sent to the in-store computer, where they are matched with pricing information. Pricing information is returned to the terminal, visually displayed, and printed on a receipt for the customer. See Figure 3.19.

FIGURE 3.19
Using an optical scanning wand to read bar coding of inventory data.

Eastman Kodak: Tradition Takes a Back Seat to the Future

The name *Kodak* has been synonymous with photography. In the early days of consumer photography, the family camera was often referred to as the "Kodak." However, evolution and technology can render even the most institutionalized tradition obsolete. The dawn of the digital camera is a prime example.

Eastman Kodak in 2004 announced its intention to stop selling traditional film cameras in the United States, Canada, and Western Europe. With sales of digital cameras poised to overtake film cameras by the end of 2004, Kodak redefined itself to keep pace with the industry. (The number-one maker of photographic film will continue to sell one-time-use cameras in the West and expand its sales of these and other film-based cameras—and film—in emerging markets where demand for them is on the rise.) This move is viewed by industry experts as evidence of Kodak's strong commitment to the future of digital photography. As an example of just how fast technology can revolutionize an industry, it was only eight years ago that Kodak unveiled the Advantix 35mm camera and hailed it as the most important photographic milestone since Instamatic cartridge-loading cameras were introduced in 1963.

According to estimates by InfoTrends Research Group, global film camera shipments in 2004 will shrink to 36 million units from 48 million in 2003, while digital camera shipments will rise to 53 million from 41 million units.

Other Input Technologies

Magnetic stripe technology is a familiar form of data entry that helps computers read credit cards. The coating of the magnetic stripe on the back of such cards can hold about 200 bytes of information. Customer account numbers can be recorded on the mag stripe so it can be read by bank ATMs, credit card authorization terminals, and many other types of magnetic stripe readers.

Smart cards that embed a microprocessor chip and several kilobytes of memory into debit, credit, and other cards are popular in Europe and becoming available in the United States. One example is in the Netherlands, where millions of smart debit cards have been issued by Dutch banks. Smart debit cards enable you to store a cash balance on the card and electronically transfer some of it to others to pay for small items and services. The balance on the card can be replenished in ATMs or other terminals. The smart debit cards used in the Netherlands feature a microprocessor and either 8 or 16 kilobytes of memory, plus the usual magnetic stripe. The smart cards are widely used to make payments in parking meters, vending machines, newsstands, pay telephones, and retail stores [5].

Digital cameras represent another fast-growing set of input technologies. Digital still cameras and digital video cameras (digital camcorders) enable you to shoot, store, and download still photos or full-motion video with audio into your PC. Then you can use image-editing software to edit and enhance the digitized images and include them in newsletters, reports, multimedia presentations, and Web pages.

The computer systems of the banking industry can magnetically read checks and deposit slips using **magnetic ink character recognition** (MICR) technology. Computers can thus sort and post checks to the proper checking accounts. Such processing is possible because the identification numbers of the bank and the customer's account are preprinted on the bottom of the checks with an iron oxide–based ink. The first bank receiving a check after it has been written must encode the amount of the check in magnetic ink on the check's lower-right corner. The MICR system uses 14 characters (the 10 decimal digits and 4 special symbols) of a standardized design. *Reader-sorter* equipment reads a check by first magnetizing the magnetic ink characters and then sensing the signal induced by each character as it passes a reading head. In this way, data are electronically captured by the bank's computer systems.

Output Technologies

Computers provide information in a variety of forms. Video displays and printed documents have been, and still are, the most common forms of output from computer systems. But other natural and attractive output technologies such as **voice response** systems and multimedia output are increasingly found along with video displays in business applications.

For example, you have probably experienced the voice and audio output generated by speech and audio microprocessors in a variety of consumer products. Voice messaging software enables PCs and servers in voice mail and messaging systems to interact with you through voice responses. And of course, multimedia output is common on the Web sites of the Internet and corporate intranets.

Video Output

Video displays are the most common type of computer output. Many desktop computers still rely on **video monitors** that use a *cathode ray tube* (CRT) technology similar to the picture tubes used in home TV sets. Usually, the clarity of the video display depends on the type of video monitor you use and the graphics circuit board installed in your computer. These can provide a variety of graphics modes of increasing capability. A high-resolution, flicker-free monitor is especially important if you spend a lot of time viewing multimedia on CDs or on the Web or the complex graphical displays of many software packages.

The biggest use of **liquid crystal displays** (LCDs) has been to provide a visual display capability for portable microcomputers and PDAs. However, the use of "flat panel" LCD video monitors for desktop PC systems has become common as their cost becomes more affordable. See Figure 3.20. These LCD displays need significantly less electric current and provide a thin, flat display. Advances in technology such as *active matrix* and *dual scan* capabilities have improved the color and clarity of LCD displays. In addition, high-clarity flat panel TVs and monitors using *plasma* display technologies are becoming popular for large-screen (42- to 80-inch) viewing.

Printed Output

Printing information on paper is still the most common form of output after video displays. Thus, most personal computer systems rely on an inkjet or laser printer to

FIGURE 3.20
The flat panel LCD video monitor is becoming the de facto standard for a desktop PC system.

produce permanent (hard-copy) output in high-quality printed form. Printed output is still a common form of business communications and is frequently required for legal documentation. Computers can produce printed reports and correspondence, documents such as sales invoices, payroll checks, bank statements, and printed versions of graphic displays. See Figure 3.21.

Inkjet printers, which spray ink onto a page, have become the most popular, low-cost printers for microcomputer systems. They are quiet, produce several pages per minute of high-quality output, and can print both black-and-white and high-quality color graphics. **Laser printers** use an electrostatic process similar to a photocopying machine to produce many pages per minute of high-quality black-and-white output. More expensive color laser printers and multifunction inkjet and laser models that print, fax, scan, and copy are other popular choices for business offices.

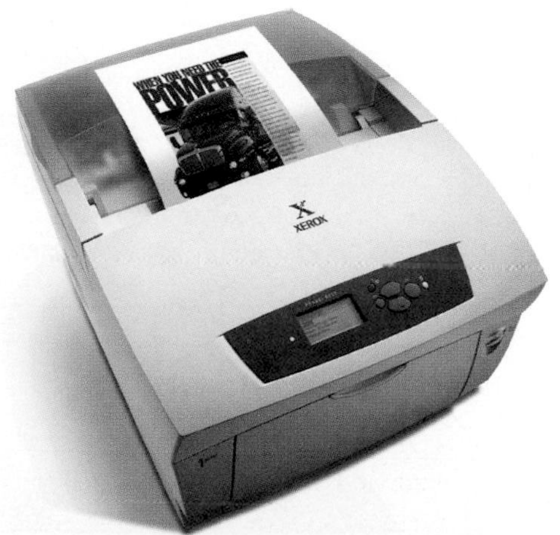

FIGURE 3.21
Modern laser printers produce high-quality color output with high speed.

Storage Trade-Offs

Data and information must be stored until needed using a variety of storage methods. For example, many people and organizations still rely on paper documents stored in filing cabinets as a major form of storage media. However, you and other computer users are more likely to depend on the memory circuits and secondary storage devices of computer systems to meet your storage requirements. Progress in very-large-scale integration (VLSI), which packs millions of memory circuit elements on tiny semiconductor memory chips, is responsible for continuing increases in the main-memory capacity of computers. Secondary storage capacities are also escalating into the billions and trillions of characters, due to advances in magnetic and optical media.

There are many types of storage media and devices. Figure 3.22 illustrates the speed, capacity, and cost relationships of several alternative primary and secondary storage media. Note the cost/speed/capacity trade-offs as you move from semiconductor memories to magnetic disks to optical disks and to magnetic tape. High-speed storage media cost more per byte and provide lower capacities. Large-capacity storage media cost less per byte but are slower. These trade-offs are why we have different kinds of storage media.

However, all storage media, especially memory chips and magnetic disks, continue to increase in speed and capacity and decrease in cost. Developments like automated high-speed cartridge assemblies have given faster access times to magnetic tape, and the speed of optical disk drives continues to increase.

Note in Figure 3.22 that semiconductor memories are used mainly for primary storage, though they are sometimes used as high-speed secondary storage devices. Magnetic disk and tape and optical disk devices, in contrast, are used as secondary storage devices to enlarge the storage capacity of computer systems. Also, because most primary storage circuits use RAM (random-access memory) chips, which lose their contents when electrical power is interrupted, secondary storage devices provide a more permanent type of storage media.

Computer Storage Fundamentals

Data are processed and stored in a computer system through the presence or absence of electronic or magnetic signals in the computer's circuitry or in the media it uses. This character is called "two-state" or **binary representation** of data, because the computer and the media can exhibit only two possible states or conditions, similar to a common light switch—ON or OFF. For example, transistors and other semiconductor circuits are in either a conducting or a nonconducting state. Media such as magnetic disks and tapes indicate these two states by having magnetized spots whose magnetic fields have one of two different directions, or polarities. This binary characteristic of computer circuitry and media is what makes the binary number system the basis for representing data in computers. Thus, for electronic circuits, the conducting

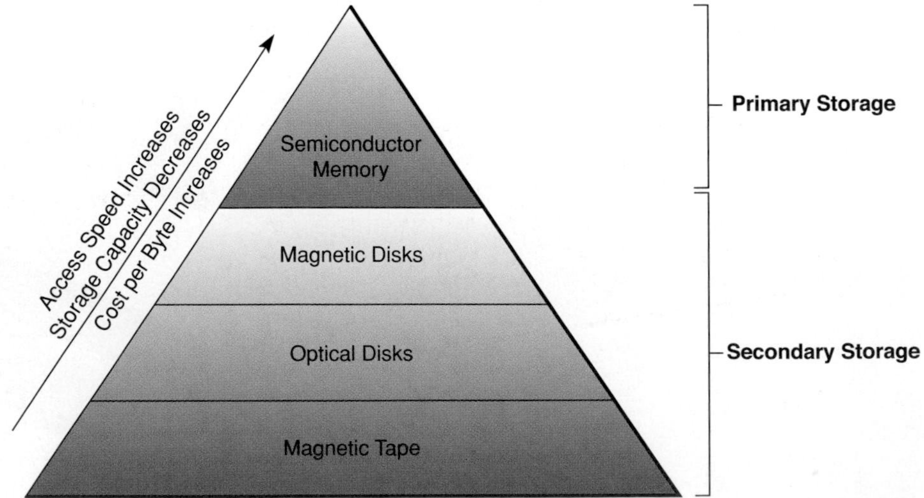

FIGURE 3.22
Storage media cost, speed, and capacity trade-offs. Note how cost increases with faster access speeds but decreases with the increased capacity of storage media.

FIGURE 3.23
Examples of the ASCII computer code that computers use to represent numbers and the letters of the alphabet.

Character	ASCII Code	Character	ASCII Code	Character	ASCII Code
0	00110000	A	01000001	N	01001110
1	00110001	B	01000010	O	01001111
2	00110010	C	01000011	P	01010000
3	00110011	D	01000100	Q	01010001
4	00110100	E	01000101	R	01010010
5	00110101	F	01000110	S	01010011
6	00110110	G	01000111	T	01010100
7	00110111	H	01001000	U	01010101
8	00111000	I	01001001	V	01010110
9	00111001	J	01001010	W	01010111
		K	01001011	X	01011000
		L	01001100	Y	01011001
		M	01001101	Z	01011010

(ON) state represents the number 1, whereas the nonconducting (OFF) state represents the number 0. For magnetic media, the magnetic field of a magnetized spot in one direction represents a 1, while magnetism in the other direction represents a 0.

The smallest element of data is called a **bit**, short for *binary digit*, which can have a value of either 0 or 1. The capacity of memory chips is usually expressed in terms of bits. A **byte** is a basic grouping of bits that the computer operates as a single unit. Typically, it consists of eight bits and represents one character of data in most computer coding schemes. Thus, the capacity of a computer's memory and secondary storage devices is usually expressed in terms of bytes. Computer codes such as ASCII (American Standard Code for Information Interchange) use various arrangements of bits to form bytes that represent the numbers 0 through 9, the letters of the alphabet, and many other characters. See Figure 3.23.

Since childhood, we have learned to do our computations using the numbers 0 through 9, the digits of the decimal number system. Although it is fine for us to use 10 digits for our computations, computers do not have this luxury. Every computer processor is made of millions of tiny switches that can be turned off or on. Because these switches have only two states, it makes sense for a computer to perform its computations with a number system that only has two digits: the **binary number system.** These digits (0 and 1) correspond to the off/on positions of the switches in the computer processor. With only these two digits, a computer can perform all the arithmetic that we can with 10 digits. Figure 3.24 illustrates the basic concepts of the binary system.

The binary system is built on an understanding of exponentiation (raising a number to a power). In contrast to the more familiar decimal system, in which each place represents the number 10 raised to a power (ones, tens, hundreds, thousands, etc.), each place in the binary system represents the number 2 raised to successive powers (2^0, 2^1, 2^2, etc.). As shown in Figure 3.24, the binary system can be used to express any integer number by using only 0 and 1.

Storage capacities are frequently measured in **kilobytes** (KB), **megabytes** (MB), **gigabytes** (GB), or **terabytes** (TB). Although *kilo* means 1,000 in the metric system, the computer industry uses *K* to represent 1,024 (or 2^{10}) storage positions. For example, a capacity of 10 megabytes is really 10,485,760 storage positions, rather than 10 million positions. However, such differences are frequently disregarded to simplify descriptions of storage capacity. Thus, a megabyte is roughly 1 million bytes of storage,

FIGURE 3.24 Computers use the binary system to store and compute numbers.

2^7	2^6	2^5	2^4	2^3	2^2	2^1	2^0
128	64	32	16	8	4	2	1
0 or 1	0 or 1	0 or 1	0 or 1	0 or 1	0 or 1	0 or 1	0 or 1

To represent any decimal number using the binary system, each place is simply assigned a value of either 0 or 1. To convert binary to decimal, simply add up the value of each place.

Example

2^7	2^6	2^5	2^4	2^3	2^2	2^1	2^0	
1	0	0	1	1	0	0	1	
128	0	0	16	8	0	0	1	
128 +	0 +	0 +	16 +	8 +	0 +	0 +	1	= 153

10011001 = 153

a gigabyte is roughly 1 billion bytes, and a terabyte represents about 1 trillion bytes, while a **petabyte** is over 1 quadrillion bytes.

To put these storage capacities in perspective, consider the following: A terabyte is equivalent to approximately 20 million typed pages, and it has been estimated that the total size of all the books, photographs, video and sound recordings, and maps in the U.S. Library of Congress approximates 3 petabytes (3,000 terabytes).

Direct and Sequential Access

Primary storage media such as semiconductor memory chips are called **direct access** memory or random-access memory (RAM). Magnetic disk devices are frequently called direct access storage devices (DASDs). In contrast, media such as magnetic tape cartridges are known as **sequential access** devices.

The terms *direct access* and *random access* describe the same concept. They mean that an element of data or instructions (such as a byte or word) can be directly stored and retrieved by selecting and using any of the locations on the storage media. They also mean that each storage position (1) has a unique address and (2) can be individually accessed in approximately the same length of time without having to search through other storage positions. For example, each memory cell on a microelectronic semiconductor RAM chip can be individually sensed or changed in the same length of time. Also, any data record stored on a magnetic or optical disk can be accessed directly in approximately the same period. See Figure 3.25.

FIGURE 3.25 Sequential versus direct access storage. Magnetic tape is a typical sequential access medium. Magnetic disks are typical direct access storage devices.

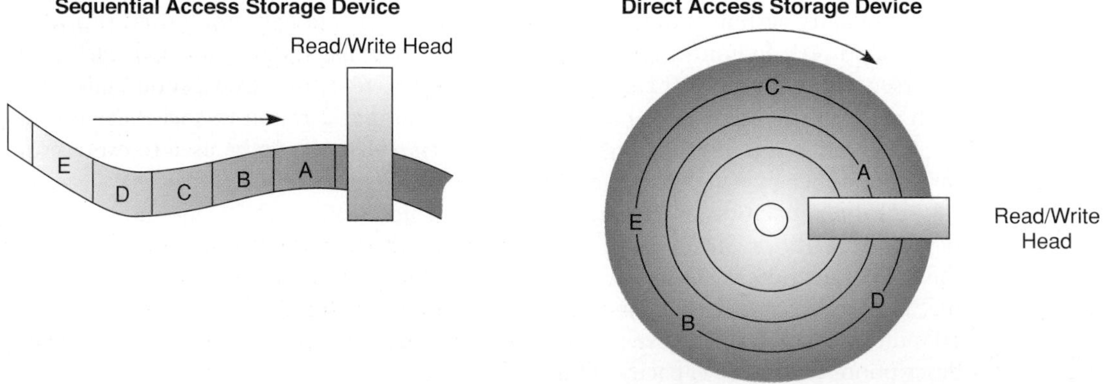

Sequential access storage media such as magnetic tape do not have unique storage addresses that can be directly addressed. Instead, data must be stored and retrieved using a sequential or serial process. Data are recorded one after another in a predetermined sequence (e.g., numeric order) on a storage medium. Locating an individual item of data requires searching the recorded data on the tape until the desired item is located.

Semiconductor Memory

Memory is the coalman to the CPU's locomotive: For maximum PC performance, it must keep the processor constantly stoked with instructions. Faster CPUs call for larger and faster memories, both in the cache where data and instructions are stored temporarily, and in the main memory [6].

The primary storage (main memory) of your computer consists of microelectronic **semiconductor memory** chips. It provides you with the working storage your computer needs to process your applications. Plug-in memory circuit boards containing 256 megabytes or more of memory chips can be added to your PC to increase its memory capacity. Specialized memory can help improve your computer's performance. Examples include external cache memory of 512 kilobytes to help your microprocessor work faster or a video graphics accelerator card with 64 megabytes or more of RAM for faster and clearer video performance. Removable credit-card-size and smaller "flash memory" RAM devices like a jump drive or a memory stick can also provide hundreds of megabytes of erasable direct access storage for PCs, PDAs, or digital cameras.

Some of the major attractions of semiconductor memory are its small size, great speed, and shock and temperature resistance. One major disadvantage of most semiconductor memory is its **volatility**. Uninterrupted electric power must be supplied, or the contents of memory will be lost. Therefore, either emergency transfer to other devices or standby electrical power (through battery packs or emergency generators) is required if data are to be saved. Another alternative is to permanently "burn in" the contents of semiconductor devices so that they cannot be erased by a loss of power.

Thus, there are two basic types of semiconductor memory: **random-access memory (RAM)** and **read-only memory (ROM)**.

- **RAM, random-access memory.** These memory chips are the most widely used primary storage medium. Each memory position can be both sensed (read) and changed (written), so it is also called read/write memory. This is a volatile memory.
- **ROM, read-only memory.** Nonvolatile random-access memory chips are used for permanent storage; ROM can be read but not erased or overwritten. Frequently used control instructions in the control unit and programs in primary storage (such as parts of the operating system) can be permanently burned into the storage cells during manufacture, sometimes called *firmware.* Variations include PROM (programmable read-only memory) and EPROM (erasable programmable read-only memory), which can be permanently or temporarily programmed after manufacture.

FIGURE 3.26
A USB flash memory drive.

One of the newest and most innovative forms of storage that uses semiconductor memory is the *flash drive* (sometimes referred to as a *jump drive*). Figure 3.26 shows a common flash memory drive.

Flash memory uses a small chip containing thousands of transistors that can be programmed to store data for virtually unlimited periods without power. The small drives can be easily transported in your pocket and are highly durable. Storage capacities currently range as high as 1 gigabyte, but newer flash technologies are making even higher storage capacities a reality.

Magnetic Disks

Multigigabyte magnetic disk drives aren't extravagant, considering that full-motion video files, sound tracks, and photo-quality images can consume colossal amounts of disk space in a blink [6].

Magnetic disks are the most common form of secondary storage for your computer system. That's because they provide fast access and high storage capacities at a reasonable cost. Magnetic disk drives contain metal disks that are coated on both sides with an iron oxide recording material. Several disks are mounted together on a vertical shaft, which typically rotates the disks at speeds of 3,600 to 7,600 revolutions per minute (rpm). Electromagnetic read/write heads are positioned by access arms between the slightly separated disks to read and write data on concentric, circular tracks. Data are recorded on tracks in the form of tiny magnetized spots to form the binary digits of common computer codes. Thousands of bytes can be recorded on each track, and there are several hundred data tracks on each disk surface, thus providing you with billions of storage positions for your software and data. See Figure 3.27.

Types of Magnetic Disks

There are several types of magnetic disk arrangements, including removable disk cartridges as well as fixed disk units. Removable disk devices are popular because they are transportable and can be used to store backup copies of your data offline for convenience and security.

- **Floppy disks**, or magnetic diskettes, consist of polyester film disks covered with an iron oxide compound. A single disk is mounted and rotates freely inside a protective flexible or hard plastic jacket, which has access openings to accommodate the read/write head of a disk drive unit. The 3 1/2-inch floppy disk, with capacities of 1.44 megabytes, is the most widely used version, with a Superdisk technology offering 120 megabytes of storage. Zip drives use a floppy-like technology to provide up to 750MB of portable disk storage.
- **Hard disk drives** combine magnetic disks, access arms, and read/write heads into a sealed module. This combination allows higher speeds, greater data recording

FIGURE 3.27 Magnetic disk media: A hard magnetic disk drive and a 3 1/2-inch floppy disk.

densities, and closer tolerances within a sealed, more stable environment. Fixed or removable disk cartridge versions are available. Capacities of hard drives range from several hundred megabytes to hundreds of gigabytes of storage.

RAID Storage

RAID computer storage equipment—big, refrigerator-size boxes full of dozens of interlinked magnetic disk drives that can store the equivalent of 100 million tax returns—hardly gets the blood rushing. But it should. Just as speedy and reliable networking opened the floodgates to cyberspace and e-commerce, ever-more-turbocharged data storage is a key building block of the Internet [8].

Disk arrays of interconnected microcomputer hard disk drives have replaced large-capacity mainframe disk drives to provide virtually unlimited online storage. Known as **RAID** (redundant arrays of independent disks), they combine from 6 to more than 100 small hard disk drives and their control microprocessors into a single unit. These RAID units provide large capacities with high access speeds because data are accessed in parallel over multiple paths from many disks. Also, RAID units provide a *fault-tolerant* capacity, in that their redundant design offers multiple copies of data on several disks. If one disk fails, data can be recovered from backup copies automatically stored on other disks. Storage area networks (SANs) are high-speed *fiber channel* local area networks that can interconnect many RAID units and thus share their combined capacity through network servers with many users.

Magnetic Tape

Tape storage is moving beyond backup. Disk subsystems provide the fastest response time for mission-critical data. But the sheer amount of data users need to access these days as part of huge enterprise applications, such as data warehouses, requires affordable [magnetic tape] storage [12].

Magnetic tape is still being used as a secondary storage medium in business applications. The read/write heads of magnetic tape drives record data in the form of magnetized spots on the iron oxide coating of the plastic tape. Magnetic tape devices include tape reels and cartridges in mainframes and midrange systems and small cassettes or cartridges for PCs. Magnetic tape cartridges have replaced tape reels in many applications and can hold over 200 megabytes.

One growing business application of magnetic tape involves the use of high-speed 36-track magnetic tape cartridges in robotic automated drive assemblies that can directly access hundreds of cartridges. These devices provide lower-cost storage to supplement magnetic disks to meet massive data warehouse and other online business storage requirements. Other major applications for magnetic tape include long-term *archival* storage and backup storage for PCs and other systems [12].

Optical Disks

Optical disk technology has become a necessity. Most software companies now distribute their elephantine programs on CD-ROMs. Many corporations are now rolling their own CDs to distribute product and corporate information that once filled bookshelves [6].

Optical disks, a fast-growing type of storage media, use several major alternative technologies. See Figure 3.28. One version is called **CD-ROM** (compact disk–read-only memory). CD-ROM technology uses 12-centimeter (4.7-inch) compact disks (CDs) similar to those used in stereo music systems. Each disk can store more than 600 megabytes. That's the equivalent of over 400 1.44-megabyte floppy disks or more than 300,000 double-spaced pages of text. A laser records data by burning permanent microscopic pits in a spiral track on a master disk from which compact disks can be mass produced. Then CD-ROM disk drives use a laser device to read the binary codes formed by those pits.

CD-R (compact disk–recordable) is another popular optical disk technology. CD-R drives or CD *burners* are commonly used to record data permanently on CDs. The major limitation of CD-ROM and CD-R disks is that recorded data cannot be

FIGURE 3.28
Comparing the capabilities of optical disk drives.

Optical Disk Drive Capabilities
• **CD-ROM** A CD-ROM drive provides a low-cost way to read data files and load software onto your computer, as well as play music CDs.
• **CD-RW** A CD-RW drive allows you to easily create your own custom data CDs for data backup or data transfer purposes. It will also allow you to store and share video files, large data files, digital photos, and other large files with other people that have access to a CD-ROM drive. This drive will also do anything your CD-ROM drive will do. It reads all your existing CD-ROMs, audio CDs, and CDs that you have created with your CD burner.
• **CD-RW/DVD** A CD-RW/DVD combination drive brings all the advantages of CD-RW, CD-ROM, and DVD-ROM to a single drive. With a CD-RW/DVD combo drive, you can read DVD-ROM disks, read CD-ROM disks, and create your own custom CDs.
• **DVD-ROM** A DVD-ROM drive allows you to enjoy the crystal clear color, picture, and sound clarity of DVD video on your PC. It will also prepare you for future software and large data files that will be released on DVD-ROM. A DVD-ROM drive can also read CD-ROM disks, effectively providing users with full optical read capability in one device.
• **DVD+RW/+R with CD-RW** A DVD-RW/R with CD-RW drive is a great all-in-one drive, allowing you to burn DVD-RW or DVD-R disks, burn CDs, and read DVDs and CDs. It enables you to create DVDs to back up and archive up to 4.7GB of data files (up to 7 times the capacity of a standard 650MB CD) and store up to 2 hours of MPEG2 digital video.

Source: Adapted from "Learn More—Optical Drives," www.dell.com.

erased. However, **CD-RW** (CD-rewritable) drives record and erase data by using a laser to heat a microscopic point on the disk's surface. In CD-RW versions using magneto-optical technology, a magnetic coil changes the spot's reflective properties from one direction to another, thus recording a binary 1 or 0. A laser device can then read the binary codes on the disk by sensing the direction of reflected light.

DVD technologies have dramatically increased optical disk capacities and capabilities. DVD (digital video disk or digital versatile disk) optical disks can hold from 3.0 to 8.5 gigabytes of multimedia data on each side. The large capacities and high-quality images and sound of DVD technology are expected to replace CD technologies for data storage and promise to accelerate the use of DVD drives for multimedia products that can be used in both computers and home entertainment systems. Thus, **DVD-ROM** disks are increasingly replacing magnetic tape videocassettes for movies and other multimedia products, while **DVD-RW** disks are being used for backup and archival storage of large data and multimedia files. See Figure 3.29.

Business Applications

One of the major uses of optical disks in mainframe and midrange systems is in **image processing,** where long-term archival storage of historical files of document images must be maintained. Financial institutions, among others, are using optical scanners to capture digitized document images and store them on optical disks as an alternative to microfilm media.

One of the major business uses of CD-ROM disks for personal computers is to provide a publishing medium for fast access to reference materials in a convenient, compact form. This material includes catalogs, directories, manuals, periodical abstracts, part listings, and statistical databases of business and economic activity. Interactive multimedia applications in business, education, and entertainment are another major use of optical disks. The large storage capacities of CD and DVD disks are a natural choice for computer video games, educational videos, multimedia encyclopedias, and advertising presentations.

FIGURE 3.29
Optical disk storage includes CD and DVD technologies.

Radio Frequency Identification

One of the newest and most rapidly growing storage technologies is **radio frequency identification (RFID)**, a system for tagging and identifying mobile objects such as store merchandise, postal packages, and sometimes even living organisms (like pets). Using a special device called an **RFID reader,** RFID allows objects to be labeled and tracked as they move from place to place.

The RFID technology works using small (sometimes smaller than a grain of sand) pieces of hardware called **RFID chips.** These chips feature an antenna to transmit and receive radio signals. Currently, there are two general types of RFID chips: *passive* and *active*. **Passive RFID** chips do not have a power source and must derive their power from the signal sent from the reader. **Active RFID** chips are self-powered and do not need to be close to the reader to transmit their signal. Any RFID chips may be attached to objects, or in the case of some passive RFID systems, injected into objects. A recent use for RFID chips is the identification of pets such as dogs or cats. By having a tiny RFID chip injected just under their skin, they can be easily identified if they become lost. The RFID chip contains contact information about the owner of the pet. Taking this a step further, the Transportation Security Administration is considering using RFID tags embedded in airline boarding passes to keep track of passengers.

Whenever a reader within range sends appropriate signals to an object, the associated RFID chip responds with the requested information, such as an identification number or product date. The reader, in turn, displays the response data to an operator. Readers may also forward data to a networked central computer system. Such RFID systems generally support storing information on the chips as well as simply reading data.

The RFID systems were created as an alternative to common bar codes. Relative to bar codes, RFID allows objects to be scanned from a greater distance, supports storing of data, and allows more information to be tracked per object.

Recently, RFID has raised some privacy concerns due to the invisible nature of the system and its capability to transmit fairly sophisticated messages. As these types of issues get worked out, we can expect to see RFID technology being used in just about every way imaginable.

Banks and Casinos Share a Common Bond

Radio tags the size of a grain of sand will be embedded in the euro note as a result of an agreement between the European Central Bank (ECB) and Japanese electronics maker Hitachi. The ECB is deeply concerned about counterfeiting and money laundering and is looking to RFID technology as a preventive measure.

In 2003, Greek authorities were confronted with 2,411 cases of counterfeit euros and seized 4,776 counterfeit banknotes, while authorities in Poland nabbed a gang suspected of making more than a million fake euros and putting them into circulation. To add to the problem, businesses find it hard to judge a note's authenticity, as current equipment cannot tell between bogus currency and old notes with worn-out security marks. Among the security features in the current euro are threads embedded in the paper which are visible under ultraviolet light.

"The main objective is to determine the authenticity of money and to stop counterfeits," Frost and Sullivan analyst Prianka Chopra said in a report published in March. "RFID tags also have the ability of recording information such as details of the transactions the paper note has been involved in. It would, therefore, also prevent money-laundering, make it possible to track illegal transactions, and even prevent kidnappers demanding unmarked bills," according to Chopra.

The RFID tags are microchips half the size of a grain of sand. They listen for a radio query and respond by transmitting their unique ID code. Most RFID tags have no batteries; they use the power from the initial radio signal to transmit their response.

In addition to acting as digital watermarks, radio chips could speed up routine bank processes such as counting. With such tags, a stack of notes can be passed through a reader and the sum added in a split second, similar to how inventory is tracked in an RFID-based system.

The euro came into circulation on January 1, 2002, with 12 countries adopting it as standard currency: Austria, Belgium, Finland, France, Germany, Greece, Ireland, Italy, Luxembourg, the Netherlands, Portugal, and Spain. In a euro note the RFID tag will contain a serial code, as well as details such as place of origin and denomination. Data can only be written on the chip's ROM during production, and not after it is out "in the wild," according to Hitachi. The same miniature RFID chip was also used in admission tickets for Japan's international expo, which was held in the country's Aichi Prefecture in 2005.

The ECB is not the only one in the business of money that sees value in RFID. A new generation of casino chips with built-in RFID tags is giving insight into the way banks and shops could keep track of real money if it were tagged. The chips, launched in 2004, will allow casino operators to spot counterfeits and thefts and to monitor the behavior of gamblers.

Counterfeit chips have long been a problem for casinos, and houses routinely mark their chips with inks visible only in infrared or ultraviolet light. Embedded RFID tags should make the chips much harder to counterfeit, and placing tag readers at staff exits could cut down on theft by employees. The tags could also help casinos manage large-scale theft. If a large stash of chips goes missing after a table is overturned during an argument, for example, casinos sometimes have to change their entire stock. This tactic is unpopular with gamblers, because any chips that they have not cashed become worthless. Instead, RFID tags would allow the casinos to identify stolen chips without the expensive process of restocking.

Aside from improving security, the tags could also be used to track how people play in a casino, says John Kendall, president of Chipco International in Raymond, Maine, which is making and selling tagged casino chips. The tagged chips would allow casino operators to keep tabs on the fortunes of every gambler on their premises, recording the stakes placed by each player along with their winnings and losses. American casino operators routinely monitor gamblers with security cameras, just as retailers monitor stores for shoplifters.

The casinos want to check that big winners are not cheating the house and identify lucrative "high rollers" and encourage them to keep playing by treating them to free meals, show tickets, or hotel rooms. But this monitoring has to be done by human observers and is haphazard and unreliable. Chip tracking could dramatically improve the process.

Although gamblers are used to having every move they, and their money, make watched and monitored in the casino, patrons of the local bank are less tolerant. "When rumours surfaced in 2003 that the European Central Bank was quietly planning to put RFID tags in euro banknotes, privacy groups balked at the possibility that anybody with an RFID reader could count the money in wallets of passers by," says Mark Roberti, editor of the *RFID Journal*, an online newsletter about the RFID industry.

And Roberti expects privacy advocates to object strongly to anything that would let people track an individual's spending. "I do not expect to see US dollars with RFID tags in my lifetime," he says. Europeans may not have so long to wait. [7]

Predictions for the Future

If Moore's law prevails and technology advancement continues, we can expect to see our lives change in remarkable and unimaginable ways. Although we cannot really predict the future, it is interesting and fun to read the predictions of futurists—people whose job it is to think about what the future might bring. Here's one man's perspective on what computing technology might do to change our lives in the decades to come.

Computers will Enable People to Live Forever

In just 15 years, we'll begin to see the merger of human and computer intelligence that ultimately will enable people to live forever. At least that's the prediction of author and futurist Ray Kurzweil.

Kurzweil suggests that nanobots will roam our bloodstreams, fixing diseased or aging organs, while computers will back up our human memories and rejuvenate our bodies by keeping us young in appearance and health.

The author of the book *The Singularity Is Near*, Kurzweil says within a quarter of a century, nonbiological intelligence will match the range and subtlety of human intelligence. He predicts that it will then soar past human ability because of the continuing acceleration of information-based technologies, as well as the ability of machines to share their knowledge instantly.

Kurzweil predicts people and computers will intermix with nanobots, blood cell-sized robots, that will be integrated into everything from our clothing to our bodies and brains. People simply need to live long enough—another 15 to 30 years—to live forever. Think of it as replacing everyone's "human body version 1.0" with *nanotechnology* that will repair or replace ailing or aging tissue, he says. Parts will become easily replaceable.

"A $1,000 worth of computation in the 2020s will be 1,000 times more powerful than the human brain," says Kurzweil, adding that in 25 years we'll have multiplied our computational power by a billion. "Fifteen years from now, it'll be a very different world. We'll have cured cancer and heart disease, or at least rendered them to manageable chronic conditions that aren't life threatening. We'll get to the point where we can stop the aging process and stave off death."

Actually, we'll hit a point where human intelligence simply can't keep up with, or even follow, the progress that computers will make, according to Kurzweil. He expects that nonbiological intelligence will have access to its own design plans and be able to improve itself rapidly. Computer, or nonbiological, intelligence created in the year 2045 will be one billion times more powerful than all human intelligence today.

"Supercomputing is behind the progress in all of these areas," Kurzweil says, adding that a prerequisite for nonbiological intelligence is to reverse-engineer biology and the human brain. That will give scientists a "toolkit of techniques" to apply when developing intelligent computers. In a written report, he said, "We won't experience 100 years of technological advance in the 21st century; we will witness on the order of 20,000 years of progress, or about 1,000 times greater than what was achieved in the 20th century."

According to Kurzweil, here's what we can expect in the not-so-distant future:

- Doctors will be doing a backup of our memories by the late 2030s.
- By the late 2020s, doctors will be sending intelligent bots, or nanobots, into our bloodstreams to keep us healthy, and into our brains to keep us young.
- In 15 years, human longevity will be greatly extended. By the 2020s, we'll be adding a year of longevity or more for every year that passes.
- In the same timeframe, we'll routinely be in virtual reality environments. Instead of making a cell call, we could "meet" someone in a virtual world and take a walk on a virtual beach and chat. Business meetings and conference calls will be held in calming or inspiring virtual locations.
- When you're walking down the street and see someone you've met before, background information about that person will pop up on your glasses or in the periphery of your vision.
- Instead of spending hours in front of a desktop machine, computers will be more ingrained in our environment. For instance, computer monitors could be replaced by projections onto our retinas or on a virtual screen hovering in the air.
- Scientists will be able to rejuvenate all of someone's body tissues and organs by transforming their skin cells into youthful versions of other cell types.
- Need a little boost? Kurzweil says scientists will be able to regrow our own cells, tissues, and even whole organs, and then introduce them into our bodies, all without surgery. As part of what he calls the "emerging field of rejuvenation medicine," new tissue and organs will be built out of cells that have been made younger.
- Got heart trouble? No problem, says Kurzweil. "We'll be able to create new heart cells from your skin cells and introduce them into your system through the bloodstream. Over time, your heart cells get replaced with these new cells, and the result is a rejuvenated, young heart with your own DNA."
- One trick we'll have to master is staying ahead of the game. Kurzweil warns that terrorists could obviously use this same technology against us. For example, they could build and spread a bioengineered biological virus that's highly powerful and stealthy.

According to Kurzweil, we're not that far away from solving a medical problem that has plagued scientists and doctors for quite some time now: the common cold. He notes that though nanotechnology could go into our bloodstreams and knock it out, before we even get to that stage, biotechnology should be able to cure the cold in just 10 years. [16]

Summary

- **Computer Systems.** Major types of computer systems are summarized in Figure 3.3. Microcomputers are used as personal computers, network computers, personal digital assistants, technical workstations, and information appliances. Midrange systems are increasingly used as powerful network servers and for many multiuser business data processing and scientific applications. Mainframe computers are larger and more powerful than most midsize systems. They are usually faster, have more memory capacity, and can support more network users and peripheral devices. They are designed to handle the information processing needs of large organizations with high volumes of transaction processing or with complex computational problems. Supercomputers are a special category of extremely powerful mainframe computer systems designed for massive computational assignments.

- **The Computer Systems Concept.** A computer is a system of information processing components that perform input, processing, output, storage, and control functions. Its hardware components include input and output devices, a central processing unit (CPU), and primary and secondary storage devices. The major functions and hardware in a computer system are summarized in Figure 3.10.
- **Peripheral Devices.** Refer to Figures 3.14 and 3.22 to review the capabilities of peripheral devices for input, output, and storage discussed in this chapter.

Key Terms and Concepts

These are the key terms and concepts of this chapter. The page number of their first explanation is given in parentheses.

1. Binary representation (96)
2. Central processing unit (83)
3. Computer system (82)
4. Computer terminal (77)
5. Cycles per second (84)
6. Direct access (98)
7. Graphical user interface (86)
8. Information appliance (77)
9. Magnetic disks (100)
    a. Floppy disk (100)
    b. Hard disk (100)
    c. RAID (redundant array of independent disks) (101)
10. Magnetic stripe (93)
11. Magnetic tape (101)
12. Mainframe system (80)
13. Microcomputer (75)
14. Midrange system (79)
15. Minicomputer (79)
16. MIPS (million instructions per second) (84)
17. Moore's law (84)
18. Network computer (77)
19. Network server (76)
20. Network terminal (77)
21. Offline (86)
22. Online (86)
23. Optical disks (101)
24. Optical scanning (92)
25. Peripherals (86)
26. Pointing devices (86)
27. Primary storage unit (84)
28. Processing speed
    a. Millisecond (84)
    b. Microsecond (84)
    c. Nanosecond (84)
    d. Picosecond (84)
29. RFID (radio frequency identification) (103)
30. Secondary storage (84)
31. Semiconductor memory (99)
    a. RAM (random-access memory) (99)
    b. ROM (read-only memory) (99)
32. Sequential access (98)
33. Speech recognition (90)
34. Storage capacity (97)
    a. Bit (97)
    b. Byte (97)
    c. Kilobyte (97)
    d. Megabyte (97)
    e. Gigabyte (97)
    f. Terabyte (97)
    g. Petabyte (98)
35. Supercomputer (81)
36. Volatility (99)
37. Workstation computer (76)

Review Quiz

Match one of the previous key terms and concepts with one of the following brief examples or definitions. Try to find the best fit for answers that seem to fit more than one term or concept. Defend your choices.

____ 1. A computer is a combination of components that perform input, processing, output, storage, and control functions.

____ 2. The main processing component of a computer system.

____ 3. A measure of computer speed in terms of processor cycles.

____ 4. Devices for consumers to access the Internet.

____ 5. The memory of a computer.

____ 6. Magnetic disks and tape and optical disks perform this function.

____ 7. Input/output and secondary storage devices for a computer system.

____ 8. Connected to and controlled by a CPU.

____ 9. Separate from and not controlled by a CPU.

____ 10. Results from the presence or absence or change in direction of electric current, magnetic fields, or light rays in computer circuits and media.

____ 11. A common computer interface using a desktop metaphor and icons.

____ 12. Can be a desktop/laptop or handheld computer.

____ 13. A computer category between microcomputers and mainframes.

____ 14. A small, portable magnetic disk encased in a thin plastic shell.

____ 15. A large-capacity disk typically found in computer systems.

____ 16. Low-cost microcomputers for use with the Internet and corporate intranets.

____ 17. A redundant array of inexpensive hard drives.

____ 18. A terminal that depends on network servers for its software and processing power.

____ 19. A computer that manages network communications and resources.

____ 20. The most powerful type of computer.

____ 21. A magnetic tape technology for credit cards.

____ 22. One billionth of a second.

____ 23. Roughly 1 billion characters of storage.

____ 24. Includes electronic mice, trackballs, pointing sticks, and touchpads.

____ 25. Smaller than a mainframe and larger than a microcomputer.

____ 26. The largest of the three main types of computers.

____ 27. Processor power measured in terms of number of instructions processed.

____ 28. Prediction that computer power will double approximately every 18 to 24 months.

____ 29. Promises to be the easiest, most natural way to communicate with computers.

____ 30. Capturing data by processing light reflected from images.

____ 31. The speed of a computer.

____ 32. One one-thousandth of a second.

____ 33. 1,024 bytes.

____ 34. A device with a keyboard and a video display networked to a computer is a typical example.

____ 35. The amount of data a storage device can hold.

____ 36. A personal computer used as a technical workstation.

____ 37. The smallest unit of data storage.

____ 38. One trillion bytes.

____ 39. You cannot erase the contents of these storage circuits.

____ 40. The memory of most computers consists of these storage circuits.

____ 41. The property that determines whether data are lost or retained when power fails.

____ 42. Each position of storage can be accessed in approximately the same time.

____ 43. Each position of storage can be accessed according to a predetermined order.

____ 44. Microelectronic storage circuits on silicon chips.

____ 45. Uses magnetic spots on metal or plastic disks.

____ 46. Uses magnetic spots on plastic tape.

____ 47. Uses a laser to read microscopic points on plastic disks.

Discussion Questions

1. What trends are occurring in the development and use of the major types of computer systems?
2. Will the convergence of PDAs, subnotebook PCs, and cell phones produce an information appliance that will make all of those categories obsolete? Why or why not?
3. Refer to the Real World Case on mobile wireless devices in the chapter. Should mobile wireless technologies be bundled together in a generic fashion (i.e., voice, video, data, messaging, etc.), or should manufacturers allow for customization of mobile devices to be more industry- or task-specific? Explain.
4. Do you think that information appliances like PDAs will replace personal computers (PCs) in business applications? Explain.
5. Are networks of PCs and servers making mainframe computers obsolete? Explain.
6. Refer to the Real World Case on Apple Computer in the chapter. What advice would you give Steve Jobs for improvements in the iPod and the Mac computer line? Defend your recommendations.
7. What are several trends that are occurring in computer peripheral devices? How do these trends affect business uses of computers?
8. What are several important computer hardware developments that you expect to happen in the next 10 years? How will these affect the business use of computers?
9. What processor, memory, magnetic disk storage, and video display capabilities would you require for a personal computer that you would use for business purposes? Explain your choices.
10. What other peripheral devices and capabilities would you want to have for your business PC? Explain your choices.

Analysis Exercises

1. **Hardware Costs**
Purchasing Computer Systems for Your Workgroup
You have been asked to get pricing information for a potential purchase of PCs for the members of your workgroup. Go to the Internet to get prices for these units from Dell and Hewlett-Packard. Look for a high-end office desktop model.

The list below shows the specifications for the basic system you have been asked to price and potential upgrades to each feature. You will want to get a price for the basic system described below and a separate price for each of the upgrades shown.

Component	Basic Unit	Upgrade
CPU (gigahertz)	2.8	3.4
Hard drive (gigabytes)	160	500
RAM (gigabytes)	1	2
Removable media	16x DVD-R/W	48x DVD-R/W
Monitor	17-inch flat screen	19-inch flat screen

Select the standard software licenses; your IT department will install the necessary software for your workgroup. Take a two-year warranty and servicing coverage offered by each supplier. If a two-year warranty is not available, simply note any differences in the coverage with the closest match.

a. Prepare a spreadsheet summarizing this pricing information and showing the cost from each supplier of the following options: (1) units with the basic configuration, (2) the incremental cost of each upgrade separately, and (3) the cost of a fully upgraded unit. If you cannot find features that exactly match the requirements, then use the next higher standard for comparison and make a note of the difference.

b. Prepare a set of PowerPoint slides summarizing your results. Include a discussion of the warranty and servicing contract options offered by each supplier.

2. **Price and Performance Trends for Computer Hardware**
Hardware Analysis
The table below details price and capacity figures for common components of personal computers. Typical prices for microprocessors, random-access memory (RAM), and hard disk storage prices are displayed.

The performance of typical components has increased substantially over time, so the speed (for the microprocessor) or the capacity (for the storage devices) is also listed for comparison purposes. Although not all improvements in these components are reflected in these capacity measures, it is interesting to examine trends in these measurable characteristics.

a. Create a spreadsheet based on the figures below and include a new row for each component, showing the price per unit of capacity (cost per megahertz of speed for microprocessors and cost per megabyte of storage for RAM and hard disk devices).

b. Create a set of graphs highlighting your results and illustrating trends in price per unit of performance (speed) or capacity.

c. Write a short paper discussing the trends you found. How long do you expect these trends to continue? Why?

d. Prepare a summary presentation outlining the points from your paper (above). Be sure to *link* your Excel chart into the PowerPoint presentation so it automatically updates when any data change in the spreadsheet.

3. **Can Computers Think Like People?**
The Turing Test
The "Turing test" is a hypothetical test to determine whether a computer system has reached the level of "artificial intelligence." If the computer can fool a person into thinking it is another person, then it has artificial intelligence. Except in very narrow areas, no computer has passed the Turing test.

Free e-mail account providers such as Hotmail or Yahoo take advantage of this fact. They need to distinguish between new account registrations generated by a person and registrations generated by spammers' software. Why? Spammers burn through thousands of e-mail accounts to send millions of e-mails. To help them, spammers need automated tools to generate these accounts. Hotmail fights this practice by requiring registrants to enter an alphanumeric code hidden within an image correctly. Spammers' programs have trouble correctly reading the code, but most humans do not. With this reverse Turing test, also called a "captcha," Hotmail can distinguish between a person and a program and allow only humans to register. As a result, spammers must look elsewhere for free accounts.

a. Aside from those mentioned above, in what applications might businesses find it useful to distinguish between a human and a computer?

	1991	1993	1995	1997	1999	2001	2003	2005
Processor: Speed, MHz	25	33	100	125	350	1000	3,000	3,800
Cost	$180	$125	$275	$250	$300	$251	$395	$549
RAM chip: MB per chip	1	4	4	16	64	256	512	2,000
Cost	$55	$140	$120	$97	$125	$90	$59	$149
Hard drive: GB per drive	.105	.250	.540	2.0	8.0	40.0	160.0	320
Cost	$480	$375	$220	$250	$220	$138	$114	$115

b. Describe a Turing test that a visually impaired person but not a computer might pass.
c. Search the Internet for the term "captcha" and describe its strengths and weaknesses.

4. **Radio Frequency Identification**
Input Device or Invasion of Privacy?
Punch cards, keyboards, bar code scanners—the trend is clear. Input devices have continued to promote faster and more accurate data entry. Key to this advance is capturing data at their source, and no tool does this better than radio frequency identification (RFID) systems. An RFID transmitter sends out a coded radio signal. An RFID tag changes and "reflects" this signal back to an antenna. The RFID system can read the reflection's unique pattern and record it in a database. Depending on the system, this pattern may be associated with a product line, shipping palette, or even a person. Although an RFID system's range is limited to a few dozen feet, this approach enables remarkable inventory tracking that doesn't rely on a human to keyboard interaction or scan. Except for the presence of a 1-inch-square (5-cm-square) RFID tag, humans may have no idea an RFID system is in operation.

Indeed, that may be part of the problem. Consumers have expressed concern that RFID chips attached to products they purchase may be used to track them. Others fear their government may require embedded RFID chips as a form of personal identification and tracking. What started as a new and improved input device has devolved into a matter of public policy.

a. How would you feel if your university used RFID tags embedded in student IDs to replace the magnetic "swipe" strip? On a campus, RFID tags might be used to control building access, manage computer access, or even automatically track class attendance.
b. Enter "RFID" into an Internet search engine and summarize the search results. Of the top 20 results, how many were positive, negative, or neutral?
c. Enter "RFID" and "privacy" into an Internet search engine, select a page expressing privacy concerns, and summarize them in a brief essay. Do you find these concerns compelling?

REAL WORLD CASE 3

E-Trade, Verizon Communications, AAA, and Others: Advances in the Business Applications of Speech Recognition Technology

As man-vs.-machine classics go, it had the crucial elements: The brash young champion. The new-and-improved computing powerhouse. That the champ was 17-year-old Ben Cook, anointed by the *Guinness Book of World Records* as the world's fastest text messager, and the machine was not a supercomputer but a cell phone, didn't detract from the drama—at least not to the crowd gathered at an Orlando voice-recognition software conference recently. Which would be faster at converting an elaborate sentence into text: Cook's flying thumbs or the elegant algorithms of new speech software from Nuance Communications?

The harrowing test phrase—"The razor-toothed piranhas of the genera Serrasalmus and Pygocentrus are the most ferocious freshwater fish in the world. In reality they seldom attack a human"—flashed on a screen. Cook thumbed furiously. A Nuance staffer calmly dictated the phrase into a cell phone. It was a blowout: Nuance's software converted the phrase flawlessly in 16 seconds; Cook trudged home in 48 seconds and was left mumbling in a dazed tone, "I don't know how you do that."

They did it with Nuance's recently launched Mobile Dictation software, but there's also a broader explanation. Speech recognition, long ridiculed as one of those perpetually just-around-the-corner technologies like the personal jet pack or Dick Tracy's wristwatch, has finally arrived. Advances in processing power, new software algorithms, and even better microphones have enabled established players like Nuance and a raft of startups to design systems that work, often at near 100 percent accuracy rates. And they're creating explosive potential for growth in markets for everything from handheld dictation devices to mobile phones to automobiles. "Speech technology," says Data Monitor analyst Daniel Hong, "is finally transitioning from a cool technology to a business solution."

In that transition, the more valuable speech recognition becomes as a business tool. Call centers and customer service departments are notorious for the infuriating "Press or say 1" purgatories that older speech-recognition technologies created, but customer outrage isn't the only penalty: The average call-center call costs $5 if handled by an employee but 50 cents with a self-service, speech-enabled system, according to Data Monitor.

Online brokerage e-Trade Financial uses Tellme Networks (which makes voice recognition software for corporate call centers and telecom directory systems) to field about 50,000 calls a day. Half of those calls never go to an e-Trade employee. The company says Tellme's system is saving it at least $30 million annually. Another example is Telecom New Zealand, which reports a tripling in call center customer satisfaction since it installed a call center speech recognition system by TuVox Inc.

TuVox, is racking up customers in the call center and corporate markets. Its VP for marketing, Azita Martin, has her team dial a call center and record the typically torturous, multistep efforts to, say, reach the billing department. Then they create an audio file that reveals what the interaction could sound like if Martin's target prospect used TuVox's software for routing calls with advanced speech-recognition technology. She e-mails the two interchanges to the CEO of a company using the call center. The contrast has helped Martin sign up numerous clients during the past few months—one reason TuVox's annual revenue is growing at double-digit rates and its customer base has quadrupled in 12 months.

Computerized speech recognition has come a long way in 20 years. The technology has become smarter, easier to use, and more integrated with other applications. Such technical advances, plus product introductions that facilitate the deployment of the technology by mainstream developers, are enabling new uses for automated speech systems.

Research in automated speech recognition (ASR) goes back to the 1930s, but serious commercialization of it didn't begin until 50 years later. In 1988, Dragon Systems Inc. demonstrated a PC-based speech recognition system with an 8,000-word vocabulary. Users had to speak slowly and clearly. One. Word. At. A. Time.

The next big step came in 1990, when Dragon demonstrated a 5,000-word continuous-speech system for PCs and a large-vocabulary, speech-to-text system for general purpose dictation. Then, in 1997, Dragon and IBM both introduced continuous speech recognition systems for general purpose use.

Meanwhile, corporations began rolling out interactive voice response (IVR) systems. The earlier ones—indeed, most in use today—are menu-driven: "For your fund balance, say or press 'one.'" A few advanced systems are more conversational: "What city are you departing from?" Despite the steady advancements to bigger vocabularies, lower error rates, and more natural interfaces, however, speech products have remained specialized tools for niche markets such as PC navigation by the disabled, medical dictation, and tightly constrained customer service interactions.

But now, previously stand-alone speech systems are linking up with enterprise systems to access other applications and spawn transactions. As a result, these speech systems—previously the domain of call center and telephony managers—are increasingly becoming something for the IT shop to worry about, if not manage.

Verizon's speech application, for example, can trigger a line test, update customer accounts, schedule repairs, and create trouble tickets—processes that require interfaces with many systems. "If you create something that's just a veneer, people get it very quickly," says Fari Ebrahimi, senior vice president for IT at Verizon. "But for customers to really get value, you need to do something with the back office."

Many of Verizon's back-office functions have been redesigned as Web services and are accessible to customers over the Web or by spoken request. The new system handles some 50,000 repair calls per day and has boosted the percentage of calls that are fully automated from 3 to 20 percent, Ebrahimi says. He won't say how much the company is saving in labor costs, but he acknowledges it's "millions and millions."

Verizon's National Operations Voice Portal is deployed across three geographically dispersed data centers, and calls are routed from point to point using voice-over-IP technology. The system uses speech recognition products and user interface designs from ScanSoft Inc. (which obtained much of Dragon's speech technology via acquisition). Telephony servers at each data center are connected to back-office application servers running BEA Systems Inc.'s BEA WebLogic Server.

"The technology that used to be in those telephone silos, managed by the call center manager, is now becoming standards-based and is being driven by the same application server that serves the Web pages," says William Meisel, president of TMA Associates, a speech-technology consulting firm in Tarzana, California. "Now the IT department can create the applications in an environment that's more familiar to them."

Organizations that have deployed speech technology say that recent advancements in natural-language understanding have made the systems more acceptable to callers. "With IVR, it was 'Touch or say three,'" says Joe Alessi, vice president for marketing and IT at AAA Minnesota/Iowa. "Now we can say, 'I'd like to change my address.'"

The organization last year replaced a Touch-Tone-based IVR member service system with a self-service system built on the Say Anything natural-language speech software engine from Nuance Communications Inc. One objective was to reduce turnover in the call center by freeing agents from handling mundane calls, such as requests for new membership cards. Another goal was to address the problem of callers bailing out of the IVR system because they found the menus confusing, Alessi says.

The new system enabled AAA to reassign 20 percent of its call center staff as the number of calls that could be completely automated increased. And the organization has reduced processing costs by $2 per call on average, for a total annual savings of $200,000, according to Alessi.

T. Rowe Price Group Inc. in Baltimore also upgraded its menu-driven IVR system to a free-form speech system based on IBM's WebSphere Voice Response and Voice Server with natural-language understanding capabilities. The investment company reports big savings in telephone charges because automated calls can be completed faster. "An area we struggled with is doing transactions in the system," says Nicholas Welsh, a vice president at T. Rowe Price. "They could take three to four minutes, because you have to go through five or six menu legs. Now the same transaction takes 30 seconds because you can speak it all in one sentence."

Source: Adapted from Jeanette Borzo, "Now You're Talking," *Business 2.0*, January–February 2007; Gary H. Anthes, "Speak Easy," *Computerworld*, July 5, 2004.

CASE STUDY QUESTIONS

1. What are the business benefits and limitations of the speech recognition systems at e-Trade, Verizon and others? How could their use of this technology be improved?
2. What types of business situations would benefit most from speech recognition technology? Which ones would benefit least? Explain your choices.
3. Given the advancements in speech recognition software over the past 20 years, what types of new applications for this technology do you see in the next 20 years? Provide examples to illustrate your answer.

REAL WORLD ACTIVITIES

1. Speech recognition technology is advancing rapidly in terms of its ability to simulate natural language conversations and accept common phrases. Using the Internet, research the state of the art in speech recognition technology. A good place to start would be the Web sites of the speech recognition system developers mentioned in the case.
2. Simply simulating natural conversations is but one capability of speech software applications. Text-to-speech, voice verification, and speech-to-text are a few others. Break into small groups with your classmates, and brainstorm about how speech recognition systems could be used in innovative and useful ways. Do you think we will eventually eliminate the need for humans in common telephone interactions? Is this good or bad?

CHAPTER 4

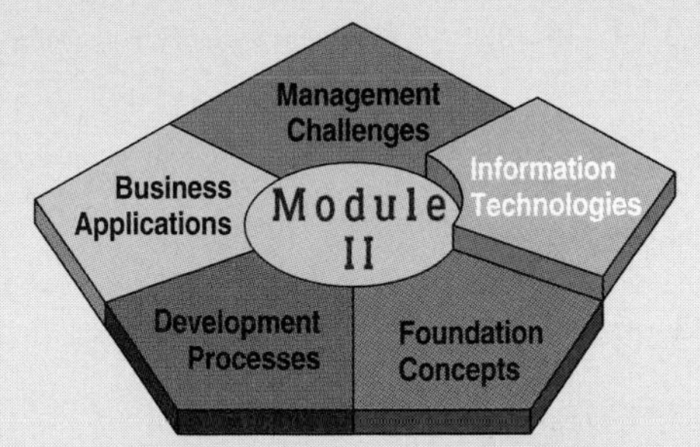

COMPUTER SOFTWARE

Chapter Highlights

Learning Objectives

After reading and studying this chapter, you should be able to:

1. Describe several important trends occurring in computer software.
2. Give examples of several major types of application and system software.
3. Explain the purpose of several popular software packages for end-user productivity and collaborative computing.
4. Define and describe the functions of an operating system.
5. Describe the main uses of computer programming software, tools, and languages.

SECTION I Application Software: End-User Applications

Introduction to Software

This chapter provides an overview of the major types of software you depend on as you work with computers and access computer networks. It discusses their characteristics and purposes and gives examples of their uses. Before we begin, let's look at an example of the changing world of software in business.

Read the Real World Case discussing software for small-to-medium businesses. We can learn a lot about the challenges and opportunities in the small business software market from this example. See Figure 4.1.

What Is Software?

To fully appreciate the need for and value of the wide variety of software available, we should be sure we understand what software is. **Software** is the general term for various kinds of programs used to operate and manipulate computers and their peripheral devices. One common way of describing hardware and software is to say that software can be thought of as the variable part of a computer and hardware the invariable part. There are many types and categories of software. We will focus our attention on the different types of software and its uses in this chapter.

Types of Software

Let's begin our analysis of software by looking at an overview of the major types and functions of **application software** and **system software** available to computer users, shown in Figure 4.2. This figure summarizes the major categories of system and application software we will discuss in this chapter. Of course, this figure is a conceptual illustration. The types of software you will encounter depend primarily on the types of computers and networks you use and on the specific tasks you want to accomplish. We will discuss application software in this section and the major types of system software in Section II.

Application Software for End Users

Figure 4.2 shows that **application software** includes a variety of programs that can be subdivided into general-purpose and function-specific application categories. **General-purpose application programs** are programs that perform common information processing jobs for end users. For example, word processing, spreadsheet, database management, and graphics programs are popular with microcomputer users for home, education, business, scientific, and many other purposes. Because they significantly increase the productivity of end users, they are sometimes known as *productivity packages*. Other examples include Web browsers, electronic mail, and groupware, which help support communication and collaboration among workgroups and teams.

An additional common way of classifying software is based on how the software was developed. **Custom software** is the term used to identify software applications that are developed within an organization for use by that organization. In other words, the organization that writes the program code is also the organization that uses the final software application. In contrast, **COTS software** (an acronym that stands for *commercial off-the-shelf*) is software developed with the intention of selling the software in multiple copies (and usually for a profit). In this case, the organization that writes the software is not the intended target audience for its use.

Several characteristics are important in describing COTS software. First, as stated in our definition, COTS software products are sold in many copies with minimal changes beyond scheduled upgrade releases. Purchasers of COTS software generally have no control over the specification, schedule, evolution, or access to either the source code or the internal documentation. A COTS product is sold, leased, or licensed to the general public, but in virtually all cases, the vendor of the product retains the intellectual property rights of the software. Custom software, in contrast, is generally owned by the organization that developed it (or that paid to have it developed),

REAL WORLD CASE 1 Wolf Peak International: Failure and Success in Application Software for the Small-to-Medium Enterprise

One of the hazards of a growing small business is a software upgrade. If you pick the wrong horse, you may find yourself riding in the wrong direction. Correcting your course may mean not only writing off your first upgrade selection but then going through the agonizing process of finding a better software solution for your company. That's what happened to Wolf Peak International of Layton, Utah, which designs and manufactures eyewear for the safety, sporting, driving, and fashion industries. Founded in 1998, the privately held small-to-midsize enterprise (SME) also specializes in overseas production, sourcing, importing, and promotional distribution services.

In Wolf Peak's early days, founder-owner Kurt Daems was happy using QuickBooks to handle accounting chores. The package is user friendly and allowed him to drill down to view transaction details or combine data in a variety of ways to create desired reports. As the company prospered, however, it quickly outgrew the capabilities of QuickBooks. "As Wolf Peak got bigger, the owner felt the need to get into a more sophisticated accounting system," says Ron Schwab, CFO at Wolf Peak International. "There were no financial people in-house at the time the decision was made to purchase a replacement for QuickBooks, and the decision was made without a finance person in place to review it."

Wolf Peak selected one of several accounting software packages promoted to growing SMEs. By the time Schwab joined the company, the package had been installed for six months, following an implementation period that lasted a full year. "The biggest difficulty for QuickBooks users is to go from a very friendly user interface and the ability to find information easily to a more sophisticated, secured, batch-oriented accounting system that became an absolute nightmare to get data out of," notes Schwab. "So the company paid a lot of money to have this new accounting system, but nobody knew how to go in and extract financial or operational data used to make critical business decisions."

FIGURE 4.1

Small-to-medium businesses are finding mission-critical support for their day-to-day activities through software designed for their size and needs.

There were other problems. Developing reusable reports was difficult, time consuming, and expensive. The company paid IT consultants to develop reports for specific needs, some of which still had not been delivered, months after they were commissioned. Ad hoc reporting was similarly intractable. Furthermore, the company's prior-year history in QuickBooks could not be converted into the new accounting package.

A situation like this creates serious problems. Accustomed to keeping close tabs on the company's operations, Daems found that he simply could not get the information he wanted. He began to lose track of his business. "He got so fed up he finally came to me and said he was ready to look at a SAP software alternative he'd heard about," Schwab recalls. "He wasn't ready to buy it, though, because he'd just sunk a lot of money into the new accounting package."

One year after Wolf Peak had switched over to the new accounting software, Schwab called the offices of JourneyTEAM, a local SAP services partner, and asked their software consultants to demonstrate the SAP Business One software suite. SAP Business One is an integrated business management software package designed specifically for SMEs like Wolf Peak: The application automates critical operations including sales, finance, purchasing, inventory, and manufacturing and delivers an accurate, up-to-the-minute view of the business. Its relative affordability promises a rapid return on investment, and its simplicity means users have a consistent, intuitive environment that they can learn quickly and use effectively.

"We had a wish list from various company employees asking for a variety of capabilities," recalls Schwab. "The JourneyTEAM people came in and demonstrated all those functionalities and more. They even generated four or five reports that we had spent several thousand dollars and several months trying to get from our other software consultants and had not yet received. Based on our data that they had input into Business One, JourneyTEAM put those reports together in an afternoon."

Daems still had a few reservations: He needed the buy-in of his VP of sales and was concerned about cost. He still wasn't ready to write off the recently installed accounting software. JourneyTEAM came in and gave another presentation for the Wolf Peak sales team and, following that, came back with an acceptable quote. With some pain, but also considerable relief, Daems wrote off the existing accounting package. "We felt the benefits of SAP Business One far outweighed the costs and time already invested in the that software system," Daems says.

Implementation of Business One took just seven weeks from the day of the initial sales presentation. "We implemented SAP Business One during our busiest period of the year with no disruptions," notes Schwab. "It went better than I expected, in particular the cutover and conversion to Business One. JourneyTEAM did an amazing job of getting all our old records converted with no real problems at all. We met our June 30 deadline and cutover during the succeeding long weekend without incident."

Schwab's enthusiasm for SAP Business One is high. "This is the best accounting program I've ever worked with," he says. "I can drill down to anything I want. And with the XL Reporter tool, I can build reports on the fly." Business One includes a seamlessly integrated reporting and financial analysis tool called XL Reporter that works with Microsoft Excel to provide instant access to financial and operational data. It reports on live data drawn from a variety of sources including general ledger, receivables, payables, sales, purchasing, and inventory software.

"Now we're building the reports we want," says Schwab. "To have a program like XL Reporter that lets us build custom reports, preset regular updates, and then work within Microsoft Excel—that's hugely valuable to us. Nobody else offers the ability to do ad hoc queries so easily. Even people who aren't serious programmers can go in and create the documents they need within the limits of their authorizations. So I highly recommend it."

For years, Daems had been running an open receivables report that presents, for example, all the invoices that are 15 days past due and greater than $450. Unfortunately, he simply could not run a report like that with the software package he bought to replace his old QuickBooks program. That situation has now changed. "With SAP Business One, we can go in there and ask for those parameters and then sort it by oldest, biggest amount, or customer," says Schwab. "And it's paperless. The accounts receivable person doesn't have to print anything out and then write a bunch of notes on it and type them into the system for someone else to find. It's all right there."

Wolf Peak also requires a very complicated commissions report, used to generate the checks that go out to the company's commissioned sales representatives, who receive individualized reports as well. The previous consultants were unable to deliver this set of reports. JourneyTEAM was able to develop it on Business One in an afternoon.

Wolf Peak is already expanding its use of SAP Business One into other areas. The company has applied the software to warehouse management, where it enables Wolf Peak to manage inventory, receiving, warehouse delivery, shipping, and all the other aspects of the warehousing task. Inventory is one of the company's biggest assets, and it has to be managed well.

"We have an audit report that lists all of the inventory, the current on-hand quantity, and the demands on it through sales orders or outstanding purchase orders," Schwab says. This report then lists the value of that inventory and allows Schwab to look at the activity against any inventory item during any period. Beyond that, it enables him to drill down to the actual invoices that affect that inventory item. "We want to minimize what we have on hand," he says, "but we always have to be sure we have enough to meet our customers' needs. Business One lets us do that."

Wolf Peak's management has also begun using the customer relationship management (CRM) functionality within Business One to assist with its collection of receivables. The company's plan is to extend its use of the software to develop and track sales opportunities as well. Three months following its installation, Wolf Peak is quite happy with its decision to go with SAP's Business One software. "Reports that used to take months to create—if we could get them at all—can now be created in minutes," says Schwab.

A less tangible but no less important benefit is the renewed confidence Business One brings to management. "A company's greatest untapped asset is its own financial information," says Schwab. "SAP Business One creates an environment where the decision makers get the information they want on a timely basis, in a format they can use. It's amazing what happens when management begins to see what is really happening inside the enterprise. Business One delivers useful information to help make good business decisions—and that's really the bottom line. This is a business management tool."

Source: Adapted from SAP America, "Wolf Peak: Making the Best Choice to Support Growth," *SAP Business Insights*, March 2007; JourneyTEAM, "Wolf Peak Success Story—SAP Business One," ABComputer.com, March 2007.

CASE STUDY QUESTIONS

1. What problems occurred when Wolf Peak upgraded from QuickBooks to a new accounting software package? How could these problems have been avoided?
2. Why did SAP's Business One prove to be a better choice for Wolf Peak's management than the new accounting software? Give several examples to illustrate your answer.
3. Should most SMEs use an integrated business software suite like SAP Business One instead of specialized accounting and other business software packages? Why or why not?

REAL WORLD ACTIVITIES

1. This case demonstrates failure and success in the software research, selection, and installation process, as well as some major differences among business application software packages in capabilities, such as ease of use and information access for employees and management. Search the Internet to find several more examples of such success and failure for software suites like SAP Business One or Oracle E-Business Suite and specialized business packages like QuickBooks or Great Plains Accounting.
2. Break into small groups with your classmates to discuss several key differences you have found on the basis of your Internet research. Then make recommendations to the class for how these differences should shape the business application software selection decision for an SME.

FIGURE 4.2 An overview of computer software. Note the major types and examples of application and system software.

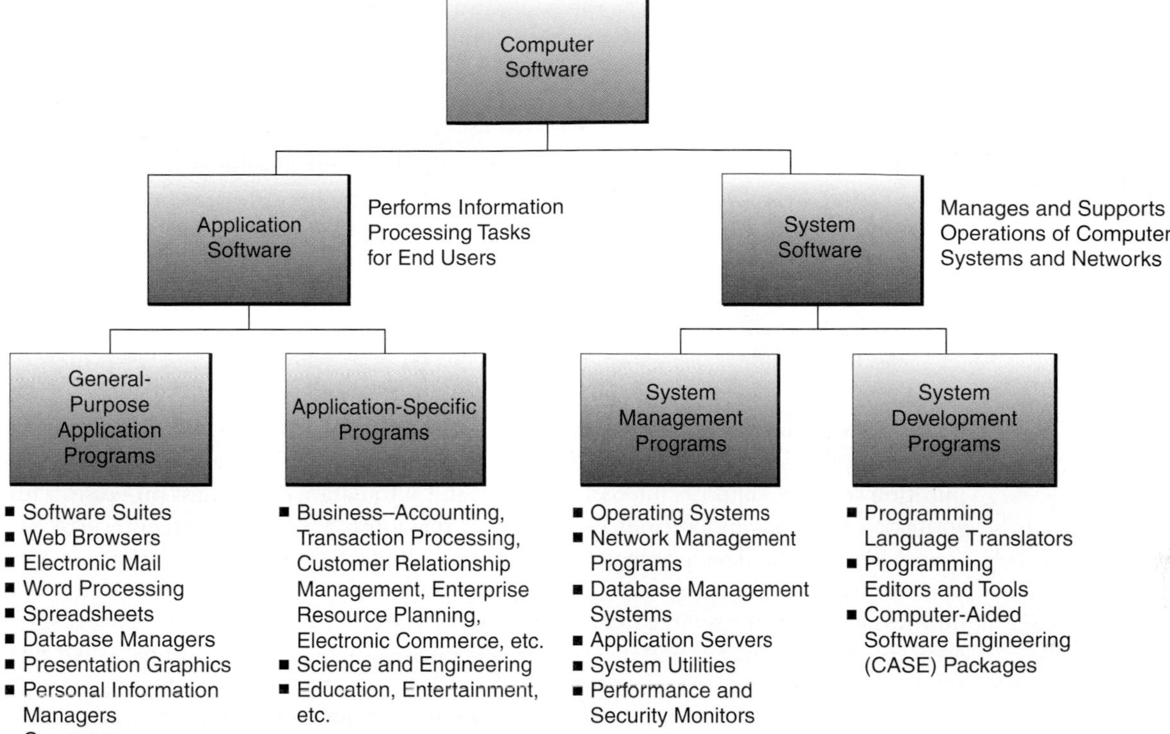

and the specifications, functionality, and ownership of the final product are controlled or retained by the developing organization.

The newest innovation in software development is called **open-source software.** In this approach, developers collaborate on the development of an application using programming standards that allow for anyone to contribute to the software. Furthermore, as each developer completes his or her project, the code for the application becomes available and free to anyone else who wishes to use it. We will discuss this new approach to software development in greater detail in Section II of this chapter.

Visa International: Implementing an e-Business Suite

Visa International is well known and respected all over the world for the innovations it has brought to global commerce with its sophisticated consumer payments processing system. But surprisingly, until recently, Visa had many outdated systems managing some of its most critical internal business processes. After an analysis by KPMG in 1999, it was determined that many of Visa's internal systems were becoming a risk to the organization.

The KPMG analysis found Visa's internal systems to be unnecessarily complex and using few of the advantages that technology can bring to an enterprise. For example, Visa's financial management infrastructure was fragmented, complex, and costly to maintain. Often, data were not standardized, resulting in many different databases generating disparate interpretations of business data. Even more surprisingly, Visa's corporate purchasing, accounts payable, and asset management functions were still being managed manually, resulting in time-consuming delays and discrepancies.

Fragmented internal systems are not unusual in a company that experiences rapid growth like Visa's double-digit growth for 11 consecutive years. After a careful review of available software solutions, Visa chose the Oracle E-Business Suite of business application software to remedy the problems that come with a complex and inefficient back office.

The results of conversion to the new software suite were spectacular. The modern financial applications in the Oracle product turned Visa's cumbersome, outdated desktop procedures into Web-based e-business solutions that met Visa's demands for all roles and processes. For example, Oracle Financials automated Visa's old organization and created a more agile system capable of accounting for the impact of financial activities on a global scale. Accounts payable was transformed from a cumbersome manual process into a streamlined system that automatically checks invoices against outgoing payments and requests reviews of any discrepancies via e-mail. And Oracle iProcurement helped automate Visa's requisitioning and purchasing system by streamlining the entire purchasing process and implementing a self-service model to increase processing efficiency [3, 9].

Business Application Software

Thousands of **function-specific application software** packages are available to support specific applications of end users in business and other fields. For example, business application software supports the reengineering and automation of business processes with strategic e-business applications like customer relationship management, enterprise resource planning, and supply chain management. Other examples are software packages that Web-enable electronic commerce applications or apply to the functional areas of business like human resource management and accounting and finance. Still other software empowers managers and business professionals with decision support tools like data mining, enterprise information portals, or knowledge management systems.

We will discuss these applications in upcoming chapters that go into more detail about these business software tools and applications. For example, data warehousing and data mining are discussed in Chapters 5 and 9; accounting, marketing, manufacturing, human resource management, and financial management applications are covered in Chapter 7. Customer relationship management, enterprise resource planning, and supply chain management are also covered in Chapter 7. Electronic commerce is the focus of Chapter 8, and decision support and data analysis applications are explored in Chapter 9. Figure 4.3 illustrates some of the many types of business application software that are available today. These particular applications are integrated in the Oracle E-Business Suite software product of Oracle Corp.

FIGURE 4.3 The business applications in Oracle's E-Business Suite software illustrate some of the many types of business application software being used today.

ORACLE E-BUSINESS SUITE

Advanced Planning	Business Intelligence	Contracts
e-Commerce	Enterprise Asset Management	Exchanges
Financials	Human Resources	Interaction Center
Manufacturing	Marketing	Order Fulfillment
Procurement	Product Development	Professional Services Automation
Projects	Sales	Service
Training	Treasury	

Source: Adapted from Oracle Corp., "E-Business Suite: Manage by Fact with Complete Automation and Complete Information," Oracle.com, 2002.

Software Suites and Integrated Packages

Let's begin our discussion of popular general purpose application software by looking at **software suites**. The most widely used productivity packages come bundled together as software suites, such as Microsoft Office, Lotus SmartSuite, Corel WordPerfect Office, and Sun's StarOffice. Examining their components gives us an overview of the important software tools that you can use to increase your productivity.

Figure 4.4 compares the basic programs that make up the top four software suites. Notice that each suite integrates software packages for word processing, spreadsheets, presentation graphics, database management, and personal information management. Microsoft, Lotus, Corel, and Sun bundle several other programs in each suite, depending on the version you select. Examples include programs for Internet access, e-mail, Web publishing, desktop publishing, voice recognition, financial management, electronic encyclopedias, and so on.

A software suite costs a lot less than the total cost of buying its individual packages separately. Another advantage is that all programs use a similar *graphical user interface* (GUI) of icons, tool and status bars, menus, and so on, which gives them the same look and feel and makes them easier to learn and use. Software suites also share common tools such as spell checkers and help wizards to increase their efficiency. Another big advantage of suites is that their programs are designed to work together seamlessly and import each other's files easily, no matter which program you are using at the time. These capabilities make them more efficient and easier to use than a variety of individual package versions.

Of course, putting so many programs and features together in one super-size package does have some disadvantages. Industry critics argue that many software suite features are never used by most end users. The suites take up a lot of disk space (often upward of 150 megabytes), depending on which version or functions you install. Because of their size, software suites are sometimes derisively called *bloatware* by their critics. The cost of suites can vary from as low as $100 for a competitive upgrade to over $700 for a full version of some editions of the suites.

These drawbacks are one reason for the continued use of **integrated packages** like Microsoft Works, Lotus eSuite WorkPlace, AppleWorks, and so on. Integrated packages combine some of the functions of several programs—word processing, spreadsheets, presentation graphics, database management, and so on—into one software package.

Because integrated packages leave out many features and functions that are in individual packages and software suites, they are considered less powerful. Their limited functionality, however, requires a lot less disk space (less than 10 megabytes), costs less than $100, and is frequently preinstalled on many low-end microcomputer systems. Integrated packages offer enough functions and features for many computer users while providing some of the advantages of software suites in a smaller package.

FIGURE 4.4 The basic program components of the top four software suites. Other programs may be included, depending on the suite edition selected.

Programs	Microsoft Office	Lotus SmartSuite	Corel WordPerfect Office	Sun StarOffice
Word Processor	Word	WordPro	WordPerfect	Writer
Spreadsheet	Excel	1–2–3	Quattro Pro	Calc
Presentation Graphics	PowerPoint	Freelance	Presentations	Impress
Database Manager	Access	Approach	Paradox	Base
Personal Information Manager	Outlook	Organizer	Corel Central	Schedule

FIGURE 4.5
Using the Microsoft Internet Explorer browser to access Google and other search engines on the Netscape.com Web site.

Web Browsers and More

The most important software component for many computer users today is the once simple and limited, but now powerful and feature-rich, **Web browser**. Browsers such as Microsoft Explorer, Netscape Navigator, Firefox, Opera, or Mozilla are software applications designed to support navigation through the point-and-click hyperlinked resources of the World Wide Web and the rest of the Internet, as well as corporate intranets and extranets. Once limited to surfing the Web, browsers are becoming the universal software platform from which end users launch information searches, e-mail, multimedia file transfers, discussion groups, and many other Internet-based applications.

Figure 4.5 illustrates the use of the Microsoft Internet Explorer browser to access search engines on the Netscape.com Web site. Netscape uses top-rated Google as its default search engine but also provides links to other popular search tools including Ask Jeeves, Look Smart, Lycos, and Overture. Using search engines to find information has become an indispensable part of business and personal Internet, intranet, and extranet applications.

Industry experts predict the Web browser will be the model for how most people use networked computers in the future. Even today, whether you want to watch a video, make a phone call, download some software, hold a videoconference, check your e-mail, or work on a spreadsheet of your team's business plan, you can use your browser to launch and host such applications. That's why browsers are sometimes called the *universal client*, that is, the software component installed on all of the networked computing and communications devices of the clients (users) throughout an enterprise.

Electronic Mail, Instant Messaging, and Weblogs

The first thing many people do at work, all over the world, is check their electronic mail. **E-mail** has changed the way people work and communicate. Millions of end users now depend on e-mail software to communicate with one another by sending and receiving electronic messages and file attachments via the Internet or their organizations' intranets or extranets. E-mail is stored on networked mail servers until you are ready. Whenever you want to, you can read your e-mail by displaying it on your workstation. So, with only a few minutes of effort (and a few microseconds of transmission time), a message to one or many individuals can be composed, sent, and received.

As we mentioned previously, e-mail software is now a mainstay component of top software suites and Web browsers. Free e-mail packages like Microsoft HotMail, Yahoo mail, and Netscape WebMail are available to Internet users from online services and Internet service providers. Most e-mail software like Microsoft Outlook Express or Netscape Messenger can route messages to multiple end users based on predefined mailing lists and provide password security, automatic message forwarding, and remote user access. They also allow you to store messages in folders and make it easy to add documents and Web file attachments to e-mail messages. E-mail packages also enable you to edit and send graphics and multimedia files as well as text and provide computer conferencing capabilities. Finally, your e-mail software may automatically filter and sort incoming messages (even news items from online services) and route them to appropriate user mailboxes and folders.

Instant messaging (IM) is an e-mail/computer-conferencing hybrid technology that has grown so rapidly that it has become a standard method of electronic messaging for millions of Internet users worldwide. By using instant messaging, groups of business professionals or friends and associates can send and receive electronic messages instantly and thus communicate and collaborate in real time in a near-conversational mode. Messages pop up instantly in an IM window on the computer screens of everyone in your business workgroup or friends on your IM "buddy list," as long as they are online, no matter what other tasks they are working on at that moment. Instant messaging software can be downloaded and IM services implemented by subscribing to many popular IM systems, including AOL's Instant Messenger and ICQ, MSN Messenger, and Yahoo Messenger. See Figure 4.6.

A **weblog** (usually shortened to **blog** or written as "web log" or "Weblog") is a **Web site** of personal or noncommercial origin that uses a dated log format updated daily or very frequently with new information about a particular subject or range of subjects. The information can be written by the site owner, gleaned from other Web sites or other sources, or contributed by users via e-mail.

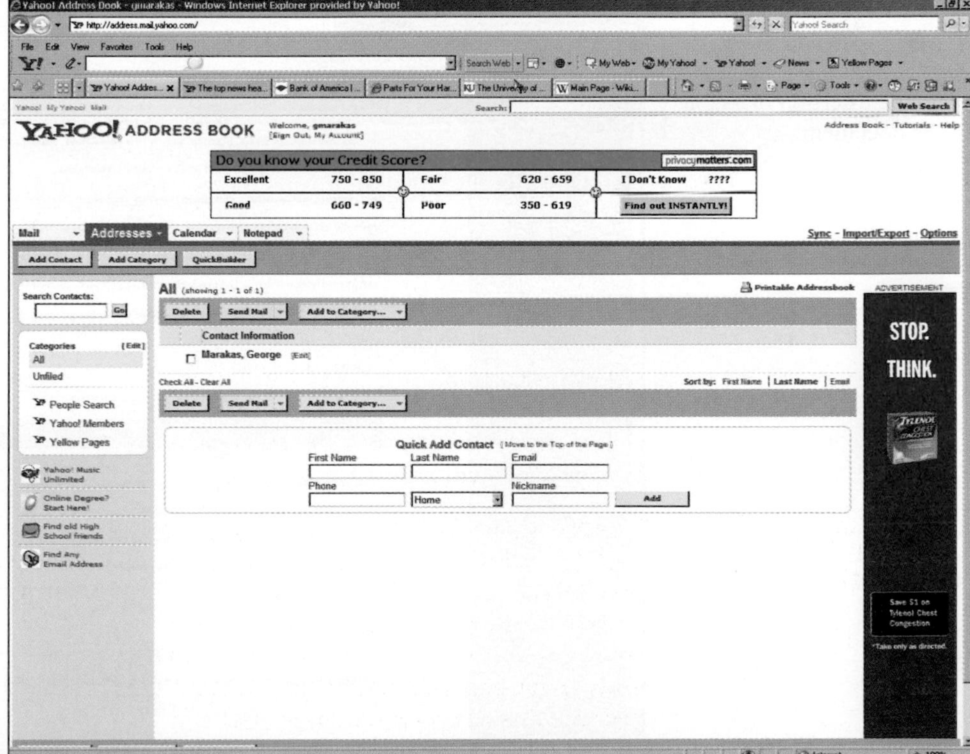

FIGURE 4.6
Using the e-mail features of the ICQ instant messaging system.

A weblog often has the quality of being a kind of "log of our times" from a particular point of view. Generally, weblogs are devoted to one or several subjects or themes, usually of topical interest. In general, weblogs can be thought of as developing commentaries, individual or collective, on their particular themes. A weblog may consist of the recorded ideas of an individual (a sort of diary) or be a complex collaboration open to anyone. Most of the latter are *moderated discussions*.

Because there are a number of variations on this idea and new variations can easily be invented, the meaning of this term is apt to gather additional connotations with time. As a formatting and content approach for a Web site, the weblog seems popular because the viewer knows that something changes every day, there is a personal (rather than bland commercial) point of view, and, on some sites, there is an opportunity to collaborate with or respond to the Web site and its participants.

Word Processing and Desktop Publishing

Software for **word processing** has transformed the process of writing just about anything. Word processing packages computerize the creation, editing, revision, and printing of *documents* (e.g., letters, memos, reports) by electronically processing *text data* (words, phrases, sentences, and paragraphs). Top word processing packages like Microsoft Word, Lotus WordPro, and Corel WordPerfect can provide a wide variety of attractively printed documents with their desktop publishing capabilities. These packages can also convert documents to HTML format for publication as Web pages on corporate intranets or the World Wide Web.

Word processing packages also provide other helpful features. For example, a *spelling checker* capability can identify and correct spelling errors, and a *thesaurus* feature helps you find a better choice of words to express ideas. You can also identify and correct grammar and punctuation errors, as well as suggest possible improvements in your writing style, with grammar and style checker functions. In addition to converting documents to HTML format, you can use the top packages to design and create Web pages from scratch for an Internet or intranet Web site. See Figure 4.7.

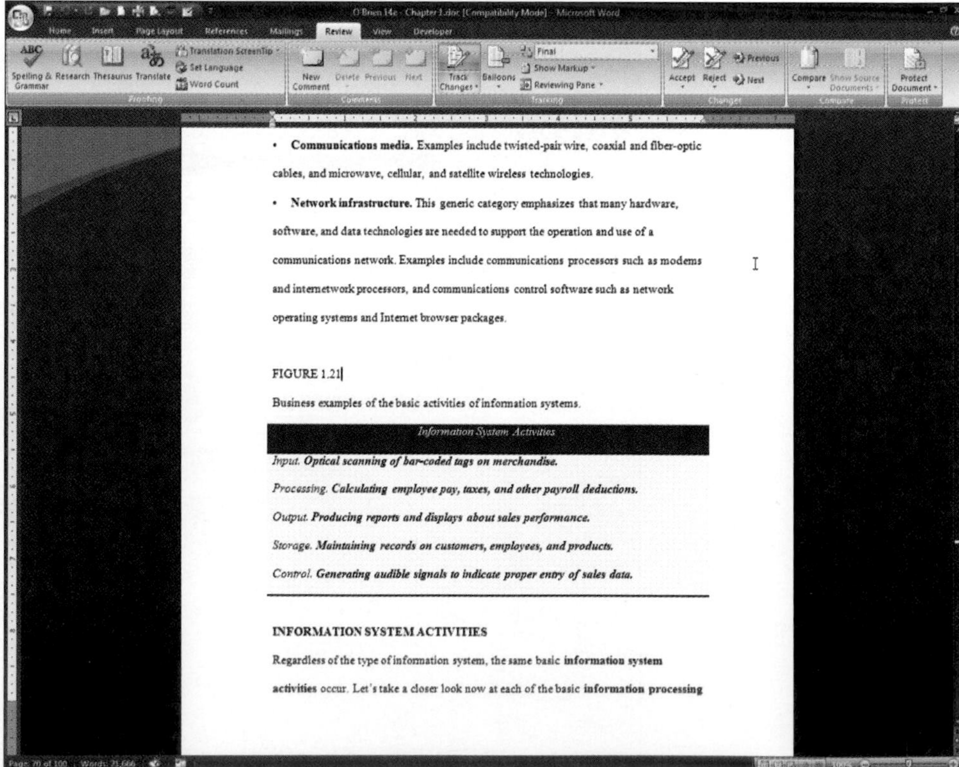

FIGURE 4.7
Using the Microsoft Word word processing package. Note the insertion of a table in the document.

End users and organizations can use **desktop publishing** (DTP) software to produce their own printed materials that look professionally published. That is, they can design and print their own newsletters, brochures, manuals, and books with several type styles, graphics, photos, and colors on each page. Word processing packages and desktop publishing packages like Adobe PageMaker, Microsoft Publisher, and QuarkXPress are used for desktop publishing. Typically, text material and graphics can be generated by word processing and graphics packages and imported as text and graphics files. Optical scanners may be used to input text and graphics from printed material. You can also use files of *clip art*, which are predrawn graphic illustrations provided by the software package or available from other sources.

Electronic Spreadsheets

Spreadsheet packages like Lotus 1-2-3, Microsoft Excel, and Corel QuattroPro are used by virtually every business for analysis, planning, and modeling. They help you develop an *electronic spreadsheet*, which is a worksheet of rows and columns that can be stored on your PC or on a network server, or converted to HTML format and stored as a Web page or *websheet* on the World Wide Web. Developing a spreadsheet involves designing its format and developing the relationships (formulas) that will be used in the worksheet. In response to your input, the computer performs necessary calculations according to the formulas you defined in the spreadsheet and displays the results immediately, whether on your workstation or Web site. Most packages also help you develop charts and graphic displays of spreadsheet results. See Figure 4.8.

For example, you could develop a spreadsheet to record and analyze past and present advertising performance for a business. You could also develop hyperlinks to a similar websheet on your marketing team's intranet Web site. Now you have a decision support tool to help you answer *what-if questions* you may have about advertising. For example, "What would happen to market share if advertising expenses

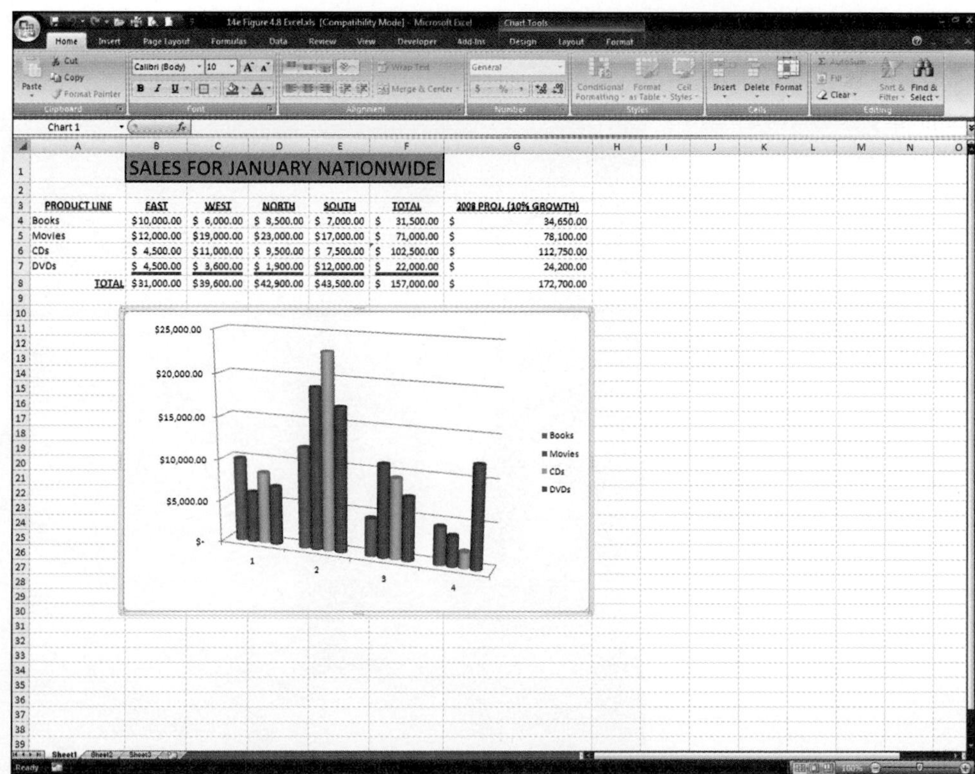

FIGURE 4.8 Using an electronic spreadsheet package, Microsoft Excel. Note the use of graphics.

were to increase by 10 percent?" To answer this question, you would simply change the advertising expense formula on the advertising performance worksheet you developed. The computer would recalculate the affected figures, producing new market share figures and graphics. You would then have better insight into the effect of advertising decisions on market share. Then you could share this insight with a note on the websheet on your team's intranet Web site.

Presentation Graphics

Presentation graphics software packages help you convert numeric data into graphics displays such as line charts, bar graphs, pie charts, and many other types of graphics. Most of the top packages also help you prepare multimedia presentations of graphics, photos, animation, and video clips, including publishing to the World Wide Web. Not only are graphics and multimedia displays easier to comprehend and communicate than numeric data, but multiple-color and multiple-media displays can more easily emphasize key points, strategic differences, and important trends in the data. Presentation graphics have proved to be much more effective than tabular presentations of numeric data for reporting and communicating in advertising media, management reports, or other business presentations. See Figure 4.9.

Presentation graphics software packages like Microsoft PowerPoint, Lotus Freelance, or Corel Presentations give you many easy-to-use capabilities that encourage the use of graphics presentations. For example, most packages help you design and manage computer-generated and orchestrated *slide shows* containing many integrated graphics and multimedia displays. Or you can select from a variety of predesigned *templates* of business presentations, prepare and edit the outline and notes for a presentation, and manage the use of multimedia files of graphics, photos, sounds, and video clips. And of course, the top packages help you tailor your graphics and multimedia presentation for transfer in HTML format to Web sites on corporate intranets or the World Wide Web.

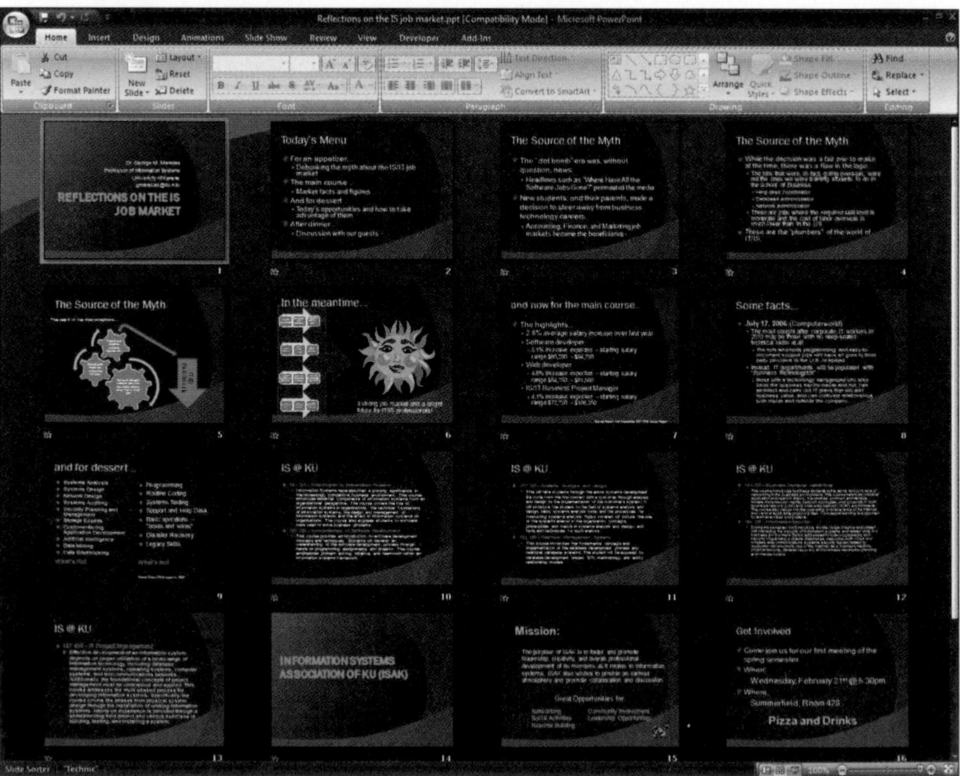

FIGURE 4.9
Using the slide preview feature of a presentation graphics package, Microsoft PowerPoint.

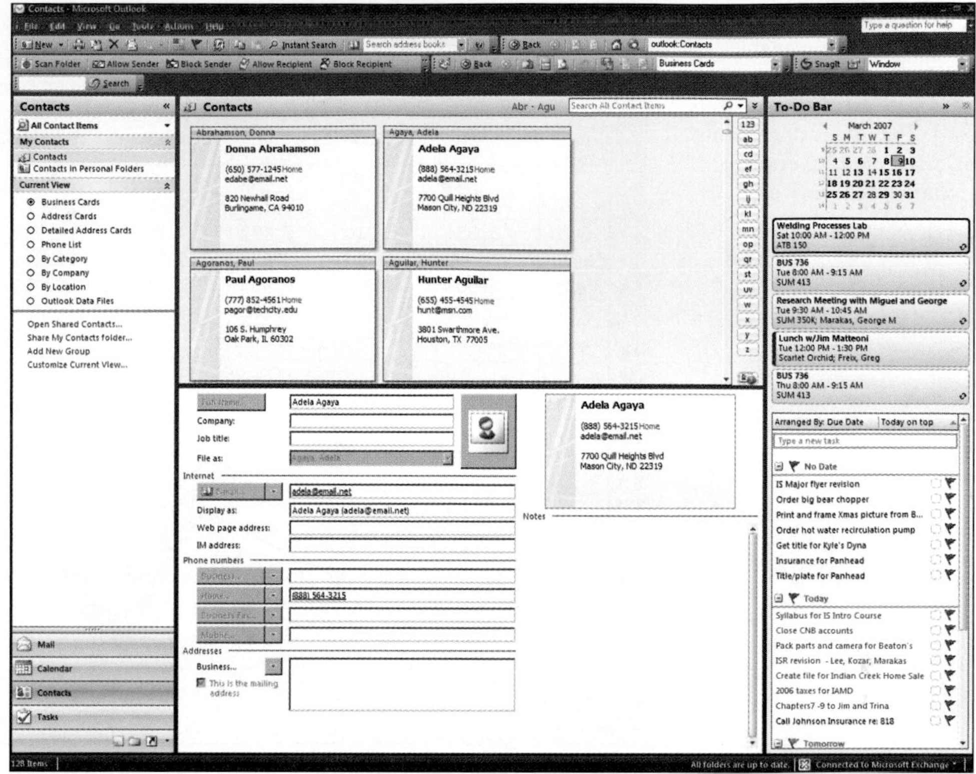

FIGURE 4.10
Using a personal information manager (PIM): Microsoft Outlook.

Personal Information Managers

The **personal information manager** (PIM) is a popular software package for end-user productivity and collaboration, as well as a popular application for personal digital assistant (PDA) handheld devices. Various PIMs such as Lotus Organizer and Microsoft Outlook help end users store, organize, and retrieve information about customers, clients, and prospects or schedule and manage appointments, meetings, and tasks. A PIM package will organize data you enter and retrieve information in a variety of forms, depending on the style and structure of the PIM and the information you want. For example, information can be retrieved as an electronic calendar or list of appointments, meetings, or other things to do; as the timetable for a project; or as a display of key facts and financial data about customers, clients, or sales prospects. Most PIMs now include the ability to access the World Wide Web and provide e-mail capability. Also, some PIMs use Internet and e-mail features to support team collaboration by sharing information such as contact lists, task lists, and schedules with other networked PIM users. See Figure 4.10.

Groupware

Groupware is software that helps workgroups and teams collaborate to accomplish group assignments. Groupware is a category of general purpose application software that combines a variety of software features and functions to facilitate collaboration. For example, groupware products like Lotus Notes, Novell GroupWise, and Microsoft Exchange support collaboration through electronic mail, discussion groups and databases, scheduling, task management, data, audio- and videoconferencing, and so on.

Groupware products rely on the Internet and corporate intranets and extranets to make collaboration possible on a global scale by *virtual teams* located anywhere in the world. For example, team members might use the Internet for global e-mail, project discussion forums, and joint Web page development. Or they might use corporate

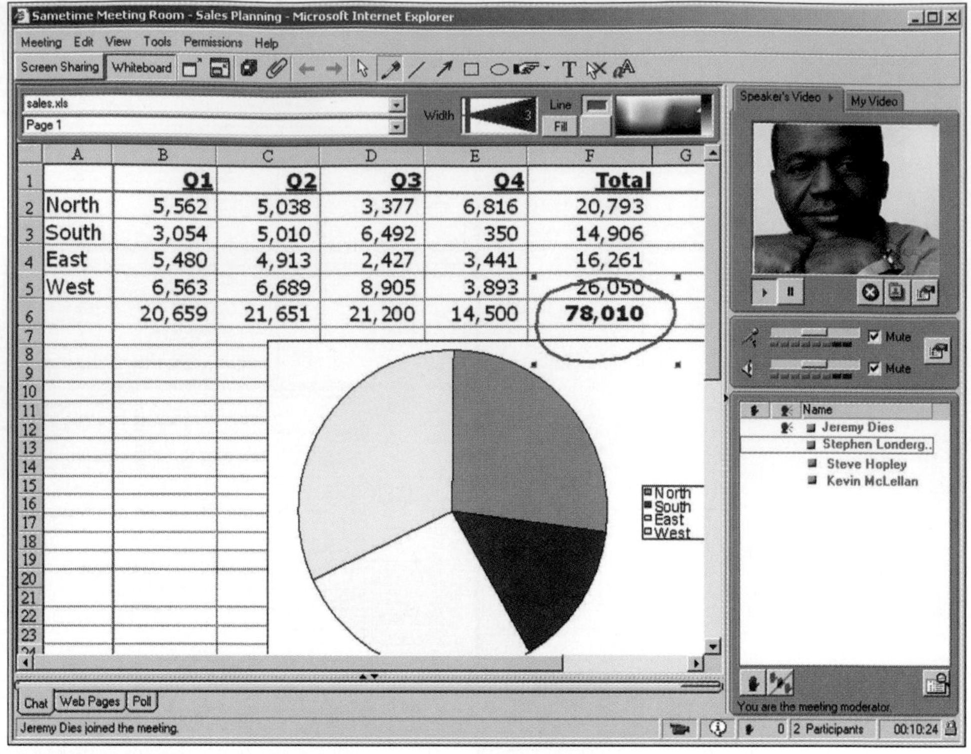

FIGURE 4.11 Lotus Sametime enables workgroups and project teams to share spreadsheets and other work documents in an interactive online collaboration process.

intranets to publish project news and progress reports and work jointly on documents stored on Web servers. See Figure 4.11.

Collaborative capabilities are also being added to other software to give it groupware-like features. For example, in the Microsoft Office software suite, Microsoft Word keeps track of who made revisions to each document, Excel tracks all changes made to a spreadsheet, and Outlook lets you keep track of tasks you delegate to other team members. Recently, the Microsoft Office suite has included functions that allow multiple people to work on and edit the same document at the same time. Using this feature, any changes made by one team member will become visible to all team members as they are being made.

Two recent additions to the collaborative software marketplace are Microsoft's Windows SharePoint Services and IBM's WebSphere. Both products allow teams to create sophisticated Web sites for information sharing and document collaboration quickly. Furthermore, businesses can use these products as a platform for application development to facilitate the efficient creation of Web-based business portals and transaction processing applications. Web sites built with collaborative development tools can integrate a wide variety of individual applications that can help increase both individual and team productivity.

Software Alternatives

Many businesses are finding alternatives to acquiring, installing, and maintaining business application software purchased from software vendors or developing and maintaining their own software in-house with their own software developer employees. For example, as we will discuss further in Chapter 10, many large companies are *outsourcing* the development and maintenance of software they need to *contract programming* firms and other software development companies, including the use of *offshore* software developers in foreign countries, and employing the Internet to communicate, collaborate, and manage their software development projects.

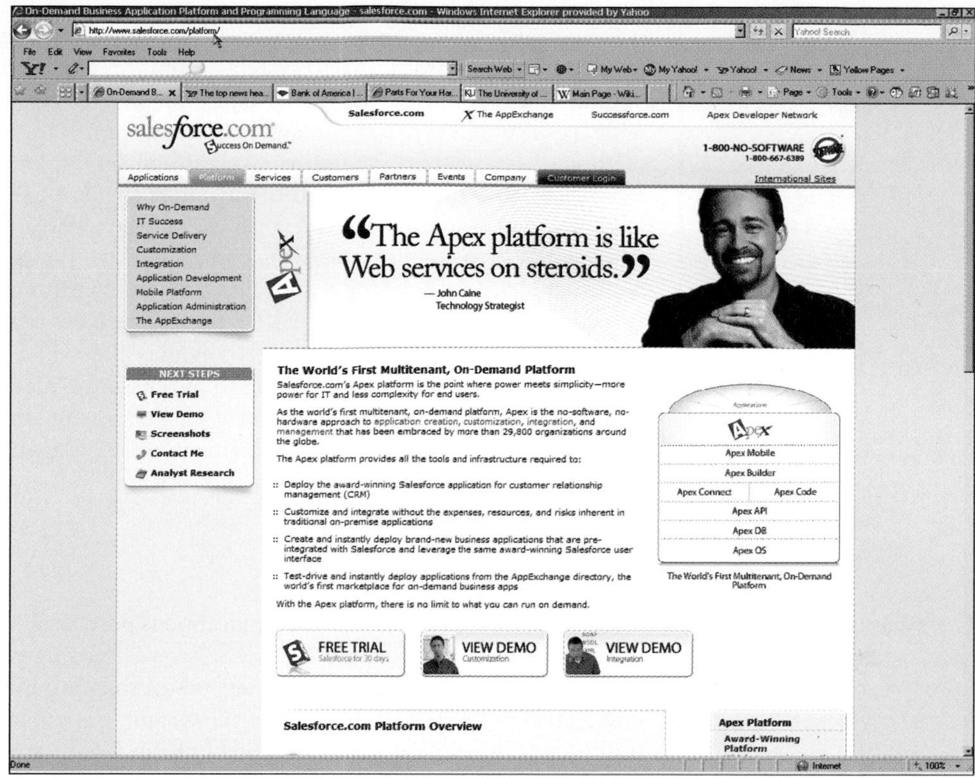

FIGURE 4.12
Salesforce.com is a leading application service provider of Web-based sales management and customer relationship management services to both large and small businesses.

Application Service Providers

A large and fast growing number of companies are turning to **application service providers** (ASPs), instead of developing or purchasing the application software they need to run their businesses. Application service providers are companies that own, operate, and maintain application software and the computer system resources (servers, system software, networks, and IT personnel) required to offer the use of the application software for a fee as a service over the Internet. The ASP can bill their customers on a per-use basis or on a monthly or annual fee basis.

Businesses are using an ASP instead of owning and maintaining their own software for many reasons. One of the biggest advantages is the low cost of initial investment, and in many cases, the short time needed to get the Web-based application set up and running. The ASP's pay-as-you-go fee structure is usually significantly less expensive than the cost of developing or purchasing, as well as running and maintaining, application software. And using an ASP eliminates or drastically reduces the need for much of the IT infrastructure (servers, system software, and IT personnel) that would be needed to acquire and support application software, including the continual challenges of distributing and managing companywide software patches and upgrades. Consequently, the use of ASPs by businesses and other organizations is expected to accelerate in the coming years [14]. See Figure 4.12.

Premiere Technologies: Vital Information and Big Savings through an ASP

In the late 1990s through 2002, Atlanta-based Premiere Technologies, a $500 million integrated personal communications services provider, acquired more than 100 small telecommunications companies throughout the world. Its goal was clear: to become a leading provider of value-added communications services, including conference calling, messaging, and Internet-based services.

Central to its aggressive growth strategy, Premiere Technologies implemented a PeopleSoft ERP system—a soup-to-nuts software suite that would provide

information vital for running nearly all aspects of Premiere's business. The enterprise resource planning (ERP) system would integrate Premiere's business processes and far-flung offices. Employees would then be able to share information companywide, resulting in cost efficiencies, productivity growth, and intelligence gains.

Such ERP systems are notoriously difficult to implement and run. As a result, Premiere Technologies decided to outsource the day-to-day management of its ERP system to Atlanta-based TransChannel Inc., whose Internet Enabled ERP (iE2) outsourcing solution delivers comprehensive PeopleSoft support, maintenance, and deployment for a fixed monthly fee. Within two months, TransChannel brought the entire PeopleSoft ERP suite online (versus an estimated 18 months for internal deployment). Premiere Technologies also saved millions of dollars through capital cost avoidance by not having to purchase the platform infrastructure and upgrade all the client hardware necessary for rolling out the ERP system internally. The bottom-line result: enormous gains in efficiency, productivity, companywide communication, and worker satisfaction through increased application reach, reliability, and flexibility [4, 13].

Software Licensing

Regardless of whether a software application is purchased COTS or accessed via an ASP, the software must be licensed for use. Software licensing is a complex topic that involves considerations of the special characteristics of software in the context of the underlying intellectual property rights, including copyright, trademark, and trade secrets, as well as traditional contract law, including the Uniform Commercial Code (UCC).

Contrary to what many believe, when an individual or company buys a software application, they have not purchased rights of ownership. Rather, they have purchased a license to use the software under the terms of the software licensing agreement. Software is generally licensed to better protect the vendor's intellectual property rights. The license often prohibits reverse engineering, modifying, disclosing, or transferring the software. In most cases, the license also gives the purchaser permission to sell or dispose of the rights provided by the license but not to duplicate or resell multiple copies of the software.

The requirement for licensing does not disappear when use of the software is obtained through an ASP. In this case, the license to dispense use of the software is granted to the ASP by the various software vendors, and in return, the ASP agrees to pay the software vendor a royalty based on the number of user accounts to which the ASP resells the rights.

Software vendors are working hard to provide easy licensing and access to their products while simultaneously preventing software piracy, which serves only to raise the ultimate cost of the product.

In the next section, we will learn about an entirely new approach to software licensing: open-source code.

SECTION II

System Software: Computer System Management

System Software Overview

System software consists of programs that manage and support a computer system and its information processing activities. For example, operating systems and network management programs serve as a vital *software interface* between computer networks and hardware and the application programs of end users.

Read the Real World Case on webtop software. We can learn a lot about the business productivity enhancements of new software developments from this example. See Figure 4.13.

Overview

We can group system software into two major categories (see Figure 4.14):

- **System management programs.** Programs that manage the hardware, software, network, and data resources of computer systems during the execution of the various information processing jobs of users. Examples of important system management programs are operating systems, network management programs, database management systems, and system utilities.
- **System development programs.** Programs that help users develop information system programs and procedures and prepare user programs for computer processing. Major software development programs are programming language translators and editors, and a variety of CASE (computer-aided software engineering) and other programming tools. We will take a closer look at CASE tools later in this chapter.

Operating Systems

The most important system software package for any computer is its operating system. An operating system is an integrated system of programs that manages the operations of the CPU, controls the input/output and storage resources and activities of the computer system, and provides various support services as the computer executes the application programs of users.

The primary purpose of an operating system is to maximize the productivity of a computer system by operating it in the most efficient manner. An operating system minimizes the amount of human intervention required during processing. It helps your application programs perform common operations such as accessing a network, entering data, saving and retrieving files, and printing or displaying output. If you have any hands-on experience with a computer, you know that the operating system must be loaded and activated before you can accomplish other tasks. This requirement emphasizes that operating systems are the most indispensable components of the software interface between users and the hardware of their computer systems.

Operating Systems Functions

An operating system performs five basic functions in the operation of a computer system: providing a user interface, resource management, task management, file management, and utilities and support services. See Figure 4.15.

The User Interface. The user interface is the part of the operating system that allows you to communicate with it so you can load programs, access files, and accomplish other tasks. Three main types of user interfaces are the *command-driven*, *menu-driven*, and *graphical user interfaces*. The trend in user interfaces for operating systems and other software is moving away from the entry of brief end-user commands, or even the selection of choices from menus of options. Instead, most software provides an easy-to-use graphical user interface (GUI) that uses icons, bars, buttons, boxes, and other images. These GUIs rely on pointing devices like the electronic mouse or touchpad to make selections that help you get things done. Currently, the most common and widely recognized GUI is the Microsoft Windows desktop.

REAL WORLD CASE 2

Google, Microsoft, and Others: Transforming the Desktop with Webtop Software Applications

It's been a long time—all the way back to the dawn of desktop computing in the early 1980s—since software developers have had as much fun as so many are having right now. Oh, building the latest version of yet another online gaming experience is challenging fun, we admit, but in productivity and business software development today, browser-based applications are where the action is. A killer webtop app no longer requires hundreds of drones slaving away on millions of lines of code. Three or four engineers and a steady supply of Red Bull are frequently all it takes to rapidly (maybe in just a few days or weeks) turn a midnight Web product brainstorm into a Web site so hot it melts the servers.

What has changed is the way today's Web-based apps can run almost as seamlessly as programs used on the desktop, with embedded audio, video, and drag-and-drop ease of use. Behind this Web-desktop fusion are technologies like Ajax (asynchronous JavaScript and XML), Macromedia's Flash, and Ruby on Rails. We'll spare you the technical details at this point; suffice it to say that these technologies are giving rise to a new webtop that may one day replace your present suite of desktop applications. Yes, that's what we said.

Hmm, we see you need convincing. Why not start with Writely, a free online word processor, which anyone who knows how to use Microsoft Word can figure out in a few clicks. Then add Zimbra, which is taking a swipe at Microsoft Outlook with an online e-mail application that has all the latest neat Ajax tricks built in. Like what? you may ask. Okay, glide your mouse over an e-mail message that includes a date, and your calendar for that day pops up. Move it over a Web site address in the message and an image of the page appears. See what we mean?

FIGURE 4.13

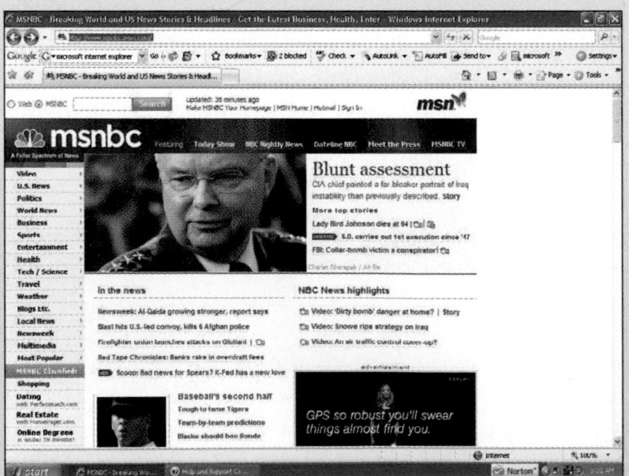

The ease and productivity enhancements of Web-based application software promises to make your webtop a powerful alternative to desktop software suites.

For an online spreadsheet, try Tracker, which becomes an interactive Web site open to viewing or changing websheets by the people you invite. Users can even subscribe to a particular spreadsheet row (say, "Sales in China") via an RSS feed, and have it automatically fed to their webtops . . . or Web sites . . . or weblogs . . . get the picture?

All of these programs link to myriad open APIs (application programming interfaces) that serve as building blocks for new applications and data on the Web from Amazon, Google, and others. Thus can the information on your desktop be fused with the entire Web through a powerful and increasingly invisible bridge between the two. Now are you impressed?

Well, Google, Microsoft, and Yahoo are energetically trying to crash this party. When the big boys start elbowing themselves to the front of the online webtop software market, you know it's more than another gee-whiz, technology passing fancy. They smell new sources of revenue from online software and webtop-presence market share gains, and they're not going to pass that up.

First out of the starting gate was Microsoft, which launched Windows Live, a personal online command center for e-mail, RSS feeds, and other content, followed quickly by Office Live, a Web site-hosting and online project management service that taps into the existing Office desktop programs and is aimed at the massive but underserved small business market. You can be sure that more webtop products are coming from a relieved Microsoft since Vista finally rolled off the assembly line.

Google answered a few months later with the Google Apps suite of webtop software products that includes e-mail, instant messaging, calendaring, collaborative word processing and spreadsheets from their popular Docs & Spreadsheets product, web page creation, and other goodies. Sorry folks, the free Standard and Student editions place text-based ads alongside e-mail, but that didn't deter their use by more than 100,000 small businesses and hundreds of universities by early 2007.

That's when the Google boys fired more directly at Microsoft Office by releasing the Google Apps Premier edition for the corporate market. Yes boss, it costs $50 per user per month, but it includes more features and capabilities than the free version, and its still a lot cheaper than the hundreds of dollars per user many firms pay for a corporate license for Microsoft's Office, whose functional overkill most of us don't need anyway.

Immediate adopters who had been working with Google included the leading ASP Salesforce.com, big Chicago real estate agency Prudential Preferred Properties, and SF Bay Pediatrics in San Francisco. The large pediatrics practice began using Google Apps two months earlier, and "the doctors learned how to use the program quickly," notes an undoubtedly relieved Andrew Johnson, CIO at SF Bay Pediatrics. "They're not technically savvy," Johnson acknowledges. "They don't want to deal with having to worry about an IT infrastructure. It just allows us to outsource things to a pretty reputable name like Google."

Obviously, the Google kids had been busy developing webtop apps and quietly buying up some of the most promising small software developers and their webtop products. At the top spot was JotSpot of Palo Alto, whose products were wikis and online collaborative spreadsheets. JotSpot, a pioneer of Web collaboration apps (a.k.a. wikis) developed the new Tracker webtop application we described previously, which provided Google with a powerful, highly collaborative online spreadsheet. Then Google scooped up the Writely online word processor and its developers, Writely Inc. of Portola Valley, California. Google loved how their software enabled online creation of documents, opened them to collaboration by anyone anywhere, and simplified publishing the end result on a Web site as a blog entry.

Many other small developers of great webtop software products remain successful and independent—until some giant company picks them up or they run out of gas. The cool Zimbra online e-mail product we mentioned was developed by Zimbra of San Mateo, California. In addition to bringing up your calendar for any date your mouse encounters in an e-mail, it can, among other things, launch Skype for any e-mail phone number or retrieve a Google map for any e-mail address it bumps into.

A popular online calendar is the product of 30Boxes of San Francisco. This Web-based software allows families and groups to create private social networks, organize events, track schedules, and share photos; it will soon allow you to save phone numbers as hyperlinks and make calls by simply clicking on a link. Our final webtop software kudos goes to 37Signals of Chicago for its Basecamp online project management product. Its Basecamp app, elegant and inexpensive, enables the creation, sharing, and tracking of to-do lists, files, performance milestones, and other key project metrics. The company's related Backpack webtop application is a powerful online organizer for individuals that can be easily added to anybody's webtop capabilities.

The business question at this point is: Why invest your time and money in a webtop product by any of the midget developers who may not survive the onslaught of giants like Google, Yahoo, and Microsoft in this market? After all, Bill Gates made it quite plain during the November 2005 launches of Windows Live and Office Live that grabbing a dominant share of the webtop is a top strategic priority for Microsoft. Of course, Google, Yahoo, and other big players vow they won't let that happen.

But not to worry. If the history of Silicon Valley is any guide, a few of the midgets will become the next big thing, and the best remaining will be bought out by giants like Google, their products reworked and renamed, and you'll be two steps ahead of your mate in the next cubicle for having had the innovative spark to be one of thousands of pioneers enjoying the ease and productivity of such software products on your personalized webtop.

Source: Adapted from Erik Schonfeld, Om Malik, and Michael V. Copeland, "The Next Net 25: The Webtop," *Business 2.0*, March 2006; Ina Fried, "Windows Live Offers Microsoft a Quick Turnaround," *CNET News.com*, March 14, 2006; Jan Brodkin, "New Business Tool: Google Apps," *PC World*, February 22, 2007; Juan Carlos Perez, "Early Google Apps Adopters Like the Price," *CIO.com*, March 29, 2007.

CASE STUDY QUESTIONS

1. Do you agree that webtop software will one day replace suites of desktop applications? Why or why not? Check out the features of a few of the webtop products mentioned in the case on the Internet to support your answer.
2. Will Microsoft succeed in dominating the webtop? Why or why not? Visit the Web sites of Windows Live, Office Live, and Google Apps and review their products and services to support your answer.
3. Should a small business invest its time and money in acquiring and learning how to use some of the webtop applications mentioned in this case? Defend your answer based on your review of the webtop products from the small developers, Google, Yahoo, and Microsoft.

REAL WORLD ACTIVITIES

1. Research the Web sites of Google and Yahoo to review the extent of their current products in the webtop application software market. Evaluate several products you find, comparing them with the offerings of Microsoft and the independent software developers mentioned in the case.
2. Try out demo versions on the Internet of several of the webtop software applications mentioned in this case, including those available from Google and Yahoo. Break into small groups with your classmates to discuss your reactions to the experience and the features you would like to see changed or added that might lure you and others into acquiring one or more of these webtop products.

FIGURE 4.14
The system and application software interface between end users and computer hardware.

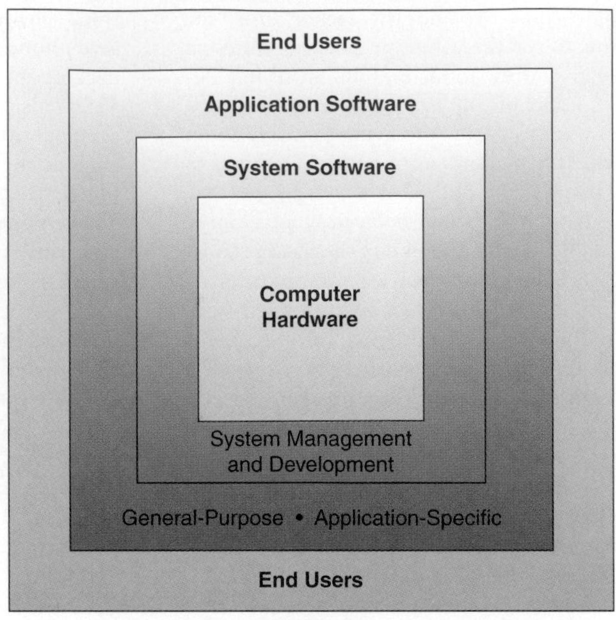

Resource Management. An operating system uses a variety of **resource management** programs to manage the hardware and networking resources of a computer system, including its CPU, memory, secondary storage devices, telecommunications processors, and input/output peripherals. For example, memory management programs keep track of where data and programs are stored. They may also subdivide memory into a number of sections and swap parts of programs and data between memory and magnetic disks or other secondary storage devices. This process can provide a computer system with a **virtual memory** capability that is significantly larger than the real memory capacity of its primary storage circuits. So, a computer with a virtual memory capability can process large programs and greater amounts of data than the capacity of its memory chips would normally allow.

File Management. An operating system contains **file management** programs that control the creation, deletion, and access of files of data and programs. File management also involves keeping track of the physical location of files on magnetic disks and other secondary storage devices. So operating systems maintain directories of information about the location and characteristics of files stored on a computer system's secondary storage devices.

FIGURE 4.15
The basic functions of an operating system include a user interface, resource management, task management, file management, and utilities and other functions.

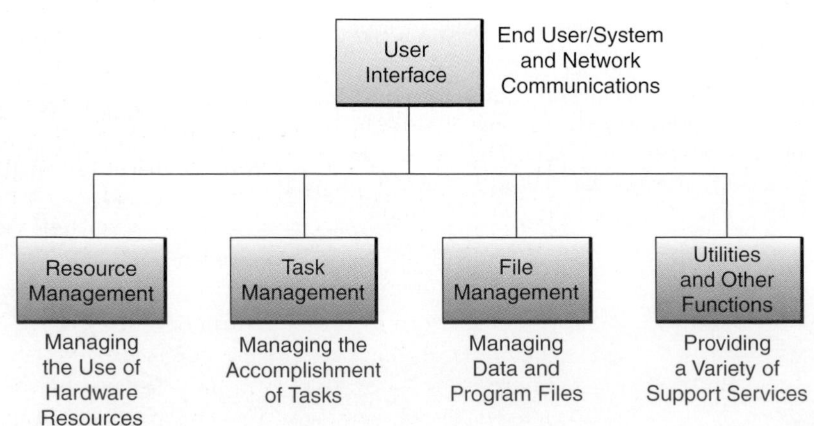

Task Management. The **task management** programs of an operating system help accomplish the computing tasks of end users. The programs control which task gets access to the CPU and for how much time. The task management functions can allocate a specific slice of CPU time to a particular task and interrupt the CPU at any time to substitute a higher priority task. Several different approaches to task management may be taken, each with advantages in certain situations.

Multitasking (sometimes referred to as *multiprogramming* or *time-sharing*) is a task management approach that allows for several computing tasks to be performed in a seemingly simultaneous fashion. In reality, multitasking assigns only one task at a time to the CPU, but it switches from one program to another so quickly that it gives the appearance of executing all of the programs at the same time. There are two basic types of multitasking: *preemptive* and *cooperative*. In preemptive multitasking, the task management functions parcel out CPU *time slices* to each program. In contrast, cooperative multitasking allows each program to control the CPU for as long as it needs it. If a program is not using the CPU, however, it can allow another program to use it temporarily. Most Windows- and Unix-based operating systems use the preemptive approach, whereas most Macintosh-style platforms use cooperative multitasking. Although the terms *multitasking* and *multiprocessing* are often used interchangeably, they are actually different concepts based on the number of CPUs being used. In multiprocessing, more than one CPU is being accessed, but in multitasking, only one CPU is in operation.

Most computers make use of some sort of multitasking. On modern microcomputers, multitasking is made possible by the development of powerful processors and their ability to address much larger memory capacities directly. This capability allows primary storage to be subdivided into several large partitions, each of which is used by a different software application.

In effect, a single computer can act as if it were several computers, or *virtual machines*, because each application program runs independently at the same time. The number of programs that can be run concurrently depends on the amount of memory that is available and the amount of processing each job demands. That's because a microprocessor (or CPU) can become overloaded with too many jobs and provide unacceptably slow response times. However, if memory and processing capacities are adequate, multitasking allows end users to switch easily from one application to another, share data files among applications, and process some applications in a *background* mode. Typically, background tasks include large printing jobs, extensive mathematical computations, or unattended telecommunications sessions.

Microsoft Windows

For many years, MS-DOS (Microsoft Disk Operating System) was the most widely used microcomputer operating system. It is a single-user, single-tasking operating system but was given a graphical user interface and limited multitasking capabilities by combining it with Microsoft **Windows.** Microsoft began replacing its DOS/Windows combination in 1995 with the Windows 95 operating system, featuring a graphical user interface, true multitasking, networking, multimedia, and many other capabilities. Microsoft introduced an enhanced Windows 98 version during 1998, and a Windows Me (Millennium Edition) consumer PC system in 2000.

Microsoft introduced its **Windows NT** (New Technology) operating system in 1995. Windows NT is a powerful, multitasking, multiuser operating system that was installed on many network servers to manage PCs with high-performance computing requirements. New Server and Workstation versions were introduced in 1997. Microsoft substantially enhanced its Windows NT products with the **Windows 2000** operating system during the year 2000.

Late in 2001, Microsoft introduced **Windows XP** Home Edition and Professional versions, and thus formally merged its two Windows operating system lines for consumer and business users, uniting them around the Windows NT and Windows 2000 code base. With Windows XP, consumers and home users finally received an enhanced

FIGURE 4.16 Comparing the purposes of the four versions of the Microsoft Windows Server 2003 operating system.

Microsoft Windows Server 2003 Comparisons
• **Windows Server 2003, Standard Edition** For smaller server applications, including file and print sharing, Internet and intranet connectivity, and centralized desktop application deployment.
• **Windows Server 2003, Enterprise Edition** For larger business applications, XML Web services, enterprise collaboration, and enterprise network support.
• **Windows Server 2003, Datacenter Edition** For business-critical and mission-critical applications demanding the highest levels of scalability and availability.
• **Windows Server 2003, Web Edition** For Web serving and hosting, providing a platform for developing and deploying Web services and applications.

Windows operating system with the performance and stability features that business users had in Windows 2000 and continue to have in Windows XP Professional. Microsoft also introduced four new **Windows Server 2003** versions in 2003, which are summarized and compared in Figure 4.16 [8].

In 2006, Microsoft released their newest operating system called Vista. Vista contains hundreds of new features; some of the most significant include an updated graphical user interface and visual style dubbed Windows Aero, improved search features, new multimedia creation tools such as Windows DVD Maker, and completely redesigned networking, audio, print, and display subsystems. Vista also aims to increase the level of communication between machines on a home network using peer-to-peer technology, making it easier to share files and digital media between computers and devices.

For developers, Vista introduced version 3.0 of the .NET Framework, which aims to make it significantly easier for developers to write high-quality applications than with the previous versions of Windows.

Microsoft's primary stated objective with Vista, however, has been to improve the state of security in the Windows operating system. One of the most common criticisms of Windows XP and its predecessors has been their commonly exploited security vulnerabilities and overall susceptibility to malware, viruses, and buffer overflows. In light of these complaints, then-Microsoft chairman Bill Gates announced in early 2002 a company-wide "Trustworthy Computing initiative" to incorporate security work into every aspect of software development at the company. Microsoft claimed that it prioritized improving the security of Windows XP and Windows Server 2003 rather than finishing Windows Vista, significantly delaying its completion.

Sometime in late 2007 or early 2008, a new server product, entitled Windows Vista Server, will emerge. This server product will be the server edition of the new Windows Vista operating system. It has been confirmed that this version of Windows Server will support both x64 (64 bit) and x86 (32 bit) processors. The IA-64 will be supported in the Datacenter Edition of the Windows Server "Longhorn" and optimized for high workload scenarios, like database servers and lines of business applications. As such, it is not optimized for use as a file or media server. Little is currently known about planned editions. Microsoft has mentioned "Cougar" as the codename for the Small Business Server product and "Centro" as the codename for a new medium-sized business product, suitable for companies with 25–500 PCs. The business products also may incorporate Exchange.

UNIX

Originally developed by AT&T, **UNIX** now is also offered by other vendors, including Solaris by Sun Microsystems and AIX by IBM. UNIX is a multitasking, multiuser, network-managing operating system whose portability allows it to run on mainframes, midrange computers, and microcomputers. UNIX is still a popular choice for Web and other network servers.

Linux

Linux is a low-cost, powerful, and reliable UNIX-like operating system that is rapidly gaining market share from UNIX and Windows servers as a high-performance operating system for network servers and Web servers in both small and large networks. Linux was developed as free or low-cost *shareware* or *open-source software* over the Internet in the 1990s by Linus Torvald of Finland and millions of programmers around the world. Linux is still being enhanced in this way but is sold with extra features and support services by software vendors such as Red Hat, Caldera, and SUSE Linux. PC versions, which support office software suites, Web browsers, and other application software, are also available.

Open-Source Software

The concept of **open-source software** (OSS) (discussed further in the Real World Case at the end of this chapter) is growing far beyond the Linux operating system. The basic idea behind open source is very simple: When programmers can read, redistribute, and modify the source code for a piece of software, the software evolves. People improve it, people adapt it, people fix bugs. And this development can happen at a speed that, if one is accustomed to the slow pace of conventional software development, seems astonishing. The open-source community of software developers has learned that this rapid evolutionary process produces better software than the traditional commercial (closed) model, in which only a very few programmers can see the source. The concept of open source, admittedly, runs counter to the highly commercial (and proprietary) world of traditional software development. Nonetheless, an increasingly large number of developers have embraced the open-source concept and come to realize that the proprietary approach to software development has hidden costs that can often outweigh its benefits.

Since 1998, the OSS movement has become a revolution in software development. This revolution, however, can actually trace its roots back more than 30 years. Typically, in the PC era, computer software had been sold only as a finished product, otherwise called a *precompiled binary*, which is installed on a user's computer by copying files to appropriate directories or folders. Moving to a new computer platform (Windows to Macintosh, for example) usually required the purchase of a new license. If the company went out of business or discontinued support of a product, users of that product had no recourse. Bug fixes were completely dependent on the organization that sold the software. In contrast, OSS is software that is licensed to guarantee free access to the programming behind the precompiled binary, otherwise called the *source code*. This access allows the user to install the software on a new platform without an additional purchase and to get support (or create a support consortium with other like-minded users) for a product whose creator no longer supports it. Those who are technically inclined can fix bugs themselves rather than waiting for someone else to do so. Generally, there is a central distribution mechanism that allows users to obtain the source code, as well as precompiled binaries in some cases. There are also mechanisms by which users may pay a fee to obtain the software, such as on a CD-ROM or DVD, which may also include some technical support. A variety of licenses are used to ensure that the source code will remain available, wherever the code is actually used.

To be clear, there are several things open source is not—it is not shareware, public-domain software, freeware, or software viewers and readers made freely available without access to source code. Shareware, whether or not the user registers it and pays the registration fee, typically allows no access to the underlying source code. Unlike freeware and public-domain software, OSS is copyrighted and distributed with license terms designed to ensure that the source code will always be available. While a fee may be charged for the software's packaging, distribution, or support, the complete package needed to create files is included, not simply a portion needed to view files created elsewhere.

The philosophy of open source is based on a variety of models that sometimes conflict; indeed, it often seems there are as many philosophies and models for developing and managing OSS as there are major products. In 1998, a small group of open-source enthusiasts decided it was time to formalize some things about open source. The newly formed group registered themselves on the Internet as www.opensource.org and began the process of defining exactly what is, and what is not, open-source software. As it stands today, open-source licensing is defined by the following characteristics:

- The license shall not restrict any party from selling or giving away the software as a component of an aggregate software distribution containing programs from several different sources.
- The program must include source code and must allow distribution in source code as well as compiled form.
- The license must allow modifications and derived works and must allow them to be distributed under the same terms as the license of the original software.
- The license may restrict source code from being distributed in modified form only if the license allows the distribution of patch files with the source code for the purpose of modifying the program at build time.
- The license must not discriminate against any person or group of persons.
- The license must not restrict anyone from making use of the program in a specific field of endeavor.
- The rights attached to the program must apply to all to whom the program is redistributed without the need for execution of an additional license by those parties.
- The license must not be specific to a product.
- The license must not contaminate other software by placing restrictions on any software distributed along with the licensed software.

This radical approach to software development and distribution is not without its detractors—most notably Microsoft. Nonetheless, the open-source movement is flourishing and stands to continue to revolutionize the way we think about software development.

Mac OS X

Actually based on a form of UNIX, the **Mac OS X** (pronounced MAC OS 10) is the latest operating system from Apple for the iMac and other Macintosh microcomputers. The Mac OS X version 10.2 Jaguar has an advanced graphical user interface and multitasking and multimedia capabilities, along with an integrated Web browser, e-mail, instant messaging, search engine, digital media player, and many other features.

Mac OS X was a radical departure from previous Macintosh operating systems; its underlying code base is completely different from previous versions. Its core, named Darwin, is an open source, UNIX-like operating system. Apple layered over Darwin a number of proprietary components, including the Aqua interface and the Finder, to complete the GUI-based operating system that is Mac OS X.

Mac OS X also included a number of features intended to make the operating system more stable and reliable than Apple's previous operating systems. Preemptive multitasking and memory protection, for example, improved the ability of the operating system to run multiple applications simultaneously without them interrupting or corrupting each other.

The most visible change was the Aqua theme. The use of soft edges, translucent colors, and pinstripes—similar to the hardware design of the first iMacs—brought more texture and color to the interface than OS 9's "Platinum" appearance had offered. Numerous users of the older versions of the operating system decried the new look as "cutesy" and lacking in professional polish. However, Aqua also has been called a bold and innovative step forward at a time when user interfaces were seen as "dull and boring." Despite the controversy, the look was instantly recognizable, and even before the first version of Mac OS X was released, third-party developers started producing skins (look and feel colors and styles for application interfaces) for customizable applications that mimicked the Aqua appearance.

Mac OS X also includes its own software development tools, most prominently an integrated development environment called Xcode. Xcode provides interfaces to compilers that support several programming languages including C, C++, Objective-C, and Java. For the Apple Intel Transition, it was modified so that developers could easily create an operating system to remain compatible with both the Intel-based and PowerPC-based Macintosh.

Orbitz and E*Trade: Switching to Linux

Chicago-based Orbitz Inc. (www.orbitz.com) is clear on the cost savings, enhanced processing power, and speed afforded by Linux. The online travel reservation company is using Linux on its 50 Sun Microsystems Java application servers running the Solaris UNIX operating system. These heavy-lifting systems feed the company's 700 Web servers—also running Linux—which dish up the screens customers interact with when they make airline, hotel, and vacation reservations online. Orbitz, founded in 2000 by five major U.S. airlines, currently tracks about 2 billion flight and fare options from more than 455 airlines in addition to 45,000 lodging properties and 23 rental car companies.

Orbitz benchmarked several vendors' latest operating systems including Linux on Intel servers, and the results were compelling. While maintaining the same capacity in terms of the number of users on its site, Orbitz was able to move from the UNIX servers to the Linux systems for about one-tenth the cost. As for the Web servers, Orbitz really sees the value of Linux's ease of maintenance. All 700 Web servers require only one administrator.

Orbitz isn't the only company enjoying the gains from converting to Linux. Take E*Trade Financial (www.etrade.com). In 1999, it paid $12 million for 60 Sun machines to run its online trading Web site. In 2002, E*Trade replaced those machines with 80 Intel-based servers running Linux for a mere $320,000. That move has enabled E*Trade to bring its tech budget down 30 percent, from $330 million in 2000 to $200 million in 2002—a big reason the company has stayed alive despite the ups and downs of the stock market and the brokerage business. On top of all that, Web site response time has improved by 30 percent [10, 6, 14].

Other System Management Programs

There are many other types of important system management software besides operating systems. These include *database management systems*, which we will cover in Chapter 5, and *network management programs*, which we will cover in Chapter 6. Figure 4.17 compares several types of system software offered by IBM and its competitors.

Several other types of system management software are marketed as separate programs or included as part of an operating system. Utility programs, or **utilities**, are an important example. Programs like Norton Utilities perform miscellaneous housekeeping and file conversion functions. Examples include data backup, data recovery, virus protection, data compression, and file defragmentation. Most operating systems also provide many utilities that perform a variety of helpful chores for computer users.

Other examples of system support programs include performance monitors and security monitors. **Performance monitors** are programs that monitor and adjust the performance and usage of one or more computer systems to keep them running efficiently. **Security monitors** are packages that monitor and control the use of computer systems and provide warning messages and record evidence of unauthorized use of computer resources. A recent trend is to merge both types of programs into operating systems like Microsoft's Windows 2003 Datacenter Server or into system management software like Computer Associates' CA-Unicenter, which can manage both mainframe systems and servers in a data center.

Another important software trend is the use of system software known as **application servers,** which provide a *middleware* interface between an operating system and the

FIGURE 4.17 Comparing system software offered by IBM and its main competitors.

Software Category	What It Does	IBM Product	Customers	Main Competitor	Customers
Network management	Monitors networks to keep them up and running.	**Tivoli**	T. Rowe Price uses it to safeguard customer records.	**HP OpenView**	Amazon.com uses it to monitor its servers.
Application server	Shuttles data between business apps and the Web.	**WebSphere**	REI uses it to serve up its Web site and distribute data.	**BEA WebLogic**	Washingtonpost.com builds news pages with it.
Database manager	Provides digital storehouses for business data.	**DB2**	Mikasa uses it to help customers find its products online.	**Oracle 9i**	It runs Southwest Airlines' frequent-flyer program.
Collaboration tools	Powers everything from e-mail to electronic calendars.	**Lotus**	Retailer Sephora uses it to coordinate store maintenance.	**Microsoft Exchange**	Time Inc. uses it to provide e-mail to its employees.
Development tools	Allows programmers to craft software code quickly.	**Rational**	Merrill Lynch used it to build code for online trading.	**Microsoft Visual Studio .NET**	Used to develop Allstate's policy management system.

Source: Adapted from Susan Orenstein, Erik Schonfeld, and Scott Herhold, "The Toughest Guy in Software," *Business 2.0*, April 2003, p. 82.

application programs of users. **Middleware** is software that helps diverse software applications and networked computer systems exchange data and work together more efficiently. Examples include application servers, Web servers, and enterprise application integration (EAI) software. Thus, for example, application servers like BEA's WebLogic and IBM's WebSphere help Web-based e-business and e-commerce applications run much faster and more efficiently on computers using Windows, UNIX, and other operating systems.

Programming Languages

To understand computer software, you need a basic knowledge of the role that programming languages play in the development of computer programs. A **programming language** allows a programmer to develop the sets of instructions that constitute a computer program. Many different programming languages have been developed, each with its own unique vocabulary, grammar, and uses.

Machine Languages

Machine languages (or *first-generation languages*) are the most basic level of programming languages. In the early stages of computer development, all program instructions had to be written using binary codes unique to each computer. This type of programming involves the difficult task of writing instructions in the form of strings of binary digits (ones and zeros) or other number systems. Programmers must have a detailed knowledge of the internal operations of the specific type of CPU they are using. They must write long series of detailed instructions to accomplish even simple processing tasks. Programming in machine language requires specifying the storage locations for every instruction and item of data used. Instructions must be included for every switch and indicator used by the program. These requirements make machine language programming a difficult and error-prone task. A machine language program to add two numbers together in the CPU of a specific computer and store the result might take the form shown in Figure 4.18.

Assembler Languages

Assembler languages (or *second-generation languages*) are the next level of programming languages. They were developed to reduce the difficulties in writing machine language programs. The use of assembler languages requires language translator programs called *assemblers* that allow a computer to convert the instructions of such

FIGURE 4.18
Examples of four levels of programming languages. These programming language instructions might be used to compute the sum of two numbers as expressed by the formula X = Y + Z.

Four Levels of Programming Languages	
• **Machine Languages:** Use binary coded instructions 1010 11001 1011 11010 1100 11011	• **High-Level Languages:** Use brief statements or arithmetic notations BASIC: X = Y + Z COBOL: COMPUTE X = Y + Z
• **Assembler Languages:** Use symbolic coded instructions LOD Y ADD Z STR X	• **Fourth-Generation Languages:** Use natural and nonprocedural statements SUM THE FOLLOWING NUMBERS

language into machine instructions. Assembler languages are frequently called symbolic languages because symbols are used to represent operation codes and storage locations. Convenient alphabetic abbreviations called *mnemonics* (memory aids) and other symbols represent operation codes, storage locations, and data elements. For example, the computation X = Y + Z in an assembler language might take the form shown in Figure 4.18.

Assembler languages are still used as a method of programming a computer in a machine-oriented language. Most computer manufacturers provide an assembler language that reflects the unique machine language instruction set of a particular line of computers. This feature is particularly desirable to *system programmers*, who program system software (as opposed to application programmers, who program application software), because it provides them with greater control and flexibility in designing a program for a particular computer. They can then produce more efficient software—that is, programs that require a minimum of instructions, storage, and CPU time to perform a specific processing assignment.

High-Level Languages

High-level languages (or *third-generation languages*) use instructions, which are called *statements*, that include brief statements or arithmetic expressions. Individual high-level language statements are actually *macroinstructions;* that is, each individual statement generates several machine instructions when translated into machine language by high-level language translator programs called *compilers* or *interpreters*. High-level language statements resemble the phrases or mathematical expressions required to express the problem or procedure being programmed. The *syntax* (vocabulary, punctuation, and grammatical rules) and *semantics* (meanings) of such statements do not reflect the internal code of any particular computer. For example, the computation X = Y + Z would be programmed in the high-level languages of BASIC and COBOL as shown in Figure 4.18.

High-level languages like BASIC, COBOL, and FORTRAN are easier to learn and program than an assembler language, because they have less rigid rules, forms, and syntaxes. However, high-level language programs are usually less efficient than assembler language programs and require a greater amount of computer time for translation into machine instructions. Because most high-level languages are machine-independent, programs written in a high-level language do not have to be reprogrammed when a new computer is installed, and programmers do not have to learn a different language for each type of computer.

Fourth-Generation Languages

The term **fourth-generation language** describes a variety of programming languages that are more nonprocedural and *conversational* than prior languages. These languages are called fourth-generation languages (4GLs) to differentiate them from machine languages (first generation), assembler languages (second generation), and high-level languages (third generation).

Most fourth-generation languages are *nonprocedural languages* that encourage users and programmers to specify the results they want, while the computer determines the sequence of instructions that will accomplish those results. Thus, fourth-generation languages have helped simplify the programming process. **Natural languages** are sometimes considered *fifth-generation* languages (5GLs) and are very close to English or other human languages. Research and development activity in artificial intelligence (AI) is developing programming languages that are as easy to use as ordinary conversation in one's native tongue. For example, INTELLECT, a natural language, would use a statement like, "What are the average exam scores in MIS 200?" to program a simple average exam score task.

In the early days of 4GLs, results suggested that high-volume transaction processing environments were not in the range of a 4GL's capabilities. Although 4GLs were characterized by their ease of use, they were also viewed as less flexible than their predecessors, primarily due to their increased storage and processing speed requirements. In today's large data volume environment, 4GLs are widely used and no longer viewed as a trade-off between ease of use and flexibility.

Object-Oriented Languages

Object-oriented languages like Visual Basic, C++, and Java are also considered fifth-generation languages and have become major tools of software development. Briefly, whereas most programming languages separate data elements from the procedures or actions that will be performed on them, object-oriented languages tie them together into **objects.** Thus, an object consists of data and the actions that can be performed on the data. For example, an object could be a set of data about a bank customer's savings account and the operations (e.g., interest calculations) that might be performed on the data. Or an object could be data in graphic form, such as a video display window plus the display actions that might be used on it. See Figure 4.19.

In procedural languages, a program consists of procedures to perform actions on each data element. However, in object-oriented systems, objects tell other objects to perform actions on themselves. For example, to open a window on a computer video display, a beginning menu object could send a window object a message to open, and a window would appear on the screen. That's because the window object contains the program code for opening itself.

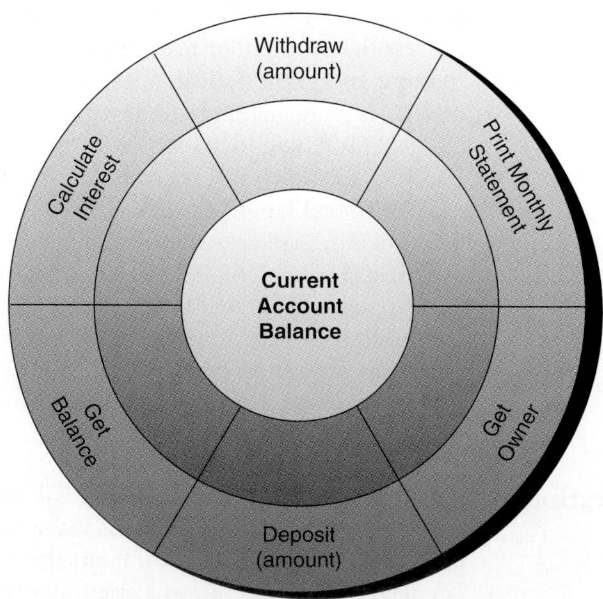

FIGURE 4.19
An example of a bank savings account object. This object consists of data about a customer's account balance and the basic operations that can be performed on those data.

FIGURE 4.20 The Visual Basic object-oriented programming environment.

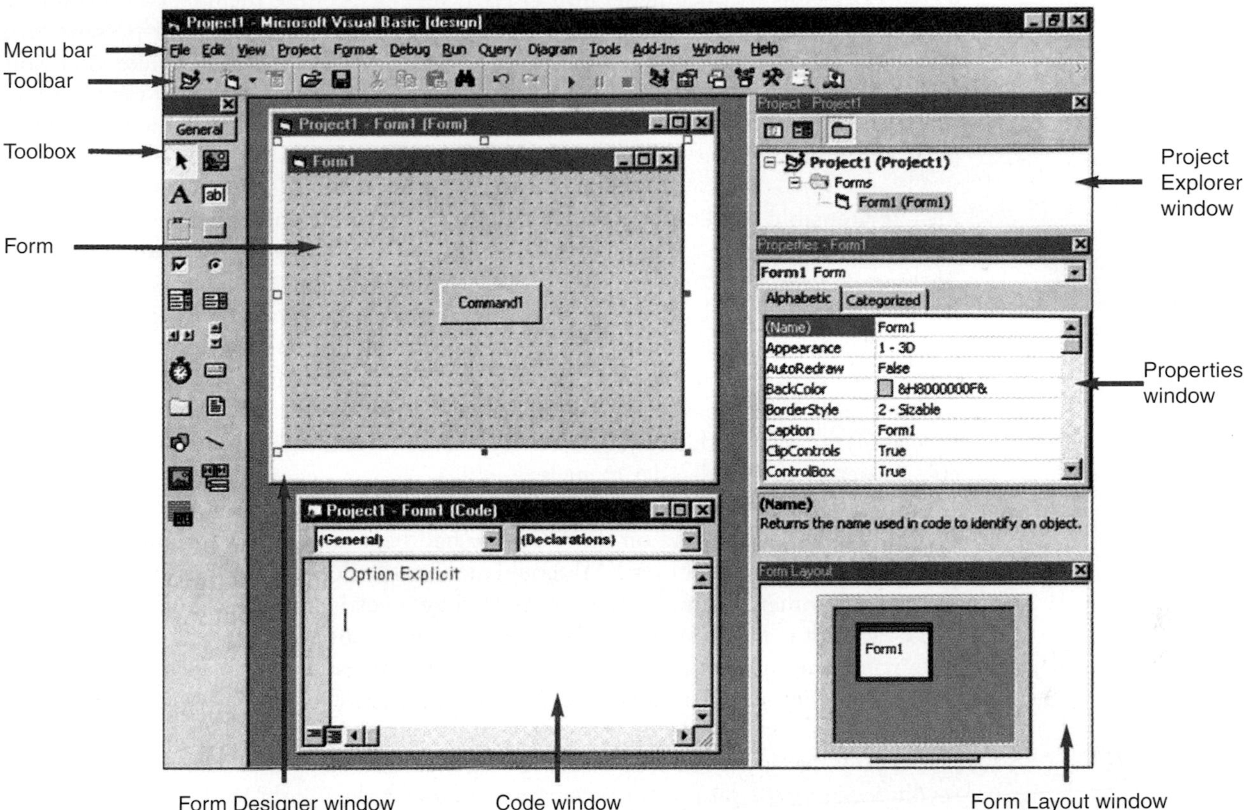

Object-oriented languages are easier to use and more efficient for programming the graphics-oriented user interfaces required by many applications. Therefore, they are the most widely used programming languages for software development today. Also, once objects are programmed, they are reusable. Therefore, reusability of objects is a major benefit of object-oriented programming. For example, programmers can construct a user interface for a new program by assembling standard objects such as windows, bars, boxes, buttons, and icons. Therefore, most object-oriented programming packages provide a GUI that supports a point-and-click, drag-and-drop visual assembly of objects known as *visual programming*. Figure 4.20 shows a display of the Visual Basic object-oriented programming environment. Object-oriented technology is discussed further in the coverage of object-oriented databases in Chapter 5.

Web Languages and Services

HTML, XML, and Java are three programming languages that are important tools for building multimedia Web pages, Web sites, and Web-based applications. In addition, XML and Java have become strategic components of the software technologies that support many Web services initiatives in business.

HTML

HTML (Hypertext Markup Language) is a page description language that creates hypertext or hypermedia documents. HTML inserts control codes within a document at points you can specify that create links (*hyperlinks*) to other parts of the document or to other documents anywhere on the World Wide Web. HTML embeds control codes in the ASCII text of a document that designate titles, headings, graphics, and multimedia components, as well as hyperlinks within the document.

As we mentioned previously, several of the programs in the top software suites automatically convert documents into HTML formats. These include Web browsers, word processing and spreadsheet programs, database managers, and presentation graphics packages. These and other specialized *Web publishing* programs like Microsoft FrontPage, Lotus FastSite, and Macromedia's DreamWeaver provide a range of features to help you design and create multimedia Web pages without formal HTML programming.

XML

XML (eXtensible Markup Language) is not a Web page format description language like HTML. Instead, XML describes the contents of Web pages (including business documents designed for use on the Web) by applying identifying tags or *contextual labels* to the data in Web documents. For example, a travel agency Web page with airline names and flight times would use hidden XML tags like "airline name" and "flight time" to categorize each of the airline flight times on that page. Or product inventory data available at a Web site could be labeled with tags like "brand," "price," and "size." By classifying data in this way, XML makes Web site information much more searchable, easier to sort, and easier to analyze.

For example, XML-enabled search software could easily find the exact product you specify if the product data on the Web site had been labeled with identifying XML tags. And a Web site that uses XML could more easily determine which Web page features its customers use and which products they investigate. Thus, XML promises to make electronic business and commerce processes a lot easier and more efficient by supporting the automatic electronic exchange of business data between companies and their customers, suppliers, and other business partners.

Java and .NET

Java is an object-oriented programming language created by Sun Microsystems that is revolutionizing the programming of applications for the World Wide Web and corporate intranets and extranets. Java is related to the C11 and Objective C programming languages but is much simpler and more secure and is computing-platform independent. Java is also specifically designed for real-time, interactive, Web-based network applications. Java applications consisting of small application programs, called *applets*, can be executed by any computer and any operating system anywhere in a network.

The ease of creating Java applets and distributing them from network servers to client PCs and network computers is one of the major reasons for Java's popularity. Applets can be small, special-purpose application programs or small modules of larger Java application programs. Java programs are platform-independent, too—they can run on Windows, UNIX, and Macintosh systems without modification.

Microsoft's **.NET** is a collection of programming support for what are known as Web services, the ability to use the Web rather than your own computer for various services (see below). .NET is intended to provide individual and business users with a seamlessly interoperable and Web-enabled interface for applications and computing devices and to make computing activities increasingly Web browser–oriented. The .NET platform includes servers, building-block services such as Web-based data storage, and device software. It also includes Passport, Microsoft's fill-in-the-form-only-once identity verification service.

The .NET platform is expected to enable the entire range of computing devices to work together and have user information automatically updated and synchronized on all of them. In addition, it will provide a premium online subscription service. The service will feature customized access to and delivery of products and services from a central starting point for the management of various applications (e.g., e-mail) or software (e.g., Office .NET). For developers, .NET offers the ability to create reusable modules, which should increase productivity and reduce the number of programming errors.

The full release of .NET is expected to take several years to complete, with intermittent releases of products such as a personal security service and new versions of Windows and Office that implement the .NET strategy coming on the market separately.

FIGURE 4.21 The benefits and limitations of the Java2 Enterprise Edition (J2EE) and Microsoft .NET software development platforms.

J2EE		.NET	
PROS	**CONS**	**PROS**	**CONS**
• Runs on any operating system and application server (may need adjustments). • Handles complex, high-volume, high-transaction applications. • Has more enterprise features for session management, fail-over, load balancing, and application integration. • Is favored by experienced enterprise vendors such as IBM, BEA, SAP, and Oracle. • Offers a wide range of vendor choices for tools and application servers. • Has a proven track record.	• Has a complex application development environment. • Tools can be difficult to use. • Java Swing environment's ability to build graphical user interfaces has limitations. • May cost more to build, deploy, and manage applications. • Lacks built-in support for Web services standards. • Is difficult to use for quick-turnaround, low-cost, and mass-market projects.	• Easy-to-use tools may increase programmer productivity. • Has a strong framework for building rich graphical user interfaces. • Gives developers choice of working in more than 20 programming languages. • Is tightly integrated with Microsoft's operating system and enterprise server software. • May cost less, due in part to built-in application server in Windows, unified management, less expensive tools. • Has built-in support for Web service standards.	• Framework runs only on Windows, restricting vendor choice. • Users of prior Microsoft tools and technology face a potentially steep learning curve. • New runtime infrastructure lacks maturity. • Questions persist about the scalability and transaction capability of the Windows platform. • Choice of integrated development environments is limited. • Getting older applications to run in new .NET environment may require effort.

Source: Carol Silwa, ".Net vs. Java," *Computerworld*, May 20, 2002, p. 31.

Visual Studio .NET is a development environment that is now available, and Windows XP supports certain .NET capabilities.

The latest version of Java is Java2 Enterprise Edition (J2EE), which has become the primary alternative to Microsoft's .NET software development platform for many organizations intent on capitalizing on the business potential of Web-based applications and Web services. Figure 4.21 compares the pros and cons of using J2EE and .NET for software development.

Web Services

Web services are software components that are based on a framework of Web and object-oriented standards and technologies for using the Web that electronically link the applications of different users and different computing platforms [4]. Thus, Web services can link key business functions for the exchange of data in real time within the Web-based applications that a business might share with its customers, suppliers, and other business partners. For example, Web services would enable the purchasing application of a business to use the Web to check the inventory of a supplier before placing a large order, while the sales application of the supplier could use Web services to automatically check the credit rating of the business with a credit-reporting agency before approving the purchase. Therefore, among both business and IT professionals, the term *Web services* is commonly used to describe the Web-based business and computing functions or services accomplished by Web services software technologies and standards.

Figure 4.22 illustrates how Web services work and identifies some of the key technologies and standards that are involved. The XML language is one of the key technologies that enable Web services to make applications work between different computing platforms. Also important are **UDDI** (Universal Description and Discovery Integration),

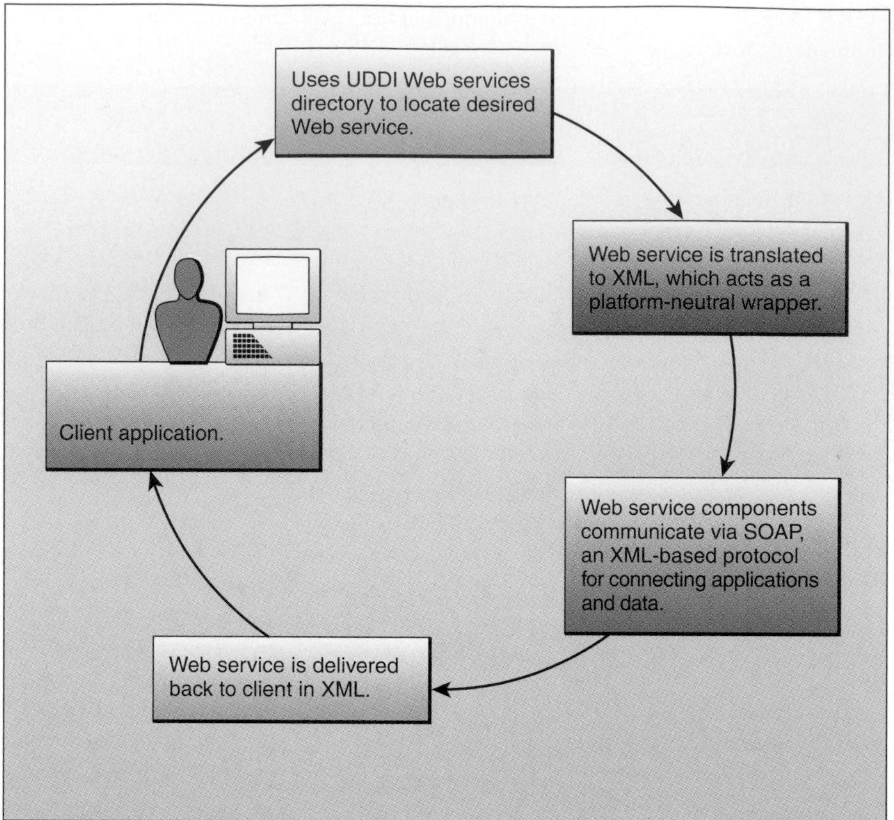

FIGURE 4.22
The basic steps in accomplishing a Web services application.

Source: Adapted from Bala Iyer, Jim Freedman, Mark Gaynor, and George Wyner, "Web Services: Enabling Dynamic Business Networks," *Communications of the Association for Information Systems* 11 (2003), p. 543.

the "yellow pages" directory of all Web services and how to locate and use them, and **SOAP** (Simple Object Access Protocol), an XML-based protocol of specifications for connecting applications to the data that they need [5].

Web services promise to be the key software technology for automating access to data and application functions between a business and its trading partners. As companies increasingly move to doing business over the Web, Web services will become essential for the development of the easy and efficient e-business and e-commerce applications that will be required. The flexibility and interoperability of Web services also will be essential for coping with the fast changing relationships between a company and its business partners that are commonplace in today's dynamic global business environment.

Wells Fargo & Co.: Developing Web Services

The term *Web services* is used to describe a collection of technologies—an alphabet soup of Web-based technical standards and communication protocols—such as XML, Universal Description Discovery and Integration (UDDI), and Simple Object Access Protocol (SOAP)—that link applications running on different computer platforms. Unlike present application integration approaches that require custom coding or expensive middleware to link individual applications, Web services aim to expose and link key functions within applications (such as the ability to see the balance in your checking account or place an order from a factory) to other applications that need them to complete business processes.

An increasing number of businesses have begun using Web services technologies developed by IBM, Microsoft, BEA Systems, and many others. Once you see one in action, you immediately know what the buzz is all about.

Wells Fargo & Co., a leading financial services provider, is using Web services to help streamline the process of initiating electronic transactions with wholesale banking customers. Its new online system, which replaced an internally developed system called Payment Manager, allows scores of customers to send data and instructions regarding wire transfers and automated clearinghouse transactions, among many other functions. While Payment Manager worked well, it required custom development to tie Wells Fargo systems to every customer who wanted to transact business electronically.

Using Web services, Wells Fargo doesn't have to custom-code at all. Now it can reuse code already built, thus making the online system easier to maintain and update with new features.

Key Web services protocols in use at Wells Fargo—including SOAP and UDDI—present standard interfaces that applications can be coded to, which facilitates data exchanges between disparate applications within the bank as well as with customers and partners. SOAP uses XML syntax to send commands between applications across the Internet. UDDI defines a universal registry or catalog of Web services. It lets software automatically discover and integrate with services on the Web when needed.

With Web services, Wells Fargo is able to accept roughly 50 different formats of files from customers; popular file types include SAP and J.D. Edwards ERP file formats. Those files are typically sent using file transfer protocol (FTP). Some of the largest customers have a direct leased line into Wells Fargo, and they send information directly into the Payment Manager transaction hub. If the file format and instructions call for a wire transfer, the information is sent to the Wells Fargo wire transfer system. Alternatively, the files could need to be sent into Wells Fargo's automated clearinghouse systems. If the file calls for cutting a check, Wells Fargo can convert the request into a written check and send it out through a third-party check processor.

Among the possibilities for future Web services are an event-notification application whereby Wells Fargo could, for example, notify customers of the arrival of information they have been awaiting. That's an improvement over the current method of customers having to log into a Wells Fargo Web site and find the information they need [8, 12].

Programming Software

Various software packages are available to help programmers develop computer programs. For example, *programming language translators* are programs that translate other programs into machine language instruction codes that computers can execute. Other software packages, such as programming language editors, are called *programming tools* because they help programmers write programs by providing a variety of program creation and editing capabilities. See Figure 4.23.

Language Translator Programs

Computer programs consist of sets of instructions written in programming languages that must be translated by a **language translator** into the computer's own machine language before they can be processed, or executed, by the CPU. Programming language translator programs (or *language processors*) are known by a variety of names. An **assembler** translates the symbolic instruction codes of programs written in an assembler language into machine language instructions, whereas a **compiler** translates high-level language statements.

An **interpreter** is a special type of compiler that translates and executes each statement in a program one at a time, instead of first producing a complete machine language program, as compilers and assemblers do. Java is an example of an interpreted language. Thus, the program instructions in Java applets are interpreted and executed *on the fly* as the applet is being executed by a client PC.

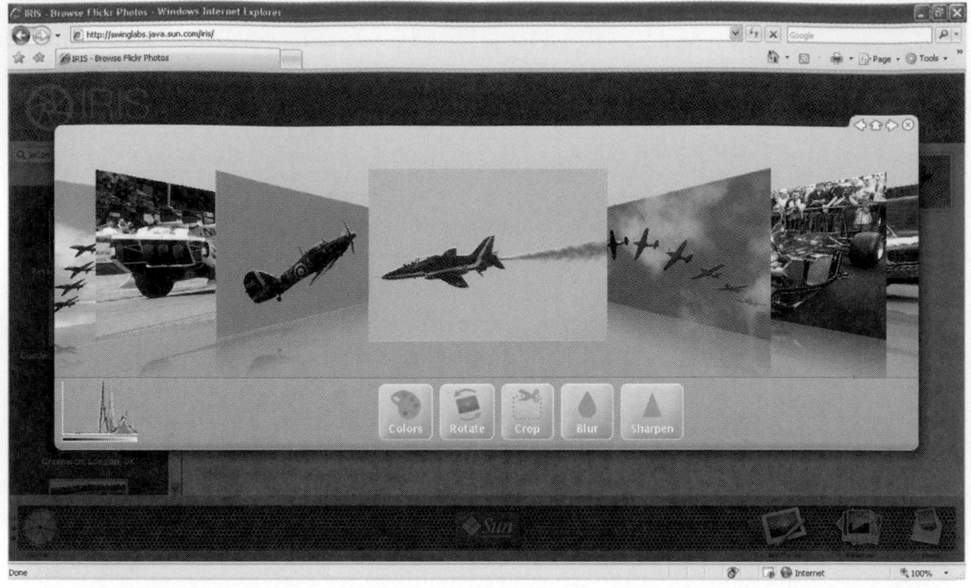

FIGURE 4.23
Using the graphical programming interface of a Java programming tool, Forte for Java, by Sun Microsystems.

Programming Tools

Software development and the computer programming process have been enhanced by adding *graphical programming interfaces* and a variety of built-in development capabilities. Language translators have always provided some editing and diagnostic capabilities to identify programming errors or *bugs*. However, most software development programs now include powerful graphics-oriented *programming editors* and *debuggers*. These **programming tools** help programmers identify and minimize errors while they are programming. Such programming tools provide a computer-aided programming environment, which decreases the drudgery of programming while increasing the efficiency and productivity of software developers. Other programming tools include diagramming packages, code generators, libraries of reusable objects and program code, and prototyping tools. All of these programming tools are an essential part of widely used programming languages like Visual Basic, C11, and Java.

CASE Tools

Since the early days of programming, software developers have needed automated tools. Initially the concentration was on program support tools such as translators, compilers, assemblers, macro processors, and linkers and loaders. However, as computers became more powerful and the software that ran on them grew larger and more complex, the range of support tools began to expand. In particular, the use of interactive time-sharing systems for software development encouraged the development of program editors, debuggers, and code analyzers.

As the range of support tools expanded, manufacturers began integrating them into a single application using a common interface. Such tools were referred to as **CASE tools** (computer-aided software engineering).

CASE tools can take a number of forms and be applied at different stages of the software development process. Those CASE tools that support activities early in the life cycle of a software project (e.g., requirements, design support tools) are sometimes called *front-end* or *upper* CASE tools. Those that are used later in the life cycle (e.g., compilers, test support tools) are called *back-end* or *lower* CASE tools.

Exploring the details of CASE tools is beyond the scope of this text, and you will encounter them again when you study systems analysis and design. For now, remember that CASE is an important part of resolving the problems of complex application development and maintenance of software applications.

Summary

- **Software.** Computer software consists of two major types of programs: (1) application software that directs the performance of a particular use, or application, of computers to meet the information processing needs of users and (2) system software that controls and supports the operations of a computer system as it performs various information processing tasks. Refer to Figure 4.2 for an overview of the major types of software.
- **Application Software.** Application software includes a variety of programs that can be segregated into general purpose and application-specific categories. General purpose application programs perform common information processing jobs for end users. Examples are word processing, electronic spreadsheet, and presentation graphics programs. Application-specific programs accomplish information processing tasks that support specific business functions or processes, scientific or engineering applications, and other computer applications in society.
- **System Software.** System software can be subdivided into system management programs and system development programs. System management programs manage the hardware, software, network, and data resources of a computer system during its execution of information processing jobs. Examples of system management programs are operating systems, network management programs, database management systems, system utilities, application servers, and performance and security monitors. Network management programs support and manage telecommunications activities and network performance telecommunications networks. Database management systems control the development, integration, and maintenance of databases. Utilities are programs that perform routine computing functions, such as backing up data or copying files, as part of an operating system or as a separate package. System development programs like language translators and programming editors help IS specialists develop computer programs to support business processes.
- **Operating Systems.** An operating system is an integrated system of programs that supervises the operation of the CPU, controls the input/output storage functions of the computer system, and provides various support services. An operating system performs five basic functions: (1) a user interface for system and network communications with users, (2) resource management for managing the hardware resources of a computer system, (3) file management for managing files of data and programs, (4) task management for managing the tasks a computer must accomplish, and (5) utilities and other functions that provide miscellaneous support services.
- **Programming Languages.** Programming languages are a major category of system software. They require the use of a variety of programming packages to help programmers develop computer programs and language translator programs to convert programming language instructions into machine language instruction codes. The five major levels of programming languages are machine languages, assembler languages, high-level languages, fourth-generation languages, and object-oriented languages. Object-oriented languages like Java and special-purpose languages like HTML and XML are being widely used for Web-based business applications and services.

Key Terms and Concepts

These are the key terms and concepts of this chapter. The page number of their first explanation is given in parentheses.

1. Application service provider (ASP) (127)
2. Application software (114)
3. Assembler language (138)
4. CASE tools (146)
5. Custom software (114)
6. COTS software (114)
7. Desktop publishing (DTP) (123)
8. E-mail (120)
9. Fourth-generation language (139)
10. Function-specific application programs (118)

11. General-purpose application programs (114)
12. Groupware (125)
13. High-level language (139)
14. HTML (141)
15. Instant messaging (IM) (121)
16. Integrated package (119)
17. Java (142)
18. Language translator (145)
19. Machine language (138)
20. Middleware (138)
21. Multitasking (133)
22. Natural language (140)
23. Object-oriented language (140)
24. Operating system (129)
25. Personal information manager (PIM) (125)
26. Presentation graphics software (124)
27. Programming language (138)
28. Software suites (119)
29. Spreadsheet package (123)
30. System software (129)
31. User interface (129)
32. Utilities (137)
33. Virtual memory (132)
34. Web browser (120)
35. Web services (143)
36. Word processing software (122)
37. XML (142)

Review Quiz

Match one of the previous key terms and concepts with one of the brief examples or definitions that follow. Try to find the best fit for answers that seem to fit more than one term or concept. Defend your choices.

____ 1. Programs that manage and support the operations of computers.

____ 2. Programs that direct the performance of a specific use of computers.

____ 3. A system of programs that manages the operations of a computer system.

____ 4. Companies that own, operate, and maintain application software and the computer system resources for a fee as a service over the Internet.

____ 5. Integrated software tool that supports the development of software applications.

____ 6. Software designed in-house for use by a specific organization or set of users.

____ 7. The function that provides a means of communication between end users and an operating system.

____ 8. Acronym meaning commercial off-the-shelf.

____ 9. Provides a greater memory capability than a computer's actual memory capacity.

____ 10. The ability to do several computing tasks concurrently.

____ 11. Still the most common programming language used on the Web.

____ 12. Converts numeric data into graphic displays.

____ 13. Translates high-level instructions into machine language instructions.

____ 14. Performs housekeeping chores for a computer system.

____ 15. A category of application software that performs common information processing tasks for end users.

____ 16. Software available for the specific applications of end users in business, science, and other fields.

____ 17. Helps you surf the Web.

____ 18. Use your networked computer to send and receive messages.

____ 19. Creates and displays a worksheet for analysis.

____ 20. Allows you to create and edit documents.

____ 21. Enables you to produce your own brochures and newsletters.

____ 22. Helps you keep track of appointments and tasks.

____ 23. A program that performs several general-purpose applications.

____ 24. A combination of individual general-purpose application packages that work easily together.

____ 25. Software to support the collaboration of teams and workgroups.

____ 26. Uses instructions in the form of coded strings of ones and zeros.

____ 27. Uses instructions consisting of symbols representing operation codes and storage locations.

____ 28. Uses instructions in the form of brief statements or the standard notation of mathematics.

____ 29. Might take the form of query languages and report generators.

____ 30. Languages that tie together data and the actions that will be performed on the data.

____ 31. As easy to use as one's native tongue.

____ 32. Includes programming editors, debuggers, and code generators.

____ 33. Produces hyperlinked multimedia documents for the Web.

____ 34. A Web document content description language.

____ 35. A popular object-oriented language for Web-based applications.

____ 36. Windows is an example of a common one of these used on most PCs.

____ 37. Software that helps diverse applications work together.

____ 38. Enables you to communicate and collaborate in real time with the online associates in your workgroup.

____ 39. Links business functions within applications for the exchange of data between companies via the Web.

Discussion Questions

1. What major trends are occurring in software? What capabilities do you expect to see in future software packages?
2. How do the different roles of system software and application software affect you as a business end user? How do you see this changing in the future?
3. Refer to the Real World Case on Wolf Peak International in the chapter. If you were starting a small business, what business application software would you choose for accounting and control of business operations and management reporting? Why?
4. Why is an operating system necessary? That is, why can't an end user just load an application program into a computer and start computing?
5. Should a Web browser be integrated into an operating system? Why or why not?
6. Refer to the Real World Case on webtop software in the chapter. What are the business incentives that lure people to start a small company to develop and market webtop software applications? Would you invest in such a company today, or any other variation in that market space? Why or why not?
7. Are software suites, Web browsers, and groupware merging together? What are the implications for a business and its end users?
8. How are HTML, XML, and Java affecting business applications on the Web?
9. Do you think Linux will surpass, in adoption and use, other operating systems for network and Web servers? Why or why not?
10. Which application software packages are the most important for a business end user to know how to use? Explain the reasons for your choices.

Analysis Exercises

Complete the following exercises as individual or group projects that apply chapter concepts to real world business situations.

1. **Desktop Application Recognition**
   Tool Selection
   ABC Department Stores would like to acquire software to do the following tasks. Identify what software packages they need.
   a. Surf the Web and their intranets and extranets.
   b. Send messages to one another's computer workstations.
   c. Help employees work together in teams.
   d. Use a group of productivity packages that work together easily.
   e. Help sales reps keep track of meetings and sales calls.
   f. Type correspondence and reports.
   g. Analyze rows and columns of sales figures.
   h. Develop a variety of graphical presentations.

2. **Y2K Revisited**
   The End of Time
   Decades ago, programmers trying to conserve valuable storage space shortened year values to two digits. This shortcut created what became known as the "Y2K" problem or "millennium bug" at the turn of the century. Programmers needed to review billions of lines of code to ensure important programs would continue to operate correctly. The Y2K problem merged with the dot-com boom and created a tremendous demand for information technology employees. Information system users spent billions of dollars fixing or replacing old software. The IT industry is only now beginning to recover from the postboom slump. Could such hysteria happen again? It can, and it likely will.

   Today, most programs use several different schemes to record dates. One scheme, POSIX time, widely employed on UNIX-based systems, requires a signed 32-bit integer to store a number representing the number of seconds since January 1, 1970. "0" represents midnight on January 1, "10" represents 10 seconds after midnight, and "–10" represents 10 seconds *before* midnight. A simple program then converts this data into any number of international date formats for display. This scheme works well because it allows programmers to subtract one date/time from another date/time and directly determine the interval between them. It also requires only 4 bytes of storage space. But 32 bits still calculates to a finite number, whereas time is infinite. As a business manager, you will need to be aware of this new threat and steer your organization away from repeating history. The following questions will help you evaluate the situation and learn from history.

a. If 1 represents 1 second and 2 represents 2 seconds, how many seconds can be represented in a binary number 32 bits long? Use a spreadsheet to show your calculations.
b. Given that POSIX time starts at midnight, January 1, 1970, in what year will time "run out"? Remember that half the available numbers represent dates before 1970. Use a spreadsheet to show your calculations.
c. As a business manager, what can you do to minimize this problem for your organization?

3. **Tracking Project Work**
Queries and Reports
You are responsible for managing information systems development projects at AAA Systems. To better track progress in completing projects, you have decided to maintain a simple database table to track the time your employees spend on various tasks and the projects with which they are associated. It will also allow you to keep track of employees' billable hours each week. The table below provides a sample data set.

a. Build a database table to store the data shown and enter the records as a set of sample data.
b. Create a query that will list the hours worked for all workers who worked more than 40 hours during production week 20.
c. Create a report grouped by project that will show the number of hours devoted to each task on the project and the subtotal number of hours devoted to each project, as well as a grand total of all hours worked.
d. Create a report grouped by employee that will show each employee's hours worked on each task and total hours worked. The user should be able to select a production week and find data for just that week presented.

4. **Matching Training to Software Use**
3-D Graphing
You have the responsibility to manage software training for Sales, Accounting, and Operations Department workers in your organization. You have surveyed the workers to get a feel for the amounts of time spent using various packages, and the results are shown below. The values shown are the total number of workers in each department and the total weekly hours the department's workers spend using each software package. You have been asked to prepare a spreadsheet summarizing these data and comparing the use of the various packages across departments.

Department	Employees	Spread-sheet	Data-base	Presentations
Sales	225	410	1,100	650
Operations	75	710	520	405
Accounting	30	310	405	50

a. Create a spreadsheet illustrating each application's average use per department. To do this, you will first enter the data shown above. Then compute the average weekly spreadsheet use by dividing spreadsheet hours by the number of Sales workers. Do this for each department. Repeat these three calculations for both database and presentation use. Round results to the nearest 1/100th.
b. Create a three-dimensional bar graph illustrating the averages by department and software package.
c. A committee has been formed to plan software training classes at your company. Prepare a slide presentation with four slides illustrating your findings. The first slide should serve as an introduction to the data. The second slide should contain a copy of the original data table (without the averages). The third slide should contain a copy of the three-dimensional bar graph from the previous answer. The fourth slide should contain your conclusions regarding key applications per department. Use professional labels, formatting, and backgrounds.

Project_Name	Task_Name	Employee_ID	Production_Week	Hours_Worked
Fin-Goods-Inv	App. Devel.	456		
Fin-Goods-Inv	DB Design	345		20
Fin-Goods-Inv	UI Design	234		16
HR	Analysis	234		24
HR	Analysis	456		48
HR	UI Design	123		8
HR	UI Design	123		40
HR	UI Design	234		32
Shipmt-Tracking	DB Design	345		24
Shipmt-Tracking	DB Design	345		16
Shipmt-Tracking	DB Development	345		20
Shipmt-Tracking	UI Design	123		32
Shipmt-Tracking	UI Design	234		24

REAL WORLD CASE 3 Microsoft and Others: Developing Software for How Companies Do Business

Microsoft, whose fortune has been built around the Windows operating system, is gaining influence over how things get done in an operating room. For the past few years, the software company has been hiring doctors, nurses, and other health-care professionals in an effort to establish internal expertise about the medical industry's IT needs. The strategy is paying off in new accounts and an expanding footprint within the sector.

Already, Matt Maynard, CIO of Pathology Associates Medical Laboratories, credits Microsoft with understanding his business "better than lots of health-care vendors." Yet others see risk in Microsoft stretching too far. "The less Microsoft knows about health care, the better it is for all of us," says Craig Feied, director of the Institute for Medical Informatics at MedStar Health. "The last thing we want is an over-engineered set of solutions built around yesterday's or today's problems."

What Microsoft is doing in health care is a sign of a major strategic shift, one that raises questions in other industries as well. From the time it was founded 28 years ago, Microsoft's focus has been on the software that goes inside computers. Increasingly, however, the company is assessing the business processes of specific industries—and writing software products to support them.

Now Microsoft is expanding the number of industries it targets, injecting industry-specific code directly into its core software platforms and hiring business-technology professionals steeped in the sectors at which it aims. Earlier this month, it hired Stuart McKee, the CIO of Washington State, to be U.S. national technology officer of its public-sector and education practice, joining a two-star general and former Coast Guard and Department of Homeland Security officials on that team.

Microsoft CEO Steve Ballmer describes a two-pronged strategy of selling customizable applications directly to small and medium companies via Microsoft's Business Solutions division, while serving larger companies through partnerships with other technology companies. In both cases, Microsoft engages its wide network of independent software vendors to build apps (applications) that run on top of its own software. What it hasn't done in the past is provide business solutions to specific industry (often referred to as *vertical*) segments.

But that's changing. Microsoft engineers are creating software add-ons, called *accelerators*, aimed at business processes common to companies in a given industry. For financial-services companies, Microsoft has an accelerator to help with the trend toward straight-through processing, an automated means of moving a transaction through multiple stages. For health-care companies, it has an accelerator to facilitate information sharing.

And Microsoft Business Solutions has begun inserting what it calls "industry-enabling layers"—software that serves the needs of a broad base of companies in a particular sector—into its enterprise applications. Its latest addition, acquired in April from Encore Business Solutions Inc., is bookkeeping software to deal with the idiosyncrasies of not-for-profits, schools, and other public-sector organizations. The new functionality will be added to the next release of Microsoft's Great Plains applications suite and is the first time Microsoft will integrate technology for the public sector into its software. It has created similar software layers for manufacturing, wholesale distribution, retail, and professional services.

The Microsoft unit that works with independent software vendors (ISVs) has reoriented around vertical industries, too. Until 18 months ago, Microsoft determined its relationships with those vendors by the type of horizontal applications they developed—say, business intelligence or enterprise resource planning. Now Microsoft identifies needs in a particular sector, recruits partners that can fill the need, and jointly creates so-called solution maps of software and services. "We've got a huge pipeline," says Mark Young, Microsoft's general manager of ISVs.

Those partners that aren't threatened by Microsoft's ISV strategy sense an opportunity. Microsoft has so far dealt with manufacturing as one sector, with the exception of specialized service for automotive companies. It's in the early stages of slicing the sector into smaller pieces, planning internal teams for sales, marketing, technology, and support to serve the aerospace, chemical, consumer packaged-goods, high-tech manufacturing, and oil and gas industries. "I'm thrilled," says Ira Dauberman, a VP at UGS PLM Solutions, of Microsoft's plans to target aerospace companies. Boeing is among UGS PLM Solutions' top accounts. "Putting a focus on aerospace is long overdue."

Microsoft is far from the only software company with a vertical strategy. IBM realigned its software division around vertical industries in December. Since then it has delivered preconfigured software bundles for 12 industries. SAP and Oracle go further, developing entire suites of vertical applications. Oracle, for instance, sells applications for real-estate companies and airports. Oracle President Charles Phillips says Microsoft "talks vertical with a horizontal product and tries to package it, twist it, and tweak it." SAP CEO Henning Kagermann contends that Microsoft's heavy reliance on independent software vendors increases complexity. "If you have too many partners in vertical applications, it's always a risk," he warns.

Yet Microsoft has a major edge in extending its strategy: Call it Microsoft's Foot In The Door advantage.

When Cooper Tire and Rubber Co., a 90-year-old maker of after-market tires, set out 18 months ago to create a product life cycle management system for designing and building new products, it assessed software from PLM specialists, custom software, and Microsoft. Cooper Tire chose a Microsoft approach, using the company's SharePoint portal software, Project project-management application, and Visio diagramming program.

It was a pragmatic decision: Cooper Tire's license agreement with Microsoft already covered the products needed, so the tire company faced development costs but no added application expense. The other approaches would have cost at least $1.5 million, and Cooper did it for less than half that. But what does Microsoft know about tire manufacturing? "That's what we were wondering, too," says Todd Wilson, project manager of technical systems in Cooper's tire division.

Microsoft brought in a systems integrator—Avanade, a joint venture between Microsoft and Accenture—and bore some of the cost. "The people they've brought in have been experienced manufacturing people. We haven't had to teach them," Wilson says. Microsoft and Avanade spent three months developing a prototype to prove its tools could meet Cooper's needs.

The resulting system helps the company get new tire designs to market in about nine months, half of what it used to take. That scored points with management because speed to market is key to Cooper's strategy of developing high-performance and racing tires to compete with Chinese tire companies. "We were a fast follower. We want to be more of a leader," Wilson says.

Another industry in which Microsoft has well-established customers is retail. It estimates 70 percent of the computing infrastructure in stores runs on Microsoft software. Yet the company is depending on creative thinking to convince retailers to use its software in more—and more strategic—ways.

An initiative called Smarter Retailing, launched in January with 17 partners, sets the lofty goal of revolutionizing the shopping experience through emerging technologies such as using a fingerprint reader in lieu of a credit-card swipe or a smart phone for one-to-one marketing in a store. Retailers have earned a reputation for treating their best customers the worst, says Janet Kennedy, managing director of Microsoft's retail and hospitality sector, which employs 170 sales, consulting, technical, and service staff to serve 105 top accounts. "The bread, milk, beer customer gets the fast lane," Kennedy says, "and the mother with three kids and $300 worth of groceries gets the slow lane."

Early participants include the A&P supermarket chain and Smart & Final, which operates a chain of warehouse stores. Smarter Retailing could serve as a model for similar undertakings in other areas. "You may see a Smarter Financial Services initiative or Smarter Manufacturing," says Gerri Elliott, VP of worldwide industry solutions.

Ballmer sums up his company's overall vertical push this way: "We've made great progress. We have great capability today that we didn't have a couple of years ago. Yet I believe there's a whole lot more that we can and need to be doing."

Microsoft has already made its mark on the technology industry. The real question is: Which industry is next?

Source: Adapted from John Foley, "Strategy Shift: Microsoft Is Looking at How Companies Do Business—and Writing Software Products to Support Those Processes," *InformationWeek*, May 31, 2004.

CASE STUDY QUESTIONS

1. A common phrase among IT professionals is, "The world views its data through Windows." Why does Microsoft dominate the desktop and networked software market? Visit its Web site at www.microsoft.com and review its broad range of software products and services to help develop your answer.
2. How successful will Microsoft be in competing with software vendors that specialize in specific market applications like health care, retail, and other specialty services? Why?
3. Do you agree with Microsoft's strategy to develop industry-specific partners to capitalize on opportunities in both large and small business sectors? Is there an advantage or a disadvantage to being one of Microsoft's partners in this type of relationship? Explain.

REAL WORLD ACTIVITIES

1. Industry-specific software applications are everywhere. However, many industries still lack a wide variety of software applications to support their needs. Using the Internet, see if you can find one example of an industry that has a wide variety of vertical applications and one industry that does not have a variety of software solutions from which to choose.
2. Using the industries that lack a wide variety of support applications, break into small groups with your classmates, and discuss what types of applications would be valuable to those industries. Why do you think the applications you came up with have not been developed?

CHAPTER 5

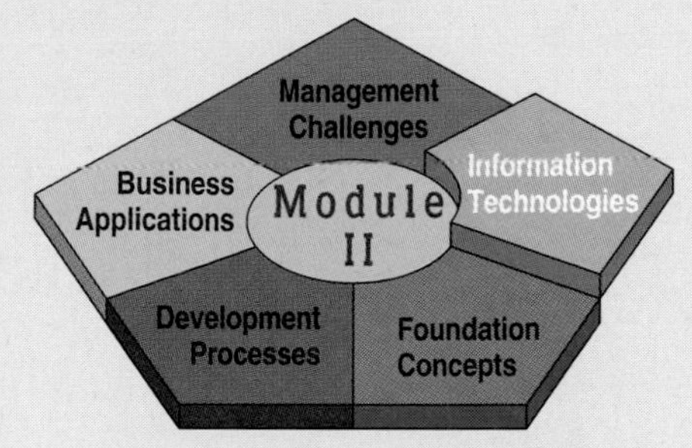

DATA RESOURCE MANAGEMENT

Chapter Highlights

Section I
Technical Foundations of Database Management

Database Management

Fundamental Data Concepts

Real World Case: Amazon, eBay, and Google: Unlocking and Sharing Business Databases

Database Structures

Database Development

Section II
Managing Data Resources

Data Resource Management

Types of Databases

Real World Case: Emerson and Sanofi: Data Stewards Seek Data Conformity

Data Warehouses and Data Mining

Traditional File Processing

The Database Management Approach

Real World Case: Acxiom Corporation: Data Demand Respect

Learning Objectives

After reading and studying this chapter, you should be able to:

1. Explain the business value of implementing data resource management processes and technologies in an organization.
2. Outline the advantages of a database management approach to managing the data resources of a business, compared with a file processing approach.
3. Explain how database management software helps business professionals and supports the operations and management of a business.
4. Provide examples to illustrate each of the following concepts:
   a. Major types of databases.
   b. Data warehouses and data mining.
   c. Logical data elements.
   d. Fundamental database structures.
   e. Database development.

SECTION I Technical Foundations of Database Management

Database Management

Just imagine how difficult it would be to get any information from an information system if data were stored in an unorganized way or if there were no systematic way to retrieve them. Therefore, in all information systems, data resources must be organized and structured in some logical manner so that they can be accessed easily, processed efficiently, retrieved quickly, and managed effectively. Data structures and access methods ranging from simple to complex have been devised to organize and access data stored by information systems efficiently. In this chapter, we will explore these concepts, as well as the managerial implications and value of data resource management. See Figure 5.1.

Read the Real World Case on the use of databases by Amazon, eBay, and Google. We can learn a lot from this case about the strategic importance of data resources to an organization.

Fundamental Data Concepts

Before we go any further, let's discuss some fundamental concepts about how data are organized in information systems. A conceptual framework of several levels of data has been devised that differentiates among different groupings, or elements, of data. Thus, data may be logically organized into characters, fields, records, files, and databases, just as writing can be organized into letters, words, sentences, paragraphs, and documents. Examples of these **logical data elements** are shown in Figure 5.2.

Character

The most basic logical data element is the **character**, which consists of a single alphabetic, numeric, or other symbol. You might argue that the bit or byte is a more elementary data element, but remember that those terms refer to the physical storage elements provided by the computer hardware, as discussed in Chapter 3. Using that understanding, one way to think of a character is that it is a byte used to represent a particular character. From a user's point of view (that is, from a *logical* as opposed to a physical or hardware view of data), a character is the most basic element of data that can be observed and manipulated.

Field

The next higher level of data is the **field**, or data item. A field consists of a grouping of related characters. For example, the grouping of alphabetic characters in a person's name may form a name field (or typically, last name, first name, and middle initial fields), and the grouping of numbers in a sales amount forms a sales amount field. Specifically, a data field represents an **attribute** (a characteristic or quality) of some **entity** (object, person, place, or event). For example, an employee's salary is an attribute that is a typical data field used to describe an entity who is an employee of a business. Generally speaking, fields are organized such that they represent some logical order. For example, last_name, first_name, address, city, state, zip code, and so on.

Record

All of the fields used to describe the attributes of an entity are grouped to form a **record**. Thus, a record represents a collection of *attributes* that describe an *entity*. An example is a person's payroll record, which consists of data fields describing attributes such as the person's name, Social Security number, and rate of pay. *Fixed-length* records contain a fixed number of fixed-length data fields. *Variable-length* records contain a variable number of fields and field lengths. Another way of looking at a record is that it represents a single *instance* of an entity. Each record in an employee file describes one specific employee.

File

A group of related records is a data **file** (sometimes referred to as a *table* or *flat file*). When thought of independent of any other files related to it, a single *table* may be referred to as a *flat file*. As a point of accuracy, the term *flat* file may be defined either narrowly or more broadly. Strictly speaking, a flat file database should consist of nothing but data and delimiters. More broadly, the term refers to any database that exists in a single file in the form of rows and columns, with no relationships or links between records and

REAL WORLD CASE 1 Amazon, eBay, and Google: Unlocking and Sharing Business Databases

The meeting had dragged on for more than an hour that rainy day in Seattle, and Jeff Bezos had heard enough. The CEO had rounded up 15 or so senior engineers and managers in one of Amazon's offices to tackle a question buzzing inside the company: Should Amazon bust open the doors of its most prized data warehouse, containing its myriad databases, and let an eager world of entrepreneurs scavenge through its data jewels?

For several years, scores of outsiders had been knocking on Amazon's door to gain access to the underlying data that powers the $7 billion retailer: product descriptions, prices, sales rankings, customer reviews, inventory figures, and countless other layers of content. In all, it was a data vault that Amazon had spent more than 10 years and a billion dollars to build, organize, and safeguard.

So why on earth would Bezos suddenly hand over the keys? Because in the hands of top Web innovators, some at the meeting argued, Amazon's data could be the dynamo of new Web sites and businesses that would expand the company's already gigantic online footprint and ultimately drive more sales. Others worried about the risks. A free-for-all, one manager warned, would "change our business in ways we don't understand."

Bezos ended the debate with characteristic gusto. He leaped from his seat, aping a flasher opening a trench coat. "We're going to aggressively expose ourselves!" he declared.

Today, there's considerable reason to cheer Bezos's exhibitionist move. Since the company opened up its data vaults in 2002, under the auspices of a project first called Amazon Web Services, more than 65,000 developers, businesses, and other entrepreneurs have tapped into the data. With it, they're building moneymaking Web sites, new online shopping interfaces, and innovative services for thousands of Amazon's independent sellers. Many have become Bezos's most ambitious business partners overnight. "Two years ago this was an experiment," says Amazon's engineering chief, Al Vermeulen. "Now it's a core part of our strategy."

FIGURE 5.1

Amazon and eBay have opened up many of their databases to developers and entrepreneurs to broaden and facilitate the buying and selling process for their associates and customers.

And that's just at Amazon. A year after Bezos's decision to open Amazon's databases to developers and business partners, eBay chief executive Meg Whitman answered a similar cry from eBay's developer community, opening the $3 billion company's database of 33 million weekly auction items to the technorati. Some 15,000 developers and others have since registered to use that prized database and access other software features. Already, 41 percent of eBay's listings are uploaded to the site using software that takes advantage of these newly accessible resources.

At Google too, the concept is finding its legs: The company parcels out some of its search-results data and recently unlocked access to its desktop and paid-search products. Now dozens of Google-driven services are cropping up, from custom Web browsers to graphical search engines. Compared with Amazon and eBay however, Google is taking baby steps. Developers can grab 1,000 search results a day for free, but anything more than that requires special permission. In January 2005, Google finally opened up its AdWords paid-search service to outside applications, allowing marketers to automate their Google ad campaigns.

What's behind the open-door policies? True to their pioneering roots, Bezos, Whitman, and the Google boys are pushing their companies into what they believe is the Web's great new beyond: an era in which online businesses operate as open-ended software platforms that can accommodate thousands of other businesses selling symbiotic products and services. Says longtime tech-book publisher Tim O'Reilly, "We can finally rip, mix, and burn each other's Web sites."

Most people think of Amazon as the world's largest retailer, or "earth's biggest bookstore," as Bezos called it in its start-up days. Inside the company, those perceptions are decidedly old school. "We are at heart a technology company," Vermeulen says. He and Bezos have begun to view Amazon as simply a big piece of software available over the Web. "Amazon.com is just another application on the platform," Vermeulen asserts.

Eric von Hippel, a business professor at MIT's Sloan School of Management, explains the old rules: "We come from a culture where if you invested in it, you kept it. That was your competitive advantage." The rise of open-source software certainly challenged that notion. The rise of open databases and Web services goes even further, holding out the promise of automating the links between online businesses by applications that depend on companies sharing their vital data.

As Vermeulen says, "Those that succeed have to think about removing walls instead of putting them up." For Amazon, there's some evidence to support that logic. Of the 65,000 people and companies that have signed up to use Amazon's free goodies, about one-third have been tinkering with software tools that help Amazon's 800,000 or so active sellers.

One of the most clever is ScoutPal, a service that turns cell phones into mobile bar-code scanners. "It's like a Geiger counter for books," founder Dave Anderson says. He came up with the idea a couple of years ago when his wife, Barbara, who sells books on Amazon, would lug home 50 pounds of titles from garage sales, only to discover that she'd paid too much for many of them to make any money. Anderson wrote an application that works in tandem with an attachable bar-code scanner. Barbara either scans in books' bar codes or punches in their 10-digit ID numbers. Then she can pull down the latest Amazon prices for the books and calculate her likely profit margin before she pays for the inventory. Anderson says his wife's sales have since tripled to about $100,000 a year, and her profit margins have jumped from 50 to 85 percent. And he's now bringing in six figures too: ScoutPal has more than 1,000 subscribers, each paying $10 a month.

Other tools are also gaining traction. Software programs like SellerEngine help merchants on the main site upload their inventory, check prices, and automate interactions such as adding new listings. Meanwhile, software from Associates Shop.com lets thousands of other Web site operators—there are more than 900,000 of these so-called Amazon associates—create customized storefronts that link back to Amazon, generating new sales for Bezos and commission revenue for the associates.

For the near term, maybe the biggest benefit to Amazon of letting folks like Anderson tinker with its platform is that it gets experimental R&D for free. "We can try to build all the applications for sellers ourselves," Vermeulen says, "or we can build a platform and let others build them." Adds Bezos, "Right now we just want to get people to use the guts of Amazon in ways that surprise us."

The experimentation at eBay has been just as ambitious. The company says that more than 1,000 new applications have emerged from its 15,000 or so registered developers. As with Amazon, the most popular are apps that help sellers automate the process of listing items on eBay or displaying them on other sites. Many of these outfits, such as ChannelAdvisor (itself a multimillion-dollar business), Marketworks, and Vendio, offer auction-listing software or services to eBay sellers. Jeff McManus, eBay's chief of platform evangelism, marvels at the benefits. "Sellers who use our APIs [application programming interfaces] become at least 50 percent more productive than those who use the Web site itself."

The data links also let companies create storefronts filled with their inventory while making transactions over eBay's network. One example is Las Vegas–based SuperPawn, which runs a chain of 46 pawnshops in Arizona, California, Nevada, Texas, and Washington. The company (recently acquired by the larger pawnshop operator Cash America International) uses eBay's APIs to automatically upload the latest pawned items from its physical stores to eBay. The system already generates more than 5 percent of SuperPawn's $40 million in annual sales and thousands more transactions for eBay.

Source: Erik Schonfeld, "The Great Giveaway," *Business 2.0*, April 2005, pp. 81–86.

CASE STUDY QUESTIONS

1. What are the business benefits to Amazon and eBay of opening up some of their databases to developers and entrepreneurs? Do you agree with this strategy? Why or why not?
2. What business factors are causing Google to move slowly in opening up its databases? Do you agree with its go-slow strategy? Why or why not?
3. Should other companies follow Amazon's and eBay's lead and open up some of their databases to developers and others? Defend your position with examples of the risks and benefits to an actual company.

REAL WORLD ACTIVITIES

1. The concept of opening up a company's product, inventory, and other databases to developers and entrepreneurs is a relatively new one. Use the Internet to find examples of companies that have adopted this strategy and the benefits they claim for doing so.
2. Opening up selective databases to outsiders is not a risk-free strategy for a company. What risks are involved? What safeguards should be put in place to guard against loss or misuse of a company's data? Break into small groups with your classmates to discuss and take a stand on these issues.

FIGURE 5.2 Examples of the logical data elements in information systems. Note especially the examples of how data fields, records, files, and databases relate.

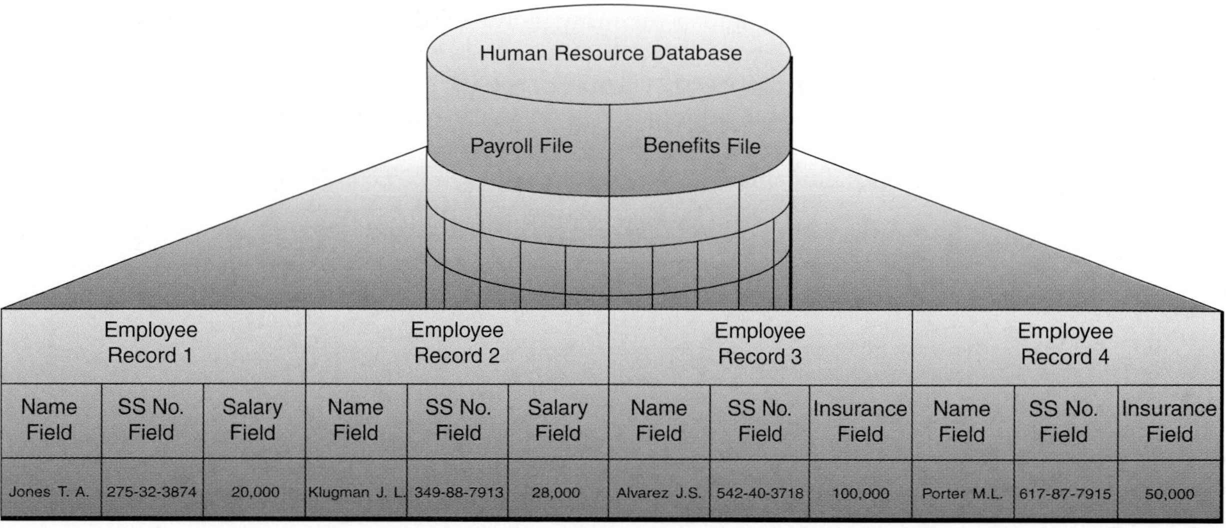

fields except the table structure. Regardless of the name used, any grouping of related records in tabular, or row and column, form is called a file. Thus, an employee file would contain the records of the employees of a firm. Files are frequently classified by the application for which they are primarily used, such as a *payroll file* or an *inventory file*, or the type of data they contain, such as a *document file* or a *graphical image* file. Files are also classified by their permanence, for example, a payroll *master file* versus a payroll weekly *transaction file*. A transaction file, therefore, would contain records of all transactions occurring during a period and might be used periodically to update the permanent records contained in a master file. A *history file* is an obsolete transaction or master file retained for backup purposes or for long-term historical storage called *archival storage*.

Database

A **database** is an integrated collection of logically related data elements. A database consolidates records previously stored in separate files into a common pool of data elements that provides data for many applications. The data stored in a database are independent of the application programs using them and of the type of storage devices on which they are stored.

Thus, databases contain data elements describing entities and relationships among entities. For example, Figure 5.3 outlines some of the entities and relationships in a

FIGURE 5.3
Some of the entities and relationships in a simplified electric utility database. Note a few of the business applications that access the data in the database.

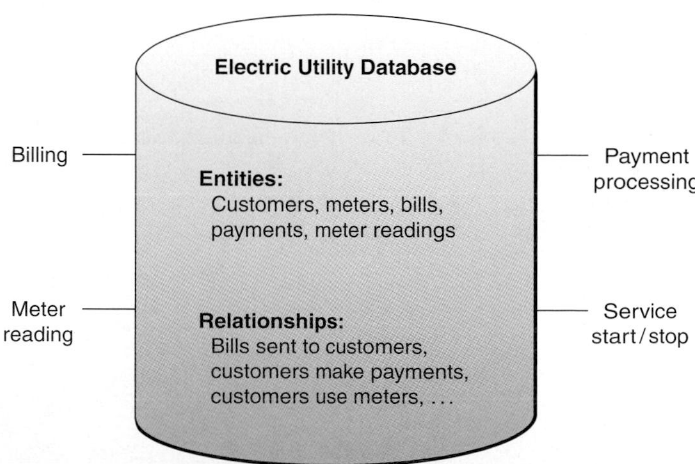

Source: Adapted from Michael V. Mannino, *Database Application Development and Design* (Burr Ridge, IL: McGraw-Hill/Irwin, 2001), p. 6.

database for an electric utility. Also shown are some of the business applications (billing, payment processing) that depend on access to the data elements in the database.

Database Structures

The relationships among the many individual data elements stored in databases are based on one of several logical data structures, or models. Database management system (DBMS) packages are designed to use a specific data structure to provide end users with quick, easy access to information stored in databases. Five fundamental **database structures** are the *hierarchical*, *network*, *relational*, *object-oriented*, and *multidimensional* models. Simplified illustrations of the first three database structures are shown in Figure 5.4.

Hierarchical Structure

Early mainframe DBMS packages used the **hierarchical structure**, in which the relationships between records form a hierarchy or treelike structure. In the traditional hierarchical model, all records are dependent and arranged in multilevel structures, consisting

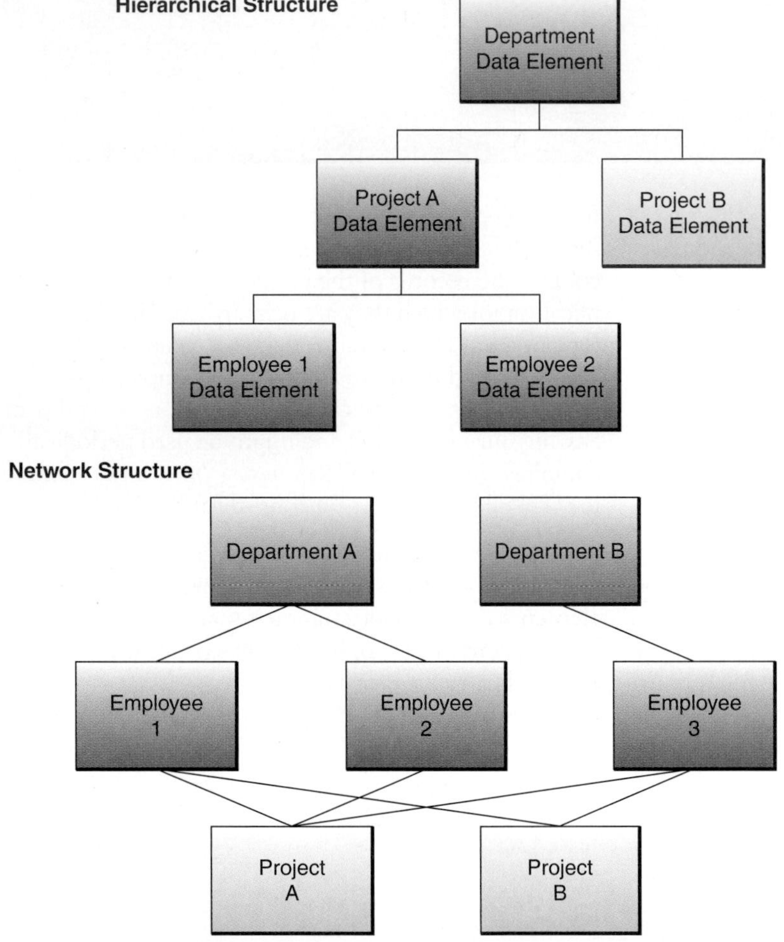

Department Table

Deptno	Dname	Dloc	Dmgr
Dept A			
Dept B			
Dept C			

Employee Table

Empno	Ename	Etitle	Esalary	Deptno
Emp 1				Dept A
Emp 2				Dept A
Emp 3				Dept B
Emp 4				Dept B
Emp 5				Dept C
Emp 6				Dept B

Source: Adapted from Michael V. Mannino, *Database Application Development and Design* (Burr Ridge, IL: McGraw-Hill/Irwin, 2001), p. 6.

FIGURE 5.4
Example of three fundamental database structures. They represent three basic ways to develop and express the relationships among the data elements in a database.

of one *root* record and any number of subordinate levels. Thus, all of the relationships among records are *one-to-many,* because each data element is related to only one element above it. The data element or record at the highest level of the hierarchy (the department data element in this illustration) is called the root element. Any data element can be accessed by moving progressively downward from a root and along the branches of the tree until the desired record (e.g., the employee data element) is located.

Network Structure

The **network structure** can represent more complex logical relationships and is still used by some mainframe DBMS packages. It allows *many-to-many* relationships among records; that is, the network model can access a data element by following one of several paths, because any data element or record can be related to any number of other data elements. For example, in Figure 5.4, departmental records can be related to more than one employee record, and employee records can be related to more than one project record. Thus, you could locate all employee records for a particular department or all project records related to a particular employee.

It should be noted that neither the hierarchical nor the network data structures are commonly found in the modern organization. The next data structure we discuss, the relational data structure, is the most common of all and serves as the foundation for most modern databases in organizations.

Relational Structure

The **relational model** is the most widely used of the three database structures. It is used by most microcomputer DBMS packages, as well as by most midrange and mainframe systems. In the relational model, all data elements within the database are viewed as being stored in the form of simple two-dimensional **tables,** sometimes referred to as *relations.* The tables in a relational database are *flat files* that have rows and columns. Each row represents a single record in the file, and each column represents a field. The major difference between a flat file and a database is that a flat file can only have data attributes specified for one file. In contrast, a database can specify data attributes for multiple files simultaneously and can relate the various data elements in one file to those in one or more other files.

Figure 5.4 illustrates the relational database model with two tables representing some of the relationships among departmental and employee records. Other tables, or relations, for this organization's database might represent the data element relationships among projects, divisions, product lines, and so on. Database management system packages based on the relational model can link data elements from various tables to provide information to users. For example, a manager might want to retrieve and display an employee's name and salary from the employee table in Figure 5.4, as well as the name of the employee's department from the department table, by using their common department number field (Deptno) to link or join the two tables. See Figure 5.5. The relational model can relate data in any one file with data in another file if both files share a common data element or field. Because of this, information can be created by retrieving data from multiple files even if they are not all stored in the same physical location.

Relational Operations

Three basic operations can be performed on a relational database to create useful sets of data. The *select* operation is used to create a subset of records that meet a stated criterion. For example, a select operation might be used on an employee database to create a subset

Department Table

Deptno	Dname	Dloc	Dmgr
Dept A			
Dept B			
Dept C			

Employee Table

Empno	Ename	Etitle	Esalary	Deptno
Emp 1				Dept A
Emp 2				Dept A
Emp 3				Dept B
Emp 4				Dept B
Emp 5				Dept C
Emp 6				Dept B

FIGURE 5.5 Joining the employee and department tables in a relational database enables you to access data selectively in both tables at the same time.

of records that contain all employees who make more than $30,000 per year and who have been with the company more than three years. Another way to think of the select operation is that it temporarily creates a table whose rows have records that meet the selection criteria.

The *join* operation can be used to temporarily combine two or more tables so that a user can see relevant data in a form that looks like it is all in one big table. Using this operation, a user can ask for data to be retrieved from multiple files or databases without having to go to each one separately.

Finally, the *project* operation is used to create a subset of the columns contained in the temporary tables created by the select and join operations. Just as the select operation creates a subset of records that meet stated criteria, the project operation creates a subset of the columns, or fields, that the user wants to see. Using a project operation, the user can decide not to view all of the columns in the table but instead only those that have the data necessary to answer a particular question or construct a specific report.

Because of the widespread use of relational models, an abundance of commercial products exists to create and manage them. Leading mainframe relational database applications include Oracle 10g from Oracle Corp. and DB2 from IBM. A very popular midrange database application is SQL server from Microsoft. The most commonly used database application for the PC is Microsoft Access.

Multidimensional Structure

The **multidimensional model** is a variation of the relational model that uses multidimensional structures to organize data and express the relationships between data. You can visualize multidimensional structures as cubes of data and cubes within cubes of data. Each side of the cube is considered a dimension of the data. Figure 5.6 is an

FIGURE 5.6 An example of the different dimensions of a multidimensional database.

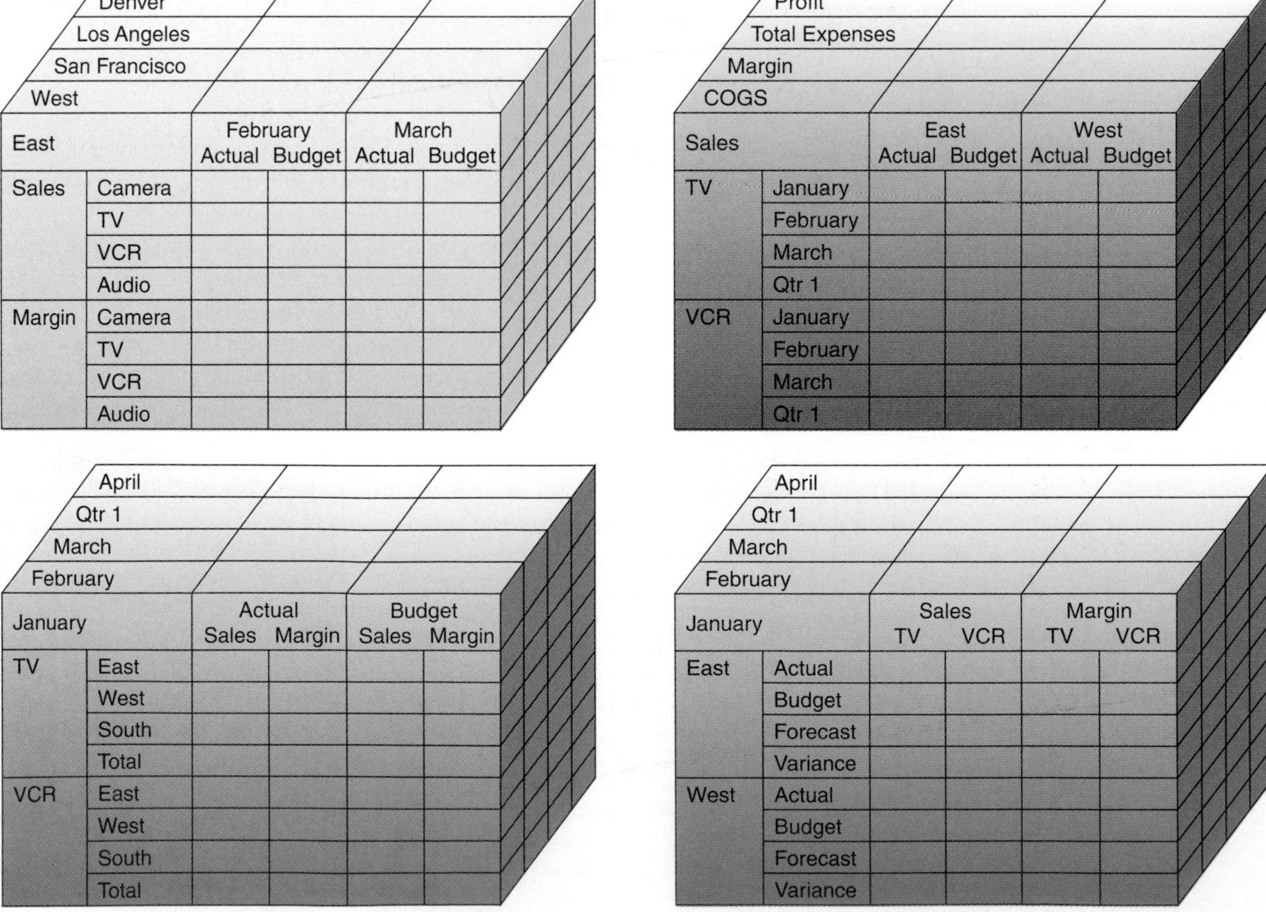

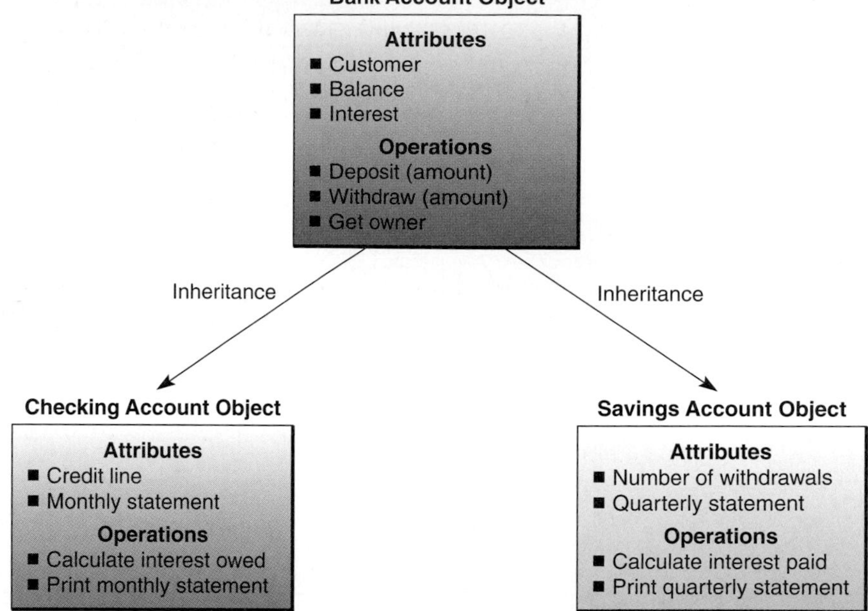

FIGURE 5.7
The checking and savings account objects can inherit common attributes and operations from the bank account object.

Source: Adapted from Ivar Jacobsen, Maria Ericsson, and Ageneta Jacobsen, *The Object Advantage: Business Process Reengineering with Object Technology* (New York: ACM Press, 1995), p. 65. Copyright © 1995, Association for Computing Machinery. Used by permission.

example that shows that each dimension can represent a different category, such as product type, region, sales channel, and time [5].

Each cell within a multidimensional structure contains aggregated data related to elements along each of its dimensions. For example, a single cell may contain the total sales for a product in a region for a specific sales channel in a single month. A major benefit of multidimensional databases is that they provide a compact and easy-to-understand way to visualize and manipulate data elements that have many interrelationships. So multidimensional databases have become the most popular database structure for the analytical databases that support *online analytical processing* (OLAP) applications, in which fast answers to complex business queries are expected. We discuss OLAP applications in Chapter 9.

Object-Oriented Structure

The **object-oriented model** is considered one of the key technologies of a new generation of multimedia Web-based applications. As Figure 5.7 illustrates, an **object** consists of data values describing the attributes of an entity, plus the operations that can be performed upon the data. This *encapsulation* capability allows the object-oriented model to handle complex types of data (graphics, pictures, voice, text) more easily than other database structures.

The object-oriented model also supports *inheritance;* that is, new objects can be automatically created by replicating some or all of the characteristics of one or more *parent* objects. Thus, in Figure 5.7, the checking and savings account objects can both inherit the common attributes and operations of the parent bank account object. Such capabilities have made *object-oriented database management systems* (OODBMS) popular in computer-aided design (CAD) and a growing number of applications. For example, object technology allows designers to develop product designs, store them as objects in an object-oriented database, and replicate and modify them to create new product designs. In addition, multimedia Web-based applications for the Internet and corporate intranets and extranets have become a major application area for object technology.

Object technology proponents argue that an object-oriented DBMS can work with *complex data types* such as document and graphic images, video clips, audio segments, and other subsets of Web pages much more efficiently than relational database

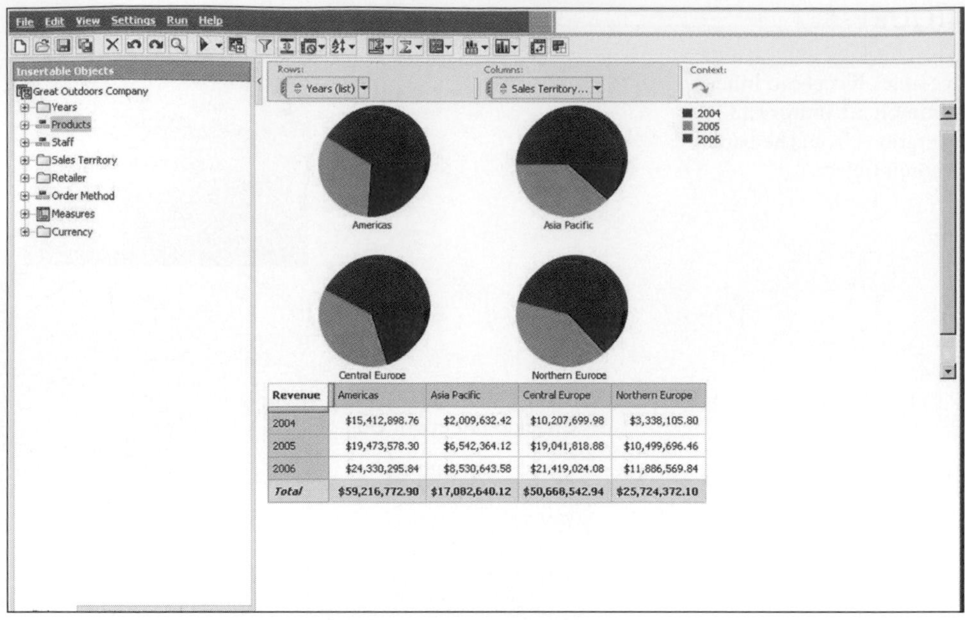

Revenue	Americas	Asia Pacific	Central Europe	Northern Europe
2004	$15,412,898.76	$2,009,632.42	$10,207,699.98	$3,338,105.80
2005	$19,473,578.30	$6,542,364.12	$19,041,818.88	$10,499,696.46
2006	$24,330,295.84	$8,530,643.58	$21,419,024.08	$11,886,569.84
Total	$59,216,772.90	$17,082,640.12	$50,668,542.94	$25,724,372.10

FIGURE 5.8
Databases can supply data to a wide variety of analysis packages allowing for data to be displayed in graphical form.

management systems. However, major relational DBMS vendors have countered by adding object-oriented modules to their relational software. Examples include multimedia object extensions to IBM's DB2 and Oracle's object-based "cartridges" for Oracle 10g. See Figure 5.8.

Evaluation of Database Structures

The hierarchical data structure was a natural model for the databases used for the structured, routine types of transaction processing characteristic of many business operations in the early years of data processing and computing. Data for these operations can easily be represented by groups of records in a hierarchical relationship. However, as time progressed, there were many cases in which information was needed about records that did not have hierarchical relationships. For example, in some organizations, employees from more than one department can work on more than one project (refer back to Figure 5.4). A network data structure could easily handle this many-to-many relationship, whereas a hierarchical model could not. As such, the more flexible network structure became popular for these types of business operations. However, like the hierarchical structure, because its relationships must be specified in advance, the network model was unable to handle ad hoc requests for information easily, which pointed to the need for the relational model.

Relational databases enable an end user to receive information easily in response to ad hoc requests. That's because not all of the relationships among the data elements in a relationally organized database need to be specified when the database is created. Database management software (such as Oracle 10g, DB2, Access, and Approach) creates new tables of data relationships by using parts of the data from several tables. Thus, relational databases are easier for programmers to work with and easier to maintain than the hierarchical and network models.

The major limitation of the relational model is that relational database management systems cannot process large amounts of business transactions as quickly and efficiently as those based on the hierarchical and network models or process complex, high-volume applications as well as the object-oriented model. This performance gap has narrowed with the development of advanced relational database software with object-oriented extensions. The use of database management software based on the object-oriented and multidimensional models is growing steadily, as these technologies are playing a greater role for OLAP and Web-based applications.

Experian Automotive: The Business Value of Relational Database Management

Experian Inc. (www.experian.com), a unit of London-based GUS PLC, runs one of the largest credit reporting agencies in the United States. But Experian wanted to expand its business beyond credit checks for automobile loans. If it could collect vehicle data from the various motor-vehicle departments in the United States and blend that with other data, such as change-of-address records, then its Experian Automotive division could sell the enhanced data to a variety of customers. For example, car dealers could use the data to make sure their inventory matches local buying preferences. And toll collectors could match license plates to addresses to find motorists who sail past tollbooths without paying.

But to offer new services, Experian first needed a way to extract, transfer, and load data from the systems of 50 different U.S. state departments of motor vehicles (DMVs), plus Puerto Rico, into a single database. That was a big challenge. "Unlike the credit industry that writes to a common format, the DMVs do not," explains Ken Kauppila, vice president of IT at Experian Automotive in Costa Mesa, California.

Of course, Experian didn't want to replicate the hodgepodge of file formats it inherited when the project began in January 1999—175 formats among 18,000 files. So Kauppila decided to transform and map the data to a common relational database format.

Fortunately, off-the-shelf software tools for extracting, transforming, and loading data (called ETL tools) make it economical to combine very large data repositories. Using ETL Extract from Evolutionary Technologies, Experian created a database that can incorporate vehicle information within 48 hours of its entry into any of the nation's DMV computers. This sector is one of the areas in which data management software tools can excel, says Guy Creese, an analyst at Aberdeen Group in Boston. "It can simplify the mechanics of multiple data feeds, and it can add to data quality, making fixes possible before errors are propagated to data warehouses," he notes.

Using the ETL extraction and transformation tools along with IBM's DB2 database system, Experian Automotive created a database that processes 175 million transactions per month and has created a variety of profitable new revenue streams. Experian's automotive database is the 10th largest database in the world—now, with up to 16 billion rows of data. But the company says the relational database is managed by just three IT professionals. Experian says it demonstrates how efficiently database software like DB2 and the ETL tools can work with a large database to handle vast amounts of data quickly.

Database Development

Database management packages like Microsoft Access or Lotus Approach allow end users to develop the databases they need easily. See Figure 5.9. However, large organizations usually place control of enterprisewide database development in the hands of **database administrators** (DBAs) and other database specialists. This delegation improves the integrity and security of organizational databases. Database developers use the *data definition language* (DDL) in database management systems like Oracle 10g or IBM's DB2 to develop and specify the data contents, relationships, and structure of each database, as well as to modify these database specifications when necessary. Such information is cataloged and stored in a database of data definitions and specifications called a *data dictionary*, or *metadata repository*, which is managed by the database management software and maintained by the DBA.

A **data dictionary** is a database management catalog or directory containing **metadata**, that is, data about data. A data dictionary relies on a specialized database software component to manage a database of data definitions, that is, metadata about the structure, data elements, and other characteristics of an organization's databases. For example, it contains the names and descriptions of all types of data records and their interrelationships, as well as information outlining requirements for end users' access and use of application programs, as well as database maintenance and security.

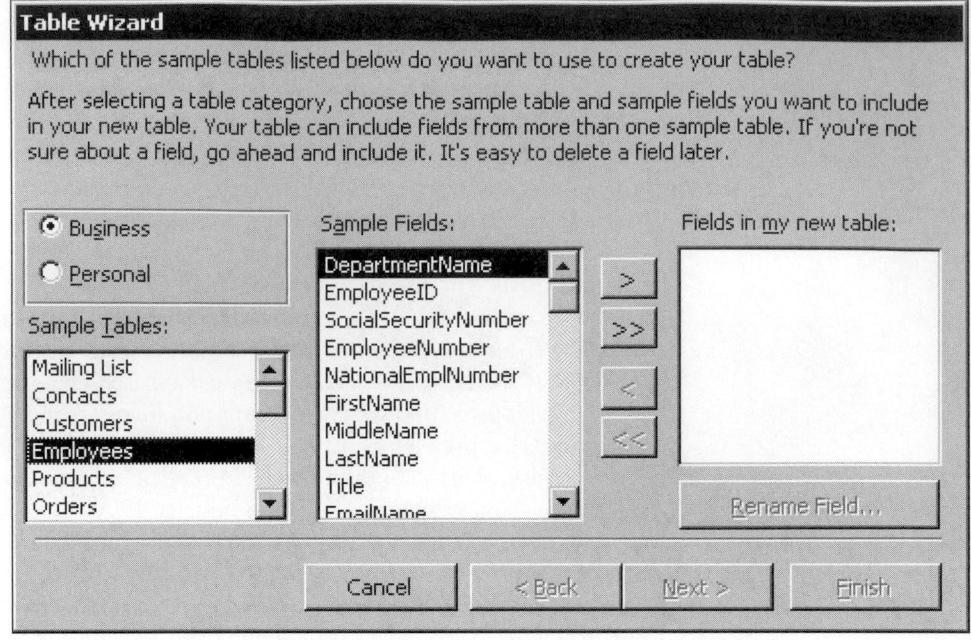

FIGURE 5.9
Creating a database table using the Table Wizard of Microsoft Access.

Data dictionaries can be queried by the database administrator to report the status of any aspect of a firm's metadata. The administrator can then make changes to the definitions of selected data elements. Some *active* (versus *passive*) data dictionaries automatically enforce standard data element definitions whenever end users and application programs access an organization's databases. For example, an active data dictionary would not allow a data entry program to use a nonstandard definition of a customer record, nor would it allow an employee to enter a name of a customer that exceeded the defined size of that data element.

Developing a large database of complex data types can be a complicated task. Database administrators and database design analysts work with end users and systems analysts to model business processes and the data they require. Then they determine (1) what data definitions should be included in the database and (2) what structures or relationships should exist among the data elements.

Data Planning and Database Design

As Figure 5.10 illustrates, database development may start with a top-down **data planning process**. Database administrators and designers work with corporate and end-user management to develop an *enterprise model* that defines the basic business process of the enterprise. They then define the information needs of end users in a business process, such as the purchasing/receiving process that all businesses have.

Next, end users must identify the key data elements that are needed to perform their specific business activities. This step frequently involves developing *entity relationship diagrams* (ERDs) that model the relationships among the many entities involved in business processes. For example, Figure 5.11 illustrates some of the relationships in a purchasing/receiving process. The ERDs are simply graphical models of the various files and their relationships, contained within a database system. End users and database designers could use database management or business modeling software to help them develop ERD models for the purchasing/receiving process, which would help identify what supplier and product data are required to automate their purchasing/receiving and other business processes using enterprise resource management (ERM) or supply chain management (SCM) software. You will learn about ERDs and other data modeling tools in much greater detail if you ever take a course in systems analysis and design.

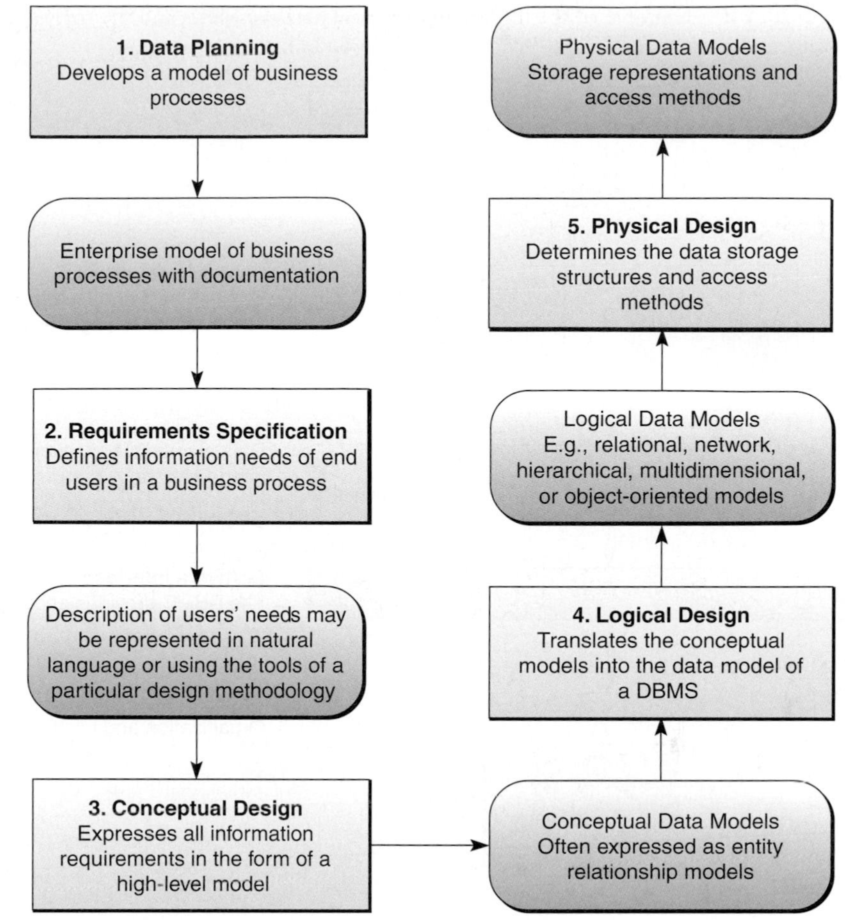

FIGURE 5.10
Database development involves data planning and database design activities. Data models that support business processes are used to develop databases that meet the information needs of users.

Such user views are a major part of a **data modeling** process, during which the relationships among data elements are identified. Each data model defines the logical relationships among the data elements needed to support a basic business process. For example, can a supplier provide more than one type of product to us? Can a customer have more than one type of account with us? Can an employee have several pay rates or be assigned to several project workgroups?

Answering such questions will identify data relationships that must be represented in a data model that supports business processes of an organization. These data models then serve as *logical design* frameworks (called *schema* and *subschema*). These frameworks determine the *physical design* of databases and the development of application programs to support the business processes of the organization. A schema is an overall logical

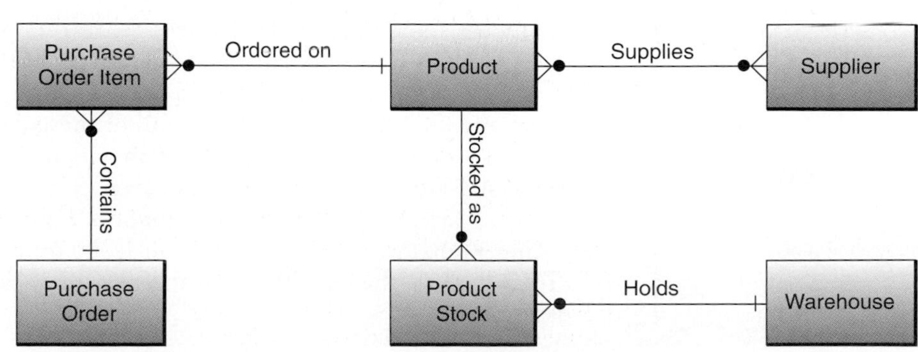

FIGURE 5.11
This entity relationship diagram illustrates some of the relationships among the entities (product, supplier, warehouse, etc.) in a purchasing/receiving business process.

FIGURE 5.12 Example of the logical and physical database views and the software interface of a banking services information system.

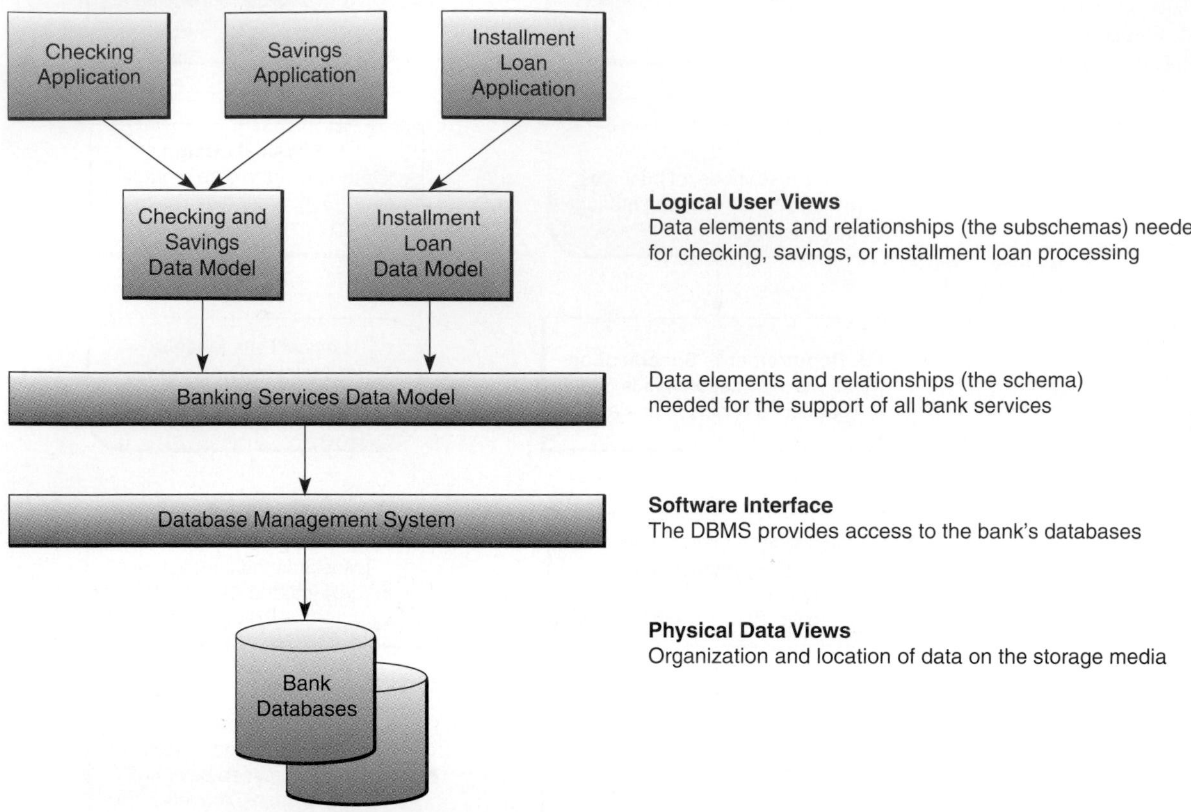

view of the relationships among the data elements in a database, whereas the subschema is a logical view of the data relationships needed to support specific end-user application programs that will access that database.

Remember that data models represent logical views of the data and relationships of the database. Physical database design takes a physical view of the data (also called the *internal view*) that describes how data are to be physically stored and accessed on the storage devices of a computer system. For example, Figure 5.12 illustrates these different database views and the software interface of a bank database processing system. In this example, checking, savings, and installment lending are the business processes whose data models are part of a banking services data model that serves as a logical data framework for all bank services.

Aetna: Insuring Tons of Data

On a daily basis, the operational services central support area at Aetna Inc. is responsible for 21.8 tons of data (174.6 terabytes [TB]). Over 119.2TB reside on mainframe-connected disk drives, while the remaining 55.4TB sit on disks attached to midrange computers. Almost all of these data are located in the company's headquarters in Hartford, Connecticut—with most of the information in relational databases. To make matters even more interesting, outside customers have access to about 20TB of the information. Four interconnected data centers containing 14 mainframes and more than 1,000 midrange servers process the data. It takes more than 4,100 direct-access storage devices to hold Aetna's key databases.

Most of Aetna's ever-growing mountain of data is health care information. The insurance company maintains records for both health maintenance organization participants and customers covered by insurance policies. Aetna has detailed records of providers, such as doctors, hospitals, dentists, and pharmacies, and it keeps track of all the claims it has processed. Some of Aetna's larger customers send tapes containing insured employee data; the firm is moving toward using the Internet to collect such data.

If managing gigabytes of data is like flying a hang glider, managing multiple terabytes of data is like piloting a space shuttle: a thousand times more complex. You can't just extrapolate from experiences with small and medium data stores to understand how to manage tons of data successfully. Even an otherwise mundane operation such as backing up a database can be daunting if the time needed to finish copying the data exceeds the time available.

Data integrity, backup, security, and availability are collectively the Holy Grail of dealing with large data stores. The sheer volume of data makes these goals a challenge, and a highly decentralized environment complicates matters even more. Developing and adhering to standardized data maintenance procedures always provide an organization with the best return on its data dollar investments [9, 11].

SECTION II Managing Data Resources

Data Resource Management

Data are a vital organizational resource that need to be managed like other important business assets. Today's business enterprises cannot survive or succeed without quality data about their internal operations and external environment.

> *With each online mouse click, either a fresh bit of data is created or already-stored data are retrieved from all those business Web sites. All that's on top of the heavy demand for industrial-strength data storage already in use by scores of big corporations. What's driving the growth is a crushing imperative for corporations to analyze every bit of information they can extract from their huge data warehouses for competitive advantage. That has turned the data storage and management function into a key strategic role of the information age* [8].

That's why organizations and their managers need to practice **data resource management**, a managerial activity that applies information systems technologies like *database management*, *data warehousing*, and other data management tools to the task of managing an organization's data resources to meet the information needs of their business stakeholders. This section will show you the managerial implications of using data resource management technologies and methods to manage an organization's data assets to meet business information requirements.

Read the Real World Case on data administration. We can learn a lot from this case about the challenges of managing the data within an organization. See Figure 5.13.

Types of Databases

Continuing developments in information technology and its business applications have resulted in the evolution of several major **types of databases**. Figure 5.14 illustrates several major conceptual categories of databases that may be found in many organizations. Let's take a brief look at some of them now.

Operational Databases

Operational databases store detailed data needed to support the business processes and operations of a company. They are also called *subject area databases* (SADB), *transaction databases*, and *production databases*. Examples are a customer database, human resource database, inventory database, and other databases containing data generated by business operations. For example, a human resource database like that shown in Figure 5.2 would include data identifying each employee and his or her time worked, compensation, benefits, performance appraisals, training and development status, and other related human resource data. Figure 5.15 illustrates some of the common operational databases that can be created and managed for a small business using Microsoft Access database management software.

Distributed Databases

Many organizations replicate and distribute copies or parts of databases to network servers at a variety of sites. These **distributed databases** can reside on network servers on the World Wide Web, on corporate intranets or extranets, or on other company networks. Distributed databases may be copies of operational or analytical databases, hypermedia or discussion databases, or any other type of database. Replication and distribution of databases improve database performance at end-user worksites. Ensuring that the data in an organization's distributed databases are consistently and concurrently updated is a major challenge of distributed database management.

Distributed databases have both advantages and disadvantages. One primary advantage of a distributed database lies with the protection of valuable data. If all of an organization's data reside in a single physical location, any catastrophic event like a fire or damage to the media holding the data would result in an equally catastrophic loss of use of that data. By having databases distributed in multiple locations, the negative impact of such an event can be minimized.

REAL WORLD CASE 2 Emerson and Sanofi: Data Stewards Seek Data Conformity

A customer is a customer is a customer, right? Actually, it's not that simple. Just ask Emerson Process Management, an Emerson Electric Co. unit in Austin that supplies process automation products. In 2000, the company attempted to build a data warehouse to store customer information from over 85 countries. The effort failed in large part because the structure of the warehouse couldn't accommodate the many variations on customers' names.

For instance, different users in different parts of the world might identify Exxon as Exxon, Mobil, Esso, or ExxonMobil, to name a few variations. The warehouse would see them as separate customers, and that would lead to inaccurate results when business users performed queries.

That's when the company hired Nancy Rybeck as a data administrator. Rybeck is now leading a renewed data warehouse project that ensures not only the standardization of customer names but also the quality and accuracy of customer data, including postal addresses, shipping addresses, and province codes.

To accomplish this task, Emerson has done something unusual: It has started to build a department with 6–10 full-time "data stewards" dedicated to establishing and maintaining the quality of data entered into the operational systems that feed the data warehouse.

The practice of having formal data stewards is uncommon. Most companies recognize the importance of data quality, but many treat it as a "find-and-fix" effort, to be conducted at the end of a project by someone in IT. Others casually assign the job to the business users who deal with the data head-on. Still others may throw resources at improving data only when a major problem occurs.

FIGURE 5.13

Modern organizations realize that managing their data resources with the same care they manage their many other valuable assets is a critical success factor in today's marketplace.

"It's usually a seesaw effect," says Chris Enger, formerly manager of information management at Philip Morris USA Inc. "When something goes wrong, they put someone in charge of data quality, and when things get better, they pull those resources away."

Creating a data quality team requires gathering people with an unusual mix of business, technology, and diplomatic skills. It's even difficult to agree on a job title. In Rybeck's department, they're called "data analysts," but titles at other companies include "data quality control supervisor," "data coordinator," or "data quality manager."

"When you say you want a data analyst, they'll come back with a DBA [database administrator]. But it's not the same at all," Rybeck says. "It's not the data structure, it's the content."

At Emerson, data analysts in each business unit review data and correct errors before the data are put into the operational systems. They also research customer relationships, locations, and corporate hierarchies; train overseas workers to fix data in their native languages; and serve as the main contact with the data administrator and database architect for new requirements and bug fixes.

As the leader of the group, Rybeck plays a role that includes establishing and communicating data standards, ensuring data integrity is maintained during database conversions, and doing the logical design for the data warehouse tables.

The stewards have their work cut out for them. Bringing together customer records from the 75 business units yielded a 75 percent duplication rate, misspellings, and fields with incorrect or missing data.

"Most of the divisions would have sworn they had great processes and standards in place," Rybeck claims. "But when you show them they entered the customer name 17 different ways, or someone had entered, 'Loading dock open 8:00–4:00' into the address field, they realize it's not as clean as they thought."

Although the data steward may report to IT—as is the case at Emerson and at the pharmaceuticals company Sanofi-Synthelabo Inc.—it's not a job for someone steeped in technical knowledge. Yet it's not right for a businessperson who's a technophobe, either.

Seth Cohen is the first data quality control supervisor at Sanofi in New York. He was hired in 2003 to help design automated processes to ensure the data quality of the customer knowledge base that Sanofi was beginning to build.

Data stewards at Sanofi need to have business knowledge because they need to make frequent judgment calls, according to Cohen. Indeed, judgment is a big part of the data steward's job—including the ability to determine when you don't need 100 percent perfection.

Cohen says that task is one of the biggest challenges of the job. "One-hundred percent accuracy is just not achievable," he argues. "Some things you're just going to have to let go or you'd have a data warehouse with only 15 to 20 records."

A good example occurs when Sanofi purchases data about doctors that includes their birth dates, Cohen says. If a birth date is given as February 31 or the number of the month is listed as 13 but the rest of the data are good, do you throw out all of the data or just figure the birth date isn't all that important?

It comes down to knowing how much it costs to fix the data versus the payback. "You can pay millions of dollars a year to get it perfect, but if the returns are in the hundreds of thousands, is it worth it?" asks Chuck Kelley, senior advisory consultant at Navigator Systems Inc., a corporate performance management consultancy in Addison, Texas.

Data stewards also need to be politically astute, diplomatic, and good at conflict resolution—in part because the environment isn't always friendly. When Cohen joined Sanofi, some questioned why he was there. In particular, IT didn't see why he was "causing them so many headaches and adding several extra steps to the process."

There are many political traps as well. Take the issue of defining "customer address." If data come from a variety of sources, you're likely to get different types of coding schemes, some of which overlap.

People may also argue about how data should be produced, Cohen says. Should field representatives enter it from their laptops? Or should it first be independently checked for quality? Should it be uploaded hourly or weekly?

Most of all, data stewards need to understand that data quality is a journey, not a destination. "It's not a one-shot deal—it's ongoing," Rybeck of Emerson says. "You can't quit after the first task."

Source: Adapted from Mary Brandel, "Data Stewards Seek Data Conformity," *Computerworld*, March 15, 2004.

CASE STUDY QUESTIONS

1. Why is the role of a data steward considered to be innovative? Explain.
2. What are the business benefits associated with the data steward program at Emerson?
3. How does effective data resource management contribute to the strategic goals of an organization? Provide examples from Emerson and others.

REAL WORLD ACTIVITIES

1. As discussed in the case, the role of data steward is relatively new, and its creation is motivated by the desire to protect the valuable data assets of the firm. There are many job descriptions in the modern organization associated with the strategic management of data resources. Using the Internet, see if you can find evidence of other job roles that are focused on the management of an organization's data. How might a person train for these new jobs?
2. As more and more data are collected, stored, processed, and disseminated by organizations, new and innovative ways to manage them must be developed. Break into small groups with your classmates, and discuss how the data resource management methods of today will need to evolve as more types of data emerge. Will we ever get to the point where we can manage our data in a completely automated manner?

FIGURE 5.14 Examples of some of the major types of databases used by organizations and end users.

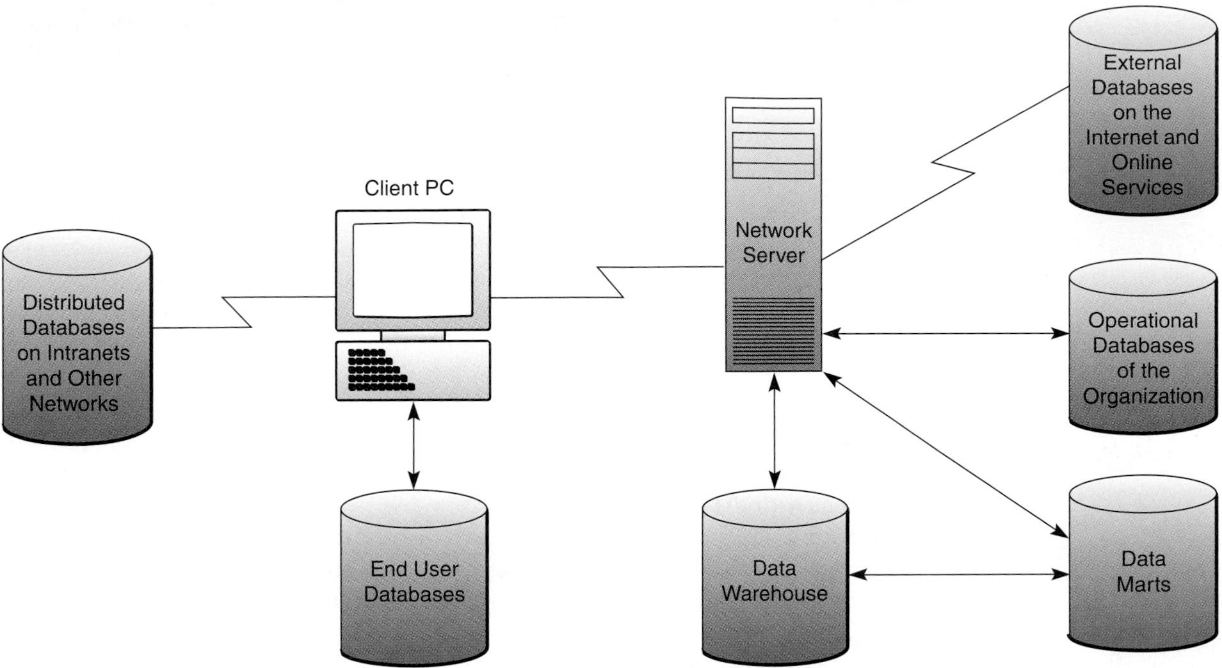

Another advantage of distributed databases is found in their storage requirements. Often, a large database system may be distributed into smaller databases based on some logical relationship between the data and the location. For example, a company with several branch operations may distribute its data so that each branch operation location is also the location of its branch database. Because multiple databases in a distributed system can be joined together, each location has control of its local data while all other locations can access any database in the company if so desired.

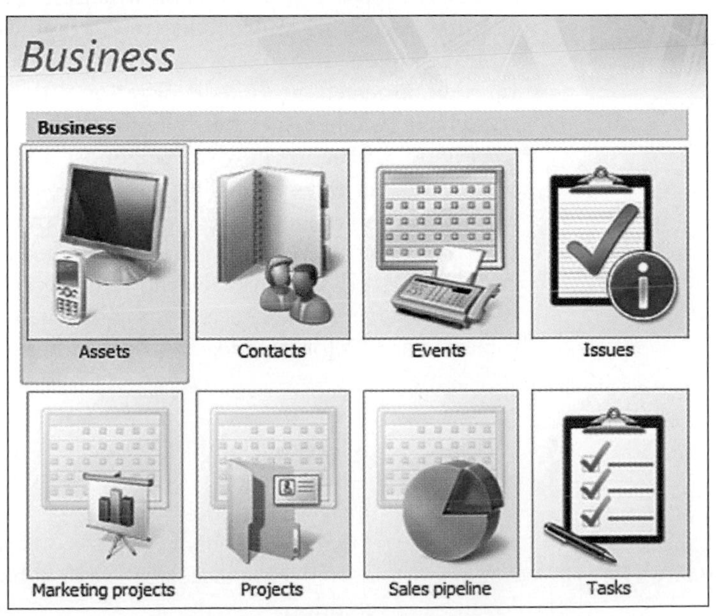

FIGURE 5.15 Examples of operational databases that can be created and managed for a small business by microcomputer database management software like Microsoft Access.

Distributed databases are not without some challenges, however. The primary challenge is the maintenance of data accuracy. If a company distributes its database to multiple locations, any change to the data in one location must somehow be updated in all other locations. This updating can be accomplished in one of two ways: *replication* or *duplication*.

Updating a distributed database using **replication** involves using a specialized software application that looks at each distributed database and then finds the changes made to it. Once these changes have been identified, the replication process makes all of the distributed databases look the same by making the appropriate changes to each one. The replication process is very complex and, depending on the number and size of the distributed databases, can consume a lot of time and computer resources.

The **duplication** process, in contrast, is much less complicated. It basically identifies one database as a master and then duplicates that database at a prescribed time after hours so that each distributed location has the same data. One drawback to the duplication process is that no changes can ever be made to any database other than the master to avoid having local changes overwritten during the duplication process. Nonetheless, properly used, duplication and replication can keep all distributed locations current with the latest data.

One additional challenge associated with distributed databases is the extra computing power and bandwidth necessary to access multiple databases in multiple locations. We will look more closely at the issue of bandwidth in Chapter 6 when we focus on telecommunications and networks.

External Databases

Access to a wealth of information from **external databases** is available for a fee from commercial online services and with or without charge from many sources on the World Wide Web. Web sites provide an endless variety of hyperlinked pages of multimedia documents in *hypermedia databases* for you to access. Data are available in the form of statistics on economic and demographic activity from *statistical* databanks. Or you can view or download abstracts or complete copies of hundreds of newspapers, magazines, newsletters, research papers, and other published material and other periodicals from *bibliographic* and *full-text* databases. Whenever you use a search engine like Google or Yahoo to look up something on the Internet, you are using an external database—a very, very large one!

Hypermedia Databases

The rapid growth of Web sites on the Internet and corporate intranets and extranets has dramatically increased the use of databases of hypertext and hypermedia documents. A Web site stores such information in a **hypermedia database** consisting of hyperlinked pages of multimedia (text, graphic, and photographic images, video clips, audio segments, and so on). That is, from a database management point of view, the set of interconnected multimedia pages on a Web site is a database of interrelated hypermedia page elements, rather than interrelated data records [2].

Figure 5.16 shows how you might use a Web browser on your client PC to connect with a Web network server. This server runs Web server software to access and transfer the Web pages you request. The Web site illustrated in Figure 5.16 uses a hypermedia database consisting of Web page content described by HTML (Hypertext Markup Language) code or XML (Extensible Markup Language) labels, image files, video files, and audio. The Web server software acts as a database management system to manage the transfer of hypermedia files for downloading by the multimedia plug-ins of your Web browser.

Land's End, Inc.: Data Warehouse Improves Inventory Analysis and Sales

At Lands' End Inc., the clothing, luggage, and home-products retailer, the number of sales lost because products were unavailable was on the rise in 2001. Whereas service and other facets of the business are important, inventory availability "is really the one that drives satisfaction for our customers," according to CIO Frank Giannantonio. Reducing lost sales not only boosts revenue, it improves customer loyalty and retention.

FIGURE 5.16 The components of a Web-based information system include Web browsers, servers, and hypermedia databases.

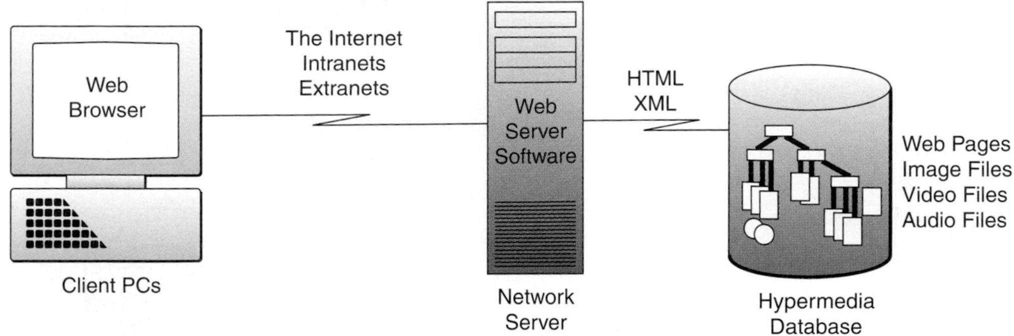

To remedy the problem, Lands' End built an inventory-management workbench, a business-intelligence and alerting system that helps inventory planners analyze and monitor the company's available stock. The system, which reduced Lands' End's lost sales by a third during the first holiday season in use, was the winner of the Data Warehousing Institute's award for best advanced-analytics system.

The inventory-management workbench—built on Business Objects SA's Application Foundation analytic engine and deployed using that vendor's WebIntelligence infrastructure—constantly monitors order-fill rates, back orders, and lost sales. Inventory managers use the system for online reporting and analysis, but it also automatically alerts them when popular items, such as white turtleneck shirts, need to be resupplied. "That's a very proactive use of business intelligence," Giannantonio says.

The data warehouse holds seven years of customer-order, shipping, and financial information, drawing data from the company's sales, order-fulfillment, inventory, and direct-marketing systems. It also has a link to a massive customer data warehouse operated by Sears, Roebuck & Co., which acquired Lands' End in 2002.

The data warehouse's effectiveness lies in its ability to combine information from different operations, such as inventory data from warehouse management and inventory turn-rate data from customer sales, for detailed analysis. It even contains regional weather information to help analysts understand why, say, raincoat sales spiked in May in the Northeast. Altogether, about 600 Lands' End employees directly access the data warehouse.

With the success of the inventory workbench, Lands' End also has built business-intelligence workbenches for business-to-business sales and to handle analytical chores such as labor scheduling for its warehouse operations. A business-intelligence workbench for sales and service is being assembled, and one for merchandising is planned. The former will provide analysis of metrics such as service levels and call-abandonment rates [12].

Data Warehouses and Data Mining

A **data warehouse** stores data that have been extracted from the various operational, external, and other databases of an organization. It is a central source of the data that have been cleaned, transformed, and cataloged so they can be used by managers and other business professionals for data mining, online analytical processing, and other forms of business analysis, market research, and decision support. (We'll talk in-depth about all of these activities in Chapter 9.) Data warehouses may be subdivided into **data marts,** which hold subsets of data from the warehouse that focus on specific aspects of a company, such as a department or a business process.

Figure 5.17 illustrates the components of a complete data warehouse system. Notice how data from various operational and external databases are captured, cleaned, and transformed into data that can be better used for analysis. This acquisition process

FIGURE 5.17 The components of a complete data warehouse system.

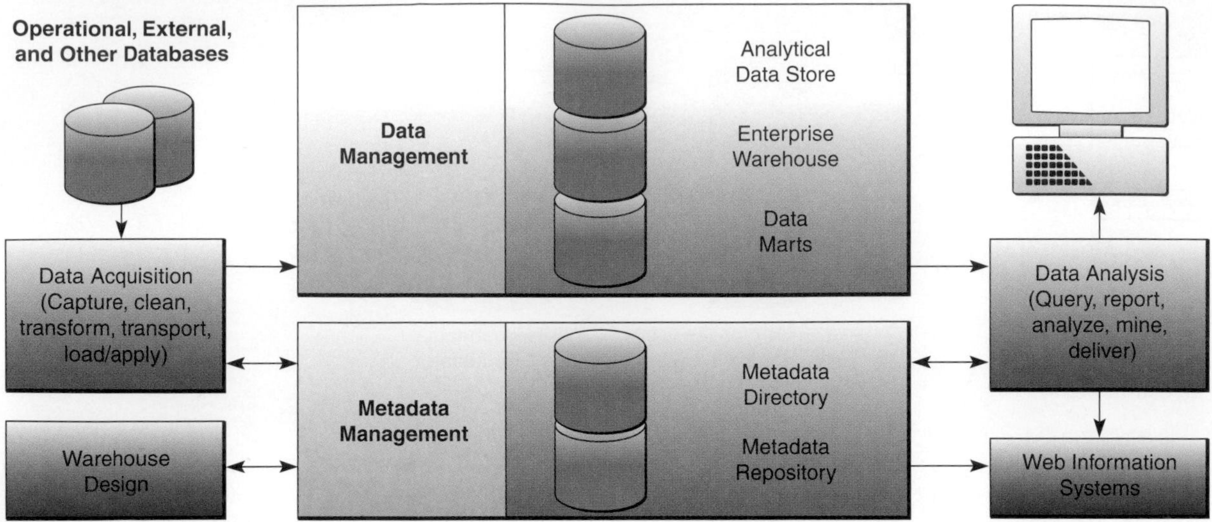

Source: Adapted, courtesy of Hewlett-Packard.

might include activities like consolidating data from several sources, filtering out unwanted data, correcting incorrect data, converting data to new data elements, or aggregating data into new data subsets.

These data are then stored in the enterprise data warehouse, from which they can be moved into data marts or to an *analytical data store* that holds data in a more useful form for certain types of analysis. *Metadata* (data that define the data in the data warehouse) are stored in a metadata repository and cataloged by a metadata directory. Finally, a variety of analytical software tools can be provided to query, report, mine, and analyze the data for delivery via Internet and intranet Web systems to business end users. See Figure 5.18.

One important characteristic about the data in a data warehouse is that, unlike a typical database in which changes can occur constantly, data in a data warehouse are *static*, which means that once the data are gathered up, formatted for storage, and stored in the data warehouse, they will never change. This restriction is so that queries can be made on the data to look for complex patterns or historical trends that might otherwise go unnoticed with dynamic data that change constantly as a result of new transactions and updates.

Data Mining

Data mining is a major use of data warehouse databases and the static data they contain. In data mining, the data in a data warehouse are analyzed to reveal hidden patterns and trends in historical business activity. This analysis can be used to help managers make decisions about strategic changes in business operations to gain competitive advantages in the marketplace [2]. See Figure 5.19.

Data mining can discover new correlations, patterns, and trends in vast amounts of business data (frequently several terabytes of data) stored in data warehouses. Data mining software uses advanced pattern recognition algorithms as well as a variety of mathematical and statistical techniques to sift through mountains of data to extract previously unknown strategic business information. For example, many companies use data mining to:

- Perform "market-basket analysis" to identify new product bundles.
- Find root causes of quality or manufacturing problems.
- Prevent customer attrition and acquire new customers.
- Cross-sell to existing customers.
- Profile customers with more accuracy [6].

FIGURE 5.18
A data warehouse and its data mart subsets hold data that have been extracted from various operational databases for business analysis, market research, decision support, and data mining applications.

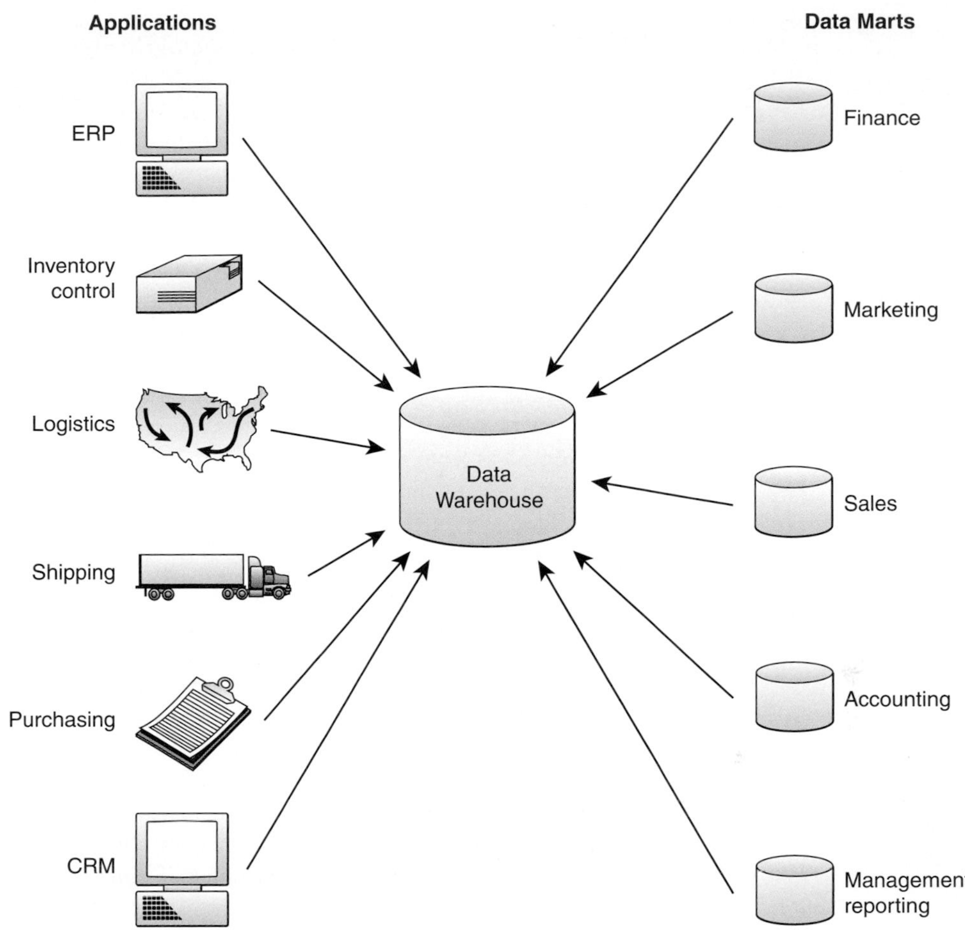

We will discuss data mining further, as well as online analytical processing (OLAP) and other technologies that analyze the data in databases and data warehouses to provide vital support for business decisions, in Chapter 9. In the meantime, let's look at a real-world example.

Bank of America: Benefits of Data Mining

In the world of banking, bigger is not always better. Bank of America (BofA) knows this all too well. A string of some 60 mergers since the mid-1980s has made BofA the nation's largest bank, servicing 27 million households with approximately 4,400 domestic offices, 13,000 ATMs, and 30 international offices in more than 150 countries. And it provides online banking access to 4 million active users.

As BofA grew, however, so did its problems with managing data across the enterprise. During its growth phase, the bank acquired at least 30 disparate,

FIGURE 5.19 How data mining extracts business knowledge from a data warehouse.

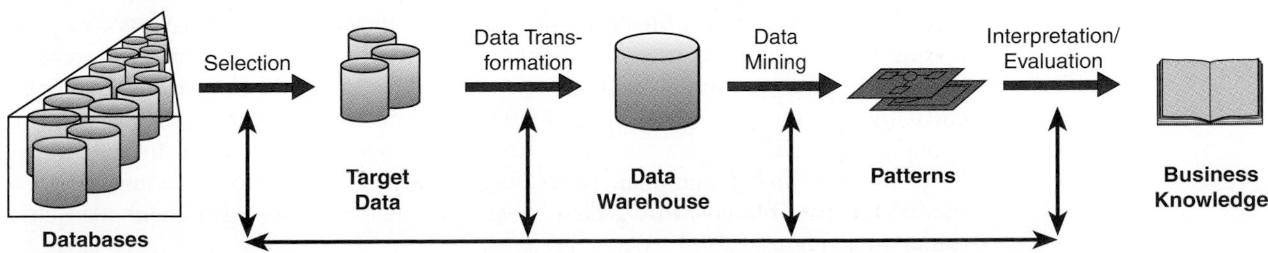

nonintegrated customer databases. One of them, a data warehouse acquired through Bank of America's merger with NationsBank in 1998, was operating completely autonomously with no integration with any other BofA system. The challenge was made greater by the fact that each data warehouse was operating in a nonstandard environment. Resources were being squandered on storing and maintaining duplicate data across these repositories.

In 2001, Bank of America decided to solve the problems by developing a central data capture and storage point. Through a single enterprise data model and standards, the bank could achieve the consistent, timely, and accurate data it was lacking across its franchise. The goal was to create a "single version of the truth" with a single source of data.

Reaching the goal of being smaller and better provided hefty operational savings. Since transitioning to a single data warehouse platform, BofA has dropped its operating costs from $11 million to $4 million per year. The savings came primarily through its new economies of scale and the elimination of duplicate technology and support staff.

Bank of America didn't stop there, though. Recently it added a business intelligence access capability to achieve greater accuracy in marketing and pricing financial products, such as home equity loans. Once BofA had all its data in one spot, it could mine those data to explore new relationships and learn more about its customers and markets.

To use the data mining function, data extracted from the data warehouse are analyzed by data mining software to discover hidden patterns. For example, data mining discovered that a certain set of customers was 15 times more likely to purchase a high-margin lending product. The bank also wanted to determine the sequence of events leading to purchasing. It fed the parameters to the data mining software and built a model for finding other customers. This model proved to be so accurate that it discovered people already in the process of applying and being approved for the lending product. Using this profile, a final list of quality prospects for solicitation was prepared. The resulting direct marketing response rates dramatically exceeded past results [1, 11].

Traditional File Processing

How would you feel if you were an executive of a company and were told that some information you wanted about your employees was too difficult and too costly to obtain? Suppose the vice president of information services gave you the following reasons:

- The information you want is in several different files, each organized in a different way.
- Each file has been organized to be used by a different application program, none of which produces the information you want in the form you need.
- No application program is available to help get the information you want from these files.

That's how end users can be frustrated when an organization relies on **file processing** systems in which data are organized, stored, and processed in independent files of data records. In the traditional file processing approach that was used in business data processing for many years, each business application was designed to use one or more specialized data files containing only specific types of data records. For example, a bank's checking account processing application was designed to access and update a data file containing specialized data records for the bank's checking account customers. Similarly, the bank's installment loan–processing application needed to access and update a specialized data file containing data records about the bank's installment loan customers. See Figure 5.20.

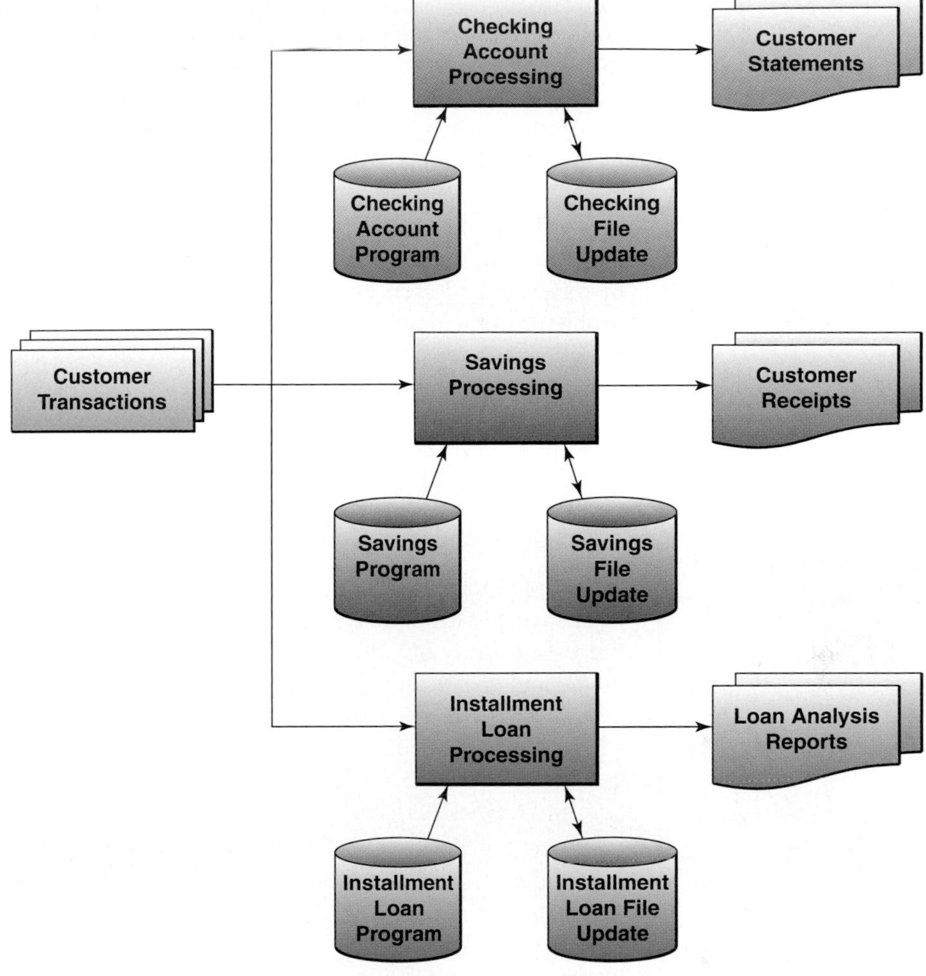

FIGURE 5.20
Examples of file processing systems in banking. Note the use of separate computer programs and independent data files in a file processing approach to the savings, installment loan, and checking account applications.

Problems of File Processing

The file processing approach finally became too cumbersome, costly, and inflexible to supply the information needed to manage modern business, and as we shall soon see, was replaced by the *database management approach*. Despite their apparent logic and simplicity, file processing systems had the following major problems:

Data Redundancy. Independent data files included a lot of duplicated data; the same data (such as a customer's name and address) were recorded and stored in several files. This **data redundancy** caused problems when data had to be updated. Separate *file maintenance* programs had to be developed and coordinated to ensure that each file was properly updated. Of course, this coordination proved difficult in practice, so a lot of inconsistency occurred among data stored in separate files.

Lack of Data Integration. Having data in independent files made it difficult to provide end users with information for ad hoc requests that required accessing data stored in several different files. Special computer programs had to be written to retrieve data from each independent file. This retrieval was so difficult, time-consuming, and costly for some organizations that it was impossible to provide end users or management with such information. End users had to manually extract the required information from the various reports produced by each separate application and prepare customized reports for management.

Data Dependence. In file processing systems, major components of a system—the organization of files, their physical locations on storage hardware, and the application software used to access those files—depended on one another in significant ways. For example, application programs typically contained references to the specific *format* of the data stored in the files they used. Thus, changes in the format and structure of data and records in a file required that changes be made to all of the programs that used that file. This *program maintenance* effort was a major burden of file processing systems. It proved difficult to do properly, and it resulted in a lot of inconsistency in the data files.

Lack of Data Integrity or Standardization. In file processing systems, it was easy for data elements such as stock numbers and customer addresses to be defined differently by different end users and applications. This divergence caused serious inconsistency problems in the development of programs to access such data. In addition, the *integrity* (i.e., the accuracy and completeness) of the data was suspect because there was no control over their use and maintenance by authorized end users. Thus, a lack of standards caused major problems in application program development and maintenance, as well as in the security and integrity of the data files needed by the organization.

Movies Go Digital with New Database

More than 100 years of motion pictures, TV broadcasts, and other images, now scattered in museums and collections around the globe, have never been cataloged in one worldwide database. That is changing however, as three U.S. universities and the U.S. Library of Congress have begun work on an online catalog of the world's movie and broadcasting treasures for researchers, historians, educators, and the public. The database will initially include information about the images, such as when they were made, who created them, and where they are kept, but some of the material also will be available for viewing online.

Jim DeRoest, assistant director of computing and communications at the University of Washington in Seattle, which is helping develop the database, says the project has long been a goal of researchers. Until now, the only catalogs of films and broadcast images have covered individual private collections or museums, which has hindered knowledge about what remains from the early days of the industry. "There are some large [collections], but there hasn't been this cross-genre type of catalog," DeRoest acknowledges.

Also participating in the project are Rutgers University Libraries in New Jersey and the Georgia Institute of Technology. A $900,000 National Science Foundation grant was commissioned by the Association of Moving Image Archivists in Hollywood through a grant from the National Film Preservation Board of the Library of Congress.

Barbara Humphrys, who works in the Library of Congress motion picture, broadcast, and recorded sound division, claims the database will make it easier for historians and researchers to find images and films. Upon its completion in early 2007, administrators can add links directly to the content so users can view images and movies, according to Humphrys. And users who find the listing of images they're seeking will be able to contact the collection owner to try to obtain viewing rights or more information.

In addition to motion pictures, TV broadcasts, and other images, the database will feature archives from the Smithsonian museums, including video from the Hubble Space Telescope and other notable or historical images.

The Library of Congress is not the only organization building digital film libraries. Lucasfilm Entertainment Co. Ltd. (the producers of *Star Wars*) has set plans in motion to create a single IT platform that provides worldwide access to all digital assets. The system will link information and art across all the company's divisions, from games to movies to animation.

Parts of the digital asset management, scheduling, budgeting, and tracking systems have been created for individual divisions. The task that remains is to take the pieces and build out a collaborative environment that centralizes digital media content for the company's offices from the United States to Singapore.

Responsible for leading the task, Lucasfilm director of information systems Lori Gianino says that many times these tools will allow "us to eliminate data entry by pulling information from other systems."

The digital asset management system will house live-action frames, stock footage, motion picture capture data, and metadata, as well as provide a production and workflow tracking system, to help artists and schedulers manage projects [4, 7].

The Database Management Approach

To solve the problems encountered with the file processing approach, the **database management approach** was conceived as the foundation of modern methods for managing organizational data. The database management approach consolidates data records, formerly held in separate files, into databases that can be accessed by many different application programs. In addition, a *database management system* (DBMS) serves as a software interface between users and databases, which helps users easily access the data in a database. Thus, database management involves the use of database management software to control how databases are created, interrogated, and maintained to provide information needed by end users.

For example, customer records and other common types of data are needed for several different applications in banking, such as check processing, automated teller systems, bank credit cards, savings accounts, and installment loan accounting. These data can be consolidated into a common *customer database*, rather than being kept in separate files for each of those applications. See Figure 5.21.

Database Management System

A **database management system** (DBMS) is the main software tool of the database management approach, because it controls the creation, maintenance, and use of the databases of an organization and its end users. As we saw in Figure 5.16, microcomputer database

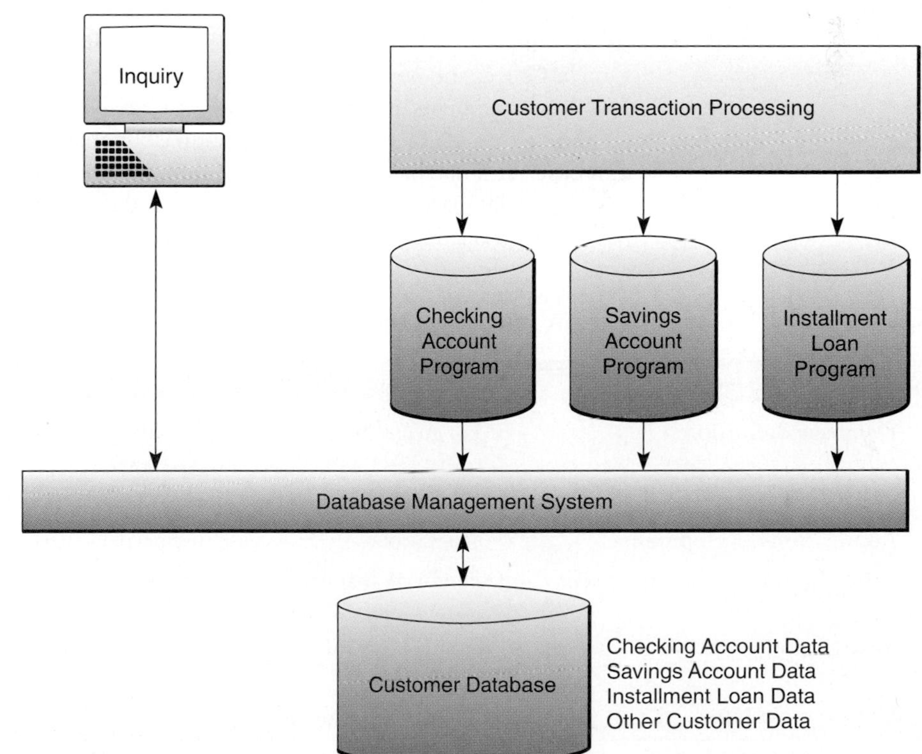

FIGURE 5.21
An example of a database management approach in a banking information system. Note how the savings, checking, and installment loan programs use a database management system to share a customer database. Note also that the DBMS allows a user to make direct, ad hoc interrogations of the database without using application programs.

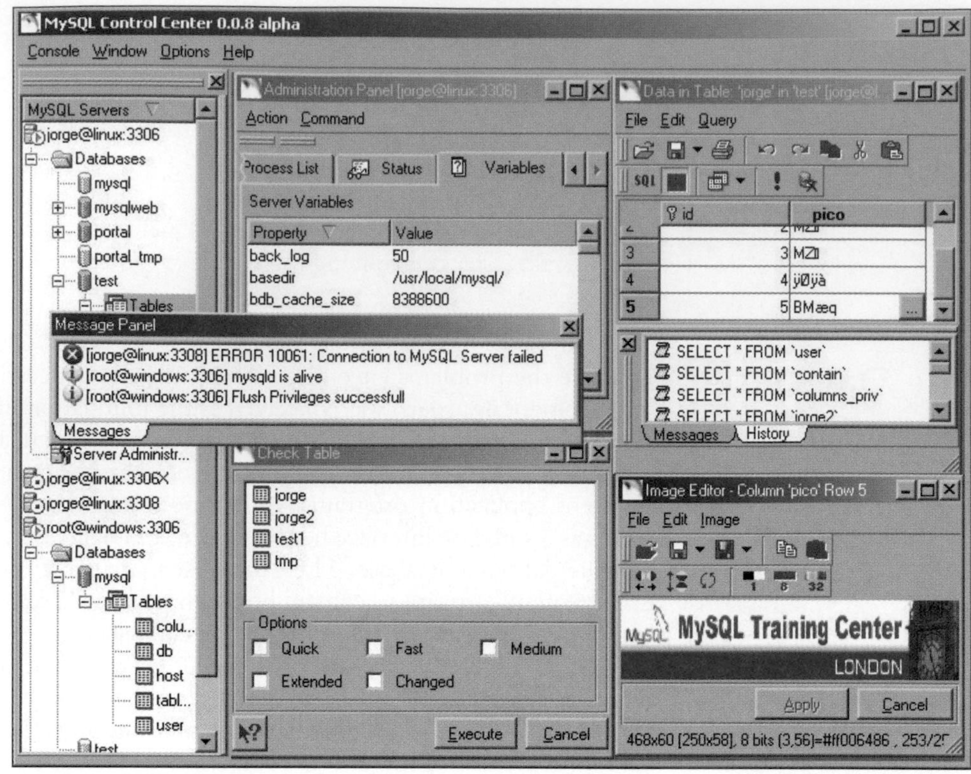

FIGURE 5.22 Database management software like MySQL, a popular open-source DBMS, supports the development, maintenance, and use of the databases of an organization.

management packages such as Microsoft Access, Lotus Approach, or Corel Paradox allow you to set up and manage databases on your PC, network server, or the World Wide Web. In mainframe and server computer systems, the database management system is an important system software package that controls the development, use, and maintenance of the databases of computer-using organizations. Examples of popular mainframe and server versions of DBMS software are IBM's DB2 Universal Database, Oracle 10g by Oracle Corp., and MySQL, a popular open-source DBMS. See Figure 5.22. Common DBMS components and functions are summarized in Figure 5.23.

The three major functions of a database management system are (1) to *create* new databases and database applications, (2) to *maintain* the quality of the data in an organization's databases, and (3) to *use* the databases of an organization to provide the information needed by its end users. See Figure 5.24.

FIGURE 5.23 Common software components and functions of a database management system.

Common DBMS Software Components	
• **Database definition**	Language and graphical tools to define entities, relationships, integrity constraints, and authorization rights.
• **Nonprocedural access**	Language and graphical tools to access data without complicated coding.
• **Application development**	Graphical tools to develop menus, data entry forms, and reports.
• **Procedural language interface**	Language that combines nonprocedural access with full capabilities of a programming language.
• **Transaction processing**	Control mechanisms to prevent interference from simultaneous users and recover lost data after a failure.
• **Database tuning**	Tools to monitor and improve database performance.

Source: Adapted from Michael V. Mannino, *Database Application Development and Design* (Burr Ridge, IL: McGraw-Hill/Irwin, 2001), p. 7.

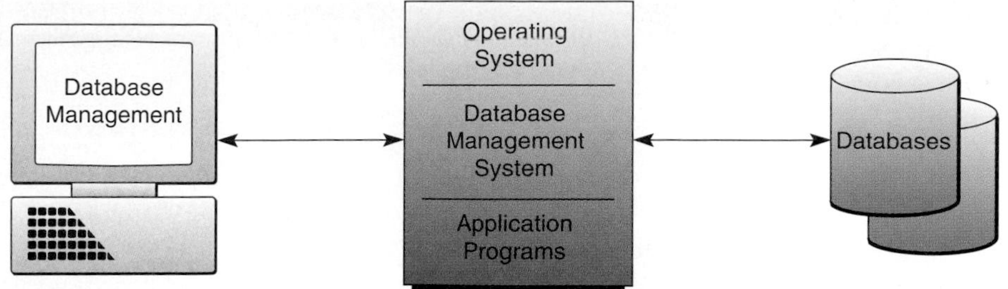

FIGURE 5.24
The three major uses of DBMS software are to create, maintain, and use the databases of an organization.

Database development involves defining and organizing the content, relationships, and structure of the data needed to build a database. **Database application development** involves using a DBMS to develop prototypes of queries, forms, reports, and Web pages for a proposed business application. **Database maintenance** involves using transaction processing systems and other tools to add, delete, update, and correct the data in a database. The primary use of a database by end users involves employing the *database interrogation* capabilities of a DBMS to access the data in a database to selectively retrieve and display information and produce reports, forms, and other documents.

Database Interrogation

A **database interrogation** capability is a major benefit of the database management approach. End users can use a DBMS by asking for information from a database using a *query* feature or a *report generator*. They can receive an immediate response in the form of video displays or printed reports. No difficult programming is required. The **query language** feature lets you easily obtain immediate responses to ad hoc data requests: You merely key in a few short inquiries—in some cases, using common sentence structures just like you would use to ask a question. The **report generator** feature allows you to specify a report format for information you want presented as a report. Figure 5.25 illustrates the use of a DBMS report generator.

SQL Queries. SQL (pronounced "see quill"), or **Structured Query Language**, is an international standard query language found in many DBMS packages. In most cases, SQL is the language structure used to "ask a question" that the DBMS will retrieve the data to answer. The basic form of a SQL query is:

SELECT . . . FROM . . . WHERE . . .

After SELECT, you list the data fields you want retrieved. After FROM, you list the files or tables from which the data must be retrieved. After WHERE, you specify

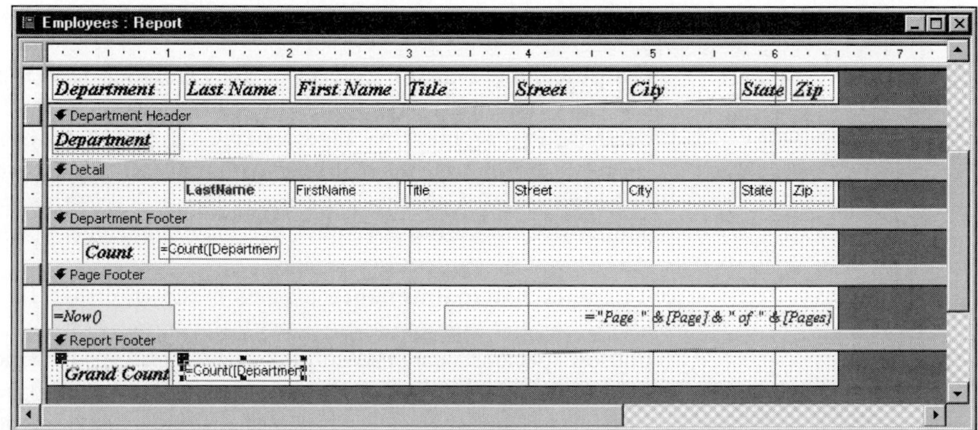

FIGURE 5.25
Using the report generator of Microsoft Access to create an employee report.

FIGURE 5.26
Comparing a natural language query with a SQL query.

A Sample Natural Language-to-SQL Translation for Microsoft Access

Natural Language

WHAT CUSTOMERS HAD NO ORDERS LAST MONTH?

SQL

```
SELECT [Customers].[Company Name],[Customers].[Contact Name]
FROM [Customers]
WHERE not Exists {SELECT [Ship Name] FROM [Orders]
  WHERE Month {[Order Date]}=l and Year {[Order Date]}=2004 and
  [Customers].[Customer ID]=[Orders].{[Customer ID]}
```

conditions that limit the search to only those data records in which you are interested. Figure 5.26 compares a SQL query to a natural language query for information on customer orders.

Boolean logic. To fully access the power of SQL, a database user needs to have a basic understanding of the concepts behind **Boolean logic**. Developed by George Boole in the mid-1800s, Boolean logic allows us to refine our searches for specific information such that only the desired information is obtained.

Boolean logic consists of three logical operators: (1) AND, (2) OR, and (3) NOT. Using these operators in conjunction with the syntax of a SQL query, a database user can refine a search to ensure only the desired data is retrieved. This same set of logical operators can be used to refine searches for information from the Internet (which is really nothing more than the world's largest database). Let's look at an example of how the three logical operators work.

Suppose we are interested in obtaining information about cats from the Internet. We could simply search on the word *cats*, and a large number of potentially useful Web sites would be retrieved. The problem is that in addition to the Web sites about cats, we would also retrieve Web sites about cats and dogs, pets in general (if the site includes the word *cats*), and probably even sites about the Broadway musical entitled *Cats*. To avoid having to sift through all the sites to find what we want, we could use Boolean logic to form a more refined query:

Cats OR felines AND NOT dogs OR Broadway

By using this search query, we would retrieve any Web site with the word *cats* or *felines* but exclude any site that also has the words *dogs* or *Broadway*. Using this approach, we would eliminate any reference to cats and dogs or to the Broadway musical entitled *Cats*. This query therefore would result in a more refined search and eliminate the need to look at Web sites that do not pertain to our specific interest.

Graphical and Natural Queries. Many end users (and IS professionals) have difficulty correctly phrasing SQL and other database language search queries. So, most end-user database management packages offer GUI (graphical user interface) point-and-click methods, which are easier to use and are translated by the software into SQL commands. See Figure 5.27. Other packages are available that use *natural language* query statements similar to conversational English (or other languages), as illustrated in Figure 5.26.

Database Maintenance

The **database maintenance** process is accomplished by *transaction processing systems* and other end user applications, with the support of the DBMS. End users and information specialists can also employ various utilities provided by a DBMS for database maintenance. The databases of an organization need to be updated continually to reflect new business transactions (e.g., sales made, products produced, inventory shipped) and other events. Other miscellaneous changes also must be made to update

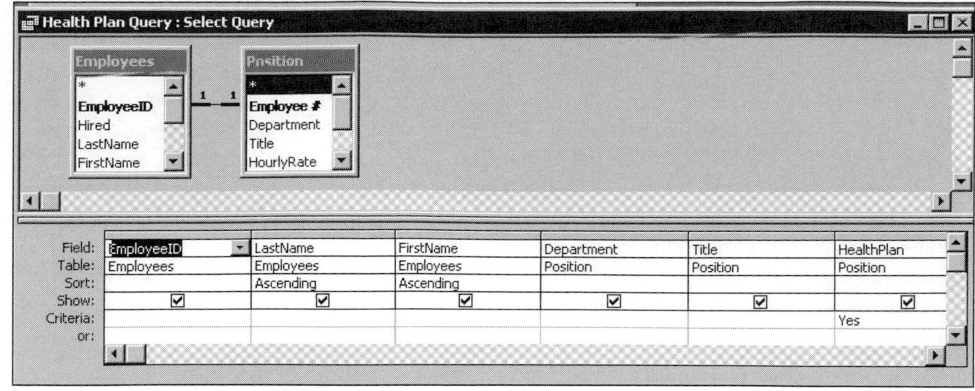

FIGURE 5.27
Using the Query Wizard of the Microsoft Access database management package to develop a query about employee health plan choices.

and correct data (e.g., customer or employee name and address changes) to ensure the accuracy of the data in the databases. We introduced transaction processing systems in Chapter 1 and will discuss them in more detail in Chapter 7.

Application Development

In addition, DBMS packages play a major role in **application development**. End users, systems analysts, and other application developers can use the internal 4GL programming language and built-in software development tools provided by many DBMS packages to develop custom application programs. For example, you can use a DBMS to develop the data entry screens, forms, reports, or Web pages of a business application that accesses a company database to find and update the data it needs. A DBMS also makes the job of application software developers easier, because they do not have to develop detailed data-handling procedures using conventional programming languages every time they write a program. Instead, they can include features such as *data manipulation language* (DML) statements in their software that call on the DBMS to perform necessary data-handling activities.

Summary

- **Data Resource Management.** Data resource management is a managerial activity that applies information technology and software tools to the task of managing an organization's data resources. Early attempts to manage data resources used a file processing approach in which data were organized and accessible only in specialized files of data records that were designed for processing by specific business application programs. This approach proved too cumbersome, costly, and inflexible to supply the information needed to manage modern business processes and organizations. Thus, the database management approach was developed to solve the problems of file processing systems.
- **Database Management.** The database management approach affects the storage and processing of data. The data needed by different applications are consolidated and integrated into several common databases instead of being stored in many independent data files. Also, the database management approach emphasizes updating and maintaining common databases, having users' application programs share the data in the database, and providing a reporting and an inquiry/response capability so end users can easily receive reports and quick responses to requests for information.
- **Database Software.** Database management systems are software packages that simplify the creation, use, and maintenance of databases. They provide software tools so end users, programmers, and database administrators can create and modify databases, interrogate a database, generate reports, do application development, and perform database maintenance.
- **Types of Databases.** Several types of databases are used by business organizations, including operational, distributed, and external databases. Data warehouses are a central source of data from other databases that have been cleaned, transformed, and cataloged for business analysis and decision support applications. That includes data mining, which attempts to find hidden patterns and trends in the warehouse data. Hypermedia databases on the World Wide Web and on corporate intranets and extranets store hyperlinked multimedia pages on a Web site. Web server software can manage such databases for quick access and maintenance of the Web database.

- **Data Access.** Data must be organized in some logical manner on physical storage devices so that they can be efficiently processed. For this reason, data are commonly organized into logical data elements such as characters, fields, records, files, and databases. Database structures, such as the hierarchical, network, relational, and object-oriented models, are used to organize the relationships among the data records stored in databases. Databases and files can be organized in either a sequential or direct manner and can be accessed and maintained by either sequential access or direct access processing methods.
- **Database Development.** The development of databases can be easily accomplished using microcomputer database management packages for small end-user applications. However, the development of large corporate databases requires a top-down data planning effort that may involve developing enterprise and entity relationship models, subject area databases, and data models that reflect the logical data elements and relationships needed to support the operation and management of the basic business processes of the organization.

Key Terms and Concepts

These are the key terms and concepts of this chapter. The page number of their first explanation is in parentheses.

1. Data dependence (177)
2. Data dictionary (163)
3. Data integration (177)
4. Data integrity (178)
5. Data mining (174)
6. Data modeling (165)
7. Data redundancy (177)
8. Data resource management (168)
9. Database administrator (DBA) (163)
10. Database interrogation (181)
11. Database management approach (179)
12. Database management system (DBMS) (179)
13. Database structures (158)
    - *a.* Hierarchical structure (158)
    - *b.* Multidimensional model (160)
    - *c.* Network structure (159)
    - *d.* Object-oriented model (161)
    - *e.* Relational model (159)
14. Duplication (172)
15. File processing (176)
16. Logical data elements (154)
    - *a.* Character (154)
    - *b.* Field (154)
    - *c.* Record (154)
    - *d.* File (154)
    - *e.* Database (157)
    - *f.* Attribute (154)
    - *g.* Entity (154)
17. Metadata (163)
18. Structured Query Language (SQL) (181)
19. Replication (172)
20. Types of databases (168)
    - *a.* Data warehouse (173)
    - *b.* Distributed (168)
    - *c.* External (172)
    - *d.* Hypermedia (172)
    - *e.* Operational (168)

Review Quiz

Match one of the key terms and concepts listed previously with one of the brief examples or definitions that follow. Try to find the best fit for answers that seem to fit more than one term or concept. Defend your choices.

____ 1. The use of integrated collections of data records and files for data storage and processing.

____ 2. A DBMS that allows you to create, interrogate, and maintain a database, create reports, and develop application programs.

____ 3. A specialist in charge of the databases of an organization.

____ 4. This DBMS feature allows users to interrogate a database easily.

____ 5. Defines and catalogs the data elements and data relationships in an organization's database.

____ 6. Helps specify and produce reports from a database.

____ 7. The main software package that supports a database management approach.

____ 8. Databases are dispersed to the Internet and corporate intranets and extranets.

____ 9. Databases that organize and store data as objects.

____ 10. Databases of hyperlinked multimedia documents on the Web.

____ 11. The management of all the data resources of an organization.

____ 12. Processing data in a data warehouse to discover key business factors and trends.

____ 13. Developing conceptual views of the relationships among data in a database.

____ 14. A customer's name.

____ 15. A customer's name, address, and account balance.

____ 16. The names, addresses, and account balances of all of your customers.

____ 17. An integrated collection of all of the data about your customers.

____ 18. Business application programs that use specialized data files.

____ 19. A treelike structure of records in a database.

____ 20. A tabular structure of records in a database.

____ 21. Records organized as cubes within cubes in a database.

____ 22. Databases that support the major business processes of an organization.

____ 23. A centralized and integrated database of current and historical data about an organization.

____ 24. Databases available on the Internet or provided by commercial information services.

Discussion Questions

1. How should a business store, access, and distribute data and information about its internal operations and external environment?
2. What role does database management play in managing data as a business resource?
3. What are the advantages of a database management approach to the file processing approach? Give examples to illustrate your answer.
4. Refer to the Real World Case on Amazon, eBay, and Google in the chapter. What does tech publisher Tim O'Reilly mean when he says, "We can finally rip, mix, and burn each other's Web sites." What are the business benefits and risks involved in this capability?
5. What is the role of a database management system in a business information system?
6. Databases of information about a firm's internal operations were formerly the only databases that were considered to be important to a business. What other kinds of databases are important for a business today?
7. Refer to the Real World Case on Emerson, Sanofi, and others in the chapter. What are the advantages to avoiding the find-it-and-fix-it approach to data resource management?
8. What are the benefits and limitations of the relational database model for business applications today?
9. Why is the object-oriented database model gaining acceptance for developing applications and managing the hypermedia databases on business Web sites?
10. How have the Internet, intranets, and extranets affected the types and uses of data resources available to business professionals? What other database trends are also affecting data resource management in business?

Analysis Exercises

Complete the following exercises as individual or group projects that apply chapter concepts to real-world businesses.

1. Joining Tables

You have the responsibility for managing technical training classes within your organization. These classes fall into two general types: highly technical training and end-user training. Software engineers sign up for the former, and administrative staff sign up for the latter. Your supervisor measures your effectiveness in part according to the average cost per training hour and type of training. In short, your supervisor expects the best training for the least cost.

To meet this need, you have negotiated an exclusive on-site training contract with Hands On Technology Transfer (HOTT), Inc. (www.traininghott.com), a high-quality technical training provider. Your negotiated rates are reproduced below in the pricing table. A separate table contains a sample list of courses you routinely make available for your organization.

a. Using these data, design and populate a table that includes basic training rate information. Designate the "Technical" field type as "Yes/No" (Boolean).

b. Using these data, design and populate a course table. Designate the CourseID field as a "Primary Key" and allow your database to automatically generate a value for this field. Designate the "Technical" field type as "Yes/No" (Boolean).

c. Prepare a query that lists each course name and its cost per day of training.

d. Prepare a query that lists the cost per student for each class. Assume maximum capacity and that you will schedule two half-day classes on the same day to take full advantage of HOTT's per-day pricing schedule.

Pricing Table

Technical	Price Per Day	Capacity
Yes	2680	15
No	2144	30

Course Table

Course ID	Course Name	Duration	Technical
1	ASP Programming	5	Yes
2	XML Programming	5	Yes
3	PHP Programming	4	Yes
4	Microsoft Word–Advanced	.5	No
5	Microsoft Excel–Advanced	.5	No
. . .			

2. **Training-Cost Management**
Having determined the cost per student for each of the classes in the previous problem, you now must carefully manage class registration. Because you pay the same flat rates no matter how many students attend (up to capacity), you want to do all you can to ensure maximum attendance. Your training provider, Hands On Technology Transfer, Inc., requires two weeks' notice in the event that you need to reschedule a class. You want to make sure your classes are at least two-thirds full before this deadline. You also want to make sure you send timely reminders to all attendees so they do not needlessly forget to show up. Use the database you created in Problem 1 to perform the following activities.
   a. Using the information provided in the sample below, add a course schedule table to your training database. Designate the ScheduleID field as a "Primary Key" and allow your database program to automatically generate a value for this field. Make the CourseID field a number field and the StartDate field a date field.
   b. Using the information provided in the sample below, add a class roster table to your training database. Make the ScheduleID field a number field. Make the Reminder and Confirmed fields both "Yes/No" (Boolean) fields.
   c. Because the Class Schedule table relates to the Course Table and the Course Table relates to the Pricing Table, why is it appropriate to record the Price Per Day information in the Class Schedule table too?
   d. What are the advantages and disadvantages of using the participant's name and e-mail address in the Class Roster table? What other database design might you use to record this information?
   e. Write a query that shows how many people have registered for each scheduled class. Include the class name, capacity, date, and count of attendees.

Class Schedule

Schedule ID	Course ID	Location	Start Date	Price Per Day
1	1	101-A	7/12/2004	2680
2	1	101-A	7/19/2004	2680
3	1	101-B	7/19/2004	2680
4	4	101-A&B	7/26/2004	2144
5	5	101-A&B	8/2/2004	2144
. . .				

Class Roster

Schedule ID	Participant	e-mail	Reminder	Confirmed
1	Linda Adams	adams.l@ . . .	Yes	Yes
1	Fatima Ahmad	ahmad.f@ . . .	Yes	No
1	Adam Alba	alba.a@ . . .	Yes	Yes
4	Denys Alyea	alyea.d@ . . .	No	No
4	Kathy Bara	bara.k@ . . .	Yes	No
. . .				

3. **Selling the Sawdust**
Selling Information By-products
Sawmill operators are in the business of turning trees into lumber. Products include boards, plywood, and veneer. For as long as there have been sawmills, there have been sawmill operators who have tried to solve the problem of what to do with their principal by-product: sawdust. Numerous creative examples abound. Likewise, businesses often generate tremendous amounts of data. The challenge then becomes what to do with this by-product. Can a little additional effort turn it into a valuable product? Research the following:
   a. What are your college's or university's policies regarding student directory data?
   b. Does your college or university sell any of its student data? If your institution sells student data, what data do they sell, to whom, and for how much?
   c. If your institution sells data, calculate the revenue earned per student. Would you be willing to pay this amount per year in exchange for maintaining your privacy?

4. **Data Formats and Manipulation**
Importing and Formatting Data into Excel
Ms. Sapper, a marketing manager in a global accounting firm, was this year's coordinator for her firm's annual partner meeting. With 400 partners from around the world, Sapper faced daunting communications tasks that she wanted to automate as much as possible. Sapper received a file containing all partners' names as well as additional, personal information from her IT department. The file ended with the extension "CSV." *Now what?* She wondered to herself.
   The CSV, or *comma separated values* format, is a very basic data format that most database applications use to import or export data. As a minimum, the CSV format groups all fields in a record into a single line of text. It then separates each field within a line with a comma or other delimiter. When the text information contains commas, the format requires this text information be placed within quotes. Sapper needed to get this data into Excel. Given how busy the IT guys appeared, she decided to do this herself.
   a. Download and save "partners.csv" from the MIS 8e OLC. Open the file using Microsoft Word. Remember to look for the "csv" file type when searching for the file to open. Describe the data's appearance.
   b. Import the "partner.csv" file into Excel. Remember to look for the "csv" file type when searching for the file to open. Does Excel automatically format the data correctly? Save your file as "partner.xls."
   c. Describe in your own words why you think database manufacturers use common formats to import and export data from their systems.

REAL WORLD CASE 3 Acxiom Corporation: Data Demand Respect

Acxiom Corp. has always been good at managing data. Lots of data. By its own estimate, Acxiom manages more than 20 billion customer and prospect records.

"We do three things really well," claims Alex Dietz, who is referred to internally as the "products and infrastructure technology leader" and functions as Acxiom's CIO. (Acxiom has no traditional titles.) Those three things, Dietz says, are managing large volumes of data; cleaning, transforming, and enhancing those data; and distilling business intelligence from the data to drive smart decisions. The data are used by Acxiom's approximately 1,000 clients for everything from developing telemarketing lists and identifying prospects for credit card offers to screening prospective employees and detecting fraudulent financial transactions.

No one at Acxiom seems to know exactly how much data the company manages in its 11 tightly guarded data centers. The company's central data center is located north of Little Rock, in Conway, Arkansas, where Acxiom was founded in 1969 as a spin-off of a local bus manufacturer. Acxiom also has data centers in Downer's Grove, Illinois, outside of Chicago, and as far away as Sunderland in the United Kingdom. The company recently opened a data center in Phoenix, and an additional facility is under construction in West Little Rock. The best estimates are that the Conway systems alone store between 1.5 and 2.0 petabytes of data, or up to 2,000 terabytes.

A portion of the data makes up Acxiom's information products, such as its InfoBase database of consumer data and its Personicx list of U.S. households segmented into 70 categories. Acxiom clients use those offerings to build marketing prospect lists, check the accuracy of names and phone numbers in their customer databases, and add demographic details or verify personnel data. Acxiom continues to add to its portfolio: In August, it debuted Personicx LifeChanges, a system that tracks U.S. households through life stages such as marriage or the purchase of a home. Those and other data products account for just over one-fifth of Acxiom's revenue.

To build its data library, Acxiom collects information from a wide range of public and private sources. The company has property deed–registration information from 930 counties across the United States, as well as from 3,500 telephone directories. It also purchases data from private sources, such as catalog and magazine subscriber lists and research from consumer surveys.

But a lot of the data Acxiom manages belongs to other companies. More than half of its revenue is generated by data-related services, such as building and hosting data warehouses, integrating and cleaning customer data, running customer relationship management applications, developing customer marketing lists, and analyzing data or providing clients with the means to analyze it themselves. Clients typically store three years of complete customer history data with Acxiom, CEO Charles Morgan says, but that's expanding to five years of data. "We like to think that these customers look at the Acxiom data center as an extension of their own data centers," he notes.

Acxiom isn't satisfied with just managing other companies' data; it wants to manage their data centers as well. In late 2004, Acxiom signed one of its most significant IT outsourcing deals, with Information Resources Inc. (IRI), which collects and sells terabytes of retail point-of-sale and consumer spending data. Under a contract potentially worth hundreds of millions of dollars, Acxiom will run IRI's data center operations and build a real-time content delivery system for the company.

Outsourcing isn't a new venture for Acxiom. Its first data center services customer was Norman Vincent Peale's Guideposts organization, some 15 years ago. Acxiom's outsourcing division was created officially in 1998, following its acquisition of May & Speh Inc., an information management services provider. Outsourcing deals now account for one-quarter of the company's sales.

Acxiom sees outsourcing as a growth area, targeting companies in data-intensive industries such as consumer packaged goods, financial services, and retail, where its data management expertise and technology give it an edge over IT-services stalwarts such as IBM and EDS, says Lee Hodges, chief operations leader. Acxiom holds up the IRI deal as emblematic of the company's outsourcing strategy. IRI collects huge amounts of product sales data from supermarkets, pharmacies, and other retailers, as well as from 70,000 volunteer households, and sells it to packaged goods manufacturers. As part of the deal, worth \$25–\$30 million a year for up to 15 years, Acxiom is developing a content-on-demand system to process retail data in near–real time, combine those data with demographic data, and sell them to IRI's clients to identify and exploit consumer buying trends as quickly as possible. IRI and Acxiom are developing applications that will help retailers and manufacturers manage new product introductions, analyze price and promotion effectiveness, and track products that are out of stock.

But its business strategy isn't what has garnered publicity for Acxiom. The company's involvement in situations that raise privacy implications has served to remind everyone that Acxiom's business, at its core, is collecting and selling data about people.

In September 2003, a controversy erupted over JetBlue turning over customer data to the federal government. A year earlier, the airline had provided data about 1.5 million passengers to Torch Concepts Inc., a military contractor developing a system for screening visitors to military bases. JetBlue and Torch Concepts were both Acxiom clients, and Acxiom provided the military contractor with demographic data and Social Security numbers to use with the passenger list provided by the airline.

The case has drawn Acxiom into the debate over when it's appropriate for companies to supply customer data to government agencies. Acxiom provides data to government agencies, acknowledges the company's privacy leader, Jennifer Barrett, though she declines to offer specifics. The company also provides privacy-consulting services to the government, Barrett notes, pointing out that the government's privacy efforts and policies lag the private sector by about 10 years. "So when government agencies ask companies for data, they often haven't thought about these issues the way Acxiom has," she says. Still, government contracts account for less than 1 percent of the company's revenue.

Acxiom considers privacy a core competency, and providing clients with privacy-consulting services is a lucrative part of its business. It was among the first companies to create a chief privacy officer post and has nine full-time employees devoted to privacy issues, along with dedicated resources in each country where Acxiom does business. Also, Acxiom is working with several members of Congress to help shape a national privacy policy, according to the company's legal leader, Jerry Jones.

Privacy's twin is security, and Acxiom is working hard on that too. The company created a security chief post in late 2003 and named Frank Caserta, a senior technical adviser in the database and data warehouse group, to the position. His job, he says, is to make sure Acxiom has a centralized, strategic view of data security and to champion the best data security practices within Acxiom and among its clients.

An increasingly security-conscious world is opening up new opportunities for Acxiom to provide data in areas such as employee background checks, compliance with regulations like the USA Patriot Act and the Do Not Call Registry, and fraud detection. In February 2004, credit data provider and Acxiom customer TransUnion LLC, together with Acxiom, introduced a system for fraud prevention and regulatory compliance for financial services, insurance, and telecommunications companies.

Acxiom has more ambitious plans on the global front. CEO Morgan says information systems for checking customer credit are woefully underdeveloped in China, where consumers can wait months to get approval for car loans. "You can imagine the fees," he exclaims. "And you wouldn't believe the paperwork."

Source: Adapted from Rick Whiting, "Data Demands Respect," *InformationWeek*, October 25, 2004.

CASE STUDY QUESTIONS

1. Acxiom is in a unique type of business. How would you describe the business of Acxiom? Is it a service- or a product-oriented business?
2. From the case, it is easy to see that Acxiom has focused on a wide variety of data from different sources. How does Acxiom decide which data to collect and for whom?
3. Acxiom's business raises many issues related to privacy. Are the data collected by Acxiom really private?

REAL WORLD ACTIVITIES

1. The case states that Acxiom started as the result of a spin-off from a bus company. Using the Internet, see if you can find the history of Acxiom. How does a bus company evolve into a data collection and dissemination company?
2. The privacy problems faced by Acxiom were associated with the accidental dissemination of data deemed sensitive by a third party. Break into small groups with your classmates, and discuss the privacy issues associated with Acxiom's business. Do you think the company is doing anything wrong?

CHAPTER 6

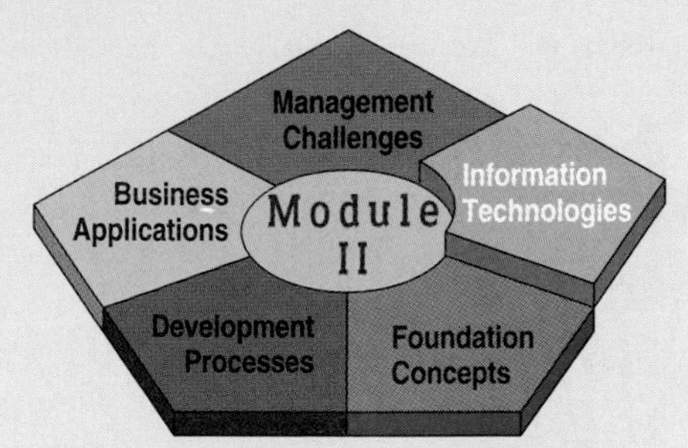

TELECOMMUNICATIONS AND NETWORKS

Chapter Highlights

Learning Objectives

After reading and studying this chapter, you should be able to:

1. Understand the concept of a network.
2. Apply Metcalfe's law in understanding the value of a network.
3. Identify several major developments and trends in the industries, technologies, and business applications of telecommunications and Internet technologies.
4. Provide examples of the business value of Internet, intranet, and extranet applications.
5. Identify the basic components, functions, and types of telecommunications networks used in business.
6. Explain the functions of major components of telecommunications network hardware, software, media, and services.
7. Explain the concept of client/server networking.
8. Understand the two forms of peer-to-peer networking.
9. Explain the difference between digital and analog signals.
10. Identify the various transmission media and topologies used in telecommunications networks.
11. Understand the fundamentals of wireless network technologies.
12. Explain the concepts behind TCP/IP.
13. Understand the seven layers of the OSI network model.

SECTION I The Networked Enterprise

Networking the Enterprise

When computers are networked, two industries—computing and communications—converge, and the result is vastly more than the sum of the parts. Suddenly, computing applications become available for business-to-business coordination and commerce, and for small as well as large organizations. The global Internet creates a public place without geographic boundaries—cyberspace—where ordinary citizens can interact, publish their ideas, and engage in the purchase of goods and services. In short, the impact of both computing and communications on our society and organizational structures is greatly magnified [16].

Telecommunications and network technologies are internetworking and revolutionizing business and society. Businesses have become **networked enterprises.** The Internet, the Web, and intranets and extranets are networking business processes and employees together and connecting them to their customers, suppliers, and other business stakeholders. Companies and workgroups can thus collaborate more creatively, manage their business operations and resources more effectively, and compete successfully in today's fast changing global economy. This chapter presents the telecommunications and network foundations for these developments.

Read the Real World Case on wireless mobile applications. We can learn a lot about the challenges and benefits of wireless mobile applications from this case. See Figure 6.1.

The Concept of a Network

Because of our focus on information systems and technologies, it is easy for us to think of networks in terms of connected computers. To understand the value of connecting computers fully however, it is important to understand the concept of a network in its broader sense.

By definition, the term **network** means an interconnected or interrelated chain, group, or system. Using this definition, we can begin to identify all kinds of networks: a chain of hotels, the road system, the names in a person's address book or PDA, the railroad system, the members of a church, club, or organization. The examples of networks in our world are virtually endless, and computer networks, though both valuable and powerful, are simply one example of the concept.

The concept of networks can be expressed as a mathematical formula that calculates the number of possible connections or interactions: $N(N - 1)$, or $N^2 - N$. In the formula, N refers to the number of *nodes* (points of connection) on the network. If only a few nodes exist on a network, the number of possible connections is quite small. Using the formula, we see that three nodes result in only six possible connections. A network of 10 nodes results in a somewhat larger number—90 connections. It's when a large number of nodes are connected that the possible number of connections grows to significant proportions. A network with 100 nodes has 9,900 possible connections, and a network with 1,000 nodes has 999,000 possible connections. This type of mathematical growth is called *exponential.* This term simply means that the growth in number of connections is many times greater than the number of nodes. Adding just one more node to a network makes the number of connections grow many times greater. Think of the effect of adding a new entry and exit ramp on highway system that connects 30,000 cities and towns. How many more connections does that one new ramp create?

Metcalfe's Law

Robert Metcalfe founded 3Com Corp. and designed the Ethernet protocol for computer networks. He used his understanding of the concept of networks to express the exponential growth in terms of potential business value. **Metcalfe's law** states that *the usefulness, or utility, of a network equals the square of the number of users.*

Metcalfe's law becomes easy to understand if you think of a common piece of technology we all use every day: the telephone. The telephone is of very limited use if only

REAL WORLD CASE 1 Best Buy, MedStar Health, and Unifi: The Challenges and Benefits of Wireless Mobile Applications

Double Agent 340 patrols Yonkers, New York, and surrounding areas looking for spyware-infected PCs and crashed hard drives. Within close reach rests his indispensable weapon, a Pocket PC phone that serves up a wealth of information and connects him wirelessly to the headquarters' IT systems.

The agent is Cristian Luzbet, dressed in a black-and-white ensemble with a matching breakaway tie, and he works for the Geek Squad, a 24-hour response unit that offers computer and network support for home PC users or businesses without an onsite IT staff. Luzbet has worked two years for the Geek Squad, a division of electronics retailer Best Buy, earning him a silver badge that he proudly displays over his belt buckle. Luzbet drives one of the Geek Squad's signature black-and-white Volkswagen Beetles. His Geek Mobile, as the cars are called, is loaded with hard drives, wireless cards, and routers. But you won't find street-map books, computer manuals, or paper stacks of customer orders. All the information Luzbet needs he can get with his Sprint PPC-6700 Smart Device, a Pocket PC/cell phone combo running Windows Mobile 5.0, which retails for about $450. Using Internet Explorer, Luzbet can link directly to Best Buy's order system.

Best Buy has about 12,000 agents like Luzbet nationwide driving Geek Mobiles and answering service calls every day. (Those who also help customers with computer problems from Geek Squad units within Best Buy stores, like Luzbet, are called double agents.) Using their mobile devices from either Sprint or Verizon Wireless, they log on to the order system, where they can adjust price quotes if necessary, enter credit card information, compose payment receipts, and complete the transaction on the spot.

FIGURE 6.1

Wireless Pocket PCs and other similar mobile devices can enable access to a company's business applications by its offsite employees.

Agents connect wirelessly through Sprint's EV-DO third-generation cellular network, one of the fastest available, and have complete Web browsing capabilities. "That sure beats asking the agents to carry laptops just for Web access," says Best Buy senior VP Sean Skelley.

Most agents service about three customers a day, with distances that can run 40 miles or so between customers. Luzbet accesses Google and Yahoo maps on the Web with his Pocket PC to look up directions to customers' homes. "It wasn't always this easy," he notes, referring to the days when the agents had to call Best Buy's dispatchers on a cell phone to get step-by-step directions.

But for the Geek Squad, mobile devices present some challenges. "Typing on our Pocket PCs' small slide-out keyboard isn't as easy as on a full-size keyboard," Luzbet says. That's why the agents often use handwriting recognition software to take notes on their Pocket PCs, such as the type of services they perform at each customer site. The agents then input the notes directly into Best Buy's order system, so the next time an agent gets a service call from a customer, he or she can refer to notes from previous visits and review past problems. In the past, agents had to wait until after the service call to type up their notes. "That's 10 to 15 extra minutes that could have otherwise been used to help the customer," Luzbet says.

While Best Buy has found a way to sidestep the problem of tiny keyboards, it isn't content to stop at handwriting recognition software. The Geek Squad is testing voice recognition software that lets agents open and close orders and auto-dial phone contacts through voice commands on their Pocket PC wireless devices. If the test is completed with flying colors, Luzbet will have an easier time keeping orders flowing and his hands on the Geek Mobile.

On one recent service call to Manhattan, a customer had trouble viewing Web pages on his laptop and couldn't get rid of a screen saver that came on every few minutes. Luzbet used his Pocket PC phone to log on to Best Buy's system, look up the customer's previous service calls, and discover he was using an outdated version of Windows. Luzbet spent about 25 minutes with the laptop, adding and removing programs and accessing Best Buy's order system to enter his notes. He then adjusted the price quote, processed the order, and e-mailed the customer a copy of the receipt, with enough time to spare for some lunch before his next service call.

Many businesses such as Best Buy that provide or manage employees' mobile devices for accessing company information find that it's worth incurring the cost and time it takes to develop software that specifically supports their business instead of buying one of the thousands of third-party, off-the-shelf software packages available. "An application to open and close orders sounds simple," Best Buy's Skelley claims, "but you won't believe how much more efficient it makes the Geek Squad."

But Best Buy and other companies have found that there's a lot more to developing business apps for mobile devices than fitting their displays on a small screen. Wireless carriers and device makers want us to believe that the high-speed, third-generation cellular networks now available will make it easy to extend applications to mobile devices. It just isn't so. Giving employees access to customer records, inventory management apps, and videoconferencing from PDAs and cell phones is far more complicated than a wireless broadband boost.

A worthwhile mobile application isn't just a shrunken version of a desktop one; it has to be formatted for display on a mobile device and easy to use without a standard keyboard. While PCs are similar enough to make one-size-fits-all desktop software, mobile devices come in all shapes and sizes. So software that works effortlessly on a Pocket PC with a touch screen could be unusable on a cell phone with a numeric keypad.

MedStar Health is facing those problems. The health care company's IT department supports thousands of doctors and nurses who use BlackBerrys, Pocket PCs, Palm Treos, and other devices to access patient records and lab images. Medical practitioners like to pick their own devices, and since there's no clear technology leader, there's not a great case for MedStar IT to push for a standard device. "There's no perfect device," acknowledges Dr. Sameer Bade, MedStar's assistant VP of clinical IT strategies. But the freedom-of-choice approach makes it difficult for the IT staff to keep up with new models and ensure that they're compatible with the company's applications.

In some cases, businesses have the motivation and resources to collaborate with vendors to develop mobile software. That's what MedStar did with Siemens Medical Solutions on PDAccess, software that lets medical practitioners access patient information from a Siemens Invision mainframe using PDAs. A business that insists on not sacrificing any functionality when developing a mobile app may be backing its IT department into a corner. "It may not be necessary for an entire application to be ported to a mobile device structure—only those parts that drive the most value," says Ben Holder, VP and CIO of Unifi. The textiles manufacturer used that approach when porting a custom-built IT services and support application to staffers' PDAs.

Also, developing mobile software that can access company applications typically requires middleware, such as Research In Motion's (RIM) Mobile Data System or Sybase's iAnywhere division's Mobile Solutions, which synchronize data between back-end systems and the devices.

Business software vendors including PeopleSoft, Salesforce.com, and Siebel Systems offer mobile versions of their applications, but they typically don't include all the functionality of the desktop versions. About 60 percent of businesses running the BlackBerry Enterprise Server deploy apps beyond e-mail, RIM says. More than 280 RIM partners have developed business applications to run on the BlackBerry. Microsoft says its Windows Mobile 5.0 operating system supports about 20,000 off-the-shelf apps.

But often the functionality of these applications doesn't match mobile workers' dreams. So off-the-shelf is often just the foundation. It's up to the IT staff to do the patchwork and integration for the various front-end and back-end applications involved in a deployment. It's usually a big effort to make an application small.

Source: Elena Malykhina, "Pocket PCs on a Mission," *InformationWeek*, February 20, 2006; "Nothing's Easy about Mobile App Development," *Information Week*, April 10, 2006.

CASE STUDY QUESTIONS

1. What are the business advantages and limitations of the Best Buy Geek Squad's use of their wireless Pocket PC mobile devices? How have they overcome the limitations of their mobile devices?
2. What are the software development challenges of wireless mobile devices? How are MedStar Health and Unifi meeting those challenges?
3. Why don't the companies in this case use some of the thousands of software packages available for their wireless mobile devices? What are the advantages and limitations of this approach?

REAL WORLD ACTIVITIES

1. Use the Internet to research wireless mobile devices like the Sprint PPC-6700. Do an analysis of the desirable features and limitations of the smart wireless mobile device you would most be willing to use in a work situation. Defend your choice.
2. While Best Buy has standardized on the Sprint PPC-6700 for its Geek Squad, MedStar Health lets their medical practitioners pick their own devices. Should companies mandate a standard wireless mobile device for their employees? Break into small groups with your classmates and discuss the pros and cons of this question; then formulate and defend a proposed solution.

you and your best friend have one. If a whole town is on the system, it becomes much more useful. If the whole world is wired, the utility of the system is phenomenal. Add the number of wireless telephone connections, and you have a massive potential for value. To reach this value, however, many people had to have access to a telephone—and they had to have used it. In other words, telephone use had to reach a critical mass of users. So it is with any technology.

Until a critical mass of users is reached, a change in technology only affects the technology. But once critical mass is attained, social, political, and economic systems change. The same is true of digital network technologies. Consider the Internet. It reached critical mass in 1993, when there were roughly 2.5 million host computers on the network. By November 1997, the vast network contained an estimated 25 million host computers. With computing costs continuing to drop rapidly (remember Moore's law from Chapter 3) and the Internet growing exponentially (Metcalfe's law), we can expect to see more and more value—conceivably for less cost—virtually every time we log on.

Trends in Telecommunications

Telecommunications is the exchange of information in any form (voice, data, text, images, audio, video) over networks. Early telecommunications networks did not use computers to route traffic and, as such, were much slower than today's computer-based networks. Major trends occurring in the field of telecommunications have a significant impact on management decisions in this area. You should thus be aware of major trends in telecommunications industries, technologies, and applications that significantly increase the decision alternatives confronting business managers and professionals. See Figure 6.2.

Industry Trends

The competitive arena for telecommunications service has changed dramatically in recent years. The telecommunications industry has changed from government-regulated monopolies to a deregulated market with fiercely competitive suppliers of telecommunications services. Numerous companies now offer businesses and consumers a choice of everything from local and global telephone services to communications satellite channels, mobile radio, cable TV, cellular phone services, and Internet access [6]. See Figure 6.3.

The explosive growth of the Internet and the World Wide Web has spawned a host of new telecommunications products, services, and providers. Driving and responding to this growth, business firms have dramatically increased their use of the Internet and

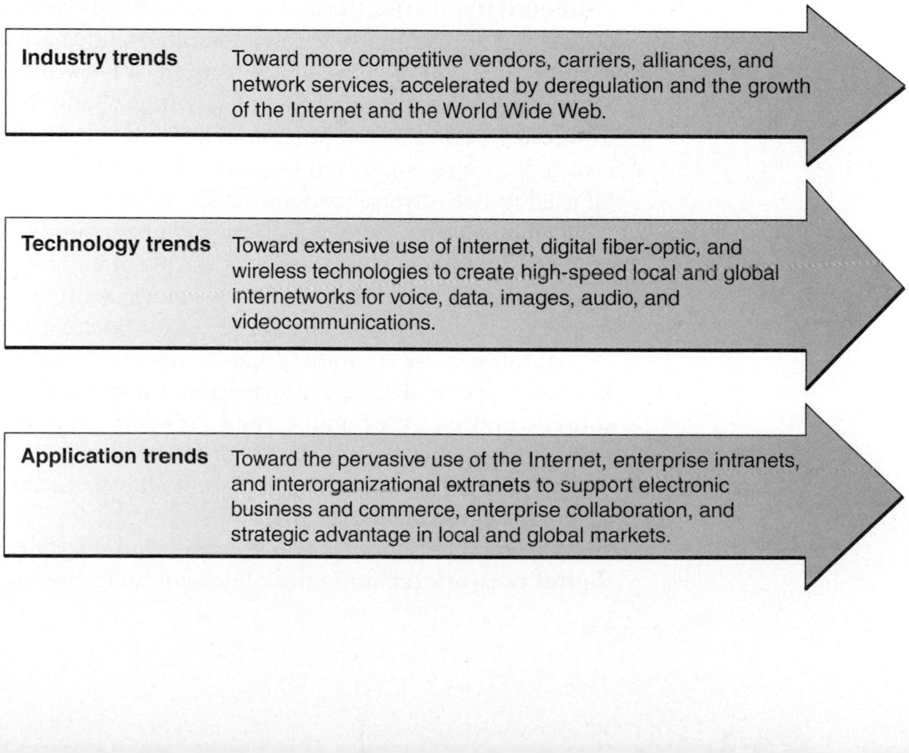

FIGURE 6.2
Major trends in business telecommunications.

Industry trends	Toward more competitive vendors, carriers, alliances, and network services, accelerated by deregulation and the growth of the Internet and the World Wide Web.
Technology trends	Toward extensive use of Internet, digital fiber-optic, and wireless technologies to create high-speed local and global internetworks for voice, data, images, audio, and videocommunications.
Application trends	Toward the pervasive use of the Internet, enterprise intranets, and interorganizational extranets to support electronic business and commerce, enterprise collaboration, and strategic advantage in local and global markets.

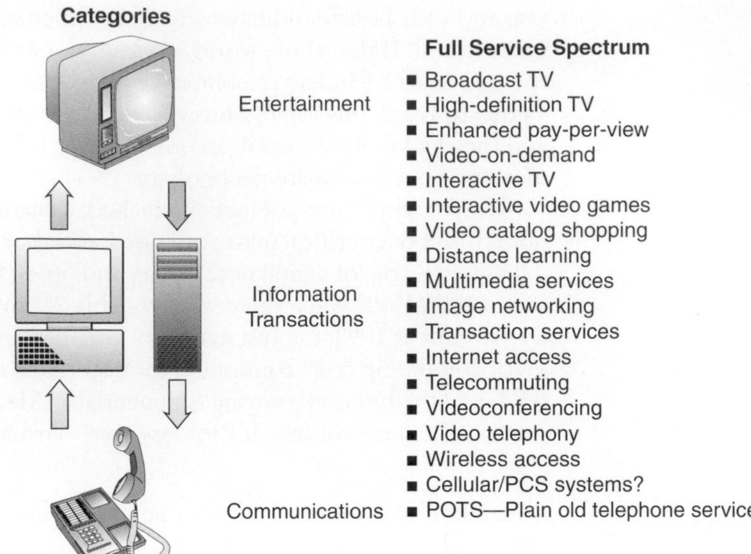

FIGURE 6.3
The spectrum of telecommunications-based services available today.

the Web for electronic commerce and collaboration. Thus, the service and vendor options available to meet a company's telecommunications needs have increased significantly, as have a business manager's decision-making alternatives.

Technology Trends

Open systems with unrestricted connectivity, using **Internet networking technologies** as their technology platform, are today's primary telecommunications technology drivers. Web browser suites, HTML Web page editors, Internet and intranet servers and network management software, TCP/IP Internet networking products, and network security firewalls are just a few examples. These technologies are being applied in Internet, intranet, and extranet applications, especially those for electronic commerce and collaboration. This trend has reinforced previous industry and technical moves toward building client/server networks based on an open-systems architecture.

Open systems are information systems that use common standards for hardware, software, applications, and networking. Open systems, like the Internet and corporate intranets and extranets, create a computing environment that is open to easy access by end users and their networked computer systems. Open systems provide greater **connectivity,** that is, the ability of networked computers and other devices to easily access and communicate with one another and share information. Any open-systems architecture also provides a high degree of network **interoperability.** That is, open systems enable the many different activities of end users to be accomplished using the different varieties of computer systems, software packages, and databases provided by a variety of interconnected networks. Frequently, software known as *middleware* may be used to help diverse systems work together.

Middleware is a general term for any programming that serves to "glue together" or mediate between two separate, and usually already existing, programs. A common application of middleware is to allow programs written for access to a particular database (e.g., DB2) to access other databases (e.g., Oracle) without the need for custom coding.

Middleware is commonly known as the "plumbing" of an information system because it routes data and information transparently between different back-end data sources and end-user applications. It's not very interesting to look at—it usually doesn't have much, if any, visible "front end" of its own—but it is an essential component of any IT infrastructure because it allows disparate systems to be joined together in a common framework.

Telecommunications is also being revolutionized by the rapid change from analog to **digital network technologies.** Telecommunications systems have always depended on voice-oriented analog transmission systems designed to transmit the variable electrical frequencies generated by the sound waves of the human voice. However, local and global telecommunications networks are rapidly converting to digital transmission technologies that transmit information in the form of discrete pulses, as computers do. This conversion provides (1) significantly higher transmission speeds, (2) the movement of larger amounts of information, (3) greater economy, and (4) much lower error rates than with analog systems. In addition, digital technologies allow telecommunications networks to carry multiple types of communications (data, voice, video) on the same circuits.

Another major trend in telecommunications technology is a change from reliance on copper wire–based media and land-based microwave relay systems to fiber-optic lines and cellular, communications satellite, and other **wireless technologies**. Fiber-optic transmission, which uses pulses of laser-generated light, offers significant advantages in terms of reduced size and installation effort, vastly greater communication capacity, much faster transmission speeds, and freedom from electrical interference. Satellite transmission offers significant advantages for organizations that need to transmit massive quantities of data, audio, and video over global networks, especially to isolated areas. Cellular, mobile radio, and other wireless systems are connecting cellular phones, PDAs, and other wireless appliances to the Internet and corporate networks.

Business Application Trends

The changes in telecommunications industries and technologies just mentioned are causing a significant change in the business use of telecommunications. The trend toward more vendors, services, Internet technologies, and open systems, and the rapid growth of the Internet, the World Wide Web, and corporate intranets and extranets, dramatically increases the number of feasible telecommunications applications. Thus, telecommunications networks are now playing vital and pervasive roles in Web-enabled e-business processes, electronic commerce, enterprise collaboration, and other business applications that support the operations, management, and strategic objectives of both large and small business enterprises.

Internet2

We cannot leave our overview of trends in telecommunications without reiterating that the Internet sits firmly in the center of the action. Despite its importance and seemingly unexplored boundaries, we are already embarking on the next generation of the "network of networks." Internet2 is a high-performance network that uses an entirely different infrastructure than the public Internet we know today. And already, more than 200 universities and scientific institutions and 60 communications corporations are part of the Internet2 network. One big misconception about Internet2 is that it's a sequel to the original Internet and will replace it someday. It never will, because it was never intended to replace the Internet. Rather, its purpose is to build a roadmap that can be followed during the next stage of innovation for the current Internet. The ideas being honed, such as new addressing protocols and satellite-quality streaming video, likely will be deployed to the Internet, but it might take close to 10 years before we see them.

Furthermore, the Internet2 network may never become totally open—it might remain solely in the domain of universities, research centers, and governments. To be sure, the lightning-fast technologies in use by Internet2 right now must eventually be turned over to the public Internet. But for now, the Internet2 project lives for the purpose of sharing, collaborating, and trying new high-speed communication ideas—interestingly, many of the same goals that shaped the early history of today's Internet.

Most of the institutions and commercial partners on the Internet2 network are connected via *Abilene*, a network backbone that will soon support throughput of 10 gigabits per second (Gbps). Several international networks are also plugged into Abilene's infrastructure, and as the project grows, more and more networks will be able to connect to the current framework. The one common denominator among all of the Internet2 partners is their active participation in the development and testing of new applications and Internet protocols with an emphasis on research and collaboration, focusing on things such as videoconferencing, multicasting, remote applications, and new protocols that take advantage of the many opportunities megabandwidth provides. In short, Internet2 is all about high-speed telecommunications and infinite bandwidth.

To give you an idea of exactly how fast this network of the future is, an international team of researchers has already used it to set a new land speed record. At the end of 2002, the team sent 6.7 gigabytes of data across 6,821 miles of fiber-optic network in less than one minute. That's roughly two full-length DVD-quality movies traveling a quarter of the way around the earth in less than one minute at an average speed of 923 million bits per second! And the same team is already hard at work attempting to break its own record.

Suffice to say that while we are exploring new ways to gain business advantage through the Internet, a significant effort is being made to make the Internet bigger and faster. In 2006, Internet2 celebrated its 10th anniversary and has significantly expanded in breadth, speed, and storage capacity since its inception in 1996. We'll look at Internet2 again later in this chapter when we discuss Internet-addressing protocols.

The Business Value of Telecommunications Networks

What *business value* is created when a company capitalizes on the trends in telecommunications we have just identified? Use of the Internet, intranets, extranets, and other telecommunications networks can dramatically cut costs, shorten business lead times and response times, support electronic commerce, improve the collaboration of workgroups, develop online operational processes, share resources, lock in customers and suppliers, and develop new products and services. These benefits make applications of telecommunications more strategic and vital for businesses that must increasingly find new ways to compete in both domestic and global markets.

Figure 6.4 illustrates how telecommunications-based business applications can help a company overcome geographic, time, cost, and structural barriers to business success. Note the examples of the business value of these four strategic capabilities of telecommunications networks. This figure emphasizes how several e-business applications can help a firm capture and provide information quickly to end users at remote geographic locations at reduced costs, as well as support its strategic organizational objectives.

For example, traveling salespeople and those at regional sales offices can use the Internet, extranets, and other networks to transmit customer orders from their laptop or desktop PCs, thus breaking geographic barriers. Point-of-sale terminals and an online sales transaction processing network can break time barriers by supporting immediate credit authorization and sales processing. Teleconferencing can be used to cut costs by reducing the need for expensive business trips, allowing customers, suppliers, and

FIGURE 6.4 Examples of the business value of business applications of telecommunications networks.

Strategic Capabilities	e-Business Examples	Business Value
Overcome geographic barriers: Capture information about business transactions from remote locations	Use the Internet and extranets to transmit customer orders from traveling salespeople to a corporate data center for order processing and inventory control	Provides better customer service by reducing delay in filling orders and improves cash flow by speeding up the billing of customers
Overcome time barriers: Provide information to remote locations immediately after it is requested	Credit authorization at the point of sale using online POS networks	Credit inquiries can be made and answered in seconds
Overcome cost barriers: Reduce the cost of more traditional means of communication	Desktop videoconferencing between a company and its business partners using the Internet, intranets, and extranets	Reduces expensive business trips; allows customers, suppliers, and employees to collaborate, thus improving the quality of decisions reached
Overcome structural barriers: Support linkages for competitive advantage	Business-to-business electronic commerce Web sites for transactions with suppliers and customers using the Internet and extranets	Fast, convenient services lock in customers and suppliers

employees to participate in meetings and collaborate on joint projects without traveling. Finally, business-to-business electronic commerce Web sites are used by businesses to establish strategic relationships with their customers and suppliers by making business transactions fast, convenient, and tailored to the needs of the business partners involved.

The Internet Revolution

The explosive growth of the **Internet** is a revolutionary phenomenon in computing and telecommunications. The Internet has become the largest and most important network of networks today and has evolved into a global *information superhighway*. We can think of the Internet as a network made up of millions of smaller private networks, each with the ability to operate independent of, or in harmony with, all the other millions of networks connected to the Internet. When this network of networks began growing in December 1991, it had about 10 servers. In January 2004, the Internet was estimated to have more than 46 million connected servers with a sustained growth rate in excess of 1 million servers per month. In January 2007, the Internet was estimated to have over one billion users with Web sites in 34 languages from English to Icelandic. Now that is some growth!

The Internet is constantly expanding as more and more businesses and other organizations and their users, computers, and networks join its global Web. Thousands of business, educational, and research networks now connect millions of computer systems and users in more than 200 countries. Internet users projected for 2010 are expected to top the 2 billion user mark, which still only represents approximately one-third of the worldwide population [10]. Apply these numbers to Metcalfe's law, and you can see the number of possible connections is extraordinary.

The Net doesn't have a central computer system or telecommunications center. There are, however, 13 servers called *root servers* that are used to handle the bulk of the routing of traffic from one computer to another. Each message sent has a unique address code so any Internet server in the network can forward it to its destination. Also, the Internet does not have a headquarters or governing body. International advisory and standards groups of individual and corporate members, such as the Internet Society (www.isoc.org) and the World Wide Web Consortium (www.w3.org), promote use of the Internet and the development of new communications standards. These common standards are the key to the free flow of messages among the widely different computers and networks of the many organizations and *Internet service providers* (ISPs) in the system.

Internet Service Providers

One of the unique aspects of the Internet is that nobody really owns it. Anyone who can access the Internet can use it and the services it offers. Because the Internet cannot be accessed directly by individuals, we need to employ the services of a company that specializes in providing easy access. An **ISP**, or **Internet service provider**, is a company that provides access to the Internet to individuals and organizations. For a monthly fee, the service provider gives you a software package, user name, password, and access phone number or access protocol. With this information (and some specialized hardware), you can then log onto the Internet, browse the World Wide Web, and send and receive e-mail.

In addition to serving individuals, ISPs also serve large companies, providing a direct connection from the company's networks to the Internet. These ISPs themselves are connected to one another through *network access points*. Through these connections, one ISP can easily connect to another ISP to obtain information about the address of a Web site or user node.

Internet Applications

The most popular Internet applications are e-mail, instant messaging, browsing the sites on the World Wide Web, and participating in *newsgroups* and *chat rooms*. Internet e-mail messages usually arrive in seconds or a few minutes anywhere in the world and can take the form of data, text, fax, and video files. Internet browser software like Netscape Navigator and Internet Explorer enables millions of users to surf the World Wide Web by clicking their way to the multimedia information resources stored on the hyperlinked pages of businesses, government, and other Web sites. Web sites offer

FIGURE 6.5
Popular uses of the Internet.

- **Surf.** Point-and-click your way to thousands of hyperlinked Web sites and resources for multimedia information, entertainment, or electronic commerce.
- **e-Mail.** Use e-mail and instant messaging to exchange electronic messages with colleagues, friends, and other Internet users.
- **Discuss.** Participate in discussion forums of special-interest newsgroups, or hold real-time text conversations in Web site chat rooms.
- **Publish.** Post your opinion, subject matter, or creative work to a Web site or weblog for others to read.
- **Buy and Sell.** Buy and sell practically anything via e-commerce retailers, wholesalers, service providers, and online auctions.
- **Download.** Transfer data files, software, reports, articles, pictures, music, videos, and other types of files to your computer system.
- **Compute.** Log onto and use thousands of Internet computer systems around the world.
- **Other Uses.** Make long-distance phone calls, hold desktop videoconferences, listen to radio programs, watch television, play video games, explore virtual worlds, etc.

information and entertainment and are the launch sites for electronic commerce transactions between businesses and their suppliers and customers. As we will discuss in Chapter 8, e-commerce Web sites offer all manner of products and services via online retailers, wholesalers, service providers, and online auctions. See Figure 6.5.

The Internet provides electronic discussion forums and bulletin board systems formed and managed by thousands of special-interest newsgroups. You can participate in discussions or post messages on a myriad of topics for other users with the same interests. Other popular applications include downloading software and information files and accessing databases provided by a variety of business, government, and other organizations. You can conduct online searches for information on Web sites in a variety of ways by using search sites and search engines such as Yahoo!, Google, and Fast Search. Logging on to other computers on the Internet and holding real-time conversations with other Internet users in *chat rooms* are also popular uses of the Internet.

Boeing 777: Using the Internet to Build a World-Class Airplane

A commercial jet airliner is arguably one of the most complicated products designed by modern engineers. It contains millions of individually designed parts that must work together to meet the very highest standards of performance, reliability, and safety. The tolerance for failure of any component of an airliner is essentially zero, and much of its complexity comes from the design and inclusion of backup systems for the backup systems. To design a commercial airliner, a monumental number of people and organizations must collaborate for hundreds of thousands of person-hours. An exemplar of modern aircraft design—the Boeing 777—is truly a model of collaborative creativity on an extraordinary scale.

The collaboration behind the Boeing 777, however, is interesting not simply for its scope but also for the pioneering communication methods it used. It was the first major aircraft designed using the Internet, along with an extensive array of private computer networks, to bring together thousands of engineers working on every phase of the project at the same time. Many of the 777's designers never met in person; while they collaborated to design an aircraft that can talk to itself, many of them would not recognize each other on the street.

The networked computer systems behind the 777's collaborative design included more than 2,200 workstations linked through eight large mainframe computers using the Internet as their communication vehicle. At the heart of the system was software called CATIA, for "Computer-Aided Three-dimensional Interactive Application." Boeing extended this with a system called EPIC, for "Electronic Pre-assembly In the Computer," enabling engineers located in different parts of the world to design and test "virtual" prototypes of crucial components of the airplane. The Boeing 777 was designed over the Internet's electronic sprawl: 250 worldwide, cross-functional teams, including suppliers and customers, linked through Internet-based computer-aided design (CAD) software. Most important, using the Internet allowed significant reductions in production costs without any compromise in quality. The virtual team approach worked so well that only a nose mock-up (to check critical wiring) was physically built before assembly of the first flight vehicle, which was only 0.03 mm out of alignment when the port wing was attached [3, 18].

Business Use of the Internet

As Figure 6.6 illustrates, business use of the Internet has expanded from an electronic information exchange to a broad platform for strategic business applications. Notice how applications such as collaboration among business partners, providing customer and vendor support, and electronic commerce have become major business uses of the Internet. Companies are also using Internet technologies for marketing, sales, and customer relationship management applications, as well as for cross-functional business applications, and applications in engineering, manufacturing, human resources, and accounting. Let's look at a real world example.

FIGURE 6.6 Examples of how a company can use the Internet for business.

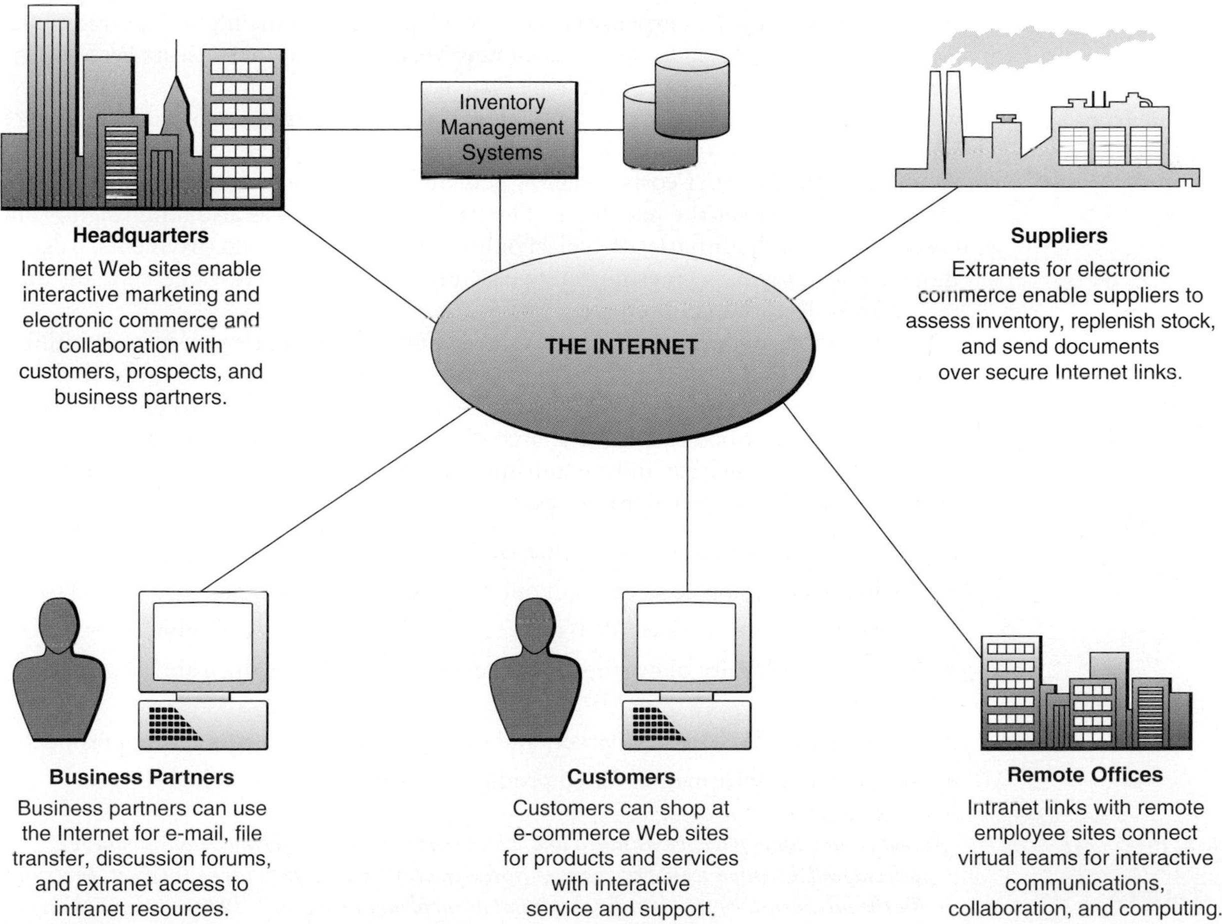
Inventory Management Systems
Headquarters
Internet Web sites enable interactive marketing and electronic commerce and collaboration with customers, prospects, and business partners.
THE INTERNET
Suppliers
Extranets for electronic commerce enable suppliers to assess inventory, replenish stock, and send documents over secure Internet links.
Business Partners
Business partners can use the Internet for e-mail, file transfer, discussion forums, and extranet access to intranet resources.
Customers
Customers can shop at e-commerce Web sites for products and services with interactive service and support.
Remote Offices
Intranet links with remote employee sites connect virtual teams for interactive communications, collaboration, and computing.

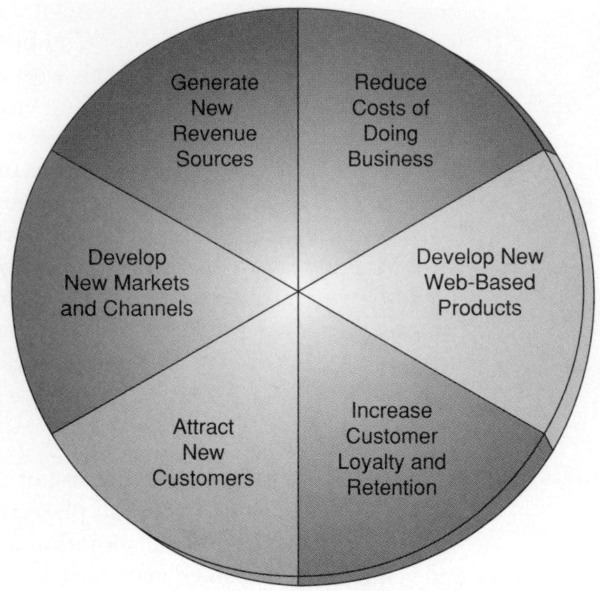

FIGURE 6.7
How companies are deriving business value from their e-business and e-commerce applications.

The Business Value of the Internet

The Internet provides a synthesis of computing and communication capabilities that adds value to every part of the business cycle [9].

What business value do companies derive from their business applications on the Internet? Figure 6.7 summarizes how many companies perceive the business value of the Internet for electronic commerce. Substantial cost savings can arise because applications that use the Internet and Internet-based technologies (like intranets and extranets) are typically less expensive to develop, operate, and maintain than traditional systems. For example, an airline saves money every time customers use its Web site instead of its customer support telephone system.

It is estimated that for certain types of transactions, the transaction cost savings are significant for online versus more traditional channels. For example, booking a reservation over the Internet costs about 90 percent less for the airline than booking the same reservation over the telephone. The banking industry has also found significant costs savings via the Internet. A typical online banking transaction (payments, balance inquiry, check payment) is estimated to cost anywhere from 50 to 95 percent less than its bricks-and-mortar counterpart.

Other primary sources of business value include attracting new customers with innovative marketing and products and retaining present customers with improved customer service and support. Of course, generating revenue through electronic commerce applications is a major source of business value, which we will discuss in Chapter 8. To summarize, most companies are building e-business and e-commerce Web sites to achieve six major business values:

- Generate new revenue from online sales.
- Reduce transaction costs through online sales and customer support.
- Attract new customers via Web marketing and advertising and online sales.
- Increase the loyalty of existing customers via improved Web customer service and support.
- Develop new Web-based markets and distribution channels for existing products.
- Develop new information-based products accessible on the Web [14].

The Role of Intranets

Many companies have sophisticated and widespread intranets, offering detailed data retrieval, collaboration tools, personalized customer profiles, and links to the Internet. Investing in the intranet, they feel, is as fundamental as supplying employees with a telephone [17].

Before we go any further, let's redefine the concept of an intranet, to emphasize specifically how intranets are related to the Internet and extranets. An **intranet** is a network inside an organization that uses Internet technologies (such as Web browsers and servers, TCP/IP network protocols, HTML hypermedia document publishing and databases, and so on) to provide an Internet-like environment within the enterprise for information sharing, communications, collaboration, and the support of business processes. An intranet is protected by security measures such as passwords, encryption, and firewalls and thus can be accessed by authorized users through the Internet. A company's intranet can also be accessed through the intranets of customers, suppliers, and other business partners via *extranet* links.

The Business Value of Intranets

Organizations of all kinds are implementing a broad range of intranet uses. One way that companies organize intranet applications is to group them conceptually into a few user services categories that reflect the basic services that intranets offer to their users. These services are provided by the intranet's portal, browser, and server software, as well as by other system and application software and groupware that are part of a company's intranet software environment. Figure 6.8 illustrates how intranets provide an *enterprise information portal* that supports communication and collaboration, Web publishing, business operations and management, and intranet portal management. Notice also how these applications can be integrated with existing IS resources and applications and extended to customers, suppliers, and business partners via the Internet and extranets.

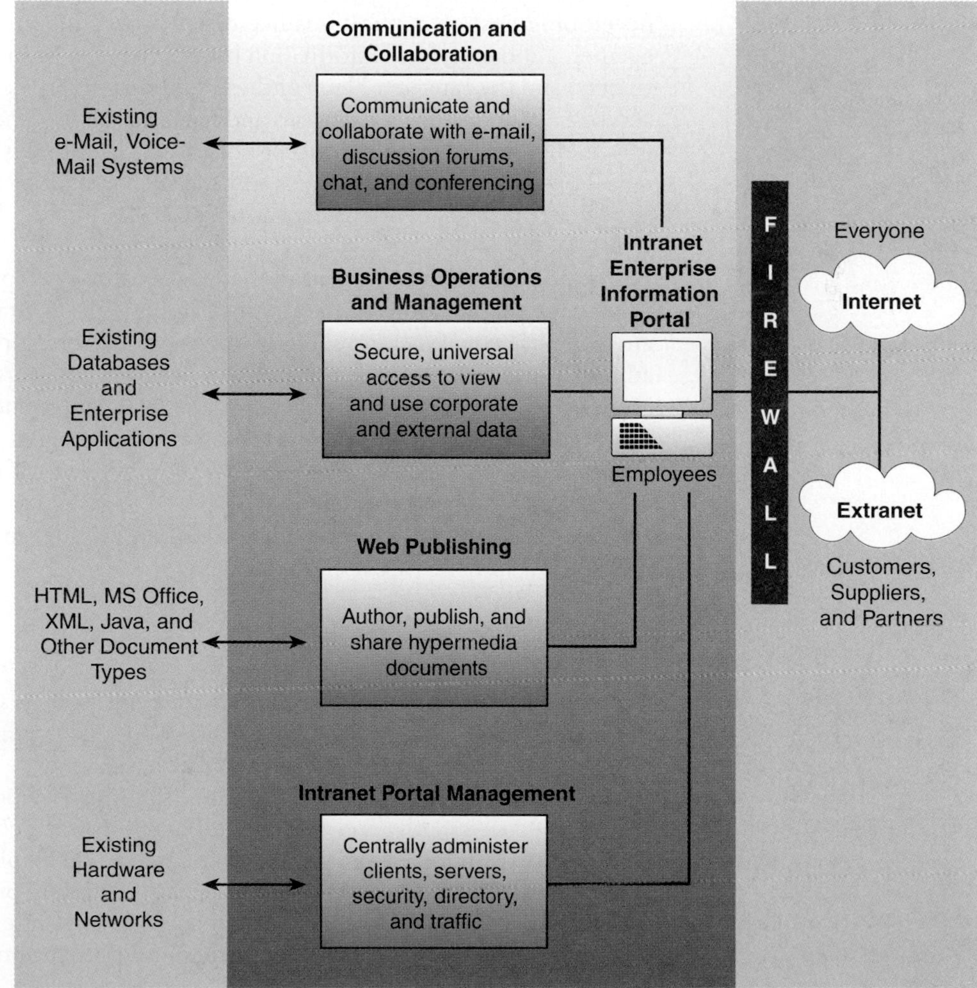

FIGURE 6.8
Intranets can provide an enterprise information portal for applications in communication and collaboration, business operations and management, Web publishing, and intranet portal management.

Communications and Collaboration. Intranets can significantly improve communications and collaboration within an enterprise. For example, you can use your intranet browser and your PC or NC workstation to send and receive e-mail, voice mail, pages, and faxes to communicate with others within your organization, as well as externally through the Internet and extranets. You can also use intranet groupware features to improve team and project collaboration with services such as discussion groups, chat rooms, and audio- and videoconferencing.

Web Publishing. The advantage of developing and publishing hyperlinked multimedia documents to hypermedia databases accessible on World Wide Web servers has moved to corporate intranets. The comparative ease, attractiveness, and lower cost of publishing and accessing multimedia business information internally via intranet Web sites have been the primary reasons for the explosive growth in the use of intranets in business. For example, information products as varied as company newsletters, technical drawings, and product catalogs can be published in a variety of ways, including hypermedia Web pages, e-mail, and net broadcasting, and as part of in-house business applications. Intranet software browsers, servers, and search engines can help you easily navigate and locate the business information you need.

Business Operations and Management. Intranets have moved beyond merely making hypermedia information available on Web servers or pushing it to users via net broadcasting. Intranets are also being used as the platform for developing and deploying critical business applications to support business operations and managerial decision making across the internetworked enterprise. For example, many companies are developing custom applications like order processing, inventory control, sales management, and enterprise information portals that can be implemented on intranets, extranets, and the Internet. Many of these applications are designed to interface with and access existing company databases and legacy systems. The software for such business uses is then installed on intranet Web servers. Employees within the company or external business partners can access and run such applications using Web browsers from anywhere on the network whenever needed.

Intranet Portal Management. Organizations must employ IT and IS professionals to manage the functions of the intranet along with maintaining the various hardware and software components necessary for successful operations. For example, a network administrator must manage the access of users via passwords and other security mechanisms to ensure each user is able to use the intranet productively while simultaneously protecting the integrity of the data resources. Included in this job are issues related to protection against unauthorized access, computer viruses, directory management, and other highly important functions.

Now let's look at one company's use of an intranet in more detail to get a better idea of how intranets are used in business.

Constellation Energy: Using an Intranet to Get Employees Working Together and More Productively

When Beth Perlman joined **Constellation Energy** as its CIO in 2002, employees of the company's four major divisions didn't do much communicating. "It was like four separate companies that never talked," she says.

Perlman herself had offices in two buildings, two Windows 95-based PCs that couldn't access the other's e-mail, and a BlackBerry that couldn't sync with them. Constellation Energy began standardizing its 10,000 employees' desktops in 2005, but that still didn't solve a lot of its information-sharing problems. "I got sick of seeing people e-mail these enormous documents" because there was no other way to electronically share ideas and information, Perlman laments. It was hard to track

versions of documents, such as when staff in different parts of the company needed to provide data for analyst presentations, she says.

What a difference a year makes. Constellation Energy in 2006 rolled out a suite of standardized, common collaboration tools throughout the company, installed wireless networks at 22 of its campuses, and redesigned its myConstellation Intranet portal.

The company's "Connect. Interact. Transform." initiative already has tremendously boosted productivity and collaboration. "It was a very quick ROI," Perlman notes. A big part of the payback has come from an enterprise software license with Microsoft that Perlman says costs "a few hundred thousand dollars," which, along with the redesigned Intranet portal, has contributed significantly to Constellation Energy's $90 million in pretax productivity savings in 2005 and 2006.

As part of the "Connect. Interact. Transform." initiative, Perlman's IT organization deployed Microsoft Live Meeting Web conferencing software; SharePoint, an information-sharing and document collaboration tool; and Windows Messenger instant messaging for use on the Intranet. To date, Live Meeting has had the biggest impact on productivity across the company, according to Perlman. More than 10,000 hours of meetings were logged in 2005 and 2006, saving the company $41 per attendee in expenses and gaining an average of 98 minutes in productivity per employee.

Now, instead of traveling to central offices for training, employees can take classes via their PCs or at kiosks with portal access that are set up in Constellation Energy's service centers for the company's 2,500 field, utility, and other workers who don't have PCs. Through Live Meeting, everyone can see the same information at the same time, Perlman says, including PowerPoint presentations. The IT organization has found this incredibly useful in its own work. "During a meeting, IT staff can look at changes to code in a program and all see the same thing," she notes.

"We thought only a few people would use SharePoint, but now it's being used by everyone. It's really ballooned," she comments. SharePoint provides a central location for documents, such as Word and Excel files, to be viewed and changed. Sharepoint also provides version control.

SharePoint's deployment has allowed Kevin Hadlock, Constellation Energy's director of investor relations, to spend more time analyzing data for the company's earnings releases and analyst presentations, as well as hundreds of fewer hours collecting the paperwork that goes into those presentations from the company's four divisions. A presentation often was revised 30 to 50 times before all changes were manually made in the final version. With SharePoint, all the information is collected electronically.

"I always know what changes have been made," says Hadlock, who says the final presentation material was completed at least one week earlier than in the past and that "the quality and accuracy of the information is greatly improved." [6, 13]

The Role of Extranets

As businesses continue to use open Internet technologies [extranets] to improve communication with customers and partners, they can gain many competitive advantages along the way—in product development, cost savings, marketing, distribution, and leveraging their partnerships [2].

As we explained previously, **extranets** are network links that use Internet technologies to interconnect the intranet of a business with the intranets of its customers, suppliers, or other business partners. Companies can establish direct private network links among themselves or create private, secure Internet links called *virtual private networks* (VPNs). (We'll look more closely at VPNs later in this chapter.) Or a company can use

FIGURE 6.9 Extranets connect the internetworked enterprise to consumers, business customers, suppliers, and other business partners.

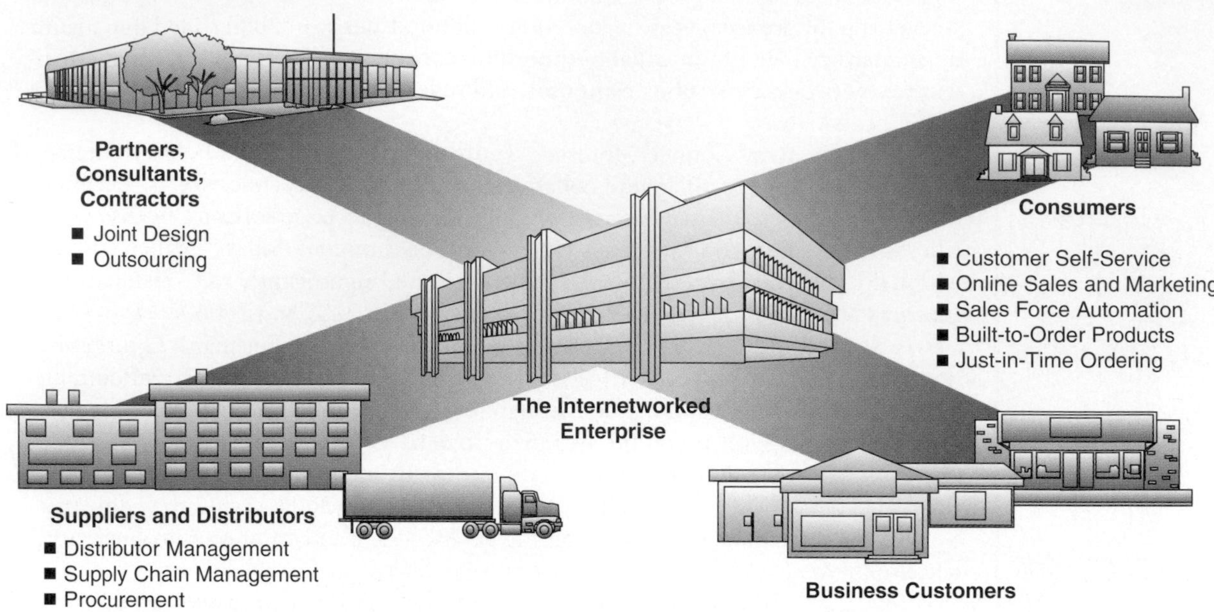

the unsecured Internet as the extranet link between its intranet and consumers and others but rely on the encryption of sensitive data and its own firewall systems to provide adequate security. Thus, extranets enable customers, suppliers, consultants, subcontractors, business prospects, and others to access selected intranet Web sites and other company databases. See Figure 6.9.

As shown in the figure, an organization's extranet can simultaneously link the organization to a wide variety of external partners. Consultants and contractors can use the extranet to facilitate the design of new systems or provide outsourcing services. The suppliers of the organization can use the extranet to ensure that the raw materials necessary for the organization to function are in stock or delivered in a timely fashion. The customers of an organization can use the extranet to access self-service functions such as ordering, order status checking, and payment. The extranet links the organization to the outside world in a manner that improves the way it does business.

The business value of extranets is derived from several factors. First, the Web browser technology of extranets makes customer and supplier access of intranet resources a lot easier and faster than previous business methods. Second, as you will see in two upcoming examples, extranets enable a company to offer new kinds of interactive Web-enabled services to their business partners. Thus, extranets are another way that a business can build and strengthen strategic relationships with its customers and suppliers. Also, extranets can enable and improve collaboration by a business with its customers and other business partners. Extranets facilitate an online, interactive product development, marketing, and customer-focused process that can bring better designed products to market faster.

Countrywide and Snap-on: Extranet Examples

Countrywide Financial has always been an industry leader in the strategic use of technology. Most recently, Countrywide continued its technology leadership through the creation of an extranet called Platinum Lender Access for its lending partners and brokers. About 500 banks and mortgage brokers can access Countrywide's intranet and selected financial databases. The extranet gives them access to

their account and transaction information, status of loans, and company announcements. Each lender or broker is automatically identified by the extranet and provided with customized information on premium rates, discounts, and any special business arrangements already negotiated with Countrywide. It's no wonder Countrywide ranks among the top five loan originators and servicers in America and is the largest online lender in the world [2, 8].

Snap-on Inc., a more than $2 billion, S&P 500 company headquartered in Kenosha, Wisconsin, is a leading global developer, manufacturer, and marketer of tool and equipment solutions for professional tool users. Products are sold through its franchise dealer vans, company direct sales, distributors, and Internet channels. To tie all of its customers and sales outlets together, Snap-on spent $300,000 to create an extranet link to its intranet called the Franchise Information Network. The extranet lets Snap-on's 4,000 independent franchises for automotive tools access a secured intranet Web site for customized information and interactive communications with Snap-on employees and other franchisees. Franchisers can get information on sales plus marketing updates. The extranet also provides tips and training programs about managing a franchise operation and discussion forums for employees and franchisees to share ideas and best practices. Finally, the Franchise Information Network provides interactive news and information on car racing and other special events sponsored by Snap-on, as well as corporate stock prices, business strategies, and other financial information [20, 22].

SECTION II Telecommunications Network Alternatives

Telecommunications Alternatives

Telecommunications is a highly technical, rapidly changing field of information systems technology. Most business professionals do not need a detailed knowledge of its technical characteristics. However, it is necessary that you understand some of the important characteristics of the basic components of telecommunications networks. This understanding will help you participate effectively in decision making regarding telecommunications alternatives.

Read the Real World Case on secure managed networks. We can learn a lot about the business value of telecommunications networks from this case. See Figure 6.10.

Figure 6.11 outlines key telecommunications component categories and examples. Remember, a basic understanding and appreciation, not a detailed knowledge, is sufficient for most business professionals.

A Telecommunications Network Model

Before we begin our discussion of telecommunications network alternatives, we should understand the basic components of a **telecommunications network**. Generally, a *communications network* is any arrangement in which a *sender* transmits a message to a *receiver* over a *channel* consisting of some type of *medium*. Figure 6.12 illustrates a simple conceptual model of a telecommunications network, which shows that it consists of five basic categories of components:

- **Terminals,** such as networked personal computers, network computers, or information appliances. Any input/output device that uses telecommunications networks to transmit or receive data is a terminal, including telephones and the various computer terminals that were discussed in Chapter 3.
- **Telecommunications processors,** which support data transmission and reception between terminals and computers. These devices, such as modems, switches, and routers, perform a variety of control and support functions in a telecommunications network. For example, they convert data from digital to analog and back, code and decode data, and control the speed, accuracy, and efficiency of the communications flow between computers and terminals in a network.
- **Telecommunications channels** over which data are transmitted and received. Telecommunications channels may use combinations of **media,** such as copper wires, coaxial cables, or fiber-optic cables, or use wireless systems like microwave, communications satellite, radio, and cellular systems to interconnect the other components of a telecommunications network.
- **Computers** of all sizes and types are interconnected by telecommunications networks so that they can carry out their information processing assignments. For example, a mainframe computer may serve as a *host computer* for a large network, assisted by a midrange computer serving as a *front-end processor*, while a microcomputer may act as a *network server* in a small network.
- **Telecommunications control software** consists of programs that control telecommunications activities and manage the functions of telecommunications networks. Examples include network management programs of all kinds, such as *telecommunications monitors* for mainframe host computers, *network operating systems* for network servers, and *Web browsers* for microcomputers.

No matter how large and complex real-world telecommunications networks may appear to be, these five basic categories of network components must be at work to support an organization's telecommunications activities. This is the conceptual framework you can use to help you understand the various types of telecommunications networks in use today.

REAL WORLD CASE 2 Metric & Multistandard Components Corp.: The Business Value of a Secure Self-Managed Network for a Small-to-Medium Business

With 22,000 customers, 48,800 catalogued parts, and 150 employees working in five U.S. locations and an office in Germany, the last thing John Bellnier needs is an unreliable network. But that's exactly what he contended with for years as IT manager at Metric & Multistandard Components Corp. (MMCC). MMCC may still be classified as a small business by some standards, but this small-to-medium business (SMB) definitely has been a big-time success story in its industry.

MMCC was founded in 1963 by three Czech immigrants in Yonkers, New York, and has grown into one of the largest U.S. distributors of metric industrial fasteners. In the last 10 years, business has doubled, reaching $20 million in sales in 2005, and growing just as fast in 2006. But the company's growth overwhelmed its telecommunications network, which was managed by an outside telecom network management company. The network crashed frequently, interrupting e-mail communications and leaving customer service representatives unable to fulfill orders promptly.

"We had locked ourselves into a three-year contract with our provider," Bellnier says. "It was a managed system and therefore we didn't have passwords to the routers. I experienced dozens of episodes of spending days on the phone trying to escalate job tickets to get the problems solved. It was a nightmare."

He recalls a particular challenge that occurred when the provider denied that its router had gone down: "Their network was broken, and we had to deal with the downtime consequences on top of spending time trying to convince someone 2,000 miles away that one of their routers needed repair."

FIGURE 6.10

Massive amounts of telecommunication activities are regularly handled via large and complex control facilities.

Several months before MMCC's contract with the provider was to expire, Bellnier began seeking a better network solution. He outlined five key requirements for a new network for the company:

- Reliability: Provide maximum network uptime to sustain business operations.
- Scalability: Grow with MMCC's increasing business demands.
- Security: Ensure confidentiality and integrity of company data.
- Economy: Reduce costs for both initial outlay and ongoing administrative and maintenance overhead.
- Responsibility: "I wanted all the hardware from one vendor so when issues come up, I know who to turn to," Bellnier adds.

Bellenier met with MMCC executives in 2004 and told them that he believed he could manage a new companywide network internally, on a limited budget, and could recoup the upfront investment by lowering operating expenses. Company executives agreed that the current network situation was intolerable and gave Bellnier the go-ahead to research and select an experienced local IT consulting firm that was certified to build telecom networks by one of the top telecom hardware and software vendors.

Bellnier selected Hi-Link Computer Corp., a Cisco Systems Premier Certified Partner that had earned Cisco specializations in wireless local area networks (LANs) and virtual private network (VPN) security. As a first step, Hi-Link audited MMCC's existing network and interviewed management about business goals and requirements. Company management was impressed with Hi-Link and agreed that Bellnier should seek a formal project proposal from the consultants.

Hi-Link's consulting engineers, led by Business Development Manager Jim Gartner, proposed to Bellnier that MMCC build a secure network foundation consisting of virtual private network links between sites. Using Cisco integrated services routers and security appliances, the network blueprint was designed to give Bellnier transparent remote access to all necessary devices, increase his control over the network, and improve network performance. Hi-Link showed Bellnier how a secure network foundation works to automate routine maintenance, monitor the network, and alert IT staff of security or performance issues.

Bellnier accepted Hi-Link's network plan and made a formal presentation outlining the proposal to company management. After discussing the business costs, risks, and benefits of Hi-Link's plan, MMCC executives agreed to the proposal and the following key project objectives:

> Goal: Create a business network for MMCC with higher reliability, security, and scalability, but lower costs, than the existing externally managed network.
>
> Strategy: Design an IP (Internet Protocol) network with advanced technologies for high availability and efficient network and security management, which can be operated by a very small IT department.
>
> Technology: Use virtual private network technologies to securely connect remote offices and users and facilitate company expansion.
>
> Support: After designing and quickly implementing a secure network foundation based on Cisco products, Hi-Link will help MMCC with technical support whenever needed.

Once the consulting contract was signed, Hi-Link began working with Cisco and the local telecom company to install the telecommunications lines needed for the new network. When those were in place, it took less than a week to deploy the Cisco routers, switches, and other telecommunications hardware preconfigured by Hi-Link. "Hi-Link made this implementation effortless by working efficiently at the best times for us," Bellnier says. "They handled all the details associated with the local telecom company, Internet providers, and project management."

After the secure, internally managed network was up and running, the following benefits soon became apparent:

- The new network eliminated MMCC's network congestion almost immediately.
- Network bandwidth, reliability, and security were significantly improved.
- The sophisticated network monitoring system greatly improved network management.
- Network downtime was reduced to nearly zero.
- The new network is saving MMCC a significant amount of money.

"The previous network had cost us just under $11,000 a month; the new high-bandwidth telecommunications lines we lease cost $4,400 per month," Bellnier explains. "We've calculated an annual savings of $77,000, which means we got our return on investment in our first six months."

Best of all, the network is transparent and easy to manage. "We can access all our Cisco routers. We can view the errors and logs. All our telecommunications lines are contracted directly with the local exchange carrier, which gives us a direct communications link to resolve troubles," Bellnier says. Hi-Link's Gartner says of MMCC's network: "Every remote office is configured in exactly the same way, and we can easily duplicate it to bring up any new location. We can easily add extra bandwidth to meet additional demands." Thus, Hi-Link is helping MMCC add wireless capability to all its warehouses, knowing that additional capacity can be provided if needed.

Gartner emphasizes that as it did for MMCC, a secure network foundation can improve a small company's operational efficiency, secure sensitive data, contain costs, and enhance employee connectivity and customer responsiveness. For example, companies with such network capabilities allow customers to securely track their orders in real time over the Web, empower customer-service agents with detailed account information even before they answer the customer's phone call, and provide easy, inexpensive videoconferencing for remote workers, vendors, and customers.

Bellnier offers advice to other IT managers in small companies that may be considering building and managing their own network: "Do not limit company expansion by thinking you cannot support or afford a self-managed system with limited resources," he says. He adds that MMCC's experience with Hi-Link shows just how quickly an SMB can "recoup the cost and implement a self-managed system with far superior performance and a lot fewer problems."

Source: Adapted from Eric J. Adams, "Creating a Foundation for Growth," *iQ Magazine*, Second Quarter 2006.

CASE STUDY QUESTIONS

1. What were the most important factors contributing to MMCC's success with its new, secure, self-managed network? Explain the reasons for your choices.
2. What are some of the business benefits and challenges of self-managed and externally managed networks?
3. Which type of network management would you advise small-to-medium business firms to use? Explain the reasons for your recommendation.

REAL WORLD ACTIVITIES

1. Use the Internet to discover more about the telecommunications products and services and current business performance and prospects of Cisco Systems and Hi-Link and some of their many competitors in the telecom industry. Which telecom hardware and software company and IT consulting firm would you recommend to a small-to-medium business with which you are familiar? Explain your reasons to the class.
2. In telecommunications network installation and management, as in many other business situations, the choice between "do it yourself" and "let the experts handle it" is a crucial business decision for many companies. Break into small groups with your classmates to debate this choice for small-to-medium businesses. See if you can agree on several key criteria that should be considered in making this decision, and report your conclusions to the class.

FIGURE 6.11 Key telecommunications network component categories and examples.

Network Alternative	Examples of Alternatives
Networks	Internet, intranet, extranet, wide area, local area, client/server, network computing, peer-to-peer
Media	Twisted-pair wire, coaxial cable, fiber optics, microwave radio, communications satellites, cellular and PCS systems, wireless mobile and LAN systems
Processors	Modems, multiplexers, switches, routers, hubs, gateways, front-end processors, private branch exchanges
Software	Network operating systems, telecommunications monitors, Web browsers, middleware
Channels	Analog/digital, switched/nonswitched, circuit/message/packet/cell switching, bandwidth alternatives
Topology/architecture	Star, ring, and bus topologies, OSI and TCP/IP architectures and protocols

Types of Telecommunications Networks

Many different types of networks serve as the telecommunications infrastructure for the Internet and the intranets and extranets of internetworked enterprises. However, from an end user's point of view, there are only a few basic types, such as wide area and local area networks and client/server, network computing, and peer-to-peer networks.

Wide Area Networks

Telecommunications networks covering a large geographic area are called **wide area networks (WANs)**. Networks that cover a large city or metropolitan area *(metropolitan area networks)* can also be included in this category. Such large networks have become a necessity for carrying out the day-to-day activities of many business and government organizations and their end users. For example, WANs are used by many multinational companies to transmit and receive information among their employees, customers, suppliers, and other organizations across cities, regions, countries, and the world. Figure 6.13 illustrates an example of a global wide area network for a major multinational corporation.

Local Area Networks

Local area networks (LANs) connect computers and other information processing devices within a limited physical area, such as an office, classroom, building, manufacturing plant, or other worksite. LANs have become commonplace in many organizations for providing telecommunications network capabilities that link end users in offices, departments, and other workgroups.

LANs use a variety of telecommunications media, such as ordinary telephone wiring, coaxial cable, or even wireless radio and infrared systems, to interconnect

FIGURE 6.12 The five basic components in a telecommunications network: (1) terminals, (2) telecommunications processors, (3) telecommunications channels, (4) computers, and (5) telecommunications software.

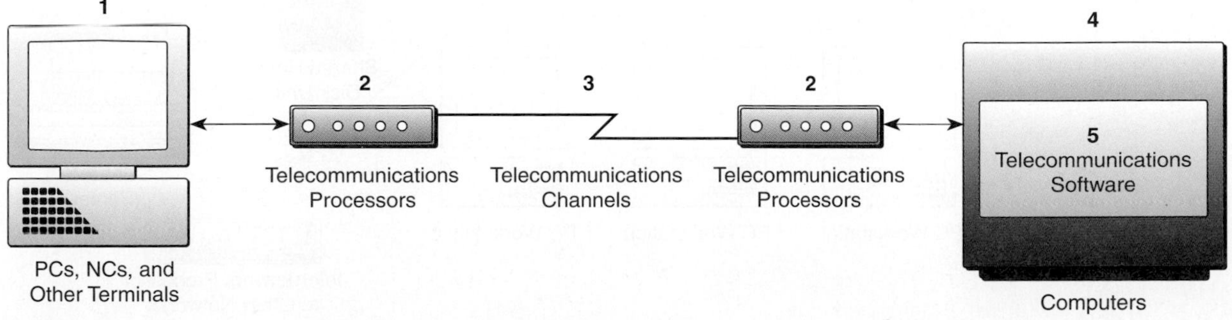

FIGURE 6.13 A global wide area network (WAN): the Chevron MPI (Multi-Protocol Internetwork).

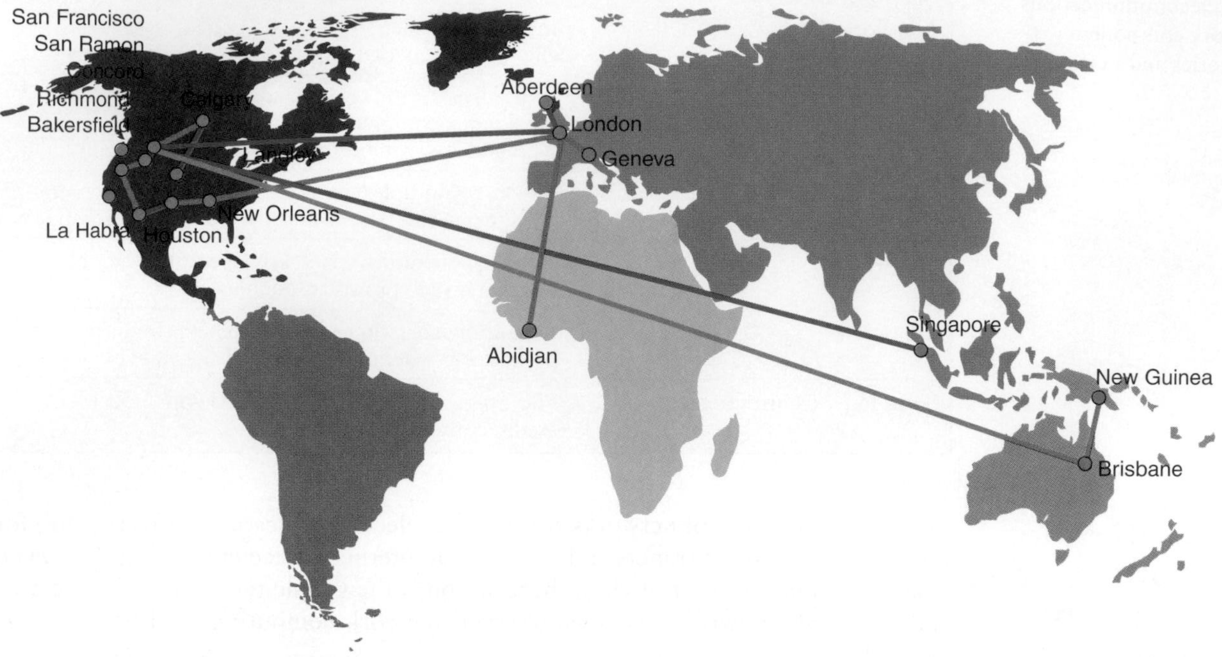

Source: Courtesy of Cisco Systems Inc.

microcomputer workstations and computer peripherals. To communicate over the network, each PC usually has a circuit board called a *network interface card.* Most LANs use a more powerful microcomputer with a large hard disk capacity, called a *file server* or **network server,** that contains a **network operating system** program that controls telecommunications and the use and sharing of network resources. For example, it distributes copies of common data files and software packages to the other microcomputers in the network and controls access to shared laser printers and other network peripherals. See Figure 6.14.

FIGURE 6.14
A local area network (LAN). Note how the LAN allows users to share hardware, software, and data resources.

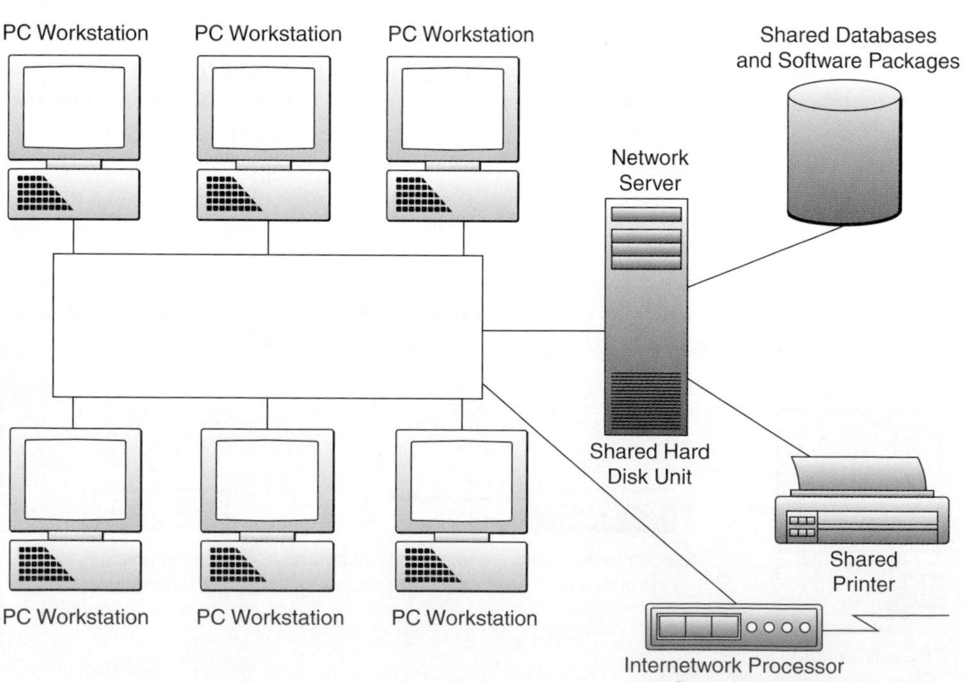

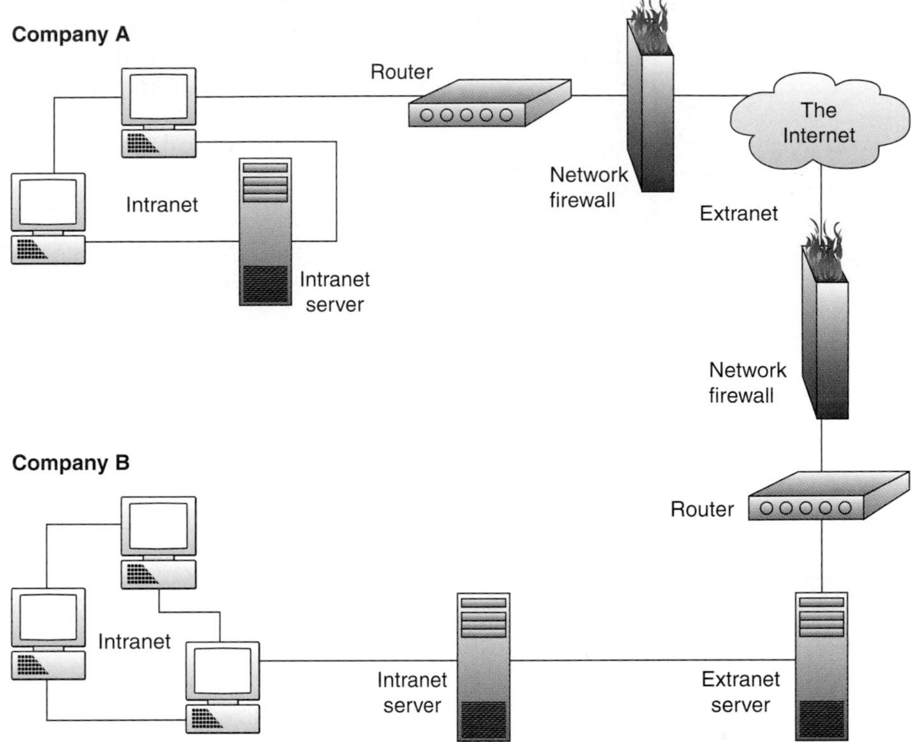

FIGURE 6.15
An example of a virtual private network protected by network firewalls.

Virtual Private Networks

Many organizations use **virtual private networks (VPNs)** to establish secure intranets and extranets. A virtual private network is a secure network that uses the Internet as its main *backbone network* but relies on network firewalls, encryption, and other security features of its Internet and intranet connections and those of participating organizations. Thus, for example, VPNs would enable a company to use the Internet to establish secure intranets between its distant branch offices and manufacturing plants and secure extranets between itself and its business customers and suppliers. Figure 6.15 illustrates a VPN in which network routers serve as firewalls to screen Internet traffic between two companies. We will discuss firewalls, encryption, and other network security features in Chapter 11. For the time being, we can think of a VPN as a pipe traveling through the Internet. Through this pipe, we can send and receive our data without anyone outside the pipe being able to see or access our transmissions. Using this approach, we can "create" a private network without incurring the high cost of a separate proprietary connection scheme. Let's look at a real-world example about the future of VPN.

Forrester: VPN to Become De Facto Access Standard

Spending on virtual private networks (VPN) will grow at a 53 percent compound annual growth rate, and VPNs will surpass traditional secured network approaches as the de facto remote access security standard by 2008, according to a report from Forrester Research.

Forrester associate analyst Robert Whiteley argues companies are attracted by the technology's application-level simplicity. Unlike traditional secure network approaches, which require special client software to access the network, VPN supports a wide range of devices, from desktop computers to PDAs, and applications, while offering network administrators greater granularity of user information and providing better endpoint security.

According to the report, some 44 percent of American businesses have deployed advanced VPNs, spending $97 million on the technology in 2005 alone. Despite the impressive adoption rate for a technology that has been in the business mainstream for less than a year, Forrester expects VPN deployments to continue to take off, with the market growing at a 53 percent compound annual growth rate.

VPNs are already well-entrenched in the financial and business services industries and in the public sector. Driven by the need to ensure endpoint security for online services, the financial services industry can boast a 56 percent penetration rate, with business services just behind at 51 percent. In both cases, Forrester predicts a compound annual growth of 34 percent to 2010 which, though impressive, pales beside the expected VPN growth in late-adopting industries.

Retail and manufacturing are poised to leap into VPN with gusto over the next few years. Retail and wholesale allocates 7.8 percent of its IT spending to security—more than even financial services. This industry shows the most VPN potential because of its eye toward security, relatively little penetration to date, and the need for large, distributed deployments—resulting in 82 percent annual market growth through 2010.

Although only 29 percent of manufacturers are currently invested in VPNs, Forrester expects that to change dramatically through 2010, predicting a phenomenal 94 percent compound annual growth rate [11, 23].

Client/Server Networks

Client/server networks have become the predominant information architecture of enterprisewide computing. In a client/server network, end-user PC or NC workstations are the **clients.** They are interconnected by local area networks and share application processing with network **servers,** which also manage the networks. (This arrangement of clients and servers is sometimes called a *two-tier* client/server architecture.) Local area networks are also interconnected to other LANs and WANs of client workstations and servers. Figure 6.16 illustrates the functions of the computer systems that may be in client/server networks, including optional host systems and superservers.

A continuing trend is the **downsizing** of larger computer systems by replacing them with client/server networks. For example, a client/server network of several interconnected local area networks may replace a large mainframe-based network with many end-user terminals. This shift typically involves a complex and costly effort to install new application software that replaces the software of older, traditional mainframe-based business information systems, now called **legacy systems**. Client/server networks are seen as more economical and flexible than legacy systems in meeting end-user, workgroup, and business unit needs and more adaptable in adjusting to a diverse range of computing workloads.

Network Computing

The growing reliance on the computer hardware, software, and data resources of the Internet, intranets, extranets, and other networks has emphasized that for many users, "the network is the computer." This **network computing** or *network-centric* concept views networks as the central computing resource of any computing environment.

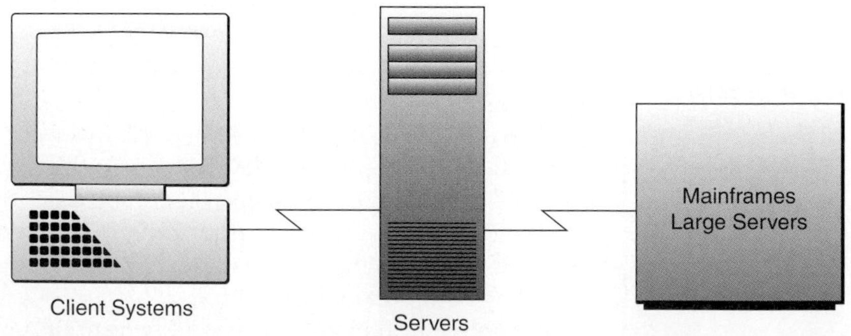
Mainframes
Large Servers
Client Systems
Servers
■ Functions: Provide user interface, perform some/most processing on an application.
■ Functions: Shared computation, application control, distributed databases.
■ Functions: Central database control, security, directory management, heavy-duty processing.

FIGURE 6.16
The functions of the computer systems in client/server networks.

FIGURE 6.17
The functions of the computer systems in network computing.

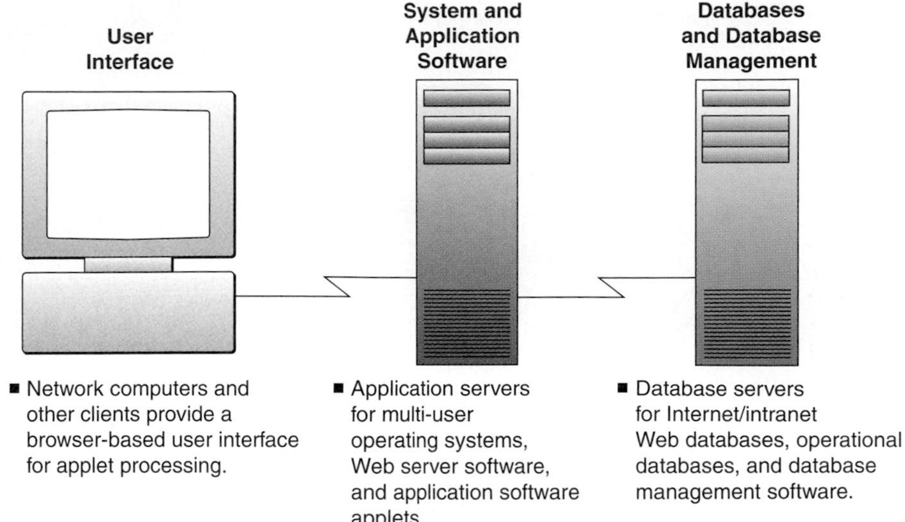
User
Interface
System and
Application
Software
Databases
and Database
Management
■ Network computers and other clients provide a browser-based user interface for applet processing.
■ Application servers for multi-user operating systems, Web server software, and application software applets.
■ Database servers for Internet/intranet Web databases, operational databases, and database management software.

Figure 6.17 illustrates that in network computing, **network computers** and other *thin clients* provide a browser-based user interface for processing small application programs called *applets*. Thin clients include network computers, Net PCs, and other low-cost network devices or information appliances. Application and database servers provide the operating system, application software, applets, databases, and database management software needed by the end users in the network. Network computing is sometimes called a *three-tier* client/server model, because it consists of thin clients, application servers, and database servers.

Peer-to-Peer Networks

The emergence of peer-to-peer (P2P) networking technologies and applications for the Internet is being hailed as a development that will have a major impact on e-business and e-commerce and the Internet itself. Whatever the merits of such claims, it is clear that peer-to-peer networks are a powerful telecommunications networking tool for many business applications.

Figure 6.18 illustrates two major models of **peer-to-peer networking** technology. In the central server architecture, P2P file-sharing software connects your PC to a central server that contains a directory of all of the other users *(peers)* in the network. When you request a file, the software searches the directory for any other users who have that file and are online at that moment. It then sends you a list of user names that are active links to all such users. Clicking on one of these user names prompts the software to connect your PC to that user's PC (making a *peer-to-peer* connection) and automatically transfers the file you want from his or her hard drive to yours.

The *pure* peer-to-peer network architecture has no central directory or server. First, the file-sharing software in the P2P network connects your PC with one of the online users in the network. Then an active link to your user name is transmitted from peer to peer to all the online users in the network that the first user (and the other online users) encountered in previous sessions. In this way, active links to more and more peers spread throughout the network the more it is used. When you request a file, the software searches every online user and sends you a list of active file names related to your request. Clicking on one of these automatically transfers the file from that user's hard drive to yours.

One of the major advantages and limitations of the central server architecture is its reliance on a central directory and server. The directory server can be slowed or overwhelmed by too many users or technical problems. However, it also provides the network with a platform that can better protect the integrity and security of the content and users of the network. Some applications of pure P2P networks, in contrast, have been plagued by slow response times and bogus and corrupted files.

FIGURE 6.18 The two major forms of peer-to-peer networks.

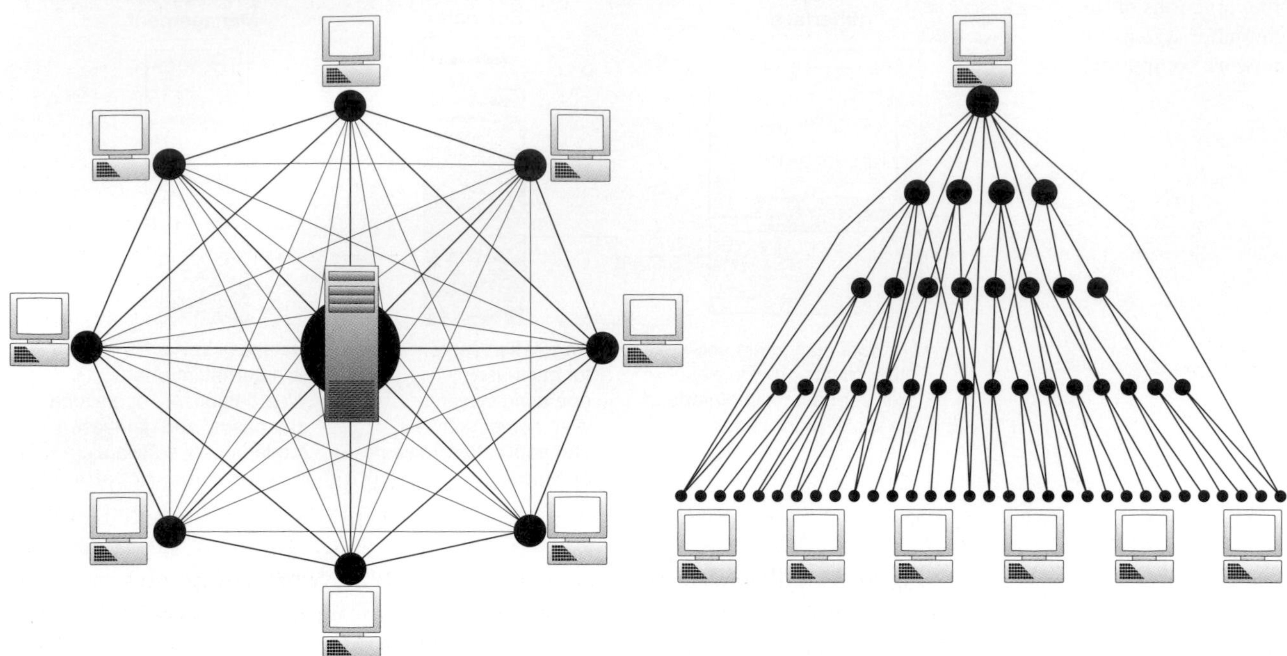

■ A peer-to-peer network architecture with a directory of all peers on a central server

■ A pure peer-to-peer network architecture with no central directory server

The Internet, as originally conceived in the late 1960s, was a peer-to-peer system. The goal of the original ARPANET (the name of the early version of today's Internet) was to share computing resources around the United States. The challenge for this effort was to integrate different kinds of existing networks as well as future technologies with one common network architecture that would allow every host to be an equal player. The first few hosts on the ARPANET—UCLA and the University of Utah, for example—were already independent computing sites with equal status. The ARPANET connected them together not in a master/slave or client/server relationship but rather as equal computing peers.

One common use for peer-to-peer networks today is the downloading and trading of files. When the term *peer-to-peer* was used to describe the *Napster* network, it implied that the peer protocol nature was important, but in reality the unique achievement of Napster was the empowerment of the peers (that is, the fringes of the network) in association with a central index that made it fast and efficient to locate available content. The peer protocol was just a common way to achieve this.

Although much media attention has focused on copyright-infringing uses of file trading networks, there are vast numbers of entirely noninfringing uses. *BitTorrent* was originally designed to keep sites from getting overwhelmed by "flash crowds" and heavy traffic. That makes it very suitable for many situations in which there are massive peaks of demand. Most Linux distributions are released via BitTorrent to help with their bandwidth needs. Another example is *Blizzard Entertainment* (http://www.blizzard.com), which uses a modified version of BitTorrent to distribute patches to its game World of Warcraft (http://www.worldofwarcraft.com). Users have often complained about BitTorrent due to a bandwidth cap that almost defeats its purpose.

Other peer-to-peer networks are emerging as well, such as *PeerCast*, which allows someone to broadcast an Internet radio or TV station with very little upstream bandwidth due to its distributed nature. Other peer-to-peer broadcast tools, sometimes called *peer-casting*, include the *IceShare* project and *FreeCast*.

Digital and Analog Signals

We regularly hear the words *analog* and *digital* associated with computers, telephones, and other hardware devices. To be sure you understand exactly what these terms mean, a short discussion may be helpful.

Basically, **analog** or **digital** refers to the method used to convert information into an electrical signal. Telephones, microphones, measuring instruments, vinyl record players, CD players, tape decks, computers, fax machines, and so on must convert information into an electrical signal in some manner so that it can be transmitted or processed. For example, a microphone must convert the pressure waves that we call *sound* into a corresponding electrical voltage or current, which can be sent down a telephone line, amplified in a sound system, broadcast on the radio, and/or recorded on some medium.

In an analog system, an electrical voltage or current is generated that is proportional to the quantity being observed. In a digital system, the quantity being observed is expressed as a number. *This is really all there is to it*, but a few details must still be discussed.

For example, in an electronic analog thermometer, if the temperature being measured is 83 degrees, then the analog system would put out, for example, 83 volts. This level could just as well be 8.3 volts or any other voltage proportional to the temperature. Thus, if the temperature doubled to 166 degrees, the output voltage would double to 166 volts (or perhaps 16.6 volts if the instrument were so scaled). The output voltage is, therefore, "analogous" to the temperature—thus the use of the term *analog*.

In the case of an electronic digital thermometer, however, the output would be the number 83 if the temperature were 83 degrees. Hence it is based on "digits." The only thing wrong with this example is that 83 is a decimal number constructed from the 10 symbols 0, 1, 2, . . . , 8, 9. We commonly use 10 symbols in our numbers for historical reasons; probably because we have 10 fingers. Ten symbols, however, is inconvenient if it is desired to express it as an electrical voltage. It is much more convenient to have only two symbols, 0 and 1. In this case, 0 could be represented by zero volts, and 1 by 5 volts, for example. Recall from Chapter 3 that this system is known as a binary (only two symbols) number system, but the principle is still the same: The output of the digital thermometer is a number, that is, "digits."

For the thermometer example above, 83 is the binary number 1010011. The electronic thermometer would send the sequence 5 volts, 0 volts, 5 volts, 0 volts, 0 volts, 5 volts, and 5 volts to express the number 83 in binary.

A digital system may seem more complicated than an analog system, but it has a number of advantages. The principal advantage is that once the measurement is expressed in digital form, it can be entered into a computer or a microprocessor and manipulated as desired. If we worked with only analog devices, we would eventually have to convert the output of the analog device into digital form if we wanted to input it into a computer. Because computer networks work primarily with digital signals, most of the hardware used by a computer network is digital.

Telecommunications Media

Telecommunications channels make use of a variety of **telecommunications media**. These include twisted-pair wire, coaxial cables, and fiber-optic cables, all of which physically link the devices in a network. Also included are terrestrial microwave, communications satellites, cellular phone systems, and packet and LAN radio, all of which use microwave and other radio waves. In addition, there are infrared systems, which use infrared light to transmit and receive data. See Figure 6.19.

Wired Technologies

Twisted-Pair Wire

Ordinary telephone wire, consisting of copper wire twisted into pairs **(twisted-pair wire)**, is the most widely used medium for telecommunications. These lines are used in established communications networks throughout the world for both voice and data transmission. Twisted-pair wiring is wrapped or shielded in a variety of forms and used extensively in home and office telephone systems and many local area networks and

FIGURE 6.19 Common telecommunications guided media: (a) Twisted-pair wire, (b) Coaxial cable, (c) Fiber-optic cable.

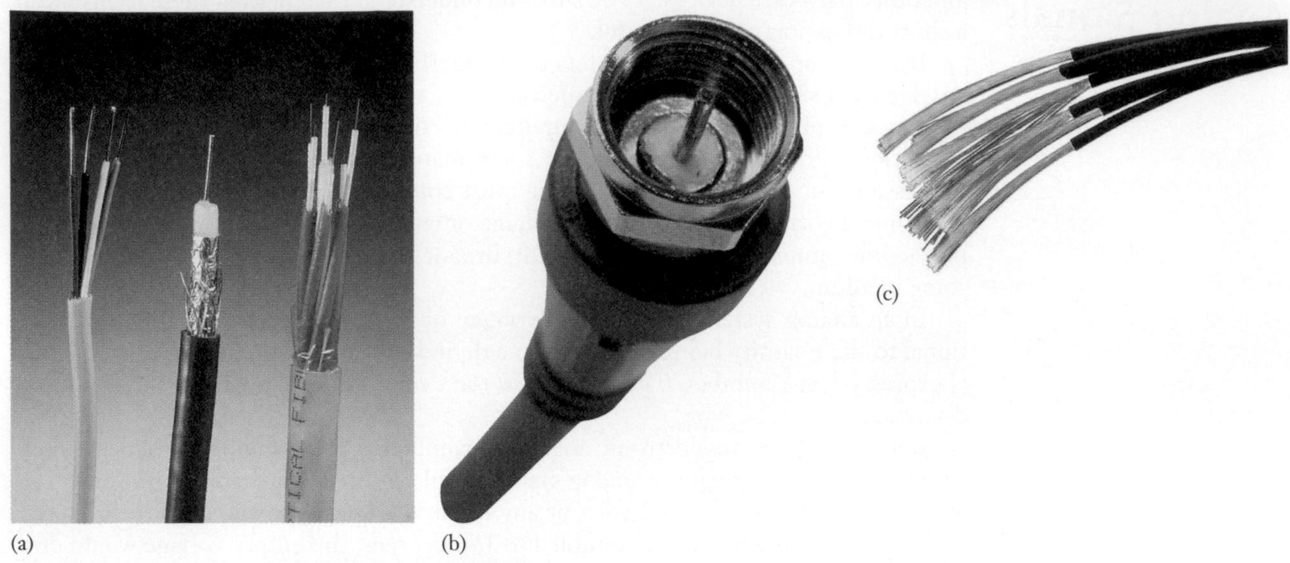

(a) (b) (c)

wide area networks. Transmission speeds can range from 2 million bits per second (unshielded) to 100 million bits per second (shielded).

Coaxial Cable

Coaxial cable consists of a sturdy copper or aluminum wire wrapped with spacers to insulate and protect it. The cable's cover and insulation minimize interference and distortion of the signals the cable carries. Groups of coaxial cables may be bundled together in a big cable for ease of installation. These high-quality lines can be placed underground and laid on the floors of lakes and oceans. They allow high-speed data transmission (from 200 million to over 500 million bits per second—200–500 Mbps) and are used instead of twisted-pair wire lines in high-service metropolitan areas, for cable TV systems, and for short-distance connections of computers and peripheral devices. Coaxial cables are also used in many office buildings and other worksites for local area networks.

Fiber Optics

Fiber optics uses cables consisting of one or more hair-thin filaments of glass fiber wrapped in a protective jacket. They can conduct pulses of visible light elements *(photons)* generated by lasers at transmission rates as high as trillions of bits per second (terabits per second, or Tbps). This speed is hundreds of times faster than coaxial cable and thousands of times better than twisted-pair wire lines. Fiber-optic cables provide substantial size and weight reductions as well as increased speed and greater carrying capacity. A half-inch-diameter fiber-optic cable can carry more than 500,000 channels, compared with about 5,500 channels for a standard coaxial cable.

Fiber-optic cables are not affected by and do not generate electromagnetic radiation; therefore, multiple fibers can be placed in the same cable. Fiber-optic cables have less need for repeaters for signal retransmissions than copper wire media. Fiber optics also has a much lower data error rate than other media and is harder to tap than electrical wire and cable. Fiber-optic cables have already been installed in many parts of the world, and they are expected to replace other communications media in many applications.

New optical technologies such as *dense wave division multiplexing* (DWDM) can split a strand of glass fiber into 40 channels, which enables each strand to carry 5 million calls. In the future, DWDM technology is expected to split each fiber into 1,000 channels, enabling each strand to carry up to 122 million calls. In addition, newly developed *optical routers* will be able to send optical signals up to 2,500 miles without needing regeneration, thus eliminating the need for repeaters every 370 miles to regenerate signals.

The Problem of "The Last Mile"

While on the subject of telecommunication media, we need to understand a pervasive problem in the telecommunications industry: the problem of **the last mile.** The last-mile problem, while simple to understand, is still one of the largest costs faced by telecommunications providers.

The basic problem goes something like this: The telecommunications provider adopts a new, faster, better technology that can provide higher bandwidths and faster telecommunication speeds to consumers. A good example of this type of situation is the invention of fiber-optic cable and its related optical technologies. Fiber can move data at lightning speed and handle a much larger volume of data than the more typical twisted-pair wiring commonly found in households. So the telecommunications provider completely reengineers the network and begins laying fiber instead of copper wire in trenches. The fiber, costing $500,000 to $1 million per mile, begins bringing all of its faster, better, and cheaper benefits to the front door of the consumer. This is where the last-mile problem begins. Out in front of the house lies enough bandwidth to handle over 100 million telephone calls or download entire movies in a few seconds. The problem is that the house it is connecting to is wired with twisted-pair wiring that simply cannot handle the bandwidth provided by fiber. This situation is analogous to hooking up a garden hose to the water volume generated by Niagara Falls. At the end of the day, the amount of water you get is whatever will come out of the garden hose and nothing more.

Many methods have been offered to solve the last mile problem. Cable companies are providing a single-wire solution to many modern households. By using sophisticated technologies, they can bring cable television, Internet access, and telephone services into a home using only the coaxial wire originally put there for cable television. Other solutions include bypassing the old wired network completely and providing high-speed services via a satellite or other wireless approach. Regardless of the solution, the problem of the last mile is still very much an issue to consider when designing a telecommunications network.

Although still in the developmental stages, one solution to the last mile problem may be **WiMax.** Defined as *Worldwide Interoperability for Microwave Access*, WiMax is intended to provide high-speed, mobile telecommunications services to diverse Internet connections and locations. There are still many issues to work out regarding WiMax, but it looks like we may be able to solve the problem of last mile connectivity somewhere in the near future.

Wireless Technologies

Wireless telecommunications technologies rely on radio wave, microwave, infrared, and visible light pulses to transport digital communications without wires between communications devices. Wireless technologies include terrestrial microwave, communications satellites, cellular and PCS telephone and pager systems, mobile data radio, wireless LANs, and various wireless Internet technologies. Each technology utilizes specific ranges within the electromagnetic spectrum (in megahertz) of electromagnetic frequencies that are specified by national regulatory agencies to minimize interference and encourage efficient telecommunications. Let's briefly review some of these major wireless communications technologies.

Terrestrial Microwave

Terrestrial microwave involves earthbound microwave systems that transmit high-speed radio signals in a line-of-sight path between relay stations spaced approximately 30 miles apart. Microwave antennas are usually placed on top of buildings, towers, hills, and mountain peaks, and they are a familiar sight in many sections of the country. They are still a popular medium for both long-distance and metropolitan area networks.

Communications Satellites

Communications satellites also use microwave radio as their telecommunications medium. Typically, high-earth orbit (HEO) communications satellites are placed in stationary geosynchronous orbits approximately 22,000 miles above the equator. Satellites are powered by solar panels and can transmit microwave signals at a rate of several hundred million bits per second. They serve as relay stations for communications signals transmitted from earth stations. Earth stations use dish antennas to beam microwave signals to the satellites that amplify and retransmit the signals to other earth stations thousands of miles away.

Whereas communications satellites were used initially for voice and video transmission, they are now also used for high-speed transmission of large volumes of data. Because of time delays caused by the great distances involved, they are not suitable for interactive, real-time processing. Communications satellite systems are operated by several firms, including Comsat, American Mobile Satellite, and Intellsat.

Various other satellite technologies are being implemented to improve global business communications. For example, many companies use networks of small satellite dish antennas known as VSAT (very small aperture terminal) to connect their stores and distant worksites via satellite. Other satellite networks use many low-earth orbit (LEO) satellites orbiting at an altitude of only 500 miles above the Earth. Companies like Globalstar offer wireless phone, paging, and messaging services to users anywhere on the globe. Let's look at a real-world example.

Bob Evans Farms: The Case for Satellite Networks

The network connecting the 459 restaurants and six food-production plants of Bob Evans Farms Inc. to one another and the Internet runs via satellite, a technology choice that came as something of a surprise to company executives. "Truthfully, we didn't want to do satellite at first," admits Bob Evans Farms CIO Larry Beckwith. The company looked at every possible offering, including a virtual private network over the Internet. But a VSAT (very small aperture terminal) communications satellite network was the only technology that supported Bob Evans's goals, was available at all sites, and was cost effective, Beckwith says.

Until 2000, the computers at Bob Evans restaurants dialed in daily over ordinary phone lines to the Columbus, Ohio, headquarters to report sales, payroll, and other data. That worked well enough, Beckwith says. But credit card authorization, especially on busy weekend mornings, was another story. "With dial-up, every time you swipe a credit card, a modem dials the credit card authorization site, makes the connection, then verifies the card, which takes another 15 seconds," Beckwith describes. If the connection fails, it restarts after timing out for 30 seconds, "a long time when you've got a line of people waiting to pay. We needed a better solution."

Satellite would give the restaurants the connection and sufficient bandwidth—8 Mbps outbound from remote sites, and 153 Kbps inbound. After talks with satellite network vendors, Beckwith ran tests for two months, first in the lab, then in one restaurant, on a Skystar Advantage system from Spacenet Inc. Only after a further month-long pilot project with 10 stores was Beckwith sold on satellite. During the next five weeks, Spacenet rolled out earth stations to 440 stores, and the network went live in September 2000.

"Average time to do a credit card authorization is about three seconds now, including getting your printed receipt," Beckwith says. Also running over satellite are nightly automatic polling of financial data from the point-of-sale (POS) systems, Lotus Notes e-mail to managers, and online manuals of restaurant procedures, restaurant POS systems, facilities, and physical plant maintenance, "things the restaurants never had live access to before," according to Beckwith.

New applications planned include online inventory management, with XML-based electronic ordering to follow. In-store audio for music and promotional messages and video broadcasting for employee training and corporate communications (Skystar supports IP multicasting) are also in the works for the near future [15].

Cellular and PCS Systems

Cellular and PCS telephone and pager systems use several radio communications technologies. However, all of them divide a geographic area into small areas, or *cells*, typically from one to several square miles in area. Each cell has its own low-power transmitter or radio relay antenna device to relay calls from one cell to another. Computers and other communications processors coordinate and control the transmissions to and from mobile users as they move from one area to another.

Cellular phone systems have long used analog communications technologies operating at frequencies in the 800–900 MHz cellular band. Newer cellular systems use digital technologies, which provide greater capacity and security, and additional services such as voice mail, paging, messaging, and caller ID. These capabilities are also available with PCS (Personal Communications Services) phone systems. PCS operates at 1,900 MHz frequencies using digital technologies that are related to digital cellular. However, PCS phone systems cost substantially less to operate and use than cellular systems and have lower power consumption requirements.

Wireless LANs

Wiring an office or a building for a local area network is often a difficult and costly task. Older buildings frequently do not have conduits for coaxial cables or additional twisted-pair wire, and the conduits in newer buildings may not have enough room to pull additional wiring through. Repairing mistakes in and damage to wiring is often difficult and costly, as are major relocations of LAN workstations and other components. One solution to such problems is installing a **wireless LAN** using one of several wireless technologies. Examples include a high-frequency radio technology similar to digital cellular and a low-frequency radio technology called *spread spectrum*.

The use of wireless LANs is growing rapidly as new high-speed technologies are implemented. A prime example is a new open-standard wireless radio-wave technology technically known as IEEE 802.11b, or more popularly as Wi-Fi (for wireless fidelity). Wi-Fi is faster (11 Mbps) and less expensive than Standard Ethernet and other common wire-based LAN technologies. Thus, Wi-Fi wireless LANs enable laptop PCs, PDAs, and other devices with Wi-Fi modems to connect easily to the Internet and other networks in a rapidly increasing number of business, public, and home environments. A faster version (802.11g) with speeds of 54 Mbps promises to make this technology even more widely used [5].

Bluetooth

A short-range wireless technology called **Bluetooth** is rapidly being built into computers and other devices. Bluetooth serves as a wire- and cable-free wireless connection to peripheral devices such as computer printers and scanners. Bluetooth operates at about 1 Mbps and has an effective range from 10 to 100 meters. Bluetooth promises to change significantly the way we use computers and other telecommunication devices.

To fully appreciate the potential value of Bluetooth, look around the space where you have your computer. You have your keyboard connected to the computer, as well as a printer, pointing device, monitor, and so on. What joins these together are their associated cables. Cables have become the bane of many offices, homes, and so on. Many of us have experienced the "joys" of trying to figure out what cable goes where and getting tangled up in the details. Bluetooth essentially aims to fix this; it is a cable-replacement technology.

Conceived initially by Ericsson and later adopted by a myriad of other companies, Bluetooth is a standard for a small, cheap radio chip to be plugged into computers, printers, mobile phones, and so forth. A Bluetooth chip is designed to replace cables by taking the information normally carried by the cable and transmitting it at a special frequency to a receiver Bluetooth chip, which will then give the information received to the computer, telephone, printer, or other Bluetooth device. Given its fairly low cost to implement, Bluetooth is set to revolutionize telecommunications.

FIGURE 6.20 The Wireless Application Protocol (WAP) architecture for wireless Internet services to mobile information appliances.

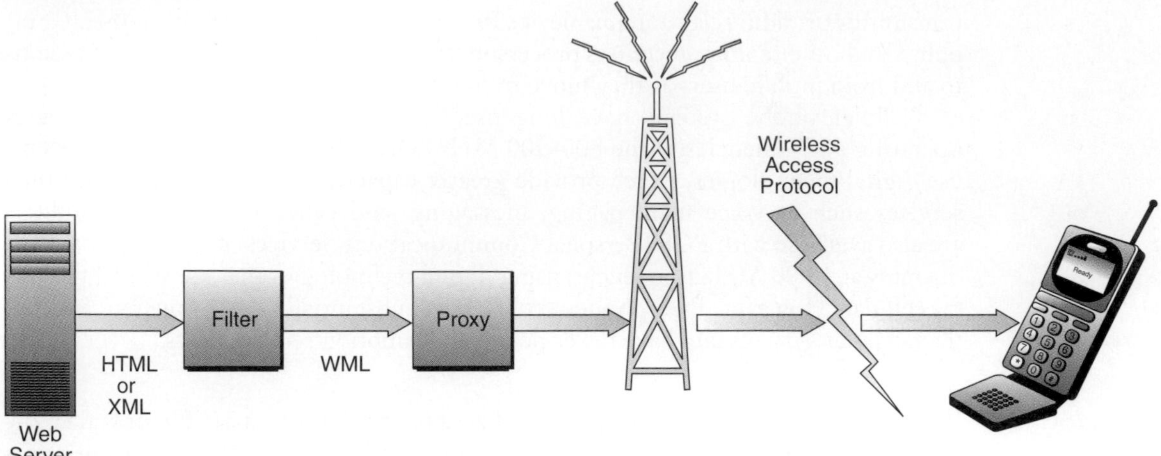

The Wireless Web

Wireless access to the Internet, intranets, and extranets is growing as more Web-enabled information appliances proliferate. Smart telephones, pagers, PDAs, and other portable communications devices have become *very thin clients* in wireless networks. Agreement on a standard *wireless application protocol* (WAP) has encouraged the development of many wireless Web applications and services. The telecommunications industry continues to work on *third-generation* (3G) wireless technologies whose goal is to raise wireless transmission speeds to enable streaming video and multimedia applications on mobile devices.

For example, the Smartphone, a PCS phone, can send and receive e-mail and provide Web access via a "Web clipping" technology that generates custom-designed Web pages from many popular financial, securities, travel, sport, entertainment, and e-commerce Web sites. Another example is the Sprint PCS Wireless Web phone, which delivers similar Web content and e-mail services via a Web-enabled PCS phone.

Figure 6.20 illustrates the wireless application protocol that is the foundation of wireless mobile Internet and Web applications. The WAP standard specifies how Web pages in HTML or XML are translated into a *wireless markup language* (WML) by *filter* software and preprocessed by *proxy* software to prepare the Web pages for wireless transmission from a Web server to a Web-enabled wireless device [16].

UPS: Wireless LANs and M-Commerce

UPS is a global company with one of the most recognized and admired brand names in the world. It has become the world's largest package delivery company and a leading global provider of specialized transportation and logistics services. Every day UPS manages the flow of goods, funds, and information in more than 200 countries and territories worldwide. A technology-driven company, UPS has over 260,000 PCs, 6,200 servers, 2,700 midrange computers, and 14 mainframes. This technology infrastructure is in place to handle the delivery and pickup of over 3.4 billion packages and documents per year, as well as the 115 million hits per day on its Web site, of which more than 9 million hits are tracking requests.

To manage all this mobile commerce (m-commerce) information, Atlanta-based UPS uses wireless as part of UPScan, a companywide, global initiative to streamline and standardize all scanning hardware and software used in its package distribution centers. For package tracking, UPScan consolidates multiple scanning applications into one wireless LAN application while maintaining interfaces with critical control and repository systems.

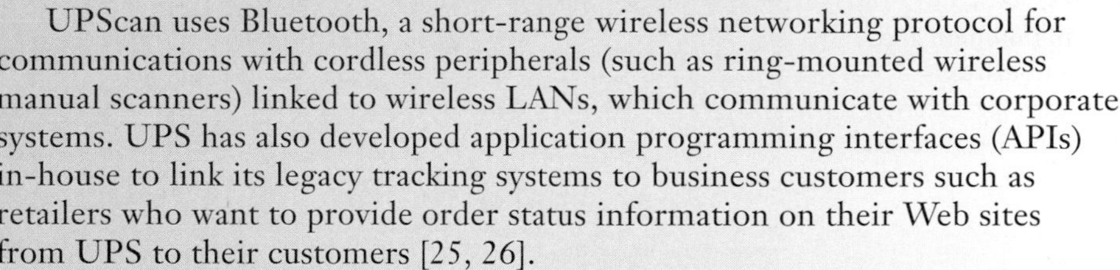

UPScan uses Bluetooth, a short-range wireless networking protocol for communications with cordless peripherals (such as ring-mounted wireless manual scanners) linked to wireless LANs, which communicate with corporate systems. UPS has also developed application programming interfaces (APIs) in-house to link its legacy tracking systems to business customers such as retailers who want to provide order status information on their Web sites from UPS to their customers [25, 26].

Telecommunications Processors

Telecommunications processors such as modems, multiplexers, switches, and routers perform a variety of support functions between the computers and other devices in a telecommunications network. Let's take a look at some of these processors and their functions. See Figure 6.21.

Modems

Modems are the most common type of communications processor. They convert the digital signals from a computer or transmission terminal at one end of a communications link into analog frequencies that can be transmitted over ordinary telephone lines. A modem at the other end of the communications line converts the transmitted data back into digital form at a receiving terminal. This process is known as *modulation* and *demodulation*, and the word *modem* is a combined abbreviation of those two words. Modems come in several forms, including small stand-alone units, plug-in circuit boards, and removable modem cards for laptop PCs. Most modems also support a variety of telecommunications functions, such as transmission error control, automatic dialing and answering, and a faxing capability. As shown in Figure 6.21, a modem is

FIGURE 6.21 Examples of some of the communications processors involved in an Internet connection.

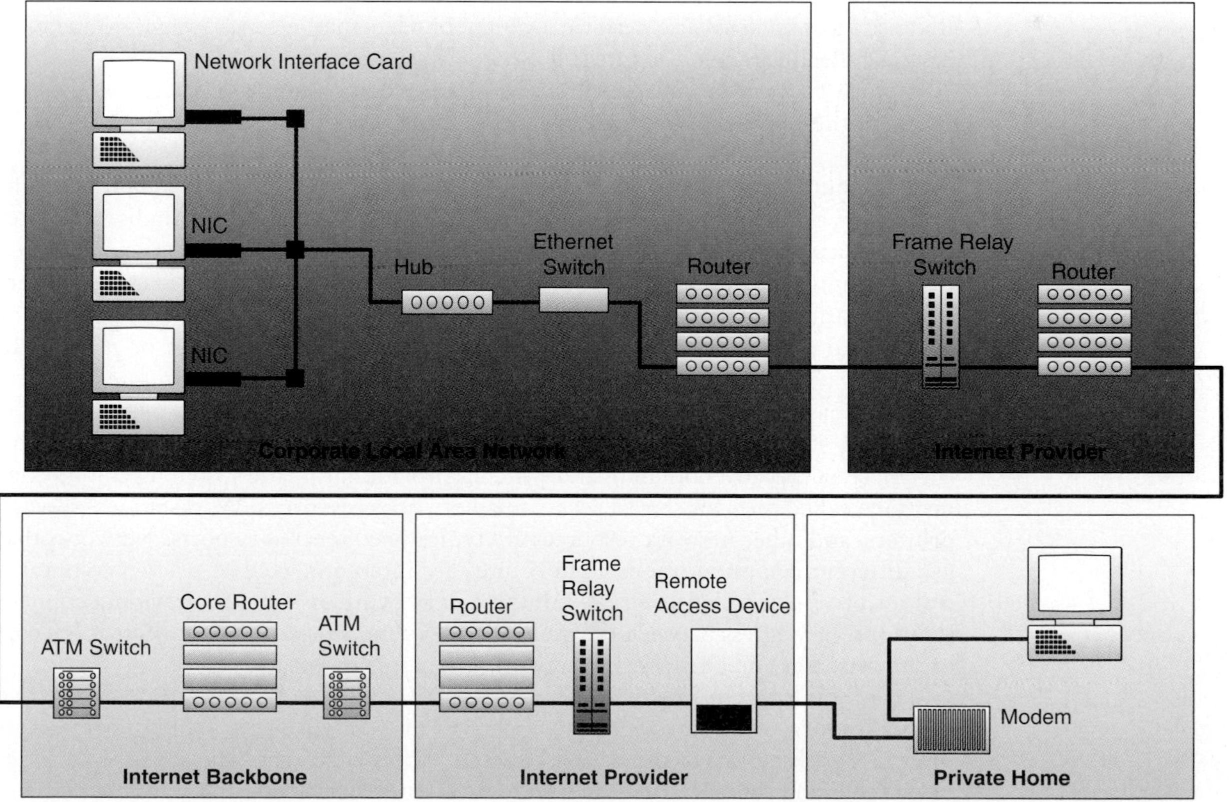

FIGURE 6.22
Comparing modem and telecommunications technologies for Internet and other network access.

Modem (56 Kbps)	DSL (Digital Subscriber Line) Modem
• Receives at 56 Kbps • Sends at 33.6 Kbps • Slowest technology	• Receives at 1.5 Mbps to 5.0 Mbps • Sends at 128 Kbps to 640 Kbps • Users must be near switching centers
ISDN (Integrated Services Digital Network)	**Cable Modem**
• Sends and receives at 128 Kbps • Users need extra lines • Becoming obsolete	• Receives at 1.5 Mbps to 5 Mbps • Sends at 128 Kbps to 2.5 Mbps • Speed degrades with many local users
Home Satellite	**Local Microwave**
• Receives at 400 Kbps • Sends via phone modem • Slow sending, higher cost	• Sends and receives at 512 Kbps to 1.4 Mbps • Higher cost • May require line of sight to base antenna

used in the private-home setting to accept the data from the Internet provider and convert it to input for a PC.

Modems are used because ordinary telephone networks were first designed to handle continuous analog signals (electromagnetic frequencies), such as those generated by the human voice over the telephone. Because data from computers are in digital form (voltage pulses), devices are necessary to convert digital signals into appropriate analog transmission frequencies and vice versa. However, digital communications networks that use only digital signals and do not need analog/digital conversion are becoming commonplace. Because most modems also perform a variety of telecommunications support functions, devices called digital modems are still used in digital networks.

Figure 6.22 compares several modem and telecommunications technologies for access to the Internet and other networks by home and business users.

Internetwork Processors

Telecommunications networks are interconnected by special-purpose communications processors called **internetwork processors**, such as switches, routers, hubs, and gateways. A *switch* is a communications processor that makes connections between telecommunications circuits in a network. Switches are now available in managed versions with network management capabilities. A bridge is a device that connects two or more local area networks that use the same communications rules or *protocol.* In contrast, a *router* is an intelligent communications processor that interconnects networks based on different rules or *protocols*, so a telecommunications message can be routed to its destination. A *hub* is a port switching communications processor. Advanced versions of both hubs and switches provide automatic switching among connections called *ports* for shared access to a network's resources. Workstations, servers, printers, and other network resources are typically connected to ports. Networks that use different communications architectures are interconnected by using a communications processor called a *gateway.* All these devices are essential to providing connectivity and easy access between the multiple LANs and wide area networks that are part of the intranets and client/server networks in many organizations.

Again referring to Figure 6.21, we can see examples of all of these elements. The corporate local area network in the upper left of the figure uses a hub to connect its multiple workstations to the network switch. The switch sends the signals to a series of switches and routers to get the data to its intended destination.

Multiplexers

A **multiplexer** is a communications processor that allows a single communications channel to carry simultaneous data transmissions from many terminals. This process is accomplished in two basic ways. In *frequency division multiplexing* (FDM), a multiplexer effectively divides a high-speed channel into multiple slow-speed channels. In *time division multiplexing* (TDM), the multiplexer divides the time each terminal can use the high-speed line into very short time slots, or time frames.

For example, if we need to have eight telephone numbers for a small business, we could have eight individual lines come into the building—one for each telephone number. Using a digital multiplexer, however, we can have one line handle all eight telephone numbers (assuming we have an eight-channel multiplexer). Mutliplexers work to increase the number of transmissions possible without increasing the number of physical data channels.

Telecommunications Software

Telecommunications software is a vital component of all telecommunications networks. Telecommunications and network management software may reside in PCs, servers, mainframes, and communications processors like multiplexers and routers. These programs are used by network servers and other computers in a network to manage network performance. Network management programs perform functions such as automatically checking client PCs for input/output activity, assigning priorities to data communications requests from clients and terminals, and detecting and correcting transmission errors and other network problems.

For example, mainframe-based wide area networks frequently use *telecommunications monitors* or *teleprocessing* (TP) monitors. The CICS (Customer Identification Control System) for IBM mainframes is a typical example. Servers in local area and other networks frequently rely on *network operating systems* like Novell NetWare or operating systems like UNIX, Linux, or Microsoft Windows 2003 Servers for network management. Many software vendors also offer telecommunications software as *middleware*, which can help diverse networks communicate with one another.

Telecommunications functions built into Microsoft Windows and other operating systems provide a variety of communications support services. For example, they work with a communications processor (such as a modem) to connect and disconnect communications links and to establish communications parameters such as transmission speed, mode, and direction.

Network Management

Network management packages such as network operating systems and telecommunications monitors determine transmission priorities, route (switch) messages, poll terminals in the network, and form waiting lines (queues) of transmission requests. They also detect and correct transmission errors, log statistics of network activity, and protect network resources from unauthorized access. See Figure 6.23.

Examples of major **network management** functions include:

- **Traffic management.** Manage network resources and traffic to avoid congestion and optimize telecommunications service levels to users.
- **Security.** Provide security as one of the top concerns of network management today. Telecommunications software must provide authentication, encryption, firewall, and auditing functions, and enforce security policies. Encryption, firewalls, and other network security defenses are covered in Chapter 11.
- **Network monitoring.** Troubleshoot and watch over the network, informing network administrators of potential problems before they occur.
- **Capacity planning.** Survey network resources and traffic patterns and users' needs to determine how best to accommodate the needs of the network as it grows and changes.

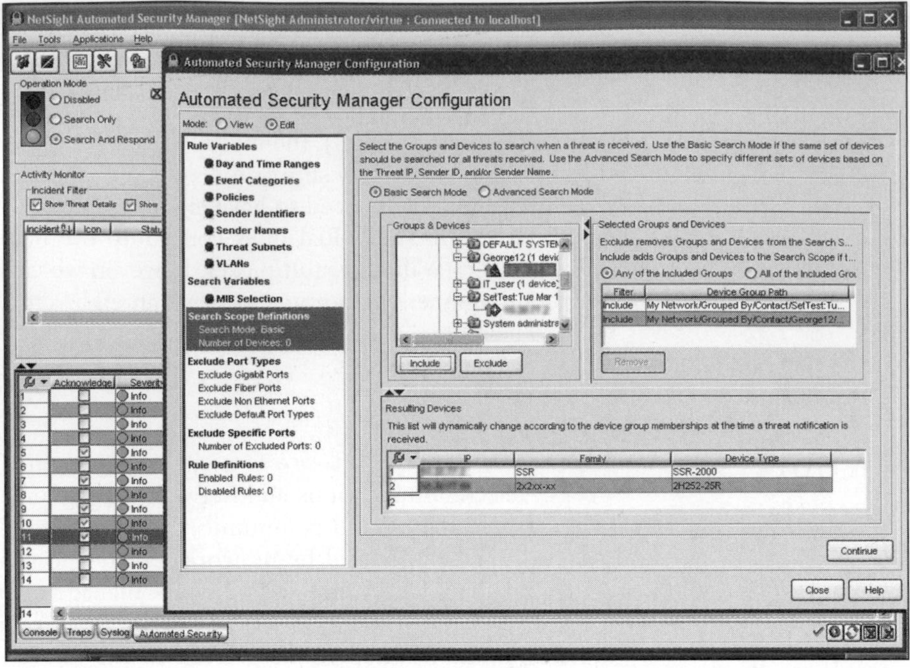

FIGURE 6.23 Network management software monitors and manages network performance.

Network Topologies

There are several basic types of **network topologies**, or structures, in telecommunications networks. Figure 6.24 illustrates three basic topologies used in wide area and local area telecommunications networks. A *star* network ties end-user computers to a central computer. A *ring* network ties local computer processors together in a ring on a more equal basis. A *bus* network is a network in which local processors share the same

FIGURE 6.24 The ring, star, and bus network topologies.

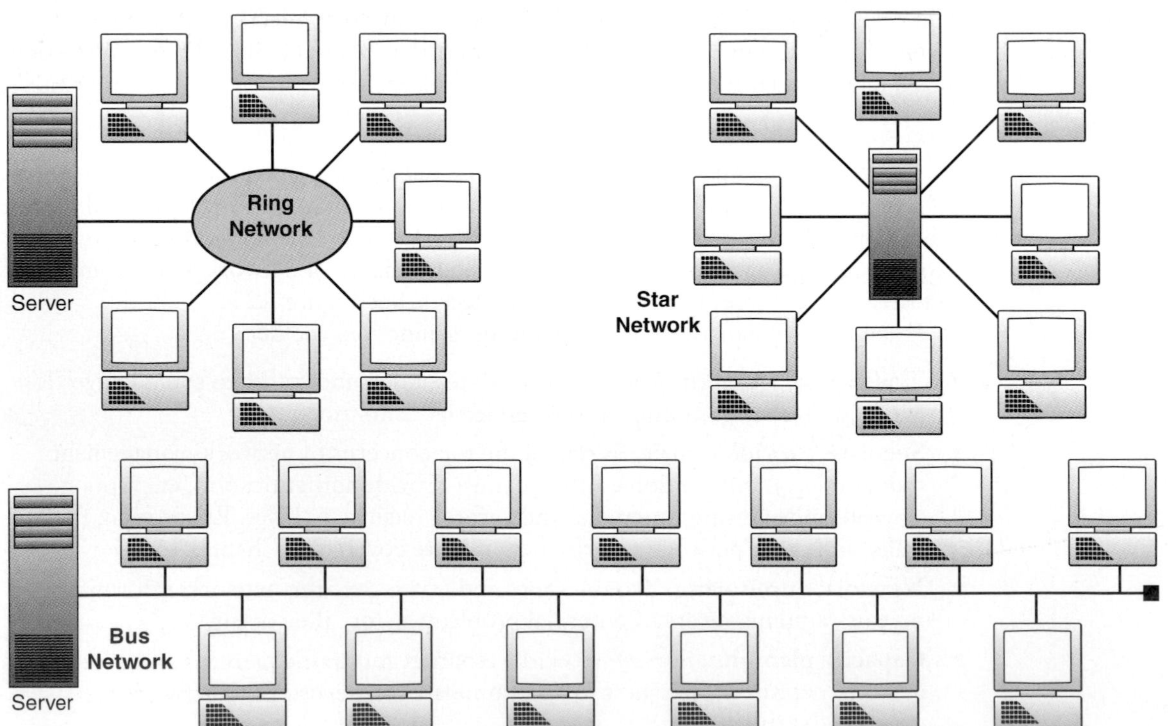

bus, or communications channel. A variation of the ring network is the *mesh* network. It uses direct communications lines to connect some or all of the computers in the ring to one another.

Wired networks may use a combination of star, ring, and bus approaches. Obviously, the star network is more centralized, whereas ring and bus networks have a more decentralized approach. However, this is not always the case. For example, the central computer in a star configuration may be acting only as a *switch*, or message-switching computer that handles the data communications between autonomous local computers. Star, ring, and bus networks differ in their performance, reliability, and cost. A pure star network is considered less reliable than a ring network, because the other computers in the star are heavily dependent on the central host computer. If it fails, there is no backup processing and communications capability, and the local computers are cut off from one another. Therefore, it is essential that the host computer be highly reliable. Having some type of multiprocessor architecture to provide a fault-tolerant capability is a common solution.

Network Architectures and Protocols

Until quite recently, sufficient standards were lacking for the interfaces among the hardware, software, and communications channels of telecommunications networks. This situation hampered the use of telecommunications, increased its costs, and reduced its efficiency and effectiveness. In response, telecommunications manufacturers and national and international organizations have developed standards called *protocols* and master plans called *network architectures* to support the development of advanced data communications networks.

Protocols

A **protocol** is a standard set of rules and procedures for the control of communications in a network. However, these standards may be limited to just one manufacturer's equipment or just one type of data communications. Part of the goal of communications network architectures is to create more standardization and compatibility among communications protocols. One example of a protocol is a standard for the physical characteristics of the cables and connectors between terminals, computers, modems, and communications lines. Other examples are the protocols that establish the communications control information needed for *handshaking*, which is the process of exchanging predetermined signals and characters to establish a telecommunications session between terminals and computers. Other protocols deal with control of data transmission reception in a network, switching techniques, internetwork connections, and so on.

Network Architectures

The goal of **network architectures** is to promote an open, simple, flexible, and efficient telecommunications environment, accomplished by the use of standard protocols, standard communications hardware and software interfaces, and the design of a standard multilevel interface between end users and computer systems.

The OSI Model

The **Open Systems Interconnection (OSI)** model is a standard description or "reference model" for how messages should be transmitted between any two points in a telecommunications network. Its purpose is to guide product implementers so that their products will consistently work with other products. The reference model defines seven layers of functions that take place at each end of a communication. Although OSI is not always strictly adhered to in terms of keeping related functions together in a well-defined layer, many, if not most, products involved in telecommunications make an attempt to describe themselves in relation to the OSI model. It is also valuable as a view of communication that furnishes a common ground for education and discussion.

Developed by representatives of major computer and telecommunication companies beginning in 1983, OSI was originally intended to be a detailed specification of interfaces. Instead, the committee decided to establish a common reference model for which others could develop detailed interfaces that in turn could become standards.

OSI was officially adopted as an international standard by the International Organization of Standards (ISO).

The main idea in OSI is that the process of communication between two endpoints in a telecommunication network can be divided into layers, with each layer adding its own set of special, related functions. Each communicating user or program is at a computer equipped with these seven layers of functions. So in a given message between users, there will be a flow of data through each layer at one end down through the layers in that computer and, at the other end, when the message arrives, another flow of data up through the layers in the receiving computer and ultimately to the end user or program. The actual programming and hardware that furnishes these seven layers of functions is usually a combination of the computer operating system, applications (e.g., your Web browser), TCP/IP or alternative transport and network protocols, and the software and hardware that enable you to put a signal on one of the lines attached to your computer.

OSI divides telecommunication into seven layers. Figure 6.25 illustrates the functions of the seven layers of the OSI model architecture.

The layers consist of two groups. The upper four layers are used whenever a message passes from or to a user. The lower three layers (up to the network layer) are used when any message passes through the host computer. Messages intended for this computer pass to the upper layers. Messages destined for some other host are not passed up to the upper layers but are forwarded to another host. The seven layers are:

Layer 1: The physical layer. This layer conveys the bit stream through the network at the electrical and mechanical level. It provides the hardware means of sending and receiving data on a carrier.

FIGURE 6.25 The seven layers of the OSI communications network architecture, and the five layers of the Internet's TCP/IP protocol suite.

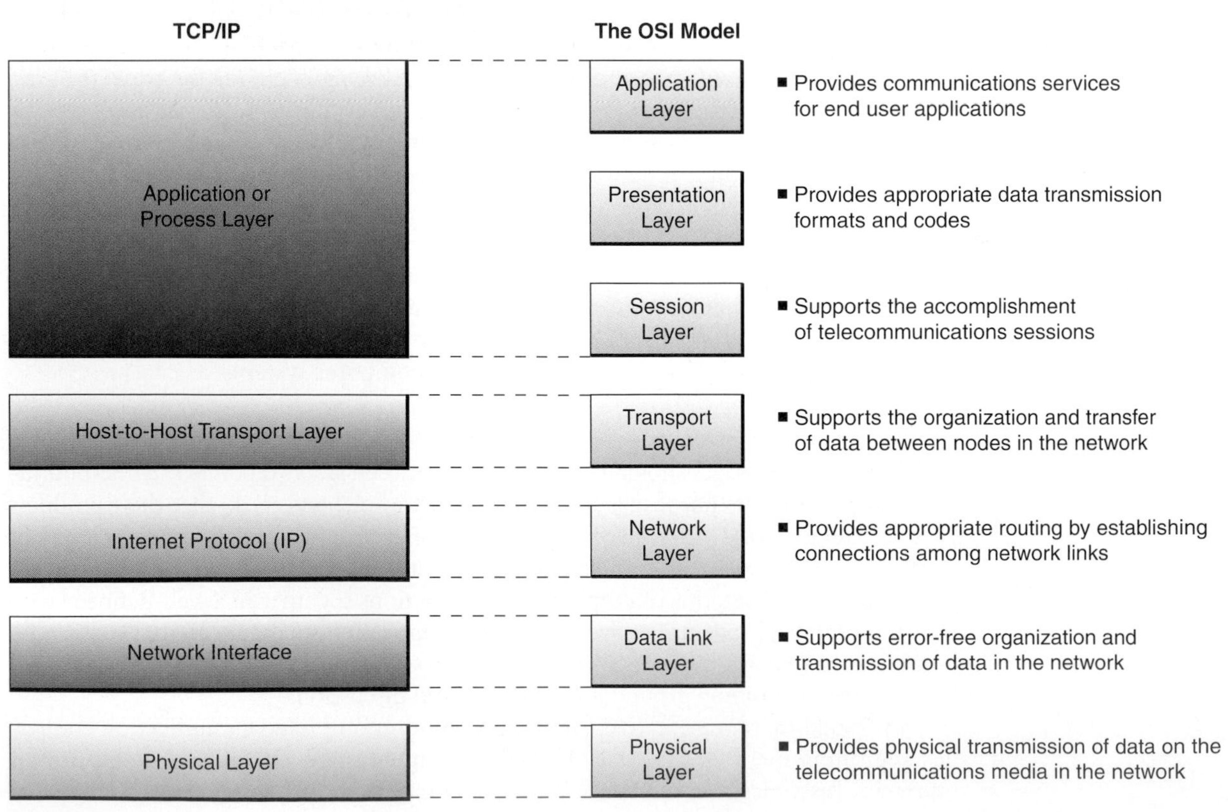

Layer 2: The data link layer. This layer provides synchronization for the physical level and does bit-stuffing for strings of 1's in excess of 5. It furnishes transmission protocol knowledge and management.

Layer 3: The network layer. This layer handles the routing of the data (sending it in the right direction to the right destination on outgoing transmissions and receiving incoming transmissions at the packet level). The network layer does routing and forwarding.

Layer 4: The transport layer. This layer manages the end-to-end control (*e.g.*, determining whether all packets have arrived) and error-checking. It ensures complete data transfer.

Layer 5: The session layer. This layer sets up, coordinates, and terminates conversations, exchanges, and dialogues between the applications at each end. It deals with session and connection coordination.

Layer 6: The presentation layer. This layer, usually part of an operating system, converts incoming and outgoing data from one presentation format to another (*e.g.*, from a text stream into a pop-up window with the newly arrived text). It's sometimes called the syntax layer.

Layer 7: The application layer. At this layer, communication partners are identified, quality of service is identified, user authentication and privacy are considered, and any constraints on data syntax are identified. (This layer is *not* the application itself, although some applications may perform application layer functions.)

The Internet's TCP/IP

The Internet uses a system of telecommunications protocols that has become so widely used that it is now accepted as a network architecture. The Internet's protocol suite is called **Transmission Control Protocol/Internet Protocol** and is known as **TCP/IP**. As Figure 6.25 shows, TCP/IP consists of five layers of protocols that can be related to the seven layers of the OSI architecture. TCP/IP is used by the Internet and by all intranets and extranets. Many companies and other organizations are thus converting their client/server and wide area networks to TCP/IP technology, which are now commonly called IP networks.

Although many of the technical aspects of the Internet can appear quite complex, the addressing, routing, and transport protocols, which make sure you get to the right Web site or your e-mail is delivered to the right place, are actually elegantly simple. TCP/IP can be thought of as analogous to how the postal system finds your house and delivers your mail. In this analogy, TCP represents the postal system and the various processes and protocols used to move the mail, while IP represents the zip code and address.

The current IP addressing protocol is called IPv4. When IP was first standardized in September 1981, the specification required that each system attached to the Internet be assigned a unique, 32-bit Internet address value. Systems that have interfaces to more than one network require a unique IP address for each network interface. The first part of an Internet address identifies the network on which the host resides, while the second part identifies the particular host on the given network. Keeping with our postal system analogy, the network address can be thought of as the zip code, and the host address represents the street address. By convention, an IP address is expressed as four decimal numbers separated by periods, such as "127.154.95.6." Valid addresses can range from 0.0.0.0 to 255.255.255.255, creating a total of about 4.3 billion addresses (4,294,967,296 to be exact). Using this two-level addressing hierarchy, any computer connected to the Internet can be located.

IP addressing can identify a specific network connected to the Internet. To provide the flexibility required to support networks of varying sizes, the Internet designers decided that the IP address space should be divided into three address classes—Classes A, B, and C. Each class fixes the boundary between the network prefix and the host number at a different point within the 32-bit address.

Class A networks are defined by the first number in an IP address. The value can range from 000 to 127, creating theoretically 128 unique networks. In reality, however, there are only 126 Class A addresses since both 0.0.0.0 and 127.0.0.0 are reserved for special use. Each Class A network address can support a total of 16,777,214 hosts per network, and they represent 50 percent of the total IPv4 address space. The Class A addresses are normally owned by large Internet service providers or well-established major corporations. For example, General Electric owns 3.0.0.0, IBM owns 9.0.0.0, Ford Motor Co. owns 19.0.0.0, and the U.S. Postal Service owns 56.0.0.0.

Class B network addresses range from 128.0 to 255.254. Using a Class B address, 16,384 networks can be identified with up to 65,534 hosts per network. Because the Class B address allocation contains slightly over 1 million addresses, it represents 25 percent of the IPv4 address space. Class B addresses are also normally owned by very large service providers and global organizations—AOL uses 205.188.0.0.

Class C addresses range from 192.0.0 to 233.255.255 and represent 12.5 percent of the available IPv4 address space. Slightly less than 2.1 million networks can be identified with a Class C address allowing approximately 537 million hosts. The remaining 12.5 percent of the IPv4 address space is reserved for special use.

You would think that 4.3 billion addresses would be sufficient for quite a while, but the Internet is running out of space. During the early days of the Internet, the seemingly unlimited address space allowed IP addresses to be allocated to an organization based on a simple request rather than on actual need. As a result, addresses were freely assigned to those who asked for them without concerns about the eventual depletion of the IP address space. Now many of the Class A and Class B host addresses are not even in use. To make matters worse, new technologies are extending IP addresses beyond computers to TVs, toasters, and coffeemakers.

This is where IPv6 comes to the rescue. Developed to work with Internet2, IPv6 increases the IP address size from 32 bits to 128 bits to support more levels of the address hierarchy and a much greater number of nodes. IPv6 supports over 340 trillion trillion trillion addresses, enough for each person in the world to be allocated 1 billion personal IP addresses! That should last for a while.

Voice Over IP

One of the newest uses for Internet protocol (IP) is *Internet telephony*—the practice of using an Internet connection to pass voice data using IP instead of using the standard public switched telephone network. Often referred to as **voice over IP** or **VoIP**, this approach makes use of a packet-based (or switched) network to carry voice calls, instead of the traditional circuit-switched network. In simpler terms, VoIP allows a person to function as if he or she were directly connected to a regular telephone network even while at home or in a remote office. As well, it skips standard long-distance charges, because the only connection is through an ISP. VoIP is being used more and more to keep corporate telephone costs down, as you can simply run two network cables to a desk instead of separate network and data cables. VoIP runs right over a standard network infrastructure, but it also demands a very well-configured network to run smoothly.

For those of us who love talking (and not having to pay for it), there is *Skype* (www.skype.com). Skype was founded in 2002 to develop the first peer-to-peer (P2P) telephony network. Today, Skype software allows telephone conversation through a PC and over the Internet instead of a separate phone connection. This proprietary freeware uses a messenger-like client and offers inbound and outbound PSTN (Public Switched Telephone Network) facilities.

Skype users can call to any non–computer-based landline or mobile telephone in the world and call other Skype users for free. The calls made to or received from traditional telephones are charged a fee, as are the voice-mail messages.

Skype software also provides features like voice mail, instant messaging, call forwarding, and conference calling. Skype users are not billed according to the distance between the two countries. Instead, the users are charged according to the prosperity of the country, the volume of calls made to and from the country, and the access charges. The latest statistical figures show that Skype is one of the fastest-growing companies on the Internet:

- Skype has 54 million members in 225 countries and territories, and the number is swelling—just through word-of-mouth marketing by satisfied users!
- Skype is adding approximately 150,000 users a day, and there are 3 million simultaneous users on the network at any given time.
- Skype has been downloaded 163 million times in 225 countries and territories.
- Skype is available in 27 languages.
- Skype has more users and serves more voice minutes than any other Internet voice communications provider.

Skype continues to grow in the consumer sector and is now offering business-specific services designed to reduce business telecommunication costs while offering more flexible alternatives to current land-line or mobile approaches. Skype also demonstrates how VoIP is fast becoming part of the telecommunications infrastructure as demonstrated in the following example.

Seaport Hotel In-Room Portal Converges Voice and Web Services

The Seaport Hotel in Boston is testing an in-room portal that enables guests to make telephone calls and access hotel services and the Internet from a touch screen.

Geared toward business travelers, the so-called SeaPortal is unique because it combines telephone and Web services over a service-oriented architecture. In addition, the new technology makes use of the hotel's existing PBX system, a less-expensive approach than replacing the in-house telephone switching system.

When a call is made in-house, a server routes it through the PBX system. If the call is outside the hotel, then the server sends it over Seaport's high-speed Internet provider as a voice over IP call, similar to services provided by Skype or Vonage.

For hotel guests, the system appears on the touch screen as a portal similar to a Web site. There's a welcome section that introduces the service; a destination guide for sports and entertainment, dining, news and weather, and other information; and a section for guest services that include hotel features and Web browsing.

The system is attached to the in-room phone, which rings when a guest presses an icon to make an in-hotel call to housecleaning, the concierge, or another service. Picking up the phone automatically makes the connection. To call outside the hotel, the guest presses on a phone link that calls up a keypad.

The portal provides Web mail access and includes a viewer for reading attachments. In addition, there are USB ports for storing messages or documents on a portable flash drive, or a guest can choose to have a document printed in the hotel's business center. All the services are available at no additional charge, including local and long-distance calls made in the continental United States [27].

Bandwidth Alternatives

The communications speed and capacity of telecommunications networks can be classified by **bandwidth**. The frequency range of a telecommunications channel, it determines the channel's maximum transmission rate. The speed and capacity of data transmission rates are typically measured in bits per second (bps). This level is sometimes referred to as the *baud* rate, though baud is more correctly a measure of signal changes in a transmission line.

Bandwidth represents the capacity of the connection. The greater the capacity, the more likely that greater performance will follow. Thus, greater bandwidth allows greater amounts of data to move from one point to another with greater speed. Although the relationship among bandwidth, data volume, and speed is theoretically

FIGURE 6.26
Examples of the telecommunications transmission speeds of various network technologies.

Network Technologies	Typical–Maximum bps
WiFi: wireless fidelity	11–54M
Standard Ethernet or token ring	10–16M
High-speed Ethernet	100M–1G
FDDI: fiber distributed data interface	100M
DDN: digital data network	2.4K–2M
PSN: packet switching network–X.25	64K–1.5M
Frame relay network	1.5M–45M
ISDN: integrated services digital network	64K/128K–2M
ATM: asynchronous transfer mode	25/155M–2.4G
SONET: synchronous optical network	45M–40G
Kbps = thousand bps or kilobits per second. Mbps = million bps or megabits per second.	Gbps = billion bps or gigabits per second.

sound, in practice, this is not always the case. A common analogy is to think of bandwidth as a pipe with water in it. The larger the pipe, the more water that can flow through it. If, however, the big pipe is connected to a small pipe, the effective amount of water that can be moved in a given time becomes severely restricted by the small pipe. The same problem occurs with network bandwidth. If a large bandwidth connection tries to move a large amount of data to a network with less bandwidth, the speed of the transmission will be determined by the speed of the smaller bandwidth.

Narrow-band channels typically provide low-speed transmission rates up to 64 Kbps but can now handle up to 2 Mbps. They are usually unshielded twisted-pair lines commonly used for telephone voice communications and for data communications by the modems of PCs and other devices. Medium-speed channels (*medium-band)* use shielded twisted-pair lines for transmission speeds up to 100 Mbps.

Broadband channels provide high-speed transmission rates at intervals from 256 Kbps to several billion bps. Typically, they use microwave, fiber optics, or satellite transmission. Examples are 1.54 Mbps for T1 and 45 Mbps for T3 communications channels, up to 100 Mbps for communications satellite channels, and between 52 Mbps and 10 Gbps for fiber-optic lines. See Figure 6.26.

Switching Alternatives

Regular telephone service relies on *circuit switching*, in which a switch opens a circuit to establish a link between a sender and receiver; it remains open until the communication session is completed. In message switching, a message is transmitted a block at a time from one switching device to another.

Packet switching involves subdividing communications messages into fixed- or variable-length groups called packets. For example, in the X.25 protocol, packets are 128 characters long, while in the *frame relay* technology, they are of variable length. Packet switching networks are frequently operated by *value-added carriers* who use computers and other communications processors to control the packet switching process and transmit the packets of various users over their networks.

Early packet switching networks were X.25 networks. The X.25 protocol is an international set of standards governing the operations of widely used, but relatively slow, packet switching networks. *Frame relay* is another popular packet switching protocol and is used by many large companies for their wide area networks. Frame relay is considerably faster than X.25 and is better able to handle the heavy telecommunications traffic of interconnected local area networks within a company's wide area client/server network. ATM *(asynchronous transfer mode)* is an emerging high-capacity *cell switching* technology. An ATM switch breaks voice, video, and other data into fixed cells of 53 bytes (48 bytes of data and 5 bytes of control information) and routes them to their next destination in the network. ATM networks are being developed by many companies needing their fast, high-capacity multimedia capabilities for voice, video, and data communications [16]. See Figure 6.27.

FIGURE 6.27
Why four large retail chains chose different network technologies to connect their stores.

Company	Technology	Why
Sears	Frame relay	Reliable, inexpensive, and accommodates mainframe and Internet protocols
Rack Room	VSAT (very small aperture terminal)	Very inexpensive way to reach small markets and shared satellite dishes at malls
Hannaford	ATM (asynchronous transfer mode)	Very high bandwidth; combines voice, video, and data
7-Eleven	ISDN (integrated services digital network)	Can use multiple channels to partition traffic among different uses

Network Interoperability

Section 256 of the Communications Act, enacted in February 1996, states two key purposes: (1) "to promote nondiscriminatory accessibility by the broadest number of users and vendors of communications products and services to public telecommunications networks used to provide telecommunications service" and (2) "to ensure the ability of users and information providers to seamlessly and transparently transmit and receive information between and across telecommunications networks." To accomplish these purposes, the Federal Communications Commission (FCC) is required to establish procedures to oversee coordinated network planning by providers of telecommunications services. It also is authorized to participate in the development, by appropriate industry standards–setting organizations of public telecommunications, of network interconnectivity standards that promote access.

As you can see, the FCC is a key regulatory agency with regard to telecommunications. While we tend to think of the FCC as the oversight body for radio and television, it is equally involved in all aspects of data and voice communications. If you reread the first paragraph of this section, it becomes clear that there is an important underlying reason for the FCC to be so involved with telecommunications. The answer lies in the importance of a concept called **network interoperability**.

This interoperability ensures that anyone anywhere on one network can communicate with anyone anywhere on another network without having to worry about speaking a common language from a telecommunications perspective. All that we have discussed in this chapter with regard to business value would not be possible without complete accessibility, transparency, and seamless interoperability across all networks. Without these things, the Internet would not be possible, nor would e-mail, instant messaging, or even common file sharing.

Fortunately for us, everyone in the telecommunications field understands the importance of network interoperability, and as such, they work together to ensure that all networks remain interoperable.

Summary

- **Telecommunications Trends.** Organizations are becoming networked enterprises that use the Internet, intranets, and other telecommunications networks to support business operations and collaboration within the enterprise and with their customers, suppliers, and other business partners. Telecommunications has entered a deregulated and fiercely competitive environment with many vendors, carriers, and services. Telecommunications technology is moving toward open, internetworked digital networks for voice, data, video, and multimedia. A major trend is the pervasive use of the Internet and its technologies to build interconnected enterprise and global networks, like intranets and extranets, to support enterprise collaboration, electronic commerce, and other e-business applications.

- **The Internet Revolution.** The explosive growth of the Internet and the use of its enabling technologies have revolutionized computing and telecommunications. The Internet has become the key platform for a rapidly expanding list of information and entertainment services and business applications, including enterprise collaboration, electronic commerce, and other e-business systems. Open systems with unrestricted connectivity using Internet technologies are the primary telecommunications technology drivers in e-business systems. Their primary goal is to promote easy and secure access by business professionals and consumers to the resources of the Internet, enterprise intranets, and interorganizational extranets.
- **The Business Value of the Internet.** Companies are deriving strategic business value from the Internet, which enables them to disseminate information globally, communicate and trade interactively with customized information and services for individual customers, and foster collaboration of people and integration of business processes within the enterprise and with business partners. These capabilities allow them to generate cost savings from using Internet technologies, revenue increases from electronic commerce, and better customer service and relationships through better supply chain management and customer relationship management.
- **The Role of Intranets.** Businesses are installing and extending intranets throughout their organizations to (1) improve communications and collaboration among individuals and teams within the enterprise; (2) publish and share valuable business information easily, inexpensively, and effectively via enterprise information portals and intranet Web sites and other intranet services; and (3) develop and deploy critical applications to support business operations and decision making.
- **The Role of Extranets.** The primary role of extranets is to link the intranet resources of a company to the intranets of its customers, suppliers, and other business partners. Extranets can also provide access to operational company databases and legacy systems to business partners. Thus, extranets provide significant business value by facilitating and strengthening the business relationships of a company with customers and suppliers, improving collaboration with its business partners, and enabling the development of new kinds of Web-based services for its customers, suppliers, and others.
- **Telecommunications Networks.** The major generic components of any telecommunications network are (1) terminals, (2) telecommunications processors, (3) communications channels, (4) computers, and (5) telecommunications software. There are several basic types of telecommunications networks, including wide area networks (WANs) and local area networks (LANs). Most WANs and LANs are interconnected using client/server, network computing, peer-to-peer, and Internet networking technologies.
- **Network Alternatives.** Key telecommunications network alternatives and components are summarized in Figure 6.11 for telecommunications media, processors, software, channels, and network architectures. A basic understanding of these major alternatives will help business end users participate effectively in decisions involving telecommunications issues. Telecommunications processors include modems, multiplexers, internetwork processors, and various devices to help interconnect and enhance the capacity and efficiency of telecommunications channels. Telecommunications networks use such media as twisted-pair wire, coaxial cables, fiber-optic cables, terrestrial microwave, communications satellites, cellular and PCS systems, wireless LANs, and other wireless technologies.
- Telecommunications software, such as network operating systems and telecom-munications monitors, controls and manages the communications activity in a telecommunications network.

Key Terms and Concepts

These are the key terms and concepts of this chapter. The page number of their first explanation is in parentheses.

1. Analog (215)
2. Bandwidth (229)
3. Bluetooth (219)
4. Client/server networks (212)
5. Coaxial cable (216)
6. Communications satellites (218)
7. Digital (215)
8. Extranets (203)
9. Fiber optics (216)
10. Internet service provider (ISP) (197)
11. Internet networking technologies (194)
12. Internetwork processors (222)
13. Intranets (201)
14. Legacy systems (212)
15. Local area networks (LAN) (209)
16. Metcalfe's law (190)
17. Middleware (194)
18. Modems (221)
19. Multiplexer (223)
20. Network (190)
21. Network architectures (225)
    - *a.* Open Systems Interconnection (OSI) (225)
    - *b.* TCP/IP (227)
22. Network computing (212)

23. Network interoperability (231)
24. Network topologies (224)
25. Open systems (194)
26. Peer-to-peer networks (213)
27. Protocol (225)
28. Telecommunications (193)
29. Telecommunications media (215)
30. Telecommunications network (206)
31. Telecommunications processors (221)
32. Telecommunications software (223)
33. Virtual private network (VPN) (211)
34. VoIP (228)
35. Wide area networks (WAN) (209)
36. Wireless LAN (219)
37. Wireless technologies (195)

Review Quiz

Match one of the key terms and concepts listed previously with one of the brief examples or definitions that follow. Try to find the best fit for answers that seem to fit more than one term or concept. Defend your choices.

____ 1. Technique for making telephone calls over the Internet.

____ 2. The ability for all networks to connect to one another.

____ 3. An interconnected or interrelated chain, group, or system.

____ 4. Software that serves to "glue together" separate programs.

____ 5. The usefulness, or utility, of a network equals the square of the number of users.

____ 6. Internet-like networks that improve communications and collaboration, publish and share information, and develop applications to support business operations and decision making within an organization.

____ 7. Provide Internet-like access to a company's operational databases and legacy systems by its customers and suppliers.

____ 8. Company that provides individuals and organizations access to the Internet.

____ 9. A communications network covering a large geographic area.

____ 10. A communications network in an office, a building, or other worksite.

____ 11. Representation of an electrical signal using binary numbers.

____ 12. Coaxial cable, microwave, and fiber optics are examples.

____ 13. A communications medium that uses pulses of laser light in glass fibers.

____ 14. A cable replacement technology for digital devices.

____ 15. Includes modems, multiplexers, and internetwork processors.

____ 16. Includes programs such as network operating systems and Web browsers.

____ 17. A common communications processor for microcomputers.

____ 18. Helps a communications channel carry simultaneous data transmissions from many terminals.

____ 19. Star, ring, and bus networks are examples.

____ 20. Representation of an electrical signal that is analogous to the signal itself.

____ 21. The communications speed and capacity of telecommunications networks.

____ 22. Intranets and extranets can use their network firewalls and other security features to establish secure Internet links within an enterprise or its trading partners.

____ 23. Sturdy cable that provides high bandwidth on a single conductor.

____ 24. Standard rules or procedures for control of communications in a network.

____ 25. An international standard, multilevel set of protocols to promote compatibility among telecommunications networks.

____ 26. The standard suite of protocols used by the Internet, intranets, extranets, and some other networks.

____ 27. Information systems with common hardware, software, and network standards that provide easy access for end users and their networked computer systems.

____ 28. Interconnected networks need communications processors such as switches, routers, hubs, and gateways.

____ 29. Web sites, Web browsers, HTML documents, hypermedia databases, and TCP/IP networks are examples.

____ 30. Networks in which end-user PCs are tied to network servers to share resources and application processing.

____ 31. Network computers provide a browser-based interface for software and databases provided by servers.

____ 32. End-user computers connect directly with each other to exchange files.

____ 33. Orbiting devices that provide multiple communication channels over a large geographical area.

____ 34. Older, traditional mainframe-based business information systems.

____ 35. Any arrangement in which a sender transmits a message to a receiver over a channel consisting of some type of medium.

____ 36. Provides wireless network access for laptop PCs in business settings.

Discussion Questions

1. The Internet is the driving force behind developments in telecommunications, networks, and other information technologies. Do you agree or disagree? Why?
2. How is the trend toward open systems, connectivity, and interoperability related to business use of the Internet, intranets, and extranets?
3. Refer to the Real World Case on Metric & Multistandard Components Corp. in the chapter. Pick a small business you would like to start. How would you handle the telecommunication needs of your company at the beginning? After your business had grown substantially a few years later? Explain the reasons for your choices.
4. How will wireless information appliances and services affect the business use of the Internet and the Web? Explain.
5. What are some of the business benefits and management challenges of client/server networks? Network computing? Peer-to-peer networks?
6. What is the business value driving so many companies to rapidly install and extend intranets throughout their organizations?
7. What strategic competitive benefits do you see in a company's use of extranets?
8. Refer to the Real World Case on Best Buy, MedStar Health, and Unifi in the chapter. Do wireless mobile devices like the Sprint PPC-6700 make laptop PCs obsolete? What do you think will be the preferred mobile computing device five years from now? Defend your answers.
9. Do you think that business use of the Internet, intranets, and extranets has changed what businesspeople expect from information technology in their jobs? Explain.
10. The insatiable demand for everything wireless, video, and Web-enabled everywhere will be the driving force behind developments in telecommunications, networking, and computing technologies for the foreseeable future. Do you agree or disagree? Why?

Analysis Exercises

1. How many addresses are enough?

The Internet Protocol version 4 assigns each connected computer a 4-byte address known as an IP address. Messages, or packets, each include this address so routers know where to forward them. They are the Internet's version of mailing addresses.

Each region of the world has been given a range of IP addresses to administer locally, with America taking the largest share. Asia, with a significantly larger population, received a disproportionately small range of numbers and fears running out.

Anticipating this problem, the Internet Engineering Task Force adopted IPv6, which uses addresses 16 bytes long. Although slow to be adopted, all Internet Root servers now support IPv6, and Internet service providers are rolling it out as needed while maintaining backward compatibility for IPv4. The U.S. federal government has mandated the change to IPv6 for all federal agencies by 2008.

a. Express as a power of 2 the number of nodes that can exist using IPv4.

b. Express as a power of 2 the number of nodes that can exist using IPv6.

2. MNO Incorporated Communications Network

Calculating Bandwidth

MNO Incorporated is considering acquiring its own leased lines to handle voice and data communications among its 14 distribution sites in three regions around the country. The peak load of communications for each site is expected to be a function of the number of phone links and the number of computers at that site. Communications data are available below. You have been asked to analyze this information.

a. Create a database table with an appropriate structure to store the data below. Enter the records shown below and get a printed listing of your table.

b. Survey results suggest that the peak traffic to and from a site will be approximately 2 kilobits per second for each phone line plus 10 kilobits per second for each computer. Create a report showing the estimated peak demand for the telecommunications system at each site in kilobits. Create a second report grouped by region and showing regional subtotals and a total for the system as a whole.

Site Location	Region	Phone Lines	Computers
Boston	East	228	95
New York	East	468	205
Richmond	East	189	84
Atlanta	East	192	88
Detroit	East	243	97
Cincinnati	East	156	62
New Orleans	Central	217	58
Chicago	Central	383	160
Saint Louis	Central	212	91
Houston	Central	238	88
Denver	West	202	77
Los Angeles	West	364	132
San Francisco	West	222	101
Seattle	West	144	54

3. Wireless Radiation

Frying Your Brains?

Radio waves, microwaves, and infrared all belong to the electromagnetic radiation spectrum. These terms reference ranges of radiation frequencies we use every day in our wireless networking environments. However, the very word *radiation* strikes fear in many people. Cell towers have sprouted from fields all along highways. Tall rooftops harbor many more cell stations in cities. Millions of cell phone users place microwave transmitters/receivers next to their heads each time they make a call. Computer network wireless access points have become ubiquitous. Even McDonald's customers can use their machines to browse the Internet as they eat burgers. With all this radiation zapping about, should we be concerned?

The electromagnetic spectrum ranges from ultra-low frequencies to radio waves, microwaves, infrared, visible light, ultraviolet, x-ray, and up to gamma ray radiation. Is radiation dangerous? The threat appears to come from two different directions, the frequency and the intensity. A preponderance of research has demonstrated the dangers of radiation at frequencies just higher than those of visible light, even including the ultraviolet light used in tanning beds, x-rays, and gamma-rays. These frequencies are high (the wavelengths are small enough) to penetrate and disrupt molecules and even atoms. The results range from burns to damaged DNA that might lead to cancer or birth defects.

However, radiation's lower frequencies ranging from visible light (the rainbow colors you can see), infrared, microwave, and radio waves have long waves unable to penetrate molecules. Indeed, microwave wave lengths are so long that microwave ovens employ a simple viewing screen that can block these long waves and yet allow visible light through. As a result, we can watch our popcorn pop without feeling any heat. Keep in mind that visible light consists of radiation frequencies closer to the "danger end" of the spectrum than microwave light.

Lower radiation frequencies can cause damage only if the *intensity* is strong enough, and that damage is limited to common burns. Microwave ovens cook food by drawing 800 or more watts and converting them into a very intense (bright) microwave light. Cellular telephones, by comparison, draw a very tiny amount of current from the phone's battery and use the resulting microwaves to transmit a signal. In fact, the heat you feel from the cell phone is not from the microwaves but rather from its discharging battery. It is extremely unlikely that either device can give the user cancer, though a microwave oven could cause serious burns if the operator disables its safety features.

a. Use an Internet search engine and report back what the World Health Organization (WHO) has had to say about microwave radiation or non-ionizing radiation.

b. Use an Internet search engine to identify the various complaints posed by stakeholders regarding cell phone towers. Write a one-page paper describing an alternative to cell phone towers that would enable cell phone use and yet mitigate all or most of these complaints.

4. Maximizing Communications

Human Networking

Ms. Sapper, this year's annual partner meeting coordinator for a global accounting firm, faced an interesting challenge. With 400 high-powered partners gathering from all around the world, she wanted to arrange meal seating in a way that maximized diversity at each table. She hoped that this seating would encourage partners to open up new lines of communication and discourage old cliques from re-forming. The banquet facility included 50 tables, each seating eight guests. Sapper had all the necessary partner data, but she found herself stumped about how to maximize diversity at each table. Let's walk her through the process.

Download and save "partners.xls" from the MIS 8e OLC. Open the file and note that in addition to partners' names, it also contains industry, region, and gender information. The Table No. column has been left blank.

a. In Excel's menu, select "Data" and then "Sort" and then press the "F1" key for help. Read through each of the topics. How would an *ascending* sort arrange the list "Smith; Jones; Zimmerman"?

b. What feature allows users to sort month lists so *January* appears before *April*?

c. Sort the partner data first on Gender, then by Industry, and then by Region, and save the file.

d. Examine the sorted results from the previous step. Notice that assigning the first eight partners to the *same* table would minimize diversity. This result should also provide a clue about how to *maximize* diversity. Using this insight, assign a table number in the range from 1 to 50 to each partner in your sorted list so to maximize diversity. Save the file as "partners_sorted.xls" and explain your logic.

REAL WORLD CASE 3 SAIC, Hewlett-Packard, GE, and Others: The Business Case for Wireless Sensor Networks

Some big companies are trying to make the world—and almost everything in it—smarter.

Science Applications International Corp. (SAIC), the big government IT contractor, is developing technology for the Departments of Defense and Homeland Security that could use hundreds of tiny, wireless sensors packed with computing power to help secure U.S. borders, bridges, power plants, and ships by detecting suspicious movements or dangerous cargo and radioing warnings back to a command center. BP plc, the world's second-largest independent oil company, aims to knock down the cost of monitoring equipment at a Washington State oil refinery, from thousands of dollars per measurement to hundreds, by replacing big, dumb, wired sensors with wireless ones in a network.

And Hewlett-Packard is experimenting with wireless networked sensors at a warehouse in Memphis, Tennessee, trying to reinvent how companies manage the flow of goods. A prototype wireless network of small video-camera sensors hooked to image-recognition software works in concert with radio-frequency identification (RFID) technology to make sure inventory is put in the right place. The cameras track goods as they move through the warehouse, and those images get matched with RFID tag numbers that describe them.

Wireless sensor devices, or "motes," package together a circuit board with networking and application software; interfaces to sensors that can detect changes in temperature, pressure, moisture, light, sound, or magnetism; and a wireless radio that can report on their findings—all powered by a pair of AA batteries. Enabled by the fusion of small, low-cost chips, low-powered radios, and the spread of wireless networking, motes are a giant leap ahead of traditional sensors that for decades have measured everything from temperature in buildings to factory machines' vibrations. Those sensors require wiring to electrical systems, which can cost $200 to $400 per sensor, and are expensive to service. Motes cost about $100 each and are much cheaper to install. That price could drop to less than $10 in a few years, as mote components follow computing's march toward higher volume, better performance, and lower prices.

One breakthrough of mote technology is special "mesh networking" software that lets each device wake up for a fraction of a second when it has an interesting result to transmit, then relay that information a few yards to its nearest neighbor. So instead of every sensor transmitting its information to a remote base station, an electronic bucket brigade moves data mote by mote until it reaches a central computer where it can be stored and analyzed. Built-in logic corrects for the failure of any sensor to transmit its data by having its neighbors cover for it. The wake-up-to-transmit feature is key, since devices need to conserve power so networks can last for years unattended in the field or anywhere data gets acquired nonstop.

"This technology enabled a major advance," claims Tom Sereno, a division manager at SAIC. Just 2 percent of the U.S. border is outfitted with ground-sensor networks that can detect illegal crossings of people or vehicles. And those sensors have shorter life spans than the wireless motes with which SAIC is developing its applications.

The potential for cost savings over traditional wired sensors is enormous. BP installed five wireless sensors at its Cherry Point refinery in Washington to monitor the temperature inside giant onsite fans. Using the motes will probably cost about $1,000 per measurement point—and maybe drop to $500 within a year or two, says Harry Cassar, technology director in BP's emerging-tech group. Each connection measured the old way cost $10,000. BP achieved the $500-per-point measurement in a test last summer to measure conditions in the engine room of an oil tanker.

And BP envisions using wireless networks of sensors to monitor industrial plants and ships, remotely adjust lighting and heat in office buildings, test soil for pollutants, and detect whether chemicals are stored properly. "Wireless mote technology has got applications in almost every part of our business," Cassar says. "We're not going to be putting in tens of these devices, or even hundreds. Ultimately, it's going to be thousands."

Intel has outfitted an Oregon chip-fabrication plant with 200 wireless sensors that constantly monitor vibration levels on some of the factory equipment and report when a measurement falls out of spec. The effort covers only a fraction of the plant's 4,000 measurable parts but has replaced some rounds by a technician who gets to each machine only every two or three months, according to Intel Research Associate Director Hans Mulder.

General Electric Co. has completed a test of sensor-outfitted shipping containers that can detect tampering, and it's developing products that could use mesh networks to secure apartment buildings and industrial areas. And Bechtel Group Inc., the largest U.S. engineering and construction company, may within a year or two start testing sensor nets that let motes self-assemble into a network without programmers specifying what route the data take. Bechtel has built wireless sensors into projects such as London's subway system and expects the technology to have applications in smart buildings, defense contracts, and chemical plants, Infrastructure Architecture Manager Fred Wettling says. "We see this just starting to take off."

By 2008 there could be 100 million wireless sensors in use, up from about 200,000 today, according to market research company Harbor Research. The worldwide market for wireless sensors, it says, will grow from $100 million in 2005 to more than $1 billion by 2009.

"For every dollar the big systems integrators and IBM make on sensors and installation, there's $10 to be made on the management of the data that comes out," promises Kris Pister, a professor of electrical engineering and computer science at UC Berkeley, who founded Dust Networks in

2002 and serves as its CTO. IBM, which plans to spend $250 million during the next five years on the technology and has created a "sensors and actuators" business unit, predicts wireless sensor nets could represent a $6 billion overall market by 2007, with the bulk of profits coming from software that helps the devices better communicate and lets customers interpret data from them.

"Sensors are just a part of an ecosystem of wireless devices," says Feng Zhao, a senior researcher at Microsoft who joined the company last year from PARC (Palo Alto Research Center) to head up a new sensor nets research group on Microsoft's Redmond, Washington, campus. His test bed is parking level P2 of building No. 112, where a handful of sensors detect the size, speed, and magnetism of everything that crosses the garage's threshold, triangulating data from video images and magnetic readings of staffers' cars. At a remote PC, a researcher can analyze the day's traffic by logging on to a Web site and posing queries using standard Web-programming techniques. The sensors work in a restricted scenario and with research prototypes, Zhao says, but "we need to figure out how to organize these systems and develop interesting applications for them" for real-world use. "For all these apps, writing software is very challenging. That will probably be a stumbling block between sensors and killer apps."

"It's kind of like the beginning of the Arpanet days for this sensor-net technology, where there's no killer app yet," argues Teresa Lunt, manager of the computer-science lab at PARC. A PARC research project called "smart matter" aims to embed sensors in the environment, and the center has done experiments with DARPA (Defense Advanced Research Projects Agency) funding, including using sensor nets to track a mock military tank based on its signature sounds. At current prices, though, minus the sensors attached to them, wireless motes are still impractical for most large networks. "But they've served as a placeholder people can use to envision applications with the understanding that they'll be replaced by better technology," Lunt says. "They've been igniting people's imaginations."

Sensor proponents predict a day when superhighways will be salted with motes that help drivers avoid collisions, bridges that report when they're seismically stressed, and networks of video cameras that pick terrorists out of a crowd. That's a long way from turning down the air conditioning when it gets too hot.

Source: Adapted from Aaron Ricadela, "Sensors Everywhere," *InformationWeek*, January 24, 2005.

CASE STUDY QUESTIONS

1. What are some of the business benefits associated with using wireless networks to collect and transmit data?
2. What are some of the challenges faced by this use of wireless technologies? What solutions can you offer?
3. The use of wireless networking as described in the case is both innovative and functional. What other business uses can you envision for this approach?

REAL WORLD ACTIVITIES

1. The companies mentioned in the case—Intel, IBM, SAIC, and GE—are all familiar names often associated with innovative approaches to technology. Using the Internet, see if you can find examples of other companies that have found ways in which to apply mote wireless technology to business needs.
2. One way of describing this use of wireless technologies is that it represents a marriage between RFID (we learned about these devices in Chapter 3) and wireless networking. This combination of enabling technologies results in an entirely new way of accomplishing an old task. Break into small groups with your classmates, and see if you can brainstorm other combinations of existing technologies to create new approaches to existing business activities.

MODULE III

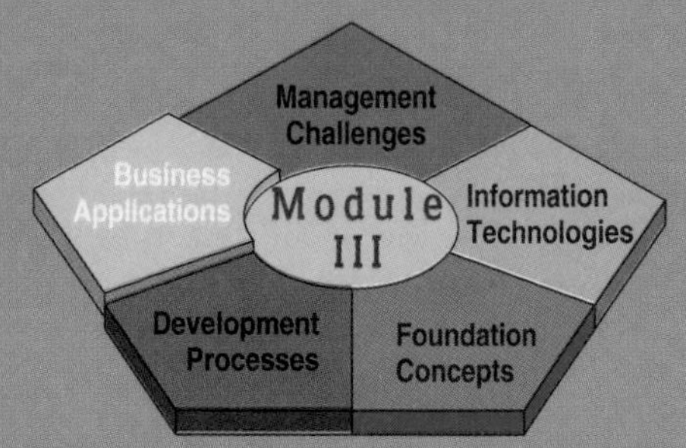

BUSINESS APPLICATIONS

How do Internet technologies and other forms of IT support business processes, electronic commerce, and business decision making? The three chapters of this module show you how such business applications of information systems are accomplished in today's networked enterprises.

- **Chapter 7: Electronic Business Systems** describes how information systems integrate and support enterprisewide business processes, especially customer relationship management, enterprise resource planning, and supply chain management, as well as the business functions of marketing, manufacturing, human resource management, accounting, and finance.
- **Chapter 8: Electronic Commerce Systems** introduces the basic process components of e-commerce systems and discusses important trends, applications, and issues in e-commerce.
- **Chapter 9: Decision Support Systems** shows how management information systems, decision support systems, executive information systems, expert systems, and artificial intelligence technologies can be applied to decision-making situations faced by business managers and professionals in today's dynamic business environment.

CHAPTER 7

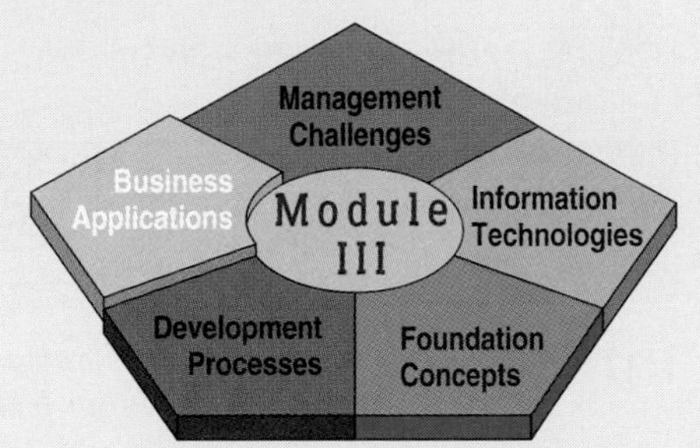

ELECTRONIC BUSINESS SYSTEMS

Chapter Highlights

Learning Objectives

After reading and studying this chapter, you should be able to:

1. Identify the following cross-functional enterprise systems, and give examples of how they can provide significant business value to a company:
   a. Enterprise resource planning.
   b. Customer relationship management.
   c. Supply chain management.
   d. Enterprise application integration.
   e. Transaction processing systems.
   f. Enterprise collaboration systems.
2. Give examples of how the Internet and other information technologies support business processes within the business functions of accounting, finance, human resource management, marketing, and production and operations management.
3. Understand the need for enterprise application integration to improve the support of business interactions across multiple e-business applications.

SECTION I Enterprise Business Systems

Introduction

Contrary to popular opinion, e-business is not synonymous with e-commerce. E-business is much broader in scope, going beyond transactions to signify use of the Net, in combination with other technologies and forms of electronic communication, to enable any type of business activity [29].

This chapter introduces the fast-changing world of business applications for the modern enterprise, which increasingly consists of what are popularly called *e-business* applications. Remember that **e-business** is the use of the Internet and other networks and information technologies to support electronic commerce, enterprise communications and collaboration, and Web-enabled business processes, both within a networked enterprise and with its customers and business partners. E-business includes *e-commerce*, which involves the buying, selling, marketing, and servicing of products, services, and information over the Internet and other networks. We will cover e-commerce in greater depth in Chapter 8.

In this chapter, we explore some of the major concepts and applications of e-business. We begin by focusing in Section I on examples of cross-functional enterprise systems, especially customer relationship management, enterprise resource planning, and supply chain management. In Section II, we explore examples of information systems that support essential processes in the functional areas of business. See Figure 7.1.

Read the Real World Case on the next page. We can learn a lot from this case about the challenges and benefits of customer relationship management systems.

Cross-Functional Enterprise Applications

Many companies today are using information technology to develop integrated **cross-functional enterprise systems** that cross the boundaries of traditional business functions to reengineer and improve vital business processes all across the enterprise. These organizations view cross-functional enterprise systems as a strategic way to use IT to share information resources and improve the efficiency and effectiveness of business processes, as well as to develop strategic relationships with customers, suppliers, and business partners. Figure 7.2 illustrates a cross-functional business process.

Many companies first moved from functional, mainframe-based *legacy systems* to integrated, cross-functional *client/server* applications. This move typically involved installing *enterprise resource planning*, *supply chain management*, or *customer relationship management* software from SAP America, Oracle, or others. Instead of focusing on the information processing requirements of business functions, such enterprise software focuses on supporting integrated clusters of business processes involved in the operations of a business.

Now, as we see continually in the Real World Cases in this text, business firms are using Internet technologies to help them reengineer and integrate the flow of information among their internal business processes and their customers and suppliers. Companies all across the globe are using the World Wide Web and their intranets and extranets as technology platforms for their cross-functional and interenterprise information systems.

Enterprise Application Architecture

Figure 7.3 presents an **enterprise application architecture**, which illustrates the interrelationships of the major cross-functional enterprise applications that many companies have or are installing today. This architecture is not intended as a detailed or exhaustive application blueprint but rather as a conceptual framework to help you visualize the basic components, processes, and interfaces of these major e-business applications, along with their interrelationships. This application architecture also spotlights the roles these business systems play in supporting the customers, suppliers, partners, and employees of a business.

REAL WORLD CASE 1 Forex Capital Markets and Wyse Technology: The Business Benefits of Customer Relationship Management

International buying and selling of global currencies comprises the largest and most liquid market in the world, with daily volumes exceeding $1.4 trillion. Since it was founded in 1999, Forex Capital Markets (FXCM) has grown into one of the largest currency trading firms in the world by offering traders direct access to this dynamic, global market. The company now boasts 12,000 clients in 70 countries and an average monthly trading volume that exceeds $20 billion.

Early in FXCM's history, the sales team tracked new leads and prospects in Excel spreadsheets. As the company grew, the team switched to Microsoft Access database software to manage increasing lead volume, but FXCM's success soon outgrew that system too. "The incredible volume was too much for Access to handle and was creating troubling inefficiencies that resulted in some leads being called twice while others were ignored," explains Marc Prosser, chief marketing officer at FXCM. "And to make matters worse, we were not able to easily share customer information as prospects moved through the pipeline. Our customers and our salespeople work around the world and around the clock, so seamless coordination is critical."

FXCM decided to purchase a CRM system to ensure that the company both capitalized on its continually increasing lead volume and retained its critical focus on building strong relationships with prospects and customers, which is critical to success in the financial marketplace. In addition to better tracking and sharing capabilities, FXCM sought a solution that it could easily customize. "We have a complex selling process that requires more flexibility than most out-of-the-box CRM solutions can provide," says Prosser. "In fact, we found that even solutions that were specifically targeted to the financial services industry could not give us what we needed without some serious tweaks." FXCM also did not want to pull IT resources away from product work to focus on a CRM implementation, so ease of installation and minimal ongoing maintenance requirements were important criteria as well.

FIGURE 7.1

CRM software enables sales and marketing professionals to increase sales revenue by providing more and better services to customers and prospects.

The company evaluated solutions from companies including Siebel, GoldMine, and SalesLogix but was most impressed with Salesforce.com. The deal was sealed during a free, 30-day test drive of the Salesforce on-demand CRM system. "With most solutions, a salesperson walks you through the demo, or you can try a generic demo on your own," explains Prosser. "With Salesforce, we were able to kick the tires in our own personal account for up to a month. We tested the functionality that was important to us and even customized the solution to match our sales process, all on our own and right within the free demo account. After we signed up, all those customizations and data rolled into our live solution."

The Salesforce CRM system was up and running at FXCM in less than two weeks. In the first two months alone, 50 sales users successfully tracked and managed more than 15,000 leads. Today, more than 100 FXCM employees around the world are using the CRM system to better track team and individual sales activities as well as marketing campaigns. "Salesforce helps us process leads much more efficiently than we did before, and we estimate that productivity is up 25 percent," says Prosser. "Our customizations put all the information that our sales team needs no more than two clicks away."

The new CRM system was integrated with internal systems—including a proprietary software application built on top of an Oracle database—putting new and updated customer information such as account transactions, balances, and contact information within easy reach of sales teams using the system. FXCM quickly and easily achieved its various integration projects through a combination of in-house FXCM resources, a third-party tool, and Salesforce.com's professional services. "Our ability to do some of our own integration work underscores a key value of the Salesforce CRM—it's very easy to install and maintain, and even integration requires few, if any, outside resources," says Prosser. "Because it's so tightly integrated, our busy teams can get a complete view of the entire customer experience simply by logging into the Salesforce CRM system."

Due to the sensitive nature of financial information, FXCM also needed tight control over security permissions and functional privileges. Salesforce allows FXCM to control data access by setting user, department, or role-based data security and sharing privileges, ensuring that information is not improperly accessed or shared. For example, sensitive data that are used by the compliance and institutional sales groups are shielded from users in other FXCM groups. Even joint venture partners have restricted access to the Salesforce system, giving them access to limited and very specific information and activities.

Wyse Technology

Like all companies, when Wyse Technology, the world leader in thin-client computing with revenues in excess of US$180 million, implemented a new customer relationship management (CRM) solution from Salesforce.com, it wanted to ensure that it derived maximum benefit from the implementation. Stephen Yeo is director of marketing for Europe, the Middle East and Asia, and Australia and New Zealand at Wyse Technology. "The first thing to say is that unlike other applications, the Salesforce system has proven to be a low-risk solution for us," he says. "It was pay as you go with no upfront investment, no servers, no software, no new network, and no consultants."

Yeo explains that the Salesforce system has made a major contribution to Wyse, helping more than double its sales volume in Europe within 12 months. "We have more than doubled lead generation and sales unit volume," he notes. "We could not have achieved such explosive growth without the help of Salesforce." One of the ways that the CRM system has helped generate leads is through the Web-to-leads functionality of the Salesforce system. "Any contacts on the Web site are automatically captured and incorporated into the system," Yeo explains. "At some points, the system has collected a lead off the Web every 15 minutes."

Not only has the new system proven to be a lead and revenue generator, but it has helped manage the doubling of business in Europe without adding additional staff. Wyse's experience with Salesforce in Europe has been so successful that the solution has also been rolled out globally to the United States, Australia, and Taiwan. There are 160 active users across all areas of the company, including sales, presales engineering, marketing, and support.

Wyse has blue-chip customers such as Federal Express and the Internal Revenue Service in the United States, Argos and the Royal Mail in the United Kingdom, Grundig in Germany, and Credit Lyonnais in France. All customer support at Wyse is managed through the Salesforce CRM system. "More and more of our enterprise accounts are demanding high-quality, pan-European or international customer care. The Salesforce system helps us deliver that. We have a 360-degree view of the customer geographically and by department," explains Yeo.

Wyse was an early adopter of Salesforce.com's Enterprise Edition CRM system, which is designed for medium to large organizations with multiple divisions or a multinational presence. Enterprise Edition provides the customization, integration, and administration functionality that large enterprises typically require, such as integrating external systems with Salesforce, as Wyse has done. Wyse is not stopping there, however. It aims to exploit the potential of the new system further to drive new leads and revenue by adding external telemarketing agencies. To date, telemarketing agencies have been appointed in France, Germany, the United Kingdom, and Australia. The external agencies make contacts using their own integrated telephony and call center management software. The results are then placed on a secure FTP server on the Internet and routed automatically into the Salesforce system to generate new leads and sales activity for Wyse. "We generated 200 leads in four weeks from one country using this new interface alone," says Yeo.

Wyse uses Salesforce's multicurrency and multilingual modules, including French and German as well as English. It is also using an offline edition so that salespeople on the road can continue to work productively with the system at times when they do not have Internet access. "Salesforce is helping us drive leads, grow revenue, and manage our rapid growth," comments Yeo. "Any CRM solution that helps us double business in 12 months without adding additional staff has more than proved itself in my eyes."

Source: "Global Currency Trading Firm Chooses World-Class CRM Solution from Salesforce.com" and "Salesforce Helps Wyse Technology Double Sales Volume in Europe within Twelve Months," Salesforce.com, 2006; Michael Hickins, "Salesforce Serves Notice," *Internetnews.com*, May 24, 2006.

CASE STUDY QUESTIONS

1. Why can't Microsoft Excel spreadsheets and Access database software handle the customer relationship needs of companies like FXCM? What functions do CRM systems like Salesforce provide to a company that these software packages do not?
2. What business benefits has the Salesforce CRM system provided to FXCM? To Wyse Technology?
3. Salesforce.com is an example of an ASP (application service provider), which we discussed in Chapter 4. What benefits do you see in this case for that method of providing a CRM system to a company versus installing a CRM software package? What disadvantages might arise? Which method would you prefer? Why?

REAL WORLD ACTIVITIES

1. The success of Salesforce.com hurt traditional software companies like Siebel Systems, which only offered CRM as a complex installed software solution. Siebel, since acquired by Oracle, responded with Siebel OnDemand, an ASP solution like Salesforce. Other companies jumped into the CRM/ASP market to compete with Salesforce.com. Use the Internet to research these companies and discover how Salesforce is responding to this intense competition for customers in the CRM market.
2. The CRM solutions in this case highlight how much information on customers and prospects is easily captured, integrated with other customer data, and accessible to company employees and even business partners. How are FXCM and Wyse securing this sensitive data? Is it enough? What else could be done to protect customer privacy and security? Break into small groups with your classmates to discuss how companies and their customers can benefit from CRM systems while still protecting customer privacy.

FIGURE 7.2 The new product development process in a manufacturing company. This is an example of a business process that must be supported by cross-functional information systems that cross the boundaries of several business functions.

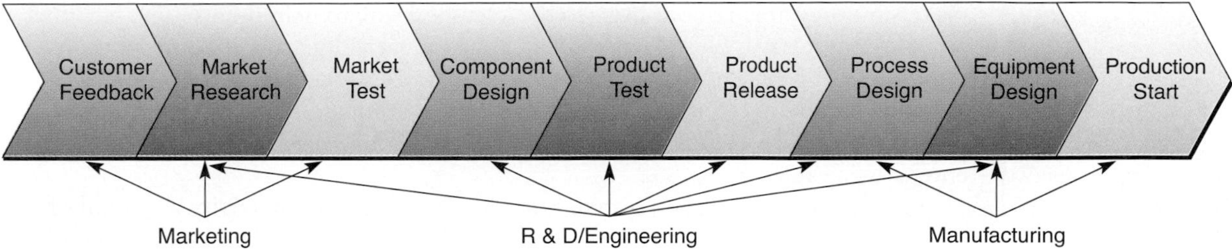

Notice that instead of concentrating on traditional business functions, or only supporting the internal business processes of a company, enterprise applications are focused on accomplishing fundamental business processes in concert with a company's customer, supplier, partner, and employee stakeholders. Thus, enterprise resource planning (ERP) concentrates on the efficiency of a firm's internal production, distribution, and financial processes. Customer relationship management (CRM) focuses on acquiring and retaining profitable customers via marketing, sales, and service processes. Partner relationship management (PRM) aims at acquiring and retaining partners who can enhance the selling and distribution of a firm's products and services. Supply chain management (SCM) focuses on developing the most efficient and effective sourcing and procurement processes with suppliers for the products and services needed by a business. Knowledge management (KM) applications focus on providing a firm's employees with tools that support group collaboration and decision support [29].

We will discuss CRM, ERP, and SCM applications in detail in this section and cover knowledge management applications in Chapter 9. Now let's look at a real-world example of a cross-functional enterprise system in action.

FIGURE 7.3
This enterprise application architecture presents an overview of the major cross-functional enterprise applications and their interrelationships.

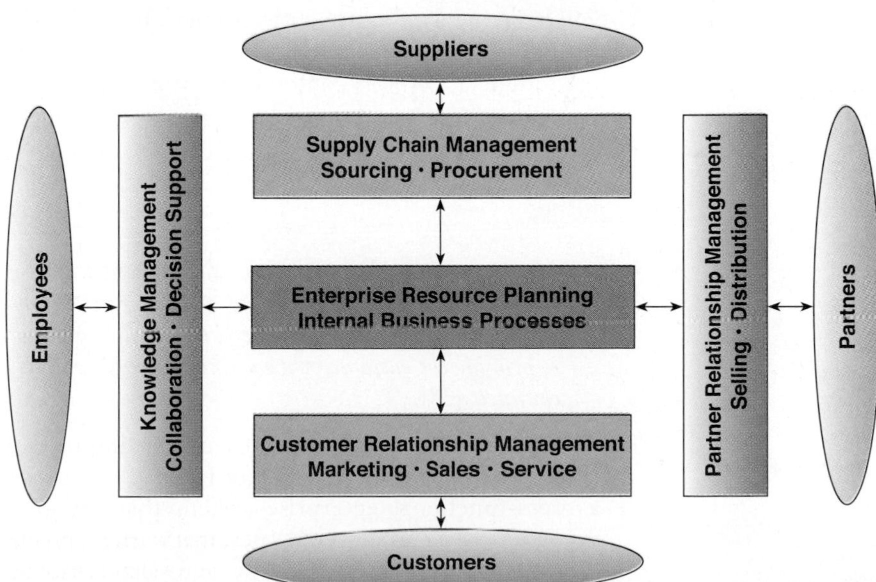

Source: Adapted from Mohan Sawhney and Jeff Zabin, *Seven Steps to Nirvana: Strategic Insights into e-Business Transformation* (New York: McGraw-Hill, 2001), p.175.

IBM and Apple: Global Cross-Functional Enterprise Systems

There is an old saying—"Physician, heal thyself." The phrase suggests that because doctors are always busy healing others, they often fail to pay attention to their own health. Every once in a while, physicians need to turn their expertise inward to make sure they are in good shape so they can be ready to help others. The personal computer industry is clearly a very busy industry, providing systems and solutions to millions of people and organizations each day. To provide a fast and effective ordering and delivery process to their customers, companies like IBM and Apple have turned their expertise and technology inward. The result is an example of an enterprise system.

An enterprise e-business system requires end-to-end connectivity across all of the different processes, from the company's legacy systems to the outer reaches of its suppliers, customers, and partners. In the personal computing world, customers want a system configured exactly the way they want it, and they want it as fast as possible. To accommodate these market pressures, PC manufacturers are developing and implementing *configure-to-order* enterprise systems.

Consider the real-time, configure-to-order system that IBM has created for its personal systems division. A customer in Europe can configure a personal computer on IBM's Web site and get real-time availability and order confirmation. Although this seems simple enough, making this action possible took a team of analysts and programmers and hundreds of person-years of effort to develop the myriad business processes and systems that need to work together.

Here's what happens when a European customer places an order with IBM: The order travels to IBM's fulfillment engine in the United Kingdom; its e-commerce engine in Boulder, Colorado; its ERP and production management systems in Raleigh, North Carolina; its sales reporting system in Southbury, Connecticut; its product database in Poughkeepsie, New York; and back to the customer's browser in Europe. Every system updates its status and communicates with every other system in real time. And each order placed in Europe zips across the Atlantic an average of four times. In its journey, it touches dozens of geographical units, legacy systems, and databases strewn across the globe.

Apple Computer's configure-to-order and manufacture-to-order systems began with over 16 legacy applications operating on a legacy platform. Upon completion of the new systems, Apple was able to offer to its customers direct buying from Apple at Apple.com, Web-enabled configure-to-order order entry and order status, and real-time credit card authorization. In addition, once the order is configured by the customer online, the manufacturing process begins automatically. Since implementing its enterprise configure-to-order system, Apple's production cycle times have shrunk by 60 percent—an improvement achieved while processing more than 6,000 orders a day [21, 29].

What Is CRM?

Managing the full range of the customer relationship involves two related objectives: one, to provide the organization and all of its customer-facing employees with a single, complete view of every customer at every touch point and across all channels; and, two, to provide the customer with a single, complete view of the company and its extended channels [25].

This quote is why companies are turning to **customer relationship management (CRM)** to improve their customer focus. CRM uses information technology to create a cross-functional enterprise system that integrates and automates many of the *customer-serving* processes in sales, marketing, and customer services that interact with a company's customers. CRM systems also create an IT framework of Web-enabled software and databases that integrates these processes with the rest of a company's business operations. CRM systems include a family of software modules that provides

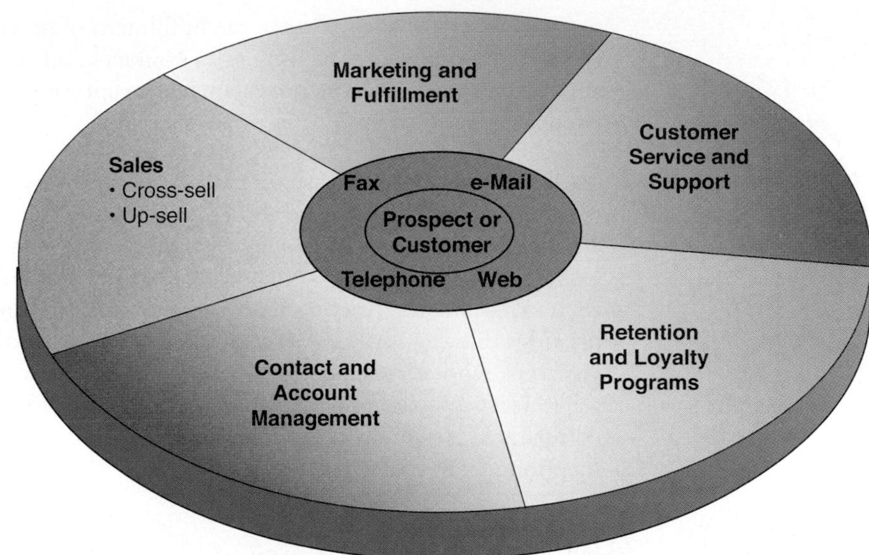

FIGURE 7.4
The major application clusters in customer relationship management.

the tools that enable a business and its employees to provide fast, convenient, dependable, and consistent service to its customers. Siebel Systems, Oracle, SAP AG, IBM, and Epiphany are some of the leading vendors of CRM software. Figure 7.4 illustrates some of the major application components of a CRM system. Let's take a look at each of them.

Contact and Account Management

CRM software helps sales, marketing, and service professionals capture and track relevant data about every past and planned contact with prospects and customers, as well as other business and life cycle events of customers. Information is captured from all customer *touchpoints*, such as telephone, fax, e-mail, the company's Web site, retail stores, kiosks, and personal contact. CRM systems store the data in a common customer database that integrates all customer account information and makes it available throughout the company via Internet, intranet, or other network links for sales, marketing, service, and other CRM applications.

Sales

A CRM system provides sales reps with the software tools and company data sources they need to support and manage their sales activities and optimize *cross-selling* and *up-selling*. Cross-selling is an approach in which a customer of one product or service, say, auto insurance, might also be interested in purchasing a related product or service, say, homeowner's insurance. By using a cross-selling technique, sales reps can better serve their customers while simultaneously improving their sales. Up-selling refers to the process of finding ways to sell a new or existing customer a better product than they are currently seeking. Examples include sales prospect and product information, product configuration, and sales quote generation capabilities. CRM also provides real-time access to a single common view of the customer, enabling sales reps to check on all aspects of a customer's account status and history before scheduling their sales calls. For example, a CRM system would alert a bank sales rep to call customers who make large deposits to sell them premier credit or investment services. Or it would alert a salesperson of unresolved service, delivery, or payment problems that could be resolved through a personal contact with a customer.

Marketing and Fulfillment

CRM systems help marketing professionals accomplish direct marketing campaigns by automating such tasks as qualifying leads for targeted marketing and scheduling and tracking direct marketing mailings. Then the CRM software helps marketing professionals capture and manage prospect and customer response data in the CRM database and analyze the customer and business value of a company's direct marketing campaigns. CRM also assists in the fulfillment of prospect and customer responses and requests by quickly scheduling sales contacts and providing appropriate information about products and services to them, while capturing relevant information for the CRM database.

Customer Service and Support

A CRM system provides service reps with software tools and real-time access to the common customer database shared by sales and marketing professionals. CRM helps customer service managers create, assign, and manage requests for service by customers. *Call center* software routes calls to customer support agents on the basis of their skills and authority to handle specific kinds of service requests. *Help desk* software provides relevant service data and suggestions for resolving problems for customer service reps who assist customers with problems with a product or service. Web-based self-service enables customers to easily access personalized support information at the company Web site, while giving them an option to receive further assistance online or by phone from customer service personnel.

Retention and Loyalty Programs

Consider the following:

- It costs six times more to sell to a new customer than to sell to an existing one.
- A typical dissatisfied customer will tell eight to ten people about his or her experience.
- A company can boost its profits 85 percent by increasing its annual customer retention by only 5 percent.
- The odds of selling a product to a new customer are 15 percent, whereas the odds of selling a product to an existing customer are 50 percent.
- Seventy percent of complaining customers will do business with the company again if it quickly takes care of a service problem [10].

Thus, enhancing and optimizing customer retention and loyalty is a major business strategy and primary objective of customer relationship management. CRM systems try to help a company identify, reward, and market to their most loyal and profitable customers. CRM analytical software includes data mining tools and other analytical marketing software, and CRM databases may consist of a customer data warehouse and CRM data marts. These tools are used to identify profitable and loyal customers and to direct and evaluate a company's targeted marketing and relationship marketing programs toward them. Figure 7.5 is an example of part of a proposed Web-based report format for evaluating Charles Schwab & Co.'s customer retention performance.

The Three Phases of CRM

Figure 7.6 illustrates another way to think about the customer and business value and components of customer relationship management. We can view CRM as an integrated system of Web-enabled software tools and databases that accomplish a variety of customer-focused business processes that support the three phases of the relationship between a business and its customers [10].

- **Acquire.** A business relies on CRM software tools and databases to help it acquire new customers by doing a superior job of contact management, sales prospecting, selling, direct marketing, and fulfillment. The goal of these CRM functions is to help customers perceive the value of a superior product offered by an outstanding company.
- **Enhance.** Web-enabled CRM account management and customer service and support tools help keep customers happy by supporting superior service from a responsive, networked team of sales and service specialists and business partners. And CRM sales force automation and direct marketing and fulfillment tools help companies cross-sell and up-sell to their customers, thus increasing their profitability to the business. The value perceived by customers is the convenience of one-stop shopping at attractive prices.

FIGURE 7.5 A proposed report format for evaluating the customer retention performance of Charles Schwab & Co.

	Navigation	Performance	Operations	Environment
Customer Retention	Customer retention rate Household retention rate Average customer tenure	Retention rate by customer cohort Retention rate by customer segment Customer loyalty rating	Percentage of customers who are active Web users Percentage of customers who interact via e-mail Decline in customer activity Propensity to defect	Competitors' offers Share of portfolio Comparative retention Comparative customer tenure
Customer Experience	Satisfaction by customer segment Satisfaction by cohort Satisfaction by customer scenario	Customer satisfaction by: • Task • Touchpoint • Channel partner End-to-end performance by scenario Customer satisfaction with quality of information provided	Elapsed time for commonly performed tasks Accuracy of Web search results Percentage of trades executed with price improvement Percentage of e-mails answered accurately in one hour	Comparative satisfaction: Competitors: • Other online brokers • Other financial service firms • All products and services
Customer Spending	Average revenue per customer Average profitability per customer Growth in customer assets Customer lifetime value	Revenues per customer segment Profits per customer segment Growth in customer assets per segment	Daily log-ins at market opening Revenue trades per day Percentage increase in customer assets Cost to serve by touchpoint	Total brokerage assets Growth in brokerage assets

- **Retain.** CRM analytical software and databases help a company proactively identify and reward its most loyal and profitable customers to retain and expand their business via targeted marketing and relationship marketing programs. The value perceived by customers is of a rewarding personalized business relationship with "their company."

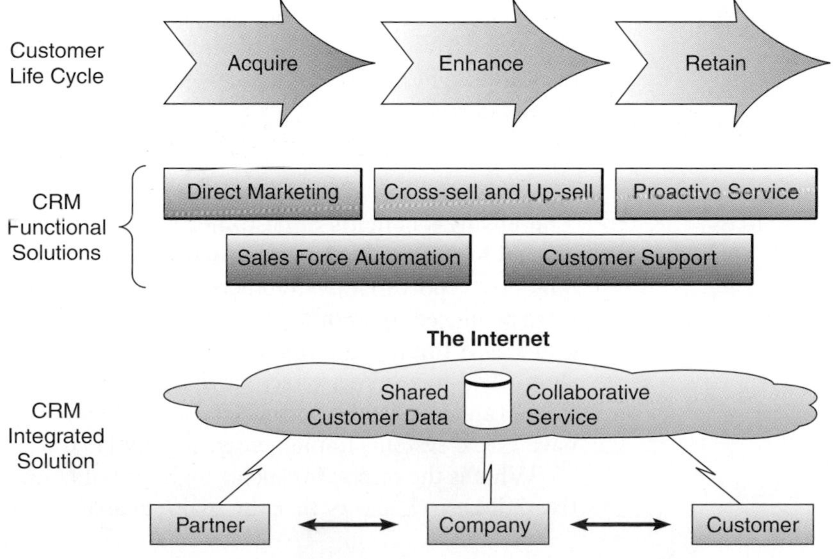

FIGURE 7.6 How CRM supports the three phases of the relationship between a business and its customers.

Benefits and Challenges of CRM

The potential business benefits of customer relationship management are many. For example, CRM allows a business to identify and target its best customers—those who are the most profitable to the business—so they can be retained as lifelong customers for greater and more profitable services. It makes possible real-time customization and personalization of products and services based on customer wants, needs, buying habits, and life cycles. CRM can also keep track of when a customer contacts the company, regardless of the contact point. And CRM systems can enable a company to provide a consistent customer experience and superior service and support across all the contact points a customer chooses. All of these benefits would provide strategic business value to a company and major customer value to its customers [7, 8, 9].

Boise Cascade: Success In Customer Service

Boise Cascade Office Products (BCOP) is a $4 billion subsidiary of paper giant Boise Cascade and a purveyor to large and midsize businesses of everything from paper to paper clips to office furniture. About two years ago, the company had a "eureka" moment: "Here we had tons of data on our customers and were doing nothing with it," says senior VP for marketing Dave Goudge, the leader of BCOP's customer data initiative. "We could distinguish ourselves in an increasingly competitive industry by collecting that data in one place, organizing it, and then using it to create great customer service."

Easier said than done. For starters, BCOP's customer information was buried in dozens of separate databases that couldn't speak to one another. Liberating that data and installing a new customer relationship management (CRM) system without disrupting BCOP's ongoing business would be challenge enough. But the organizational hurdles were higher still. For BCOP to make full use of its data, service representatives would have to learn to sell, territorial sales reps would have to share data on their clients, and once-autonomous brands within BCOP would have to be consolidated.

Still, phase one of the initiative dubbed One Boise went into effect on time and within 1 percent of the $20 million the firm had budgeted—and life began to get dramatically easier for BCOP clients. Now when you call to place an order (or log on—about 18 percent of sales come via the Web), you key up an identifying number and are soon greeted by name by a rep whose screen shows all of your most recent BCOP interactions. Depending on your past dealings with the company, your call might get special routing—to a specialist in a particular kind of merchandise, say, or to a Spanish-speaking rep—all before the rep even picks up the phone.

Lost on the Web site? Click "Need Assistance?" and a pop-up screen asks whether you would like help by instant message or by phone. Choose the former and a rep will be on your screen immediately. Choose the latter and the phone will ring within 30 seconds. "BCOP has taken much of the aggravation out of ordering supplies," says Bob Powell, purchasing manager at Citizens Banking Corp., an $8 billion Midwestern bank [22].

CRM Failures

The business benefits of customer relationship management are not guaranteed but instead have proven elusive for many companies. Surveys by industry research groups include a report that over 50 percent of CRM projects did not produce the results that were promised. In another research report, 20 percent of businesses surveyed reported that CRM implementations had actually damaged long-standing customer relationships. And in a survey of senior management satisfaction with 25 management tools, CRM ranked near the bottom in user satisfaction, even though 72 percent expected to have CRM systems implemented shortly [17].

What is the reason for such a high rate of failure or dissatisfaction with CRM initiatives? Research shows that the major reason is a familiar one: lack of understanding and preparation. That is, too often business managers rely on a major new application of information technology (like CRM) to solve a business problem without first developing the business process changes and change management programs that are required. For example, in many cases, failed CRM projects were implemented without the participation of the business stakeholders involved. Therefore, employees and customers were not prepared for the new processes or challenges that were part of the new CRM implementation. We will discuss the topic of failures in information technology management, system implementation, and change management further in subsequent chapters.

Gevity HR and Monster.com: Failures in CRM Implementation

No amount of high-level cooperation will protect a CRM project from rank-and-file employees who hate it. Lisa Harris, CIO at the HR services firm Gevity HR, based in Bradenton, Florida, faced rebellion from the staff when she installed Oracle CRM software that helped solve some customers' problems online—without the help of a live operator. Call-center employees felt that the software threatened their jobs, so they quietly discouraged customers from using it. "Our operators would say, 'Wouldn't you rather call up? I'll take care of everything you need,'" Harris says. She stuck with the online CRM but also belatedly began talking to employees about software. She changed their work routines to include more customer handholding and less data entry, which was increasingly done online.

CRM software is complex to install because it often touches many different legacy systems. Harris says she spent millions of dollars integrating a CRM application in 1997 for a previous employer. But when the project was finished, it took operators too long to get data onscreen. The company had bogged down the performance of the new CRM implementation by trying to integrate too many complex business systems. The project ended up a total failure, she acknowledges [3].

And when Monster.com rolled out a CRM program, it was sure it had a new money-making strategy on its hands. The Massachusetts-based job-listings company had invested over $1 million in customized software and integrated all its computer systems in an attempt to boost the efficiency of its sales force. These CRM applications had been specially developed to allow Monster.com's sales representatives instant access to data for prospective customers.

However, the new system proved to be frighteningly slow—so slow, in fact, that salespeople in the field found themselves unable to download customer information from the company's databases onto their laptops. Every time they tried, their machines froze. Eventually, Monster.com was forced to rebuild the entire system. It lost millions of dollars along the way, not to mention the goodwill of both customers and employees [17].

What Is ERP?

ERP is the technological backbone of e-business, an enterprisewide transaction framework with links into sales order processing, inventory management and control, production and distribution planning, and finance [10].

Enterprise resource planning (ERP) is a cross-functional enterprise system driven by an integrated suite of software modules that supports the basic internal business processes of a company. For example, ERP software for a manufacturing company will typically process the data from, and track the status of, sales, inventory, shipping, and invoicing, as well as forecast raw material and human resource requirements. Figure 7.7 presents the major application components of an ERP system.

ERP gives a company an integrated real-time view of its core business processes, such as production, order processing, and inventory management, tied together by the ERP application software and a common database maintained by a database management system. ERP systems track business resources (e.g., cash, raw materials, production capacity) and the status of commitments made by the business (e.g., customer orders,

FIGURE 7.7
The major application components of enterprise resource planning demonstrate the cross-functional approach of ERP systems.

purchase orders, employee payroll), no matter which department (e.g., manufacturing, purchasing sales, accounting) has entered the data into the system [20].

ERP software suites typically consist of integrated modules of manufacturing, distribution, sales, accounting, and human resource applications. Examples of manufacturing processes supported are material requirements planning, production planning, and capacity planning. Some of the sales and marketing processes supported by ERP are sales analysis, sales planning, and pricing analysis, while typical distribution applications include order management, purchasing, and logistics planning. ERP systems support many vital human resource processes, from personnel requirements planning to salary and benefits administration, and accomplish most required financial recordkeeping and managerial accounting applications. Figure 7.8 illustrates the processes supported by the ERP system installed by Colgate-Palmolive Co. Let's take a closer look at its experience with ERP.

Colgate-Palmolive: The Business Value of ERP

Colgate-Palmolive is a global consumer products company that implemented the SAP R/3 enterprise resource planning system. Colgate embarked on an implementation of SAP R/3 to allow the company to access more timely and accurate data, get the most out of working capital, and reduce manufacturing costs. An important factor for Colgate was whether it could use the software across the entire spectrum of its business. Colgate needed the ability to coordinate globally and act locally. The implementation of SAP across the Colgate supply chain contributed to increased profitability. Now installed in operations that produce most of Colgate's worldwide sales, SAP was expanded to all Colgate divisions worldwide. Global efficiencies in purchasing—combined with product and packaging standardization—also produced large savings.

- Before ERP, it took Colgate U.S. anywhere from one to five days to acquire an order and another one to two days to process the order. Now, order acquisition and processing combined take four hours, not up to seven days. Distribution planning and picking used to take up to four days; today, they take 14 hours. In total, the order-to-delivery time has been cut in half.
- Before ERP, on-time deliveries used to occur only 91.5 percent of the time, and cases ordered were delivered correctly 97.5 percent of the time. After R/3, the figures are 97.5 percent and 99.0 percent, respectively.
- After ERP, domestic inventories have dropped by one-third and receivables outstanding have dropped to 22.4 days from 31.4. Working capital as a percentage of sales has plummeted to 6.3 percent from 11.3 percent. Total delivered cost per case has been reduced by nearly 10 percent [10].

FIGURE 7.8 The business processes and functions supported by the ERP system implemented by Colgate-Palmolive Co.

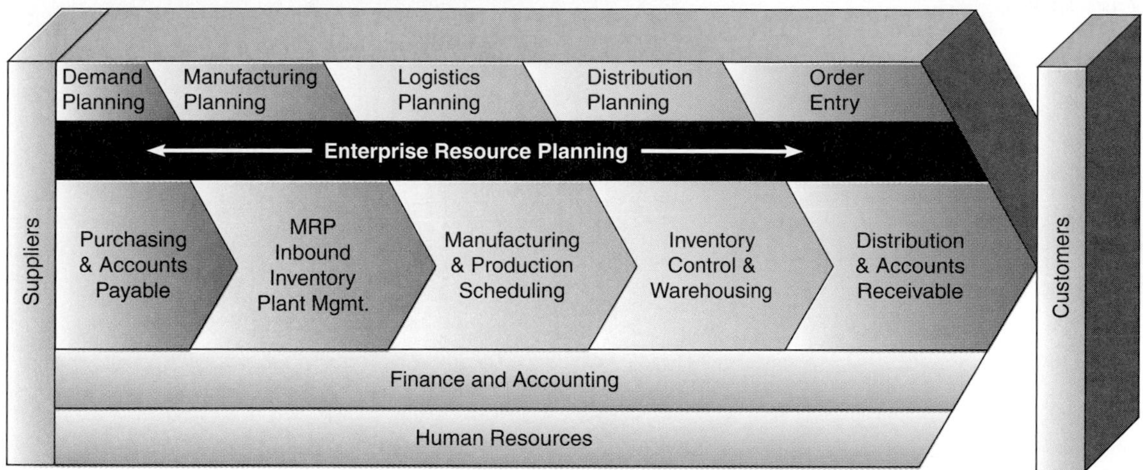

Benefits and Challenges of ERP

As the example of Colgate-Palmolive illustrates, ERP systems can generate significant business benefits for a company. Many other companies have found major business value in their use of ERP in several basic ways [14].

- **Quality and Efficiency.** ERP creates a framework for integrating and improving a company's internal business processes that results in significant improvements in the quality and efficiency of customer service, production, and distribution.
- **Decreased Costs.** Many companies report significant reductions in transaction processing costs and hardware, software, and IT support staff compared with the nonintegrated legacy systems that were replaced by their new ERP systems.
- **Decision Support.** ERP quickly provides vital, cross-functional information on business performance to managers, which significantly improves their ability to make better decisions in a timely manner across the entire business enterprise.
- **Enterprise Agility.** Implementing ERP systems breaks down many former departmental and functional walls or "silos" of business processes, information systems, and information resources. This agility results in more flexible organizational structures, managerial responsibilities, and work roles and therefore a more agile and adaptive organization and workforce that can more easily capitalize on new business opportunities.

The Costs of ERP

An ERP implementation is like the corporate equivalent of a brain transplant. We pulled the plug on every company application and moved to PeopleSoft software. The risk was certainly disruption of business, because if you do not do ERP properly, you can kill your company, guaranteed [10].

So says Jim Prevo, CIO of Green Mountain Coffee Roasters in Vermont, commenting on its successful implementation of an ERP system. Although the benefits of ERP are many, the costs and risks are also considerable, as we will continue to see in some of the real-world cases and examples in the text. Figure 7.9 illustrates the relative size and types of costs of implementing an ERP system in a company. Notice that hardware and software costs are a small part of total costs, and the costs of developing new business processes (reengineering) and preparing employees for the new system (training and change management) make up the bulk of implementing a new ERP system. Converting data from previous legacy systems to the new cross-functional ERP system is another major category of ERP implementation costs [12].

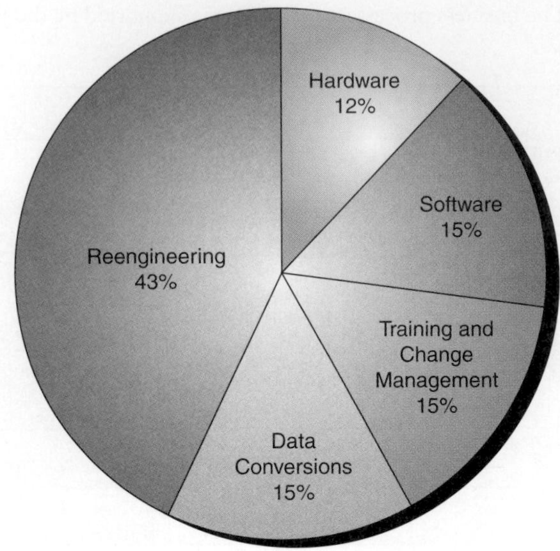

FIGURE 7.9
Typical costs of implementing a new ERP system.

The costs and risks of failure in implementing a new ERP system are substantial. Most companies have had successful ERP implementations, but a sizable minority of firms experienced spectacular and costly failures that heavily damaged their overall business. Big losses in revenue, profits, and market share resulted when core business processes and information systems failed or did not work properly. In many cases, orders and shipments were lost, inventory changes were not recorded correctly, and unreliable inventory levels caused major stock-outs to occur for weeks or months. Companies like Hershey Foods, Nike, A-DEC, and Connecticut General sustained losses running into hundreds of millions of dollars in some instances. In the case of FoxMeyer Drugs, a $5 billion pharmaceutical wholesaler, the company had to file for bankruptcy protection and then was bought out by its arch competitor McKesson Drugs [10].

Whirlpool Corporation: Rush to ERP Leads to Shipping Snafus

Whirlpool Corp. is the world's leading manufacturer and marketer of major home appliances, with annual sales of over $11 billion, 68,000 employees, and nearly 50 manufacturing and technology research centers around the globe. While it may be an expert on gentle spin cycles that cause no damage to your clothes, it was less facile at recognizing the dangers of moving too fast in an ERP implementation. When it was announced that the ERP system was almost ready to implement, Whirlpool executives made a risky and ultimately damaging business decision by going live with an SAP R/3 enterprise resource planning (ERP) application over the three-day Labor Day holiday, though several small problems with the software remained unaddressed. Fixing the problems would have delayed Whirlpool's "go live" date by only one week, but pressures to take advantage of the long weekend and get off the legacy systems pushed the appliance maker to go ahead with its original plan.

The rush to implement resulted in a crippled shipping system that left appliances sitting in warehouses and stores with six- to eight-week delays for receiving orders. The important issue, however, is that the problem could have been avoided. Three months before Whirlpool was scheduled to go live, SAP assigned a postimplementation consultant to check for any functionality problems that might affect the launch. The testing raised two red flags. Two batch-processing transactions were taking a long time to feed into the decision-support database and customer service system. Although recommendations on how to fix the issues were made, Whirlpool managers decided to hold off on the fix. They reasoned that a lot of ERP systems go live with minor bugs without any problems.

The Labor Day weekend system launch went well, and things seemed to be running smoothly for several days after the launch when 1,000 system users processed appliance orders. But by the middle of the month, with 4,000 users, performance started to deteriorate. That's when stores selling Whirlpool appliances started feeling the pinch. Foremost Appliance in Chantilly, Virginia, which gets one-third of its revenue from Whirlpool sales, suffered when shipments from Whirlpool's distribution center in Carlisle, Pennsylvania, were delayed for six to eight weeks. Whirlpool appliance distributors were forced to advise customers who needed their appliances quickly to look at other brands. This failure cost Whirlpool large losses of potential sales [5, 30].

Causes of ERP Failures

What have been the major causes of failure in ERP projects? In almost every case, the business managers and IT professionals of these companies underestimated the complexity of the planning, development, and training that were needed to prepare for a new ERP system that would radically change their business processes and information systems. Failure to involve affected employees in the planning and development phases and to change management programs, or trying to do too much too fast in the conversion process, also were typical causes of failed ERP projects. Insufficient training in the new work tasks required by the ERP system, and failure to do enough data conversion and testing, were other causes of failure. In many cases, ERP failures were also due to overreliance by company or IT management on the claims of ERP software vendors or on the assistance of prestigious consulting firms hired to lead the implementation [11]. The following experiences of companies that did it right give us a helpful look at what is needed for a successful ERP implementation.

Reebok and Home Depot: Success with ERP

SAP Retail is a good ERP product, argues Kevin Restivo, a Canada-based analyst who works for IDC in Framingham, Massachusetts. But technology is never a "silver bullet, just part of a larger puzzle" that includes making sure internal business processes are in tune with the software's capabilities. That's especially true given the processing complexities faced by retailers, he adds.

In late 1998, Reebok International Ltd. was the first U.S. company to go live with SAP Retail, which now supports 115 outlet stores run by the Stoughton, Massachusetts–based footwear maker. Peter Burrows, Reebok's chief technology officer, says the SAP ERP system is producing "a very high level of stock accuracy" in the stores. But the yearlong development and installation process wasn't easy and required some adjustments as the project went along, Burrows notes.

Home Depot Inc. recently completed a SAP ERP installation in the company's Argentina operations. Gary Cochran, vice president of information services at the Atlanta-based home improvement retailer, claims he made "limited use" of SAP's consulting services. Instead, Cochran put together a team of 50 top employees—IT personnel and end users. Because of the team's familiarity with traditional legacy systems, it didn't have to "face some of the configuration issues that have been problematic for other people," according to Cochran. "It went so smoothly there was literally no ripple in corporate organization" [14].

What Is SCM?

Legacy supply chains are clogged with unnecessary steps and redundant stockpiles. For instance, a typical box of breakfast cereal spends an incredible 104 days getting from factory to supermarket, struggling its way through an unbelievable maze of wholesalers, distributors, brokers, and consolidators, each of which has a warehouse. The e-commerce opportunity

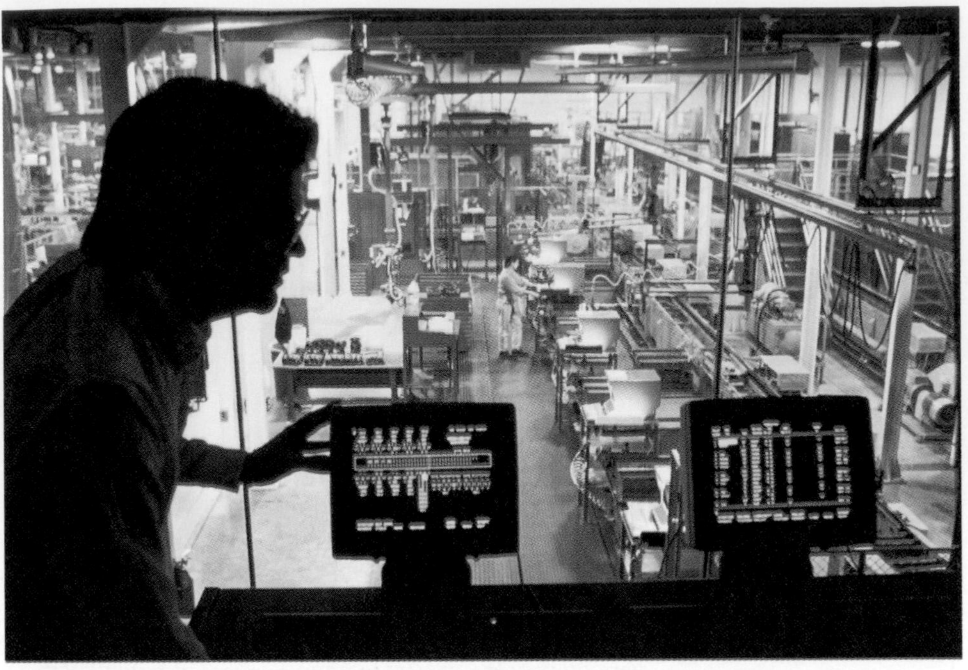

FIGURE 7.10
Computer-based supply chain management systems are enabling reduced cycle times, increased revenues, and a competitive edge in fast-paced retail markets.

lies in the fusing of each company's internal systems to those of its suppliers, partners, and customers. This fusion forces companies to better integrate interenterprise supply chain processes to improve manufacturing efficiency and distribution effectiveness [10].

Supply chain management (SCM) is a cross-functional interenterprise system that uses information technology to help support and manage the links between some of a company's key business processes and those of its suppliers, customers, and business partners. The goal of SCM is to create a fast, efficient, and low-cost network of business relationships, or **supply chain**, to get a company's products from concept to market (see Figure 7.10).

What exactly is a company's supply chain? Let's suppose a company wants to build and sell a product to other businesses. To accomplish this, it must buy raw materials and a variety of contracted services from other companies. The interrelationships with suppliers, customers, distributors, and other businesses that are needed to design, build, and sell a product make up the network of business entities, relationships, and processes that is called a supply chain. And because each supply chain process should add value to the products or services a company produces, a supply chain is frequently called a *value chain*, a different but related concept we discussed in Chapter 2. In any event, many companies today are using Internet technologies to create interenterprise e-business systems for supply chain management that help a company streamline its traditional supply chain processes.

Figure 7.11 illustrates the basic business processes in the supply chain life cycle and the functional SCM processes that support them. It also emphasizes how many companies today are reengineering their supply chain processes, aided by Internet technologies and supply chain management software. For example, the demands of today's competitive business environment are pushing manufacturers to use their intranets, extranets, and e-commerce Web portals to help them reengineer their relationships with their suppliers, distributors, and retailers. The objective is to significantly reduce costs, increase efficiency, and improve their supply chain cycle times. SCM software can also help improve interenterprise coordination among supply chain process players. The result is much more effective distribution and channel networks among business partners. The Web initiatives of Moen Inc. illustrate these developments.

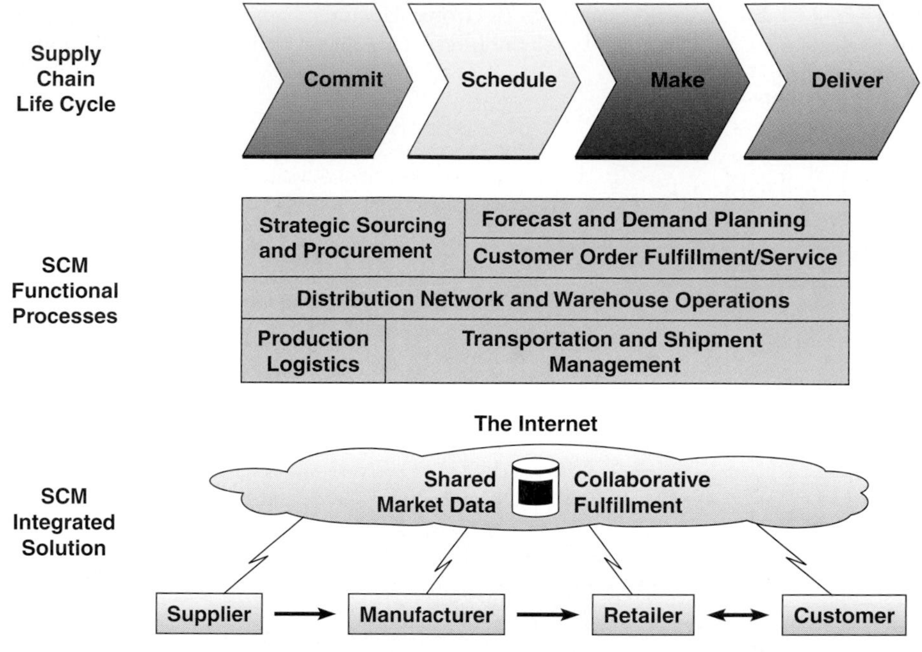

FIGURE 7.11
Supply chain management software and Internet technologies can help companies reengineer and integrate the functional SCM processes that support the supply chain life cycle.

Moen Inc.: Web-Enabling the Supply Chain

In late 1998, faucet maker Moen Inc. started sending electronic files of new product designs by e-mail. A few months later, it launched ProjectNet, an online extranet site where Moen can share digital designs simultaneously with suppliers worldwide. Every supplier can make changes immediately. Moen consolidates all the design changes in a master Web file. That way, design problems are discovered instantly, and adjustments can be made just as fast, cutting the time it takes to lock in a final design to three days.

Next the company attacked the cumbersome process of ordering parts from suppliers and updating them by fax or phone. In October 2000, the company launched its SupplyNet extranet site that allows parts suppliers to check the status of Moen's orders online. Every time Moen changes an order, the supplier receives an e-mail. If a supplier can't fill an order in time, it can alert Moen right away so the faucet maker can search elsewhere for the part. Today, the 40 key suppliers who make 80 percent of the parts that Moen buys use SupplyNet. The result: The company has shaved $3 million, or almost 6 percent, off its raw materials and work-in-progress inventories since October.

Moen's approach is high-speed compared with that of competitors. Many still rely on fax machines to do most of their business. The percentage of companies using the Internet to speed the supply chain in the construction/home improvement field, which includes plumbing, rose to 8.4 percent in 2004 up from 3.2 percent in 2000 and is expected to continue a steady upward trend, according to Forrester Research. "Moen is a step ahead of its peers in embracing Internet technologies," notes analyst Navi Radjou of Forrester Research.

Moen may be ahead of its peers, but there's plenty of work to do. Its Technology Chief's most sensitive task is CustomerNet, the company's attempt to wire wholesalers, who account for 50 percent of the company's business. Unlike suppliers, who depend on Moen for most of their business, the company has little sway with wholesalers that buy plumbing, heating, and other products—not just faucets—from many manufacturers. Most still order by fax, even though that process causes errors up to 40 percent of the time. Moen execs are undaunted. They're courting wholesalers with the same methodical determination that has made Moen a Web-smart company [21].

FIGURE 7.12 A typical example of electronic data interchange activities, an important form of business-to-business electronic commerce. EDI over the Internet is a major B2B e-commerce application.

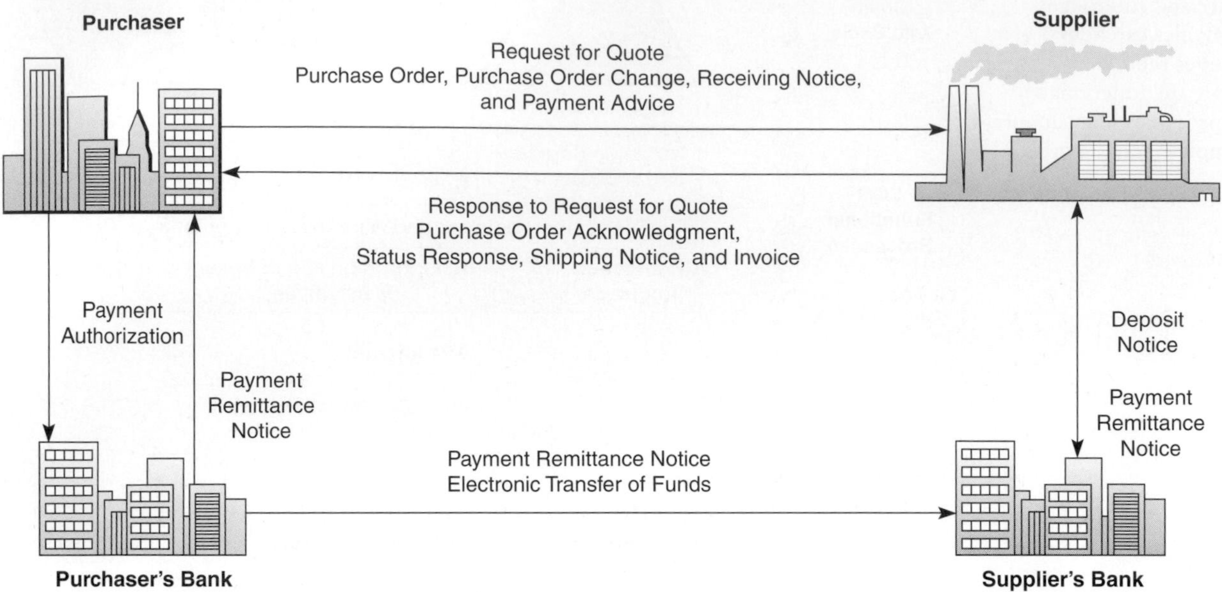

Electronic Data Interchange

Electronic data interchange (EDI) was one of the earliest uses of information technology for supply chain management. EDI involves the electronic exchange of business transaction documents over the Internet and other networks between supply chain trading partners (organizations and their customers and suppliers). Data representing a variety of business transaction documents (e.g., purchase orders, invoices, requests for quotations, shipping notices) are automatically exchanged between computers using standard document message formats. Typically, EDI software is used to convert a company's own document formats into standardized EDI formats specified by various industry and international protocols. Thus, EDI is an example of the almost complete automation of an e-commerce supply chain process. And EDI over the Internet, using secure *virtual private networks*, is a growing B2B e-commerce application.

Formatted transaction data are transmitted over network links directly between computers without paper documents or human intervention. In addition to direct network links between the computers of trading partners, third-party services are widely used. Value-added network companies like GE Global Exchange Services and Computer Associates offer a variety of EDI services for relatively high fees. But many EDI service providers now offer secure, lower cost EDI services over the Internet. Figure 7.12 illustrates a typical EDI system [23].

EDI is still a popular data-transmission format among major trading partners, primarily to automate repetitive transactions, though it is increasingly being replaced by XML-based Web services. EDI automatically tracks inventory changes; triggers orders, invoices, and other documents related to transactions; and schedules and confirms delivery and payment. By digitally integrating the supply chain, EDI streamlines processes, saves time, and increases accuracy. And by using Internet technologies, lower cost Internet-based EDI services are now available to smaller businesses [27].

The Role of SCM

Figure 7.13 helps us understand the role and activities of supply chain management in business more clearly. The top three levels of Figure 7.13 show the strategic, tactical, and operational objectives and outcomes of SCM planning, which are then accomplished by the business partners in a supply chain at the execution level of SCM. The role of information technology in SCM is to support these objectives with interenterprise

FIGURE 7.13 The objectives and outcomes of supply chain management are accomplished for a business with the help of interenterprise SCM information systems.

SCM Objectives		SCM Outcomes
What? Establish objectives, policies, and operating footprint	**Strategic**	• Objectives • Supply policies (service levels) • Network design
How much? Deploy resources to match supply to demand	**Tactical**	• Demand forecast • Production, procurement, logistics plan • Inventory targets
When? Where? Schedule, monitor, control, and adjust production	**Operational**	• Work center scheduling • Order/inventory tracking
Do Build and transport	**Execution**	• Order cycle • Material movement

Source: Adapted from Keith Oliver, Anne Chung, and Nick Samanach, "Beyond Utopia: The Realist's Guide to Internet-Enabled Supply Chain Management," *Strategy and Business*, Second Quarter, 2001, p. 99.

information systems that produce many of the outcomes a business needs to effectively manage its supply chain. That's why many companies today are installing SCM software and developing Web-based SCM information systems [15].

Until recently, SCM software products typically were developed for either supply chain planning or execution applications. SCM planning software from vendors such as i2 and Manugistics supports a variety of applications for supply and demand forecasting. SCM execution software from vendors such as EXE Technologies and Manhattan Associates supports applications like order management, logistics management, and warehouse management. However, big ERP vendors like Oracle and SAP are now offering Web-enabled software suites of e-business applications that include SCM modules. Examples include Oracle's e-Business Suite and SAP AG's mySAP [4].

Benefits and Challenges of SCM

Creating a real-time SCM infrastructure is a daunting and ongoing issue and quite often a point of failure for several reasons. The chief reason is that the planning, selection, and implementation of SCM solutions is becoming more complex as the pace of technological change accelerates and the number of a company's partners increases [9].

The promised outcomes that are outlined in Figure 7.14 emphasize the major business benefits that are possible with effective supply chain management systems. Companies know that SCM systems can provide them with key business benefits such as faster, more accurate order processing, reductions in inventory levels, quicker times to market, lower transaction and materials costs, and strategic relationships with their suppliers. All of these benefits of SCM are aimed at helping a company achieve agility and responsiveness in meeting the demands of its customers and the needs of its business partners.

But developing effective SCM systems has proven to be a complex and difficult application of information technology to business operations. So achieving the business value and customer value goals and objectives of supply chain management, as illustrated in Figure 7.15, has been a major challenge for most companies.

What are the causes of problems in supply chain management? Several reasons stand out. A lack of proper demand-planning knowledge, tools, and guidelines is a major source of SCM failure. Inaccurate or overoptimistic demand forecasts will cause major production, inventory, and other business problems, no matter how efficient the

FIGURE 7.14 The supply chain management functions and potential benefits offered by the SCM module in the mySAP e-business software suite.

SCM Functions	SCM Outcomes
Planning	
Supply chain design	• Optimize network of suppliers, plants, and distribution centers.
Collaborative demand and supply planning	• Develop an accurate forecast of customer demand by sharing demand and supply forecasts instantaneously across multiple tiers. • Internet-enable collaborative scenarios, such as collaborative planning, forecasting, and replenishment (CPFR), and vendor-managed inventory.
Execution	
Materials management	• Share accurate inventory and procurement order information. • Ensure materials required for production are available in the right place at the right time. • Reduce raw material spending, procurement costs, safety stocks, and raw material and finished goods inventory.
Collaborative manufacturing	• Optimize plans and schedules while considering resource, material, and dependency constraints.
Collaborative fulfillment	• Commit to delivery dates in real time. • Fulfill orders from all channels on time with order management, transportation planning, and vehicle scheduling. • Support the entire logistics process, including picking, packing, shipping, and delivery in foreign countries.
Supply chain event management	• Monitor every stage of the supply chain process, from price quotation to the moment the customer receives the product, and receive alerts when problems arise.
Supply chain performance management	• Report key measurements in the supply chain, such as filling rates, order cycle times, and capacity utilization.

rest of the supply chain management process. Inaccurate production, inventory, and other business data provided by a company's other information systems are a frequent cause of SCM problems. And the lack of adequate collaboration among marketing, production, and inventory management departments within a company, and with suppliers, distributors, and others, will sabotage any SCM system. Even the SCM software tools themselves are considered to be immature, incomplete, and hard to implement by many companies that are installing SCM systems [2].

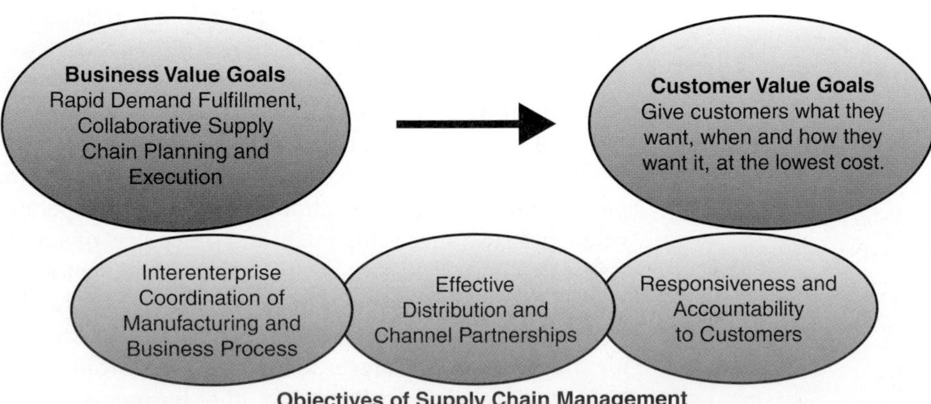

FIGURE 7.15 Achieving the goals and objectives of supply chain management is a major challenge for many companies today.

Enterprise Application Integration

How does a business interconnect its cross-functional enterprise systems? **Enterprise application integration (EAI)** software is being used by many companies to connect their major e-business applications. See Figure 7.16. EAI software enables users to model the business processes involved in the interactions that should occur between business applications. EAI also provides *middleware* that performs data conversion and coordination, application communication and messaging services, and access to the application interfaces involved. Thus, EAI software can integrate a variety of enterprise application clusters by letting them exchange data according to rules derived from the business process models developed by users. For example, a typical rule might be:

When an order is complete, have the order application tell the accounting system to send a bill and alert shipping to send out the product.

Thus, as Figure 7.16 illustrates, EAI software can integrate the front-office and back-office applications of a business so they work together in a seamless, integrated way [18]. This vital capability provides real business value to a business enterprise that must respond quickly and effectively to business events and customer demands. For example, the integration of enterprise application clusters has been shown to dramatically improve customer call center responsiveness and effectiveness. That's because EAI integrates access to everything the customer and product data customer reps need to serve customers quickly. EAI also streamlines sales order processing so products and services can be delivered faster. Thus, EAI improves customer and supplier experience with the business because of its responsiveness [18, 26]. See Figure 7.17.

Dell Inc.: Enterprise Application Integration

In a survey of just 75 companies it deals with, Dell Inc. found they used 18 different software packages, says Terry Klein, vice president of e-business for Dell's "relationship group." This lack of integration means that companies aren't getting the seamless processing that reduces costs and speeds up customer responsiveness.

Dell knew that figuring out how to get its system to talk to each of those 18 different systems in its partners' back offices, one at a time, would be impractical, to say the least. So Dell installed software from webMethods, a maker of industrial-strength business-to-business integration software, based in Fairfax, Virginia. webMethods' enterprise application integration (EAI) technology acts as a software translator and creates a kind of hub that, using the Web, allows instantaneous communication among networked companies' internal business systems.

For Dell, the first fruit of installing the webMethods software is what Dell calls e-procurement, and it goes like this: A business customer pulls product information directly from Dell's server into the customer's purchasing system, which creates an electronic requisition. After the requisition is approved online by the customer, a computer-generated purchase order shoots over the Internet back to Dell.

The entire process can take 60 seconds. Dell says the system, which went live in the spring of 2000, has automatically cut errors in its procurement processes from about 200 per million transactions to 10 per million. And Dell has been able to

FIGURE 7.16
Enterprise application integration software connects front-office and back-office applications.

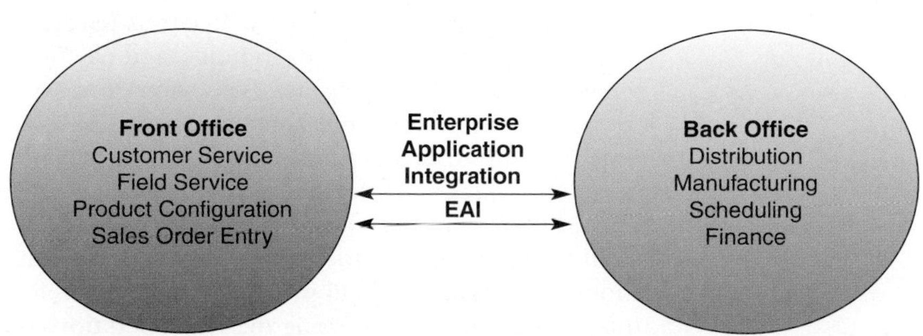

FIGURE 7.17 An example of a new customer order process showing how EAI middleware connects several business information systems within a company.

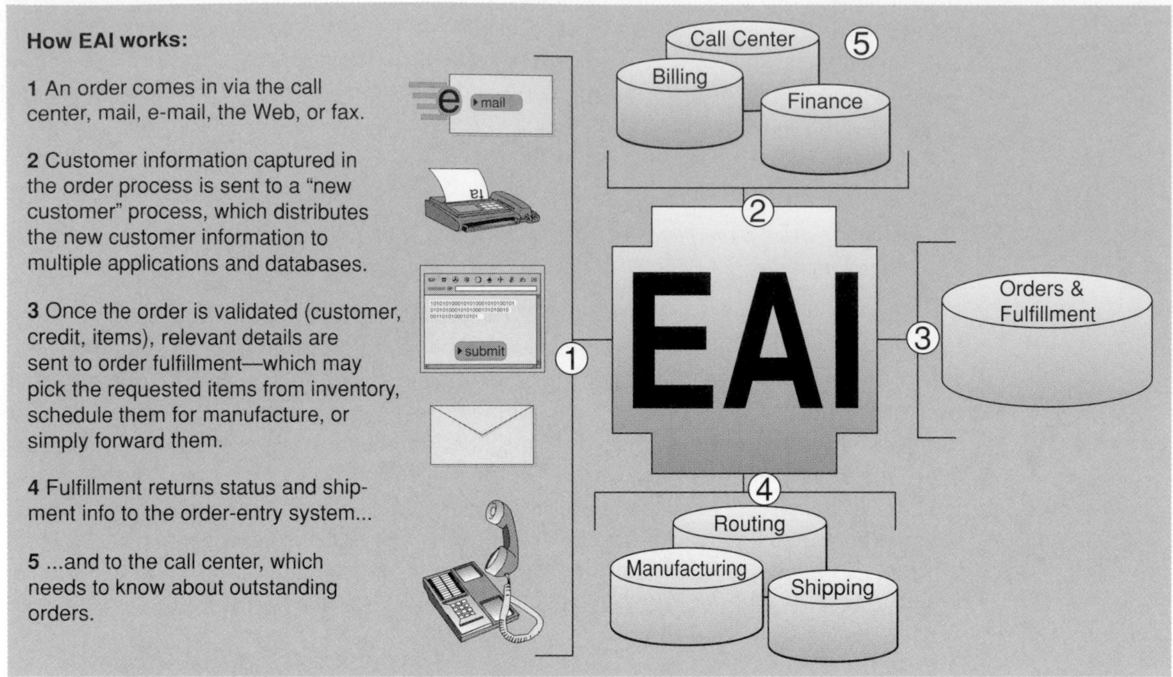

shave $40 to $50 off the cost of processing each order. That adds up to $5 million a year in cost savings, since thousands of orders flow to Dell through its webMethods system daily.

The EAI software also enabled Dell to build links to 40 or so of its biggest customers, allowing a customer to buy, say, a truckload of new laptops online while Dell simultaneously enters the order for those laptops into the customer's procurement system. Think of it as one-click shopping for corporate buyers. Just as Amazon.com automates the process of entering credit card information to speed purchases by consumers, Dell is able to update its customers' procurement tracking systems every time they make a purchase [6].

How EAI works:
1 An order comes in via the call center, mail, e-mail, the Web, or fax.
2 Customer information captured in the order process is sent to a "new customer" process, which distributes the new customer information to multiple applications and databases.
3 Once the order is validated (customer, credit, items), relevant details are sent to order fulfillment—which may pick the requested items from inventory, schedule them for manufacture, or simply forward them.
4 Fulfillment returns status and shipment info to the order-entry system...
5 ...and to the call center, which needs to know about outstanding orders.
mail
submit
Call Center
Billing
Finance
EAI
Orders & Fulfillment
Routing
Manufacturing
Shipping

Transaction Processing Systems

Transaction processing systems (TPS) are cross-functional information systems that process data resulting from the occurrence of business transactions. We introduced transaction processing systems in Chapter 1 as one of the major application categories of information systems in business.

Transactions are events that occur as part of doing business, such as sales, purchases, deposits, withdrawals, refunds, and payments. Think, for example, of the data generated whenever a business sells something to a customer on credit, whether in a retail store or at an e-commerce site on the Web. Data about the customer, product, salesperson, store, and so on must be captured and processed. This need prompts additional transactions, such as credit checks, customer billing, inventory changes, and increases in accounts receivable balances, which generate even more data. Thus, transaction processing activities are needed to capture and process such data, or the operations of a business would grind to a halt. Therefore, transaction processing systems play a vital role in supporting the vital operations of most companies today.

FIGURE 7.18 The Syntellect pay-per-view online transaction processing system.

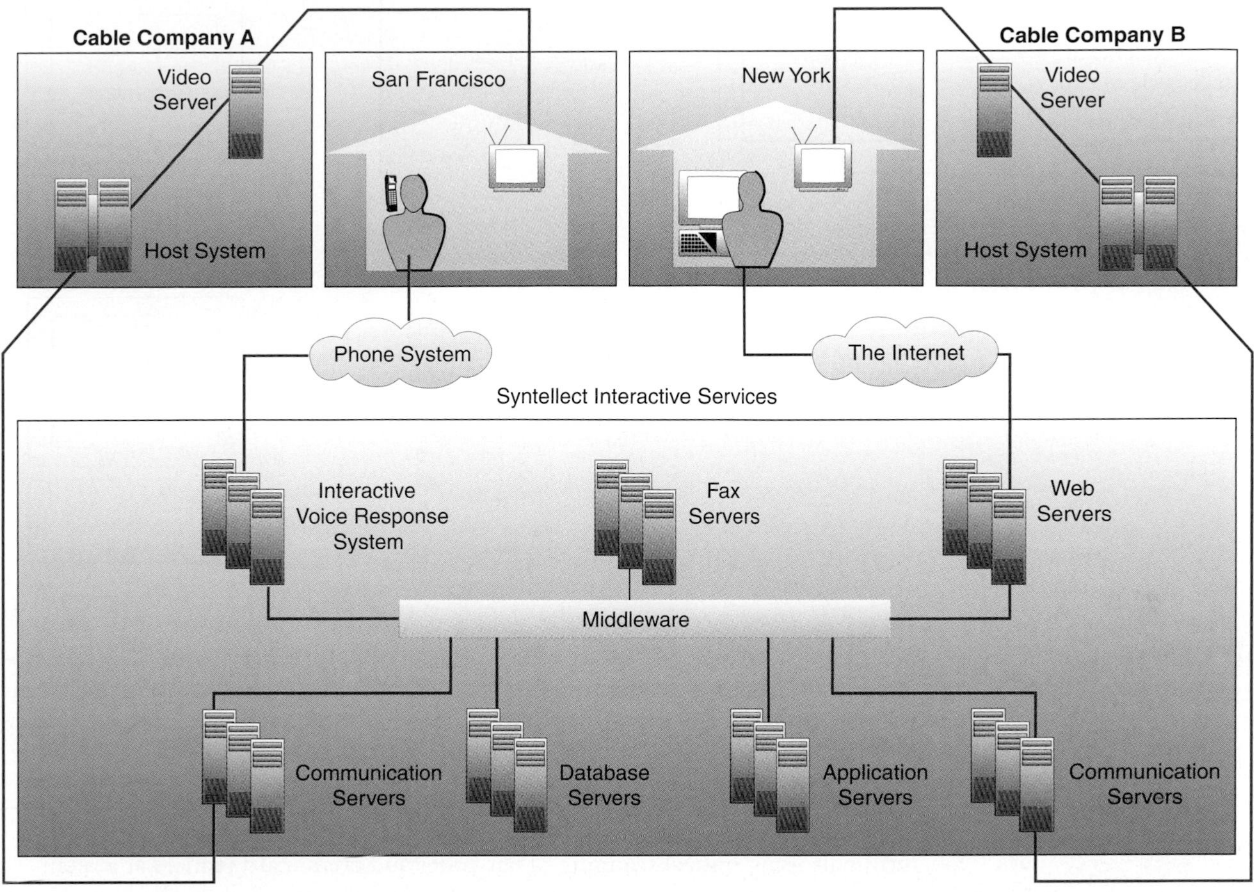

Online transaction processing systems play a strategic role in Web-enabled business processes and electronic commerce. Many firms are using the Internet and other networks that tie them electronically to their customers or suppliers for online transaction processing (OLTP). Such *real-time* systems, which capture and process transactions immediately, can help firms provide superior service to customers and other trading partners. This capability adds value to their products and services and thus gives them an important way to differentiate themselves from their competitors.

Syntellect's Online Transaction Processing

Figure 7.18 illustrates an online transaction processing system for cable pay-per-view systems developed by Syntellect Interactive Services. Cable TV viewers can select pay-per-view events offered by their cable companies using the phone or the World Wide Web. The pay-per-view order is captured by Syntellect's interactive voice response system or Web server, then transported to Syntellect database application servers. There the order is processed, customer and sales databases are updated, and the approved order is relayed back to the cable company's video server, which transmits the video of the pay-per-view event to the customer. Thus, Syntellect teams with over 700 cable companies to offer a very popular and very profitable service [18].

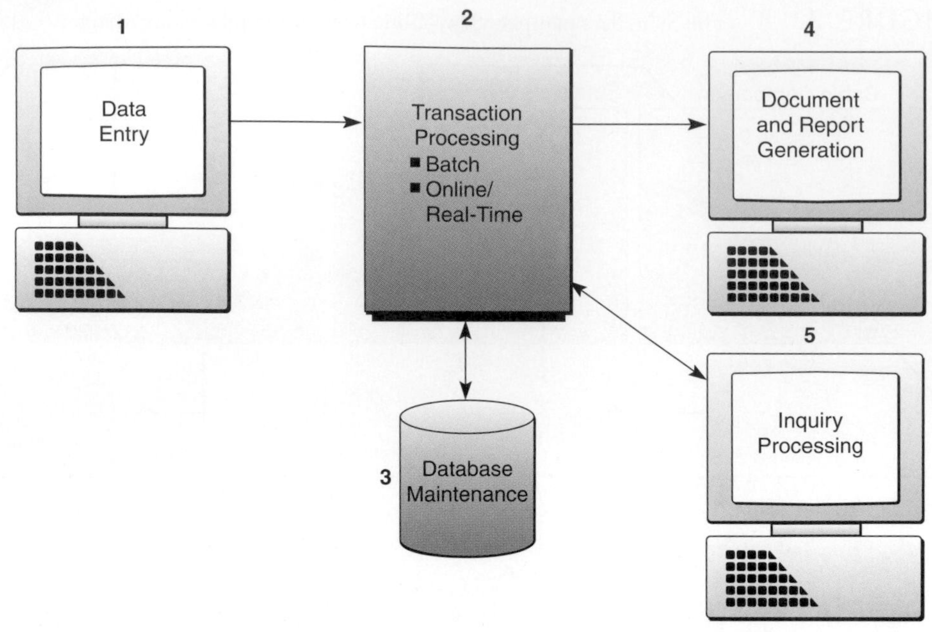

FIGURE 7.19
The transaction processing cycle. Note that transaction processing systems use a five-stage cycle of data entry, transaction processing, database maintenance, document and report generation, and inquiry processing activities.

The Transaction Processing Cycle

Transaction processing systems, such as Syntellect's, capture and process data describing business transactions, update organizational databases, and produce a variety of information products. You should understand this as a **transaction processing cycle** of several basic activities, as illustrated in Figure 7.19.

- **Data Entry**. The first step of the transaction processing cycle is the capture of business data. For example, transaction data may be collected by point-of-sale terminals using optical scanning of bar codes and credit card readers at a retail store or other business. Or transaction data can be captured at an electronic commerce Web site on the Internet. The proper recording and editing of data so they are quickly and correctly captured for processing is one of the major design challenges of information systems discussed in Chapter 12.
- **Transaction Processing.** Transaction processing systems process data in two basic ways: (1) **batch processing**, where transaction data are accumulated over a period of time and processed periodically, and (2) **real-time processing** (also called online processing), where data are processed immediately after a transaction occurs. All online transaction processing systems incorporate real-time processing capabilities. Many online systems also depend on the capabilities of *fault tolerant* computer systems that can continue to operate even if parts of the system fail. We will discuss this fault tolerant concept in Chapter 11.
- **Database Maintenance.** An organization's databases must be maintained by its transaction processing systems so that they are always correct and up-to-date. Therefore, transaction processing systems update the corporate databases of an organization to reflect changes resulting from day-to-day business transactions. For example, credit sales made to customers will cause customer account balances to be increased and the amount of inventory on hand to be decreased. Database maintenance ensures that these and other changes are reflected in the data records stored in the company's databases.
- **Document and Report Generation.** Transaction processing systems produce a variety of documents and reports. Examples of transaction documents include purchase orders, paychecks, sales receipts, invoices, and customer statements. Transaction reports might take the form of a transaction listing such as a payroll register or edit reports that describe errors detected during processing.

- **Inquiry Processing.** Many transaction processing systems allow you to use the Internet, intranets, extranets, and Web browsers or database management query languages to make inquiries and receive responses regarding the results of transaction processing activity. Typically, responses are displayed in a variety of prespecified formats or screens. For example, you might check on the status of a sales order, the balance in an account, or the amount of stock in inventory and receive immediate responses at your PC.

Enterprise Collaboration Systems

Really difficult business problems always have many aspects. Often a major decision depends on an impromptu search for one or two key pieces of auxiliary information and a quick ad hoc analysis of several possible scenarios. You need software tools that easily combine and recombine data from many sources. You need Internet access for all kinds of research. Widely scattered people need to be able to collaborate and work the data in different ways [13].

Enterprise collaboration systems (ECS) are cross-functional information systems that enhance communication, coordination, and collaboration among the members of business teams and workgroups. Information technology, especially Internet technologies, provides tools to help us collaborate—to communicate ideas, share resources, and coordinate our work efforts as members of the many formal and informal process and project teams and workgroups that make up many of today's organizations. Thus, the goal of ECS is to enable us to work together more easily and effectively by helping us:

- **Communicate:** Sharing information with each other.
- **Coordinate:** Coordinating our individual work efforts and use of resources with each other.
- **Collaborate:** Working together cooperatively on joint projects and assignments.

For example, engineers, business specialists, and external consultants may form a virtual team for a project. The team may rely on intranets and extranets to collaborate via e-mail, videoconferencing, discussion forums, and a multimedia database of work-in-progress information at a project Web site. The enterprise collaboration system may use PC workstations networked to a variety of servers on which project, corporate, and other databases are stored. In addition, network servers may provide a variety of software resources, such as Web browsers, groupware, and application packages, to assist the team's collaboration until the project is completed.

Tools for Enterprise Collaboration

The capabilities and potential of the Internet as well as intranets and extranets are driving the demand for better enterprise collaboration tools in business. However, it is Internet technologies like Web browsers and servers, hypermedia documents and databases, and intranets and extranets that provide the hardware, software, data, and network platforms for many of the groupware tools for enterprise collaboration that business users want. Figure 7.20 provides an overview of some of the software tools for electronic communication, electronic conferencing, and collaborative work management.

Electronic communication tools include electronic mail, voice mail, faxing, Web publishing, bulletin board systems, paging, and Internet phone systems. These tools enable you to electronically send messages, documents, and files in data, text, voice, or multimedia over computer networks. This capability helps you share everything from voice and text messages to copies of project documents and data files with your team members, wherever they may be. The ease and efficiency of such communications are major contributors to the collaboration process.

Electronic conferencing tools help people communicate and collaborate while working together. A variety of conferencing methods enables the members of teams

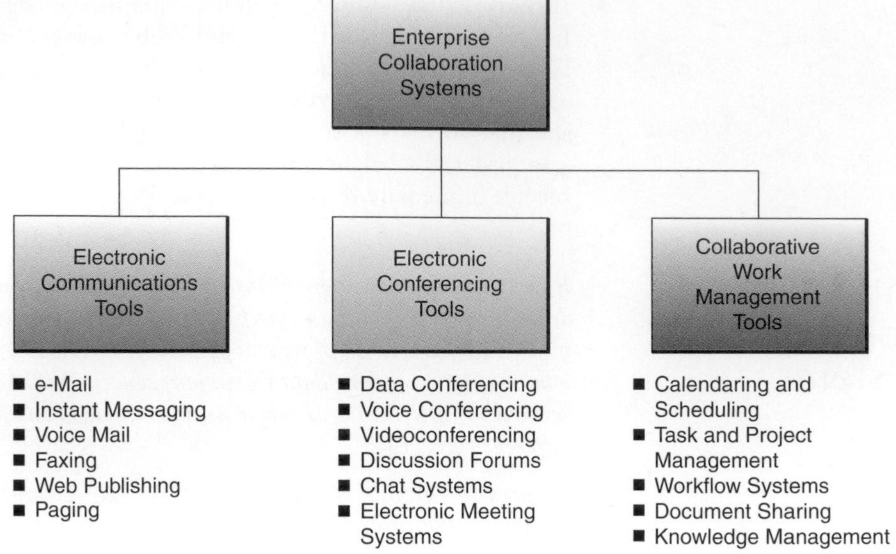

FIGURE 7.20
Electronic communications, conferencing, and collaborative work software tools enhance enterprise collaboration.

and workgroups at different locations to exchange ideas interactively at the same time or at different times at their convenience. These methods include data and voice conferencing, videoconferencing, chat systems, and discussion forums. Electronic conferencing options also include *electronic meeting systems* and other *group support systems* where team members can meet at the same time and place in a *decision room* setting or use the Internet to work collaboratively anywhere in the world. See Figure 7.21.

Collaborative work management tools help people accomplish or manage group work activities. This category of software includes calendaring and scheduling tools, task and project management, workflow systems, and knowledge management tools. Other tools for joint work, such as joint document creation, editing, and revision, are found in the software suites discussed in Chapter 4.

General Electric Co.: Committed to Enterprise Collaboration

GE has made a huge commitment to the Lotus Development tools QuickPlace (which lets employees set up Web-based work spaces) and Sametime (for real-time online meetings), which permit ad hoc collaboration without help from the IT department. These tools streamline the company's communication in myriad ways. Thus, GE's recruiting teams can set up QuickPlaces to trade information about prospective hires. And GE engineers share drawings, design requirements, and production schedules with supervisors on manufacturing floors. In all, GE has created almost 18,000 QuickPlaces for 250,000 users, says CTO Larry Biagini. "And if we have an engineering project with someone outside the company, we'll set up a QuickPlace or Sametime session and invite outside people."

There's also Support Central, a companywide knowledge management system developed using software from GE's Fanuc division. Employees sign on and complete a survey about their areas of expertise. The responses are added to a knowledge base so people with questions anywhere in GE can find people with answers. "Someone may have a question about, say, titanium metallurgy, and they'll be able to find documents about it, or send e-mail or initiate an online chat with someone who can help," says Stuart Scott, CIO of GE Industrial Systems. The result of all this collaboration? Faster workflow and quicker, smarter decisions, according to GE executives [18].

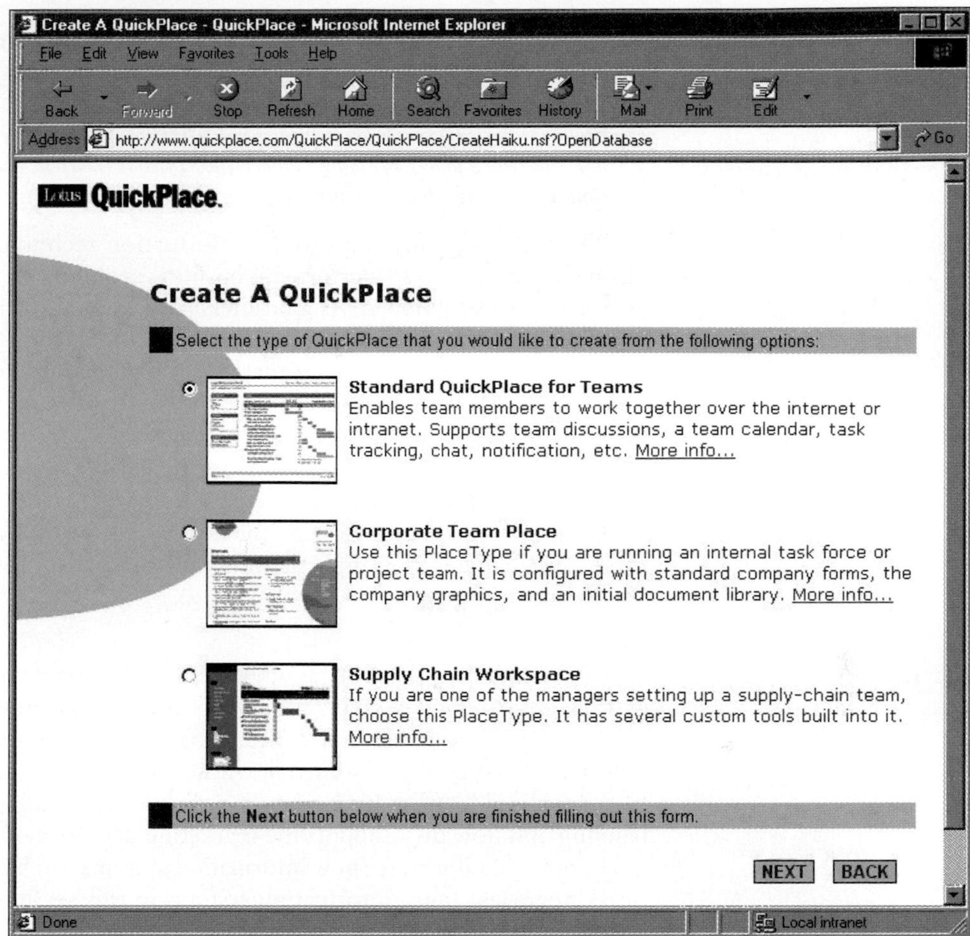

FIGURE 7.21
QuickPlace by Lotus Development helps virtual workgroups set up Web-based work spaces for collaborative work assignments.

SECTION II Functional Business Systems

Business managers are moving from a tradition where they could avoid, delegate, or ignore decisions about IT to one where they cannot create a marketing, product, international, organization, or financial plan that does not involve such decisions [19].

There are as many ways to use information technology in business as there are business activities to be performed, business problems to be solved, and business opportunities to be pursued. As a business professional, you should have a basic understanding and appreciation of the major ways information systems are used to support each of the functions of business that must be accomplished in any company that wants to succeed. Thus, in this section, we discuss **functional business systems**, that is, a variety of types of information systems (transaction processing, management information, decision support, etc.) that support the business functions of accounting, finance, marketing, operations management, and human resource management.

Read the Real World Case on the next page. We can learn a lot about the business value and challenges of implementing Web-based marketing systems from this case. See Figure 7.22.

IT in Business

It is also important that you, as a business professional, have a specific understanding of how information systems affect a particular business function—marketing, for example—or a particular industry (e.g., banking) that is directly related to your career objectives. For example, someone whose career objective is a marketing position in banking should have a basic understanding of how information systems are used in banking and how they support the marketing activities of banks and other firms.

Figure 7.23 illustrates how information systems can be grouped into business function categories. Thus, information systems in this section will be analyzed according to the business function they support by looking at a few key examples in each functional area. This approach should give you an appreciation of the variety of functional business systems that both small and large business firms may use.

Marketing Systems

The business function of marketing is concerned with the pricing, promotion, and sale of existing products in existing markets, as well as the development of new products and new markets to better attract and serve present and potential customers. Thus, marketing performs a vital function in the operation of a business enterprise. Business firms have increasingly turned to information technology to help them perform vital marketing functions in the face of the rapid changes of today's environment.

Figure 7.24 illustrates how **marketing information systems** provide information technologies that support major components of the marketing function. For example, Internet/intranet Web sites and services make an *interactive marketing* process possible, in which customers can become partners in creating, marketing, purchasing, and improving products and services. *Sales force automation* systems use mobile computing and Internet technologies to automate many information-processing activities for sales support and management. Other marketing information systems assist marketing managers in customer relationship management, product planning, pricing and other product management decisions, advertising, sales promotion, targeted marketing strategies, and market research and forecasting. Let's take a closer look at three of these marketing applications.

Interactive Marketing

The term **interactive marketing** has been coined to describe a customer-focused marketing process that is based on using the Internet, intranets, and extranets to establish two-way transactions between a business and its customers or potential customers. The goal of interactive marketing is to enable a company to use those networks profitably

REAL WORLD CASE 2 Yahoo, Google, and Chrysler: How the Internet Is Changing Advertising and Marketing

Advertising has always been the glamour child of marketing. From the moment consumer-product companies started placing ads in mid-19th century newspapers, mass media advertising has been about making connections. But while the modern world knits itself ever more closely together with telecommunications and the Internet, advertising is becoming increasingly disconnected—from its historical base, its business models, and its audiences. Thanks to the Internet, advertising is going through its first true paradigm shift since the advent of television half a century ago. As a result, your average executive in the ad or media business is feeling as lonely and unstable as a 30-foot sailboat with a broken keel foundering in the swells of a Category 2 hurricane. Let's look at a prime example.

Chrysler has more than $2 billion to spend each year, and the way it is spending it worries executives at News Corp., the Washington Post Co., and virtually every other media company on the planet. Chrysler's director of marketing communications oversees a budget that *Advertising Age* ranks as the sixth-largest pool of ad dollars in the nation. Whoever has that job decides how many minutes of the carmaker's commercials appear on networks and cable channels nationwide and how many pages of its ads turn up in magazines like *Fortune* and newspapers such as *USA Today*.

Julie Roehm, Chrysler's former director of marketing communications, was hired away from Chrysler by Wal-Mart to make its advertising decisions at the beginning of 2006, resigned at the end of the year, and sued Wal-Mart for breach of contract at the beginning of 2007. But here's the scary part for traditional media: Roehm rarely missed a chance to talk about how delighted she was with online advertising. She spent 10 percent of the budget online in 2004, allotted closer to 18 percent for 2005, and had allocated more than 20 percent for 2006. Do the math: In 2006, roughly $400 million of Chrysler's money that used to go into TV, newspaper, and magazine ads was spent on the Internet. Said Roehm: "I hate to sound like such a marketing geek, but we like to fish where the fish are."

No wonder media executives are concerned. One of their headaches is Googlemania. Google effectively reinvented online advertising with the targeted, classified-like text links that you now see everywhere. Soaring profits from selling those ads (net revenue in the first quarter of 2005 alone was a staggering $794 million) helped drive Google's stock market capitalization to all time highs, making Google the most highly prized media company in the world. But while the old guard is keeping a watchful eye on Google, the company it really fears, and the one advertisers like Chrysler increasingly love, is Yahoo.

It's been easy for most people to overlook the media and advertising juggernaut that Terry Semel, Yahoo's CEO, has assembled since he arrived from Hollywood four years ago. That's partly because Semel makes himself easy to overlook. He's not a showman like Apple's Steve Jobs or a high-tech rock star like Google's Larry Page or Sergey Brin. When Semel speaks, he says bland things that go to the core of his view of the marketing opportunity of the Internet, like: "The great part about the Internet of all the existing mediums from before is that it's the first one that is truly global, and its impact is massive."

Like many good negotiators, Semel knows that the more he says publicly, the less he's likely to win. Twenty years of doing movie deals as co-CEO of Warner Bros. taught him that. At 62, Semel's a behind-the-scenes guy, a strategist with a bold master plan: to transform Yahoo into the 21st century's first media titan. He has surrounded himself not with nerdy brainiacs but with veteran advertising and media executives adept at building bridges to the powerful businesses that feel the most threatened by the Internet.

So far, Semel has put together one of the Web's hottest winning streaks. When he took over in 2001, the Yahoo! portal—founded in 1994 by Jerry Yang and David Filo—was a mess. The dot-com bubble had burst, revenues had fallen by half, and red ink flooded the bottom line. As the founders took a back seat (today Yang acts as the resident visionary, and Filo works in IT), Semel and his enforcer, COO Dan Rosenzweig, set about diversifying sales beyond the banner ads Yahoo had lived off.

He added search advertising, online classifieds, and a host of commission-generating businesses such as selling SBC and Verizon broadband subscriptions. The moves transformed a

FIGURE 7.22

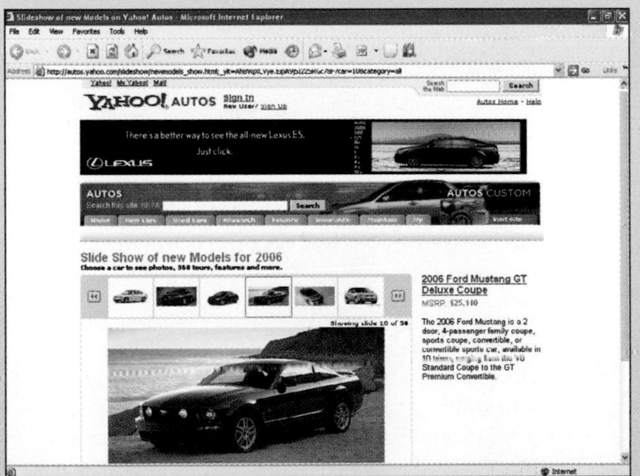

Yahoo has led the way in persuading large companies to use online advertising instead of traditional media.

money loser into a $3-billion-a-year company that posted operating incomes in 2005 in excess of $1 billion, a near-Microsoftian operating margin of some 30 percent. Today Yahoo arguably offers the online world's broadest array of information and entertainment for users, married to the Web's most sophisticated collection of offerings for advertisers. Each month more than 430 million people worldwide typically visit one of its myriad sites.

Until recently Semel's grand plan was missing a crucial strand: widespread use of online advertising by big marketers like Chrysler. Burned or disillusioned by the dot-com bubble, they questioned whether online advertising would ever match the effectiveness of commercials or print ads. Sure, Google's text ads work, because you throw them in front of users, just as they are looking to buy or research something online, like a smart, aggressive Yellow Pages. But using the Internet to sell something like "that Pepsi feeling"—creating and fostering an emotional attachment to a brand—was a challenge of an entirely different order. Most marketers doubted that it could be done.

But lately decision makers like Chrysler's former director Roehm are seeing the Internet in a new light. Their conversion can be explained in one word: broadband. Because of rapid developments in computer networking and telecommunications, roughly one-third of U.S. households now have high-speed Internet connections, which has done two things that advertisers like. It has caused the average time Americans spend online to grow 50 percent. According to several research firms and advertisers, surfing the Internet now takes up to 30 percent of the time Americans spend with all media. And instead of handcuffing advertisers to the banner ads of the Internet bubble years, broadband has freed them to fashion creative messages that are more like TV commercials.

In May 2005, Forrester Research surveyed 99 major advertisers and 20 ad agencies and found that nearly 85 percent of them planned to expand their online ad budgets that year. More significant, it reported a radical shift from the belief that brand building and the Internet don't mix. Sixty-three percent of those surveyed said that online advertising was a brand-building tool "equal to or better than" advertising on TV or in print. Anecdotal evidence supports that. Not a week goes by, it seems, without a big advertiser—P&G, Pepsi, and Georgia Pacific are recent examples—announcing plans to expand promotion of its products online. The trend means that a huge volume of brand advertising will flow into the online world—$8 billion to $12 billion a year by 2010, depending on whom you ask, up from less than $5 billion in 2005, about 3.5 percent of total U.S. spending on brand advertising.

For Semel and Yahoo, that is the best possible news. It's true that Google leads the pack in the $5-billion-a-year market for search-related ads and Yahoo is lagging in second place. But in the scrum for online brand advertising—almost as large a market—Yahoo is poised to grab the biggest share. Its 181 million active registered users are probably the largest online clientele, which means Yahoo can tell advertisers it knows the habits of more users than any other portal—or any traditional media company.

Says Brian McAndrews, CEO of Aquantive, one of the largest advertising firms specializing in Internet distribution: "Yahoo's opportunity is massive." And while its online rivals like Google and Microsoft's MSN are ramping up to attract brand advertising too, Morgan Stanley Internet analyst Mary Meeker says the advantage right now is Yahoo's: "If you're new to online advertising (and a lot of companies and their ad agencies are), Yahoo is your first call because they do everything."

Source: Adapted from Fred Vogelstein, "Yahoo's Brilliant Solution," and Daniel Gross, "Birth of a Salesman," *Fortune*, August 8, 2005; Catherine Holahan, "Google's Revolution May Not Be Televised," *BusinessWeek*, April 4, 2007; Sandra O'Laughlin, "Bell Sounds for Next Round in Roehm vs. Wal-Mart," *Brandweek*, April 6, 2007.

CASE STUDY QUESTIONS

1. Why are companies like Chrysler now looking more favorably at the Internet as a great medium for their advertising dollars? What has happened to change their view?
2. How do Google's online ad revenue sources and strategy differ from Yahoo's? Which online ad strategy is superior for attracting advertising from small companies? For attracting advertising from large companies? Defend your position.
3. If you were director of marketing communications at Chrysler, how would you distribute Chrysler's advertising dollars among online and traditional TV and print media? Defend your position.

REAL WORLD ACTIVITIES

1. Google and Microsoft's MSN realize that they must move beyond search advertising revenue to block Yahoo's attempt to dominate the move of big advertisers to online advertising. Use the Internet to discover how the three rivals are faring in the battle for online advertising and the reasons for any changes you find.
2. Online advertising can be viewed as an entertainment experience, as a helpful source of clues to find what you and other customers want, or as a bothersome intrusion into your online experience and right to privacy. Break into small groups with your classmates to discuss this issue. Attempt to formulate a joint position on these aspects of online advertising to present to the rest of the class.

FIGURE 7.23 Examples of functional information systems. Note how they support the major functional areas of business.

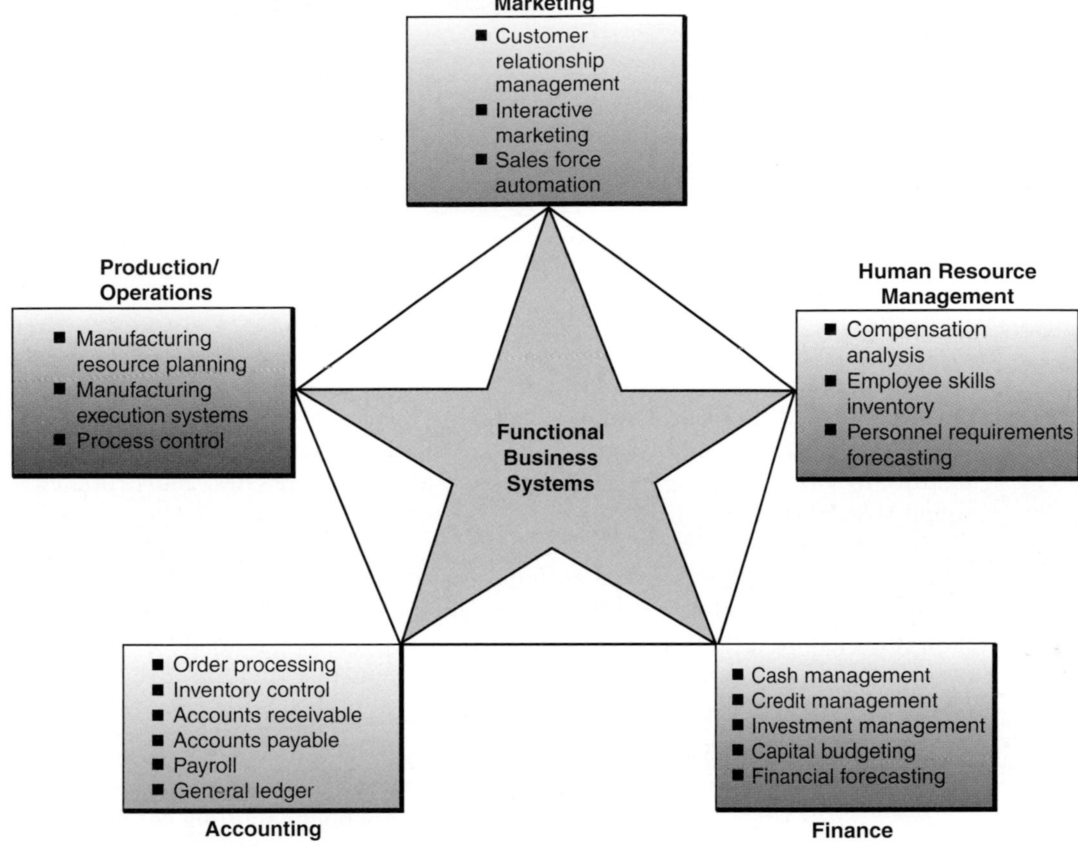

to attract and keep customers who will become partners with the business in creating, purchasing, and improving products and services.

In interactive marketing, customers are not just passive participants who receive media advertising prior to purchase but are actively engaged in network-enabled proactive and interactive processes. Interactive marketing encourages customers to

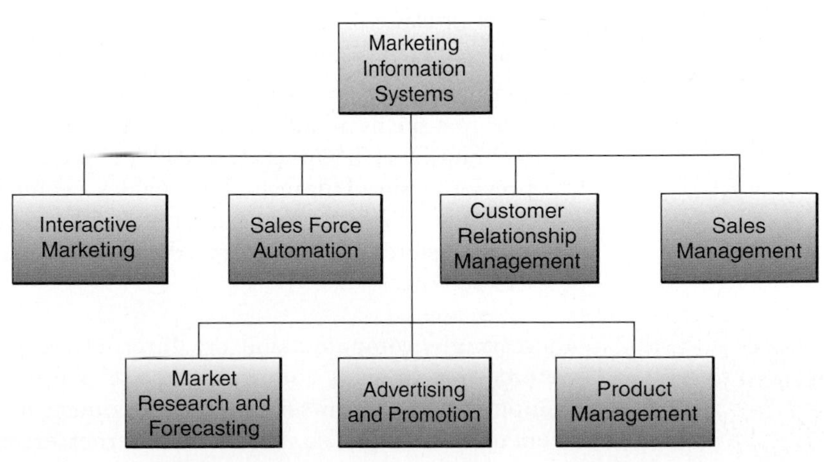

FIGURE 7.24 Marketing information systems provide information technologies to support major components of the marketing function.

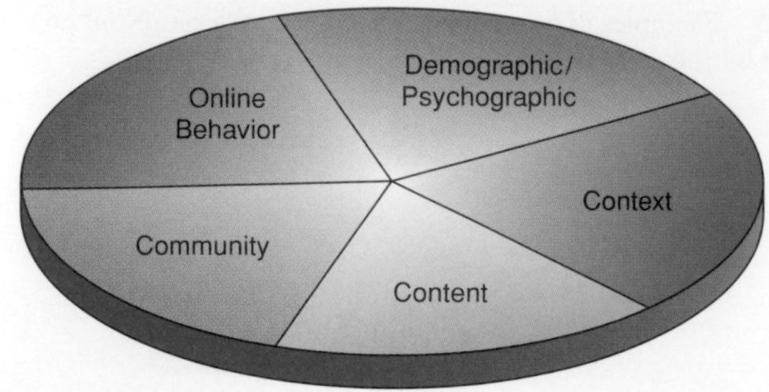

FIGURE 7.25
The five major components of targeted marketing for electronic commerce.

become involved in product development, delivery, and service issues. This involvement is enabled by various Internet technologies, including chat and discussion groups, Web forms and questionnaires, instant messaging, and e-mail correspondence. Finally, the expected outcomes of interactive marketing are a rich mixture of vital marketing data, new product ideas, volume sales, and strong customer relationships.

Targeted Marketing

Targeted marketing has become an important tool in developing advertising and promotion strategies to strengthen a company's e-commerce initiatives, as well as its traditional business venues. As illustrated in Figure 7.25, targeted marketing is an advertising and promotion management concept that includes five targeting components [24].

- **Community.** Companies can customize their Web advertising messages and promotion methods to appeal to people in specific communities. They can be *communities of interest*, such as *virtual communities* of online sporting enthusiasts or arts and crafts hobbyists, or geographic communities formed by the Web sites of a city or other local organization.
- **Content.** Advertising such as electronic billboards or banners can be placed on a variety of selected Web sites, in addition to a company's Web site. The content of these messages is aimed at the targeted audience. An ad for a product campaign on the opening page of an Internet search engine is a typical example.
- **Context.** Advertising appears only in Web pages that are relevant to the content of a product or service. So advertising is targeted only at people who are already looking for information about a subject (e.g., vacation travel) that is related to a company's products (e.g., car rental services).
- **Demographic/Psychographic.** Web marketing efforts can be aimed at specific types or classes of people—unmarried, twenty-something, middle income, male college graduates, for example.
- **Online Behavior.** Advertising and promotion efforts can be tailored to each visit to a site by an individual. This strategy is based on a variety of tracking techniques, such as Web "cookie" files recorded on the visitor's disk drive from previous visits. This technique enables a company to track a person's online behavior at a Web site so it can target marketing efforts (e.g., coupons redeemable at retail stores or e-commerce Web sites) to that individual during each visit to its Web site.

Sales Force Automation

Increasingly, computers and the Internet are providing the basis for sales force automation. In many companies, the sales force is being outfitted with notebook computers, Web browsers, and sales contact management software that connect them to marketing Web sites on the Internet, extranets, and their company intranets.

FIGURE 7.26
This Web-based sales force automation package supports sales lead management of qualified prospects and the management of current customer accounts.

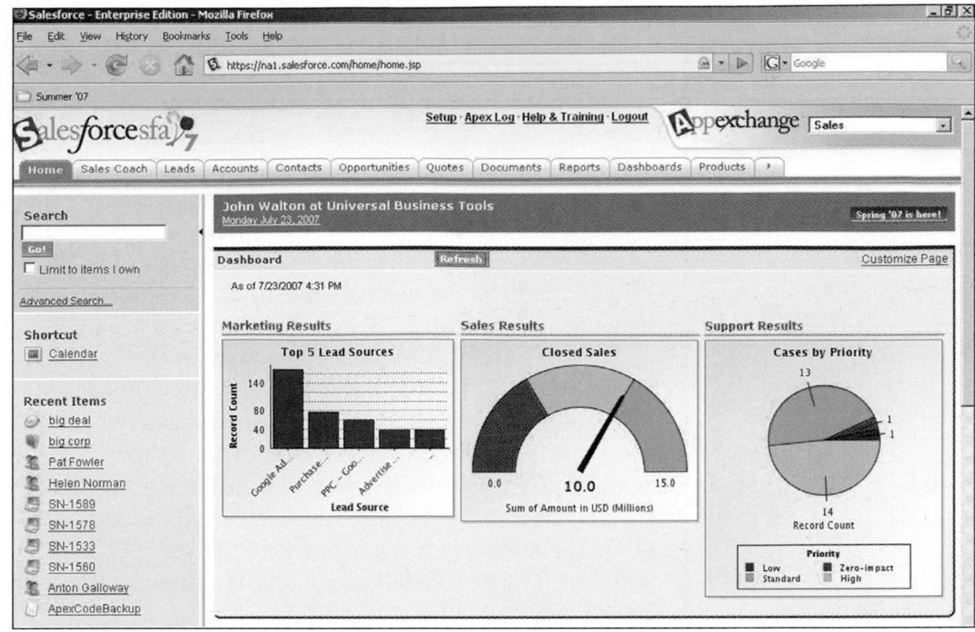

This connectivity not only increases the personal productivity of salespeople but dramatically speeds up the capture and analysis of sales data from the field to marketing managers at company headquarters. In return, it allows marketing and sales management to improve the delivery of information and the support they provide to their salespeople. Therefore, many companies are viewing sales force automation as a way to gain a strategic advantage in sales productivity and marketing responsiveness. See Figure 7.26.

For example, salespeople use their PCs to record sales data as they make their calls on customers and prospects during the day. Then each night, sales reps in the field can connect their computers by modem and telephone links to the Internet and extranets, which can access intranet or other network servers at their company. They can upload information about sales orders, sales calls, and other sales statistics, as well as send electronic mail messages and access Web site sales support information. In return, the network servers may download product availability data, lists of information about good sales prospects, and e-mail messages.

Baker Tanks: Web-Based Sales Force Automation

Baker Tanks, a nationwide leader in rentals of industrial containment and transfer equipment, serves customers throughout the country in industries ranging from construction to aerospace. Because of this varied client base, it's especially important—and challenging—for salespeople to be aware of the specifics of each account every time they speak to customers. The company's 50 sales professionals are on the road four days a week visiting customers on location. That creates additional challenges when it comes to keeping track of customer information and accessing it when needed.

In the past, salespeople filled out paper forms to track customer information, which was later entered into an electronic database. This process left the reps with less time to do what they do best—selling. Even worse, the traveling representatives had no way of connecting to the electronic database from the customer's location.

They were collecting plenty of information, but they couldn't access and use it effectively.

"They were recording everything on paper, and that's a very unproductive way of getting things done," says Scott Whitford, systems administrator and lead on the wireless Salesforce.com solution. "We were looking for a solution that would improve our communications, not only between corporate and field people, but between field people and our customers." Adds Darrell Yoshinaga, marketing manager at Baker Tanks, "We were looking for a tool we could implement quickly, but that would still give us the flexibility we needed to become more efficient."

Baker Tanks was immediately drawn to the Web-based functionality, quick implementation time, and low capital investment of a sales force automation system. The ability to connect to sales information anywhere at any time was also an attractive feature. So Baker Tanks moved from a paper-based system to a Web-based system, eliminating the extra step of transferring information from paper documents to the database. Next, sales reps were outfitted with personal digital assistants (PDAs) enabled with the Salesforce.com service. "Our salespeople are real road warriors, and we needed to extend the system to them rather than make them come to the system," Whitford reflects.

Each PDA is equipped with a wireless modem that allows the salesperson to connect to Salesforce.com for customer contact information, as well as sales history and anecdotal notes on the customer—all with read and write access. Salespeople can also use the PDAs to e-mail responses to customers more promptly and improve time management by integrating appointment scheduling and calendar viewing. Says Yoshinaga: "We have achieved our main objective of communicating better with our customers. And our salespeople have become more productive because they have instant access to information and electronic reporting capabilities" [1].

Manufacturing Systems

Manufacturing information systems support the *production/operations* function that includes all activities associated with the planning and control of the processes that produce goods or services. Thus, the production/operations function is concerned with the management of the operational processes and systems of all business firms. Information systems used for operations management and transaction processing support all firms that must plan, monitor, and control inventories, purchases, and the flow of goods and services. Therefore, firms such as transportation companies, wholesalers, retailers, financial institutions, and service companies must use production/operations information systems to plan and control their operations. In this section, we will concentrate on computer-based manufacturing applications to illustrate information systems that support the production/operations function.

Computer-Integrated Manufacturing

Once upon a time, manufacturers operated on a simple build-to-stock model. They built 100 or 100,000 of an item and sold them via distribution networks. They kept track of the stock of inventory and made more of the item once inventory levels dipped below a threshold. Rush jobs were both rare and expensive, and configuration options limited. Things have changed. Concepts like just-in-time inventory, build-to-order (BTO) manufacturing, end-to-end supply chain visibility, the explosion in contract manufacturing, and the development of Web-based e-business tools for collaborative manufacturing have revolutionized plant management [28].

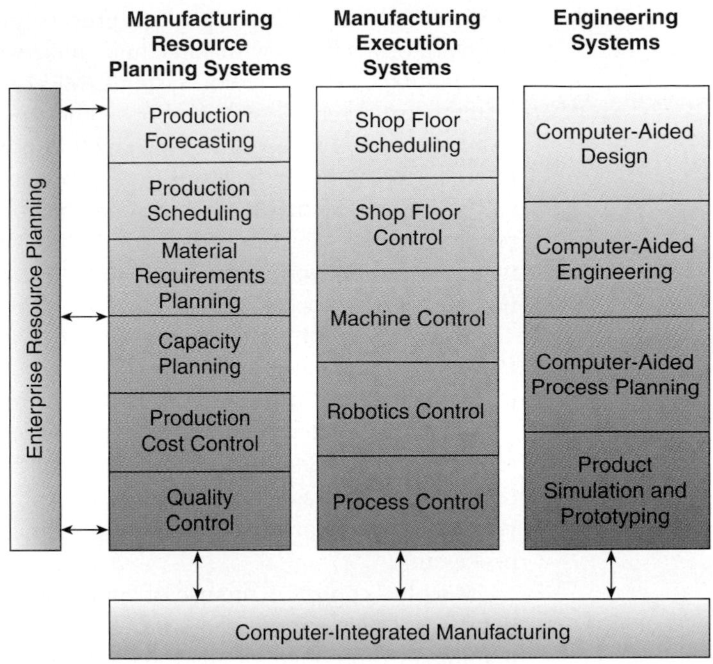

FIGURE 7.27
Manufacturing information systems support computer-integrated manufacturing. Note that manufacturing resources planning systems are one of the application clusters in an ERP system.

Various manufacturing information systems, many of them Web enabled, are used to support **computer-integrated manufacturing (CIM)**. See Figure 7.27. CIM is an overall concept that stresses that the objectives of computer-based systems in manufacturing must be to:

- **Simplify** (reengineer) production processes, product designs, and factory organization as a vital foundation to automation and integration.
- **Automate** production processes and the business functions that support them with computers, machines, and robots.
- **Integrate** all production and support processes using computer networks, cross-functional business software, and other information technologies.

The overall goal of CIM and other such manufacturing information systems is to create flexible, agile, manufacturing processes that efficiently produce products of the highest quality. Thus, CIM supports the concepts of *flexible manufacturing systems*, *agile manufacturing*, and *total quality management*. Implementing such manufacturing concepts enables a company to respond quickly to and fulfill customer requirements with high-quality products and services.

Manufacturing information systems help companies simplify, automate, and integrate many of the activities needed to produce products of all kinds. For example, computers are used to help engineers design better products using both *computer-aided engineering* (CAE) and *computer-aided design* (CAD) systems and achieve better production processes with *computer-aided process planning*. They are also used to help plan the types of material needed in the production process, which is called *material requirements planning* (MRP), and to integrate MRP with production scheduling and shop floor operations, which is known as *manufacturing resource planning*. Many of the processes within manufacturing resource planning systems are included in the manufacturing modules of enterprise resource planning (ERP) software, as discussed in the first section of this chapter.

Computer-aided manufacturing (CAM) systems are those that automate the production process. For example, this automation could be accomplished by monitoring and controlling the production process in a factory (manufacturing execution systems) or by directly controlling a physical process (process control), a machine tool (machine control), or machines with some humanlike work capabilities (robots).

Manufacturing execution systems (MES) are performance-monitoring information systems for factory floor operations. They monitor, track, and control the five essential components involved in a production process: materials, equipment, personnel, instructions and specifications, and production facilities. MES includes shop floor scheduling and control, machine control, robotics control, and process control systems. These manufacturing systems monitor, report, and adjust the status and performance of production components to help a company achieve a flexible, high-quality manufacturing process.

Process control is the use of computers to control an ongoing physical process. Process control computers control physical processes in petroleum refineries, cement plants, steel mills, chemical plants, food product manufacturing plants, pulp and paper mills, electric power plants, and so on. A process control computer system requires the use of special sensing devices that measure physical phenomena such as temperature or pressure changes. These continuous physical measurements are converted to digital form by analog-to-digital converters and relayed to computers for processing.

Machine control is the use of computers to control the actions of machines, also popularly called *numerical control.* The computer-based control of machine tools to manufacture products of all kinds is a typical numerical control application used by many factories throughout the world.

Human Resource Systems

The human resource management (HRM) function involves the recruitment, placement, evaluation, compensation, and development of the employees of an organization. The goal of human resource management is the effective and efficient use of the human resources of a company. Thus, **human resource information systems** are designed to support (1) planning to meet the personnel needs of the business, (2) development of employees to their full potential, and (3) control of all personnel policies and programs. Originally, businesses used computer-based information systems to (1) produce paychecks and payroll reports, (2) maintain personnel records, and (3) analyze the use of personnel in business operations. Many firms have gone beyond these traditional *personnel management* functions and developed human resource information systems (HRIS) that also support (1) recruitment, selection, and hiring; (2) job placement; (3) performance appraisals; (4) employee benefits analysis; (5) training and development; and (6) health, safety, and security. See Figure 7.28.

HRM and the Internet

The Internet has become a major force for change in human resource management. For example, **online HRM systems** may involve recruiting employees through recruitment sections of corporate Web sites. Companies are also using commercial recruiting services and databases on the World Wide Web, posting messages in selected Internet newsgroups, and communicating with job applicants via e-mail.

The Internet has a wealth of information and contacts for both employers and job hunters. Top Web sites for job hunters and employers on the World Wide Web include Monster.com, HotJobs.com, and CareerBuilder.com. These Web sites are full of reports, statistics, and other useful HRM information, such as job reports by industry or listings of the top recruiting markets by industry and profession.

HRM and Corporate Intranets

Intranet technologies allow companies to process most common HRM applications over their corporate intranets. Intranets allow the HRM department to provide around-the-clock services to their customers: the employees. They can also disseminate valuable information faster than through previous company channels. Intranets can collect information online from employees for input to their HRM files, and they

FIGURE 7.28 Human resource information systems support the strategic, tactical, and operational use of the human resources of an organization.

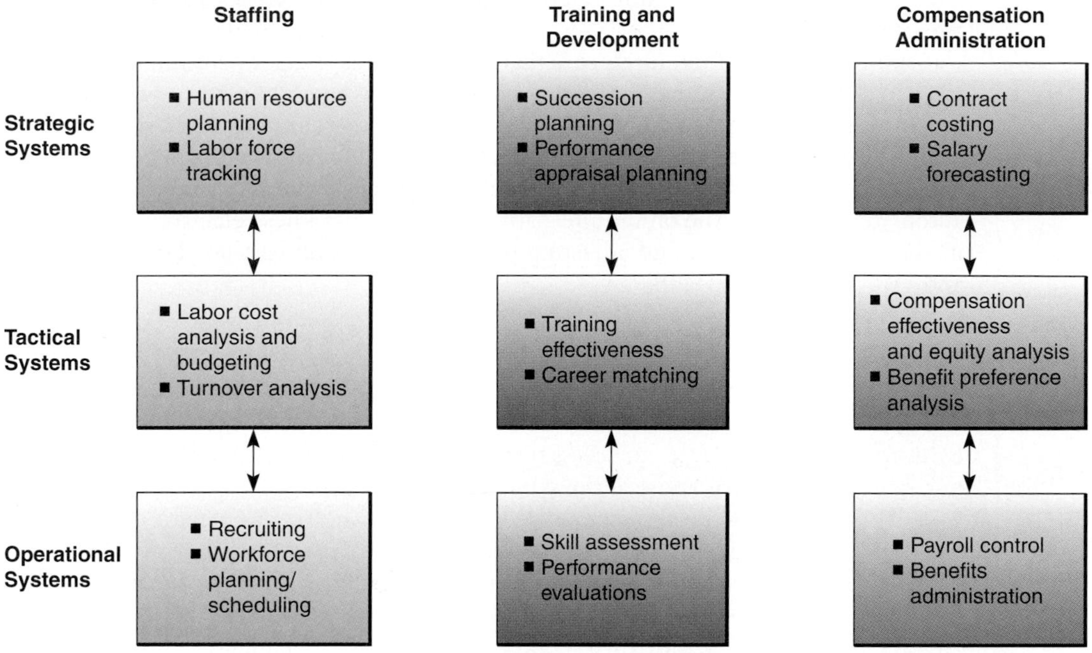

can enable managers and other employees to perform HRM tasks with little intervention by the HRM department. See Figure 7.29.

For example, *employee self-service* (ESS) intranet applications allow employees to view benefits, enter travel and expense reports, verify employment and salary information, access and update their personal information, and enter data that has a time

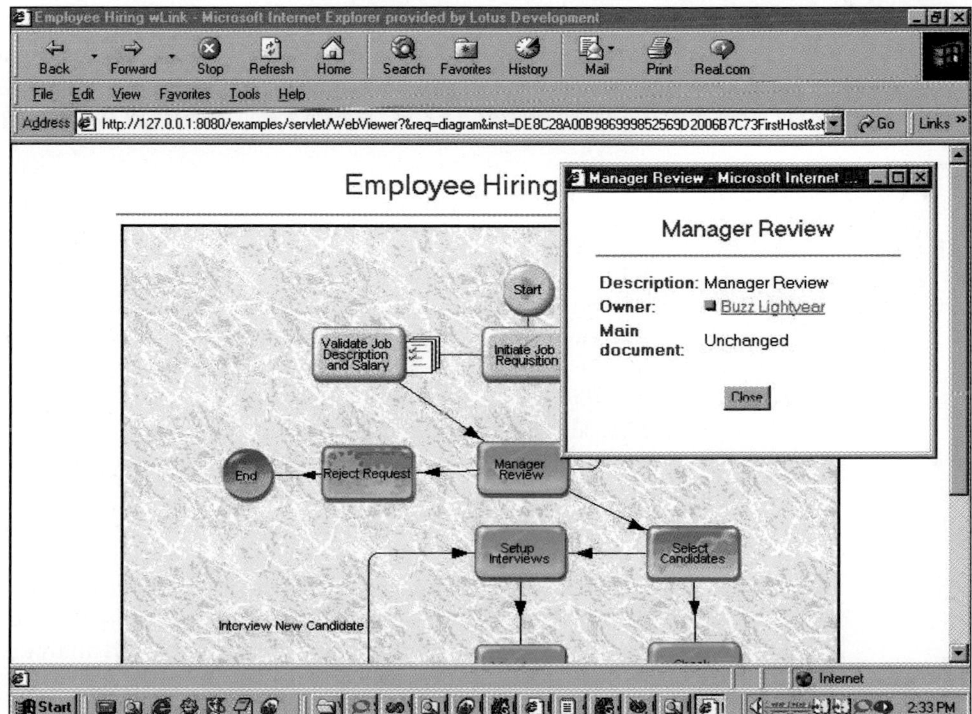

FIGURE 7.29
An example of an employee hiring review system.

constraint. Through this completely electronic process, employees can use their Web browsers to look up individual payroll and benefits information online, right from their desktop PCs, mobile computers, or intranet kiosks located around a worksite.

Another benefit of the intranet is that it can serve as a superior training tool. Employees can easily download instructions and processes to get the information or education they need. In addition, employees using new technology can view training videos over the intranet on demand. Thus, the intranet eliminates the need to loan out and track training videos. Employees can also use their corporate intranets to produce automated paysheets, the online alternative to time cards. These electronic forms have made viewing, entering, and adjusting payroll information easy for both employees and HRM professionals [16].

Charles Schwab & Co.: Web-Based Human Resource Systems

It receives 1.3 million page views per day, but it's not Yahoo or America Online or even CNN.com. It's an intranet created by Charles Schwab & Co. that enables Schwab's 23,000 employees to access detailed HR information about benefits, training, computer support, and scads of company information.

"As a company, we're very committed to using technology to benefit our customers and to provide good services to our employees," says Anne Barr, vice president of the intranet initiative known throughout the company as the "Schweb." The Schweb provides managers with online access to accurate information about employees. Because the directory is online, it's a lot easier to update and maintain than a set of desktop applications, notes Barr.

The intranet provides employees with more personalized information about themselves, their roles, and the organization than they'd otherwise be able to obtain from the company's human resources department. "The other benefit is that it helps employees find the information they need faster and serve customers faster, more effectively," says Barr. There are now 30 HR applications that link into the Schweb, including the Learning Intranet, an application that helps manage training for Schwab's customer-facing employees, and eTimesheets, which employees use to manage their own vacation time.

The productivity benefits alone from the use of the Schweb are huge. Schwab is saving hundreds of thousands of dollars annually by having employees fill out benefit forms online using an application called eForms, says Barr [16].

Accounting Systems

Accounting information systems are the oldest and most widely used information systems in business. Computer-based accounting systems record and report the flow of funds through an organization on a historical basis and produce important financial statements such as balance sheets and income statements. Such systems also produce forecasts of future conditions, including projected financial statements and financial budgets. A firm's financial performance is measured against such forecasts by other analytical accounting reports.

Operational accounting systems emphasize legal and historical record-keeping and the production of accurate financial statements. Typically, these systems include transaction processing systems such as order processing, inventory control, accounts receivable, accounts payable, payroll, and general ledger systems. Management accounting systems focus on the planning and control of business operations. They emphasize cost accounting reports, the development of financial budgets and projected financial statements, and analytical reports comparing actual to forecasted performance.

FIGURE 7.30 Important accounting information systems for transaction processing and financial reporting. Note how they are related to each other in terms of input and output flows.

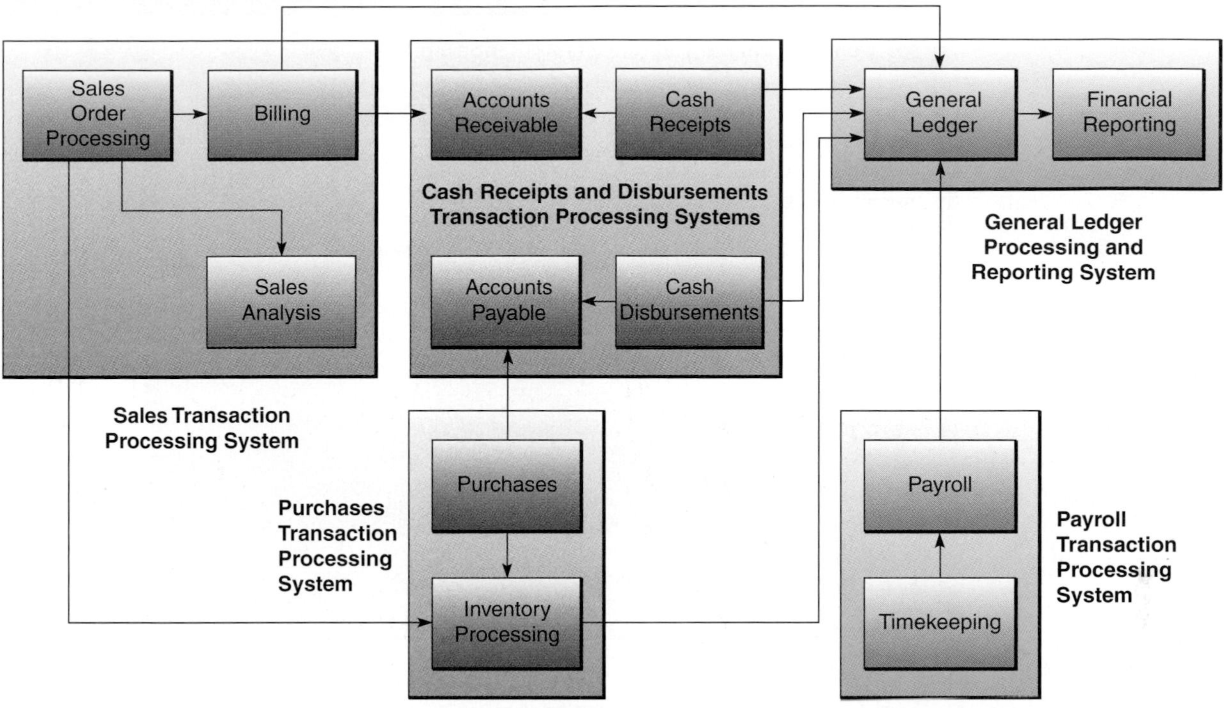

Figure 7.30 illustrates the interrelationships of several important accounting information systems commonly computerized by both large and small businesses. Many accounting software packages are available for these applications. Figure 7.31 summarizes the essential purpose of six common, but important, accounting information systems used by both large and small business firms.

FIGURE 7.31 A summary of six essential accounting information systems used in business.

Common Business Accounting Systems
• **Order Processing** Captures and processes customer orders and produces data for inventory control and accounts receivable.
• **Inventory Control** Processes data reflecting changes in inventory and provides shipping and reorder information.
• **Accounts Receivable** Records amounts owed by customers and produces customer invoices, monthly customer statements, and credit management reports.
• **Accounts Payable** Records purchases from, amounts owed to, and payments to suppliers, and produces cash management reports.
• **Payroll** Records employee work and compensation data and produces paychecks and other payroll documents and reports.
• **General Ledger** Consolidates data from other accounting systems and produces the periodic financial statements and reports of the business.

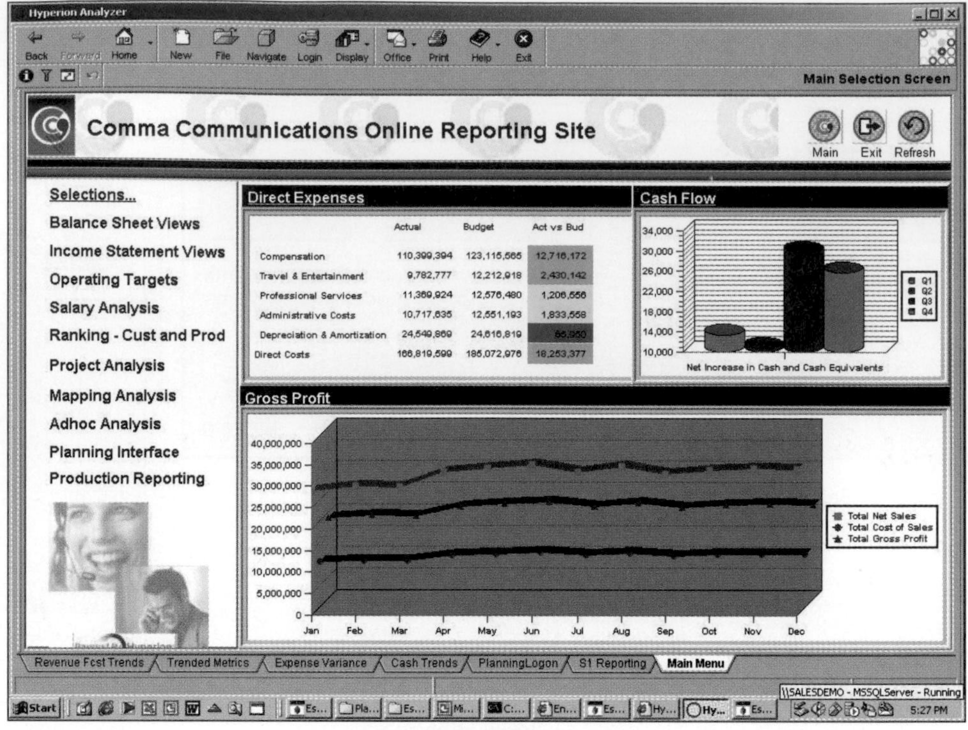

FIGURE 7.32
An example of an online accounting report.

Online Accounting Systems

It should come as no surprise that the accounting information systems illustrated in Figures 7.30 and 7.31 are being transformed by Internet technologies. Using the Internet and other networks changes how accounting information systems monitor and track business activity. The online, interactive nature of such networks calls for new forms of transaction documents, procedures, and controls. This demand particularly applies to systems like order processing, inventory control, accounts receivable, and accounts payable. As outlined in Figure 7.31, these systems are directly involved in the processing of transactions between a business and its customers and suppliers. So naturally, many companies are using Internet and other network links to these trading partners for such online transaction processing systems, as discussed in Section I. Figure 7.32 is an example of an online accounting report.

Financial Management Systems

Computer-based **financial management systems** support business managers and professionals in decisions regarding (1) the financing of a business and (2) the allocation and control of financial resources within a business. Major financial management system categories include cash and investment management, capital budgeting, financial forecasting, and financial planning. See Figure 7.33.

For example, the **capital budgeting** process involves evaluating the profitability and financial impact of proposed capital expenditures. Long-term expenditure proposals for facilities and equipment can be analyzed using a variety of return on investment (ROI) evaluation techniques. This application makes heavy use of spreadsheet models that incorporate present value analysis of expected cash flows and probability analysis of risk to determine the optimum mix of capital projects for a business.

Financial analysts also typically use electronic spreadsheets and other **financial planning** software to evaluate the present and projected financial performance of a business. They also help determine the financing needs of a business and analyze

FIGURE 7.33
Examples of important financial management systems.

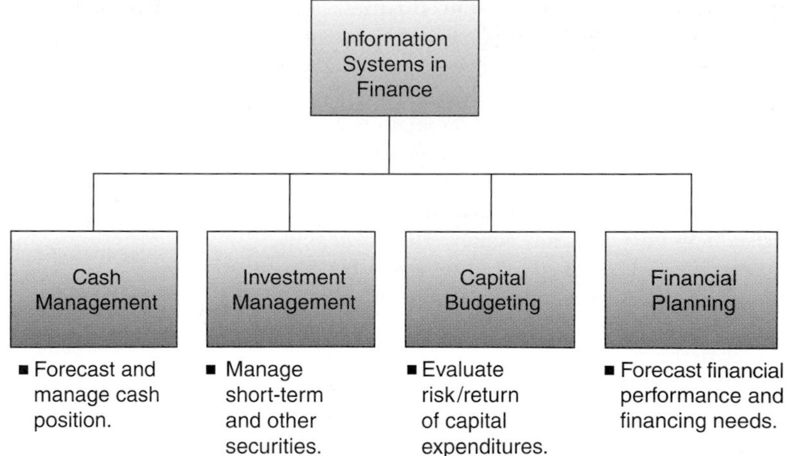

alternative methods of financing. Financial analysts use financial forecasts of the economic situation, business operations, types of financing available, interest rates, and stock and bond prices to develop an optimal financing plan for the business. Electronic spreadsheet packages, DSS software, and Web-based groupware can be used to build and manipulate financial models. Answers to what-if and goal-seeking questions can be explored as financial analysts and managers evaluate their financing and investment alternatives. We will discuss such applications further in Chapter 9.

Summary

- **Cross-Functional Enterprise Systems.** Major e-business applications and their interrelationships are summarized in the enterprise application architecture of Figure 7.3. These applications include integrated cross-functional enterprise systems such as enterprise resource planning (ERP), customer relationship management (CRM), and supply chain management (SCM).
- These applications may be interconnected by enterprise application integration (EAI) systems so that business professionals can more easily access the information resources they need to support the demands of customers, suppliers, and business partners. Enterprise collaboration systems (ECS) are cross-functional systems that support and enhance communication and collaboration among the teams and workgroups in an organization. Refer to Figures 7.16 and 7.20 for summary views of the business applications in EAI systems and enterprise collaboration systems.
- **Transaction Processing Systems.** Online transaction processing systems play a vital role in business. Transaction processing involves the basic activities of (1) data entry, (2) transaction processing, (3) database maintenance, (4) document and report generation, and (5) inquiry processing. Many firms are using the Internet, intranets, extranets, and other networks for online transaction processing to provide superior service to their customers and suppliers. Figure 7.19 illustrates the basic activities of transaction processing systems.
- **Customer Relationship Management: The Business Focus.** Customer relationship management is a cross-functional enterprise system that integrates and automates many of the customer-serving processes in sales, marketing, and customer services that interact with a company's customers. CRM systems use information technology to support the many companies who are reorienting themselves into customer-focused businesses as a top business strategy. The major application components of CRM include contact and account management, sales, marketing and fulfillment, customer service and support, and retention and loyalty programs, all aimed at helping a company acquire, enhance, and retain profitable relationships with its customers as a primary business goal. However, many companies have found CRM systems difficult to implement properly due to lack of adequate understanding and preparation by management and affected employees. Finally, many companies are moving toward collaborative CRM systems that support the collaboration of employees, business partners, and the customers themselves in enhancing profitable customer relationships.

- **Enterprise Resource Planning: The Business Backbone.** Enterprise resource planning is a cross-functional enterprise system that integrates and automates many of the internal business processes of a company, particularly those within the manufacturing, logistics, distribution, accounting, finance, and human resource functions of the business. Thus, ERP serves as the vital backbone information system of the enterprise, helping a company achieve the efficiency, agility, and responsiveness required to succeed in a dynamic business environment. ERP software typically consists of integrated modules that give a company a real-time cross-functional view of its core business processes, such as production, order processing, and sales, and its resources, such as cash, raw materials, production capacity, and people. However, properly implementing ERP systems is a difficult and costly process that has caused serious business losses for some companies that underestimated the planning, development, and training that were necessary to reengineer their business processes to accommodate their new ERP systems. However, continuing developments in ERP software, including Web-enabled modules and e-business software suites, have made ERP more flexible and user-friendly, as well as extending it outward to a company's business partners.
- **Supply Chain Management: The Business Network.** Supply chain management is a cross-functional interenterprise system that integrates and automates the network of business processes and relationships between a company and its suppliers, customers, distributors, and other business partners. The goal of SCM is to help a company achieve agility and responsiveness in meeting the demands of their customers and needs of their suppliers by enabling it to design, build, and sell its products using a fast, efficient, and low-cost network of business partners, processes, and relationships, or supply chain. SCM is frequently subdivided into supply chain planning applications, such as demand and supply forecasting, and supply chain execution applications, such as inventory management, logistics management, and warehouse management. Developing effective supply chain systems and achieving the business goals of SCM has proven to be a complex and difficult challenge for many firms. But SCM continues to be a major concern and top e-business initiative as companies increase their use of Internet technologies to enhance integration and collaboration with their business partners and improve the operational efficiency and business effectiveness of their supply chains.
- **Functional Business Systems.** Functional business information systems support the business functions of marketing, production/operations, accounting, finance, and human resource management through a variety of e-business operational and management information systems summarized in Figure 7.23.
- **Marketing.** Marketing information systems support traditional and e-commerce processes and management of the marketing function. Major types of marketing information systems include interactive marketing on e-commerce Web sites, sales force automation, customer relationship management, sales management, product management, targeted marketing, advertising and promotion, and market research. Thus, marketing information systems assist marketing managers in electronic commerce product development and customer relationship decisions, as well as in planning advertising and sales promotion strategies and developing the e-commerce potential of new and present products, and new channels of distribution.
- **Manufacturing.** Computer-based manufacturing information systems help a company achieve computer-integrated manufacturing (CIM) and thus simplify, automate, and integrate many of the activities needed to quickly produce high-quality products to meet changing customer demands. For example, computer-aided design using collaborative manufacturing networks helps engineers collaborate on the design of new products and processes. Then manufacturing resource planning systems help plan the types of resources needed in the production process. Finally, manufacturing execution systems monitor and control the manufacture of products on the factory floor through shop floor scheduling and control systems, controlling a physical process (process control), a machine tool (numerical control), or machines with some humanlike work capabilities (robotics).
- **Human Resource Management.** Human resource information systems support human resource management in organizations. They include information systems for staffing the organization, training and development, and compensation administration. HRM Web sites on the Internet or corporate intranets have become important tools for providing HR services to present and prospective employees.
- **Accounting and Finance.** Accounting information systems record, report, and analyze business transactions and events for the management of the business enterprise. Figure 7.31 summarizes six essential accounting systems: order processing, inventory control, accounts receivable, accounts payable, payroll, and general ledger. Information systems in finance support managers in decisions regarding the financing of a business and the allocation of financial resources within a business. Financial information systems include cash management, online investment management, capital budgeting, and financial forecasting and planning.

Key Terms and Concepts

These are the key terms and concepts of this chapter. The page number of their first explanation is in parentheses.

1. Accounting information systems (276)
2. Batch processing (262)
3. Computer-aided manufacturing (CAM) (273)
4. Computer-integrated manufacturing (CIM) (273)
5. Cross-functional enterprise systems (240)
6. Customer relationship management (CRM) (244)
7. E-business (240)
8. Electronic data interchange (EDI) (256)
9. Enterprise application architecture (240)
10. Enterprise application integration (EAI) (259)
11. Enterprise collaboration systems (ECS) (263)
12. Enterprise resource planning (ERP) (249)
13. Financial management systems (278)
14. Functional business systems (266)
15. Human resource information systems (274)
16. Interactive marketing (266)
17. Machine control (274)
18. Manufacturing execution systems (MES) (274)
19. Manufacturing information systems (272)
20. Marketing information systems (266)
21. Online transaction processing systems (261)
22. Process control (274)
23. Real-time processing (262)
24. Sales force automation (270)
25. Supply chain (254)
26. Supply chain management (SCM) (254)
27. Targeted marketing (270)
28. Transaction processing cycle (262)
29. Transaction processing systems (TPS) (260)

Review Quiz

Match one of the key terms and concepts listed previously with one of the brief examples or definitions that follow. Try to find the best fit for the answers that seem to fit more than one term or concept. Defend your choices.

____ 1. Using the Internet and other networks for e-commerce, enterprise collaboration, and Web-enabled business processes.

____ 2. Information systems that cross the boundaries of the functional areas of a business to integrate and automate business processes.

____ 3. Information systems that support marketing, production, accounting, finance, and human resource management.

____ 4. Many business applications of IT today fit into a framework of interrelated cross-functional enterprise applications.

____ 5. Software that interconnects enterprise application systems.

____ 6. Information systems for customer relationship management, sales management, and promotion management.

____ 7. Collaborating interactively with customers in creating, purchasing, servicing, and improving products and services.

____ 8. Using mobile computing networks to support salespeople in the field.

____ 9. Information systems that support manufacturing operations and management.

____ 10. A conceptual framework for simplifying and integrating all aspects of manufacturing automation.

____ 11. Using computers in a variety of ways to help manufacture products.

____ 12. Use electronic communications, conferencing, and collaborative work tools to support and enhance collaboration among teams and workgroups.

____ 13. Using computers to operate a petroleum refinery.

____ 14. Using computers to help operate machine tools.

____ 15. Information systems to support staffing, training and development, and compensation administration.

____ 16. The automatic exchange of electronic business documents between the networked computers of business partners.

____ 17. Accomplishes legal and historical recordkeeping and gathers information for the planning and control of business operations.

____ 18. Information systems for cash management, investment management, capital budgeting, and financial forecasting.

____ 19. Performance monitoring and control systems for factory floor operations.

____ 20. Customizing advertising and promotion methods to fit their intended audience.

____ 21. A cross-functional system that helps a business develop and manage its customer-facing business processes.

____ 22. A cross-functional enterprise system that helps a business integrate and automate many of its internal business processes and information systems.

____ 23. A cross-functional interenterprise system that helps a business manage its network of relationships and processes with its business partners.

____ 24. A network of business partners, processes, and relationships that supports the design, manufacture, distribution, and sale of a company's products.

____ 25. Collecting and periodically processing transaction data.

____ 26. Processing transaction data immediately after they are captured.

____ 27. A sequence of data entry, transaction processing, database maintenance, document and report generation, and inquiry processing activities.

____ 28. Systems that immediately capture and process transaction data and update corporate databases.

Discussion Questions

1. Refer to the Real World Case on FXCM and Wyse in the chapter. How could CRM systems like Salesforce.com help a business you deal with provide you with better service?
2. Why is there a strong trend toward cross-functional integrated enterprise systems in the business use of information technology?
3. Which of the 13 tools for accounting information systems summarized in Figure 7.28 do you feel are essential for any business to have today? Which of them do you feel are optional, depending on the type of business or another factor? Explain.
4. Refer to the example about Dell Computer in the chapter. What other solutions could there be for the problem of information systems incompatibility in business besides EAI systems?
5. Refer to the example about Charles Schwab & Co. in the chapter. What are the most important HR applications a company should offer to its employees via a Web-based system? Why?
6. How could sales force automation affect salesperson productivity, marketing management, and competitive advantage?
7. How can Internet technologies be involved in improving a process in one of the functions of business? Choose one example and evaluate its business value.
8. Refer to the Real World Case on Yahoo, Google, and Chrysler in the chapter. What other information technology changes do you feel will influence the use of traditional versus online media for advertising in the future, besides those mentioned in the case?
9. What are several e-business applications that you might recommend to a small company to help it survive and succeed in challenging economic times? Why?
10. Refer to the example about General Electric in the chapter. Do enterprise collaboration systems contribute to bottom-line profits for a business? Discuss the reasons for your answer.

Analysis Exercises

1. **Application Service Provider Marketplace**
The traditional ASP definition includes Web interface (or thin client) and external, Internet-based, server-side processing and data storage. However, the business world hasn't always felt constrained by these definitions. Microsoft, McAfee, QuickBooks, and others are providing Internet-based application services without meeting these exact criteria.

Microsoft provides automatic Internet-based application maintenance as part of its one-time licensing fee. Through "automatic updates," Microsoft provides updates, fixes, and security patches to its software without IT staff involvement and minimal end user inconvenience.

McAfee, in contrast, charges an annual maintenance fee that includes daily application and virus definition updates. McAfee provides it for one year as part of its license. After the first year, license holders may continue to use the software, but they must pay a subscription fee if they want updates. Customers tend to pay for this subscription service to protect themselves from new virus threats.

a. Would you use or recommend any of Intuit's online application services (www.intuit.com) to a small business? Why or why not?

b. America Online provides a free instant messaging service (AIM, for AOL Instant Messenger). This service enables instant messaging, file sharing, and voice and video conferencing through a free application anyone can download and install. Is AOL operating as an ASP? How so?

c. Visit AOL's "Enterprise AIM services" Web site (enterprise.aim.com). What additional features does AOL provide to enterprises? Why do you suppose AOL moved away from the ASP model for its enterprise solution?

2. eWork Exchange and eLance.com: Online Job Matching and Auctions

Many opportunities await those who troll the big job boards, the free-agent sites, the auction services where applicants bid for projects, and the niche sites for specialized jobs and skills. Examples of top job matching and auction sites are eWorkExchange and eLance.com.

eWork Exchange (www.ework.com). No more sifting through irrelevant search results; fill out a list of your skills and let eWork Exchange's proprietary technology find the most suitable projects for you—no bidding required.

eLance.com (www.elance.com). This global auction marketplace covers more than just IT jobs; it runs the gamut from astrology and medicine to corporate work and cooking projects. Register a description of your services, or go straight to browsing the listings of open projects—and then start bidding. A feedback section lets both employers and freelancers rate one another.

a. Check out eWork Exchange, eLance, and other online job sites on the Web.

b. Evaluate several sites on the basis of their ease of use and their value to job seekers and employers.

c. Which Web site was your favorite? Why?

3. Job Search Database

Visit Web sites like Monster.com and others mentioned in this chapter to gather information about available jobs. Look up and record the relevant data for at least 10 current job openings that are of interest to you or that meet criteria provided by your instructor.

a. Create a database table to store key characteristics of these job opportunities. Include all of the job characteristics shown in the list that follows as fields in your table, but feel free to add fields of interest to you. If data are not available for some fields (e.g., salary range) for a particular job, leave that field blank.

b. Write a query that sorts jobs by region and then business function.

c. Create a report that groups jobs by region and sorts jobs within each region by business function.

Table: Jobs

Field	Sample Data (find your own for this exercise)
Employer	Techtron Inc.
Job Title	Systems Analyst
Region	North East
Location	Springfield, MA
Business Function	Information Technology
Description	Work with team to analyze, design, and develop e-commerce systems. Skills in systems analysis, relational database design, and programming in Java are required.
Qualifications	Bachelors degree in Information Systems or Computer Sciences, two years Java programming experience.
Salary Range	$48,000–60,000 depending on experience

4. Performing an Industry Financial Analysis

Employees apply their skills for the benefit of their organization. In addition to skills specific to their business function, employees need a keen understanding of their business environment. This environment includes their organization's business and financial structure as well as its relationships with competitors, customers, and relevant regulatory agencies.

Interviewers expect job candidates to have basic knowledge in of each of these areas. Developing such an understanding demonstrates the candidate's interest in the position and helps assure the interviewer that the candidate knows what he or she is getting into. Indeed, after a modest amount of research, job hunters may rule out certain opportunities based on what they discover. The Internet combined with good database skills can help simplify these tasks.

a. Go to the Web sites of at least three firms you identified in problem 3. Obtain information about their financial operations, including net sales (or net revenue), after-tax income, and any current information affecting the organization or industry.

b. Using the same database you created in problem 3, create a new table that includes the fields described next. Add fields that may interest you as well.

c. Add a field called OrganizationID to the Jobs table you created in the previous exercise. Make its field type Number (long integer). Write an update query that populates this new field with the appropriate values from the Organizations table's OrganizationID field. To do this, join the Jobs table and the Organizations table using the Employer/Organization Name fields. This join will only work if the names used are identical, so be sure you've typed them in that way. Execute the query to complete the update. The tables already join using the Employer/Organization Name fields, so why might you want to also join them on the OrganizationID field? Is the Employer field in the Jobs table still necessary?

d. Create a report that shows job opportunities by industry. Within each industry, sort the records by the organization's name. Include Job Title, Globalization, Net Income, and Competitors in each record. Be sure to join the Jobs table and the Organizations table using the OrganizationID field.

Table: Organizations

Field	Sample Data (find your own for this exercise)
OrganizationID	Set this as your primary key and let the database automatically generate the value.
Organization Name	Be sure to spell the name exactly as you did in the job opportunity table (copy and paste works best for this).
Industry	Legal, medical, consulting, education, etc.
Globalization	Local, regional, national, international
Revenue	Net sales or revenue from the most current financial reports
Net Income (after tax)	From the most current financial reports
Competitors	Names of key competitors
Employees	Number of employees

REAL WORLD CASE 3 Tesco: Applying Lean Logistics to Supply Chain Management

The Tesco supermarket chain in Britain has been a pioneer in retailing for more than a decade. In the mid-1990s, as he looked at the opportunities for retailers provided by the emergence of lean logistics, Graham Booth, Tesco's supply chain management director (now retired), had a very simple insight: A rapid replenishment system triggered by the customer would work in any retail format. What's more, it would work even better if the same replenishment system, using the same suppliers, cross-dock distribution centers, and vehicles serving many stores, could supply every retail store format.

Booth saw that there might be very little difference in real costs in supplying the same item through any store format, because the purchase price from the supplier could be negotiated for the whole network, not by format, and the same replenishment system making frequent milk runs to larger stores could also stop at small stores to share logistics costs. The cost disadvantage of smaller outlets, due to weak supplier leverage and expensive logistics, would largely disappear.

Booth approached Dan Jones and his research group at the Cardiff Business School in Wales, asking how Tesco could benefit from Toyota's supplier logistics methods to reduce time and effort. Jones suggested "taking a walk"—examining a typical provision stream, in this case the one for cola soft drink products. He urged Booth to invite the other functional directors at Tesco—retail, purchasing, distribution, and finance—along with the operations and supply chain directors of Britvic, the company supplying the cola.

On a cold day in January 1997, this group set out, walking back through the provision stream for cola from the checkout counter of the grocery store through Tesco's regional distribution center (RDC), Britvic's RDC, the warehouse at the Britvic bottling plant, the filling lines for cola destined for Tesco, and the warehouse of Britvic's can supplier. Along the way, Jones and his team from Cardiff kept asking simple questions: "Why are products missing from the shelves? Why does a sales associate need to re-sort products from roll cages that have just come off the truck from the RDC? Why is so much stock needed in the back of the grocery store, at the Tesco RDC, and at Britvic's RDC? Why are there huge warehouses of cans waiting to be filled near the bottling plants?"

And so on. The walk was an eye-opener. When Tesco and Britvic directors analyzed the map they drew of the process as they walked, they could see waste at every step, along with huge opportunities for saving costs while increasing the satisfaction of the end customer. As Booth looked at the situation, he realized that practically all of Tesco's practices for getting goods from the supplier to the shelf would need to change.

The first step was to hook the point-of-sale data in the store directly to a shipping decision in Tesco's RDC. This step made the end customer at the checkout point the "pacemaker" regulating the provision stream. Tesco then increased the frequency of deliveries to the retail stores. After several years of experimentation, Tesco's trucks now leave the RDCs for each store every few hours, around the clock, carrying an amount of cola proportional to what was sold in the last few hours. At the RDC, cola is now received directly from the supplier's bottling plant in wheeled dollies. They are rolled directly from the supplier into the delivery truck to the stores. And once at the stores, the dollies are rolled directly to the point of sale, where they take the place of the usual sales racks.

This innovation eliminates several "touches," in which employees moved cola from large pallets to roll cages, to the stores, and then onto dollies to reach the shelves, where they were handled one last time. (In drawing the provision stream maps of the original process, Tesco discovered that half its cost in operating this provision stream was the labor required to fill the shelves in the store.)

For fast-moving products like cola, the Tesco RDC is now a cross-dock rather than a warehouse product, with goods from suppliers spending only a few hours between their receipt and their dispatch to the stores. To guard against sudden spikes in demand, a buffer stock of full dollies is still held aside. But because of the frequency of replenishment, the buffer is very small. Back at the cola supplier, even larger changes have taken place. Britvic improved the flexibility of its filling lines, so it can now make what the customer has just requested in small batches with very high reliability. This capability means that there are practically no finished goods awaiting shipment in Britvic's filling plant.

The final logistics step is for Tesco's delivery truck to take the dollies several times a day from the RDC on a milk run to a series of Tesco stores. At each store it collects the empty dollies and then visits several suppliers to return them. At each stop it also picks up full dollies and then returns to the Tesco RDC to restart the cycle. That may sound like a good way to increase truck miles and logistics costs, and many traditional managers, including those at Tesco and Britvic, have assumed it must. However, in practice, these methods substantially reduce the total miles driven along with freight costs, while also reducing total inventories in the system.

The consequence, in terms of performance, is remarkable. Total "touches" on the product (each of which involves costly human effort) have been reduced from 150 to 50. The total throughput time, from the filling line at the supplier to the customer leaving the store with the cola, has declined from 20 days to 5 days. The number of inventory stocking points has been reduced from five to two (the small buffer in the RDC and the roller racks in the store), and the supplier's distribution center for the items has disappeared.

As he grasped the logic of lean logistics, Booth realized that his simple insight was valid: A rapid-replenishment system triggered by the customer would work in any retail format. What was more, it would work even better if the same replenishment system, using the same suppliers, cross-dock distribution centers, and vehicles serving many stores, could supply every retail format.

Using those insights, Tesco set out to create a range of formats, beginning in Britain, so that households could obtain fast-moving consumer goods from a complete variety of outlets. This experiment has led to tiny Tesco Express convenience stores at gas stations and in busy urban intersections; Tesco Metro stores (at the small end of the "supermarket" range) on busy streets and in high-density urban areas; traditional Tesco supermarkets in urban and suburban areas; Tesco Extra on the suburban perimeter as an answer to "big boxes" retail stores operated in Britain by Wal-Mart's ASDA subsidiary; and Tesco.com for the Web shopper.

The strategy has worked brilliantly, permitting Tesco to establish the lowest cost position among British retailers (including Wal-Mart) while posting progressively higher margins and steadily increasing its share in every format. But this is just the beginning. By offering households a range of formats for every circumstance and pioneering the use of loyalty cards, which give discounts to frequent shoppers, Tesco is in a position to know everything a household buys during the course of a year at all formats, and where and when consumers buy it. In fact, 80 percent of items currently bought in Tesco stores are bought by loyalty-card holders. These loyal customers obtain close to 100 percent of their needs at the range of Tesco outlets.

Source: James P. Womack and Daniel T. Jones, "Teaching the Big Box New Tricks," *Fortune*, November 14, 2005.

CASE STUDY QUESTIONS

1. What key insights of Tesco's SCM director Graham Booth helped revolutionize Tesco's supply chain and range of retail store formats? Can these insights be applied to any kind of retail business? Why or why not?
2. How did Dan Jones and his research group from the Cardiff Business School of Wales demonstrate the inefficiencies of the Tesco and Britvic supply chains? Can this methodology be applied to the supply chain of any kind of business? Why or why not?
3. What are the major business and competitive benefits gained by Tesco as the result of its supply chain initiatives? Can other retail chains and retail stores achieve some or all of the same results? Defend your position with examples of actual retail chains and stores you know.

REAL WORLD ACTIVITIES

1. Use the Internet to investigate Tesco's present financial success and competitive position and what other retailers in Britain are doing to compete with Tesco. Then investigate if other retail chains or stores in the United States or any other country seem to be applying a supply chain management strategy similar to Tesco's.
2. Many retail chains and stores have loyalty cards similar to Tesco's. Use the Internet to research the loyalty-card performance of these companies. Break into small groups with your classmates to discuss how these and other retail stores you know could improve their loyalty-card performance compared with Tesco's stellar performance with its customers.

CHAPTER 8

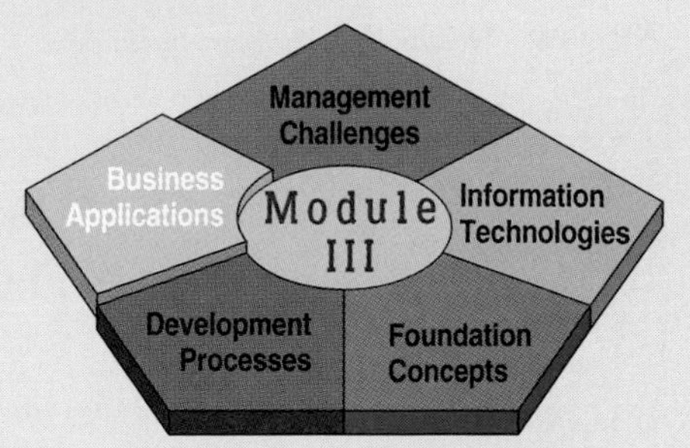

ELECTRONIC COMMERCE SYSTEMS

Chapter Highlights

Section I
Electronic Commerce Fundamentals

Introduction to Electronic Commerce

The Scope of e-Commerce

Real World Case: eBay versus Google and Microsoft: The Competitive Battle for e-Commerce Supremacy

Essential e-Commerce Processes

Electronic Payment Processes

Section II
e-Commerce Applications and Issues

Real World Case: Entellium, Digg, Peerflix, Zappos, and Jigsaw: Success for Second Movers in e-Commerce

Business-to-Consumer e-Commerce

Web Store Requirements

Business-to-Business e-Commerce

e-Commerce Marketplaces

Clicks and Bricks in e-Commerce

Real World Case: Yahoo and Flickr: Will Social Media and Social Networking Give Yahoo a Competitive Edge on the Web?

Learning Objectives

After reading and studying this chapter, you should be able to:

1. Identify the major categories and trends of e-commerce applications.
2. Identify the essential processes of an e-commerce system and give examples of how it is implemented in e-commerce applications.
3. Identify and give examples of several key factors and Web store requirements needed to succeed in e-commerce.
4. Identify and explain the business value of several types of e-commerce marketplaces.
5. Discuss the benefits and trade-offs of several e-commerce clicks and bricks alternatives.

SECTION I Electronic Commerce Fundamentals

Introduction to Electronic Commerce

E-commerce is changing the shape of competition, the speed of action, and the streamlining of interactions, products, and payments from customers to companies and from companies to suppliers [13].

For most companies today, **electronic commerce** is more than just buying and selling products online. Instead, it encompasses the entire online process of developing, marketing, selling, delivering, servicing, and paying for products and services transacted on internetworked, global marketplaces of customers, with the support of a worldwide network of business partners. In fact, many consider the term "e-commerce" to be somewhat antiquated. Given that many young businesspeople have grown up in a world in which online commerce has always been available, it may soon be time to eliminate the distinction between e-commerce and e-business and simply accept that it is all "just business as usual." Until then, we will retain the term "e-commerce" because it allows for a clearer picture of the differences between online and more traditional business transactions.

As we will see in this chapter, electronic commerce systems rely on the resources of the Internet and many other information technologies to support every step of this process. We will also see that most companies, large and small, are engaged in some form of e-commerce activities. Therefore, developing an e-commerce capability has become an important option that should be considered by most businesses today.

Read the Real World Case on the next page. We can learn a lot about the challenges and opportunities in the field of electronic commerce from this example. See Figure 8.1.

The Scope of e-Commerce

Figure 8.2 illustrates the range of business processes involved in the marketing, buying, selling, and servicing of products and services in companies that engage in e-commerce [7]. Companies involved in e-commerce as either buyers or sellers rely on Internet-based technologies and e-commerce applications and services to accomplish marketing, discovery, transaction processing, and product and customer service processes. For example, electronic commerce can include interactive marketing, ordering, payment, and customer support processes at e-commerce catalog and auction sites on the World Wide Web. But e-commerce also includes e-business processes such as extranet access of inventory databases by customers and suppliers (transaction processing), intranet access of customer relationship management systems by sales and customer service reps (service and support), and customer collaboration in product development via e-mail exchanges and Internet newsgroups (marketing/discovery).

The advantages of e-commerce allow a business of virtually any size and located virtually anywhere on the planet to conduct business with just about anyone, anywhere. Imagine a small olive oil manufacturer in a remote village in Italy selling its wares to major department stores and specialty food shops in New York, London, Tokyo, and other large metropolitan markets. The power of e-commerce allows for geophysical barriers to disappear, making all consumers and businesses on Earth potential customers and suppliers.

e-Commerce Technologies

What technologies are necessary for electronic commerce? The short answer is that most information technologies and Internet technologies that we discuss in this text are, in some form, involved in electronic commerce systems. A more specific answer is illustrated in Figure 8.3, which gives an example of the technology resources required by

REAL WORLD CASE 1 eBay versus Google and Microsoft: The Competitive Battle for e-Commerce Supremacy

For most of its existence, eBay has enjoyed a virtual monopoly. It now commands more than 90 percent of the online auction market, and from 1999 to 2004, it posted at least 40 percent annual profit growth every year, even as brawny competitors like Amazon and Yahoo were taking runs at its core business. Yet for all its phenomenal success, in 2006 eBay began to face the toughest challenges of its 10-year history. The armies massing on its borders hail from Google and Microsoft, but rather than aim for eBay's auction business, the two behemoths want to use their strength in search and advertising to build dominance in online classifieds—the format that many analysts think will define the future of e-commerce.

"Ebay auctions are still too hard for many consumers to navigate," says Safa Rashtchy, senior analyst covering e-commerce and search at Piper Jaffray. "Overall, people prefer to buy locally, but there hasn't been an efficient way for them to find each other."

Fans of the populist Web site Craigslist, in which eBay owns a 25 percent stake, might disagree. With dedicated sites in many cities across the world, Craigslist is an online classifieds meeting place for millions of people looking to share ideas, meet a friend, find a job, or locate an apartment. Meg Whitman, CEO of eBay notes, "Craigslist is an excellent example of how the Internet brings people together to trade goods, help neighbors, or speak out on important issues. Craigslist has become the online gathering place for local communities." But Craigslist doesn't have an online payment system—it doesn't use eBay's PayPal—or an industrial-strength shopping search engine that could help it grow into a major global player. Not to mention that founder Craig Newmark and CEO Jim Buckmaster seem in no hurry to expand too quickly on that global scale.

FIGURE 8.1

Windows Live Expo is Microsoft's competitive weapon in its battle with eBay and Google for the online classifieds market.

Two of the most formidable companies on the planet, however, are in more of a rush. Google and Microsoft certainly have the resources; some say the invasion into eBay's turf began when Louis Monier, former director of advanced technology at eBay and the wizard behind its search innovations, was poached by Google last summer. The challengers also have a motive: The burgeoning online classifieds business is growing at a far faster clip than auctions.

Microsoft launched its listings service, Windows Live Expo, in February 2006 as yet another of its Windows Live initiatives. Users are able to post classifieds for free, limit access by buddy lists, and focus listings geographically; a tie-in to MSN's Virtual Earth mapping service helps buyers and sellers find each other easily. Says Gary Wiseman, product unit manager, "What sets Windows Live Expo apart is that people can set their own search parameters for goods and services. They can define their own marketplace universe."

Most classified advertising services generalize product location by a predefined city location, regardless of where in the city the product is located. However, all products and services listed in Windows Live Expo are geographically identified, or geo-tagged, by zip code, not city, which specifically defines where the product is located. Windows Live Expo customers also have the option to search for items within a radius as small as 25 miles or as large as the entire United States, making it easier to define a search. Windows Live Expo listings are also integrated with MSN's satellite-image–based Windows Live Local so customers can view maps and aerial imagery of neighborhoods they may want to live in or see exactly where this weekend's garage sale is.

Google's foray, called Google Base, went live in mid-November 2005, a powerful foundation on which Google could build any number of products that compete with eBay. A massive, searchable database, the free service allows users to post everything from recipes and concert dates to used cars and job listings, and local merchants can upload inventory listings. Users are able to post classifieds data so buyers can see what's on the shelves in the bricks-and-mortar stores in their neighborhoods. With eBay acquiring nearly half of its new buyers and sellers in the United States through paid listings, mostly on Google and Yahoo, it could lose buyers if Google puts its own search results first.

Google Base users can submit all types of online and offline content, which becomes searchable on Google. Users can describe any item with *attributes,* which will help people find it when they do related searches. Based on an item's relevance, users may find their results for searches on Froogle, Google Maps, or the main Google search engine. The more popular individual attributes become, the more often Google suggests them when others post the same items.

"People could bypass eBay altogether," claims Scot Wingo, CEO of ChannelAdvisor, which helps big eBay sellers like Best Buy maximize online sales. One of Wingo's clients, online shoe retailer Grapevinehill, recently started listing its inventory on Google Base in addition to eBay. Owner Mark Fitzgerald says he made the move to reach Google's broader audience and that the new listings are already driving traffic to his store: "We definitely see some momentum building."

eBay isn't blind to this shift in e-commerce. Its recent acquisitions and launches—comparison site Shopping.com and international online classifieds sites Kijiji, Gumtree, and LoQUo—lend themselves to the online listings business. Kijiji, which means "village" in Swahili, and the others provide international online classifieds Web sites that offer a place for people in many cities in Asia, Europe, the United Kingdom, Australia, Canada, New Zealand, and South Africa to meet via personals, share ideas, buy or trade goods and services, find accommodations, or share information on housing, real estate, jobs, and other topics.

Then in September 2005, eBay acquired Luxembourg-based Skype Technologies SA, the global Internet communications company, for approximately \$2.6 billion in upfront cash and eBay stock. eBay claimed that that Skype, eBay, and PayPal create an unparalleled e-commerce and communications engine for buyers and sellers around the world.

eBay defended the huge premium it paid for Skype (the *Economist* noted that Skype had yet to make a dime's worth of profit) by emphasizing that online shopping depends on a number of factors to function well and that communications, like payments and shipping, is a critical part of this process. Skype will streamline and improve communications between buyers and sellers as it is integrated into the eBay marketplace, argues eBay. Buyers will gain an easy way to talk to sellers quickly and get the information they need to buy, and sellers can more easily build relationships with customers and close sales. As a result, eBay hopes that Skype (which then had 54 million members in 225 countries, was adding about 150,000 users every day, and was the market leader in nearly all countries it does business) will increase the velocity of trade on eBay, especially in categories that require more involved communications such as used cars, business and industrial equipment, and high-end collectibles.

eBay CEO Meg Whitman struck back again in mid-2006 with an alliance of sorts with Yahoo, which will sell ads for eBay's sites and promote eBay's PayPal payment service as a way for consumers to pay for Yahoo services. That undoubtedly led to a surprise deal with Google later that year, in which Google agreed to promote Skype calls on its Web site, while eBay will allow Google to place ads on eBay's Web sites in markets outside the United States.

Actually, say some analysts, eBay's strongest defense could turn out to be its PayPal fraud and payment staff—more than 1,000 employees—which Google and Microsoft have yet to match. "It's a huge advantage," says analyst David Edwards of American Technology Research. "People overlook how complicated eBay's business is."

Source: Adapted from Michael V. Copeland, "The Big Guns' Next Target: eBay," *Business 2.0 Online*, January 31, 2006; Microsoft Corporation, "Windows Live Expo Now Available to U.S. Consumers," February 28, 2006; Google.com, "About Google Base," May 19, 2006; Kevin J. Delaney, Mylene Mangalindan, and Robert A. Guth, "New Tech Alliances Signal More Scrambling Ahead, *The Wall Street Journal*, May 26, 2006; Cooley Godward LLP, "eBay's Kijiji Acquires Classifieds Web Sites," May 18, 2005; Skype.com, "eBay to Acquire Skype," September 12, 2005; eBay.com; Adam Lashinsky, "Building eBay 2.0," *Fortune*, October 16, 2006.

CASE STUDY QUESTIONS

1. Do you agree with Google and Microsoft that eBay is now vulnerable to their assaults via Google Base and Windows Live Expo? Why or why not?
2. What are the major advantages and limitations of Google Base and Windows Live Expo? Which do you prefer, or would you use both? Why? Go to their Internet Web sites and read reviews at other sites to help you answer.
3. Are eBay's development of Kijiji, acquisition of Skype, alliance with Yahoo, and other acquisitions as noted in this case enough to ward off the competitive assaults of Google and Microsoft? Defend your position.

REAL WORLD ACTIVITIES

1. Go to the Internet to discover the latest developments in eBay's auctions performance and its use of its acquisitions in its battle for the online classifieds market with Google and Microsoft. Have any new entrants appeared to seriously challenge these major players, including Craigslist? Which players appear to be the winners and losers in this competition? Defend your position to the class.
2. Personalized online classifieds Web pages that are accessible to others online have a great potential for serious security, privacy, fraud, and spam assaults by online criminals, hackers, and spammers. Use the Internet to research how the companies in this case are protecting users of their products from such assaults. Break into small groups with your classmates to discuss this issue, your research results, and other steps that users and the companies could take to improve the security of online classifieds.

FIGURE 8.2 E-commerce involves accomplishing a range of business processes to support the electronic buying and selling of goods and services.

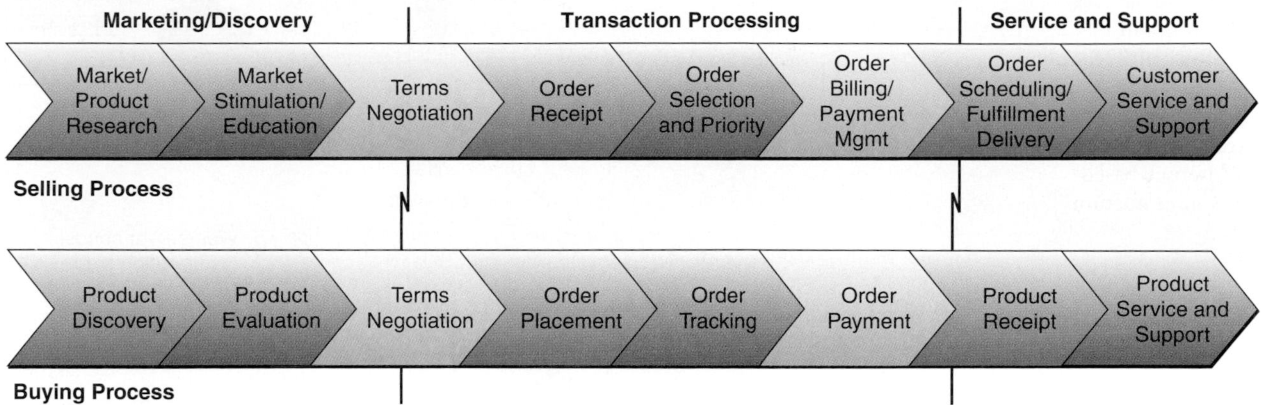

many e-commerce systems. The figure illustrates some of the hardware, software, data, and network components used by FreeMarkets Inc. to provide business-to-business (B2B) online auction e-commerce services [5].

Categories of e-Commerce

Many companies today are participating in or sponsoring four basic categories of electronic commerce applications: **business-to-consumer**, **business-to-business**, **consumer-to-consumer**, and business-to-government e-commerce. Note: We do not explicitly cover business-to-government (B2G) and *e-government* applications because they are beyond the scope of this text. Suffice to say that many e-commerce concepts apply to such applications.

Business-to-Consumer (B2C) e-Commerce In this form of electronic commerce, businesses must develop attractive electronic marketplaces to sell products and services to consumers. For example, many companies offer e-commerce Web sites that provide virtual storefronts and multimedia catalogs, interactive order processing, secure electronic payment systems, and online customer support. The B2C marketplace is growing like a wildfire but still remains the tip of the iceberg when compared with all online commerce.

Consumer-to-Consumer (C2C) e-Commerce The huge success of online auctions like eBay, where consumers (as well as businesses) can buy from and sell to one another in an auction process at an auction Web site, makes this e-commerce model an important e-commerce business strategy. Thus, participating in or sponsoring consumer or business auctions is an important e-commerce alternative for B2C, C2B (consumer-to-business), or B2B e-commerce. Electronic personal advertising of products or services to buy or sell by consumers at electronic newspaper sites, consumer e-commerce portals, or personal Web sites is also an important form of C2C e-commerce.

Business-to-Business (B2B) e-Commerce If B2C activities are the tip of the iceberg, B2B represents the part of the iceberg that is under the water—the biggest part. This category of electronic commerce involves both electronic business marketplaces and direct market links between businesses. For example, many companies offer secure Internet or extranet e-commerce catalog Web sites for their business customers and suppliers. Also very important are B2B e-commerce portals that provide auction and exchange marketplaces for businesses. Others may rely on electronic data interchange (EDI) via the Internet or extranets for computer-to-computer exchange of e-commerce documents with their larger business customers and suppliers.

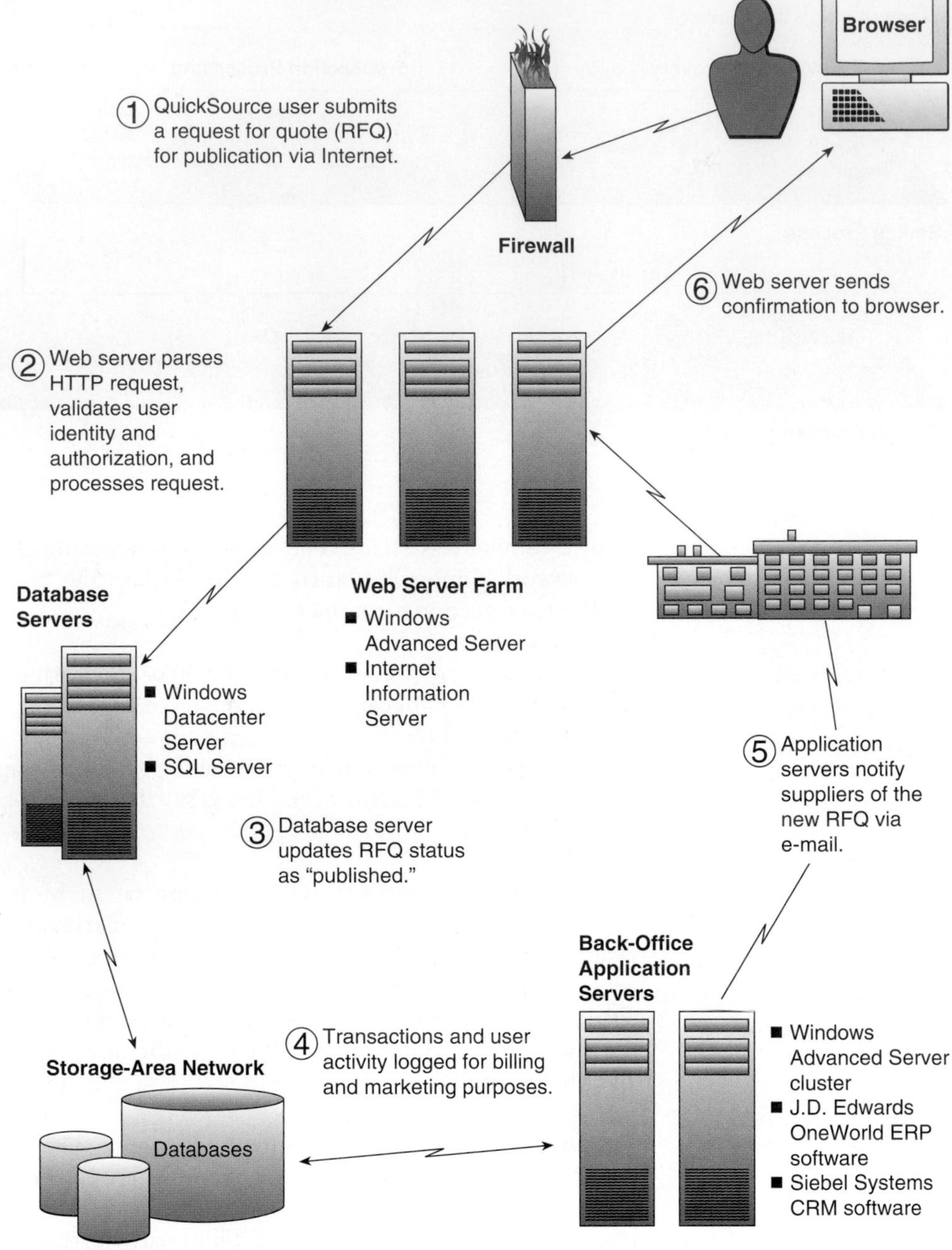

Browser
Firewall
① QuickSource user submits a request for quote (RFQ) for publication via Internet.
② Web server parses HTTP request, validates user identity and authorization, and processes request.
③ Database server updates RFQ status as "published."
④ Transactions and user activity logged for billing and marketing purposes.
⑤ Application servers notify suppliers of the new RFQ via e-mail.
⑥ Web server sends confirmation to browser.
Web Server Farm
■ Windows Advanced Server
■ Internet Information Server
Database Servers
■ Windows Datacenter Server
■ SQL Server
Storage-Area Network
Databases
Back-Office Application Servers
■ Windows Advanced Server cluster
■ J.D. Edwards OneWorld ERP software
■ Siebel Systems CRM software

FIGURE 8.3
The hardware, software, network, and database components and IT architecture of B2B online auctions provider FreeMarkets Inc. are illustrated in this example of its Internet-based QuickSource auction service.

Essential e-Commerce Processes

The essential **e-commerce processes** required for the successful operation and management of e-commerce activities are illustrated in Figure 8.4. This figure outlines the nine key components of an *e-commerce process architecture* that is the foundation of the e-commerce initiatives of many companies today [11]. We concentrate on the role these processes play in e-commerce systems, but you should recognize that many of these components may also be used in internal, noncommerce e-business applications. An example would be an intranet-based human resource system used by a company's employees, which might use all but the catalog management and product payment processes shown in Figure 8.4. Let's take a brief look at each essential process category.

Access Control and Security

E-commerce processes must establish mutual trust and secure access between the parties in an e-commerce transaction by authenticating users, authorizing access,

FIGURE 8.4 This e-commerce process architecture highlights nine essential categories of e-commerce processes.

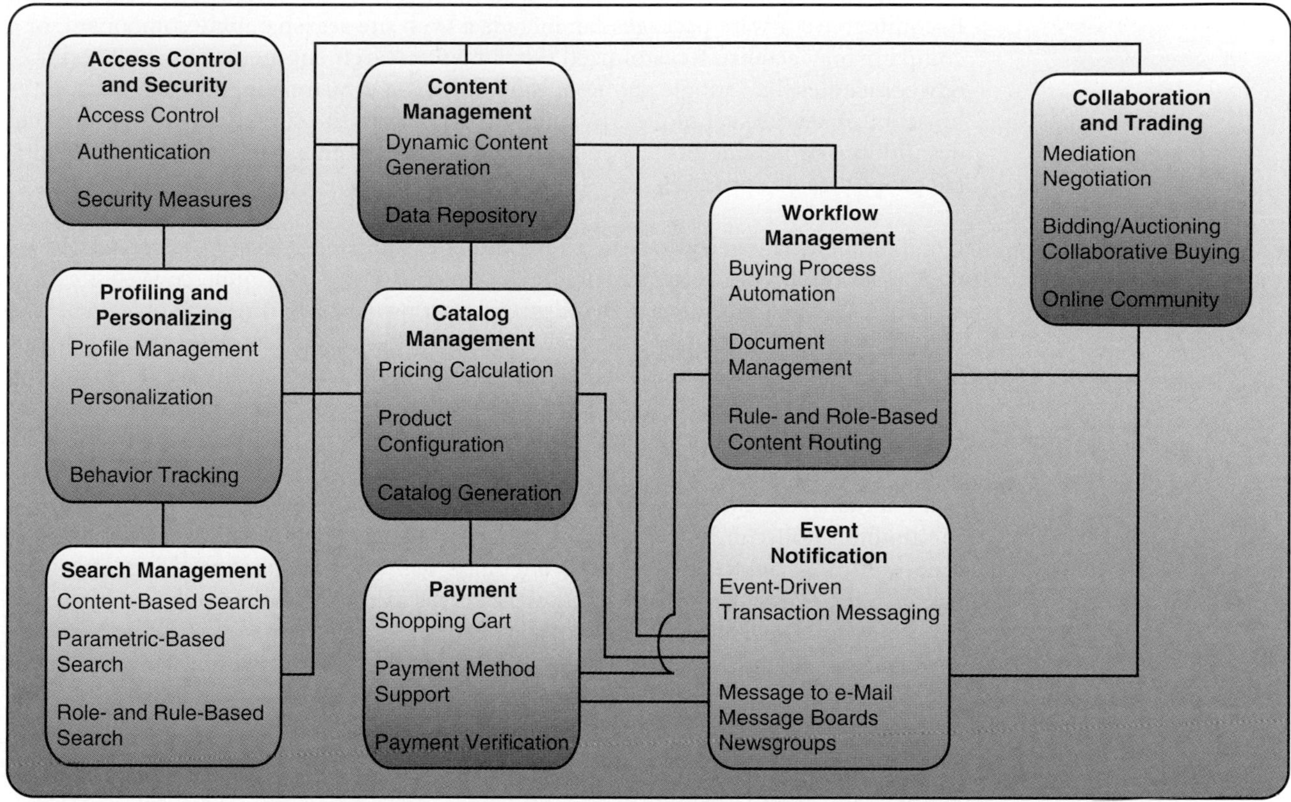

and enforcing security features. For example, these processes establish that a customer and e-commerce site are who they say they are through user names and passwords, encryption keys, or digital certificates and signatures. The e-commerce site must then authorize access to only those parts of the site that an individual user needs to accomplish his or her particular transactions. Thus, you usually will be given access to all resources of an e-commerce site except for other people's accounts, restricted company data, and Web master administration areas. Companies engaged in B2B e-commerce may rely on secure industry exchanges for procuring goods and services or Web trading portals that allow only registered customers to access trading information and applications. Other security processes protect the resources of e-commerce sites from threats such as hacker attacks, theft of passwords or credit card numbers, and system failures. We discuss many of these security threats and features in Chapter 11.

Profiling and Personalizing

Once you have gained access to an e-commerce site, profiling processes can occur that gather data on you and your Web site behavior and choices, as well as build electronic profiles of your characteristics and preferences. User profiles are developed using profiling tools such as user registration, cookie files, Web site behavior tracking software, and user feedback. These profiles are then used to recognize you as an individual user and provide you with a personalized view of the contents of the site, as well as product recommendations and personalized Web advertising as part of a *one-to-one marketing* strategy. Profiling processes are also used to help authenticate your identity for account management and payment purposes and gather data for customer relationship management, marketing planning, and Web site management. Some of the ethical issues in user profiling are discussed in Chapter 11.

Search Management

Efficient and effective search processes provide a top e-commerce Web site capability that helps customers find the specific product or service they want to evaluate or buy. E-commerce software packages can include a Web site search engine component, or a company may acquire a customized e-commerce search engine from search technology companies like Google and Requisite Technology. Search engines may use a combination of search techniques, including searches based on content (e.g., a product description) or parameters (e.g., above, below, or between a range of values for multiple properties of a product).

Content and Catalog Management

Content management software helps e-commerce companies develop, generate, deliver, update, and archive text data and multimedia information at e-commerce Web sites. For example, German media giant Bertelsmann, part owner of BarnesandNoble.com, uses StoryServer content manager software to generate Web page templates that enable online editors from six international offices to easily publish and update book reviews and other product information, which are sold (syndicated) to other e-commerce sites.

E-commerce content frequently takes the form of multimedia catalogs of product information. As such, generating and managing catalog content is a major subset of content management, or **catalog management**. For example, W.W. Grainger & Co., a multibillion-dollar industrial parts distributor, uses the CenterStage catalog management software suite to retrieve data from more than 2,000 supplier databases, standardize the data, translate it into HTML or XML for Web use, and organize and enhance the data for speedy delivery as multimedia Web pages at its www.grainger.com Web site.

Content and catalog management software works with the profiling tools we mentioned previously to personalize the content of Web pages seen by individual users. For example, Travelocity.com uses OnDisplay content manager software to push personalized promotional information about other travel opportunities to users while they are involved in an online travel-related transaction.

Finally, content and catalog management may be expanded to include *product configuration* processes that support Web-based customer self-service and the *mass customization* of a company's products. Configuration software helps online customers select the optimum feasible set of product features that can be included in a finished product. For example, both Dell Computer and Cisco Systems use configuration software to sell built-to-order computers and network processors to their online customers [3].

Cabletron Systems: e-Commerce Configuration

When $3 billion network equipment maker Cabletron Systems began selling its wares online, its sales reps knew full well that peddling made-to-order routers was not as simple as the mouse-click marvel of online book selling. Cabletron's big business customers—whether ISP EarthLink or motorcycle maker Harley-Davidson—did not have the technical expertise to build their own routers (which can be as small as a breadbox or as large as a television, depending on the customer, and can include hundreds of components). Worse, Cabletron's Web site listed thousands of parts that presented users with nearly infinite combinations, most of which would work only when assembled in a certain way.

That's why part of Cabletron's new online sales team consists of a set of complex Web-based product configuration tools made by PeopleSoft Inc. Called eSales Configuration Workbench, the system prompts customers the same way a salesperson might: It walks them through product features; analyzes their needs, budgets, and time constraints; and considers only components and options compatible with existing systems. The configurator also suggests various options—different kinds of backup power, the number of parts, types of connecting wires—and generates price quotes for up to 500 concurrent online users. When a customer clicks the Buy button, the configurator generates an order that is passed on to Cabletron's back-end order fulfillment systems, which update inventory, accounting, and shipping databases.

Within the first year of using the eSales Configuration Workbench, Cabletron saw staggering results. Some 60 percent of the businesses using its Web site now use the configurator. Cabletron estimates the system saved $12 million in one year by whittling down the number of misconfigured orders—and subsequent returns—to nearly nothing. Cabletron considers the system to be 98.8 percent accurate. Order processing costs also dropped 96 percent, and customers can now place online orders in 10 to 20 minutes—a fraction of the two to three days it takes through a sales rep. As they say, however, "all good things must come to an end." Since Cabletron's merger with Enterasys, the online configurator has been retired, and the old sales rep–driven configurator method is back. Cabletron is working on an expert system version of the old eSales system that is expected to be 100 percent accurate. The new system will be able to configure entire system solutions instead of just routers [2, 6].

Workflow Management

Many of the business processes in e-commerce applications can be managed and partially automated with the help of workflow management software. E-business workflow systems for enterprise collaboration help employees electronically collaborate to accomplish structured work tasks within knowledge-based business processes. Workflow management in both e-business and e-commerce depends on a *workflow software engine* containing software models of the business processes to be accomplished. The workflow models express the predefined sets of business rules, roles of stakeholders, authorization requirements, routing alternatives, databases used, and sequence of tasks required for each e-commerce process. Thus, workflow systems ensure that the proper transactions, decisions, and work activities are performed, and the correct data and documents are routed to the right employees, customers, suppliers, and other business stakeholders.

As many of you begin your business careers, you will be charged with the responsibility of driving cost out of existing business processes while maintaining or improving the effectiveness of those processes. As you continue to acquire a greater appreciation for, and understanding of, how technology can benefit business, you will explore workflow management as the key to this optimization of cost and effectiveness throughout the business.

For example, Figure 8.5 illustrates the e-commerce procurement processes of the MS Market system of Microsoft Corp. Microsoft employees use its global intranet and the catalog/content management and workflow management software engines built into MS Market to electronically purchase more than $3 billion annually of business supplies and materials from approved suppliers connected to the MS Market system by their corporate extranets [13].

Microsoft Corporation: e-Commerce Purchasing Processes

MS Market is an internal e-commerce purchasing system that works on Microsoft's intranet. MS Market has drastically reduced the personnel required to manage low-cost requisitions and gives employees a quick, easy way to order materials without being burdened with paperwork and bureaucratic processes. These high-volume, low-dollar transactions represent about 70 percent of total volume but only 3 percent of Microsoft's accounts payable. Employees were wasting time turning requisitions into purchase orders (POs) and trying to follow business rules and processes. Managers wanted to streamline this process, so the decision was made to create a requisitioning tool that would take all the controls and validations used by requisition personnel and push them onto the Web. Employees wanted an easy-to-use

FIGURE 8.5
The role of catalog/content management and workflow management in a Web-based procurement process: the MS Market system used by Microsoft Corp.

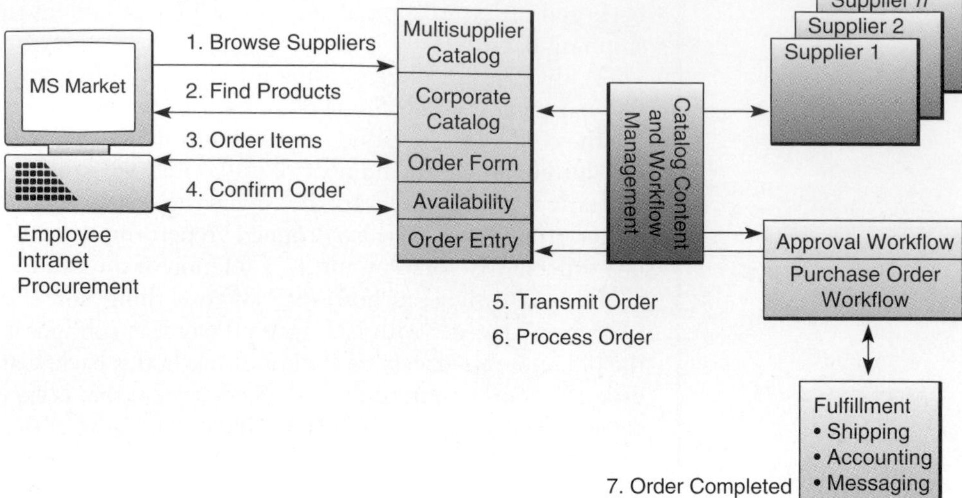

online form for ordering supplies that included extranet interfaces to procurement partners, such as Boise Cascade and Marriott.

How does this system work? Let's say a Microsoft employee wants a technical book. He goes to the MS Market site on Microsoft's intranet, and MS Market immediately identifies his preferences and approval code through his log-on ID. The employee selects the Barnes & Noble link, which brings up a catalog, order form, and a list of hundreds of books with titles and prices that have been negotiated between Microsoft buyers and Barnes & Noble. He selects a book, puts it in the order form, and completes the order by verifying his group's cost center number and manager's name.

The order is transmitted immediately to the supplier, cutting down on delivery time as well as accounting for the payment of the supplies. Upon submission of the order, MS Market generates an order tracking number for reference, sends notification via e-mail to the employee's manager, and transmits the order over the Internet to Barnes & Noble for fulfillment. In this case, since the purchase total is only $40, the manager's specific approval is not required. Two days later the book arrives at the employee's office. Thus, MS Market lets employees easily order low-cost items in a controlled fashion at a low cost, without going through a complicated PO approval process [13, 17].

Event Notification

Most e-commerce applications are *event-driven* systems that respond to a multitude of events—from a new customer's first Web site access, to payment and delivery processes, to innumerable customer relationship and supply chain management activities. That is why event notification processes play an important role in e-commerce systems; customers, suppliers, employees, and other stakeholders must be notified of all events that might affect their status in a transaction. Event notification software works with workflow management software to monitor all e-commerce processes and record all relevant events, including unexpected changes or problem situations. Then it works with user-profiling software to automatically notify all involved stakeholders of important transaction events using appropriate user-preferred methods of electronic messaging, such as e-mail, newsgroup, pager, and fax communications. This notification includes a company's management, who then can monitor their employees' responsiveness to e-commerce events and customer and supplier feedback.

For example, when you purchase a product at a retail e-commerce Web site like Amazon.com, you automatically receive an e-mail record of your order. Then you may receive e-mail notifications of any change in product availability or shipment status and, finally, an e-mail message notifying you that your order has been shipped and is complete.

Collaboration and Trading

This major category of e-commerce processes consists of those that support the vital collaboration arrangements and trading services needed by customers, suppliers, and other stakeholders to accomplish e-commerce transactions. Thus, in Chapter 2 we discussed how a customer-focused e-business uses tools such as e-mail, chat systems, and discussion groups to nurture online *communities of interest* among employees and customers to enhance customer service and build customer loyalty in e-commerce. The essential collaboration among business trading partners in e-commerce may also be provided by Internet-based trading services. For example, B2B e-commerce Web portals provided by companies like Ariba and Commerce One support matchmaking, negotiation, and mediation processes among business buyers and sellers. In addition, B2B e-commerce is heavily dependent on Internet-based trading platforms and portals that provide online exchange and auctions for e-business enterprises. Therefore, the online auctions and exchanges developed by companies like FreeMarkets are revolutionizing the procurement processes of many major corporations. We will discuss these and other e-commerce applications in Section II.

Electronic Payment Processes

Payment for the products and services purchased is an obvious and vital set of processes in electronic commerce transactions. But payment processes are not simple, because of the nearly anonymous electronic nature of transactions taking place between the networked computer systems of buyers and sellers and the many security issues involved. Electronic commerce payment processes are also complex because of the wide variety of debit and credit alternatives and financial institutions and intermediaries that may be part of the process. Therefore, a variety of **electronic payment systems** have evolved over time. In addition, new payment systems are being developed and tested to meet the security and technical challenges of electronic commerce over the Internet.

Web Payment Processes

Most e-commerce systems on the Web involving businesses and consumers (B2C) depend on credit card payment processes. But many B2B e-commerce systems rely on more complex payment processes based on the use of purchase orders, as was illustrated in Figure 8.5. However, both types of e-commerce typically use an electronic *shopping cart* process, which enables customers to select products from Web site catalog displays and put them temporarily in a virtual shopping basket for later checkout and processing. Figure 8.6 illustrates and summarizes a B2C electronic payment system with several payment alternatives.

Electronic Funds Transfer

Electronic funds transfer (EFT) systems are a major form of electronic payment systems in banking and retailing industries. EFT systems use a variety of information technologies to capture and process money and credit transfers between banks and businesses and their customers. For example, banking networks support teller terminals at all bank offices and automated teller machines (ATMs) at locations throughout the world. Banks, credit card companies, and other businesses may support pay-by-phone services. Very popular also are Web-based payment services, such as PayPal and BillPoint for cash transfers and CheckFree and Paytrust for automatic bill payment, that enable the customers of banks and other bill payment services to use the Internet to electronically pay bills. In addition, most point-of-sale terminals in retail stores are networked to bank EFT systems, which makes it possible for you to use a credit card or debit card instantly to pay for gas, groceries, or other purchases at participating retail outlets.

FIGURE 8.6
An example of a secure electronic payment system with many payment alternatives.

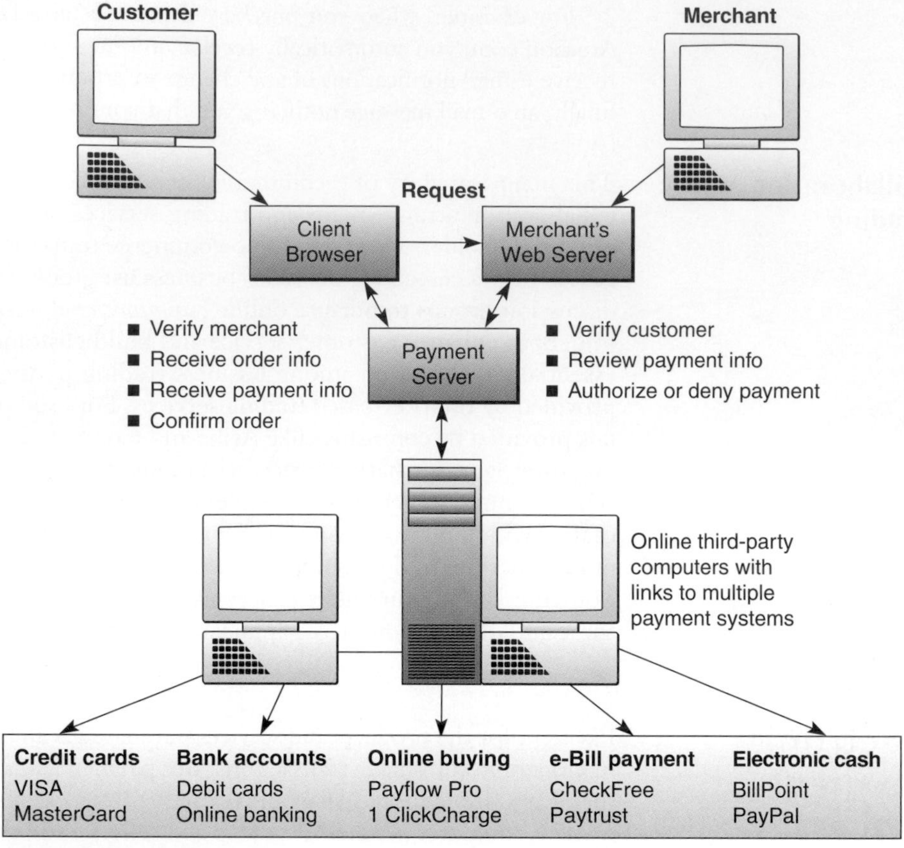

Secure Electronic Payments

When you make an online purchase on the Internet, your credit card information is vulnerable to interception by *network sniffers*, software that easily recognizes credit card number formats. Several basic security measures are being used to solve this security problem: (1) encrypt (code and scramble) the data passing between the customer and merchant, (2) encrypt the data passing between the customer and the company authorizing the credit card transaction, or (3) take sensitive information offline. (Note: Because encryption and other security issues are discussed in Chapter 11, we will not explain how they work in this section.)

For example, many companies use the Secure Socket Layer (SSL) security method developed by Netscape Communications that automatically encrypts data passing between your Web browser and a merchant's server. However, sensitive information is still vulnerable to misuse once it's decrypted (decoded and unscrambled) and stored on a merchant's server. So a digital wallet payment system was developed. In this method, you add security software add-on modules to your Web browser. That enables your browser to encrypt your credit card data in such a way that only the bank that authorizes credit card transactions for the merchant gets to see it. All the merchant is told is whether your credit card transaction is approved or not.

The Secure Electronic Transaction (SET) standard for electronic payment security extends this digital wallet approach. In this method, software encrypts a digital envelope of digital certificates specifying the payment details for each transaction. SET has been agreed to by VISA, MasterCard, IBM, Microsoft, Netscape, and most other industry players. Therefore, a system like SET may become the standard for secure electronic payments on the Internet. See Figure 8.7.

FIGURE 8.7
VeriSign provides electronic payment, security, and many other e-commerce services.

SECTION II e-Commerce Applications and Issues

e-commerce is here to stay. The Web and e-commerce are key industry drivers. It's changed how many companies do business. It's created new channels for our customers. Companies are at the e-commerce crossroads and there are many ways to go [13].

Thus, e-commerce is changing how companies do business both internally and externally with their customers, suppliers, and other business partners. How companies apply e-commerce to their businesses is also subject to change as managers confront a variety of e-commerce alternatives. The applications of e-commerce by many companies have gone through several major stages as e-commerce matures in the world of business. For example, e-commerce between businesses and consumers (B2C) moved from merely offering multimedia company information at corporate Web sites *(brochureware)*, to offering products and services at Web storefront sites via electronic catalogs and online sales transactions. B2B e-commerce, in contrast, started with Web site support to help business customers serve themselves, and then moved toward automating intranet and extranet procurement systems.

Read the Real World Case on the next page. We can learn a lot from this example about the challenges and opportunities faced by new companies that compete against a well-established Web-based businesses. See Figure 8.8.

e-Commerce Trends

Figure 8.9 illustrates some of the trends taking place in the e-commerce applications that we introduced at the beginning of this section. Notice how B2C e-commerce moves from simple Web storefronts to interactive marketing capabilities that provide a personalized shopping experience for customers, and then toward a totally integrated Web store that supports a variety of customer shopping experiences. B2C e-commerce is also moving toward a self-service model in which customers configure and customize the products and services they wish to buy, aided by configuration software and online customer support as needed.

B2B e-commerce participants moved quickly from self-service on the Web to configuration and customization capabilities and extranets connecting trading partners. As B2C e-commerce moves toward full-service and wide-selection retail Web portals, B2B is also trending toward the use of e-commerce portals that provide catalog, exchange, and auction markets for business customers within or across industries. Of course, both of these trends are enabled by e-business capabilities like customer relationship management and supply chain management, which are the hallmarks of the customer-focused and internetworked supply chains of a fully e-business-enabled company [23].

Business-to-Consumer e-Commerce

e-commerce applications that focus on the consumer share an important goal: to attract potential buyers, transact goods and services, and build customer loyalty through individual courteous treatment and engaging community features [11].

What does it take to create a successful B2C e-commerce business venture? That's the question that many are asking in the wake of the failures of many pure B2C *dot-com* companies. One obvious answer would be to create a Web business initiative that offers attractive products or services of great customer value, with a business plan based on realistic forecasts of profitability within the first year or two of operation—a condition that was lacking in many failed dot-coms. But such failures have not stemmed the tide of millions of businesses, both large and small, that are moving at least part of their business to the Web. So let's take a look at some essential success factors and Web site capabilities for companies engaged in either B2C or B2B e-commerce. Figure 8.10 provides examples of a few top-rated retail Web companies.

REAL WORLD CASE 2 Entellium, Digg, Peerflix, Zappos, and Jigsaw: Success for Second Movers in e-Commerce

Anyone who has watched short-track speed skating during the Winter Olympics knows that skating with the lead is no easy task. The No. 2 skater gets to conserve precious energy by drafting behind the leader. No. 2 watches the frontrunner's every move, gauging when and where to make a bid for the gold. Now corporate America and speed skating have much in common. There are no safe leads.

For companies that use the Internet as the home base for their businesses, the second-mover advantage seems even more substantial. That's why Paul Johnston is deeply grateful to Marc Benioff. Johnston's Seattle-based start-up, Entellium, has won hundreds of contracts against Benioff's Salesforce.com and other competitors since it moved from Malaysia in 2004, and its revenues grew fivefold in 2005. But what Johnston really likes is not having to sell companies on the concept of letting an outsider host their customer relationship management software.

What makes fast-following the hot strategy of the moment is the relative ease with which founders can get a start-up out on the track and send it chasing the competition. Cheap open-source tools can help you deploy new business software quickly. Offshore manufacturers can quickly churn out anything from semiconductors to engine parts. The Web connects marketers to a vast pool of beta testers, while angel investors and venture capitalists, flush with new funds, stand at the ready.

Of course, fast-following isn't as simple as saying "Me too." To battle established leaders, you need the right product and strategy, and a big dose of savvy. Here's how to show up after the starting gun and still come out on top.

FIGURE 8.8

Entellium is an example of a company that successfully implemented a second mover strategy on the Web.

Number 1: Be better, faster, cheaper, easier

To steal business from Benioff, Johnston knew that Entellium had to offer something different. "This is true for any follower," he says. It's what Johnston calls the "awesome, awesome, not totally xxxx-ed up" approach. The first "awesome" is how Entellium's software works. Johnston, formerly an Apple sales exec, aims to bring to the stodgy world of enterprise software the ease of use of consumer-directed offerings like Google Maps and the role-playing game Everquest. He even hired developers from the gaming industry to borrow interface tricks.

After appealing to customers on usability, Johnston hits them with the price: about 40 percent less than the competition. That's the second "awesome." The last part is making Entellium a less risky decision. Who wants to put their job on the line for a start-up the boss has never heard of? Johnston offers free 24/7 service to make it easier for new customers to stick their necks out.

Number 2: Trip up incumbents with tactics from other fields

Common wisdom would say that the last thing the world needs is another technology news Web site. But Digg founders Jay Adelson and Kevin Rose are uncommonly wise. A year ago, inspired by social-networking sites like MySpace—whose users rank everything from people to music—Adelson and Rose decided to use the same approach to build a better version of tech news site Slashdot. Digg lets readers submit news stories and vote for the ones they think are most important. The top 15 vote-getters make it to the front page.

The formula is working. Between May and November, the number of monthly unique visitors to Digg surged 284 percent to 404,000, eclipsing Slashdot's 367,000, according to ComScore Media Metrix. And Adelson and Rose recently landed $2.8 million from investors, including eBay founder Pierre Omidyar and Netscape cofounder Marc Andreessen.

Moving forward, Adelson and Rose won't be shy about borrowing even more from seemingly unrelated companies. Soon they'll start tracking what members read and offer story recommendations a la Amazon. Digg is also set to branch out into nontechnology stories, which readers will be able to categorize with Del.icio.us-style tags. "A lot of companies are afraid to touch their original technology, to reconsider the premise on which they started the business," Adelson notes. "But when you stop doing that, that's when you get lapped."

Number 3: Swipe their business models and start your own race

When Billy McNair and Danny Robinson were hatching the idea for a new DVD company, Netflix handed them part of their business plan: Consumers had already learned that renting by mail was easy. But McNair and Robinson believed they could do better than rentals. After all, eBay had shown them how.

By mixing together the best of two worlds, the founders came up with Peerflix, a Web site on which people exchange DVDs for a 99-cent transaction fee. Like eBay, Peerflix sits in the middle, linking movie fans and taking a piece of the action. Eager to avoid going head-to-head with eBay, however, McNair and Robinson are starting with lower-ticket items—those that sell for less than $25—for which auctions may not be worth the hassle.

"We've married the best of online rental services and online secondary markets," McNair claims. Since launching in September, Peerflix has helped trade nearly 200,000 DVDs, and the founders are now talking about extending the idea to video games and other items.

Number 4: Follow the biggest leader you can find

When he hatched Zappos six years ago, Nick Swinmum put other online shoe sellers in his cross-hairs. Web-based competitors typically carried a limited number of brands and catered to small niches—say, women's dress shoes or men's outdoor boots. Zappos would crush them, Swinmum reasoned, with an online store that offered every conceivable make and model.

That was the right idea, but it focused on the wrong competitors. The online shoe market was so tiny that even if Zappos dominated it, there wouldn't be enough business for the company to thrive. To grow, it had to steal customers from bricks-and-mortar stores. Before 2001, Zappos didn't carry inventory; rather, the company asked distributors to "drop-ship" directly to consumers. It was an easy, cheap arrangement, but the problem was that Zappos couldn't guarantee service; eight percent of the time customers tried to buy shoes, the desired pair was out of stock. In other words, the experience was nothing like walking into a shoe store. "We realized then who our real competition was, and that we had to find a way to make an inventory model work," Swinmum says.

So Zappos began cozying up to suppliers. Contrary to industry practice, Swinmum shared data with manufacturers on exactly how well their shoes were selling. "Traditionally the vendor-retail relationship was adversarial," he recognizes. "We thought, 'Instead of trying to hide this information from the brands, let's open everything up. They can help us build the business.'" Did they ever. Grateful shoe reps helped Zappos craft promotions to goose sales.

Since targeting traditional shoe stores, Zappos has thrived. In 2001, the company did $8.6 million in sales; the next year it did $32 million. In 2005, Zappos posted more than $300 million in revenues from an expanding line of shoes, handbags, and other leather goods.

Number 5: Aim for the leader's Achilles' heel

When he was VP for sales at online marketing shop Digital Impact, Jim Fowler watched his field reps fail with a growing sense of frustration. Their problem? The leading online databases of corporate information, such as Dun & Bradstreet subsidiary Hoover's, didn't offer the deep, up-to-date contact lists that salespeople need to close deals. But rather than complain about those vendors, Fowler decided to improve on them.

His company, Jigsaw, is a new kind of contact subscription service: All of the names and addresses in Jigsaw's database come from its users. Sales reps pay a minimum of $25 per month to access contacts at thousands of companies—or pay nothing if they contribute 25 contacts per month themselves. Users police the listings to ensure they're current.

Since Jigsaw's launch in December 2004, its database has surged from 200,000 contacts to more than 2 million; some 38,000 subscribers are adding 10,000 new contacts a day. Through Jigsaw you can find more than 16,000 contacts at Medtronic, for example; Hoover's, meanwhile, offers extensive research on the company but only about 30 contacts. According to Fowler, "It's never too late if you are smarter and better than everyone else."

Source: Adapted from Jon Birger, "Second-Mover Advantage," *Fortune*, March 20, 2006; Michael V. Copeland, "Start Last, Finish First," *Business 2.0*, February 2, 2006; Sidra Durst, "Shoe In," *Business 2.0*, December 2006.

CASE STUDY QUESTIONS

1. Is the second-mover advantage always a good business strategy? Defend your answer with examples of the companies in this case.
2. What can a front-runner business do to foil the assaults of second movers? Defend your answer using the examples of the front-runner companies in the case.
3. Do second movers always have the advantage in Web-based business success? Why or why not? Evaluate the five strategies given in the case and the companies that used them to help defend your answer.

REAL WORLD ACTIVITIES

1. Use the Internet to research the current business status of all of the many companies in this case. Are the second movers still successfully using their strategies, or have the first movers foiled their attempts? Have new strong players entered the markets of the first and second movers, or have business, economic, or societal developments occurred to change the nature of competition in these markets?
2. Assume you will start an Internet-based business similar to one of those mentioned in this case or another one of your choice. Would you be a first, second, or later mover in the market you select? How would you differentiate yourself from other competitors or prospective new entrants? Break into small groups to share your ideas and attempt to agree on the best Web-based business opportunity of the group.

FIGURE 8.9 Trends in B2C and B2B e-commerce, and the business strategies and value driving these trends.

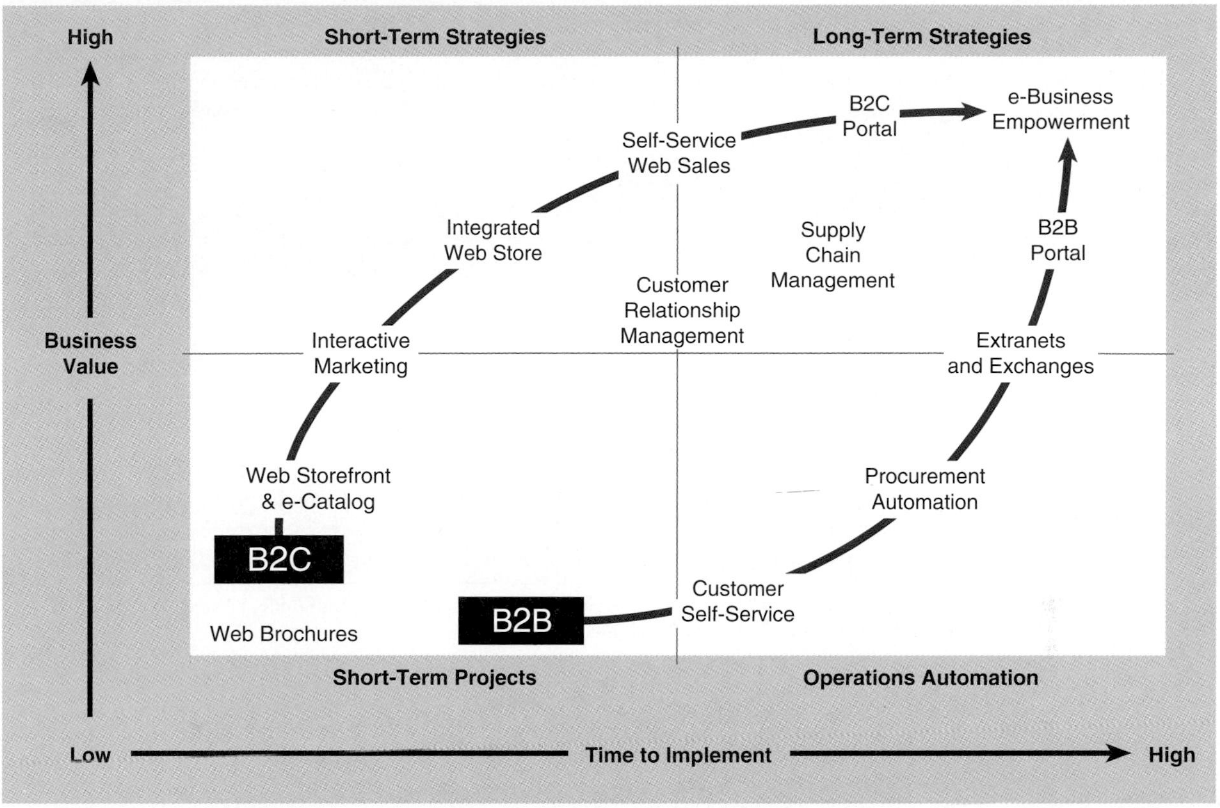

Source: Adapted from Jonathan Rosenoer, Douglas Armstrong, and J. Russell Gates, *The Clickable Corporation: Successful Strategies for Capturing the Internet Advantage* (New York: The Free Press, 1999), p. 24.

e-Commerce Success Factors

On the Internet, the barriers of time, distance, and form are broken down, and businesses are able to transact the sale of goods and services 24 hours a day, 7 days a week, 365 days a year with consumers all over the world. In certain cases, it is even possible to convert a physical good (CDs, packaged software, a newspaper) to a virtual good (MP3 audio, downloadable software, information in HTML format) [11].

A basic fact of Internet retailing is that all retail Web sites are created equal as far as the "location, location, location" imperative of success in retailing is concerned. No site is any closer to its Web customers, and competitors offering similar goods and services may be only a mouse click away. This scenario makes it vital that businesses find ways to build customer satisfaction, loyalty, and relationships, so customers keep coming back to their Web stores. Thus, the key to e-tail success is to optimize several key factors such as selection and value, performance and service efficiency, the look and feel of the site, advertising and incentives to purchase, personal attention, community relationships, and security and reliability. Let's briefly examine each of these factors that are essential to the success of a B2C Web business. See Figure 8.11.

Selection and Value Obviously, a business must offer Web shoppers a good selection of attractive products and services at competitive prices, or the shoppers will quickly click away from a Web store. But a company's prices don't have to be the lowest on the Web if it builds a reputation for high quality, guaranteed satisfaction, and top customer support while shopping and after the sale. For example, top-rated e-tailer REI.com helps you select quality outdoor gear for hiking and other activities with a "How to Choose" section and gives a money-back guarantee on your purchases.

FIGURE 8.10
Examples of a few top-rated retail Web sites.

Top Retail Web Sites
• **Amazon.com** **www.amazon.com** Amazon.com is the exception to the rule that consumers prefer to shop "real world" retailers online. The mother of all shopping sites, Amazon features a vast selection of books, videos, DVDs, CDs, toys, kitchen items, electronics, and even home and garden goods sold to millions of loyal customers.
• **eBay** **www.ebay.com** The fabled auction site operates the world's biggest electronic flea market, with everything from antiques, computers, and coins to Pez dispensers and baseball cards. This site boasts billions of page views per month, and millions of items for sale in thousands of categories supported by thousands of special-interest groups.
• **Eddie Bauer** **www.eddiebauer.com** Sportswear titan Eddie Bauer has integrated its retail channels-store, Web site, and catalog. Shoppers can return an item to any Eddie Bauer store, no matter where it was purchased—a policy other merchants should follow.
• **Lands' End** **www.landsend.com** With several seasons as an online retailer, Lands' End is a pro at meeting shoppers' expectations. One of the best features: Specialty Shoppers. A customer service rep will help you make your selections and answer questions by phone or via a live chat.

Source: Adapted from "Tech Lifestyles: Shopping," Technology Buyers Guide, *Fortune*, Winter 2001, pp. 288–90.

Performance and Service People don't want to be kept waiting when browsing, selecting, or paying in a Web store. A site must be efficiently designed for ease of access, shopping, and buying, with sufficient server power and network capacity to support Web site traffic. Web shopping and customer service must also be friendly and helpful, as well as quick and easy. In addition, products offered should be available in inventory for prompt shipment to the customer.

Look and Feel B2C sites can offer customers an attractive Web storefront, shopping areas, and multimedia product catalogs. These could range from an exciting shopping

FIGURE 8.11
Some of the key factors for success in e-commerce.

e-Commerce Success Factors
• **Selection and Value.** Attractive product selections, competitive prices, satisfaction guarantees, and customer support after the sale.
• **Performance and Service.** Fast, easy navigation, shopping, and purchasing, and prompt shipping and delivery.
• **Look and Feel.** Attractive Web storefront, Web site shopping areas, multimedia product catalog pages, and shopping features.
• **Advertising and Incentives.** Targeted Web page advertising and e-mail promotions, discounts and special offers, including advertising at affiliate sites.
• **Personal Attention.** Personal Web pages, personalized product recommendations, Web advertising and e-mail notices, and interactive support for all customers.
• **Community Relationships.** Virtual communities of customers, suppliers, company representatives, and others via newsgroups, chat rooms, and links to related sites.
• **Security and Reliability.** Security of customer information and Web site transactions, trustworthy product information, and reliable order fulfillment.

FIGURE 8.12 How traditional and Web marketing communications differ in supporting each step of the buying process.

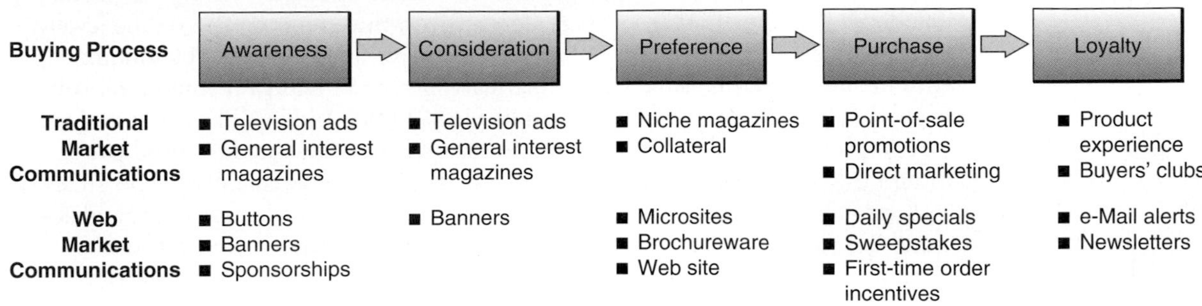

experience with audio, video, and moving graphics to a more simple and comfortable look and feel. Thus, most retail e-commerce sites let customers browse product sections, select products, drop them into a virtual shopping cart, and go to a virtual checkout station when they are ready to pay for their order.

Advertising and Incentives Some Web stores may advertise in traditional media, but most advertise on the Web with targeted and personalized banner ads and other Web page and e-mail promotions. Most B2C sites also offer shoppers incentives to buy and return. Typically, these incentives mean coupons, discounts, special offers, and vouchers for other Web services, sometimes with other e-tailers at cross-linked Web sites. Many Web stores also increase their market reach by being part of Web banner advertising exchange programs with thousand of other Web retailers. Figure 8.12 compares major marketing communications choices in traditional and e-commerce marketing to support each step of the buying process [21].

Personal Attention Personalizing your shopping experience encourages you to buy and make return visits. Thus, e-commerce software can automatically record details of your visits and build user profiles of you and other Web shoppers. Many sites also encourage you to register with them and fill out a personal interest profile. Then, whenever you return, you are welcomed by name or with a personal Web page, greeted with special offers, and guided to those parts of the site in which you are most interested. This *one-to-one marketing* and relationship building power is one of the major advantages of personalized Web retailing.

Community Relationships Giving online customers with special interests a feeling of belonging to a unique group of like-minded individuals helps build customer loyalty and value. Thus, Web site relationship and affinity marketing programs build and promote virtual communities of customers, suppliers, company representatives, and others via a variety of Web-based collaboration tools. Examples include discussion forums or newsgroups, chat rooms, message board systems, and cross-links to related Web site communities.

Security and Reliability As a customer of a successful Web store, you must feel confident that your credit card, personal information, and details of your transactions are secure from unauthorized use. You must also feel that you are dealing with a trustworthy business whose products and other Web site information you can trust to be as advertised. Having your orders filled and shipped as you requested, in the time frame promised, and with good customer support are other measures of an e-tailer's reliability.

Amazon.com: B2C Retailing from A to Z

Amazon (www.amazon.com) is arguably one of the biggest and best virtual retailers on the Web. In 2004, Amazon enjoyed a sales volume in excess of $6.5 billion and expanded its "soup-to-nuts" product offerings with the opening of an online jewelry store. This new Amazon division offers a selection of more than 75,000 unique items, including sterling silver, blue topaz earrings for $15 and a platinum, radiant-cut diamond necklace totaling 31.74 carats for $93,000. And just like the rest of the Amazon product lines, everything about Amazon.com is designed to speed you through the process of browsing, selecting, and ordering merchandise while giving you personalized service at discount prices. Searching for products is quick and accurate, the ordering process easy and fast, confirmation is quick, notifications are accurate and friendly, and delivery is prompt. For most e-buyers, Amazon.com is the first stop when looking for just about anything.

In creating this potential powerhouse of retail services, Amazon.com wants to be more than a Wal-Mart of the Web. Rather, Amazon wants to be a next-generation retail commerce portal. Imagine a customized site where—through a personalized shopping service and alliances with thousands of other dealers—you can shop easily with a trusted brand as you research the features, prices, and availability of millions of products from a single storefront that has Amazon's—and your—name on it.

That's what has brought Amazon this far in its first years of business: an exhaustive focus on convenience, selection, and personalization. It has lived up to its billing as having "Earth's Biggest Selection" by building an inventory of millions of products. It was also among the first Net stores to facilitate credit card purchases, greet customers by name and offer customized home pages, send purchase recommendations via e-mail, and number and explain each step in the purchasing process. This combination of vast selection, efficiency, discount prices, and personal service is why Amazon is thought of as the B2C Web site that has everything from A to Z [4, 25].

Web Store Requirements

Most business-to-consumer e-commerce ventures take the form of retail business sites on the World Wide Web. Whether a huge retail Web portal like Amazon.com or a small specialty Web retailer, the primary focus of such e-tailers is to develop, operate, and manage their Web sites so they become high-priority destinations for consumers who will repeatedly choose to go there to buy products and services. Thus, these Web sites must be able to demonstrate the key factors for e-commerce success that we have just covered. In this section, let's discuss the essential Web store requirements that you would have to implement to support a successful retail business on the Web, as summarized and illustrated in Figure 8.13.

Developing a Web Store

Before you can launch your own retail store on the Internet, you must build an e-commerce Web site. Many companies use simple Web site design software tools and predesigned templates provided by their Web site hosting service to construct their Web retail store. That includes building your Web storefront and product catalog Web pages, as well as tools to provide shopping cart features, process orders, handle credit card payments, and so forth. Of course, larger companies can use their own software developers or hire an outside Web site development contractor to build a custom-designed e-commerce site. Also, like most companies, you can contract with your ISP (Internet service provider) or a specialized Web hosting company to operate and maintain your B2C Web site.

Once you build your Web site, it must be developed as a retail Web business by marketing it in a variety of ways that attract visitors to your site and transform them

FIGURE 8.13 To develop a successful e-commerce business, these Web store requirements must be implemented by a company or its Web site hosting service.

Developing a Web Store		
• **Build**	• **Market**	
Web site design tools	Web page advertising	
Site design templates	E-mail promotions	
Custom design services	Web advertising exchanges with affiliate sites	
Web site hosting	Search engine registrations	
Serving Your Customers		
• **Serve**	• **Transact**	• **Support**
Personalized Web pages	Flexible order process	Web site online help
Dynamic multimedia catalog	Credit card processing	Customer service e-mail
Catalog search engine	Shipping and tax calculations	Discussion groups and chat rooms
Integrated shopping cart	E-mail order notifications	Links to related sites
Managing a Web Store		
• **Manage**	• **Operate**	• **Protect**
Web site usage statistics	24×7 Web site hosting	User password protection
Sales and inventory reports	Online tech support	Encrypted order processing
Customer account management	Scalable network capacity	Encrypted Web site administration
Links to accounting system	Redundant servers and power	Network firewalls and security monitors

into loyal Web customers. So your Web site should include Web page and e-mail advertising and promotions for Web visitors and customers, as well as Web advertising exchange programs with other Web stores. Also, you can register your Web business with its own domain name (e.g., yourstore.com), as well as registering your Web site with the major Web search engines and directories to help Web surfers find your site more easily. In addition, you might consider affiliating as a small business partner with large Web portals like Yahoo! and Netscape, large e-tailers and auction sites like Amazon and eBay, and small business e-commerce portals like Microsoft's Small Business Center.

Freemerchant and Google AdWords: In the Business of Helping Businesses Get Business

Freemerchant and Google AdWords are just two examples of the many companies that help small businesses get on, and get business from, the Web. Freemerchant.com enables you to set up a Web store for free by choosing from over 60 design templates. Its service includes Web hosting on secure networks, shopping cart and order processing, and providing common database software for importing product catalog data. Additional fee-based services include banner ad exchanges, domain and search engine registrations, and enabling product data to be listed on eBay and sales data exported to the QuickBooks accounting system (see Figure 8.14).

Google AdWords is where e-businesses turn when they have their store ready to open and they want to advertise their products and services. AdWords advertisers have the ability to target their advertisements to over 225 countries in six languages with support for up to six international currencies. Once the account has been set up and the keywords selected, ads go live instantly.

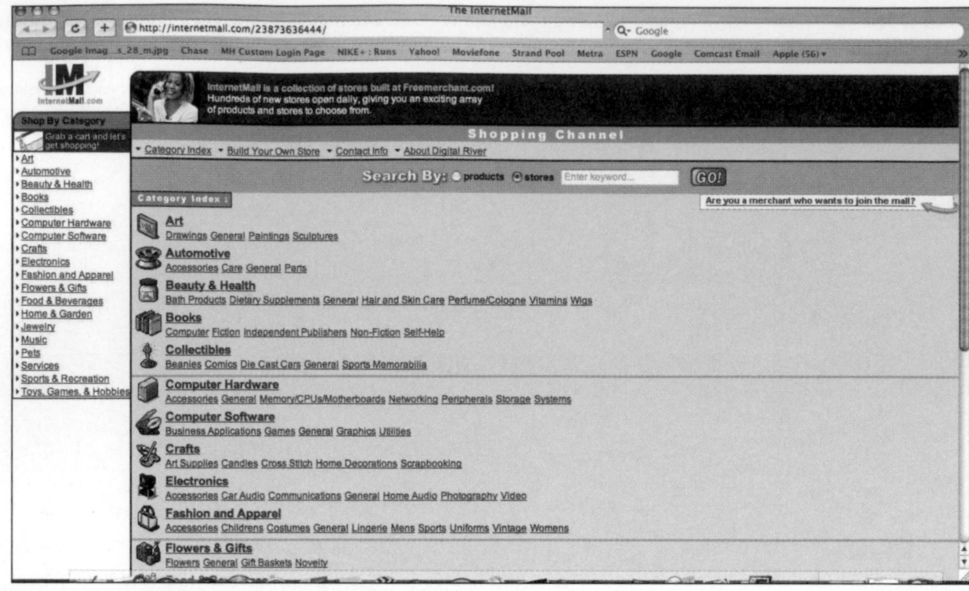

FIGURE 8.14
FreeMerchant is one of many companies offering retail Web site development and hosting services.

Ads on AdWords are ranked on the page based on a formula of cost-per-click times the clickthrough rate, which enables an ad's rank to improve without costing more. Advertisers who use the AdWords program enjoy a strong and growing distribution network not only from Google but also through affiliates like America Online, Ask.com, EarthLink, Lycos Canada, Netscape, CompuServe, AT&T Worldnet, and NYTimes.com.

Google recently started serving Google AdWords on content sites (such as HowStuffWorks.com) and via ad networks like Fastclick and BurstNet, as well as on Google search results, in an attempt to improve the program's reach and get better results for advertisers. It doesn't cost any extra. The Google AdWords shown on content sites is highly targeted and is a "feather in the cap" of Google. No other search engine has achieved this kind of global reach. You pick the keywords, and AdWords gets the results [20, 24].

Serving Your Customers

Once your retail store is on the Web and receiving visitors, the Web site must help you welcome and serve them personally and efficiently so that they become loyal customers. So most e-tailers use several Web site tools to create user profiles, customer files, and personal Web pages and promotions that help them develop a one-to-one relationship with their customers. This effort includes creating incentives to encourage visitors to register, developing *Web cookie files* to automatically identify returning visitors, or contracting with Web site tracking companies like DoubleClick and others for software to automatically record and analyze the details of the Web site behavior and preferences of Web shoppers.

Of course, your Web site should have the look and feel of an attractive, friendly, and efficient Web store. That means having e-commerce features like a dynamically changing and updated multimedia catalog, a fast catalog search engine, and a convenient shopping cart system that is integrated with Web shopping, promotions, payment, shipping, and customer account information. Your e-commerce order processing software should be fast and able to adjust to personalized promotions and customer options like gift handling, special discounts, credit card or other payments, and shipping and tax alternatives. Also, automatically sending your customers e-mail notices to document when orders are processed and shipped is a top customer service feature of e-tail transaction processing.

Providing customer support for your Web store is an essential Web site capability. Thus, many e-tail sites offer help menus, tutorials, and lists of FAQs (frequently asked questions) to provide self-help features for Web shoppers. Of course, e-mail correspondence with customer service representatives of your Web store offers more personal assistance to customers. Establishing Web site discussion groups and chat rooms for your customers and store personnel to interact helps create a more personal community that can provide invaluable support to customers, as well as build customer loyalty. Providing links to related Web sites from your Web store can help customers find additional information and resources, as well as earning commission income from the affiliate marketing programs of other Web retailers. For example, the Amazon.com Affiliate program pays commissions of up to 15 percent for purchases made by Web shoppers clicking to its Web store from your site.

Managing a Web Store

A Web retail store must be managed as both a business and a Web site, and most e-commerce hosting companies offer software and services to help you do just that. For example, companies like Freemerchant, Prodigy Biz, and Verio provide their hosting clients with a variety of management reports that record and analyze Web store traffic, inventory, and sales results. Other services build customer lists for e-mail and Web page promotions or provide customer relationship management features to help retain Web customers. Also, some e-commerce software includes links to download inventory and sales data into accounting packages like QuickBooks for bookkeeping and preparation of financial statements and reports.

Of course, Web hosting companies must enable their Web store clients to be available online 24 hours a day and seven days a week all year. This availability requires them to build or contract for sufficient network capacity to handle peak Web traffic loads and redundant network servers and power sources to respond to system or power failures. Most hosting companies provide e-commerce software that uses passwords and encryption to protect Web store transactions and customer records and employ network firewalls and security monitors to repel hacker attacks and other security threats. Many hosting services also offer their clients 24-hour tech support to help them with any technical problems that arise. We will discuss these and other e-commerce security management issues in Chapter 11.

Verio Inc.: Web Site Management

Verio Inc. (www.verio.com) is an example of one of the world's leading Web hosting companies. Verio provides complete software, computing, and network resources to Web hosting companies, as well as offering e-commerce development and hosting services to Web retailers. Verio also offers a Web start-up and development service for small businesses called SiteMerlin (www.sitemerlin.com). Verio guarantees 98.9 percent Web site uptime to its e-commerce customers, with 24/7 server monitoring and customer support. Verio hosts more than 10,000 small- and medium-sized Web businesses; has a network hosting alliance with Sun Microsystems and an Oracle Web database application service; and provides hosting services to Terra Lycos and other Web hosting companies [24].

Business-to-Business e-Commerce

Business-to-business electronic commerce is the wholesale and supply side of the commercial process, where businesses buy, sell, or trade with other businesses. B2B electronic commerce relies on many different information technologies, most of which are implemented at e-commerce Web sites on the World Wide Web and corporate intranets and extranets. B2B applications include electronic catalog systems, electronic trading systems such as exchange and auction portals, electronic data interchange, electronic funds transfers, and so on. All of the factors for building a successful retail

Web site we discussed previously also apply to wholesale Web sites for business-to-business electronic commerce.

In addition, many businesses are integrating their Web-based e-commerce systems with their e-business systems for supply chain management, customer relationship management, and online transaction processing, as well as with their traditional, or legacy, computer-based accounting and business information systems. This integration ensures that all electronic commerce activities are integrated with e-business processes and supported by up-to-date corporate inventory and other databases, which in turn are automatically updated by Web sales activities. Let's look at a successful example.

Cisco Systems: B2B Marketplace Success

The e-commerce Web site operated by Cisco Systems enables corporate users to purchase routers, switches, and other hardware that customers need to build high-speed information networks. Over 70 percent of Cisco's sales take place using this method.

So what has made Cisco so successful? Some would argue that its market—networking hardware—is a prime product to sell online because the customer base is composed almost entirely of IT department staffers and consultants. To some degree, this is certainly true. On the other hand, competitors initially scoffed at Cisco's efforts due to the inherent complexity of its product. However, it's difficult to dispute that Cisco has built an online store with functionality and usefulness that is a model of success in the B2B commerce world.

Cisco was able to achieve success largely due to the variety of service offerings made available throughout its purchasing process. In addition to simply providing a catalog and transaction processing facilities, Cisco includes a personalized interface for buyers and an extensive customer support section with contact information, technical documents, software updates, product configuration tools, and even online training and certification courses for Cisco hardware. Also, Cisco provides direct integration with its internal back-end systems for frequent customers and makes software available that customers can use to design custom links to their own line-of-business software from such players as SAP America, PeopleSoft, and Oracle.

Cisco has also made a concerted effort to ensure that postsale customer support is available to buyers of every kind. For most large corporations, this support means diligent account management and dedicated support representatives to troubleshoot problems and aid in complex network design. For smaller businesses that may be installing their first routers or switches, Cisco includes recommended configurations and simple FAQs to get users up and running.

Like any mature virtual marketplace, Cisco's online presence integrates directly with Cisco's internal applications and databases to automatically manage inventory and production. Cisco even allows vendors such as HP, PeopleSoft, and IBM to exchange design data to enable easy network configuration troubleshooting online [11].

e-Commerce Marketplaces

The latest e-commerce transaction systems are scaled and customized to allow buyers and sellers to meet in a variety of high-speed trading platforms: auctions, catalogs, and exchanges [15].

Businesses of any size can now buy everything from chemicals to electronic components, excess electrical energy, construction materials, or paper products at business-to-business **e-commerce marketplaces**. Figure 8.15 outlines five major types of e-commerce marketplaces used by businesses today. However, many B2B **portals** provide several types of marketplaces. Thus, they may offer an electronic **catalog** shopping and ordering site for products from many suppliers in an industry. Or they may serve as an **exchange** for

FIGURE 8.15
Types of e-commerce marketplaces.

e-Commerce Marketplaces
• **One to many:** Sell-side marketplaces. Host one major supplier, who dictates product catalog offerings and prices. Examples: Cisco.com and Dell.com.
• **Many to one:** Buy-side marketplaces. Attract many suppliers that flock to these exchanges to bid on the business of a major buyer like GE or AT&T.
• **Some to many:** Distribution marketplaces. Unite major suppliers who combine their product catalogs to attract a larger audience of buyers. Examples: VerticalNet and Works.com.
• **Many to some:** Procurement marketplaces. Unite major buyers who combine their purchasing catalogs to attract more suppliers and thus more competition and lower prices. Examples: the auto industry's Covisint and energy industry's Pantellos.
• **Many to many:** Auction marketplaces used by many buyers and sellers that can create a variety of buyers' or sellers' auctions to dynamically optimize prices. Examples are eBay and FreeMarkets.

buying and selling via a bid-ask process or at negotiated prices. Very popular are electronic **auction** Web sites for B2B auctions of products and services. Figure 8.16 illustrates a B2B trading system that offers exchange, auction, and reverse auction (where sellers bid for the business of a buyer) electronic markets [15].

Many of these B2B **e-commerce portals** are developed and hosted by third-party *market-maker* companies who serve as **infomediaries** that bring buyers and sellers together in catalog, exchange, and auction markets. Infomediaries are companies that serve as intermediaries in e-business and e-commerce transactions. Examples are Ariba, Commerce One, and VerticalNet, to name a few successful companies. All provide e-commerce marketplace software products and services to power business Web portals for e-commerce transactions.

These B2B e-commerce sites make business purchasing decisions faster, simpler, and more cost-effective, because companies can use Web systems to research and transact with many vendors. Business buyers get one-stop shopping and accurate purchasing information. They also get impartial advice from infomediaries that they can't get from the sites hosted by suppliers and distributors. Thus, companies can negotiate

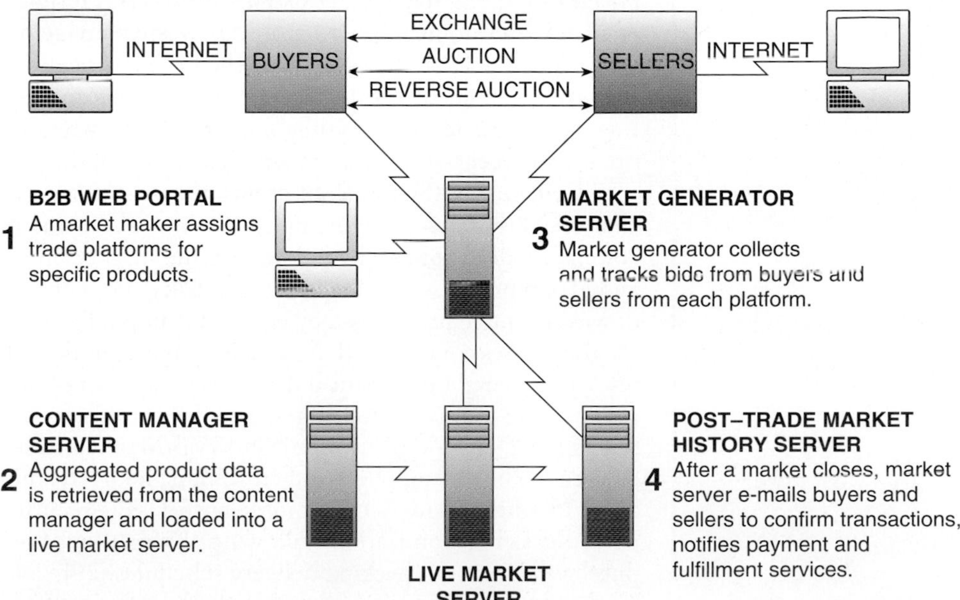

FIGURE 8.16
An example of a B2B e-commerce Web portal that offers exchange, auction, and reverse auction electronic markets.

or bid for better prices from a larger pool of vendors. And of course, suppliers benefit from easy access to customers from all over the globe [15]. Now, let's look at a real world example.

ChemConnect and Heritage Services: Public and Private B2B Exchanges

Public B2B Exchanges The pricing was becoming cutthroat in the closing minutes of the online auction. A North American chemical producer offered to sell a plastics stabilizer to a *Fortune* 20 firm for $4.35 per kilogram. But with two minutes left, a lower price from a Chinese company flashed across the computer screens at ChemConnect (www.chemconnect.com), the San Francisco operator of a public online marketplace for the chemical industry. The North American producer lowered its price. Back and forth the two firms went as ChemConnect officials saw the price drop penny by penny. The Chinese offered $4.23. Finally, the North American company won the $500,000 contract with an offer of $4.20. The auction was just one of 20 taking place on ChemConnect's Web site one August morning, as companies from North America, Europe, and Asia bid on the lucrative six-month contracts.

ChemConnect hosted the event during several hours on a recent Monday morning. The same bidding process without the online auction would have taken at least three months, according to the company that held the event—even using e-mail. In the past, this company sent e-mails to all the suppliers it wanted to bid on its business. Then in a few days those companies would respond with their opening bids. The buyer would counter. Up to a week elapsed between every round.

Not only does ChemConnect help save companies time when they're buying, but it offers a central hub in a fragmented industry. More than 89,000 companies around the world produce chemicals, according to the American Chemical Council. ChemConnect, housed on one floor of a San Francisco high-rise, allows many of them to find suppliers or buyers they did not know existed.

Private B2B Exchanges Heritage Environmental Services President Ken Price agreed to enter two B2B Web public auctions, hosted by FreeMarkets (now owned by Ariba), to bid on contracts in 2001. But Heritage didn't end up winning. Not only that, the online auction process emphasized price, meaning Heritage had to lower its fees to compete.

Heritage managers quickly concluded that this flavor of Net commerce wasn't for them. Instead, they decided on a different strategy: building their own online portal to link Heritage with existing customers. Heritage's B2B Web-based exchange lets customers order hazardous-waste management services and keep tabs on their accounts. It also speeds up the billing process because it accepts payment for services online. "What we've got is a nice central focal point where everyone in the process can see what's going on," says Price, who expects his company to book up to 15 percent of its business this year through the private portal.

Heritage is at the forefront of business-to-business e-commerce: private exchanges. This form of online link appeals to a growing number of large and small companies disappointed by public Internet markets intended to facilitate auctions and group purchasing. Like Heritage, many suppliers have been unhappy with the downward price pressures they encounter in public Internet markets.

Businesses concerned that participating in public B2B exchanges would put sales information and other critical data in the hands of customers and competitors are also turning to private exchanges. Smaller companies such as Heritage, as well as giants like Dell Computer, Intel, and Wal-Mart, have set up private online exchanges to link to suppliers and customers, help streamline the business, and boost sales. Private exchanges offer more control, say executives at these companies, and permit easier customization—allowing automation of processes such as sending purchase orders or checking delivery schedules [29].

Clicks and Bricks in e-Commerce

Companies are recognizing that success will go to those who can execute clicks-and-mortar strategies that bridge the physical and virtual worlds. Different companies will need to follow very different paths in deciding how closely—or loosely—to integrate their Internet initiatives with their traditional operations [9].

Figure 8.17 illustrates the spectrum of alternatives and benefit trade-offs that e-business enterprises face when choosing an e-commerce **clicks-and-bricks strategy**. E-business managers must answer this question: Should we integrate our e-commerce virtual business operations with our traditional physical business operations or keep them separate? As Figure 8.17 shows, companies have been implementing a range of integration/separation strategies and made key benefits trade-offs in answering that question. Let's take a look at several alternatives [10].

e-Commerce Integration

The Internet is just another channel that gets plugged into the business architecture [10].

So says CIO Bill Seltzer of the office supply retailer Office Depot, which fully integrates its OfficeDepot.com e-commerce sales channel into its traditional business operations. Thus, Office Depot is a prime example of why many companies have chosen integrated clicks-and-bricks strategies, where their e-commerce business is integrated in some major ways into the traditional business operations of a company. The business case for such strategies rests on:

- Capitalizing on any unique strategic capabilities that may exist in a company's traditional business operations that could be used to support an e-commerce business.
- Gaining several strategic benefits of integrating e-commerce into a company's traditional business, such as sharing established brands and key business information, joint buying power, and distribution efficiencies.

For example, Office Depot already had a successful catalog sales business with a professional call center and a fleet of over 2,000 delivery trucks. Its 1,825 stores and 30 warehouses were networked by a sophisticated information system that provided complete customer, vendor, order, and product inventory data in real time. These business resources made an invaluable foundation for coordinating Office Depot's e-commerce activities and customer services with its catalog business and physical

FIGURE 8.17 Companies have a spectrum of alternatives and benefit trade-offs when deciding on an integrated or separate e-commerce business.

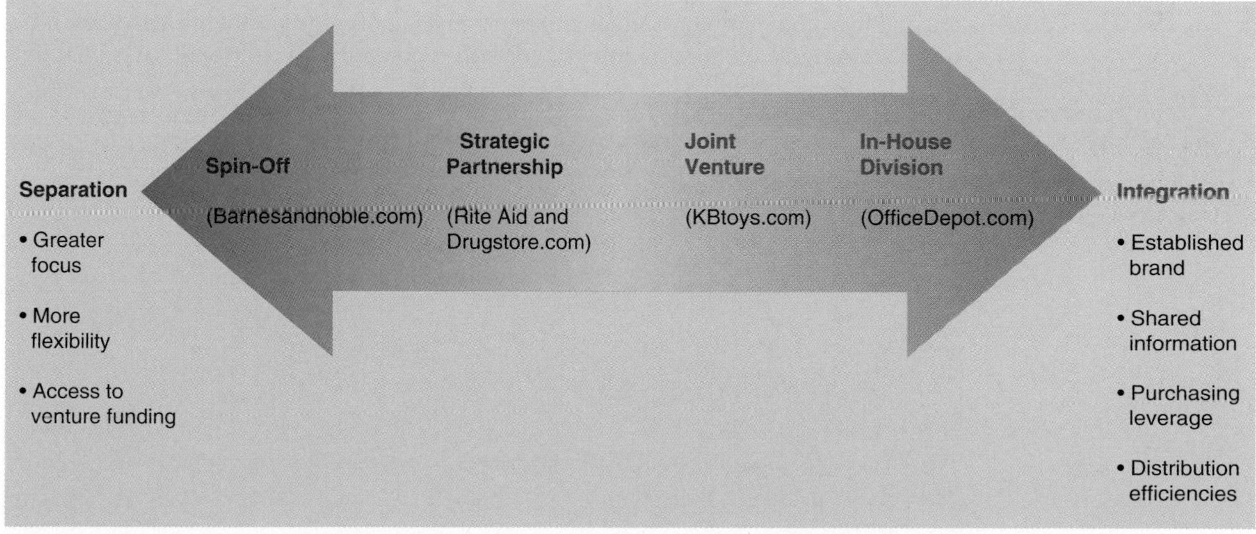

stores. Thus, customers can shop at OfficeDepot.com at their home or business or at in-store kiosks. Then they can choose to pick up their purchases at the stores or have them delivered. In addition, the integration of Web-enabled e-commerce applications within Office Depot's traditional store and catalog operations has helped increase the traffic at their physical stores and improved the catalog operation's productivity and average order size.

Other Clicks-and-Bricks Strategies

As Figure 8.17 illustrates, other clicks-and-bricks strategies range from partial e-commerce integration using joint ventures and strategic partnerships to complete separation via the spin-off of an independent e-commerce company.

For example, KBtoys.com is an e-commerce joint venture of KB Online Holdings LLC, created by toy retailer KB Toys and BrainPlay.com, formerly an e-tailer of children's products. The company is 80 percent owned by KB Toys but has independent management teams and separate distribution systems. However, KBtoys.com has successfully capitalized on the shared brand name and buying power of KB Toys, as well as the ability of its customers to return purchases to over 1,300 KB Toys stores, which also heavily promotes the e-commerce site.

The strategic partnership of the Rite-Aid retail drugstore chain and Drugstore.com is a good example of a less integrated e-commerce venture. Rite-Aid only owns about 25 percent of Drugstore.com, which has an independent management team and a separate business brand. However, both companies share the decreased costs and increased revenue benefits of joint buying power, an integrated distribution center, co-branded pharmacy products, and joint prescription fulfillment at Rite-Aid stores.

Finally, let's look at an example of the benefits and challenges of a completely separate clicks-and-bricks strategy. Barnesandnoble.com was created as an independent e-commerce company that was spun off by the Barnes & Noble book retail chain. This status enabled it to gain several hundred million dollars in venture capital funding, create an entrepreneurial culture, attract quality management, maintain a high degree of business flexibility, and accelerate decision making. But the book e-retailer has done poorly since its founding and failed to gain market share from Amazon.com, its leading competitor. Many business analysts say that the failure of Barnes & Noble to integrate some of the marketing and operations of Barnesandnoble.com within their thousands of bookstores meant it forfeited a key strategic business opportunity.

e-Commerce Channel Choices

Some of the key questions that the management of companies must answer in making a clicks-and-bricks decision and developing the resulting e-commerce channel are outlined in Figure 8.18. An **e-commerce channel** is the marketing or sales channel created by a company to conduct and manage its chosen e-commerce activities. How this e-commerce channel is integrated with a company's traditional sales channels

FIGURE 8.18
Key questions for developing an e-commerce channel strategy.

A Checklist for Channel Development

1. What audiences are we attempting to reach?
2. What action do we want those audiences to take? To learn about us, to give us information about themselves, to make an inquiry, to buy something from our site, to buy something through another channel?
3. Who owns the e-commerce channel within the organization?
4. Is the e-commerce channel planned alongside other channels?
5. Do we have a process for generating, approving, releasing, and withdrawing content?
6. Will our brands translate to the new channel or will they require modification?
7. How will we market the channel itself?

(e.g., retail/wholesale outlets, catalog sales, direct sales) is a major consideration in developing its e-commerce strategy [16].

Thus, the examples in this section emphasize that there is no universal clicks-and-bricks e-commerce strategy or e-commerce channel choice for every company, industry, or type of business. Both e-commerce integration and separation have major business benefits and shortcomings. Deciding on a clicks-and-bricks strategy and e-commerce channel depends heavily on whether a company's unique business operations provide strategic capabilities and resources to successfully support a profitable business model for its e-commerce channel. As these examples show, most companies are implementing some measure of clicks-and-bricks integration, because "the benefits of integration are almost always too great to abandon entirely" [10].

Citigroup: Think Business Issues First, Technology Second

Despite massive spending on digital technologies in the last few years, few financial services firms have succeeded in translating their digital investments into customer and shareholder value. To reap the huge potential benefits of the new digital technologies, companies must look beyond such unfocused goals as "establishing a Web presence" and concentrate instead on reinventing their business designs. In addition, organizations must redirect their fascination with new technologies toward an honest assessment of the important business issues and goals that need to be addressed.

Why have financial services firms failed to translate digital investments into value? Many have been rushing onto the Web and installing related technologies without first asking whether moving online can address their most pressing business issues or help them take advantage of specific business opportunities. Citigroup's e-Citi initiative provides a striking case study in this regard. From 1997 through 1999, Citigroup invested over $1 billion in e-Citi. Formed with ambitious goals for complementing current businesses, creating new ones, and capturing new customers and profits, e-Citi took a centralized approach to e-commerce that failed to create attractive e-commerce offerings for the business units. It took three years of steadily increasing losses before Citigroup finally decentralized e-Citi and its resources and established, for example, a consumer e-business unit and a parallel e-business effort focused on corporate customers.

e-Citi's job was to keep all of Citigroup on its toes—partly by competing with the very bank, credit card company, and other businesses that made Citigroup a $230 billion giant. There was to be an e-Citibank called Citi f/i and a financial portal called Finance.com. The e-Citi unit soon had 1,600 employees and more than 100 U.S. Web sites. The idea: to cannibalize their business before someone else did.

The only thing e-Citi was successful at was spending money. In online banking, for example, Citigroup was so determined to make Citi f/i an independent operation that customers of the online bank weren't considered the same as regular Citibank customers and therefore couldn't use Citibank branches. Depositors of the new Citi f/i felt betrayed and quickly became dissatisfied. The online bank drew a mere 30,000 accounts versus 146 million for the rest of Citigroup's banking operations. By March 2000, word came down from Citigroup Chairman Sandy Weill: e-commerce initiatives must be part of the existing business, not self-appointed upstarts trying to be competitors. The most interesting part of this directive was its direct contradiction of the original e-Citi mandate issued by Chairman Weill less than 36 months earlier. Several worldwide divisions of Citigroup, such as Asia-Pacific, expressed open disapproval of the e-Citi initiative and began forming their own regional e-commerce initiatives. As an example, Citibank Asia-Pacific broke away from the e-Citi initiative in early 2000 and, in contrast to e-Citi's $1 billion spent over three years with no marketable products, generated 10 new profitable e-financial products for around $1.4 million in less than 10 months!

Following the refocusing of e-Citi, by early 2001, the results were easy to see. The number of online customers was up 80 percent because Citibank's and e-Citi's credit card operations were pushing Web services themselves, instead of leaving that mostly to e-Citi. Citigroup now serves 10 million customers online. e-Citi's staff was scaled back to only 100 people, and it was limited to facilitating the implementation of projects proposed by the various regional Internet operating groups. The more than 100 Web sites were trimmed to 38, and the reported loss for online efforts in the first half of 2001 was down 41 percent, to $67 million, from a loss of $114 million a year before. By shifting its attention from the latest and greatest technologies to the latest and greatest business initiatives, Citigroup turned e-failure into e-success [14, 22].

Summary

- **Electronic Commerce.** Electronic commerce encompasses the entire online process of developing, marketing, selling, delivering, servicing, and paying for products and services. The Internet and related technologies and e-commerce Web sites on the World Wide Web and corporate intranets and extranets serve as the business and technology platforms for e-commerce marketplaces for consumers and businesses in the basic categories of business-to-consumer (B2C), business-to-business (B2B), and consumer-to-consumer (C2C) e-commerce. The essential processes that should be implemented in all e-commerce applications—access control and security, personalizing and profiling, search management, content management, catalog management, payment systems, workflow management, event notification, and collaboration and trading—are summarized in Figure 8.4.
- **e-Commerce Issues.** Many e-business enterprises are moving toward offering full-service B2C and B2B e-commerce portals supported by integrated customer-focused processes and internetworked supply chains, as illustrated in Figure 8.9. In addition, companies must evaluate a variety of e-commerce integration or separation alternatives and benefit trade-offs when choosing a clicks-and-bricks strategy and e-commerce channel, as summarized in Figures 8.17 and 8.18.
- **B2C e-Commerce.** Businesses typically sell products and services to consumers at e-commerce Web sites that provide attractive Web pages, multimedia catalogs, interactive order processing, secure electronic payment systems, and online customer support. However, successful e-tailers build customer satisfaction and loyalty by optimizing factors outlined in Figure 8.11, such as selection and value, performance and service efficiency, the look and feel of the site, advertising and incentives to purchase, personal attention, community relationships, and security and reliability. In addition, a Web store has several key business requirements, including building and marketing a Web business, serving and supporting customers, and managing a Web store, as summarized in Figure 8.13.
- **B2B e-Commerce.** Business-to-business applications of e-commerce involve electronic catalog, exchange, and auction marketplaces that use Internet, intranet, and extranet Web sites and portals to unite buyers and sellers, as summarized in Figure 8.15 and illustrated in Figure 8.16. Many B2B e-commerce portals are developed and operated for a variety of industries by third-party market-maker companies called infomediaries, which may represent consortiums of major corporations.

Key Terms and Concepts

These are the key terms and concepts of this chapter. The page number of their first explanation is in parentheses.

1. Clicks-and-bricks strategy (313)
2. e-commerce channel (314)
3. e-commerce marketplaces (310)
   a. Auction (311)
   b. Catalog (310)
   c. Exchange (310)
   d. Portal (310)
4. Electronic commerce (288)
   a. Business-to-business (B2B) (291)
   b. Business-to-consumer (B2C) (291)
   c. Consumer-to-consumer (C2C) (291)
5. Electronic funds transfer (EFT) (297)

6. e-commerce processes (292)
   a. Access control and security (292)
   b. Content and catalog management (294)
   c. Collaboration and trading (297)
   d. Electronic payment systems (297)
   e. Event notification (296)
   f. Profiling and personalizing (293)
   g. Search management (294)
   h. Workflow management (295)
7. Infomediaries (311)

Review Quiz

Match one of the key terms and concepts listed previously with each of the brief examples or definitions that follow. Try to find the best fit for the answers that seem to fit more than one term or concept. Defend your choices.

____ 1. The online process of developing, marketing, selling, delivering, servicing, and paying for products and services.

____ 2. Business selling to consumers at retail Web stores is an example.

____ 3. Using an e-commerce portal for auctions by business customers and their suppliers is an example.

____ 4. Using an e-commerce Web site for auctions among consumers is an example.

____ 5. E-commerce applications must implement several major categories of interrelated processes such as search management and catalog management.

____ 6. Helps to establish mutual trust between you and an e-tailer at an e-commerce site.

____ 7. Tracks your Web site behavior to provide you with an individualized Web store experience.

____ 8. Develops, generates, delivers, and updates information to you at a Web site.

____ 9. Ensures that proper e-commerce transactions, decisions, and activities are performed to better serve you.

____ 10. Sends you an e-mail when what you ordered at an e-commerce site has been shipped.

____ 11. Includes matchmaking, negotiation, and mediation processes among buyers and sellers.

____ 12. Companies that serve as intermediaries in e-commerce transactions.

____ 13. A Web site for e-commerce transactions.

____ 14. An e-commerce marketplace that may provide catalog, exchange, or auction service for businesses or consumers.

____ 15. Buyers bidding for the business of a seller.

____ 16. Marketplace for bid (buy) and ask (sell) transactions.

____ 17. The most widely used type of marketplace in B2C e-commerce.

____ 18. The marketing or sales channel created by a company to conduct and manage its e-commerce activities.

____ 19. The processing of money and credit transfers between businesses and financial institutions.

____ 20. Ways to provide efficient, convenient, and secure payments in e-commerce.

____ 21. Companies can evaluate and choose from several e-commerce integration alternatives.

Discussion Questions

1. Most businesses should engage in electronic commerce on the Internet. Do you agree or disagree with this statement? Explain your position.
2. Are you interested in investing in, owning, managing, or working for a business that is primarily engaged in electronic commerce on the Internet? Explain your position.
3. Refer to the Real World Case on eBay versus Google and Microsoft in the chapter. What recent or new consumer uses of the Internet may these companies be overlooking or underutilizing that would help their competitive positions? Defend your proposals.
4. Why do you think there have been so many business failures among "dot-com" companies that were devoted only to retail e-commerce?
5. Do the e-commerce success factors listed in Figure 8.11 guarantee success for an e-commerce business venture? Give a few examples of what else could go wrong and how you would confront such challenges.
6. If personalizing a customer's Web site experience is a key success factor, then electronic profiling processes to track visitor Web site behavior are necessary. Do you agree or disagree with this statement? Explain your position.

7. All corporate procurement should be accomplished in e-commerce auction marketplaces, instead of using B2B Web sites that feature fixed-price catalogs or negotiated prices. Explain your position on this proposal.
8. Refer to the Real World Case on Entellium, Digg, Peerflix, Zappos, and Jigsaw in the chapter. Assume you are starting a Web-based business. Are any economic, business, or societal developments occurring that are being overlooked as new Web-based business opportunities, or would you choose a second-mover strategy against an established Web-business? Discuss the reasons for your choice of a Web-based business.
9. If you were starting an e-commerce Web store, which of the business requirements summarized in Figure 8.13 would you primarily do yourself, and which would you outsource to a Web development or hosting company? Why?
10. Refer to the Real World Case on Yahoo and Flickr at the end of this chapter. Can social networking help a Web-based business be more successful? Why or why not?

Analysis Exercises

Complete the following exercises as individual or group projects that apply chapter concepts to real-world business situations.

1. **Small Business e-Commerce Portals**

On the net, small businesses have become big business. And a really big business, Microsoft, wants a piece of the action. The company's Small Business Center (www.microsoft.com/smallbusiness) is one of many sites offering advice and services for small businesses moving online. Most features, whether free or paid, are what you'd expect: lots of links and information along the lines established by Prodigy Biz (www.prodigybiz.com) or Entrabase.com. Small Business Center, however, stands out for its affordable advertising and marketing services. See Figure 8.19.

One program helps businesses create banner ads and places them on a collection of Web sites that it claims are visited by 60 percent of the Web surfing community. With its "Banner Network Ads" program, buyers don't pay a huge fee upfront, and they don't run the risk that a huge number of visitors will unexpectedly drive up clickthrough commissions. Instead, this program allows small business to pay a small, fixed fee

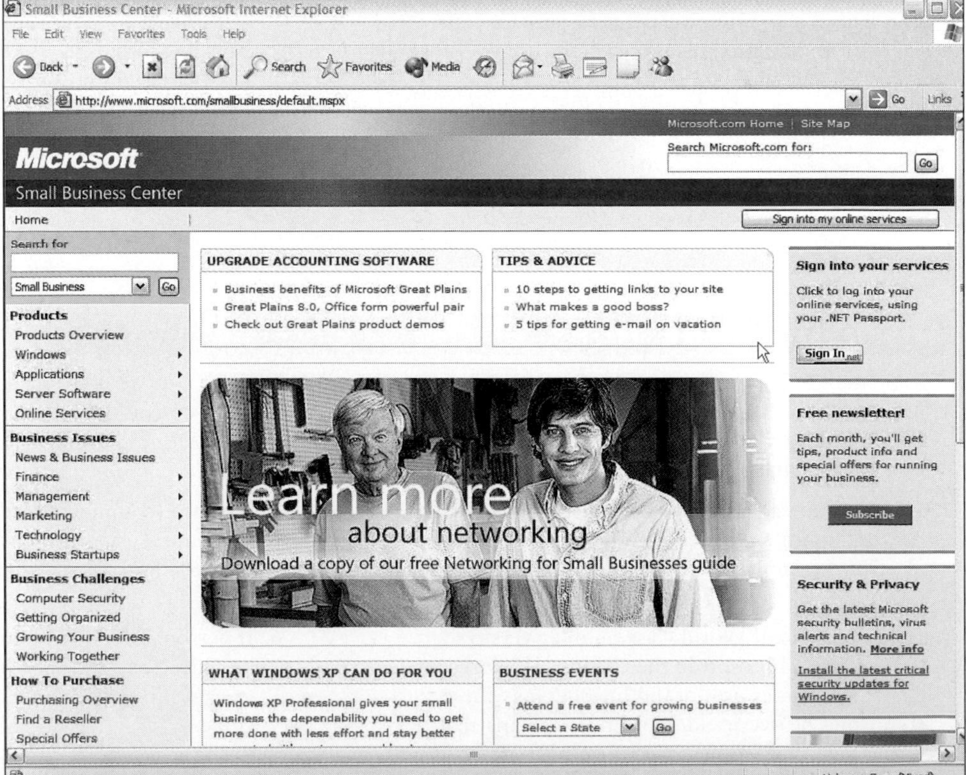

FIGURE 8.19 Microsoft's Small Business Center is a small business e-commerce portal.

for a guaranteed number of clickthroughs (people who click on your banner ad to visit your Web site). Small Business Center rotates these banner ads around a network of participating Web sites and removes the ad as soon as it has received the guaranteed number of clickthrough visitors. This action eliminates the guesswork regarding both traffic and fees. The three packages, 100, 250, and 1,000 visitors, break down to 50 cents per visitor.

a. Check out Small Business Center and the other e-commerce portals mentioned. Identify several benefits and limitations for a business using these Web sites.

b. Which Web site is your favorite? Why?

c. Which site would you recommend or use to help a small business wanting to get into e-commerce? Why?

2. e-Commerce Web Sites for Car Buying

Nowadays new car buyers can configure the car of their dreams on Microsoft's MSN Autos Web site, as well as those of Ford, GM, and other auto giants. Many independent online car purchase and research companies offer similar services. See Figure 8.20. Car buying information provided by manufacturers, brokerage sites, car dealers, financial institutions, and consumer advocate Web sites has exploded in the past few years.

Yet in the age of the Internet, the auto industry remains a steadfast holdout to innovations that might threaten the well-established and well-connected supply chain, the car dealership. American new car buyers simply cannot skip the middleperson and purchase an automobile directly from the manufacturer. That's not simply a business decision by the manufacturers either; that's the law.

Even so, many car buyers use the Internet as a place to research their purchases. Instead of selling new cars directly, Web sites such as Autobytel.com of Irvine, California, simply put consumers in touch with a local dealer where they test drive a vehicle and negotiate a price. Autobytel.com has been referring buyers to new and used car dealers since 1995. It also offers online financing and insurance.

Online car buying sites on the Web make consumers less dependent on what cars a dealer has on the lot. At online sites, buyers can customize a car—or van, truck, or sport utility vehicle—by selecting trim, paint, color, and other options before purchase. They can also use Web sites such as CarBuyingTips.com to help prepare for the final negotiating process.

a. Check out several of the Web sites shown in Figure 8.20. Evaluate them based on ease of use, relevance of information provided, and other criteria you feel are important. Don't forget the classic: "Did they make you want to buy?"

FIGURE 8.20
Table for Problem 2

Top Car Buying Web Sites	
Autobytel.com	**www.autobytel.com**
Enter make and model, and a local dealer will contact you with a price offer. Home delivery is an option.	
AutoNation	**www.autonation.com**
Every make and model available, as well as financing and insurance information, home delivery, and test drives.	
Microsoft MSN Autos	**www.autos.msn.com**
Auto reviews, detailed vehicle specifications, safety ratings, and buying services for new and used cars, including customizing your very own Ford.	
cars.com	**www.cars.com**
Research tools include automotive reviews, model reports, dealer locators, and financing information.	
CarsDirect.com	**www.carsdirect.com**
Research price and design, and then order your car. CarsDirect will deliver it to your home. A top-rated site.	
Edmunds.com	**www.edmunds.com**
For an objective opinion, Edmunds.com provides reviews, safety updates, and rebate news for car buyers.	
FordVehicles.com	**www.fordvehicles.com**
Research, configure, price, and order your new Ford car, minivan, truck, or SUV at this Web site.	
GM BuyPower	**www.gmbuypower.com**
With access to nearly 6,000 GM dealerships, car shoppers can get a price quote, schedule a test drive, and buy.	

b. Which sites would you use or recommend if you or a friend actually wanted to buy a car? Why?
c. Check out the Consumer Federation of America's study on anticompetitive new car buying state laws or similar studies online. How much does it estimate consumers would save if they could purchase cars directly from manufacturers online?

3. **Comparing e-Commerce Sites**
In this exercise, you will experiment with electronic shopping and compare alternative electronic commerce sites. First, you will need to select a category of product widely available on the Web, such as books, CDs, or toys. Second, select five specific products to price on the Internet, for example, five specific CDs you might be interested in buying. Third, search three prominent e-commerce sites selling this type of product and record the price charged for each product by each site.
   a. Using a spreadsheet, record a set of information similar to that shown for each product. (Categories describing the product will vary depending on the type of product you select—CDs might require the title of the CD and the performer[s], whereas toys or similar products would require the name of the product and its description.) See Figure 8.21.
   b. For each product, rank each company on the basis of the price charged. Give a rating of 1 for the lowest price and 3 for the highest, and split the ratings for ties—two sites tying for the lowest price would each receive a 1.5. If a site does not have one of the products available for sale, give that site a rating of 4 for that product. Add the ratings across your products to produce an overall price/availability rating for each site.
   c. Based on your experience with these sites, rate them on their ease of use, completeness of information, and order-filling and shipping options. As in part (b), give a rating of 1 to the site you feel is best in each category, a 2 to the second best, and a 3 to the poorest site.
   d. Prepare a set of PowerPoint slides or similar presentation materials summarizing the key results and including an overall assessment of the sites you compared.

4. **e-Commerce: The Dark Side**
Anonymous transactions on the Internet can have a dark side. Research each of the terms below on the Web. Prepare a one-page report for each term researched. Your paper should describe the problem and provide examples and illustrations where possible. Conclude each paper with recommendations on how to guard against each type of fraud.
   a. Search using the terms "Ponzi Scheme" or "Pyramid Scheme." To find current examples in action, try searching for "plasma TV $50," "cash matrix," "e-books" and "matrix," or "gifting" through a search engine or action site.
   b. Search using the terms "phishing" and "identity." If possible, include a printout of a real-world example that you or an acquaintance may have received via e-mail.
   c. Search using the term "third-party escrow." What legitimate function does this serve? Provide an example of a legitimate third-party escrow service for Internet transactions. How has the third-party escrow system been used to commit fraud on the Internet?
   d. Prepare a one-page paper describing a type of online fraud not covered in the previous questions. Prepare presentation materials and present your findings to the class. Be sure to include a description of the fraud, how to detect it, and how to avoid it. Use real-world illustrations if possible.

FIGURE 8.21 Table for Problem 3

		Price			Rating		
Title of Book	**Author**	**Site A**	**Site B**	**Site C**	**A**	**B**	**C**
The Return of Little Big Man	Berger, T.	15.00	16.95	14.50	2	3	1
Learning Perl/Tk	Walsh, N. & Mui, L.	26.36	25.95	25.95	3	1.5	1.5
Business at the Speed of Thought	Gates, W.	21.00	22.95	21.00	1.5	3	1.5
Murders for the Holidays	Smith, G.		8.25	7.95	4	2	1
Designs for Dullards	Jones	17.95	18.50	18.50	1	2.5	2.5
Sum of ratings (low score represents most favorable rating)					11.5	12	7.5

REAL WORLD CASE 3 Yahoo and Flickr: Will Social Media and Social Networking Give Yahoo a Competitive Edge on the Web?

"I have never seen so many people with cameras," says Jerry Yang. "It is kind of scary." It was a perfect September evening in 2005 at Yahoo headquarters in Sunnyvale, California. Yang, cofounder and chief Yahoo, was surrounded by roughly 250 photographers. But these were not paparazzi angling to profile the billionaire. They are, in fact, far more interested in taking digital snapshots of one another.

This act of mass photography is a party for Flickr, the rapidly growing photo-sharing site acquired by Yahoo in March 2005. Flickr cofounder Stewart Butterfield posted an open invitation on the Flickr blog, and all of these people—customers, really—just showed up. Butterfield and his cofounder and wife, Caterina Fake, have quite a fan club. "Flickr has changed so many lives. The number of friends I have has exploded," enthuses Deborah Lattimore, an entrepreneur who owns a transcription service.

Behind Lattimore is a huge screen with hundreds of constantly changing photos, a sample of the 14,000 or so images uploaded to Flickr every hour. Peer closely and you'll see snaps of the party that guests have already sent in via cell phone. "I look at Flickr with envy," Yang says. "It feels like where the Web is going."

What Yang envies is the community of 1.5 million rabidly loyal users Flickr has cultivated and the vast amount of content they've created. Of the 60 million photos uploaded to the site so far, more than 80 percent are public, meaning that anyone can look at them. More than half have been "tagged" with user-created labels, making them searchable. To use Flickr is to belong to the culture of participation sweeping the Web—write your own blog, produce your own podcast, and post your personal photos for all to see. If this is where the Web is going, Yang wants to make sure Yahoo gets there first. However, you can be sure that Google and Microsoft have the same idea.

Indeed, the Flickr purchase helped ignite a larger strategy. Thanks to a new generation of managers like Butterfield and Fake, Yahoo is starting to see how user-generated content, or "social media," that provides an information sharing and personal connecting experience many users love, called "social networking," is a key weapon in its war against Google. That upstart in neighboring Mountain View may have a better reputation for search, it may dominate online advertising, and it may always win when it comes to machines and math. But Yahoo has 191 million *registered* users. What would happen if it could form deep, lasting, Flickr-like social-networking bonds with them—and get them to apply tags not just to photos but to the entire Web?

For one thing, the company could make a lot more money. More rabid users mean more ads and more premium subscriptions such as Flickr Pro, whose users pay $25 a year to take their photo-uploading allowance from 20 megabytes to 2 gigabytes a month. Such user fees account for 13 percent of Yahoo's revenues. Together, ads and fees added up to $3.8 billion in revenues and $1.2 billion in profits for the first nine months of this year.

It's a strategy that comes right from the top. Social media "is going to be a gigantic piece of what we do," says Yahoo CEO Terry Semel. "I don't think old media is what people are going to spend most of their time doing on the Internet. This paradigm needs its own inventions, its own methods, its own way to go forward." That doesn't mean Yahoo isn't ignoring traditional mass media—quite the opposite, in fact—but when it comes to the future of social media and social networking on the Web, Semel has been praised as one of Silicon Valley's savviest CEOs.

Of course, the News Corp.'s canny Robert Murdoch gets social networking too, paying a whopping $580 million in 2005 for the top social-networking site MySpace.com. Murdoch must be smiling all the way to the bank after MySpace was rated America's most popular Web site in June 2006, with almost 5 percent of all Internet traffic during the month. Not to be outdone, Google snapped up another top social networking site in November 2006, paying $1.65 billion in stock for the phenomenal popularity and growth of the video Web site YouTube. That leaves premier college social-networking site Facebook available, but Facebook reportedly turned down a $750 million offer from Yahoo in 2005, then refused to reopen negotiations when Yahoo was prepared to offer $1.65 billion in the first quarter of 2006.

Semel may get it, but if you want to see his revolution in action, you have to talk to the young guns he's been hiring. Many of the champions of social media inside Yahoo—including Flickr's Butterfield and Fake, senior technologist Bradley Horowitz, and the head of Yahoo's developer network Toni Schneider—are former start-up founders recently acquired or hired. These entrepreneurs are sprinkling their social media DNA all over the company, in a process some insiders are calling the "Flickrization" of Yahoo. The Flickrizers' most ambitious goal is to turn Web searching itself into a social event—the idea being that you can find what you're looking for faster if you first see pages saved and tagged by people you know and trust. Done well, it could play as the triumph of the humans over Google's cold, mechanical approach.

But there were moments when Yahoo was decidedly unfriendly toward users' content. In 1999, it bought GeoCities, the popular purveyor of personal homepages, and proceeded to raze the 41 virtual neighborhoods into which its sites were clustered. Worse, Yahoo's new terms of service said the company owned rights to all GeoCities content, even members' photographs. Thousands of GeoCities residents left in protest. Yahoo quickly rescinded the terms of service.

Still, the company has managed to get the user-generated formula right most of the time. It has a forum for special interests in Yahoo Groups, which now boasts 70 million members. And asking people to post their own reviews, as

Amazon and Netflix know, is one of the best ways to grow your site's social value; Yahoo has more than 6 billion user-generated ratings on Yahoo Music alone.

Flickr began in a New York hotel in November 2003. That's where Butterfield was suffering from food poisoning when he had a feverish dream about a multiplayer game built around sharing digital photographs. The vision stuck with him. Three months later, Butterfield and Fake, a former art director at Salon.com, built the first version of Flickr in a Vancouver, British Columbia, loft. At first, the site centered on instant messaging, with a tray of photos that could be dragged into the conversation. Early members were gamers, bloggers, and digital-camera enthusiasts who set the tone by posting captivating pictures. They started to arrange local meetings to take more. Butterfield tweaked the technology, Fake nurtured the community, and membership went up to 250,000 people by the time Yahoo came knocking a year later.

The feature that first caught the eye of Horowitz, senior director of Yahoo's technology development group, was all that voluntary tagging Flickr users were doing. Instead of teaching computers to identify images, Flickr gets people to do the heavy lifting. Most users describe their photos with tags and make them public for the benefit of friends and family, without realizing that they're greasing the wheels of a great social media machine. Add together all those labels and you have millions of keywords, a gold mine of image search. For a good time, try sampling the 94,000 photos Flickr users have tagged with the word "fun."

Encouraged to look at the start-up by an e-mail from a Yahoo engineer and Flickr fanatic in Bangalore, India, Horowitz invited Butterfield and Fake to Silicon Valley in late 2004. They had lunch in the Yahoo cafeteria and immediately hit it off. The feeling was mutual. By March, Horowitz had persuaded his top brass to buy Flickr for an undisclosed sum, estimated to be around $30 million. But first, COO Dan Rosensweig had to overcome a lot of internal grumbling. There was no real business behind Flickr, and no unique technology either. So why did Yahoo need it? Says Rosensweig, "We could only justify it when we realized how big the vision could be if applied to the Yahoo network."

Such was the hunger for social media projects that Butterfield and Fake were in high demand from the moment they arrived in Sunnyvale. The pair were pulled into meetings with other groups—Yahoo Travel, Shopping, Local—that wanted help becoming more Flickrized. Fake spoke to the folks at Yahoo Autos about the best ways to build a community around custom rides for auto enthusiasts. The travel group, which has more than 250,000 in-depth travel guides written by readers, wanted to tap the knowledge of its audience even further.

If social search pans out, it could give Yahoo a much-needed edge over Google. Google takes an automated approach to search, throwing armies of Ph.D.s and thousands of servers at the problem. It wants to make search more relevant by creating better algorithms. Yahoo also does algorithmic search, but it can't beat Google at that game. So it's gambling that tapping into the collective intelligence of its audience will produce more relevant search results. "It is not who has the bigger index," Horowitz says, taking a swipe at his rival. "We hear a lot about efforts to index all the artifacts of human knowledge, but the actual bulk of human knowledge lives in people's heads."

Source: Adapted from Erick Schonfeld, "The Flickrization of Yahoo!" *Business 2.0*, December 2005; Steve Rosenbush, "Facebook's on the Block," *BusinessWeek Online*, March 28, 2006 Nicholas Carlson, "Yahoo 'Faced' in Social Network Indecision?" *Internetnews.com*, April 7, 2007.

CASE STUDY QUESTIONS

1. How does the Web foster the growth of social media and social networking Web sites? What potential benefits could such Web sites offer a business? Visit several sites like Flickr, MySpace, Facebook, and YouTube to support your answer.
2. What business benefits does Yahoo hope to gain from its acquisition of Flickr and drive to "Flickrize" its business? How realistic are such planned benefits for Yahoo at the present time, given the acquisition of MySpace by News Corp. and YouTube by Google? Defend your position.
3. Can social media and social networking serve as a strategic competitive differentiator for Yahoo, enabling it to overtake Google in the multibillion-dollar targeted search ads market? Why or why not?

REAL WORLD ACTIVITIES

1. Visit the main Yahoo Web site and evaluate the status of Yahoo's current integration of social networking into its many Web-based businesses such as Yahoo Autos, Local, Shopping, Travel, My Web, and Yahoo Search. Is such integration easily apparent? Does it seem to improve the value of the services offered? Present your findings to the class.
2. How are News Corp. and Google capitalizing on their respective acquisitions of MySpace and YouTube? Visit their Web sites and search the Internet for information that will enable you evaluate how these companies are integrating social networking into their business initiatives.
3. As in personalized online classifieds Web pages, social media and social networking sites offer personalized Web pages that are accessible to others online. Unfortunately, this ability may provide the potential for serious security, privacy, fraud, and spam assaults by online criminals, hackers, and spammers. Use the Internet to research how Yahoo and others are protecting users of their social networking sites from such assaults. Break into small groups with your classmates to discuss this issue, your research results, and other steps that users and the companies could take to improve the security of social networking sites.

CHAPTER 9

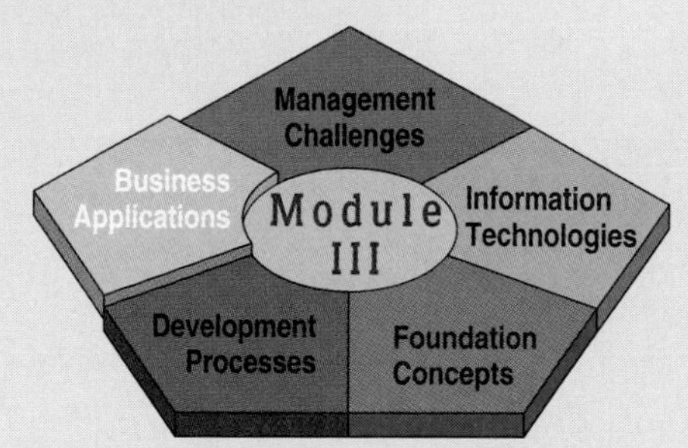

DECISION SUPPORT SYSTEMS

Chapter Highlights

Learning Objectives

After reading and studying this chapter, you should be able to:

1. Identify the changes taking place in the form and use of decision support in business.
2. Identify the role and reporting alternatives of management information systems.
3. Describe how online analytical processing can meet key information needs of managers.
4. Explain the decision support system concept and how it differs from traditional management information systems.
5. Explain how the following information systems can support the information needs of executives, managers, and business professionals:
   a. Executive information systems.
   b. Enterprise information portals.
   c. Knowledge management systems.
6. Identify how neural networks, fuzzy logic, genetic algorithms, virtual reality, and intelligent agents can be used in business.
7. Give examples of several ways expert systems can be used in business decision-making situations.

SECTION I Decision Support in Business

Introduction

As companies migrate toward responsive e-business models, they are investing in new data-driven decision support application frameworks that help them respond rapidly to changing market conditions and customer needs [27].

To succeed in business today, companies need information systems that can support the diverse information and decision-making needs of their managers and business professionals. In this section, we will explore in more detail how this is accomplished by several types of management information, decision support, and other information systems. We concentrate our attention on how the Internet, intranets, and other Web-enabled information technologies have significantly strengthened the role that information systems play in supporting the decision-making activities of every manager and knowledge worker in business.

Read the Real World Case on the next page. We can learn a lot from this case about the decision-making value of dashboards in business. See Figure 9.1.

Information, Decisions, and Management

Figure 9.2 emphasizes that the type of information required by decision makers in a company is directly related to the **level of management decision making** and the amount of structure in the decision situations they face. It is important to understand that the framework of the classic *managerial pyramid* shown in Figure 9.2 applies even in today's *downsized organizations* and *flattened* or nonhierarchical organizational structures. Levels of management decision making still exist, but their size, shape, and participants continue to change as today's fluid organizational structures evolve. Thus, the levels of managerial decision making that must be supported by information technology in a successful organization are:

- **Strategic Management.** Typically, a board of directors and an executive committee of the CEO and top executives develop overall organizational goals, strategies, policies, and objectives as part of a strategic planning process. They also monitor the strategic performance of the organization and its overall direction in the political, economic, and competitive business environment.
- **Tactical Management.** Increasingly, business professionals in self-directed teams as well as business unit managers develop short- and medium-range plans, schedules, and budgets and specify the policies, procedures, and business objectives for their subunits of the company. They also allocate resources and monitor the performance of their organizational subunits, including departments, divisions, process teams, project teams, and other workgroups.
- **Operational Management.** The members of self-directed teams or operating managers develop short-range plans such as weekly production schedules. They direct the use of resources and the performance of tasks according to procedures and within budgets and schedules they establish for the teams and other workgroups of the organization.

Information Quality

What characteristics of information products make them valuable and useful to you? To answer this important question, we must first examine the characteristics or attributes of **information quality.** Information that is outdated, inaccurate, or hard to understand is not very meaningful, useful, or valuable to you or other business professionals. People need information of high quality, that is, information products whose characteristics, attributes, or qualities make the information more valuable to them. It is useful to think of information as having the three dimensions of time, content, and form. Figure 9.3 summarizes the important attributes of information quality and groups them into these three dimensions.

REAL WORLD CASE 1

Oracle Corporation and Others: Dashboards for Executives and Business Professionals: The Power and the Challenge

Oracle CEO Lawrence J. Ellison was on his honeymoon. The billionaire and his bride, romance novelist Melanie Craft, were relaxing on his 243-foot Katana yacht off St. Barts, the Caribbean island known as a haven for movie moguls and rock stars. But Ellison, for the umpteenth time, couldn't help himself. He climbed to his office on the upper deck of the Katana, fired up his computer, and logged on to the Web site of a small company called NetSuite. It was the last day of the fiscal year, and Ellison, the cofounder of NetSuite and its largest investor, needed to know if the start-up was going to meet its numbers.

Before the Internet, Ellison says, taking the pulse of a company was sort of ridiculous to get the latest sales information. He would call several people and wait days for them to process financial reports that often were out of date by the time he got them. "You would use your cell phone and work on feelings," he says.

But thanks to a new Web-based management tool known as a "dashboard," Ellison had the information he needed in seconds. Like the instrument panel in a car, the computer version displays critical info in easy-to-read graphics, assembled from data pulled in real time from corporate software and databases. Logging on to his dashboard for NetSuite, Ellison reviewed the financial data and saw surprisingly strong sales. He quickly called NetSuite CEO Zachary A. Nelson. Recalls Nelson: "The first thing he screams is: 'Are the numbers on my dashboard right?'" Nelson looked at his own dashboard, but his sales data were lower. So he pushed a refresh button. "The information came up with the new orders, and it was the exact same number," says Nelson. "It was a very big high-five call."

FIGURE 9.1

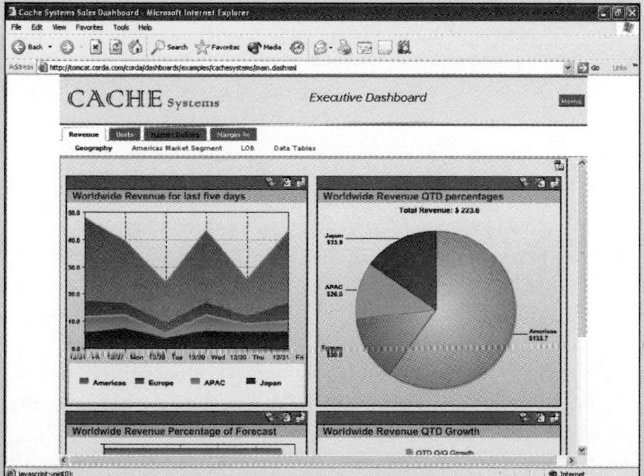

Dashboards provide key business information to executives, small business managers, and many business professionals.

The dashboard has become the CEO's killer app, making the gritty details of a business that are often buried deep within a large organization accessible at a glance to senior executives. So powerful are the programs that they're beginning to change the nature of management, from an intuitive art into more of a science. Managers can see key changes in their businesses almost instantaneously—when salespeople falter or quality slides—and take quick, corrective action.

At Verizon, CEO Ivan Seidenberg and other executives can choose from among 300 metrics to put on their dashboards, from broadband sales to wireless subscriber defections. At General Electric, James P. Campbell, chief of the Consumer & Industrial division, which makes appliances and lighting products, tracks the number of orders coming in from each customer every day and compares that with targets. "I look at the digital dashboard the first thing in the morning so I have a quick global view of sales and service levels across the organization," notes Campbell. "It's a key operational tool in our business."

The technology is particularly valuable to small companies, since most of them couldn't afford sophisticated software in the past. Until about five years ago, dashboards had to be custom built, so the expense could run into the millions of dollars. Now, NetSuite and others offer products that run $1,000 to $2,000 a year per user. "NetSuite brought on a total change in the way the company works and thinks," indicates Nate Porter, vice president of American Reporting, a Kirkland, Washington, provider of credit reports and other mortgage services.

Still, dashboards have drawn some flak. Critics say CEOs can miss the big picture if they're glued to their computer screens. Other critics fear dashboards are an alluring but destructive force, the latest incarnation of Big Brother. The concern is that companies will use the technology to invade the privacy of workers and wield it as a whip to keep them in line. Even managers who use dashboards admit the tools can raise pressure on employees, create divisions in the office, and lead workers to hoard information.

One common concern is that dashboards can hurt morale. Consider the case of Little Earth Productions Inc., a Pittsburgh clothing manufacturer. The company uses NetSuite's tools to monitor the amount of business each salesperson has brought in and then displays it publicly. "You do feel bummed out sometimes if you are low on the list," agrees Ronisue Koller, a Little Earth salesperson.

Those pressures can lead to even bigger disruptions. NetSuite CEO Nelson says his dashboard allows him to read every e-mail sent by the sales staff and inspect the leads of each salesperson. "It's frightening," he says. And it can have serious consequences. Once a month, Nelson plays "lead fairy" and looks at which sales leads have been followed up on and which ones haven't. One salesman quit when Nelson wrested away his sales leads that were not being used and gave them to others who were out of leads. "This raised enormous hackles in the company," acknowledges Nelson. "That's fine with me because he wasn't doing his job anyway."

Jeff Raikes, president of the Microsoft division that makes Microsoft Office software, says that more than half of Microsoft's employees use dashboards, including CEO Steve Ballmer. "Every time I go to see Ballmer, it's an expectation that I bring my dashboard with me," says Raikes. Ballmer, he adds, reviews the dashboards of his seven business heads during one-on-one meetings, zeroing in on such metrics as sales, customer satisfaction, and the status of key products under development.

In manufacturing, GE execs use them to follow the production of everything from light bulbs to dishwashers, making sure production lines are running smoothly. In the software business, Raikes uses his dashboard to track the progress of the upcoming version of Office. Shaygan Kheradpir, the chief information officer at Verizon, has on his dashboard what coworkers call the Wall of Shaygan, a replica of every single node on the telecom giant's network. All green is good. Yellow or red merits a click. Red means an outage somewhere. "It makes you move where you need to move," he says.

Dashboard technology can help keep customers happy, too. Before NetSuite, American Reporting's Porter says customer service reps just answered the phone and had no place to store client requests. Now the company's entire customer service team uses the software. As a result, customer service managers can see who is responding to calls. And service reps have access to every repair ticket, making it easier to handle customer problems.

American Reporting isn't the only small business that's benefiting. Jerry Driggs, chief operating officer of Little Earth, took four months to move his business data onto the NetSuite system. Little Earth sells funky eco-fashion products, such as a handbag made with recycled license plates. Today half of the company's 50 employees use the system to manage their production, sales, and financial operations. "Once you see it is so intuitive, you wonder how we ran the business before," claims Driggs.

Back then, the company had no system to measure its production requirements or level of raw materials, much of which came from China. It took about six weeks to make and ship a handbag. And Little Earth constantly struggled with cash problems because Driggs would often buy more trim pieces and twist-knob closures than he needed. Now, using NetSuite, Driggs can monitor his purchase orders and inventory levels, and the system even alerts him when he is running low on closures and other parts. The result: Little Earth has slashed its shipping time to three days. "All of those things that used to drive us crazy are literally at our fingertips," says Driggs.

If it's near the end of a financial quarter, Oracle's Ellison tracks his customers like a hawk. "I want to know what our five biggest deals are three days before the quarter closes," he asserts. "I look at the dashboard several times a day. So much of our sales activity gets compressed into a few days." Ellison will then call the companies himself or figure out another way to seal the deal.

Ellison is more convinced than ever that dashboards are the way of the future. He just wishes more of his employees thought the way he does. One continuing frustration is that though all of Oracle's 20,000 salespeople use dashboards, Ellison says some 20 percent of them refuse to enter their sales leads into the system. Salespeople don't want to be held accountable for a lead that isn't converted into a sale. That makes it hard to get a true picture of the demand for Oracle's products.

Ellison has considered refusing to pay commissions on a sale if the order is not entered into a dashboard, but for now he thinks such a move might prove to be a bit draconian. "The salespeople are the last of the independents," notes Ellison. "They think their Rolodex is private." Even Ellison, one of the world's richest men, concedes that technology—and the power it gives him—has it limits. "People have to be persuaded that it's right," he says.

Source: Adapted from Spencer E. Ante and Jena McGregor, "Giving the Boss the Big Picture," *BusinessWeek*, February 13, 2006.

CASE STUDY QUESTIONS

1. What is the attraction of dashboards to CEOs and other executives? What real business value do they provide to executives?
2. The case emphasizes that managers of small businesses and many business professionals now rely on dashboards. What business benefits do dashboards provide to this business audience?
3. What are several reasons for criticism of the use of dashboards by executives? Do you agree with any of this criticism? Why or why not?

REAL WORLD ACTIVITIES

1. Use the Internet to research makers of dashboards for large and small business. For example, try NetSuite, Hyperion Solutions, and Salesforce.com for relatively inexpensive versions and Microsoft, Oracle, and SAP for more costly corporate dashboards. Evaluate the dashboard examples and demos you experience. Pick your favorites and explain your reasons for doing so to the class.
2. How would you like to work for an executive whose dashboard provides the level of information about company and employee performance described in this case? Would you want that level of information when you enter the executive ranks? Break into small groups with your classmates to discuss this issue, and formulate suggestions on any changes or safeguards you would propose for the business use of dashboards.

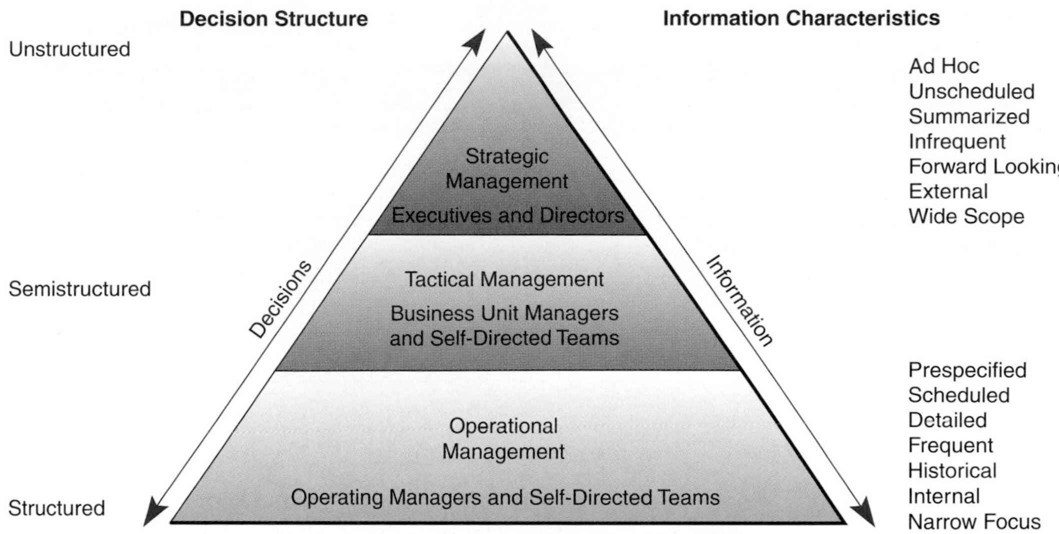

FIGURE 9.2
Information requirements of decision makers. The type of information required by directors, executives, managers, and members of self-directed teams is directly related to the level of management decision making involved and the structure of decision situations they face.

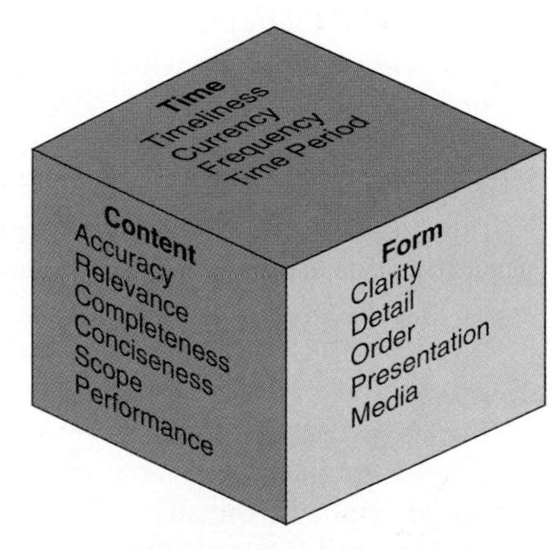

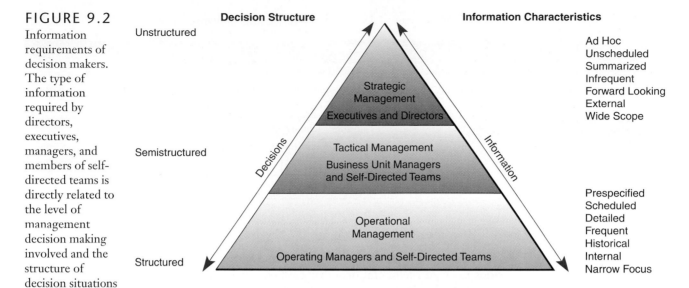

FIGURE 9.3
A summary of the attributes of information quality. This figure outlines the attributes that should be present in high-quality information products.

Time Dimension	
Timeliness	Information should be provided when it is needed.
Currency	Information should be up-to-date when it is provided.
Frequency	Information should be provided as often as needed.
Time Period	Information can be provided about past, present, and future time periods.
Content Dimension	
Accuracy	Information should be free from errors.
Relevance	Information should be related to the information needs of a specific recipient for a specific situation.
Completeness	All the information that is needed should be provided.
Conciseness	Only the information that is needed should be provided.
Scope	Information can have a broad or narrow scope, or an internal or external focus.
Performance	Information can reveal performance by measuring activities accomplished, progress made, or resources accumulated.
Form Dimension	
Clarity	Information should be provided in a form that is easy to understand.
Detail	Information can be provided in detail or summary form.
Order	Information can be arranged in a predetermined sequence.
Presentation	Information can be presented in narrative, numeric, graphic, or other forms.
Media	Information can be provided in the form of printed paper documents, video displays, or other media.

FIGURE 9.4 Examples of decisions by the type of decision structure and level of management.

Decision Structure	Operational Management	Tactical Management	Strategic Management
Unstructured	Cash management	Business process reengineering Workgroup performance analysis	New e-business initiatives Company reorganization
Semistructured	Credit management Production scheduling Daily work assignment	Employee performance appraisal Capital budgeting Program budgeting	Product planning Mergers and acquisitions Site location
Structured	Inventory control	Program control	

Decision Structure

One way of understanding decision making is by looking at **decision structure**. Decisions made at the operational management level tend to be more *structured*, those at the tactical level more *semistructured*, and those at the strategic management level more *unstructured*. Structured decisions involve situations in which the procedures to follow, when a decision is needed, can be specified in advance. The inventory reorder decisions faced by most businesses are a typical example. Unstructured decisions involve decision situations in which it is not possible to specify in advance most of the decision procedures to follow. Most decisions related to long-term strategy can be thought of as unstructured (e.g., "What product lines should we develop over the next five years?"). Most business decision situations are semistructured. That is, some decision procedures can be prespecified but not enough to lead to a definite recommended decision. For example, decisions involved in starting a new line of e-commerce services or making major changes to employee benefits would probably range from unstructured to semistructured. Finally, decisions that are unstructured are those for which no procedures or rules exist to guide the decision makers toward the correct decision. In these types of decisions, many sources of information must be accessed, and the decision often rests on experience and "gut feeling." One example of an unstructured decision might be the answer to the question, "What business should we be in 10 years from now?" Figure 9.4 provides a variety of examples of business decisions by type of decision structure and level of management [22].

Therefore, information systems must be designed to produce a variety of information products to meet the changing needs of decision makers throughout an organization. For example, decision makers at the strategic management level may look to *decision support systems* to provide them with more summarized, ad hoc, unscheduled reports, forecasts, and external intelligence to support their more unstructured planning and policymaking responsibilities. Decision makers at the operational management level, in contrast, may depend on *management information systems* to supply more prespecified internal reports emphasizing detailed current and historical data comparisons that support their more structured responsibilities in day-to-day operations. Figure 9.5 compares the information and decision support capabilities of management information systems and decision support systems, which we will explore in this chapter.

Decision Support Trends

The emerging class of applications focuses on personalized decision support, modeling, information retrieval, data warehousing, what-if scenarios, and reporting [27].

As we discussed in Chapter 1, using information systems to support business decision making has been one of the primary thrusts of the business use of information technology. However, during the 1990s, both academic researchers and business practitioners began reporting that the traditional managerial focus originating in classic

FIGURE 9.5
Comparing the major differences in the information and decision support capabilities of management information systems and decision support systems.

	Management Information Systems	Decision Support Systems
• Decision support provided	Provide information about the performance of the organization	Provide information and decision support techniques to analyze specific problems or opportunities
• Information form and frequency	Periodic, exception, demand, and push reports and responses	Interactive inquiries and responses
• Information format	Prespecified, fixed format	Ad hoc, flexible, and adaptable format
• Information processing methodology	Information produced by extraction and manipulation of business data	Information produced by analytical modeling of business data

management information systems (1960s), decision support systems (1970s), and executive information systems (1980s) was expanding. The fast pace of new information technologies like PC hardware and software suites, client/server networks, and networked PC versions of DSS software made decision support available to lower levels of management, as well as to nonmanagerial individuals and self-directed teams of business professionals [18, 40, 45].

This trend has accelerated with the dramatic growth of the Internet and of intranets and extranets that internetwork companies and their stakeholders. The e-business and e-commerce initiatives that are being implemented by many companies are also expanding the information and decision support uses and the expectations of a company's employees, managers, customers, suppliers, and other business partners. Figure 9.6 illustrates that all business stakeholders expect easy and instant access to information and Web-enabled self-service data analysis [27]. Today's businesses are responding with a variety of personalized and proactive Web-based analytical techniques to support the decision-making requirements of all of their constituents.

Thus, the growth of corporate intranets and extranets, as well as the Web, has accelerated the development and use of "executive-class" information delivery and decision support software tools by lower levels of management and by individuals and teams of business professionals. In addition, this dramatic expansion has opened the door to the use of such **business intelligence (BI)** tools by the suppliers, customers, and other business stakeholders of a company for customer relationship management, supply chain management, and other e-business applications.

Figure 9.7 highlights several major information technologies that are being customized, personalized, and Web-enabled to provide key business information and

FIGURE 9.6
A business must meet the information and data analysis requirements of its stakeholders with more personalized and proactive Web-based decision support.

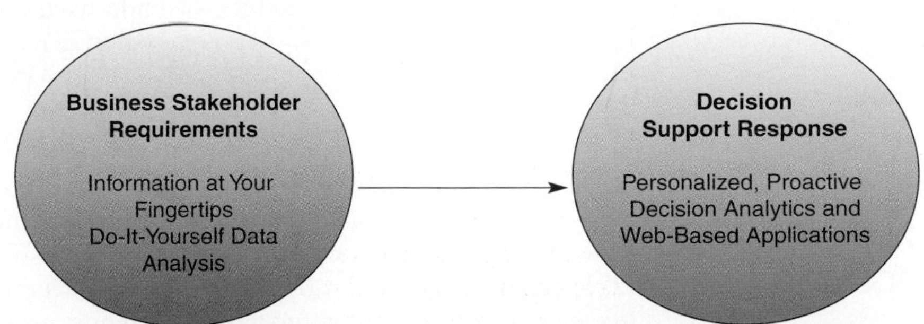

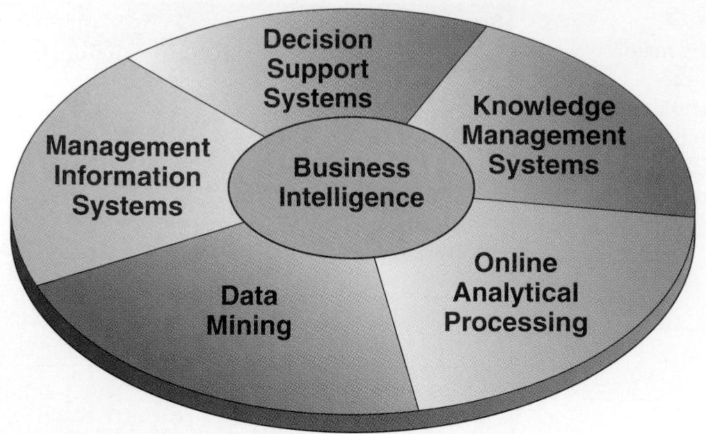

FIGURE 9.7
Business intelligence applications are based on personalized and Web-enabled information analysis, knowledge management, and decision support technologies.

analytical tools for managers, business professionals, and business stakeholders [25, 26, 33, 48]. We highlight the trends toward such business intelligence applications in the various types of information and decision support systems that are discussed in this chapter.

Cisco Systems: MIS Dashboard

At Cisco (www.cisco.com), company executives say that ideally, everyone in the business should have access to real-time information. "The whole corporation is moving to real time," says Mike Zill, director of sales and finance IT at Cisco. "It's difficult to have applications stay in batch mode when the business architecture is message-based."

Channel account managers in the sales department use a Web-based "dashboard," or graphical user interface–based view, from OneChannel Inc. that gives them real-time views of their accounts' activities. When a business condition hits a predetermined threshold, the software triggers an alert, sending a message or warning to the user's dashboard. For example, if Cisco's sales department has a top-10 list of new products it wants sold through, say, Ingram Micro, the application will let the Cisco channel manager know the instant the distributor's sales fall outside target levels.

To achieve this system, Cisco had to build deep hooks into its supply chain, which wasn't easy to develop. The firm has established agreements with its partners to receive point-of-sale data via the Internet or, in some cases, through electronic data interchange. However, most of the data are batched. Few partners will feed real-time point-of-sale data to the company, according to Zill.

Once it receives the data, Cisco couples it with real-time, Web-based inventory information and processes it using analytics software from Hyperion Solutions Corp. Channel managers can then query the Hyperion software in detail through the OneChannel dashboard to find the underlying causes of any distribution problem. "The response time is fast enough so you're not waiting," Zill says. And that's the essence of real time for any user [23].

Decision Support Systems

Decision support systems are computer-based information systems that provide interactive information support to managers and business professionals during the decision-making process. Decision support systems use (1) analytical models, (2) specialized databases, (3) a decision maker's own insights and judgments, and (4) an interactive, computer-based modeling process to support semistructured business decisions.

Example

An example might help at this point. Sales managers typically rely on management information systems to produce sales analysis reports. These reports contain sales performance figures by product line, salesperson, sales region, and so on. A decision support system, however, would also interactively show a sales manager the effects on sales performance of changes in a variety of factors (e.g., promotion expense, salesperson compensation). The DSS could then use several criteria (e.g., expected gross margin, market share) to evaluate and rank alternative combinations of sales performance factors.

Therefore, DSS systems are designed to be ad hoc, quick-response systems that are initiated and controlled by business decision makers. Decision support systems are thus able to directly support the specific types of decisions and the personal decision-making styles and needs of individual executives, managers, and business professionals.

DSS Components

Unlike management information systems, decision support systems rely on **model bases** as well as databases as vital system resources. A DSS model base is a software component that consists of models used in computational and analytical routines that mathematically express relationships among variables. For example, a spreadsheet program might contain models that express simple accounting relationships among variables, such as Revenue 2 Expenses 5 Profit. Or a DSS model base could include models and analytical techniques used to express much more complex relationships. For example, it might contain linear programming models, multiple regression forecasting models, and capital budgeting present value models. Such models may be stored in the form of spreadsheet models or templates or statistical and mathematical programs and program modules [28]. See Figure 9.8.

In addition, DSS software packages can combine model components to create integrated models that support specific types of decisions [13]. DSS software typically contains built-in analytical modeling routines and also enables you to build your own models. Many DSS packages are now available in microcomputer and Web-enabled versions. Of course, electronic spreadsheet packages also provide some of the model building (spreadsheet models) and analytical modeling (what-if and goal-seeking analysis) offered by more powerful DSS software. As businesses become more aware of the power of decision support systems, they are using them in ever-increasing areas of the business. See Figure 9.9.

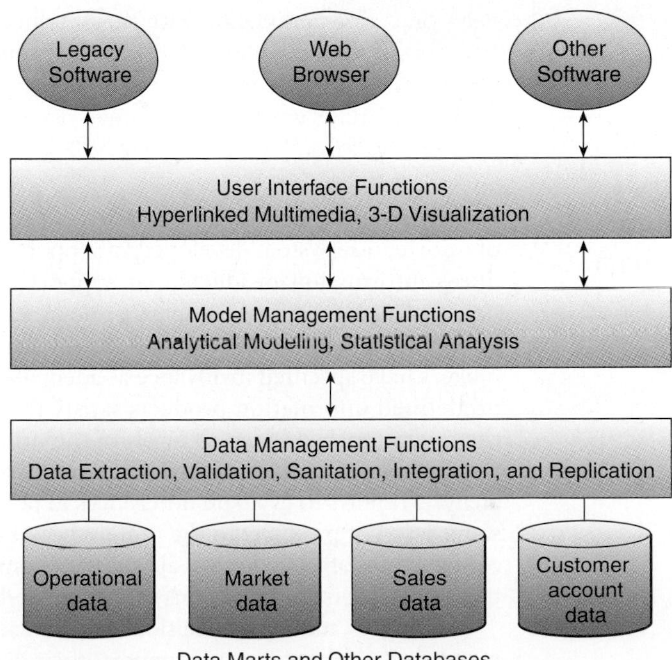

FIGURE 9.8
Components of a Web-enabled marketing decision support system. Note the hardware, software, model, data, and network resources involved.

FIGURE 9.9 Many businesses are turning to decision support systems and their underlying models to improve a wide variety of business functions.

Analytics competitors make expert use of statistics and modeling to improve a wide variety of functions. Here are some common applications:		
Function	**Description**	**Exemplars**
Supply chain	Simulate and optimize supply chain flows; reduce inventory and stock-outs.	Dell, Wal-Mart, Amazon
Customer selection, loyalty, and service	Identify customers with the greatest profit potential; increase likelihood that they will want the product or service offering; retain their loyalty.	Harrah's, Capital One, Barclays
Pricing	Identify the price that will maximize yield or profit.	Progressive, Marriott
Human capital	Select the best employees for particular tasks or jobs at particular compensation levels.	New England Patriots, Oakland A's, Boston Red Sox
Product and service quality	Detect quality problems early and minimize them.	Honda, Intel
Financial performance	Better understand the drivers of financial performance and the effects of nonfinancial factors.	MCI, Verizon
Research and development	Improve quality, efficacy, and, where applicable, safety of products and services.	Novartis, Amazon, Yahoo

Source: Adapted from Thomas H. Davenport, "Competing on Analytics," *Harvard Business Review*, January 2006.

Web-Enabled DSS at PepsiCo

PepsiCo and Sedgwick James Inc., the world's second-largest insurance broker, developed a risk management DSS to help minimize PepsiCo's losses from accidents, theft, and other causes. Every week, Sedgwick loads the latest casualty claims data from the nation's leading insurance carriers into a DSS database resident on IBM RS/6000 servers in the PepsiCo intranet. The database is then accessed by managers and analysts using desktop PCs and remote laptops equipped with the INFORM risk management system. Both the RS/6000 servers and local PCs use Information Builders' middleware to provide PepsiCo managers and business analysts with transparent data access from a variety of hardware/software configurations.

The INFORM risk management system combines the analytical power of focus decision support modeling with the graphical analysis capabilities of Focus/EIS for Windows. As a result, PepsiCo managers and business analysts at all levels can pinpoint critical trends, drill down for detailed backup information, identify potential problems, and plan ways to minimize risks and maximize profits [33].

Management Information Systems

Recall from Chapter 1 that **management information systems** were the original type of information system developed to support managerial decision making. An MIS produces information products that support many of the day-to-day decision-making needs of managers and business professionals. Reports, displays, and responses produced by management information systems provide information that these decision makers have specified in advance as adequately meeting their information needs. Such predefined information products satisfy the information needs of decision makers at the operational and tactical levels of the organization who are faced with more structured types of decision situations. For example, sales managers rely heavily on sales analysis reports to evaluate differences in performance among salespeople who sell the same types of products to the same types of customers. They have a pretty good idea of the kinds of information about sales results (by product line, sales territory, customer, salesperson, and so on) that they need to manage sales performance effectively.

Managers and other decision makers use an MIS to request information at their networked workstations that supports their decision-making activities. This information takes the form of periodic, exception, and demand reports and immediate responses to inquiries. Web browsers, application programs, and database management software provide access to information in the intranet and other operational databases of the organization. Remember, operational databases are maintained by transaction processing systems. Data about the business environment are obtained from Internet or extranet databases when necessary.

Management Reporting Alternatives

Management information systems provide a variety of information products to managers. Four major **reporting alternatives** are provided by such systems.

- **Periodic Scheduled Reports.** This traditional form of providing information to managers uses a prespecified format designed to provide managers with information on a regular basis. Typical examples of such periodic scheduled reports are daily or weekly sales analysis reports and monthly financial statements.
- **Exception Reports.** In some cases, reports are produced only when exceptional conditions occur. In other cases, reports are produced periodically but contain information only about these exceptional conditions. For example, a credit manager can be provided with a report that contains only information on customers who have exceeded their credit limits. Exception reporting reduces *information overload* instead of overwhelming decision makers with periodic detailed reports of business activity.
- **Demand Reports and Responses.** Information is available whenever a manager demands it. For example, Web browsers and DBMS query languages and report generators enable managers at PC workstations to get immediate responses or to find and obtain customized reports as a result of their requests for the information they need. Thus, managers do not have to wait for periodic reports to arrive as scheduled.
- **Push Reporting.** Information is *pushed* to a manager's networked workstation. Thus, many companies are using Webcasting software to selectively broadcast reports and other information to the networked PCs of managers and specialists over their corporate intranets. See Figure 9.10.

FIGURE 9.10 An example of the components in a marketing intelligence system that uses the Internet and a corporate intranet system to "push" information to employees.

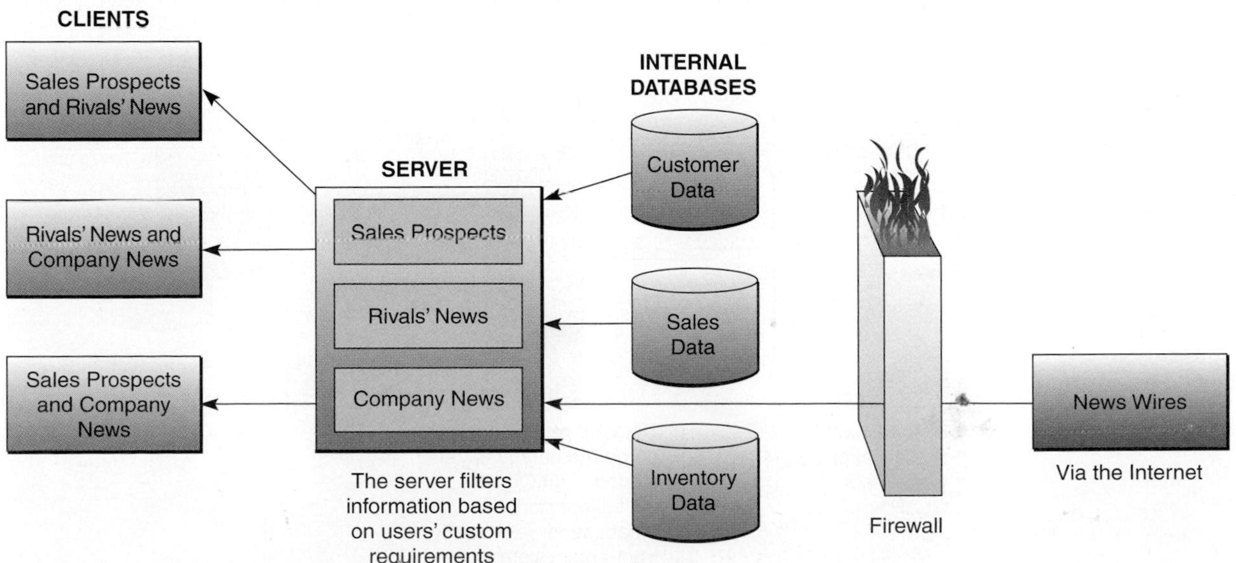

Online Analytical Processing

At a recent stockholder meeting, the CEO of PepsiCo, D. Wayne Calloway, said: "Ten years ago I could have told you how Doritos were selling west of the Mississippi. Today, not only can I tell you how well Doritos sell west of the Mississippi, I can also tell you how well they are selling in California, in Orange County, in the town of Irvine, in the local Vons supermarket, in the special promotion, at the end of Aisle 4, on Thursdays." [49].

The competitive and dynamic nature of today's global business environment is driving demands by business managers and analysts for information systems that can provide fast answers to complex business queries. The IS industry has responded to these demands with developments like analytical databases, data marts, data warehouses, data mining techniques, and multidimensional database structures (discussed in Chapter 5), and with specialized servers and Web-enabled software products that support **online analytical processing (OLAP)**.

Online analytical processing enables managers and analysts to interactively examine and manipulate large amounts of detailed and consolidated data from many perspectives. OLAP involves analyzing complex relationships among thousands or even millions of data items stored in data marts, data warehouses, and other multidimensional databases to discover patterns, trends, and exception conditions. An OLAP session takes place online in real time, with rapid responses to a manager's or analyst's queries, so that the analytical or decision-making process is undisturbed. See Figure 9.11.

Online analytical processing involves several basic analytical operations, including consolidation, "drill-down," and "slicing and dicing." See Figure 9.12.

- **Consolidation.** Consolidation involves the aggregation of data, which can involve simple roll-ups or complex groupings involving interrelated data. For example, data about sales offices can be rolled up to the district level, and district-level data can be rolled up to provide a regional-level perspective.
- **Drill-Down.** OLAP can also go in the reverse direction and automatically display detailed data that comprise consolidated data. This process is called drill-down. For example, the sales by individual products or sales reps that make up a region's sales totals could be easily accessed.
- **Slicing and Dicing.** Slicing and dicing refers to the ability to look at the database from different viewpoints. One slice of the sales database might show all sales of a product type within regions. Another slice might show all sales by sales channel within each product type. Slicing and dicing is often performed along a time axis to analyze trends and find time-based patterns in the data.

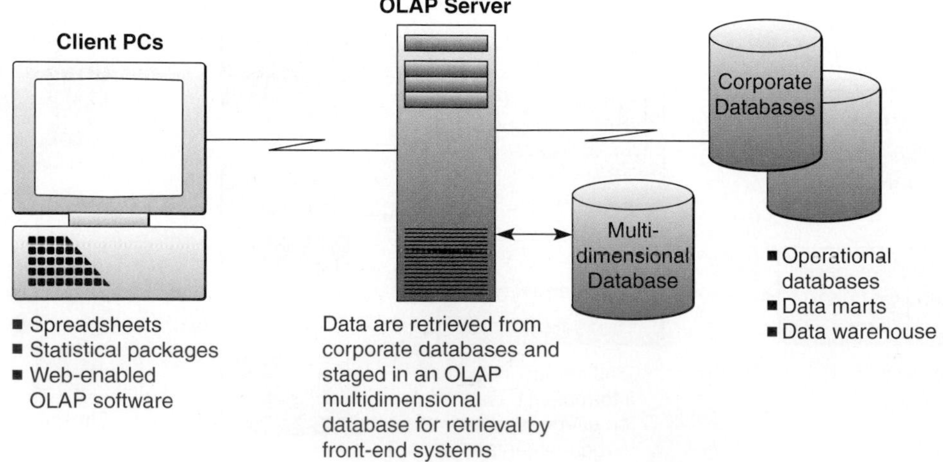

FIGURE 9.11
Online analytical processing may involve the use of specialized servers and multidimensional databases. OLAP provides fast answers to complex queries posed by managers and analysts using traditional and Web-enabled OLAP software.

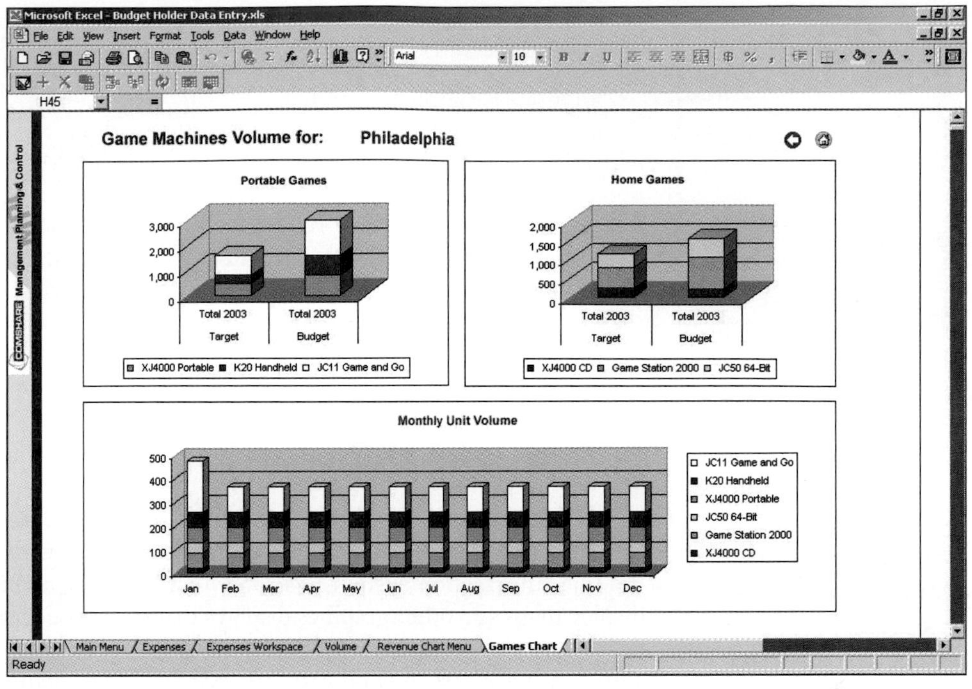

FIGURE 9.12
Comshare's Management Planning and Control software enables business professionals to use Microsoft Excel as their user interface for Web-enabled online analytical processing.

The GAP: Using OLAP to Analyze Key Measures in a Retail Environment

GAP Inc., headquartered in San Francisco, is a leading international specialty retailer with over 3,000 stores worldwide offering clothing, accessories, and personal care products for men, women, children, and babies under The Gap, Banana Republic, and Old Navy brand names. Customers can shop at The Gap stores in every state in the United States, as well as in the United Kingdom, Canada, France, Japan, and Germany.

Along with its global successes come global-size problems. To maintain competitive pricing in all their product lines, GAP Inc. needs to constantly look for ways to improve the profitability of individual stores, improve inventory management by store and brand, and track and understand seasonality trends by brand.

GAP managers know that to improve profitability, they need to accurately and efficiently report and analyze a set of key business measures, which in turn will allow them to better match their inventory levels to individual store sales, thereby improving inventory turnover. Although these are important issues in any industry, they are particularly critical in retail.

To fulfill these requirements, GAP business managers must track these metrics down to and including the level of every combination of store, product, style, and color by week—a breakdown that yields over 3 billion combinations!

To make the job somewhat easier, GAP analysts have determined that tracking two of GAP's major store chains, The Gap and Old Navy, provides a sufficient level of accuracy to make decisions for the entire company. Nonetheless, each store chain needs to track approximately 200 measures, 100 time elements, 200 season members, and a dozen fiscal and price information points. Furthermore, Old Navy must keep track of 1,500 store locations and 150,000 products. The Gap stores must track 3,000 store locations and 350,000 products. In addition, both store chains need to track currency for foreign exchange transactions. In total, their tracking system supports over 1,000 users accessing the information.

It is easy to imagine the complexity of such a decision support system, but things get even more complex when you consider the fact that GAP Inc. needed to design such a system to support the use of MS Excel as the primary reporting tool, because most managers were already trained in its use. Finally, the system response time has to be fast, regardless of the volume of data and the number of users.

So, how is this all accomplished?—OLAP, of course!

Data are loaded weekly into a multidimensional system that contains approximately 7,501gb of data. The business managers use MS Excel as the primary reporting and analysis tool, and retrieval times are as fast as three seconds. The secret to the success of this system centers on an Essbase model spanning 15 physical Essbase databases, linked to form four "virtual" cubes. Each virtual cube represents a single store chain. Together, they represent a single view or solution to gap's reporting and analysis needs. GAP business managers have at their disposal the information they need to make better and faster decisions that enable them to monitor and improve profitability to a finite level [3, 19].

Geographic Information and Data Visualization Systems

Geographic information systems (GIS) and **data visualization systems (DVS)** are special categories of DSS that integrate computer graphics with other DSS features. A geographic information system is a DSS that uses *geographic databases* to construct and display maps and other graphics displays that support decisions affecting the geographic distribution of people and other resources. Many companies are using GIS technology along with *global positioning system* (GPS) devices to help them choose new retail store locations, optimize distribution routes, or analyze the demographics of their target audiences. For example, companies like Levi Strauss, Arby's, Consolidated Rail, and Federal Express use GIS packages to integrate maps, graphics, and other geographic data with business data from spreadsheets and statistical packages. GIS software such as MapInfo and Atlas GIS is used for most business GIS applications. See Figure 9.13.

Data visualization systems represent complex data using interactive, three-dimensional, graphical forms such as charts, graphs, and maps. DVS tools help users interactively sort, subdivide, combine, and organize data while the data are in their

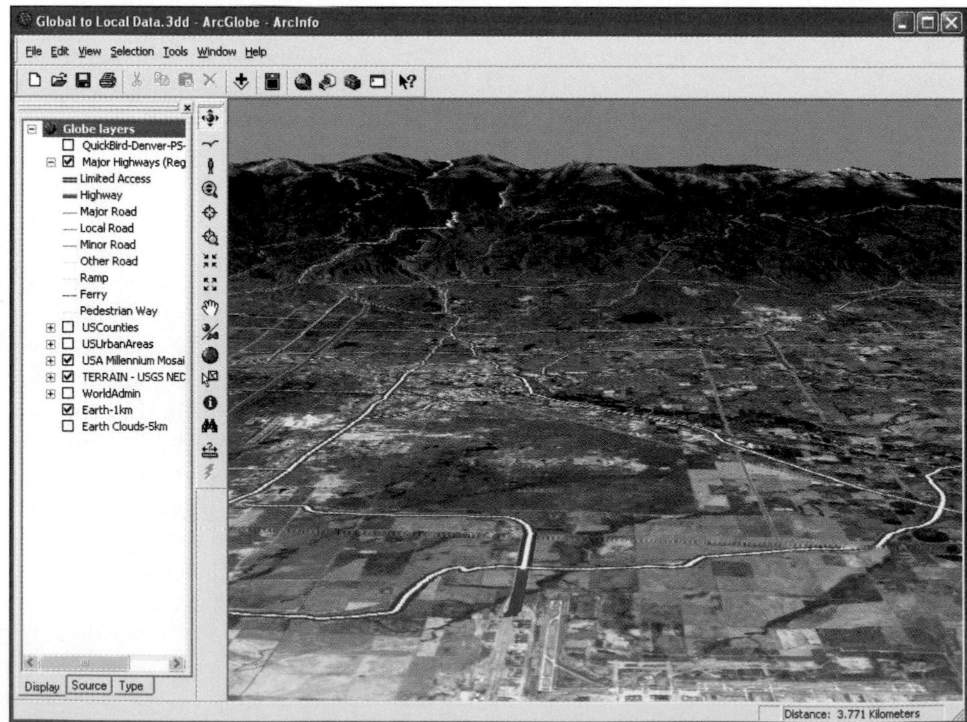

FIGURE 9.13
Geographic information systems facilitate the mining and visualization of data associated with a geophysical location.

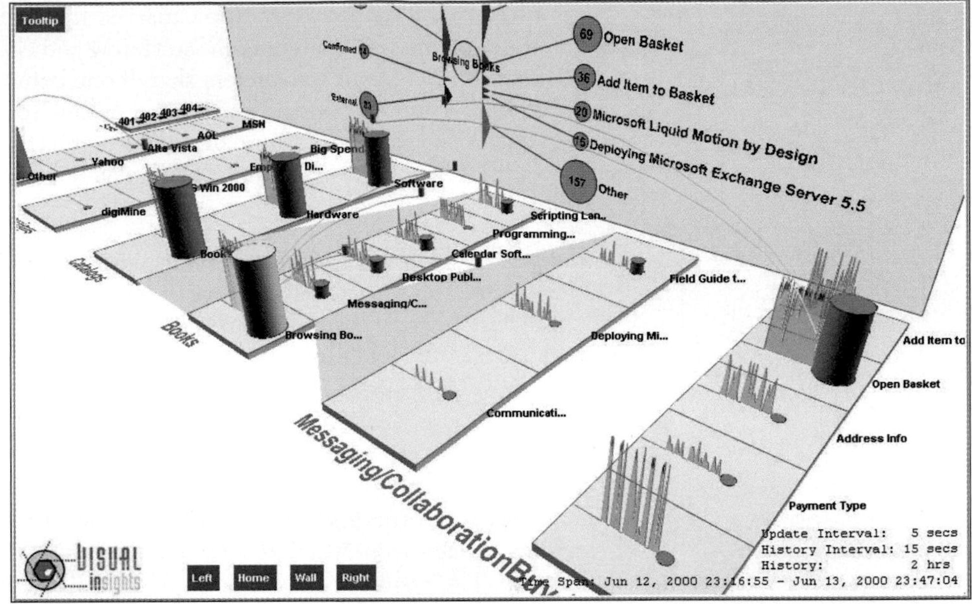

FIGURE 9.14
Using a data visualization system to analyze user activity on an e-commerce Web site.

graphical form. This assistance helps users discover patterns, links, and anomalies in business or scientific data in an interactive knowledge discovery and decision support process. Business applications like data mining typically use interactive graphs that let users drill down in real time and manipulate the underlying data of a business model to help clarify their meaning for business decision making [14, 24]. Figure 9.14 is an example of Web site activity data displayed by a data visualization system.

The concept of the geographic information system and data visualization is not a new one. One of the first recorded uses of the concept occurred in September 1854. During a 10-day period, 500 people, all from the same section of London, England, died of cholera. Dr. John Snow, a local physician, had been studying this cholera epidemic for some time. In trying to determine the source of the cholera, Dr. Snow located every cholera death in the Soho district of London by marking the location of the home of each victim with a dot on a map he had drawn. Figure 9.15 contains a replica of his original map.

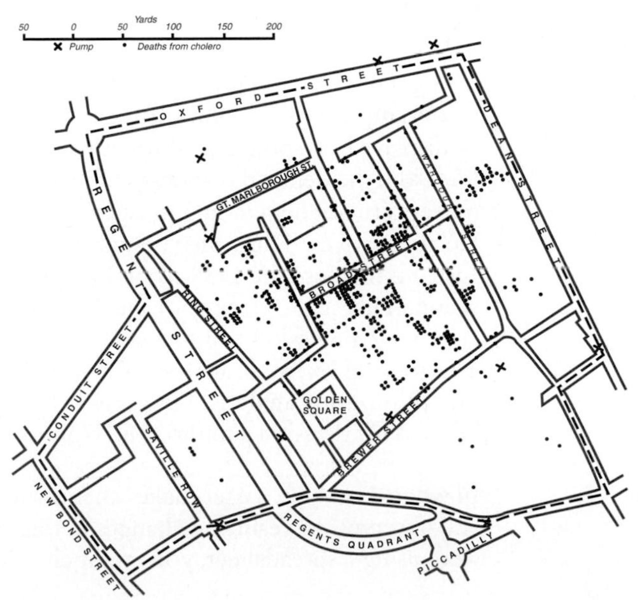

FIGURE 9.15
Replica of Dr. John Snow's cholera epidemic map.

As can be seen on the map, Dr. Snow marked the deaths with dots, and the 11 *X*s represent water pumps. By examining the scattering and clustering of the dots, Dr. Snow observed that the victims of the cholera shared one common attribute: They all lived near—and drank from—the Broad Street water pump. To test his hypothesis, Dr. Snow requested that the handle of the pump be removed, thus rendering it inoperable. Within a very short time, the cholera epidemic, which claimed more than 500 lives, was over.

Eli Lilly: Data Visualization for Decision Support

A new idea in software is beginning to help companies reduce the time and money they spend searching for patterns and meaning in their data oceans. It's an approach that started as a doctoral thesis by Christopher Ahlberg, the 32-year-old Swedish-born founder of software company Spotfire, in Somerville, Massachusetts.

Spotfire's software is the first to combine both "data visualization" and a powerful database querying flexibility. Known as DecisionSite, the data visualization system (DVS) software isn't cheap—installations start at $100,000. That hasn't stopped customers in a wide range of industries from buying more than 16,000 licenses.

The magic in Spotfire's software is that it lets users easily do what-if queries and comparisons of data from different sources by moving sliders on a computer screen with a mouse. The results appear as brightly colored bar graphs, pie charts, scatter plots, and even maps.

When Spotfire rolled out its software in 1997, it aimed first at the drug industry, where the data explosion has been immense. An early adopter was Sheldon Ort, Eli Lilly's information officer for manufacturing and supply services. Ort now has some 1,500 company scientists around the world hooked up to Spotfire's software. "We primarily use it to facilitate decision making," Ort says. "With its ability to represent multiple sources of information and interactively change your view, it's helpful for homing in on specific molecules and deciding whether we should be doing further testing on them."

Using Spotfire, researchers avoid having to construct multiple queries in perfect syntax. Dragging the sliders to and fro, the user is actually launching a sequence of queries in rapid succession and seeing the outcomes expressed graphically onscreen. Lilly uses the software to conduct meetings among researchers at multiple sites who are linked on a computer network. As the person making a presentation moves the sliders on his or her screen, everyone can see the families, clusters, outliers, gaps, anomalies, and other statistical nuggets that database users fish for. Ideas can be tried out collaboratively in real time [10].

Using Decision Support Systems

Using a decision support system involves an interactive **analytical modeling** process. For example, using a DSS software package for decision support may result in a series of displays in response to alternative what-if changes entered by a manager. This differs from the demand responses of management information systems, because decision makers are not demanding prespecified information. Rather, they are exploring possible alternatives. Thus, they do not have to specify their information needs in advance. Instead, they use the DSS to find the information they need to help them make a decision. That is the essence of the decision support system concept.

Using a decision support system involves four basic types of analytical modeling activities: (1) what-if analysis, (2) sensitivity analysis, (3) goal-seeking analysis, and (4) optimization analysis. Let's briefly look at each type of analytical modeling that can be used for decision support. See Figure 9.16.

What-If Analysis

In **what-if analysis**, a user makes changes to variables, or relationships among variables, and observes the resulting changes in the values of other variables. For example, if you were using a spreadsheet, you might change a revenue amount (a variable) or a tax rate

FIGURE 9.16
Activities and examples of the major types of analytical modeling.

Type of Analytical Modeling	Activities and Examples
What-if analysis	Observing how changes to selected variables affect other variables. *Example:* What if we cut advertising by 10 percent? What would happen to sales?
Sensitivity analysis	Observing how repeated changes to a single variable affect other variables. *Example:* Let's cut advertising by $100 repeatedly so we can see its relationship to sales.
Goal-seeking analysis	Making repeated changes to selected variables until a chosen variable reaches a target value. *Example:* Let's try increases in advertising until sales reach $1 million.
Optimization analysis	Finding an optimum value for selected variables, given certain constraints. *Example:* What's the best amount of advertising to have, given our budget and choice of media?

formula (a relationship among variables) in a simple financial spreadsheet model. Then you could command the spreadsheet program to instantly recalculate all affected variables in the spreadsheet. A managerial user would be very interested in observing and evaluating any changes that occurred to the values in the spreadsheet, especially to a variable such as net profit after taxes. To many managers, net profit after taxes is an example of the *bottom line*, that is, a key factor in making many types of decisions. This type of analysis would be repeated until the manager was satisfied with what the results revealed about the effects of various possible decisions. Figure 9.17 is an example of what-if analysis.

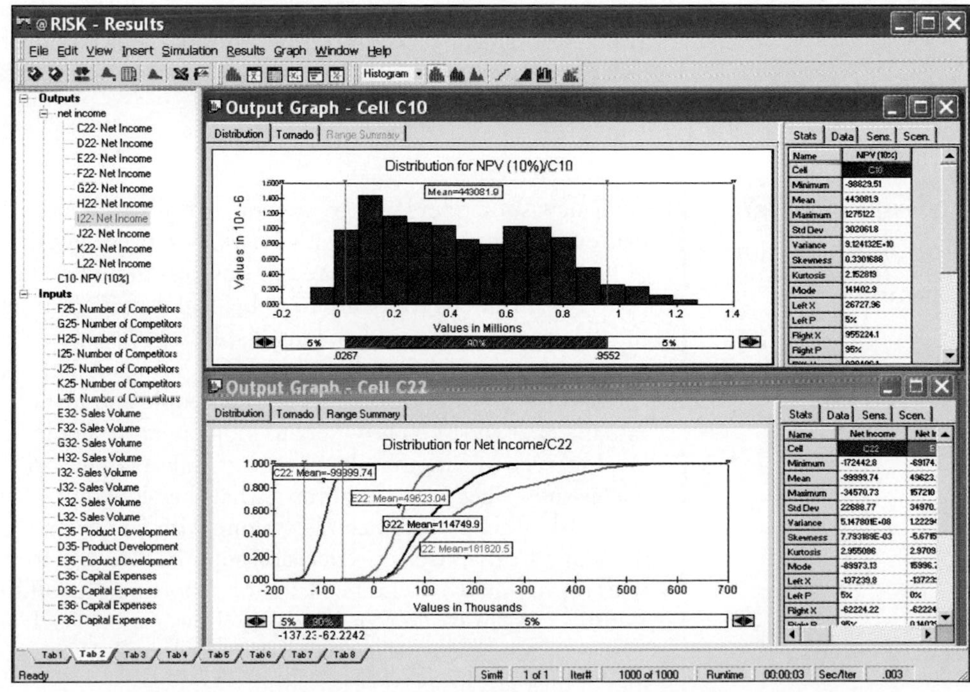

FIGURE 9.17
This what-if analysis involves the evaluation of probability distributions of net income and net present value (NPV) generated by changes to values for sales, competitors, product development, and capital expenses.

Sensitivity Analysis

Sensitivity analysis is a special case of what-if analysis. Typically, the value of only one variable is changed repeatedly, and the resulting changes on other variables are observed. As such, sensitivity analysis is really a case of what-if analysis involving repeated changes to only one variable at a time. Some DSS packages automatically make repeated small changes to a variable when asked to perform sensitivity analysis. Typically, sensitivity analysis is used when decision makers are uncertain about the assumptions made in estimating the value of certain key variables. In our previous spreadsheet example, the value of revenue could be changed repeatedly in small increments, and the effects on other spreadsheet variables observed and evaluated. This process would help a manager understand the impact of various revenue levels on other factors involved in decisions being considered.

Goal-Seeking Analysis

Goal-seeking analysis reverses the direction of the analysis done in what-if and sensitivity analyses. Instead of observing how changes in a variable affect other variables, goal-seeking analysis (also called *how can* analysis) sets a target value (goal) for a variable and then repeatedly changes other variables until the target value is achieved. For example, you could specify a target value (goal) of $2 million in net profit after taxes for a business venture. Then you could repeatedly change the value of revenue or expenses in a spreadsheet model until a result of $2 million is achieved. Thus, you would discover what amount of revenue or level of expenses the business venture needs to achieve to reach the goal of $2 million in after-tax profits. Therefore, this form of analytical modeling would help answer the question, "How can we achieve $2 million in net profit after taxes?" instead of the question, "What happens if we change revenue or expenses?" Thus, goal-seeking analysis is another important method of decision support.

Optimization Analysis

Optimization analysis is a more complex extension of goal-seeking analysis. Instead of setting a specific target value for a variable, the goal is to find the optimum value for one or more target variables, given certain constraints. Then one or more other variables are changed repeatedly, subject to the specified constraints, until the best values for the target variables are discovered. For example, you could try to determine the highest possible level of profits that could be achieved by varying the values for selected revenue sources and expense categories. Changes to such variables could be subject to constraints such as the limited capacity of a production process or limits to available financing. Optimization typically is accomplished using software like the Solver tool in Microsoft Excel and other software packages for optimization techniques such as linear programming.

Lexis-Nexis: Web Tools for Decision Support

"Our new subscribers will grow geometrically with Web-based access to our information services," explains Keith Hawk, vice president of sales for the Nexis division of Lexis-Nexis. "And therefore our business model is changing from selling primarily to organizations to selling to individual users." To track its 1.7 million subscribers of legal and news documents, Lexis-Nexis replaced its old decision support system with new DSS tools and an NCR Teradata data warehouse system. The new customer data warehouse lets 475 salespeople and in-house analysts use the corporate intranet and Web browsers to look up daily detailed customer usage data.

The type of data that the company's salespeople sort through and analyze includes subscriber usage patterns—what they look up, what sources they use most often, when they're connecting—along with customer contract details. To get to that data, Lexis-Nexis uses decision support software from Microstrategy Inc. Field sales representatives who need ad hoc reporting capabilities use Microstrategy DSS WebPE, a Web-based reporting tool. Power users, such as market research analysts, use DSS Agent, an analytical modeling tool with Web access, to closely analyze and model business processes [15, 18].

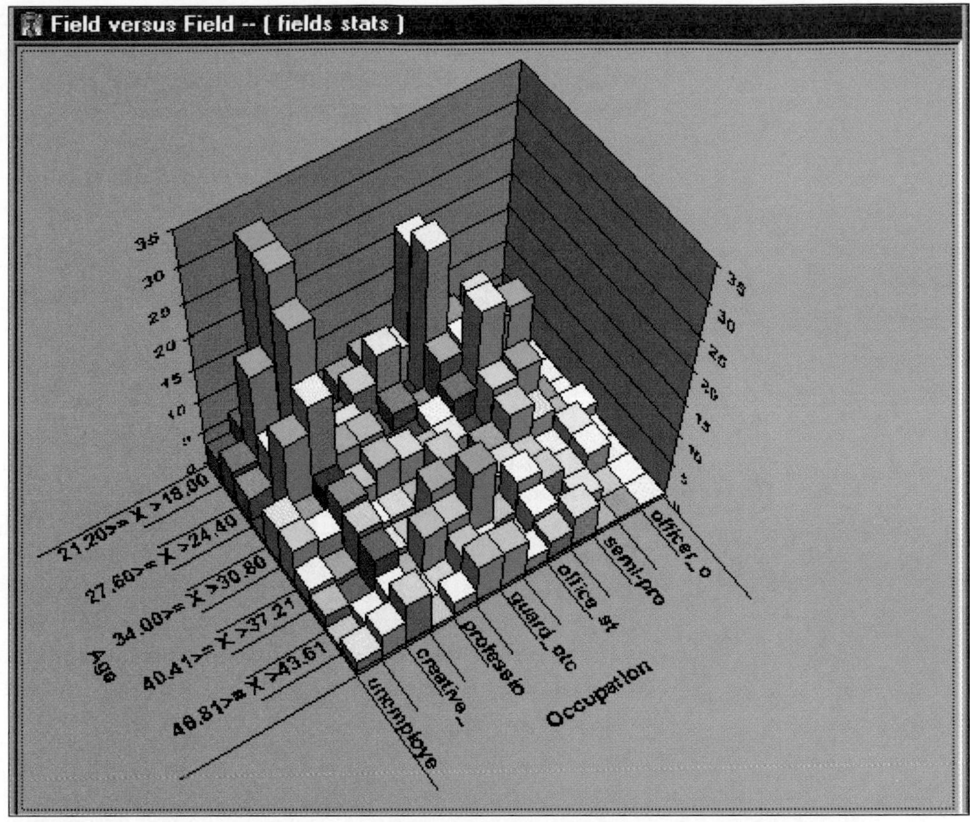

FIGURE 9.18
Data mining software helps discover patterns in business data, like this analysis of customer demographic information.

Data Mining for Decision Support

We discussed **data mining** and data warehouses in Chapter 5 as vital tools for organizing and exploiting the data resources of a company. Thus, data mining's main purpose is to provide decision support to managers and business professionals through a process referred to as *knowledge discovery.* Data mining software analyzes the vast stores of historical business data that have been prepared for analysis in corporate data warehouses and tries to discover patterns, trends, and correlations hidden in the data that can help a company improve its business performance.

Data mining software may perform regression, decision tree, neural network, cluster detection, or market basket analysis for a business. See Figure 9.18. The data mining process can highlight buying patterns, reveal customer tendencies, cut redundant costs, or uncover unseen profitable relationships and opportunities. For example, many companies use data mining to find more profitable ways to perform successful direct mailings, including e-mailings, or discover better ways to display products in a store, design a better e-commerce Web site, reach untapped profitable customers, or recognize customers or products that are unprofitable or marginal [16].

Market basket analysis (MBA) is one of the most common and useful types of data mining for marketing. The purpose of market basket analysis is to determine what products customers purchase together with other products. MBA takes its name from the concept of customers throwing all their purchases into a shopping cart (a market basket) during grocery shopping. Knowing what products people purchase as a group can be very helpful to a retailer or any other company. A store could use this information to place products frequently sold together into the same area, and a catalog or World Wide Web merchant could use it to determine the layouts of a catalog and order form. Direct marketers could use the basket analysis results to determine what new products to offer their prior customers.

In some cases, the fact that items sell together is obvious—every fast-food restaurant asks their customers "Would you like fries with that?" whenever a customer orders a sandwich. However, sometimes the fact that certain items would sell well together is far from obvious. A well-known example is the relationship between beer and diapers. A supermarket performing a basket analysis discovered that diapers and beer sell well together on Thursdays. While the result makes some sense—couples stocking up on supplies for themselves and for their children before the weekend starts—it's far from intuitive. The strength of market basket analysis is as follows: By using computer data mining tools, it's not necessary for a person to think of what products consumers would logically buy together; instead, the customers' sales data speak for themselves. This is a good example of data-driven marketing.

Once it is known that customers who buy one product are likely to buy another, it is possible for a company to market the products together or make the purchasers of one product target prospects for another. If customers who purchase diapers are already likely to purchase beer, they'll be even more likely to buy beer if there happens to be a beer display just outside the diaper aisle. Likewise, if it's known that customers who buy a sweater from a certain mail-order catalog have a propensity toward buying a jacket from the same catalog, sales of jackets can be increased by having the telephone representatives describe and offer the jacket to anyone who calls in to order the sweater. By targeting customers who are already known to be likely buyers, the effectiveness of a given marketing effort is significantly increased—regardless of whether the marketing takes the form of in-store displays, catalog layout design, or direct offers to customers.

Data mining can be used in any situation in which hidden patterns need to be revealed. Here's a real-world example in which data mining is used to help coaches win basketball games.

National Basketball Association: Playing "Mine" Games

The job of a coach in the National Basketball Association (NBA) is an exciting job to be sure. It is also a job where winning is expected, and too much losing is simply not tolerated. So what can an NBA coach do to help bring his team to victory? Naturally, there are the full-court press, the pick and roll, the fast break, the low post, and, of course, multimillion-dollar players. But to help develop the strategy necessary to win on any given day, NBA coaches also have a different kind of weapon in their arsenal: data mining. About 20 NBA teams have been using Advanced Scout, a data mining application developed by IBM, to hone their game plans.

Advanced Scout is a data analysis tool that coaches use on laptops both at home and on road trips to mine data housed on the NBA's central server. The events of each game are categorized statistically—by points, assists and fouls, and so on—and time stamped, allowing coaches to easily search NBA game videos to give meaning to statistical findings. So, for instance, if a coach finds via Advanced Scout that a star opposing player has trouble scoring against certain players on his team, he can pinpoint the times on the game tapes when the opposing star goes head-to-head with those players and devise a defensive strategy.

The results from Advanced Scout are presented to the coach in one of two forms: a text description or a graph. Automatically generated text describes the patterns found for the situation under analysis. An example report might look something like this:

> *When Price was point-guard, J. Williams missed 0 percent (0) of his jump field-goal attempts and made 100 percent (4) of his jump field-goal attempts. The total number of such field-goal attempts was 4. This is a different pattern than the norm which shows that Cavaliers' players missed 50.70 percent of their total field-goal attempts. Cavaliers' players scored 49.30 percent of their total field-goal attempts.*

Results in a natural language form can be more easily understood by the coach. The text presentation also offers a suggestion as to why the particular pattern is interesting—explicitly pointing out the ways that this particular pattern deviates from an expected norm—in essence presenting an initial argument and easily interpretable justification of the relative importance of this finding. Advanced Scout also allows for "what-if" analysis to investigate different combinations of players to improve a given situation. For example, if plays designed for former Pistons power forward Ben Wallace were less successful when Chauncey Billups played point guard, coach Flip Saunders could issue a query for the identical circumstances, except with Lindsey Hunter or Rip Hamilton as point guards. Data mining takes the excitement of the NBA to a higher level by allowing coaches to play the best against the best [20, 44].

Executive Information Systems

Executive information systems (EIS) are information systems that combine many of the features of management information systems and decision support systems. When they were first developed, their focus was on meeting the strategic information needs of top management. Thus, the first goal of executive information systems was to provide top executives with immediate and easy access to information about a firm's *critical success factors* (CSFs), that is, key factors that are critical to accomplishing an organization's strategic objectives. For example, the executives of a retail store chain would probably consider factors such as its e-commerce versus traditional sales results or its product line mix to be critical to its survival and success.

However, executive information systems are becoming so widely used by managers, analysts, and other knowledge workers that they are sometimes humorously called "everyone's information systems." More popular alternative names are enterprise information systems (EIS) and executive support systems (ESS). These names also reflect the fact that more features, such as Web browsing, electronic mail, groupware tools, and DSS and expert system capabilities, are being added to many systems to make them more useful to managers and business professionals [18, 45].

Features of an EIS

In an EIS, information is presented in forms tailored to the preferences of the executives using the system. For example, most executive information systems stress the use of a graphical user interface and graphics displays that can be customized to the information preferences of executives using the EIS. Other information presentation methods used by an EIS include exception reporting and trend analysis. The ability to *drill down*, which allows executives to quickly retrieve displays of related information at lower levels of detail, is another important capability.

Figure 9.19 shows one of the displays provided by the Web-enabled Hyperion executive information system. Notice how simple and brief this display is. Also note how it provides users of the system with the ability to drill down quickly to lower levels of detail in areas of particular interest to them. Beside the drill-down capability, the Hyperion EIS also stresses trend analysis and exception reporting. Thus, a business user can quickly discover the direction key factors are heading and the extent to which critical factors are deviating from expected results.

Executive information systems have spread into the ranks of middle management and business professionals as their feasibility and benefits have been recognized and as less expensive systems for client/server networks and corporate intranets became available. For example, one popular EIS software package reports that only 3 percent of its users are top executives. Another example is the EIS of Conoco, one of the world's largest oil companies. Conoco's EIS is used by most senior managers and by over 4,000 employees located at corporate headquarters in Houston and throughout the world [5, 46, 48].

EIS at Conoco and KeyCorp

As we just mentioned, Conoco Inc. has a widely used EIS. Conoco's EIS is a large system with 75 different applications and hundreds of screen displays. Senior executives and over 4,000 managers and analysts worldwide use EIS applications ranging

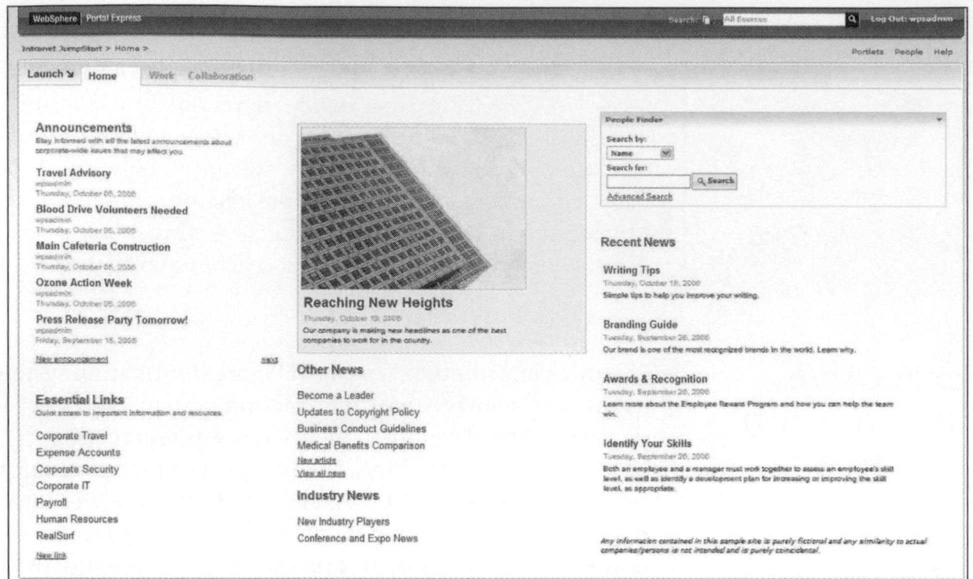

FIGURE 9.19
This Web-based executive information system provides managers and business professionals with a variety of personalized information and analytical tools for decision support.

from analyzing internal operations and financial results to viewing external events that affect the petroleum industry. Conoco's EIS is popular with its users and has resulted in improved employee productivity and decision making and significant cost savings compared with alternative methods of generating information for managers and analysts [5].

KeyCorp is a large banking and financial services holding company. It developed Keynet, a corporate intranet that transformed its mainframe-based EIS into a new EIS—a Web-enabled system it calls "everyone's information system." Now more than 1,000 managers and analysts have Web access to 40 major business information areas within Keynet, ranging from sales and financial statistics to human resource management [40].

Enterprise Portals and Decision Support

Don't confuse portals with the executive information systems that have been used in some industries for many years. Portals are for everyone in the company, and not just for executives. You want people on the front lines making decisions using browsers and portals rather than just executives using specialized executive information system software [40].

We mentioned previously in this chapter that major changes and expansions are taking place in traditional MIS, DSS, and EIS tools for providing the information and modeling managers need to support their decision making. Decision support in business is changing, driven by rapid developments in end-user computing and networking; Internet and Web technologies; and Web-enabled business applications. One of the key changes taking place in management information and decision support systems in business is the rapid growth of enterprise information portals.

Enterprise Information Portals

A user checks his e-mail, looks up the current company stock price, checks his available vacation days, and receives an order from a customer—all from the browser on his desktop. That is the next-generation intranet, also known as a corporate or enterprise information portal. With it, the browser becomes the dashboard to daily business tasks [39].

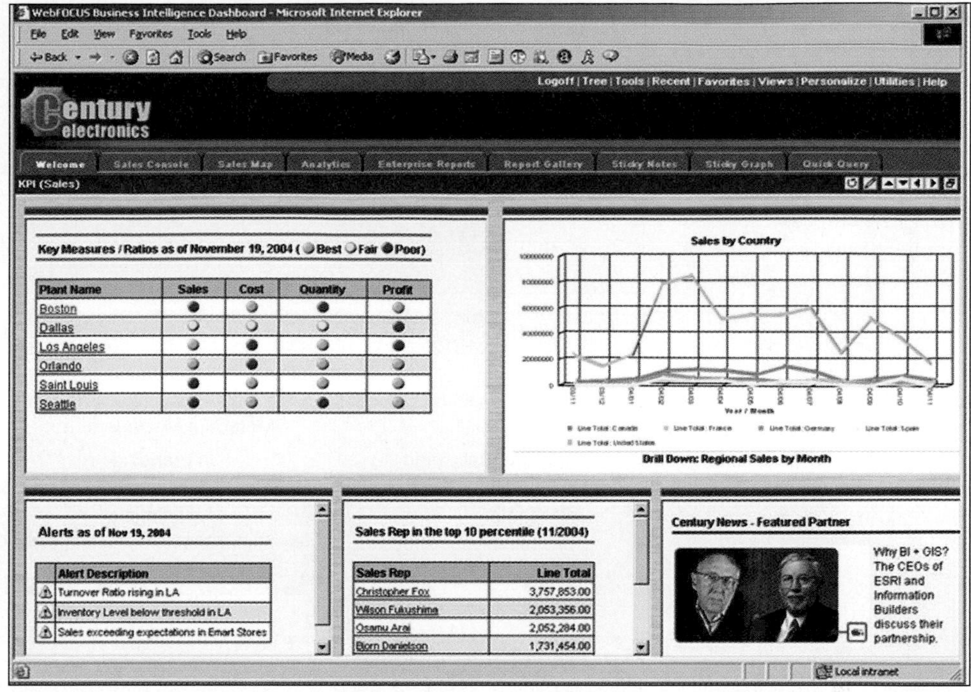

FIGURE 9.20
An enterprise information portal can provide a business professional with a personalized workplace of information sources, administrative and analytical tools, and relevant business applications.

An **enterprise information portal (EIP)** is a Web-based interface and integration of MIS, DSS, EIS, and other technologies that gives all intranet users and selected extranet users access to a variety of internal and external business applications and services. For example, internal applications might include access to e-mail, project Web sites, and discussion groups; human resources Web self-services; customer, inventory, and other corporate databases; decision support systems; and knowledge management systems. External applications might include industry, financial, and other Internet news services; links to industry discussion groups; and links to customer and supplier Internet and extranet Web sites. Enterprise information portals are typically tailored or personalized to the needs of individual business users or groups of users, giving them a personalized *digital dashboard* of information sources and applications. See Figure 9.20.

The business benefits of enterprise information portals include providing more specific and selective information to business users, providing easy access to key corporate intranet Web site resources, delivering industry and business news, and providing better access to company data for selected customers, suppliers, or business partners. Enterprise information portals can also help avoid excessive surfing by employees across company and Internet Web sites by making it easier for them to receive or find the information and services they need, thus improving the productivity of a company's workforce [40].

Figure 9.21 illustrates how companies are developing enterprise information portals as a way to provide Web-enabled information, knowledge, and decision support to their executives, managers, employees, suppliers, customers, and other business partners. The enterprise information portal is a customized and personalized Web-based interface for corporate intranets, which gives users easy access to a variety of internal and external business applications, databases, and services. For example, the EIP in Figure 9.20 might give a qualified user secure access to DSS, data mining, and OLAP tools; the Internet and the Web; the corporate intranet; supplier or customer extranets; operational and analytical databases; a data warehouse; and a variety of business applications [36, 39, 40].

FIGURE 9.21
The components of this enterprise information portal identify it as a Web-enabled decision support system that can be personalized for executives, managers, employees, suppliers, customers, and other business partners.

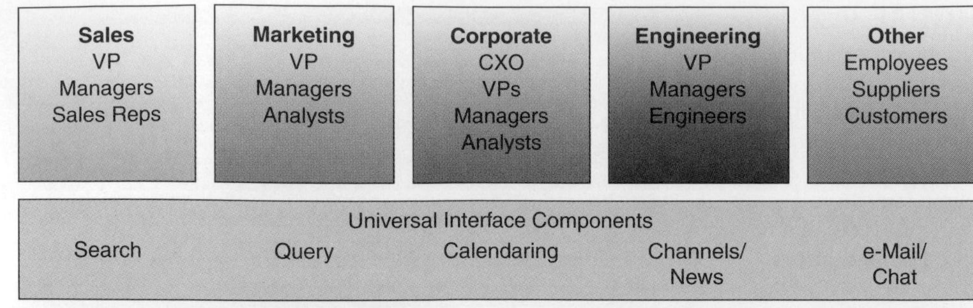

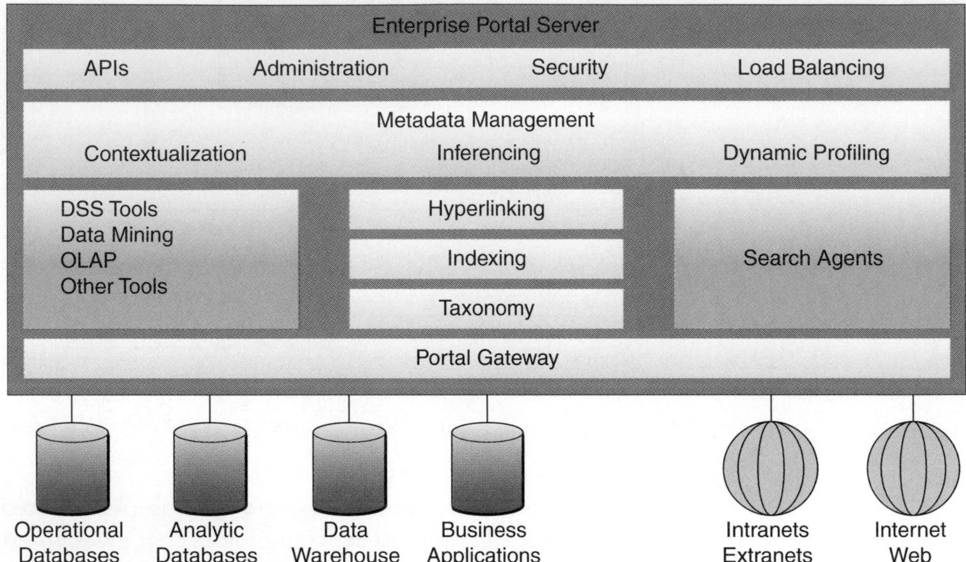

Knowledge Management Systems

We introduced **knowledge management systems** in Chapter 2 as the use of information technology to help gather, organize, and share business knowledge within an organization. In many organizations, hypermedia databases at corporate intranet Web sites have become the *knowledge bases* for storage and dissemination of business knowledge. This knowledge frequently takes the form of best practices, policies, and business solutions at the project, team, business unit, and enterprise levels of the company.

For many companies, enterprise information portals are the entry to corporate intranets that serve as their knowledge management systems. That's why such portals are called **enterprise knowledge portals** by their vendors. Thus, enterprise knowledge portals play an essential role in helping companies use their intranets as knowledge management systems to share and disseminate knowledge in support of business decision making by managers and business professionals [35, 36]. See Figure 9.22. Now let's look at an example of a Web-enabled knowledge management system in business.

Qwest Communications: Web Knowledge Management System

At Qwest Communications, knowledge management (KM) was the only way to be sure that call center representatives had the information they needed, when they needed it. Relying on print documentation or a supervisor's directive did not ensure cross-company accuracy or even that the information was delivered to all who needed it. Knowledge management was the only way to ensure that support would be available for every conceivable situation and that the information was accurate and complete. Qwest has had an online procedures database for quite some time, but it was just online documentation. Each document looked different. Design was in the hands of the individual author, and there were lots of authors. Compounding the problem, authors had their own views about the content and the appropriate level of detail. Generally speaking, they wrote what *they* thought the representative needed to know, not necessarily what the representative *actually* needed to know.

In 1999 the old system was replaced by *InfoBuddy*, Qwest's Web-based knowledge management system. It supports a wide variety of job functions in addition to customer service representatives, including technical repair, installation and maintenance, and so on. InfoBuddy uses a methods and procedures database with intelligent KM capabilities such as searching, tagging, and customizable interface. It can reorder the information presentation based on who the user is.

When users identify themselves and their job function or role, the InfoBuddy intranet portal knows how to configure its user interface to provide information of most value to each person. In addition, users have the ability to personalize their portal through the "MyBuddy" feature, enabling representatives to place bookmarks on their home pages to the information they feel is most important. Over time, as users "learn" from the system, they can replace learned material with new, usually more advanced information.

In addition, the InfoBuddy system "pushes" information to specific users based on their needs. For example, if a new promotion were initiated, specific information—products, pricing, and so on—would appear on the "desktop" of those representatives who are involved in the marketing initiative [42].

FIGURE 9.22 This example of the capabilities and components of an enterprise knowledge portal emphasizes its use as a Web-based knowledge management system.

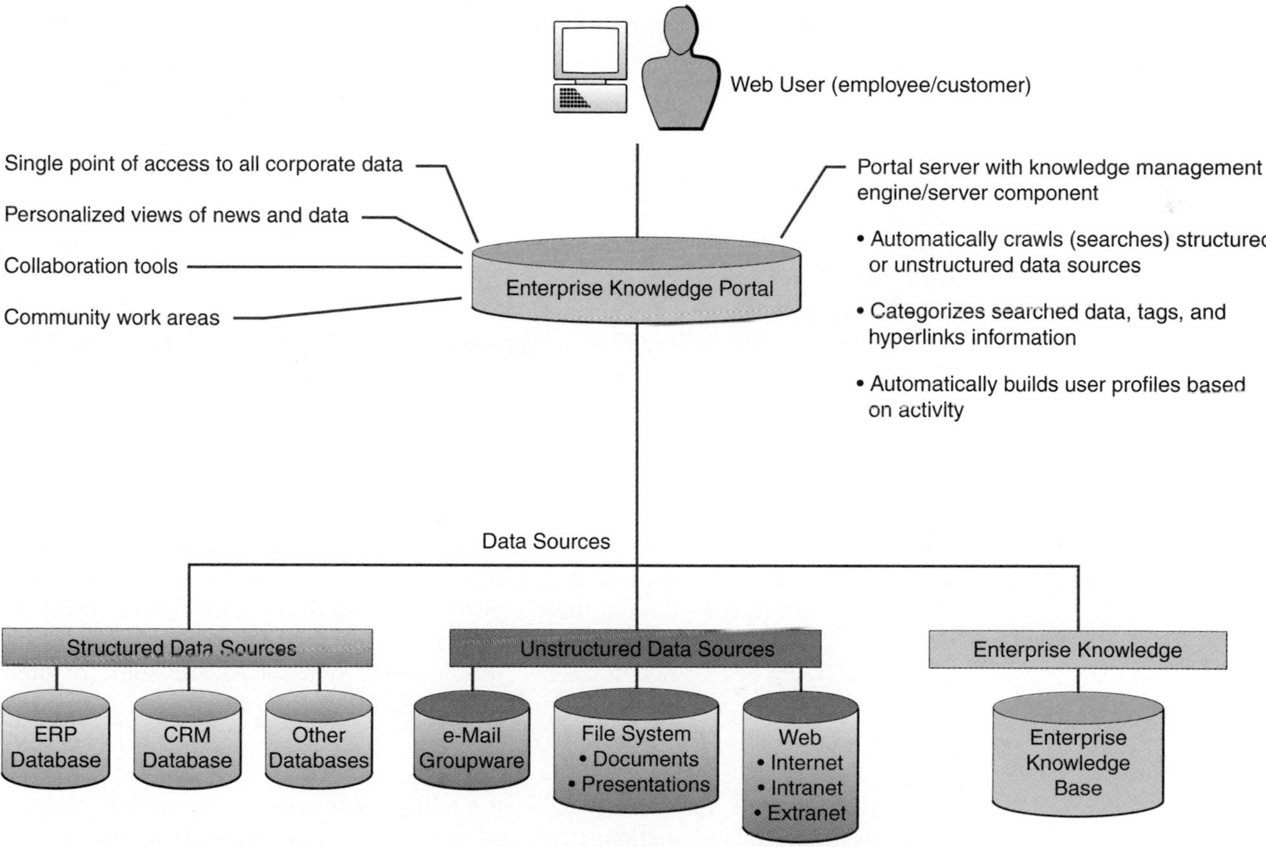

SECTION II Artificial Intelligence Technologies in Business

Business and AI

Artificial intelligence (AI) technologies are being used in a variety of ways to improve the decision support provided to managers and business professionals in many companies. See Figure 9.23. For example:

> *AI-enabled applications are at work in information distribution and retrieval, database mining, product design, manufacturing, inspection, training, user support, surgical planning, resource scheduling, and complex resource management.*
>
> *Indeed, for anyone who schedules, plans, allocates resources, designs new products, uses the Internet, develops software, is responsible for product quality, is an investment professional, heads up IT, uses IT, or operates in any of a score of other capacities and arenas, AI technologies already may be in place and providing competitive advantage* [50].

Read the Real World Case on the next page. We can learn a lot about artificial intelligence applications in business from this example.

An Overview of Artificial Intelligence

What is artificial intelligence? **Artificial intelligence (AI)** is a field of science and technology based on disciplines such as computer science, biology, psychology, linguistics, mathematics, and engineering. The goal of AI is to develop computers that can simulate the ability to think, as well as see, hear, walk, talk, and feel. A major thrust of artificial intelligence is the simulation of computer functions normally associated with human intelligence, such as reasoning, learning, and problem solving, as summarized in Figure 9.24.

Debate has raged around artificial intelligence since serious work in the field began in the 1950s. Not only technological but moral and philosophical questions abound about the possibility of intelligent, thinking machines. For example, British AI pioneer Alan Turing in 1950 proposed a test for determining if machines could think. According to the Turing test, a computer could demonstrate intelligence if a human interviewer, conversing with an unseen human and an unseen computer, could not tell which was which [30, 45].

Although much work has been done in many of the subgroups that fall under the AI umbrella, critics believe that no computer can truly pass the Turing test. They claim that developing intelligence to impart true humanlike capabilities to computers is simply not possible. But progress continues, and only time will tell if the ambitious goals of artificial intelligence will be achieved and equal the popular images found in science fiction.

The Domains of Artificial Intelligence

Figure 9.25 illustrates the major **domains** of AI research and development. Note that AI **applications** can be grouped under three major areas—cognitive science, robotics, and natural interfaces—though these classifications do overlap, and other classifications can be used. Also note that expert systems are just one of many important AI applications. Let's briefly review each of these major areas of AI and some of their current technologies. Figure 9.26 outlines some of the latest developments in commercial applications of artificial intelligence.

Cognitive Science This area of artificial intelligence is based on research in biology, neurology, psychology, mathematics, and many allied disciplines. It focuses on researching how the human brain works and how humans think and learn. The results of such research in *human information processing* are the basis for the development of a variety of computer-based applications in artificial intelligence.

REAL WORLD CASE 2

Harrah's Entertainment, LendingTree, DeepGreen Financial, and Cisco Systems: Successes and Challenges of Automated Decision Making

For over half a century, the field of artificial intelligence (AI) has promised that computers would relieve managers and professionals of the need to make certain types of decisions. Computer programs would analyze data and make sound judgments, whether it be to configure a complex computer, diagnose and treat a patient's illness, or determine when to stir a big vat of soup, with little or no human help.

But automated decision making has been slow to materialize. Many early artificial intelligence applications were just solutions looking for problems, contributing little to improved organizational performance. In medicine, for example, doctors showed little interest in having machines diagnose their patients' diseases. In the business sector, even when expert systems were directed at real issues, extracting the right kind of specialized knowledge from seasoned decision makers and maintaining it over time proved to be more difficult than anticipated.

But now, automated decision making is finally coming of age. The new generation of applications, however, differs from prior AI-based decision support systems in several important respects. To begin with, the new systems are easier to create and manage than earlier ones, which leaned heavily on the expertise of knowledge engineers. What's more, the new applications do not require anyone to identify the problems or to initiate the analysis. Indeed, decision-making capabilities are embedded into the normal flow of work, and they are typically triggered without human intervention: They sense online data or conditions, apply codified knowledge or logic and make decisions—all with minimal amounts of human intervention. And finally, unlike earlier systems, the new ones are designed to translate decisions into action quickly, accurately, and efficiently.

Of course, there is still a role for people. Managers still need to be involved in reviewing and confirming decisions and, in exceptional cases, in making the actual decisions. Also, even the most automated systems rely on experts and managers to create and maintain rules and monitor the results.

Today's automated decision systems are best suited for decisions that must be made frequently and rapidly, using information that is available electronically. The knowledge and decision criteria used in these systems need to be highly structured, and the factors that must be taken into account must be well understood. If experts can readily codify the decision rules and if high-quality data are available, the conditions are ripe for automating the decision.

Bank credit decisions are a good example: They are repetitive, are susceptible to uniform criteria, and can be made by drawing on the vast supply of consumer credit data that are available. A decision about whom to hire as CEO, by contrast, would be a poor choice. It occurs only rarely, and different observers are apt to apply their own criteria, such as personal chemistry, which cannot be easily captured in a computer model.

The transportation industry was one of the first to employ automated decision making on a large scale. After being used initially by airlines to optimize seat pricing, decision-making technology has since been applied to a variety of areas, including flight scheduling and crew and airport staff scheduling.

Yield-management programs have also been adopted in related businesses, such as lodging. For example, Harrah's Entertainment, the world's largest casino operator, makes several million dollars a month in incremental revenue by optimizing room rates at its hotels and offering different rates to members of its loyalty program based on projected demand. The use of yield-management systems for hotel room pricing is common, but combining it with loyalty management programs is unusual. The combination ensures that the best customers get the best prices and, in turn, these customers will reward the company with their loyalty.

Investment firms have relied upon AI-based decision-making technology extensively for program trading and arbitrage. But much of the recent activity within the financial industry has revolved around creating new applications aimed at finding good banking and insurance customers and

FIGURE 9.23

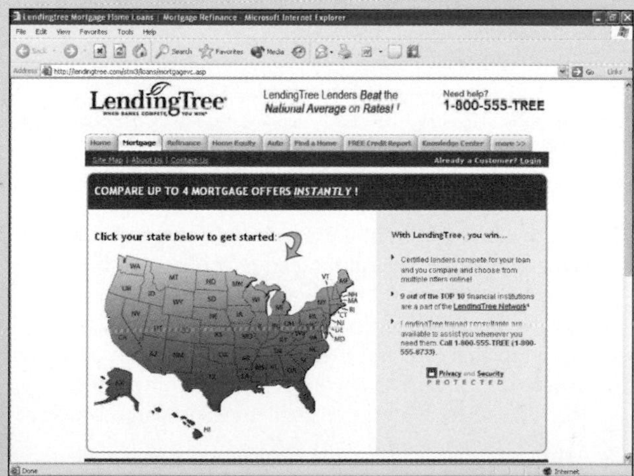

Business uses of artificial intelligence include Web-based automated decision-making applications in mortgage banking.

serving their needs. The widespread availability of online credit information and financial history, the need for differentiation through rapid customer service, and the rapid growth of online financial services providers have led to increases in automated decisions.

To compete in the same arena as LendingTree, lenders are forced to be more highly automated and are implementing automated decision engines to help them remain competitive. For example, DeepGreen Financial in Cleveland, Ohio, was created from the ground up to make use of automated decision technology. DeepGreen originates loans in 46 states through its Web site and through partnerships with LendingTree, priceline.com, and MortgageIT.com, based in New York City. It also offers home equity lending services for mortgage brokers and private-label or co-branded home equity lending technology and fulfillment services. Since its inception in 2000, DeepGreen's Internet technology has been used to process more than 325,000 applications and originate more than $4.4 billion of home equity lines of credit, according to Jerry Selitto, the bank's founding chief executive officer.

DeepGreen created an Internet-based system that makes credit decisions within minutes by skimming off the customers with the best credit, enabling just eight employees to process some 400 applications a day. Instead of competing on the basis of interest rates, DeepGreen's drawing card is ease of application and speedy approval. The company provides nearly instantaneous, unconditional decisions without requiring traditional appraisals or upfront paperwork from borrowers.

Customers can complete the application within five minutes, at which point the automated process begins: A credit report is pulled, the credit is scored, a property valuation is completed using online data, confirmations are made concerning fraud and flood insurance, and a final decision is made on the loan. In about 80 percent of the cases, customers receive a final decision within two minutes. (In some cases, DeepGreen is only able to offer a conditional commitment because some of the information—usually the valuation—is not available online.) After approval, the system selects a notary public located near the customer's home and the customer chooses a closing date. All the loan documents are automatically generated and express-mailed to the notary.

DeepGreen's competitive strategy is driven by the convergence of several factors. At its core, it relies on the advancement of analytic and rule-based AI-technologies without which the business would not be possible. It also leverages the bank's deep understanding of changing market conditions and pricing dynamics. Together with DeepGreen's extensive use of online information, these factors enable the company to tailor loan terms to the needs of individual borrowers. Moreover, the company's focus on high-end customers makes it possible to offer speed, service, and convenience. Credit decisions involving affluent, low-risk borrowers are relatively easy to make. Finally, high-end borrowers tend to be Internet-savvy; if you build an online service that meets their specific needs, they will come.

The consequences of not defining limits can be huge. Several years ago, during the e-commerce boom, Cisco Systems, based in San Jose, California, belatedly found out that it was relying too heavily on its automated ordering and supply chain systems. Management realized that many of the orders that had been entered on the books were not as firm as they assumed and, in all likelihood, would never be shipped. This glitch eventually forced Cisco to write off more than $2 billion in excess inventory.

Over and above their close monitoring of risk levels, managers in charge of automated decision systems must also develop processes for managing exceptions. Among other things, they need to determine in advance what happens when the computer has too little data on which to make a decision (a frequent reason for allowing exceptions). Companies should have clear criteria for determining when cases cannot be addressed through automation and who should deal with the exceptions. They should also ensure that exceptions are viewed internally as opportunities to learn, rather than as failures of the system.

Source: Adapted from Thomas H. Davenport and Jeanne G. Harris, "Automated Decision Making Comes of Age," *MIT Sloan Management Review*, Summer 2005; Thomas H. Davenport, "Competing on Analytics," *Harvard Business Review*, January 2006.

CASE STUDY QUESTIONS

1. Why did some previous attempts to use artificial intelligence technologies fail? What key differences of the new AI-based applications versus the old cause the authors to declare that automated decision making is finally coming of age?
2. What types of decisions are best suited for automated decision making? Provide several examples of successful applications from the companies in this case to illustrate your answer.
3. What role do humans play in automated decision-making applications? What are some of the challenges faced by managers where automated decision-making systems are being used? What solutions are needed to meet such challenges?

REAL WORLD ACTIVITIES

1. Use the Internet to find examples of companies that are using automated decision making or other business applications of artificial intelligence. You might begin by looking for such information on the companies mentioned in this case and their main competitors, and then widen your search to encompass other companies. What business benefits or challenges do you discover?
2. Artificial intelligence applications in business such as automated decision making pose potential business risks, as evidenced by the Cisco Systems experience, and have the potential for other risks to business and human security and safety, for example. Break into small groups with your classmates to discuss such risks and propose controls and safeguards to lessen the possibility of such occurrences.

FIGURE 9.24
Some of the attributes of intelligent behavior. AI is attempting to duplicate these capabilities in computer-based systems.

Attributes of Intelligent Behavior
• Think and reason.
• Use reason to solve problems.
• Learn or understand from experience.
• Acquire and apply knowledge.
• Exhibit creativity and imagination.
• Deal with complex or perplexing situations.
• Respond quickly and successfully to new situations.
• Recognize the relative importance of elements in a situation.
• Handle ambiguous, incomplete, or erroneous information.

Applications in the cognitive science area of AI include the development of *expert systems* and other *knowledge-based systems* that add a knowledge base and some reasoning capability to information systems. Also included are *adaptive learning systems* that can modify their behaviors on the basis of information they acquire as they operate. Chess-playing systems are primitive examples of such applications, though many more applications are being implemented. *Fuzzy logic* systems can process data that are incomplete or ambiguous, that is, *fuzzy data*. Thus, they can solve semistructured problems with incomplete knowledge by developing approximate inferences and answers, as humans do. *Neural network* software can learn by processing sample problems and their solutions. As neural nets start to recognize patterns, they can begin to program themselves to solve such problems on their own. *Genetic algorithm* software uses Darwinian (survival of the fittest), randomizing, and other mathematics functions to simulate evolutionary processes that can generate increasingly better solutions to problems. And *intelligent agents* use expert system and other AI technologies to serve as software surrogates for a variety of end-user applications.

Robotics AI, engineering, and physiology are the basic disciplines of **robotics**. This technology produces robot machines with computer intelligence and computer-controlled, humanlike physical capabilities. This area thus includes applications designed to give robots the powers of sight, or visual perception; touch, or tactile capabilities; dexterity, or skill in handling and manipulation; locomotion, or the physical ability to move over any terrain; and navigation, or the intelligence to properly find one's way to a destination [30].

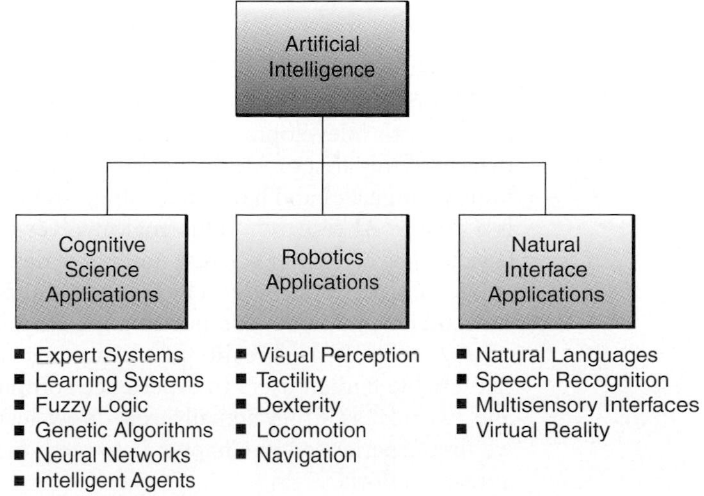

FIGURE 9.25
The major application areas of artificial intelligence. Note that the many applications of AI can be grouped into the three major areas of cognitive science, robotics, and natural interfaces.

FIGURE 9.26
Examples of some of the latest commercial applications of AI.

Commercial Applications of AI

Decision Support

- Intelligent work environment that will help you capture the *why* as well as the *what* of engineered design and decision making.
- Intelligent human-computer interface (HCI) systems that can understand spoken language and gestures and facilitate problem solving by supporting organizationwide collaborations to solve particular problems.
- Situation assessment and resource allocation software for uses that range from airlines and airports to logistics centers.

Information Retrieval

- AI-based intranet and Internet systems that distill tidal waves of information into simple presentations.
- Natural language technology to retrieve any sort of online information, from text to pictures, videos, maps, and audio clips, in response to English questions.
- Database mining for marketing trend analysis, financial forecasting, maintenance cost reduction, and more.

Virtual Reality

- X-raylike vision enabled by enhanced-reality visualization that allows brain surgeons to "see through" intervening tissue to operate, monitor, and evaluate disease progression.
- Automated animation interfaces that allow users to interact with virtual objects via touch (e.g., medical students can "feel" what it's like to suture severed aortas).
- A virtual walk-through by a potential buyer of a new condominium property that has yet to be built. Pre-sales can be accomplished before the construction even begins.
- Training individuals to perform safely and effectively in hazardous environments such as jet fighters, nuclear environments, and hazardous industrial situations.
- Addition of smell, taste, and touch to sight and hearing along with motion tracking and 3D capabilities so users can experience all relevant sensory stimuli when operating in virtual environments.

Robotics

- Machine-vision inspections systems for gauging, guiding, identifying, and inspecting products and providing competitive advantage in manufacturing.
- Cutting-edge robotics systems, from micro robots and hands and legs, to cognitive robotic and trainable modular vision systems.

Natural Interfaces The development of natural interfaces is considered a major area of AI applications and is essential to the natural use of computers by humans. For example, the development of *natural languages* and speech recognition are major thrusts of this area of AI. Being able to talk to computers and robots in conversational human languages and have them "understand" us as easily as we understand each other is a goal of AI research. This goal involves research and development in linguistics, psychology, computer science, and other disciplines. Other natural interface research applications include the development of multisensory devices that use a variety of body movements to operate computers, which is related to the emerging application area of *virtual reality*. Virtual reality involves using multisensory human-computer interfaces that enable human users to experience computer-simulated objects, spaces, activities, and "worlds" as if they actually exist. Now, let's look again at BAE Systems (a company we first experienced in Chapter 2) to see how AI is assisting with its knowledge management efforts.

BAE Systems: Using AI for Knowledge Management

It's one of those blue-sky goals to which many big companies only aspire: capturing the seemingly infinite amount of intellectual capital that's carried by tens of thousands of employees around the world and using it to achieve competitive advantage. But it's a flight that's well under way at London-based BAE Systems PLC (www.baesystems.com), formerly British Aerospace, which is getting solid returns on a knowledge management intranet-based system. Thousands of BAE engineers scattered across five continents in 100 offices are using the system to search for information that may be vital to big initiatives and to identify and eliminate redundant project work.

Like other far-flung multinationals, the $20 billion-plus aerospace and engineering giant suspected that its engineers and other workers might be wasting a lot of time searching for information scattered across the enterprise. So BAE Systems invested roughly $150,000 to study its global operations to see whether "we had the right information to support decision-making processes and if people had the right learning systems to help them support their day-to-day jobs," according to Richard West, BAE's organizational and e-learning manager in Farnborough, England.

The results, says West, "were certainly eye-opening." BAE Systems discovered that nearly two-thirds of its top 120 decision makers didn't have the right information at key stages. The company also found that 80 percent of employees were "wasting" an average of 30 minutes each day trying to find the information they needed to do their jobs. Another 60 percent were spending an hour or more duplicating the work of others.

One of the problems BAE Systems officials discovered through the study was information overload on its intranets. The information itself was often unstructured, and the search engines were inadequate for conducting keyword searches to find information, says West. The company decided to test two or three of the top intranet search engines over three months and compare their ability to find information, says West.

One of the search engines BAE Systems tested was from San Francisco–based Autonomy Inc. The Autonomy search engine uses advanced pattern matching, intelligent agents, and other artificial intelligence (AI) technologies whose "ability to retrieve information was second to none," says West. What sold BAE Systems on Autonomy's AI-based technology was its ability to flag whether other people in the organization are searching against similar information and, perhaps, working on common problems.

That kind of matching identification helped the Autonomy system pay for itself just seven months after it was installed. One of the system's first big payoffs came when two disparate groups of engineers in the United Kingdom were working on wing construction issues for the company's Harrier 2 military aircraft. After using the Autonomy system to search for wing specification information across the company's intranet, one of the engineering groups discovered that the other group was working on the same problem. Catching the redundancy early in the cycle helped save the company millions, says West. And a year into using the Autonomy search engine, BAE Systems evaluated its performance and determined that it was able to reduce the time needed to retrieve information from its intranet by 90 percent [25].

Expert Systems

One of the most practical and widely implemented applications of artificial intelligence in business is the development of expert systems and other knowledge-based information systems. A knowledge-based information system (KBIS) adds a knowledge base to the major components found in other types of computer-based information systems. An **expert system (ES)** is a knowledge-based information system that uses its knowledge about a specific, complex application area to act as an expert consultant to end users. Expert systems provide answers to questions in a very specific problem area

FIGURE 9.27 Components of an expert system. The software modules perform inferences on a knowledge base built by an expert and/or knowledge engineer. This provides expert answers to an end user's questions in an interactive process.

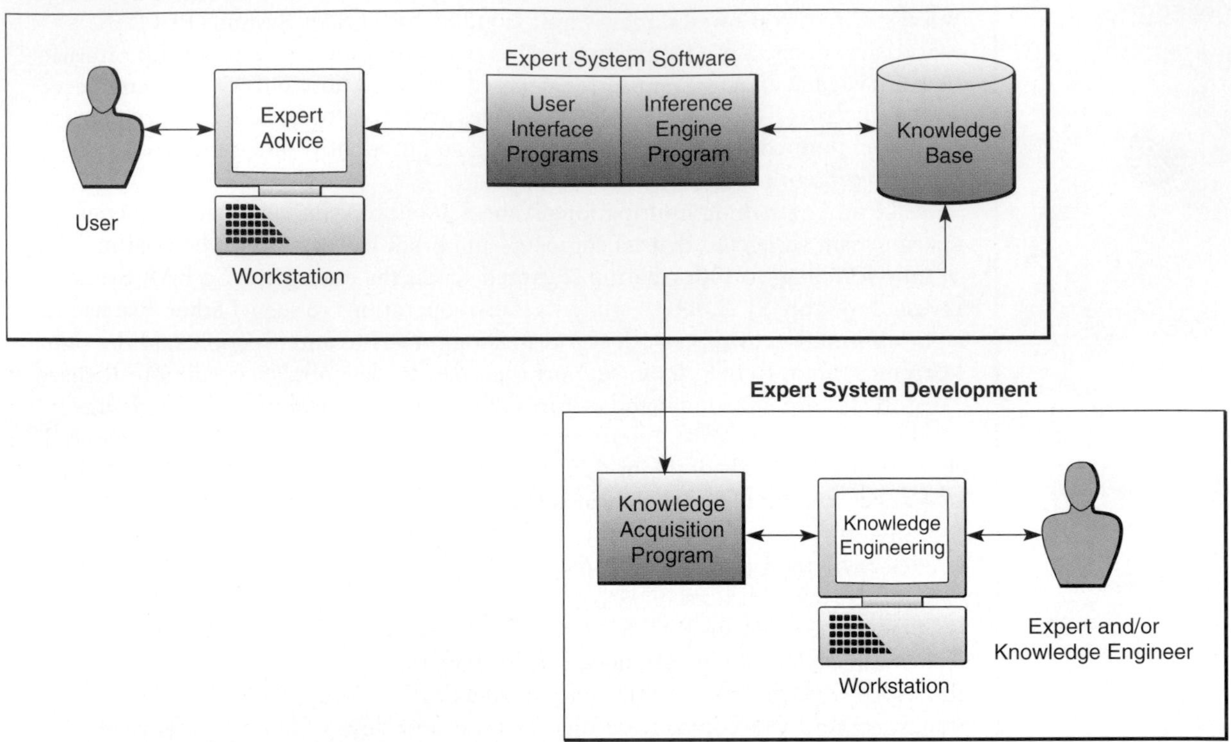

by making humanlike inferences about knowledge contained in a specialized knowledge base. They must also be able to explain their reasoning process and conclusions to a user. So expert systems can provide decision support to end users in the form of advice from an expert consultant in a specific problem area [30].

Components of an Expert System

The components of an expert system include a knowledge base and software modules that perform inferences on the knowledge in the knowledge base and communicate answers to a user's questions. Figure 9.27 illustrates the interrelated components of an expert system. Note the following components:

- **Knowledge Base.** The knowledge base of an expert system contains (1) facts about a specific subject area (e.g., *John is an analyst*) and (2) heuristics (rules of thumb) that express the reasoning procedures of an expert on the subject (e.g., *IF John is an analyst, THEN he needs a workstation*). There are many ways that such knowledge is represented in expert systems. Examples are *rule-based, frame-based, object-based,* and *case-based* methods of knowledge representation. See Figure 9.28.
- **Software Resources.** An expert system software package contains an inference engine and other programs for refining knowledge and communicating with users. The **inference engine** program processes the knowledge (such as rules and facts) related to a specific problem. It then makes associations and inferences resulting in recommended courses of action for a user. User interface programs for communicating with end users are also needed, including an explanation program to explain the reasoning process to a user if requested. Knowledge acquisition programs are not part of an expert system but are software tools for knowledge base development, as are *expert system shells,* which are used for developing expert systems.

FIGURE 9.28
A summary of four ways that knowledge can be represented in an expert system's knowledge base.

Methods of Knowledge Representation

- **Case-Based Reasoning.** Representing knowledge in an expert system's knowledge base in the form of cases, that is, examples of past performance, occurrences, and experiences.
- **Frame-Based Knowledge.** Knowledge represented in the form of a hierarchy or network of *frames*. A frame is a collection of knowledge about an entity consisting of a complex package of data values describing its attributes.
- **Object-Based Knowledge.** Knowledge represented as a network of objects. An object is a data element that includes both data and the methods or processes that act on those data.
- **Rule-Based Knowledge.** Knowledge represented in the form of rules and statements of fact. Rules are statements that typically take the form of a premise and a conclusion such as: If (condition), Then (conclusion).

Expert System Applications

Using an expert system involves an interactive computer-based session in which the solution to a problem is explored, with the expert system acting as a consultant to an end user. The expert system asks questions of the user, searches its knowledge base for facts and rules or other knowledge, explains its reasoning process when asked, and gives expert advice to the user in the subject area being explored. For example, Figure 9.29 illustrates an expert system application.

Expert systems are being used for many different types of applications, and the variety of applications is expected to continue to increase. However, you should realize that expert systems typically accomplish one or more generic uses. Figure 9.30 outlines five generic categories of expert system activities, with specific examples of actual expert system applications. As you can see, expert systems are being used in many different fields, including medicine, engineering, the physical sciences, and business. Expert systems now help diagnose illnesses, search for minerals, analyze compounds, recommend repairs, and do financial planning. So from a strategic business standpoint, expert systems can be and are being used to improve every step of the product cycle of a business, from finding customers to shipping products to providing customer service.

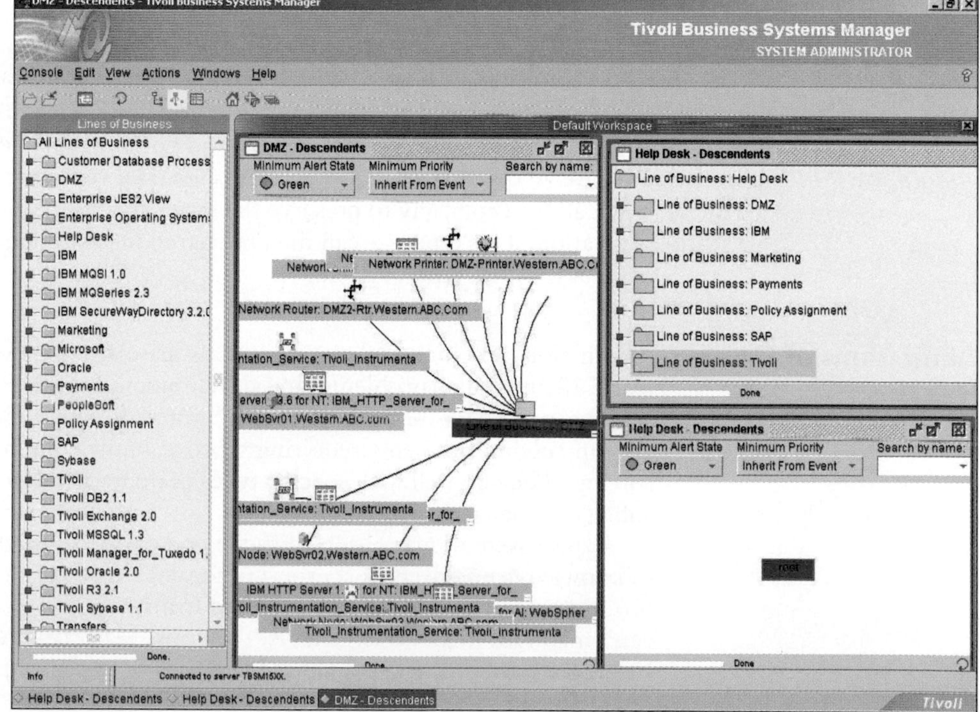

FIGURE 9.29
Tivoli Business Systems Manager by IBM automatically monitors and manages the computers in a network with proactive expert system software components based on IBM's extensive mainframe systems management expertise.

FIGURE 9.30
Major application categories and examples of typical expert systems. Note the variety of applications that can be supported by such systems.

Application Categories of Expert Systems
• **Decision management**—Systems that appraise situations or consider alternatives and make recommendations based on criteria supplied during the discovery process: Loan portfolio analysis. Employee performance evaluation. Insurance underwriting. Demographic forecasts.
• **Diagnostic/troubleshooting**—Systems that infer underlying causes from reported symptoms and history: Equipment calibration. Help desk operations. Software debugging. Medical diagnosis.
• **Design/configuration**—Systems that help configure equipment components, given existing constraints: Computer option installation. Manufacturability studies. Communications networks. Optimum assembly plan.
• **Selection/classification**—Systems that help users choose products or processes, often from among large or complex sets of alternatives: Material selection. Delinquent account identification. Information classification. Suspect identification.
• **Process monitoring/control**—Systems that monitor and control procedures or processes: Machine control (including robotics). Inventory control. Production monitoring. Chemical testing.

Benefits of Expert Systems

An expert system captures the expertise of an expert or group of experts in a computer-based information system. Thus, it can outperform a single human expert in many problem situations. That's because an expert system is faster and more consistent, can have the knowledge of several experts, and does not get tired or distracted by overwork or stress. Expert systems also help preserve and reproduce the knowledge of experts. They allow a company to preserve the expertise of an expert before she leaves the organization. This expertise can then be shared by reproducing the software and knowledge base of the expert system.

Limitations of Expert Systems

The major limitations of expert systems arise from their limited focus, inability to learn, maintenance problems, and developmental cost. Expert systems excel only in solving specific types of problems in a limited domain of knowledge. They fail miserably in solving problems requiring a broad knowledge base and subjective problem solving. They do well with specific types of operational or analytical tasks but falter at subjective managerial decision making.

Expert systems may also be difficult and costly to develop and maintain. The costs of knowledge engineers, lost expert time, and hardware and software resources may be too high to offset the benefits expected from some applications. Also, expert systems can't maintain themselves. That is, they can't learn from experience but instead must be taught new knowledge and modified as new expertise is needed to match developments in their subject areas.

Cutler-Hammer: Strategic Expert System

Cutler-Hammer's IT people were pioneers when they began work in 1995 on an expert system software program called Bid Manager. Its original purpose was to let customers' engineers deal more directly with the factory. Today Bid Manager has grown into a giant software package with 6 million lines of code, a far-reaching, all-embracing, e-manufacturing weapon with a sharp competitive edge. Not surprisingly, Cutler-Hammer has kept it largely under wraps.

To start with, the program allows a customer, a distributor, or one of the company's sales engineers in the field to easily configure the sometimes devilishly complex innards of Cutler-Hammer equipment with its convoluted wiring patterns and precise placement of dozens of electronic and electrical components. The software automatically checks that the engineers do everything right. If they place a switch or a wire in the wrong spot, they get a gentle electronic slap on the wrist—an onscreen message pointing out the mistake. Bid Manager contains thousands of rules to ensure that designs are done correctly; at the same time, it allows for idiosyncrasies—a user may want the equipment to turn on electric motors in a certain way, for instance.

"No outsider could possibly know an industry such as ours well enough to cover it the way Bid Manager does," claims Barbara J. Riesmeyer, manager of IT at Cutler-Hammer's power and control systems division and a developer of Bid Manager. To create the software, the company enlisted not only 15 software writers but also experts at the plants, sales engineers, and many others. Director of e-business Ray L. Huber led the team and, with Riesmeyer, created what they call the design-to-delivery (D2D) vision.

With more than 61,000 orders processed electronically in one year at Cutler-Hammer, the expert system unquestionably has proved itself. Plant managers Frank C. Campbell at Sumter and Steven R. Kavanaugh at Fayetteville overflow with praise for the software. It's easy to see why. Whereas in the past paperwork stifled production flow, now Bid Manager takes care of even small but significant details. What's more, says Huber, "Bid Manager has helped us think differently about products." For example, Cutler-Hammer has standardized its products and models, slimming down the number of steel enclosure sizes from more than 400 to only 100.

There's no question that the expert system has decisively helped Cutler-Hammer's business. CEO Randy Carson reports that Bid Manager has increased Cutler-Hammer's market share for configured products—motor control centers, control panels, and the like—by 15 percent. He adds that Bid Manager has boosted sales of the larger assemblies by 20 percent, doubling profits, increasing productivity by 35 percent, and reducing quality costs by 26 percent. He concludes, "Bid Manager has transformed Cutler-Hammer into a customer-driven company" [11].

Developing Expert Systems

What types of problems are most suitable to expert system solutions? One way to answer this question is to look at examples of the applications of current expert systems, including the generic tasks they can accomplish, as were summarized in Figure 9.30. Another way is to identify criteria that make a problem situation suitable for an expert system. Figure 9.31 outlines some important criteria.

Figure 9.31 emphasizes that many real-world situations do not fit the suitability criteria for expert system solutions. Hundreds of rules may be required to capture the assumptions, facts, and reasoning that are involved in even simple problem situations. For example, a task that might take an expert a few minutes to accomplish might require an expert system with hundreds of rules and take several months to develop [45].

The easiest way to develop an expert system is to use an **expert system shell** as a developmental tool. An expert system shell is a software package consisting of an expert system without its kernel, that is, its knowledge base. This leaves a *shell* of software (the

FIGURE 9.31
Criteria for applications that are suitable for expert systems development.

Suitability Criteria for Expert Systems

- **Domain:** The domain, or subject area, of the problem is relatively small and limited to a well-defined problem area.
- **Expertise:** Solutions to the problem require the efforts of an expert. That is, a body of knowledge, techniques, and intuition is needed that only a few people possess.
- **Complexity:** Solution of the problem is a complex task that requires logical inference processing, which would not be handled as well by conventional information processing.
- **Structure:** The solution process must be able to cope with ill-structured, uncertain, missing, and conflicting data, and a problem situation that changes with the passage of time.
- **Availability:** An expert exists who is articulate and cooperative, and who has the support of the management and end users involved in the development of the proposed system.

inference engine and user interface programs) with generic inferencing and user interface capabilities. Other development tools (e.g., rule editors, user interface generators) are added in making the shell a powerful expert system development tool.

Expert system shells are now available as relatively low-cost software packages that help users develop their own expert systems on microcomputers. They allow trained users to develop the knowledge base for a specific expert system application. For example, one shell uses a spreadsheet format to help end users develop IF-THEN rules, automatically generating rules based on examples furnished by a user. Once a knowledge base is constructed, it is used with the shell's inference engine and user interface modules as a complete expert system on a specific subject area. Other software tools may require an IT specialist to develop expert systems. See Figure 9.32.

Knowledge Engineering

A **knowledge engineer** is a professional who works with experts to capture the knowledge (facts and rules of thumb) they possess. The knowledge engineer then builds the knowledge base (and the rest of the expert system if necessary), using an iterative, prototyping process until the expert system is acceptable. Thus, knowledge engineers perform a role similar to that of systems analysts in conventional information systems development.

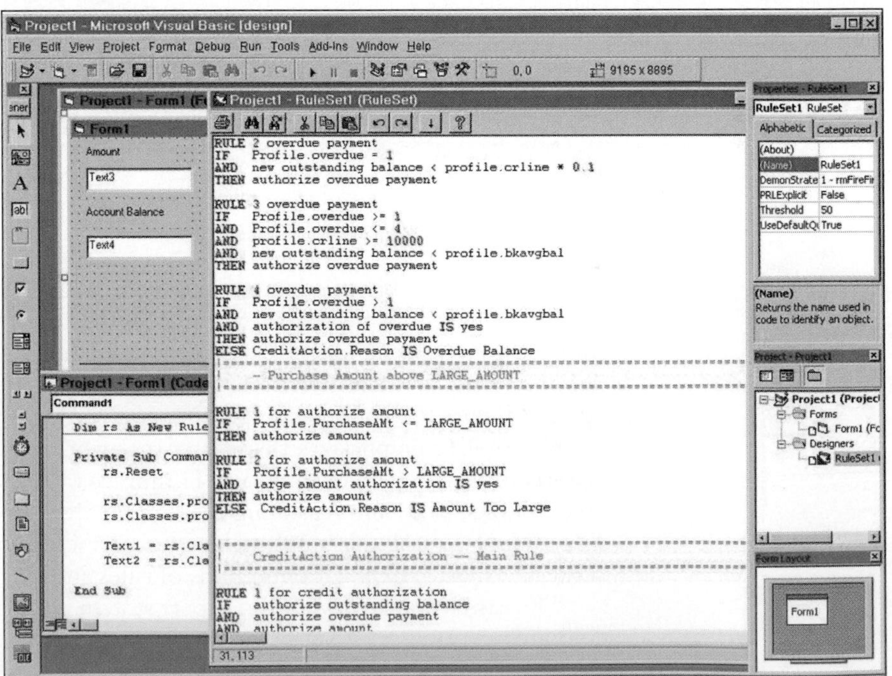

FIGURE 9.32
Using the Visual Rule Studio and Visual Basic to develop rules for a credit management expert system.

Once the decision is made to develop an expert system, a team of one or more domain experts and a knowledge engineer may be formed. Or experts skilled in the use of expert system shells could develop their own expert systems. If a shell is used, facts and rules of thumb about a specific domain can be defined and entered into a knowledge base with the help of a rule editor or other knowledge acquisition tool. A limited working prototype of the knowledge base is then constructed, tested, and evaluated using the inference engine and user interface programs of the shell. The knowledge engineer and domain experts can modify the knowledge base, then retest the system and evaluate the results. This process is repeated until the knowledge base and the shell result in an acceptable expert system.

Neural Networks

Neural networks are computing systems modeled after the brain's meshlike network of interconnected processing elements, called *neurons*. Of course, neural networks are a lot simpler in architecture (the human brain is estimated to have over 100 billion neuron brain cells!). However, like the brain, the interconnected processors in a neural network operate in parallel and interact dynamically. This interaction enables the network to "learn" from data it processes. That is, it learns to recognize patterns and relationships in this data. The more data examples it receives as input, the better it can learn to duplicate the results of the examples it processes. Thus, the neural network will change the strengths of the interconnections between the processing elements in response to changing patterns in the data it receives and the results that occur [8, 45]. See Figure 9.33.

For example, a neural network can be trained to learn which credit characteristics result in good or bad loans. Developers of a credit evaluation neural network could provide it with data from many examples of credit applications and loan results to process, with opportunities to adjust the signal strengths between its neurons. The neural network would continue to be trained until it demonstrated a high degree of accuracy in correctly duplicating the results of recent cases. At that point it would be trained enough to begin making credit evaluations of its own.

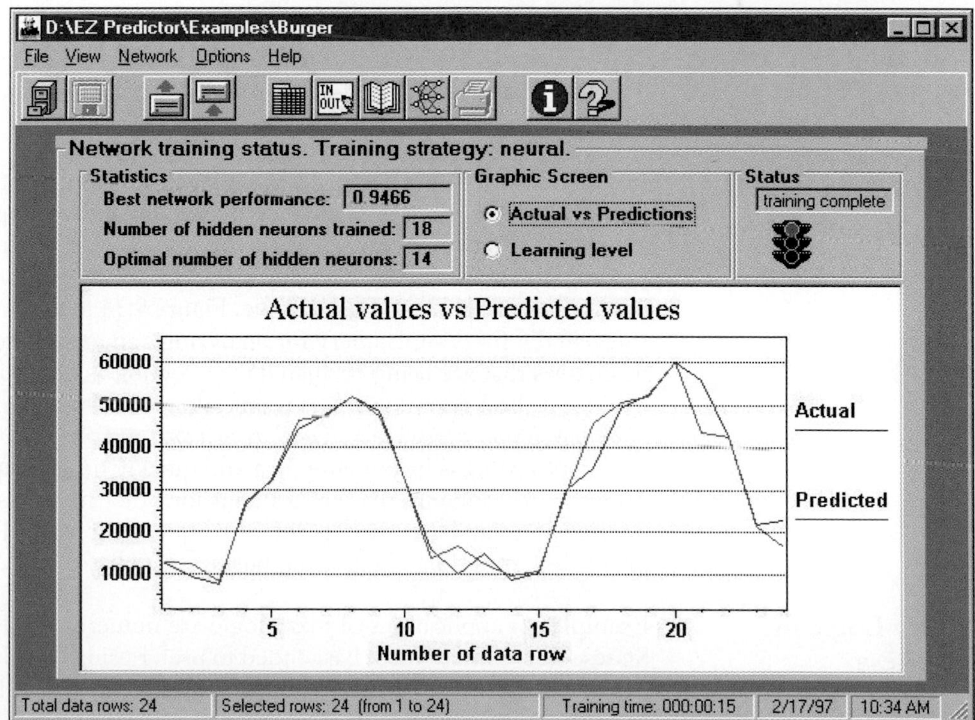

FIGURE 9.33 Evaluating the training status of a neural network application.

Modern Neurosurgery: Neural Nets Help Save Lives

Neurosurgery, surgery performed on the brain and spinal cord, has advanced to extraordinary levels of skill and success in just the last decade. One of the most common applications of neurosurgical techniques is the removal of brain tumors. Currently, surgeons search for tumors manually using a metal biopsy needle inserted into the brain. Guided by ultrasound and modern imaging techniques such as MRI/CT scans, they primarily use tactile feedback to localize the tumor. This method, however, can be imprecise, as the tumors can easily shift during surgery, causing healthy tissue to be mistakenly treated as tumorous tissue. This inaccuracy can increase the risk of a stroke should a needle accidentally sever an artery.

A new technique, which is a combination of hardware and software, has been developed that gives neurosurgeons the ability to find their way through the brain while doing less damage as they operate. The primary piece of the hardware is a robotic probe that has on its tip several miniature sensors: an endoscope that transmits images and instruments that measure tissue density and blood flow. This probe is inserted into the brain and guided through it by a robotic mechanism that is more precise and accurate than human hands.

The real power in this miracle technique, however, is the sophisticated, adaptable neural network software that provides an instant in-depth analysis of the data gathered by the probe. Surgeons are able to look at a computer screen in the operating room and see a vast array of useful real-time information about what is going on in the patient's brain, such as whether the probe is encountering healthy tissue, blood vessels, or a tumor. The neural net software is adaptable in that it learns from experience the difference between normal tissue and tumorous tissue. Laboratory biopsy test results are used to validate the data used for training the neural net software. Once trained, the neural net can be used to identify in real time abnormal tissues encountered during surgical operations. Once learned, the probe is robotically advanced and stops immediately when it detects a signature significantly different from what was learned to be normal tissue. At this point, tissue identification is performed automatically, and the results presented to the surgeon. The surgeon can then treat the abnormal tissue appropriately and without delay.

This new technique gives surgeons finer control of surgical instruments during delicate brain operations. Overall, the new technique will increase the safety, accuracy, and efficiency of surgical procedures [6, 37].

Fuzzy Logic Systems

In spite of their funny name, **fuzzy logic** systems represent a small but serious application of AI in business. Fuzzy logic is a method of reasoning that resembles human reasoning, in that it allows for approximate values and inferences (fuzzy logic) and incomplete or ambiguous data (fuzzy data) instead of relying only on *crisp data*, such as binary (yes/no) choices. For example, Figure 9.34 illustrates a partial set of rules (fuzzy rules) and a fuzzy SQL query for analyzing and extracting credit risk information on businesses that are being evaluated for selection as investments.

Notice how fuzzy logic uses terminology that is deliberately imprecise, such as *very high*, *increasing*, *somewhat decreased*, *reasonable*, and *very low*. This language enables fuzzy systems to process incomplete data and quickly provide approximate, but acceptable, solutions to problems that are difficult for other methods to solve. Thus, fuzzy logic queries of a database, such as the SQL query shown in Figure 9.34, promise to improve the extraction of data from business databases [12, 26].

Fuzzy Logic in Business

Examples of applications of fuzzy logic are numerous in Japan but rare in the United States. The United States has tended to prefer using AI solutions like expert systems or neural networks. But Japan has implemented many fuzzy logic applications, especially the use of special-purpose fuzzy logic microprocessor chips, called fuzzy process

FIGURE 9.34 An example of fuzzy logic rules and a fuzzy logic SQL query in a credit risk analysis application.

Fuzzy Logic Rules

Risk should be acceptable
If debt-equity is very high
then risk is positively increased
If income is increasing
then risk is somewhat decreased
If cash reserves are low to very low
then risk is very increased
If PE ratio is good
then risk is generally decreased

Fuzzy Logic SQL Query

```
Select companies
   from financials
      where revenues are very large
         and pe_ratio is acceptable
         and profits are high to very high
         and (income/employee_tot) is reasonable
```

controllers. Thus, the Japanese ride on subway trains, use elevators, and drive cars that are guided or supported by fuzzy process controllers made by Hitachi and Toshiba. Many models of Japanese-made products also feature fuzzy logic microprocessors. The list is growing and includes autofocus cameras, autostabilizing camcorders, energy-efficient air conditioners, self-adjusting washing machines, and automatic transmissions [34].

Genetic Algorithms

The use of **genetic algorithms** is a growing application of artificial intelligence. Genetic algorithm software uses Darwinian (survival of the fittest), randomizing, and other mathematical functions to simulate an evolutionary process that can yield increasingly better solutions to a problem. Genetic algorithms were first used to simulate millions of years in biological, geological, and ecosystem evolution in just a few minutes on a computer. Genetic algorithm software is being used to model a variety of scientific, technical, and business processes [4, 21].

Genetic algorithms are especially useful for situations in which thousands of solutions are possible and must be evaluated to produce an optimal solution. Genetic algorithm software uses sets of mathematical process rules *(algorithms)* that specify how combinations of process components or steps are to be formed. This process may involve trying random process combinations *(mutation)*, combining parts of several good processes *(crossover)*, and selecting good sets of processes and discarding poor ones *(selection)* to generate increasingly better solutions. Figure 9.35 illustrates a business use of genetic algorithm software.

GE's Engeneous

General Electric's design of a more efficient jet engine for the Boeing 777 is a classic example of a genetic algorithm application in business. A major engineering challenge was to develop more efficient fan blades for the engine. GE's engineers estimated that it would take billions of years, even with a supercomputer, to mathematically evaluate the astronomical number of performance and cost factors and combinations involved. Instead, GE used a hybrid genetic algorithm/expert system, called Engeneous, that produced an optimal solution in less than a week [4].

Virtual Reality

Virtual reality (VR) is computer-simulated reality. Virtual reality is a fast-growing area of artificial intelligence that had its origins in efforts to build more natural, realistic, multisensory human-computer interfaces. So virtual reality relies on multisensory input/output devices such as a tracking headset with video goggles and stereo earphones, a *data glove* or jumpsuit with fiber-optic sensors that track your body movements, and a *walker* that monitors the movement of your feet. Then you can experience

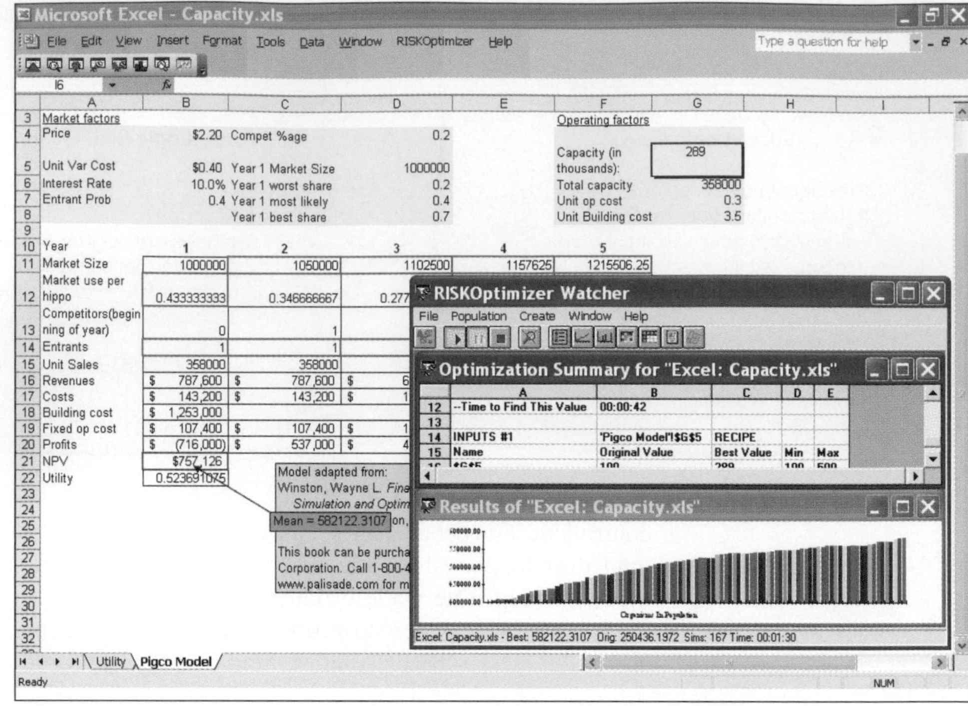

FIGURE 9.35
Risk Optimizer software combines genetic algorithms with a risk simulation function in this airline yield optimization application.

computer-simulated "virtual worlds" three-dimensionally through sight, sound, and touch. Virtual reality is also called *telepresence*. For example, you can enter a computer-generated virtual world, look around and observe its contents, pick up and move objects, and move around in it at will. Thus, virtual reality allows you to interact with computer-simulated objects, entities, and environments as if they actually exist [2, 41]. See Figure 9.36.

VR Applications

Current applications of virtual reality are wide-ranging and include computer-aided design (CAD), medical diagnostics and treatment, scientific experimentation in many physical and biological sciences, flight simulation for training pilots and

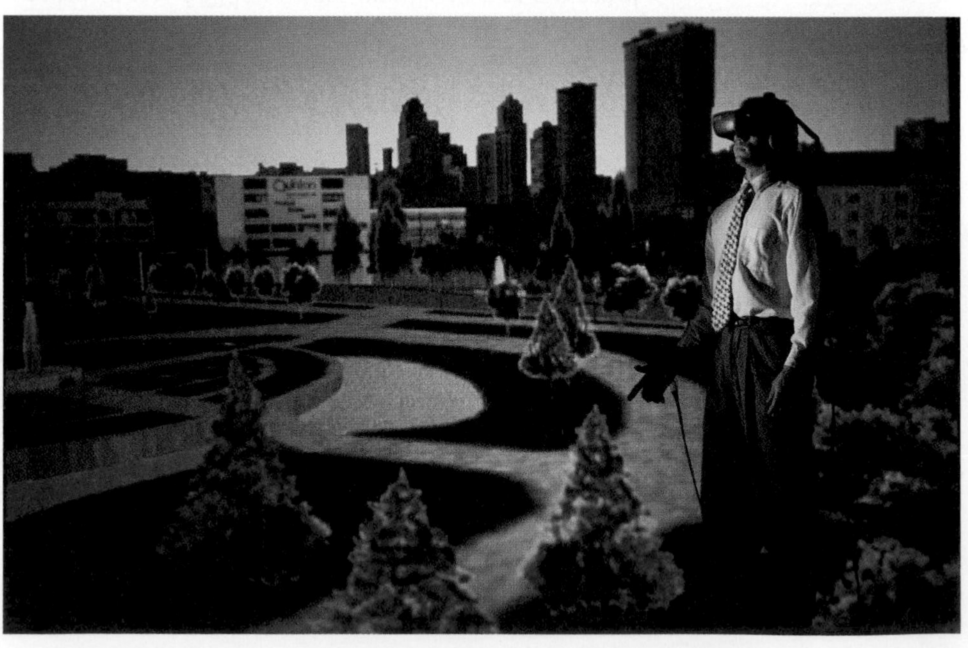

FIGURE 9.36
This landscape architect uses a virtual reality system to view and move through the design of the Seattle Commons, an urban design proposal for downtown Seattle.

astronauts, product demonstrations, employee training, and entertainment, especially 3D video arcade games. CAD is the most widely used industrial VR application. It enables architects and other designers to design and test electronic 3D models of products and structures by entering the models themselves and examining, touching, and manipulating sections and parts from all angles. This scientific-visualization capability is also used by pharmaceutical and biotechnology firms to develop and observe the behavior of computerized models of new drugs and materials and by medical researchers to develop ways for physicians to enter and examine a virtual reality of a patient's body.

VR becomes *telepresence* when users, who can be anywhere in the world, use VR systems to work alone or together at a remote site. Typically, this involves using a VR system to enhance the sight and touch of a human who is remotely manipulating equipment to accomplish a task. Examples range from virtual surgery, where surgeon and patient may be on either side of the globe, to the remote use of equipment in hazardous environments such as chemical plants or nuclear reactors.

Norsk Hydro: Drilling Decisions Made in a Virtual Oil Field

Norsk Hydro, based in Oslo, Norway, is a *Fortune* 500 energy and aluminum supplier operating in more than 40 countries worldwide. It is a leading offshore producer of oil and gas, the world's third-largest aluminum supplier, and a leader in the development of renewable energy sources. Norsk Hydro is also an innovator in the use of virtual reality technology. It uses VR to make decisions that, if wrong, could cost the company millions in lost revenues and, more important, could harm the environment. One example of its successful use of VR is the Troll Oil Field project.

The Troll Oil Field is located in the North Sea. The eastern part of the field has an oil column only 12 to 14 meters wide, but with in-place reserves of approximately 2.2 billion barrels. The oil is produced by horizontal wells located 0.5 to 1.5 meters above the point where the oil and seawater make contact.

During one drilling of a horizontal well, the drill bit was in sand of relatively low quality. No further good-quality reservoir sands were predicted from the geological model along the planned well track. Approximately 250 meters remained to the planned total depth, so a major decision to terminate the well-required confirmation. If the decision to terminate the well was the right decision, the cost of drilling to that date would be lost, but no further loss or damage to the environment would occur. If, however, the decision to terminate the well was the wrong decision, valuable oil reserves would be lost forever.

Virtual reality technology was fundamental in deciding whether to terminate the well. All relevant data were loaded into the system for review. During a virtual reality session, the well team discovered a mismatch between the seismic data and the geological model. Based on this observation, they made a quick reinterpretation of some key seismic horizons and updated the geological model locally around the well.

The updated model changed the prognosis for the remaining section of the well from poor-quality sand to high-quality sand. It was decided to continue drilling, and the new prognosis was proven correct. As a result, 175 meters of extra-high-quality sand with an estimated production volume of 100,000 standard cubic meters of oil were drilled in the last section of the well [38, 43].

Intelligent Agents

Intelligent agents are growing in popularity as a way to use artificial intelligence routines in software to help users accomplish many kinds of tasks in e-business and e-commerce. An intelligent agent is a *software surrogate* for an end user or a process that fulfills a stated need or activity. An intelligent agent uses its built-in and learned knowledge base about a person or process to make decisions and accomplish tasks in a way that fulfills the

FIGURE 9.37
Examples of different types of intelligent agents.

Types of Intelligent Agents
User Interface Agents
• **Interface Tutors.** Observe user computer operations, correct user mistakes, and provide hints and advice on efficient software use.
• **Presentation Agents.** Show information in a variety of reporting and presentation forms and media based on user preferences.
• **Network Navigation Agents.** Discover paths to information and provide ways to view information that are preferred by a user.
• **Role-Playing Agents.** Play what-if games and other roles to help users understand information and make better decisions.
Information Management Agents
• **Search Agents.** Help users find files and databases, search for desired information, and suggest and find new types of information products, media, and resources.
• **Information Brokers.** Provide commercial services to discover and develop information resources that fit the business or personal needs of a user.
• **Information Filters.** Receive, find, filter, discard, save, forward, and notify users about products received or desired, including e-mail, voice mail, and all other information media.

intentions of a user. Sometimes an intelligent agent is given a graphic representation or persona, such as Einstein for a science advisor, Sherlock Holmes for an information search agent, and so on. Thus, intelligent agents (also called *software robots* or "bots") are special-purpose, knowledge-based information systems that accomplish specific tasks for users. Figure 9.37 summarizes major types of intelligent agents [32].

The wizards found in Microsoft Office and other software suites are among the most well-known examples of intelligent agents. These wizards are built-in capabilities that can analyze how an end user is using a software package and offer suggestions on how to complete various tasks. Thus, wizards might help you change document margins, format spreadsheet cells, query a database, or construct a graph. Wizards and other software agents are also designed to adjust to your way of using a software package so that they can anticipate when you will need their assistance. See Figure 9.38.

The use of intelligent agents is growing rapidly as a way to simplify software use, search Web sites on the Internet and corporate intranets, and help customers do comparison shopping among the many e-commerce sites on the Web. Intelligent agents are becoming necessary as software packages become more sophisticated and powerful, as the Internet and the World Wide Web become more vast and complex, and as information sources and e-commerce alternatives proliferate exponentially. In fact, some commentators forecast that much of the future of computing will consist of intelligent agents performing their work for users.

Dow Jones & Co.: Intelligent Web Agents

Web sites such as Amazon.com's Shop the Web, Excite's Jango.com, and MySimon.com use intelligent agent technology to help users compare prices for fragrances, book titles, or other items on multiple sites. Other types of agents can answer e-mail, conduct intelligent searches, or help users find news reports and useful sites based on stated preferences.

For example, dozens of sites can show you the news, but Dow Jones & Co.'s Dow Jones Interactive (www.djinteractive.com) is different. Nearly 600,000 customers pay to search through stories from its 6,000 licensed and internal publications.

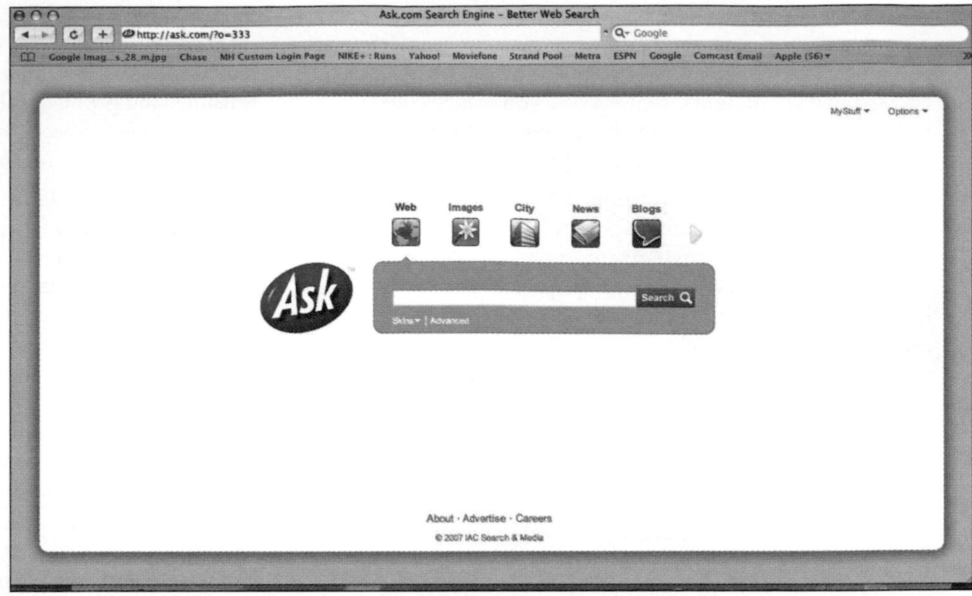

FIGURE 9.38
Intelligent agents help you find information in a variety of categories from many online sources.

That's a huge amount of data to filter, and the company has applied intelligent agent and other artificial intelligence technologies to manage the task.

One of the site's most important features is Custom Clips, which allows users to create folders based on predefined topics—such as agribusiness or IBM—or to build their own using custom key words. When the site IS agent retrieves relevant articles, it can post them to a database-generated Web page or send the stories to the user's e-mail address [31, 32].

Summary

- **Information, Decisions, and Management.** Information systems can support a variety of management decision-making levels and decisions. These include the three levels of management activity (strategic, tactical, and operational decision making) and three types of decision structures (structured, semistructured, and unstructured). Information systems provide a wide range of information products to support these types of decisions at all levels of the organization.
- **Decision Support Trends.** Major changes are taking place in traditional MIS, DSS, and EIS tools for providing the information and modeling managers need to support their decision making. Decision support in business is changing, driven by rapid developments in end-user computing and networking; Internet and Web technologies; and Web-enabled business applications. The growth of corporate intranets and extranets, as well as the Web, has accelerated the development of "executive-class" interfaces like enterprise information portals and Web-enabled business intelligence software tools, as well as their use by lower levels of management and individuals and teams of business professionals. In addition, the growth of e-commerce and e-business applications has expanded the use of enterprise portals and DSS tools by the suppliers, customers, and other business stakeholders of a company.
- **Management Information Systems.** Management information systems provide prespecified reports and responses to managers on a periodic, exception, demand, or push reporting basis to meet their need for information to support decision making.
- **OLAP and Data Mining.** Online analytical processing interactively analyzes complex relationships among large amounts of data stored in multidimensional databases. Data mining analyzes the vast amounts of historical data that have been prepared for analysis in data warehouses. Both technologies discover patterns, trends, and exception conditions in a company's data that support business analysis and decision making.
- **Decision Support Systems.** Decision support systems are interactive, computer-based information systems

that use DSS software and a model base and database to provide information tailored to support semistructured and unstructured decisions faced by individual managers. They are designed to use a decision maker's own insights and judgments in an ad hoc, interactive, analytical modeling process leading to a specific decision.

- **Executive Information Systems.** Executive information systems are information systems originally designed to support the strategic information needs of top management. However, their use is spreading to lower levels of management and business professionals. EIS are easy to use and enable executives to retrieve information tailored to their needs and preferences. Thus, EIS can provide information about a company's critical success factors to executives to support their planning and control responsibilities.
- **Enterprise Information and Knowledge Portals.** Enterprise information portals provide a customized and personalized Web-based interface for corporate intranets to give their users easy access to a variety of internal and external business applications, databases, and information services that are tailored to their individual preferences and information needs. Thus, an EIP can supply personalized Web-enabled information, knowledge, and decision support to executives, managers, and business professionals, as well as to customers, suppliers, and other business partners. An enterprise knowledge portal is a corporate intranet portal that extends the use of an EIP to include knowledge management functions and knowledge base resources so that it becomes a major form of knowledge management system for a company.
- **Artificial Intelligence.** The major application domains of artificial intelligence (AI) include a variety of applications in cognitive science, robotics, and natural interfaces. The goal of AI is the development of computer functions normally associated with human physical and mental capabilities, such as robots that see, hear, talk, feel, and move, and software capable of reasoning, learning, and problem solving. Thus, AI is being applied to many applications in business operations and managerial decision making, as well as in many other fields.
- **AI Technologies.** The many application areas of AI are summarized in Figure 9.25, including neural networks, fuzzy logic, genetic algorithms, virtual reality, and intelligent agents. Neural nets are hardware or software systems based on simple models of the brain's neuron structure that can learn to recognize patterns in data. Fuzzy logic systems use rules of approximate reasoning to solve problems when data are incomplete or ambiguous. Genetic algorithms use selection, randomizing, and other mathematic functions to simulate an evolutionary process that can yield increasingly better solutions to problems. Virtual reality systems are multisensory systems that enable human users to experience computer-simulated environments as if they actually existed. Intelligent agents are knowledge-based software surrogates for a user or process in the accomplishment of selected tasks.
- **Expert Systems.** Expert systems are knowledge-based information systems that use software and a knowledge base about a specific, complex application area to act as expert consultants to users in many business and technical applications. Software includes an inference engine program that makes inferences based on the facts and rules stored in the knowledge base. A knowledge base consists of facts about a specific subject area and heuristics (rules of thumb) that express the reasoning procedures of an expert. The benefits of expert systems (such as preservation and replication of expertise) must be balanced with their limited applicability in many problem situations.

Key Terms and Concepts

These are the key terms and concepts of this chapter. The page number of their first explanation is in parentheses.

1. Analytical modeling (338)
   a. Goal-seeking analysis (340)
   b. Optimization analysis (340)
   c. Sensitivity analysis (340)
   d. What-if analysis (338)
2. Artificial intelligence (348)
3. Business intelligence (329)
4. Data mining (341)
5. Data visualization system (336)
6. Decision structure (328)
7. Decision support system (330)
8. Enterprise information portal (345)
9. Enterprise knowledge portal (346)
10. Executive information system (343)
11. Expert system (353)
12. Expert system shell (357)
13. Fuzzy logic (360)
14. Genetic algorithms (361)
15. Geographic information system (336)
16. Inference engine (354)
17. Intelligent agent (363)
18. Knowledge base (354)
19. Knowledge engineer (358)
20. Knowledge management system (346)
21. Management information system (332)
22. Model base (311)
23. Neural network (359)
24. Online analytical processing (334)
25. Robotics (351)
26. Virtual reality (361)

Review Quiz

Match one of the key terms and concepts listed previously with one of the brief examples or definitions that follow. Try to find the best fit for answers that seem to fit more than one term or concept. Defend your choices.

____ 1. Decision-making procedures cannot be specified in advance for some complex decision situations.

____ 2. Information systems for the strategic information needs of top and middle managers.

____ 3. Systems that produce predefined reports for management.

____ 4. Provide an interactive modeling capability tailored to the specific information needs of managers.

____ 5. Provides business information and analytical tools for managers, business professionals, and business stakeholders.

____ 6. A collection of mathematical models and analytical techniques.

____ 7. Analyzing the effect of changing variables and relationships and manipulating a mathematical model.

____ 8. Changing revenues and tax rates to see the effect on net profit after taxes.

____ 9. Changing revenues in many small increments to see revenue's effect on net profit after taxes.

____ 10. Changing revenues and expenses to find how you could achieve a specific amount of net profit after taxes.

____ 11. Changing revenues and expenses subject to certain constraints to achieve the highest profit after taxes.

____ 12. Real-time analysis of complex business data.

____ 13. Attempts to find patterns hidden in business data in a data warehouse.

____ 14. Represents complex data using three-dimensional graphical forms.

____ 15. A customized and personalized Web interface to internal and external information resources available through a corporate intranet.

____ 16. Using intranets to gather, store, and share a company's best practices among employees.

____ 17. An enterprise information portal that can access knowledge management functions and company knowledge bases.

____ 18. Information technology that focuses on the development of computer functions normally associated with human physical and mental capabilities.

____ 19. Development of computer-based machines that possess capabilities such as sight, hearing, dexterity, and movement.

____ 20. Computers that can provide you with computer-simulated experiences.

____ 21. An information system that integrates computer graphics, geographic databases, and DSS capabilities.

____ 22. A knowledge-based information system that acts as an expert consultant to users in a specific application area.

____ 23. A collection of facts and reasoning procedures in a specific subject area.

____ 24. A software package that manipulates a knowledge base and makes associations and inferences leading to a recommended course of action.

____ 25. A software package consisting of an inference engine and user interface programs used as an expert system development tool.

____ 26. An analyst who interviews experts to develop a knowledge base about a specific application area.

____ 27. AI systems that use neuron structures to recognize patterns in data.

____ 28. AI systems that use approximate reasoning to process ambiguous data.

____ 29. Knowledge-based software surrogates that do things for you.

____ 30. Software that uses mathematical functions to simulate an evolutionary process.

Discussion Questions

1. Are the form and use of information and decision support systems for managers and business professionals changing and expanding? Why or why not?
2. Has the growth of self-directed teams to manage work in organizations changed the need for strategic, tactical, and operational decision making in business?
3. What is the difference between the ability of a manager to retrieve information instantly on demand using an MIS and the capabilities provided by a DSS?
4. Refer to the Real World Case on Oracle Corporation and others in the chapter. What are the key indicators that you would want in a dashboard for a business you

would like to start or a job you would like to have? Defend your choices.

5. In what ways does using an electronic spreadsheet package provide you with the capabilities of a decision support system?
6. Are enterprise information portals making executive information systems unnecessary? Explain your reasoning.
7. Refer to the Real World Case on Harrah's Entertainment, LendingTree, DeepGreen Financial, and Cisco Systems in the chapter. What other Web-based applications of automated decision making can you propose that would have a high chance of business success? Defend your proposals.
8. Can computers think? Will they ever be able to? Explain why or why not.
9. Which applications of AI have the most potential value for use in the operations and management of a business? Defend your choices.
10. What are some of the limitations or dangers you see in the use of AI technologies such as expert systems, virtual reality, and intelligent agents? What could be done to minimize such effects?

Analysis Exercises

1. **eCommerce Web Site Reviews**
   BizRate.com
   BizRate (www.bizrate.com) instantly provides information about hundreds of online stores. Supported product lines include books, music, electronics, clothes, hardware, gifts, and more. Customer reviews help shoppers select products and retailers with confidence. BizRate also features a "Smart Choice" tag that balances retailer reviews, price, and other variables to recommend a "best buy."
   a. Use BizRate.com to check out a product of interest. How thorough, valid, and valuable were the product and retailer reviews to you? Explain.
   b. How could nonretail businesses use a similar Web-enabled review system? Give an example.
   c. How is BizRate's Web site functionality similar to a decision support system (DSS)?

2. **Enterprise Application Integration**
   Digital Desktops
   Information coming from a variety of business systems can appear on the executive desktop as a consolidated whole. Often referred to as a "digital dashboard," the information contained in such a view might include the executive's schedule, current e-mail, a brief list of production delays, major accounts past due, current sales summaries, and a financial market summary. Although it isn't possible to fit all an organization's information on a single screen, it is possible to summarize data in ways specified by the executive and then act as a launching point or portal for further point-and-click enquiries.

   How might such a system look? Portals such as my.Excite.com, my.MSN.com, "I, Google" (www.google.com/ig), and my.Yahoo.com make good general-purpose information portals. These Web sites contain characteristics in common with their business-oriented brethren. They provide information from many different sources such as e-mail, instant messages, calendars, tasks lists, stock quotes, weather, and news. They allow users to determine what information sources they see. For example, a user may choose to list only business-related news and omit sports, lottery results, and horoscopes. They allow users to filter the information they see. For example, a user may choose to view only local weather, news containing specific keywords, or market results only for stocks she owns. They allow users to arrange their own information space so that information a user finds most important appears in the right place. Finally, they allow users to drill down into the information they find important to receive more detail.

   Once a user has set up an account and identified his or her preferences, these public portals remember the user's preferences and deliver only what the user has requested. Users may change their preferences as often as they wish, and the controls to make these changes require only point-and-click programming skills.
   a. Visit one of the portal sites listed above. Configure the site to meet your own information needs. Provide a printout of the result.
   b. Look up "Digital Dashboard" on the 20/20 Software Web site (www.2020software), read about products with this feature, and describe these products in your own words.

3. **Case-Based Marketing**
   Selling on Amazon.com
   A case-based reasoning system is a type of "expert system." It attempts to match the facts on hand to a database of prior "cases." When a case-based reasoning system finds one or more cases in its database that closely matches the facts at hand, it then evaluates and reports the most common outcomes. Given enough cases, such a system can prove very useful. Even better, if a case-based system automatically captures cases as they occur, then it will become a powerful tool that continually fine-tunes its results as it gains "experience."

Amazon.com relies on just such a system to refer books to its customers. Like many e-commerce sites, Amazon allows visitors to search for, buy, and review books. Amazon.com takes its database interactivity a step further. Given a particular book title, its case-based reasoning engine examines all past sales of that book to see if the customers who bought that book shared other book purchases in common. It then produces a short list and presents that list to the user. The overall effect approaches that of a sales clerk who says, "Oh! If you like this book, then you'll really like reading these as well." However, Amazon's system has the experience of hundreds of millions more transactions than even the most wizened and well-read sales clerk.

Equipped with this information, customers may consider purchasing additional books, or the information may increase customers' confidence that they have selected the right book. Better information increases customers' confidence in their purchases and encourages additional sales.

a. What is the source of expertise behind Amazon's online book recommendations?

b. How do you feel about online merchants tracking your purchases and using this information to recommend additional purchases?

c. What measures protect consumers from the government's obtaining their personal shopping histories maintained by Amazon?

d. Although Amazon doesn't share personal information, it still capitalizes on its customers' shopping data. Is this ethical? Should Amazon offer its customers the right to opt out of this information gathering?

4. Palm City Police Department
Goal Seeking
The Palm City Police Department has eight defined precincts. The police station in each precinct has primary responsibility for all activities in its precinct area. The table lists the current population of each precinct, the number of violent crimes committed in each precinct, and the number of officers assigned to each precinct. The department has established a goal of equalizing access to police services. Ratios of population per police officer and violent crimes per police officer should be calculated for each precinct. These ratios for the city as a whole are shown below.

a. Build a spreadsheet to perform this analysis and print it out.

b. Currently, no funds are available to hire additional officers. Based on the citywide ratios, the department has decided to develop a plan to shift resources as needed to ensure that no precinct has more than 1,100 residents per police officer and no precinct has more than seven violent crimes per police officer. The department will transfer officers from precincts that easily meet these goals to precincts that violate one or both of these ratios. Use "goal seeking" on your spreadsheet to move police officers between precincts until the goals are met. You can use the goal seek tool to see how many officers would be required to bring each precinct into compliance and then judgmentally reduce officers in precincts that are substantially within the criteria. Print out a set of results that allow the departments to comply with these ratios and a memorandum to your instructor summarizing your results and the process you used to develop them.

	Violent	**Police**	
Precinct	**Population**	**Crimes**	**Officers**
Shea Blvd.	96,552	318	85
Lakeland Heights	99,223	582	108
Sunnydale	68,432	206	77
Old Town	47,732	496	55
Mountainview	101,233	359	82
Financial District	58,102	511	70
Riverdale	78,903	537	70
Cole Memorial	75,801	306	82
Total	**625,978**	**3,315**	**629**
Per Officer	**995.196**	**5.270**	

REAL WORLD CASE 3 IBM, Linden Labs, and Others: The Business Case for Virtual Worlds in a 3D Internet

Last November in Beijing, IBM gathered 2,000 employees, with 5,000 more watching on the Web, to unveil a series of global initiatives on digital storage, branchless banking, and the like. During the presentation, CEO Sam Palmisano walked up to an onstage PC, logged onto the online three-dimensional virtual world called Second Life, and took command of the cartoon-like "avatar" that represents him there. He then visited a version of Beijing's Forbidden City built on virtual real estate and dropped by an IBM meeting where avatars controlled by employees in Australia, Florida, India, Ireland, and elsewhere were discussing supercomputing. Among the initiatives announced by Palmisano that day was a $10 million project to help build out the "3-D Internet" exemplified by Second Life.

By early January 2007, more than 3,000 IBM employees had acquired their own avatars, and about 300 were routinely conducting company business inside Second Life. "The 3-D Internet may at first appear to be eye candy," Palmisano writes in an e-mail interview, "but don't get hung up on how frivolous some of its initial uses may seem." He calls 3D realms such as Second Life the "next phase of the Internet's evolution" and says they may have "the same level of impact" as the first Web explosion.

There's no question that Second Life's initial uses have gotten a lot of media attention in recent months. And indeed, Second Life's admixture of fantasy and reality is intoxicating. The software you download from secondlife.com lets you imagine you're stepping inside your PC's screen to inhabit and move about in a brightly colored, three-dimensional world that resembles *Grand Theft Auto* crossed with *Lord of the Rings.* Within that digital realm, you can go anywhere (though some areas are private). There are stores, beaches, golf courses, bars, ski areas, high-rise office buildings, fantastical anime cities, medieval role-playing regions, and, yes, sex clubs. None of this is created by Linden Labs, the 110-employee San Francisco company behind Second Life. It's all created by the users.

This virtual world—don't call it a game—has become a phenomenon: Second Life, which is free for casual use, has about 334,000 regular visitors. More than 2.6 million have checked it out, a figure that in mid-January 2007 was growing by about 20,000 per day. But what's beginning to catch the attention of IBM and other huge corporations is something potentially far more profound than a new online pastime. It's the ability to use Second Life as a platform for a whole new Net—this one in 3D and even more social than the original—with huge opportunities to sell products and services. Bill Gurley, a venture capitalist with Benchmark Capital, says he invested in Second Life because it's like Microsoft or eBay—a venue in which thousands of ancillary businesses can sprout.

The company's backers include some of the world's smartest, richest, and most successful tech entrepreneurs. The chairperson and first big outside investor is Mitch Kapor, creator of Lotus 1-2-3, the spreadsheet application that helped begin the PC software revolution. Other investors include eBay founder Pierre Omidyar, Amazon CEO Jeff Bezos, and Microsoft chief technology architect (and inventor of Lotus Notes) Ray Ozzie, each credited with a seminal networked product of our age. They think Second Life may be next, and some respected tech pundits agree. Says Mark Anderson, author of the *Strategic News Service* newsletter: "In two years I think Second Life will be huge, probably as large as the entire gaming community is today."

In the case of IBM, it's not just a matter of touting the wonders of Second Life; it's really using it, both as a business opportunity and as an internal tool. Ian Hughes, one of the company's "metaverse evangelists"—an actual title—says Second Life stimulates collaboration among a dispersed workforce. ("Metaverse," a word coined by Neal Stephenson in his 1992 novel, *Snow Crash*, is gaining currency as the generic name for virtual worlds.) "We're all used to teleconferences," says Hughes. "But in Second Life we gather and mingle before the meeting, and when it finishes, some people stop and talk again. We start to form social networks and the kinds of bonds you make in real life." Hughes, whose Second Life handle is "Predator Potato," often attends IBM meetings as a pudgy avatar with spiky green hair.

The immersive 3D environment Second Life is pioneering could shape the way we interact online, especially if combined with motion capture technologies that are migrating from movie special effects into business products (exemplified by the motion-tracking capabilities responsible for the runaway success of Nintendo's Wii game system).

But it's far from certain that Linden Lab will be the main beneficiary. Second Life's software is so hard to use that fewer than one in six people who try it are still online 30 days later. Linden's servers frequently falter under the weight of its growing audience, and critical functions such as search sometimes break down. Although Second Life is the biggest virtual world, the company remains minuscule—2006 revenues were less than $11 million—and competitors are nipping at its heels. They too smell opportunity.

Second Life, which opened in June 2003 and almost died a few months later, relaunched in January 2004, this time with more focus on user creativity and in-world entrepreneurship. Linden took the advice of Lawrence Lessig, the Stanford Law School intellectual property guru, who recommended letting users own their own content. That, he argued, would encourage them to create more. The company also made it possible to exchange Second Life's currency, called Linden dollars, for the real thing (for a fee, of course). Residents could thus build, own, or sell their digital creations. Second Life had become a real economy.

And Linden changed its business model. It began generating revenues primarily from the sale of virtual land. So far Linden has sold 3,500 private islands, each equivalent to

16 acres in the real world. (The world inside Second Life currently occupies about 150 square miles. But it's growing, and as population increases, Linden simply creates more digital real estate.) Each island costs $1,675 to purchase and $295 monthly to maintain; some buyers subdivide their land and rent or sell it at a profit. In essence, customers are renting space on the 1,750 servers that store the digital representation of the land. One of the biggest landowners is IBM, which rules over 24 islands.

Since Linden revamped its business model to focus on real estate, users and revenues have grown at least 10 percent every month. These days, about $600,000 is spent daily throughout Second Life, for an annual gross domestic product of about $220 million. Some of that money is going to Nike, Sony BMG, Toyota, Sun, Starwood, and many others that have operations in Second Life. Some sell virtual clothing and other merchandise for avatars; some even move real product. IBM has built stores for Circuit City and Sears, where, for example, you can mock up a kitchen with Sears appliances to see how it would look. ABN Amro, the Dutch bank, recently opened an office in Second Life that offers information about products and services, as well as job openings.

All these enterprises need guidance and help building things. Linden Lab counts 65 companies that have sprung up inside Second Life to serve real-world business customers. CTO Cory Ondrejka says about 350 people work full-time for such companies, and there are at least $10 million worth of such projects underway.

CEO Rosedale hopes that other companies' virtual worlds will interoperate with Second Life. That could benefit Linden, so long as it remains the biggest operator. "Say IBM uses our code to build its own intranet version that's somewhat different from Second Life," he says. "A user may say 'Wow, this virtual thing IBM has built is pretty cool. Now I want to go to the mainland.' And we have another customer." In effect, Linden hopes to control the standards for virtual worlds so that they become the equivalent of the HTTP and HTML standards that define the Web.

That could lead to what Rosedale thinks will be Linden's greatest long-term opportunity: running some of the lucrative services necessary to keep all these linked virtual worlds functioning smoothly. "We can recreate Google's business in this environment," Rosedale claims, not to mention Network Solutions' Web-address registration business and Paypal's online-payments system.

Easier said than done, of course. Metaverses will become a very competitive field, says Irving Wladawsky-Berger, vice president for technical strategy at IBM. These are just the earliest days of exploration, and needless to say, the outcome is anything but certain. "Today," notes Wladawsky-Berger, "virtual worlds are where video and VCRs were in the early 1980s, or where the Web was in 1993."

Source: Adapted from David Kirkpatrick, "It's Not a Game," *Fortune*, February 5, 2007; Aili McConnon, "The Mind-Bending World of Work," *BusinessWeek*, April 2, 2007.

CASE STUDY QUESTIONS

1. What are the most important business benefits and limitations of 3D virtual worlds like Second Life to real-world companies such as those mentioned in this case?
2. Why do you think IBM is taking a leadership role in promoting and using 3D metaverses like Second Life? What business benefits might it expect to gain from its involvement in developing a 3D Internet? Explain your reasoning.
3. Are 3D virtual worlds like Second Life "solutions in search of a problem" at this stage of their development, in that do not satisfy any vital business need? Why or why not?

REAL WORLD ACTIVITIES

1. Search the Internet to determine how Second Life, Linden Labs, IBM, and other companies mentioned in this case are doing in terms of the growth and business success of their development or use of 3D virtual worlds. Have new competitors successfully entered the 3D Internet market? If so, how do they differ in the products and services they offer?
2. Visit the Second Life Web site and evaluate the experience in terms of level of difficulty, response times, operation of basic functions, realism, and so forth. Are 3D virtual worlds like Second Life ready for widespread use as an important form of social networking? How could they improve what they offer to make it more appealing and successful? Break into small groups with your classmates to debate these issues.

MODULE IV

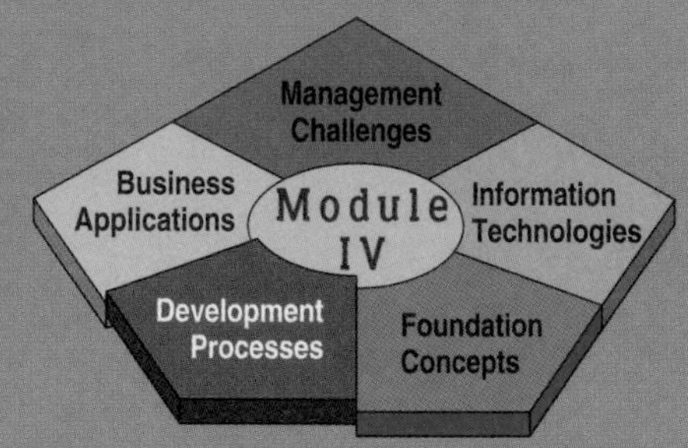

DEVELOPMENT PROCESSES

How can business professionals plan, develop, and implement solutions that use information technologies to help meet the challenges and opportunities they face in today's business environment? Answering that question is the goal of the chapter in this module, which concentrates on the processes for planning, developing, and implementing IT-based business applications.

- **Chapter 10: Developing Business/IT Solutions** introduces the traditional, prototyping, and end-user approaches to the development of information systems and discusses the processes and managerial issues in the implementation of new business applications of information technology, including the topics of user resistance and involvement and change management.

CHAPTER 10

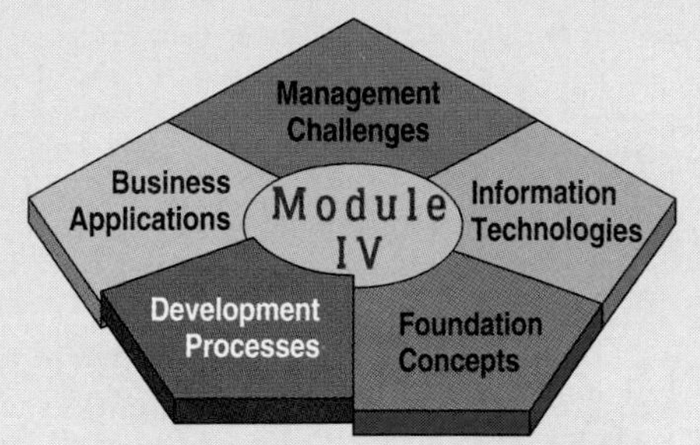

DEVELOPING BUSINESS/IT SOLUTIONS

Chapter Highlights

Section I
Developing Business Systems

IS Development

The Systems Approach

Real World Case: Intuit Inc.: Innovation in Customer-Driven Development of Small Business and Consumer Software

Systems Analysis and Design

The Systems Development Life Cycle

Starting the Systems Development Process

Systems Analysis

Systems Design

End-User Development

Technical Note: Overview of Object-Oriented Analysis and Design

Section II
Implementing Business Systems

Implementation

Implementing New Systems

Project Management

Real World Case: Infosys Technologies: The Implementation Challenges of Knowledge Management Initiatives

Evaluating Hardware, Software, and Services

Other Implementation Activities

Implementation Challenges

User Resistance and Involvement

Change Management

Real World Case: Indiana University: Financial Aid System Implementation: Success or Failure?

Learning Objectives

After reading and studying this chapter, you should be able to:

1. Use the systems development process outlined in this chapter and the model of IS components from Chapter 1 as problem-solving frameworks to help you propose information systems solutions to simple business problems.
2. Describe and give examples to illustrate how you might use each of the steps of the information systems development cycle to develop and implement a business information system.
3. Explain how prototyping can be used as an effective technique to improve the process of systems development for end users and IS specialists.
4. Understand the basics of project management and their importance to a successful system development effort.
5. Identify the activities involved in the implementation of new information systems.
6. Compare and contrast the four basic system conversion strategies.
7. Describe several evaluation factors that should be considered in evaluating the acquisition of hardware, software, and IS services.
8. Identify several change management solutions for user resistance to the implementation of new information systems.

SECTION I Developing Business Systems

IS Development

Suppose the chief executive of the company where you work asks you to find a Web-enabled way to get information to and from the salespeople in your company. How would you start? What would you do? Would you just plunge ahead and hope you could come up with a reasonable solution? How would you know whether your solution was a good one for your company? Do you think there might be a systematic way to help you develop a good solution to the CEO's request? There is. It's a problem-solving process called *the systems approach*.

When the systems approach to problem solving is applied to the development of information systems solutions to business problems, it is called *information systems development* or *application development*. This section will show you how the systems approach can be used to develop business systems and applications that meet the business needs of a company and its employees and stakeholders.

Refer to the Real World Case on the next page. We can learn a lot about the challenges of application development from this example. See Figure 10.1.

The Systems Approach

The **systems approach** to problem solving uses a systems orientation to define problems and opportunities and then develop appropriate, feasible solutions in response. Analyzing a problem and formulating a solution involves the following interrelated activities:

1. Recognize and define a problem or opportunity using *systems thinking*.
2. Develop and evaluate alternative system solutions.
3. Select the system solution that best meets your requirements.
4. Design the selected system solution.
5. Implement and evaluate the success of the designed system.

Systems Thinking

Using **systems thinking** to understand a problem or opportunity is one of the most important aspects of the systems approach. Management consultant and author Peter Senge calls systems thinking *the fifth discipline*. Senge argues that mastering systems thinking (along with the disciplines of personal mastery, mental models, shared vision, and team learning) is vital to personal fulfillment and business success in a world of constant change. The essence of the discipline of systems thinking is "seeing the forest *and* the trees" in any situation by:

- Seeing *interrelationships* among *systems* rather than linear cause-and-effect chains whenever events occur.
- Seeing *processes* of change among *systems* rather than discrete "snapshots" of change, whenever changes occur [27].

One way of practicing systems thinking is to try to find systems, subsystems, and components of systems in any situation you are studying. This approach is also known as using a *systems context* or having a *systemic view* of a situation. For example, the business organization or business process in which a problem or opportunity arises could be viewed as a system of input, processing, output, feedback, and control components. Then to understand a problem and solve it, you would determine if these basic systems functions are being properly performed. See Figure 10.2.

Example

The sales process of a business can be viewed as a system. You could then ask: Is poor sales performance (output) caused by inadequate selling effort (input), out-of-date sales procedures (processing), incorrect sales information (feedback), or inadequate sales management (control)? Figure 10.2 illustrates this concept.

REAL WORLD CASE 1 Intuit Inc.: Innovation in Customer-Driven Development of Small Business and Consumer Software

The shrink reminds the geeks to play nice. "If somebody has an idea, don't stomp on it," says Anthony Creed, psychologist and full-time developer of new ideas at Intuit, the software company. "It's more important to get the stupidest idea out there and build on it than not to have it in the first place." The group of eight software development managers has just started brainstorming the next generation of the company's hit income tax preparation product, TurboTax.

"How about a tax-preparation product you could customize based on your emotional state?" suggests a product developer. "It could have a control bar showing how angry or happy you are." Another, more senior executive suggests a Three Stooges–themed product. "We don't have a funny tax product right now," muses Creed. "What about putting a 'wild' into the software?" suggests a product manager in a fleece jacket. "Then the customers could write content themselves."

If you find it weird that such far-out thinking is being applied to improving tax software, you don't know Intuit. These free-association sessions happen at least once a week at the offices of Intuit's tax division in San Diego, and similar gatherings are routine throughout the Silicon Valley–based company. In fact, they're just one stage in a systematic process of innovation created—and nurtured, fine-tuned, and evangelized—by Scott Cook, Intuit's cofounder and spiritual leader.

It's a process that features near-maniacal focus on the customer. Before Creed even put marker to whiteboard, employees had conducted about 100 interviews with potential customers and visited 25 homes in Atlanta, Baltimore, and other cities to watch how real people prepared their taxes. At the end of the idea session, Creed whips out his PDA and photographs the board so that he and another team have a record they can use to flesh out the concepts. Then it's back to the customers, whose reactions will be analyzed. The process iterates until the company hammers out a product that people will pay for, use, and like.

FIGURE 10.1

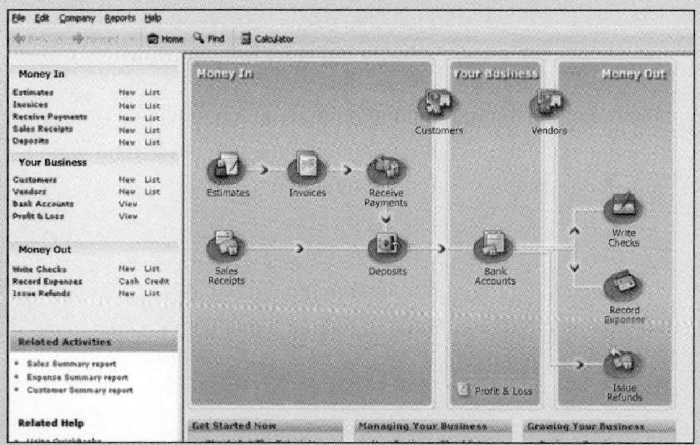

Intuit's exhaustive customer-driven application development process helped make its new QuickBooks: Simple Start Edition a runaway success in small business accounting software.

Actually, *like* may be too strong a word. Few people truly *enjoy* financial software, which is part of the challenge facing Intuit. Ever since Cook launched the company in 1983, he has made it his mission to remove the agony from necessary but odious tasks such as bookkeeping and tax preparation. At Intuit they call them "pain points." Today the company dominates the retail software market for tax preparation and small business accounting, at 79 percent and 85 percent, respectively, according to the NPD Group.

But Intuit knows there's still a tantalizingly large number of Americans who don't use financial software. In the case of tax prep, about 20 million hardy souls use neither tax software nor a professional tax preparer. In other words, Intuit's biggest competitor isn't other software companies but rather, well, nothing. To keep growing, the company has to come up with ways to get at those 20 million people, many of whom would just as soon eat packing materials as use a tax program.

Cook always knew he was good at the creative stuff, but it took CEO Steve Bennett's managerial chops to codify his ideas into a system. In 2000, Cook, then chairman, and Bill Campbell, then CEO, recruited Bennett from General Electric, where he was executive vice president of GE Capital, because they felt the company needed a leader with more experience managing large operations. Revenues were nearing $1 billion, and the company had 4,000 employees. "We had struck out at several businesses because we couldn't operate them," says Cook.

One key way the new CEO got things out of the founder's brain was by pushing Cook to boil down his ideas into coherent, repeatable phrases. Perhaps the most crucial is "savoring the surprise," an expression that comes from the origin of Intuit's successful small business accounting software, QuickBooks.

Cook started the company with Quicken, software to help individuals manage their personal finances. By the early 1990s, Quicken was taking off in the market, but a survey showed that almost half of its customers were using it to manage the finances of some kind of business. Cook dismissed it as a research anomaly. It wasn't until another survey a year later found an even higher number of business Quicken users that Cook saw an opportunity to build accounting software for small companies.

"Savor the surprise" is what Cook did once he finally accepted the market research. (QuickBooks' annual revenues now total $753 million.) It's a way of looking at business that Cook has spread around the company. In fact, it's the principle behind one of Intuit's signature tactics for getting inside the heads of customers: dispatching employees to visit users at their homes or offices, or both, and watch them work.

Such visits, called "follow-me-homes," in Intuit parlance, are central to the company's processes, both for developing new products and learning how to improve old ones.

"What Intuit does in the field is wonderful," says Clayton Christensen, the Harvard Business School professor who wrote the bestseller *The Innovator's Dilemma.* "When a market is not well defined, the only way you get insights about what customers will buy is to go out and see what people are trying to get done in their lives."

Two years ago, the QuickBooks division sent more than 500 employees on follow-me-homes for three days. Even CEO Bennett tells of visiting a San Francisco woman who runs a small construction company and listening to her complain about QuickBooks as four cats crawled over him. Rick Jensen, who heads product development in Intuit's tax product group, recalls one light bulb experience at a customer's home: "She got a screen about charitable donations, which asked if they were 'cash' or 'noncash.' She said, 'I wrote a check, so it must be noncash.'" Afterward, Intuit changed that language. Says Brad Henske, who oversees the entire tax group: "I read the other day that Microsoft hires anthropologists to study how people work. We have those people here—we call them employees."

After Intuit's research found that more than half of American small businesses that own computers still keep their books with simple spreadsheets or pencil and paper, developers in 2003 set out to learn how they might get those people to use QuickBooks. The 10-person team began with 40 follow-me-homes. "Small businesses told us, 'I don't need no stinkin' accounting!'" says Terry Hicks, who ran the project. "Many of them didn't even associate the benefits of good financial management with accounting."

So Hicks and his team decided to keep it simple. They built a stripped-down prototype of QuickBooks and tried that with the customers during some follow-me-homes. Still no go. "It was still accounting software, just with fewer features," says Hicks.

"Customers told us they wanted to track the money coming in and the money going out. So we said, 'Got it! You want accounts receivable and accounts payable.' But when many of them hear the word 'account,' they think of their bank account. So in the second prototype we stopped using accounting terminology at all. Accounts payable became 'money out.' This was a case of savoring the surprise. It wasn't until we tried and failed with a prototype that the entire team was like 'Okay, *now* I get it,'" says Hicks.

The first prototype required users to go through 125 setup screens just to get started, already far fewer than a regular QuickBooks product; Hicks and his team eventually reduced that to 3. In those last weeks of fine-tuning, the product that became QuickBooks: Simple Start Edition finally got simple enough. A few more traces of accounting jargon were removed. And the results in the marketplace after it was launched in September 2004 proved all the care had been worth it: In its first year, it outsold all accounting software in the United States except QuickBooks itself. But to get to that final product, Intuit had to cycle through its interview process with customers six separate times.

A touchstone of Intuit's approach to innovation is the acceptance of failure. "I've had my share of really bad ideas," admits Cook. At a recent companywide marketing meeting, he presented an award for "the Failure We Learned the Most From." Failure, in fact, is more than just tolerated—it's an important part of the process. It's simply a reason to pick a customer's brain some more, mark up another whiteboard, and get down to business. As far as Scott Cook is concerned, if at first you don't fail, you're not doing your damn job.

Source: Adapted from David Kirkpatrick, "Throw It at the Wall and See If It Sticks," *Fortune*, December 12, 2005.

CASE STUDY QUESTIONS

1. Should Intuit's "far-out thinking" and acceptance of failure as part of the application software development process be duplicated at large software development companies like Microsoft and at the thousands of small independent software companies that exist? Why or why not?
2. Which do you prefer? Intuit's customer-driven development process, in which hundreds of employees and managers are sent to consult with customers in their homes or places of business, or Microsoft's process of using professional anthropologists do such research? Why?
3. Intuit developed the wildly successful QuickBooks: Simple Start Edition, which eliminated all accounting jargon. Could this idea be the foundation of a new version of Intuit's top-selling TurboTax software, which removed all tax accounting jargon from that product to reach a major segment of the 20 million Americans who do not use tax preparation software or a professional tax preparer? Would such a product be possible or successful? Why or why not?

REAL WORLD ACTIVITIES

1. Use the Internet to analyze the current market leaders in personal finance products like Quicken and small business accounting software like QuickBooks. Is Intuit still the dominant market leader? Are there any old players losing market share to Intuit or to new entrants in the market? Conduct research to discover the reasons for any such developments.
2. Do you agree with Scott Cook's belief that if at first you don't fail, you're not doing your job, and with his "savoring the surprise" credo? Why or why not? Break into small groups with your classmates to discuss your positions on these issues and if they could be applied successfully to other jobs or businesses.

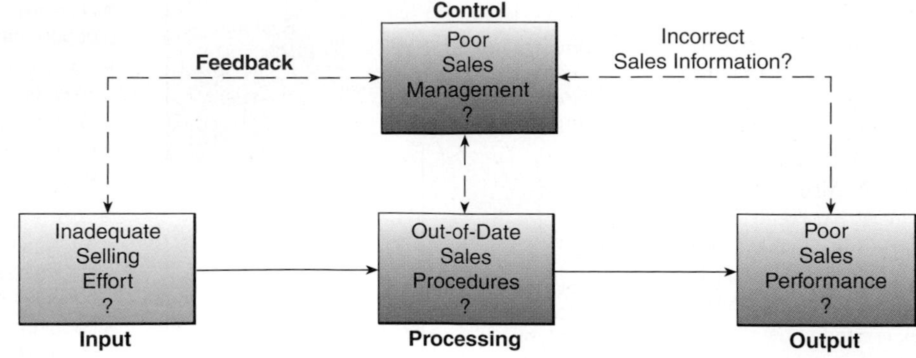

FIGURE 10.2
An example of systems thinking. You can better understand a sales problem or opportunity by identifying and evaluating the components of a sales system.

Systems Analysis and Design

The overall process by which information systems are designed and implemented within organizations is referred to as **systems analysis and design (SA&D)**. Within this process are contained activities that include the identification of business problems; the proposed solution, in the form of an information system (IS), to one or more of the problems identified; and the design and implementation of that proposed solution to achieve the desired and stated goals of the organization.

Today, there are many approaches to SA&D. The two most common approaches are **object-oriented analysis and design** and the **life cycle approach.** Although each has its advantages and disadvantages, and the two approaches differ in many respects, they both are concerned with the analysis and design of a successful information system. In most cases, the choice of approach will depend on the type of system under study and the degree to which users are able to specify their needs and requirements clearly. A thorough discussion of both approaches is beyond the scope of this text, but we provide a brief overview of the object-oriented approach, with a focus on the most common method: the life cycle approach.

The Systems Development Life Cycle

One method of using the systems approach to develop information system solutions, and the one that is most prevalent in organization systems analysis and design, can be viewed as a multistep, iterative process called the **systems development life cycle (SDLC)**. Figure 10.3 illustrates what goes on in each stage of this process: (1) investigation, (2) analysis, (3) design, (4) implementation, and (5) maintenance.

It is important to realize, however, that all of the activities involved in the SDLC are highly related and interdependent. Therefore, in actual practice, several developmental activities may be occurring at the same time, and certain activities within a given step may be repeated. Therefore, both users and systems analysts may recycle back at any time to repeat previous activities to modify and improve a system under development. We discuss the activities and products of each step of the systems development cycle in this chapter.

Starting the Systems Development Process

Do we have business opportunities? What are our business priorities? How can information technologies provide information system solutions that address our business priorities? These are the questions that have to be answered in the **systems investigation stage**—the first step in the systems development process. This stage may involve consideration of proposals generated by a company's business/IT planning process, which we will discuss in Chapter 12. Typically, the IT function performs feasibility studies to evaluate proposed information system solutions to meet a company's business priorities and opportunities, as identified in its strategic planning process [11].

Feasibility Studies

Because the process of development can be costly, the systems investigation stage typically requires the development of a **feasibility study**. At this stage, the feasibility study is a preliminary study that determines the information needs of prospective users and

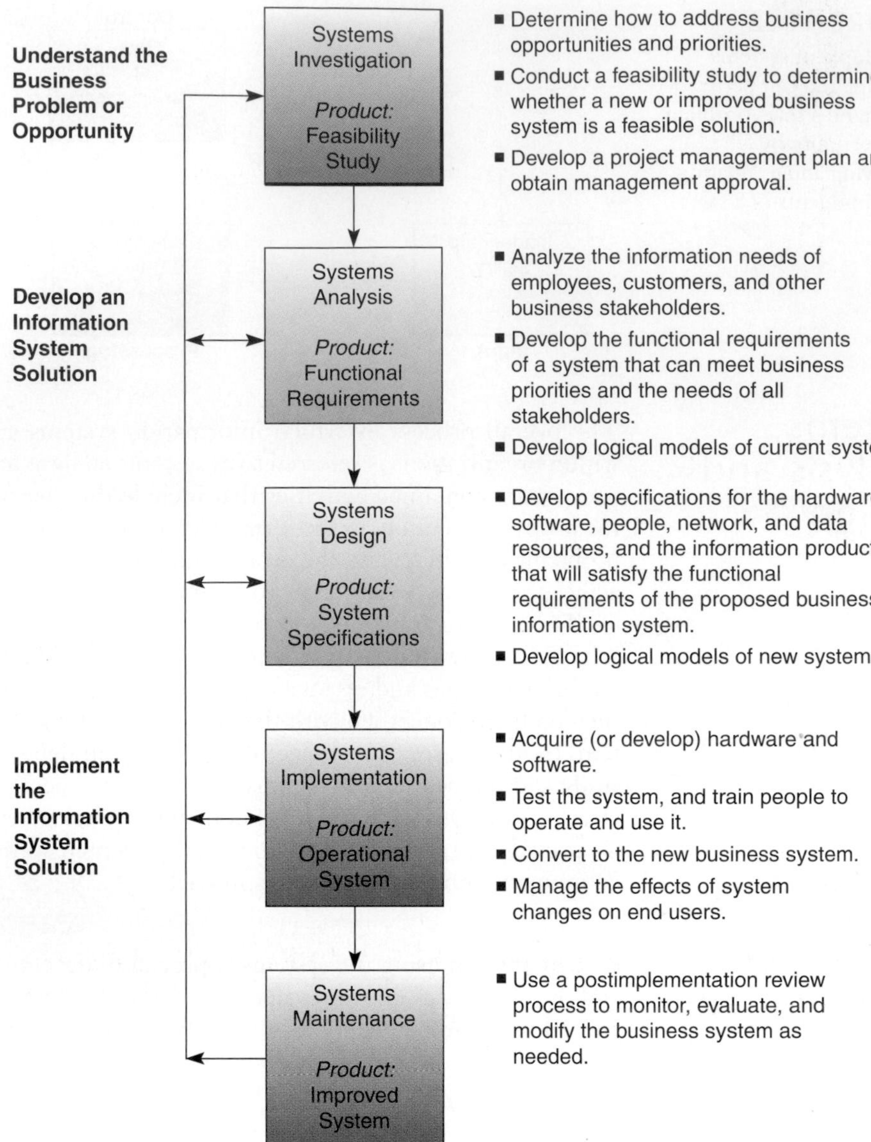
Understand the Business Problem or Opportunity
Systems Investigation
Product: Feasibility Study
■ Determine how to address business opportunities and priorities.
■ Conduct a feasibility study to determine whether a new or improved business system is a feasible solution.
■ Develop a project management plan and obtain management approval.
Develop an Information System Solution
Systems Analysis
Product: Functional Requirements
■ Analyze the information needs of employees, customers, and other business stakeholders.
■ Develop the functional requirements of a system that can meet business priorities and the needs of all stakeholders.
■ Develop logical models of current system.
Systems Design
Product: System Specifications
■ Develop specifications for the hardware, software, people, network, and data resources, and the information products that will satisfy the functional requirements of the proposed business information system.
■ Develop logical models of new system.
Implement the Information System Solution
Systems Implementation
Product: Operational System
■ Acquire (or develop) hardware and software.
■ Test the system, and train people to operate and use it.
■ Convert to the new business system.
■ Manage the effects of system changes on end users.
Systems Maintenance
Product: Improved System
■ Use a postimplementation review process to monitor, evaluate, and modify the business system as needed.

FIGURE 10.3
The traditional information systems development life cycle. Note how the five steps of the cycle are based on the stages of the systems approach. Also note the products that result from each step in the cycle and that you can recycle back to any previous step if more work is needed.

the resource requirements, costs, benefits, and feasibility of a proposed project. Then a team of business professionals and IS specialists might formalize the findings of this study in a written report that includes preliminary specifications and a developmental plan for a proposed business application. If the management of the company approves the recommendations of the feasibility study, the development process can continue.

By design, the preliminary feasibility study of a project is a very rough analysis of its viability that must be continually refined over time. It is, nonetheless, a necessary first step in making the final commitment of organizational resources to the development of the proposed system. In some cases, however, the preliminary feasibility assessment is unnecessary. For extremely small or obvious projects, it may actually represent a waste of valuable time. Also, certain changes in the business environment may dictate the need for change, regardless of the assessed feasibility of such change. If the government changes the tax structure for employee income, an organization has no choice but to make the necessary changes to its payroll system. If a critical program has a major bug in it, the organization has no choice but to address and resolve it. In other words, there is little point in assessing the feasibility of a problem that must be solved. In these cases, the feasibility assessment may be better directed to the analysis

FIGURE 10.4
Operational, economic, technical, human, and legal/political factors. Note that there is more to feasibility than cost savings or the availability of hardware and software.

Operational Feasibility	Economic Feasibility
• How well the proposed system supports the business priorities of the organization. • How well the proposed system will solve the identified problem. • How well the proposed system will fit with the existing organizational structure.	• Cost savings. • Increased revenue. • Decreased investment requirements. • Increased profits. • Cost/benefit analysis.
Technical Feasibility	**Human Factors Feasibility**
• Hardware, software, and network capability, reliability, and availability.	• Employee, customer, supplier acceptance. • Management support. • Determining the right people for the various new or revised roles.
Legal/Political Feasibility	
• Patent, copyright, and licensing. • Governmental restrictions. • Affected stakeholders and reporting authority.	

of alternative approaches to the solution rather than the problem itself. Regardless, however, the conduct of a thorough preliminary feasibility study should be the default standard in the organization, and a decision to eliminate this first step in the process should always be carefully scrutinized and justified.

Thus, the goal of the preliminary feasibility study is to evaluate alternative system solutions and propose the most feasible and desirable business application for development. The feasibility of a proposed business system can be evaluated in terms of five major categories, as illustrated in Figure 10.4.

Operational Feasibility

The **operational feasibility** assessment focuses on the degree to which the proposed development project fits with the existing business environment and objectives with regard to development schedule, delivery date, corporate culture, and existing business processes. Furthermore, this assessment determines the degree to which the project meets the specific business objectives set forth during the proposal phase. In the early stages of operational feasibility assessment, we are primarily interested in determining whether the identified problem is worth solving or the proposed solution actually solves the problem at hand. In addition, we must concern ourselves with an initial assessment of **schedule feasibility**—can we identify and solve the problem at hand within a reasonable time period? In the latter stages of operational feasibility assessment, such as during the physical design phase of the SDLC, we shift focus to one of strategic fit and organizational impact, such as determining to what degree the proposed physical system will require changes in the organizational structure or what changes in the current spans of authority need to be made to accommodate the new system.

Economic Feasibility

The purpose of the **economic feasibility** assessment is to determine the extent to which the proposed system will provide positive economic benefits to the organization. This determination involves the identification and quantification of all benefits expected from the system, as well as the explicit identification of all expected costs of the

FIGURE 10.5
Possible benefits of new information systems, with examples. Note that an opposite result for each of these benefits would be a cost or disadvantage of new systems.

Tangible Benefits	Example
• Increase in sales or profits.	• Development of IT-based products.
• Decrease in information processing costs.	• Elimination of unnecessary documents.
• Decrease in operating costs.	• Reduction in inventory carrying costs.
• Decrease in required investment.	• Decrease in inventory investment required.
• Increased operational efficiency.	• Less spoilage, waste, and idle time.
Intangible Benefits	**Example**
• Improved information availability.	• More timely and accurate information.
• Improved abilities in analysis.	• OLAP and data mining.
• Improved customer service.	• More timely service response.
• Improved employee morale.	• Elimination of burdensome job tasks.
• Improved management decision making.	• Better information and decision analysis.
• Improved competitive position.	• Systems that lock in customers.
• Improved business image.	• Progressive image as perceived by customers, suppliers, and investors.

project. In the early stages of the project, it is impossible to define and assess accurately all of the benefits and costs associated with the new system. Thus, the economic feasibility assessment is an ongoing process in which the definable short-term costs are constantly being weighed against the definable long-term benefits. If a project cannot be accurately judged as economically feasible using hard costs, then the project should not proceed, regardless of the other assessment category outcomes.

The assessment of economic feasibility typically involves the preparation of a **cost/benefit analysis**. If costs and benefits can be quantified with a high degree of certainty, they are referred to as *tangible;* if not, they are called *intangible*. Examples of **tangible costs** are the costs of hardware and software, employee salaries, and other quantifiable costs needed to develop and implement an IS solution. **Intangible costs** are difficult to quantify; they include the loss of customer goodwill or employee morale caused by errors and disruptions arising from the installation of a new system.

Tangible benefits are favorable results, such as the decrease in payroll costs caused by a reduction in personnel or a decrease in inventory carrying costs caused by reduction in inventory. **Intangible benefits** are harder to estimate. Such benefits as better customer service or faster and more accurate information for management fall into this category. Figure 10.5 lists typical tangible and intangible benefits with examples. Possible tangible and intangible costs would be the opposite of each benefit shown.

Technical Feasibility

The assessment of **technical feasibility** is focused on gaining an understanding of the present technical resources of the organization and their applicability to the expected needs of the proposed system. The analyst must assess the degree to which the current technical resources, including hardware, software, and operating environments, can be upgraded or added to, such that the needs of the proposed system can be met. If the current technology is deemed sufficient, then the technical feasibility of the project is clear. If this is not the case however, the analyst must determine whether the technology necessary to meet the stated specifications exists. The danger here is that the project may require technology that does not yet exist in a stable form. Despite the claims of vendors that they can supply whatever is required, the analyst must be able to accurately assess the degree to which the needed technology exists in a form suitable for the proposed project. See Figure 10.6.

FIGURE 10.6
Examples of how a feasibility study might measure the feasibility of a proposed e-commerce system for a business.

Operational Feasibility	Economic Feasibility
• How well a proposed e-commerce system fits the company's plans for developing Web-based sales, marketing, and financial systems.	• Savings in labor costs. • Increased sales revenue. • Decreased investment in inventory. • Increased profits. • Acceptable return on investment.
Technical Feasibility	**Human Factors Feasibility**
• Capability, reliability, and availability of Web store hardware, software, and management services.	• Acceptance of employees. • Management support. • Customer and supplier acceptance. • Staff developers have necessary skills.
Legal/Political Feasibility	
• No patent or copyright violations. • Software licensing for developer side only. • No governmental restrictions. • No changes to existing reporting authority.	

Human Factors Feasibility

It is one thing to assess the degree to which a proposed system can work and quite another to evaluate whether the system will work. The **human factors feasibility** assessment focuses on the most important components of a successful system implementation: the managers and end users. No matter how elegant the technology, the system will not work if the end users and managers do not perceive it to be relevant and therefore do not support it. In this category, we assess the degree of resistance to the proposed system, the perceived role of end users in the development process, the degree of change to the end users' working environment as a result of the new system, and the current state of human resources available to conduct the project and manage and use the system on completion.

Legal/Political Feasibility

This category of assessment is often overlooked during the early stages of project initiation and analysis. The **legal/political feasibility** of a proposed project includes a thorough analysis of any potential legal ramifications resulting from the construction and implementation of the new system. Such legal issues include copyright or patent infringements, violation of existing antitrust laws (e.g., the antitrust suit brought against Microsoft Corporation over Windows and Internet Explorer by the U.S. Justice Department in 1998), foreign trade restrictions, or any existing contractual obligations of the organization.

The political side of the assessment focuses on gaining an understanding of who the key stakeholders within the organization are and the degree to which the proposed system may positively or negatively affect the distribution of power. Such distribution can have major political repercussions and may cause disruption or failure of an otherwise relevant development effort.

Systems Analysis

What is **systems analysis**? Whether you want to develop a new application quickly or are involved in a long-term project, you will need to perform several basic activities of systems analysis. Many of these activities are extensions of those used in conducting a feasibility study. However, systems analysis is not a preliminary study. It is an in-depth study of end-user information needs that produces *functional requirements* that are u-as the basis for the design of a new information system. Systems analysis traditionally involves a detailed study of:

- The information needs of a company and end users like yourself.
- The activities, resources, and products of one or more of the present information systems being used.
- The information system capabilities required to meet your information needs and those of other business stakeholders that may use the system.

Organizational Analysis

An **organizational analysis** is an important first step in systems analysis. How can people improve an information system if they know very little about the organizational environment in which that system is located? They can't. That's why the members of a development team have to know something about the organization, its management structure, its people, its business activities, the environmental systems it must deal with, and its current information systems. Someone on the team must know this information in more detail for the specific business units or end-user workgroups that will be affected by the new or improved information system being proposed. For example, a new inventory control system for a chain of department stores cannot be designed unless someone on a development team understands a great deal about the company and the types of business activities that affect its inventory. That's why business end users are frequently added to systems development teams.

Analysis of the Present System

Before you design a new system, it is important to study the system that will be improved or replaced (assuming there is one). You need to analyze how this system uses hardware, software, network, and people resources to convert data resources, such as transactions data, into information products, such as reports and displays. Then you should document how the information system activities of input, processing, output, storage, and control are accomplished.

For example, you might evaluate the format, timing, volume, and quality of input and output activities. Such *user interface* activities are vital to effective interaction between end users and a computer-based system. Then, in the systems design stage, you can specify what the resources, products, and activities should be to support the user interface in the system you are designing.

BuyerZone and OfficeMax: Evaluating Customer Web Site Experiences

Customers of business-to-business sites are faced with much more difficult decisions than the customers of business-to-consumer sites. Jakob Nielsen of Nielsen Norman Group recently studied the reactions of users who were trying to decide whether to lease or buy office equipment.

BuyerZone.com and OfficeMax both failed in the study because they didn't support users going through a process. To support a customer's process, businesses need to understand it from the user's perspective. If users feel pushed through a process or can't figure out what to do next, you're skipping steps that matter to them. Don't just design Web pages. Design support for users' tasks. Here's how:

- **Support Processes before Pushing Transactions.** Customers need compelling reasons to complete complex tasks on the Web. It's usually easier to pick up the phone and deal with a salesperson than to go it alone on the Web. Users often say that the Web is fine for preliminary research but useless for closing deals. Most B2B sites overlook their users' perspectives in their eagerness to move them to the checkout line. For example, users don't want to click Buy Now until they select their payment options on BuyerZone.com. Unfortunately, clicking Buy Now is the only way to see both leasing and purchase prices.
- **Provide the Right Tools at the Right Time.** Complex processes require different tools for different stages of the process. Early in a process, customers

need ways to look quickly at their purchasing options in many ways, without commitment. Let users easily manipulate data they care about, and carry that forward to their transaction when they're ready. For example, though it's good that BuyerZone.com offers a calculator to explore leasing prices, users struggle to understand the leasing terminology and want more guidance and recommendations from the tool.

- **Integrate Related Tasks.** From a customer's prospective, leasing is just a payment option and part of a larger acquisition process, not a separate task. Yet OfficeMax separates leasing from purchasing, as if a user would get leases in an independent project. A user who has selected office equipment on OfficeMax's Web site can't explore how to lease that equipment. Instead, she must abandon her selection, find leasing services from the site's Business Services section, and then suffer through an awkward registration process [19, 20].

Logical Analysis

One of the primary activities that occurs during the analysis phase is the construction of a **logical model** of the current system. The logical model can be thought of as a blueprint of the current system that displays only *what* the current system does without regard to *how* it does it. By constructing and analyzing a logical model of the current system, a systems analyst can more easily understand the various processes, functions, and data associated with the system without getting bogged down with all the issues surrounding the hardware or the software. Also, by creating a logical model, the various noncomputer components of a system can be incorporated, analyzed, and understood. For example, in the physical version of a system, a person's inbox may be the location where new orders are stored until they have been entered into the computer. In the logical model, that inbox is treated just like a computer hard drive or other electronic storage media. In a logical sense, it is just another place to store data.

Functional Requirements Analysis and Determination

This step of systems analysis is one of the most difficult. You may need to work as a team with IS analysts and other end users to determine your specific business information needs. For example, first you need to determine what type of information each business activity requires; what its format, volume, and frequency should be; and what response times are necessary. Second, you must try to determine the information processing capabilities required for each system activity (input, processing, output, storage, control) to meet these information needs. *As with the construction of the logical model, your main goal is to identify what should be done, not how to do it.*

When this step of the life cycle is complete, a set of **functional requirements** for the proposed new system will exist. Functional requirements are end-user information requirements that are not tied to the hardware, software, network, data, and people resources that end users presently use or might use in the new system. That is left to the design stage to determine. For example, Figure 10.7 shows examples of functional requirements for a proposed e-commerce application for a business.

FIGURE 10.7
Examples of functional requirements for a proposed e-commerce system for a business.

Examples of Functional Requirements
• **User Interface Requirements** Automatic entry of product data and easy-to-use data entry screens for Web customers.
• **Processing Requirements** Fast, automatic calculation of sales totals and shipping costs.
• **Storage Requirements** Fast retrieval and update of data from product, pricing, and customer databases.
• **Control Requirements** Signals for data entry errors and quick e-mail confirmation for customers.

FIGURE 10.8 Systems design can be viewed as the design of user interfaces, data, and processes.

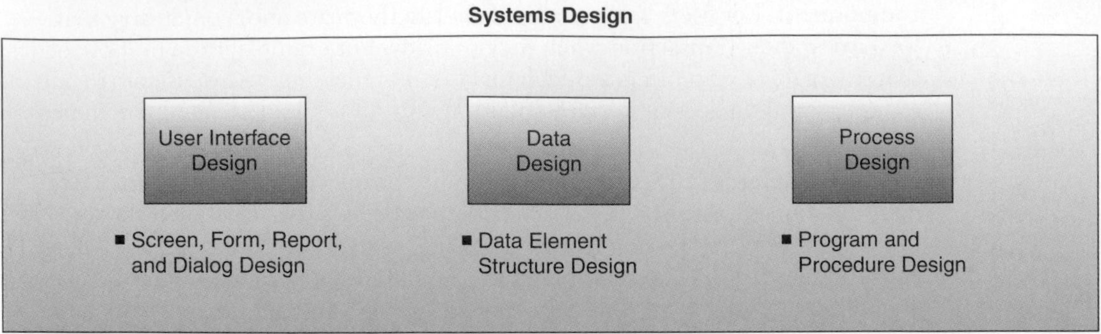

Systems Design

Once the analysis portion of the life cycle is complete, the process of **systems design** can begin. Here is where the logical model of the current system is modified until it represents the blueprint for the new system. This version of the logical model represents what the new system will do. During the **physical** design portion of this step, users and analysts focus on determining *how* the system will accomplish its objectives. This point is where issues related to hardware, software, networking, data storage, security, and many others will be discussed and determined. As such, systems design consists of design activities that ultimately produce physical system specifications satisfying the functional requirements that were developed in the systems analysis process.

A useful way to look at systems design is illustrated in Figure 10.8. This concept focuses on three major products, or *deliverables,* that should result from the design stage. In this framework, systems design consists of three activities: user interface, data, and process design. This framework results in specifications for user interface methods and products, database structures, and processing and control procedures.

Prototyping

During the design phase, the development process frequently takes the form of, or includes, a *prototyping* approach. **Prototyping** is the rapid development and testing of working models, or **prototypes,** of new applications in an interactive, iterative process that can be used by both IS specialists and business professionals. Prototyping, as a development tool, makes the development process faster and easier, especially for projects for which end-user requirements are hard to define. Prototyping has also opened up the application development process to end users because it simplifies and accelerates systems design. Thus prototyping has enlarged the role of the business stakeholders affected by a proposed system and helps enable a quicker and more responsive development process called *agile systems development* (ASD). See Figure 10.9.

The Prototyping Process

Prototyping can be used for both large and small applications. Typically, large business systems still require using a traditional systems development approach, but parts of such systems can frequently be prototyped. A prototype of a business application needed by an end user is developed quickly using a variety of application development software tools. The prototype system is then repeatedly refined until it is acceptable.

As Figure 10.9 illustrates, prototyping is an iterative, interactive process. End users with sufficient experience with application development tools can do prototyping themselves. Alternatively, you could work with an IS specialist to develop a prototype system in a series of interactive sessions. For example, you could develop, test, and refine prototypes of management reports, data entry screens, or output displays.

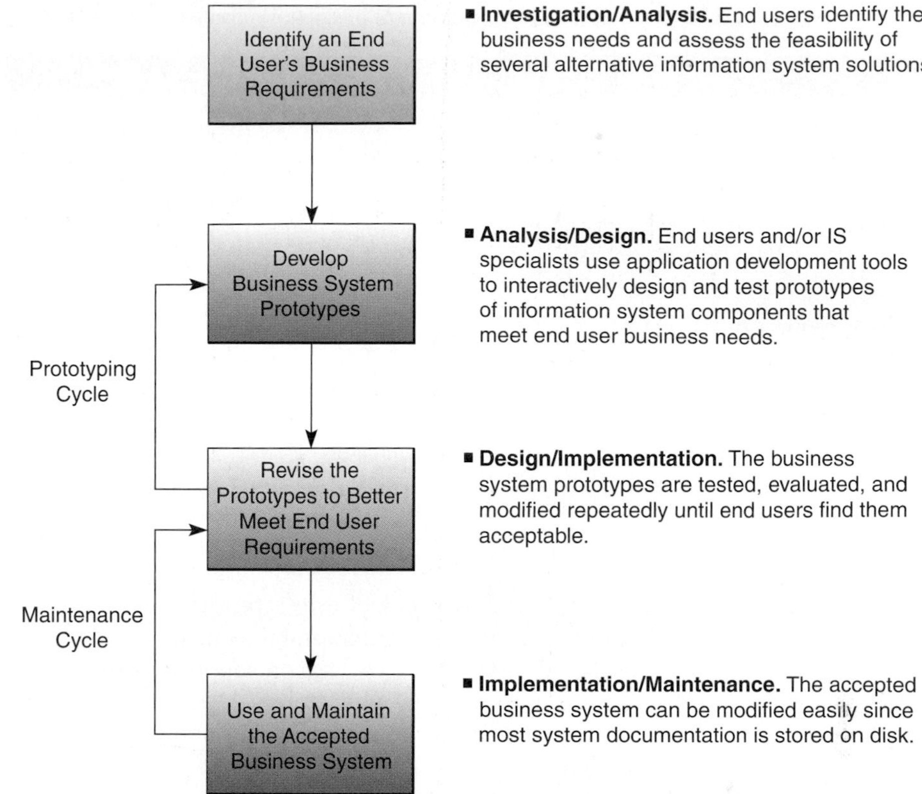
Identify an End User's Business Requirements
Develop Business System Prototypes
Revise the Prototypes to Better Meet End User Requirements
Use and Maintain the Accepted Business System
Prototyping Cycle
Maintenance Cycle
■ **Investigation/Analysis.** End users identify their business needs and assess the feasibility of several alternative information system solutions.
■ **Analysis/Design.** End users and/or IS specialists use application development tools to interactively design and test prototypes of information system components that meet end user business needs.
■ **Design/Implementation.** The business system prototypes are tested, evaluated, and modified repeatedly until end users find them acceptable.
■ **Implementation/Maintenance.** The accepted business system can be modified easily since most system documentation is stored on disk.

FIGURE 10.9
Application development using prototyping. Note how prototyping combines the steps of the systems development cycle and changes the traditional roles of IS specialists and end users.

Usually, a prototype is modified several times before end users find it acceptable. Program modules are then generated by application development software using conventional programming languages. The final version of the application system is turned over to its end users for operational use. Although prototyping is a useful method of allowing an end user to develop small software applications, its real power is as a development tool, within a life cycle project, to assist analysts and users in finalizing the various interfaces and functions of a large business system. Figure 10.10 outlines a typical prototyping-based systems development process for a business application.

FIGURE 10.10
An example of a typical application of prototyping during a software development project.

Example of Prototyping Development
• **Team.** A few end users and IS developers form a team to develop a business application.
• **Schematic.** The initial prototype schematic design is developed.
• **Prototype.** The schematic is converted into a simple point-and-click prototype using prototyping tools.
• **Presentation.** A few screens and routine linkages are presented to users.
• **Feedback.** After the team gets feedback from users, the prototype is reiterated.
• **Reiteration.** Further presentations and reiterations are made.
• **Consultation.** Consultations are held with IT consultants to identify potential improvements and conformance to existing standards.
• **Completion.** The prototype is used as a model to create a finished application.
• **Acceptance.** Users review and sign off on their acceptance of the new business system.
• **Installation.** The new business software is installed on network servers.

FIGURE 10.11 Useful guidelines for the design of business Web sites.

Checklist for Corporate Web Sites

- **Remember the Customer:** Successful Web sites are built solely for the customer, not to make company vice presidents happy.
- **Aesthetics:** Successful designs combine fast-loading graphics and simple color palettes for pages that are easy to read.
- **Broadband Content:** The Web's coolest stuff can't be accessed by most Web surfers. Including a little streaming video isn't bad, but don't make it the focus of your site.
- **Easy to Navigate:** Make sure it's easy to get from one part of your site to another. Providing a site map, accessible from every page, helps.
- **Searchability:** Many sites have their own search engines; very few are actually useful. Make sure yours is.
- **Incompatibilities:** A site that looks great on a PC using Internet Explorer can often look miserable on an iBook running Netscape.
- **Registration Forms:** Registration forms are a useful way to gather customer data. But make your customers fill out a three-page form, and watch them flee.
- **Dead Links:** Dead links are the bane of all Web surfers—be sure to keep your links updated. Many Web-design software tools can now do this for you.

User Interface Design

Let's take a closer look at **user interface design**, because it is the system component closest to business end users and the one they will most likely help design. The user interface design activity focuses on supporting the interactions between end users and their computer-based applications. Designers concentrate on the design of attractive and efficient forms of user input and output, such as easy-to-use Internet or intranet Web pages.

As we mentioned previously, user interface design is frequently a *prototyping* process, in which working models or prototypes of user interface methods are designed and modified several times with feedback from end users. The user interface design process produces detailed design specifications for information products such as display screens, interactive user/computer dialogues (including the sequence or flow of dialogue), audio responses, forms, documents, and reports. Figure 10.11 gives examples of user interface design elements and other guidelines suggested for the multimedia Web pages of e-commerce Web sites [7]. Figure 10.12 presents actual before and after screen displays of the user interface design process for a work scheduling application of State Farm Insurance Company [21].

FIGURE 10.12 An example of the user interface design process. State Farm developers changed this work scheduling and assignment application's interface after usability testing showed that end users working with the old interface (at left) didn't realize that they had to follow a six-step process. If users jumped to a new page out of order, they would lose their work. The new interface (at right) made it clearer that a process had to be followed.

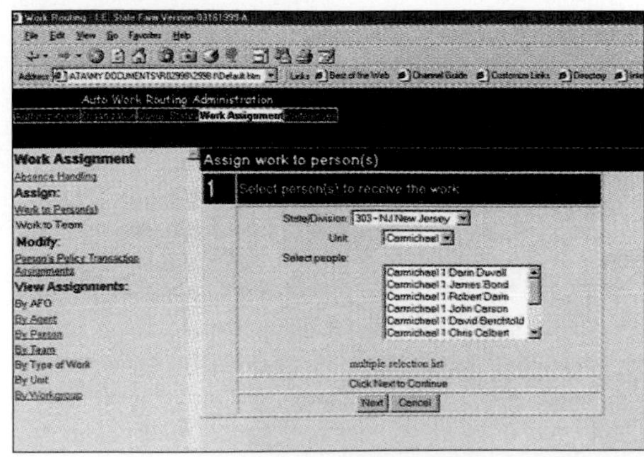

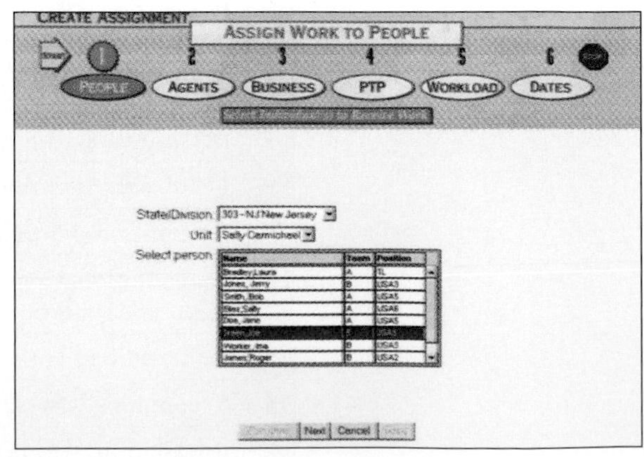

Google: Evaluating User Interface Design

Google's weekly user interface design meeting is a no-bumbling zone. Run by Marissa Mayer, the company's VP of search products and user experience, it's the meeting during which the look and feel of Google's products are hammered out. For two hours, Mayer evaluates a stream of design proposals ranging from minor tweaks to the whole layout of a new product. Each presentation is allotted a specific amount of time, which a giant digital clock on the wall ticks off in seconds. On a split screen at the left, notes from the meeting appear in real time, and designers around the world drop in by videoconference. On the right, graph after graph of usability test results data are projected: What do users do when a tab is moved from the side of the page to the top? What if a box is tinted gray? In Mayer's UI group, it's all about the numbers. No one, it is guaranteed, will attempt to justify a design by proclaiming, "I think it looks better this way."

The first presenters, a young, hip-looking pair of guys, are reporting the results of a four-month usability experiment. Which part of the page caught users' attention? How long did they stay there? Which elements did they skip right by? Why? "We have over 100 slides," one of the presenters tells Mayer as the lights dim, "so we're going to skip a few." To the uninitiated, the design revisions they show look like a slam dunk. Masses of numbers are being presented on the fly, and the graphs trend upward at nice angles.

Mayer, however, is unconvinced. "It looks pretty noisy if you look at the base data," she says, leaning back in her chair, and then she asks if a searches/per user/per day graph is available. There is an uncomfortable pause. "Uh, no," they say. "Well," Mayer replies, "that's a good macro statistic that indicates user happiness. So can we see that one soon?" The men nod.

As the stopwatch hits its mark, another team steps up. Its design is less polished, and Mayer thoroughly but politely takes it apart. The page is trying to do too much, she tells the group. Better to back off and do a few things really well. "If you give users more to choose from," she says, "they'll actually choose worse."

By the meeting's end, Mayer has said no a lot more than yes, but the presenters have taken her judgments evenly. They clearly prize brevity: The shorter the meeting, the sooner everyone can get back to their pet projects [33].

System Specifications

System specifications formalize the design of an application's user interface methods and products, database structures, and processing and control procedures. Therefore, systems designers frequently develop hardware, software, network, data, and personnel specifications for a proposed system. Figure 10.13 shows examples of system specifications that could be developed for an e-commerce system of a company.

End-User Development

In a traditional systems development cycle, your role as a business end user is similar to that of a customer or a client. Typically, you make a request for a new or improved system, answer questions about your specific information needs and information processing problems, and provide background information on your existing business systems. Then IS professionals work with you to analyze your problem and suggest alternative solutions. When you approve the best alternative, it is designed and implemented. Here again, you may be involved in a prototyping design process or be on an implementation team with IS specialists.

However, in **end-user development**, IS professionals play a consulting role while you do your own application development. Sometimes a staff of user consultants may be available to help you and other end users with your application development efforts. This help may include training in the use of application packages; selection of hardware and software; assistance in gaining access to organization databases; and, of course, assistance in analysis, design, and implementing the business application of IT that you need.

FIGURE 10.13
Examples of system specifications for a new e-commerce system for a business.

Examples of System Specifications
• **User Interface Specifications** Use personalized screens that welcome repeat Web customers and make product recommendations.
• **Database Specifications** Develop databases that use object/relational database management software to organize access to all customer and inventory data and to multimedia product information.
• **Software Specifications** Acquire an e-commerce software engine to process all e-commerce transactions with fast responses—i.e., retrieve necessary product data and compute all sales amounts in less than one second.
• **Hardware and Network Specifications** Install redundant networked Web servers and sufficient high-bandwidth telecommunications lines to host the company e-commerce Web site.
• **Personnel Specifications** Hire an e-commerce manager and specialists and a Webmaster and Web designer to plan, develop, and manage e-commerce operations.

Focus on IS Activities

It is important to remember that end-user development should focus on the fundamental activities of any information system: input, processing, output, storage, and control, as we described in Chapter 1. Figure 10.14 illustrates these system components and the questions they address.

In analyzing a potential application, you should focus first on the *output* to be produced by the application. What information is needed, and in what form should it be presented? Next, look at the *input* data to be supplied to the application. What data are available? From what sources? In what form? Then you should examine the *processing*

FIGURE 10.14 End-user development should focus on the basic information processing activity components of an information system.

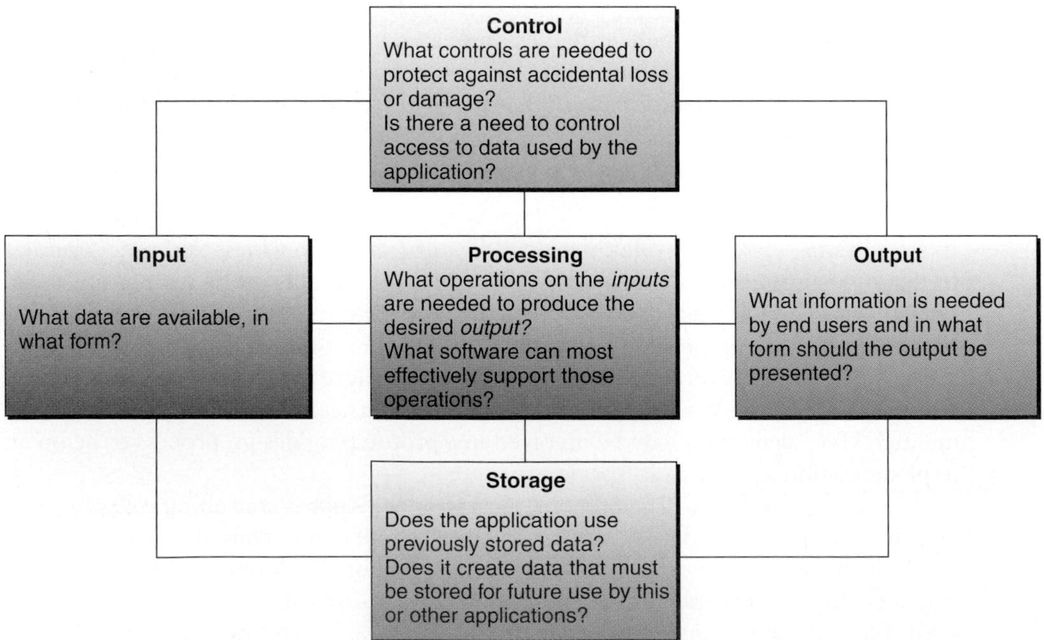

Source: Adapted from James N. Morgan, *Application Cases in MIS*, 4th ed. (New York: Irwin/McGraw-Hill, 2002), p. 31.

requirements. What operations or transformation processes will be required to convert the available inputs into the desired output? Among software packages the developer is able to use, which package can best perform the operations required?

You may find that the desired output cannot be produced from the inputs that are available. If this is the case, you must either make adjustments to the output expected or find additional sources of input data, including data stored in files and databases from external sources. The *storage* component will vary in importance in end-user applications. For example, some applications require extensive use of stored data or the creation of data that must be stored for future use. These are better suited for database management development projects than for spreadsheet applications.

Necessary *control* measures for end-user applications vary greatly depending on the scope and duration of the application, the number and nature of the users of the application, and the nature of the data involved. For example, control measures are needed to protect against accidental loss or damage to end-user files. The most basic protection against this type of loss is simply to make backup copies of application files on a frequent and systematic basis. Another example is the cell protection feature of spreadsheets that protects key cells from accidental erasure by users.

Doing End-User Development

In end-user development, you and other business professionals can develop new or improved ways to perform your jobs without the direct involvement of IS specialists. The application development capabilities built into a variety of end-user software packages have made it easier for many users to develop their own computer-based solutions. For example, Figure 10.15 illustrates a Web site development tool you could use to help you develop, update, and manage an intranet Web site for your business unit. Or you might use an electronic spreadsheet package as a tool to develop an easy way to analyze weekly sales results for the sales managers in a company. Or you could use a Web site development package to design Web pages for a small business Web store or a departmental intranet Web site. Let's take a look at a real-world example of how many companies are encouraging business end users to do their own Web site development [22]. See Figure 10.16.

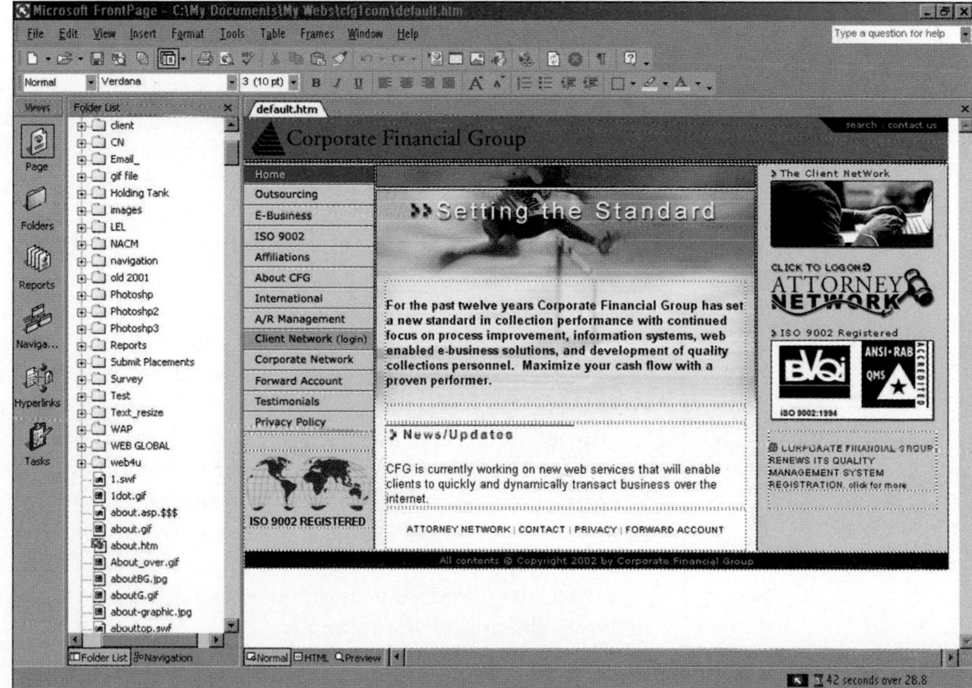

FIGURE 10.15
Microsoft FrontPage is an example of an easy-to-use end-user Web site development tool.

FIGURE 10.16
How companies are encouraging and managing intranet Web site development by business end users.

Encouraging End User Web Development
• **Look for Tools that Make Sense** Some Web development tools may be more powerful and more costly than what your business end users really need.
• **Spur Creativity** Consider a competition among business departments for the best Web site to help spur users to more creative uses of their intranet sites.
• **Set Some Limits** Yes, you have to keep some control. Consider putting limits on exactly what parts of a Web page users can change and who can change what pages. You still want some consistency across the organization.
• **Give Managers Responsibility** Make business unit managers sign off on who will be Web publishing from their groups, and make the managers personally responsible for the content that goes on their Web sites. That will help prevent the publishing of inappropriate content by some users.
• **Make Users Comfortable** Training users well on the tools will help them become confident in their ability to properly manage and update their sites—and save IT the trouble of fixing problems later on or providing continuous support for minor problems.

End User Applications Development: 99 Percent Accuracy Is Not Enough

A typical oil and gas company acquisition deal is worth millions of dollars. One Dallas firm made a great deal on an oil and gas acquisition, lost millions of dollars, and ultimately fired the executives who made this great deal. What went wrong? Their end-user–developed spreadsheet model contained a single error, and the executives had based their actions on their spreadsheet data.

Are such errors common? Only a few cases of spreadsheet disasters like this have been made public, but consultants and independent audits have found errors in as many as 30 percent of the spreadsheet models that are created with today's ubiquitous, off-the-shelf spreadsheet applications. Because a typical organization can have literally tens of thousands of user-developed spreadsheets in use, a 1 percent error rate can range from creating a minor nuisance to catastrophic results. In several experiments, mechanical errors were found in about 1 percent of spreadsheet cells. Although this number may seem high, it actually compares favorably with the typically undetected error rates among expert typists.

Even more important than mechanical errors are logic errors—those that involve an incorrect formula. Logic errors are bad for two reasons. First, they are difficult for the model's developer to detect. Second, tests have found undetected logic errors in about 4 percent of all cells. This rate actually corresponds favorably to error rates in software development. Numerous studies have shown that even experienced professional programmers make undetected mistakes in 3 to 7 percent of all lines of code before they begin the debugging stage. Add the inexperience of the typical end-user developer, and you have a recipe for disaster.

Professional programmers have procedures in place to reduce errors to about 2 in every 1,000 lines of code, but error reduction efforts among end-user developers are often cursory. Surveys have shown that most spreadsheet models have design flaws that are likely to lead to long-term errors. The surveys also found only about 1 in 10 companies have policies for producing spreadsheet models. Even when policies exist, they are rarely enforced. Crucially, the external audits so important in program debugging are quite rare.

So what can be done to ensure your spreadsheet models are accurate? Above all other approaches, have your models audited by a professional programmer before putting them to use. If you conduct your own audit, be sure to look for numerical errors, qualitative errors, and unusual results from test data. In software development, we have learned the hard way that we have to treat programming errors as things that are bound to occur, even with the best developers. By adopting the practice of conscientious audits, end-user–developed spreadsheets can become valuable and reliable components in an organization's application architecture [24, 25].

Technical Note: Overview of Object-Oriented Analysis and Design

As stated at the beginning of this chapter, there are two common approaches to analysis and design: SDLC and object-oriented. Whereas the SDLC remains the predominant approach to software development, the object-oriented approach is gaining favor, particularly among programmers focusing on complex systems that require handling a wide variety of complex data structures, such as audio, video, images, documents, Web pages, and other types of data.

We introduced the concepts of objects and object oriented databases in Chapter Five. Thorough coverage of the object-oriented approach to analysis and design is beyond the scope of this text, but a brief overview is presented here. Let's begin with a simple definition of anything object-oriented.

An **object-oriented system** is composed of *objects*. An object can be anything a programmer wants to manage or manipulate—cars, people, animals, savings accounts, food products, business units, organizations, customers—literally anything. Once an object is defined by a programmer, its characteristics can be used to allow one object to interact with another object or pass information to another object. The behavior of an object-oriented system entails collaboration between these objects, and the state of the system is the combined state of all the objects in it.

Collaboration between objects requires them to send messages or information to one another. The exact semantics of message sending between objects varies, depending on the kind of system being modeled. In some systems, "sending a message" is the same as "invoking a method." In others, "sending a message" might involve sending data using a pre-prescribed media. The three areas of interest to us in an object-oriented system are object-oriented programming, object-oriented analysis, and object-oriented design.

Object-oriented programming (OOP) is the programming paradigm that uses "objects" to design applications and computer programs. It employs several techniques from previously established paradigms, including

- **Inheritance:** The ability of one object to inherit the characteristics of a higher-order object. For example, all cars have wheels; therefore, an object defined as a *sports car* and as a special type of the object *cars* must also have wheels.
- **Modularity:** The extent to which a program is designed as series of interlinked yet stand-alone modules.
- **Polymorphism:** The ability of an object to behave differently depending on the conditions in which its behavior is invoked. For example, two objects that inherit the behavior *speak* from an object class *animal* might be a dog object and a cat object. Both have a behavior defined as *speak*. When the dog object is commanded to speak, it will *bark*, whereas when the cat object is commanded to speak, it will *meow*.
- **Encapsulation:** Concealing all of the characteristics associated with a particular object inside the object itself. This paradigm allows objects to inherit characteristics simply by defining a subobject. For example, the object *airplane* contains all of the characteristics of an airplane: wings, tail, rudder, pilot, speed, altitude, and so forth.

Even though it originated in the 1960s, OOP was not commonly used in mainstream software application development until the 1990s. Today, many popular programming languages (e.g., ActionScript, Ada 95/2005, C#, C++, Delphi, Java, JavaScript, Lisp, Objective-C, Perl, PHP, Python, RealBasic, Ruby, Squeak, VB.Net, Visual FoxPro, and Visual Prolog) support OOP.

Object-oriented analysis (OOA) aims to model *the problem domain*, that is, the problem we want to solve, by developing an object-oriented (OO) system. The source of the analysis is a set of written requirement statements and/or diagrams that illustrates the statements.

Similar to the SDLC-developed model, an object-oriented analysis model does not take into account implementation constraints, such as concurrency, distribution, persistence, or inheritance, nor how the system will be built. Because object-oriented systems are modular, the model of a system can be divided into multiple domains, each of which are separately analyzed and represent separate business, technological, or conceptual areas of interest. The result of object-oriented analysis is a description of what is to be built, using concepts and relationships between concepts, often expressed as a conceptual model. Any other documentation needed to describe what is to be built is also included in the result of the analysis.

Object-oriented design (OOD) describes the activity when designers look for logical solutions to solve a problem using objects. Object-oriented design takes the conceptual model that results from the object-oriented analysis and adds implementation constraints imposed by the environment, the programming language, and the chosen tools, as well as architectural assumptions chosen as the basis of the design.

The concepts in the conceptual model are mapped to concrete classes, abstract interfaces, and roles that the objects take in various situations. The interfaces and their implementations for stable concepts can be made available as reusable services. Concepts identified as unstable in object-oriented analysis will form the basis for policy classes that make decisions and implement environment- or situation-specific logics or algorithms. The result of the object-oriented design is a detailed description of how the system can be built, using objects.

Thus, the object-oriented world bears many similarities to the more conventional SDLC approach. This approach simply takes a different view of the programming domain and thus approaches the problem-solving activities inherent in system development from a different direction.

In the next section, we will continue looking at systems development by changing our focus from design to implementation.

SECTION II Implementing Business Systems

Implementation

Once a new information system has been designed, it must be implemented as a working system and maintained to keep it operating properly. The implementation process we will cover in this section follows the investigation, analysis, and design stages of the systems development cycle we discussed in Section I. Implementation is a vital step in the deployment of information technology to support the employees, customers, and other business stakeholders of a company.

Read the Real World Case in this chapter. We can learn a lot from this case about the challenges of implementing information systems that attempt to change how employees obtain and share knowledge and information. See Figure 10.17.

Implementing New Systems

Figure 10.18 illustrates that the **systems implementation** stage involves hardware and software acquisition, software development, testing of programs and procedures, conversion of data resources, and a variety of conversion alternatives. It also involves the education and training of end users and specialists who will operate a new system.

Implementation can be a difficult and time-consuming process. However, it is vital in ensuring the success of any newly developed system, for even a well-designed system will fail if it is not properly implemented. That is why the **implementation process** typically requires a **project management** effort on the part of IT and business unit managers. They must enforce a project plan that includes job responsibilities, timelines for major stages of development, and financial budgets. This plan is necessary if a project is to be completed on time and within its established budget while still meeting its design objectives. Figure 10.19 illustrates the activities and timelines that might be required to implement an intranet for a new employee benefits system in the human resource department of a company [10].

Zurich North America: IT Project Management

Dave Patterson is a big believer in what he describes as full project transparency. "Every project we're working on and its status is reported through the intranet," notes Patterson, vice president of IT at Zurich North America, the Baltimore-based insurance arm of Zurich Financial Services (www.zurich.com). "The status of projects is all very fact-based. You're either making your dates or you're not; you're on budget or you're not; you either have an issue or you don't."

Patterson claims Zurich applies the same black-and-white, fact-based thinking when it comes to paying salaries and bonuses to members of an IT project team. The bulk of each project team member's salary is based on market pay rates and the worker's competency. "But about 10 to 20 percent of compensation is based on whether the company makes money and whether we deliver a project as promised," Patterson says.

His other financial rule of thumb is to always get the budget and funding arrangements of a project in writing. "At the start of every project, there is a project agreement," Patterson promises. "It needs to contain the full scope of the project plans, risk analysis, costs and benefits, and it has to be signed by the business partners willing to pay for the project. I will not allow a project to initiate if I don't have a customer who is willing to pay for it [12]."

Project Management

Any discussion of information systems design and development would be incomplete without including a discussion of basic **project management** concepts, techniques, and tools. So, before we progress any further into our discussion of implementation, we need to understand how our project got to this point, hopefully on time and on budget.

REAL WORLD CASE 2 Infosys Technologies: The Implementation Challenges of Knowledge Management Initiatives

Infosys Technologies, headquartered in Bangalore, India, is one of the world's largest software development contractors, with revenue of $1.6 billion in fiscal 2005 and employing over 50,000 software engineers and other staff in early 2006. The company has a long history of trying to leverage knowledge created by its employees for corporate advantage. Its adage "learn once, use anywhere" reinforces the continual learning and reflection required for knowledge accumulation and reuse. It also draws attention to a core belief that knowledge belongs not only to those employees who create it but to the entire company.

Infosys began efforts to transform its employees' knowledge into an organizationwide resource in the early 1990s. In 1999, a central knowledge management (KM) group was created to facilitate a companywide KM program, including the creation of an intranet knowledge portal called KShop for the accumulation and reuse of organizational knowledge.

But by early 2000, patronage of KShop by employees remained low. Employees within various project teams and practice communities continued to use their informal networks to access knowledge in times of need. Local repositories of specialized knowledge continued to proliferate within project teams and practice communities. In other words, processes at different levels of the knowledge system were not coupling and reinforcing one another.

In response, during the first quarter of 2001, the KM group implemented a major initiative called "the knowledge currency unit (KCU) incentive" scheme to jump-start contributions to KShop. According to the scheme, Infosys employees who contributed or reviewed contributions to KShop would be awarded KCUs, which they could accumulate and exchange for monetary rewards or prizes. In addition, employees' cumulative KCU scores would be displayed on a scoreboard on KShop, thereby increasing the visibility and standing of prolific contributors.

FIGURE 10.17

Infosys Technologies is one of the world's largest and most successful software development contractors.

These initiatives began yielding results, especially after the KCU incentive scheme was introduced. For instance, within a year of introduction of the KCU scheme, more than 2,400 new knowledge assets project proposals, case studies, and reusable software codes were contributed to KShop, with nearly 20 percent of Infosys employees contributing at least one knowledge asset. Over 130,000 KCUs were generated by the KM group and distributed among contributing and reviewing employees.

Even as these events unfolded, the KM group began wondering if the KCU incentive scheme had become *too* successful. One concern had to do with employees experiencing information overload and, consequently, higher search costs for reusable knowledge. As a member of the KM team commented: "Some people have told us informally that they are finding it faster to do things on their own or to ask someone they know instead of searching the repository for reusable content."

Complicating matters, the explosive growth in the number of contributions began placing a heavy burden on the limited number of volunteer reviewers. A shortage of reviewers made it difficult for the KM group to ensure that contributions were reviewed for quality and relevance before being published on KShop. With review processes still struggling to keep pace with the accelerating pace of contributions, assets of uncertain quality began appearing on KShop. When even contributions of questionable quality began receiving high-quality ratings from colleagues, the rating scheme itself came under scrutiny.

Concerns also began emerging about the possible impacts of the KCU scheme on knowledge processes at the other levels of the organization. One such concern was the potential for the KCU incentive scheme to destroy the spirit of community and the asking culture within the company. What employees would have given freely to one another previously was now being monetized through the KCU incentive scheme. "Why not gain some rewards and recognition for my knowledge contributions, especially when others are doing so?" was the question being asked by employees who had shared their knowledge earlier for free. An additional concern was the real possibility that some project teams and practice groups, disappointed with KShop, could revert to building and relying on their own local repositories instead of contributing to the central portal.

Sensing the potential of the KCU incentive scheme to compromise the companywide KM program, the KM group took several actions. First, it intervened to decouple knowledge sharing from the economic incentives that threatened the spirit of community and the perceived utility of KShop. Specifically, in April 2002, the KM group modified the KCU incentive scheme to emphasize recognition and personal visibility for knowledge-sharing contributions more than monetary rewards. It formulated a new composite KCU score that emphasized the usefulness and benefit of contributions to Infosys as rated not just by volunteer reviewers or colleagues but also by actual users. Moreover, to increase the accountability of reviewers and users who rated contributions to KShop, the KM group began demanding tangible proof to justify any high ratings. Finally, the KM group significantly reduced the number of KCUs awarded for reviewing contributions to KShop and raised the bar for cashing in the KCU incentive points for monetary rewards. The KM group hoped that these steps would shift the motivation to share knowledge away from monetary rewards.

A second set of initiatives focused on improving KM practices within project teams and practice communities. Intense time pressure in completing projects within stringent deadlines reduced knowledge codification efforts within teams. To address this issue, the KM group modified forms and project templates to facilitate extraction of knowledge using automated tools. The group also implemented a project-tracking tool on KShop to log details and deliverables pertaining to every project within Infosys. The objective of these initiatives was to enable the codification and extraction of knowledge even as teams carried out their routine project-related tasks.

Despite these attempts, knowledge codification continued to vary across project teams. To address this shortcoming, the KM group introduced a hierarchy of roles to broker knowledge sharing among project teams, practice communities, and the wider organization. Within each project team, one volunteer member would be designated as the KM prime. The KM prime would be responsible for identifying and facilitating the fulfillment of the team's knowledge needs for each project. The KM prime would also ensure that, after the completion of each project, the team codified and shared critical knowledge gained during the project with the rest of the company. At the practice community and wider organizational levels, the KM group created the role of knowledge champions to spearhead and facilitate knowledge sharing and reuse in critical or emerging technologies and methodologies. Furthermore, the KM group encouraged employees to swap stories on KShop with the view of promoting widespread sharing of tacit individual and team-level knowledge and experiences.

After the modified KCU scheme was introduced, those who had contributed to KShop just to secure monetary rewards reduced their participation. For instance, in the two quarters immediately following the introduction of the modified KCU scheme, the number of new contributors per quarter declined by nearly 37 percent, whereas the number of new knowledge assets contributed to KShop per quarter declined by approximately 26 percent. After this significant initial decline, however, the number of new knowledge assets contributed to KShop slowly stabilized and then increased at a more manageable pace. Finally, users of KShop reported lower search costs and significant increases in the quality and utility of knowledge assets available through the portal.

Looking into the future, the KM group was optimistic that the KM prime and knowledge champion roles in project groups and development communities would yield positive outcomes. A manager who had been associated with the KM initiative from the beginning reflected on the challenges faced in the implementation process at Infosys:

> *We are coming to realize that knowledge management requires much more than just technology. We have to pay attention to the cultural and social facets of knowledge management as well. We have to continually campaign and evangelize besides investing the time and resources to manage the content. Knowledge management initially appears to be a deceptively simple task. But, make just one wrong move, and it is difficult to convince people to come back.*

Source: Raghu Garud and Arun Kumaraswamy, "Vicious and Virtuous Circles in the Management of Knowledge: The Case of Infosys Technologies," *MIS Quarterly*, March 2005; Julie Schlosser, "Infosys U.," *Fortune*, March 20, 2006.

CASE STUDY QUESTIONS

1. Why do you think the knowledge management system at Infosys faced such serious implementation challenges? Defend your answer with examples from the case.
2. What steps did the KM group at Infosys take to improve participation in the KM system? Why were some of these initiatives counterproductive? The KM group responded with corrective initiatives. Do you think these will succeed? Why or why not?
3. What change management initiatives should the KM group have initiated at Infosys before attempting to develop and implement knowledge management at the company? Defend your proposals, paying particular attention to the final quote in the case by a long-time KM manager at Infosys.

REAL WORLD ACTIVITIES

1. Research the Internet to find examples of successful implementations of knowledge management systems. What successes do these companies claim, and what reasons do they give for their successful KM initiatives?
2. If knowledge management would succeed anywhere, one would think it would be a smashing success at a progressive successful IT company like Infosys. Break into small groups with your classmates to discuss what change management and other implementation strategies and tactics you would use to ensure a successful KM initiative at Infosys, one of the companies you found in your previous Internet research, or a company of your choice.

FIGURE 10.18 An overview of the implementation process. Implementation activities are needed to transform a newly developed information system into an operational system for end users.

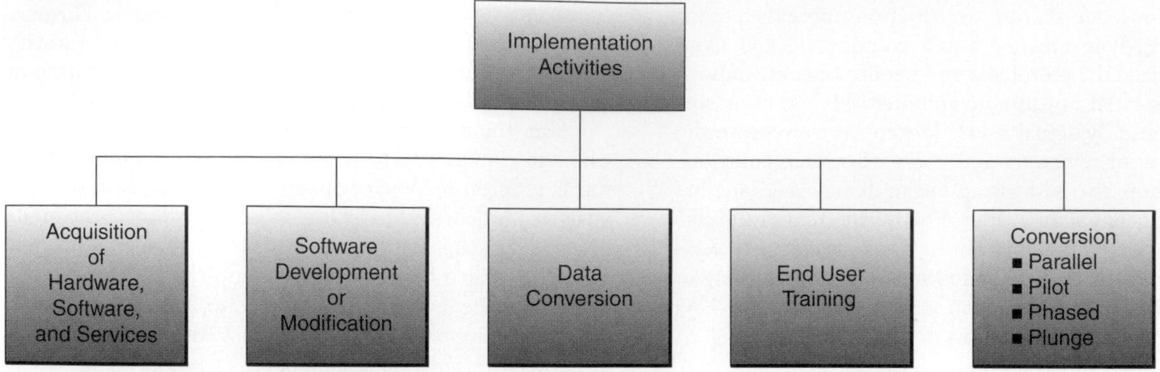

Although a thorough discussion of project management is far beyond the scope of this text, we can nonetheless look at the big picture and acquaint ourselves with the necessary steps in the process. It is important to note that the skills and knowledge necessary to be a good project manager will translate into virtually any project environment, and people who have acquired them are regularly sought after by most organizations.

What Is a Project?

A **project** is a special set of activities with a clear beginning and end. Every project has a set of *goals*, *objectives*, and *tasks*. Also, every project must deal with a set of *limitations* or *constraints*. Finally, though the content can vary from one project to the next, there are many important similarities in the process. The first, and probably the greatest, contribution of the modern project management approach is to identify the project as a series of steps or phases. The SDLC is a project management approach tailored toward the design and development of information systems. Before we return our focus to a specific project management approach such as the SDLC, let's look at a more generic picture of project management and see how it compares. No matter what the project, three elements will be necessary to manage it effectively and efficiently: *process*, *tools*, and *techniques*.

The Process of Project Management

The modern project management approach has identified five phases in the process. Figure 10.20 illustrates the five phases.

FIGURE 10.19 An example of the implementation process activities and timelines for a company installing an intranet-based employee benefits system in its human resource management department.

Intranet Implementation Activities	Month 1	Month 2	Month 3	Month 4
Acquire and install server hardware and software				
Train administrators				
Acquire and install browser software				
Acquire and install publishing software				
Train benefits employees on publishing software				
Convert benefits manuals and add revisions				
Create Web-based tutorials for the intranet				
Hold rollout meetings				

FIGURE 10.20
The five phases of project management.

Project Management Phase	Example Activities
Initiating/Defining	• State the problem(s)/goal(s). • Identify the objectives. • Secure resources. • Explore costs/benefits in feasibility study.
Planning	• Identify and sequence activities. • Identify the "critical path." • Estimate time and resources needed for completion. • Write a detailed project plan.
Executing	• Commit resources to specific tasks. • Add additional resources/personnel if necessary. • Initiate project work.
Controlling	• Establish reporting obligations. • Create reporting tools. • Compare actual progress with a baseline. • Initiate control interventions if necessary.
Closing	• Install all deliverables. • Finalize all obligations/commitments. • Meet with stakeholders. • Release project resources. • Document the project. • Issue final report.

Initiating and Defining The first phase of the project management process serves as a foundation for all that follows. The most important objective to achieve during this phase is the clear and succinct statement of the problem that the project is to solve or the goals that the project is to achieve. Any ambiguity at this point often spells doom for even the best executed projects. Also during this phase, it is necessary to identify and secure the resources necessary to execute the project, explore the costs and benefits, and identify any risks. As you have probably recognized, this is exactly what happens during the systems investigation phase of the SDLC.

Planning The next phase in the project management process involves planning the project. Here, every project objective and every activity associated with that objective must be identified and sequenced. Several tools have been created to assist in the sequencing of these activities, including simple *dependence diagrams*, *program evaluation and review* (PERT), *critical path method* (CPM), and a commonly used timeline diagram known as a *Gantt chart*. All of these tools have a particular use in project management, but their common goal is to assist in the planning and sequencing of activities associated with the objectives of the project, such that nothing is left out, performed out of logical order, or done twice. These same tools also assist the project manager in determining how long each activity is going to take and thus how long the project is going to take. Finally, later in the project process, the tools will be used to see if the project is on schedule and, if not, where the delays occurred and what might be done to remedy the delay.

Executing Once all of the activities in the planning phase are complete and all detailed plans have been created and approved, the execution phase of the project can begin. It is here that all of the plans are put into motion. Resources, tasks, and schedules are brought together, and the necessary work teams are created and set forth on their assigned paths. In many respects, this is the most exciting part of the project management process. The phases of systems analysis and system design are the primary phases associated with project execution in the SDLC.

Controlling Some project management experts suggest that controlling is simply an integral part of the execution phase of project management. Others suggest it must be viewed as a separate set of activities that, admittedly, occur simultaneous to the execution phase. In either case, it is important to give sufficient attention to the controlling activities to ensure the project objectives and deadlines are met.

Probably the single most important tool for project control is the report. Three common types of reports are generated to assist with project control. The *variance report* contains information related to the difference between actual and planned project progress. It is useful in identifying when a project is off track but provides little evidence as to what is causing the delay.

The second and third types of reports are more helpful in determining the cause of delays and the appropriate corrections. The *status report* is an open-ended report that details the process that led to the current project state. By analyzing this report, a project manager can pinpoint where the delay began and create a plan to get past it and possibly make up for lost time. This is where the *resource allocation* report becomes useful. This report identifies the various resources (e.g., people, equipment) that are being applied to specific project activities and where currently unused, or *slack*, resources may be available.

Closing This last phase of the project management process focuses on bringing a project to a successful end. The beginning of the end of a project is the implementation and installation of all of the project deliverables. The next step is the formal release of the project resources so they can be redeployed into other projects or job roles. The final step in this phase is to review the final documentation and publish the final project report. Here is where the good, and bad, news concerning the project is documented, and the elements necessary for a postproject review are identified.

Many airline pilots (and passengers, for that matter) identify the final approach and landing as one of the most critical elements of any flight. It is during those remaining moments that even the smoothest of flights can come to an undesirable conclusion. Projects are quite similar in this regard. The most beautifully planned, executed, and controlled project can be deemed a failure if it is poorly implemented. As such, we must turn our attention back to the issues of systems implementation, hopefully with a clearer understanding of how we arrived at this point and the process we will follow to do it again in another project.

Evaluating Hardware, Software, and Services

A major activity during the implementation phase of the SDLC is the acquisition of the hardware and software necessary to implement the new system. How do companies evaluate and select hardware, software, and IT services, such as those shown in Figure 10.21? Large companies may require suppliers to present bids and proposals based on system specifications developed during the design stage of systems development. Minimum acceptable physical and performance characteristics for all hardware and software requirements are established. Most large business firms and all government agencies formalize these requirements by listing them in a document called an RFP (request for proposal) or RFQ (request for quotation). Then they send the RFP or RFQ to appropriate vendors, which use it as the basis for preparing a proposed purchase agreement.

Companies may use a *scoring* system of evaluation when there are several competing proposals for a hardware or software acquisition. They give each **evaluation factor** a certain number of maximum possible points. Then they assign each competing

FIGURE 10.21
Examples from IBM Corporation of the kinds of hardware, software, and IS services that many companies are evaluating and acquiring to support their e-commerce initiatives.

Hardware
Full range of offerings, including xSeries servers, iSeries midrange servers for small and midsize businesses, RS/6000 servers for UNIX customers and z900 mainframes for large enterprises. Also has full range of storage options.
Software
Web server: Lotus DominoGo Web server. **Storefront:** WebSphere Commerce Suite (formerly known as Net.Commerce) for storefront and catalog creation, relationship marketing, and order management. Can add Commerce Integrator to integrate with back-end systems and Catalog Architect for content management. **Middleware/transaction services:** WebSphere application server manages transactions. MQ Series queues messages and manages connections. CICS processes transactions. **Database:** DB2 Universal Database. **Tools:** WebSphere Studio includes set of predefined templates and common business logic. **Other applications:** IBM Payment Suite for handling credit cards and managing digital certificates.
Services
IBM Global Services, which includes groups organized by each major industry, including retail and financial. Can design, build, and host e-commerce applications.

proposal points for each factor, depending on how well it meets the user's specifications. Scoring evaluation factors for several proposals helps organize and document the evaluation process. It also spotlights the strengths and weaknesses of each proposal.

Whatever the claims of hardware manufacturers and software suppliers, the performance of hardware and software must be demonstrated and evaluated. Independent hardware and software information services (e.g., Datapro, Auerbach) may be used to gain detailed specification information and evaluations. Other users are frequently the best source of information needed to evaluate the claims of manufacturers and suppliers. That's why Internet newsgroups and Weblogs established to exchange information about specific software or hardware vendors and their products have become one of the best sources for obtaining up-to-date information about the experiences of users of the products.

Large companies frequently evaluate proposed hardware and software by requiring the processing of special *benchmark* test programs and test data. Benchmarking simulates the processing of typical jobs on several computers and evaluates their performances. Users can then evaluate test results to determine which hardware device or software package display the best performance characteristics.

Hardware Evaluation Factors

When you evaluate the hardware needed by a new business application, you should investigate specific physical and performance characteristics for each computer system or peripheral component to be acquired. Specific questions must be answered concerning many important factors. Ten of these **hardware evaluation factors** and questions are summarized in Figure 10.22.

Notice that there is much more to evaluating hardware than determining the fastest and cheapest computing device. For example, the question of obsolescence must be addressed by making a technology evaluation. The factor of ergonomics is also very important. Ergonomic factors ensure that computer hardware and software are user friendly, that is, safe, comfortable, and easy to use. Connectivity is another important evaluation factor, because so many network technologies and bandwidth alternatives are available to connect computer systems to the Internet, intranet, and extranet networks.

FIGURE 10.22
A summary of 10 major hardware evaluation factors. Notice how you can use this to evaluate a computer system or a peripheral device.

Hardware Evaluation Factors	Rating
Performance What is its speed, capacity, and throughput?	
Cost What is its lease or purchase price? What will be its cost of operation and maintenance?	
Reliability What are the risks of malfunction and its maintenance requirements? What are its error control and diagnostic features?	
Compatibility Is it compatible with existing hardware and software? Is it compatible with hardware and software provided by competing suppliers?	
Technology In what year of its product life cycle is it? Does it use a new untested technology, or does it run the risk of obsolescence?	
Ergonomics Has it been "human factors engineered" with the user in mind? Is it user-friendly, designed to be safe, comfortable, and easy to use?	
Connectivity Can it be easily connected to wide area and local area networks that use different types of network technologies and bandwidth alternatives?	
Scalability Can it handle the processing demands of a wide range of end users, transactions, queries, and other information processing requirements?	
Software Is system and application software available that can best use this hardware?	
Support Are the services required to support and maintain it available?	
Overall Rating	

Software Evaluation Factors

You should evaluate software according to many factors that are similar to those used for hardware evaluation. Thus, the factors of performance, cost, reliability, availability, compatibility, modularity, technology, ergonomics, and support should be used to evaluate proposed software acquisitions. In addition, however, the **software evaluation factors** summarized in Figure 10.23 must also be considered. You should answer the questions they generate to evaluate software purchases properly. For example, some software packages are notoriously slow, hard to use, bug-filled, or poorly documented. They are not a good choice, even if offered at attractive prices.

Evaluating IS Services

Most suppliers of hardware and software products and many other firms offer a variety of **IS services** to end users and organizations. Examples include assistance in developing a company Web site, installation or conversion of new hardware and software, employee training, and hardware maintenance. Some of these services are provided without cost by hardware manufacturers and software suppliers.

Other types of IS services needed by a business can be outsourced to an outside company for a negotiated price. For example, *systems integrators* take over complete responsibility for an organization's computer facilities when an organization outsources its computer operations. They may also assume responsibility for developing and implementing large systems development projects that involve many vendors and subcontractors. Value-added resellers (VARs) specialize in providing industry-specific hardware, software, and services from selected manufacturers.

FIGURE 10.23
A summary of selected software evaluation factors. Note that most of the hardware evaluation factors in Figure 10.22 can also be used to evaluate software packages.

Software Evaluation Factors	Rating
Quality Is it bug free, or does it have many errors in its program code?	
Efficiency Is the software a well-developed system of program code that does not use much CPU time, memory capacity, or disk space?	
Flexibility Can it handle our business processes easily, without major modification?	
Security Does it provide control procedures for errors, malfunctions, and improper use?	
Connectivity Is it Web-enabled so it can easily access the Internet, intranets, and extranets on its own or by working with Web browsers or other network software?	
Maintenance Will new features and bug fixes be easily implemented by our own software developers?	
Documentation Is the software well documented? Does it include help screens and helpful software agents?	
Hardware Does existing hardware have the features required to best use this software?	
Other Factors What are its performance, cost, reliability, availability, compatibility, modularity, technology, ergonomics, scalability, and support characteristics? (Use the hardware evaluation factor questions in Figure 10.22.)	
Overall Rating	

Many other services are available to end users, including systems design, contract programming, and consulting services. Evaluation factors and questions for IS services are summarized in Figure 10.24.

Other Implementation Activities

Testing, data conversion, documentation, and training are keys to successful implementation of a new business system.

Testing

System testing may involve testing and debugging software, testing Web site performance, and testing new hardware. An important part of testing is the review of prototypes of displays, reports, and other output. Prototypes should be reviewed by end users of the proposed systems for possible errors. Of course, testing should not occur only during the system's implementation stage but throughout the system's development process. For example, you might examine and critique prototypes of input documents, screen displays, and processing procedures during the systems design stage. Immediate end user testing is one of the benefits of a prototyping process.

Data Conversion

Implementing new information systems for many organizations today frequently involves replacing a previous system and its software and databases. One of the most important implementation activities required when installing new software in such cases is called **data conversion**. For example, installing new software packages may require converting the data elements in databases that are affected by a new application into new data formats. Other data conversion activities that are typically required include

FIGURE 10.24
Evaluation factors for IS services. These factors focus on the quality of support services business users may need.

Evaluation Factors for IS Services	Rating
Performance What has been their past performance in view of their past promises?	
Systems Development Are Web site and other e-business developers available? What are their quality and cost?	
Maintenance Is equipment maintenance provided? What are its quality and cost?	
Conversion What systems development and installation services will they provide during the conversion period?	
Training Is the necessary training of personnel provided? What are its quality and cost?	
Backup Are similar computer facilities available nearby for emergency backup purposes?	
Accessibility Does the vendor provide local or regional sites that offer sales, systems development, and hardware maintenance services? Is a customer support center at the vendor's Web site available? Is a customer hotline provided?	
Business Position Is the vendor financially strong, with good industry market prospects?	
Hardware Do they provide a wide selection of compatible hardware devices and accessories?	
Software Do they offer a variety of useful e-business software and application packages?	
Overall Rating	

correcting incorrect data, filtering out unwanted data, consolidating data from several databases, and organizing data into new data subsets, such as databases, data marts, and data warehouses. A good data conversion process is essential, because improperly organized and formatted data are frequently reported to be one of the major causes of failures in implementing new systems.

During the design phase, the analysts create a data dictionary that not only describes the various data elements contained in the new system but also specifies any necessary conversions from the old system. In some cases, only the name of the data element is changed, such as if the old system field CUST_ID becomes CLIENT_ID in the new system. In other cases, the actual format of the data is changed, thus requiring some conversion application to be written to filter the old data and put them into the new format. An example of this might be the creation of a new CUSTOMER_ID format to allow for expansion or make two merged systems compatible with each other. This type of data element conversion requires additional time to occur, because each element must pass through the conversion filter before being written into the new data files.

Yet another issue is the time necessary to transfer the data from the old data files into the files for the new system. Although it is possible that the new system may have been designed to use the existing data files, this is not normally the case, especially in situations when a new system is replacing a legacy system that is fairly old. The time necessary to transfer the old data can have a material impact on the conversion process and on the strategy that is ultimately selected. Consider the following situation.

Suppose the conversion to the new system requires the transfer of data from 10 different data files. The average record length across the 10 files is 1,780 bytes, and the total number of records contained in the 10 files is 120 million. With this information and an estimate of the transfer time in bytes per minute, the total transfer time can be easily calculated as follows: Assume a transfer rate of 10.5 megabytes per second (Mbps) (Fast Ethernet) with no conversion algorithm. Then,

1,780 bytes × 120 million records = 213,600,000,000 bytes.

213,600,000,000 bytes/10.5 Mbps = 20,343 seconds.

20,343 seconds = 5.65 hours.

Although the preceding calculations appear to be such that the conversion process does not take an inordinate amount of time, we must also be aware that they assume an error-free transfer, no format conversion, and 100 percent use of available network bandwidth. If the transfer is done using a slower communication medium, say 1.25 Mbps, the time jumps to 47.47 hours (just under two days).

The important consideration here is not simply the time necessary to effect the transfer but the preservation of the integrity of the current system data files during the process. If the transfer turns out to be around 4.5 hours, then it could theoretically occur after business hours and be easily accomplished by the opening of the next day's business. If, however, the process takes two full days, then it would need to begin at the close of business on Friday and would not be complete until late Sunday afternoon. Should any glitches show up in the process, either the transfer would have to wait a week to be rerun or the possibility of disrupting daily operations or losing new data would be very real. As you can see, careful thought about the logistics associated with data transfer must be given when recommending the most appropriate conversion strategy for the new system.

Documentation

Developing good user **documentation** is an important part of the implementation process. Sample data entry display screens, forms, and reports are good examples of documentation. When *computer-aided systems engineering* methods are used, documentation can be created and changed easily because it is stored and accessible on disk in a *system repository*. Documentation serves as a method of communication among the people responsible for developing, implementing, and maintaining a computer-based system. Installing and operating a newly designed system or modifying an established application requires a detailed record of that system's design. Documentation is extremely important in diagnosing errors and making changes, especially if the end users or systems analysts who developed a system are no longer with the organization.

Training

Training is a vital implementation activity. IS personnel, such as user consultants, must be sure that end users are trained to operate a new business system, or its implementation will fail. Training may involve only activities like data entry, or it may involve all aspects of the proper use of a new system. In addition, managers and end users must be educated in how the new technology affects the company's business operations and management. This knowledge should be supplemented by training programs for any new hardware devices, software packages, and their use for specific work activities. Figure 10.25 illustrates how one business coordinated its end-user training program with each stage of its implementation process for developing intranet and Internet access within the company [5].

System Conversion Strategies

The initial operation of a new business system can be a difficult task. It typically requires a **conversion** process from the use of a present system to the operation of a new or improved application. Conversion methods can soften the impact of introducing new information technologies into an organization. Four major forms of system conversion are illustrated in Figure 10.26. They include:

- Parallel conversion.
- Pilot conversion.
- Phased conversion.
- Direct conversion.

FIGURE 10.25 How one company developed training programs for the implementation of an e-commerce Web site and intranet access for its employees.

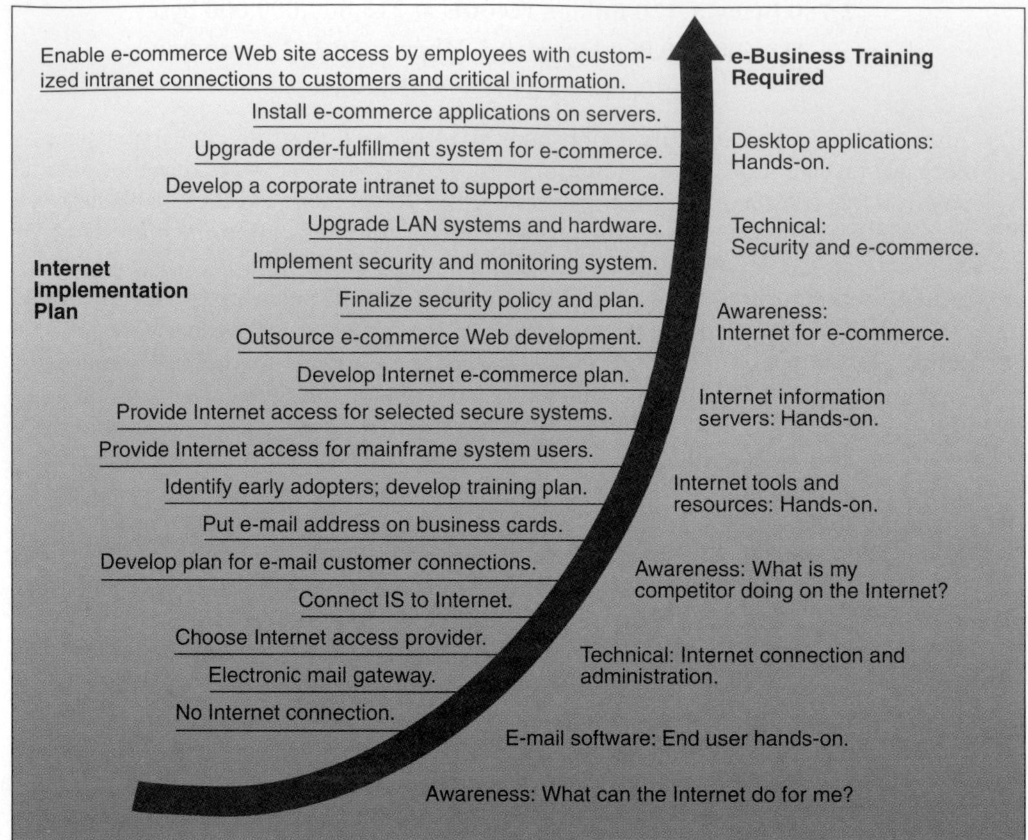

Direct Conversion The simplest conversion strategy, and probably the most disruptive to the organization, is the **direct cutover** approach. This method, sometimes referred to as the **slam dunk** or **cold-turkey strategy,** is as abrupt as its name implies. Using this approach, the old system is simply turned off, and the new system is turned on in its place. Although this method is the least expensive of all available strategies and may be the only viable solution in situations in which activating the new system is an emergency or when the two systems cannot coexist under any conditions, it is also

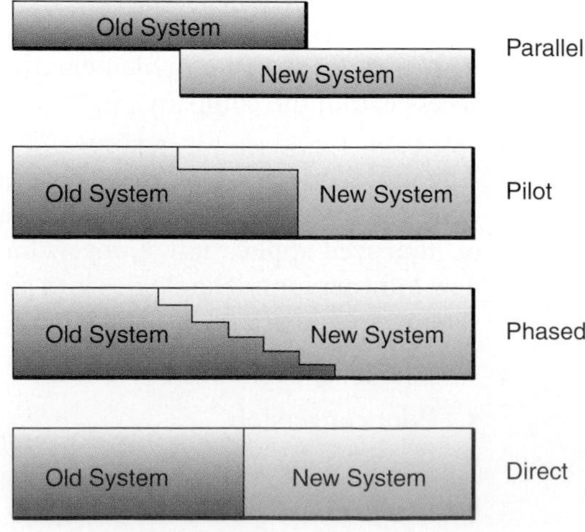

FIGURE 10.26 The four major forms of conversion to a new system.

the one that poses the greatest risk of failure. Once the new system becomes operational, the end users must cope with any errors or dysfunctions, and depending on the severity of the problem, this approach can have a significant effect on the quality of the work performed. Direct conversion should be considered only in extreme circumstances, when no other conversion strategy is viable.

Parallel Conversion At the opposite end of the risk spectrum is the **parallel conversion** strategy. Here, the old and new systems are run simultaneously until the end users and project coordinators are fully satisfied that the new system is functioning correctly and the old system is no longer necessary. Using this approach, a parallel conversion can be effected with either a **single cutover,** with a set, predetermined date for stopping the parallel operation, or a **phased cutover,** which uses some predetermined method of phasing in each piece of the new system and turning off a similar piece of the old system.

Although clearly having the advantage of low risk, the parallel approach also brings with it the highest cost. To execute a parallel approach properly, the end users must literally perform all daily functions with both systems, thus creating a massive redundancy in activities and literally double the work. In fact, unless the operational costs of the new system are significantly less than the old system, the cost of parallel operation can be as much as three to four times greater than the old system alone. During a parallel conversion, all outputs from both systems are compared for concurrency and accuracy, until it is determined that the new system is functioning at least as well as the one it is replacing. Parallel conversion may be the best choice in situations in which an automated system is replacing a manual one. In certain circumstances when end users cannot cope with the often confusing redundancy of two systems, the parallel conversion strategy may not be viable. Also, parallel conversion may not be possible if the organization does not have the available computing resources to operate two systems at the same time.

Pilot Conversion In some situations, the new system may be installed in multiple locations, such as a series of bank branches or retail outlets. In other cases, the conversion may be able to be planned from a geographic perspective. When these types of scenarios exist, the possibility for using a **pilot conversion** strategy exists. This approach allows for the conversion to the new system, using either a direct or parallel method, at a single location. The advantage to this approach is a location can be selected that best represents the conditions across the organization but also may be less risky in terms of any loss of time or delays in processing. Once the installation is complete at the pilot site, the process can be evaluated and any changes to the system made to prevent problems encountered at the pilot site from reoccurring at the remaining installations. This approach may also be required if the individual sites or locations have certain unique characteristics or idiosyncrasies that make either a direct or parallel approach infeasible.

Phased Conversion A **phased** or **gradual conversion** strategy attempts to take advantage of the best features of both the direct and parallel approaches while minimizing the risks involved. This incremental approach to conversion allows for the new system to be brought online as a series of functional components that are logically ordered to minimize disruption to end users and the flow of business.

Phased conversion is analogous to the release of multiple versions of an application by a software developer. Each version of the software should correct any known bugs and allow for 100 percent compatibility with data entered into or processed by the previous version. Although having the advantage of lower risk, the phased approach takes the most time and thus creates the most disruption to the organization over time.

Postimplementation Activities

When all is said and done, the single most costly activity occurs after the system implementation is complete: the **postimplementation maintenance phase.** The primary objectives associated with systems maintenance are to correct errors or faults in the system, provide changes to effect performance improvement, or adapt the system to changes in the operating or business environment. In a typical organization, more programmers and analysts are assigned to application maintenance activities than to application development. Furthermore, though a new system can take several months or years to design and build and cost hundreds of thousands or millions of dollars, the resulting system can operate around the clock and last for five to ten years, or longer. One major activity in postimplementation involves making changes to the system as a result of the users finally having an opportunity to use it. These are called **change requests.** Such requests can range from fixing a software bug not found during testing to designing an enhancement to an existing process or function.

Systems Maintenance

Managing and implementing change requests is only one aspect of the systems maintenance phase activities. In some ways, once the maintenance phase begins, the life cycle starts over again. New requirements are articulated, analyzed, designed, checked for feasibility, tested, and implemented. Although the range and nature of specific maintenance requests vary from system to system, four basic categories of maintenance can be identified: (1) corrective, (2) adaptive, (3) perfective, and (4) preventive.

The activities associated with **corrective maintenance** are focused on fixing bugs and logic errors not detected during the implementation testing period. **Adaptive maintenance** refers to those activities associated with modifying existing functions or adding new functionality to accommodate changes in the business or operating environments. **Perfective maintenance** activities involve changes made to an existing system that are intended to improve the performance of a function or interface. The final category of maintenance activities, **preventive maintenance,** involves those activities intended to reduce the chances of a system failure or extend the capacity of a current system's useful life. Although often the lowest-priority maintenance activity, preventive maintenance is nonetheless a high value-adding function and vital to an organization's ability to realize the full value of its investment in the system.

Postimplementation Review

The maintenance activity also includes a postimplementation review process to ensure that newly implemented systems meet the business objectives established for them. Errors in the development or use of a system must be corrected by the maintenance process. This process includes a periodic review or audit of a system to ensure that it is operating properly and meeting its objectives. This audit occurs in addition to continually monitoring a new system for potential problems or necessary changes.

Aviall Inc.: System Implementation Failure and Success

When Joe Lacik arrived at Aviall as Chief Information Officer (CIO), the supplier of airplane parts and components had lost control of its inventory. The installation of new software systems to keep track of the availability and prices of the 360,000 parts it buys and then supplies to airplane operators and owners had failed. The company couldn't count on the price-tracking software to work with its warehouse management and inventory control software or its order fulfillment software. The result? The wrong parts got to the wrong customers, and the company's sales fell 8 percent in one year.

Obviously, Aviall hadn't figured out what it needed to get the new software products to work together during the implementation process. But the wounds were self-inflicted. Aviall's own IT staff had picked the software and installed it. So Lacik's first job was to find a way to get the software IT had acquired to exchange data. And while tackling that task, he had to make sure the data could be swapped with other key applications, like its new customer relationship management and Web commerce software.

Lacik's answer was to hire a developer of software adapters to help him integrate his software systems. Simply put, when two pieces of software call the same piece of data, a software adapter figures out what has to be done. The adapter transfers that piece of data between the two programs, making sure it ends up in the right place. Then each program that receives it can process the data further. For example, one of the most important connections would be between the inventory control software and the CRM software, enabling a sales representative to draw information on the prices and availability of parts and assure a customer that an order could be filled.

Developing and implementing that adapter took two years—and Lacik even brought in IT consultants to help. But when the moment of truth arrived, nothing much happened. Eventually though, the software adapters got fixed. Then Lacik found out that "technology is the easy part" when implementing something like a customer relationship management (CRM) application.

First, he now says, you have to change the sales force. Or at least how it conducts business. "The vast majority of CRM projects fail, and the reason is you have to change the behavior of the sales force," he argues. In this case, Aviall's sales force needed to get accustomed to having their actions measured. For the first time, the number of sales calls a month, the types of customers called on, and the reasons why would be tracked.

And mimicking the system the 250 inside sales, branch, and customer service people used to manage orders was not an overnight proposition. "We didn't want to re-create the order-entry process," acknowledges Lacik. In this case, the IT staff "didn't even know the right questions to ask" to create a new computer-based system. It took about 20 "yeah, but" sessions with salespeople to figure out what was needed. And it took nearly three years to develop and implement the new order processing system, because issues as simple as whether a customer has sufficient credit to make a purchase had to be handled deftly.

But the resuscitation of Aviall's sales didn't depend solely on the implementation of a new order processing system. With adapters in place, salespeople working the CRM system could immediately check prices and availability of parts by querying the inventory control system. Then the order fulfillment software made sure that the right parts got to the right customers at the right time.

The result? Aviall's sales almost doubled three years after Lacik's arrival, as the newly integrated software systems he had implemented operated almost flawlessly, thus playing a big part in making those sales happen [34].

Implementation Challenges

Implementing new business/IT strategies, particularly when they involve large-scale innovative technologies, involves major organizational change. For many organizations, moving into e-business represents the fourth or fifth major change they have experienced, and endured, since the early 1980s. Successful implementation of these new strategies and applications requires managing the effects of changes in key organizational dimensions such as business processes, organizational structures, managerial roles, work assignments, and stakeholder relationships. Figure 10.27 emphasizes the variety and extent of the challenges reported by 100 companies that developed and implemented new enterprise information portals and ERP systems.

User Resistance and Involvement

Any new way of doing things generates some resistance from the people affected. For example, the implementation of new work support technologies can generate fear and resistance to change in employees. One of the keys to solving problems of **user resistance** to new information technologies is proper education and training. Even more

FIGURE 10.27
The 10 greatest challenges of developing and implementing intranet enterprise portals and enterprise resource planning systems reported by 100 companies.

Intranet Enterprise Portal Challenges	Enterprise Resource Planning Challenges
• Security, security, security. • Defining the scope and purpose of the portal. • Finding the time and the money. • Ensuring consistent data quality. • Getting employees to use it. • Organizing the data. • Finding technical expertise. • Integrating the pieces. • Making it easy to use. • Providing all users with access.	• Getting end user buy-in. • Scheduling/planning. • Integrating legacy systems/data. • Getting management buy-in. • Dealing with multiple/international sites and partners. • Changing culture/mind-sets. • IT training. • Getting, keeping IT staff. • Moving to a new platform. • Performance/system upgrades.

important is **user involvement** in organizational changes and the development of new information systems. Organizations have a variety of strategies to help manage business change, and one basic requirement is the involvement and commitment of top management and all business stakeholders affected by the new system.

Direct end-user participation in business planning and application development projects before a new system is implemented is especially important in reducing the potential for end-user resistance. That is why end users frequently are members of systems development teams or do their own development work. Such involvement helps ensure that end users assume ownership of a system and that its design meets their needs. Systems that tend to inconvenience or frustrate users cannot be effective systems, no matter how technically elegant they are or how efficiently they process data. For example, Figure 10.28 illustrates some of the major obstacles to knowledge management systems in business. Notice that end-user resistance to sharing knowledge is the biggest obstacle to the implementation of knowledge management applications. Let's look at a real-world example that spotlights end-user resistance and some of its solutions.

Qwest and Others: User Resistance and Involvement

In the mid-1980s, Shirley Wong was part of a team developing software for an automated 411 system at a large West Coast telephone company that is now part of Qwest Communications. After a great deal of work, the team unveiled the system to telephone operators and were greeted with universal hisses and boos. "The operators didn't want it," recalls Wong, who is now the Webmaster at Optodyne, Inc. The company had wasted at least $1 million on the effort, and as a result of the fiasco, the project director and three managers were fired.

The problem: The operators who would be using the system were never consulted about their needs.

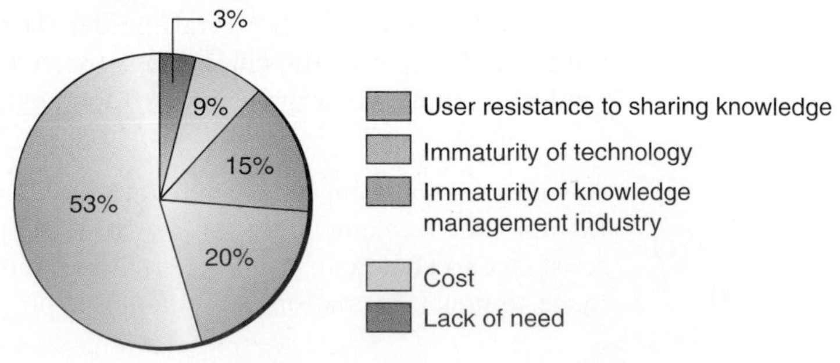

FIGURE 10.28
Obstacles to knowledge management systems. Note that end-user resistance to knowledge sharing is the biggest obstacle.

Times change, and many IT project managers realize how crucial users are to a project's success. But how do you get users to take system requirements seriously? "This is probably the biggest problem at most companies," argues Bill Berghel, a project manager at FedEx Corp. in Memphis.

To get users engaged, start by educating their bosses, says Naomi Karten, president of Karten Associates, a customer service consulting firm. Demonstrate how important user input is to the success of systems. Use real examples to show the benefits of doing things right and the consequences of doing things wrong. Once they get it, make sure they buy in on every project, she recommends. "Senior managers have to make sure that people below them make the time," says Peter Goundry, MIS manager at Aircast Inc., a medical device maker in Summit, New Jersey.

Don't just ask what users want; find out what they need. "Focus on what ails the user, not just what the user wants in a system," suggests Rob Norris, CIO at Pinocol Assurance in Denver. "Users don't always know what they want," notes Sue McKay, CIO at Aircast. "Sometimes, you have to help them understand that what they think they want won't give them what they need." For example, end users may have heard about some cool system to produce management reports and may not realize the same information is already easily available through existing databases.

And don't make the mistake Wong's group made. Talk with enough people to really understand the business process you're trying to facilitate. "If you are creating a new sales system and you're only dealing with the VP of sales, you're doomed," warns Aircast's McKay. Don't forget the sales representatives, sales assistants, and customers.

One of the best ways to get users interested and keep them engaged is to make them partners in application development. "We show a series of prototypes to the users and work toward what they do want," says Berghel of FedEx. And each iteration should take only a few days, to keep up the momentum, he adds.

Change Management

Figure 10.29 illustrates some of the key dimensions of **change management** and the level of difficulty and business impact involved. Notice some of the people, process, and technology factors involved in the implementation of business/IT strategies and applications or other changes caused by introducing new information technologies into a company. Some of the technical factors listed, such as systems integrators and outsourcing, will be discussed in more detail in the next few chapters. For example, systems integrators are consulting firms or other outside contractors that may be paid to assume the responsibility for developing and implementing a new e-business application, including designing and leading its change management activities. And notice that people factors have the highest level of difficulty and longest time to resolve of any dimension of change management.

Thus, people are a major focus of organizational change management. This focus includes activities such as developing innovative ways to measure, motivate, and reward performance, as well as designing programs to recruit and train employees in the core competencies required in a changing workplace. Change management also involves analyzing and defining all changes facing the organization and developing programs to reduce the risks and costs and maximize the benefits of change. For example, implementing a new e-business application such as customer relationship management might involve developing a *change action plan*, assigning selected managers as *change sponsors*, developing employee *change teams*, and encouraging open communications and feedback about organizational changes. Some key tactics change experts recommend include:

- Involve as many people as possible in e-business planning and application development.
- Make constant change an expected part of the culture.

FIGURE 10.29 Some of the key dimensions of change management. Examples of the people, process, and technology factors involved in managing the implementation of IT-based changes to an organization.

Impact on Business (Low → High)	Technology	Process	People
Strategic	• Enterprise Architecture • Supplier Partnership • Systems Integrators • Outsourcing	• Ownership • Design • Enterprisewide Processes • Interenterprise Processes	• Change Leaders • Loose/Tight Controls • Executive Sponsorship and Support • Aligning on Conditions of Satisfaction
Operational	• Technology Selection • Technology Support • Installation Requirements	• Change Control • Implementation Management • Support Processes	• Recruitment • Retention • Training • Knowledge Transfer

Low — Level of Difficulty/Time to Resolve — High

Source: Adapted from Grant Norris, James Hurley, Kenneth Hartley, John Dunleavy, and John Balls, *E-Business and ERP: Transforming the Enterprise* (New York, John Wiley & Sons, 2000), p. 120. Reprinted by permission.

- Tell everyone as much as possible about everything as often as possible, preferably in person.
- Make liberal use of financial incentives and recognition.
- Work within the company culture, not around it [22].

A Change Management Process

An eight-level process of change management for organizations is illustrated in Figure 10.30. This change management model is only one of many that could be applied to manage organizational changes caused by new business/IT strategies and applications and other changes in business processes. For example, this model suggests that the business vision created in the strategic planning phase should be communicated in a compelling *change story* to the people in the organization. Evaluating the readiness for changes within an organization and then developing change strategies and choosing and training change leaders and champions based on that assessment could be the next steps in the process.

These change leaders are the change agents who then are able to lead change teams of employees and other business stakeholders in building a business case for changes in technology, business processes, job content, and organizational structures. They also communicate the benefits of these changes and lead training programs on the details of new business applications. Of course, many change management models include methods for performance measurement and rewards to provide financial incentives for employees and stakeholders to cooperate with changes that may be required. In addition, fostering a new e-business culture within an organization by establishing communities of interest for employees and other business stakeholders via Internet, intranet, and extranet discussion groups could be a valuable change management strategy. Such groups encourage stakeholder involvement and buy-in for the changes brought about by implementing new e-business applications of information technology.

FIGURE 10.30 A process of change management. Examples of the activities involved in succ organizational change caused by the implementation of new business processes.

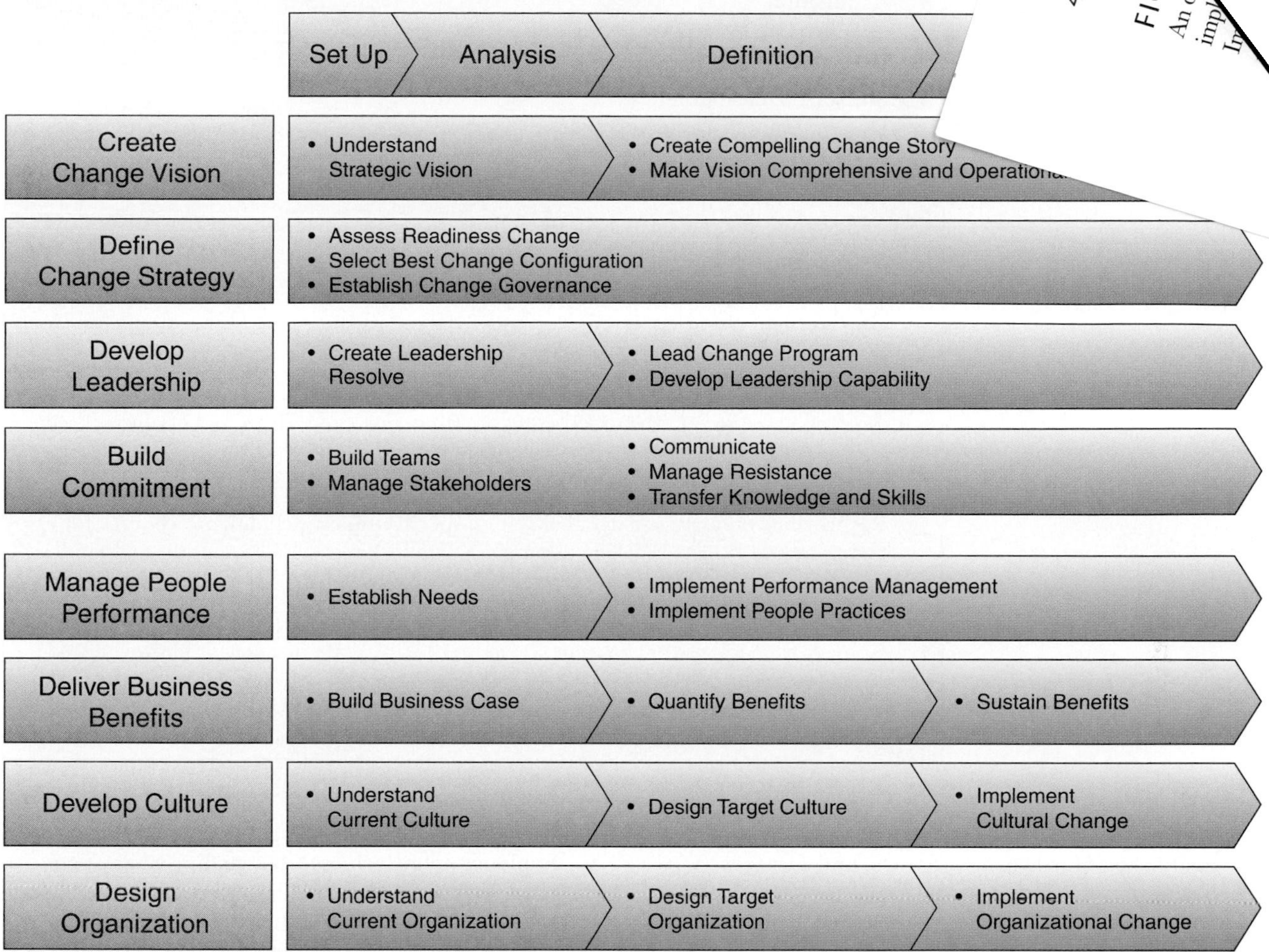

Source: Adapted from Martin Diese, Conrad Nowikow, Patric King, and Amy Wright, *Executive's Guide to E-Business: From Tactics to Strategy*, p. 190. Copyright © 2000 by John Wiley & Sons Inc. Reprinted by permission.

Summary

- **The Systems Development Cycle.** Business end users and IS specialists may use a systems approach to help them develop information system solutions to meet business opportunities. This approach frequently involves a systems development cycle in which IS specialists and end users conceive, design, and implement business systems. The stages, activities, and products of the information systems development cycle are summarized in Figure 10.3.
- **Prototyping.** Prototyping is a major alternative methodology to the traditional information systems development cycle. It includes the use of prototyping tools and methodologies, which promote an iterative, interactive process that develops prototypes of user interfaces and other information system components. See Figure 10.9.
- **End-User Development.** The application development capabilities built into many end-user software packages have made it easier for end users to develop their own business applications. End users should focus their development efforts on the system components of business processes that can benefit from the use of information technology, as summarized in Figure 10.14.
- **Implementing IS.** The implementation process for information system projects is summarized in Figure 10.27. Implementation involves acquisition, testing, documentation, training, installation, and conversion activities that transform a newly designed business system into an operational system for end users.

…E 10.31

…rview of the …ementation process. …plementation activities are …eeded to transform a newly developed information system into an operational system for end users.

Implementing New Systems
• **Acquisition** Evaluate and acquire necessary hardware and software resources and information system services. Screen vendor proposals.
• **Software Development** Develop any software that will not be acquired externally as software packages. Make any necessary modifications to software packages that are acquired.
• **Data Conversion** Convert data in company databases to new data formats and subsets required by newly installed software.
• **Training** Educate and train management, end users, customers, and other business stakeholders. Use consultants or training programs to develop user competencies.
• **Testing** Test and make necessary corrections to the programs, procedures, and hardware used by a new system.
• **Documentation** Record and communicate detailed system specifications, including procedures for end users and IS personnel and examples of input screens and output displays and reports.
• **Conversion** Convert from the use of a present system to the operation of a new or improved system.This conversion may involve operating both new and old systems in *parallel* for a trial period, operation of a *pilot* system on a trial basis at one location, *phasing* in the new system one location at a time, or a *direct cutover* to the new system.

- **Evaluating Hardware, Software, and Services.** Business professionals should know how to evaluate the acquisition of information system resources. IT vendors' proposals should be based on specifications developed during the design stage of systems development. A formal evaluation process reduces the possibility of incorrect or unnecessary purchases of hardware or software. Several major evaluation factors, summarized in Figures 10.22, 10.23, and 10.24, can be used to evaluate hardware, software, and IS services.
- **Implementing Business Change.** Implementation activities include managing the introduction and implementation of changes in business processes, organizational structures, job assignments, and work relationships resulting from business/IT strategies and applications such as e-business initiatives, reengineering projects, supply chain alliances, and the introduction of new technologies. Companies use change management tactics such as user involvement in business/IT planning and development to reduce end-user resistance and maximize acceptance of business changes by all stakeholders.

Key Terms and Concepts

These are the key terms and concepts of this chapter. The page number of their first explanation is in parentheses.

1. Change management (409)
2. Conversion (403)
3. Cost/benefit analysis (380)
4. Data conversion (401)
5. Documentation (403)
6. Economic feasibility (379)
7. End-user development (387)
8. Feasibility study (377)
9. Functional requirements (383)
10. Human factors feasibility (381)
11. Implementation process (393)
12. Intangible (380)
    a. Benefits (380)
    b. Costs (380)
13. Legal/political feasibility (381)
14. Logical model (383)
15. Operational feasibility (379)
16. Organizational analysis (382)
17. Postimplementation review (406)
18. Project management (393)
19. Prototyping (384)

20. Systems analysis and design (377)
21. Systems approach (374)
22. Systems development life cycle (377)
23. Systems implementation (393)
24. Systems maintenance (406)
25. Systems specifications (387)
26. System testing (401)
27. Systems thinking (374)
28. Tangible (380)
    a. Benefits (380)
    b. Costs (380)
29. Technical feasibility (380)
30. User interface design (386)
31. User involvement (408)
32. User resistance (407)

Review Quiz

Match one of the key terms and concepts listed previously with each of the brief examples or definitions that follow. Try to find the best fit for answers that seem to fit more than one term or concept. Defend your choices.

____ 1. Using an organized sequence of activities to study a problem or opportunity using systems thinking.

____ 2. Trying to recognize systems and the new interrelationships and components of systems in any situation.

____ 3. Evaluating the success of a solution after it has been implemented.

____ 4. Your evaluation shows that benefits outweigh costs for a proposed system.

____ 5. The costs of acquiring computer hardware, software, and specialists.

____ 6. Loss of customer goodwill caused by errors in a new system.

____ 7. Increases in profits caused by a new system.

____ 8. Improved employee morale caused by efficiency and effectiveness of a new system.

____ 9. A multistep process to conceive, design, and implement an information system.

____ 10. A diagram or blueprint of a system that shows what it does without regard to how it does it.

____ 11. Determines the organizational, economic, technical, and operational feasibility of a proposed information system.

____ 12. Cost savings and additional profits will exceed the investment required.

____ 13. Reliable hardware and software are available to implement a proposed system.

____ 14. Determining whether any copyright or patent infringements exist as the result of a new system.

____ 15. Do we have the right people to operate the new system?

____ 16. Studying in detail the information needs of users and any information systems presently used and then developing a system to correct a problem or improve operations.

____ 17. A detailed description of user information needs and the input, processing, output, storage, and control capabilities required to meet those needs.

____ 18. Systems design should focus on developing user-friendly input and output methods for a system.

____ 19. A detailed description of the hardware, software, people, network, and data resources and information products required by a proposed system.

____ 20. Acquiring hardware and software, testing and documenting a proposed system, and training people to use it.

____ 21. Making improvements to an operational system.

____ 22. An interactive and iterative process of developing and refining information system prototypes.

____ 23. Managers and business specialists can develop their own e-business applications.

____ 24. Includes acquisition, testing, training, and conversion to a new system.

____ 25. Operate in parallel with the old system, use a test site, switch in stages, or cut over immediately to a new system.

____ 26. Checking whether hardware and software work properly for end users.

____ 27. A user manual communicates the design and operating procedures of a system.

____ 28. Keeping an IS project on time and within its budget would be a major goal.

____ 29. Common response to major changes in organizational structures, roles, and stakeholder relationships.

____ 30. Participation in business planning and application development projects before a new system is implemented is one example.

____ 31. Among other things, it involves analyzing and defining all changes facing an organization and developing programs to reduce risks and maximize benefits.

Discussion Questions

1. Why has prototyping become a popular way to develop business applications? What are prototyping's advantages and disadvantages?
2. Refer to the Real World Case on Intuit Inc. in the chapter. Intuit is an innovative software developer in its market niche. Could Intuit be as successful in other software markets? If so, which ones, and why? If not, why not?
3. Review the BuyerZone and OfficeMax real world example in the chapter. What design changes should BuyerZone and OfficeMax make to correct the design flaws at their sites? Explain your reasoning.
4. What are the three most important factors you would use in evaluating computer hardware? Computer software? Explain why.
5. Assume that in your first week on a new job you are asked to use a type of business software that you have never used before. What kind of user training should your company provide to you before you start?
6. Refer to the Real World Case on Infosys Technologies in the chapter. The participants in social networking Web sites like MySpace and Facebook don't seem to have a problem sharing knowledge. Could any concepts of social networking help make corporate knowledge management initiatives more successful? Why or why not?
7. What is the difference among the parallel, direct, phased, and pilot forms of IS conversion? Which conversion strategy is best? Explain why.
8. Review the Google real world example in the chapter. How might you change the user interface of Google's search pages and those of some of its other products on the Web? Defend your proposals.
9. Review the Aviall, Inc. real world example in the chapter. Why would a company's IT staff acquire and install new software systems that would not work together when implemented? What should they have done? Outline the reasons for your answer.
10. Pick a business task you would like to computerize. How could you use the steps of the information systems development cycle as illustrated in Figure 10.3 to help you? Use examples to illustrate your answer.

Analysis Exercises

1. SDLC in Practice

Community Action

The Systems Development Life Cycle (SDLC) provides a structured problem-solving software development methodology. However, what works for information system–related problems also works for many business problems too. The SDLC provides a framework that requires adherents to follow a logical sequence. This sequence promotes careful analysis and helps ensure you are doing the right thing as well as doing the thing right.

You can apply the SDLC to address many business problems. Think about a problem in your community. Your community may include your campus, your work, or your neighborhood. Your instructor may provide additional guidelines. Select a problem, complete each step in turn, and prepare a report detailing each step. Due to the location-specific nature of this exercise, expect to conduct first-hand research and interviews.

a. Select a problem and quantify its effects.
b. Identify the cause or causes of the problem.
c. Describe various solutions to this problem. Include estimated costs and benefits for each solution.
d. Select a solution and prepare a plan for its implementation.
e. Identify the parties responsible for monitoring and maintaining the solution. What metrics should they use to monitor the results?

2. Planning for Success

Project Planning

Projects have many dependencies, any of which could become points of failure. Without the cooperation or input from even one vital resource, a project may fail to meet its objectives. Effective project planning helps project managers think through a project before it starts and prepare communication strategies in advance.

a. Read the article "How to Create a Clear Project Plan," *Darwin Magazine*, August 2004 (www.darwinmag.com/read/080104/project.html), and summarize its main points.
b. Read through the "SDLC in Practice" exercise and select a problem as directed by your professor.
c. Prepare a project plan for the problem you selected.
d. Present your project plan to your class. Solicit your peers' suggestions for improvement.

3. Americans with Disabilities Act

Enabling Technologies

The Americans with Disabilities Act prohibits discrimination on the basis of disability in public accommodations and commercial facilities. This act has been interpreted to include certain information systems as well. All information systems development projects should take ADA issues into consideration during development. Accommodating disabled employees and customers must never become an afterthought.

Even if you do not presently experience physical limitations, you may in the future, or you may have employees under your supervision who require special tools to enable access to information systems. Research information systems access solutions. Be sure to include a detailed description of the hardware or software solution, solution provider, and cost of accommodating each limitation listed next.

a. Partial visual impairment.
b. Total visual impairment.
c. Manual dexterity impairment.

4. Central London Congestion Charging Scheme
Conversion Strategies
The city of London is well known for its many historic sites, live theater, and heavy traffic. Despite a sophisticated underground subway system known locally as the "tube," traffic delays, car exhaust, noise pollution, and vehicle–pedestrian accidents have plagued Londoners for decades. After long deliberation, London's city government adopted the Central London Congestion Charging Scheme. This plan involved establishing a toll perimeter around London's center. Rather than stopping cars to collect tolls, however, London set up video cameras at each toll zone crossing. These cameras link to a billing system that charges each vehicle's registered owner a one-day access toll with same-day reentrance privileges. The steep toll, approximately $8, discourages vehicle traffic into London's city center.

Londoners who live within the toll zone receive a special discount, as do residents living near the toll zone boundary, certain government workers, and businesses operating fleets of vehicles. Tolls remain in effect during working hours on workdays. Car owners have until the end of the day to pay their toll through e-mail, SMS messaging, telephone, Web site, or kiosk.

The tolls have resulted in a significant decrease in automobile traffic, increased use of mass transit, fewer accidents, and faster driving times. The tolls have had a negligible effect on business operations and most residents. They have also generated significant revenue that London uses to maintain the system and enhance public transportation.

Consider the massive work involved in educating the public, marking all streets entering the toll zone, setting up cameras, and building the information systems. The information systems alone must process the raw images, match license plates to a payment database, receive payments, send out nonpayment notices, and process appeals. Police also use the system's databases for a variety of law enforcement–related work.

a. Briefly describe the advantages and disadvantages of each conversion strategy (parallel, pilot, phased, and plunge) as they apply to the Central London Congestion Charging Scheme project.
b. Which conversion strategy would you recommend for this project?
c. Defend your recommendation in detail.

REAL WORLD CASE 3 Indiana University: Financial Aid System Implementation: Success or Failure?

Successful system implementation is always the goal of any software development project. Literally volumes have been written about an implementation's critical success factors and the importance of "getting it right." Despite all this preaching about how critical implementation is to the overall success of the project, failures still occur and implementations still go awry. The question is whether anything can be learned from the adventure.

The following description of a recent system implementation represents two sides of the same issue. One side sees the glass half full, the other half empty. Maybe they're both right—you decide.

Half Full

Glitches encountered during a $52 million PeopleSoft Inc. software implementation at a major eight-campus Midwestern university system have left thousands of students without their promised financial aid, requiring a number of stopgap measures and frustrating students just as school was getting under way.

Staffers at Indiana University, whose flagship campus is in Bloomington, are scrambling to manually work around the system bugs, which began cropping up in late August 2004 just as classes began. Officials estimate that about 3,000 students out of 60,000, or 5 percent, were denied financial aid that was already pledged to them. The majority of those students attend the Indiana University–Purdue University campus in Indianapolis.

Since 1998, Indiana University has been working to retire systems, some of which are more than 20 years old, in favor of PeopleSoft Enterprise. The loan problems arose during the installation of the financial aid module, part of the Campus Solutions 8 package.

"As is often the case with a systems implementation of this size and scope, the first time some modules have been used [has] not been without complications," acknowledges Norma Holland, associate vice president at Indiana University, in an e-mail statement. She notes the glitches aren't the "result of the system proper" but apparently surfaced "at those places where fine-tuning was needed to align the university's business processes to the system specifications and functionality."

She also says the start of classes limited the time for comprehensive testing of the software and staff training.

To compensate for the unexpected shortfall of funds, the university has had to dip into its reserve accounts and issue no-interest, short-term loans to students for things such as tuition, says Sue Williams, a university spokeswoman. Other measures included getting landlords to promise not to charge students interest on late rent and letting students draw from the bursar's office account for textbook purchases.

The origins of the financial aid problems are still under investigation. But it appears that most of the problems were caused by interface issues between the loan systems at lending institutions such as the Student Loan Marketing Association (Sallie Mae) and the PeopleSoft application. Without offering the technical details, Williams claims that the financial aid module is as big and complex as all the other installed modules combined. It's also more "sensitive" to exceptions than the legacy system was. For instance, if there was a discrepancy between the amount the lending system issued and what the university had already earmarked, the financial aid application would block the transaction.

In addition, though the system is centralized, it has to take into account variables throughout the different campuses, including the differences between part-time and full-time students or multiple lenders. Despite these problems, the staff has manually been able to clear up about 300 accounts per day and hopes to have them all corrected within three weeks, Williams promises.

PeopleSoft officials remained upbeat. "Indiana University is a happy customer, and they're saying it's an internal issue and not a problem with the software," says spokesman Steve Swasey. "It's a complex rollout, and we're working very closely with them. We have our consulting group in there and will continue to support them in every phase of the implementation."

Half Empty

There we go again. "Technical glitches in a $52 million installation of PeopleSoft Inc.'s applications at Indiana University have left thousands of students without access to promised financial aid . . . "

What is the explanation? According to university spokeswoman Norma Holland, "The glitches were not caused by the system proper." According to this statement, Holland seems to think that software is the "system proper." She doesn't realize that a system is the *amalgamation* of software, processes, and people.

Any project manager worth her work-breakdown structure knows that for a system to be successful, it is imperative that the work processes be aligned to the system processes and that users be trained in a timely manner—*far ahead of the delivery of the technology*. As part of due diligence for any proposed system, the project manager must ask the following questions:

- What degree of change will the new system bring to the processes currently being followed?
- Will the users be willing to make the necessary changes?
- Are the users ready to make the necessary changes?
- What is the latest time by which the users must be made ready?

Obviously, either these questions weren't asked, or if they were asked, no follow-up plans were put into place at the university. As a result, with classes looming, the IT team ran out of time for system testing and user training.

Was the date for the start of classes an unknown? If the team had any project management sense, it would have established "runaway triggers" for system testing and end-user training. Those would have made the project manager aware of the impending delays, and the team could have done one of the following:

- Speed up the project to finish the system testing and user training in a timely manner.
- Implement contingency procedures and work-arounds.
- Suspend the project in an orderly way until the following semester.

Obviously, IT staffers didn't have a systematic status-tracking process in place and simply ran into the start-of-classes wall. Then they blamed the wall for being there. And apparently they waited until the end of the project to start training the users. Smart project managers (and sponsors) know that user training must begin well in advance of the system implementation.

But there's more. Another university spokeswoman, Sue Williams, claims, "Most problems were caused by interface issues between the PeopleSoft application and the loan systems at lending institutions." Is one to believe that the interface was unexpected and sprung onto the university's PeopleSoft system out of left field? The data interface with external systems, a perennial problem, must be investigated as a part of the project planning process. These questions should have been asked:

- What is the quality of incoming data?
- What volumes of data will need to be handled?
- What will be the frequency of data transmission?
- Will there be any media/infrastructure incompatibility?
- Will the data be available in a timely manner?
- Are there any cross-system data dependencies?

Obviously, none of that took place, or this fiasco wouldn't have happened.

Williams calls the financial aid module "big and complex." That is what scope parsing is all about: chunking a big project into smaller, progressive scope modules. Why didn't the sponsor (if there was one) make sure that the complex project was broken into smaller chunks? Instead, the IT team brought all eight campuses live in a single cycle, knowing very well the inherent complexity of the endeavor. As a result, 3,000 students, many of their parents, and hundreds of landlords were left in the lurch.

How many ways did this project violate project management best practices?

1. Poor or no due diligence.
2. No user training.
3. Absence of system status alerts.
4. System interface problems ignored.
5. The complex project wasn't broken down into progressively delivered smaller chunks.

If after all these missteps the university is still a "happy customer," as stated by PeopleSoft, then the university officials and staff involved obviously have not listened to their "customers," the 3,000 students who were negatively affect by the failure of the financial aid system.

Source: Adapted from Marc L. Songini, "ERP System Doesn't Make Grade in Indiana," *Computerworld*, September 13, 2004; Gopal K. Kapur, "Opinion: One Born Every Minute," *Computerworld*, November 29, 2004.

CASE STUDY QUESTIONS

1. As with any story, there are always two sides. Indiana University sees the problem as a surprise; outside observers see the problem as predictable and preventable. What do you think? Why?
2. Is it possible that some implementation problems cannot be easily foreseen or prevented? Give some examples.
3. What could Indiana University have done differently to prevent this unfortunate event from occurring? Is there evidence to suggest that it learned from this experience?

REAL WORLD ACTIVITIES

1. In many cases, we hear about implementation failures more often than implementation successes. Using the Internet, see if you can find some examples of implementation success stories. Why were they successful?
2. The project described in the case was an example of a large-scale software deployment of vendor software. Break into small groups with your classmates and discuss the differences between implementing vendor-supplied software and in-house developed software. Should an in-house project be implemented differently than a vendor supplied application? Why or why not?

MODULE V

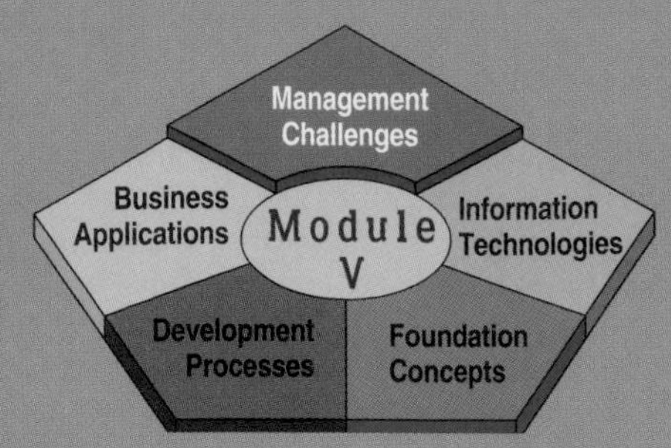

MANAGEMENT CHALLENGES

What managerial challenges do information systems pose for today's business enterprises? The two chapters of this module emphasize how managers and business professionals can manage the successful use of information technologies in a global economy.

- **Chapter 11: Security and Ethical Challenges** discusses the threats against and defenses needed for the performance and security of business information systems, as well as the ethical implications and societal impacts of information technology.
- **Chapter 12: Enterprise and Global Management of Information Technology** discusses the major challenges that information technology presents to business managers, the components of information systems management, and the managerial implications of the use of information technology in global business.

CHAPTER 11

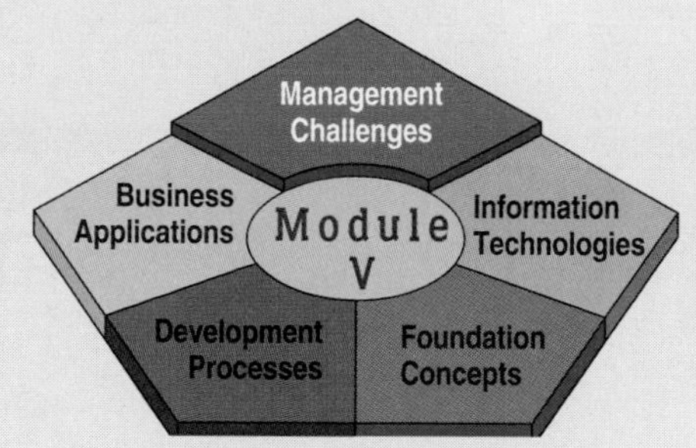

SECURITY AND ETHICAL CHALLENGES

Chapter Highlights

Learning Objectives

After reading and studying this chapter, you should be able to:

1. Identify several ethical issues regarding how the use of information technologies in business affects employment, individuality, working conditions, privacy, crime, health, and solutions to societal problems.
2. Identify several types of security management strategies and defenses and explain how they can be used to ensure the security of business applications of information technology.
3. Propose several ways that business managers and professionals can help lessen the harmful effects and increase the beneficial effects of the use of information technology.

SECTION I Security, Ethical, and Societal Challenges of IT

Introduction

There is no question that the use of information technology in business presents major security challenges, poses serious ethical questions, and affects society in significant ways. Therefore, in this section, we explore the threats to businesses and individuals posed by many types of computer crime and unethical behavior. In Section II, we will examine a variety of methods that companies use to manage the security and integrity of their business systems. Now let's look at a real-world example.

Read the Real World Case on the next page. We can learn a lot from this case about the security and ethical issues in business that arise from the challenges caused by cybercriminals. See Figure 11.1.

Business/IT Security, Ethics, and Society

The use of information technologies in business has had major impacts on society and thus raises ethical issues in the areas of crime, privacy, individuality, employment, health, and working conditions. See Figure 11.2.

It is important to understand that information technology has had beneficial results as well as detrimental effects on society and people in each of these areas. For example, computerizing a manufacturing process may have the beneficial result of improving working conditions and producing products of higher quality at less cost but also the adverse effect of eliminating people's jobs. So your job as a manager or business professional should involve managing your work activities and those of others to minimize the detrimental effects of business applications of information technology and optimize their beneficial effects. That would represent an ethically responsible use of information technology.

Ethical Responsibility of Business Professionals

As a business professional, you have a responsibility to promote ethical uses of information technology in the workplace. Whether or not you have managerial responsibilities, you should accept the ethical responsibilities that come with your work activities. That includes properly performing your role as a vital human resource in the business systems you help develop and use in your organization. As a manager or business professional, it will be your responsibility to make decisions about business activities and the use of information technologies that may have an ethical dimension that must be considered.

For example, should you electronically monitor your employees' work activities and electronic mail? Should you let employees use their work computers for private business or take home copies of software for their personal use? Should you electronically access your employees' personnel records or workstation files? Should you sell customer information extracted from transaction processing systems to other companies? These are a few examples of the types of decisions you will have to make that have an ethical dimension. So let's take a closer look at several **ethical foundations** in business and information technology.

Business Ethics

Business ethics is concerned with the numerous ethical questions that managers must confront as part of their daily business decision making. For example, Figure 11.3 outlines some of the basic categories of ethical issues and specific business practices that have serious ethical consequences. Notice that the issues of intellectual property rights, customer and employee privacy, security of company records, and workplace safety are highlighted because they have been major areas of ethical controversy in information technology [17].

How can managers make ethical decisions when confronted with business issues such as those listed in Figure 11.3? Several important alternatives based on theories of corporate social responsibility can be used [22, 30]. For example, in business ethics, the *stockholder theory* holds that managers are agents of the stockholders, and their only ethical responsibility is to increase the profits of the business without violating the law or engaging in fraudulent practices.

REAL WORLD CASE 1

Cyberscams: Four Top Cybercriminals: Who They Are and What They Do

Cyberscams are today's fastest growing criminal niche. Scores of banks and e-commerce giants, from JPMorgan Chase & Co. to Wal-Mart.com, have been hit, sometimes repeatedly, by hackers and online fraud schemes. The 2005 FBI Computer Crime Survey estimated annual losses to all types of computer crime—including attacks of viruses and other "malware," financial fraud, and network intrusions—at $67 billion a year. Of the 2,066 companies responding to the survey, 87 percent reported a security incident. And the U.S. Federal Trade Commission says identity theft is its top complaint.

To track cybercrime, law enforcement officers work with companies such as eBay or Microsoft, as well as with legal authorities around the globe. eBay has 60 people combating fraud, while Microsoft's Internet Safety Enforcement team has 65 operatives, including former law enforcement agents and federal prosecutors. To document the extent of the activity, *BusinessWeek* reporters scoured underground Web sites where stolen data are swapped like so many baseball cards on eBay.

Consider this e-mail promoting the launch of an online crime trading bazaar, vendorsname.ws, last year: "During the battle with US Secret Service, we !@# &! all those bastards and now are running a brand new, improved and the biggest carders' forum you ever seen." The message brags about its array of stolen goods: U.S. and European credit card data, "active and wealthy" PayPal accounts, and Social Security numbers. Those who "register today" get a "bonus" choice of "one Citybank account with online access with 3K on board" or "25 credit cards with PINs for online carding."

FIGURE 11.1

Web sites like eBay's PayPal payment service must defend themselves from frequent attempts at fraudulent transactions by cyberscammers.

What follows is a look at four individuals who have been identified by multiple law enforcement authorities as high-priority targets in their investigations. It's no coincidence that all are Russian. Strong technical universities, comparatively low incomes, and an unstable legal system make the former Soviet Union an ideal breeding ground for cyberscams. Also, tense political relations sometimes complicate efforts to obtain cooperation with local law enforcement. "The low standard of living and high savviness is a bad combination," argues Robert C. Chesnut, a former federal prosecutor who is a senior vice president directing antifraud efforts at eBay.

Among the most pernicious scams to emerge in the last few years are so-called reshipping rings. And the king of these is a Russian-born hacker who goes by the name Shtirlitz—a sly reference to a fictional Soviet secret agent who spied on the Nazis. In real life, Shtirlitz is being investigated by the U.S. Postal Inspection Service in connection with tens of millions of dollars worth of fraud in which Americans signed up to serve as unwitting collaborators in converting stolen credit card data into tangible goods that can be sold for cash. "We think he is involved in the recruitment of hundreds of people," says William A Schambura, an analyst with the U.S. Postal Inspection Service.

Investigators believe that people like Shtirlitz use stolen credit cards to purchase goods they send to Americans whose homes serve as drop-off points. The Americans send the goods overseas, before either the credit card owner or the online merchant catches on. Then the goods are fenced on the black market.

BusinessWeek found that reshipping groups take out advertisements in newspapers and spoof ads from online job sites. "We have a promotional job offer for you!!" beckons one e-mail for a "shipping-receiving position" from UHM Cargo that appeared to come from Monster.com. It states that "starting salary is $70–$80 per processed shipment. Health and life benefits after 90 days."

Officials do not know Shterlitz's real name but believe he is 25–27 years old and lived in the San Francisco area at one time after his parents emigrated. They do not know where he is now but believe he is active. In one forum of CardingWorld.cc, a person with the alias iNFERNis, posted this request on December 23, 2005: "Hi, I need eBay logins with mail access, please icq 271-365-234." A few hours later, Shtirlitz replied: "I know good vendor. ICQ me: 80-911."

Once equipped, someone could log into those eBay accounts and use them to buy goods with the owners' money while emptying the money out of their PayPal accounts. "The Web sites are more like a dating service," notes Yohai Einav, an analyst at RSA Security Inc. "Then you can conduct transactions in private chat rooms. I can click on someone's name and start doing business with them."

The technical tools to steal credit card numbers and online bank account log-in data are often just as valuable as the stolen goods themselves. A cybercriminal known as "Smash" is being investigated by the Postal Inspection Service on the suspicion that he helps hackers hack. The picture, or avatar, that accompanies Smash's posts in online chat rooms shows a fallen angel. Around 25–30 years old and based in Moscow, he is believed to be an expert in building spyware programs, malicious code that can track Web surfers' keystrokes and is often hidden in corrupted Web sites and spam e-mail.

The U.S. enforcement officials say Smash's Russia-based company, RAT Systems, openly hawks spyware on the Web at www.ratsystems.org. On its home page, RAT Systems denies any malicious intent: "In-general, we're against destructive payloads and the spreading of viruses. Coding spyware is not a crime." But the "terms of service" guarantee that its spyware products will be undetectable by the antivirus software made by security companies such as McAfee Inc. and Symantec Corp. One product, called the TAN Systems Security Leak, created to attack German companies, sells for $834.

Postal Inspection Service officials are also investigating Smash's activity as a senior member of the International Association for the Advancement of Criminal Activity, which they describe as a loose-knit network of hackers, identity thieves, and financial fraudsters. Smash and another sought-after hacker named ZoOmer jointly operate IAAcA's Web site, www.theftservices.com, one of the most popular and virulent stolen-data trading sites, according to U.S. officials.

On May 11, 2005, Massachusetts Attorney General Tom Reilly filed a lawsuit against Leo Kuvayev and six accomplices, accusing them of sending millions of spam e-mails to peddle counterfeit drugs, pirated software, fake watches, and pornography. Kuvayev, a 34-year-old native of Russia who uses the nickname BadCow, is one of the world's top three spammers, according to antispam group Spamhaus. State officials allege that Kuvayev and his associates used a number of Web-hosting services from the United States and around the world to launch attacks.

Massachusetts was able to go after Kuvayev because he listed a Massachusetts address on his driver's license and conducted business using a Boston post office box. On October 11, 2005, after none of the defendants appeared to answer the charges, a Superior Court judge issued a default judgment against them. The judge found the spammers in violation of state and federal consumer protection laws and ordered a permanent shutdown of dozens of illegal Web sites. Kuvayev and his codefendants were ordered to pay $37 million in civil penalties for sending nearly 150,000 illegal e-mails.

Federal law enforcement officials believe Kuvayev's operation was pulling in more than $30 million a year. State officials suspect Kuvayev fled to Russia before he was sued. "The problem is, Russia does not have any anti-spamming laws at the moment," says U.S. Postal Inspection Service senior investigator Gregory Crabb. "It's hard to catch someone who isn't breaking the law."

Bank robbers rob banks because that's where the money is. For cybercriminals, the best loot is often found inside the networks of credit card processors, the middlemen that handle card transactions for merchants and banks. Postal Inspection Service officials say they are investigating Roman Khoda, aka MyO, on the strong suspicion that he is connected to the theft of a million credit card numbers in recent years.

A 26-year-old Russian with a university degree in physics, Khoda once worked with the leading members of carderplanet, one of the largest online marketplaces used to buy and sell pilfered bank account and card data, until it was broken up by U.S. and foreign officials in August 2004. But Khoda is unlike some cocky hackers who often write their own digital signatures into malicious code, says Crabb; Khoda operates with stealth. At carderplanet and successor Web sites, he has not left a detailed trail connecting him directly to stolen data.

But Crabb says officials know that Khoda and two accomplices conducted extensive due diligence on the computer networks of recent targets they intended to break into, even setting up fake companies with accounts at the credit card processors to test for holes in their systems. Then they lugged PCs to a rented apartment on the Mediterranean island of Malta, according to Crabb. Using proxy servers in the United States, China, and Ukraine to hide their Internet connection, Khoda & Co. then unleashed their break-in attacks.

Source: Adapted from Spencer E. Ante and Brian Grow, "Meet the Hackers," *BusinessWeek*, May 29, 2006.

CASE STUDY QUESTIONS

1. List several reasons "cyberscams are today's fastest-growing criminal niche." Explain why the reasons you give contribute to the growth of cyberscams.
2. What are several security measures that could be implemented to combat the spread of cyberscams? Explain why your suggestions would be effective in limiting the spread of cyberscams.
3. Which of the four top cybercriminals described in this case poses the biggest threat to businesses? To consumers? Explain the reasons for your choices, and describe how businesses and consumers can protect themselves from these cyberscammers.

REAL WORLD ACTIVITIES

1. Note: It is not advisable to visit any of the cyberscam Web sites mentioned in this case or any others you discover. To do so could make you, your computer, and your network vulnerable to various forms of cybercrime. Search other sites on the Internet for the latest information on cyberscams, the cybercriminals mentioned in this case, and ways to combat cyberscams. What are some of the new developments you find in each of these areas?
2. How can you protect yourself from cyberscams and other forms of cybercrime? Break into small groups with your classmates to discuss this issue and formulate some key protective recommendations. Include all forms of cybercrime mentioned in this case in your recommendations, as well as those you uncover in your Internet research.

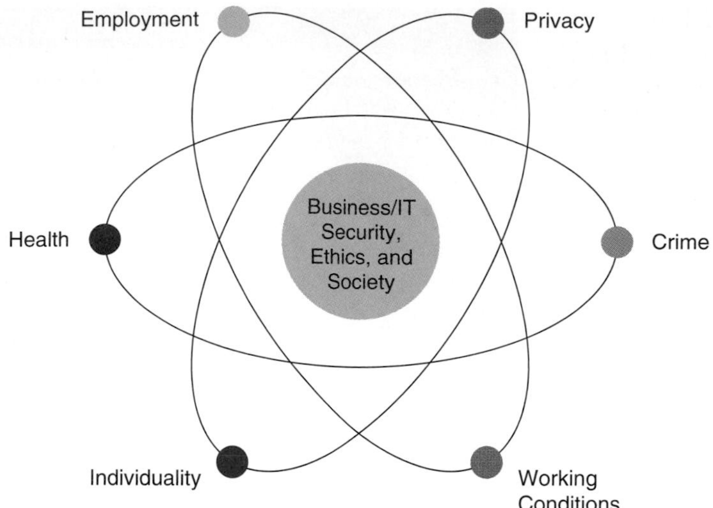

FIGURE 11.2
Important aspects of the security, ethical, and societal dimensions of the use of information technology in business. Remember that information technologies can support both beneficial and detrimental effects on society in each of the areas shown.

However, the *social contract theory* states that companies have ethical responsibilities to all members of society, which allows corporations to exist according to a social contract. The first condition of the contract requires companies to enhance the economic satisfaction of consumers and employees. They must do that without polluting the environment or depleting natural resources, misusing political power, or subjecting their employees to dehumanizing working conditions. The second condition requires companies to avoid fraudulent practices, show respect for their employees as human beings, and avoid practices that systematically worsen the position of any group in society.

The *stakeholder theory* of business ethics maintains that managers have an ethical responsibility to manage a firm for the benefit of all its stakeholders, that is, all individuals and groups that have a stake in, or claim on, a company. These stakeholders usually include the corporation's stockholders, employees, customers, suppliers, and the local community. Sometimes the term is broadened to include all groups who can affect or be affected by the corporation, such as competitors, government agencies, and special-interest groups. Balancing the claims of conflicting stakeholders is obviously not an easy task for managers.

Technology Ethics

Another important ethical dimension deals specifically with the ethics of the use of any form of technology. For example, Figure 11.4 outlines four principles of technology ethics. These principles can serve as basic ethical requirements that companies should

FIGURE 11.3 Basic categories of ethical business issues. Information technology has caused ethical controversy in the areas of intellectual property rights, customer and employee privacy, security of company information, and workplace safety.

Equity	Rights	Honesty	Exercise of Corporate Power
Executive salaries Comparable worth Product pricing **Intellectual property rights** Noncompetitive agreements	Corporate due process Employee health screening **Customer privacy** **Employee privacy** Sexual harassment Affirmative action Equal employment opportunity Shareholder interests Employment at will Whistle-blowing	Employee conflicts of interest **Security of company information** Inappropriate gifts Advertising content Government contract issues Financial and cash management procedures Questionable business practices in foreign countries	Product safety Environmental issues Disinvestment Corporate contributions Social issues raised by religious organizations Plant/facility closures and downsizing Political action committees **Workplace safety**

FIGURE 11.4
Ethical principles to help evaluate the potential harms or risks of the use of new technologies.

Principles of Technology Ethics
• **Proportionality.** The good achieved by the technology must outweigh the harm or risk. Moreover, there must be no alternative that achieves the same or comparable benefits with less harm or risk.
• **Informed Consent.** Those affected by the technology should understand and accept the risks.
• **Justice.** The benefits and burdens of the technology should be distributed fairly. Those who benefit should bear their fair share of the risks, and those who do not benefit should not suffer a significant increase in risk.
• **Minimized Risk.** Even if judged acceptable by the other three guidelines, the technology must be implemented so as to avoid all unnecessary risk.

meet to help ensure the ethical implementation of information technologies and information systems in business.

One common example of technology ethics involves some of the health risks of using computer workstations for extended periods in high-volume data entry job positions. Many organizations display ethical behavior by scheduling work breaks and limiting the exposure of data entry workers to staring at a computer monitor to minimize their risk of developing a variety of work-related health disorders, such as hand or eye injuries. The health impact of information technology is discussed later in this chapter.

Ethical Guidelines

We have outlined a few ethical principles that can serve as the basis for ethical conduct by managers, end users, and IS professionals. But what more specific guidelines might help your ethical use of information technology? Many companies and organizations answer that question today with detailed policies for ethical computer and Internet usage by their employees. For example, most policies specify that company computer workstations and networks are company resources that must be used only for work-related uses, whether using internal networks or the Internet.

Another way to answer this question is to examine statements of responsibilities contained in codes of professional conduct for IS professionals. A good example is the code of professional conduct of the Association of Information Technology Professionals (AITP), an organization of professionals in the computing field. Its code of conduct outlines the ethical considerations inherent in the major responsibilities of an IS professional. Figure 11.5 is a portion of the AITP code of conduct.

Business and IS professionals can live up to their ethical responsibilities by voluntarily following such guidelines. For example, you can be a **responsible professional** by (1) acting with integrity, (2) increasing your professional competence, (3) setting high standards of personal performance, (4) accepting responsibility for your work, and (5) advancing the health, privacy, and general welfare of the public. Then you would be demonstrating ethical conduct, avoiding computer crime, and increasing the security of any information system you develop or use.

Enron Corporation: Failure in Business Ethics

Much has been said about the driven, cultlike ethos of the organization that styled itself "the world's leading company." Truth be told, for all its razzle-dazzle use of Internet technology, a lot of the things Enron did weren't so very exceptional: paying insanely large bonuses to executives, for example, often in the form of stock options (a practice that not only hid true compensation costs but also encouraged managers to keep the stock price up by any means necessary); promising outlandish growth, year after year, and making absurdly confident predictions about every new market it entered, however untested; scarcely ever admitting a weakness to the outside world; and showing scant interest in the questions or doubts of some in its own ranks about its questionable, unethical, and even illegal business and accounting practices.

FIGURE 11.5
Part of the AITP standards of professional conduct. This code can serve as a model for ethical conduct by business end users as well as IS professionals.

AITP Standards of Professional Conduct

In recognition of my obligation to my employer I shall:

- Avoid conflicts of interest and ensure that my employer is aware of any potential conflicts.
- Protect the privacy and confidentiality of all information entrusted to me.
- Not misrepresent or withhold information that is germane to the situation.
- Not attempt to use the resources of my employer for personal gain or for any purpose without proper approval.
- Not exploit the weakness of a computer system for personal gain or personal satisfaction.

In recognition of my obligation to society I shall:

- Use my skill and knowledge to inform the public in all areas of my expertise.
- To the best of my ability, ensure that the products of my work are used in a socially responsible way.
- Support, respect, and abide by the appropriate local, state, provincial, and federal laws.
- Never misrepresent or withhold information that is germane to a problem or a situation of public concern, nor will I allow any such known information to remain unchallenged.
- Not use knowledge of a confidential or personal nature in any unauthorized manner to achieve personal gain.

Credibility comes hard in business. You earn it slowly, by conducting yourself with integrity year in and year out, or by showing exceptional leadership in exceptional circumstances, such as on September 11, 2001. The surest way to lose it, short of being caught in an outright lie, is to promise much and deliver little. Those, at least, are two conclusions suggested by an exclusive survey of executives conducted by Clark, Martire, and Bartolomeo for *Business 2.0*.

Executives rated Enron Chairman and CEO Ken Lay least credible of the business figures in the survey. Perhaps it had something to do with statements like:

- "Our performance has never been stronger; our business model has never been more robust; our growth has never been more certain . . . I have never felt better about the prospects for the company." —E-mail to employees, August 14, 2001
- "The company is probably in the strongest and best shape that it has ever been in." —Interview in *BusinessWeek*, August 24, 2001
- "Our 26 percent increase in [profits] shows the very strong results of our core wholesale and retail energy businesses and our natural gas pipelines." —Press release, October 16, 2001

But three weeks later, Enron admitted that it had overstated earnings by $586 million since 1997. Within a few more weeks, Enron also disclosed a stunning $638 million third-quarter loss, and then filed for Chapter 11 bankruptcy [15].

Dick Hudson, former CIO of Houston-based oil drilling company Global Marine Inc. and now president of Hudson & Associates, an executive IT consulting firm in Katy, Texas, thinks Enron started with a good business strategy and that if it hadn't pushed the envelope, it could well have been a successful *Fortune* 1000 firm. But its sights were set on the *Fortune* 10, so it got into markets such as broadband, which is a tough nut to crack even for the industry's leaders. "Those good old boys in Houston, they had to walk with the big dogs," accuses Hudson. "They are a textbook case of greed and mismanagement" [31].

On May 25, 2006, Kenneth Lay was convicted on six counts of securities and wire fraud and faced a total of 45 years in prison. Lay died July 5, 2006, before sentencing could be passed.

FIGURE 11.6
How large companies are protecting themselves from cybercrime.

Security Technologies Used	Security Management
Antivirus 96% Virtual private networks 86% Intrusion-detection systems 85% Content filtering/monitoring 77% Public-key infrastructure 45% Smart cards 43% Biometrics 19%	▪ Security is about 6 to 8% of the IT budget in developed countries. ▪ 63% currently have or plan to establish in the next two years the position of chief security officer or chief information security officer. ▪ 40% have a chief privacy officer, and another 6% intend to appoint one within the next two years. ▪ 39% acknowledged that their systems had been compromised in some way within the past year. ▪ 24% have cyber risk insurance, and another 5% intend to acquire such coverage.

Source: 2003 Global Security Survey by Deloitte Touche Tohmatsu, New York, June 2003, cited in Mitch Betts, "The Almanac," *Computerworld*, July 14, 2003, p. 42.

Computer Crime

Cybercrime is becoming one of the Net's growth businesses. Today, criminals are doing everything from stealing intellectual property and committing fraud to unleashing viruses and committing acts of cyber terrorism [27].

Computer crime, a growing threat to society, is caused by the criminal or irresponsible actions of individuals who are taking advantage of the widespread use and vulnerability of computers and the Internet and other networks. It presents a major challenge to the ethical use of information technologies. Computer crime also poses serious threats to the integrity, safety, and survival of most business systems and thus makes the development of effective security methods a top priority [12]. See Figure 11.6.

Computer crime is defined by the Association of Information Technology Professionals (AITP) as including (1) the unauthorized use, access, modification, and destruction of hardware, software, data, or network resources; (2) the unauthorized release of information; (3) the unauthorized copying of software; (4) denying an end user access to his or her own hardware, software, data, or network resources; and (5) using or conspiring to use computer or network resources to illegally obtain information or tangible property. This definition was promoted by the AITP in a Model Computer Crime Act and is reflected in many computer crime laws.

PayPal Inc.: Cybercrime on the Internet

At PayPal Inc. (www.paypal.com), an online payment processing company, now a subsidiary of eBay, security specialists noticed one day that there were too many Hudsens and Stivensons opening accounts with the company. John Kothanek, PayPal's lead fraud investigator (and a former military intelligence officer), discovered 10 names opening batches of 40 or more accounts that were being used to buy high-value computer goods in auctions on eBay.com. So PayPal froze the funds used to pay for the eBay goods (all to be shipped to an address in Russia) and started an investigation. Then one of PayPal's merchants reported that it had been redirected to a mock site called PayPal.

Kothanek's team set up sniffer software, which catches packet traffic, at the mock site. The software showed that operators of the mock site were using it to capture PayPal user log-ins and passwords. Investigators also used the sniffer to log the perpetrators' own IP address, which they then used to search against PayPal's database. It turned out that all of the accounts under scrutiny were opened by the same Internet address.

Using two freeware network-discovery tools, TraceRoute and Sam Spade, PayPal found a connection between the fake PayPal server address and the shipping address in Russia to which the accounts were trying to send goods. Meanwhile, calls were pouring in from credit card companies disputing the charges made from the suspect PayPal accounts. The perpetrators had racked up more than $100,000 in fraudulent charges using stolen credit cards—and PayPal was fully liable to repay them.

"Carders typically buy high-value goods like computers and jewelry so they can resell them," comments Ken Miller, PayPal's fraud control director. PayPal froze the funds in those accounts and began to receive e-mail and phone calls from the perpetrators, who demanded that the funds be released. "They were blatant," says Kothanek. "They thought we couldn't touch them because they were in Russia."

Then PayPal got a call from the FBI. The FBI had lured the suspects into custody by pretending to be a technology company offering them security jobs. Using a forensics tool kit called EnCase, Kothanek's team helped the FBI tie its case to PayPal's by using keyword and pattern searches familiar to the PayPal investigators to analyze the slack and ambient space—where deleted files remain until overwritten—on a mirror-image backup of the suspects' hard drives.

"We were able to establish a link between their machine's IP address, the credit cards they were using in our system, and the Perl scripts they were using to open accounts on our system," describes Kothanek. The alleged perpetrators, Alexey Ivanov and Vasili Gorchkov, were charged with multiple counts of wire fraud and convicted in fall 2001 [23].

Hacking and Cracking

Cyber thieves have at their fingertips a dozen dangerous tools, from "scans" that ferret out weaknesses in Web site software programs to "sniffers" that snatch passwords [36].

Hacking, in computerese, is the obsessive use of computers or the unauthorized access and use of networked computer systems. Hackers can be outsiders or company employees who use the Internet and other networks to steal or damage data and programs. One of the issues in hacking is what to do about a hacker who commits only *electronic breaking and entering*, that is, gets access to a computer system and reads some files but neither steals nor damages anything. This situation is common in computer crime cases that are prosecuted. In most cases, courts have found that the typical computer crime statute language prohibiting malicious access to a computer system did apply to anyone gaining unauthorized access to another's computer networks [27]. See Figure 11.7.

Hackers can monitor e-mail, Web server access, or file transfers to extract passwords or steal network files or to plant data that will cause a system to welcome intruders. A hacker may also use remote services that allow one computer on a network to execute programs on another computer to gain privileged access within a network. Telnet, an Internet tool for interactive use of remote computers, can help hackers discover information to plan other attacks. Hackers have used Telnet to access a computer's e-mail port, for example, to monitor e-mail messages for passwords and other information about privileged user accounts and network resources. These are just some of the typical types of computer crimes that hackers commit on the Internet on a regular basis. That's why Internet security measures like encryption and firewalls, as discussed in the next section, are so vital to the success of electronic commerce and other e-business applications.

The hacking community is quick to make the distinction between hacking and cracking. A cracker (also called a black hat or darkside hacker) is a malicious or criminal hacker. This term is seldom used outside of the security industry and by some modern programmers. The general public uses the term *hacker* to refer to the same thing. In computer jargon, the meaning of *hacker* can be much more broad. The name comes from the opposite of white hat hackers.

FIGURE 11.7
Examples of common hacking tactics to assault companies through the Internet and other networks.

Common Hacking Tactics

Denial of Service. This is becoming a common networking prank. By hammering a Web site's equipment with too many requests for information, an attacker can effectively clog the system, slowing performance or even crashing the site. This method of overloading computers is sometimes used to cover up an attack.

Scans. Widespread probes of the Internet to determine types of computers, services, and connections. That way the bad guys can take advantage of weaknesses in a particular make of computer or software program.

Sniffer. Programs that covertly search individual packets of data as they pass through the Internet, capturing passwords or the entire contents.

Spoofing. Faking an e-mail address or Web page to trick users into passing along critical information like passwords or credit card numbers.

Trojan Horse. A program that, unknown to the user, contains instructions that exploit a known vulnerability in some software.

Back Doors. In case the original entry point has been detected, having a few hidden ways back makes reentry easy—and difficult to detect.

Malicious Applets. Tiny programs, sometimes written in the popular Java computer language, that misuse your computer's resources, modify files on the hard disk, send fake e-mail, or steal passwords.

War Dialing. Programs that automatically dial thousands of telephone numbers in search of a way in through a modem connection.

Logic Bombs. An instruction in a computer program that triggers a malicious act.

Buffer Overflow. A technique for crashing or gaining control of a computer by sending too much data to the buffer in a computer's memory.

Password Crackers. Software that can guess passwords.

Social Engineering. A tactic used to gain access to computer systems by talking unsuspecting company employees out of valuable information such as passwords.

Dumpster Diving. Sifting through a company's garbage to find information to help break into its computers. Sometimes the information is used to make a stab at social engineering more credible.

Usually a cracker is a person who maintains knowledge of the vulnerabilities and exploits he or she finds for private advantage, not revealing them to either the general public or the manufacturer for correction. Many crackers promote individual freedom and accessibility over privacy and security. Crackers may seek to expand holes in systems; any attempts made to patch software are generally to prevent others from also compromising a system they have already obtained secure control over. In the most extreme cases, a cracker may work to cause damage maliciously or make threats to do so for blackmail purposes.

The term *cracker* was coined by Richard Stallman to provide an alternative to abusing the existing word *hacker* for this meaning. This term's use is limited (as is "black hat"), mostly to some areas of the computer and security field and, even there, is considered controversial. One group that refers to themselves as hackers consists of skilled computer enthusiasts. The other, and more common usage, refers to people who attempt to gain unauthorized access to computer systems. Many members of the first group attempt to convince people that intruders should be called crackers rather than hackers, but the common usage remains ingrained.

Cyber Theft

Many computer crimes involve the theft of money. In the majority of cases, they are "inside jobs" that involve unauthorized network entry and fraudulent alteration of computer databases to cover the tracks of the employees involved. Of course, many computer crimes involve the use of the Internet. One early example was the theft of $11 million from Citibank in late 1994. Russian hacker Vladimir Levin and his accomplices in St. Petersburg used the Internet to electronically break into Citibank's mainframe systems in New York. They then succeeded in transferring the funds from several Citibank accounts to their own accounts at banks in Finland, Israel, and California.

In most cases, the scope of such financial losses is much larger than the incidents reported. Most companies don't reveal that they have been targets or victims of computer crime. They fear scaring off customers and provoking complaints by shareholders. In fact, several British banks, including the Bank of London, paid hackers more than a half million dollars not to reveal information about electronic break-ins [25].

Citibank: Getting "Phished"

Fraudwatch International, an Australia-based Internet fraud investigation organization, maintains information on Internet fraud schemes across the globe. The latest and fastest growing Internet scam monitored by Fraudwatch is called "phishing." The term (pronounced "fishing") refers to an Internet scam that is exactly that—fishing for information—usually personal information such as credit card, bank account, or Social Security numbers.

Scammers "phish" for your personal information in a variety of ways but most commonly through fraudulent e-mails claiming to be from your bank or another institution that already has your personal details, asking you to confirm these details.

Once scammers have phished out your information, they can use it in a number of ways. Your credit card could be used for unauthorized purchases, or your bank account could be cleared out, or they might simply gather the information for an identity theft scam or sell your information to identity theft rings.

Phishing e-mails are commonly used in association with a fake Web site that looks very similar to a real Web site from the relevant institution.

This new Internet scam is spreading at an alarming rate. In the first half of 2004, Fraudwatch reported over 30 new companies targeted by phishing scams, and Bankers Online.com reported over 1,000 unique phishing campaigns in April 2004 alone.

One of the largest, and most widely publicized, phishing scams focused on customers of Citibank, one of the world's largest consumer and commercial banks. The phishing e-mail, purporting to be from Citibank, said that on January 10, 2004, the bank blocked some accounts "connected with money laundering, credit card fraud, terrorism, and check fraud activity." It said the bank had sent account data to government authorities and might have changed some accounts.

"Citibank notifies all it's [sic] customers in cases of high fraud or criminal activity and asks you to check your account's balances," the e-mail said. It provided a link, "if you suspect or have found any fraud activity on your account."

The return address on the scam was citibank64541@yahoo.co.uk, with a subject line "Important Fraud Alert from Citibank" [28, 40].

Unauthorized Use at Work

The **unauthorized use** of computer systems and networks can be called *time and resource theft*. A common example is unauthorized use of company-owned computer networks by employees. This use may range from doing private consulting or personal finances to playing video games to unauthorized use of the Internet on company networks. Network monitoring software, called *sniffers*, is frequently used to monitor network traffic to evaluate network capacity, as well as to reveal evidence of improper use. See Figures 11.8 and 11.9.

According to one survey, 90 percent of U.S. workers admit to surfing recreational sites during office hours, and 84 percent say they send personal e-mail from work. So this kind of activity alone may not get you fired from your job. However, other Internet activities at work can bring instant dismissal. For example, *The New York Times* fired 23 workers because they were distributing racist and sexually offensive jokes on the company's e-mail system [39].

Xerox Corp. fired more than 40 workers for spending up to eight hours a day on pornography sites on the Web. Several employees even downloaded pornographic videos, which took so much network bandwidth that it choked the company network

FIGURE 11.8
Internet abuses in the workplace.

Internet Abuses	Activity
General e-Mail Abuses	Include spamming, harassments, chain letters, solicitations, spoofing, propagations of viruses/worms, and defamatory statements.
Unauthorized Usage and Access	Sharing of passwords and access into networks without permission.
Copyright Infringement/ Plagiarism	Using illegal or pirated software that costs organizations millions of dollars because of copyright infringements. Copying of Web sites and copyrighted logos.
Newsgroup Postings	Posting of messages on various non-work-related topics from sex to lawn care advice.
Transmission of Confidential Data	Using the Internet to display or transmit trade secrets.
Pornography	Accessing sexually explicit sites from the workplace as well as the display, distribution, and surfing of these offensive sites.
Hacking	Hacking of Web sites, ranging from denial-of-service attacks to accessing organizational databases.
Non-Work-Related Download/Upload	Propagation of software that ties up office bandwidth. Use of programs that allow the transmission of movies, music, and graphical materials.
Leisure Use of the Internet	Loafing around the Internet, which includes shopping, sending e-cards and personal e-mail, gambling online, chatting, game playing, auctioning, stock trading, and doing other personal activities.
Usage of External ISPs	Using an external ISP to connect to the Internet to avoid detection.
Moonlighting	Using office resources such as networks and computers to organize and conduct personal business (side jobs).

Source: Adapted from Keng Fiona Fui-Hoon Nah and Limei Teng, "Acceptable Internet Use Policy," *Communications of the ACM*, January 2002, p. 76.

and prevented coworkers from sending or receiving e-mail. Xerox instituted an eight-member SWAT team on computer abuse that uses software to review every Web site its 40,000 computer users view each day. Other companies clamp down even harder by installing software like SurfWatch, which enables them to block and monitor access to off-limit Web sites [20].

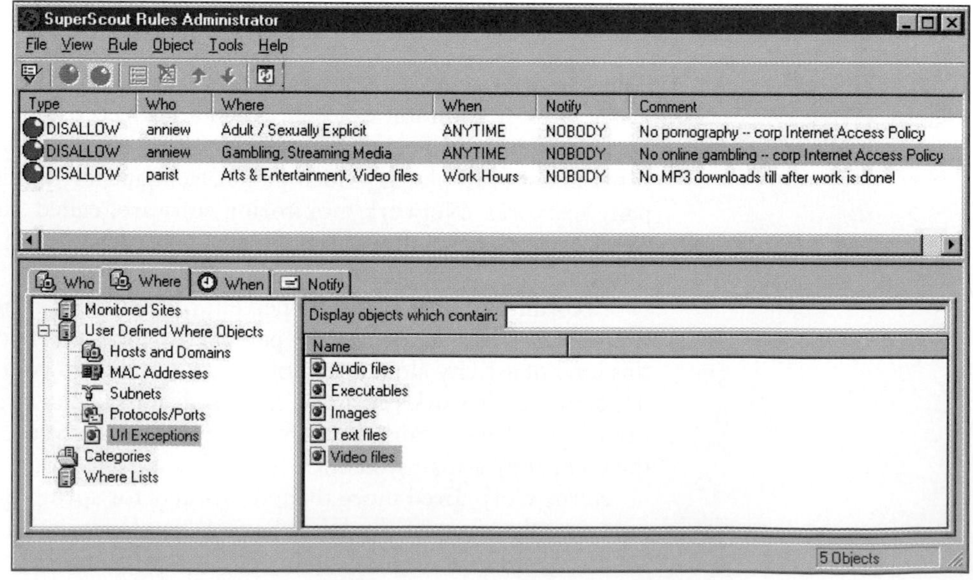

FIGURE 11.9
Network monitoring software (sniffers) like SurfWatch is used to monitor the use of the Internet by employees at work. SurfWatch can also block access to unauthorized Web sites.

AGM Container Controls: Stealing Time and Resources

It's not hard to see why the Net provides all kinds of productivity-frittering distractions—from instant messaging socializing to eBay, pornography, and sports scores. Worse, company secrets may be floating across your firewall. And what you dismiss as simple time wasting could be setting you up for harassment, discrimination, copyright infringement, and other lawsuits. Lawsuits are not the only risk that employers face. Intellectual property can make its way out of the office more easily than ever with the help of electronic communications.

There are two ways to remedy cyberslacking: monitoring Internet use (and making sure employees know you're doing it) or simply blocking sites deemed unrelated to work. Neither is an easy—or bulletproof—fix. If nothing else, a monitoring system with the right amount of follow-up can help employees realize how much company time they waste on the Internet—and help get them back on track.

Howard Stewart, president of AGM Container Controls in Tucson, Arizona, had a feeling that one of his employees was using her PC for personal use a little too much. "When I talked to the employee, she denied she was using e-mail or the Internet for personal use," he says, explaining that the company has a written policy against using the Internet for anything other than work. "However, I knew that this policy was ineffective because a few of my employees had come to the realization that I couldn't monitor their usage."

Stewart chose a simple program from Strategic Business Solutions called Resource Monitor. "Was that employee ever surprised when I was able to negate point-by-point each of her denials that she was using the computer for personal business," Stewart exclaims. "She was shocked to discover that I could give her the exact dates and times she was on and how long she had been at inappropriate sites. Up to that point, she had claimed that she didn't have enough time to take on additional projects at work" [35].

Software Piracy

Computer programs are valuable property and thus the subject of theft from computer systems. However, unauthorized copying of software, or **software piracy**, is also a major form of software theft. Widespread unauthorized copying of software by company employees is a major form of software piracy. This activity has resulted in lawsuits by the Software Publishers Association, an industry association of software developers, against major corporations that allowed unauthorized copying of their programs.

Unauthorized copying is illegal because software is intellectual property that is protected by copyright law and user licensing agreements. For example, in the United States, commercial software packages are protected by the Computer Software Piracy and Counterfeiting Amendment to the Federal Copyright Act. In most cases, the purchase of a commercial software package is really a payment to license its fair use by an individual end user. Therefore, many companies sign *site licenses* that allow them to legally make a certain number of copies for use by their employees at a particular location. Other alternatives are *shareware*, which allows you to make copies of software for others, and *public domain software*, which is not copyrighted.

A 2004 study by the Business Software Alliance, an antipiracy group whose members include Apple Computer, IBM, Intel, and Microsoft, shows that pirated software accounts for 36 percent of software in use worldwide. Reported losses from software piracy in 2003 were nearly $29 billion. "That's over a third of the industry's revenue," says Bob Kruger, the group's VP for enforcement. According to the findings, only $51 billion of the $80 billion in software purchased in 2003 was legally acquired.

Theft of Intellectual Property

Software is not the only property that is subject to computer-based piracy. Other **intellectual property theft** occurs in the form of infringements of copyrighted material, such as music, videos, images, articles, books, and other written works, which most courts have deemed illegal. Digitized versions can easily be captured by computer systems and made available for people to access or download at Internet Web sites or can be readily disseminated by e-mail as file attachments. The development of peer-to-peer (P2P) networking technologies (discussed in Chapter 6) has made digital versions of copyrighted material even more vulnerable to unauthorized use. For example, P2P file-sharing software enables direct MP3 audio file transfers of specified tracks of music between your PC and those of other users on the Internet. Thus, such software creates a *peer-to-peer network* of millions of Internet users who electronically trade digital versions of copyrighted or public domain music stored on their PC's hard drives. More recently, music publishers and manufacturers are offering legal, and relatively inexpensive, methods to access online music in a variety of formats. Because of this proactive posture, the music industry reports that illegal downloading of music and video properties is down and continuing to drop significantly. Let's look at the ongoing debate in this controversial area more closely with a real-world example that emphasizes the threat of developments in IT to intellectual property rights.

Copying Music CDs: Intellectual Property Controversy

Only a few years after Napster's launch, online song-swapping floats dead in the water. A dogged legal campaign by the Recording Industry Association of America (RIAA) shut down the top services, Napster and Audiogalaxy. The others—Kazaa and Morpheus—are on the run, as are their users, who are being sued by the RIAA.

Others, like Gnutella, have been built to withstand legal assault. By avoiding centralized servers and spreading the goods around the globe, the free-music hackers hope their networks will be impossible to shut down. Too bad they're also impossible to use. Shawn Fanning had a hit because Napster provided quick and easy access to a huge trove of music. His deservedly nameless imitators require us to do far more work to find far fewer tunes, all in the name of playing keep-away from the Man.

Why bother? The P2P music fanatics are wasting their time fighting a battle that no longer matters. The real action in music sharing isn't online. It's on foot.

Look at the numbers: Industry estimates say over 6 billion blank CDs will be sold worldwide in 2003—that's one for every person alive today—along with 44 million drives on which to burn them. And 140 million people now own writable drives—far more than the most optimistic membership claims made by Napster or any of its heirs. "You'll find one on nearly every consumer PC," cites Gartner analyst Mary Craig, one of the more bearish forecasters in the business. "They're not using them for backups."

A previous generation of computer junkies called it sneakernet. Rather than relying on the slow, buggy network connections of the day, we hand-carried tapes and floppies to one another's mainframes. Now, sneakernet is in the schoolyard, bringing reluctant musicians to fans royalty-free, without the Net's assistance [5].

Computer Viruses and Worms

One of the most destructive examples of computer crime involves the creation of a **computer virus** or *worm. Virus* is the more popular term, but technically, a virus is a program code that cannot work without being inserted into another program. A worm is a distinct program that can run unaided. In either case, these programs copy annoying or destructive routines into the networked computer systems of anyone who accesses computers infected with the virus or who uses copies of magnetic disks taken from infected computers. Thus, a computer virus or worm can spread destruction among many users. Although they sometimes display only humorous messages, they more often destroy the contents of memory, hard disks, and other storage devices. Copy routines in the virus or worm spread the virus and destroy the data and software of many computer users [36]. See Figure 11.10.

Computer viruses typically enter a computer system through e-mail and file attachments via the Internet and online services or through illegal or borrowed copies of software. Copies of *shareware* software downloaded from the Internet can be another

FIGURE 11.10 The top 5 virus families of all time. Note that three of the five occurred during 2004.

Top Five Virus Families of All Time

MyDoom **First Discovered: 1/26/2004**

- Spreads both by e-mail and over the Kazaa file-sharing network. It appears to install some form of backdoor component on compromised machines, as well as effecting a denial of service attack on the SCO Group's Web site.
- The e-mail poses either as a returned message or as a Unicode message that can't be rendered properly and urges the target to click on the attachment to see the message.
- This worm also has a backdoor component, which opens up two TCP ports—that stay open even after the worm's termination date (February 12, 2004).
- Upon executing the virus, a copy of Notepad is opened, filled with lots of nonsense characters.

Netsky **First Discovered: 3/3/2004**

- A mass-mailing worm that spreads by e-mailing itself to all e-mail addresses found in files on all local and mapped network drives.
- It also tries to spread via peer-to-peer file sharing applications by copying itself into the shared folder used by the file-sharing applications (it searches for folders whose name contains the string "share" or "sharing"), renaming itself to pose as one of 26 other common files along the way.

SoBig **First Discovered: 6/25/2003**

- A mass-mailing e-mail worm that arrives in the form of an e-mail attachment named "Movie_0074.mpeg.pif," "Document003.pif," "Untitled1.pif," or "Sample.pif." The message subject title will read "Re: Movies," "Re: Sample," "Re: Document," or "Re: Here is that sample," and it will appear to originate from big@boss.com.
- The worm will scan all .WAB, .DBX, .HTML, .HTM, .EML, and .TXT files on the victim's machine looking for e-mail addresses to which it can send itself and attempt to spread over the local network.
- It will also attempt to download updates for itself.

Klez **First Discovered: 4/17/2002**

- A mass-mailing e-mail worm that arrives in the form of an e-mail attachment with a random file name. The worm exploits a known vulnerability in MS Outlook to auto-execute on unpatched clients. Once run, the worm will try to disable a selection of security applications—specifically virus scanners—and tries to copy itself to all local and networked drives, renaming itself with a random file name.
- Virus has a very damaging payload; it drops the W32/Elkern virus, which will delete all files it can find on the infected machine and any mapped network drives on the 13th of all even-numbered months.

Sasser **First Discovered: 8/24/2004**

- Spreads by exploiting a recent Microsoft vulnerability, spreading from machine to machine with no user intervention required.
- The worm spawns multiple threads, some of which scan the local class A subnet, others the class B subnet, and others completely random subnets. The worm scans public ranges like 10.0.0.0 and 192.168.0.0 only if they are part of the local subnet.

The Cost of All This...

- Nearly 115 million computers across 200 countries were infected at one time or another in 2004 by rapidly proliferating software agents including Trojans, viruses, and worms.
- As many as 11 million computers worldwide—mostly within homes and small organizations—are now believed to be permanently infected and used by criminal syndicates or malevolents to send out spam; mount distributed denial of service (DDoS) attacks; carry out extortion, identity theft, and phishing scams; or disseminate new viruses.
- The total economic damage worldwide from virus proliferation—with an additional 480 new species in 2004 alone—is now estimated to lie between $166 billion and $202 billion for 2004 by the mi2g Intelligence Unit.
- With an installed base of around 600 million Windows-based computers worldwide, average damage per installed machine is between $277 and $336.

Source: Mi2g.com, "2004: Year of the Global Malware Epidemic—Top Ten Lessons," November 21, 2004.

source of viruses. A virus usually copies itself into the files of a computer's operating system. Then the virus spreads to the main memory and copies itself onto the computer's hard disk and any inserted floppy disks. The virus spreads to other computers through e-mail, file transfers, other telecommunications activities, or floppy disks from infected computers. Thus, as a good practice, you should avoid using software from questionable sources without checking for viruses. You should also regularly use *antivirus programs* that can help diagnose and remove computer viruses from infected files on your hard disk. We will discuss virus defenses further in Section II.

University of Chicago: The Nimda Worm Privacy Issues

The Nimda worm—reports of which first began flooding into mailing lists and security firms on September 18, 2001—is a mass-mailed piece of malicious code that infects systems running Microsoft Corp.'s Windows 95, 98, Me, NT, and 2002. Unlike other worms and viruses, Nimda is capable of spreading via both network-based e-mail and Web browsers. It was also written to scan for and exploit back doors left behind by previous viruses such as Code Red and Sadmind.

"The newness of this is that it leverages a number of different vulnerabilities in order to propagate itself," according to Allen Householder, an analyst at the CERT Coordination Center at Carnegie Mellon University in Pittsburgh. Nimda propagates by various means, including modifying Web content on vulnerable systems running Microsoft's Internet Information Server software. In the process, Nimda clogs part of the Internet, slowing down or even stopping Web traffic for some users. Many sites also experience high volumes of e-mail and network traffic as a result of the worm.

In a four-hour period, the University of Chicago's Web servers were scanned by almost 7,000 unique IP addresses looking for vulnerabilities to exploit, recalls Larry Lidz, a senior network security officer at the school. As a result of the attacks, about 20 university servers were infected with the Nimda worm and had to be disconnected from the network. Lidz recommended to school officials that those systems be reformatted and all software reinstalled. "If somebody has used a back door left by worms such as Code Red to infect your systems, you never really know what they have done to the system," Lidz warns [36].

Adware and Spyware

Two more recent entries into the computer vulnerabilities arena are **adware** and **spyware**. By definition, adware is software that, while purporting to serve some useful function and often fulfilling that function, also allows Internet advertisers to display advertisements as banners and pop-up ads without the consent of the computer user. In the extreme, adware can also collect information about the user of its host computer and send it over the Internet to its owner. This special class of adware is called **spyware** and is defined as any software that employs users' Internet connection in the background without their knowledge or explicit permission. Spyware programs collect specific information about you, ranging from general demographics like name, address, and Internet surfing habits to credit card, Social Security number, user names, passwords, or other personal information. It is important to understand that not all adware programs are spyware. Proper adware represents a viable, albeit sometimes irritating, revenue model for many software companies that allows you to get products for free and, when used correctly, does not pose any significant privacy threat. In contrast, spyware is and should be considered a clear threat to your privacy.

Whereas proper adware generally allows the computer user to opt in to its use in exchange for free use of a piece of software, spyware operates under a rather bizarre ethical model. Consider the following:

- You illegally enter a bank's computer system and place a stealth piece of software in their system. If you are detected or caught, you might be prosecuted and may go to jail.

- You write a worm or virus and spread it around the Internet or other networks. If you are detected or caught, you might be prosecuted and may go to jail.
- You write a program that spreads a spyware agent across computer systems connected to the Internet that steals the private information of the users it infects, manipulates their Internet experience, and uses other people's Web sites and browsers to display your advertising. If you are detected or caught, you may get rich, you don't go to jail, and the computer users are left with possibly rebuilding their computer system to get rid of your spyware.

Spyware has a variety of characteristics, beyond its potential for stealing valuable private information, which make it undesirable to most computer users. At the very least, it plagues the user of the infected machine with unwanted advertising. More often, it watches everything a user does online and sends that information back to the marketing company that created the spyware. Often, spyware applications add advertising links to Web pages owned by other people, for which the Web page owner does not get paid, and may even redirect the payments from legitimate affiliate-fee advertisers to the makers of the spyware. Other undesirable characteristics include setting an infected system's browser home page and search settings to point to the spyware owner's Web sites (generally loaded with advertising), often in a manner that prevents you from changing back the settings (referred to as home-page hijacking). In the extremes, spyware can make a dial-up modem continually call premium-rate phone numbers, thus causing large telephone charges (and usually fees to the spyware owner) or leave security holes in an infected system allowing the makers of the spyware—or, in particularly bad cases, anyone at all—to download and run software on the infected machine (such downloads are called *Trojans*). In almost all cases, spyware severely degrades system performance. As you can see, spyware doesn't have any redeeming features except for the benefits to its owner. Its use is pervasive, and failing to protect against it virtually ensures your system will eventually become infected.

Protecting against adware and spyware generally requires the purchase and installation of one of a variety of programs designed to prevent the software from being downloaded and installed. Once a computer is infected, however, removal programs are often not completely successful in eliminating the nuisance.

Trends in Virus and Spam Attacks

Commtouch, a developer of technology for real-time antispam and virus protection, reports a variety of spam and computer virus statistics on a monthly basis. Its data are based on information gathered by the Commtouch Detection Center, which recently analyzed more than 2 billion messages from over 130 countries during the month of January, 2006.

"The number of massive attacks grew in January," points out Amir Lev, president and CTO. "In large part due to the speed of distribution, they succeeded in reaching many of their targets despite the presence of traditional anti-virus programs."

The numbers are indeed alarming: 19 new e-mail-born significant virus attacks, of which a troubling 8 (42 percent) were graded "low intensity," 7 (37 percent) considered "medium intensity," and 4 (21 percent) massive attacks a rare phenomenon for a single month.

One outbreak of specific interest, consisting of 7 variants, illustrates how viruses are growing in sophistication. The first variant was launched around December 25 as a low intensity virus; however, with subsequently released variants, the attack's intensity grew into a massive outbreak by the end of the month.

The biggest virus attacks are the quickest, so fast moving solutions are required. One of the factors measured by Commtouch is the speed of distribution. "We consider attacks that peak within eight hours to have 'short spans,' since it takes an average of 8–10 hours for a traditional anti-virus vendor to release an updated signature blocking a new virus," explains Lev.

Computer virus statistics indicate that 40 percent of attacks during January met this profile. Also, there is a clear connection between the attack's speed and its intensity: Faster attacks are bigger ones. The average distribution time of low intensity attacks is a "leisurely" 27 hours, and medium intensity attacks can take 17 hours. But massive attacks take as little as 5.5 hours to spread through hundreds of millions of e-mails.

"The conclusion is clear," adds Lev. "Without a reliable solution for early hour protection that complements the old-fashioned anti-virus solutions, users are unprotected from the most massive attacks."

Based in part on a reliable third-party lab test, Commtouch compared detection times of 21 leading AV engines against 19 new viruses in January. The results:

- On average, each AV completely missed 6.2 viruses (the attack was completed, and a signature was not yet available).
- The average response time to new viruses among all AV engines was 8.12 hours.

As Lev warns, "The data should be of great concern to AV vendors and IT managers alike. An eight-hour response spells [out] a simple truth—a traditional AV solution does not stand a chance against massive attacks that end before a signature is even released."

Spam distribution patterns on a global level for January show that 43.18 percent of global spam comes from U.S.-based sources (down from approximately 50 percent). China represents another significant launching pad for 12.89 percent of the spam. Korean and German sources each distribute about 4 percent of global spam, and the rest of spam originates from around the globe.

Although spammers make every effort to use diverse domains, in a sample of 256 million messages, Commtouch found that some domains are used significantly more than others. Leading the list are hotmail.com (4.7 million), yahoo.com (4.2 million), msn.com (2.1 million), cisco.com (1.9 million), and gmail.com (1.5 million). Spammers have deduced that to avoid being blocked by the simplest mail server rules, they need to use a valid domain. However, if the domain is unique and used only for spam, they might easily be blacklisted. The result: Spammers often use popular domains that blacklists do not block.

Major spam categories include the following:

Category	% of Spam	Popular Products/Subjects
Pharmaceutical	52.46%	Medical offering
Gifts	14.08	Rolex replicas
Enhancers & diets	13.38	Lose weight, etc;
Finance	7.57	Refinance your home, Your loan is approved
Software	6.34	Windows XP Pro, Photoshop, MS-Office
Porn & dating	5.28	Date sites
Fraud	.88	eBay Inc., Urgent Security Notification

[41]

Privacy Issues

Information technology makes it technically and economically feasible to collect, store, integrate, interchange, and retrieve data and information quickly and easily. This characteristic has an important beneficial effect on the efficiency and effectiveness of computer-based information systems. However, the power of information technology to store and retrieve information can have a negative effect on the **right to privacy** of every individual. For example, confidential e-mail messages by employees are monitored by many companies. Personal information is being collected about individuals every time they visit a site on the World Wide Web. Confidential information on individuals contained in centralized computer databases by credit bureaus, government agencies, and private business firms has been stolen or misused, resulting in the invasion of privacy, fraud, and other injustices. The unauthorized use of such information has badly damaged the privacy of individuals. Errors in such databases could seriously hurt the credit standing or reputation of an individual.

Governments around the world, but none more than in the United States, are debating privacy issues and considering various forms of legislation. With regard to the Internet, **opt-in** versus **opt-out** is central to the debate over privacy legislation. Consumer protection groups typically endorse an opt-in standard, making privacy the default. An opt-in system automatically protects consumers who do not specifically allow data to be compiled about them. Most business interests back opt-out, arguing it doesn't disrupt the flow of e-commerce. Interestingly, current laws in this regard differ between the United States and Europe. In the United States, opt-out is the default position, whereas in Europe, consumers must opt-in or their information cannot be used.

Additional privacy issues under debate include:

- Accessing private e-mail conversations and computer records and collecting and sharing information about individuals gained from their visits to Internet Web sites and newsgroups (violation of privacy).
- Always knowing where a person is, especially as mobile and paging services become more closely associated with people rather than places (computer monitoring).
- Using customer information gained from many sources to market additional business services (computer matching).
- Collecting telephone numbers, e-mail addresses, credit card numbers, and other personal information to build individual customer profiles (unauthorized personal files).

Privacy on the Internet

If you don't take the proper precautions, any time you send an e-mail, access a Web site, post a message to a newsgroup, or use the Internet for banking and shopping . . . whether you're online for business or pleasure, you're vulnerable to anyone bent on collecting data about you without your knowledge. Fortunately, by using tools like encryption and anonymous remailers—and by being selective about the sites you visit and the information you provide—you can minimize, if not completely eliminate, the risk of your privacy being violated [26].

The Internet is notorious for giving its users a feeling of anonymity when in reality they are highly visible and open to violations of their privacy. Most of the Internet and its World Wide Web, e-mail, chat, and newsgroups are still a wide open, unsecured electronic frontier, with no tough rules on what information is personal and private. Information about Internet users is captured legitimately and automatically each time you visit a Web site or newsgroup and is recorded as a "cookie file" on your hard disk. Then the Web site owners or online auditing services like DoubleClick may sell the information from cookie files and other records of your Internet use to third parties. To make matters worse, much of the Net and Web is an easy target for the interception or theft by hackers of private information furnished to Web sites by Internet users.

Of course, you can protect your privacy in several ways. For example, sensitive e-mail can be protected by encryption, if both e-mail parties use compatible encryption software built into their e-mail programs. Newsgroup postings can be made privately by sending them through *anonymous remailers* that protect your identity when you add your comments to a discussion. You can ask your Internet service provider not to sell your name and personal information to mailing list providers and other marketers. Finally, you can decline to reveal personal data and interests on online service and Web site user profiles to limit your exposure to electronic snooping [26].

ID Analytics Study: Identity Theft Often Goes Unrecognized by Both Consumers and Businesses

Robert K. was home having an early Christmas dinner with his family on December 23 when there was an unexpected knock at the front door. It was a delivery service with an urgent package—but this was no holiday gift. It was a notice that Robert was being sued by Homecomings Financial Network Inc. for $75,000, plus attorneys' fees.

Robert's story had a typical beginning. In April 2001, as he and his wife applied to refinance their home mortgage, they noticed disturbing entries on their credit report. There were some $75,000 in unsettled debts on a line of credit they once held with Homecomings. But the couple had settled their debt and had closed the account the year before.

After some frantic phone calls and a lot of paperwork, the matter had apparently been cleared up. It was discovered that an imposter had managed to gain control of the line of credit and had switched the address on the account to Houston, Texas—so Robert had never received notice of the outstanding bills.

By July 2001, Robert held paperwork from Homecomings indicating he and his wife were not responsible for the debt, and they moved on with their lives, believing the episode was over.

That is, until Christmas 2003, when the messenger arrived with a lawsuit filed in Texas.

Homecomings, a subsidiary of GMAC Financial Services that originated $18 billion in residential mortgages last year, claimed Robert had been negligent. They claimed Robert was slow to discover and report the identity theft, which "caused the injury to Homecomings," according to the lawsuit. "As such, [Robert] is liable for any and all sums attributed to his negligence."

While Robert was eventually able to get Homecomings to drop the suit, he and his wife nonetheless sustained significant losses in both time and attorneys' fees.

The theft of personal information has become an immense problem for both individuals and companies. A 2003 study conducted by ID Analytics Inc. involved a number of major companies, including Citibank, Dell Computer, and Bank of America. Of the 200 million new credit cards, checking accounts, and cell phone accounts that were opened in 2001, seven out of eight identity thefts were incorrectly categorized as simple credit losses by lenders.

An overall key finding was that a surprising portion of the identity fraud cases perpetrated against businesses were actually without a consumer victim because the fraudulent identity was simply fabricated. The study went on to find that in many identity theft cases, by the time the consumer has complained and the problem has been discovered, the bank has already written it off as a credit loss. Because of the criminals' ability to obfuscate traces of the crime, 88.4 percent of identity frauds discovered through the research were not originally reported as such by businesses.

Of the 200 million accounts the study surveyed, 100 million were for credit card applications, while 100 million other accounts were from a variety of companies extending credit to consumers, including Dell Financial Services, JPMorgan Chase, Sprint, T-Mobile, Circuit City, and First North American National Bank.

The companies that agreed to be part of the study said they had losses of $85 million from ID theft and fraud in 2001. ID Analytics said the study put total ID theft losses at $1.07 billion for 2001. While it is extremely difficult to ascertain the exact revenue losses resulting from identity theft, the ID Analytics study was corroborated with information also released by the Federal Trade Commission (FTC) in 2003. The FTC study showed that close to 10 million consumers were victims of some type of identity theft in 2002.

The ID Analytics study showed the total fraud rate of all the applications reviewed to be 2 percent, a much higher figure than the banking and credit card industries had previously recognized. The study also found that identity theft was much more prevalent among what it called "instant credit grantors." ID Analytics pointed specifically to Web-based wireless phone sellers. The study said that any company soliciting fast credit approval is much more likely to be connected to identity theft and fraud cases.

One of the key findings of the study was that "fraud rates vary greatly by the type of application, depending on whether it's a face-to-face transaction (e.g., in a store or bank) versus a 'faceless' transaction (e.g., online, by telephone, or via postal mail), in combination with whether it is instant credit granted at the point of initial purchase versus noninstant credit where there is a waiting period (e.g., a checking account). The highest rate of fraud detected was among instant credit transactions, at 6 percent, and also among faceless transactions, at 4.4 percent. By comparison, lenders had tagged instant credit fraud at .46 percent and faceless fraud .23 percent."

The authors of the study urged cross-industry collaboration to prevent ID theft in the future, saying that "no single corporation or industry has sufficient visibility to identify fraudulent patterns based on analysis of its applications alone" [4, 33].

Computer Matching

Computer profiling and mistakes in the **computer matching** of personal data are other controversial threats to privacy. Individuals have been mistakenly arrested and jailed and people have been denied credit because their physical profiles or personal data have been used by profiling software to match them incorrectly or improperly with the wrong individuals. Another threat is the unauthorized matching of computerized information about you extracted from the databases of sales transaction processing systems and sold to information brokers or other companies. A more recent threat is the unauthorized matching and sale of information about you collected from Internet Web sites and newsgroups you visit, as we discussed previously. You are then subjected to a barrage of unsolicited promotional material and sales contacts as well as having your privacy violated [26].

Privacy Laws

Many countries strictly regulate the collection and use of personal data by business corporations and government agencies. Many government *privacy laws* attempt to enforce the privacy of computer-based files and communications. For example, in the United States, the Electronic Communications Privacy Act and the Computer Fraud and Abuse Act prohibit intercepting data communications messages, stealing or destroying data, or trespassing in federal-related computer systems. Because the Internet includes federal-related computer systems, privacy attorneys argue that the laws also require notifying employees if a company intends to monitor Internet usage. Another example is the U.S. Computer Matching and Privacy Act, which regulates the matching of data held in federal agency files to verify eligibility for federal programs.

More recently, new legislation intended to protect individual privacy has created some new challenges for organizations. Sarbanes-Oxley, the Health Insurance Portability and Accountability Act (HIPAA), Gramm-Leach-Bliley, the USA Patriot Act, the California Security Breach Law, and Securities and Exchange Commission rule 17a-4 are but a few of the compliance challenges facing organizations. In an effort to comply with these new privacy laws, it is estimated that a typical company will spend 3–4 percent of its IT budget on compliance applications and projects.

Computer Libel and Censorship

The opposite side of the privacy debate is the right of people to know about matters others may want to keep private (freedom of information), the right of people to express their opinions about such matters (freedom of speech), and the right of people to publish those opinions (freedom of the press). Some of the biggest battlegrounds in the debate are the bulletin boards, e-mail boxes, and online files of the Internet and public information networks such as America Online and the Microsoft Network.

The weapons being used in this battle include *spamming*, *flame mail*, libel laws, and censorship.

Spamming is the indiscriminate sending of unsolicited e-mail messages *(spam)* to many Internet users. Spamming is the favorite tactic of mass mailers of unsolicited advertisements, or *junk e-mail.* Spamming has also been used by cybercriminals to spread computer viruses or infiltrate many computer systems.

Flaming is the practice of sending extremely critical, derogatory, and often vulgar e-mail messages *(flame mail)* or newsgroup postings to other users on the Internet or online services. Flaming is especially prevalent on some of the Internet's special-interest newsgroups.

There have been many incidents of racist or defamatory messages on the Web that have led to calls for censorship and lawsuits for libel. In addition, the presence of sexually explicit material at many World Wide Web locations has triggered lawsuits and censorship actions by various groups and governments.

The Current State of Cyberlaw

Cyberlaw is the term used to describe laws intended to regulate activities over the Internet or via the use of electronic data communications. Cyberlaw encompasses a wide variety of legal and political issues related to the Internet and other communications technologies, including intellectual property, privacy, freedom of expression, and jurisdiction.

The intersection of technology and the law is often controversial. Some feel that the Internet should not (or possibly cannot) be regulated in any form. Furthermore, the development of sophisticated technologies, such as encryption and cryptography, make traditional forms of regulation extremely difficult. Finally, the fundamental end-to-end nature of the Internet means that if one mode of communication is regulated or shut down, another method will be devised and spring up in its place. In the words of John Gilmore, founder of the Electronic Frontier Foundation, "the Internet treats censorship as damage and simply routes around it."

Cyberlaw is a new phenomenon, having emerged after the onset of Internet. As we know, the Internet grew in a relatively unplanned and unregulated manner. Even the early pioneers of the Internet could not have anticipated the scope and far-reaching consequences of the cyberspace of today and tomorrow. Although major legal disputes related to cyber activities certainly arose in the early 1990s, it was not until 1996 and 1997 that an actual body of law began to emerge. The area, clearly in its infancy, remains largely unsettled. The debate continues regarding the applicability of analogous legal principles derived from prior controversies that had nothing to do with cyberspace. As we progress in our understanding of the complex issues in cyberspace, new and better laws, regulations, and policies likely will be adopted and enacted.

Other Challenges

Let's now explore some other important challenges that arise from the use of information technologies in business, as illustrated in Figure 11.2. These challenges include the potential ethical and societal impacts of business applications of IT in the areas of employment, individuality, working conditions, and health.

Employment Challenges

The impact of information technologies on employment is a major ethical concern and directly related to the use of computers to achieve automation of work activities. There can be no doubt that the use of information technologies has created new jobs and increased productivity while also causing a significant reduction in some types of job opportunities. For example, when computers are used for accounting systems or the automated control of machine tools, they are accomplishing tasks formerly performed by many clerks and machinists. Also, jobs created by information technology may require different types of skills and education than do the jobs that are eliminated. Therefore, people may become unemployed unless they can be retrained for new positions or new responsibilities.

However, there can be no doubt that Internet technologies have created a host of new job opportunities. Many new jobs, including Internet Webmasters, e-commerce directors, systems analysts, and user consultants, have been created to support e-business and e-commerce applications. Additional jobs have been created because information technologies make possible the production of complex industrial and technical goods and services that would otherwise be impossible to produce. Thus, jobs have been created by activities that are heavily dependent on information technology, in such areas as space exploration, microelectronic technology, and telecommunications.

Computer Monitoring

One of the most explosive ethical issues concerning workplace privacy and the quality of working conditions in business is **computer monitoring**. That is, computers are being used to monitor the productivity and behavior of millions of employees while they work. Supposedly, computer monitoring occurs so employers can collect productivity data about their employees to increase the efficiency and quality of service. However, computer monitoring has been criticized as unethical because it monitors individuals, not just work, and is done continually, which violates workers' privacy and personal freedom. For example, when you call to make a reservation, an airline reservation agent may be timed on the exact number of seconds he or she took per caller, the time between calls, and the number and length of breaks taken. In addition, your conversation may be monitored. See Figure 11.11.

Computer monitoring has been criticized as an invasion of the privacy of employees because, in many cases, they do not know that they are being monitored or don't know how the information is being used. Critics also say that an employee's right of due process may be harmed by the improper use of collected data to make personnel decisions. Because computer monitoring increases the stress on employees who must work under constant electronic surveillance, it has also been blamed for causing health problems among monitored workers. Finally, computer monitoring has been blamed for robbing workers of the dignity of their work. In its extremes, computer monitoring can create an "electronic sweatshop," in which workers are forced to work at a hectic pace under poor working conditions.

FIGURE 11.11
Computer monitoring can be used to record the productivity and behavior of people while they work.

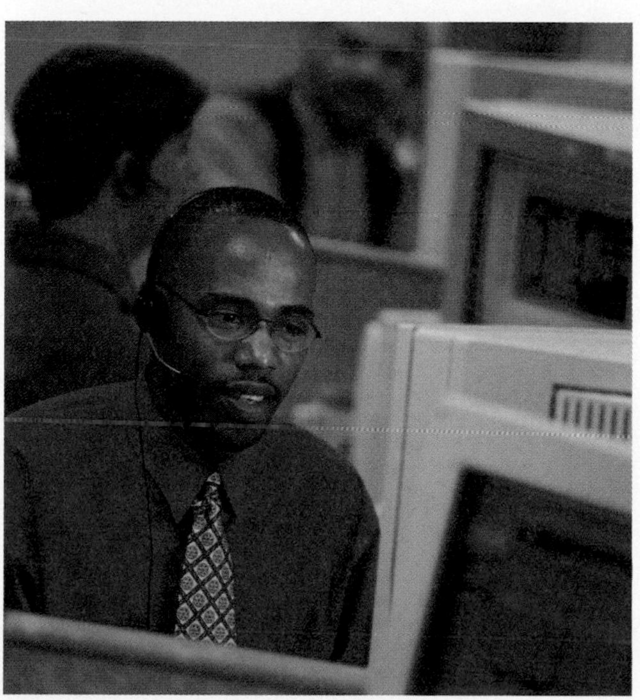

Political pressure is building to outlaw or regulate computer monitoring in the workplace. For example, public advocacy groups, labor unions, and many legislators are pushing for action at the state and federal level in the United States. The proposed laws would regulate computer monitoring and protect the worker's right to know and right to privacy. In the meantime, lawsuits by monitored workers against employers are increasing. So computer monitoring of workers is one ethical issue in business that won't go away.

Challenges in Working Conditions

Information technology has eliminated monotonous or obnoxious tasks in the office and the factory that formerly had to be performed by people. For example, word processing and desktop publishing make producing office documents a lot easier to do, and robots have taken over repetitive welding and spray painting jobs in the automotive industry. In many instances, this shift allows people to concentrate on more challenging and interesting assignments, upgrades the skill level of the work to be performed, and creates challenging jobs requiring highly developed skills in the computer industry and computer-using organizations. Thus, information technology can be said to upgrade the quality of work because it can upgrade the quality of working conditions and the content of work activities.

Of course, some jobs in information technology—data entry, for example—are quite repetitive and routine. Also, to the extent that computers are utilized in some types of automation, IT must take some responsibility for the criticism of assembly-line operations that require the continual repetition of elementary tasks, thus forcing a worker to work like a machine instead of like a skilled craftsperson. Many automated operations are also criticized for relegating people to a "do-nothing" standby role, where workers spend most of their time waiting for infrequent opportunities to push some buttons. Such effects do have a detrimental effect on the quality of work, but they must be compared against the less burdensome and more creative jobs created by information technology.

Challenges to Individuality

A frequent criticism of information systems centers on their negative effect on the individuality of people. Computer-based systems are criticized as impersonal systems that dehumanize and depersonalize activities that have been computerized, because they eliminate the human relationships present in noncomputer systems.

Another aspect of the loss of individuality is the regimentation that seems required by some computer-based systems. These systems do not appear to possess any flexibility. They demand strict adherence to detailed procedures if the system is to work. The negative impact of IT on individuality is reinforced by horror stories that describe how inflexible and uncaring some organizations with computer-based processes are when it comes to rectifying their own mistakes. Many of us are familiar with stories of how computerized customer billing and accounting systems continued to demand payment and send warning notices to a customer whose account had already been paid, despite repeated attempts by the customer to have the error corrected.

However, many business applications of IT are designed to minimize depersonalization and regimentation. For example, many e-commerce systems stress personalization and community features to encourage repeated visits to e-commerce Web sites. Thus, the widespread use of personal computers and the Internet has dramatically improved the development of people-oriented and personalized information systems.

Health Issues

The use of information technology in the workplace raises a variety of health issues. Heavy use of computers is reportedly causing health problems like job stress, damaged arm and neck muscles, eyestrain, radiation exposure, and even death by computer-caused accidents. For example, computer monitoring is blamed as a major cause of computer-related job stress. Workers, unions, and government officials criticize computer monitoring as putting so much stress on employees that it leads to health problems.

People who sit at PC workstations or visual display terminals (VDTs) in fast-paced, repetitive keystroke jobs can suffer a variety of health problems known collectively as *cumulative trauma disorders* (CTDs). Their fingers, wrists, arms, necks, and backs may become so weak and painful that they cannot work. Strained muscles, back pain, and nerve damage may result. In particular, some computer workers may suffer from *carpal tunnel syndrome*, a painful, crippling ailment of the hand and wrist that typically requires surgery to cure.

Prolonged viewing of video displays causes eyestrain and other health problems in employees who must do this all day. Radiation caused by the cathode ray tubes (CRTs) that produce video displays is another health concern. CRTs produce an electromagnetic field that may cause harmful radiation of employees who work too close for too long in front of video monitors. Some pregnant workers have reported miscarriages and fetal deformities due to prolonged exposure to CRTs at work. However, several studies have failed to find conclusive evidence concerning this problem. Still, several organizations recommend that female workers minimize their use of CRTs during pregnancy [7, 9].

Ergonomics

Solutions to some of these health problems are based on the science of **ergonomics**, sometimes called *human factors engineering*. See Figure 11.12. The goal of ergonomics is to design healthy work environments that are safe, comfortable, and pleasant for people to work in, thus increasing employee morale and productivity. Ergonomics stresses the healthy design of the workplace, workstations, computers and other machines, and even software packages. Other health issues may require ergonomic solutions emphasizing job design rather than workplace design. For example, this approach may require policies providing for work breaks from heavy video monitor use every few hours, while limiting the CRT exposure of pregnant workers. Ergonomic job design can also provide more variety in job tasks for those workers who spend most of their workday at computer workstations.

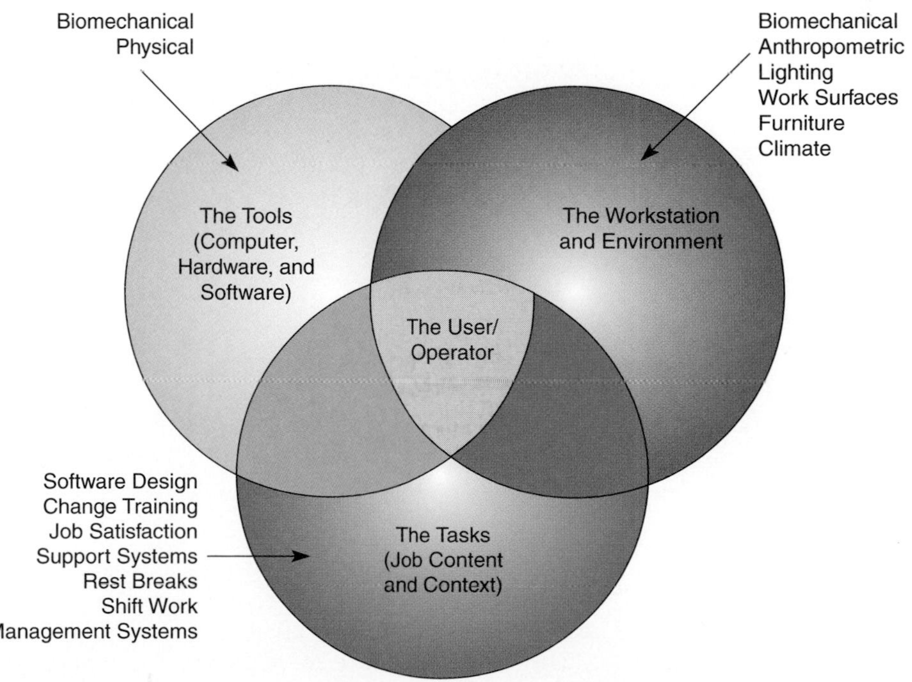

FIGURE 11.12
Ergonomic factors in the workplace. Note that good ergonomic design considers tools, tasks, the workstation, and the environment.

Societal Solutions

As we noted at the beginning of the chapter, the Internet and other information technologies can have many beneficial effects on society. We can use information technologies to solve human and social problems through **societal solutions** such as medical diagnosis, computer-assisted instruction, governmental program planning, environmental quality control, and law enforcement. For example, computers can help diagnose an illness, prescribe necessary treatment, and monitor the progress of hospital patients. Computer-assisted instruction (CAI) and computer-based training (CBT) enable interactive instruction tailored to the needs of students. Distance learning is supported by telecommunications networks, video conferencing, e-mail, and other technologies.

Information technologies can be used for crime control through various law enforcement applications. For example, computerized alarm systems allow police to identify and respond quickly to evidence of criminal activity. Computers have been used to monitor the level of pollution in the air and in bodies of water, detect the sources of pollution, and issue early warnings when dangerous levels are reached. Computers are also used for the program planning of many government agencies in such areas as urban planning, population density and land use studies, highway planning, and urban transit studies. Computers are being used in job placement systems to help match unemployed persons with available jobs. These and other applications illustrate that information technology can be used to help solve the problems of society.

Obviously, many of the detrimental effects of information technology are caused by individuals or organizations that do not accept ethical responsibility for their actions. Like other powerful technologies, information technology possesses the potential for great harm or great good for all humankind. If managers, business professionals, and IS specialists accept their ethical responsibilities, then information technology can help improve living and working conditions for all of society.

SECTION II Security Management of Information Technology

Introduction

With Internet access proliferating rapidly, one might think that the biggest obstacle to electronic commerce would be bandwidth. But it's not; the number one problem is security. And part of the problem is that the Internet was developed for interoperability, not impenetrability [35].

As we saw in Section I, there are many significant threats to the security of information systems in business. That's why this section is dedicated to exploring the methods that companies can use to manage their security. Business managers and professionals alike are responsible for the security, quality, and performance of the business information systems in their business units. Like any other vital business assets, hardware, software, networks, and data resources need to be protected by a variety of security measures to ensure their quality and beneficial use. That's the business value of security management.

Read the Real World Case on the next page. We can learn a lot about the causes of failures in proper security for vital data on customers and other business information from this case. See Figure 11.13.

Tools of Security Management

The goal of **security management** is the accuracy, integrity, and safety of all information system processes and resources. Thus, effective security management can minimize errors, fraud, and losses in the information systems that interconnect today's companies and their customers, suppliers, and other stakeholders. As Figure 11.14 illustrates, security management is a complex task. As you can see, security managers must acquire and integrate a variety of security tools and methods to protect a company's information system resources. We discuss many of these security measures in this section.

Providence Health and Cervalis: Security Management

The need for security management is being driven by both the increasing threat of cybercrimes and the growing use of the Internet to link companies with partners and customers, argues David Rymal, director of technology at Providence Health System (www.providence.org) in Everett, Washington. "There is an increasing pressure to enable wide and unfettered access from our business units. We are getting so many requests to open up ports in our firewall that pretty soon it is going to look like Swiss cheese," Rymal says. "The more of them you have open, the more vulnerabilities you create."

The whole notion of "Web services," in which companies use common Web protocols to link their business systems with those of external partners and suppliers, is only going to increase the need for better security, according to users. Adding to the pressure is the growing number of remote workers and the trend toward wireless applications, which has meant finding better ways to identify and authenticate users and controlling the access they have on the network. "You have to keep in mind that the minute you open your servers or services to the Internet, you are going to have bad people trying to get in," warns Edward Rabbinovitch, vice president of global networks and infrastructure operations at Cervalis Inc. (www.cervalis.com), a Stamford, Connecticut–based Internet hosting service.

While it's impossible to guarantee 100 percent security, companies should make things as difficult as possible for outsiders or insiders trying to steal or damage IT assets, IT managers say. Cervalis's security, for instance, begins at its ingress points—where the Internet meets its networks. The company uses strict port control and

REAL WORLD CASE 2 Lowe's, TCI, Bank of America, ChoicePoint, and Others: Failures in Data Security Management

In February 2005, data aggregator ChoicePoint acknowledged that identity thieves had stolen vital information on 145,000 people. Less than two weeks later, Bank of America admitted it had lost backup tapes that held the account information of 1.2 million credit card holders. In March, shoe retailer DSW said its stores' credit card data had been breached; the U.S. Secret Service estimated that at least 100,000 valuable numbers had been accessed. More than a month later, DSW released the real number: 1.4 million. Reed Elsevier's LexisNexis, a ChoicePoint rival, followed suit, revealing first that unauthorized users had compromised 32,000 identities, then upping the number to 310,000.

Corporate America is finally owning up to a long-held secret: It can't safeguard some of its most valuable data. Let's look at four examples in more detail.

On the evening of November 7, 2003, two computer geeks named Adam Botbyl and Brian Salcedo pulled into the parking lot of a Lowe's Home Improvement store in Southfield, Michigan. From the comfort of Botbyl's white Pontiac Grand Prix, the duo opened a WiFi-equipped laptop and logged on to a wireless access point meant for Lowe's employees to connect phones and scanners to the store's computer system. Once Salcedo and Botbyl had hopped onto the company's network, they tried to install a homemade version of Lowe's credit card–processing program. Their aim: to capture the credit card numbers of thousands of Lowe's customers.

Over a period of several days, Salcedo gained access not only to the Southfield store but to Lowe's corporate data center in North Carolina. Once inside, he learned how the retailer approved and processed credit cards, then wrote his own version of Lowe's proprietary credit card transaction software. In Salcedo's version, according to a later indictment, the information would be saved in a file that he could later access.

What Salcedo apparently didn't realize is that many corporate computer systems are getting better at telling when someone's messing with them. Lowe's network engineers, from the company's data center in North Carolina, were able to piece together the timing of the various break-ins. On November 6, 2003, Lowe's officials called the Charlotte office of the FBI. Doris Gardner and members of her cybercrime squad arrived at Lowe's data center almost immediately. Agents took their places around the edge of the room while the Lowe's tech staff sought to zero in on the origin of the break-ins.

Using system-monitoring tools, the Lowe's team soon determined a security breach was happening that very moment in Southfield. On November 7, Gardner had agents stake out the store there. That evening, the FBI caught a break. One of the agents noticed an eerie glow coming from the front seat of a Pontiac Grand Prix. It was the laptop. The FBI ran the license plate and came up with Botbyl's name.

Within days the geeks had been caught—before they were able to capitalize on any credit card information. Botbyl, 21, pleaded guilty to one count of conspiracy and is serving a two-year sentence. Salcedo, 22, was sentenced to nine years. Today he sits in a prison in Lewis Run, Pennsylvania. The FBI says he hacked other companies that didn't stop him in time. "He definitely gained financially from other hacks," says the FBI's Gardner.

If Botbyl was caught by Lowe's security, shouldn't strong intrusion detection be enough to stop data leakage? Not by a long shot. Witness Teledata Communications International— a company that prided itself on its security. In 1999, Philip Cummings landed a job with TCI as a lowly help-desk worker. The company, now in Hauppauge, New York, makes devices used by banks, doctor's offices, and car dealerships that allow instant credit checks by connecting to credit agencies like Experian or Equifax. When customers had problems logging on to one of the agencies from a TCI box, they would call in for help. Cummings would answer, ask them for their user code and password (TCI didn't keep the information itself, ironically, for security's sake), and help them fix their problem. Then he pocketed the information.

Outside work, Cummings struck a deal with a man he knew in New Rochelle, New York, named Linus Baptiste. Baptiste would give Cummings names of wealthy people and ask him to pull their confidential credit information. According to the indictment, Cummings would log in to the credit-reporting agencies using one of TCI's client passwords, find personal data such as Social Security and bank account numbers, and hand them over. Baptiste knew people

FIGURE 11.13

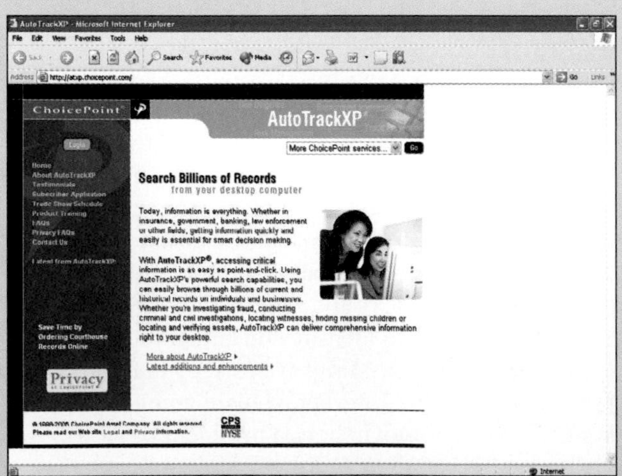

ChoicePoint is a data resource for billions of records about businesses and individuals. Its lack of adequate safeguards led to the theft of thousands of individual records in 2005.

in Brooklyn and the Bronx willing to pay $60 for each name; he and Cummings split the cash.

Cummings soon quit TCI and in 2001 moved to Georgia. He worked off a stolen TCI laptop and a roster of TCI client passwords. When a TCI client changed passwords, Cummings would move down his list, find another, and give it to Baptiste. Prosecutors say the two accessed some 30,000 names, all of which they sold to others. They continued doing that for two years; TCI never had any idea.

The first inkling of Cummings's doings came in early 2002, when Ford Motor, one of TCI's clients, couldn't account for 15,000 credit checks that Experian said the company had made with it. Soon the FBI was involved. Experian kept digging, as did Equifax. Both found that the requests seemed to be originating from one number in New Rochelle. On October 29, 2002, FBI agents raided Baptiste's home and found three computers under two beds and credit reports hidden all over his bedroom. With Baptiste's help, the Feds eventually fingered Cummings, who is now serving a 14-year sentence in federal prison.

But surely security is much tighter in the banking industry. Well, not necessarily. In late December 2004, Bank of America employees packed up and sent to its backup data center tapes containing information on government workers enrolled in a charge card account. Or at least, that's where they were supposed to go. The tapes—none of which were encrypted—shipped via commercial air. But just after New Year's, bank officials realized that the tapes had never arrived. They scrambled to see what might be lost. It wasn't pretty: more than a million names, addresses, account numbers, and Social Security numbers. On January 10, the bank called in the Secret Service.

For the next month, the bank and the investigators worked in silence. Account holders had no idea that their information might be on the loose. Bank of America says the Secret Service asked it to keep quiet while it investigated. The bank kept monitoring the accounts, looking for any funny business, but found none—and still hasn't, it says. In mid-February, the bank finally went public, promising that it had changed its ways (backup tapes no longer go by commercial air, for instance) and offering free credit reports and fraud monitoring to affected consumers.

Bank of America might have escaped serious damage, but security experts were left gasping at what it calls its "industry standard" methods of backing up and shipping customer data. "The Bank of America incident was absolute stupidity," exclaims Jim Stickley, the CTO of TraceSecurity, a threat-management company based in Baton Rouge. Even though Stickley has seen plenty of gaping security holes, he can't stop talking about Bank of America. "Everything you want to protect is on those tapes. If they're not encrypted, strike No. 1. Then they're using commercial carriers to transfer the tapes, and they're like, 'Everybody does that.' But that's not the case. It's not like it's a surprise that stuff can be stolen from commercial airlines. I think there were several bad choices they made there that could have been avoided."

And then there's ChoicePoint, Enemy No. 1 to privacy advocates. Since spinning off from credit bureau Equifax in 1997, it has been buying up databases and data mining operations. Businesses, individuals, and even the FBI now rely on its storehouse of billions of pieces of information on practically everybody. Other customers: Nigerian scammers who apparently used the data to rip off people's identities.

The problem was unreliable safeguards. To ensure that only certain businesses had access to its data, ChoicePoint set up certain requirements that potential customers must meet. A man named Olatunji Oluwatosin—and possibly others—used fake names and a Hollywood copy shop fax machine to create fictitious small businesses requesting ChoicePoint service. Before Oluwatosin was caught—after someone at Choice Point grew suspicious about one of his applications—he accessed at least 145,000 names.

After news of the security breach leaked out, ChoicePoint's stock hit the rocks. At least three class-action suits have been filed, including one that accuses the company of concealing material information and allowing executives to sell $20 million worth of ChoicePoint shares before the news broke. Lesson to all companies: The business cost of poor data security can be quite high, as the ChoicePoint fallout demonstrates.

Source: Adapted from Daniel Roth and Stephanie Mehta, "The Great Data Heist," *Fortune*, May 16, 2005.

CASE STUDY QUESTIONS

1. Why have there been so many recent incidents of data security breaches and loss of customer data by reputable companies? Provide several possible reasons for this development.
2. What security safeguards must companies have to deter electronic break-ins into their computer networks, business applications, and data resources, like the incident at Lowe's? Defend your proposed security measures.
3. What security safeguards would have deterred the loss of customer data at TCI, Bank of America, and ChoicePoint? Defend your proposed security measures to avoid the incidents that occurred at each company.

REAL WORLD ACTIVITIES

1. Search the Internet for the latest information on computer security developments for the four main companies in this case and any other companies that have reported major data losses or other computer security problems. Then research information on the latest developments in security measures to protect companies from data theft and losses. Report some of your findings to the class.
2. Break into small groups with your classmates to share the information you have found in your Internet research on data losses, other computer security problems, and the latest developments in computer security measures. Develop several key computer security recommendations for companies to implement to avoid many of the problems you discovered.

FIGURE 11.14
Examples of important security measures that are part of the security management of information systems.

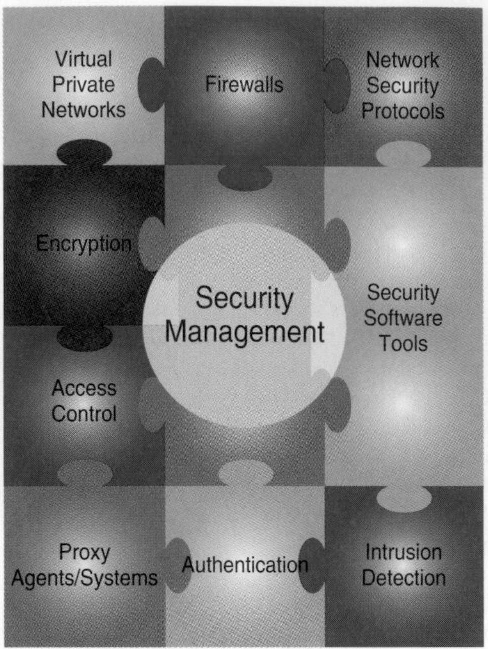

management on all of its Internet-facing routers to ensure that open ports don't provide easy access for malicious attackers. Redundant, load-balanced firewalls that are sandwiched between two layers of content switches filter all traffic coming in from the Internet. Network-based intrusion-detection systems are sprinkled throughout the Cervalis network [37].

Internetworked Security Defenses

Few professionals today face greater challenges than those IT managers who are developing Internet security policies for rapidly changing network infrastructures. How can they balance the need for Internet security and Internet access? Are the budgets for Internet security adequate? What impact will intranet, extranet, and Web application development have on security architectures? How can they come up with best practices for developing Internet security policy? [35]

The security of today's networked business enterprises is a major management challenge. Many companies are still in the process of getting fully connected to the Web and the Internet for e-commerce and are reengineering their internal business processes with intranets, e-business software, and extranet links to customers, suppliers, and other business partners. Vital network links and business flows need to be protected from external attack by cybercriminals and from subversion by the criminal or irresponsible acts of insiders. This protection requires a variety of security tools and defensive measures and a coordinated security management program. Let's take a look at some of these important security defenses.

Encryption

Encryption of data has become an important way to protect data and other computer network resources, especially on the Internet, intranets, and extranets. Passwords, messages, files, and other data can be transmitted in scrambled form and unscrambled by computer systems for authorized users only. Encryption involves using special mathematical algorithms, or keys, to transform digital data into a scrambled code before they are transmitted and decode the data when they are received. The most widely used encryption method uses a pair of public and private keys unique to each

FIGURE 11.15 How public key/private key encryption works.

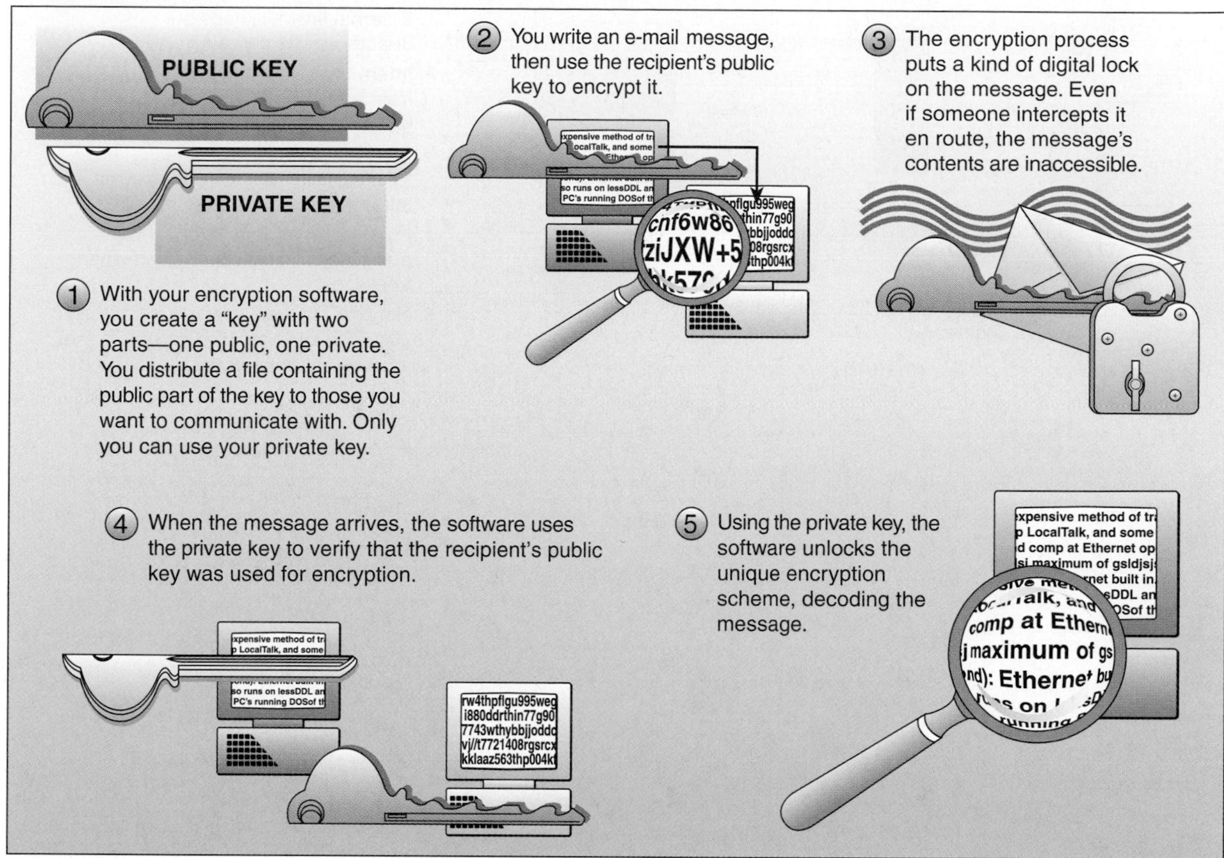

individual. For example, e-mail could be scrambled and encoded using a unique *public key* for the recipient that is known to the sender. After the e-mail is transmitted, only the recipient's secret *private key* could unscramble the message [26]. See Figure 11.15.

Encryption programs are sold as separate products or built into other software used for the encryption process. There are several competing software encryption standards, but the top two are RSA (by RSA Data Security) and PGP (pretty good privacy), a popular encryption program available on the Internet. Software products including Microsoft Windows XP, Novell NetWare, and Lotus Notes offer encryption features using RSA software.

Firewalls

Another important method for control and security on the Internet and other networks is the use of **firewall** computers and software. A network firewall can be a communications processor, typically a *router*, or a dedicated server, along with firewall software. A firewall serves as a "gatekeeper" system that protects a company's intranets and other computer networks from intrusion by providing a filter and safe transfer point for access to and from the Internet and other networks. It screens all network traffic for proper passwords or other security codes and only allows authorized transmissions in and out of the network. Firewall software has also become an essential computer system component for individuals connecting to the Internet with DSL or cable modems, because of their vulnerable, "always-on" connection status. Figure 11.16 illustrates an Internet/intranet firewall system for a company [15].

Firewalls can deter, but not completely prevent, unauthorized access (hacking) into computer networks. In some cases, a firewall may allow access only from trusted locations on the Internet to particular computers inside the firewall. Or it may allow only

FIGURE 11.16 An example of the Internet and intranet firewalls in a company's networks.

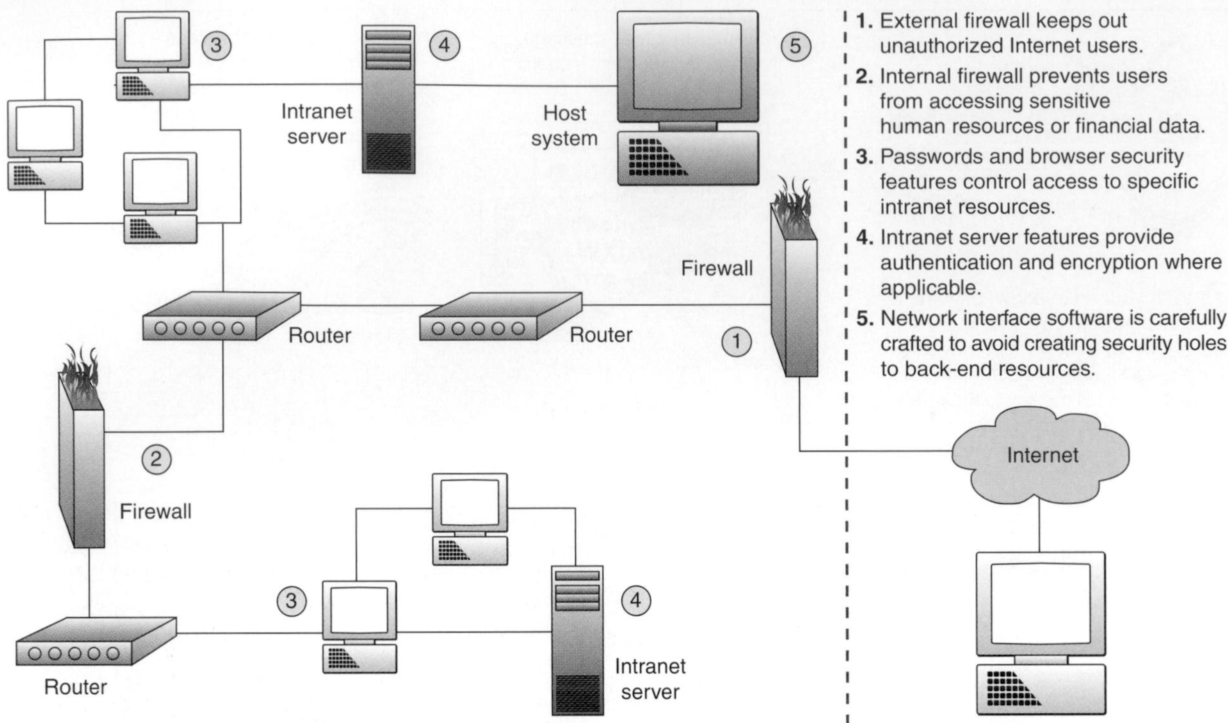
③
④
Intranet server
Host system
⑤
Firewall
Router
Router
①
②
Firewall
③
④
Intranet server
Router
Internet
1. External firewall keeps out unauthorized Internet users.
2. Internal firewall prevents users from accessing sensitive human resources or financial data.
3. Passwords and browser security features control access to specific intranet resources.
4. Intranet server features provide authentication and encryption where applicable.
5. Network interface software is carefully crafted to avoid creating security holes to back-end resources.

"safe" information to pass. For example, a firewall may permit users to read e-mail from remote locations but not run certain programs. In other cases, it is impossible to distinguish the safe use of a particular network service from unsafe use, and so all requests must be blocked. The firewall may then provide substitutes for some network services (such as e-mail or file transfers) that perform most of the same functions but are not as vulnerable to penetration.

Barry Nance: Testing PC Firewall Security

From all over the world, and even from your hometown, the bad guys' software is constantly probing the Internet, examining consecutive IP addresses for information. Ah! The software finds an active IP address. What sort of device is it? Does it have a network management agent? Whose protocol stack is the device running? Is the IP address permanently assigned? Might the device be a good target for a virus, Trojan, or worm? Is port 23, used by Telnet, open? Might it be worth flooding the device with denial-of-service packets? Does the IP address correspond to a registered domain name? Is the network node running Web server, FTP server, database server, or file sharing software?

A sophisticated probe can discover a staggering amount of data and store it for future use. If an employee's home PC has a persistent Internet connection via Digital Subscriber Line (DSL) or cable, the probe's database almost certainly contains the IP address and network node data. Even dial-up users with dynamically assigned IP addresses can be at risk if connections last more than a half day. An employee who routinely handles company business and confidential data from his or her home computer is also at risk.

A number of companies offer personal firewall products to help block Internet-based intruders. Software developer Barry Nance tested some of the best known, including Norton Personal Firewall and Black Ice Defender, to find out which offers the best deterrent to Internet probes.

A software firewall to protect your home PC intercepts and examines each inbound or outbound Internet message. It distinguishes, for example, between legitimate messages that are responses to your Web browsing and illegitimate messages that you never asked for. The software also uses network address translation to substitute a bogus IP address inside your computer's outgoing Internet messages. When the bad guys don't know who you are, they can't penetrate your PC.

Nance used many tools to test security by trying to penetrate each firewall and scan for ports. He also launched a 10-minute barrage of network request messages on all common ports and measured the time it took each firewall to resolve the requests.

The results were gratifying for anyone concerned about Internet security. All of the firewalls successfully blocked unsolicited Internet messages, port scans, and denial of service attacks. They slowed Internet access only slightly as they protected the computer from Nance's hacking efforts [19].

Denial of Service Attacks

Major attacks against e-commerce and corporate Web sites in the past few years have demonstrated that the Internet is extremely vulnerable to a variety of assaults by criminal hackers, especially **distributed denial of service (DDOS)** attacks. Figure 11.17 outlines the steps organizations can take to protect themselves from DDOS attacks.

Denial of service assaults via the Internet depend on three layers of networked computer systems: (1) the victim's Web site, (2) the victim's Internet service provider (ISP), and (3) the sites of "zombie" or slave computers that were commandeered by the cybercriminals. For example, in early 2000, hackers broke into hundreds of servers, mostly poorly protected servers at universities, and planted Trojan horse .exe programs, which were then used to launch a barrage of service requests in a concerted attack on e-commerce Web sites like Yahoo! and eBay [16].

As Figure 11.17 shows, defensive measures and security precautions must be taken at all three levels of the computer networks involved. These are the basic steps companies and other organizations can take to protect their Web sites from denial of service and other hacking attacks. Now let's take a look at a real-world example of a more sophisticated defense technology.

MTV Networks: Denial of Service Defenses

MTV.com, the Web site for the cable TV music channel, is the target of distributed denial of service (DDOS) attacks each fall when the MTV Video Music Awards are televised. But the attacks, in which MTV.com's network servers are deliberately overloaded by massive automated requests for service by hackers, are now blunted because New York–based Viacom International's (www.viacom.com) MTV Networks division is protecting its 15 entertainment Web sites (including the MTV,

FIGURE 11.17
How to defend against denial of service attacks.

Defenses against Denial of Service
• **At the zombie machines:** Set and enforce security policies. Scan regularly for Trojan horse programs and vulnerabilities. Close unused ports. Remind users not to open .exe mail attachments.
• **At the ISP:** Monitor and block traffic spikes. Filter spoofed IP addresses. Coordinate security with network providers.
• **At the victim's Web site:** Create backup servers and network connections. Limit connections to each server. Install multiple intrusion-detection systems and multiple routers for incoming traffic to reduce choke points.

VH-1, and Nickelodeon sites) with Enforcer, a network security software tool from Mazu Networks Inc. in Cambridge, Massachusetts.

"During the MTV Awards and other highly publicized TV events, some folks try to knock us out of the water," acknowledges Brian Amirian, director of Web hosting and development at MTV Networks Online Technology. So last year, MTV attached Mazu's Enforcer to telecom uplinks between the MTV Web sites and the company's Internet service provider.

Amirian says one reason he selected Mazu's product is the efficient way it uses proprietary hardware to filter out DDOS attacks. Some other products that he evaluated, but rejected, used software that relied on the more limited filtering capabilities of existing network routers. Mazu's Enforcer builds a statistical model of Web site traffic when no attack is occurring, touts Carty Castaldi, vice president of engineering at Mazu Networks. During a DDOS attack, Enforcer identifies data packets associated with the attack based on their statistical differences from the norm and recommends a filter that typically blocks 80 percent of the attack packets and about 5 percent of nonattack packets, he says.

In any event, MTV Networks' Amirian is happy. According to his calculations, he recouped the $32,000 investment in Enforcer within about two months, because the Mazu device kept MTV's Web site from being disrupted during the heavy advertising period surrounding the Video Music Awards [1].

e-Mail Monitoring

Spot checks just aren't good enough anymore. The tide is turning toward systematic monitoring of corporate e-mail traffic using content-monitoring software that scans for troublesome words that might compromise corporate security. The reason: Users of monitoring software said they're concerned about protecting their intellectual property and guarding themselves against litigation [6].

As we mentioned in Section I, Internet and other online e-mail systems are one of the favorite avenues of attack by hackers for spreading computer viruses or breaking into networked computers. E-mail is also the battleground for attempts by companies to enforce policies against illegal, personal, or damaging messages by employees versus the demands of some employees and others who see such policies as violations of privacy rights.

Sonalysts, Inc.: Corporate e-Mail Monitoring

John Conlin is browsing around some company's network again. This time he's searching employees' e-mail by keywords. But he can also sniff out which Web sites workers have visited and see how long they were there and at what time. All this snooping leaves no tracks. What Conlin does is not illegal. In fact, it's probably already happening at your company. If not, just wait. Conlin's company, eSniff, sells an electronic monitoring device that allows businesses to spy on their workers. It may sound like a scene from a movie, but as either an employee or a manager, you'd better get used to it. Some 82 percent of businesses monitor their employees in some way, according to the American Management Association.

eSniff logs all Internet traffic, recording and reporting anything that's been labeled as suspicious. For example, an administrator can view e-mail log summaries and quickly drill down to the actual content of any questionable e-mail to make sure it hasn't fallen into the wrong inbox. "It's rare for eSniff to be installed on a network and not find a lot of inappropriate activity," Conlin says, adding that close to 100 percent of workers register some kind of improper use.

But Randy Dickson, a systems analyst for the Connecticut-based multimedia production firm Sonalysts Inc., found different results. His firm uses eSniff to monitor all Internet activity. Dickson was pleased to find there was less abuse going on than he thought. For instance, Dickson had been concerned about time wasted using instant messaging but found that most employee IM activity was for legitimate business use and was actually saving the company money on phone bills [35].

Virus Defenses

Is your PC protected from the latest viruses, worms, Trojan horses, and other malicious programs that can wreak havoc on your PC? Chances are it is, if it's periodically linked to the corporate network. These days, corporate antivirus protection is a centralized function of information technology. Someone installs it for you on your PC and notebook or, increasingly, distributes it over the network. The antivirus software runs in the background, popping up every so often to reassure you. The trend right now is to automate the process entirely [10].

Many companies are building defenses against the spread of viruses by centralizing the distribution and updating of **antivirus software** as a responsibility of their IS departments. Other companies are outsourcing the virus protection responsibility to their Internet service providers or telecommunications or security management companies.

One reason for this trend is that the major antivirus software companies like Trend Micro (eDoctor and PC-cillin), McAfee (VirusScan), and Symantec (Norton Antivirus) have developed network versions of their programs, which they are marketing to ISPs and others as a service they should offer to all their customers. The antivirus companies are also marketing *security suites* of software that integrate virus protection with firewalls, Web security, and content-blocking features [11]. See Figure 11.18.

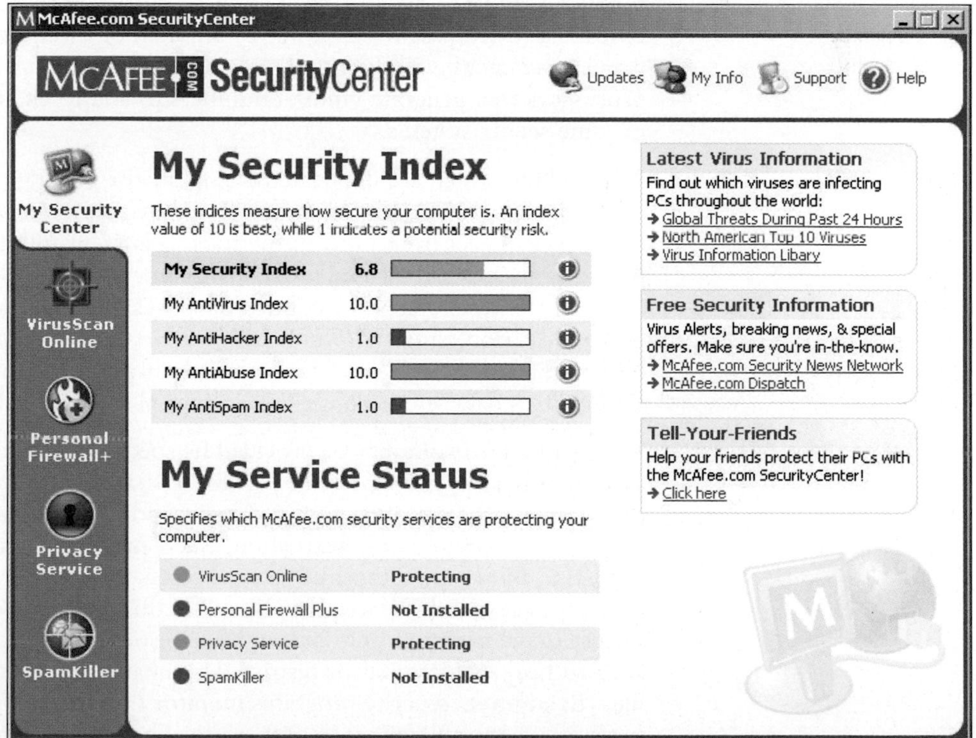

FIGURE 11.18
An example of security suite PC software that includes antivirus and firewall protection.

TruSecure and 724 Inc.: Limitations of Antivirus Software

Much of the standard antivirus software that was available at the time the Nimda worm struck failed to keep the worm from spreading, users and analysts said. The worm does a number of insidious things, such as modifying critical system files and registry keys, making every directory available as a file share, and creating a guest account with administrator privileges, recounts Russ Cooper, an analyst at TruSecure Corp., a Reston, Virginia–based security firm. "These characteristics make it incredibly difficult to clean the worm from an infected system," he notes.

"Running antivirus software alone will not fix the problem," warns Edward York, chief technical officer at 724 Inc., an application hosting service in Lompoc, California. "The server must be secured all over again, all open shares closed, the hot fixes reapplied, the guest account disabled again and all traces of any file called root.exe or admin.dll deleted from the system." Administrators also need to ensure that any registry items added by Nimda have been removed, he indicates. And, says York, until more sophisticated fixes become available, the only sure course is to disconnect infected systems from the network, reformat their hard drives, reinstall software from a clean source, and apply the appropriate security patches [36].

Other Security Measures

Let's now briefly examine a variety of security measures that are commonly used to protect business systems and networks. These include both hardware and software tools, like fault-tolerant computers and security monitors, and security policies and procedures, like passwords and backup files. All are part of an integrated security management effort at many companies today.

Security Codes

Typically, a multilevel **password** system is used for security management. First, an end user logs on to the computer system by entering his or her unique identification code, or user ID. Second, the end user is asked to enter a password to gain access into the system. (Passwords should be changed frequently and consist of unusual combinations of upper- and lowercase letters and numbers.) Third, to access an individual file, a unique file name must be entered. In some systems, the password to read the contents of a file is different from that required to write to a file (change its contents). This feature adds another level of protection to stored data resources. However, for even stricter security, passwords can be scrambled, or *encrypted*, to avoid their theft or improper use, as we will discuss shortly. In addition, *smart cards*, which contain microprocessors that generate random numbers to add to an end user's password, are used in some secure systems.

Backup Files

Backup files, which are duplicate files of data or programs, are another important security measure. Files can also be protected by *file retention* measures that involve storing copies of files from previous periods. If current files are destroyed, the files from previous periods can be used to reconstruct new current files. Sometimes, several generations of files are kept for control purposes. Thus, master files from several recent periods of processing (known as *child*, *parent*, and *grandparent* files) may be kept for backup purposes. Such files may be stored off-premises, that is, in a location away from a company's data center, sometimes in special storage vaults in remote locations.

Security Monitors

Security of a network may be provided by specialized system software packages known as **system security monitors**. See Figure 11.19. System security monitors are programs that monitor the use of computer systems and networks and protect them from unauthorized use, fraud, and destruction. Such programs provide the security measures needed to allow only authorized users to access the networks. For example, identification codes and passwords are frequently used for this purpose. Security monitors also control the use of the hardware, software, and data resources of a computer system. For example, even authorized users may be restricted to the use of certain devices, programs, and data files. In addition, security programs monitor the use of computer networks and collect statistics on any attempts at improper use. They then produce reports to assist in maintaining the security of the network.

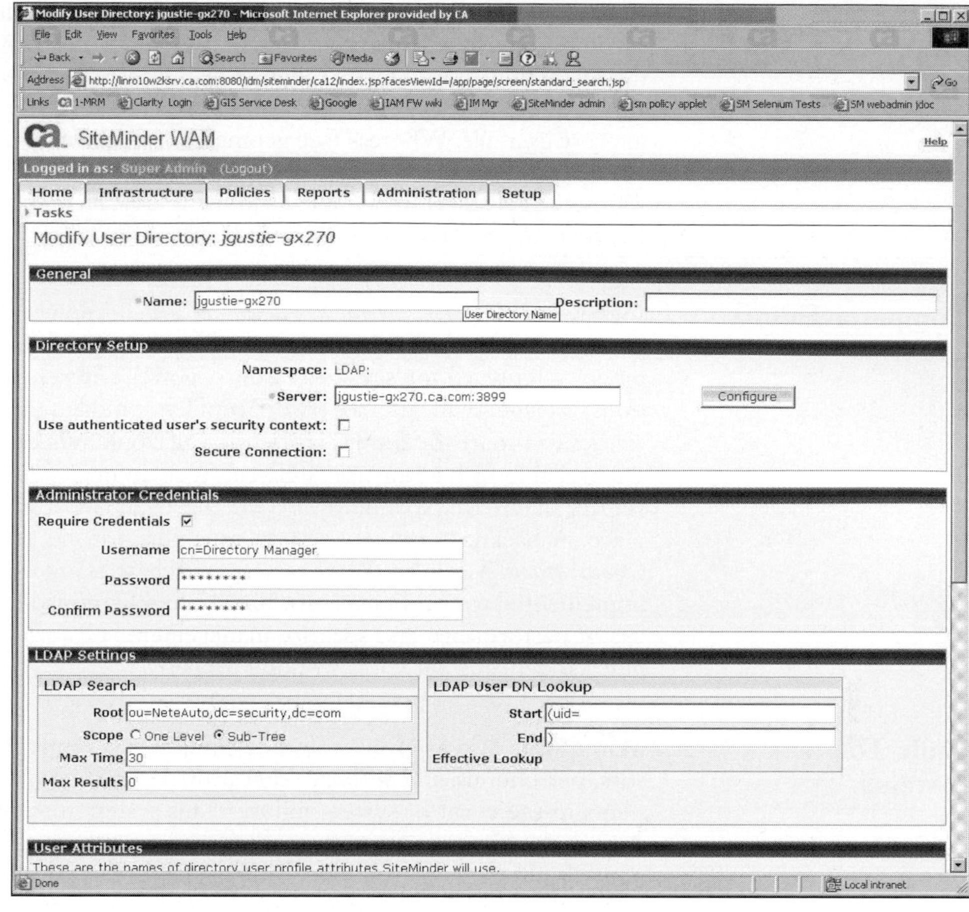

FIGURE 11.19
The eTrust security monitor manages a variety of security functions for major corporate networks, including monitoring the status of Web-based applications throughout a network.

Biometric Security

Biometric security is a fast-growing area of computer security. These are security measures provided by computer devices that measure physical traits that make each individual unique, such as voice verification, fingerprints, hand geometry, signature dynamics, keystroke analysis, retina scanning, face recognition, and genetic pattern analysis. Biometric control devices use special-purpose sensors to measure and digitize a biometric profile of a person's fingerprints, voice, or other physical trait. The digitized signal is processed and compared to a previously processed profile of the individual stored on magnetic disk. If the profiles match, the individual is allowed entry into a computer network and given access to secure system resources [2]. See Figure 11.20.

FIGURE 11.20
An evaluation of common biometric security techniques based on user requirements, accuracy, and cost.

Evaluation of Biometric Techniques

	User Criteria		System Criteria	
	Intrusiveness	Effort	Accuracy	Cost
Dynamic signature verification	Excellent	Fair	Fair	Excellent
Face geometry	Good	Good	Fair	Good
Finger scan	Fair	Good	Good	Good
Hand geometry	Fair	Good	Fair	Fair
Passive iris scan	Poor	Excellent	Excellent	Poor
Retina scan	Poor	Poor	Very good	Fair
Voice print	Very good	Poor	Fair	Very good

Notice that the examples of biometric security listed in Figure 11.20 are rated according to the degree of intrusiveness (how much the technique interrupts a user) and the relative amount of effort required by the user to authenticate. Also, the relative accuracy and cost of each are assessed. As you can see, trade-offs in these four areas exist in every example. Whereas face geometry is judged easy on the user in terms of intrusiveness and effort, its accuracy is not considered as high as that of other methods. Biometrics is still in its infancy, and many new technologies are being developed to improve on accuracy while minimizing user effort.

Computer Failure Controls

"Sorry, our computer systems are down" is a well-known phrase to many end users. A variety of controls can prevent such computer failure or minimize its effects. Computer systems fail for several reasons—power failures, electronic circuitry malfunctions, telecommunications network problems, hidden programming errors, computer viruses, computer operator errors, and electronic vandalism. For example, computers are available with automatic and remote maintenance capabilities. Programs of preventive maintenance of hardware and management of software updates are commonplace. A backup computer system capability can be arranged with *disaster recovery organizations.* Major hardware or software changes are usually carefully scheduled and implemented to avoid problems. Finally, highly trained data center personnel and the use of performance and security management software help keep a company's computer system and networks working properly.

Fault-Tolerant Systems

Many firms also use **fault-tolerant** computer systems that have redundant processors, peripherals, and software that provide a *fail-over* capability to back up components in the event of system failure. This system may provide a *fail-safe* capability, so that the computer system continues to operate at the same level even if there is a major hardware or software failure. However, many fault-tolerant computer systems offer a *fail-soft* capability, so the computer system can continue to operate at a reduced but acceptable level in the event of a major system failure. Figure 11.21 outlines some of the fault-tolerant capabilities used in many computer systems and networks [21].

FIGURE 11.21
Methods of fault tolerance in computer-based information systems.

Layer	Threats	Fault-Tolerant Methods
Applications	Environment, hardware, and software faults	Application-specific redundancy and rollback to previous checkpoint
Systems	Outages	System isolation, data security, system integrity
Databases	Data errors	Separation of transactions and safe updates, complete transaction histories, backup files
Networks	Transmission errors	Reliable controllers; safe asynchrony and handshaking; alternative routing; error-detecting and error-correcting codes
Processes	Hardware and software faults	Alternative computations, rollback to checkpoints
Files	Media errors	Replication of critical data on different media and sites; archiving, backup, retrieval
Processors	Hardware faults	Instruction retry; error-correcting codes in memory and processing; replication; multiple processors, and memories

Visa International: Fault-Tolerant Systems

"There is no such thing as 99.9 percent reliability; it has to be 100 percent," demands Richard L. Knight, senior vice president for operations at Inovant Inc., the Visa International subsidiary that runs its data centers. "Anything less than 100 percent, and I'm looking for a job." The company has had 98 minutes of downtime in 12 years. Visa fights the battle against outages and defects on two broad fronts: Its physical processing plant is protected by multiple layers of redundancy and backups, and the company's IT shop has raised software testing to a fine art.

There are more than 1 billion Visa payment cards outstanding around the world, spawning $2 trillion in transactions per year for 23 million merchants and automated teller machines and Visa's 21,000 member financial institutions. "We run the biggest payments engine in the world," says Sara Garrison, senior vice president for systems development at Visa U.S.A. Inc. in Foster City, California. "If you took all the traffic on all the stock markets in the world in 24 hours, we do that on a coffee break. And our capacity grows at 20 to 30 percent year to year, so every three years, our capacity doubles."

Visa has four global processing centers to handle that load, but the Washington, D.C., facility is the largest, with half of all global payment transactions flowing through the building. It shares U.S. traffic with a center in San Mateo, California, but it can instantly pick up the full United States if San Mateo goes down.

Indeed, everything in Visa's processing infrastructure—from entire data centers to computers, individual processors, and communications switches—has a backup. Even the backups have backups [3].

Disaster Recovery

Natural and human-made disasters do happen. Hurricanes, earthquakes, fires, floods, criminal and terrorist acts, and human error can all severely damage an organization's computing resources and thus the health of the organization itself. Many companies, especially online e-commerce retailers and wholesalers, airlines, banks, and Internet service providers, for example, are crippled by losing even a few hours of computing power. Many firms could survive only a few days without computing facilities. That's why organizations develop **disaster recovery** procedures and formalize them in a *disaster recovery plan*. It specifies which employees will participate in disaster recovery and what their duties will be; what hardware, software, and facilities will be used; and the priority of applications that will be processed. Arrangements with other companies for use of alternative facilities as a disaster recovery site and off-site storage of an organization's databases are also part of an effective disaster recovery effort.

System Controls and Audits

Two final security management requirements that need to be mentioned are the development of information system controls and auditing business systems. Let's take a brief look at these two security measures.

Information System Controls

Information system controls are methods and devices that attempt to ensure the accuracy, validity, and propriety of information system activities. Information system (IS) controls must be developed to ensure proper data entry, processing techniques, storage methods, and information output. Thus, IS controls are designed to monitor and maintain the quality and security of the input, processing, output, and storage activities of any information system. See Figure 11.22.

For example, IS controls are needed to ensure the proper entry of data into a business system and thus avoid the garbage in, garbage out (GIGO) syndrome. Examples include passwords and other security codes, formatted data entry screens, and audible error signals. Computer software can include instructions to identify

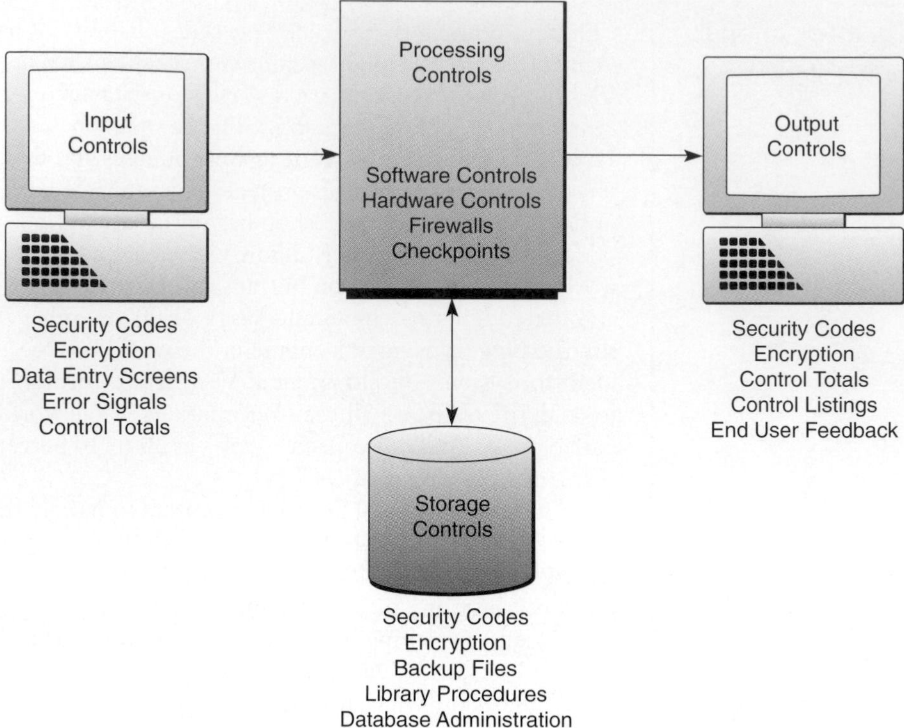

FIGURE 11.22
Examples of information system controls. Note that they are designed to monitor and maintain the quality and security of the input, processing, output, and storage activities of an information system.

incorrect, invalid, or improper input data as it enters the computer system. For example, a data entry program can check for invalid codes, data fields, and transactions, and conduct "reasonableness checks" to determine if input data exceed specified limits or are out of sequence.

Auditing IT Security

IT security management should be periodically examined, or audited, by a company's internal auditing staff or external auditors from professional accounting firms. Such audits review and evaluate whether proper and adequate security measures and management policies have been developed and implemented. This process typically involves verifying the accuracy and integrity of the software used, as well as the input of data and output produced by business applications. Some firms employ special computer security auditors for this assignment. They may use special test data to check processing accuracy and the control procedures built into the software. The auditors may develop special test programs or use audit software packages.

Another important objective of business system audits is testing the integrity of an application's *audit trail.* An **audit trail** can be defined as the presence of documentation that allows a transaction to be traced through all stages of its information processing. This journey may begin with a transaction's appearance on a source document and end with its transformation into information in a final output document or report. The audit trail of manual information systems is quite visible and easy to trace. However, computer-based information systems have changed the form of the audit trail. Now auditors must know how to search electronically through disk and tape files of past activity to follow the audit trail of today's networked computer systems.

Many times, this *electronic audit trail* takes the form of *control logs* that automatically record all computer network activity on magnetic disk or tape devices. This audit feature can be found on many online transaction processing systems, performance and security monitors, operating systems, and network control programs. Software that records all network activity is also widely used on the Internet, especially the World

FIGURE 11.23
How to protect yourself from cybercrime and other computer security threats.

Security Management for Internet Users

1. Use antivirus and firewall software and update it often to keep destructive programs off your computer.
2. Don't allow online merchants to store your credit card information for future purchases.
3. Use a hard-to-guess password that contains a mix of numbers and letters, and change it frequently.
4. Use different passwords for different Web sites and applications to keep hackers guessing.
5. Install all operating system patches and upgrades.
6. Use the most up-to-date version of your Web browser, e-mail software, and other programs.
7. Send credit card numbers only to secure sites; look for a padlock or key icons at the bottom of the browser.
8. Use a security program that gives you control over "cookies" that send information back to Web sites.
9. Install firewall software to screen traffic if you use DSL or a cable modem to connect to the Net.
10. Don't open e-mail attachments unless you know the source of the incoming message.

Wide Web, as well as on corporate intranets and extranets. Such an audit trail helps auditors check for errors or fraud but also helps IS security specialists trace and evaluate the trail of hacker attacks on computer networks.

Figure 11.23 summarizes 10 security management steps you can take to protect your computer system resources from hacking and other forms of cybercrime [13].

Summary

- **Ethical and Societal Dimensions.** The vital role of information technologies and systems in society raises serious ethical and societal issues in terms of their impact on employment, individuality, working conditions, privacy, health, and computer crime, as illustrated in Figure 11.2.

  Employment issues include the loss of jobs due to computerization and automation of work versus the jobs created to supply and support new information technologies and the business applications they make possible. The impact on working conditions involves the issues of computer monitoring of employees and the quality of the working conditions of jobs that make heavy use of information technologies. The effect of IT on individuality addresses the issues of the depersonalization, regimentation, and inflexibility of some computerized business systems.

  Health issues are raised by heavy use of computer workstations for long periods by employees, which may cause work-related health disorders. Serious privacy issues are raised by the use of IT to access or collect private information without authorization, as well as for computer profiling, computer matching, computer monitoring, and computer libel and censorship. Computer crime issues surround activities such as hacking, computer viruses and worms, cyber theft, unauthorized use at work, software piracy, and piracy of intellectual property.

  Managers, business professionals, and IS specialists can help solve the problems of improper use of IT by assuming their ethical responsibilities for the ergonomic design, beneficial use, and enlightened management of information technologies in our society.

- **Ethical Responsibility in Business.** Business and IT activities involve many ethical considerations. Basic principles of technology and business ethics can serve as guidelines for business professionals when dealing with ethical business issues that may arise in the widespread use of information technology in business and society. Examples include theories of corporate social responsibility, which outline the ethical responsibility of management and employees to a company's stockholders, stakeholders, and society, and the four principles of technology ethics summarized in Figure 11.4.

- **Security Management.** One of the most important responsibilities of the management of a company is to ensure the security and quality of its IT-enabled business activities. Security management tools and policies can ensure the accuracy, integrity, and safety of the information systems and resources of a company and thus minimize errors, fraud, and security losses in its business activities. Examples mentioned in the chapter include the use of encryption of confidential business data, firewalls, e-mail monitoring, antivirus software, security codes, backup files, security monitors, biometric security measures, computer failure controls, fault-tolerant systems, disaster recovery measures, information system controls, and security audits of business systems.

Key Terms and Concepts

These are the key terms and concepts of this chapter. The page number of their first explanation is in parentheses.

1. Antivirus software (453)
2. Audit trail (458)
3. Backup files (454)
4. Biometric security (455)
5. Business ethics (420)
6. Computer crime (426)
7. Computer matching (439)
8. Computer monitoring (441)
9. Computer virus (432)
10. Cyberlaw (440)
11. Distributed denial of service (451)
12. Disaster recovery (457)
13. Encryption (448)
14. Ergonomics (443)
15. Ethical foundations (420)
16. Fault tolerant (456)
17. Firewall (449)
18. Flaming (440)
19. Hacking (427)
20. Information system controls (457)
21. Intellectual property theft (431)
22. Opt-in/Opt-out (437)
23. Passwords (454)
24. Security management (445)
25. Software piracy (431)
26. Spamming (440)
27. Spyware/Adware (434)
28. System security monitor (454)
29. Unauthorized use (429)

Review Quiz

Match one of the key terms and concepts listed previously with one of the brief examples or definitions that follow. Try to find the best fit for the answers that seem to fit more than one term or concept. Defend your choices.

____ 1. Ensuring the accuracy, integrity, and safety of business/IT activities and resources.

____ 2. Control totals, error signals, backup files, and security codes are examples.

____ 3. Software that can control access and use of a computer system.

____ 4. A computer system can continue to operate even after a major system failure if it has this capability.

____ 5. A computer system that serves as a filter for access to and from other networks by a company's networked computers.

____ 6. Laws and regulations focused on issues related to the Internet and other forms of networked communications.

____ 7. The presence of documentation that allows a transaction to be traced through all stages of information processing.

____ 8. Using your voice or fingerprints to identify you electronically.

____ 9. A plan to continue IS operations during an emergency.

____ 10. Scrambling data during its transmission.

____ 11. Ethical choices may result from decision-making processes, cultural values, or behavioral stages.

____ 12. Managers must confront numerous ethical questions in their businesses.

____ 13. Sending unsolicited e-mail indiscriminately.

____ 14. Software that can infect a machine and transmit private information back to its owner.

____ 15. Two different perspectives on the use of private information.

____ 16. Using computers to identify individuals that fit a certain profile.

____ 17. Using computers to monitor the activities of workers.

____ 18. Overwhelming a Web site with requests for service from captive computers.

____ 19. Using computers and networks to steal money, services, software, or data.

____ 20. Using company computers to access the Internet during work hours for personal business.

____ 21. Unauthorized copying of software.

____ 22. Unauthorized copying of copyrighted material.

____ 23. Electronic breaking and entering into a computer system.

____ 24. A program makes copies of itself and destroys data and programs.

____ 25. Finds and eliminates computer viruses.

____ 26. Sending extremely critical, derogatory, and vulgar e-mail messages.

____ 27. Designing computer hardware, software, and workstations that are safe, comfortable, and easy to use.

Discussion Questions

1. What can be done to improve the security of business uses of the Internet? Give several examples of security measures and technologies you would use.
2. What potential security problems do you see in the increasing use of intranets and extranets in business? What might be done to solve such problems? Give several examples.
3. Refer to the Real World example about copying CDs and music downloading in the chapter. Is copying music CDs an ethical practice? How about Internet music downloading? Explain.
4. What are your major concerns about computer crime and privacy on the Internet? What can you do about it? Explain.
5. What is disaster recovery? How could it be implemented at your school or work?
6. Refer to the Real World Case on cyberscams and cybercriminals and the real world example about PayPal in the chapter. What are some of the possible clues that PayPal's security team and software must look for and guard against to rebuff cyberscammers? Defend your assumptions.
7. Is there an ethical crisis in business today? What role does information technology play in unethical business practices?
8. What are several business decisions that you will have to make as a manager that have both ethical and IT dimensions? Give examples to illustrate your answer.
9. Refer to the Real World Case on Lowe's, TCI, Bank of America, and ChoicePoint in the chapter. How high on the list of strategic objectives for a company do you think computer and data security should be for most companies today? Is it, in your opinion? Defend your positions based on your Internet research as well as your own experiences.
10. What would be examples of one positive and one negative effect of the use of information technologies in each of the ethical and societal dimensions illustrated in Figure 11.2? Explain several of your choices.

Analysis Exercises

1. Problems with Passwords

Authentication

Network and application managers need to know who is accessing their systems to determine appropriate access levels. Typically, they require that users create secret passwords. A secret password, known only to the user, allows an administrator to feel confident a user is who the user says he or she is. Systems administrators even have the authority to determine the characteristics of passwords. For example, they may set a minimum length and require that a password include numbers, symbols, or mixed letter case. They may also require that a user change his or her password every few weeks or months. These approaches have numerous problems:

- Users often forget complicated or frequently changing passwords, resulting in frequent calls to a help desk. The help-desk employee then faces the burden of identifying the employee by some other means and resetting the password. This process takes time and is subject to social engineering.
- Users may write down their passwords. However, this leaves passwords subject to discovery and theft.
- Users often pick the same password for many different accounts. However, someone who discovers one of these passwords then has the "keys" to all the accounts.
- Users may pick an easy-to-remember password. However, such passwords are easy to anticipate and therefore to guess. Password cracking programs cycle through entire dictionaries of English language words and common word/number combinations such as "smart1" or "2smart4U."
- Users may give away their passwords over the phone (social engineering) or via e-mail (phishing, a type of social engineering) to individuals representing themselves as a system administrator. Perhaps you have already received e-mails purportedly from a financial institution claiming identity or account difficulties and asking you to "reconfirm" your account information on their authentic-looking Web site.

As you can see, using passwords to identify a person is fraught with problems. Here are some alternatives to explore. Look up each authentication approach listed below on the Internet, describe the method in your own words (be sure to cite your sources), and briefly list the advantages and disadvantages.

a. Biometrics (biological measuring).
b. Smart cards.
c. Bio chips.

2. Your Internet Job Rights

Three Ethical Scenarios

Whether you're an employer or an employee, you should know what your rights are when it comes to Internet use in the workplace. Mark Grossman, a Florida attorney who specializes in computer and Internet law, gives answers to some basic questions.

- **Scenario 1:** Nobody told you that your Internet use in the office was being monitored. Now you've been warned you'll be fired if you use the Internet for recreational surfing again. What are your rights?

  Bottom line: When you're using your office computer, you have virtually no rights. You'd have a tough time convincing a court that the boss invaded your privacy by monitoring your use of the company PC on company time. You should probably be grateful you got a warning.

- **Scenario 2:** Your employees are abusing their Internet privileges, but you don't have an Internet usage policy. What do you do?

  Bottom line: Although the law isn't fully developed in this area, courts are taking a straightforward approach: If it's a company computer, the company can control the way it's used. You don't need an Internet usage policy to prevent inappropriate use of your company computers. To protect yourself in the future, distribute an Internet policy to your employees as soon as possible.

- **Scenario 3:** Employee John Doe downloads adult material to his PC at work, and employee Jane Smith sees it. Smith then proceeds to sue the company for sexual harassment. As the employer, are you liable?

  Bottom line: Whether it comes from the Internet or from a magazine, adult material simply has no place in the office. So Smith could certainly sue the company for allowing a sexually hostile environment. The best defense is for the company to have an Internet usage policy that prohibits visits to adult sites. Of course, you have to follow through. If someone is looking at adult material in the office, you must at least send the offending employee a written reprimand. If the company lacks a strict Internet policy, though, Smith could prevail in court.

a. Do you agree with the advice of attorney Mark Grossman in each of the scenarios? Why or why not?

b. What would your advice be? Explain your positions.

c. Identify any ethical principles you may be using in explaining your position in each of the scenarios.

3. Exploiting Security Weaknesses

Social Engineering

An employee who needs permission to access an electronic workspace, database, or other information systems resource typically fills in a request form and obtains approval from the responsible manager. The manager then routes the request to one of the system's administrators.

Highly trusted and well-trained systems administrators spend a significant amount of time doing nothing more technical than adding or removing names from access control lists. In large organizations, it's not unusual for systems administrators to have never met any of the people involved in a specific request. The administrators may not even work in the same office.

Hackers have learned to take advantage of this approach to access authorization. They begin by "probing" an organization. The hacker doesn't expect to compromise the system during this initial probe. He or she simply starts by making a few phone calls to learn who is responsible for granting access and how to apply. A little more probing helps the hacker learn who's who within the organization's structure. Some organizations even post this information online in the form of employee directories. With this information in hand, the hacker knows who to talk to, what to ask for, and what names to use to sound convincing. The hacker is now ready to try to impersonate an employee and trick a systems administrator into revealing a password and unwittingly granting unauthorized access.

Organizations determine who needs access to what applications. They also need a system through which they can authenticate the identity of an individual making a request. Finally, they need to manage this process both effectively and inexpensively.

a. Describe the business problems presented by this exercise.

b. Suggest several ways to reduce an organization's exposure to social engineering.

c. Prepare an orientation memo to new hires in your IT department describing "social engineering." Suggest several ways employees can avoid being tricked by hackers.

4. Privacy Statements

The Spyware Problem

Web surfers may feel anonymous as they use the Internet, but that feeling isn't always justified. IP addresses, cookies, site log-in procedures, and credit card purchases all help track how often users visit a site and what pages they view. Some companies go further.

Some free screensaver software and peer-to-peer file sharing come with "spyware" embedded within their applications. Once loaded, these applications run in the background. What they actually track depends on the specific software. To stay on the "right side" of U.S. law, these companies outline their software's functions in general terms and include this information in the small print within their end-user licensing agreement (EULA) and/or privacy policy. In fact, these agreements may even include a stipulation that users not disable any part of their software as a condition for free use.

Because most users don't read these policies, they have no idea what privacy rights they may have given up. They indeed get their free file sharing program or screen saver, but they may be getting a lot more. Some spyware programs even remain on hard drives and stay active after users have uninstalled their "free" software.

a. Use a search engine to search for "spyware," "spyware removal," "adware," or other related terms. Prepare a one-page summary of your results. Include URLs for online sources.

b. Select three of your favorite Web sites and print out their privacy policies. What do they share in common? How do they differ?

c. Write your own Web site privacy policy, striking a balance between customer and business needs.

REAL WORLD CASE 3 Western Corporate Federal Credit Union and Others: Managing Information Security

Christofer Hoff is on a mission. As the director of information security at Western Corporate Federal Credit Union (WesCorp), Hoff has launched an initiative to quantify the benefits of information security spending for business executives at the San Dimas, California–based company.

The constantly evolving technology and threat environment and the difficulty of attaching a specific monetary value to information assets make it hard to come up with traditional return-on-investment numbers, Hoff says. So the focus instead is on gathering corporate metrics that show how the company can reduce risk exposure and avoid costs—such as those related to virus attacks—by implementing the appropriate security measures.

As part of this effort, Hoff's team is implementing a process methodology called OCTAVE from Carnegie Mellon University's Software Engineering Institute. OCTAVE helps companies identify infrastructure vulnerabilities, prioritize information assets, and create asset-specific threat profiles and mitigation plans.

The OCTAVE (Operationally Critical Threat, Asset and Vulnerability Evaluation) methodology rests on three sets of principles:

Risk Evaluation

- **Self-direction** by people in the organization who take responsibility.
- **Adaptable measures** that can change with technology.
- **A defined process** and standard evaluation procedures.
- **A foundation for a continual process** that improves security over time.

Risk Management

- **A forward-looking view** that explores changing relationships among assets, threats, and vulnerabilities.
- **A focus on a "critical few"** security issues.
- **Integrated management** of security policies and strategies with those of the organization.

Organizational and Cultural

- **Open communication** of risk information and activities built around collaboration.
- **A global perspective** on risk in the context of the organization's mission and business objectives.
- **Teamwork** for an interdisciplinary approach.

It's all about showing "reduction of risk on investment," according to Hoff. "I'm not interested in showing that I've improved the bottom line. What I can show is how we have managed risk on behalf of the company and reduced our risk exposure."

Hoff is among a growing number of security managers who say it's time to approach information security as an operational risk management issue rather than a function focused solely on implementing tactical fixes for every new threat that surfaces.

The need to comply with regulations such as the Sarbanes-Oxley Act, the Health Insurance Portability and Accountability Act, and California's SB 1386 is one of the primary factors pushing companies to take a more business-oriented look at their information security measures. Also lending urgency to the situation is a wave of legislation that lawmakers are considering in response to a series of well-publicized data compromises at Bank of America Corp., ChoicePoint Inc., and LexisNexis Group.

Evolving threats and a greater exposure to risk are also pushing the need for a more strategic view of security. The growing use of wireless and handheld technologies and the tendency to connect internal networks with those of suppliers, partners, and customers have dramatically increased security risks and the potential consequences of a breach.

"All of a sudden, there are a lot of new stakeholders in information security," including regulators, shareholders, customers, employees, and business partners, recognizes Carolee Birchall, vice president and senior risk officer at BMO Bank of Montreal in Toronto. "All of these groups have different expectations of IT, and they all come to a head around information security."

The trend calls for a fundamental rethinking of security objectives, say security managers such as Hoff. The goal isn't to completely eliminate all risk, because that is unrealistic, acknowledges Kirk Herath, chief privacy officer at Nationwide Mutual Insurance Co. in Columbus, Ohio. Rather, it's to understand the broad nature and scope of the threats to your specific situation.

You should base mitigation measures on the probability of loss or disruption from those risks. The focus is not on point technologies but rather on higher-level issues such as system availability, recovery, and incident response, according to Herath.

A risk-mitigation approach starts with a detailed understanding of the information assets that you want to protect and what exactly you want to protect them against, recommends Vinnie Cottone, vice president of infrastructure services at Eaton Vance Distributors Inc., a financial services firm in Boston. The company is currently implementing security changes aimed at addressing five specific issues identified during a corporatewide IT and business risk-assessment exercise. The issues include a need for stronger user authentication and measures for securing and enforcing policies on all endpoint devices—such as laptops and wireless systems—that attempt to log in to the Eaton Vance network.

"We took a look at every possible [information security] threat to Eaton Vance, and from there we came out with a lot of 'what if' scenarios and then determined what we should do" to deal with them, Cottone describes.

But most security managers acknowledge that the daily tasks of dealing with unreliable software code and chasing the latest viruses, worms, and spyware leave little time or resources to focus on such big-picture strategies.

Changing business requirements and the growing complexity of threats can also keep security managers tied to tactical issues, even if they don't want to be. Adding to the challenge is a troubling disconnect between security organizations and business units, security managers complain.

Lloyd Hession, chief information security officer at Radianz Inc., a New York–based provider of communications services to the financial services industry, says a common view of executives is, "We have spent all this money on antivirus tools, Web filters, and firewalls, and why hasn't that stopped this problem?" Security managers claim they're too often seen as purveyors of fear, uncertainty, and doubt who have little understanding of business requirements.

To change that image, they need to help business managers understand the trade-offs that have to be made to accommodate a new security measure. And that means no geekspeak, says Cottone. "You really can't talk technical or any kind of jargon" when communicating security strategy to the business side, he urges.

The key message, says Hession, is that information security is a business problem that is "not addressed simply by the firewalls and antivirus [tools] that are already in place."

Source: Adapted from Jaikumar Vijayan, "Strategic Security" and "The OCTAVE Approach," *Computerworld*, April 11, 2005.

CASE STUDY QUESTIONS

1. Why is information security a major concern for many companies today? What are security managers doing to improve their companies' information security? What else should they be doing?
2. Why does the OCTAVE methodology promise to improve security in organizations? Does it work? Explain your answer with examples from the case or other sources on the Internet.
3. What does Lloyd Hession mean when he says information security is "not addressed simply by the firewalls and antivirus [tools] that are already in place"? What other security measures does he recommend to improve information security? What would you add to his recommendations? Explain your reasoning.

REAL WORLD ACTIVITIES

1. The focus on information security is an important one for modern organizations of all sizes. Use the Internet to find examples of companies that are striving to improve their information security. What approaches and methods are they using to improve the security of their companies?
2. Private and corporate information is under attack from a wide variety of sources. Break into small groups with your classmates and discuss the various threats to information security. Are you doing your share to protect your information?

CHAPTER 12

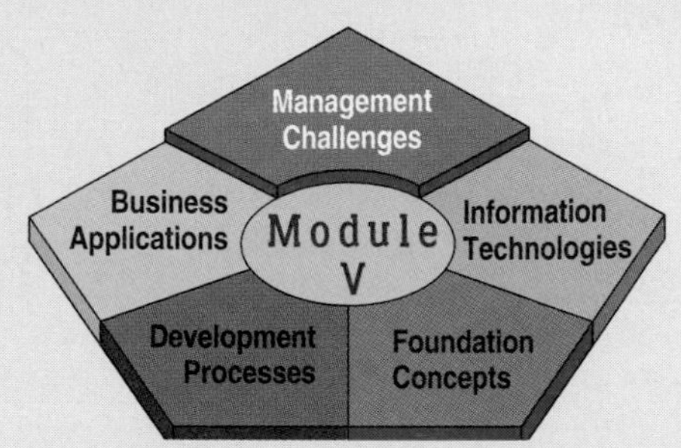

ENTERPRISE AND GLOBAL MANAGEMENT OF INFORMATION TECHNOLOGY

Chapter Highlights

Learning Objectives

After reading and studying this chapter, you should be able to:

1. Identify each of the three components of information technology management and use examples to illustrate how they might be implemented in a business.
2. Explain how failures in IT management can be reduced by the involvement of business managers in IT planning and management.
3. Identify several cultural, political, and geoeconomic challenges that confront managers in the management of global information technologies.
4. Explain the effect on global business/IT strategy of the trend toward a transnational business strategy by international business organizations.
5. Identify several considerations that affect the choice of IT applications, IT platforms, data access policies, and systems development methods by a global business enterprise.
6. Understand the fundamental concepts of outsourcing and offshoring, as well as the primary reasons for selecting such an approach to IS/IT management.

SECTION I Managing Information Technology

Business and IT

The strategic and operational importance of information technology in business is no longer questioned. As the 21st century unfolds, many companies throughout the world are intent on transforming themselves into global business powerhouses through major investments in global e-business, e-commerce, and other IT initiatives. Thus, there is a real need for business managers and professionals to understand how to manage this vital organizational function. In this section, we explore how the IS function can be organized and managed and stress the importance of a customer and business value focus for the management of information technologies. Whether you plan to be an entrepreneur and run your own business, a manager in a corporation, or a business professional, managing information systems and technologies will be one of your major responsibilities. See Figure 12.1.

Read the Real World Case on the next page. We can learn a lot from this case about how business and IT executives meet the challenges of successfully managing information technology in business.

Managing Information Technology

As we have seen throughout this text, information technology is an essential component of business success for companies today. But information technology is also a vital business resource that must be properly managed. Thus, we have also seen many real-world examples in which the management of information technologies plays a pivotal role in ensuring the success or contributing to the failure of a company's strategic business initiatives. Therefore, managing the information systems and technologies that support the modern business processes of companies today is a major challenge for both business and IT managers and professionals.

How should information technology be managed? Figure 12.2 illustrates one popular approach to **managing information technology** in a large company [4]. This managerial approach has three major components:

- **Managing the joint development and implementation of business/IT strategies.** Led by the CEO (chief executive officer) and CIO (chief information officer), proposals are developed by business and IT managers and professionals regarding the use of IT to support the strategic business priorities of the company. This business/IT planning process *aligns* IT with strategic business goals. The process also includes evaluating the business case for investing in the development and implementation of each proposed business/IT project.
- **Managing the development and implementation of new business/IT applications and technologies.** This step is the primary responsibility of the CIO and CTO (chief technology officer). This area of IT management involves managing the processes for information systems development and implementation we discussed in Chapter 10, as well as the responsibility for research into the strategic business uses of new information technologies.
- **Managing the IT organization and the IT infrastructure.** The CIO and IT managers share responsibility for managing the work of IT professionals who are typically organized into a variety of project teams and other organizational subunits. In addition, they are responsible for managing the IT infrastructure of hardware, software, databases, telecommunications networks, and other IT resources, which must be acquired, operated, monitored, and maintained.

Let's look at a real-world example.

REAL WORLD CASE 1 Hewlett-Packard: Managing Radical Change in IT to Support New Business Goals

When Randy Mott joined Wal-Mart fresh out of college in 1978, its in-house tech staff had only 30 members, and company founder Sam Walton had not yet become a believer in the power of computing to revolutionize retailing. But Mott and his cohorts developed a network of computerized distribution centers that made it simple to open and run new stores with cookie-cutter efficiency.

Then in the early 1990s, Mott, by this time chief information officer, persuaded higher-ups to invest in a so-called data warehouse. That let the company collect and sift customer data to analyze buying trends as no company ever had—right down to which flavor of Pop-Tarts sells best at a given store. "Information technology wasn't Mr. Sam's favorite topic. He viewed it as a necessary evil," recalls fellow Wal-Mart Stores alumnus Charlie McMurtry, who has worked with Mott for years. "But later, Randy got [Walton's] ultimate compliment. He said, 'Man, you'd make a great store manager.'"

By the time Mott took his latest job in the summer of 2005 as CIO of Hewlett-Packard Co., he had become a rock star of sorts among the corporate techie set—an executive who understood not only technology and how it could be used to improve a business but also how to deliver those benefits. In addition to his 22-year stint at Wal-Mart, Mott moved to Dell for 5 years to help the top PC maker hone its already huge IT advantage. By melding nearly 100 separate systems into a single data warehouse, Mott's team enabled Dell to quickly spot rising inventory for a particular chip, for instance, so the company could offer online promotions for devices containing that part before the price fell too steeply.

FIGURE 12.1

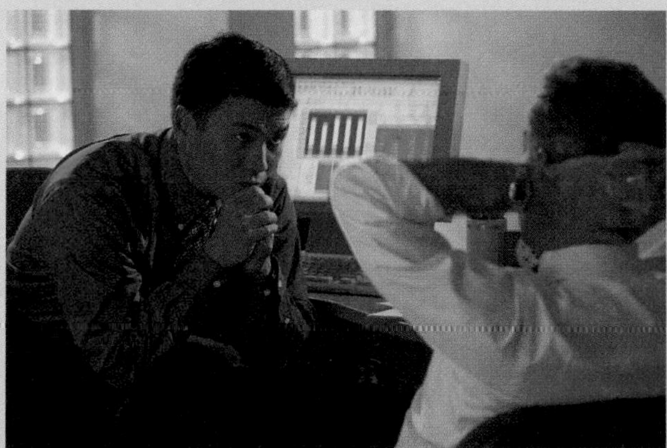

Companies like Hewlett-Packard face major challenges when implementing changes to make the IT function a more efficient and vital contributor to their business success.

Now Mott, 49, is embarking on his boldest and most challenging project yet: a three-year, $1 billion-plus makeover of HP's internal tech systems. On May 17, 2006, the company announced it would replace 85 loosely connected data centers around the world with six cutting-edge facilities—two each in Austin, Atlanta, and Houston. Mott is pushing sweeping changes in the way HP/IT operates, slashing thousands of smaller projects at the decentralized company to focus on a few corporatewide initiatives, including scrapping 784 isolated databases for one companywide data warehouse. Says Mott: "We want to make HP the envy of the technology world."

If it works, Mott's makeover could have more impact than any new HP advertising campaign, printer, or PC and could turbocharge the company's already impressive turnaround since new CEO Mark Hurd took over in April 2005 after leaving his job as head of NCR. If Mott is successful, HP's annual spending on tech should be cut in half in the years ahead, from $3.5 billion in 2005, say insiders.

More important, a Wal-Mart–style data warehouse could help HP make headway on its most vexing problem in recent years: how to capitalize on its vast breadth. Although HP sells everything from $10 ink cartridges to multimillion-dollar supercomputers, the company has operated more like a conglomerate of separate companies than a one-stop tech superstore. "We shipped 55 million printers, 30 million PCs, and 2 million servers last year," says CEO Hurd. "If we can integrate all that information, it would enable us to know exactly how we're doing in Chicago on a given day, or whether the CIO of a big customer also happens to own any of our products at home."

It's a gargantuan challenge, even for someone with the credentials of Randall D. Mott. For one, this will be his first real fix-it job. FedEx CIO Rob Carter, who counts himself a big fan, points out that Mott had the advantage at Wal-Mart and Dell of building infrastructure largely from scratch. "Randy never had to go corral all the horses that had gotten out of the barn," comments Carter.

Also, Mott's initiatives may stir up a hornet's nest within HP. They will likely require thousands of layoffs in the IT function, while demanding the support of remaining staffers in a company that has long resisted centralized control. Mott is testing the limits of the HP culture, taking away the right of thousands of IT workers to purchase their own tech equipment and, for some, their ability to telecommute. That's not to mention the stress of tearing up the tech infrastructure—and putting many existing IT initiatives on hold—at the same time that CEO Hurd is demanding a revamp of everything from sales to product lines. "Everyone is already averaging 60 hours a week," gripes one veteran HP manager, who requested anonymity. "At some point, you hit a breaking point."

But Mott has the absolute backing of Hurd, who began recruiting him shortly after arriving at HP in February 2005.

The pair have known each other for years. At both Wal-Mart and Dell, Mott bought NCR data warehousing gear from Hurd, who was a leading evangelist for the technology during his years at the helm of NCR. Hurd eventually wooed Mott in July on the strength of a $15 million pay package and a promise to support him if he'd sign on for the aggressive three-year transformation.

Since then, Mott has been methodically building his team. He has quietly added nearly a dozen respected executives from his days at Wal-Mart and Dell, including McMurtry and Ron Griffin, the former CIO of Home Depot who is now HP's senior vice president in charge of application development and support. A key turning point came in September 2005, when Mott won the HP board's commitment to buy or build the new data centers and the servers, storage banks, and networking gear to fill them.

"Randy is the right leader at the right time for HP," argues Michele Goins, a long-time HP executive who now reports to Mott and who runs the IT systems for the huge printer division. "If he'd come here three years ago, he would have left. Carly [former CEO Carleton S. Fiorina] didn't understand IT. She had a lot of things she was focused on, but IT wasn't one of them."

Still, Mott's greatest strength may be that while a technologist, he has the management skills to actually make IT take root in a company's culture. Linda M. Dillman, a one-time Wal-Mart CIO and now its executive vice president for risk management and benefits administration, recalls how Mott championed the deployment of IT by showing how it achieved Wal-Mart's business goals. "Randy is very, very pragmatic," explains Dillman. "He understands you can't just follow a dream."

Underlings say Mott's low-key Southern charm belies an intensity that typically brings him into the office by 6:15 a.m. He has no patience for quick summaries during grueling, two-day business reviews he convenes once a month. But he disdains long picture shows too. "People will want to give him 50,000-foot PowerPoint presentations, but he wants the numbers—not the pictures," says Sue Braun, another new HP arrival who worked with Mott at Wal-Mart and Dell.

That certainly jibes with CEO Hurd's view of the world, which is why he's backing the centralizing of HP's balkanized information systems, even while working to decentralize the operational control grabbed by Fiorina during her tenure. The idea is to make sure all of HP's businesses are working off the same set of data and to give them the tools to make the best decisions quickly for the entire company—say, a single customer management system, so executives can know the full breadth of what any account buys from HP.

But Hurd and Mott also believe in speed over endless analysis. So within months of his arrival, Mott had trimmed 1,200 individual projects—such as an e-learning application for new hires—to just 500. But he also imposed real deadlines to make sure projects were completed. That way, teams could reap real benefits, then move on to the next priority. "In the past, there was never any end date, just lots of phases," describes Mott. Whereas HP previously had five or more IT workers in 100 different locations, he decided to reduce that to 25. To break the news of impending layoffs, Mott held close to 20 "coffee talks" with HP employees in various countries. "I tell them that part of the reason we need to move so fast is that the problem doesn't get better with time," Mott comments.

No doubt, that could lead to some trying times in the next year. But the benefits may be surprising. For example, HP has already built its own fiber-optic network to connect the six new data centers to outposts around the globe—an approach that should cut its monthly networking bill to phone companies by 40 percent. It's enough to prompt HP veterans such as Goins to wonder if Mott can do for his new employer what he did for his first one. "When I listen to Randy, I think 'Why can't we have the kind of success that Wal-Mart has had?'"

Source: Adapted from Peter Burrows, "Stopping the Sprawl at HP," *BusinessWeek*, May 29, 2006.

CASE STUDY QUESTIONS

1. Will the initiatives being undertaken by CIO Randy Mott to implement major changes to the IT function at HP make IT a more efficient and vital contributor to HP's business success? Defend your position on each of the major initiatives he is implementing.
2. Do you approve of the change management job Mott is doing, including his meetings with HP employees throughout the world and having "coffee talks" with them? Why or why not?
3. Assume you have been hired as a management consultant or coach to CIO Mott. What are several suggestions you might give him to help him successfully implement his ambitious plans for IT changes at HP? Defend your proposals.

REAL WORLD ACTIVITIES

1. Use the Internet to discover the current financial performance of HP and determine if HP's major changes and spending on IT are being viewed as a positive or negative contributor to its performance. Then investigate HP's competitive performance in market share, units sold, and other areas compared with Dell, Lenovo, Sun, IBM, and any other competitors you find, as well as the reasons given for HP's current competitive stance.
2. Implementing major changes as CIO Mott is doing causes many employees to lose their jobs and much angst on the part of some of those who remain, whose jobs and work styles may also change. Break into small groups with your classmates to discuss how you would handle a change management process at HP or any other company faced with implementing similar decisions.

FIGURE 12.2
The major components of information technology management. Note the executives with primary responsibilities in each area.

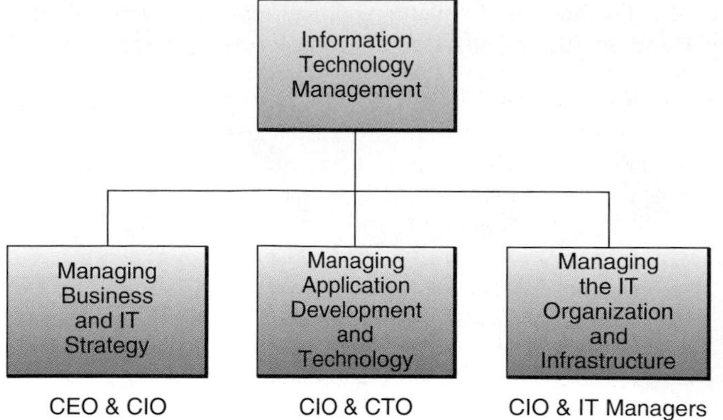

Avnet Marshall: Managing IT

Figure 12.3 contrasts how Avnet Marshall's information technology management differs from conventional IT management [4]. Notice that it uses the model of IT management illustrated in Figure 12.2. For example, in technology management, Avnet Marshall uses a best-of-breed approach that supports business needs instead of enforcing a standardized and homogeneous choice of hardware, software, database, and networking technologies. In managing its IT organization, Avnet Marshall hires IS professionals who can integrate IT with business. These IS professionals are organized in workgroups around business/IT initiatives that focus on building IT-enabled business services for customers.

Business/IT Planning

Figure 12.4 illustrates the **business/IT planning process**, which focuses on discovering innovative approaches to satisfying a company's customer value and business value goals [10]. This planning process leads to the development of strategies and business models for new business applications, processes, products, and services. Then a company

FIGURE 12.3
Comparing conventional and e-business-driven IT management approaches.

IT Management	Conventional Practices	Avnet Marshall's Business/IT Practices
Technology Management	• Approach to IT infrastructure may sacrifice match with business needs for vendor homogeneity and technology platform choices.	• Best-of-breed approach to IT infrastructure in which effective match with business needs takes precedence over commitment to technology platform choices and vendor homogeneity.
Managing the IT Organization	• Hire "best by position" who can bring specific IT expertise. • Departments organized around IT expertise with business liaisons and explicit delegation of tasks. • IT projects have separable cost/value considerations. Funding typically allocated within constraints of yearly budget for IT function.	• Hire "best athletes," IS professionals who can flexibly integrate new IT and business competencies. • Evolving workgroups organized around emerging IT-intensive business initiatives with little explicit delegation of tasks. • IT funding typically based on value proposition around business opportunity related to building services for customers. IT project inseparable part of business initiative.

FIGURE 12.4 The business/IT planning process emphasizes a customer and business value focus for developing business strategies and models and an IT architecture for business applications.

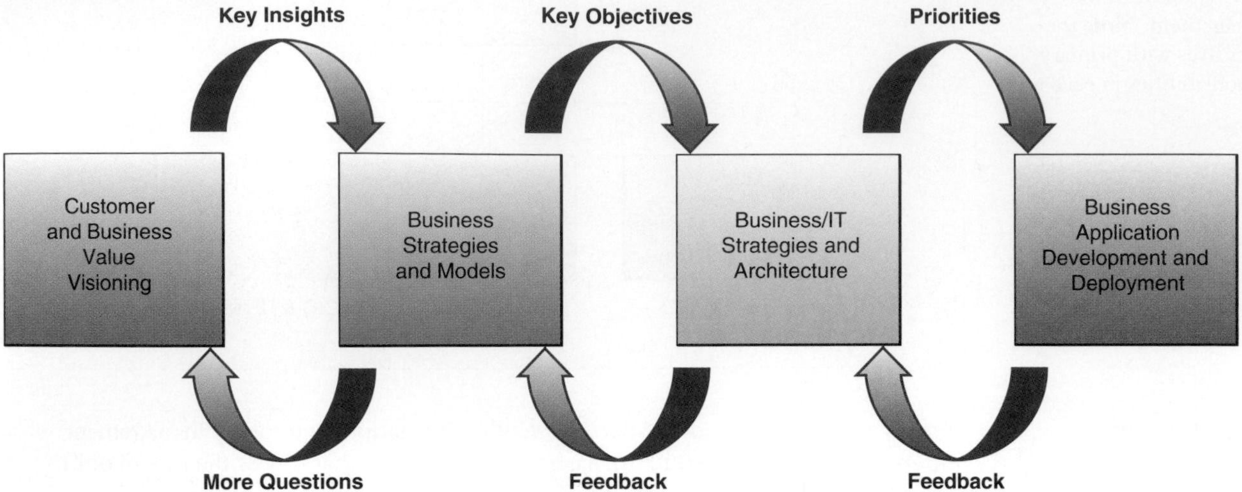

can develop IT strategies and an IT architecture that supports building and implementing its newly planned business applications.

Both the CEO and the CIO of a company must manage the development of complementary business and IT strategies to meet its customer value and business value vision. This *co-adaptation* process is necessary because, as we have seen so often in this text, information technologies are a fast changing but vital component in many strategic business initiatives. The business/IT planning process has three major components:

- **Strategy development.** Developing business strategies that support a company's business vision. For example, using information technology to create innovative e-business systems that focus on customer and business value. We will discuss this process in more detail shortly.
- **Resource management.** Developing strategic plans for managing or outsourcing a company's IT resources, including IS personnel, hardware, software, data, and network resources.
- **Technology architecture.** Making strategic IT choices that reflect an information technology architecture designed to support a company's business/IT initiatives.

Information Technology Architecture

The IT architecture created by the strategic business/IT planning process is a conceptual design, or blueprint, that includes the following major components:

- **Technology platform.** The Internet, intranets, extranets, and other networks, computer systems, system software, and integrated enterprise application software provide a computing and communications infrastructure, or platform, that supports the strategic use of information technology for e-business, e-commerce, and other business/IT applications.
- **Data resources.** Many types of operational and specialized databases, including data warehouses and Internet/intranet databases (as reviewed in Chapter 5), store and provide data and information for business processes and decision support.
- **Applications architecture.** Business applications of information technology are designed as an integrated architecture *or portfolio* of enterprise systems that support strategic business initiatives, as well as cross-functional business processes. For example, an applications architecture should include support for developing

FIGURE 12.5
Comparing business/IT strategic and application planning approaches.

Conventional IT Planning	Avnet Marshall's Business/IT Planning
• Strategic alignment: IT strategy tracks specified enterprise strategy. • CEO endorses IT vision shaped through CIO. • IT application development projects functionally organized as technological solutions to business issues. • Phased application development based on learning from pilot projects.	• Strategic improvisation: IT strategy and enterprise business strategy co-adaptively unfold based on the clear guidance of a focus on customer value. • CEO proactively shapes IT vision jointly with CIO as part of e-business strategy. • IT application development projects colocated with e-business initiatives to form centers of IT-intensive business expertise. • Perpetual application development based on continuous learning from rapid deployment and prototyping with end user involvement.

and maintaining the inter-enterprise supply chain applications and integrated enterprise resource planning and customer relationship management applications discussed in Chapter 7.

- **IT organization.** The organizational structure of the IS function within a company and the distribution of IS specialists are designed to meet the changing strategies of a business. The form of the IT organization depends on the managerial philosophy and business/IT strategies formulated during the strategic planning process.

Avnet Marshall: Business/IT Planning

Figure 12.5 outlines Avnet Marshall's planning process for business/IT initiatives and compares it with conventional IT planning approaches [4]. Avnet Marshall weaves both business and IT strategic planning together *coadaptively* under the guidance of the CEO and the CIO instead of developing IT strategy by just tracking and supporting business strategies. Avnet Marshall also locates IT application development projects within the business units that are involved in an e-business initiative to form centers of business/IT expertise throughout the company. Finally, Avnet Marshall uses a prototyping application development process with rapid deployment of new business applications instead of a traditional systems development approach. This application development strategy trades the risk of implementing incomplete applications with the benefits of gaining competitive advantages from early deployment of new e-business services to employees, customers, and other stakeholders and of involving them in the "fine-tuning" phase of application development.

Managing the IT Function

A radical shift is occurring in corporate computing—think of it as the recentralization of management. It's a step back toward the 1970s, when a data-processing manager could sit at a console and track all the technology assets of the corporation. Then came the 1980s and early 1990s. Departments got their own PCs and software; client/server networks sprang up all across companies.

Three things have happened in the past few years: The Internet boom inspired businesses to connect all those networks; companies put on their intranets essential applications without which their businesses could not function; and it became apparent that maintaining PCs on a network is very, very expensive. Such changes create an urgent need for centralization [12].

Organizing IT

In the early years of computing, the development of large mainframe computers and telecommunications networks and terminals caused a **centralization** of computer hardware and software, databases, and information specialists at the corporate level of organizations. Next, the development of minicomputers and microcomputers accelerated a **downsizing** trend, which prompted a move back toward **decentralization** by many business firms. Distributed client/server networks at the corporate, department, workgroup, and team levels came into being, which promoted a shift of databases and information specialists to some departments and the creation of *information centers* to support end-user and workgroup computing.

Lately, the trend is to establish more centralized control over the management of the IT resources of a company while still serving the strategic needs of its business units, especially their e-business and e-commerce initiatives. This trend has resulted in the development of hybrid structures with both centralized and decentralized components. See Figure 12.6. For example, the IT function at Avnet Marshall is organized into several business-focused development groups, as well as operations management and planning groups [5].

Some companies spin off their information systems function into IS *subsidiaries* that offer IS services to external organizations as well as to their parent company. Other companies create or spin off their e-commerce and Internet-related business units or IT groups into separate companies or business units. Other corporations **outsource**, that is, turn over all or parts of their IS operations to outside contractors known as *systems integrators*. In addition, some companies are outsourcing software procurement and support to *application service providers* (ASPs), which provide and support business application and other software via the Internet and intranets to all of a company's employee workstations. We will discuss outsourcing in greater detail later in this section. In the meantime, let's take a few minutes to review, and expand on, what we know about managing the various functions and activities in IS.

Managing Application Development

Application development management involves managing activities such as systems analysis and design, prototyping, applications programming, project management, quality assurance, and system maintenance for all major business/IT development projects. Managing application development requires managing the activities of teams of systems analysts, software developers, and other IS professionals working on a variety of information systems development projects. Thus, project management is a key IT management responsibility if business/IT projects are to be completed on time and within their budgets and meet their design objectives. In addition, some systems development groups have established *development centers* staffed with IS professionals.

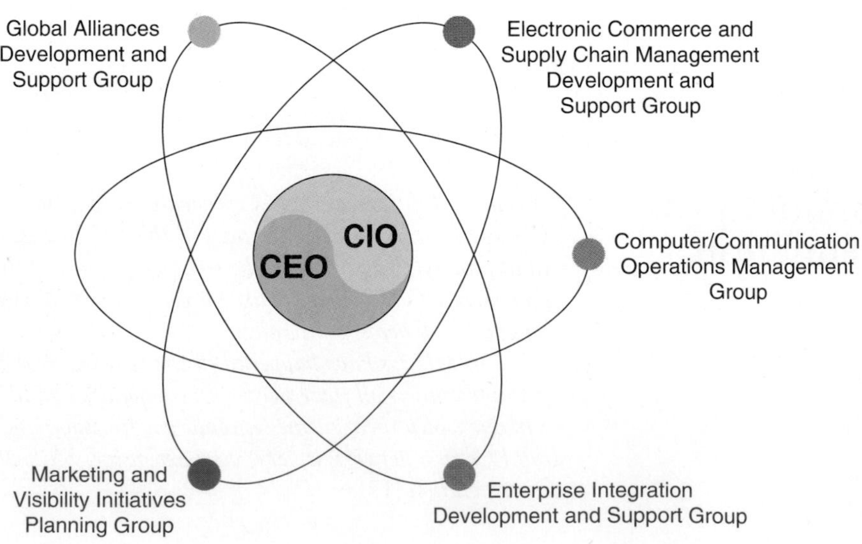

FIGURE 12.6
The organizational components of the IT function at Avnet Marshall.

Their role is to evaluate new application development tools and help information systems specialists use them to improve their application development efforts.

Managing IS Operations

IS operations management is concerned with the use of hardware, software, network, and personnel resources in the corporate or business unit **data centers** (computer centers) of an organization. Operational activities that must be managed include computer system operations, network management, production control, and production support.

Most operations management activities are being automated by the use of software packages for computer system performance management. These **system performance monitors** look after the processing of computer jobs, help develop a planned schedule of computer operations that can optimize computer system performance, and produce detailed statistics that are invaluable for effective planning and control of computing capacity. Such information evaluates computer system utilization, costs, and performance. This evaluation provides information for capacity planning, production planning and control, and hardware/software acquisition planning. It is also used in quality assurance programs, which stress the quality of services to business end users. See Figure 12.7.

System performance monitors also supply information needed by **chargeback systems** that allocate costs to users on the basis of the information services rendered. All costs incurred are recorded, reported, allocated, and charged back to specific end-user business units, depending on their use of system resources. When companies use this arrangement, the information services department becomes a service center whose costs are charged directly to business units rather than being lumped with other administrative service costs and treated as overhead costs.

Many performance monitors also feature **process control** capabilities. Such packages not only monitor but also automatically control computer operations at large data centers. Some use built-in expert system modules that are based on knowledge gleaned from experts in the operations of specific computer systems and operating systems. These performance monitors provide more efficient computer operations than human-operated systems. They also enable "lights out" data centers at some companies, where computer systems are operated unattended, especially after normal business hours.

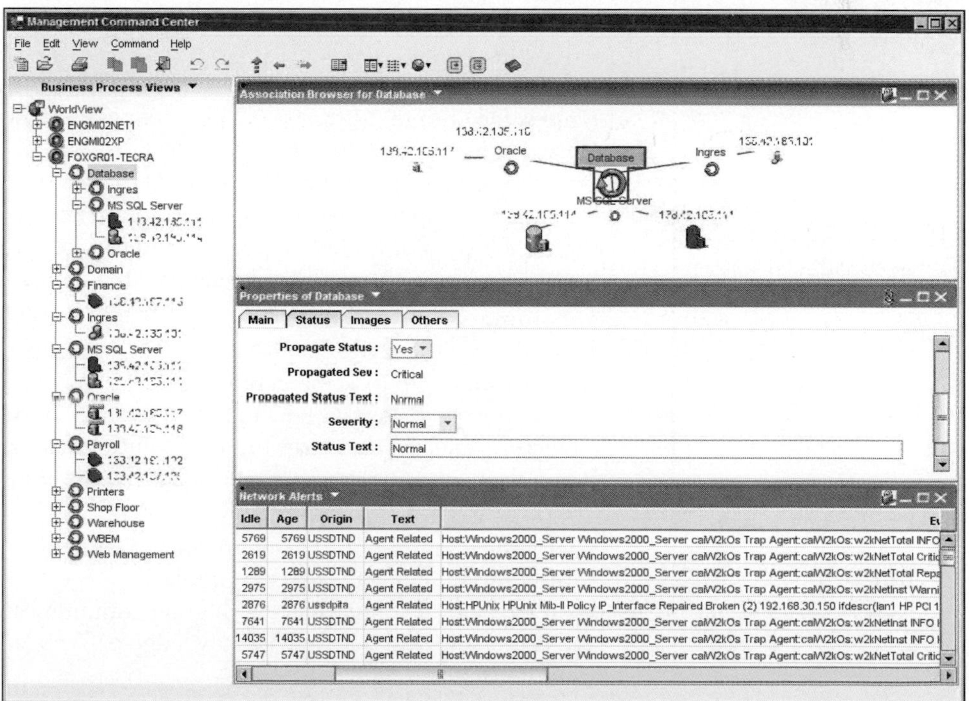

FIGURE 12.7 The CA-Unicenter TNG system performance monitor includes an Enterprise Management Portal module that helps IT specialists monitor and manage a variety of networked computer systems and operating systems.

IT Staff Planning

The success or failure of an information services organization rests primarily on the quality of its people. Many firms consider **IT staff planning**, or recruiting, training, and retaining qualified IS personnel, as one of their greatest challenges. Managing information services functions involves the management of managerial, technical, and clerical personnel. One of the most important jobs of information services managers is to recruit qualified personnel and develop, organize, and direct the capabilities of existing personnel. Employees must be continually trained to keep up with the latest developments in a fast moving and highly technical field. Employee job performances must be continually evaluated and outstanding performances rewarded with salary increases or promotions. Salary and wage levels must be set, and career paths must be designed so individuals can move to new jobs through promotion and transfer as they gain in seniority and expertise.

The CIO and Other IT Executives

The **chief information officer (CIO)** oversees all use of information technology in many companies and brings it into alignment with strategic business goals. Thus, all traditional computer services, Internet technology, telecommunications network services, and other IS technology support services are the responsibility of this executive. The CIO does not direct day-to-day information services activities however. Instead, CIOs concentrate on business/IT planning and strategy. They also work with the CEO and other top executives to develop strategic uses of information technology in electronic business and commerce that help make the firm more competitive in the marketplace. Many companies have also filled the CIO position with executives from the business functions or units outside the IS field. Such CIOs emphasize that the chief role of information technology is to help a company meet its strategic business objectives.

Top IT Jobs: Requirements and Compensation

- **Chief information officer**
  Base salary range: $184,000–$293,000+; varies by location
  Bonus range: Up to 40 percent of salary
  The top position in IT isn't all about technology. To land this job, you need to be a Business Technologist with a big "B" and a big "T." If you understand the business, the organization's strategy, and the broad spectrum of technologies, systems, applications, and people necessary to execute it, you will be in great demand by organizations.
- **Chief technology officer**
  Base salary range: $148,000–$240,000+; varies by location
  Bonus range: Up to 40 percent of salary
  If you're second-in-command to the CIO or chief technology officer and you have years of applications development experience, your next move should be into the chief technology officer's spot. To land this job, you'll need to be a passionate problem solver with a demonstrated record of reducing development time.
- **E-commerce architect**
  Base salary range: $115,000–$170,000+; varies by location
  Bonus range: Up to 15 percent of salary
  If you know Java, Perl, C++, and Web services; have experience in systems architecture; and can design an Internet solution from concept through implementation, many companies want you to plan and develop their e-commerce sites.
- **Technical team leader**
  Base salary range: $75,000–$100,000+; varies by location
  Bonus range: Up to 20 percent of salary
  Senior technical team leaders with good communication, project management, and leadership skills, as well as knowledge of Web languages and databases, are still highly sought after.

- **Practice manager**
  Base salary range: \$70,000–\$100,000+; varies by location
  Bonus range: Up to 20 percent of salary
  If you've got a background in IT assessment and a pedigree in business development (MBA preferred), you can land a job as a point person for big projects. You'll need skills in IT operations and software assessment, as well as in marketing, staffing, budgeting, and building customer relationships.
- **Systems analyst**
  Base salary range: \$56,000–\$100,000+; varies by location
  Bonus range: Up to 25 percent of salary
  If you have problem-solving skills and a degree in information systems (BS or MBA), you can be assured of finding a good job as a systems analyst. You'll need to have excellent interpersonal skills, good technical skills, and an ability to apply your problem-solving and critical-thinking skills to the design of new systems.

Source: www.salary.com.

Technology Management

The management of rapidly changing technology is important to any organization. Changes in information technology, like the rise of the PC, client/server networks, and the Internet and intranets, have come swiftly and dramatically and are expected to continue into the future. Developments in information systems technology have had, and will continue to have, a major impact on the operations, costs, management work environment, and competitive position of many organizations.

Thus, all information technologies must be managed as a technology platform for integrating internally focused or externally facing business applications. Such technologies include the Internet, intranets, and a variety of electronic commerce and collaboration technologies, as well as integrated enterprise software for customer relationship management, enterprise resource planning, and supply chain management. In many companies, **technology management** is the primary responsibility of a **chief technology officer (CTO)**, who is in charge of all information technology planning and deployment.

Managing User Services

Teams and workgroups of business professionals commonly use PC workstations, software packages, and the Internet, intranets, and other networks to develop and apply information technology to their work activities. Thus, many companies have responded by creating **user services**, or *client services*, functions to support and manage end-user and workgroup computing.

End-user services provide both opportunities and problems for business unit managers. For example, some firms create an *information center* group staffed with user liaison specialists or Web-enabled intranet help desks. IS specialists with titles such as user consultant, account executive, or business analyst may also be assigned to end-user workgroups. These specialists perform a vital role by troubleshooting problems, gathering and communicating information, coordinating educational efforts, and helping business professionals with application development.

In addition to these measures, most organizations still establish and enforce policies for the acquisition of hardware and software by end users and business units. This process ensures their compatibility with company standards for hardware, software, and network connectivity. Also important is the development of applications with proper security and quality controls to promote correct performance and safeguard the integrity of corporate and departmental networks and databases.

Outsourcing and Offshoring IT and IS

An increasingly popular approach to managing the IS and IT functions of the organization is to adopt an outsourcing strategy. **Outsourcing**, in broad terms, is the purchase of goods or services that were previously provided internally from third-party partners. Outsourcing is a generic term used for a broad range of information technology functions that are selectively contracted to an external service provider.

Outsourcing

A commonly outsourced IS function is software application development. This process includes contracting (or subcontracting) with an external organization for the development of complete or partial software products/projects, the purchase of packaged or customized package software products, or activities and/or resources that aid in the software development life cycle. Figure 12.8 lists the functions typically outsourced, the reasons behind the decision to outsource, and several aspects associated with successful vendor selection and a successful outsourcing effort.

Although companies can, theoretically, choose to outsource any organization function, and do so for any reason, there are five main categories of reasons behind a decision to outsource:

Save Money—Achieve Greater ROI.

- Outsourcing IS/IT functions to skilled service providers is often a strategic approach to stretching strained budgets. Companies that take a well-managed approach to outsourcing can gain cost savings of upwards of 40–80 percent.

FIGURE 12.8 Outsourcing's Top 10. Notice, despite all of the media coverage, application development is No. 3.

Top 10 Reasons Companies Outsource	Top 10 Factors in Vendor Selection
1. Reduce and control operating costs.	1. Commitment to quality.
2. Improve company focus.	2. Price.
3. Gain access to world-class capabilities.	3. References/reputation.
4. Free internal resources for other purposes.	4. Flexible contract terms.
5. Necessary resources are not available internally.	5. Scope of resources.
6. Accelerate reengineering benefits.	6. Additional value-added capability.
7. Function is difficult to manage internally or is out of control.	7. Cultural match.
8. Make capital funds available.	8. Existing relationship.
9. Share risks.	9. Location.
10. Cash infusion.	10. Other.

Top 10 Factors for Successful Outsourcing	Top 10 IT Areas Being Outsourced
1. Understand company goals and objectives.	1. Maintenance and repair.
2. A strategic vision and plan.	2. Training.
3. Select the right vendor.	3. Applications development.
4. Ongoing management of the relationships.	4. Consulting and reengineering.
5. A properly structured contract.	5. Mainframe data centers.
6. Open communication with affected individuals/groups.	6. Client/server services and administration.
7. Senior executive support and involvement.	7. Network administration.
8. Careful attention to personnel issues.	8. Desktop services.
9. Near term financial justification.	9. End-user support.
10. Use of outside expertise.	10. Total IT outsourcing.

Source: The Outsourcing Institute.

Focus on Core Competencies.

- Outsourced professionals allow an organization and its employees to focus on the business they are in rather than a business in which they are not. By utilizing an outsourcing strategy for application development, an organization can focus its IS professionals on identifying and solving business problems rather than on programming and prototyping new applications.

Achieve Flexible Staffing Levels.

- Strategic use of an outsourcing approach to IS/IT functions can result in business growth without increasing overhead. Outsourcing provides a pool of qualified professionals available for unique, niche, or overflow projects. If the unique skill set required by an organization is difficult to find or expensive to maintain in-house, outsourcing can allow for the acquisition of the needed expertise.

Gain Access to Global Resources.

- The Outsourcing Institute asserts that the rules for successfully growing a business have changed: "It's no longer about what you own or build. . . . [Instead] success is hinged to resources and talent you can access." Using global expertise allows an organization to gain the advantage of skilled labor, regardless of location, and significantly increase the quality of its deliverables. As such, outsourcing can create opportunities for smaller businesses that might not otherwise be possible due to costs or geophysical constraints.

Decrease Time to Market.

- Outsourcing extends the traditional small business benefits of flexibility and responsiveness, allowing smaller organizations to effectively compete against bigger firms. Supplementing an existing workforce with offshore support could allow for productivity 24 hours a day. Having access to resources able to work on key projects even while local employees are asleep can serve to accelerate time to market and provide for a key competitive advantage.

Offshoring

Although often confused with outsourcing, offshoring is also increasingly becoming part of a strategic approach to IS/IT management. **Offshoring** can be defined as a relocation of an organization's business processes (including production/manufacturing) to a lower-cost location, usually overseas. Offshoring can be considered in the context of either *production* offshoring or *services* offshoring. After its accession to the World Trade Organization (WTO), China emerged as a prominent destination for production offshoring. After technical progress in telecommunications improved the possibilities of trade in services, India became a country that chose to focus on this domain.

The growth of services offshoring in information systems is linked to the availability of large amounts of reliable and affordable communication infrastructure following the telecom bust of the late 1990s. Coupled with the digitization of many services, it became possible to shift the actual delivery location of services to low-cost locations in a manner theoretically transparent to end users.

India, the Philippines, Ireland, and Eastern European countries benefited greatly from this trend due to their large pool of English-speaking and technically qualified workers. India's offshoring industry took root in IT functions in the 1990s and has since moved to back-office processes, such as call centers and transaction processing, as well as high-end jobs, such as application development.

Offshoring is often enabled by the transfer of valuable information to the offshore site. Such information and training enables the remote workers to produce results of comparable value previously produced by internal employees. When such transfer includes proprietary materials, such as confidential documents and trade secrets, protected by nondisclosure agreements, then intellectual property has been transferred or exported. The documentation and valuation of such exports is quite difficult but should be considered because it comprises items that may be regulated or taxable.

Offshoring has been a controversial issue with heated debates. On one hand, it is seen as benefiting both the origin and destination country through free trade. On the other hand, job losses in developed countries have sparked opposition to offshoring. Some critics agree that both sides will benefit in terms of overall production and numbers of jobs created but that the subjective quality of the new jobs will be less than the previous ones. While this debate continues, companies continue to use offshoring as a viable IS/IT management approach. Let's look at a real-world example of offshore outsourcing.

Delta Airlines: IT Outsourcing Keeps it Flying

Faced with declining passenger revenues and rising costs, Delta Air Lines Inc. launched a plan in early 2003 to cut operating expenses (with the exception of fuel) by 15 percent by the end of 2005. Cutting its unionized flight crew and maintenance personnel would involve thorny labor issues, so the airline—which posted a total net loss of $2.5 billion over 2001 and 2002—looked to support operations for savings. In January 2004, Delta moved part of its call center reservations operations to service centers in India.

Delta says the move will save the company $12 to $15 million, including IT-related service costs. It's an example of how more companies are willing to accept the greater risk of outsourcing revenue-generating processes offshore. Traditional outsourcing of application development to far-flung places might mean a project gets delayed if technology, miscommunication, or political upheaval causes a disruption. But as more businesses look for further cost savings, they're beginning to farm out entire operational departments—ranging from call centers to human resources support to accounting—to contractors with facilities in lower-wage countries such as India.

The Delta effort took meticulous planning. Delta knew that revenue could be lost if customers were frustrated with the offshore service provider. But factors such as a robust communications infrastructure in India and the ability to monitor operator performance remotely from Delta headquarters helped alleviate its concerns. Dedicated voice and data connections tied the Mumbai (formerly Bombay), India, operations to Delta's U.S. operations. Customer calls to Delta's toll-free number are routed to the Indian facilities and transferred to the agent with the skills most appropriate to serve a particular customer's needs.

To control quality of an operation that's thousands of miles away from its Atlanta headquarters, Delta uses contact-center management software from Witness Systems Inc. The vendor's eQuality Suite automatically creates voice and screen data captures from individual agents' workstations that can be viewed in real time or archived. The call center performance thus far has exceeded learning-curve expectations, and target call-handling times exceeded specific targets in the first three weeks of operations.

But not all of Delta's plans have proceeded as smoothly as the India call center project. Delta had planned to open another call center in the Philippines and expected to build a high-speed data network between the Indian and Philippines locations so each site could act as a backup for the other. But in late 2003, Delta canceled plans to open the Philippines center. Delta's security people decided it wouldn't be a good move, given the turbulent political environment in that country.

Some IT outsourcing comes with higher risk. In typical application-development outsourcing, a project might get derailed by a political disruption, but business carries on. With business-process outsourcing, an entire department can be put at risk, which, in the case of a call center, can mean a cut in revenue. The Philippines isn't the only country requiring an assessment of political stability. Brazil, India, and Russia—all increasingly popular destinations for such outsourcing—have problems related to political instability or military tension in at least some regions. The offshore business-process outsourcing trend has grown enough that a few insurance companies now offer political risk coverage for companies engaged in it [4, 15].

Failures in IT Management

Managing information technology is not an easy task. The information systems function often has performance problems in many organizations. The promised benefits of information technology have not occurred in many documented cases. Studies by management consulting firms and university researchers have shown that many businesses have not been successful in managing their use of information technology. Thus, it is evident that in many organizations, information technology is not being used effectively and efficiently, and there have been **failures in IT management.** For example:

- Information technology is not being used *effectively* by companies that use IT primarily to computerize traditional business processes instead of developing innovative e-business processes involving customers, suppliers, and other business partners, electronic commerce, and Web-enabled decision support.
- Information technology is not being used *efficiently* by information systems that provide poor response times and frequent downtimes or IS professionals and consultants who do not properly manage application development projects.

Let's look more closely, using a real-world example.

PeopleFirst Finance: Failure of a CRM Project

You've been warned: Putting in a decent customer relationship management (CRM) system is as perilous as installing enterprise resource planning (ERP) systems used to be. CRM projects fail more often than not, analysts say. The software is hard to install. It forces a lot of change, quickly, on business units. And even when companies manage to install and link applications that hold client information, they often don't serve customers any better, reports Gartner Inc. Mercer Management Consulting calls CRM a "money pit."

But some companies have gotten CRM to work well—on the second or third try. Some of the disappointment can be chalked up to classic bad habits in IT, such as not listening—sometimes not even talking—to end users about what they want. Or the CRM team may try to do too much at once, which almost guarantees delays and cost overruns.

PeopleFirst Finance LLC (www.peoplefirst.com), an online car loan company in San Diego, dived into CRM in June 2000, when it tried to install a complete CRM suite. It was clear about three months into the installation that things weren't going well, acknowledges Sharon Spooler, vice president of business intelligence at PeopleFirst. For example, there was no easy, automated way to manage bounce-backs from e-mail sales pitches that didn't reach intended recipients, she notes. Also, the software couldn't properly track multiple versions of e-mail sales letters. The result: PeopleFirst couldn't get an accurate view of which campaigns worked.

"We tried problem solving with the vendor. We tried a lot of different things to make it work. Every time you'd think you had a problem solved, another one would pop up," Spooler says. "It was like a game of whack-a-mole." Spooler declined to name the vendor, citing a deal struck when PeopleFirst killed the project in March 2001 [21].

Management Involvement and Governance

What is the solution to failures in the information systems function? There are no quick and easy answers. However, the experiences of successful organizations reveal that extensive and meaningful **managerial and end user involvement** is the key ingredient of high-quality information systems performance. Involving business managers in the governance of the IS function and business professionals in the development of IS applications should thus shape the response of management to the challenge of improving the business value of information technology [5, 10]. See Figure 12.9.

FIGURE 12.9 Senior management needs to be involved in critical business/IT decisions to optimize the business value and performance of the IT function.

IT Decision	Senior Management's Role	Consequences of Abdicating the Decision
• **How much should we spend on IT?**	Define the strategic role that IT will play in the company, and then determine the level of funding needed to achieve that objective.	The company fails to develop an IT platform that furthers its strategy, despite high IT spending.
• **Which business processes should receive our IT dollars?**	Make clear decisions about which IT initiatives will and will not be funded.	A lack of focus overwhelms the IT unit, which tries to deliver many projects that may have little companywide value or can't be implemented well simultaneously.
• **Which IT capabilities need to be companywide?**	Decide which IT capabilities should be provided centrally and which should be developed by individual businesses.	Excessive technical and process standardization limit the flexibility of business units, or frequent exceptions to the standards increase costs and limit business synergies.
• **How good do our IT services really need to be?**	Decide which features—for example, enhanced reliability or response time—are needed on the basis of their costs and benefits.	The company may pay for service options that, given its priorities, aren't worth their costs.
• **What security and privacy risks will we accept?**	Lead the decision making on the trade-offs between security and privacy on one hand and convenience on the other.	An overemphasis on security and privacy may inconvenience customers, employees, and suppliers; an underemphasis may make data vulnerable.
• **Whom do we blame if an IT initiative fails?**	Assign a business executive to be accountable for every IT project; monitor business metrics.	The business value of systems is never realized.

Source: Jeanne W. Ross and Peter Weill, "Six IT Decisions Your IT People Shouldn't Make," *Harvard Business Review*, November 2002, p. 87.

Involving managers in the management of IT (from the CEO to the managers of business units) requires the development of *governance structures* (e.g., executive councils, steering committees) that encourage their active participation in planning and controlling the business uses of IT. Thus, many organizations have policies that require managers to be involved in IT decisions that affect their business units. This requirement helps managers avoid IS performance problems in their business units and development projects. With this high degree of involvement, managers can improve the strategic business value of information technology [20]. Also, as we noted in Chapter 10, the problems of employee resistance and poor user interface design can only be solved by direct end-user participation in system development projects. Overseeing such involvement is another vital management task.

SECTION II Managing Global IT

The International Dimension

Whether they are in Berlin or Bombay, Kuala Lumpur or Kansas, San Francisco or Seoul, companies around the globe are developing new models to operate competitively in a digital economy. These models are structured, yet agile; global, yet local; and they concentrate on maximizing the risk-adjusted return from both knowledge and technology assets [10].

International dimensions have become a vital part of managing a business enterprise in the internetworked global economies and markets of today. Whether you become a manager in a large corporation or the owner of a small business, you will be affected by international business developments and deal in some way with people, products, or services whose origin is not your home country.

Read the Real World Case on the next page. We can learn a lot about the ways companies are responding to the challenges of the globalization of IT from this case. See Figure 12.11.

Global IT Management

Figure 12.9 illustrates the major dimensions of the job of managing global information technology that we cover in this section. Notice that all global IT activities must be adjusted to take into account the cultural, political, and geoeconomic challenges that exist in the international business community. Developing appropriate business and IT strategies for the global marketplace should be the first step in **global information technology management**. Once that is done, end users and IS managers can move on to developing the portfolio of business applications needed to support business/IT strategies; the hardware, software, and Internet-based technology platforms to support those applications; the data resource management methods to provide necessary databases; and finally the systems development projects that will produce the global information systems required.

Cendant Corp.: Global IT Management's Cultural, Political, and Geoeconomic Challenges

Lawrence Kinder faced a typical kind of global challenge. He is executive vice president and CIO with global responsibility for IT at Cendant Corp., which recently acquired Avis Group holdings. His company, a service and information provider for automotive transportation and vehicle management in Garden City, New York, grew internationally in 1999 by acquiring the United Kingdom's PHH Vehicle Management Services, the world's second-largest vehicle leasing and fleet management company, and Wright Express LLC, the world's largest credit card and information services provider.

"We grew organically in North America and built a solid and stable IT foundation that we have been able to leverage in Europe," Kinder says. The key is to take the time to understand the day-to-day workings of each local IT group, he claims, and to put strategic IT planning on the back burner until all groups can focus on leveraging their cultures and talents.

Kinder regularly brings together company leaders with similar roles from the United States, Canada, and Europe to "give each other a shot of adrenaline." He posits that developing and supporting global businesses is more demanding than even strategic planning. But, he says, "Giving my global IT leaders the opportunity to think more broadly about their applications and solve international business problems has created a true learning organization" [14].

REAL WORLD CASE 2 IBM Corporation: Competing Globally by Offshoring IT Workers and Giving Away Technology

It's IBM's nightmare. In a conference room in Bangalore, a team of retail experts at software company Wipro are redesigning the consumer experience for a major U.S. retail chain. They're methodically evaluating the checkout area. The client wants its processes to be state of the art, and Srikant Shankaranarayana, Wipro's brainy, intense, 44-year-old general manager for retail solutions, is pushing his consultants and engineers to ask tough questions: Should salesclerks carry handheld transaction devices or stand at cash registers? Which merchandise should be tracked electronically? How much information needs to be in the database to ensure that discount promotions don't last longer than necessary?

Those are exactly the kinds of questions that IBM wants to be asking its retail customers, and the fact that such companies as Louis Vuitton and Target are turning to India for answers is not a good thing for IBM. Almost half of IBM's revenues now come from such business/IT services. And only services promise to provide growth on the massive scale that IBM needs to make shareholders happy. Luckily for IBM, Wipro has only 100 retail consultants. So far.

Meanwhile, IBM's costs remain those of a mature First World corporation. It has about 260,000 expensive employees in the United States and other developed countries (the other 60,000 are in lower-cost regions) and 164,000 pensioned retirees, all quarterbacked from a gleaming modern headquarters on 432 acres of pricey Westchester County real estate.

But though they don't put it quite this boldly, CEO Sam Palmisano and other top IBMers think they're well on the way to having the problem licked. Interviews with the CEO's lieutenants reveal a strategy that not only challenges upstarts like Wipro directly by taking the low-cost model right back at them but also includes a dimension that is so original and so bold that it will either reenergize Big Blue's profits or undermine its vaunted status as the biggest company in IT.

FIGURE 12.10

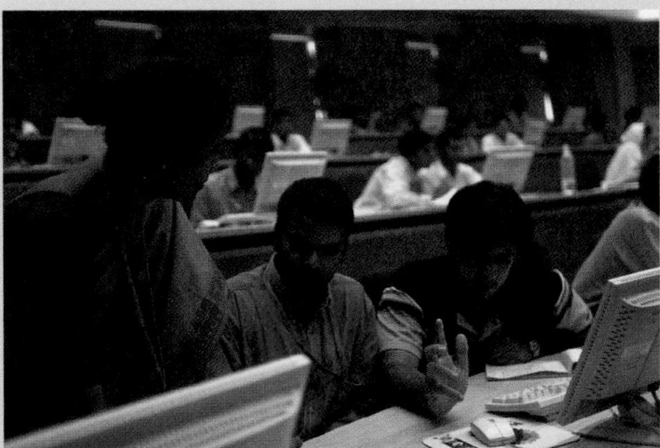

Software development contractors in India like Wipro are establishing IT consulting groups, causing IBM to expand its IT consulting workforce in that country to compete better for global business.

Simply put, IBM is gambling that it can win by giving away crown jewels—precious intellectual property in the form of software, patents, and ideas. Spread enough of those riches around, the theory goes, and the entire industry will grow faster, opening new frontiers. That, in turn, should create opportunities for IBM to sell high-value products and services that meet the new demand.

IBM's response to the India threat has been swift. In April 2005, after first-quarter revenues from services came in unexpectedly weak and IBM disappointed Wall Street's earnings expectations, the company eliminated 14,500 jobs, mostly in Europe. It was the biggest job cut in three years: The company shut its European headquarters and moved most of the surviving employees out to the field, to what Palmisano calls "client-facing positions."

Next, *The New York Times* reported having obtained an internal IBM memo saying the company would hire 14,000 people in India this year. IBM calls the figure "exaggerated," but newcomers in any number would add to an already surprisingly large roster in developing countries. Of the programmers who write custom code for IBM's services group, about half—26,000 or so—are in India, Brazil, or China. "Strategic low-cost geographies" is the IBM lingo for such places.

India already accounts for the largest number of IBMers outside the United States (it recently surpassed Japan). In 2004, Big Blue acquired India's Daksh eServices, whose 6,000 employees operate call centers for companies like Amazon.com and Citicorp. Goldman Sachs calculates that by the end of next year, IBM Services' head count in India will top 52,000. That would be more than one-fourth of all its services personnel and about one-sixth of IBMers worldwide. It would put IBM in India on a par with Wipro, the largest local software company, and make it bigger than Infosys and Tata Consultancy Services.

Growth in the developing world is a natural part of implementing a "global delivery model" for services, says senior vice president Bob Moffat. In July, Palmisano reorganized services, naming the 49-year-old Moffat one of three executives who will run it jointly. While the other two will oversee the delivery of services to clients, Moffat's job is to find efficiencies. He spent the past three years taking billions of dollars in costs out of IBM's physical supply chain—the delivery of parts and goods to and from factories and on to the customer. His mission now is to cut the cost of delivering services, even high-value ones, by tightening the "services supply chain." That mostly means people—getting the right ones to the right place at the right time. He has to extract every last penny of value from IBM's 260,000 developed-country employees if they're going to stay on the payroll.

And man, does Palmisano sound confident. In an e-mail to *Fortune*, he makes a remarkable claim: that by adopting the strategy he calls simply "openness," IBM has tapped a major new "spur to innovation itself." The company lavishes some $5.7 billion a year on R&D. By sharing its discoveries wisely, Palmisano says, IBM will "make the pie bigger," and the entire industry will grow faster.

Collaborating with customers and even rivals to invent new technologies is a big part of this sharing plan, whose first fruits are already apparent. In hardware, IBM has codeveloped with Sony and Toshiba a breakthrough chip called the Cell, which could eventually help transform all of IBM's computers. In software, embracing Linux and other open-source technology has given IBM new platforms on which it is building almost all its high-growth applications.

The idea that giving things away makes the pie bigger for everybody is not IBM's invention, of course. The open-source software movement that developed Linux is a good example. Says Palmisano: "This isn't theory for us. Collaborative innovation today is crucial to every aspect of our business. We've learned how to deliver value within this kind of business system and how to make money."

A walking, talking embodiment of that is Jim Stallings, Palmisano's vice president for intellectual property and standards—a job Palmisano invented when he tapped Stallings for it last September. Stallings, 49, used to manage IBM's work with the Linux community; now he's the guy who figures out what Big Blue should give away and what it should keep. A buttoned-down former Marine Corps captain and 14-year IBM veteran, he's not the most likely high-tech Santa. Yet he's almost hypnotically good at explaining how IBM's plan works. The giveaways to open-source software groups, customer groups, universities, and other IT companies are surprisingly extensive and diverse.

IBM says there's no way to attach a precise dollar value to its giveaways—but *Fortune* calculates they're worth at least $150 million a year. And while sharing is not yet a universal part of its culture, the company has come a long way from the arrogant, standoffish, monopolistic IBM of yore.

What's in it for IBM? Big Blue seldom gives away a technology unless it has intellectual property and expertise that will enable it to make money if the technology is widely adopted. When IBM hands out tools to retailers, it often sells them additional software and consulting services. What's more, freebies themselves can be a potent weapon. Application-related software from Microsoft can be costly. An open-source version like Apache Geronimo is free and is the latest salvo in IBM's open-source challenge to Microsoft. It has also embraced the Linux operating system, a formidable rival to Windows, and Firefox, a popular challenger to the Internet Explorer Web browser.

IBM has also found giveaways to be a potent door opener abroad, where the company derives 63 percent of its revenues. Stallings has been to China four times this year and plans to go again in September, twice. He's working to convince policymakers and business leaders that using open-source software makes more sense than buying Microsoft's. This IBMer bearing gifts has found a receptive audience. Now IBM is helping build a giant network based largely on Linux to connect all of China's libraries.

All this sounds well and good, but the outcome is far from certain. IBM is in a brutally competitive marketplace with a long list of rivals going after the same customer dollar. But Palmisano argues that IBM will be able to create products and services that capitalize on new markets as they emerge.

Yet even his own executives need periodic convincing. Two years ago, some insiders fretted that IBM might be "shooting itself in the foot" by giving its ideas away. But in the end, company researchers concluded that as long as IT remains hard to use, expensive, and labor intensive, with customers continuing to need help solving business problems—and any business computer user would guess that means forever—IBM will have the opportunity to thrive.

Source: Adapted from David Kirkpatrick, "IBM Shares Its Secrets," *Fortune*, September 5, 2005.

CASE STUDY QUESTIONS

1. Do you agree with IBM's employment response to competition from software development contractors in India, like Wipro, that are expanding into IT consulting services? Why or why not?
2. Will IBM's plan to give away some of its IT assets and intellectual property and increase its support of open-source software products like Linux be a successful growth strategy in the "brutally competitive marketplace" in which it operates? Why or why not?
3. Do you agree with IBM researchers' assumption that IT will remain "hard to use, expensive, and labor-intensive, with customers continuing to need help solving business problems" for a long time to come? Should IBM bet its business on that assumption? Defend your answers to both questions.

REAL WORLD ACTIVITIES

1. Use the Internet to research news on the latest developments in the competition to provide IT consulting services to businesses and governments. Check out IBM's performance, as well as major players like HP and Accenture, new entrants like Dell, and international competitors like Wipro. Who appears to be winning or losing in this arena? What reasons can you uncover for the results you find?
2. IBM eliminated 14,500 jobs, mostly in Europe, and then reportedly hired thousands of additional IT workers in India. Such cutting of high-cost jobs and offshoring jobs to a subsidiary in a lower-cost country is a controversial business strategy being used by other global companies. Break into small groups with your classmates to discuss the implications of this issue for your current or future career choices and the kinds of companies or organizations you would want to work for.

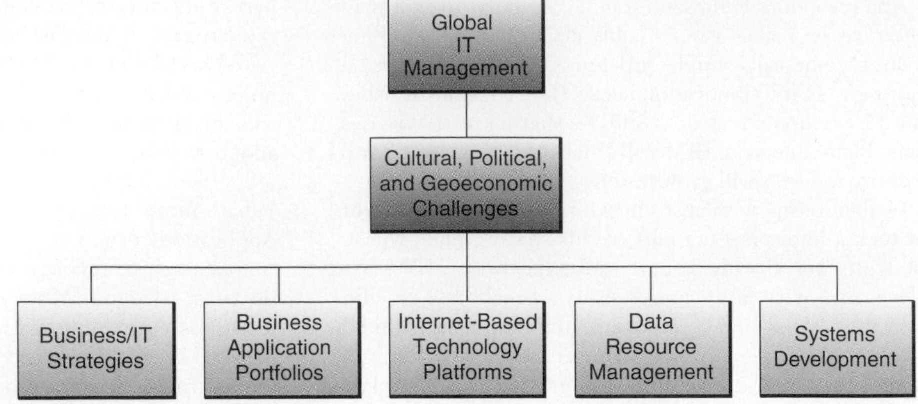

FIGURE 12.11
The major dimensions of global e-business technology management.

Cultural, Political, and Geoeconomic Challenges

"Business as usual" is not good enough in global business operations. The same holds true for global e-business technology management. There are too many cultural, political, and geoeconomic (geographic and economic) realities that must be confronted for a business to succeed in global markets. As we have just mentioned, global information technology management must focus on developing global business IT strategies and managing global e-business application portfolios, Internet technologies, platforms, databases, and systems development projects. But managers must also accomplish this task from a perspective and through methods that take into account the cultural, political, and geoeconomic differences that exist when doing business internationally.

For example, a major **political challenge** is that many countries have rules regulating or prohibiting transfer of data across their national boundaries (transborder data flows), especially personal information such as personnel records. Others severely restrict, tax, or prohibit imports of hardware and software. Still others have local content laws that specify the portion of the value of a product that must be added in that country if it is to be sold there. Other countries have reciprocal trade agreements that require a business to spend part of the revenue it earns in a country in that nation's economy [18].

Geoeconomic challenges in global business and IT refer to the effects of geography on the economic realities of international business activities. The sheer physical distances involved are still a major problem, even in this day of Internet telecommunications and jet travel. For example, it may still take too long to fly in specialists when IT problems occur in a remote site. It is still difficult to communicate in real time across the world's 24 time zones. It is still difficult to get good-quality telephone and telecommunications service in many countries. There are still problems finding the job skills required in some countries or enticing specialists from other countries to live and work there. Finally, there are still problems (and opportunities) in the great differences in the cost of living and labor costs in various countries. All of these geoeconomic challenges must be addressed when developing a company's global business and IT strategies.

Cultural challenges facing global business and IT managers include differences in languages, cultural interests, religions, customs, social attitudes, and political philosophies. Obviously, global IT managers must be trained and sensitized to such cultural differences before they are sent abroad or brought into a corporation's home country. Other cultural challenges include differences in work styles and business relationships. For example, should you take your time to avoid mistakes or hurry to get something done early? Should you go it alone or work cooperatively? Should the most experienced person lead, or should leadership be shared? The answers to such questions depend on the culture you are in and highlight the cultural differences that might exist in the global workplace. Let's take a look at a real-world example involving the global IT talent pool.

Global Competition for IT Talent

Opportunity for professional growth is a major element of the competition between global businesses and governments for IT talent. Many IT workers understand that their résumé is their most important asset and seek positions in which they can work with modern or leading-edge technologies. Although many countries offer opportunities to work in emerging technologies, the United States leads in the sheer number and variety of IT jobs working with résumé-enhancing technologies. The question that faces policymakers in other countries is where their nation has room to improve their competitiveness by attracting or retaining skilled IT talent.

Australia, for example, has a literate and affluent population, with higher per capita Internet use than the United States, but it lacks the market size and concentration of investment capital to compete with the United States in providing IT employment opportunities. As a result, there are thousands of Australians working in Silicon Valley despite a shortage of over 30,000 IT professionals at home. Some Latin American and other countries suffer because of their limited telecommunications infrastructures. Although countries like Chile have modern systems with competitive telecommunications pricing and Internet access, others have government-run telephone companies with service levels that do not support modern e-commerce development. For example, in some countries, dedicated Internet connections are not available, and all telephone calls, including Internet connectivity, are priced by the duration of the connection.

With worldwide competition for IT professionals and unprecedented mobility in the IT workforce, it seems that the best method for attracting or retaining IT workers involves the development of an overall program of economic, social, and technical opportunity. India and China, for example, seem to be experiencing a reverse brain drain as skilled IT professionals return home to take leadership roles in new ventures. Increased domestic demand, fueled by a combination of new domestic software needs, increased Internet connectivity, new e-commerce ventures, and local software shops developing for foreign customers are all attracting experienced managers and entrepreneurs back home and providing rewarding employment for local entry-level technologists.

Canada, Japan, and even India have all taken recent steps to facilitate the entry of foreign professional workers, especially IT specialists. Australia and New Zealand recruit foreign professionals, including those from the United States, by promoting the natural beauty of their countries and the relaxed lifestyles. Australia has considered easing the immigration process for IT specialists and already relaxed its rules for foreign students who wish to remain to work. Other countries are taking steps to address the outflow of companies and talented individuals.

Thus, Costa Rica has parlayed political stability, a growing educational infrastructure, and an aggressive program to recruit foreign firms such as Intel into an unemployment rate of less than 5 percent and wage and job opportunities that tend to keep talented citizens at home. And Trinidad and Tobago have created a foreign investment zone aimed at high-tech industries and eliminated import duties on computer equipment in an attempt to increase foreign investment and encourage a generation of domestic computer users [24].

Global Business/IT Strategies

Businesses are moving away from *international* strategies in which foreign subsidiaries are autonomous but depend on headquarters for new processes, products, and ideas, or *global* strategies, in which a company's worldwide operations are closely managed by corporate headquarters. Instead, companies are moving toward a **transnational strategy**, where the company's business depends heavily on its information systems and Internet technologies to help it integrate its global business activities. Instead of having independent IS units at its subsidiaries, or even a centralized IS operation directed

FIGURE 12.12 Companies operating internationally are moving toward transnational business and IT strategies. Note some of the chief differences among international, global, and transnational business and IT strategies.

Comparing Global Business/IT Strategies		
International	**Global**	**Transnational**
• Autonomous operations. • Region specific. • Vertical integration. • Specific customers. • Captive manufacturing. • Customer segmentation and dedication by region and plant.	• Global sourcing. • Multiregional. • Horizontal integration. • Some transparency of customers and production. • Some cross regionalization.	• Virtual business operations via global alliances. • World markets and mass customization. • Global e-commerce and customer service. • Transparent manufacturing. • Global supply chain and logistics. • Dynamic resource management.
Information Technology Characteristics		
• Stand-alone systems. • Decentralized/no standards. • Heavy reliance on interfaces. • Multiple systems, high redundancy, and duplication of services and operations. • Lack of common systems and data.	• Regional decentralization. • Interface dependent. • Some consolidation of applications and use of common systems. • Reduced duplication of operations. • Some worldwide IT standards.	• Logically consolidated, physically distributed, Internet connected. • Common global data resources. • Integrated global enterprise systems. • Internet, intranet, extranet, and Web-based applications. • Transnational IT policies and standards.

from its headquarters, a transnational business tries to develop an integrated and cooperative worldwide hardware, software, and Internet-based architecture for its IT platform. Figure 12.12 compares the three approaches to global business/IT strategy [17]. Figure 12.13 illustrates how transnational business and IT strategies have been implemented by global companies [23].

FIGURE 12.13 Examples of how transnational business and IT strategies were implemented by global companies.

Tactic	Global Alliances	Global Sourcing and Logistics	Global Customer Service
Examples	British Airways/US Airways KLM/Northwest Qantas/American	Benetton	American Express
IT Environment	Global network (online reservation system).	Global network, EPOS terminals in 4,000 stores, CAD/CAM in central manufacturing, robots and laser scanner in automated warehouse.	Global network linked from local branches and local merchants to the customer database and medical or legal referrals database.
Results	• Coordination of schedules. • Code sharing. • Coordination of flights. • Co-ownership.	• Produce 2,000 sweaters per hour using CAD/CAM. • Quick response (in stores in 10 days). • Reduced inventories (just-in-time).	• Worldwide access to funds. • "Global Assist" hotline. • Emergency credit card replacement. • 24-hour customer service.

FIGURE 12.14
Some of the business reasons driving global business applications.

Business Drivers of Global IT
• **Global customers.** Customers are people who may travel anywhere or companies with global operations. Global IT can help provide fast, convenient service.
• **Global products.** Products are the same throughout the world or are assembled by subsidiaries throughout the world. Global IT can help manage worldwide marketing and quality control.
• **Global operations.** Parts of a production or assembly process are assigned to subsidiaries based on changing economic or other conditions. Only global IT can support such geographic flexibility.
• **Global resources.** The use and cost of common equipment, facilities, and people are shared by subsidiaries of a global company. Global IT can keep track of such shared resources.
• **Global collaboration.** The knowledge and expertise of colleagues in a global company can be quickly accessed, shared, and organized to support individual or group efforts. Only global IT can support such enterprise collaboration.

Global Business/IT Applications

The applications of information technology developed by global companies depend on their **global business/IT strategies** and their expertise and experience in IT. However, their IT applications also depend on a variety of **global business drivers**, that is, business requirements caused by the nature of the industry and its competitive or environmental forces. One example would be companies like airlines or hotel chains that have global customers who travel widely or have global operations. Such companies need global IT capabilities for online transaction processing so they can provide fast, convenient service to their customers—or face losing them to their competitors. The economies of scale provided by global business operations are other business drivers that require the support of global IT applications. Figure 12.14 summarizes some of the business requirements that make global IT a competitive necessity [9].

Of course, many global IT applications, particularly finance, accounting, and office applications, have been in operation for many years. For example, most multinational companies have global financial budgeting and cash management systems and office automation applications such as fax and e-mail systems. However, as global operations expand and global competition heats up, there is increasing pressure for companies to install global e-commerce and e-business applications for their customers and suppliers. Examples include global e-commerce Web sites and customer service systems for customers, and global supply chain management systems for suppliers. In the past, such systems relied almost exclusively on privately constructed or government-owned telecommunications networks. But the explosive business use of the Internet, intranets, and extranets for electronic commerce has made such applications much more feasible for global companies.

TRW Inc.: Global Business/IT Challenges, Global IT Platforms

In the world of global IT operations, timing is everything. And so is knowing the ropes of the country you're in. Take, for example, Cleveland-based TRW Inc., a $17 billion technology, manufacturing, and services company with operations in 35 countries. When TRW's plant in Poland experiences a problem with its enterprise resource planning system or its global wide area network, the first wave of support comes from the local IT team. If that group is unsuccessful in righting the situation, backup is called in from a second team and even a third in the same time zone in either the United Kingdom or Germany.

Speed is of the essence, and local support means faster access to end users and resources, such as service providers, telephone companies, and equipment. This clustering of quick-response IT support teams by time zones and proximity is just one of the lessons learned by Mostafa Mehrabani, who has served as vice president and CIO at TRW for three years and for the past two years has developed the company's global IT operations.

"For a while, we were trying to perform day-to-day support of LANs and IT development for our Asian operations from the U.S.," he admits. "We came to the conclusion that while you can get someone on the phone, it isn't the same as being there and understanding the culture." So TRW developed centers of excellence, which are groups of subject-matter experts who assist employees throughout the company with their problems and requirements. "Often, we don't have the luxury of certain technical expertise in every part of the world, and we don't have the need for full-time experts in every region. Pooling resources to solve global IT issues is a major advantage," says Mehrabani [14].

Global IT Platforms

The management of technology platforms (also called the technology infrastructure) is another major dimension of global IT management—that is, managing the hardware, software, data resources, telecommunications networks, and computing facilities that support global business operations. The management of a global IT platform is not only technically complex but also has major political and cultural implications.

For example, hardware choices are difficult in some countries because of high prices, high tariffs, import restrictions, long lead times for government approvals, lack of local service or spare parts, and lack of documentation tailored to local conditions. Software choices can also present unique problems. Software packages developed in Europe may be incompatible with American or Asian versions, even when purchased from the same hardware vendor. Well-known U.S. software packages may be unavailable because there is no local distributor or because the software publisher refuses to supply markets that disregard software licensing and copyright agreements [9].

Managing international data communications networks, including Internet, intranet, extranet, and other networks, is a key global IT challenge. Figure 12.15 outlines the top

FIGURE 12.15
The top 10 issues in managing international data communications.

International Data Communications Issues
Network Management Issues
• Improving the operational efficiency of networks.
• Dealing with different networks.
• Controlling data communication security.
Regulatory Issues
• Dealing with transborder data flow restrictions.
• Managing international telecommunication regulations.
• Handling international politics.
Technology Issues
• Managing network infrastructure across countries.
• Managing international integration of technologies.
Country-Oriented Issues
• Reconciling national differences.
• Dealing with international tariff structures.

Source: Adapted from Vincent S. Lai and Wingyan Chung, "Managing International Data Communications," *Communications of the ACM*, March 2002, p. 91.

10 international data communications issues as reported by IS executives at 300 *Fortune* 500 multinational companies. Notice how political issues dominate the top 10 listing over technology issues, clearly emphasizing their importance in the management of global telecommunications.

Establishing computing facilities internationally is another global challenge. Companies with global business operations usually establish or contract with systems integrators for additional data centers in their subsidiaries in other countries. These data centers meet local and regional computing needs and even help balance global computing workloads through communications satellite links. However, offshore data centers can pose major problems in headquarters' support, hardware and software acquisition, maintenance, and security. That's why many global companies turn to application service providers or systems integrators like EDS or IBM to manage their overseas operations.

Citibank: Consolidating Global IT Platforms

A $100 million-plus global IT consolidation project has enabled Citibank (www.citibank.com) to replace a decades-old set of back-office corporate banking systems in all of its overseas corporate offices with a single global system with standard user interfaces and business processes. The New York–based bank completed changeover projects in the Asia-Pacific region, Western and Eastern Europe, and Latin America. The changeover, which began in early 2000, was completed in mid-2004 with rollouts in more than 100 countries.

The bank said the project pays for itself by letting the company avoid development costs related to a clunky legacy back-office system. Developed in-house in the 1970s, the old system has morphed into 58 disparate software applications, according to Jeff Berg, executive director of program management at Citibank's parent, New York–based Citigroup Inc. "In the '70s, we were growing rapidly in countries around the world. To get up and running quickly, we'd use this system called Cosmos [Consolidated Online Modulated Operating System]," recounts Berg. "As the bank grew, we did make a mistake in that we released the source code to each of the countries, and they changed it."

Berg notes Citibank now has a single system, customized for each country in which it operates, using each nation's language, regulatory rules, and business processes. Citibank reduced the number of its data centers in Europe from 18 to about 4 by standardizing on the new banking software from i-Flex Solutions Inc. in Bangalore, India. The bank anticipates an 18-month return on investment, says Berg. The software, called Flexcube, is based on an Oracle database. It automates the general ledger as well as customer accounting, deposits and withdrawals, and interest on accounts, among other services. Citibank will be able to simply change parameters in the new software to incorporate a particular country's language, regulations, and currency conversions [16].

The Internet as a Global IT Platform

What makes the Internet and the World Wide Web so important for international business? This interconnected matrix of computers, information, and networks that reaches tens of millions of users in over one hundred countries is a business environment free of traditional boundaries and limits. Linking to an online global infrastructure offers companies unprecedented potential for expanding markets, reducing costs, and improving profit margins at a price that is typically a small percentage of the corporate communications budget. The Internet provides an interactive channel for direct communication and data exchange with customers, suppliers, distributors, manufacturers, product developers, financial backers, information providers—in fact, with all parties involved in a given business venture [3].

So the Internet and the World Wide Web have now become vital components in international business and commerce. Within a few years, the Internet, with its interconnected network of thousands of networks of computers and databases, has established

Key Questions
• Will you have to develop a new navigational logic to accommodate cultural preferences?
• What content will you translate, and what content will you create from scratch to address regional competitors or products that differ from those in the United States?
• Should your multilingual effort be an adjunct to your main site, or will you make it a separate site, perhaps with a country-specific domain name?
• What kinds of traditional and new media advertising will you have to do in each country to draw traffic to your site?
• Will your site get so many hits that you'll need to set up a server in a local country?
• What are the legal ramifications of having your Web site targeted at a particular country, such as laws on competitive behavior, treatment of children, or privacy?

FIGURE 12.16 Key questions for companies establishing global Internet Web sites.

itself as a technology platform free of many traditional international boundaries and limits. By connecting their businesses to this online global infrastructure, companies can expand their markets, reduce communications and distribution costs, and improve their profit margins without massive cost outlays for new telecommunications facilities. Figure 12.16 outlines key considerations for global e-commerce Web sites [13].

The Internet, along with its related intranet and extranet technologies, provides a low-cost interactive channel for communications and data exchange with employees, customers, suppliers, distributors, manufacturers, product developers, financial backers, information providers, and so on. In fact, all parties involved can use the Internet and other related networks to communicate and collaborate to bring a business venture to its successful completion. However, as Figure 12.17 illustrates, much work needs to be done to bring secure Internet access and electronic commerce to more people in more countries. But the trend is clearly toward continued expansion of the Internet as it becomes a pervasive IT platform for global business.

Global Data Access Issues

Global **data access issues** have been a subject of political controversy and technology barriers in global business operations for many years but have become more visible with the growth of the Internet and the pressures of e-commerce. A major example is the issue of **transborder data flows (TDF)**, in which business data flow across

FIGURE 12.17 Current numbers of Internet users by world region. Note: Internet usage and population statistics, updated on March 24, 2005.

World Internet Usage and Population Statistics						
World Regions	Population (2005 Est.)	Population % of World	Internet Usage, Latest Data	Usage Growth 2000–2005	Penetration (% Population)	World Users %
Africa	900,465,411	14.0 %	13,468,600	198.3%	1.5%	1.5%
Asia	3,612,363,165	56.3	302,257,003	164.4	8.4	34.0
Europe	730,991,138	11.4	259,653,144	151.9	35.5	29.2
Middle East	259,499,772	4.0	19,370,700	266.5	7.5	2.2
North America	328,387,059	5.1	221,437,647	104.9	67.4	24.9
Latin America/Caribbean	546,917,192	8.5	56,224,957	211.2	10.3	6.3
Oceania/Australia	33,443,448	0.5	16,269,080	113.5	48.6	1.8
WORLD TOTAL	**6,412,067,185**	**100.0**	**888,681,131**	**146.2**	**13.9**	**100.0**

Source: www.internetworldstats.com.

FIGURE 12.18
Key data privacy provisions of the agreement to protect the privacy of consumers in e-commerce transactions between the United States and the European Union.

U.S.–EU Data Privacy Requirements
• Notice of purpose and use of data collected.
• Ability to opt out of third-party distribution of data.
• Access for consumers to their information.
• Adequate security, data integrity, and enforcement provisions.

international borders over the telecommunications networks of global information systems. Many countries view TDF as violating their national sovereignty because these data flows avoid customs duties and regulations for the import or export of goods and services. Others view TDF as violating their laws to protect the local IT industry from competition or their labor regulations for protecting local jobs. In many cases, the data flow business issues that seem especially politically sensitive are those that affect the movement out of a country of personal data in e-commerce and human resource applications.

Many countries, especially those in the European Union, may view transborder data flows as a violation of their privacy legislation because, in many cases, data about individuals are being moved out of the country without stringent privacy safeguards. For example, Figure 12.18 outlines the key provisions of a data privacy agreement between the United States and the European Union [22]. The agreement exempts U.S. companies engaging in international e-commerce from EU data privacy sanctions if they join a self-regulatory program that provides EU consumers with basic information about, and control over, how their personal data are used. Thus, the agreement is said to provide a "safe harbor" for such companies from the requirements of the EU's Data Privacy Directive, which bans the transfer of personal information on EU citizens to countries that do not have adequate data privacy protection [22].

Council of Europe: Global Cybercrime Treaty

Some information technology managers fear that the Council of Europe's controversial cybercrime treaty, which was approved by 26 member states, plus the United States, Canada, Japan, and South Africa, in November 2001, will affect their businesses from both a liability and a security perspective. But before getting all worked up over liability issues, American IT leaders need to remember that European nation-states are cooperating with the United States in terms of cyberlegislation and law enforcement, explains Martha Stansell-Gamm, chief of the Computer Crime and Intellectual Property Section at the U.S. Department of Justice (DOJ). Stansell-Gamm was the DOJ's representative in the drafting of the treaty. The United States participated because it has observer status within the Council of Europe.

"We already have many treaties—bilateral and multilateral—on law enforcement matters like extradition, mutual assistance, money laundering, and corruption," she notes. "An awful lot of what's going into this treaty is not new; this just combines technology and criminal law and international law."

Just as in other international law enforcement pacts, the primary objective of the treaty is to break the bottlenecks in international cyber investigations, says Stansell-Gamm.

The new Convention on Cybercrime treaty contains provisions that regulate illegal access, illegal interception of electronic communications, data interference, system interference, misuse of devices, computer-related forgery and fraud, child pornography, copyright violations, and corporate liability. Treaty backers say it will serve as a foundation for legislation on such issues by the European Union and its member states and for cooperative agreements with other countries [19].

FIGURE 12.19
Countries that restrict or forbid Internet access by their citizens.

Global Government Restrictions on Internet Access
• **High Government Access Fees** Kazakhstan, Kyrgyzstan
• **Government-Monitored Access** China, Iran, Saudi Arabia, Azerbaijan, Uzbekistan
• **Government-Filtered Access** Belarus, Cuba, Iraq, Tunisia, Sierra Leone, Tajikistan, Turkmenistan, Vietnam
• **No Public Access Allowed** Burma, Libya, North Korea

Internet Access Issues

The Paris-based organization Reporters Without Borders (RSF) reports that there are 45 countries that "restrict their citizens' access to the Internet." At its most fundamental, the struggle between Internet censorship and openness at the national level revolves around three main means: controlling the conduits, filtering the flows, and punishing the purveyors. In countries such as Burma, Libya, North Korea, Syria, and the countries of Central Asia and the Caucasus, Internet access is either banned or subject to tight limitations through government-controlled ISPs, says the RSF [25].

Figure 12.19 outlines the restrictions to public **Internet access** by the governments of the 20 countries deemed most restrictive by the Paris-based Reporters Without Borders (RSF) [25]. See their Web site at www.rsf.fr.

So the Internet has become a global battleground over public access to data and information at business and private sites on the World Wide Web. Of course, this becomes a business issue because restrictive access policies severely inhibit the growth of e-commerce with such countries. Most of the rest of the world has decided that restricting Internet access is not a viable policy but in fact would hurt their countries' opportunities for economic growth and prosperity. Instead, national and international efforts are being made to rate and filter Internet content deemed inappropriate or criminal, such as Web sites for child pornography or terrorism. In any event, countries that significantly restrict Internet access are also choosing to restrict their participation in the growth of electronic commerce [25].

To RSF and others, these countries' rulers face a lose–lose struggle against the Information Age. By denying or limiting Internet access, they stymie a major engine of economic growth. But by easing access, they expose their citizenry to ideas that potentially might destabilize to the status quo. Either way, many people will get access to the electronic information they want. "In Syria, for example, people go to Lebanon for the weekend to retrieve their e-mail," says Virginie Locussol, RSF's desk officer for the Middle East and North Africa [25].

Global Systems Development

Just imagine the challenges of developing efficient, effective, and responsive applications for business end users domestically. Then multiply that by the number of countries and cultures that may use a global e-business system. That's the challenge of managing global systems development. Naturally, there are conflicts over local versus global system requirements and difficulties in agreeing on common system features such as multilingual user interfaces and flexible design standards. And all of this effort must take place in an environment that promotes involvement and "ownership" of a system by local end users.

Other **systems development issues** arise from disturbances caused by systems implementation and maintenance activities. For example, "An interruption during a third shift in New York City will present midday service interruptions in Tokyo." Another major development issue relates to the trade-offs between developing one system that can run on multiple computer and operating system platforms or letting each local site customize the software for its own platform [9].

Other important global systems development issues are concerned with global standardization of data definitions. Common data definitions are necessary for sharing data among the parts of an international business. Differences in language, culture, and technology platforms can make global data standardization quite difficult. For example, a sale may be called "an 'order booked' in the United Kingdom, an 'order scheduled' in Germany, and an 'order produced' in France" [18]. However, businesses are moving ahead to standardize data definitions and structures. By moving their subsidiaries into data modeling and database design, they hope to develop a global data architecture that supports their global business objectives.

Systems Development Strategies

Several strategies can be used to solve some of the systems development problems that arise in global IT. First is transforming an application used by the home office into a global application. However, often the system used by a subsidiary that has the best version of an application will be chosen for global use. Another approach is setting up a *multinational development team* with key people from several subsidiaries to ensure that the system design meets the needs of local sites as well as corporate headquarters.

A third approach is called *parallel development.* That's because parts of the system are assigned to different subsidiaries and the home office to develop at the same time, based on the expertise and experience at each site. Another approach is the concept of *centers of excellence.* In this approach, an entire system may be assigned for development to a particular subsidiary based on its expertise in the business or technical dimensions needed for successful development. A final approach that has rapidly become a major development option is to outsource the development work to global or *offshore* development companies that have the skills and experience required to develop global business/IT applications. Obviously, all of these approaches require development team collaboration and managerial oversight to meet the global needs of a business. So, global systems development teams are making heavy use of the Internet, intranets, groupware, and other electronic collaboration technologies [9]. See Figure 12.20.

DHL Worldwide: Global Systems Development

San Francisco–based DHL Worldwide Express Inc. has opened development centers in the United Kingdom and in Malaysia, India, and other parts of Asia. The international delivery giant is able to take advantage of time differences between these locations and California to create an extended workday.

"For us, large-scale development is not a hothouse environment; it's an everyday reality," says Colum Joyce, a global e-business strategy manager based in DHL's offices in Brussels. That means establishing development facilities around the world, as well as working with outsourcers where necessary. These realities, combined with the lower turnover rates and salaries in many foreign countries—the average salary for a skilled programmer in India, for example, is about $30,000—are driving global companies to open offshore facilities.

DHL's offshore developers tailor e-business applications to country-specific requirements and even take lead roles in some development efforts, such as a wireless service applications project that's under way in Europe and Asia. According to Joyce, the company looks at several factors when hiring in these locations, including the technical and linguistic skills of local workers, long-term business viability, and knowledge transfer. "A mastery of English is a key skill set, as it is the operating

FIGURE 12.20 An example of Internet-enabled collaboration in global IT systems development. Note the roles played by the client company, offshore outsource developer, global open-source community, and just-in-time development team.

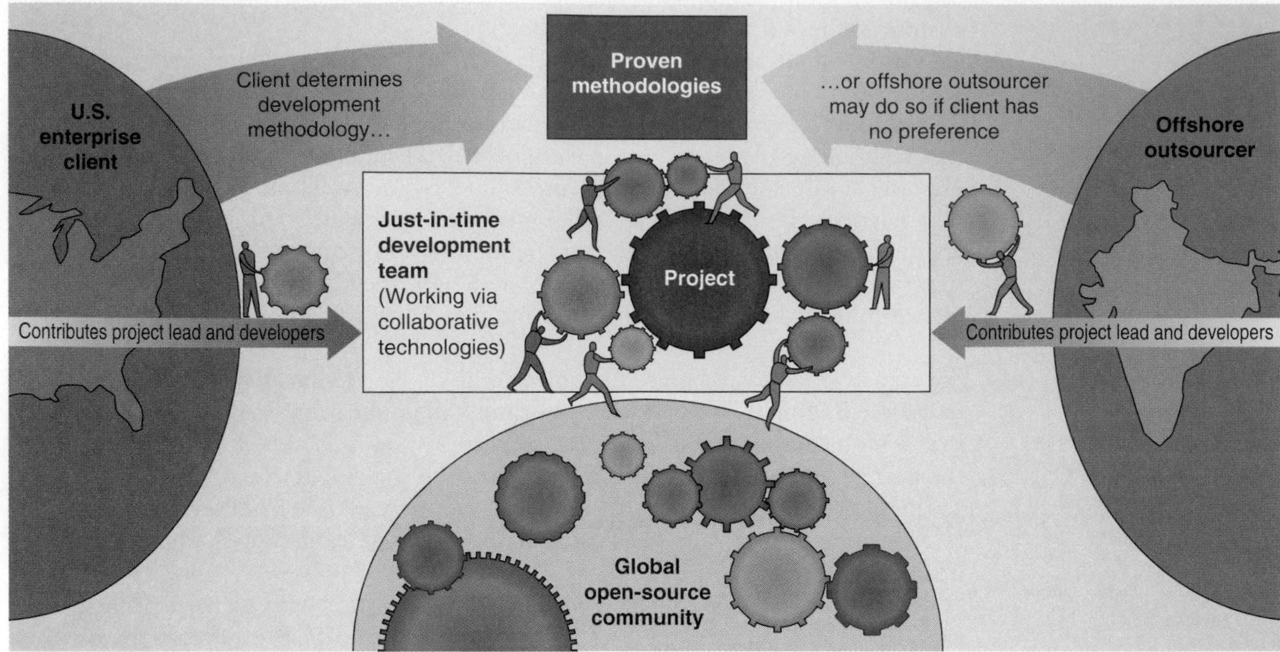

Source: Adapted from Jon Udell, "Leveraging a Global Advantage," *Infoworld*, April 21, 2003, p. 35.

language of all cross-group communication for all development, whether it be verbal, hard copy, or electronic communication," Joyce explains.

"It is not so much the knowledge but the willingness and flexibility to learn that is important in hiring global IT workers," Joyce continues. "In an incredibly dynamic environment, it is the attitude, rather than gross development capability, that counts the most in recruitment." Nonetheless, Joyce acknowledges that success in such endeavors depends heavily on adopting market standards in technology infrastructures and ensuring continual communication among development teams in disparate locations. To that end, DHL puts a great deal of effort into developing what Joyce calls "hybrid managers" who are heavily immersed in both IT and business.

"This has been a process we have engaged in for over 15 years," Joyce says. "The boundaries are really transparent now, and managers and personnel are cross-comfortable with the global business and its supporting infrastructure." [6]

Summary

- **Managing Information Technology.** Managing IT can be viewed as having three major components: (1) managing the joint development and implementation of e-business and IT strategies, (2) managing the development of e-business applications and the research and implementation of new information technologies, and (3) managing IT processes, professionals, and subunits within a company's IT organization and IS function.
- **Failures in IT Management.** Information systems are not being used effectively or efficiently by many organizations. The experiences of successful organizations reveal that the basic ingredient of high-quality information system performance is extensive and meaningful management and user involvement in the governance and development of IT applications. Thus, managers may serve on executive IT groups

and create IS management functions within their business units.

- **Managing Global IT.** The international dimensions of managing global information technologies include dealing with cultural, political, and geoeconomic challenges posed by various countries; developing appropriate business and IT strategies for the global marketplace; and developing a portfolio of global e-business and e-commerce applications and an Internet-based technology platform to support them. In addition, data access methods have to be developed and systems development projects managed to produce the global e-business applications that are required to compete successfully in the global marketplace.
- **Global Business and IT Strategies and Issues.** Many businesses are becoming global companies and moving toward transnational business strategies in which they integrate the global business activities of their subsidiaries and headquarters. This transition requires that they develop a global IT platform—that is, an integrated worldwide hardware, software, and Internet-based network architecture. Global companies are increasingly using the Internet and related technologies as a major component of this IT platform to develop and deliver global IT applications that meet their unique global business requirements. Global IT and end-user managers must deal with limitations to the availability of hardware and software; restrictions on transborder data flows, Internet access, and movement of personal data; and difficulties with developing common data definitions and system requirements.

Key Terms and Concepts

These are the key terms and concepts of this chapter. The page number of their first explanation is in parentheses.

1. Application development management (472)
2. Business/IT planning process (469)
3. Centralization or decentralization of IT (472)
4. Chargeback systems (473)
5. Chief information officer (474)
6. Chief technology officer (475)
7. Data center (473)
8. Downsizing (472)
9. Global business drivers (487)
10. Global information technology management (481)
    - *a.* Data access issues (490)
    - *b.* Systems development issues (492)
11. IS operations management (473)
12. IT architecture (470)
13. IT staff planning (474)
14. Management involvement (479)
15. Managing information technology (466)
16. Offshoring (477)
17. Outsourcing (476)
18. System performance monitor (473)
19. Technology management (475)
20. Transborder data flows (490)
21. Transnational strategy (485)
22. User services (475)

Review Quiz

Match one of the key terms and concepts listed previously with one of the brief examples or definitions that follow. Try to find the best fit for the answers that seem to fit more than one term or concept. Defend your choices.

____ 1. Focuses on discovering innovative approaches to satisfying a company's customer value and business value goals with the support of IT.

____ 2. Concerned with the use of hardware, software, network, and IS personnel resources within the corporate or business unit.

____ 3. Managing business/IT planning and the IS function within a company.

____ 4. A conceptual design, or blueprint, of an organization's IS/IT functions, hardware, and software created by a strategic business/IT planning process.

____ 5. Many organizations have both centralized and decentralized IT units.

____ 6. Managing the creation and implementation of new business applications.

____ 7. End users need liaison, consulting, and training services.

____ 8. Involves recruiting, training, and retaining qualified IS personnel.

____ 9. Corporate locations for computer system operations.

____ 10. Rapidly changing technological developments must be anticipated, identified, and implemented.

____ 11. A relocation of an organization's business processes (including production/manufacturing) to a lower cost location, usually overseas.

____ 12. The executive responsible for strategic business/IT planning and IT management.

____ 13. The executive in charge of researching and implementing new information technologies.

____ 14. Software that helps monitor and control computer systems in a data center.

____ 15. The cost of IS services may be allocated back to end users.

____ 16. Many business firms are replacing their mainframe systems with networked PCs and servers.

____ 17. The purchase of goods or services from third-party partners that were previously provided internally.

____ 18. Managing IT to support a company's international business operations.

____ 19. A business depends heavily on its information systems and Internet technologies to help it integrate its global business activities.

____ 20. Global customers, products, operations, resources, and collaboration.

____ 21. Global telecommunications networks like the Internet move data across national boundaries.

____ 22. Agreement is needed on common user interfaces and Web site design features in global IT.

____ 23. Security requirements for personal information in corporate databases within a host country are a top concern.

____ 24. Business managers should oversee IT decision making and projects that are critical to their business units' success.

Discussion Questions

1. What has been the impact of information technologies on the work relationships, activities, and resources of managers?
2. What can business unit managers do about performance problems in the use of information technology and the development and operation of information systems in their business units?
3. Refer to the Real World Case on Hewlett-Packard in the chapter. Would you like to be the CIO of a company today? Would you want to serve on an executive steering committee of business managers that makes decisions on the use of IT within a company? Explain your answers to both questions.
4. How are Internet technologies affecting the structure and work roles of modern organizations? For example, will middle management wither away? Will companies consist primarily of self-directed project teams of knowledge workers? Explain your answers.
5. Should the IS function in a business be centralized or decentralized? Use the Internet to find recent developments to support your answer.
6. Refer to the Real World Case on the IBM Corporation in the chapter. Do you agree with CEO Sam Palmisano that if IBM shares its discoveries wisely, "it will make the pie bigger," and IBM and the whole IT industry will grow faster? Why or why not?
7. How will the Internet, intranets, and extranets affect each of the components of global information technology management, as illustrated in Figure 12.11? Give several examples.
8. How might cultural, political, or geoeconomic challenges affect a global company's use of the Internet? Give several examples.
9. Will the increasing use of the Internet by firms with global business operations change their move toward a transnational business strategy? Explain.
10. How might the Internet, intranets, and extranets affect the business drivers or requirements responsible for a company's use of global IT, as shown in Figure 12.14? Give several examples to illustrate your answer.

Analysis Exercises

1. **Top-Rated Web Sites for Executives**
   CEO Express
   Check out CEO Express (www.ceoexpress.com), a top-rated Web portal for busy executives. See Figure 12.21. The site provides links to top U.S. and international newspapers, business and technology magazines, and news services. Hundreds of links to business and technology research sources and references are provided, as well as travel services, online shopping, and recreational Web sites. Premium services include e-mail, contact management, calendaring and scheduling, community networking, and powerful information organizing and sharing tools.

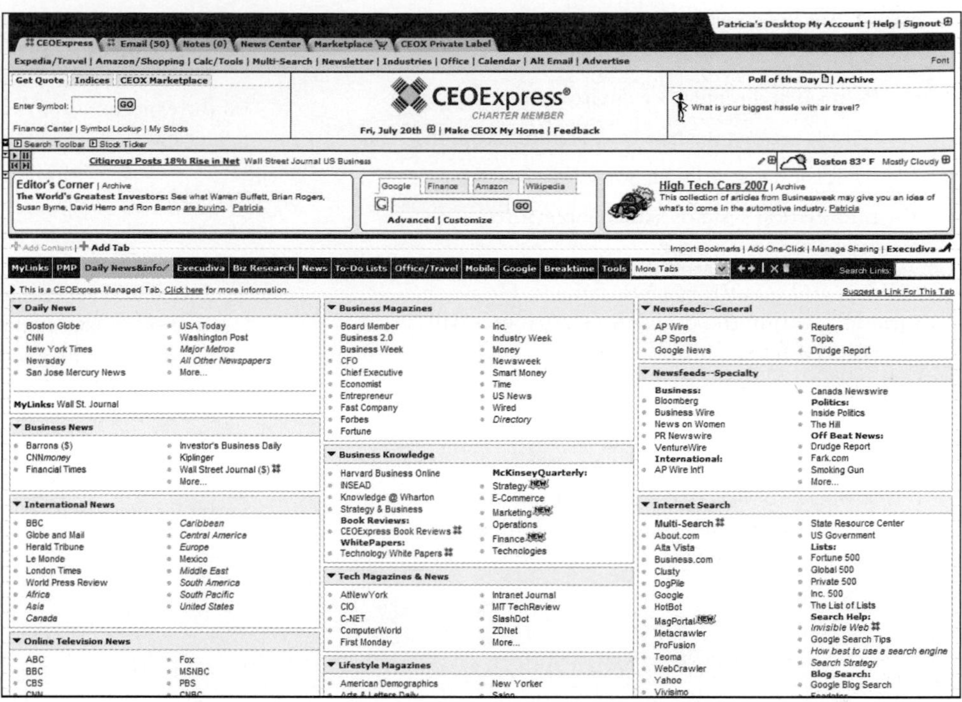

FIGURE 12.21
The CEO Express Web site.

a. Evaluate the CEO Express Web site as a source of useful links to business and technology news, analysis, and research sources for business executives and professionals.

b. Compare CEO Express with Google News (news.google.com) and Google IG (www.google.com/ig). What advantages does CEO Express provide?

c. Select the featured article from the "Editor's Corner." What was the source? Summarize the article. Was it useful to you?

2. **Information and Communications for Development**
Assessing Global Capabilities
Over one billion people take their electrical and telecommunications systems for granted. However, for billions more, the service-on-demand mentality remains a distant dream and Internet access only a rumor. Recognizing the need to promote global information and communications technologies (GICT), the World Bank has undertaken numerous technology infrastructure assessment and development projects.

a. What is the World Bank (www.worldbank.org) doing to address third-world computer literacy needs?

b. What is MIT (www.mit.edu) doing to help increase global computer literacy?

3. **Overseas Assignments**
Incompatible Electricity?
Traveling outside their home country poses special challenges for business travelers who need to remain connected, especially those working out of their hotel rooms. Electricity varies by voltage, cycles, and electric-plug shape. Likewise, telephone jacks may vary from country to country, and American cell phones work pretty much only in America.

If you find yourself on an overseas assignment, how will you keep your laptop computer charged? How will you access the Internet? Can you free yourself from expensive hotel telephone surcharges?

Pick a country to "visit" (your professor may assign one instead), and report on specific solutions to each question. Be sure to include the manufacturer and model number of any hardware you may require. Cite all your sources.

a. What do you need to bring with you to keep your laptop computer charged?

b. What do you need to bring with you to connect your laptop's modem to the local telephone network?

c. What will you use in place of your handy cell phone?

d. Use a collaboration-enabled system such as Blackboard, Web CT, Dreamweaver, or Front Page to merge, organize, and publish your results with the rest of your class to create an online resource.

4. **Knowledge Work on the Move**
Business Process Outsourcing
Having discovered knowledge work's location independence, many organizations seek to lower their labor costs by moving their digital operations overseas. When evaluating such opportunities,

managers must consider the following regional attributes:

- Political and regulatory environment.
- Infrastructure (electrical, telecommunications).
- Professionally skilled labor force.
- Information systems skilled labor force.

All prospective locations must have a supportive political and regulatory environment. However, variations within the other three attributes will pose special limitations. For example, India has millions of well-educated workers but notoriously unreliable telecommunications and electrical grids. Organizations setting up outsourcing operations in India build their own islands of stability with backup power and satellite telecommunications systems. A region with a shortage of professionally skilled labor may offer labor-intensive activities such as call centers or data entry instead, yet even these jobs require basic computer literacy.

The value of services provided depends primarily on the expertise or creativity involved in its performance. List suitable job titles for each work characteristic below. Rank each item in order of the value provided.

a. Digitize: Convert data or information into a digital form.

b. Distribute: Process information in one direction or another based on strict rules and nondigital inputs (if the inputs were digital, a computer could probably do the job).

c. Analyze: Process information based on human expertise.

d. Create: Create new information or products based on human expertise.

REAL WORLD CASE 3 Northwestern Mutual Life, GE, and Boeing: The Business Challenges of Outsourcing

There is certainly no shortage of advice when it comes to discussing the keys to a successful outsourcing effort. Furthermore, it seems that for every company facing the issue, there exist only a few simple guidelines for it to use in managing the effort. Some companies are focused on privacy and security. Others seem more concerned with reengineering, while still others tend to focus on the effective management of the outsourcing relationship. Each of these perspectives is important, but it is clear that the key issues to successful outsourcing are often unique to the company and its needs.

For example, concerns about privacy and security have kept many financial-services companies from moving customer data files offshore, limiting their ability to reap cost savings offered by outsourcing vendors in low-cost countries. Executives at Northwestern Mutual Life Insurance Co. believe they've solved the problem.

Since late 2004, the diversified insurance and financial-services company has given IT workers at Infosys Technologies Ltd. in India access to applications containing sensitive customer data, including Social Security numbers. The employees use dumb terminals that limit users' ability to alter, record, or print the data. "The machines don't even have hard drives," Northwestern Mutual CIO Barbara Piehler notes in an interview at the Gartner outsourcing conference. The terminals are linked via secure, high-speed phone lines to Northwestern Mutual's servers in Milwaukee. Infosys staffers use them to test and maintain a number of the company's business applications.

Northwestern Mutual executives came up with the plan after deciding they weren't getting the most out of their offshore contractors, Piehler recalls. The company previously sent to India only the IT applications that didn't involve customer data. "But that limits what you can do offshore," she said.

Financial-services companies have a lot to gain by moving IT work offshore. They can cut the cost of IT work by 39 percent by outsourcing it abroad, Deloitte Consulting estimates.

But some federal regulators believe the practice carries privacy risks. In a study released last year, the Federal Deposit Insurance Corp. noted that "background checks of [services firms'] employees involving credit-bureau information, criminal records, or even drug-testing results are standard requirements in the United States. The ability to obtain the same types of reviews in many other countries is questionable." For now, the government hasn't imposed any significant restrictions on offshoring personal data, though lawmakers in some states, such as California, have proposed them.

Northwestern Mutual's safeguards are more than adequate to protect customer data, Piehler argues. Beyond secure lines and dumb terminals, the company insists that Infosys put additional physical security measures in place. A guard is posted on the floor of the Infosys facility where Northwestern Mutual's work is performed, and employees aren't allowed to take any documents or media with them after they clock out. "Nobody cares about protecting our customers more than I do," Piehler asserts.

Northwestern Mutual doesn't inform its 3 million policyholders that their personal data are, in some cases, viewed by offshore workers. "It's just the way we do business now," Piehler says. Some analysts, however, say that it's good business practice for companies to inform customers if their personal data are accessed offshore. "Beyond any ethical responsibility, you don't want your customers to have a nasty surprise if something goes wrong," warns Phil Fersht, research VP at the Yankee Group.

Under the Gramm-Leach-Bliley Act of 1999, financial-services companies must explain their privacy policies to customers. However, the law doesn't prevent financial-services companies from transferring customer data to offshore third parties for processing. It also doesn't provide customers with the right to opt out of such activity.

Beyond privacy issues, opponents of moving data offshore say the practice threatens U.S. jobs. Piehler counters that Northwestern Mutual, which employs about 1,000 technology workers, hasn't cut any domestic IT staff since it began sending work to India.

When it comes to outsourcing, privacy concerns are not always the primary motivation. In fact, there could be a $1 billion sale out there for a lucky enterprise-software vendor and perhaps an outsourcing-services partner if the right solution can be found for General Electric Co. GE would like to implement a massive enterprise resource planning system to tie together its 11 business units and countless divisions. "We have looked at it, and we'll continue to look at it," acknowledges Richard Dobbs, financial-services leader at the diversified consumer and business-to-business manufacturing and services company.

GE uses ERP applications from PeopleSoft, SAP, and a number of other vendors. The company ideally would like to "rationalize" its ERP systems, Dobbs agrees, and he put the cost of such an effort "north of $1 billion."

However, integrating the entire company's operations through a single ERP system could ultimately prove too expensive and complicated an effort to undertake. "It would be hard to get our hands around that," Dobbs acknowledges. As an alternative, Dobbs would like to see a major outsourcing company pair up with a major ERP vendor to provide GE with a "wing-to-wing" ERP offering on an outsourced basis.

GE is embracing outsourcing in a big way. It was one of the first major companies to employ IT staff in low-cost countries such as India using so-called captive operations—facilities located abroad but company owned and operated. Now GE has come full circle to embrace outsourcing as the best means to access low-cost labor and efficient IT and business-process services.

"Outsourcing is the way of business now," Dobbs proclaims. Last year, GE spun off its India-based business-process-out-sourcing arm, General Electric Capital International Services, for about $500 million to private investors. The company also sold, to Affiliated Computer Services Inc., a number of other BPO facilities, which that company now operates on behalf of GE under a 10-year outsourcing contract.

Executives at Boeing Co. are telling a tale of two outsourcing projects that show the importance of preparation to the success of an IT services engagement. The company's decision in 2003 to outsource a range of technology operations to several vendors is returning greater savings than expected because Boeing IT executives followed a meticulous transition plan, claims Philip Harris, the aerospace company's director of IT sourcing and benchmarking. By contrast, the company's rushed effort to turn over IT operations to a single vendor in 1998 following its merger with McDonnell Douglas resulted in numerous foul-ups. "There were a lot of bumps," Harris says.

Boeing outsources the bulk of its IT operations to Computer Sciences Corp., Dell, and IBM. The move has since helped the company keep IT costs in check and operate more efficiently. "The best-of-breed model has delivered the anticipated savings, plus more," Harris promises. He didn't provide specifics, but even a small percentage of extra savings could yield big dollars for Boeing, which spends more than $1 billion annually on IT.

Boeing awarded CSC two six-year contracts worth a total of $150 million to manage its servers and mainframes. IBM received a three-year, $160 million deal to run Boeing's voice network, and Dell won a five-year contract to operate the company's desktop systems for an undisclosed sum.

The success of the deals is in large part because of the extensive preparatory work that Boeing undertook before signing, according to Harris. Among other things, the company formed a transition committee, led by Harris, charged with ensuring that even the smallest details of the handover—such as sending the right contractors to the right buildings—were planned. Boeing also insisted that vendors competing for the contracts include detailed plans for transitioning the company's employees to the outsourcing company in their bids. Harris claims his job depended on a smooth transfer. "If it wasn't a seamless transition, then I would have been explaining to my successor why it wasn't successful."

Boeing's current low-turbulence IT outsourcing engagements stand in stark contrast to its earlier effort to hand over technology operations to IBM following the merger with McDonnell Douglas. IBM had previously signed a groundbreaking, 10-year, $3 billion outsourcing deal with McDonnell Douglas that Boeing inherited. But Boeing didn't take enough time to prepare for the transition, which went badly, Harris notes. "There were help-desk tickets piling up on the floor," he recalls.

Harris doesn't blame IBM for the problems, which also included an executive secretary losing all communication with her boss. Rather, Boeing's lack of preparation was at fault, he says.

Source: Adapted from Paul McDougall, "The Hard Road to Outsourcing," *InformationWeek*, April 11, 2005.

CASE STUDY QUESTIONS

1. The law does not require companies to disclose to their customers that they have outsourced or offshored access to their data. Is this a potential problem for either the company or the customer? Why or why not?
2. What is meant by the term "best-of-breed model"? Why has this approach worked for Boeing?
3. GE wants to outsource its entire ERP system based, in part, on its successes with other outsourcing projects. Is it possible to outsource too much?

REAL WORLD ACTIVITIES

1. Each of the companies in the case shares a common goal but from a different perspective. As we learned in the chapter, there are a variety of reasons a company may choose to outsource. Using the Internet and Figure 12.6 as your guide, see if you can find examples of companies that have chosen to outsource for reasons different from the three outlined in the case. What were their reasons?
2. Outsourcing and offshoring are controversial issues—particularly when it comes to jobs. Break into small groups with your classmates and discuss the pros and cons of this issue. Should we curtail outsourcing and offshoring to protect jobs? Are new jobs being created to replace the ones lost?

Review Quiz Answers

Chapter 1

Foundations of Information Systems in Business

1. 20
2. 18
3. 23
4. 23*a*
5. 23*b*
6. 23*c*
7. 15
8. 1
9. 22*b*
10. 8
11. 9
12. 10
13. 25
14. 12
15. 2
16. 3
17. 14
18. 4
19. 17
20. 13
21. 13*a*
22. 13*b*
23. 24
24. 24*a*
25. 24*b*
26. 22
27. 16*a*
28. 16*b*
29. 16*c*
30. 16*d*
31. 16*e*
32. 26
33. 26*c*
34. 26*b*
35. 26*a*
36. 19
37. 11
38. 7
39. 26*d*
40. 5
41. 6
42. 14*a*
43. 21
44. 22*a*

Chapter 2

Competing with Information Technology

1. 3
2. 4
3. 12
4. 11
5. 5
6. 13
7. 6
8. 14
9. 10
10. 2
11. 1
12. 15
13. 8
14. 9
15. 7

Chapter 3

Computer Hardware

1. 3
2. 2
3. 5
4. 8
5. 27
6. 30
7. 25
8. 22
9. 21
10. 1
11. 7
12. 13
13. 14
14. 9*a*
15. 9*b*
16. 18
17. 9*c*
18. 20
19. 19
20. 35
21. 10
22. 28*c*
23. 34*e*
24. 26
25. 15
26. 12
27. 16
28. 17
29. 33
30. 24
31. 28
32. 28*a*
33. 34*c*
34. 4
35. 34
36. 37
37. 34*a*
38. 34*f*
39. 31*b*
40. 31*a*
41. 36
42. 6
43. 32
44. 31
45. 9
46. 11
47. 23

Chapter 4

Computer Software

1. 30
2. 2
3. 24
4. 1
5. 4
6. 5
7. 31
8. 6
9. 33
10. 21
11. 14
12. 26
13. 18
14. 32
15. 11
16. 10
17. 34
18. 8
19. 29
20. 36
21. 7
22. 25
23. 16
24. 28
25. 12
26. 19
27. 3
28. 13
29. 9
30. 23
31. 22
32. 27
33. 14
34. 37
35. 17
36. 24
37. 20
38. 15
39. 35

Chapter 5

Data Resource Management

1. 11
2. 10
3. 9
4. 18
5. 2
6. 3
7. 12
8. 20*b*
9. 13*d*
10. 20*d*
11. 8
12. 5
13. 6
14. 16*b*
15. 16*c*
16. 16*d*
17. 16*e*
18. 15
19. 13*a*
20. 13*e*
21. 13*b*
22. 20*e*
23. 20*a*
24. 20*c*

Chapter 6

Telecommunications and Networks

1. 34
2. 23
3. 20
4. 17
5. 16
6. 13
7. 8
8. 10
9. 35
10. 15
11. 7
12. 29
13. 9
14. 3
15. 31
16. 32
17. 18
18. 19
19. 24
20. 1
21. 2
22. 33
23. 5
24. 27
25. 21*a*
26. 21*b*
27. 25
28. 12
29. 11
30. 4
31. 22
32. 26
33. 6
34. 14
35. 30
36. 36

Chapter 7

Electronic Business Systems

1. 7
2. 5
3. 14
4. 9
5. 10
6. 20
7. 16
8. 24
9. 19
10. 4
11. 3
12. 11
13. 22
14. 17
15. 15
16. 8
17. 1
18. 13
19. 18
20. 27
21. 6
22. 12
23. 26
24. 25
25. 2
26. 23
27. 28
28. 21

Chapter 8

Electronic Commerce Systems

1. 6
2. 6*b*
3. 6*a*
4. 6*c*
5. 5
6. 8
7. 8*a*
8. 8*g*
9. 8*d*
10. 8*i*
11. 8*f*
12. 8*c*
13. 9
14. 3*d*
15. 3
16. 3*a*
17. 3*c*
18. 3*b*
19. 2
20. 7
21. 8*e*
22. 10
23. 1
24. 4
25. 11

Chapter 9

Decision Support Systems

1. 6
2. 10
3. 21
4. 7
5. 3
6. 22
7. 1
8. 1*d*
9. 1*c*
10. 1*a*
11. 1*b*
12. 24
13. 4
14. 5
15. 8
16. 20
17. 9
18. 2
19. 25
20. 26
21. 15
22. 11
23. 18
24. 16
25. 12
26. 19
27. 23
28. 13
29. 17
30. 14

Chapter 10

Developing Business/IT Solutions

1. 20
2. 26
3. 16
4. 3
5. 27*b*
6. 12*b*
7. 27*a*
8. 12*a*
9. 21
10. 14
11. 8
12. 6
13. 28
14. 13
15. 10
16. 19
17. 9
18. 29
19. 24
20. 22
21. 23
22. 18
23. 7
24. 11
25. 2
26. 25
27. 5
28. 17
29. 31
30. 30
31. 1

Chapter 11

Security and Ethical Challenges

1. 24
2. 20
3. 28
4. 16
5. 17
6. 10
7. 2
8. 4
9. 12
10. 13
11. 15
12. 5
13. 26
14. 27
15. 22
16. 7
17. 8
18. 11
19. 6
20. 29
21. 25
22. 21
23. 19
24. 9
25. 1
26. 18
27. 14

Chapter 12

Enterprise and Global Management of Information Technology

1. 2
2. 11
3. 15
4. 12
5. 3
6. 1
7. 22
8. 13
9. 7
10. 19
11. 16
12. 5
13. 6
14. 18
15. 4
16. 8
17. 17
18. 10
19. 21
20. 9
21. 20
22. 10b
23. 10a
24. 14

Selected References

Preface

Sawhney, Mohan; and Jeff Zabin. *The Seven Steps to Nirvana: Strategic Insights into e-Business Transformation.* New York: McGraw-Hill, 2001.

Chapter 1—Foundations of Information Systems in Business

1. Melymuka, Kathleen. "Profiting from Mistakes." *Computerworld*, April 20, 2001.
2. Kalakota, Ravi; and Marcia Robinson. *E-Business 2.0: Roadmap for Success*. Reading, MA: Addison-Wesley, 2001.
3. Institute for Development Policy and Management, http://www.egov4dev.org/home.htm and http://www.e-devexchange.org/eGov/home.htm, March 2004.
4. "Citibank E-Mail Hoax and Webpage Scam," http://www.millersmiles.co.uk/identitytheft/citibank-email-verification-hoax.htm, November 2003.
5. Lee, Allen. "Inaugural Editor's Comments." *MIS Quarterly*, March 1999.
6. Norris, Grant; James Hurley; Kenneth Hartley; John Dunleavy; and John Balls. *E-Business and ERP: Transforming the Enterprise*. New York: John Wiley & Sons, 2000.
7. Radcliff, Deborah. "Aligning Marriott." *Computerworld*, April 20, 2000.
8. Rosencrance, L. "Citibank Customers Hit with E-Mail Scam." *Computerworld*, October 24, 2003.
9. Steadman, Craig. "Failed ERP Gamble Haunts Hershey." *Computerworld*, November 1, 1999.
10. Weiss, Todd. "Hershey Upgrades R/3 ERP System without Hitches." *Computerworld*, September 9, 2002.
11. Williams, Lisa. "EMC Keeps Red Sox in the Game." *ITworldcanada.com*. 2006.
12. Thibodeau, Patrick. "Want to Win in Vegas? Bet on an IT Job, Not the Super Bowl." *Computerworld*, Feb. 02, 2007.

Chapter 2—Competing with Information Technology

1. "Agilent Technologies ERP Information for Customers," http://www.tmintl.agilent.com/model/index.shtml, n.d.
2. Applegate, Lynda; Robert D. Austin; and F. Warren McFarlan. *Corporate Information Systems Management: Text and Cases*. 6th ed. Burr Ridge, IL: Irwin/McGraw-Hill, 2003.
3. Bowles, Jerry. "Best Practices for Global Competitiveness." *Fortune*, Special Advertising Section, November 24, 1997.
4. Caron, J. Raymond; Sirkka Jarvenpaa; and Donna Stoddard. "Business Reengineering at CIGNA Corporation: Experiences and Lessons from the First Five Years." *MIS Quarterly*, September 1994.
5. Christensen, Clayton. *The Innovators Dilemma: When New Technologies Cause Great Firms to Fail*. Boston: Harvard Business School Press, 1997.
6. Cronin, Mary. *The Internet Strategy Handbook*. Boston: Harvard Business School Press, 1996.
7. Davenport, Thomas H. *Process Innovation: Reengineering Work through Information Technology*. Boston: Harvard Business School Press, 1993.
8. El Sawy, Omar; and Gene Bowles. "Redesigning the Customer Support Process for the Electronic Economy: Insights from Storage Dimensions." *MIS Quarterly*, December 1997.
9. El Sawy, Omar; Arvind Malhotra; Sanjay Gosain; and Kerry Young. "IT-Intensive Value Innovation in the Electronic Economy: Insights from Marshall Industries." *MIS Quarterly*, September 1999.
10. Frye, Colleen. "Imaging Proves Catalyst for Reengineering." *Client/Server Computing*, November 1994.
11. Garner, Rochelle. "Please Don't Call IT Knowledge Management!" *Computerworld*, August 9, 1999.
12. Goldman, Steven; Roger Nagel; and Kenneth Preis. *Agile Competitors and Virtual Organizations: Strategies for Enriching the Customer*. New York: Van Nostrand Reinhold, 1995.
13. Grover, Varun; and Pradipkumar Ramanlal. "Six Myths of Information and Markets: Information Technology Networks, Electronic Commerce, and the Battle for Consumer Surplus." *MIS Quarterly*, December 1999.

14. Hamm, Steve; and Marcia Stepaneck. "From Reengineering to E-Engineering." *BusinessWeek e.biz*, March 22, 1999.

15. Hoffman, T. "In the Know: Knowledge Management Case Study Pays Off for BAE Systems." *Computerworld*, October 14, 2002.

16. "Intel Telecom Case Studies, Best Known Call Center Practices," http://www.intel.com/network/csp/resources/case_studies/enterprise/7867web.htm, n.d.

17. Kalakota, Ravi; and Marcia Robinson. *E-Business 2.0: Roadmap for Success*. Reading, MA: Addison-Wesley, 2001.

18. Kettinger, William; Varun Grover; and Albert Segars. "Do Strategic Systems Really Pay Off? An Analysis of Classic Strategic IT Cases." *Information Systems Management*, Winter 1995.

19. Kettinger, William; James Teng; and Subashish Guha. "Business Process Change: A Study of Methodologies, Techniques, and Tools." *MIS Quarterly*, March 1997.

20. Nonaka, Ikujiro. "The Knowledge Creating Company." *Harvard Business Review*, November–December 1991.

21. Porter, Michael, and Victor Millar. "How Information Gives You Competitive Advantage." *Harvard Business Review*, July–August 1985.

22. Prokesch, Steven. "Unleashing the Power of Learning: An Interview with British Petroleum's John Browne." *Harvard Business Review*, September–October 1997.

23. Sambamurthy, V.; Anandhi Bharadwaj; and Varun Grover. "Shaping Agility through Digital Options: Reconceptualizing the Role of Information Technology in Contemporary Firms." *MIS Quarterly*, June 2003.

24. Seybold, Patricia. *Customers.com: How to Create a Profitable Business Strategy for the Internet and Beyond*. New York: Times Books, 1998.

25. Shapiro, Carl; and Hal Varian. *Information Rules: A Strategic Guide to the Network Economy*. Boston: Harvard Business School Press, 1999.

26. Siekman, Philip. "Why Infotech Loves Its Giant Job Shops." *Fortune*, May 12, 1997.

27. Songini, Marc. "ERP Effort Sinks Agilent Revenue." *Computerworld*, August 26, 2002.

28. Strategy Works, "Retrieval Is the Key to the New Economy," http://www.thestrategyworks.com/articles/knowledge2.htm, August 31, 2000.

29. Babcock, Charles. "Evolve Business Processes, Don't Reengineer Them." *InformationWeek*, November 11, 2004.

30. Weill, Peter; and Michael Vitale. *Place to Space: Migrating to E-Business Models*. Boston: Harvard Business School Press, 2001.

Chapter 3—Computer Hardware

1. *Computerworld*, *PC Week*, *PC Magazine*, and *PC World* are just a few examples of many good magazines for current information on computer systems hardware and its use in end-user and enterprise applications.

2. The World Wide Web sites of computer manufacturers such as Apple Computer, Dell Computer, Gateway, IBM, Hewlett-Packard, Compaq, and Sun Microsystems are good sources of information about computer hardware developments.

3. Alexander, Steve. "Speech Recognition." *Computerworld*, November 8, 1999.

4. "Computing in the New Millennium." *Fortune*, Technology Buyers Guide, Winter 2000.

5. Guyon, Janet. "Smart Plastic." *Fortune*, October 13, 1997.

6. "Hardware." *Fortune*, Technology Buyer's Guide, Winter 1999.

7. Hecht, Jeff. "Casino Chips to Carry RFID Tags." *New Scientist*, January 2004.

8. Joch, Alan. "Fewer Servers, Better Service." *Computerworld*, June 4, 2001.

9. Kennedy, Ken, et al. "A Nationwide Parallel Computing Environment." *Communications of the ACM*, November 1997.

10. Messerschmitt, David. *Networked Applications: A Guide to the New Computing Infrastructure*. San Francisco: Morgan Kaufmann, 1999.

11. Ouellette, Tim. "Goodbye to the Glass House." *Computerworld*, May 26, 1997.

12. Ouellette, Tim. "Tape Storage Put to New Enterprise Uses." *Computerworld*, November 10, 1997.

13. Reimers, Barbara. "Blades Spin ROI Potential." *Computerworld*, February 11, 2002.

14. Simpson, David. "The Datamation 100." *Datamation*, July 1997.

15. "Top 500 Supercomputer Sites: ASCII White," www.top500.org, May 18, 2003.

16. Gaudin, Sharon. "Kurzweil: Computers Will Enable People to Live Forever." *Informationweek*, November 21, 2006.

Chapter 4—Computer Software

1. Examples of many good magazines for current information and reviews of computer software for business applications can be found at ZD Net, the Web site for ZD Publications (www.zdnet.com), including *PC Magazine, PC Week, PC Computing, Macworld, Inter@ctive week,* and *Computer Shopper.*
2. The Web sites of companies like Microsoft, Sun Microsystems, Lotus, IBM, Apple Computer, and Oracle are good sources of information about computer software developments.
3. Ascent Solutions Inc., http://www.ascentsolutionsus.com/erp.htm.
4. Citrix i-Business Report. "Achieving Business Transformation through Application Service Providers." *Business Communications Review,* May 3, 2002.
5. Iyer, Bala; Jim Freedman; Mark Gaynor; and George Wyner. "Web Services: Enabling Dynamic Business Networks." *Communications of the Association for Information Systems* 11, 2003.
6. Gonsalves, A. "At Orbitz, Linux Delivers Double the Performance at One-Tenth the Cost." *InternetWeek.com,* July 1, 2003.
7. Mearian, Lucas. "Fidelity Makes Big XML Conversion." *Computerworld,* October 1, 2001.
8. Microsoft Corporation, "Introducing the Windows 2003 Family," www.microsoft.com, July 1, 2003.
9. Oracle Corporation, "Visa to Save Millions a Year by Automating Back-Office Processes with Oracle E-Business Suite," Customer Profile, www.oracle.com, September 13, 2002.
10. Orbitz Corporate, http://www.orbitz.com/App/about/about.jsp?z=63z0&r=42.
11. Sliwa, Carol. ".Net vs. Java." *Computerworld,* May 20, 2002.
12. Smith, T. "How Web Services Help Wells Fargo Customers." *InternetWeek,* May 13, 2003.
13. Transchannel, LLC., "Transchannel Announces ie2 for People-Soft," http://www.prnewswire.com/, 2002.
14. Vogelstein, Fred. "Servers with a Smile." *Fortune,* September 30, 2002.
15. Wainewright, Ivan. "An Introduction to Application Service Providers (ASPs)." *TechSoup,* May 1, 2000.

Chapter 5—Data Resource Management

1. Amato-McCoy, D. "Enterprise Data Solution Finds a Home at BofA." *Financial Technology Network,* http://www.financetech.com/story/BNK/BNK20021210S0030, December 10, 2002.
2. Fox, Pimm. "Extracting Dollars from Data." *Computerworld,* April 15, 2002.
3. Jacobsen, Ivar; Maria Ericsson; and Ageneta Jacobsen. *The Object Advantage: Business Process Reengineering with Object Technology.* New York: ACM Press, 1995.
4. Weiss, Todd. "IBM to Play Lead Role in Creation of Global Film Database," *Computerworld,* September 3, 2003.
5. IBM Corporation, "DB2 Business Intelligence," www.ibm.com, July 27, 2003.
6. Kalakota, Ravi; and Marcia Robinson. *E-Business 2.0: Roadmap for Success.* Reading, MA: Addison-Wesley, 2002.
7. Sullivan, Laurie. "Lucasfilm Linking Movies, Games, Animation with IT," *InformationWeek,* August 7, 2006.
8. Lorents, Alden; and James Morgan. *Database Systems: Concepts, Management and Applications.* Fort Worth, TX: Dryden Press, 1998.
9. MacSweeney, G. "Aetna Mines Ethnic Health Data." *InsuranceTech,* April 1, 2003.
10. Mannino, Michael. *Database Application Development and Design.* Burr Ridge, IL: McGraw-Hill/Irwin, 2001.
11. Nance, Barry. "Managing Tons of Data." *Computerworld,* April 23, 2001.
12. Whiting, Rick. "The Data-Warehouse Advantage," *InformationWeek,* July 28, 2003.

Chapter 6—Telecommunications and Networks

1. Armor, Daniel. *The E-Business (R)Evolution: Living and Working in an Interconnected World.* Upper Saddle River, NJ: Prentice Hall, 2000.
2. Barksdale, Jim. "The Next Step: Extranets." *Netscape Columns: The Main Thing,* December 3, 1996.
3. "Boeing 777: A Case Study," http://www.eweek.org/2002/nbm/collaborate/collab01.html, n.d.
4. Bresnick, Alan. "Verizon Turns Up Heat in Online Data Wars." *Cable Datacom News,* June 1, 2003.
5. "Cable Modem Info Center," www.cabledatacomnews.com, July 26, 2003.
6. McGee, Marianne Kolbasuk. "Constellation Energy Use IT to Get Employees Working Together and More Productively." *InformationWeek,* September 12, 2006.
7. Chatterjee, Samir. "Requirements for Success in Gigabit Networking." *Communications of the ACM,* July 1997.

8. "Countrywide Home Loans Uses Netscape Platform to Develop Extensive Internet and Intranet Solutions." Netscape Corporate Public Relations Press Release, August 15, 1996.
9. Cronin, Mary. *Doing More Business on the Internet*. New York: Van Nostrand Reinhold, 1995.
10. www.internetworldstats.com, February 19, 2007.
11. Friedman, Matthew. "SSL VPNs Will Grow 54% a Year, Become Defacto Access Standard: Report. *InformationWeek*, January 5, 2005.
12. Housel, Thomas; and Eric Skopec. *Global Telecommunications Revolution: The Business Perspective*. New York: McGraw-Hill/Irwin, 2001.
13. Garevy, Martin J. "Threats Bring IT and Operations Together." *InformationWeek*, September 19, 2005.
14. Kalakota, Ravi; and Marcia Robinson. *E-Business 2.0: Roadmap for Success*. Reading, MA: Addison-Wesley, 2001.
15. Lais, Sami. "Satellites Link Bob Evans Farms." *Computerworld*, July 2, 2001.
16. Messerschmitt, David. *Network Applications: A Guide to the New Computing Infrastructure*. San Francisco: Morgan Kaufmann, 1999.
17. Murphy, Kate. "Cruising the Net in Hyperdrive." *BusinessWeek*, January 24, 2000.
18. Norris, G., "Boeing's Seventh Wonder," *IEEE Spectrum*, http://www.spectrum.ieee.org/publicaccess/1095b777.html, 1995.
19. O'Brien, Atiye. "Friday Intranet Focus." Upside.com: Hot Private Companies. Upside, 1996.
20. Orenstein, David. "Price, Speed, Location All Part of Broadband Choice." *Computerworld*, July 26, 1999.
21. Papows, Jeff. "Endquotes." NetReady Adviser, Winter 1997.
22. "Snap-On Tools Company Uses Netscape Software for Extranet Solution." Netscape Corporate Public Relations Press Release, March 6, 1997.
23. Hamblen, Matthew. "Carriers See Big Growth in IP-based VPN Services." *Computerworld*, January 6, 2005.
24. Stuart, Anne. "Cutting the Cord." *Inc. Tech*, March 2001.
25. UPS corporate Web site, "About UPS," http://www.ups.com/content/us/en/about/index.html, n.d.
26. Farber, Dan. "UPS Takes Wireless to the Next Level." ZDNet Tech Update, http://techupdate.zdnet.com/techupdate/stories/main/0,14179,2913461,00.html, February 19, 2007.
27. Gonsalves, Antone. "Seaport Hotel In-Room Portal Converges Voice, Web Services." *InformationWeek*. January 24, 2007.

Chapter 7—Electronic Business Systems

1. "Baker Tanks Leverages salesforce.com's Wireless Access to Extend Range of Customer Service." Salesforce.com, 2002.
2. Afuah, Allan; and Christopher Tucci. *Internet Business Models and Strategies*. New York: McGraw-Hill/Irwin, 2001.
3. Clark, Charles; Nancy Cavanaugh; Carol Brown; and V. Sambamurthy. "Building Change-Readiness Capabilities in the IS Organization: Insights from the Bell Atlantic Experience." *MIS Quarterly*, December 1997.
4. Cole-Gomolski, Barb. "Users Loath to Share Their Know-How." *Computerworld*, November 17, 1997.
5. Collett, S. "SAP: Whirlpool's Rush to Go Live Leads to Shipping Snafus." *Computerworld*, November 4, 1999.
6. "Communications Leader Becomes Customer-Focused E-Business," *Siebel.com*, March 12, 2001.
7. Cronin, Mary. *The Internet Strategy Handbook*. Boston: Harvard Business School Press, 1996.
8. Cross, John; Michael Earl; and Jeffrey Sampler. "Transformation of the IT Function at British Petroleum." *MIS Quarterly*, December 1997.
9. Das, Sidhartha; Shaker Zahra; and Merrill Warkentin. "Integrating the Content and Process of Strategic MIS Planning with Competitive Strategy." *Decision Sciences Journal*, November–December 1991.
10. De Geus, Arie. "Planning as Learning." *Harvard Business Review*, March–April 1988.
11. Earl, Michael. "Experiences in Strategic Information Systems Planning." *MIS Quarterly*, March 1993.
12. El Sawy, Omar; and Gene Bowles. "Redesigning the Customer Support Process for the Electronic Economy: Insights from Storage Dimensions." *MIS Quarterly*, December 1997.
13. Gates, Bill. *Business @ the Speed of Thought*. New York: Warner Books, 1999.
14. Grover, Varun; James Teng; and Kirk Fiedler. "IS Investment Priorities in Contemporary Organizations." *Communications of the ACM*, February 1998.
15. Hawson, James; and Jesse Beeler. "Effects of User Participation in Systems Development: A Longitudinal Field Experiment." *MIS Quarterly*, December 1997.
16. Hoffman, Thomas. "Intranet Helps Workers Navigate Corporate Maze." *Computerworld*, June 4, 2001.
17. Kettinger, William; James Teng; and Subashish Guha. "Business Process Change: A Study of Methodologies, Techniques, and Tools." *MIS Quarterly*, March 1997.
18. Kalakota, Ravi; and Marcia Robinson, *E-Business 2.0: Roadmap for Success*. Reading, MA: Addison-Wesley, 2001.
19. Keen, Peter; and Craigg Ballance. *Online Profits: A Manager's Guide to Electronic Commerce*. Boston: Harvard Business School Press, 1997.

20. Koudsi, Suzanne. "Actually, It Is Like Brain Surgery." *Fortune*, March 20, 2000.

21. KPMG Case Study. "Think Different: Apple Americas Transforms Its US Business with SAP/R3 in Just Twelve Months." 1999.

22. Levinson, M. "Cleared for Takeoff." *CIO*, April 1, 2002.

23. Martin, Chuck. *The Digital Estate: Strategies for Competing, Surviving, and Thriving in an Internetworked World.* New York: McGraw-Hill, 1997.

24. Orenstein, David. "Enterprise Application Integration." *Computerworld*, October 4, 1999.

25. Robb, Drew. "Rediscovering Efficiency." *Computerworld*, July 16, 2001.

26. Sawhney, Mohan, and Jeff Zabin. *The Seven Steps to Nirvana: Strategic Insights into e-Business Transformation*. New York: McGraw-Hill, 2001.

Chapter 8—Electronic Commerce Systems

1. Armor, Daniel. The *E-Business (R)Evolution: Living and Working in an Interconnected World*. Upper Saddle River, NJ: Prentice Hall, 2000.

2. Cross, Kim. "Need Options? Go Configure." *Business 2.0*, February 2000.

3. Davis, Jeffrey. "How IT Works." *Business 2.0*, February 2000.

4. Davis, Jeffrey. "Mall Rats." *Business 2.0*, January 1999.

5. Essex, David. "Betting on Win 2K." *Computerworld*, February 26, 2001.

6. Enterasys Company Info., http://www.enterasys.com/corporate, n.d.

7. Fellenstein, Craig; and Ron Wood. *Exploring E-Commerce, Global E-Business, and E-Societies*. Upper Saddle River, NJ: Prentice Hall, 2000.

8. Fingar, Peter; Harsha Kumar; and Tarun Sharma. *Enterprise E-Commerce*. Tampa, FL: Meghan-Kiffer Press, 2000.

9. Georgia, Bonnie. "Give Your E-Store an Edge." *Smart Business*, October 2001.

10. Gulati, Ranjay; and Jason Garino. "Get the Right Mix of Clicks and Bricks." *Harvard Business Review*, May–June 2000.

11. Hoque, Faisal. *E-Enterprise: Business Models, Architecture and Components*. Cambridge, UK: Cambridge University Press, 2000.

12. Kalakota, Ravi; and Marcia Robinson. *E-Business 2.0: Roadmap for Success*. Reading, MA: Addison-Wesley, 2001.

13. Kalakota, Ravi; and Andrew Whinston. *Electronic Commerce: A Manager's Guide*. Reading, MA: Addison-Wesley, 1997.

14. Keenan, Faith; and Timothy Mullaney. "Let's Get Back to Basics." *BusinessWeek e.biz*, October 29, 2001.

15. Leon, Mark. "Trading Spaces." *Business 2.0*, February 2000.

16. May, Paul. *The Business of E-Commerce: From Corporate Strategy to Technology*. Cambridge, UK: Cambridge University Press, 2001.

17. Microsoft IT Showcase, "MS Market: Business Case Study," http://download.microsoft.com/download/6/5/9/659955d7-0cb7-42b6-8e78-daf1e9c49a75/MSMarketBCS.doc, 2002.

18. Morgan, Cynthia. "Dead Set against SET?" *Computerworld*, March 29, 1999.

19. Nesdore, P., "Customer Relationship Management: Getting Personal," *e-commerceIQ.com*, http://www.ecommerceiq.com/special_interests/crm/80-eCommerceIQ_crm.html, 2003.

20. "Pay-Per-Click Marketing," http://www.pay-per-click-adwords.com/pay-per-click-adwords.html, n.d.

21. Rayport, Jeffrey; and Bernard Jaworski. *Introduction to e-Commerce*. New York: McGraw-Hill/Irwin, 2001.

22. Riley, M.; S. Laiken; and J. Williams; "Digital Business Designs in Financial Services," Mercer Management Consulting Commentary, http://www.mercermc.com/Perspectives/WhitePapers/Commentaries/Comm00DBDinFinancialServices.pdf, 2002.

23. Rosenoer, Jonathan; Douglas Armstrong; and J. Russell Gates. *The Clickable Corporation: Successful Strategies for Capturing the Internet Advantage*. New York: The Free Press, 1999.

24. "Servers with a Smile." *Fortune*, Technology Buyers Guide, Summer 2000.

25. Seybold, Patricia; with Ronnie Marshak. *Customers.Com: How to Create a Profitable Business Strategy for the Internet and Beyond*. New York: Times Business, 1998.

26. Sliwa, Carol. "Users Cling to EDI for Critical Transactions." *Computerworld*, March 15, 1999.

27. "Tech Lifestyles: Shopping." *Fortune*, Technology Buyers Guide, Winter 2001.

28. "Telefónica Servicios Avanzados De Informació Leads Spain's Retail Industry into Global Electronic Commerce," www.netscape.com/solutions/business/profiles, March 1999.

29. Young, Eric. "Web Marketplaces That Really Work." *Fortune/CNET Tech Review*, Winter 2002.

Chapter 9—Decision Support Systems

1. "AmeriKing," Customer Profile, Plumtree.com, October 25, 2002.
2. Ashline, Peter; and Vincent Lai. "Virtual Reality: An Emerging User-Interface Technology." *Information Systems Management*, Winter 1995.
3. Beacon Analytics Case Study, "Analyzing Key Measures in a Retail Environment," http://www.beaconus.com/downloads/Beacon%20Case%20Study-The%20GAP.pdf, 2003.
4. Begley, Sharon. "Software au Naturel." *Newsweek*, May 8, 1995.
5. Belcher, Lloyd; and Hugh Watson. "Assessing the Value of Conoco's EIS." *MIS Quarterly*, September 1993.
6. Bioluminate Inc. press release, "Bioluminate to Develop 'Smart Probe' for Early Breast Cancer Detection," http://www.bioluminate.com/press_rel1.html, December 5, 2000.
7. Bose, Ranjit; and Vijayan Sugumaran. "Application of Intelligent Agent Technology for Managerial Data Analysis and Mining." *The Data Base for Advances in Information Systems*, Winter 1999.
8. Botchner, Ed. "Data Mining: Plumbing the Depths of Corporate Databases." *Computerworld*, Special Advertising Supplement, April 21, 1997.
9. Brown, Eryn. "Slow Road to Fast Data." *Fortune*, March 18, 2002.
10. Brown, Stuart. "Making Decisions in a Flood of Data." *Fortune*, August 13, 2001.
11. Bylinsky, Gene. "The e-Factory Catches On." *Fortune*, August 13, 2001.
12. Cox, Earl. "Relational Database Queries Using Fuzzy Logic." *AI Expert*, January 1995.
13. Darling, Charles. "Ease Implementation Woes with Packaged Datamarts." *Datamation*, March 1997.
14. Deck, Stewart. "Data Visualization." *Computerworld*, October 11, 1999.
15. Deck, Stewart. "Data Warehouse Project Starts Simply." *Computerworld*, February 15, 1999.
16. Deck, Stewart. "Early Users Give Nod to Analysis Package." *Computerworld*, February 22, 1999.
17. Freeman, Eva. "Desktop Reporting Tools." *Datamation*, June 1997.
18. Gantz, John. "The New World of Enterprise Reporting Is Here." *Computerworld*, February 1, 1999.
19. "GAP, Inc. at a Glance," http://www.gapinc.com/about/At_A_Glance.pdf, Summer 2004.
20. Glode, M. "Scans: Most Valuable Player." *Wired Magazine*, July 22, 1997.
21. Goldberg, David. "Genetic and Evolutionary Algorithms Come of Age." *Communications of the ACM*, March 1994.
22. Gorry, G. Anthony; and Michael Scott Morton. "A Framework for Management Information Systems." *Sloan Management Review*, Fall 1971; republished Spring 1989.
23. Hall, Mark. "Get Real." *Computerworld*, April 1, 2002.
24. Hall, Mark. "Supercomputing: From R&D to P&L." *Computerworld*, December 13, 1999.
25. Hoffman, Thomas. "In the Know." *Computerworld*, October 14, 2002.
26. Jablonowski, Mark. "Fuzzy Risk Analysis: Using AI Systems." *AI Expert*, December 1994.
27. Kalakota, Ravi; and Marcia Robinson. *E-Business 2.0: Roadmap for Success*. Reading, MA: Addison-Wesley, 2001.
28. Kalakota, Ravi; and Andrew Whinston. *Electronic Commerce: A Manager's Guide*. Reading, MA: Addison-Wesley, 1997.
29. King, Julia. "Sharing GIS Talent with the World." *Computerworld*, October 6, 1997.
30. Kurszweil, Raymond. *The Age of Intelligent Machines*. Cambridge, MA: The MIT Press, 1992.
31. Lundquist, Christopher. "Personalization in E-Commerce." *Computerworld*, March 22, 1999.
32. Machlis, Sharon. "Agent Technology." *Computerworld*, March 22, 1999.
33. Mailoux, Jacquiline. "New Menu at PepsiCo." *Computerworld*, May 6, 1996.
34. McNeill, F. Martin; and Ellen Thro. *Fuzzy Logic: A Practical Approach*. Boston: AP Professional, 1994.
35. Mitchell, Lori. "Enterprise Knowledge Portals Wise Up Your Business." *Infoworld.com*, December 2000.
36. Murray, Gerry. "Making Connections with Enterprise Knowledge Portals." White Paper. *Computerworld*, September 6, 1999.
37. "NASA Ames Research Center Report," Smart Surgical Probe, Bioluminate Inc., http://technology.arc.nasa.gov/success/probe.html, 2003.
38. Norsk Hydro Corporate Background, http://www.hydro.com/en/about/index.html, 2004.
39. Orenstein, David. "Corporate Portals." *Computerworld*, June 28, 1999.
40. Ouellette, Tim. "Opening Your Own Portal." *Computerworld*, August 9, 1999.
41. Pimentel, Ken; and Kevin Teixeira. *Virtual Reality through the New Looking Glass*. 2nd ed. New York: Intel/McGraw-Hill, 1995.
42. Rosenberg, Marc. *e-Learning: Strategies for Delivering Knowledge in the Digital Age*. New York: McGraw-Hill, 2001.
43. Schlumberger Information Solutions, "Norsk Hydro Makes a Valuable Drilling Decision," Schlumberger Technical Report GMP-5911, http://www.sis.slb.com/media/software/success/ir_drillingdecision.pdf, 2002.

44. Shay, S. "Trendlines." *CIO Magazine*, February 1, 1998.

45. Turban, Efraim; and Jay Aronson. *Decision Support Systems and Intelligent Systems*. Upper Saddle River, NJ: Prentice Hall, 1998.

46. Vandenbosch, Betty; and Sid Huff. "Searching and Scanning: How Executives Obtain Information from Executive Information Systems." *MIS Quarterly*, March 1997.

47. Wagner, Mitch. "Reality Check." *Computerworld*, February 26, 1997.

48. Watson, Hugh; and John Satzinger. "Guidelines for Designing EIS Interfaces." *Information Systems Management*, Fall 1994.

49. Watterson, Karen. "Parallel Tracks." *Datamation*, May 1997.

50. Winston, Patrick. "Rethinking Artificial Intelligence." Program Announcement, Massachusetts Institute of Technology, September 1997.

51. Wreden, Nick. "Enterprise Portals: Integrating Information to Drive Productivity." *Beyond Computing*, March 2000.

Chapter 10—Developing Business/IT Solutions

1. Anthes, Gary. "The Quest for IT E-Quality." *Computerworld*, December 13, 1999.

2. Clark, Charles; Nancy Cavanaugh; Carol Brown; and V. Sambamurthy. "Building Change-Readiness Capabilities in the IS Organization: Insights from the Bell Atlantic Experience." *MIS Quarterly*, December 1997.

3. Cole-Gomolski, Barbara. "Companies Turn to Web for ERP Training." *Computerworld*, February 8, 1999.

4. Cole-Gomolski, Barbara. "Users Loath to Share Their Know-How." *Computerworld*, November 17, 1997.

5. Cronin, Mary. *The Internet Strategy Handbook*. Boston: Harvard Business School Press, 1996.

6. Diese, Martin; Conrad Nowikow; Patrick King; and Amy Wright. *Executive's Guide to E-Business: From Tactics to Strategy*. New York: John Wiley & Sons, 2000.

7. "Design Matters." *Fortune*, Technology Buyers Guide, Winter 2001.

8. Casey, Susan. "On the Hot Seat." *Fortune*, January 22, 2007.

9. Hawson, James; and Jesse Beeler. "Effects of User Participation in Systems Development: A Longitudinal Field Experiment." *MIS Quarterly*, December 1997.

10. Hills, Melanie. *Intranet Business Strategies*. New York: John Wiley & Sons, 1997.

11. Kalakota, Ravi; and Marcia Robinson. *E-Business 2.0: Roadmap for Success*. Reading, MA: Addison-Wesley, 2001.

12. King, Julia. "Back to Basics." *Computerworld*, April 22, 2002.

13. Lazar, Jonathan. *User-Centered Web Development*. Sudbury, MA: Jones and Bartlett, 2001.

14. McDonnel, Sharon. "Putting CRM to Work." *Computerworld*, March 12, 2001.

15. Melymuka, Kathleen. "An Expanding Universe." *Computerworld*, September 14, 1998.

16. Melymuka, Kathleen. "Energizing the Company." *Computerworld*, August 13, 2001.

17. Melymuka, Kathleen. "Profiting from Mistakes." *Computerworld*, April 20, 2001.

18. Morgan, James N. *Application Cases in MIS*. 4th ed. New York: Irwin/McGraw-Hill, 2002.

19. Neilsen, Jakob. "Better Data Brings Better Sales." *Business 2.0*, May 15, 2001.

20. Nielsen, Jakob. "Design for Process, Not for Products." *Business 2.0*, July 10, 2001.

21. Orenstein, David. "Software Is Too Hard to Use." *Computerworld*, August 23, 1999.

22. Ouellette, Tim. "Giving Users the Key to Their Web Content." *Computerworld*, July 26, 1999.

23. Ouellette, Tim. "Opening Your Own Portal." *Computerworld*, August 9, 1999.

24. Panko, R. "Application Development: Finding Spreadsheet Errors." *InformationWeek*, May 29, 1995.

25. Panko, R. "What We Know about Spreadsheet Errors." *Journal of End-User Computing* 10, no. 2, 1998, pp. 15–21.

26. Schwartz, Matthew. "Time for a Makeover." *Computerworld*, August 19, 2002.

27. Senge, Peter. *The Fifth Discipline: The Art and Practice of the Learning Organization*. New York: Currency Doubleday, 1994.

28. Sliwa, Carol. "E-Commerce Solutions: How Real?" *Computerworld*, February 28, 2000.

29. Solomon, Melissa. "Filtering Out the Noise." *Computerworld*, February 25, 2002.

30. Songini, Marc. "GM Locomotive Unit Puts ERP Rollout Back on Track." *Computerworld*, February 11, 2002.

31. Steinert-Thelkeld, Tom. "Aviall Thinks Outside the Box." *Baseline*, January 17, 2003.

32. Whitten, Jeffrey, and Lonnie Bentley. *Systems Analysis and Design Methods*. 5th ed. New York: McGraw-Hill/Irwin, 2000.

Chapter 11—Security and Ethical Challenges

1. Alexander, Steve, and Matt Hamblen. "Top-Flight Technology." *Computerworld*, September 23, 2002.
2. Anthes, Gary. "Biometrics." *Computerworld*, October 12, 1998.
3. Anthes, Gary. "When Five 9s Aren't Enough." *Computerworld*, October 8, 2001.
4. Berniker, M., "Study: ID Theft Often Goes Unrecognized," *Internetnews.com*, http://www.internetnews.com/ec-news/article.php/3081881, 2003.
5. Boutin, Paul. "Burn Baby Burn." *Wired*, December 2002.
6. Deckmyn, Dominique. "More Managers Monitor E-Mail." *Computerworld*, October 18, 1999.
7. Dejoie, Roy; George Fowler; and David Paradice, eds. *Ethical Issues in Information Systems*. Boston: Boyd & Fraser, 1991.
8. Donaldson, Thomas. "Values in Tension: Ethics Away from Home." *Harvard Business Review*, September–October 1996.
9. Dunlop, Charles; and Rob Kling, eds. *Computerization and Controversy: Value Conflicts and Social Choices*. San Diego: Academic Press, 1991.
10. Elias, Paul. "Paid Informant." *Red Herring*, January 16, 2001.
11. Harrison, Ann. "Virus Scanning Moving to ISPs." *Computerworld*, September 20, 1999.
12. "In Depth: Security." *Computerworld*, July 9, 2001.
13. Joy, Bill. "Report from the Cyberfront." *Newsweek*, February 21, 2000.
14. Johnson, Deborah. "Ethics Online." *Communications of the ACM*, January 1997.
15. Lardner, James. "Why Should Anyone Believe You?" *Business 2.0*, March 2002.
16. Levy, Stephen; and Brad Stone. "Hunting the Hackers." *Newsweek*, February 21, 2000.
17. Madsen, Peter; and Jay Shafritz. *Essentials of Business Ethics*. New York: Meridian, 1990.
18. McCarthy, Michael. "Keystroke Cops." *The Wall Street Journal*, March 7, 2000.
19. Nance, Barry. "Sending Firewalls Home." *Computerworld*, May 28, 2001.
20. Naughton, Keith. "CyberSlacking." *Newsweek*, November 29, 1999.
21. Neumann, Peter. *Computer-Related Risks*. New York: ACM Press, 1995.
22. Phillips, Robert. *Stakeholder Theory and Organizational Ethics*. San Francisco: Berrett-Koehler, 2003.
23. Radcliff, Deborah. "Cybersleuthing Solves the Case." *Computerworld*, January 14, 2002.
24. Robinson, Lori. "How It Works: Viruses." *Smart Computing*, March 2000.
25. Rothfeder, Jeffrey. "Hacked! Are Your Company Files Safe?" *PC World*, November 1996.
26. Rothfeder, Jeffrey. "No Privacy on the Net." *PC World*, February 1997.
27. Sager, Ira; Steve Hamm; Neil Gross; John Carey; and Robert Hoff. "Cyber Crime." *BusinessWeek*, February 21, 2000.
28. Schoepke, P., and G. Milner, "Phishing Scams Increase 180% in April Alone!" *BankersOnline.com*, http://www.bankersonline.com/technology/tech_phishing052404.html, 2004.
29. Smith, H. Jefferson; and John Hasnas. "Debating the Stakeholder Theory." *Beyond Computing*, March–April 1994.
30. Smith, H. Jefferson; and John Hasnas. "Establishing an Ethical Framework." *Beyond Computing*, January–February 1994.
31. Solomon, Melissa; and Michael Meehan. "Enron Lesson: Tech Is for Support." *Computerworld*, February 18, 2002.
32. Spinello, Richard. *Cyberethics: Morality and Law in Cyberspace*. 2nd ed. Sudbury, MA: Jones and Bartlett, 2003.
33. Sullivan, B. "ID Theft Victims Face Tough Bank Fights." MSNBC.com, http://msnbc.msn.com/id/4264051/, 2004.
34. Verton, Dan. "Insider Monitoring Seen as Next Wave in IT Security." *Computerworld*, March 19, 2001.
35. VanScoy, Kayte. "What Your Workers Are Really Up To." *Ziff Davis Smart Business*, September 2001.
36. Vijayan, Jaikumar. "Nimda Needs Harsh Disinfectant." *Computerworld*, September 24, 2001.
37. Vijayan, Jaikumar. "Securing the Center." *Computerworld*, May 13, 2002.
38. Willard, Nancy. *The Cyberethics Reader*. Burr Ridge, IL: Irwin/McGraw-Hill, 1997.
39. York, Thomas. "Invasion of Privacy? E-Mail Monitoring Is on the Rise." *InformationWeek Online*, February 21, 2000.
40. Youl, T. "Phishing Scams: Understanding the Latest Trends." *FraudWatch International*, White Paper, 2004.
41. Commtouch Press release, Feb. 15, 2006. http://www.commtouch.com/Site/News_Events/pr_content.asp?news_id=602&cat_id=1.

Chapter 12—Enterprise and Global Management of Information Technology

1. Bryan, Lowell; Jane Fraser; Jeremy Oppenheim; and Wilhelm Rall. *Race for the World: Strategies to Build a Great Global Firm*. Boston: Harvard Business School Press, 1999.
2. Christensen, Clayton. *The Innovators Dilemma: When New Technologies Cause Great Firms to Fail*. Boston: Harvard Business School Press, 1997.
3. Cronin, Mary. *Global Advantage on the Internet*. New York: Van Nostrand Reinhold, 1996.
4. "Delta Signs Offshore Call Center Agreement." *South Florida Business Journal*, October 7, 2002.
5. El Sawy, Omar; Arvind Malhotra; Sanjay Gosain; and Kerry Young. "IT-Intensive Value Innovation in the Electronic Economy: Insights from Marshall Industries." *MIS Quarterly*, September 1999.
6. Gilhooly, Kym. "The Staff That Never Sleeps." *Computerworld*, June 25, 2001.
7. Grover, Varun; James Teng; and Kirk Fiedler. "IS Investment Opportunities in Contemporary Organizations." *Communications of the ACM*, February 1998.
8. Hall, Mark. "Service Providers Give Users More IT Options." *Computerworld*, February 7, 2000.
9. Ives, Blake, and Sirkka Jarvenpaa. "Applications of Global Information Technology: Key Issues for Management." *MIS Quarterly*, March 1991.
10. Kalakota, Ravi, and Marcia Robinson. *E-Business 2.0: Roadmap for Success*. Reading, MA: Addison-Wesley, 2001.
11. Kalin, Sari. "The Importance of Being Multiculturally Correct." Global Innovators Series, *Computerworld*, October 6, 1997.
12. Kirkpatrick, David. "Back to the Future with Centralized Computing." *Fortune*, November 10, 1997.
13. LaPlante, Alice. "Global Boundaries.com." Global Innovators Series, *Computerworld*, October 6, 1997.
14. Leinfuss, Emily. "Blend It, Mix It, Unify It." *Computerworld*, March 26, 2001.
15. McDougall, P. "Opportunity on the Line." *InformationWeek*, October 20, 2003.
16. Mearian, Lucas. "Citibank Overhauls Overseas Systems." *Computerworld*, February 4, 2002.
17. Mische, Michael. "Transnational Architecture: A Reengineering Approach." *Information Systems Management*, Winter 1995.
18. Palvia, Prashant; Shailendra Palvia; and Edward Roche, eds. *Global Information Technology and Systems Management*. Marietta, GA: Ivy League, 1996.
19. Radcliff, Deborah. "Playing by Europe's Rules." *Computerworld*, July 9, 2001.
20. Ross, Jeanne; and Peter Weill. "Six IT Decisions Your IT People Shouldn't Make." *Harvard Business Review*, November 2002.
21. Songini, Marc; and Kim Nash. "Try, Try Again." *Computerworld*, February 18, 2002.
22. Thibodeau, Patrick. "Europe and U.S. Agree on Data Rules." *Computerworld*, March 20, 2000.
23. Vitalari, Nicholas; and James Wetherbe. "Emerging Best Practices in Global Systems Development." In *Global Information Technology and Systems Management*, ed. Prashant Palvia et al. Marietta, GA: Ivy League, 1996.
24. West, Lawrence; and Walter Bogumil. "Immigration and the Global IT Workforce." *Communications of the ACM*, July 2001.
25. Reporters Without Borders. "The 15 Enemies of the Internet and Other Countries to Watch." www.rsf.org. November, 17, 2005.

Glossary for Business Professionals

Accounting Information Systems Information systems that record and report business transactions and the flow of funds through an organization, then produce financial statements. These statements provide information for the planning and control of business operations, as well as for legal and historical recordkeeping.

Ada A programming language named after Augusta Ada Byron, considered the world's first computer programmer. Developed for the U.S. Department of Defense as a standard high-order language.

Ad Hoc Inquiries Unique, unscheduled, situation-specific information requests.

Agile Competition The ability of a company to operate profitably in a competitive environment of continual and unpredictable changes in customer preferences, market conditions, and business opportunities.

Algorithm A set of well-defined rules or processes for solving a problem in a finite number of steps.

Analog Computer A computer that operates on data by measuring changes in continuous physical variables such as voltage, resistance, and rotation. Contrast with Digital Computer.

Analytical Database A database of data extracted from operational and external databases to provide data tailored to online analytical processing, decision support, and executive information systems.

Analytical Modeling Interactive use of computer-based mathematical models to explore decision alternatives using what-if analysis, sensitivity analysis, goal-seeking analysis, and optimization analysis.

Applet A small, limited-purpose application program or small, independent module of a larger application program.

Application Development See Systems Development.

Application Generator A software package that supports the development of an application through an interactive terminal dialogue, where the programmer/analyst defines screens, reports, computations, and data structures.

Application Portfolio A planning tool used to evaluate present and proposed information systems applications in terms of the amount of revenue or assets invested in information systems that support major business functions and processes.

Applications Architecture A conceptual planning framework in which business applications of information technology are designed as an integrated architecture of enterprise systems that support strategic business initiatives and cross-functional business processes.

Application Server System software that provides a middleware interface between an operating system and the application programs of users.

Application Software Programs that specify the information processing activities required for the completion of specific tasks of computer users. Examples are electronic spreadsheet and word processing programs or inventory or payroll programs.

Application-Specific Programs Application software packages that support specific applications of end users in business, science and engineering, and other areas.

Arithmetic-Logic Unit (ALU) The unit of a computing system containing the circuits that perform arithmetic and logical operations.

Artificial Intelligence (AI) A science and technology whose goal is to develop computers that can think, as well as see, hear, walk, talk, and feel. A major thrust is the development of computer functions normally associated with human intelligence, for example, reasoning, inference, learning, and problem solving.

ASCII: American Standard Code for Information Interchange A standard code used for information interchange among data processing systems, communication systems, and associated equipment.

Assembler A computer program that translates an assembler language into machine language.

Assembler Language A programming language that utilizes symbols to represent operation codes and storage locations.

Asynchronous A sequence of operations without a regular or predictable time relationship. Thus, operations do not happen at regular timed intervals, but an operation will begin only after a previous operation is completed. In data transmission, involves the use of start and stop bits with each character to indicate the beginning and end of the character being transmitted. Contrast with Synchronous.

Audit Trail The presence of media and procedures that allow a transaction to be traced through all stages of information processing, beginning with its appearance on a source document and ending with its transformation into information in a final output document.

Automated Teller Machine (ATM) A special-purpose transaction terminal used to provide remote banking services.

Back-End Processor Typically, a smaller, general-purpose computer dedicated to database processing using a database management system (DBMS). Also called a database machine or server.

Background Processing The automatic execution of lower-priority computer programs when higher-priority programs are not using the resources of the computer system. Contrast with Foreground Processing.

Backward-Chaining An inference process that justifies a proposed conclusion by determining if it will result when rules are applied to the facts in a given situation.

Bandwidth The frequency range of a telecommunications channel, which determines its maximum transmission rate. The speed and capacity of transmission rates are typically measured in bits per second (bps). Bandwidth is a function of the telecommunications hardware, software, and media used by the telecommunications channel.

Bar Codes Vertical marks or bars placed on merchandise tags or packaging that can be sensed and read by optical character-reading devices. The width and combination of vertical lines are used to represent data.

Barriers to Entry Technological, financial, or legal requirements that deter firms from entering an industry.

BASIC: Beginner's All-Purpose Symbolic Instruction Code A programming language developed at Dartmouth College and designed for programming by end users.

Batch Processing A category of data processing in which data are accumulated into batches and processed periodically. Contrast with Real-Time Processing.

Baud A unit of measurement used to specify data transmission speeds. It is a unit of signaling speed equal to the number of discrete conditions or signal events per second. In many data communications applications, it represents one bit per second.

Binary Pertaining to a characteristic or property involving a selection, choice, or condition in which there are two possibilities, or pertaining to the number system that utilizes a base of 2.

Biometric Controls Computer-based security methods that measure physical traits and characteristics such as fingerprints, voice prints, retina scans, and so on.

Bit A contraction of "binary digit." It can have the value of either 0 or 1.

Block A grouping of contiguous data records or other data elements that are handled as a unit.

Branch A transfer of control from one instruction to another in a computer program that is not part of the normal sequential execution of the instructions of the program.

Browser See Web Browser.

Buffer Temporary storage used when transmitting data from one device to another to compensate for a difference in rate of flow of data or time of occurrence of events.

Bug A mistake or malfunction.

Bulletin Board System (BBS) A service of online computer networks in which electronic messages, data files, or programs can be stored for other subscribers to read or copy.

Bundling The inclusion of software, maintenance, training, and other products or services in the price of a computer system.

Bus A set of conducting paths for movement of data and instructions that interconnects the various components of the CPU.

Business Ethics An area of philosophy concerned with developing ethical principles and promoting ethical behavior and practices in the accomplishment of business tasks and decision making.

Business Intelligence (BI) A term primarily used in industry that incorporates a range of analytical and decision support applications in business including data mining, decision support systems, knowledge management systems, and online analytical processing.

Business/IT Planning The process of developing a company's business vision, strategies, and goals, as well as how they will be supported by the company's information technology architecture and implemented by its business application development process.

Business Process Reengineering (BPR) Restructuring and transforming a business process by a fundamental rethinking and redesign to achieve dramatic improvements in cost, quality, speed, and so on.

Byte A sequence of adjacent binary digits operated on as a unit and usually shorter than a computer word. In many computer systems, a byte is a grouping of eight bits that can represent one alphabetic or special character or that can be packed with two decimal digits.

C A low-level structured programming language that resembles a machine-independent assembler language.

C++ An object-oriented version of C that is widely used for software package development.

Cache Memory A high-speed temporary storage area in the CPU for storing parts of a program or data during processing.

Capacity Management The use of planning and control methods to forecast and control information processing job loads, hardware and software usage, and other computer system resource requirements.

Case-Based Reasoning Representing knowledge in an expert system's knowledge base in the form of cases, that is, examples of past performance, occurrences, and experiences.

Cathode Ray Tube (CRT) An electronic vacuum tube (television picture tube) that displays the output of a computer system.

CD-ROM An optical disk technology for microcomputers featuring compact disks with a storage capacity of over 500 megabytes.

Cellular Phone Systems A radio communications technology that divides a metropolitan area into a honeycomb of cells to greatly increase the number of frequencies and thus the users that can take advantage of mobile phone service.

Central Processing Unit (CPU) The unit of a computer system that includes the circuits that control the interpretation and execution of instructions. In many computer systems, the CPU includes the arithmetic-logic unit, the control unit, and the primary storage unit.

Change Management Managing the process of implementing major changes in information technology, business processes, organizational structures, and job assignments to reduce the risks and costs of change and optimize its benefits.

Channel (1) A path along which signals can be sent. (2) A small special-purpose processor that controls the movement of data between the CPU and input/output devices.

Chargeback Systems Methods of allocating costs to end-user departments on the basis of the information services rendered and information system resources utilized.

Chat Systems Software that enables two or more users at networked PCs to carry on online, real-time text conversations.

Check Bit A binary check digit; for example, a parity bit.

Check Digit A digit in a data field that is utilized to check for errors or loss of characters in the data field as a result of data transfer operations.

Checkpoint A place in a program where a check or a recording of data for restart purposes is performed.

Chief Information Officer A senior management position that oversees all information technology for a firm concentrating on long-range information system planning and strategy.

Client (1) An end user. (2) The end user's networked microcomputer in client/server networks. (3) The version of a software package designed to run on an end user's networked microcomputer, such as a Web browser client, a groupware client, and so on.

Client/Server Network A computer network where end-user workstations (clients) are connected via telecommunications links to network servers and possibly to mainframe superservers.

Clock A device that generates periodic signals utilized to control the timing of a computer. Also, a register whose contents change at regular intervals in such a way as to measure time.

Coaxial Cable A sturdy copper or aluminum wire wrapped with spacers to insulate and protect it. Groups of coaxial cables may also be bundled together in a bigger cable for ease of installation.

COBOL: COmmon Business Oriented Language A widely used business data processing programming language.

Code Computer instructions.

Cognitive Science An area of artificial intelligence that focuses on researching how the human brain works and how humans think and learn, to apply such findings to the design of computer-based systems.

Cognitive Styles Basic patterns in how people handle information and confront problems.

Cognitive Theory Theories about how the human brain works and how humans think and learn.

Collaborative Work Management Tools Software that helps people accomplish or manage joint work activities.

Communications Satellite Earth satellites placed in stationary orbits above the equator that serve as relay stations for communications signals transmitted from earth stations.

Competitive Advantage Developing products, services, processes, or capabilities that give a company a superior business position relative to its competitors and other competitive forces.

Competitive Forces A firm must confront (1) rivalry of competitors within its industry, (2) threats of new entrants, (3) threats of substitutes, (4) the bargaining power of customers, and (5) the bargaining power of suppliers.

Competitive Strategies A firm can develop cost leadership, product differentiation, and business innovation strategies to confront its competitive forces.

Compiler A program that translates a high-level programming language into a machine-language program.

Computer A device that has the ability to accept data; internally store and execute a program of instructions; perform mathematical, logical, and manipulative operations on data; and report the results.

Computer-Aided Design (CAD) The use of computers and advanced graphics hardware and software to provide interactive design assistance for engineering and architectural design.

Computer-Aided Engineering (CAE) The use of computers to simulate, analyze, and evaluate models of product designs and production processes developed using computer-aided design methods.

Computer-Aided Manufacturing (CAM) The use of computers to automate the production process and operations of a manufacturing plant. Also called factory automation.

Computer-Aided Planning (CAP) The use of software packages as tools to support the planning process.

Computer-Aided Software Engineering (CASE) Same as Computer-Aided Systems Engineering, but emphasizing the importance of software development.

Computer-Aided Systems Engineering (CASE) Using software packages to accomplish and automate many of the activities of information systems development, including software development or programming.

Computer Application The use of a computer to solve a specific problem or accomplish a particular job for an end user. For example, common business computer applications include sales order processing, inventory control, and payroll.

Computer-Assisted Instruction (CAI) The use of computers to provide drills, practice exercises, and tutorial sequences to students.

Computer-Based Information System An information system that uses computer hardware and software to perform its information processing activities.

Computer Crime Criminal actions accomplished through the use of computer systems, especially with intent to defraud, destroy, or make unauthorized use of computer system resources.

Computer Ethics A system of principles governing the legal, professional, social, and moral responsibilities of computer specialists and end users.

Computer Generations Major stages in the historical development of computing.

Computer Graphics Using computer-generated images to analyze and interpret data, present information, and create computer-aided design and art.

Computer Industry The industry composed of firms that supply computer hardware, software, and services.

Computer-Integrated Manufacturing (CIM) An overall concept that stresses that the goals of computer use in factory automation should be to simplify, automate, and integrate production processes and other aspects of manufacturing.

Computer Matching Using computers to screen and match data about individual characteristics provided by a variety of computer-based information systems and databases to identify individuals for business, government, or other purposes.

Computer Monitoring Using computers to monitor the behavior and productivity of workers on the job and in the workplace.

Computer Program A series of instructions or statements in a form acceptable to a computer, prepared to achieve a certain result.

Computer System Computer hardware as a system of input, processing, output, storage, and control components. Thus, a computer system consists of input and output devices, primary and secondary storage devices, the central processing unit, the control unit within the CPU, and other peripheral devices.

Computer Terminal Any input/output device connected by telecommunications links to a computer.

Computer Virus or Worm Program code that copies its destructive program routines into the computer systems of anyone who accesses computer systems that have used the program, or anyone who uses copies of data or programs taken from such computers. This spreads the destruction of data and programs among many computer users. Technically, a virus will not run unaided but must be inserted into another program, whereas a worm is a distinct program that can run unaided.

Concurrent Processing The generic term for the capability of computers to work on several tasks at the same time, that is, concurrently. This may involve specific capabilities such as overlapped processing, multiprocessing, multiprogramming, multitasking, parallel processing, and so on.

Connectivity The degree to which hardware, software, and databases can be easily linked together in a telecommunications network.

Control (1) The systems component that evaluates feedback to determine whether the system is moving toward the achievement of its goal and then makes any necessary adjustments to the input and processing components of the system to ensure that proper output is produced. (2) A management function that involves observing and measuring organizational performance and environmental activities and modifying the plans and activities of the organization when necessary.

Control Listing A detailed report that describes each transaction occurring during a period.

Control Totals Accumulating totals of data at multiple points in an information system to ensure correct information processing.

Control Unit A subunit of the central processing unit that controls and directs the operations of the computer system. The control unit retrieves computer instructions in proper sequence, interprets each instruction, and then directs the other parts of the computer system in their implementation.

Conversion The process in which the hardware, software, people, network, and data resources of an old information system must be converted to the requirements of a new information system. This usually involves a parallel, phased, pilot, or plunge conversion process from the old to the new system.

Cooperative Processing Information processing that allows the computers in a distributed processing network to share the processing of parts of an end user's application.

Cost/Benefit Analysis Identifying the advantages or benefits and the disadvantages or costs of a proposed solution.

Critical Success Factors A small number of key factors that executives consider critical to the success of the enterprise. These are key areas in which successful performance will assure the success of the organization and attainment of its goals.

Cross-Functional Information Systems Information systems that are integrated combinations of business information systems, thus sharing information resources across the functional units of an organization.

Cursor A movable point of light displayed on most video display screens to assist the user in the input of data.

Customer Relationship Management (CRM) A cross-functional e-business application that integrates and automates many customer serving processes in sales, direct marketing, account and order management, and customer service and support.

Cybernetic System A system that uses feedback and control components to achieve a self-regulating capability.

Cylinder An imaginary vertical cylinder consisting of the vertical alignment of tracks on each surface of magnetic disks that are accessed simultaneously by the read/write heads of a disk drive.

Data Facts or observations about physical phenomena or business transactions. More specifically, data are objective measurements of the attributes (characteristics) of entities such as people, places, things, and events.

Data Administration A data resource management function that involves the establishment and enforcement of policies and procedures for managing data as a strategic corporate resource.

Database An integrated collection of logically related data elements. A database consolidates many records previously stored in separate files so that a common pool of data serves many applications.

Database Administration A data resource management function that includes responsibility for developing and maintaining the organization's data dictionary, designing and monitoring the performance of databases, and enforcing standards for database use and security.

Database Administrator A specialist responsible for maintaining standards for the development, maintenance, and security of an organization's databases.

Database Maintenance The activity of keeping a database up to date by adding, changing, or deleting data.

Database Management Approach An approach to the storage and processing of data in which independent files are consolidated into a common pool, or database, of records available to different application programs and end users for processing and data retrieval.

Database Management System (DBMS) A set of computer programs that controls the creation, maintenance, and utilization of the databases of an organization.

Database Processing Utilizing a database for data processing activities such as maintenance, information retrieval, or report generation.

Data Center An organizational unit that uses centralized computing resources to perform information processing activities for an organization. Also known as a computer center.

Data Conferencing Users at networked PCs can view, mark up, revise, and save changes to a shared whiteboard of drawings, documents, and other material.

Data Conversion Converting data into new data formats required by a new business application and its software and databases. Also includes correcting incorrect data, filtering out unwanted data, and consolidating data into new databases and other data subsets.

Data Design The design of the logical structure of databases and files to be used by a proposed information system. This design produces detailed descriptions of the entities, relationships, data elements, and integrity rules for system files and databases.

Data Dictionary A software module and database containing descriptions and definitions concerning the structure, data elements, interrelationships, and other characteristics of a database.

Data Entry The process of converting data into a form suitable for entry into a computer system. Also called data capture or input preparation.

Data Flow Diagram A graphic diagramming tool that uses a few simple symbols to illustrate the flow of data among external entities, processing activities, and data storage elements.

Data Management Control program functions that provide access to data sets, enforce data storage conventions, and regulate the use of input/output devices.

Data Mining Using special purpose software to analyze data from a data warehouse to find hidden patterns and trends.

Data Model A conceptual framework that defines the logical relationships among the data elements needed to support a basic business or other process.

Data Modeling A process in which the relationships between data elements are identified and defined to develop data models.

Data Planning A corporate planning and analysis function that focuses on data resource management. It includes the responsibility for developing an overall information policy and data architecture for the firm's data resources.

Data Processing The execution of a systematic sequence of operations performed on data to transform them into information.

Data Resource Management A managerial activity that applies information systems technology and management tools to the task of managing an organization's data resources. Its three major components are database administration, data administration, and data planning.

Data Warehouse An integrated collection of data extracted from operational, historical, and external databases and cleaned, transformed, and cataloged for retrieval and analysis (*data mining*) to provide business intelligence for business decision making.

Debug To detect, locate, and remove errors from a program or malfunctions from a computer.

Decision Support System (DSS) An information system that utilizes decision models, a database, and a decision maker's own insights in an ad hoc, interactive analytical modeling process to reach a specific decision by a specific decision maker.

Demand Reports and Responses Information provided whenever a manager or end user demands it.

Desktop Publishing The use of microcomputers, laser printers, and page makeup software to produce a variety of printed materials that were formerly produced only by professional printers.

Desktop Videoconferencing The use of end-user computer workstations to conduct two-way interactive video conferences.

Development Centers Systems development consultant groups formed to serve as consultants to the professional programmers and systems analysts of an organization to improve their application development efforts.

Digital Computer A computer that operates on digital data by performing arithmetic and logical operations on the data. Contrast with Analog Computer.

Digitizer A device that is used to convert drawings and other graphic images on paper or other materials into digital data that are entered into a computer system.

Direct Access A method of storage in which each storage position has a unique address and can be individually accessed in approximately the same period without having to search through other storage positions. Same as Random Access. Contrast with Sequential Access.

Direct Access Storage Device (DASD) A storage device that can directly access data to be stored or retrieved, for example, a magnetic disk unit.

Direct Data Organization A method of data organization in which logical data elements are distributed randomly on or within the physical data medium. For example, logical data records distributed randomly on the surfaces of a magnetic disk file. Also called direct organization.

Direct Input/Output Methods such as keyboard entry, voice input/output, and video displays that allow data to be input into or output from a computer system without the use of machine-readable media.

Disaster Recovery Methods for ensuring that an organization recovers from natural and human-caused disasters that have affected its computer-based operations.

Discussion Forum An online network discussion platform to encourage and manage online text discussions over a period among members of special interest groups or project teams.

Distributed Databases The concept of distributing databases or portions of a database at remote sites where the data are most frequently referenced. Sharing of data is made possible through a network that interconnects the distributed databases.

Distributed Processing A form of decentralization of information processing made possible by a network of computers dispersed throughout an organization. Processing of user applications is accomplished by several computers interconnected by a telecommunications network, rather than relying on one large centralized computer facility or on the decentralized operation of several independent computers.

Document (1) A medium on which data have been recorded for human use, such as a report or invoice. (2) In word processing, a generic term for text material such as letters, memos, reports, and so on.

Documentation A collection of documents or information that describes a computer program, information system, or required data processing operations.

Downsizing Moving to smaller computing platforms, such as from mainframe systems to networks of personal computers and servers.

Downtime The time interval during which a device is malfunctioning or inoperative.

DSS Generator A software package for a decision support system that contains modules for database, model, and dialogue management.

Duplex In communications, pertains to a simultaneous two-way independent transmission in both directions.

EBCDIC: Extended Binary Coded Decimal Interchange Code An eight-bit code that is widely used by mainframe computers.

Echo Check A method of checking the accuracy of data transmission in which the received data are returned to the sending device for comparison with the original data.

e-Commerce Marketplaces Internet, intranet, and extranet Web sites and portals hosted by individual companies, consortiums of organizations, or third-party intermediaries providing electronic catalog, exchange, and auction markets to unite buyers and sellers to accomplish e-commerce transactions.

Economic Feasibility Whether expected cost savings, increased revenue, increased profits, and reductions in required investment exceed the costs of developing and operating a proposed system.

EDI: Electronic Data Interchange The automatic electronic exchange of business documents between the computers of different organizations.

Edit To modify the form or format of data. For example, to insert or delete characters such as page numbers or decimal points.

Edit Report A report that describes errors detected during processing.

EFT: Electronic Funds Transfer The development of banking and payment systems that transfer funds electronically instead of using cash or paper documents such as checks.

Electronic Business (e-Business) The use of Internet technologies to internetwork and empower business processes, electronic commerce, and enterprise communication and collaboration within a company and with its customers, suppliers, and other business stakeholders.

Electronic Commerce (e-Commerce) The buying and selling, marketing and servicing, and delivery and payment of products, services, and information over the Internet, intranets, extranets, and other networks, between an internetworked enterprise and its prospects, customers, suppliers, and other business partners. Includes business-to-consumer (B2C), business-to-business (B2B), and consumer-to-consumer (C2C) e-commerce.

Electronic Communications Tools Software that helps communicate and collaborate with others by electronically sending messages, documents, and files in data, text, voice, or multimedia over the Internet, intranets, extranets, and other computer networks.

Electronic Conferencing Tools Software that helps networked computer users share information and collaborate while working together on joint assignments, no matter where they are located.

Electronic Data Processing (EDP) The use of electronic computers to process data automatically.

Electronic Document Management An image processing technology in which an electronic document may consist of digitized voice notes and electronic graphics images, as well as digitized images of traditional documents.

Electronic Mail Sending and receiving text messages between networked PCs over telecommunications networks. E-mail can also include data files, software, and multimedia messages and documents as attachments.

Electronic Meeting Systems (EMS) Using a meeting room with networked PCs, a large-screen projector, and EMS software to facilitate communication, collaboration, and group decision making in business meetings.

Electronic Payment Systems Alternative cash or credit payment methods using various electronic technologies to pay for products and services in electronic commerce.

Electronic Spreadsheet Package An application program used as a computerized tool for analysis, planning, and modeling that allows users to enter and manipulate data into an electronic worksheet of rows and columns.

Emulation To imitate one system with another so that the imitating system accepts the same data, executes the same programs, and achieves the same results as the imitated system.

Encryption To scramble data or convert them, prior to transmission, to a secret code that masks the meaning of the data to unauthorized recipients. Similar to enciphering.

End User Anyone who uses an information system or the information it produces.

End-User Computing Systems Computer-based information systems that directly support both the operational and managerial applications of end users.

Enterprise Application Integration (EAI) A cross-functional e-business application that integrates front-office applications like customer relationship management with back-office applications like enterprise resource management.

Enterprise Collaboration Systems The use of groupware tools and the Internet, intranets, extranets, and other computer networks to support and enhance communication, coordination, collaboration, and resource sharing among teams and workgroups in an internetworked enterprise.

Enterprise Information Portal A customized and personalized Web-based interface for corporate intranets and extranets that gives qualified users access to a variety of internal and external e-business and e-commerce applications, databases, software tools, and information services.

Enterprise Knowledge Portal An enterprise information portal that serves as a knowledge management system by providing users with access to enterprise knowledge bases.

Enterprise Model A conceptual framework that defines the structures and relationships of business processes and data elements, as well as other planning structures, such as critical success factors and organizational units.

Enterprise Resource Planning (ERP) Integrated cross-functional software that reengineers manufacturing, distribution, finance, human resources, and other basic business processes of a company to improve its efficiency, agility, and profitability.

Entity Relationship Diagram (ERD) A data planning and systems development diagramming tool that models the relationships among the entities in a business process.

Entropy The tendency of a system to lose a relatively stable state of equilibrium.

Ergonomics The science and technology emphasizing the safety, comfort, and ease of use of human-operated machines such as computers. The goal of ergonomics is to produce systems that are user friendly: safe, comfortable, and easy to use. Ergonomics is also called human factors engineering.

Exception Reports Reports produced only when exceptional conditions occur, or reports produced periodically that contain information only about exceptional conditions.

Executive Information System (EIS) An information system that provides strategic information tailored to the needs of executives and other decision makers.

Executive Support System (ESS) An executive information system with additional capabilities, including data analysis, decision support, electronic mail, and personal productivity tools.

Expert System (ES) A computer-based information system that uses its knowledge about a specific complex application area to act as an expert consultant to users. The system consists of a knowledge base and software modules that perform inferences on the knowledge and communicate answers to a user's questions.

Extranet A network that links selected resources of a company with its customers, suppliers, and other business partners, using the Internet or private networks to link the organizations' intranets.

Facilities Management The use of an external service organization to operate and manage the information processing facilities of an organization.

Fault Tolerant Systems Computers that have multiple central processors, peripherals, and system software and that are able to continue operations even if there is a major hardware or software failure.

Faxing (Facsimile) Transmitting and receiving images of documents over the telephone or computer networks using PCs or fax machines.

Feasibility Study A preliminary study that investigates the information needs of end users and the objectives, constraints, basic resource requirements, cost/benefits, and feasibility of proposed projects.

Feedback (1) Data or information concerning the components and operations of a system. (2) The use of part of the output of a system as input to the system.

Fiber Optics The technology that uses cables consisting of very thin filaments of glass fibers that can conduct the light generated by lasers for high-speed telecommunications.

Field A data element that consists of a grouping of characters that describe a particular attribute of an entity. For example, the name field or salary field of an employee.

Fifth Generation The next generation of computers. Major advances in parallel processing, user interfaces, and artificial intelligence may provide computers that will be able to see, hear, talk, and think.

File A collection of related data records treated as a unit. Sometimes called a data set.

File Management Controlling the creation, deletion, access, and use of files of data and programs.

File Processing Organizing data into specialized files of data records designed for processing only by specific application programs. Contrast with Database Management Approach.

Financial Management Systems Information systems that support financial managers in the financing of a business and the allocation and control of financial resources. These include cash and securities management, capital budgeting, financial forecasting, and financial planning.

Firewall Computers, communications processors, and software that protect computer networks from intrusion by screening all network traffic and serving as a safe transfer point for access to and from other networks.

Firmware The use of microprogrammed read-only memory circuits in place of hard-wired logic circuitry. See also Microprogramming.

Floating Point Pertaining to a number representation system in which each number is represented by two sets of digits. One set represents the significant digits or fixed-point "base" of the number, while the other set of digits represents the "exponent," which indicates the precision of the number.

Floppy Disk A small plastic disk coated with iron oxide that resembles a small phonograph record enclosed in a protective envelope. It is a widely used form of magnetic disk media that provides a direct access storage capability for microcomputer systems.

Flowchart A graphical representation in which symbols are used to represent operations, data, flow, logic, equipment, and so on. A program flowchart illustrates the structure and sequence of operations of a program, whereas a system flowchart illustrates the components and flows of information systems.

Foreground Processing The automatic execution of the computer programs that have been designed to preempt the use of computing facilities. Contrast with Background Processing.

Format The arrangement of data on a medium.

FORTRAN: FORmula TRANslation A high-level programming language widely utilized to develop computer programs that perform mathematical computations for scientific, engineering, and selected business applications.

Forward Chaining An inference strategy that reaches a conclusion by applying rules to facts to determine if any facts satisfy a rule's conditions in a particular situation.

Fourth-Generation Languages (4GL) Programming languages that are easier to use than high-level languages like BASIC, COBOL, or FORTRAN. They are also known as nonprocedural, natural, or very-high-level languages.

Frame A collection of knowledge about an entity or other concept consisting of a complex package of slots, that is, data values describing the characteristics or attributes of an entity.

Frame-Based Knowledge Knowledge represented in the form of a hierarchy or network of frames.

Front-End Processor Typically a smaller, general-purpose computer that is dedicated to handling data communications control functions in a communications network, thus relieving the host computer of these functions.

Functional Business Systems Information systems within a business organization that support one of the traditional functions of business such as marketing, finance, or production. Functional business systems can be either operations or management information systems.

Functional Requirements The information system capabilities required to meet the information needs of end users. Also called system requirements.

Fuzzy Logic Systems Computer-based systems that can process data that are incomplete or only partially correct, that is, fuzzy data. Such systems can solve unstructured problems with incomplete knowledge, as humans do.

General Purpose Application Programs Programs that can perform information processing jobs for users from all application areas. For example, word processing programs, electronic spreadsheet programs, and graphics programs can be used by individuals for home, education, business, scientific, and many other purposes.

General-Purpose Computer A computer that is designed to handle a wide variety of problems. Contrast with Special-Purpose Computer.

Generate To produce a machine-language program for performing a specific data processing task based on parameters supplied by a programmer or user.

Genetic Algorithm An application of artificial intelligence software that uses Darwinian (survival of the fittest) randomizing and other functions to simulate an evolutionary process that can yield increasingly better solutions to a problem.

Gigabyte One billion bytes. More accurately, 2 to the 30th power, or 1,073,741,824 in decimal notation.

GIGO An acronym of "Garbage In, Garbage Out," which emphasizes that information systems will produce erroneous and invalid output when provided with erroneous and invalid input data or instructions.

Global Company A business that is driven by a global strategy so that all of its activities are planned and implemented in the context of a whole-world system.

Global e-Business Technology Management Managing information technologies in a global e-business enterprise, amid the cultural, political, and geoeconomic challenges involved in developing e-business/IT strategies, global e-business and e-commerce applications portfolios, Internet-based technology platforms, and global data resource management policies.

Global Information Technology The use of computer-based information systems and telecommunications networks using a variety of information technologies to support global business operations and management.

Globalization Becoming a global enterprise by expanding into global markets, using global production facilities, forming alliances with global partners, and so on.

Goal-Seeking Analysis Making repeated changes to selected variables until a chosen variable reaches a target value.

Graphical User Interface A software interface that relies on icons, bars, buttons, boxes, and other images to initiate computer-based tasks for users.

Graphics Pertaining to symbolic input or output from a computer system, such as lines, curves, and geometric shapes, using video display units or graphics plotters and printers.

Graphics Pen and Tablet A device that allows an end user to draw or write on a pressure-sensitive tablet and have the handwriting or graphics digitized by the computer and accepted as input.

Graphics Software A program that helps users generate graphics displays.

Group Decision Making Decisions made by groups of people coming to an agreement on a particular issue.

Group Decision Support System (GDSS) A decision support system that provides support for decision making by groups of people.

Group Support Systems (GSS) An information system that enhances communication, coordination, collaboration, decision making, and group work activities of teams and workgroups.

Groupware Software to support and enhance the communication, coordination, and collaboration among networked teams and workgroups, including software tools for electronic communications, electronic conferencing, and cooperative work management.

Hacking (1) Obsessive use of a computer. (2) The unauthorized access and use of computer systems.

Handshaking Exchange of predetermined signals when a connection is established between two communications terminals.

Hard Copy A data medium or data record that has a degree of permanence and that can be read by people or machines.

Hardware (1) Machines and media. (2) Physical equipment, as opposed to computer programs or methods of use. (3) Mechanical, magnetic, electrical, electronic, or optical devices. Contrast with Software.

Hash Total The sum of numbers in a data field that are not normally added, such as account numbers or other identification numbers. It is utilized as a control total, especially during input/output operations of batch processing systems.

Header Label A machine-readable record at the beginning of a file containing data for file identification and control.

Heuristic Pertaining to exploratory methods of problem solving in which solutions are discovered by evaluation of the progress made toward the final result. It is an exploratory trial-and-error approach guided by rules of thumb. Opposite of algorithmic.

Hierarchical Data Structure A logical data structure in which the relationships between records form a hierarchy or tree structure. The relationships among records are one to many, because each data element is related only to one element above it.

High-Level Language A programming language that utilizes macro instructions and statements that closely resemble human language or mathematical notation to describe the problem to be solved or the procedure to be used. Also called a compiler language.

Homeostasis A relatively stable state of equilibrium of a system.

Host Computer Typically a larger central computer that performs the major data processing tasks in a computer network.

Human Factors Hardware and software capabilities that can affect the comfort, safety, ease of use, and user customization of computer-based information systems.

Human Information Processing A conceptual framework about the human cognitive process that uses an information processing context to explain how humans capture, process, and use information.

Human Resource Information Systems (HRIS) Information systems that support human resource management activities such as recruitment, selection and hiring, job placement and performance appraisals, and training and development.

Hybrid AI Systems Systems that integrate several AI technologies, such as expert systems and neural networks.

Hypermedia Documents containing multiple forms of media, including text, graphics, video, and sound, that can be interactively searched, like Hypertext.

Hypertext Text in electronic form that has been indexed and linked (hyperlinks) by software in a variety of ways so that it can be randomly and interactively searched by a user.

Hypertext Markup Language (HTML) A popular page description language for creating hypertext and hypermedia documents for World Wide Web and intranet Web sites.

Icon A small figure on a video display that looks like a familiar office or other device such as a file folder (for storing a file) or a wastebasket (for deleting a file).

Image Processing A computer-based technology that allows end users to electronically capture, store, process, and retrieve images that may include numeric data, text, handwriting, graphics, documents, and photographs. Image processing makes heavy use of optical scanning and optical disk technologies.

Impact Printers Printers that form images on paper through the pressing of a printing element and an inked ribbon or roller against the face of a sheet of paper.

Index An ordered reference list of the contents of a file or document together with keys or reference notations for identification or location of those contents.

Index Sequential A method of data organization in which records are organized in sequential order and also referenced by an index. When utilized with direct access file devices, it is known as index sequential access method, or ISAM.

Inference Engine The software component of an expert system, which processes the rules and facts related to a specific problem and makes associations and inferences resulting in recommended courses of action.

Infomediaries Third-party market-maker companies that serve as intermediaries to bring buyers and sellers together by developing and hosting electronic catalog, exchange, and auction markets to accomplish e-commerce transactions.

Information Data placed in a meaningful and useful context for an end user.

Information Appliances Small Web-enabled microcomputer devices with specialized functions, such as handheld PDAs, TV set–top boxes, game consoles, cellular and PCS phones, wired telephone appliances, and other Web-enabled home appliances.

Information Architecture A conceptual framework that defines the basic structure, content, and relationships of the organizational databases that provide the data needed to support the basic business processes of an organization.

Information Center A support facility for the end users of an organization. It allows users to learn to develop their own application programs and accomplish their own information processing tasks. End users are provided with hardware support, software support, and people support (trained user consultants).

Information Float The time that a document is in transit between the sender and receiver and thus unavailable for any action or response.

Information Processing A concept that covers both the traditional concept of processing numeric and alphabetic data and the processing of text, images, and voices. It emphasizes that the production of information products for users should be the focus of processing activities.

Information Quality The degree to which information has content, form, and time characteristics that give it value for specific end users.

Information Resource Management (IRM) A management concept that views data, information, and computer resources (computer hardware, software, networks, and personnel) as valuable organizational resources that should be efficiently, economically, and effectively managed for the benefit of the entire organization.

Information Retrieval The methods and procedures for recovering specific information from stored data.

Information Superhighway An advanced high-speed Internet-like network that connects individuals, households, businesses, government agencies, libraries, schools, universities, and other institutions with interactive voice, video, data, and multimedia communications.

Information System (1) A set of people, procedures, and resources that collects, transforms, and disseminates information in an organization. (2) A system that accepts data resources as input and processes them into information products as output.

Information System Model A conceptual framework that views an information system as a system that uses the resources of hardware (machines and media), software (programs and procedures), people (users and specialists), and networks (communications media and network support) to perform input, processing, output, storage, and control activities that transform data resources (databases and knowledge bases) into information products.

Information Systems Development See Systems Development.

Information System Specialist A person whose occupation is related to the providing of information system services. For example, a systems analyst, programmer, or computer operator.

Information Technology (IT) Hardware, software, telecommunications, database management, and other information processing technologies used in computer-based information systems.

Information Technology Architecture A conceptual blueprint that specifies the components and interrelationships of a company's technology infrastructure, data resources, applications architecture, and IT organization.

Information Technology Management Managing information technologies by (1) the joint development and implementation of business and IT strategies by business and IT executives, (2) managing the research and implementation of new information technologies and the development of business applications, and (3) managing the IT processes, professionals, subunits, and infrastructure within a company.

Information Theory The branch of learning concerned with the likelihood of accurate transmission or communication of messages subject to transmission failure, distortion, and noise.

Input Pertaining to a device, process, or channel involved in the insertion of data into a data processing system. Opposite of Output.

Input/Output (I/O) Pertaining to either input or output, or both.

Input/Output Interface Hardware Devices such as I/O ports, I/O buses, buffers, channels, and input/output control units, which assist the CPU in its input/output assignments. These devices make it possible for modern computer systems to perform input, output, and processing functions simultaneously.

Inquiry Processing Computer processing that supports the real-time interrogation of online files and databases by end users.

Instruction A grouping of characters that specifies the computer operation to be performed.

Intangible Benefits and Costs The nonquantifiable benefits and costs of a proposed solution or system.

Integrated Circuit A complex microelectronic circuit consisting of interconnected circuit elements that cannot be disassembled because they are placed on or within a "continuous substrate" such as a silicon chip.

Integrated Packages Software that combines the ability to do several general-purpose applications (such as word processing, electronic spreadsheet, and graphics) into one program.

Intelligent Agent A special-purpose knowledge-based system that serves as a software surrogate to accomplish specific tasks for end users.

Intelligent Terminal A terminal with the capabilities of a microcomputer that can thus perform many data processing and other functions without accessing a larger computer.

Interactive Marketing A dynamic collaborative process of creating, purchasing, and improving products and services that builds close relationships between a business and its customers, using a variety of services on the Internet, intranets, and extranets.

Interactive Processing A type of real-time processing in which users can interact with a computer on a real-time basis.

Interactive Video Computer-based systems that integrate image processing with text, audio, and video processing technologies, which makes interactive multimedia presentations possible.

Interface A shared boundary, such as the boundary between two systems. For example, the boundary between a computer and its peripheral devices.

Internet A rapidly growing computer network of millions of business, educational, and governmental networks connecting hundreds of millions of computers and their users in over 200 countries.

Internetwork Processor Communications processors used by local area networks to interconnect them with other local area and wide area networks. Examples include switches, routers, hubs, and gateways.

Internetworks Interconnected local area and wide area networks.

Interoperability Being able to accomplish end-user applications using different types of computer systems, operating systems, and application software, interconnected by different types of local and wide area networks.

Interorganizational Information Systems Information systems that interconnect an organization with other organizations, such as a business and its customers and suppliers.

Interpreter A computer program that translates and executes each source language statement before translating and executing the next one.

Interrupt A condition that causes an interruption in a processing operation during which another task is performed. At the conclusion of this new assignment, control may be transferred back to the point at which the original processing operation was interrupted or to other tasks with a higher priority.

Intranet An Internet-like network within an organization. Web browser software provides easy access to internal Web sites established by business units, teams, and individuals, and other network resources and applications.

Inverted File A file that references entities by their attributes.

IT Architecture A conceptual design for the implementation of information technology in an organization, including its hardware, software, and network technology platforms, data resources, application portfolio, and IS organization.

Iterative Pertaining to the repeated execution of a series of steps.

Java An object-oriented programming language designed for programming real-time, interactive, Web-based applications in the form of applets for use on clients and servers on the Internet, intranets, and extranets.

Job A specified group of tasks prescribed as a unit of work for a computer.

Job Control Language (JCL) A language for communicating with the operating system of a computer to identify a job and describe its requirements.

Joystick A small lever set in a box used to move the cursor on the computer's display screen.

K An abbreviation for the prefix *kilo*, which is 1,000 in decimal notation. When referring to storage capacity, it is equivalent to 2 to the 10th power, or 1,024 in decimal notation.

Key One or more fields within a data record that are used to identify it or control its use.

Keyboarding Using the keyboard of a microcomputer or computer terminal.

Knowledge Base A computer-accessible collection of knowledge about a subject in a variety of forms, such as facts and rules of inference, frames, and objects.

Knowledge-Based Information System An information system that adds a knowledge base to the database and other components found in other types of computer-based information systems.

Knowledge Engineer A specialist who works with experts to capture the knowledge they possess to develop a knowledge base for expert systems and other knowledge-based systems.

Knowledge Management Organizing and sharing the diverse forms of business information created within an organization. Includes managing project and enterprise document libraries, discussion databases, intranet Web site databases, and other types of knowledge bases.

Knowledge Workers People whose primary work activities include creating, using, and distributing information.

Language Translator Program A program that converts the programming language instructions in a computer program into machine language code. Major types include assemblers, compilers, and interpreters.

Large-Scale Integration (LSI) A method of constructing electronic circuits in which thousands of circuits can be placed on a single semiconductor chip.

Legacy Systems The older, traditional, mainframe-based business information systems of an organization.

Light Pen A photoelectronic device that allows data to be entered or altered on the face of a video display terminal.

Liquid Crystal Displays (LCDs) Electronic visual displays that form characters by applying an electrical charge to selected silicon crystals.

List Organization A method of data organization that uses indexes and pointers to allow for nonsequential retrieval.

List Processing A method of processing data in the form of lists.

Local Area Network (LAN) A communications network that typically connects computers, terminals, and other computerized devices within a limited physical area such as an office, building, manufacturing plant, or other worksite.

Locking In Customers and Suppliers Building valuable relationships with customers and suppliers that deter them from abandoning a firm for its competitors or intimidating it into accepting less profitable relationships.

Logical Data Elements Data elements that are independent of the physical data media on which they are recorded.

Logical System Design Developing general specifications for how basic information systems activities can meet end-user requirements.

Loop A sequence of instructions in a computer program that is executed repeatedly until a terminal condition prevails.

Machine Cycle The timing of a basic CPU operation as determined by a fixed number of electrical pulses emitted by the CPU's timing circuitry or internal clock.

Machine Language A programming language in which instructions are expressed in the binary code of the computer.

Macro Instruction An instruction in a source language that is equivalent to a specified sequence of machine instructions.

Magnetic Disk A flat, circular plate with a magnetic surface on which data can be stored by selective magnetization of portions of the curved surface.

Magnetic Ink An ink that contains particles of iron oxide that can be magnetized and detected by magnetic sensors.

Magnetic Ink Character Recognition (MICR) The machine recognition of characters printed with magnetic ink. Primarily used for check processing by the banking industry.

Magnetic Tape A plastic tape with a magnetic surface on which data can be stored by selective magnetization of portions of the surface.

Mag Stripe Card A plastic, wallet-size card with a strip of magnetic tape on one surface; widely used for credit/debit cards.

Mainframe A larger computer system, typically with a separate central processing unit, as distinguished from microcomputer and minicomputer systems.

Management Information System (MIS) A management support system that produces prespecified reports, displays, and responses on a periodic, exception, demand, or push reporting basis.

Management Support System (MSS) An information system that provides information to support managerial decision making. More specifically, an information-reporting system, executive information system, or decision support system.

Managerial End User A manager, entrepreneur, or managerial-level professional who personally uses information systems. Also, the manager of the department or other organizational unit that relies on information systems.

Managerial Roles Management of the performance of a variety of interpersonal, information, and decision roles.

Manual Data Processing Data processing that requires continual human operation and intervention and that utilizes simple data processing tools such as paper forms, pencils, and filing cabinets.

Manufacturing Information Systems Information systems that support the planning, control, and accomplishment of manufacturing processes. This includes concepts such as computer-integrated manufacturing (CIM) and technologies such as computer-aided manufacturing (CAM) or computer-aided design (CAD).

Marketing Information Systems Information systems that support the planning, control, and transaction processing required for the accomplishment of marketing activities, such as sales management, advertising, and promotion.

Mass Storage Secondary storage devices with extra-large storage capacities, such as magnetic or optical disks.

Master File A data file containing relatively permanent information that is utilized as an authoritative reference and is usually updated periodically. Contrast with Transaction File.

Mathematical Model A mathematical representation of a process, device, or concept.

Media All tangible objects on which data are recorded.

Megabyte One million bytes. More accurately, 2 to the 20th power, or 1,048,576 in decimal notation.

Memory See Storage.

Menu A displayed list of items (usually the names of alternative applications, files, or activities) from which an end user makes a selection.

Menu Driven A characteristic of interactive computing systems that provides menu displays and operator prompting to assist an end user in performing a particular job.

Metadata Data about data; data describing the structure, data elements, interrelationships, and other characteristics of a database.

Microcomputer A very small computer, ranging in size from a "computer on a chip" to handheld, laptop, and desktop units, and servers.

Micrographics The use of microfilm, microfiche, and other microforms to record data in greatly reduced form.

Microprocessor A microcomputer central processing unit (CPU) on a chip. Without input/output or primary storage capabilities in most types.

Microprogram A small set of elementary control instructions called microinstructions or microcode.

Microprogramming The use of special software (microprograms) to perform the functions of special hardware (electronic control circuitry). Microprograms stored in a read-only storage module of the control unit interpret the machine language instructions of a computer program and decode them into elementary microinstructions, which are then executed.

Microsecond A millionth of a second.

Middleware Software that helps diverse software programs and networked computer systems work together, thus promoting their interoperability.

Midrange Computer A computer category between microcomputers and mainframes. Examples include minicomputers, network servers, and technical workstations.

Millisecond A thousandth of a second.

Minicomputer A type of midrange computer.

Model Base An organized software collection of conceptual, mathematical, and logical models that express business relationships, computational routines, or analytical techniques.

Modem (MOdulator-DEModulator) A device that converts the digital signals from input/output devices into appropriate frequencies at a transmission terminal and converts them back into digital signals at a receiving terminal.

Monitor Software or hardware that observes, supervises, controls, or verifies the operations of a system.

Mouse A small device that is electronically connected to a computer and is moved by hand on a flat surface to move the cursor on a video screen in the same direction. Buttons on the mouse allow users to issue commands and make responses or selections.

Multidimensional Structure A database model that uses multidimensional structures (such as cubes or cubes within cubes) to store data and relationships between data.

Multimedia Presentations Providing information using a variety of media, including text and graphics displays, voice and other audio, photographs, and video segments.

Multiplex To interleave or simultaneously transmit two or more messages on a single channel.

Multiplexer An electronic device that allows a single communications channel to carry simultaneous data transmissions from many terminals.

Multiprocessing Pertaining to the simultaneous execution of two or more instructions by a computer or computer network.

Multiprocessor Computer Systems Computer systems that use a multiprocessor architecture in the design of their central processing units. This includes the use of support microprocessors and multiple instruction processors, including parallel processor designs.

Multiprogramming Pertaining to the concurrent execution of two or more programs by a computer by interleaving their execution.

Multitasking The concurrent use of the same computer to accomplish several different information processing tasks. Each task may require the use of a different program or the concurrent use of the same copy of a program by several users.

Nanosecond One billionth of a second.

Natural Language A programming language that is very close to human language. Also called very-high-level language.

Network An interconnected system of computers, terminals, and communications channels and devices.

Network Architecture A master plan designed to promote an open, simple, flexible, and efficient telecommunications environment through the use of standard protocols, standard communications hardware and software interfaces, and the design of a standard multilevel telecommunications interface between end users and computer systems.

Network Computer A low-cost networked microcomputer with no or minimal disk storage, which depends on Internet or intranet servers for its operating system and Web browser, Java-enabled application software, and data access and storage.

Network Computing A network-centric view of computing in which "the network is the computer," that is, the view that computer networks are the central computing resource of any computing environment.

Network Data Structure A logical data structure that allows many-to-many relationships among data records. It allows entry into a database at multiple points, because any data element or record can be related to many other data elements.

Neural Networks Computer processors or software whose architecture is based on the human brain's meshlike neuron structure. Neural networks can process many pieces of information simultaneously and learn to recognize patterns and programs to solve related problems on their own.

Node A terminal point in a communications network.

Nonprocedural Languages Programming languages that allow users and professional programmers to specify the results they want without specifying how to solve the problem.

Numerical Control Automatic control of a machine process by a computer that makes use of numerical data, generally introduced as the operation is in process. Also called machine control.

Object A data element that includes both data and the methods or processes that act on those data.

Object-Based Knowledge Knowledge represented as a network of objects.

Object-Oriented Language An object-oriented programming (OOP) language used to develop programs that create and use objects to perform information processing tasks.

Object Program A compiled or assembled program composed of executable machine instructions. Contrast with Source Program.

OEM: Original Equipment Manufacturer A firm that manufactures and sells computers by assembling components produced by other hardware manufacturers.

Office Automation (OA) The use of computer-based information systems that collect, process, store, and transmit electronic messages, documents, and other forms of office communications among individuals, workgroups, and organizations.

Offline Pertaining to equipment or devices not under control of the central processing unit.

Offshoring A relocation of an organization's business processes to a lower cost location overseas.

Online Pertaining to equipment or devices under control of the central processing unit.

Online Analytical Processing (OLAP) A capability of some management, decision support, and executive information systems that supports interactive examination and manipulation of large amounts of data from many perspectives.

Online Transaction Processing (OLTP) A real-time transaction processing system.

Open Systems Information systems that use common standards for hardware, software, applications, and networking to create a computing environment that allows easy access by end users and their networked computer systems.

Operand That which is operated upon. That part of a computer instruction that is identified by the address part of the instruction.

Operating Environment Software packages or modules that add a graphics-based interface among end users, the operating system, and their application programs and that may also provide multitasking capability.

Operating System The main control program of a computer system. It is a system of programs that controls the execution of computer programs and may provide scheduling, debugging, input/output control, system accounting, compilation, storage assignment, data management, and related services.

Operational Feasibility The willingness and ability of management, employees, customers, and suppliers to operate, use, and support a proposed system.

Operation Code A code that represents specific operations to be performed upon the operands in a computer instruction.

Operations Support System (OSS) An information system that collects, processes, and stores data generated by the operations systems of an organization and produces data and information for input into a management information system or for the control of an operations system.

Operations System A basic subsystem of the business firm that constitutes its input, processing, and output components. Also called a physical system.

Optical Character Recognition (OCR) The machine identification of printed characters through the use of light-sensitive devices.

Optical Disks A secondary storage medium using CD (compact disk) and DVD (digital versatile disk) technologies to read tiny spots on plastic disks. The disks are currently capable of storing billions of characters of information.

Optical Scanner A device that optically scans characters or images and generates their digital representations.

Optimization Analysis Finding an optimum value for selected variables in a mathematical model, given certain constraints.

Organizational Feasibility How well a proposed information system supports the objectives of an organization's strategic plan for information systems.

Output Pertaining to a device, process, or channel involved with the transfer of data or information out of an information processing system. Opposite of Input.

Outsourcing Turning over all or part of an organization's information systems operation to outside contractors, known as systems integrators or service providers.

Packet A group of data and control information in a specified format that is transmitted as an entity.

Packet Switching A data transmission process that transmits addressed packets such that a channel is occupied only for the duration of transmission of the packet.

Page A segment of a program or data, usually of fixed length.

Paging A process that automatically and continually transfers pages of programs and data between primary storage and direct access storage devices. It provides computers with multiprogramming and virtual memory capabilities.

Parallel Processing Executing many instructions at the same time, that is, in parallel. Performed by advanced computers using many instruction processors organized in clusters or networks.

Parity Bit A check bit appended to an array of binary digits to make the sum of all the binary digits, including the check bit, always odd or always even.

Pascal A high-level, general-purpose, structured programming language named after Blaise Pascal. It was developed by Niklaus Wirth of Zurich in 1968.

Pattern Recognition The identification of shapes, forms, or configurations by automatic means.

PCM: Plug-Compatible Manufacturer A firm that manufactures computer equipment that can be plugged into existing computer systems without requiring additional hardware or software interfaces.

Peer-to-Peer Network (P2P) A computing environment in which end-user computers connect, communicate, and collaborate directly with one another via the Internet or other telecommunications network links.

Pen-Based Computers Tablet-style microcomputers that recognize handwriting and hand drawing done by a pen-shaped device on their pressure-sensitive display screens.

Performance Monitor A software package that monitors the processing of computer system jobs, helps develop a planned schedule of computer operations that can optimize computer system performance, and produces detailed statistics that are used for computer system capacity planning and control.

Periodic Reports Providing information to managers using a prespecified format designed to provide information on a regularly scheduled basis.

Peripheral Devices In a computer system, any unit of equipment, distinct from the central processing unit, that provides the system with input, output, or storage capabilities.

Personal Digital Assistant (PDA) Handheld microcomputer devices that enable you to manage information such as appointments, to-do lists, and sales contacts, send and receive e-mail, access the Web, and exchange such information with your desktop PC or network server.

Personal Information Manager (PIM) A software package that helps end users store, organize, and retrieve text and numerical data in the form of notes, lists, memos, and a variety of other forms.

Physical System Design Design of the user interface methods and products, database structures, and processing and control procedures for a proposed information system, including hardware, software, and personnel specifications.

Picosecond One trillionth of a second.

Plasma Display Output devices that generate a visual display with electrically charged particles of gas trapped between glass plates.

Plotter A hard-copy output device that produces drawings and graphical displays on paper or other materials.

Pointer A data element associated with an index, a record, or other set of data that contains the address of a related record.

Pointing Devices Devices that allow end users to issue commands or make choices by moving a cursor on the display screen.

Pointing Stick A small buttonlike device on a keyboard that moves the cursor on the screen in the direction of the pressure placed upon it.

Point-of-Sale (POS) Terminal A computer terminal used in retail stores that serves the function of a cash register as well as collecting sales data and performing other data processing functions.

Port (1) Electronic circuitry that provides a connection point between the CPU and input/output devices. (2) A connection point for a communications line on a CPU or other front-end device.

Postimplementation Review Monitoring and evaluating the results of an implemented solution or system.

Presentation Graphics Using computer-generated graphics to enhance the information presented in reports and other types of presentations.

Prespecified Reports Reports whose format is specified in advance to provide managers with information periodically, on an exception basis, or on demand.

Private Branch Exchange (PBX) A switching device that serves as an interface between the many telephone lines within a work area and the local telephone company's main telephone lines or trunks. Computerized PBXs can handle the switching of both voices and data.

Procedure-Oriented Language A programming language designed for the convenient expression of procedures used in the solution of a wide class of problems.

Procedures Sets of instructions used by people to complete a task.

Process Control The use of a computer to control an ongoing physical process, such as petrochemical production.

Process Design The design of the programs and procedures needed by a proposed information system, including detailed program specifications and procedures.

Processor A hardware device or software system capable of performing operations on data.

Program A set of instructions that causes a computer to perform a particular task.

Programmed Decision A decision that can be automated by basing it on a decision rule that outlines the steps to take when confronted with the need for a specific decision.

Programmer A person mainly involved in designing, writing, and testing computer programs.

Programming The design, writing, and testing of a program.

Programming Language A language used to develop the instructions in computer programs.

Programming Tools Software packages or modules that provide editing and diagnostic capabilities and other support facilities to assist the programming process.

Project Management Managing the accomplishment of an information system development project according to a specific project plan, in order that a project is completed on time and within its budget and meets its design objectives.

Prompt Messages that assist a user in performing a particular job. This would include error messages, correction suggestions, questions, and other messages that guide an end user.

Protocol A set of rules and procedures for the control of communications in a communications network.

Prototype A working model. In particular, a working model of an information system that includes tentative versions of user input and output, databases and files, control methods, and processing routines.

Prototyping The rapid development and testing of working models, or prototypes, of new information system applications in an interactive, iterative process involving both systems analysts and end users.

Pseudocode An informal design language of structured programming that expresses the processing logic of a program module in ordinary human language phrases.

Pull Marketing Marketing methods that rely on the use of Web browsers by end users to access marketing materials and resources at Internet, intranet, and extranet Web sites.

Push Marketing Marketing methods that rely on Web broadcasting software to push marketing information and other marketing materials to end users' computers.

Quality Assurance Methods for ensuring that information systems are free from errors and fraud and provide information products of high quality.

Query Language A high-level, humanlike language provided by a database management system that enables users to easily extract data and information from a database.

Queue (1) A waiting line formed by items in a system waiting for service. (2) To arrange in or form a queue.

RAID Redundant array of independent disks. Magnetic disk units that house many interconnected microcomputer hard disk drives, thus providing large, fault-tolerant storage capacities.

Random Access Same as Direct Access. Contrast with Sequential Access.

Random-Access Memory (RAM) One of the basic types of semiconductor memory used for temporary storage of data or programs during processing. Each memory position can be directly sensed (read) or changed (written) in the same length of time, regardless of its location on the storage medium.

Reach and Range Analysis A planning framework that contrasts a firm's ability to use its IT platform to reach its stakeholders with the range of information products and services that can be provided or shared through IT.

Read-Only Memory (ROM) A basic type of semiconductor memory used for permanent storage. Can only be read, not "written," that is, changed. Variations are Programmable Read-Only Memory (PROM) and Erasable Programmable Read-Only Memory (EPROM).

Real Time Pertaining to the performance of data processing during the actual time a business or physical process transpires, in order that results of the data processing can be used to support the completion of the process.

Real-Time Processing Data processing in which data are processed immediately rather than periodically. Also called online processing. Contrast with Batch Processing.

Record A collection of related data fields treated as a unit.

Reduced Instruction Set Computer (RISC) A CPU architecture that optimizes processing speed by the use of a smaller number of basic machine instructions than traditional CPU designs.

Redundancy In information processing, the repetition of part or all of a message to increase the chance that the correct information will be understood by the recipient.

Register A device capable of storing a specified amount of data, such as one word.

Relational Data Structure A logical data structure in which all data elements within the database are viewed as being stored in the form of simple tables. DBMS packages based on the relational model can link data elements from various tables as long as the tables share common data elements.

Remote Access Pertaining to communication with the data processing facility by one or more stations that are distant from that facility.

Remote Job Entry (RJE) Entering jobs into a batch processing system from a remote facility.

Report Generator A feature of database management system packages that allows an end user to quickly specify a report format for the display of information retrieved from a database.

Reprographics Copying and duplicating technology and methods.

Resource Management An operating system function that controls the use of computer system resources such as primary storage, secondary storage, CPU processing time, and input/output devices by other system software and application software packages.

Robotics The technology of building machines (robots) with computer intelligence and humanlike physical capabilities.

Routine An ordered set of instructions that may have some general or frequent use.

RPG: Report Program Generator A problem-oriented language that utilizes a generator to construct programs that produce reports and perform other data processing tasks.

Rule Statements that typically take the form of a premise and a conclusion, such as if–then rules: If (condition), Then (conclusion).

Rule-Based Knowledge Knowledge represented in the form of rules and statements of fact.

Scalability The ability of hardware or software to handle the processing demands of a wide range of end users, transactions, queries, and other information processing requirements.

Scenario Approach A planning approach in which managers, employees, and planners create scenarios of what an organization will be like three to five years or more into the future and identify the role IT can play in those scenarios.

Schema An overall conceptual or logical view of the relationships between the data in a database.

Scientific Method An analytical methodology that involves (1) recognizing phenomena, (2) formulating a hypothesis about the causes or effects of the phenomena, (3) testing the hypothesis through experimentation, (4) evaluating the results of such experiments, and (5) drawing conclusions about the hypothesis.

Secondary Storage Storage that supplements the primary storage of a computer. Synonymous with auxiliary storage.

Sector A subdivision of a track on a magnetic disk surface.

Security Codes Passwords, identification codes, account codes, and other codes that limit the access and use of computer-based system resources to authorized users.

Security Management Protecting the accuracy, integrity, and safety of the processes and resources of an internetworked e-business enterprise against computer crime, accidental or malicious destruction, and natural disasters, using security measures such as encryption, firewalls, antivirus software, fault tolerant computers, and security monitors.

Security Monitor A software package that monitors the use of a computer system and protects its resources from unauthorized use, fraud, and vandalism.

Semiconductor Memory Microelectronic storage circuitry etched on tiny chips of silicon or other semiconducting material. The primary storage of most modern computers consists of microelectronic semiconductor storage chips for random-access memory (RAM) and read-only memory (ROM).

Semistructured Decisions Decisions involving procedures that can be partially prespecified but not enough to lead to a definite recommended decision.

Sensitivity Analysis Observing how repeated changes to a single variable affect other variables in a mathematical model.

Sequential Access A sequential method of storing and retrieving data from a file. Contrast with Random Access and Direct Access.

Sequential Data Organization Organizing logical data elements according to a prescribed sequence.

Serial Pertaining to the sequential or consecutive occurrence of two or more related activities in a single device or channel.

Server (1) A computer that supports applications and telecommunications in a network, as well as the sharing of peripheral devices, software, and databases among the workstations in the network. (2) Versions of software for installation on network servers designed to control and support applications on client microcomputers in client/server networks. Examples include multiuser network operating systems and specialized software for running Internet, intranet, and extranet Web applications, such as electronic commerce and enterprise collaboration.

Service Bureau A firm offering computer and data processing services. Also called a computer service center.

Smart Products Industrial and consumer products, with "intelligence" provided by built-in microcomputers or microprocessors that significantly improve the performance and capabilities of such products.

Software Computer programs and procedures concerned with the operation of an information system. Contrast with Hardware.

Software Package A computer program supplied by computer manufacturers, independent software companies, or other computer users. Also known as canned programs, proprietary software, or packaged programs.

Software Piracy Unauthorized copying of software.

Software Suites A combination of individual software packages that share a common graphical user interface and are designed for easy transfer of data between applications.

Solid State Pertaining to devices such as transistors and diodes whose operation depends on the control of electric or magnetic phenomena in solid materials.

Source Data Automation The use of automated methods of data entry that attempt to reduce or eliminate many of the activities, people, and data media required by traditional data entry methods.

Source Document A document that is the original formal record of a transaction, such as a purchase order or sales invoice.

Source Program A computer program written in a language that is subject to a translation process. Contrast with Object Program.

Special-Purpose Computer A computer designed to handle a restricted class of problems. Contrast with General-Purpose Computer.

Speech Recognition Direct conversion of spoken data into electronic form suitable for entry into a computer system. Also called voice data entry.

Spooling Simultaneous peripheral operation online. Storing input data from low-speed devices temporarily on high-speed secondary storage units, which can be quickly accessed by the CPU. Also, writing output data at high speeds onto magnetic tape or disk units from which it can be transferred to slow-speed devices such as a printer.

Stage Analysis A planning process in which the information system needs of an organization are based on an analysis of its current stage in the growth cycle of the organization and its use of information systems technology.

Standards Measures of performance developed to evaluate the progress of a system toward its objectives.

Storage Pertaining to a device into which data can be entered, in which they can be held, and from which they can be retrieved at a later time. Same as Memory.

Strategic Information Systems Information systems that provide a firm with competitive products and services that give it a strategic advantage over its competitors in the marketplace. Also, information systems that promote business innovation, improve business processes, and build strategic information resources for a firm.

Strategic Opportunities Matrix A planning framework that uses a matrix to help identify opportunities with strategic business potential, as well as a firm's ability to exploit such opportunities with IT.

Structure Chart A design and documentation technique to show the purpose and relationships of the various modules in a program.

Structured Decisions Decisions that are structured by the decision procedures or decision rules developed for them. They involve situations in which the procedures to follow when a decision is needed can be specified in advance.

Structured Programming A programming methodology that uses a top-down program design and a limited number of control structures in a program to create highly structured modules of program code.

Structured Query Language (SQL) A query language that is becoming a standard for advanced database management system packages. A query's basic form is SELECT ... FROM ... WHERE.

Subroutine A routine that can be part of another program routine.

Subschema A subset or transformation of the logical view of the database schema that is required by a particular user application program.

Subsystem A system that is a component of a larger system.

Supercomputer A special category of large computer systems that are the most powerful available. They are designed to solve massive computational problems.

Superconductor Materials that can conduct electricity with almost no resistance. This allows the development of extremely fast and small electronic circuits. Formerly only possible at supercold temperatures near absolute zero. Recent developments promise superconducting materials near room temperature.

Supply Chain The network of business processes and interrelationships among businesses that are needed to build, sell, and deliver a product to its final customer.

Supply Chain Management Integrating management practices and information technology to optimize information and product flows among the processes and business partners within a supply chain.

Switch (1) A device or programming technique for making a selection. (2) A computer that controls message switching among the computers and terminals in a telecommunications network.

Switching Costs The costs in time, money, effort, and inconvenience that it would take a customer or supplier to switch its business to a firm's competitors.

Synchronous A characteristic in which each event, or the performance of any basic operation, is constrained to start on, and usually to keep in step with, signals from a timing clock. Contrast with Asynchronous.

System (1) A group of interrelated or interacting elements forming a unified whole. (2) A group of interrelated components working together toward a common goal by accepting inputs and producing outputs in an organized transformation process. (3) An assembly of methods, procedures, or techniques unified by regulated interaction to form an organized whole. (4) An organized collection of people, machines, and methods required to accomplish a set of specific functions.

System Flowchart A graphic diagramming tool used to show the flow of information processing activities as data are processed by people and devices.

Systems Analysis (1) Analyzing in detail the components and requirements of a system. (2) Analyzing in detail the information needs of an organization, the characteristics and components of presently utilized information systems, and the functional requirements of proposed information systems.

Systems Approach A systematic process of problem solving that defines problems and opportunities in a systems context. Data are gathered describing the problem or opportunity, and alternative solutions are identified and evaluated. Then the best solution is selected and implemented, and its success is evaluated.

Systems Design Deciding how a proposed information system will meet the information needs of end users. Includes logical and physical design activities and user interface, data, and process design activities that produce system specifications that satisfy the system requirements developed in the systems analysis stage.

Systems Development (1) Conceiving, designing, and implementing a system. (2) Developing information systems by a process of investigation, analysis, design, implementation, and maintenance. Also called the systems development life cycle (SDLC), information systems development, or application development.

Systems Development Tools Graphical, textual, and computer-aided tools and techniques used to help analyze, design, and document the development of an information system. Typically used to represent (1) the components and flows of a system, (2) the user interface, (3) data attributes and relationships, and (4) detailed system processes.

Systems Implementation The stage of systems development in which hardware and software are acquired, developed, and installed; the system is tested and documented; people are trained to operate and use the system; and an organization converts to the use of a newly developed system.

Systems Investigation The screening, selection, and preliminary study of a proposed information system solution to a business problem.

Systems Maintenance The monitoring, evaluating, and modifying of a system to make desirable or necessary improvements.

System Software Programs that control and support operations of a computer system. System software includes a variety of programs, such as operating systems, database management systems, communications control programs, service and utility programs, and programming language translators.

System Specifications The product of the systems design stage. It consists of specifications for the hardware, software, facilities, personnel, databases, and the user interface of a proposed information system.

Systems Thinking Recognizing systems, subsystems, components of systems, and system interrelationships in a situation. Also known as a systems context or a systemic view of a situation.

System Support Programs Programs that support the operations, management, and users of a computer system by providing a variety of support services. Examples are system utilities and performance monitors.

Tangible Benefits and Costs The quantifiable benefits and costs of a proposed solution or system.

Task and Project Management Managing team and workgroup projects by scheduling, tracking, and charting the completion status of tasks within a project.

Task Management A basic operating system function that manages the accomplishment of the computing tasks of users by a computer system.

TCP/IP Transmission control protocol/Internet protocol. A suite of telecommunications network protocols used by the Internet, intranets, and extranets that has become a de facto network architecture standard for many companies.

Technical Feasibility Whether reliable hardware and software capable of meeting the needs of a proposed system can be acquired or developed by an organization in the required time.

Technology Management The organizational responsibility to identify, introduce, and monitor the assimilation of new information system technologies into organizations.

Telecommunications Pertaining to the transmission of signals over long distances, including not only data communications but also the transmission of images and voices using radio, television, and other communications technologies.

Telecommunications Channel The part of a telecommunications network that connects the message source with the message receiver. It includes the hardware, software, and media used to connect one network location to another for the purpose of transmitting and receiving information.

Telecommunications Controller A data communications interface device (frequently a special purpose mini- or microcomputer) that can control a telecommunications network containing many terminals.

Telecommunications Control Program A computer program that controls and supports the communications between the computers and terminals in a telecommunications network.

Telecommunications Monitors Computer programs that control and support the communications between the computers and terminals in a telecommunications network.

Telecommunications Processors Internetwork processors such as switches and routers and other devices such as multiplexers and communications controllers that allow a communications channel to carry simultaneous data transmissions from many terminals. They may also perform error monitoring, diagnostics and correction, modulation-demodulation, data compression, data coding and decoding, message switching, port contention, and buffer storage.

Telecommuting The use of telecommunications to replace commuting to work from one's home.

Teleconferencing The use of video communications to allow business conferences to be held with participants who are scattered across a country, continent, or the world.

Telephone Tag The process that occurs when two people who wish to contact each other by telephone repeatedly miss each other's phone calls.

Teleprocessing Using telecommunications for computer-based information processing.

Terabyte One trillion bytes. More accurately, 2 to the 40th power, or 1,009,511,627,776 in decimal notation.

Text Data Words, phrases, sentences, and paragraphs used in documents and other forms of communication.

Throughput The total amount of useful work performed by a data processing system during a given period.

Time Sharing Providing computer services to many users simultaneously while providing rapid responses to each.

Total Quality Management Planning and implementing programs of continuous quality improvement, where quality is defined as meeting or exceeding the requirements and expectations of customers for a product or service.

Touch-Sensitive Screen An input device that accepts data input by the placement of a finger on or close to the CRT screen.

Track The portion of a moving storage medium, such as a drum, tape, or disk, that is accessible to a given reading head position.

Trackball A rollerball device set in a case used to move the cursor on a computer's display screen.

Transaction An event that occurs as part of doing business, such as a sale, purchase, deposit, withdrawal, refund, transfer, payment, and so on.

Transaction Document A document produced as part of a business transaction. For example, a purchase order, paycheck, sales receipt, or customer invoice.

Transaction File A data file containing relatively transient data to be processed in combination with a master file. Contrast with Master File.

Transaction Processing Cycle A cycle of basic transaction processing activities including data entry, transaction processing, database maintenance, document and report generation, and inquiry processing.

Transaction Processing System (TPS) An information system that processes data arising from the occurrence of business transactions.

Transaction Terminals Terminals used in banks, retail stores, factories, and other worksites to capture transaction data at their point of origin. Examples are point-of-sale (POS) terminals and automated teller machines (ATMs).

Transborder Data Flows (TDF) The flow of business data over telecommunications networks across international borders.

Transform Algorithm Performing an arithmetic computation on a record key and using the result of the calculation as an address for that record. Also known as key transformation or hashing.

Transnational Strategy A management approach in which an organization integrates its global business activities through close cooperation and interdependence among its headquarters, operations, and international subsidiaries and its use of appropriate global information technologies.

Turnaround Document Output of a computer system (such as customer invoices and statements) that is designed to be returned to the organization as machine-readable input.

Turnaround Time The elapsed time between submission of a job to a computing center and the return of the results.

Turnkey Systems Computer systems in which all of the hardware, software, and systems development needed by a user are provided.

Unbundling The separate pricing of hardware, software, and other related services.

Uniform Resource Locator (URL) An access code (such as http://www.sun.com) for identifying and locating hypermedia document files, databases, and other resources at Web sites and other locations on the Internet, intranets, and extranets.

Universal Product Code (UPC) A standard identification code using bar coding printed on products that can be read by optical scanners such as those found at a supermarket checkout.

Unstructured Decisions Decisions that must be made in situations in which it is not possible to specify in advance most of the decision procedures to follow.

User Friendly A characteristic of human-operated equipment and systems that makes them safe, comfortable, and easy to use.

User Interface That part of an operating system or other program that allows users to communicate with it to load programs, access files, and accomplish other computing tasks.

User Interface Design Designing the interactions between end users and computer systems, including input/output methods and the conversion of data between human-readable and machine-readable forms.

Utility Program A standard set of routines that assists in the operation of a computer system by performing some frequently required process such as copying, sorting, or merging.

Value-Added Carriers Third-party vendors who lease telecommunications lines from common carriers and offer a variety of telecommunications services to customers.

Value-Added Resellers (VARs) Companies that provide industry-specific software for use with the computer systems of selected manufacturers.

Value Chain Viewing a firm as a series, chain, or network of basic activities that adds value to its products and services and thus adds a margin of value to the firm.

Videoconferencing Real-time video and audio conferencing (1) among users at networked PCs (desktop videoconferencing) or (2) among participants in conference rooms or auditoriums in different locations (teleconferencing). Videoconferencing can also include whiteboarding and document sharing.

Virtual Communities Groups of people with similar interests who meet and share ideas on the Internet and online services and develop a feeling of belonging to a community.

Virtual Company A form of organization that uses telecommunications networks and other information technologies to link the people, assets, and ideas of a variety of business partners, no matter where they may be, to exploit a business opportunity.

Virtual Machine Pertaining to the simulation of one type of computer system by another computer system.

Virtual Mall An online multimedia simulation of a shopping mall with many different interlinked retail Web sites.

Virtual Memory The use of secondary storage devices as an extension of the primary storage of the computer, thus giving the appearance of a larger main memory than actually exists.

Virtual Private Network A secure network that uses the Internet as its main backbone network to connect the intranets of a company's different locations or to establish extranet links between a company and its customers, suppliers, or other business partners.

Virtual Reality The use of multisensory human/computer interfaces that enable human users to experience computer-simulated objects, entities, spaces, and "worlds" as if they actually existed.

Virtual Storefront An online multimedia simulation of a retail store shopping experience on the Web.

Virtual Team A team whose members use the Internet, intranets, extranets, and other networks to communicate, coordinate, and collaborate with one another on tasks and projects, even though they may work in different geographic locations and for different organizations.

VLSI: Very-Large-Scale Integration Semiconductor chips containing hundreds of thousands of circuits.

Voice Conferencing Telephone conversations shared among several participants via speaker phones or networked PCs with Internet telephone software.

Voice Mail Unanswered telephone messages that are digitized, stored, and played back to the recipient by a voice messaging computer.

Volatile Memory Memory (such as electronic semiconductor memory) that loses its contents when electrical power is interrupted.

Wand A handheld optical character recognition device used for data entry by many transaction terminals.

Web Browser A software package that provides the user interface for accessing Internet, intranet, and extranet Web sites. Browsers are becoming multifunction universal clients for sending and receiving e-mail, downloading files, accessing Java applets, participating in discussion groups, developing Web pages, and other Internet, intranet, and extranet applications.

Web Publishing Creating, converting, and storing hyperlinked documents and other material on Internet or intranet Web servers so they can easily be shared via Web browsers with teams, workgroups, or the enterprise.

Web Services A collection of Web and object-oriented technologies for linking Web-based applications running on different hardware, software, database, or network platforms. For example, Web services could link key business functions within the applications a business shares with its customers, suppliers, and business partners.

What-If Analysis Observing how changes to selected variables affect other variables in a mathematical model.

Whiteboarding See Data Conferencing.

Wide Area Network (WAN) A data communications network covering a large geographic area.

Window One section of a computer's multiple-section display screen, each section of which can have a different display.

Wireless LANs Using radio or infrared transmissions to link devices in a local area network.

Wireless Technologies Using radio wave, microwave, infrared, and laser technologies to transport digital communications without wires between communications devices. Examples include terrestrial microwave, communications satellites, cellular and PCS phone and pager systems, mobile data radio, and various wireless Internet technologies.

Word (1) A string of characters considered as unit. (2) An ordered set of bits (usually larger than a byte) handled as a unit by the central processing unit.

Word Processing The automation of the transformation of ideas and information into a readable form of communication. It involves the use of computers to manipulate text data to produce office communications in the form of documents.

Workgroup Computing Members of a networked workgroup may use groupware tools to communicate, coordinate, and collaborate and to share hardware, software, and databases to accomplish group assignments.

Workstation (1) A computer system designed to support the work of one person. (2) A high-powered computer to support the work of professionals in engineering, science, and other areas that require extensive computing power and graphics capabilities.

World Wide Web (WWW) A global network of multimedia Internet sites for information, education, entertainment, e-business, and e-commerce.

XML (Extensible Markup Language) A Web document content description language that describes the content of Web pages by applying hidden identifying tags or contextual labels to the data in Web documents. By categorizing and classifying Web data this way, XML makes Web content easier to identify, search, analyze, and selectively exchange between computers.

Photo Credits

Chapter One

Manchan / Getty Images, p. 5
© 2007 Intuit Inc. All rights reserved, p. 15
Courtesy of Infor, p. 16
© Patrice Latron / Corbis, p. 26

Chapter Two

© Kate Medley / The New York Times / Redux, p. 43
© Royalty Free / Corbis, p. 54

Chapter Three

© Comstock / PunchStock, p. 71
Photo courtesy of United States Army, p. 73
Hewlett-Packard Company, p. 75
© Royalty Free / Corbis, p. 75
Hewlett-Packard Company, p. 75
Courtesy of Sun Microsystems, Inc., p. 78
China Foto Press / Getty Images, p. 79
© Royalty Free / Corbis, p. 81
Image courtesy of Silicon Graphics, Inc., p. 82
Courtesy of Intel, p. 83
McGraw-Hill Companies, Inc. / John Flournoy, photographer, p. 87
Courtesy of Logitech, p. 89
Courtesy of Microsoft, p. 89
Courtesy of International Business Machines Corporation. Unauthorized use not permitted, p. 89
© AP / Wide World Photos, p. 89
© Comstock / PunchStock, p. 90
Courtesy of Philips Speech Recognition Systems, p. 91
Courtesy of Xerox, p. 92
© Jeff Smith / The Image Bank / Getty Images, p. 93
Hewlett Packard Company, p. 95
Courtesy of Xerox, p. 95
Courtesy of Lexar Media, p. 99
© Stockbyte / PunchStock, p. 100
© Royalty Free / Corbis, p. 100
Photodisc / Getty Images, p. 103

Chapter Four

© Chuck Savage / Corbis, p. 115
Netscape and the "N" Logo are registered trademarks of Netscape Communications Corporation. Netscape content © 2007. Used with permission, p. 120
2007 by Yahoo! Inc. YAHOO! and the YAHOO! logo are trademarks of Yahoo! Inc. © Reproduced with permission of Yahoo! Inc., p. 121
Microsoft product screen shot reprinted with permission from Microsoft Corporation, p. 122
Microsoft product screen shot reprinted with permission from Microsoft Corporation, p. 123
Microsoft product screen shot reprinted with permission from Microsoft Corporation, p. 124
Microsoft product screen shot reprinted with permission from Microsoft Corporation, p. 125
Courtesy of International Business Machines Corporation. Unauthorized use not permitted, p. 126
Courtesy of Salesforce.com, p. 127
Courtesy of MSNBC.com, p. 130
Microsoft product screen shot reprinted with permission from Microsoft Corporation, p. 141
Courtesy of Sun Microsystems, p. 146

Chapter Five

McGraw-Hill Companies, Inc. / John Flournoy, photographer, p. 155
Courtesy of Cognos, p. 162
Microsoft product screen shot reprinted with permission from Microsoft Corporation, p. 164
© Digital Vision / Getty Images, p. 169
Microsoft product screen shot reprinted with permission from Microsoft Corporation, p. 171
Courtesy of MySQL.com, p. 180
Microsoft product screen shot reprinted with permission from Microsoft Corporation, p. 181
Microsoft product screen shot reprinted with permission from Microsoft Corporation, p. 183

Chapter Six

Courtesy of Nokia, p. 191
© Kevin Moloney / The New York Times / Redux, p. 207
Phil Degginger / Getty Images, p. 216
Ryan McVay / Getty Images, p. 216
CMCD / Getty Images, p. 216
© Enterasys Networks, Inc. All Rights Reserved, p. 224

Chapter Seven

© Simon Dearden / Corbis, p. 241
Gary Gladstone Studio Inc. / Getty Images, p. 254
Courtesy of International Business Machines Corporation. Unauthorized use not permitted, p. 265
2007 by Yahoo! Inc. YAHOO! and the YAHOO! logo are trademarks of Yahoo! Inc. © Reproduced with permission of Yahoo! Inc., p. 267
Courtesy of salesforce.com, p. 271
Courtesy of International Business Machines Corporation. Unauthorized use not permitted, p. 275
Hyperion, p. 278

Chapter Eight

Microsoft product screen shot reprinted with permission from Microsoft Corporation, p. 289
Courtesy of VeriSign Inc., p. 299
Courtesy of Entellium, Inc., p. 301
Courtesy of Digital River, Inc., p. 308
Microsoft product screen shot reprinted with permission from Microsoft Corporation, p. 318

Chapter Nine

© 2007 CORDA Technologies Inc.®; All rights Reserved, p. 325
Courtesy of Microsoft, p. 335
Copyright © ESRI, USGS, DigitalGlobe. All rights reserved. Used by permission, p. 336
Courtesy of ADVIZOR Solutions, Inc., p. 337
Courtesy of Palisade Software, p. 339
© XpertRule Software Ltd.; www.xpertrule.com http://www.xpertrule.com, p. 341
Courtesy of International Business Machines Corporation. Unauthorized use not permitted, p. 344
Courtesy of Information Builders, p. 345
Courtesy of Lending Tree, p. 349
Courtesy of International Business Machines Corporation. Unauthorized use not permitted, p. 355
Microsoft product screen shot reprinted with permission from Microsoft Corporation, p. 358
Courtesy of Trading Solutions at www.tradingsolutions.com http://www.tradingsolutions.com, p. 359
Courtesy of Palisade Software, p. 362
© George Steinmetz/Corbis, p. 362
Courtesy of Ask Jeeves, p. 365

Chapter Ten

QuickBooks® Screen Shots © Intuit Inc. All Rights Reserved, p. 375
Courtesy of the Usability Lab of State Farm, p. 386
Courtesy of the Usability Lab of State Farm, p. 386
Courtesy of Microsoft, p. 389
© Lynsey Addario/Corbis, p. 394

Chapter Eleven

These materials have been reproduced with the permission of eBay Inc. © 2007 eBay Inc. All Rights Reserved, p. 421
Courtesy of SurfControl, p. 430
© Charles Gupton, p. 441
Courtesy of Choice Point, p. 446
Courtesy of McAfee, p. 453
Courtesy CA, Inc., p. 455

Chapter Twelve

© Comstock Images / AgeFotostock, p. 467
Courtesy CA, Inc., p. 473
© Christopher Brown / Polaris, p. 482
Courtesy of CEO Express, p. 497

Name Index

Company Index

Subject Index